This is Volume 23 of WEST'S NEW YORK PRACTICE SERIES

West's New York Practice Series

Vol. 1	Walker, et al., New York Limited Liability Companies and Partnerships: A Guide to Law and Practice
Vols. 2-4	Haig, et al., Commercial Litigation in New York State Courts
Vol. 5	Barker and Alexander, Evidence in New York State and Federal Courts
Vol. 6	Greenberg, Marcus, et al., New York Criminal Law
Vol. 7	Marks, et al., New York Pretrial Criminal Procedure
Vol. 8	Davies, Stecich, Gold, et al., New York Civil Appellate Practice
Vol. 9	Ginsberg, Weinberg, et al., Environmental Law and Regulation in New York
Vol. 10	Sobie, et al., New York Family Court Practice
Vols. 11-12	Scheinkman, et al., New York Law of Domestic Relations

Vol. 13	Taber, et al., Employment Litigation in New York
Vols. 14-16	Kreindler, Rodriguez, et al., New York Law of Torts
Vols. 17-19	Field, Moskin, et al., New York and Delaware Business Organizations: Choice, Formation, Operation, Financing and Acquisitions
Vols. 20-25	Ostertag, Benson, et al., General Practice in New York
Vol. 26	Borchers, Markell, et al., New York State Administrative Procedure and Practice
Vol. A	Borges, et al., Enforcing Judgments and Collecting Debts in New York
Vols. B-C	Bensel, Frank, McKeon, et al., Personal Injury Practice in New York
Vols. D-E	Preminger, et al., Trusts and Estates Practice in New York
Vols. F-G	Finkelstein and Ferrara, Landlord and Tenant Practice in New York

COORDINATED RESEARCH IN NEW YORK FROM WEST

New York Practice 2d
David D. Siegel

Handling the DWI Case in New York
Peter Gerstenzang

New York Elder Law Practice
Vincent J. Russo and Marvin Rachlin

WEST'S McKINNEY'S FORMS
Civil Practice Law and Rules

Uniform Commercial Code

Business Corporation Law

Matrimonial and Family Law

Real Property Practice

Estates and Surrogate Practice

Criminal Procedure Law

Not-For-Profit Corporation Law

Tax Practice and Procedure

Local Government Forms

Selected Consolidated Law Forms

McKinney's Consolidated Laws of New York Annotated

West's New York Legal Update

New York Digest

New York Law Finder

PAMPHLETS
New York Civil Practice Law and Rules

New York Sentence Charts

WESTLAW®

COORDINATED RESEARCH FROM WEST

WEST*Check*® and WESTMATE®

West CD–ROM Libraries™

To order any of these New York practice tools, call your West Representative or 1–800–328–9352.

> **NEED RESEARCH HELP?**
>
> **If you have research questions concerning WESTLAW or West Publications, call West's Reference Attorneys at 1–800–733–2889.**

GENERAL PRACTICE IN NEW YORK

By

ROBERT L. OSTERTAG
HON. JAMES D. BENSON

Sections 21.1 to 27.58

ST. PAUL, MINN.
WEST GROUP
1998

GENERAL PRACTICE IN NEW YORK
FORMS ON DISK™

The **Forms on Disk**™ which accompany these volumes provide instant access to WordPerfect 5.1/5.2 versions of the forms included in *General Practice in New York*. These electronic forms will save you hours of time drafting legal documents. The electronic forms can be loaded into your word processing software and formatted to match the document style of your law firm. These electronic forms become templates for you to use over and over without having to retype them each time.

The forms in Volumes 20, 21, 22, 23, 24 and 25 that are included on the accompanying disks are marked with the following disk icon for easy identification. 💾

COPYRIGHT © 1998 By WEST GROUP
610 Opperman Drive
P.O. Box 64526
St. Paul, MN 55164–0526
1–800–328–9352

All rights reserved
Printed in the United States of America
ISBN 0–314–23144–7

TEXT IS PRINTED ON 10% POST CONSUMER RECYCLED PAPER

WESTLAW® ELECTRONIC RESEARCH GUIDE

Coordinating Legal Research with WESTLAW

The *New York Practice Series* is an essential aid to legal research. WESTLAW provides a vast, online library of over 8000 collections of documents and services that can supplement research begun in this publication, encompassing:

- Federal and state primary law (statutes, regulations, rules, and case law), including West's editorial enhancements, such as headnotes, Key Number classifications, annotations

- Secondary law resources (texts and treatises published by West Group and by other publishers, as well as law reviews)

- Legal news

- Directories of attorneys and experts

- Court records and filings

- Citators

Specialized topical subsets of these resources have been created for more than thirty areas of practice.

In addition to legal information, there are general news and reference databases and a broad array of specialized materials frequently useful in connection with legal matters, covering accounting, business, environment, ethics, finance, medicine, social and physical sciences.

This guide will focus on a few aspects of WESTLAW use to supplement research begun in this publication, and will direct you to additional sources of assistance.

Databases

A database is a collection of documents with some features in common. It may contain statutes, court decisions, administrative materials, commentaries, news or other information. Each database has a unique identifier, used in many WESTLAW commands to select a database of interest. For example, the database containing New York cases has the identifier NY-CS.

The WESTLAW Directory is a comprehensive list of databases with information about each database, including the types of documents each

WESTLAW ELECTRONIC RESEARCH GUIDE

contains. The first page of a standard or customized WESTLAW Directory is displayed upon signing on to WESTLAW, except when prior, saved research is resumed. To access the WESTLAW Directory at any time, enter DB.

Databases of potential interest in connection with your research include:

NY-AG	New York Attorney General Opinions
NYETH-EO	New York Ethics Opinions
NYETH-CS	Legal Ethics & Professional Responsibility - New York Cases
WLD-NY	West's Legal Directory - New York
LAWPRAC	The Legal Practice Database

For information as to currentness and search tips regarding any WESTLAW database, enter the SCOPE command SC followed by the database identifier (e.g., SC NY-CS). It is not necessary to include the identifier to obtain scope information about the currently selected database.

WESTLAW Highlights

Use of this publication may be supplemented through the WESTLAW Bulletin (WLB), the WESTLAW New York State Bulletin (WSB-NY) and various Topical Highlights. Highlights databases contain summaries of significant judicial, legislative and administrative developments and are updated daily; they are searchable both from an automatic list of recent documents and using general WESTLAW search methods for documents accumulated over time. The full text of any judicial decision may be retrieved by entering FIND.

Consult the WESTLAW Directory (enter DB) for a complete, current listing of highlights databases.

Retrieving a Specific Case

The FIND command can be used to quickly retrieve a case whose citation is known. For example:

FI 616 A.2d 1336

Updating Case Law Research

There are a variety of citator services on WESTLAW for use in updating research.

Insta-Cite® may be used to verify citations, find parallel citations, ascertain the history of a case, and see whether it remains valid law. References are also provided to secondary sources, such as Corpus Juris Secundum®, that cite the case. To view the Insta-Cite history of a displayed

WESTLAW ELECTRONIC RESEARCH GUIDE

case, simply enter the command IC. To view the Insta-Cite history of a selected case, enter a command in this form:

IC 574 A.2d 502

Shepard's® Citations provides a comprehensive list of cases and publications that have cited a particular case, with explanatory analysis to indicate how the citing cases have treated the case, e.g., "followed," "explained." To view the Shepard's Citations about a displayed case, enter the command SH. Add a case citation, if necessary, as in the prior Insta-Cite example.

For the latest citing references, not yet incorporated in Shepard's Citations, use Shepard's PreView® (SP command) and QuickCite™ (QC command), in the same way.

To see a complete list of publications covered by any of the citator services, enter its service abbreviation (IC, SH, SP or QC) followed by PUBS. To ascertain the scope of coverage for any of the services, enter the SCOPE command (SC) followed by the appropriate service abbreviation. For the complete list of commands available in a citator service, enter its service abbreviation (IC, SH, SP or QC) followed by CMDS.

Retrieving Statutes, Court Rules and Regulations

Annotated and unannotated versions of the New York statutes are searchable on WESTLAW (identifiers NY-ST-ANN and NY-ST), as are New York court rules (NY-RULES) and New York Administrative Code (NY-ADC).

The United States Code and United States Code - Annotated are searchable databases on WESTLAW (identifiers USC and USCA, respectively), as are federal court rules (US-RULES) and regulations (CFR).

In addition, the FIND command may be used to retrieve specific provisions by citation, obviating the need for database selection or search. To FIND a desired document, enter FI, followed by the citation of the desired document, using the full name of the publication, or one of the abbreviated styles recognized by WESTLAW.

If WESTLAW does not recognize the style you enter, you may enter one of the following, using US, NY, or any other state code in place of XX:

FI XX-ST	Displays templates for codified statutes
FI XX-LEGIS	Displays templates for legislation
FI XX-RULES	Displays templates for rules
FI XX-ORDERS	Displays templates for court orders

Alternatively, entering FI followed by the publication's full name or an accepted abbreviation will normally display templates, useful jump

WESTLAW ELECTRONIC RESEARCH GUIDE

possibilities, or helpful information necessary to complete the FIND process. For example:

FI USCA	Displays templates for United States Code - Annotated
FI FRAP	Displays templates for Federal Rules of Appellate Procedure
FI FRCP	Displays templates for Federal Rules of Civil Procedure
FI FRCRP	Displays templates for Federal Rules of Criminal Procedure
FI FRE	Displays templates for Federal Rules of Evidence
FI CFR	Displays templates for Code of Federal Regulations
FI FR	Displays templates for Federal Register

To view the complete list of FINDable documents and associated prescribed forms, enter FI PUBS.

Updating Research in re Statutes, Rules and Regulations

When viewing a statute, rule or regulation on WESTLAW after a search or FIND command, it is easy to update your research. A message will appear on the screen if relevant amendments, repeals or other new material are available through the UPDATE feature. Entering the UPDATE command will display such material.

Documents used to update New York statutes are also searchable in New York Legislative Service (NY-LEGIS). Those used to update rules are searchable in New York Orders (NY-ORDERS).

Documents used to update federal statutes, rules, and regulations are searchable in the United States Public Laws (US-PL), Federal Orders (US-ORDERS) and Federal Register (FR) databases, respectively.

When documents citing a statute, rule or regulation are of interest, Shepard's Citations on WESTLAW may be of assistance. That service covers federal constitutional provisions, statutes and administrative provisions, and corresponding materials from many states. The command SH PUBS displays a directory of publications which may be Shepardized on WESTLAW. Consult the WESTLAW manual for more information about citator services.

Using WESTLAW as a Citator

For research beyond the coverage of any citator service, go directly to the databases (cases, for example) containing citing documents and use standard WESTLAW search techniques to retrieve documents citing specific constitutional provisions, statutes, standard jury instructions or other authorities.

Fortunately, the specific portion of a citation is often reasonably distinctive, such as 22:636.1, 301.65, 401(k), 12-21-5, 12052. When it is, a search on that specific portion alone may retrieve applicable documents without any substantial number of inapplicable ones (unless the number happens to be coincidentally popular in another context).

Similarly, if the citation involves more than one number, such as 42 U.S.C.A. §1201, a search containing both numbers (e.g., 42 +5 1201) is likely to produce mostly desired information, even though the component numbers are common.

If necessary, the search may be limited in several ways:

A. Switch from a general database to one containing mostly cases within the subject area of the cite being researched;

B. Use a connector (&, /S, /P, etc.) to narrow the search to documents including terms which are highly likely to accompany the correct citation in the context of the issue being researched;

C. Include other citation information in the query. Because of the variety of citation formats used in documents, this option should be used primarily where other options prove insufficient. Below are illustrative queries for any database containing New York cases:

N.Y.Const.! Const.! Constitution /s 6 VI +3 3

will retrieve cases citing the New York State Constitution, Art. 6, §3; and

"Criminal Procedure Law" CPL /s 30.30

will retrieve cases citing Criminal Procedure Law §30.30.

Alternative Retrieval Methods

WIN® (WESTLAW Is Natural™) allows you to frame your issue in plain English to retrieve documents:

Does new trial motion extend (toll) the time for filing (taking) appeal?

Alternatively, retrieval may be focused by use of the Terms and Connectors method:

TO(30) /P DI(NEW +1 TRIAL /P EXTEND!
EXTENSION TOLL! /P APPEAL)

In databases with Key Numbers, either of the above examples will identify Appeal and Error ⌫345.1 as a Key Number collecting headnotes relevant to this issue if there are pertinent cases.

Since the Key Numbers are affixed to points of law by trained specialists based on conceptual understanding of the case, relevant cases that were not retrieved by either of the language-dependent methods will often be found at a Key Number.

Similarly, citations in retrieved documents (to cases, statutes, rules, etc.) may suggest additional, fruitful research using other WESTLAW databases (e.g., annotated statutes, rules) or services (e.g., citator services).

Key Number Search

Frequently, case law research rapidly converges on a few topics, headings and Key Numbers within West's Key Number System that are likely to contain relevant cases. These may be discovered from known, relevant reported cases from any jurisdiction; Library References in West publications; browsing in a digest; or browsing the Key Number System on WESTLAW using the JUMP feature or the KEY command.

Once discovered, topics, subheadings or Key Numbers are useful as search terms (in databases containing reported cases) alone or with other search terms,to focus the search within a narrow range of potentially relevant material.

For example, to retrieve cases with at least one headnote classified to Appeal and Error ⚲345.1, sign on to a caselaw database and enter

    30k345.1   [use with other search terms, if desired]

The topic name (Appeal and Error) is replaced by its numerical equivalent (30) and the ⚲ by the letter k. A list of topics and their numerical equivalents is in the WESTLAW Reference Manual and is displayed in WESTLAW when the KEY command is entered.

Using JUMP

WESTLAW's JUMP feature allows you to move from one document to another or from one part of a document to another, then easily return to your original place, without losing your original result. Opportunities to move in this manner are marked in the text with a JUMP symbol (▶). Whenever you see the JUMP symbol, you may move to the place designated by the adjacent reference by using the Tab, arrow keys or mouse click to position the cursor on the JUMP symbol, then pressing Enter or clicking again with the mouse.

Within the text of a court opinion, JUMP arrows are adjacent to case cites and federal statute cites, and adjacent to parenthesized numbers marking discussions corresponding to headnotes.

On a screen containing the text of a headnote, the JUMP arrows allow movement to the corresponding discussion in the text of the opinion,

   ▶ (3)

WESTLAW ELECTRONIC RESEARCH GUIDE

and allow browsing West's Key Number System beginning at various heading levels:

- 30   APPEAL AND ERROR
- 30VII   Transfer of Cause
- 30VII(A)   Time of Taking Proceedings
- 30k343   Commencement of Period of Limitation
- 30k345.1 k.   Motion for new trial.

To return from a JUMP, enter GB (except for JUMPs between a headnote and the corresponding discussion in opinion, for which there is a matching number in parenthesis in both headnote and opinion). Returns from successive JUMPs (e.g., from case to cited case to case cited by cited case) without intervening returns may be accomplished by repeated entry of GB or by using the MAP command.

General Information

The information provided above illustrates some of the ways WESTLAW can complement research using this publication. However, this brief overview illustrates only some of the power of WESTLAW. The full range of WESTLAW search techniques is available to support your research.

Please consult the WESTLAW Reference Manual for additional information or assistance or call West's Reference Attorneys at 1-800-REF-ATTY (1-800-733-2889).

For information about subscribing to WESTLAW, please call 1-800-328-9352.

*

SUMMARY OF CONTENTS

Volume 20

Chapter   **Page**

1. Business Organizations: Corporations — 2
2. Non-corporate Entities: Limited Liability Companies and Partnerships — 253
3. Municipal Law — 403
4. Administrative Law — 468
5. Commercial Sales Contracts — 594
6. Buying and Selling a Small Business — 670

Volume 21

7. Consumer Law — 2
8. Enforcement of Money Judgments — 181
9. Bankruptcy — 253
10. Mechanic's Liens — 541
11. Mortgage Foreclosure — 683
12. Purchase and Sale of Real Estate — 792

Volume 22

13. Landlord–Tenant Law — 2
14. Eminent Domain — 108
15. Environmental Law — 212
16. New York Land Use Law — 296
17. New York Employment Law — 467
18. Civil Rights Law — 609
19. Immigration and Nationality Law—Permanent Residence Applications — 733
20. Adoptions — 857

Volume 23

21. Domestic Relations — 2
22. Guardianship — 162
23. Elder Law — 329
24. Estate Planning — 448
25. Probate and Estate Administration — 545
26. Personal Injury — 638

xv

SUMMARY OF CONTENTS

Chapter | **Page**
27. Products Liability — 722

Volume 24

28. Legal Malpractice — 2
29. Medical Malpractice — 92
30. Damages — 166
31. Insurance — 251
32. Workers' Compensation — 315
33. Local Criminal Court Practice — 382
34. Social Security Disability Cases — 452
35. Income Tax — 551
36. Alcoholic Beverage Control Law — 653
37. Civil Appellate Practice Before the Appellate Division and Other Intermediate Appellate Courts — 738

Volume 25

38. Criminal Appellate Practice Before the Appellate Division and Other Intermediate Appelllate Courts — 2
39. Civil and Criminal Appeals to the Court of Appeals — 145

Table of Jury Instructions — 235
Table of Forms — 236
Table of Statutes — iii
Table of Rules — iii
Table of Cases — iii
Index — iii

XVI

TABLE OF CONTENTS

Volume 20

CHAPTER 1. BUSINESS ORGANIZATIONS: CORPORATIONS

Sec.
1.1	Scope Note.
1.2	Strategy.
1.3	Strategy Checklist.
1.4	Overview.
1.5	Definitions.
1.6	Formation of Corporations.
1.7	____ Certificates; Notices.
1.8	____ Corporate Seal.
1.9	____ Corporate Purposes.
1.10	____ ____ Upholding and Disregarding the Corporate Entity.
1.11	____ ____ General Powers.
1.12	____ ____ Defense of *Ultra Vires*.
1.13	____ Corporate Name.
1.14	____ ____ Reservation of Name.
1.15	____ Service of Process.
1.16	____ ____ Records and Certificates of Department of State.
1.17	____ ____ Statutory Designation of Secretary of State as Agent for Service of Process.
1.18	____ ____ Registered Agent for Service of Process.
1.19	____ ____ Upon Unauthorized Foreign Corporation.
1.20	____ Incorporators and Promoters.
1.21	____ Certificate of Incorporation.
1.22	____ Bylaws.
1.23	____ Organization Meeting; Biennial Statement; Franchise Tax.
1.24	____ Formation of Corporations Summary.
1.25	____ Formation of Corporations Checklist.
1.26	Capital Structure.
1.27	____ Authorized Shares.
1.28	____ Preferred Shares in Series.
1.29	____ Subscription for Shares.
1.30	____ Consideration and Payment for Shares.
1.31	____ Rights to Purchase Shares.
1.32	____ Stated Capital.
1.33	____ Corporate Bonds; Convertible Securities.
1.34	____ Federal Income Taxation Aspects.
1.35	____ Capital Structure Summary.
1.36	____ Capital Structure Checklist.
1.37	Distributions.
1.38	____ Dividends; Share Distributions and Changes.
1.39	____ Purchase or Redemption of Shares.

TABLE OF CONTENTS

Sec.
1.40 ____ Federal Income Tax Aspects.
1.41 ____ Distributions Summary.
1.42 ____ Distributions Checklist.
1.43 Shareholders' Meetings and Agreements—Generally.
1.44 ____ Notice Requirements.
1.45 ____ Voting.
1.46 ____ Quorum Requirements.
1.47 ____ Agreements; Voting Trusts.
1.48 ____ Action Without a Meeting.
1.49 Shareholders' Meetings and Agreements Summary.
1.50 Shareholders' Meetings and Agreements Checklist.
1.51 Shareholders' Rights.
1.52 ____ Preemptive Rights.
1.53 ____ Inspection of Books and Records.
1.54 ____ Shareholders' Rights Summary.
1.55 ____ Shareholders' Rights Checklist.
1.56 Shareholders' Liabilities.
1.57 ____ Shareholders' Liabilities Summary.
1.58 ____ Shareholders' Liabilities Checklist.
1.59 Directors.
1.60 ____ Vacancies; New Directorships.
1.61 ____ Removal.
1.62 ____ Meetings.
1.63 ____ ____ Quorum and Voting Requirements.
1.64 ____ Executive Committee; Other Committees.
1.65 ____ Fiduciary Duties.
1.66 ____ Liabilities.
1.67 ____ Directors Summary.
1.68 ____ Directors Checklist.
1.69 Officers.
1.70 ____ Officers Summary.
1.71 ____ Officers Checklist.
1.72 Amendment of Certificate of Incorporation.
1.73 ____ Procedure.
1.74 ____ Class Vote.
1.75 ____ Certificate of Amendment.
1.76 ____ Certificate of Change.
1.77 ____ Restated Certificate of Incorporation.
1.78 ____ Reorganization Under Act of Congress.
1.79 Amendment of Certificate of Incorporation Summary.
1.80 Amendment of Certificate of Incorporation Checklist.
1.81 Business Combinations.
1.82 ____ Mergers and Consolidations.
1.83 ____ ____ Procedures.
1.84 ____ ____ Effect.
1.85 ____ Sale, Lease, Exchange, or Other Disposition of Assets.
1.86 ____ ____ Mortgage or Security Interest in Assets.
1.87 ____ ____ Guarantee Authorized by Shareholders.
1.88 ____ Share Exchanges.
1.89 ____ Takeover Bids.

TABLE OF CONTENTS

Sec.
1.90 ____ Right of Shareholder to Receive Payment for Shares.
1.91 ____ Federal Income Taxation Aspects.
1.92 Business Combinations Summary.
1.93 Business Combinations Checklist.
1.94 Dissolution.
1.95 ____ Non-judicial Dissolution.
1.96 ____ ____ Authorization.
1.97 ____ ____ Certificate of Dissolution.
1.98 ____ ____ Notice to Creditors.
1.99 ____ Judicial Dissolution.
1.100 ____ ____ Attorney General's Action.
1.101 ____ ____ Directors' Petition.
1.102 ____ ____ Shareholders' Petition.
1.103 ____ ____ Petition Upon Deadlock Among Directors or Shareholders and in Other Circumstances.
1.104 ____ ____ Procedures.
1.105 ____ ____ Preservation of Assets; Appointment of Receiver.
1.106 ____ ____ Certain Transfers and Judgments Void; Injunction.
1.107 ____ Liquidation Distributions.
1.108 ____ ____ Federal Income Tax Aspects.
1.109 ____ Dissolution Summary.
1.110 ____ Dissolution Checklist.
1.111 Receivership.
1.112 Receivership—Summary.
1.113 ____ Checklist.
1.114 Foreign Corporations.
1.115 ____ Authorization to Do Business in New York.
1.116 ____ Application for Authority.
1.117 ____ ____ Effect of Filing.
1.118 ____ Surrender of Authority.
1.119 ____ Termination of Existence.
1.120 Foreign Corporations Summary.
1.121 Foreign Corporations Checklist.
1.122 Professional Service Corporations.
1.123 Professional Service Corporations Summary.
1.124 Professional Service Corporations Checklist.
1.125 Foreign Professional Service Corporations.
1.126 Foreign Professional Service Corporations Summary.
1.127 Foreign Professional Service Corporations Checklist.
1.128 Transactional Checklist—Generally.
1.129 ____ Formation ("Birth").
1.130 ____ Operation ("Growth").
1.131 ____ Business Combinations ("Marriage").
1.132 ____ Spin-offs and Split-offs ("Children" and "Divorce").
1.133 ____ Repurchase of Shares ("Redemption").
1.134 ____ Dissolution; Liquidation ("Death").
1.135 Procedural Checklist—Generally.
1.136 ____ Notices.
1.137 ____ Reservation of Corporate Name.
1.138 ____ ____ Foreign Corporations.

XIX

TABLE OF CONTENTS

Sec.
1.139	____ Mandatory and Permissive Provisions in Certificate of Incorporation.
1.140	____ Incorporation.
1.141	____ Filing Certificate of Incorporation.
1.142	____ Bylaws.
1.143	____ Organization Meetings.
1.144	____ Share Certificate.
1.145	____ Shareholder Approval Requirements.
1.146	____ Shareholder's Right to Receive Payment for Shares.
1.147	____ Close Corporations.
1.148	____ Foreign Corporations.
1.149	Drafting Checklist.
1.150	Form—Application to Reserve Corporate Name. 💾
1.151	____ Certificate of Incorporation. 💾
1.152	____ Bylaws. 💾
1.153	____ Subscription Agreement. 💾
1.154	____ Certificate of Amendment. 💾
1.155	____ Certificate of Dissolution. 💾

CHAPTER 2. NON-CORPORATE ENTITIES: LIMITED LIABILTY COMPANIES AND PARTNERSHIPS

2.1	Scope Note.
2.2	Strategy—Choice of Entity.
2.3	Tax Classification.
2.4	____ Eagerly–Awaited Simplification.
2.5	____ Former Corporate Characteristics Test.
2.6	____ ____ Limited Liability.
2.7	____ ____ Continuity of Life.
2.8	____ ____ Free Transferability of Interests.
2.9	____ ____ Centralized Management.
2.10	Partnership vs. LLC.
2.11	____ Tax Implications.
2.12	____ Liability.
2.13	____ Flexibility.
2.14	Limited Liability Companies.
2.15	____ Governing Law.
2.16	____ Formation.
2.17	____ ____ Articles of Organization.
2.18	____ ____ Publication.
2.19	____ ____ Operating Agreement.
2.20	____ ____ Other Issues.
2.21	____ Members.
2.22	____ ____ Admission of New Members.
2.23	____ ____ Liability.
2.24	____ ____ One-member LLCs.
2.25	____ Management.
2.26	____ ____ Members vs. Managers.
2.27	____ ____ Voting: Members.
2.28	____ ____ Voting: Managers.

TABLE OF CONTENTS

Sec.
2.29 — — Non-waivable Requirements.
2.30 — — Delegation of Responsibility.
2.31 — — Standard of Care.
2.32 — — Agency Authority.
2.33 — Assignment of Interests.
2.34 — — Default Rules.
2.35 — — Vote Required to Admit Assignee as Member.
2.36 — Dissolution.
2.37 — — Events.
2.38 — — Continuation of Business after Dissolution Event.
2.39 — — Winding Up.
2.40 — Conversions/Mergers.
2.41 — — Procedures.
2.42 — — Dissenters' Rights.
2.43 — PLLCs.
2.44 General Partnerships.
2.45 — Governing Law.
2.46 — Formation.
2.47 — — Agreement.
2.48 — — Business Certificate.
2.49 — — Publication.
2.50 — — Other Issues.
2.51 — Partners.
2.52 — — Admission of New Partners.
2.53 — — Liability.
2.54 — — Contribution Issues.
2.55 — Management.
2.56 — — Voting.
2.57 — — Non-waivable Requirements.
2.58 — — Delegation of Responsibility.
2.59 — — Standard of Care.
2.60 — — Agency Authority.
2.61 — Assignment of Interests.
2.62 — — Default Rules.
2.63 — — Vote Required to Admit New Partner.
2.64 — Dissolution.
2.65 — — Events.
2.66 — — Continuation of Business after Dissolution Event.
2.67 — — Winding Up.
2.68 — Conversions/Mergers.
2.69 — — Procedures.
2.70 — — Dissenters' Rights.
2.71 — Professional Organizations.
2.72 Limited Liability Partnerships.
2.73 — Governing Law.
2.74 — Comparison with General Partnerships.
2.75 — Formation/Registration.
2.76 — Other Issues.
2.77 Limited Partnerships.
2.78 — Governing Law.

XXI

TABLE OF CONTENTS

Sec.
2.79 ____ Formation.
2.80 ____ ____ Certificate of Limited Partnership.
2.81 ____ ____ Publication.
2.82 ____ ____ Agreement.
2.83 ____ ____ Other Issues.
2.84 ____ Partners.
2.85 ____ ____ Admission of New Partners.
2.86 ____ ____ Liability.
2.87 ____ Contribution Issues.
2.88 ____ Management.
2.89 ____ ____ Voting: General Partners.
2.90 ____ ____ Voting: Limited Partners.
2.91 ____ ____ Delegation of Responsibility.
2.92 ____ ____ Standard of Care.
2.93 ____ ____ Agency Authority.
2.94 ____ Assignment of Interests.
2.95 ____ ____ Default Rules.
2.96 ____ ____ Vote Required to Admit New Partner.
2.97 ____ Dissolution.
2.98 ____ ____ Events.
2.99 ____ ____ Continuation of Business after Dissolution Event.
2.100 ____ ____ Winding Up.
2.101 ____ Conversions/Mergers.
2.102 ____ ____ Procedures.
2.103 ____ ____ Dissenters' Rights.
2.104 ____ Professional Organizations.
2.105 Due Diligence Issues.
2.106 Securities Laws Issues.
2.107 Summary.
2.108 Chart Comparing New York Entities.
2.109 Drafting Checklist.
2.110 Forms.
2.111 ____ LLC Articles of Organization. 💾
2.112 ____ Operating Agreement: Member–Managed LLC. 💾
2.113 ____ Registration as LLP. 💾
2.114 ____ Certificate of Limited Partnership. 💾
2.115 ____ Limited Partnership Agreement. 💾

CHAPTER 3. MUNICIPAL LAW

3.1 Scope Note.
3.2 Strategy.
3.3 Municipal Corporations.
3.4 ____ Creation.
3.5 ____ Consolidation, Annexation and Dissolution.
3.6 ____ ____ Annexation Checklist.
3.7 Powers of Municipal Corporations.
3.8 ____ Governmental v. Proprietary Powers.
3.9 ____ Police Powers.
3.10 Legislative Enactments.

TABLE OF CONTENTS

Sec.
- 3.11 ____ Resolutions.
- 3.12 ____ Ordinances.
- 3.13 ____ Rules and Regulations.
- 3.14 ____ Local Laws.
- 3.15 ____ Referendum Requirements.
- 3.16 Acquisition and Disposition of Property.
- 3.17 Officers and Employees.
- 3.18 ____ Qualifications.
- 3.19 ____ Terms.
- 3.20 ____ Removal.
- 3.21 ____ Collective Bargaining.
- 3.22 ____ Conflicts of Interest.
- 3.23 ____ ____ Checklist.
- 3.24 Contracts.
- 3.25 ____ Competitive Bidding.
- 3.26 Municipal Finance.
- 3.27 ____ Municipal Borrowing.
- 3.28 Public Meetings.
- 3.29 Access to Records.
- 3.30 Tort Claims Against Municipalities.
- 3.31 ____ Checklist.
- 3.32 Challenges to Governmental Determinations.
- 3.33 Special Purpose Units of Government.
- 3.34 ____ Industrial Development Agencies.
- 3.35 ____ Public Authorities.
- 3.36 Forms.
- 3.37 ____ Notice of Claim.
- 3.38 ____ Verified Complaint in Tort Action.

CHAPTER 4. ADMINISTRATIVE LAW

- 4.1 Scope Note.
- 4.2 Strategy.
- 4.3 ____ Checklist.
- 4.4 Procedural Due Process.
- 4.5 ____ Individualized State Action.
- 4.6 ____ Protected Interests.
- 4.7 ____ The Process Due.
- 4.8 ____ Summary.
- 4.9 ____ Checklist.
- 4.10 Adjudicatory Proceedings.
- 4.11 ____ Definition of an Adjudicatory Proceeding.
- 4.12 ____ Notice.
- 4.13 ____ Discovery.
- 4.14 ____ Right to Counsel.
- 4.15 ____ Evidence.
- 4.16 ____ Cross-Examination and Witness Attendance.
- 4.17 ____ Official Notice.
- 4.18 ____ Statement of Decision and Decisional Record.
- 4.19 ____ Burden of Proof.

TABLE OF CONTENTS

Sec.
4.20 ____ Intervention.
4.21 ____ Unreasonable Agency Delay.
4.22 ____ Agency Duty to Decide Consistently.
4.23 ____ Intra-agency Review.
4.24 ____ Checking Agency Bias.
4.25 ____ *Res Judicata* and Collateral Estoppel Effect.
4.26 ____ Special Rules Applicable to Licensing Matters.
4.27 ____ Special Issues in Handling Licensing Matters.
4.28 ____ ____ Basic License Information.
4.29 ____ ____ The Role of SAPA and SEQRA in the Licensing Process.
4.30 ____ ____ Accuracy and Completeness in Applications.
4.31 ____ ____ Opportunities to Expedite the Process.
4.32 ____ ____ Opportunities for Variances from Standard Approaches.
4.33 ____ ____ Renewal, Suspension and Revocation Issues.
4.34 ____ Special Issues in Handling Enforcement Matters.
4.35 ____ ____ Strategies to Minimize Violations.
4.36 ____ ____ Agency Fact–Finding in the Pre-enforcement Phase.
4.37 ____ ____ Agency Enforcement Options.
4.38 ____ ____ The Settlement Process.
4.39 ____ ____ The Hearing Process.
4.40 ____ ____ Post–Hearing Issues.
4.41 ____ Summary.
4.42 ____ Checklist.
4.43 Administrative Rulemaking.
4.44 ____ Rulemaking Compared With Other Agency Action.
4.45 ____ Rulemaking Notice.
4.46 ____ Comments and Agency Assessment of Comments.
4.47 ____ Agency Duty to Reveal Underlying Information.
4.48 ____ Notice of Adoption and Effective Date of Rules.
4.49 ____ Ancillary Documentation and the Role of GORR.
4.50 ____ Rule Filing and Publication.
4.51 ____ Declaratory Rulings Regarding Rules.
4.52 ____ Overlapping State and Federal Rules.
4.53 ____ Special Strategic Considerations in Handling Administrative Rulemaking Matters.
4.54 ____ ____ Basic Sources of Information on Rulemaking.
4.55 ____ ____ Participating in the Rulemaking Process.
4.56 ____ ____ Special Issues in Negotiated Rulemakings.
4.57 ____ ____ Special Issues in Emergency Rulemakings.
4.58 ____ ____ Agency Guidance Documents.
4.59 ____ Summary.
4.60 ____ Checklist.
4.61 Agency Information–Gathering.
4.62 ____ Administrative Searches.
4.63 ____ Administrative Subpoenas.
4.64 ____ Reporting and Recordkeeping Requirements.
4.65 ____ Summary.
4.66 ____ Checklist.
4.67 Judicial Review.
4.68 ____ Delegation of Authority to Agencies.

TABLE OF CONTENTS

Sec.
4.69 —— Standing to Seek Judicial Review.
4.70 —— Ripeness.
4.71 —— Final Order and Relief in the Nature of Prohibition.
4.72 —— Exhaustion of Administrative Remedies.
4.73 —— Primary Jurisdiction.
4.74 —— Statutory Preclusion of Judicial Review.
4.75 —— Article 78 and the Consolidation of the Common Law Prerogative Writs.
4.76 —— Standards of Review.
4.77 —— —— Review of Agency Determinations of Law.
4.78 —— —— Review of Agency Determinations of Fact Under the Substantial Evidence Test.
4.79 —— —— Review of Agency Determinations of Fact Under the Arbitrary and Capricious Test.
4.80 —— —— Review of Administrative Rules.
4.81 —— —— Review of Administrative Discretion.
4.82 —— Statutes of Limitation Applicable to Judicial Review of Agency Action.
4.83 —— Venue in Article 78 Proceedings.
4.84 —— Subject Matter Jurisdiction in Article 78 Proceedings.
4.85 —— Summary.
4.86 —— Checklist.
4.87 Forms.
4.88 —— Notice of Appearance in Licensing or Permitting Matter. 💾
4.89 —— Notice for Discovery and Inspection in an Administrative Proceeding. 💾
4.90 —— Notice of Deposition in an Administrative Proceeding. 💾
4.91 —— Notice to Permit Entry Upon Real Property. 💾

CHAPTER 5. COMMERCIAL SALES CONTRACTS

5.1 Scope Note.
5.2 Strategy.
5.3 Transactional Checklist—Breach of Contract.
5.4 Defining a Contract.
5.5 Governing Law.
5.6 —— Freedom to Contract—Generally.
5.7 —— —— Presumption of Legality.
5.8 —— —— —— Burden of Proof.
5.9 —— —— —— Determining the Contract's Validity.
5.10 —— —— —— —— Not All Illegal Contracts Are Unenforceable.
5.11 —— Public Policy Issues.
5.12 —— Unconscionability.
5.13 —— —— Elements.
5.14 —— —— Codification in UCC.
5.15 —— Duty of Good Faith—Generally.
5.16 —— —— Codification in UCC.
5.17 The Written Contract—Statute of Frauds.
5.18 —— —— General Rules.
5.19 —— —— Formal Requirements.

XXV

TABLE OF CONTENTS

Sec.
5.20 ____ ____ Nature of the Writing.
5.21 ____ Parol or Extrinsic Evidence.
5.22 ____ Offer.
5.23 ____ Acceptance.
5.24 ____ ____ Additional Terms.
5.25 ____ Indefiniteness.
5.26 ____ Use of Open Terms.
5.27 Warranties.
5.28 ____ Warranty of Title Against Infringement.
5.29 ____ Express Warranty.
5.30 ____ Implied Warranty of Merchantability.
5.31 ____ Implied Warranty of Fitness for a Particular Purpose.
5.32 Assumption of the Risk of Loss.
5.33 ____ In the Absence of Breach.
5.34 ____ In the Event of a Breach.
5.35 Performance.
5.36 ____ Buyer's Response to Tender of Delivery.
5.37 ____ ____ Acceptance.
5.38 ____ ____ Rejection.
5.39 ____ ____ Revocation of Acceptance.
5.40 Breach of Contract.
5.41 ____ Seller's Remedies.
5.42 ____ ____ Action for the Price.
5.43 ____ ____ Withholding the Goods and Stopping Delivery.
5.44 ____ ____ Recovery of Goods Delivered.
5.45 ____ ____ Resale.
5.46 ____ ____ Damages for Non-acceptance or Repudiation.
5.47 ____ Buyer's Remedies.
5.48 ____ ____ Cover.
5.49 ____ ____ Damages for Non-delivery.
5.50 ____ ____ Damages for Breach Regarding Accepted Goods.
5.51 ____ ____ Specific Performance or Replevin.
5.52 ____ Liquidated Damages.
5.53 ____ Mitigation of Damages.
5.54 Third-Party Interests.
5.55 ____ Subsequent Buyers.
5.56 ____ Other Creditors.
5.57 Drafting Checklists—Order of Goods for Resale by Buyer.
5.58 ____ Verified Complaint On Account Stated for Goods, Services and Wares Delivered.
5.59 ____ Plaintiff's Notice of Motion for Summary Judgment in Contract Action.
5.60 ____ Affidavit of Officer of Plaintiff Company in Support of Summary Judgment Motion in Contract Action.
5.61 ____ Notice of Petition for Order Staying Arbitration in Dispute Over Contract for Sale of Goods.
5.62 ____ Petition for Order Staying Arbitration in Dispute Over Contract for Sale of Goods.
5.63 ____ Affidavit in Opposition to Petition for Order Staying Arbitration in Dispute Over Contract for Sale of Goods.

TABLE OF CONTENTS

Sec.
- 5.64 ____ Answer to Petition for Order Staying Arbitration in Dispute Over Contract for Sale of Goods.
- 5.65 Forms—Order of Goods for Resale by Buyer. 💾
- 5.66 ____ Verified Complaint On Account Stated for Goods, Services and Wares Delivered. 💾
- 5.67 ____ Plaintiff's Notice of Motion for Summary Judgment in Contract Action. 💾
- 5.68 ____ Affidavit of Vice President of Plaintiff Purchaser in Support of Summary Judgment Motion in Contract Action. 💾
- 5.69 ____ Notice of Petition for Order Staying Arbitration in Dispute Over Contract for Sale of Goods. 💾
- 5.70 ____ Petition for Order Staying Arbitration in Dispute Over Contract for Sale of Goods. 💾
- 5.71 ____ Affidavit in Opposition to Petition for Order Staying Arbitration in Dispute Over Contract for Sale of Goods. 💾
- 5.72 ____ Answer to Petition for Order Staying Arbitration in Dispute Over Contract for Sale of Goods. 💾

CHAPTER 6. BUYING AND SELLING A SMALL BUSINESS

- 6.1 Scope Note.
- 6.2 Strategy: Representing the Buyer—Introduction.
- 6.3 ____ The Attorney's Role.
- 6.4 ____ Different Considerations Depending on the Type of Transaction.
- 6.5 ____ General Stages of the Transaction.
- 6.6 Representing the Buyer—Investigating the Business.
- 6.7 ____ Nature and Operation of Business.
- 6.8 ____ Geographic Location.
- 6.9 ____ The Negotiating Team.
- 6.10 ____ The Letter of Intent.
- 6.11 ____ Confidentiality Agreements.
- 6.12 ____ Drafting the Agreement.
- 6.13 Due Diligence Investigation.
- 6.14 ____ Legal Issues.
- 6.15 ____ ____ Organizational Documents.
- 6.16 ____ ____ Ownership Documents.
- 6.17 ____ ____ Existing Contracts.
- 6.18 ____ ____ Liens and Security Interests.
- 6.19 ____ ____ Corporate and Trade Names.
- 6.20 ____ ____ Real Estate.
- 6.21 ____ ____ Compliance With Law.
- 6.22 ____ ____ Litigation Investigation.
- 6.23 ____ Financial Issues—General Considerations.
- 6.24 ____ ____ Seller's Records From the Buyer's Position.
- 6.25 ____ ____ Buyer's Records From the Seller's Position.
- 6.26 ____ ____ Public Records.
- 6.27 ____ ____ Financial Statements.
- 6.28 ____ ____ The Need for Other Professionals.
- 6.29 ____ ____ Valuation of the Business.

TABLE OF CONTENTS

Sec.	
6.30	____ ____ Tax Returns.
6.31	Tax Issues for Buyer.
6.32	____ Asset Purchase.
6.33	____ ____ Allocation of Purchase Price.
6.34	____ ____ Depreciation of Assets.
6.35	____ ____ Land.
6.36	____ ____ Good Will and Covenants Not to Compete.
6.37	____ ____ Inventory.
6.38	____ ____ Cash.
6.39	____ ____ Supplies.
6.40	____ ____ Patents, Franchises, Trademarks, Trade Names.
6.41	____ Stock Purchase.
6.42	____ ____ Basis of Stock.
6.43	____ ____ Basis of Corporate Assets.
6.44	____ ____ Election to Treat Stock Purchase as Asset Purchase.
6.45	____ Mergers, Consolidations, and Exchanges.
6.46	Structuring the Buyer's Transaction.
6.47	____ Type of Payment.
6.48	____ Assumption of Seller's Liabilities.
6.49	____ Security to Seller.
6.50	____ Notes.
6.51	____ Escrow Arrangements and Agreements.
6.52	Drafting the Buyer's Asset Purchase Agreement.
6.53	____ Identification of the Parties.
6.54	____ Recitals.
6.55	____ Assets and Property to Be Conveyed.
6.56	____ Retained Assets of Seller.
6.57	____ Purchase Price and Method of Payment.
6.58	____ Closing.
6.59	____ Representations, Warranties and Covenants of Seller.
6.60	____ Representations, Warranties and Covenants of Buyer.
6.61	____ Conduct of Business Prior to Closing.
6.62	____ Indemnifications.
6.63	____ Corporate or Other Name.
6.64	____ ____ Notice to Customers and Suppliers.
6.65	____ ____ UCC Bulk Sale Notices or Escrow Agreement in Lieu of UCC Bulk Sale Notice.
6.66	____ ____ NYS Sales Tax and Bulk Sale Notification.
6.67	____ ____ Covenant Not to Compete.
6.68	____ Matters Respecting Real Property.
6.69	____ Conditions Precedent to Purchaser's Obligations.
6.70	____ Conditions Precedent to Seller's Obligations.
6.71	____ Nature and Survival of Representations and Warranties.
6.72	____ Non-disclosure Provisions.
6.73	____ Miscellaneous Agreements Between Buyer and Seller.
6.74	____ Documents to Be Delivered to Purchaser at Closing.
6.75	____ Documents to Be Delivered to Seller at Closing.
6.76	____ Notices, Severability and Other General Provisions.
6.77	____ Documents to Be Prepared or Reviewed Prior to Closing.
6.78	Drafting the Buyer's Stock Purchase Agreement.

TABLE OF CONTENTS

Sec.	
6.79	____ Identification of the Parties.
6.80	____ Recitals.
6.81	____ Sale of Shares.
6.82	____ Purchase Price and Method of Payment.
6.83	____ Closing.
6.84	____ Representations, Warranties and Covenants of Seller.
6.85	____ Representations, Warranties and Covenants of Buyer.
6.86	____ Conduct of Business Prior to Closing.
6.87	____ Indemnifications.
6.88	____ Covenant Not to Compete.
6.89	____ Matters Respecting Real Property.
6.90	____ Nondisclosure Provisions.
6.91	____ Conditions Precedent to Purchaser's Obligations.
6.92	____ Conditions Precedent to Seller's Obligations.
6.93	____ Nature and Survival of Representations and Warranties.
6.94	____ Documents to Be Delivered to Purchaser at Closing.
6.95	____ Documents to Be Delivered to Seller at Closing.
6.96	____ Notices, Severability and Other General Provisions.
6.97	____ Documents to Be Prepared or Reviewed Prior to Closing.
6.98	Post–Contract and Pre-closing.
6.99	____ Bulk Sales Act—UCC Article 6.
6.100	____ NYS Sales Tax and Bulk Sale Notification.
6.101	____ Plant Closing Notice.
6.102	____ Environmental Searches and Testing.
6.103	____ Certificate of Good Standing.
6.104	____ Real Property Transfer Gains Tax.
6.105	Closing and Post–Closing.
6.106	Strategy: Representing the Seller—Introduction.
6.107	____ The Attorney's Role.
6.108	____ Different Considerations Depending on the Type of Transaction.
6.109	____ General Stages of the Transaction.
6.110	Representing the Seller—General Investigation.
6.111	____ Investigating the Buyer.
6.112	____ The Negotiating Team.
6.113	____ The Letter of Intent.
6.114	____ Confidentiality Agreements.
6.115	____ Drafting the Agreement.
6.116	Tax Issues for the Seller—General Overview.
6.117	____ Asset Sale.
6.118	____ ____ Allocation of Purchase Price.
6.119	____ ____ Depreciation Recapture.
6.120	____ ____ Capital Gains or Losses.
6.121	____ ____ Ordinary Income.
6.122	____ ____ Income to Corporation.
6.123	____ ____ Real Property Transfer Gains Tax.
6.124	____ ____ Covenant Not to Compete and Consulting Agreements.
6.125	____ Stock Sale—General Advantages.
6.126	____ ____ Capital Gain or Loss.
6.127	____ ____ No Concern for Income to a Corporate Entity.

TABLE OF CONTENTS

Sec.
6.128 ____ ____ Real Property Transfer Gains Tax.
6.129 ____ ____ Consulting and Non-compete Agreements.
6.130 ____ ____ I.R.C. § 1244 Stock and Qualified Small Business Stock.
6.131 ____ ____ Stock Transfer Tax.
6.132 ____ ____ Collapsible Corporation.
6.133 ____ ____ Mergers, Consolidations and Exchanges.
6.134 Structuring the Seller's Transaction—General Overview.
6.135 ____ Purchase Price and Payment Terms.
6.136 ____ Security to Seller.
6.137 ____ Notes.
6.138 ____ Escrow Arrangements.
6.139 Drafting the Seller's Asset Sale Agreement.
6.140 ____ Identification of the Parties.
6.141 ____ Recitals.
6.142 ____ Assets and Property to Be Conveyed.
6.143 ____ Assets Retained by Seller.
6.144 ____ Sale Price and Method of Payment.
6.145 ____ Closing.
6.146 ____ Representations, Warranties and Covenants of Buyer.
6.147 ____ Representations, Warranties and Covenants of Seller.
6.148 ____ Conduct of Business Prior to Closing.
6.149 ____ Indemnifications.
6.150 ____ Matters Respecting Real Property.
6.151 ____ Notice to Customers and Suppliers.
6.152 ____ Covenant Not to Compete and Consulting Agreements.
6.153 ____ UCC Bulk Sale Notices or Escrow Agreements in Lieu of UCC Bulk Sale Notice.
6.154 ____ New York State Sales Tax and Bulk Sale Notification.
6.155 ____ Nature and Survival of Representations and Warranties.
6.156 ____ Non-disclosure Provisions.
6.157 ____ Conditions Precedent to Seller's Obligations.
6.158 ____ Conditions Precedent to Buyer's Obligations.
6.159 ____ Documents to Be Delivered to Seller at Closing.
6.160 ____ Documents to Be Delivered to Buyer at Closing.
6.161 ____ Notices, Severability and Other General Provisions.
6.162 ____ Documents to Be Prepared or Reviewed Prior to Closing.
6.163 Drafting the Seller's Stock Sale Agreement.
6.164 ____ Identification of the Parties.
6.165 ____ Recitals.
6.166 ____ Sale of Shares.
6.167 ____ Sale Price and Method of Payment.
6.168 ____ Closing.
6.169 ____ Representations, Warranties and Covenants of Buyer.
6.170 ____ Representations, Warranties and Covenants of Seller.
6.171 ____ Conduct of Business Prior to Closing.
6.172 ____ Indemnifications.
6.173 ____ Matters Respecting Real Property.
6.174 ____ Non-disclosure Provisions.
6.175 ____ Covenants Not to Compete and Consulting Agreements.
6.176 ____ Notice to Customers and Suppliers.

TABLE OF CONTENTS

Sec.
6.177 —— Conditions Precedent to Seller's Obligations.
6.178 —— Conditions Precedent to Buyer's Obligations.
6.179 —— Nature and Survival of Representations and Warranties.
6.180 —— Documents to Be Delivered to Seller at Closing.
6.181 —— Documents to Be Delivered to Buyer at Closing.
6.182 —— Notices, Severability and Other General Provisions.
6.183 —— Documents to Be Prepared or Reviewed Prior to Closing.
6.184 Post–contract and Pre-closing.
6.185 Closing and Post–Closing.
6.186 Forms.
6.187 —— Asset Purchase and Sale Agreement. 💾
6.188 —— Agreement of Purchase and Sale of Stock. 💾

Volume 21

CHAPTER 7. CONSUMER LAW

7.1 Scope Note.
7.2 Strategy—Generally.
7.3 —— Automobile Sales Cases.
7.4 —— Automobile Leasing Cases.
7.5 —— Credit Reporting.
7.6 —— Debt Collection.
7.7 —— Deceptive Business Practices.
7.8 —— Information to Obtain at Outset of Case.
7.9 Lemon Laws.
7.10 —— New Cars.
7.11 —— Used Cars.
7.12 —— Arbitration or Plenary Action?
7.13 —— Arbitration Procedure.
7.14 —— —— Preparation for the Hearing.
7.15 —— —— The Hearing.
7.16 —— —— Appeals and Confirmation Proceedings.
7.17 —— —— Scope of Review.
7.18 —— Source Materials.
7.19 Automobile Leasing—Overview.
7.20 —— Statutory Protection Overview.
7.21 —— The Consumer Leasing Act.
7.22 —— The Motor Vehicle Retail Leasing Act.
7.23 Motor Vehicle Installment Sales.
7.24 Repossession—Overview.
7.25 —— Prevention and Avoidance.
7.26 —— Defending Deficiency Claims.
7.27 Automobile Repairs.
7.28 Automobile Repair Shop Liens—Overview.
7.29 —— Statutory Challenges.
7.30 Credit Reporting—Overview.
7.31 —— Consumer Rights.
7.32 —— Non-litigation Strategies.
7.33 —— Litigating Credit Reporting Matters.

XXXI

TABLE OF CONTENTS

Sec.
- 7.34 Debt Collection—History and Overview.
- 7.35 ___ Claims for Intentional Infliction of Emotional Distress.
- 7.36 ___ Statutory Overview.
- 7.37 ___ FDCPA—Contacts With Third Parties.
- 7.38 ___ ___ Contacts With a Debtor.
- 7.39 ___ ___ Prohibited Tactics.
- 7.40 ___ ___ Improper Omissions and Disclosures.
- 7.41 ___ ___ Harassment or Abuse.
- 7.42 ___ ___ Improper Demands.
- 7.43 ___ ___ Judicial Enforcement.
- 7.44 ___ State Law.
- 7.45 Deceptive Practices Act—Overview.
- 7.46 ___ Elements of the Claim.
- 7.47 ___ Types of Recovery Available.
- 7.48 Drafting Checklist—List of Essential Allegations.
- 7.49 Forms—Lemon Law Document Request Pursuant to 13 NYCRR § 300.9(a).
- 7.50 ___ Notice of Petition to Vacate Lemon Law Arbitration Award Pursuant to CPLR Article 75.
- 7.51 ___ Petition to Vacate Lemon Law Arbitration Award Pursuant to CPLR Article 75.
- 7.52 ___ Complaint for Fraud, Breach of Warranties, Deceptive Business Practices, Used Car Lemon Law, Rescission and Revocation of Acceptance for Fraudulent Leasing Practices.
- 7.53 ___ Answer and Third-party Complaint Alleging Fraud, Deceptive Practices, Breach of Warranty, and Federal Odometer Law Claims in Fraudulent Automobile Lease Case.
- 7.54 ___ Answer to Complaint by Automobile Leasing Company for Deficiency Following Repossession, Alleging Commercially Unreasonable Resale and Deceptive Business Practices.
- 7.55 ___ Affirmation in Opposition to Lessor's Motion for Summary Judgment and in Support of Lessee's Cross-motion for Summary Judgment Alleging Commercially Unreasonable Resale.
- 7.56 ___ Notice of Rescission And/or Revocation of Acceptance and Demand for Restitution Pursuant to UCC 2–601 and 2–608.
- 7.57 ___ Order to Show Cause in Proceeding under Lien Law § 201–a to Vacate Garageman's Lien.
- 7.58 ___ Verified Petition in Proceeding under Lien Law § 201–a to Vacate Garageman's Lien.
- 7.59 ___ Affirmation in Support of Petition in Proceeding under Lien Law § 201–a to Vacate Garageman's Lien.
- 7.60 ___ Complaint Against Credit Reporting Agency Alleging Violations of the Fair Credit Reporting Act and the New York State Fair Credit Reporting Act and Deceptive Business Practices.
- 7.61 ___ Stipulation of Settlement of Plaintiff's Lemon Law Claims Providing for Cancellation of Lease and Deletion of Any Derogatory Credit Information.

TABLE OF CONTENTS

Sec.
7.62 ____ Complaint Alleging Violations of the Fair Debt Collection Practices Act and the Deceptive Practices Act. 💾
7.63 ____ Order to Show Cause with Temporary Restraining Order, Seeking Preliminary Injunction in Action Alleging Fraud, Deceptive Business Practices and Breach of Warranties. 💾
7.64 ____ Affirmation in Support of Temporary Restraining Order and Preliminary Injunction in Action Alleging Fraud, Deceptive Business Practices and Breach of Warranties. 💾
7.65 ____ Complaint in Action Alleging Fraud, Deceptive Business Practices and Breach of Warranties. 💾

CHAPTER 8. ENFORCEMENT OF MONEY JUDGMENTS

8.1 Scope Note.
8.2 Strategy.
8.3 Judgments—Generally.
8.4 ____ Methods to Obtain.
8.5 Form of Judgment—Judgment–Roll.
8.6 ____ Interest.
8.7 ____ Fees, Costs and Disbursements.
8.8 ____ Entry.
8.9 ____ Transcript of Judgment.
8.10 Matters Affecting Judgment—Vacatur.
8.11 ____ Satisfaction By Payment or Otherwise.
8.12 ____ Assignment.
8.13 ____ Death of Judgment Debtor.
8.14 ____ Amendment or Correction.
8.15 Actions on Judgments.
8.16 Entry of a Foreign Judgment—Sister–State Judgments.
8.17 ____ Federal Court Judgments.
8.18 ____ Foreign Country Judgments.
8.19 Judgment Enforcement Against Property—Definition of Property.
8.20 ____ Exemptions.
8.21 ____ Property in the Possession of Others.
8.22 ____ Disclosure of Property.
8.23 ____ ____ Subpoenas.
8.24 Article 52 Enforcement Devices—Introduction.
8.25 ____ Restraining Notices—Nature and Use.
8.26 ____ ____ Formal Requirements.
8.27 ____ ____ Service and Punishment for Disobedience.
8.28 ____ Execution.
8.29 ____ ____ Property Execution With Regard to Personal Property.
8.30 ____ ____ ____ Sale, Distribution and Priority In Proceeds.
8.31 ____ ____ Property Execution With Regard to Real Property.
8.32 ____ ____ ____ Notice and Sale of Real Property.
8.33 ____ ____ ____ Distribution of Proceeds of Sale and Conveyance of Title.
8.34 ____ Income Execution.
8.35 ____ Installment Payment Order—Nature and Purpose.
8.36 ____ ____ Form of Application and Service.

XXXIII

TABLE OF CONTENTS

Sec.
- 8.37 ____ Receiver.
- 8.38 ____ ____ Application, Appointment and Extension.
- 8.39 ____ Turnover Orders For Property or Debts.
- 8.40 ____ ____ Turnover Against the Judgment Debtor.
- 8.41 ____ ____ Turnover Against A Garnishee.
- 8.42 ____ Contempt.
- 8.43 ____ Arrest of the Judgment Debtor.
- 8.44 Protective Orders.
- 8.45 Proceeding To Determine Adverse Claims.
- 8.46 Forms.
- 8.47 ____ Statement For Judgment (Default Judgment), Affidavit of Facts Constituting the Claim, the Default and the Amount Due.
- 8.48 ____ Affidavit of Confession of Judgment and Judgment by Confession.
- 8.49 ____ Notice to Judgment Debtor [or Obligor].
- 8.50 ____ Subpoena (*Duces Tecum*) To Take Deposition of Judgment Debtor With Restraining Notice.
- 8.51 ____ Subpoena (*Duces Tecum*) To Take Deposition of Witness With Restraining Notice.
- 8.52 ____ Information Subpoena.
- 8.53 ____ Restraining Notice to Judgment Debtor.
- 8.54 ____ Execution.
- 8.55 ____ Income Execution.
- 8.56 ____ Affirmation and Order To Show Cause To Punish Judgment Debtor—Witness For Contempt.

CHAPTER 9. BANKRUPTCY

- 9.1 Scope Note.
- 9.2 Strategy.
- 9.3 ____ Checklist for Representing a Debtor.
- 9.4 ____ Checklist for Representing a Creditor.
- 9.5 Governing Law.
- 9.6 Nature of Cases Under Each Chapter of the Bankruptcy Code.
- 9.7 Eligibility to File.
- 9.8 Commencement of a Case—Voluntary Cases.
- 9.9 ____ Involuntary Cases.
- 9.10 ____ ____ Procedure.
- 9.11 ____ Additional Requirements.
- 9.12 ____ First–Day Orders.
- 9.13 Joint Administration.
- 9.14 Substantive Consolidation.
- 9.15 Types of Proceedings in Cases Under the Bankruptcy Code.
- 9.16 ____ Adversary Proceedings.
- 9.17 ____ Contested Matters.
- 9.18 Jurisdiction of the Bankruptcy Court.
- 9.19 ____ Types of Jurisdiction.
- 9.20 ____ Case Ancillary to Foreign Proceedings.
- 9.21 Venue.
- 9.22 Withdrawal of Reference.

XXXIV

TABLE OF CONTENTS

Sec.
9.23 Abstention.
9.24 Removal.
9.25 Appeals—To District Court and Bankruptcy Appellate Panel From Bankruptcy Court.
9.26 ___ To Court of Appeals From District Court.
9.27 The Debtor in Possession.
9.28 ___ Rights, Powers and Duties.
9.29 Employment of Professionals.
9.30 ___ Compensation.
9.31 ___ ___ Fee Applications.
9.32 U.S. Trustee.
9.33 ___ Duties Owed by Debtors and Trustees.
9.34 Bankruptcy Trustee.
9.35 Mediators.
9.36 Creditors.
9.37 ___ Meeting of Creditors.
9.38 ___ ___ Scope of Examination.
9.39 Examinations Under Bankruptcy Rule 2004.
9.40 ___ Notice Requirements.
9.41 ___ Subpoena.
9.42 Right of Parties in Interest to Be Heard.
9.43 Statutory Committees.
9.44 ___ Function and Duties.
9.45 ___ Right to Bring Litigation.
9.46 ___ Fiduciary Duty.
9.47 ___ Removal of Members.
9.48 ___ Organizational Meeting.
9.49 Property of the Estate.
9.50 Automatic Stay.
9.51 ___ Exceptions.
9.52 ___ Obtaining Relief.
9.53 ___ ___ Strategy.
9.54 ___ ___ Hearing.
9.55 ___ ___ Single Asset Real Estate Debtor.
9.56 Adequate Protection.
9.57 ___ Types.
9.58 ___ Strategy.
9.59 ___ Objections and Hearing.
9.60 Use, Sale, or Lease of Property.
9.61 ___ Ordinary Course of Business.
9.62 ___ Outside Ordinary Course of Business.
9.63 ___ Sales Free and Clear of Liens.
9.64 ___ Appeals from Order Authorizing Sale.
9.65 Cash Collateral.
9.66 ___ Strategy.
9.67 ___ Hearing.
9.68 ___ Postpetition Proceeds.
9.69 ___ ___ Security Interests in Rents and Hotel Revenues.
9.70 Abandonment of Property.
9.71 Postpetition Financing.

TABLE OF CONTENTS

Sec.
9.72 —— Hearing.
9.73 —— Appeals From Order Authorizing.
9.74 Executory Contracts and Unexpired Leases.
9.75 —— Strategy.
9.76 —— Time for Assumption or Rejection.
9.77 —— Nonresidential Real Property Leases.
9.78 —— Assumption by the Debtor.
9.79 —— Assumption and Assignment.
9.80 —— Exceptions to Assumption and Assignment.
9.81 —— Rejection by Debtor.
9.82 —— Damages Arising From Rejection: Debtor as Tenant/Lessee.
9.83 —— Calculation of Allowed Real Property Lease Rejection Damages.
9.84 —— Debtor as Landlord/Lessor.
9.85 —— Unexpired Personal Property Leases.
9.86 Collective Bargaining Agreements.
9.87 Retired Employees' Insurance Benefits.
9.88 —— Procedure for Modifying.
9.89 Utility Services.
9.90 Claims Procedures.
9.91 —— Filing Proofs of Claim or Interest.
9.92 —— —— Bar Dates.
9.93 —— Late-Filed Proofs of Claim.
9.94 —— Amendment of Proofs of Claim or Interest.
9.95 —— Withdrawal of Claims.
9.96 —— Allowance of, and Objections to, Claims or Interests.
9.97 —— Compromise and Settlement of Claims.
9.98 —— Allowance of Administrative Expense Claims.
9.99 —— Secured Claims.
9.100 —— —— Bifurcation of Claims.
9.101 —— —— Avoidance of Liens.
9.102 —— Interest on Claims and Charges Against Secured Claims.
9.103 —— Valuation of Collateral.
9.104 —— —— Methods of Valuation.
9.105 —— Reclamation Claims.
9.106 Priorities.
9.107 Subordination.
9.108 —— Strategy.
9.109 Setoff.
9.110 —— Strategy.
9.111 —— Characteristics of Claims.
9.112 Recoupment.
9.113 The Avoiding Powers.
9.114 —— Strategy.
9.115 —— Strong Arm Powers.
9.116 —— Avoidance of Certain Statutory Liens.
9.117 —— Preferences.
9.118 —— Exceptions to the Avoidance of Preferential Transfers.
9.119 —— Fraudulent Conveyances.
9.120 —— Liability of Transferee of Avoided Transfer.

XXXVI

TABLE OF CONTENTS

Sec.

9.121 —— Statute of Limitations and Standing.
9.122 —— Relation–Back Provision.
9.123 —— Reclamation.
9.124 Return of Goods by Debtor.
9.125 Exemptions.
9.126 —— Procedure.
9.127 —— Objections.
9.128 —— Lien Avoidance.
9.129 —— Liens on Exempt Property.
9.130 Reaffirmation of Debts.
9.131 —— Strategy.
9.132 Protection Against Discriminatory Treatment.
9.133 Tax Considerations.
9.134 Conversion and Dismissal of Cases Under Title 11.
9.135 Effect of Conversion.
9.136 Effect of Dismissal.
9.137 Closing and Reopening Cases.
9.138 Chapter 11—Appointment of a Trustee.
9.139 —— Duties of a Trustee.
9.140 —— Appointment of an Examiner.
9.141 —— Duties of an Examiner.
9.142 —— Exclusivity—Right to File a Plan.
9.143 —— —— Small Businesses.
9.144 —— —— Strategy: Representing a Debtor.
9.145 —— —— Strategy: Representing a Creditor.
9.146 —— —— Appealability of Orders.
9.147 —— Plan.
9.148 —— —— Mandatory Provisions.
9.149 —— —— Discretionary Provisions.
9.150 —— —— Exemption from Securities Registration.
9.151 —— —— Retention of Jurisdiction by the Court.
9.152 —— Classification of Claims.
9.153 —— —— Effect on Voting.
9.154 —— —— Substantially Similar Claims.
9.155 —— —— Convenience Class.
9.156 —— Recourse and Nonrecourse Claims: The § 1111(b) Election.
9.157 —— —— Strategy.
9.158 —— Impairment of Claims or Interests.
9.159 —— —— Rights Are Altered.
9.160 —— —— Defaults Are Not Cured.
9.161 —— Disclosure and Solicitation.
9.162 —— Acceptance of a Plan.
9.163 —— Prepackaged and Prenegotiated Plans.
9.164 —— Modification of a Plan.
9.165 —— Confirmation.
9.166 —— Cramdown.
9.167 —— Effect of Confirmation.
9.168 —— Discharge.
9.169 —— —— Limitations.
9.170 —— —— Release of Nondebtor.

XXXVII

TABLE OF CONTENTS

Sec.
9.171 ____ Channelling Injunctions: Asbestos–Related Cases.
9.172 ____ Plan Implementation.
9.173 ____ Small Business Reorganizations.
9.174 ____ Conversion or Dismissal of Cases.
9.175 ____ ____ Procedure.
9.176 ____ Closing and Reopening Cases.
9.177 Chapter 7—Overview.
9.178 ____ Commencement of a Case.
9.179 ____ Fees.
9.180 ____ Appointment of an Interim Trustee.
9.181 ____ Election of a Permanent Trustee.
9.182 ____ Duties of a Trustee.
9.183 ____ Employment of Professionals.
9.184 ____ Creditors' Committee.
9.185 ____ Protection Against Discriminatory Treatment.
9.186 ____ The Debtor's Statement of Intention.
9.187 ____ Exemptions.
9.188 ____ Redemption of Property.
9.189 ____ ____ Procedure.
9.190 ____ Reaffirmation of Debts.
9.191 ____ Abandonment of Property.
9.192 ____ Debtor's Surrender of Property and Records.
9.193 ____ Trustee's Turnover Powers.
9.194 ____ Liability of General Partners.
9.195 ____ Trustee's Operation of the Business.
9.196 ____ Executory Contracts.
9.197 ____ Adversary Proceedings to Avoid Liens and Transfers.
9.198 ____ ____ Statute of Limitations.
9.199 ____ Treatment of Certain Liens.
9.200 ____ Trustee's Sale of Assets.
9.201 ____ Disposition of Property Subject to the Interest of Another.
9.202 ____ Priorities.
9.203 ____ Special Tax Provisions.
9.204 ____ Discharge.
9.205 ____ ____ Exceptions to General Discharge of the Debtor.
9.206 ____ ____ Procedure for Objections to General Discharge of the Debtor.
9.207 ____ ____ Exceptions to Discharge of Particular Debts.
9.208 ____ ____ Procedure for Objections to Discharge of Particular Debts.
9.209 ____ Conversion or Dismissal of Cases.
9.210 ____ ____ Procedure.
9.211 ____ Closing and Reopening Cases.
9.212 Chapter 12—Overview.
9.213 ____ Rights and Powers of Debtor.
9.214 ____ Appointment of a Trustee.
9.215 ____ Duties of a Trustee.
9.216 ____ Automatic Stay.
9.217 ____ Property of the Estate.
9.218 ____ Sales Free of Interests.

XXXVIII

TABLE OF CONTENTS

Sec.
9.219 ____ Adequate Protection.
9.220 ____ Exclusivity—Right to File a Plan.
9.221 ____ Plan.
9.222 ____ ____ Mandatory Provisions.
9.223 ____ ____ Discretionary Provisions.
9.224 ____ ____ Modification.
9.225 ____ ____ Confirmation.
9.226 ____ ____ Confirmation: Objections.
9.227 ____ Disbursements.
9.228 ____ Effect of Confirmation.
9.229 ____ Discharge.
9.230 ____ Modification after Confirmation.
9.231 ____ Special Tax Provisions.
9.232 ____ Revocation of Confirmation Order.
9.233 ____ Conversion or Dismissal of Cases.
9.234 ____ ____ Procedure.
9.235 ____ Closing and Reopening Cases.
9.236 Chapter 13—Overview.
9.237 ____ Eligibility.
9.238 ____ Rights and Powers of Debtor.
9.239 ____ Appointment of a Trustee.
9.240 ____ Duties of a Trustee.
9.241 ____ Automatic Stay.
9.242 ____ ____ Relief.
9.243 ____ Property of the Estate.
9.244 ____ ____ Use, Sale, or Lease.
9.245 ____ Exclusivity—Right to File a Plan.
9.246 ____ Plan.
9.247 ____ ____ Mandatory Provisions.
9.248 ____ ____ Discretionary Provisions.
9.249 ____ ____ Discretionary Provisions: Debtor's Principal Residence.
9.250 ____ ____ Modification.
9.251 ____ ____ Confirmation.
9.252 ____ ____ Confirmation: Objections.
9.253 ____ ____ Confirmation: Effect.
9.254 ____ Payments.
9.255 ____ Discharge.
9.256 ____ ____ Exceptions.
9.257 ____ ____ Objections.
9.258 ____ ____ Revocation.
9.259 ____ Postconfirmation Modification of a Plan.
9.260 ____ Revocation of Confirmation Order.
9.261 ____ Conversion or Dismissal of Cases.
9.262 ____ ____ Procedure.
9.263 ____ Closing and Reopening Cases.
9.264 Procedural Checklist—Commencing a Voluntary Case.
9.265 ____ Lists and Schedules to be Filed at the Commencement of a Case Under Chapter 7, 11, 12, or 13.
9.266 ____ Commencing an Adversary Proceeding.
9.267 ____ Commencing a Contested Matter.

TABLE OF CONTENTS

Sec.
9.268 ___ Appeal from an Interlocutory Judgment, Order, or Decree of a Bankruptcy Judge.
9.269 ___ Creditor's Motion to Request Relief from the Automatic Stay.
9.270 ___ Creditor's Motion to Obtain Adequate Protection.
9.271 ___ Debtor's Motion to Use, Sell, or Lease Property of the Estate.
9.272 ___ Debtor's Motion to Request Use of Cash Collateral.
9.273 ___ Cash Collateral Stipulation.
9.274 ___ Debtor's Motion to Obtain Postpetition Financing.
9.275 ___ Request to Assume, Reject, or Assign an Executory Contract or Unexpired Nonresidential Real Property Lease.
9.276 ___ Debtor's Motion to Reject or Modify a Collective Bargaining Agreement.
9.277 ___ Debtor's Motion to Obtain Approval of a Compromise and Settlement of a Claim.
9.278 ___ Claiming Exemptions.
9.279 ___ Debtor's Motion to Avoid a Judicial Lien or a Nonpossessory, Nonpurchase–Money Security Interest that Impairs Exempt Property.
9.280 ___ Debtor's Motion to Obtain Court Approval of a Reaffirmation Agreement.
9.281 ___ Debtor's Motion to Request an Extension of Exclusivity.
9.282 ___ Filing a Chapter 11 Plan and Disclosure Statement.
9.283 ___ Soliciting Acceptance of a Chapter 11 Plan.
9.284 ___ Filing a Chapter 12 or 13 Plan of Debt Adjustment.
9.285 ___ Objection to a Chapter 12 or 13 Plan.
9.286 ___ Debtor's Motion to Request Modification of a Chapter 12 or 13 Plan after Confirmation
9.287 Drafting Checklist—General Rules for all Motions, Applications, and Complaints.
9.288 ___ Complaint in an Adversary Proceeding.
9.289 ___ Motion for Leave to Appeal From an Interlocutory Judgment, Order, or Decree of a Bankruptcy Judge.
9.290 ___ Motion for a Stay of a Bankruptcy Court Judgment or Order Pending Appeal.
9.291 ___ Application of Debtor or Statutory Committee to Retain Professionals.
9.292 ___ Creditor's Motion to Request Relief From the Automatic Stay.
9.293 ___ Creditor's Motion to Obtain Adequate Protection.
9.294 ___ Debtor's Motion to Use, Sell, or Lease Property of the Estate.
9.295 ___ Debtor's Motion to Request Use of Cash Collateral.
9.296 ___ Cash Collateral Stipulation.
9.297 ___ Debtor's Motion to Obtain Postpetition Financing.
9.298 ___ Motion to Assume or Reject an Executory Contract or Unexpired Non-residential Real Property Lease.
9.299 ___ Debtor's Motion to Reject or Modify a Collective Bargaining Agreement (CBA).
9.300 ___ Debtor's Motion to Obtain Approval of a Compromise and Settlement of a Claim.

TABLE OF CONTENTS

Sec.
9.301 ____ Debtor's Motion to Avoid a Judicial Lien or a Nonpossessory, Nonpurchase–Money Security Interest that Impairs Exempt Property.
9.302 ____ Reaffirmation Agreement.
9.303 ____ Debtor's Motion for Approval of a Reaffirmation Agreement.
9.304 ____ Debtor's Motion to Request an Extension of Exclusivity.
9.305 Forms—Notice of Appearance and Demand for Service of Documents. 💾
9.306 ____ Contested Matter—Motion. 💾
9.307 ____ ____ Notice of Motion. 💾
9.308 ____ ____ Proposed Order. 💾
9.309 ____ Adversary Proceeding—Complaint. 💾
9.310 ____ Retention of Professionals—Application. 💾
9.311 ____ ____ Affidavit. 💾
9.312 ____ Plan Provision for Retention of Jurisdiction. 💾

CHAPTER 10. MECHANIC'S LIENS

10.1 Scope Note.
10.2 Strategy.
10.3 Nature of Mechanic's Lien.
10.4 Creation of Mechanic's Lien—Elements.
10.5 ____ ____ Protected Class.
10.6 ____ ____ Improvements to Real Property.
10.7 ____ ____ Consent or Request of Owner.
10.8 Extent of Lien—Ownership Interest at Time of Filing.
10.9 ____ Sale of Property.
10.10 ____ Insurance Proceeds.
10.11 ____ Amount.
10.12 ____ Loss of Profits.
10.13 Subcontractors and Materialmen—Derivative Rights.
10.14 ____ ____ Statutory Protections.
10.15 Procedure—Notice of Lien.
10.16 ____ ____ Contents.
10.17 ____ ____ Filing.
10.18 ____ ____ Service.
10.19 Amendment of Notice of Lien.
10.20 Lien for Private Improvements—Checklist.
10.21 Liens Under Contract for Public Improvements—Extent of Lien.
10.22 ____ Notice of Lien.
10.23 ____ Filing of Notice of Lien.
10.24 ____ Notice of Completion and Acceptance.
10.25 ____ Checklist.
10.26 Lien Priorities—Private Improvements—Parity of Mechanic's Liens.
10.27 ____ ____ Assignments of Contract Rights.
10.28 ____ ____ Building Loan Mortgages.
10.29 ____ ____ Contracts of Sale.
10.30 ____ ____ Seller's Mortgage.
10.31 ____ ____ Deeds.

XLI

TABLE OF CONTENTS

Sec.

10.32	——— Contracts for Public Improvements.
10.33	Assignment of Liens.
10.34	Assignments of Contracts for Private Improvements and Orders to be Filed—Filing of Notice of Assignment.
10.35	——— Contents of Notice of Assignment.
10.36	——— Extension of Term of Notice of Assignment.
10.37	Assignment of Contracts and Orders for Public Improvements.
10.38	Duration of Lien for Private Improvements—Notice of Pendency.
10.39	——— Extensions.
10.40	Duration of Lien Under Contract for a Public Improvement—Notice of Pendency.
10.41	——— Extension of Lien.
10.42	Discharge of Lien for Private Improvement—Satisfaction of Lien.
10.43	——— Expiration of Term.
10.44	——— Termination of Notice of Pendency.
10.45	——— Failure to Prosecute.
10.46	——— Undertaking.
10.47	——— Judgment.
10.48	——— Defective Lien.
10.49	——— Deposit of Money with County Clerk or Court.
10.50	Discharge of Lien for Public Improvement—Satisfaction of Lien.
10.51	——— Expiration of Lien.
10.52	——— Satisfaction of Judgment.
10.53	——— Deposit of Money.
10.54	——— Undertaking.
10.55	——— Retention of Credit.
10.56	——— Invalidity of Lien.
10.57	——— Failure to Prosecute.
10.58	——— Procedures.
10.59	Building Loan Contracts—Filing Requirements.
10.60	——— Checklist.
10.61	Subordination of Liens—Agreement with Owner.
10.62	——— ——— Postponement of Judgments.
10.63	Subordination of Liens to Subsequent Mortgage.
10.64	Subordination of Notices of *Lis Pendens*.
10.65	Discharge of Liens on Sale of Real Property.
10.66	Limitations on Waiver of Mechanic's Lien.
10.67	Effect of Filing of Notice of Lien on Right of Arbitration.
10.68	Bond to Discharge Liens—Effect of Bond.
10.69	——— Requirements of Bond.
10.70	——— Claim Against Bond.
10.71	——— Notice of Claim.
10.72	——— Action on Bond.
10.73	——— Discharge of Liens and Notices of Claims.
10.74	Protecting the Owner—Itemized Statement.
10.75	——— Lien Wilfully Exaggerated.
10.76	Repossession of Materials Not Used.
10.77	Enforcement of Mechanic's Liens—Courts.
10.78	——— Courts of Record—Procedures.
10.79	——— ——— Necessary Parties.

TABLE OF CONTENTS

Sec.
10.80 ___ Actions in a Court Not of Record—Summons and Complaint.
10.81 ___ ___ Proceedings Upon Return of Summons.
10.82 ___ ___ Judgments and Transcripts.
10.83 ___ Costs and Disbursements.
10.84 ___ Effect of Failure to Establish Lien.
10.85 ___ Deposit of Money or Securities to Discharge Lien—Procedures.
10.86 ___ ___ Effect of Order.
10.87 ___ ___ Preference Over Contractors.
10.88 ___ ___ Delivery of Property in Lieu of Money.
10.89 ___ Deficiency Judgment.
10.90 ___ Vacating of Mechanic's Lien, Cancellation of Bond or Return of Deposit.
10.91 ___ Public Improvements.
10.92 ___ New Parties.
10.93 ___ Service of Answer on State or Public Corporation.
10.94 Trust Funds—Purpose.
10.95 ___ Creation.
10.96 ___ Contractors and Subcontractors.
10.97 ___ Beneficiaries.
10.98 Diversion of Trust Assets.
10.99 Notice of Lending.
10.100 Record Keeping Obligations.
10.101 Right of Beneficiaries to Examine Books or Records.
10.102 Action to Enforce Trust—Standing and Procedure.
10.103 ___ Remedies.
10.104 ___ Preferences.
10.105 Relief After Judgment on Obligation Constituting Trust Claim; Effect on Mechanic's Liens.
10.106 Misappropriation of Trust Funds.
10.107 Procedural Checklist.
10.108 Forms.
10.109 ___ Notice of Mechanic's Lien—General Form.
10.110 ___ Notice of Lien for Public Improvement.
10.111 ___ Form For Demand for Terms of Contract.
10.112 ___ Demand for Notice of Completion and Acceptance of Public Improvement.
10.113 ___ Petition to Amend Notice of Mechanic's Lien—Correct Name of Owner of Property.
10.114 ___ Assignment of Lien for Public Improvement.
10.115 ___ Assignment of Mechanic's Lien.
10.116 ___ Assignment of Moneys Due or to Become Due Under Public Improvement Contract.
10.117 ___ Affidavit for Continuance of Mechanic's Lien.
10.118 ___ Affidavit for Continuance of Lien for Public Improvement.
10.119 ___ Petition to Discharge Mechanic's Lien Where Notice of Lien Defective.
10.120 ___ Petition for Order Discharging Mechanic's Lien Upon Filing of Undertaking.

XLIII

TABLE OF CONTENTS

Sec.
10.121 ____ Undertaking to Discharge Mechanic's Lien. 💾
10.122 ____ Petition for Order Fixing Amount of Undertaking to Discharge Mechanic's Lien. 💾
10.123 ____ Approval by Lienors of Subordination of Mechanic's Liens to Trust Bond or Note and Mortgage. 💾
10.124 ____ Affidavit for Order Fixing Amount of Bond to Discharge All Mechanic's Liens. 💾
10.125 ____ Petition for Order Requiring Itemized Statement. 💾
10.126 ____ Notice of Application for Order Requiring Itemized Statement. 💾
10.127 ____ Demand for Itemized Statement. 💾
10.128 ____ Affidavit in Support of Application to Cancel Mechanic's Lien for Failure to Furnish Itemized Statement. 💾
10.129 ____ Notice Requiring Lienor to Commence Action to Enforce Mechanic's Lien. 💾
10.130 ____ Affidavit in Support of Application to Cancel Notice of Mechanic's Lien for Failure to Commence Action. 💾
10.131 ____ Notice Requiring Lienor to Commence Action to Enforce Lien for Public Improvement. 💾
10.132 ____ Affidavit in Support of Application to Cancel Notice of Lien for Public Improvement for Failure to Commence Action. 💾
10.133 ____ Complaint for Foreclosure of Lien for Public Improvement. 💾
10.134 ____ Complaint for Foreclosure of Mechanic's Lien—Contractor. 💾
10.135 ____ Defense and Counterclaim Based on Wilful Exaggeration of Mechanic's Lien. 💾
10.136 ____ Affidavit in Support of Motion to Consolidate Actions for Foreclosure of Mechanic's Liens. 💾
10.137 ____ Notice of Motion to Consolidate Actions to Foreclose Mechanic's Liens. 💾
10.138 ____ Acceptance of Offer to Pay Money Into Court in Discharge of Mechanic's Lien. 💾
10.139 ____ Offer to Pay Money Into Court in Discharge of Mechanic's Lien. 💾
10.140 ____ Judgment of Foreclosure and Sale—Mechanic's Lien. 💾
10.141 ____ Judgment of Foreclosure—Lien for Public Improvement—Where Lien Discharged and Fund Retained for Payment. 💾
10.142 ____ Affidavit in Support of Motion for Summary Judgment—Foreclosure of Lien for Public Improvement. 💾
10.143 ____ Demand for Verified Statement from Trustee. 💾
10.144 ____ Petition for Verified Statement from Trustee of Trust Funds. 💾
10.145 ____ Complaint by Subcontractor to Enforce Trust Against Funds Received by Contractor or Assignee of Contractor. 💾
10.146 ____ Complaint by Surety to Have Parties Declared Trustees of Subcontract Moneys and for Accounting. 💾
10.147 ____ Affidavit in Support of Motion to Determine if Class Action Can be Maintained—Action to Impress and Enforce Trust. 💾

TABLE OF CONTENTS

CHAPTER 11. MORTGAGE FORECLOSURE

Sec.
11.1	Scope Note.
11.2	Strategy—Initial Client Interview.
11.3	___ First Review of Loan Documents.
11.4	___ Foreclosure Title Certificate.
11.5	New York Mortgage Foreclosure Law.
11.6	___ Choice of Remedies: Foreclosure Action or Money Action.
11.7	___ Partial Foreclosure Action.
11.8	___ Non-Judicial Foreclosure.
11.9	Representing Subordinate Lienors.
11.10	Pre-commencement Procedure.
11.11	___ Notice of Default.
11.12	___ Notice of Acceleration.
11.13	___ Foreclosure Title Certificate.
11.14	Determining the Necessary Defendants.
11.15	___ The United States As a Necessary Defendant.
11.16	Starting the Foreclosure Action.
11.17	___ Notice of Pendency of Action.
11.18	Summons.
11.19	___ Venue.
11.20	Complaint.
11.21	___ Allegations Regarding Parties.
11.22	___ Allegations Regarding Loan, Note and Mortgage.
11.23	___ References to Pertinent Terms of Note and Mortgage.
11.24	___ Asserting Default(s).
11.25	___ Reserving Right to Add Advances Made by Plaintiff to Indebtedness Secured by Mortgage.
11.26	___ Allegation Regarding Subordinate Interest of Defendant(s).
11.27	___ Whether There Has Been or is Pending Another Action Regarding the Mortgage Debt.
11.28	___ Amendments.
11.29	Receivers.
11.30	___ Considerations in Determining Whether to Seek Appointment of Receiver.
11.31	___ *Ex Parte* Motion for Appointment of Receiver.
11.32	___ Compensation.
11.33	___ Opposing Appointment of Receiver.
11.34	___ Discharging Receiver.
11.35	Defendant's Response.
11.36	___ Motion to Dismiss Complaint.
11.37	___ Answer and Defenses.
11.38	___ Notice of Appearance and Waiver.
11.39	Obtaining Judgment.
11.40	___ Motion for Judgment.
11.41	___ Opposing Motion for Judgment.
11.42	Reference to Compute.
11.43	___ Hearing Before Referee to Compute.
11.44	___ Report of Referee to Compute.
11.45	___ Motion to Confirm Referee's Computation Report and for Judgment of Foreclosure and Sale.

TABLE OF CONTENTS

Sec.
11.46 Judgment of Foreclosure and Sale.
11.47 Foreclosure Sale.
11.48 ____ Noticing and Advertising the Sale.
11.49 ____ Conducting the Sale.
11.50 ____ Vacating the Sale.
11.51 Referee's Deed, Other Closing Documents and Referee's Report of Sale.
11.52 Deficiency Judgment.
11.53 Surplus Money Proceedings.
11.54 Eviction of Tenants and Other Occupants After Foreclosure Sale.
11.55 Drafting Checklists.
11.56 ____ Notice of Default.
11.57 ____ Notice of Acceleration.
11.58 ____ Notice of Pendency of Action.
11.59 ____ Summons.
11.60 ____ Complaint.
11.61 ____ Order Appointing Receiver.
11.62 ____ Affidavit in Support of *Ex Parte* Application for Receiver.
11.63 ____ Notice of Motion for Summary Judgment and Related Relief.
11.64 ____ Affidavit of Regularity and in Support of Plaintiff's Motion for Summary Judgment and Related Relief.
11.65 ____ Judgment of Foreclosure and Sale.
11.66 ____ Notice of Sale.
11.67 ____ Terms and Memorandum of Sale.
11.68 Forms.
11.69 ____ Notice of Default. 💾
11.70 ____ Notice of Acceleration. 💾
11.71 ____ Notice of Pendency of Action. 💾
11.72 ____ Summons. 💾
11.73 ____ Verified Complaint for Foreclosure of Mortgage Affecting Single Family Residence. 💾
11.74 ____ Verified Complaint for Foreclosure of Mortgage Affecting Commercial, Multi–Unit Residential or Mixed Property. 💾
11.75 ____ Order Appointing Receiver. 💾
11.76 ____ Affidavit in Support of Motion for Appointment of Receiver. 💾
11.77 ____ Notice of Motion for Summary Judgment and Related Relief. 💾
11.78 ____ Affidavit of Regularity and in Support of Motion for Summary Judgment. 💾
11.79 ____ Judgment of Foreclosure and Sale. 💾
11.80 ____ Notice of Sale. 💾
11.81 ____ Terms and Memorandum of Sale. 💾

CHAPTER 12. PURCHASE AND SALE OF REAL ESTATE

12.1 Scope Note.
12.2 Strategy.
12.3 ____ Pre-contract Checklist.
12.4 Contract of Sale.

TABLE OF CONTENTS

Sec.
12.5 ____ Preparation and Delivery
12.6 ____ Recordation.
12.7 Residential Contract of Sale.
12.8 ____ Parties.
12.9 ____ Premises.
12.10 ____ Personal Property.
12.11 ____ Purchase Price and Method of Payment.
12.12 ____ ____ Down Payment.
12.13 ____ ____ Assumption of Existing Mortgage.
12.14 ____ ____ Purchase Money Mortgage.
12.15 ____ ____ Mortgage Contingency.
12.16 ____ ____ Acceptable Funds.
12.17 ____ Permitted Exceptions.
12.18 ____ Governmental Violations and Orders.
12.19 ____ Seller's Representations.
12.20 ____ Condition of Property.
12.21 ____ Insurable and Marketable Title.
12.22 ____ Closing, Deed and Title.
12.23 ____ Closing Date and Place.
12.24 ____ Conditions to Closing.
12.25 ____ Deed Transfer and Recording Taxes.
12.26 ____ Apportionments.
12.27 ____ Allowance for Unpaid Taxes.
12.28 ____ Title Examination; Seller's Inability to Convey; Limitation of Liability.
12.29 ____ Defaults and Remedies.
12.30 ____ Assignment.
12.31 ____ Broker.
12.32 ____ Risk of Loss.
12.33 Condominium Contract of Sale.
12.34 ____ Comparisons to the Residential Contract of Sale.
12.35 ____ Homeowner's Associations.
12.36 Contract of Sale for Office, Commercial and Multi-family Residential Premises.
12.37 Contract of Sale for Cooperative Apartment
12.38 ____ Standard Form.
12.39 Contract of Sale for New Construction.
12.40 Title Insurance.
12.41 ____ The Buyer's Obligation.
12.42 ____ Role of the Title Insurer.
12.43 ____ Duration and Cost.
12.44 ____ Basic and Extended Coverage.
12.45 Title Insurance Policy.
12.46 ____ Loan Policy Coverage.
12.47 ____ New York Modifications of Loan Policy.
12.48 ____ Owner's Policy Coverage.
12.49 ____ New York Modifications of Owner's Policy.
12.50 ____ Standard Exceptions.
12.51 ____ Endorsements.
12.52 ____ Exclusions.

TABLE OF CONTENTS

Sec.
12.53 Title Examination: Recording Title and the Torrens System.
12.54 ___ Objections to Be Disposed of Prior to Closing.
12.55 ___ ___ Checklist.
12.56 The Survey Map.
12.57 ___ What it May Disclose.
12.58 ___ Effect on Marketability of Title.
12.59 ___ ___ Where Contract Is Silent on the Matter of Survey.
12.60 ___ ___ Where Contract Subject to Any State of Facts an Accurate Survey May Show.
12.61 ___ ___ Where Contract Subject to Any State of Facts an Accurate Survey May Show Provided Same Does Not Render Title Unmarketable.
12.62 ___ ___ Where Contract Subject to Specific Encroachments or to Facts Shown on a Specific Survey.
12.63 ___ ___ Suggested Clause.
12.64 Marketability of Title.
12.65 ___ What Renders Title Unmarketable.
12.66 ___ ___ Encroachments Due to Adverse Possession.
12.67 ___ ___ Party Walls.
12.68 ___ Driveway Easements.
12.69 ___ Other Covenants and Restrictions.
12.70 ___ Reservations for Public Utilities.
12.71 ___ Land Abutting Bodies of Water and the Federal Navigational Servitude.
12.72 Closing of Title.
12.73 ___ Checklist.
12.74 ___ Recording Fees and Filings.
12.75 ___ Disclosure and Other Requirements.
12.76 ___ ___ Foreign Investors Real Property Tax.
12.77 ___ ___ Form 1099–S Federal Requirement for One to Four Family Residence.
12.78 ___ ___ Form 1099–S Federal Requirement for One to Four Family Residence—Checklist.
12.79 ___ ___ Cash Payments Received by Businesses in Excess of $10,000.
12.80 ___ ___ Lead Paint Hazards.
12.81 ___ ___ Agricultural Foreign Investment Disclosure Act.
12.82 ___ Payment of Taxes.
12.83 ___ ___ New York State Real Estate Transfer Tax and Mansion Tax.
12.84 ___ ___ Article 31–B—Real Property Transfer Gains Tax.
12.85 ___ ___ New York City Real Property Transfer Tax.
12.86 ___ ___ Cities of Mount Vernon and Yonkers.
12.87 ___ ___ Real Estate Investment Trusts.
12.88 ___ ___ Mortgage Recording Tax Outside New York City.
12.89 ___ ___ Mortgage Recording Tax Rate in New York City.
12.90 ___ Method of Payment.
12.91 ___ Other Required Forms and Information.
12.92 Forms.
12.93 ___ Residential Contract of Sale.

TABLE OF CONTENTS

Sec.
12.94 ___ Contract of Sale—Condominium Unit.
12.95 ___ ___ Office, Commercial and Multi–Family Residential Premises.
12.96 ___ ___ Cooperative Apartment.
12.97 ___ Durable General Power of Attorney. 💾
12.98 ___ Power of Attorney to Take Effect at a Later Time. 💾

Volume 22

CHAPTER 13. LANDLORD–TENANT LAW

13.1 Scope Note.
13.2 Strategy.
13.3 ___ Checklists.
13.4 Summary Proceedings.
13.5 ___ Venue and Jurisdiction.
13.6 ___ Service of Process.
13.7 ___ ___ Personal Delivery.
13.8 ___ ___ Substituted Service.
13.9 ___ ___ Conspicuous Place Service.
13.10 ___ ___ New York City Civil Court "Postcard Requirement."
13.11 Non-payment Proceedings.
13.12 ___ Rent Demands.
13.13 ___ Notice of Petition.
13.14 ___ ___ Form of Notice.
13.15 ___ ___ Content of Notice.
13.16 ___ ___ Defects in the Notice.
13.17 ___ The Petition.
13.18 ___ ___ Defects in the Petition.
13.19 ___ ___ Verification.
13.20 ___ ___ Defects in the Verification.
13.21 Responding to the Non-payment Petition.
13.22 ___ The Answer.
13.23 ___ The Motion to Dismiss.
13.24 ___ The RPAPL § 755 Motion to Stay.
13.25 Tenant Defenses to the Non-payment Proceeding.
13.26 ___ No Landlord Tenant Relationship.
13.27 ___ Tenant Out of Possession.
13.28 ___ Statutory Noncompliance.
13.29 ___ Illegal Rent.
13.30 ___ Actual Eviction.
13.31 ___ Constructive Eviction.
13.32 ___ Warranty of Habitability.
13.33 ___ Laches.
13.34 ___ Payment.
13.35 Holdover Proceedings.
13.36 ___ Predicate Notices.
13.37 ___ ___ Month-to-Month Tenants.
13.38 ___ ___ Illegal Use.
13.39 ___ ___ Rent–Controlled Tenants.

XLIX

TABLE OF CONTENTS

Sec.
13.40 ____ ____ Rent–Stabilized Tenants.
13.41 ____ The Notice of Petition.
13.42 ____ ____ Defects in the Notice.
13.43 ____ ____ Holdover Petition—Form and Content.
13.44 ____ ____ Defects in the Petition.
13.45 ____ ____ Verification and Verification Defects.
13.46 Responding to the Holdover Petition.
13.47 ____ The Answer.
13.48 ____ The Motion to Dismiss.
13.49 Tenant Defenses to the Holdover Proceeding.
13.50 ____ Acceptance of Rent After Expiration or Termination of Tenancy.
13.51 ____ Defective Predicate Notice.
13.52 ____ ____ Rent–Regulated Apartments.
13.53 ____ Waiver.
13.54 ____ Equitable Estoppel.
13.55 ____ Succession Rights to Rent–Regulated Apartments.
13.56 Counterclaims.
13.57 Bill of Particulars.
13.58 Discovery.
13.59 ____ Notice to Admit.
13.60 ____ Freedom of Information Law.
13.61 The Trial—Adjournments.
13.62 ____ Amending Petition and Burden of Proof.
13.63 Stipulations—Overview.
13.64 ____ Non-payment Proceedings.
13.65 ____ Holdover Proceedings.
13.66 ____ Enforcement and Vacatur.
13.67 The Judgment and Warrant.
13.68 ____ Staying the Warrant in Non-payment Proceedings.
13.69 ____ Staying the Warrant in New York City Residential Holdover Proceedings.
13.70 Yellowstone Actions.
13.71 ____ Obtaining the Injunction.
13.72 Article 7–A Proceedings.
13.73 Rent Regulatory Proceedings.
13.74 ____ Rent Overcharge.
13.75 ____ Service Reduction.
13.76 ____ Major Capital Improvement Rent Increase.
13.77 Checklist of Essential Allegations.
13.78 ____ Petition Non-payment.
13.79 ____ Holdover Petition.
13.80 ____ Stipulation Settling Non-payment Proceeding.
13.81 ____ Stipulation Settling Holdover Proceeding.
13.82 Forms.
13.83 ____ Petition Non-payment. 💾
13.84 ____ Petition Holdover. 💾
13.85 ____ Individual Verification. 💾
13.86 ____ Corporate Officer Verification. 💾
13.87 ____ Partnership Verification. 💾

L

TABLE OF CONTENTS

Sec.
13.88 ____ Attorney Verification.
13.89 ____ Stipulations.
13.90 ____ ____ Settling Non-payment Proceeding.
13.91 ____ ____ Settling Non-payment Proceeding With Final Judgment in Favor of Petitioner.
13.92 ____ ____ Settling Holdover Proceeding Where Tenant Agrees to Cure Lease Violation.
13.93 ____ ____ Settling Holdover Proceeding Where Tenant–Respondent Agrees to Vacate Premises.

CHAPTER 14. EMINENT DOMAIN

14.1 Scope Note.
14.2 Strategies for Condemnors and Condemnees.
14.3 Exercise of the Power of Eminent Domain.
14.4 ____ The State as Condemnor.
14.5 ____ Other Public Entities as Condemnor.
14.6 ____ Private Entities.
14.7 Property Rights Subject to Acquisition.
14.8 ____ Real Property.
14.9 ____ Easements.
14.10 ____ Leases.
14.11 ____ Personal Property.
14.12 ____ Public Property/Priority of Taking.
14.13 ____ Excess Property.
14.14 *De Facto* Taking.
14.15 Public Use, Benefit or Purpose.
14.16 ____ Particular Uses.
14.17 ____ Incidental Private Benefit.
14.18 Just Compensation.
14.19 Summary.
14.20 The First Stage: The Condemnation Phase.
14.21 Public Hearing.
14.22 Exemptions From the Public Hearing Requirement.
14.23 ____ Overlap with Other Governmental Requirements.
14.24 ____ Overlap with Issuance of a Certificate of Environmental Compatibility and Public Need.
14.25 ____ Alternate Public Hearing.
14.26 ____ *De Minimis* Acquisition or Emergency Situation.
14.27 ____ Section 41.34 of the Mental Hygiene Law.
14.28 Notice.
14.29 Conduct of the Public Hearing and Requirement of a Record.
14.30 Determination and Findings.
14.31 ____ Publication of Synopsis.
14.32 ____ Interplay with SEQRA.
14.33 ____ Amendments for Field Conditions.
14.34 Judicial Review of Determination and Findings.
14.35 ____ Prerequisite Determination.
14.36 ____ Persons Entitled to Review.
14.37 ____ 30–Day Statute of Limitations.

TABLE OF CONTENTS

Sec.
14.38 ____ Scope of Review.
14.39 Summary.
14.40 The Second Stage—The "Offer and Negotiation" Phase.
14.41 ____ Pretaking Appraisals.
14.42 ____ Pretaking Discovery.
14.43 ____ Offer as Payment in Full.
14.44 ____ Advance Payment.
14.45 Use and Occupancy by Condemnee After Taking.
14.46 Summary.
14.47 The Third Stage—The Acquisition Phase.
14.48 ____ Court of Claims v. Supreme Court Jurisdiction.
14.49 ____ Statute of Limitations for Bringing an Acquisition Proceeding.
14.50 ____ ____ Acquisition in Stages.
14.51 ____ Acquisition Map.
14.52 Acquisition of Property—Court of Claims Jurisdiction.
14.53 ____ Condemnors Subject to Court of Claims Jurisdiction.
14.54 ____ Filing and Notice Requirements.
14.55 ____ Vesting of Title.
14.56 Acquisition of Property—Supreme Court Jurisdiction.
14.57 ____ Notice of Pendency.
14.58 ____ Petition in Condemnation.
14.59 ____ ____ Content.
14.60 ____ ____ Additional Content Rules for Certain Non-governmental Condemnors.
14.61 ____ Notice.
14.62 ____ ____ Certification of Names of Reputed Condemnees.
14.63 ____ Answer by Condemnee.
14.64 ____ ____ Defenses.
14.65 ____ Vesting of Title and Order of Condemnation.
14.66 Notice of Acquisition.
14.67 Immediate Entry.
14.68 Summary.
14.69 The Fourth Stage—The Compensation Phase.
14.70 ____ Court of Claims.
14.71 ____ ____ Time to File Claim.
14.72 ____ ____ Service.
14.73 ____ Supreme Court.
14.74 ____ ____ Time to File Claim.
14.75 ____ ____ Service.
14.76 Content of Claim.
14.77 Scope of Just Compensation.
14.78 ____ "Highest and Best Use."
14.79 ____ Total Taking.
14.80 ____ ____ Direct Damages.
14.81 ____ ____ Improvements.
14.82 ____ Partial Taking.
14.83 ____ Temporary Taking.
14.84 ____ ____ Easements.
14.85 Methods of Valuation to Determine Compensation.

LII

TABLE OF CONTENTS

Sec.
14.86 ____ Market Approach to Value.
14.87 ____ Income Approach to Value.
14.88 ____ Cost Approach to Value.
14.89 Specialty Property.
14.90 Effect of Environmental Contamination on Property Value.
14.91 Fixtures.
14.92 ____ Compensable Fixtures.
14.93 ____ Valuation of Fixtures.
14.94 Leasehold Interests.
14.95 ____ Valuation and Compensation.
14.96 Loss of Business and Goodwill.
14.97 Going Concern Value.
14.98 Moving and Relocation Expenses.
14.99 Conflicting Claims by Condemnees.
14.100 ____ Conflicting Claims to the Condemnor's Offer.
14.101 ____ Conflicting Claims to the Award.
14.102 The Trial on Compensation.
14.103 ____ Preference.
14.104 ____ Filing and Exchange of Appraisals.
14.105 ____ Expert Testimony.
14.106 ____ Viewing of the Property.
14.107 ____ Joint or Consolidated Trials.
14.108 ____ Interest.
14.109 Setoff for Indirect Benefit.
14.110 Incidental Expenses and Proration of Taxes.
14.111 Abandonment of Procedure by Condemnor.
14.112 Finding that Condemnor is Not Legally Authorized to Acquire the Property.
14.113 Finding Contrary to Claim by Condemnor That it Did Not Take Property.
14.114 Decision By the Court and Entry of Judgment.
14.115 Additional Allowances for Costs and Expenses.
14.116 Payment Pending Appeal.
14.117 Small Claims Proceedings.
14.118 Summary.
14.119 Procedural Checklist.
14.120 Forms—Demand on Condemnor to File Copy of Proceedings to Determine Need and Location of Public Project with Appellate Division for Purpose of Judicial Review.
14.121 ____ Petition for Review of Determination and Finding that Public Use, Benefit or Purpose Will be Served by Proposed Acquisition.
14.122 ____ Judgment of Appellate Division Rejecting the Determination and Finding that Public Use, Benefit or Purpose Will be Served by Proposed Acquisition.
14.123 ____ Complaint by Condemnee to Establish Fair and Reasonable Value for Temporary Use and Occupancy After Acquisition by Eminent Domain.

LIII

TABLE OF CONTENTS

Sec.
14.124 ____ Notice of Pendency of Proceeding in Supreme Court to Acquire Property by Eminent Domain and File Acquisition Map.
14.125 ____ Notice of Petition in Proceeding in Supreme Court to Acquire Property by Eminent Domain and File Acquisition Map.
14.126 ____ Petition in Proceeding in Supreme Court to Acquire Property by Eminent Domain and File Acquisition Map.
14.127 ____ Petition in Proceeding in Supreme Court to Acquire Property by Eminent Domain and File Acquisition Map—Petitioner Exempt from Compliance with Eminent Domain Procedure Law Article 2.
14.128 ____ Answer to Petition in Proceeding in Supreme Court to Acquire Property by Eminent Domain and File Acquisition Map.
14.129 ____ Order to Show Cause Why Condemnor Should Not be Permitted to Enter Immediately upon Real Property and Devote It Temporarily to Public Use Specified in Petition Upon Deposit of a Fixed Sum with the Court.
14.130 ____ Order to Show Cause Why Condemnor Should Not be Permitted to File Acquisition Maps or Enter upon Real Property.
14.131 ____ Order in Proceeding in Supreme Court to Acquire Property by Eminent Domain and File Acquisition Map.
14.132 ____ Notice of Acquisition by Eminent Domain Where Supreme Court Has Jurisdiction.
14.133 ____ Claim for Damages Arising from Acquisition by Eminent Domain—General Form.
14.134 ____ Judgment Awarding Compensation in Claim for Acquisition of Property by Eminent Domain.
14.135 ____ Notice of Motion for Additional Allowance to Condemnee for Expert Witnesses.
14.136 ____ Affidavit in Support of Motion for Additional Allowance to Condemnee for Expert Witnesses.
14.137 ____ Order Granting Additional Allowance to Condemnee for Expert Witnesses.

CHAPTER 15. ENVIRONMENTAL LAW

15.1 Scope Note.
15.2 Strategy.
15.3 State Environmental Quality Review Act.
15.4 ____ Determination of Significance.
15.5 ____ The Environmental Impact Statement and Findings Statement.
15.6 ____ Judicial Review.
15.7 ____ Checklist.
15.8 Water Pollution Control.
15.9 ____ SPDES Permit Program.
15.10 ____ Stormwater Discharges and Oil Spills.
15.11 ____ Enforcement.

TABLE OF CONTENTS

Sec.

15.12 ___ Strategy: Clean Water Act Citizen Suit Checklist.
15.13 Wetlands Protection.
15.14 ___ Strategy: Checklist.
15.15 ___ The Federal Scheme.
15.16 ___ New York Tidal and Freshwater Wetlands Law.
15.17 ___ Permit Procedure and Criteria.
15.18 ___ Penalties.
15.19 Air Pollution Control.
15.20 ___ The 1990 CAA Amendments.
15.21 ___ New York State Requirements.
15.22 ___ Enforcement.
15.23 Regulation of Solid and Hazardous Waste.
15.24 ___ New York Hazardous Waste Regulation.
15.25 ___ Enforcement.
15.26 Regulation of Underground Storage Tanks and Petroleum Storage Tanks—Federal Law.
15.27 ___ New York Law.
15.28 Regulation of Inactive Hazardous Waste Sites—CERCLA.
15.29 ___ CERCLA Section 107(a).
15.30 ___ Lender Liability, Contribution and Indemnification Under CERCLA.
15.31 ___ New York Law.
15.32 Relevant Common Law Doctrines—Nuisance.
15.33 Common Law Doctrines—Trespass.
15.34 Regulatory Takings.
15.35 Drafting Checklist—Clean Water Act Citizen Suit Notice Letter.
15.36 ___ Clean Water Act and Resource Conservation and Recovery Act Citizen Suit Notice Letter.
15.37 ___ Clean Water Act Complaint.
15.38 ___ Nuisance and Trespass Complaint.
15.39 ___ Oil Spill Complaint.
15.40 Forms—Clean Water Act Citizen Suit Notice Letter. 💾
15.41 ___ Clean Water Act and Resource Conservation and Recovery Act Citizen Suit Notice Letter. 💾
15.42 ___ Clean Water Act Complaint. 💾
15.43 ___ Nuisance and Trespass Complaint. 💾
15.44 ___ Oil Spill Complaint. 💾

CHAPTER 16. LAND USE LAW

16.1 Scope Note.
16.2 Strategy.
16.3 Local Land Use Law.
16.4 ___ Delegated Authority.
16.5 ___ Enabling Acts.
16.6 ___ ___ New York City.
16.7 ___ Home Rule Authority.
16.8 ___ ___ Flexibility.
16.9 ___ ___ Floating Zone.
16.10 ___ Summary.

TABLE OF CONTENTS

Sec.
16.11	Comprehensive Plan.
16.12	___ Judicial Definition.
16.13	___ Statutory Definition.
16.14	___ Preparation and Adoption.
16.15	___ Protects Zoning Against Challenge.
16.16	___ Summary.
16.17	Substantive Limits—Illustrative Case.
16.18	___ Substantive Due Process.
16.19	___ Procedural Due Process.
16.20	___ Equal Protection.
16.21	___ *Ultra Vires*.
16.22	___ Regulatory Takings.
16.23	___ Vested Rights.
16.24	___ Preemption.
16.25	___ First Amendment.
16.26	___ Summary.
16.27	Local Process.
16.28	___ Structure of Local Regulations.
16.29	___ Adoption.
16.30	___ Amendment.
16.31	___ Other Regulations/Official Map.
16.32	___ Building Regulations and Permits.
16.33	___ Summary.
16.34	Local Boards and Practices.
16.35	___ Local Legislature.
16.36	___ Planning Board.
16.37	___ Zoning Board of Appeals.
16.38	___ Freedom of Information.
16.39	___ Open Meetings.
16.40	___ Conflict of Interests.
16.41	___ Summary.
16.42	Judicial Review.
16.43	___ Procedures.
16.44	___ Standards.
16.45	___ ___ Local Legislature.
16.46	___ ___ Zoning Board of Appeals.
16.47	___ ___ Planning Board.
16.48	___ Standing.
16.49	___ Exhaustion.
16.50	___ Remedies.
16.51	___ Summary.
16.52	Local Environmental Review.
16.53	___ Actions Subject to SEQRA.
16.54	___ ___ Building Permits.
16.55	___ ___ Variances.
16.56	___ ___ Subdivisions.
16.57	___ ___ Site Plans.
16.58	___ ___ Rezoning.
16.59	___ Summary.
16.60	Zoning Law—In General.

LVI

TABLE OF CONTENTS

Sec.	
16.61	As of Right Use.
16.62	Nonconforming Use—Definition and Application.
16.63	___ Changes.
16.64	___ Reconstruction and Restoration.
16.65	___ Enlargement, Alteration or Extension.
16.66	___ Changes to Another Nonconforming Use.
16.67	___ Termination.
16.68	___ Abandonment.
16.69	___ Amortization.
16.70	___ Transfer of Ownership.
16.71	___ Procedures.
16.72	___ Summary.
16.73	Use Variance.
16.74	___ Statutory Standard.
16.75	___ ___ Reasonable Return.
16.76	___ ___ Unique Hardship.
16.77	___ ___ Protect Essential Neighborhood Character.
16.78	___ ___ Self-Created Hardship.
16.79	___ Minimum Variance Needed.
16.80	___ Procedure.
16.81	___ Summary.
16.82	Area Variance.
16.83	___ Statutory Balancing Test.
16.84	___ ___ Guiding Principles from Case Law.
16.85	___ ___ Balancing Factors.
16.86	___ Minimum Variance Needed.
16.87	___ Procedure.
16.88	___ Summary.
16.89	Conditions Imposed on Use and Area Variances.
16.90	Special Use Permits.
16.91	___ Imposition and Use of Standards.
16.92	___ Findings and Determination of Board.
16.93	___ Limitation on Imposition of Conditions.
16.94	___ Procedure.
16.95	___ Summary.
16.96	Subdivision Approval.
16.97	___ Procedure.
16.98	___ ___ How Affected By SEQRA.
16.99	___ Provision of Essential Services.
16.100	___ Parkland.
16.101	___ Decisions and Conditions.
16.102	___ Summary.
16.103	Site Plans.
16.104	___ Responsible Agency.
16.105	___ ___ Procedure.
16.106	___ ___ Standards for Review.
16.107	___ ___ Conditions Imposed.
16.108	___ Summary.
16.109	Particularized Actions.
16.110	___ Spot Zoning.

TABLE OF CONTENTS

Sec.
16.111 _____ _____ Challenge Dismissed.
16.112 _____ _____ Challenge Successful.
16.113 _____ Rezoning.
16.114 _____ _____ Conditions.
16.115 _____ _____ Contract Zoning.
16.116 _____ _____ Development Agreements.
16.117 _____ Summary.
16.118 Special Regulations.
16.119 _____ Accessory Uses.
16.120 _____ Accessory Apartments.
16.121 _____ Home Offices.
16.122 _____ Definition of Family.
16.123 _____ Affordable Housing.
16.124 _____ Mobile Homes.
16.125 _____ Aesthetics.
16.126 _____ _____ Architectural Review.
16.127 _____ _____ Historic Preservation.
16.128 _____ Public Uses.
16.129 _____ _____ Public Utilities.
16.130 _____ _____ Cellular Transmission Facilities.
16.131 _____ _____ Religious Uses.
16.132 _____ Summary.
16.133 Forms—Environmental Assessment—Short Form. 💾
16.134 _____ Environmental Assessment—Long Form. 💾

CHAPTER 17. EMPLOYMENT LAW

17.1 Scope Note.
17.2 Strategy.
17.3 _____ Plaintiff's Counsel's Investigation.
17.4 _____ Defendant's Counsel's Investigation.
17.5 _____ Pre-litigation Settlement Process.
17.6 _____ Negotiating With Opposing Counsel.
17.7 _____ Alternative Dispute Resolution ("ADR").
17.8 _____ _____ Mediation.
17.9 _____ _____ Arbitration.
17.10 _____ Settlement and Severance Agreements.
17.11 _____ _____ Older Workers Benefit Protection Act ("OWBPA").
17.12 _____ _____ COBRA.
17.13 _____ _____ Pay.
17.14 _____ _____ Income Taxes.
17.15 _____ _____ Benefits.
17.16 _____ Other Severance Issues.
17.17 _____ Independent Contractor vs. Employee.
17.18 _____ Checklist: Initial Considerations for Plaintiff.
17.19 _____ Checklist: Terminating an Employee.
17.20 Causes of Action.
17.21 _____ Tort–Assault.
17.22 _____ _____ Battery.
17.23 _____ _____ Conspiracy.

LVIII

TABLE OF CONTENTS

Sec.
17.24 ___ ___ Conversion.
17.25 ___ ___ Defamation.
17.26 ___ ___ False Imprisonment; Malicious Prosecution.
17.27 ___ ___ Fraud, Negligent Misrepresentation and Fraudulent Inducement.
17.28 ___ ___ Intentional Infliction of Emotional Distress.
17.29 ___ ___ Interference with Business Relations.
17.30 ___ ___ Negligence.
17.31 ___ ___ *Prima Facie* Tort.
17.32 ___ ___ Wrongful Discharge.
17.33 ___ Contract.
17.34 ___ ___ Express Promises.
17.35 ___ ___ Implied Promises.
17.36 ___ ___ Estoppel.
17.37 Statutory Causes of Action—Age Discrimination.
17.38 ___ Anti-reprisal Provisions of Various Statutes.
17.39 ___ Arrest Records.
17.40 ___ Bankruptcy.
17.41 ___ Convictions.
17.42 ___ Credit Information.
17.43 ___ Disability.
17.44 ___ Equal Pay.
17.45 ___ Family and Medical Leave Act (FMLA).
17.46 ___ Health Plan Coverage (COBRA).
17.47 ___ Legal Off Duty Activities.
17.48 ___ Marital Status Discrimination.
17.49 ___ Discrimination on the Basis of Race, Color or National Origin.
17.50 ___ Pension Plans.
17.51 ___ Plant Closing, Mass Layoffs.
17.52 ___ Polygraphs.
17.53 ___ Public Employees.
17.54 ___ Pregnancy.
17.55 ___ Privacy.
17.56 ___ Religious Discrimination.
17.57 ___ Sex Discrimination, Harassment.
17.58 ___ Sexual Orientation Discrimination.
17.59 ___ Title VII, Burdens of Proof.
17.60 ___ Unemployment Insurance.
17.61 ___ Unionization, Rights Within Unions.
17.62 ___ Unsafe Workplace.
17.63 ___ Wages; Unpaid Compensation; Overtime.
17.64 ___ Whistleblowing/*Qui Tam*.
17.65 ___ Workers' Compensation.
17.66 Procedure—Anti-discrimination Agency Practice.
17.67 ___ Filing and Responding to Administrative Charges.
17.68 ___ Election of Remedies.
17.69 ___ Statutes of Limitations and Prerequisites to Private Lawsuits.
17.70 Private Lawsuits.

TABLE OF CONTENTS

Sec.
17.71 ____ Discovery—General Considerations.
17.72 ____ ____ Plaintiff's Strategy.
17.73 ____ Summary Judgment.
17.74 ____ Trial.
17.75 ____ Fee Application.
17.76 ____ Post-Trial Motions and Appeal.
17.77 ____ Checklist: Statutes of Limitations.
17.78 ____ Checklist: Commencement of New York State Actions.
17.79 ____ Checklist: Commencement of Federal Court Actions.
17.80 Miscellaneous Practice Issues—OFCCP/Glass Ceiling Audits.
17.81 ____ Employment Policies and Handbooks.
17.82 Drafting the Complaint.
17.83 Drafting Checklist—Complaint.
17.84 Drafting the Answer.
17.85 Drafting Checklist—Answer.
17.86 Forms—Client (Plaintiff) Intake Questionnaire.
17.87 ____ Severance/Release Agreement.
17.88 ____ Letter to EEOC Requesting "Mohasco" Waiver of State Processing.
17.89 ____ Charge of Discrimination—New York State Division of Human Rights (Official Form).
17.90 ____ Information Sheet—New York State Division of Human Rights (Official Form).
17.91 ____ SDHR Information Sheet.
17.92 ____ Charge of Discrimination—Equal Employment Opportunity Commission (Official Form).
17.93 ____ Affidavit for a Charge of Discrimination—Equal Employment Opportunity Commission (Official Form).
17.94 ____ EEOC Filing Cover Letter Requesting EEOC Processing of Dual-filed Charge.
17.95 ____ Letter Requesting Administrative Convenience Dismissal from State or City Administrative Agency.
17.96 ____ Pleadings—New York State Complaint.
17.97 ____ ____ New York State Answer.
17.98 ____ ____ Federal Complaint.
17.99 ____ ____ Federal Answer.

CHAPTER 18. CIVIL RIGHTS

18.1 Scope Note.
18.2 Strategy.
18.3 ____ Checklist.
18.4 Overview of New York and Federal Civil Rights Provisions.
18.5 Jurisdiction over Civil Rights Actions.
18.6 New York Bill of Rights.
18.7 ____ Overview.
18.8 ____ Comparison With Federal Bill of Rights.
18.9 ____ Search and Seizure.
18.10 ____ ____ Civil Liability.
18.11 ____ ____ Return of Seized Property.

LX

TABLE OF CONTENTS

Sec.
18.12 —— Rights of Persons Accused of Crimes.
18.13 —— —— Public Trial/Closure of Courtroom.
18.14 —— —— Exclusion of Public or Press.
18.15 —— Rights of Jurors.
18.16 General Federal Civil Rights Provisions.
18.17 —— 42 U.S.C.A. § 1981.
18.18 —— 42 U.S.C.A. § 1983.
18.19 —— Other Federal Civil Rights Provisions.
18.20 Police and Prosecutorial Misconduct.
18.21 —— Excessive Force.
18.22 —— False Arrest.
18.23 —— False Imprisonment.
18.24 —— Search and Seizure.
18.25 —— Malicious Prosecution.
18.26 First Amendment.
18.27 —— Freedom of Speech.
18.28 —— Freedom of Religion.
18.29 Rights of Prisoners.
18.30 Defenses to Federal Actions.
18.31 —— Absolute Immunity.
18.32 —— Qualified Immunity.
18.33 —— Eleventh Amendment.
18.34 —— *Monell* and Its Progeny.
18.35 —— *Respondeat Superior*.
18.36 —— Abstention.
18.37 —— *Res Judicata* and Collateral Estoppel.
18.38 —— Statute of Limitations.
18.39 Housing.
18.40 —— Prohibition Against Discrimination in Publicly Assisted Housing.
18.41 —— —— Owners and Lessors.
18.42 —— —— Real Estate Agents and Brokers.
18.43 —— —— Remedies for Discrimination.
18.44 —— Prohibition Against Discrimination in Private Housing.
18.45 —— —— Owners and Lessors.
18.46 —— —— Real Estate Agents and Brokers.
18.47 —— —— Cooperatives.
18.48 —— —— Remedies for Discrimination.
18.49 —— —— —— Administrative Proceedings.
18.50 —— —— —— Actions in State and Federal Court.
18.51 —— *Prima Facie* Case and Burden of Proof.
18.52 —— Summary of Procedure for Filing an Administrative Claim and Challenging an SDHR Order.
18.53 Education.
18.54 Equal Rights in Places of Public Accommodation and Amusement.
18.55 —— General Provisions.
18.56 —— Private Clubs.
18.57 —— Persons With Disabilities Accompanied by a Guide Dog, Hearing Dog or Service Dog.
18.58 —— Remedies for Discrimination.

LXI

TABLE OF CONTENTS

Sec.
18.59 Employment Discrimination Provisions Exclusive to the New York Civil Rights Law.
18.60 ___ In General.
18.61 ___ Persons With Disabilities.
18.62 ___ Persons With Genetic Disorders.
18.63 Right of Privacy.
18.64 ___ Generally.
18.65 ___ Police Officers, Corrections Officers and Firefighters.
18.66 ___ Victims of Sex Offenses.
18.67 Changing One's Name.
18.68 ___ Procedure for Petition to Change Name.
18.69 ___ ___ Contents of Petition.
18.70 ___ ___ Special Procedures for Infants.
18.71 ___ Factors to Be Considered by the Court.
18.72 ___ Publication Requirement.
18.73 ___ Checklist.
18.74 Heart Balm Statute.
18.75 ___ Penalty for Bringing Action.
18.76 ___ Action for Return of Gifts Made in Contemplation of Marriage.
18.77 ___ ___ Procedure.
18.78 Miscellaneous Rights and Immunities.
18.79 ___ Frivolous Litigation.
18.80 ___ ___ Protection from SLAPP Suits.
18.81 ___ Libel and Slander.
18.82 ___ ___ Defenses.
18.83 ___ Breast Feeding.
18.84 ___ Suspension of Rights Due to Imprisonment.
18.85 ___ Shield Law.
18.86 ___ Performing Abortion.
18.87 ___ "Good Samaritan" Law Provisions.
18.88 Drafting Checklists.
18.89 ___ Framing the Federal Court § 1983 Complaint.
18.90 ___ Petition to Change One's Name.
18.91 Forms.
18.92 ___ Complaint for False Arrest, False Imprisonment and Malicious Prosecution. 💾
18.93 ___ Complaint for Excessive Force.
18.94 ___ Complaint for Return of Seized Property. 💾
18.95 ___ Complaint Against Landlord for Housing Discrimination. 💾
18.96 ___ Complaint Against Cooperative for Discrimination. 💾
18.97 ___ Notice of Commencement of Action for Discrimination. 💾
18.98 ___ Complaint for Discrimination in Place of Public Accommodation. 💾
18.99 ___ Petition to Change Name. 💾

CHAPTER 19. IMMIGRATION AND NATIONALITY LAW —PERMANENT RESIDENCE APPLICATIONS

19.1 Scope Note.

LXII

TABLE OF CONTENTS

Sec.	
19.2	Strategy.
19.3	___ Flowchart.
19.4	Overview of the U.S. Immigration System.
19.5	___ Numerical Limitations on Immigrant Selection.
19.6	___ Implementation: Foreign State Chargeability and Quota Allocation.
19.7	Family–Based Immigration.
19.8	___ Immediate Relative Categories.
19.9	___ Family Preference Categories.
19.10	___ Qualifying as a Relation.
19.11	___ ___ "Child" and "Parent" Issues.
19.12	___ ___ "Marriage" Issues.
19.13	___ Petitioning Procedures and Documentation.
19.14	___ ___ I–130 Petition.
19.15	___ Orphans and Amerasians.
19.16	___ Abused Spouse and Children.
19.17	Employment–Based Immigration.
19.18	___ First Employment Preference Applicants (Priority Workers).
19.19	___ ___ Extraordinary Ability Aliens.
19.20	___ ___ Outstanding Professors and Researchers.
19.21	___ ___ Managerial or Executive Intracompany Transferees.
19.22	___ Second Employment Preference Applicants.
19.23	___ ___ Exceptional Ability Aliens.
19.24	___ ___ Advanced Degree Professionals.
19.25	___ ___ The Role of "National Interest."
19.26	___ Third Employment Preference Applicants.
19.27	___ ___ Professional and Skilled Workers.
19.28	___ ___ Unskilled Workers.
19.29	___ I–140 Petition, Procedures and Documentation.
19.30	___ ___ Checklist.
19.31	___ Labor Certification.
19.32	___ ___ Procedures.
19.33	___ ___ Legal Issues.
19.34	___ ___ Job Description.
19.35	___ ___ Business Necessity.
19.36	___ ___ Recruitment.
19.37	___ ___ Approvals.
19.38	___ ___ Notices of Findings.
19.39	___ ___ Denials and Administrative Appeal.
19.40	___ Fourth Employment Preference Applicants.
19.41	___ ___ Religious Workers and Ministers.
19.42	___ Fifth Employment Preference Applicants (Immigrant Investors).
19.43	___ Petition Procedures and Requirements.
19.44	___ ___ Special Immigrant Investor Programs.
19.45	Special Categories.
19.46	___ The Diversity (Lottery) Program.
19.47	___ Registry.
19.48	___ Cancellation of Removal.
19.49	___ Legislatively Created Programs.

TABLE OF CONTENTS

Sec.
19.50 ____ Asylum and Refugee Status.
19.51 Applying for Permanent Residence.
19.52 ____ Exclusionary Grounds.
19.53 ____ Immigrant Visa Processing.
19.54 ____ ____ Framework of the Immigrant Visa Processing System.
19.55 ____ ____ Special Requirements, Public Law No. 103–317.
19.56 ____ ____ Checklist of Required Documents.
19.57 ____ Adjustment of Status.
19.58 ____ ____ General Requirements.
19.59 ____ ____ Special Provisions of Section 245(i).
19.60 ____ ____ Discretionary Factors.
19.61 ____ ____ Application Process.
19.62 ____ ____ Concurrent Filing of Petition and Adjustment of Status.
19.63 ____ ____ Completion of the Process.
19.64 ____ ____ Administrative and Judicial Review.
19.65 ____ ____ Checklist.
19.66 ____ Tactical Considerations.
19.67 ____ ____ Nonimmigrant Status as a Factor.
19.68 ____ ____ Immigrant Visa Processing Versus Adjustment of Status.
19.69 ____ ____ Flowchart.
19.70 The Green Card and its Limitations.
19.71 ____ Conditional Residence.
19.72 ____ ____ Marriage Cases, Removal of Condition.
19.73 ____ ____ Immigrant Investors, Removal of Condition.
19.74 ____ Unconditional Permanent Residence.
19.75 Forms.
19.76 ____ Form I–130.
19.77 ____ Form I–140.
19.78 ____ Form I–485.
19.79 ____ Form OF–230.

CHAPTER 20. ADOPTIONS

20.1 Scope Note.
20.2 Strategy.
20.3 ____ Checklist: Pre-adoption—Counsel for Parents.
20.4 ____ Checklist: Interview With Birth Mother.
20.5 Adoptions—Generally.
20.6 ____ Defined.
20.7 ____ Rationale.
20.8 ____ Judicial Construction of Statutes.
20.9 ____ Concurrent Jurisdiction.
20.10 ____ ____ Where to File Adoption Proceedings.
20.11 ____ Choice of Venue.
20.12 ____ Types.
20.13 ____ Effect of Adoption.
20.14 ____ Who May Adopt—Statutory Mandates.
20.15 ____ ____ Separated Persons.

LXIV

TABLE OF CONTENTS

Sec.
20.16 ____ ____ Foster Parents: Preference to Adopt.
20.17 ____ ____ Second Parent Adoptions.
20.18 ____ ____ Unwed Putative Fathers.
20.19 ____ ____ Citizens and Aliens.
20.20 ____ ____ Age as a Factor.
20.21 ____ ____ Extended Family as Factor.
20.22 ____ ____ Adult Unmarried Person.
20.23 ____ Who May Be Adopted—In General.
20.24 ____ ____ Adult Adoptions.
20.25 ____ ____ Aliens.
20.26 ____ ____ Non-marital Children.
20.27 ____ ____ Interracial Adoptions.
20.28 ____ ____ Religion as a Factor.
20.29 ____ Consents Required—Statutory Mandate.
20.30 ____ ____ Rights of Unwed Fathers.
20.31 ____ ____ When Consent Not Required.
20.32 ____ ____ Notice of a Proposed Adoption.
20.33 ____ ____ Checklist of Fathers to Receive Notice of Adoption.
20.34 ____ Persons Excluded from Notice.
20.35 ____ Purpose of Notice.
20.36 ____ Procedure.
20.37 Private Placement Adoptions—In General.
20.38 ____ Terminating Parental Rights Based Upon Abandonment.
20.39 ____ Terminating Parental Rights Based Upon Mental Retardation.
20.40 ____ Dual Representation Prohibited.
20.41 ____ Independent Counsel.
20.42 ____ Permissible Dual Representation.
20.43 ____ Independent Representation of the Child.
20.44 ____ The Attorney's Fee.
20.45 ____ Locating an Infant for Adoption—The Attorney's Responsibility.
20.46 ____ Illegal Sale of Babies.
20.47 ____ Advertisement.
20.48 ____ Foreign Infants.
20.49 ____ Readoption of Foreign Infants.
20.50 ____ Native American Children.
20.51 ____ Residency Requirements.
20.52 ____ Permissible Payments by Adoptive Parents.
20.53 ____ Interstate Compact on the Placement of Children.
20.54 ____ Pre-certification of Adoptive Parents—In General.
20.55 ____ ____ Requirement of Pre-certification.
20.56 ____ ____ Procedure.
20.57 ____ ____ Checklist of Documents Needed for Certification.
20.58 ____ Hospital Procedures—Physical Transfer of Custody of the Infant to the Adoptive Parents.
20.59 ____ ____ Certification Procedures.
20.60 ____ Petition for Temporary Guardianship—Legislative Background.
20.61 ____ ____ Impact of Pre–placement Certification.

TABLE OF CONTENTS

Sec.
20.62 ____ Procedure Upon Filing Petition for Temporary Guardianship.
20.63 ____ Consent of Birth Parents.
20.64 ____ ____ Extra–Judicial Consent.
20.65 ____ ____ Judicial Consents.
20.66 ____ ____ Personal Appearances Required.
20.67 ____ ____ Step-Parent Adoptions.
20.68 ____ Foreign Born Children.
20.69 ____ Petition for Adoption.
20.70 ____ The Agreement of Adoption.
20.71 ____ Affidavit of Attorney Representing Adoptive Parents.
20.72 ____ Confidential Affidavit.
20.73 ____ Attorney's Affidavit of Financial Disclosure.
20.74 ____ Notification of Order of Adoption; Report of Adoption.
20.75 ____ Order of Adoption.
20.76 ____ Birth Mother's Affidavit Regarding Putative Father.
20.77 ____ Affidavit of Intermediary.
20.78 ____ Attorney's Affidavit Regarding Legal Fees.
20.79 ____ Affidavit of Explanation of Criminal Activity.
20.80 ____ Investigation by Disinterested Person.
20.81 ____ The Hearing.
20.82 ____ Certificate of Adoption.
20.83 ____ The New Birth Certificate.
20.84 ____ Checklist of Documents Required for Private Placement Adoption.
20.85 Agency Adoptions—Defined.
20.86 ____ Definition of "Authorized Agency."
20.87 ____ Venue.
20.88 ____ Child's Entry into the System.
20.89 ____ ____ Voluntary Transfer of Legal Custody of Children to the Authorized Agency.
20.90 ____ ____ Judicial Surrender.
20.91 ____ ____ Extra–Judicial Surrender.
20.92 ____ ____ Court Approval of Extra–Judicial Surrender.
20.93 ____ ____ Assigned Counsel.
20.94 ____ ____ Required Notice of Application.
20.95 ____ ____ Notification to Court.
20.96 ____ ____ Court Order.
20.97 ____ ____ Conditional Surrender.
20.98 ____ ____ Recording a Surrender.
20.99 ____ ____ Revocation of Surrender.
20.100 ____ ____ Proceedings Subsequent to Execution of Extra–Judicial Surrender.
20.101 ____ ____ Court Ordered Transfer of Children to Authorized Agency.
20.102 ____ Procedures.
20.103 ____ The Petition.
20.104 ____ The Agreement of Adoption.
20.105 ____ Verified Schedule.
20.106 ____ Affidavit of Financial Disclosure.
20.107 ____ Confidential Affidavit.

TABLE OF CONTENTS

Sec.
- 20.108 ____ Marital Affidavit.
- 20.109 ____ Child's Medical History.
- 20.110 ____ Supplemental Affidavit.
- 20.111 ____ Notification of Order of Adoption; Report of Adoption.
- 20.112 ____ Doctor's Certificate of Health.
- 20.113 ____ Authorization and Approval for Subsidized Adoption.
- 20.114 ____ Adoption Homestudy.
- 20.115 ____ Affidavit Identifying Party.
- 20.116 ____ Order of Adoption.
- 20.117 ____ Certificate of Adoption.
- 20.118 ____ Abuse Clearance Form.
- 20.119 ____ Unavailability of Abuse Clearance Form and Criminal Conviction Check.
- 20.120 ____ Attorney's Affidavit of Legal Fees.
- 20.121 ____ Checklist of Other Required Supporting Documentation.
- 20.122 ____ The Adoption Hearing.
- 20.123 Post-adoption Issues—The Open Adoption.
- 20.124 ____ Visitation With Siblings.
- 20.125 ____ Sealing Adoption Records.
- 20.126 ____ ____ Constitutionality of Laws Relating to Sealing Records.
- 20.127 ____ ____ Good Cause for Unsealing Records.
- 20.128 ____ ____ ____ Criminal Investigation and Probation Department.
- 20.129 ____ ____ ____ Requirement of Medical Information.
- 20.130 ____ ____ ____ Religion.
- 20.131 ____ Abrogation of Order.
- 20.132 Checklist of Facts and Allegations to be Included in the Petition for a Private Placement Adoption.
- 20.133 Forms—Private Placement Adoptions—Petition for Certification as a Qualified Adoptive Parent. 💾
- 20.134 ____ ____ Petition for Temporary Guardianship. 💾
- 20.135 ____ ____ Judicial Consent of Natural Parent. 💾
- 20.136 ____ ____ Extra-Judicial Consent of Natural Parent. 💾
- 20.137 ____ ____ Petition for Adoption. 💾
- 20.138 ____ ____ Order of Adoption (Private Placement). 💾
- 20.139 ____ Agency Adoptions—Petition for Adoption. 💾
- 20.140 ____ ____ Verified Schedule. 💾
- 20.141 ____ ____ Marital Affidavit. 💾
- 20.142 ____ ____ Marital Affidavit Dispensing With Consent of Spouse After Three Year Separation. 💾
- 20.143 ____ ____ Confidential Affidavit. 💾
- 20.144 ____ ____ Affidavit Pursuant to Section 111–a of the Domestic Relations Law. 💾
- 20.145 ____ ____ Agreement of Adoption and Consent. 💾
- 20.146 ____ ____ Affidavit Identifying Party. 💾
- 20.147 ____ ____ Affidavit of Financial Disclosure by Parents. 💾
- 20.148 ____ ____ Order of Adoption. 💾

Volume 23

CHAPTER 21. DOMESTIC RELATIONS

21.1   Scope Note.

TABLE OF CONTENTS

Sec.
21.2 Strategy.
21.3 Jurisdiction.
21.4 —— Residence Requirements.
21.5 —— Uniform Child Custody Jurisdiction Act.
21.6 Competency of the Court to Grant Relief.
21.7 —— Equitable Distribution.
21.8 —— Support.
21.9 —— Custody and Visitation.
21.10 Jurisdiction Over the Defendant's Person or Property.
21.11 —— Personal Jurisdiction.
21.12 —— Long Arm Jurisdiction.
21.13 —— *In Rem* Jurisdiction.
21.14 *Quasi in Rem* Jurisdiction.
21.15 Venue.
21.16 —— Changing Venue.
21.17 Joinder, Consolidation and Joint Trials.
21.18 Grounds for Divorce.
21.19 —— No Official No–Fault Ground.
21.20 —— Cruel and Inhuman Treatment.
21.21 —— —— Defenses.
21.22 —— Abandonment.
21.23 —— —— Defenses.
21.24 —— —— Effect of Separation Agreement.
21.25 —— Imprisonment.
21.26 —— Adultery.
21.27 —— —— Defenses.
21.28 —— —— Effect of Separation Agreement.
21.29 —— Divorce Action Based Upon Living Apart Pursuant to Separation Decree or Judgment.
21.30 —— Divorce Action Based Upon Living Apart Pursuant to Separation Agreement.
21.31 —— Dual Divorce.
21.32 Effect of Sister State Divorce Judgment.
21.33 Equitable Distribution.
21.34 —— When Available.
21.35 —— Identification of Property.
21.36 —— Characterization of Property.
21.37 —— —— Marital Property.
21.38 —— —— —— Pensions.
21.39 —— —— —— Professional Practices, Licenses, Degrees and Careers.
21.40 —— —— Separate Property.
21.41 —— —— —— Increase in Value of Separate Property.
21.42 —— Valuation Dates.
21.43 —— Valuation Methods.
21.44 —— Distribution Factors.
21.45 —— Tax Considerations.
21.46 Maintenance.
21.47 —— Legislative Factors.
21.48 —— Effect of Fault.

LXVIII

TABLE OF CONTENTS

Sec.	
21.49	____ Current Trends.
21.50	____ Payments Fixed by Agreement.
21.51	____ Tax Consequences.
21.52	Child Support.
21.53	____ Child Support Standards Act.
21.54	____ ____ Where Statutory Percentages Are Unfair or Inappropriate.
21.55	____ ____ Recent Trends.
21.56	____ Effect of Agreement or Stipulation.
21.57	Health and Life Insurance.
21.58	Custody.
21.59	____ Visitation.
21.60	____ Relocation of Custodial Parent With the Child.
21.61	____ Joint Custody.
21.62	____ Proceedings in Which Custody Dispositions Are Available.
21.63	Financial Disclosure.
21.64	Disclosure on Matters Going to the Merits of the Case.
21.65	Net Worth Statement.
21.66	Statement of Proposed Disposition.
21.67	Findings of Fact and Conclusions of Law; Judgments.
21.68	Modification.
21.69	____ Maintenance.
21.70	____ Child Support.
21.71	____ Custody.
21.72	Enforcement.
21.73	____ Plenary Action to Enforce Agreement.
21.74	____ Defenses.
21.75	Practice Considerations.
21.76	____ Procedure for Attorneys in Domestic Relations Matters.
21.77	____ Disciplinary Rules.
21.78	____ Fee Arbitration Rules.
21.79	____ Rules Regarding Case Management.
21.80	Procedural Checklist—Calendar Control.
21.81	Drafting Checklist—Retainer Agreements.
21.82	_____ Complaint in Action for Divorce.
21.83	_____ Statement of Proposed Disposition.
21.84	Forms.
21.85	____ Retainer Agreement. 💾
21.86	____ Complaint for Divorce. 💾
21.87	____ Statement of Net Worth. 💾
21.88	____ Statement of Proposed Disposition. 💾
21.89	____ Findings of Fact and Conclusions of Law. 💾
21.90	____ Matrimonial Judgments. 💾
21.91	____ Referee's Report on Findings of Fact and Conclusions of Law. 💾
21.92	____ Matrimonial Judgment Entered Upon Referee's Report. 💾

CHAPTER 22. GUARDIANSHIP

22.1	Scope Note.

LXIX

TABLE OF CONTENTS

Sec.
22.2 Strategy.
22.3 Checklists.
22.4 Prior Law—Generally.
22.5 ____ Role of Committees and Conservators.
22.6 ____ Problems Encountered.
22.7 ____ Impact of *Matter of Grinker (Rose)*.
22.8 Legislative Purpose of Mental Hygiene Law Article 81.
22.9 Definitions.
22.10 Summary.
22.11 Power to Appoint Guardian—Generally.
22.12 ____ Elements.
22.13 ____ Incapacity.
22.14 ____ Primary Considerations.
22.15 ____ Jurisdiction.
22.16 ____ Venue.
22.17 ____ Standing to Commence Proceeding.
22.18 ____ Summary.
22.19 Proceeding to Appoint Guardian.
22.20 ____ Time and Method of Service of Notice.
22.21 ____ Persons Entitled to Notice.
22.22 ____ Notice Requirements.
22.23 ____ Petition.
22.24 ____ Summary.
22.25 Court Evaluator—Persons Eligible for Appointment.
22.26 ____ Duties.
22.27 ____ Compensation.
22.28 ____ Appointment of Counsel for the Alleged Incapacitated Person.
22.29 ____ Summary.
22.30 Hearing and Order—An Overview.
22.31 ____ Procedure.
22.32 ____ Presence of Person Alleged to be Incapacitated.
22.33 ____ Evidence.
22.34 ____ Findings of the Court.
22.35 ____ ____ Voluntary Appointment.
22.36 ____ ____ Personal Needs.
22.37 ____ ____ Property Management.
22.38 ____ Dispositional Alternatives.
22.39 ____ Award of Counsel Fees to Petitioner.
22.40 ____ Person to be Appointed Guardian.
22.41 ____ Priority and Criteria for Appointment.
22.42 ____ Requirement of Bond.
22.43 ____ Designation of Clerk and Issuance of Commission.
22.44 ____ Summary.
22.45 Role of Guardian—Overview.
22.46 ____ Duties.
22.47 ____ Powers; Property Management.
22.48 ____ Substituted Judgment.
22.49 ____ Petition for Authorization to Transfer Property.
22.50 ____ ____ Notice of Application.

TABLE OF CONTENTS

Sec.
22.51 ____ ____ Considerations of Court.
22.52 ____ ____ Granting Petition.
22.53 ____ Powers; Personal Needs.
22.54 ____ Effect of Appointment on Incapacitated Person.
22.55 ____ Summary.
22.56 Provisional Remedies.
22.57 ____ Temporary Guardian.
22.58 ____ Injunction and Temporary Restraining Orders.
22.59 ____ Notice of Pendency.
22.60 ____ Summary.
22.61 Compensation of Guardian.
22.62 Reports by Guardian.
22.63 ____ Initial Report.
22.64 ____ Annual Report.
22.65 ____ Examination; Court Examiners.
22.66 ____ Intermediate and Final Reports.
22.67 ____ Decree Upon Approving Accounts.
22.68 ____ Summary.
22.69 Removal, Discharge and Resignation of Guardian—Removal.
22.70 ____ Discharge or Modification of Powers.
22.71 ____ Resignation or Suspension of Powers.
22.72 ____ Vacancy in Office; Appointment of Interim and Successor Guardians.
22.73 ____ Standby Guardian.
22.74 ____ Summary.
22.75 Education Requirements—Generally.
22.76 ____ Guardian Training.
22.77 ____ Court Evaluator Training.
22.78 ____ Court Examiner Training.
22.79 ____ Compliance.
22.80 ____ Summary.
22.81 Proceedings to Discover Property Withheld.
22.82 ____ Petition and Supporting Papers.
22.83 ____ Grounds For Inquiry.
22.84 ____ Answer.
22.85 ____ Trial.
22.86 ____ Decree.
22.87 ____ Summary.
22.88 Drafting Checklists.
22.89 ____ Order to Show Cause.
22.90 ____ Petition.
22.91 ____ Court Evaluator's Report.
22.92 ____ Order and Judgment.
22.93 ____ Initial Report of the Guardian.
22.94 ____ Annual Report.
22.95 ____ Decree Approving Accounts.
22.96 ____ Petition on Proceeding to Discover Property Withheld.
22.97 Forms.
22.98 ____ Order to Show Cause. 🖫
22.99 ____ Petition. 🖫

TABLE OF CONTENTS

Sec.
22.100 ____ Court Evaluator's Report. 💾
22.101 ____ Order and Judgment Appointing Guardian of the Person and Property. 💾
22.102 ____ Oath and Designation of Guardian. 💾
22.103 ____ Commission of Guardian. 💾
22.104 ____ Initial Report of Guardian. 💾
22.105 ____ Annual Report and Inventory of Guardian. 💾
22.106 ____ Decree Upon Approving Accounts. 💾
22.107 ____ Petition on Proceeding to Discover Property Withheld. 💾

CHAPTER 23. ELDER LAW

23.1 Scope Note.
23.2 Strategy.
23.3 Ethical Considerations.
23.4 ____ Identifying the Client.
23.5 ____ Confidentiality.
23.6 ____ Diminished Capacity.
23.7 Social Security Benefits.
23.8 ____ Quarters of Coverage.
23.9 ____ Insured Status.
23.10 ____ Calculation of Benefits.
23.11 ____ Retirement Benefits.
23.12 ____ Benefits for Spouses, Survivors and Dependents.
23.13 ____ Reduction in Benefits Due to Earned Income.
23.14 ____ Overpayments and Underpayments.
23.15 ____ Administrative and Judicial Appeals.
23.16 ____ Representation by Attorneys.
23.17 Supplemental Security Income for the Elderly.
23.18 ____ Categorical Eligibility.
23.19 ____ Financial Eligibility.
23.20 ____ Benefit Calculation.
23.21 ____ Underpayments and Overpayments.
23.22 ____ Administrative and Judicial Appeals.
23.23 ____ Representation by Attorneys.
23.24 Retirement Income from Qualified Plans.
23.25 ____ Eligibility, Vesting and Accrual.
23.26 ____ Contribution Limitations.
23.27 ____ Payment of Benefits.
23.28 ____ Alienation and Assignment.
23.29 ____ Spousal Rights.
23.30 ____ Qualified Domestic Relations Orders.
23.31 ____ Waiver of Spousal Rights.
23.32 ____ Taxation of Contributions.
23.33 ____ Distributions.
23.34 ____ Termination or Merger.
23.35 ____ Appeals.
23.36 Railroad Retirement Benefits.
23.37 Benefits for Federal Employees.
23.38 ____ Federal Employees Retirement System ("FERS").

TABLE OF CONTENTS

Sec.
23.39	____ Civil Service Retirement Act ("CSRA").
23.40	____ Appeals.
23.41	Veterans' Benefits.
23.42	Medicare.
23.43	____ Eligibility and Enrollment.
23.44	____ Part A Benefits.
23.45	____ ____ Hospital Services.
23.46	____ ____ Skilled Nursing Facilities.
23.47	____ ____ Home Health Care.
23.48	____ ____ Hospice Care.
23.49	____ Part B Supplementary Medical Insurance.
23.50	____ ____ Deductibles and Coinsurance.
23.51	____ ____ Assignment of Claims/Participating Physicians.
23.52	____ ____ Limitations on Balance Billing.
23.53	____ ____ Administrative and Judicial Appeals.
23.54	____ ____ Eligibility for Benefits.
23.55	____ ____ Part A Fiscal Intermediary Decisions.
23.56	____ ____ Part A Peer Review Organization Decisions.
23.57	____ ____ Part B Determinations.
23.58	Supplemental Medical Insurance (Medigap Plans).
23.59	____ Gaps in Medicare Coverage.
23.60	____ Federal and State Regulation of the Industry.
23.61	____ Ten Standard Plans.
23.62	____ Criteria for Choosing the Right Plan.
23.63	Long Term Care Insurance.
23.64	____ Regulation Under New York Law.
23.65	____ Relationship to Medicaid Eligibility.
23.66	____ The Partnership For Long Term Care/Robert Wood Johnson Program.
23.67	____ Choosing a Policy.
23.68	____ Tax Issues.
23.69	Medicaid.
23.70	____ Covered Services.
23.71	____ Basic Eligibility Requirements.
23.72	____ Surplus Income Program for the "Medically Needy."
23.73	____ Income.
23.74	____ Resources.
23.75	____ Exempt Resources.
23.76	____ Transfer of Resources.
23.77	____ Treatment of Trusts.
23.78	____ ____ Self Settled Trusts.
23.79	____ ____ Third Party Trusts.
23.80	____ Spousal Budgeting: Protection of Resources and Income for the Community Spouse.
23.81	____ Recoveries Against Estates.
23.82	____ Liens.
23.83	____ Administrative and Judicial Appeals.
23.84	Home Care Coverage.
23.85	____ Medicare.
23.86	____ Medicaid.

TABLE OF CONTENTS

Sec.

23.87	—— Expanded In–Home Services for the Elderly Program ("EI-SEP").
23.88	—— Private Insurance.
23.89	Hospital Patients Rights.
23.90	—— Bill of Rights.
23.91	—— Discharge Planning.
23.92	Nursing Home Resident Rights.
23.93	—— Admission to a Facility.
23.94	—— Bill of Rights.
23.95	—— Financial Rights.
23.96	—— Transfer and Discharge.
23.97	—— Bed Hold Policy.
23.98	—— Remedies for Violation of Rights or Improper Treatment.
23.99	Housing Issues.
23.100	—— Real Property Tax Exemption.
23.101	—— Real Property Tax Credit.
23.102	—— Tax Assistance Loans.
23.103	—— Home Repair Assistance.
23.104	—— Reverse Mortgages and Home Equity Loans.
23.105	—— Home Energy Assistance Program ("HEAP").
23.106	—— Tenant Protections.
23.107	—— Life Care Retirement Communities.
23.108	—— Community Based Services.
23.109	Health Care Decision Making.
23.110	—— Health Care Proxy.
23.111	—— The Living Will.
23.112	—— Do Not Resuscitate Orders.
23.113	—— Physician Assisted Suicide.
23.114	Tax Issues.
23.115	—— Additional Standard Deduction for the Aged and Blind.
23.116	—— Incapacity.
23.117	—— Sale of a Principal Residence.
23.118	—— Medical Deductions.
23.119	Miscellaneous Programs.
23.120	—— Elderly Pharmaceutical Insurance Coverage ("EPIC").
23.121	—— Life Line Telephone Service.
23.122	Forms.
23.123	—— Documentation Letter.
23.124	—— Consultation Letter.
23.125	—— Health Care Proxy Statutory Form.
23.126	—— Sample Living Will.

CHAPTER 24. ESTATE PLANNING

24.1	Scope Note.
24.2	Strategy.
24.3	Wills.
24.4	—— Execution Requirements.
24.5	—— —— Signature.
24.6	—— —— Publication.

TABLE OF CONTENTS

Sec.	
24.7	_____ _____ Witnesses.
24.8	_____ _____ Self Proving Affidavit.
24.9	_____ Provisions—Personal Property Dispositions.
24.10	_____ _____ Debts and Taxes.
24.11	_____ _____ Real Property.
24.12	_____ _____ Residuary Estate.
24.13	_____ _____ Dispositions in Trust.
24.14	_____ _____ Guardianships.
24.15	_____ _____ Appointment of Executors and Trustees.
24.16	_____ _____ Fiduciary Powers.
24.17	_____ _____ Miscellaneous.
24.18	Federal Estate and Gift Taxes.
24.19	_____ Rates.
24.20	New York State Estate and Gift Tax.
24.21	Estate Tax Planning—Utilizing the Unified Credit.
24.22	_____ Utilizing the Marital Deduction.
24.23	_____ Formula Clauses.
24.24	Generation Skipping Transfer Tax.
24.25	_____ Taxable Termination.
24.26	_____ Direct Skip.
24.27	_____ Taxable Distribution.
24.28	_____ Generation Assignment.
24.29	_____ Multiple Skips.
24.30	_____ Exemption.
24.31	_____ "Reverse QTIP."
24.32	Charitable Bequests.
24.33	Planning With Certain Assets.
24.34	_____ Life Insurance.
24.35	_____ _____ Life Insurance Trusts.
24.36	_____ _____ _____ "Crummey Powers."
24.37	_____ Retirement Benefits.
24.38	_____ Closely Held Business Interests.
24.39	_____ _____ Buy-Sell Agreements.
24.40	_____ _____ Liquidity Issues.
24.41	_____ _____ Minority Discounts.
24.42	_____ Farms and Business Real Property.
24.43	_____ Installment Obligations.
24.44	Lifetime Planning.
24.45	_____ Valuation of Gifts.
24.46	_____ _____ Grantor Retained Trusts.
24.47	_____ _____ Residence Trusts.
24.48	_____ _____ _____ Income Tax Considerations.
24.49	_____ Annual Gift Tax Exclusion.
24.50	_____ _____ Section 2503(c) Trusts.
24.51	_____ _____ Uniform Transfers to Minor's Act Accounts.
24.52	_____ _____ Crummey Trusts.
24.53	_____ _____ Family Limited Partnerships.
24.54	_____ Charitable Remainder Trusts.
24.55	_____ Charitable Lead Trusts.
24.56	Planning in Special Situations—Terminally Ill.

LXXV

TABLE OF CONTENTS

Sec.
24.57 __ __ Self-Canceling Installment Notes.
24.58 __ Non-citizen Spouses.
24.59 __ Multiple Marriages.
24.60 __ __ Spousal Rights.
24.61 __ __ __ Joint Wills and Contracts to Make Wills.
24.62 __ __ Long Term Care.
24.63 __ Separation.
24.64 __ Divorce.
24.65 __ __ Death During Divorce Proceeding.
24.66 __ Unmarried Couples.
24.67 Postmortem Planning.
24.68 __ Disclaimers.
24.69 __ __ Disclaimer Trusts.
24.70 __ __ Creditor Avoidance.
24.71 __ __ New York Statutory Requirements.
24.72 __ Partial QTIP Election.
24.73 __ Electing Alternate Valuation Date.
24.74 __ Allocation of Income and Expenses.
24.75 __ __ U.S. Savings Bonds.
24.76 __ __ Expenses.
24.77 __ Choosing the Fiscal Year of the Estate.
24.78 __ Electing to File Joint Return with Decedent's Spouse.
24.79 __ Waiving Commissions.
24.80 Probate Avoidance.
24.81 __ Revocable Trusts.
24.82 __ Totten Trusts.
24.83 __ Jointly Held Assets.
24.84 Asset Protection.
24.85 __ Statutory Exemptions.
24.86 __ Family Partnerships.
24.87 __ Domestic Trusts.
24.88 __ Foreign Trusts.
24.89 Powers of Attorney.
24.90 Advance Directives.
24.91 __ Health Care Proxy.
24.92 __ Living Will.
24.93 Ethical Considerations in Estate Planning.
24.94 __ Multiple Clients.
24.95 __ Attorney/Draftsman as Fiduciary or Beneficiary.
24.96 Forms
24.97 __ Estate Planner's Checklist.
24.98 __ Sample Information Request Letter.
24.99 __ Client Questionnaire.
24.100 __ "Durable" Power of Attorney Form.
24.101 __ Crummey Notice.
24.102 __ Spousal Conflicts Letter.

CHAPTER 25. PROBATE AND ESTATE ADMINISTRATION

25.1 Scope Note.

TABLE OF CONTENTS

Sec.
25.2 Explanation of Basic Legal Terms in Estate Practice.
25.3 Strategy.
25.4 Who May Commence the Estate of a Person Who Dies Without a Will.
25.5 Who Is Entitled to Letters of Administration.
25.6 Who May Commence the Estate of a Person Who Dies With a Will.
25.7 Documents Required on Application for Letters of Administration.
25.8 Who Must Be Cited on an Application for Letters of Administration.
25.9 When a Guardian *Ad Litem* Must be Appointed.
25.10 Denial or Revocation of Letters of Administration.
25.11 Letters of Temporary Administration.
25.12 Venue.
25.13 Duty of the Fiduciary to Expeditiously Seek Probate.
25.14 When a Beneficiary Should Petition for Probate.
25.15 When a Creditor Should Petition for Probate.
25.16 When a Person in Litigation with an Estate Should Petition for Probate.
25.17 Information to Be Gathered by Attorney.
25.18 Contents of Petition for Probate.
25.19 Documents Required to Accompany Probate Petition.
25.20 What to Do If Your Client Cannot Produce the Original Will.
25.21 Requirements and Procedure for Proving a Will Where the Original Is Lost.
25.22 How to Get a Will Admitted to Probate If None of the Witnesses to the Will are Available.
25.23 When a Court Must Appoint a Guardian *Ad Litem* in a Probate Proceeding.
25.24 Who May Oppose the Admission to Probate of a Will By Filing Objections.
25.25 When Objections Must Be Filed.
25.26 How to Start an Estate Administration Where There Will Be a Delay in Getting a Will Admitted to Probate.
25.27 Form of Objections to Probate.
25.28 Burden of Proof
25.29 Requirement of a Notice of Objections to Complete Jurisdiction in a Contested Probate.
25.30 Right to a Trial by Jury.
25.31 Right to Discovery in a Probate, Administration or Accounting Proceeding.
25.32 Who Is Entitled to Letters of Administration When a Person Dies Without a Will.
25.33 Procedures to Follow in Administering the Estate.
25.34 How to Force an Estate Administration to Be Completed—Compelling an Accounting.
25.35 Concluding an Estate Administration Without an Accounting Proceeding.
25.36 Obtaining a Decree Concluding the Estate Based on Filed Receipts and Releases.
25.37 Concluding an Estate by a Formal Judicial Accounting.

TABLE OF CONTENTS

Sec.
25.38 Objections to an Account.
25.39 Prosecuting Objections to an Account.
25.40 Claims Against an Estate by a Creditor.
25.41 Representing a Claimant Against an Estate.
25.42 Obtaining Information About Estate Assets and Recovering Estate Property.
25.43 How to Proceed When Your Client Has a Claim Against an Estate.
25.44 A Special Provision for an Estate Beneficiary Obtaining Funds for Education.
25.45 Who Is Entitled to Assets When Two or More Fiduciaries Are in Dispute.
25.46 Compensation of Executor and Administrator, When Payable.
25.47 Attorney's Fees.
25.48 Declining to Serve as an Executor or Trustee.
25.49 Renouncing an Inheritance.
25.50 Construction of a Will.
25.51 Forms.
25.52 ____ Probate Petition.
25.53 ____ Affidavit Proving Correct Copy of Will.
25.54 ____ Citation in Probate.
25.55 ____ Affidavit of Service of Citation.
25.56 ____ Affidavit of Mailing Notice of Application for Letters of Administration.
25.57 ____ Waiver and Consent.
25.58 ____ Notice of Probate.
25.59 ____ Deposition Affidavit of Subscribing Witness.
25.60 ____ Objections to Probate.
25.61 ____ Decree Granting Probate.
25.62 ____ Receipt and Release Agreement Concluding an Estate Without an Accounting Proceeding.
25.63 ____ Receipt and Release (Legacy).
25.64 ____ Petition to Judicially Settle Executor's Account.
25.65 ____ Citation to Executor to Show Cause Why Judicially Executor Should Not Account.
25.66 ____ Accounting Form.
25.67 ____ Petition for Letters of Administration or Limited Letters of Administration or Temporary Administration.
25.68 ____ Decree Appointing Administrator.
25.69 ____ Affidavit Asking Court to Fix Amount of Administrator's Bond.
25.70 ____ Waiver of Citation, Renunciation of Signer's Claim to Letters and Consent to Appointment of Administrator.
25.71 ____ Notice of Application for Letters of Administration.
25.72 ____ Citation That Can Be Adopted for Use in Any Proceeding.

CHAPTER 26. PERSONAL INJURY

26.1 Scope Note.
26.2 Strategy.

LXXVIII

TABLE OF CONTENTS

Sec.
26.3	____ Client Interview.
26.4	____ Valuing the Case.
26.5	____ Skills and Ethics.
26.6	____ Retainer.
26.7	____ ____ Retainer Statement.
26.8	____ Expenses.
26.9	Investigation.
26.10	____ Premises Liability.
26.11	____ Medical Malpractice.
26.12	____ ____ Hospital.
26.13	____ ____ Dental and Podiatric Malpractice.
26.14	____ Products Liability.
26.15	____ Dog Bites.
26.16	____ Chemical Exposure.
26.17	____ Automobile Accidents.
26.18	____ ____ Police Report.
26.19	____ ____ Witness Statements.
26.20	____ ____ MV104.
26.21	____ ____ Application of No–Fault.
26.22	____ ____ Medical Records.
26.23	____ ____ Photographs.
26.24	____ ____ Insurance Policies and Coverage.
26.25	Claims Procedure for Automobile Accidents.
26.26	____ Filing Notice of Claim With the Motor Vehicle Accident Indemnity Corporation.
26.27	____ ____ Procedure for Cases in Which There Is No Insurance.
26.28	____ ____ Procedure for Cases in Which There Is No Insurance and the Identity of the Wrongdoer Is Not Ascertainable (Hit and Run).
26.29	____ ____ Procedure for Cases in Which Insurance Initially Is Believed to Exist, But There Is No Insurance After Later Disclaimer.
26.30	____ ____ Late Claims.
26.31	Theories of Liability.
26.32	Filing the Action.
26.33	____ When.
26.34	____ Where.
26.35	____ Potential Defendants.
26.36	The Summons and the Complaint.
26.37	The Answer.
26.38	Actions Against Municipal Corporations.
26.39	____ Notice of Claim.
26.40	____ ____ Content.
26.41	Actions Against the State.
26.42	Discovery—Generally.
26.43	____ Depositions.
26.44	____ Interrogatories.
26.45	____ Document Discovery and Inspection.
26.46	____ Bills of Particulars.
26.47	____ Demand for a Bill of Particulars.

LXXIX

TABLE OF CONTENTS

Sec.
26.48 Settlement.
26.49 Liens.
26.50 Alternative Dispute Resolution.
26.51 Trial Preparation: Introductory Note.
26.52 Trial.
26.53 ____ Subpoenas.
26.54 ____ Exhibits.
26.55 ____ *Voir Dire.*
26.56 Disbursement of Proceeds of Settlement or Recovery.
26.57 Drafting Checklists.
26.58 ____ Complaint.
26.59 ____ Answer.
26.60 ____ Demand for Bill of Particulars.
26.61 ____ Responses to Demand for Bill of Particulars.
26.62 Forms—Client's Retainer Agreement.
26.63 ____ Retainer Statement.
26.64 ____ Department of Motor Vehicles MV104 Form.
26.65 ____ Summons and Complaint.
26.66 ____ Amended Answer, Counterclaim and Cross Claim.
26.67 ____ Defendant's Demand for a Verified Bill of Particulars.
26.68 ____ Defendant's CPLR 3101 Demands.
26.69 ____ Plaintiff's Demand for a Verified Bill of Particulars.
26.70 ____ Plaintiff's CPLR 3101 Demands.
26.71 ____ Closing Statement.

CHAPTER 27. PRODUCTS LIABILITY

27.1 Scope Note.
27.2 Strategy.
27.3 Historical Overview.
27.4 Bases of a Products Liability Claim.
27.5 Theories of Liability.
27.6 ____ Manufacturing Defect or Mistake in the Manufacturing Process.
27.7 ____ Defective Design.
27.8 ____ ____ Burden of Proof.
27.9 ____ ____ Defense.
27.10 ____ Failure to Warn or Inadequate Warnings.
27.11 ____ ____ Burden of Proof.
27.12 ____ ____ Duty to Warn.
27.13 ____ ____ Adequacy of Warning.
27.14 ____ ____ Jury Question.
27.15 ____ ____ Informed Intermediary Defense.
27.16 ____ ____ Duty to Warn the Unusually Sensitive.
27.17 ____ ____ Non-Commercial Cases.
27.18 ____ Failure to Test.
27.19 ____ ____ FDA Approval.
27.20 ____ ____ Jury Question.
27.21 ____ ____ Preemption Defense.
27.22 Distributors' or Sellers' Liability.

TABLE OF CONTENTS

Sec.
27.23 ____ Sale Must Be Part of Ordinary Business.
27.24 ____ Service v. Sales.
27.25 ____ Medical Care Providers.
27.26 Successor Liability.
27.27 ____ Burden of Proof.
27.28 ____ Punitive Damages.
27.29 Liability of the Manufacturer of Component Parts.
27.30 Liability of the Manufacturer of the Complete Product.
27.31 Introducing Evidence of Post Accident Modification or Repairs.
27.32 Introducing Evidence of Other Incidents.
27.33 Effect of Destruction of the Product Upon Plaintiff's Ability to Prove a Defect.
27.34 Proof of Causation.
27.35 ____ Question for the Jury or Question for the Judge.
27.36 Foreseeability of Harm.
27.37 Discovery Issues.
27.38 ____ Confidentiality Orders or Stipulations.
27.39 Statute of Limitations.
27.40 Intervening Acts of Negligence—Plaintiff's Misuse of the Product.
27.41 ____ Alteration of the Product After it Has Left the Hands of the Manufacturer.
27.42 Preemption of Private Claims.
27.43 ____ Old Rule.
27.44 ____ New Rule.
27.45 ____ National Traffic & Motor Vehicle Safety Act and Its Savings Clause.
27.46 ____ Public Health Cigarette Labeling & Advertising Act of 1965 and the Public Health Cigarette Smoking Act of 1969—The *Cipollone* Decision.
27.47 ____ Federal Insecticide, Fungicide and Rodenticide Act (FIFRA) and Its Impact on Labeling Requirements.
27.48 ____ Medical Device Amendments to FDA Regulations.
27.49 ____ Limits on Preemption and Statutory Defenses.
27.50 ____ Validity of the Safety Standard or Regulatory Statute.
27.51 ____ Checklist.
27.52 Imposing Liability when the Manufacturer of a Fungible or Generic Product Is Unknown (Concert of Action/Market Share Liability).
27.53 Collateral Estoppel in Products Liability Cases.
27.54 Proof of Allegations Checklist.
27.55 Drafting Checklist—Complaint.
27.56 ____ Answer.
27.57 Forms—Products Liability Complaint.
27.58 ____ Products Liability Answer.

Volume 24

CHAPTER 28. LEGAL MALPRACTICE

28.1 Scope Note.

TABLE OF CONTENTS

Sec.
- 28.2 Strategy.
- 28.3 The Duty of Care.
- 28.4 ──── Specific Acts—Erroneous Advice.
- 28.5 ──── ──── Incompetent Tax Advice.
- 28.6 ──── ──── Proper Withdrawal.
- 28.7 ──── ──── Detecting Fraud.
- 28.8 ──── Causation.
- 28.9 ──── ──── The Doctrine of Compelled Settlement.
- 28.10 ──── Damages.
- 28.11 ──── Defenses—The Privity Rule.
- 28.12 ──── ──── Lawyer's Judgment Rule.
- 28.13 ──── ──── Statute of Limitations.
- 28.14 ──── ──── Continuous Representation Tolling Doctrine.
- 28.15 ──── ──── Extension by Estoppel.
- 28.16 ──── ────Standard Negligence Defenses of Lack of Foreseeability and Supervening Act.
- 28.17 ──── ──── Concealment of Malpractice Not a Separate Cause of Action.
- 28.18 ──── ──── Need for Consistent Positions.
- 28.19 The Duty of Loyalty.
- 28.20 ──── Conflict of Interest.
- 28.21 ──── Disqualification.
- 28.22 ──── Misappropriation of Client Funds.
- 28.23 Liability for Negligence of Independent Contractors.
- 28.24 Statutory Liability Under Judiciary Law § 487.
- 28.25 Vicarious Liability for Partner's Misdeeds.
- 28.26 Liability for Indemnity and Contribution.
- 28.27 Fee Disputes.
- 28.28 ──── Alternative Dispute Resolution.
- 28.29 ──── ──── Retainer Agreements Given Strict Scrutiny.
- 28.30 ──── ──── Arbitration Clause in Retainer Agreement May Waive Other Client Rights.
- 28.31 ──── Statutory Limitations.
- 28.32 ──── Account Stated.
- 28.33 ──── A Standard of Reasonableness.
- 28.34 Limited Liability Companies and Limited Liability Partnerships.
- 28.35 Lawyers Professional Liability Insurance.
- 28.36 ──── Extended Reporting Period.
- 28.37 ──── What Is a "Claim" and When Is It "Made"?
- 28.38 ──── Professional Capacity and Typical Exclusions.
- 28.39 ──── Limits, Deductibles and Defense.
- 28.40 ──── Notice of Claim and Notice of Occurrence.
- 28.41 ──── Cancellation.
- 28.42 ──── Innocent Partner Coverage.
- 28.43 ──── Application for Coverage and Rescission of Policy.
- 28.44 ──── Bad Faith.
- 28.45 ──── Cautions for Dissolving Law Firms.
- 28.46 Conclusion.
- 28.47 Drafting Checklist—Retainer Agreement.
- 28.48 ──── Malpractice Complaint Against Attorney.

TABLE OF CONTENTS

Sec.
28.49 ____ Answer to Malpractice Complaint on Behalf of Attorney.
28.50 Forms—Retainer Agreement With ADR Clause. 🖫
28.51 ____ Retainer Agreement Without ADR Clause. 🖫
28.52 ____ Complaint for Malpractice: Commercial Transaction. 🖫
28.53 ____ Complaint for Malpractice: Personal Injury Action. 🖫
28.54 ____ Answer: Commercial Transaction. 🖫
28.55 ____ Answer: Personal Injury Action. 🖫

CHAPTER 29. MEDICAL MALPRACTICE

29.1 Scope Note.
29.2 Strategy.
29.3 ____ Determining the Presence or Absence of Medical Malpractice.
29.4 ____ The Nature and Degree of Damages.
29.5 ____ Interviewing the Client.
29.6 ____ ____ History of the Current Condition.
29.7 ____ ____ Past Medical Conditions.
29.8 ____ ____ Current Medical Condition.
29.9 ____ ____ Miscellaneous Issues.
29.10 The Common Law Standards.
29.11 ____ The Standard of Care.
29.12 ____ ____ Hospitals' *Respondeat-Superior* Liability.
29.13 ____ ____ Hospitals' Direct Liability.
29.14 ____ Informed Consent.
29.15 ____ Health Maintenance Organizations.
29.16 ____ Expert Witnesses.
29.17 ____ Defenses in Medical Malpractice Cases.
29.18 Regulatory Standards.
29.19 ____ Qualifications of Nurse Midwives.
29.20 ____ Clinical Laboratories.
29.21 ____ Blood Banks.
29.22 ____ Testing for Phenylketonuria and Other Diseases and Conditions/Early Intervention Program.
29.23 ____ Hospitals.
29.24 Damages.
29.25 Procedure.
29.26 ____ Statutes of Limitation.
29.27 ____ Steps for Filing an Action.
29.28 ____ ____ Certificate of Merit.
29.29 ____ ____ Notice of Medical Malpractice Action.
29.30 ____ ____ Pre-calendar Conferences.
29.31 ____ Periodic Payment of Large Verdicts.
29.32 Hospital Operations and Medical Negligence—Credentialling of Physicians.
29.33 ____ Quality Assurance and Risk Management.
29.34 ____ Departmentalization of Services—Departmental Chairs.
29.35 Training and Education of Physicians.
29.36 ____ Medical School.
29.37 ____ PGY–1 (Internship).
29.38 ____ Residency.

TABLE OF CONTENTS

Sec.
29.39 ____ Fellowships.
29.40 ____ Board Certification & Re-certification.
29.41 ____ Associations, Societies, and Continuing Medical Education.
29.42 ____ National Practitioner Data Bank.
29.43 Medical Literature.
29.44 ____ Obtaining Medical Literature.
29.45 ____ Sources.
29.46 ____ Using Medical Literature to Evaluate a Case.
29.47 ____ Preparing for Depositions.
29.48 ____ Preparing for Trial.
29.49 ____ Use of Treatises in State Court.
29.50 ____ Use of Treatises in Federal Court.
29.51 Evaluating and Understanding Medical Records—Physician's Records.
29.52 ____ Hospital Records.
29.53 ____ ____ Informed Consent Forms.
29.54 ____ ____ Progress Notes.
29.55 ____ ____ Order Sheets.
29.56 ____ ____ Consultation Records.
29.57 ____ ____ Operative Records.
29.58 ____ ____ Medication Records.
29.59 ____ ____ Intake and Output Records.
29.60 ____ ____ Radiographic Records.
29.61 ____ ____ Obstetrical Records.
29.62 ____ ____ ICU/CCU Records.
29.63 ____ ____ Nurses' Notes.
29.64 Discovery.
29.65 ____ Obtaining and Identifying Relevant Records.
29.66 ____ ____ Physician's Records.
29.67 ____ ____ Hospital Records.
29.68 ____ ____ Billing Records.
29.69 ____ ____ Pharmacy Records.
29.70 ____ ____ Allied Health Provider Records.
29.71 ____ ____ Workers' Compensation Claims File.
29.72 ____ ____ Autopsy Report.
29.73 ____ ____ Workers' Compensation Actions.
29.74 ____ ____ Medical Malpractice Actions.
29.75 Trial Preparation.
29.76 Drafting Checklists.
29.77 ____ Order to Show Cause to Obtain Medical Records.
29.78 ____ Affirmation in Support of Order to Show Cause.
29.79 ____ Certificate of Merit.
29.80 Forms
29.81 ____ Order to Show Cause to Obtain Medical Records. 💾
29.82 ____ Affirmation in Support of Order to Show Cause. 💾
29.83 ____ Certificate of Merit. 💾

CHAPTER 30. DAMAGES

30.1 Scope Note.

TABLE OF CONTENTS

Sec.
30.2 Strategy.
30.3 ____ Pretrial Stage.
30.4 ____ Trial Stage.
30.5 The Nature of Damages.
30.6 Compensatory Damages.
30.7 ____ Personal Injury.
30.8 ____ ____ Physical Pain and Suffering.
30.9 ____ ____ Mental or Emotional Pain and Suffering.
30.10 ____ ____ Loss of Earnings and Impairment of Future Earning Ability.
30.11 ____ ____ Aggravation of Pre-existing Injuries.
30.12 ____ Wrongful Death.
30.13 ____ ____ Damages Sustained Before Death.
30.14 ____ ____ Damages Sustained After Death.
30.15 ____ Loss of Consortium.
30.16 ____ Property Damage.
30.17 ____ ____ Real Property.
30.18 ____ Personal Property.
30.19 ____ Breach of Contract.
30.20 ____ ____ Contract Price and Actual Loss.
30.21 ____ ____ Delay in Performance.
30.22 ____ ____ Defective Performance.
30.23 ____ ____ Anticipatory Breach.
30.24 ____ ____ Damages Within the Contemplation of the Parties, and Loss of Profits.
30.25 ____ ____ Building and Construction.
30.26 ____ Minimizing and Mitigating Damages.
30.27 ____ ____ Contracts.
30.28 ____ ____ Personal Injury.
30.29 ____ ____ Excessive or Inadequate Damages.
30.30 ____ ____ Specific Awards.
30.31 Punitive Damages.
30.32 ____ Intentional Torts.
30.33 ____ Negligence.
30.34 ____ Contract.
30.35 ____ Awards.
30.36 ____ Mitigation.
30.37 Nominal Damages.
30.38 Statutory Damages.
30.39 Liquidated Damages and Penalties.
30.40 Interest.
30.41 Attorney Fees.
30.42 ____ Statutory.
30.43 ____ Agreements and Miscellaneous.
30.44 Periodic Payment of Judgments.
30.45 Forms.
30.46 ____ *Ad Damnum* Clause in Ordinary Complaint.
30.47 ____ *Ad Damnum* Clause in Complaint in Medical or Dental Malpractice Action or in Action Against Municipal Government (Supreme Court).

LXXXV

TABLE OF CONTENTS

Sec.
30.48 —— Clauses in Complaint in Action Involving Automobile Accident. 💾
30.49 —— Request for Supplemental Demand for Relief in Medical or Dental Malpractice Action or Action Against Municipal Corporation. 💾
30.50 —— Defense of Culpable Conduct in Answer. 💾
30.51 —— Defense of Failure to Use Seat Belt Contained in Answer. 💾
30.52 —— Defense of Indemnification From Collateral Sources. 💾
30.53 —— Partial Defense; Mitigation of Damages. 💾
30.54 —— Partial Defense; Mitigation of Damages in Libel Action. 💾
30.55 —— Partial Defense; Inability to Convey Property. 💾
30.56 —— Notice of Motion to Amend Verdict (or Judgment) to Add Interest. 💾
30.57 —— Affidavit in Support of Motion to Amend Verdict (or Judgment) to Add Interest. 💾
30.58 —— Notice of Motion to Fix Date From Which Interest is to Be Computed. 💾
30.59 —— Affidavit in Support of Motion to Fix Date From Which Interest is to Be Computed. 💾
30.60 Pattern Jury Instructions.
30.61 —— Personal Injury—Subsequent Injury, Accident.
30.62 —— —— Loss of Earnings.
30.63 —— Damages—Personal Injury—Shock and Fright and Physical Consequences.
30.64 —— —— Aggravation of Injury.
30.65 —— Payment of Income Taxes on Damages for Personal Injury.
30.66 —— Reduction to Present Value.
30.67 —— Wrongful Death—Conscious Pain and Suffering.
30.68 —— Personal Injury—Collateral Sources—Itemized Verdict (CPLR 4111).
30.69 —— Damages—Property Without Market Value.
30.70 —— Damages—Property With Market Value.
30.71 —— Contracts—Damages—Generally.
30.72 —— —— Damages—Employment Contract.

CHAPTER 31. INSURANCE

31.1 Scope Note.
31.2 Strategy.
31.3 —— Checklist.
31.4 Sources of New York Insurance Law.
31.5 Third Parties Involved in the Placement and Administration of the Insurance Contract.
31.6 —— Insurance Brokers.
31.7 —— Insurance Agents.
31.8 Nature of Insurance.
31.9 Interpreting an Insurance Policy.
31.10 Notice.
31.11 The Cooperation Clause.

TABLE OF CONTENTS

Sec.
31.12 The Insurer's Duty to Defend.
31.13 ____ Responding to a Request for a Defense.
31.14 ____ Damages for Breach of the Duty.
31.15 Reservations of Rights By an Insurer.
31.16 Disclaiming/Denying Coverage.
31.17 The Insurer's Duty of Good Faith and Fair Dealing.
31.18 Rescission of Insurance Policies.
31.19 Reformation.
31.20 Lost Policies.
31.21 Nature of Relief.
31.22 Service of Process.
31.23 Pre-answer Security.
31.24 Arbitration Clauses.
31.25 Choice of Law.
31.26 Statutes of Limitation.
31.27 Burden of Proof.
31.28 Insolvent Insurers.
31.29 Subrogation.
31.30 Allocation of Losses Between Co-insurers.
31.31 Checklist of Essential Allegations.
31.32 Forms—Complaint By Policyholder for Declaratory Relief and Breach of Contract. 💾
31.33 ____ Complaint By Insurer for Declaratory Relief. 💾
31.34 ____ Complaint By Insurer for Rescission. 💾
31.35 ____ Affirmative Defenses Asserted By Insurer in a Coverage Action. 💾

CHAPTER 32. WORKERS' COMPENSATION

32.1 Scope Note.
32.2 Strategy.
32.3 ____ Employer's Counsel's Checklist.
32.4 ____ Employee's Counsel's Checklist.
32.5 Introduction to The Workers' Compensation Law.
32.6 ____ History and Theory.
32.7 ____ ____ Workmen's Compensation Law of 1910.
32.8 ____ ____ Constitutional Amendment.
32.9 ____ ____ Workmen's Compensation Law of 1914.
32.10 ____ ____ Statutory Changes.
32.11 Workers' Compensation Board.
32.12 Employer's Obligations and Methods of Coverage.
32.13 Compensable Injury.
32.14 Exclusive Remedy Doctrine.
32.15 ____ Exceptions.
32.16 Pre-hearing Conference.
32.17 Hearings.
32.18 ____ Statute of Limitations.
32.19 ____ Burden of Proof, Presumptions and Defenses.
32.20 ____ Conciliation Process.
32.21 Benefits.

TABLE OF CONTENTS

Sec.
- 32.22 ____ Classification of Disability.
- 32.23 ____ Wage Replacement.
- 32.24 ____ ____ Schedule vs. Non-schedule Awards.
- 32.25 ____ ____ Rehabilitation.
- 32.26 ____ ____ Industrially Disabled.
- 32.27 ____ ____ Special Disability Fund.
- 32.28 ____ Medical Benefits.
- 32.29 ____ Facial Disfigurement.
- 32.30 ____ Death Awards.
- 32.31 ____ ____ Funeral Expenses.
- 32.32 ____ Assignments, Liens and Lump-sum Settlements.
- 32.33 Board Review of Decisions, Orders and Awards.
- 32.34 Appeal to Court.
- 32.35 Reopening Closed Claims.
- 32.36 Discrimination.
- 32.37 Licensed Representative.
- 32.38 Attorney's Fees.
- 32.39 Posted Notice of Coverage.
- 32.40 Uninsured Employers' Fund.
- 32.41 Insurance Policy for Workers' Compensation.
- 32.42 State Insurance Fund.
- 32.43 Federal Workers' Compensation Laws and Benefits.
- 32.44 Disability Benefits Law.
- 32.45 ____ Employer's Obligations.
- 32.46 ____ Exempt Employees.
- 32.47 ____ Benefits and Employee Contribution.
- 32.48 ____ Special Fund.
- 32.49 ____ Employee Eligibility.
- 32.50 ____ Claim Filing.
- 32.51 ____ Pregnancy.
- 32.52 ____ End Note.
- 32.53 Forms.
- 32.54 ____ Workers' Compensation Board Employee's Claim For Compensation. (C–3 7–97)
- 32.55 ____ Workers' Compensation Board Employer's Report of Work–Related Accident/Occupational Disease. (C–2 10–97)
- 32.56 ____ Workers' Compensation Board Attending Doctor's Report and Carrier/Employer Billing. (C–4 3–97)
- 32.57 ____ Workers' Compensation Board Notice that Right to Compensation is Controverted. (C–7 2–97)
- 32.58 ____ Workers' Compensation Board Notice that Payment of Compensation for Disability has Been Stopped or Modified. (C–8/8.6 4–97)
- 32.59 ____ Notice and Proof of Claim for Disability Benefits. (DB-450 3–97)
- 32.60 ____ Notice of Total or Partial Rejection of Claim for Disability Benefits. (DB–451 3–97)

CHAPTER 33. LOCAL CRIMINAL COURT PRACTICE

- 33.1 Scope Note.

TABLE OF CONTENTS

Sec.
33.2 Strategy.
33.3 Overview of Local Criminal Court Process.
33.4 Police/Citizen Encounters.
33.5 ____ Vehicle Stops.
33.6 ____ The Parked Car.
33.7 ____ Arrest Without Warrant.
33.8 Accusatory Instruments.
33.9 ____ Information.
33.10 ____ Simplified Information.
33.11 ____ Prosecutor's Information.
33.12 ____ Misdemeanor and Felony Complaints.
33.13 ____ Supporting Depositions.
33.14 ____ ____ Procedure.
33.15 ____ ____ When Must They Be Provided?
33.16 ____ ____ Who Must Be Served?
33.17 ____ ____ Service of Request Must be Timely.
33.18 ____ ____ Request By Attorney Requires Service on Counsel.
33.19 ____ ____ Dismissal For Failure to Serve.
33.20 ____ ____ Motion Must Be In Writing.
33.21 ____ ____ Motion to Dismiss Must Be Timely.
33.22 ____ ____ Factual Insufficiency Not Jurisdictional: Plea Waives Defect.
33.23 ____ ____ Superseding Information Disallowed.
33.24 ____ ____ People May File New Information Upon Dismissal of Supporting Deposition.
33.25 ____ ____ Failure to Serve Not An Amendable Defect.
33.26 ____ ____ Verification.
33.27 Probable Cause Hearing.
33.28 Plea Bargaining.
33.29 ____ Plea Bargain Can Be Conditioned Upon Waiver of Right to Appeal.
33.30 ____ Plea Bargaining—No Penalty for Asserting Right to Trial.
33.31 Pretrial Discovery.
33.32 ____ Applicable to Simplified Informations.
33.33 ____ Applicable to Traffic Infractions.
33.34 ____ Subpoenas.
33.35 ____ Demands to Produce/Bills of Particulars.
33.36 ____ ____ Must Be Filed Within 30 Days.
33.37 ____ ____ Response Within 15 Days.
33.38 ____ ____ People's Failure to Comply With Time Limits.
33.39 ____ *Brady* Material.
33.40 ____ ____ Prosecutor Need Not Be Aware of Evidence.
33.41 ____ ____ Timely Disclosure.
33.42 Evidence.
33.43 ____ Motions to Suppress.
33.44 ____ *Sandoval* Issues—Prior Convictions.
33.45 ____ ____ Procedure.
33.46 ____ ____ *Sandoval* Criteria.
33.47 ____ ____ Defendant's Presence at *Sandoval* Hearing.
33.48 ____ *Miranda*.

LXXXIX

TABLE OF CONTENTS

Sec.	
33.49	__ __ Applicable to Misdemeanor Traffic Offenses.
33.50	__ __ Stop and Frisk Does Not Constitute Custodial Interrogation.
33.51	__ __ Sobriety Checkpoint Stops Are Non-custodial.
33.52	__ __ Interrogation Defined.
33.53	__ __ Public Safety Exception.
33.54	__ __ Pedigree Exception.
33.55	__ __ Waiver Following Assertion of Right to Remain Silent.
33.56	__ __ Waiver Following Request for Counsel.
33.57	__ Involuntary Statements.
33.58	__ __ May Not Be Used to Impeach.
33.59	__ __ Applicability of Harmless Error Doctrine.
33.60	__ The Use of Defendant's Pre-arrest Silence.
33.61	__ Corroboration of Admission or Confession Required.
33.62	Trial.
33.63	__ Modes of Trial.
33.64	__ Order of Jury Trial Proceedings.
33.65	__ Order of Bench Trial Proceedings.
33.66	__ Trial of Speeding Tickets.
33.67	__ __ Discovery.
33.68	__ __ People's *Prima Facie* Case.
33.69	__ __ When Not to Request a Supporting Deposition.
33.70	__ __ Speeding Trial Summary.
33.71	Speedy Trial Pursuant to CPL § 30.20.
33.72	__ Application to Traffic Infractions.
33.73	__ Criteria.
33.74	CPL § 30.30.
33.75	__ Vehicle and Traffic Law Violations Generally Excluded.
33.76	__ __ Unless Combined With Felony, Misdemeanor or Violation.
33.77	__ People's Readiness Rule.
33.78	__ Requirements for An Assertion of Readiness.
33.79	__ __ Actual Readiness for Trial.
33.80	__ Guilty Plea Waives CPL § 30.30 Motion.
33.81	__ Burden of Proof.
33.82	__ Commencement of Criminal Action—Appearance Tickets.
33.83	__ Uniform Traffic Tickets.
33.84	__ Excludable Time.
33.85	__ __ Motions.
33.86	__ __ Defective Accusatory Instrument.
33.87	__ __ Adjournments.
33.88	__ __ Delays by the Court.
33.89	__ __ Effect of Defendant's Unavailability.
33.90	__ Post Readiness Delay.
33.91	Procedural Checklists.
33.92	__ Notice of Motion to Dismiss For Failure to Serve a Timely Supporting Deposition/Attorney Affirmation in Support of Motion.
33.93	__ Demand to Produce: Speeding Ticket.
33.94	Drafting Checklists.

TABLE OF CONTENTS

Sec.
33.95 ____ Notice of Motion to Dismiss For Failure to Serve a Timely Supporting Deposition.
33.96 ____ Attorney Affirmation in Support of Motion to Dismiss For Failure to Serve a Timely Supporting Deposition.
33.97 ____ Demand to Produce: Speeding Ticket.
33.98 Forms.
33.99 ____ Notice of Motion to Dismiss For Failure to Serve a Timely Supporting Deposition. 💾
33.100 ____ Attorney Affirmation in Support of Motion to Dismiss For Failure to Serve a Timely Supporting Deposition. 💾
33.101 ____ Demand to Produce: Speeding Ticket. 💾

CHAPTER 34. SOCIAL SECURITY DISABILITY CASES

34.1 Scope Note.
34.2 Strategy.
34.3 The Law of Disability.
34.4 ____ Statutory Definition of Disability.
34.5 ____ Judicial Definitions.
34.6 ____ Durational Requirements.
34.7 ____ Comparison to Workers' Compensation.
34.8 ____ Assessing Disability: The Sequential Evaluation.
34.9 ____ ____ Substantial Gainful Activity.
34.10 ____ ____ Severity.
34.11 ____ ____ Listings of Impairments.
34.12 ____ ____ Ability to Do Past Relevant Work.
34.13 ____ ____ Ability to Do Other Work.
34.14 ____ ____ Dispensing With Individualized Assessment.
34.15 Financial Consideration of The Two Federal Programs: Social Security Disability Insurance Benefits and Supplemental Security Income.
34.16 ____ Income.
34.17 ____ Assets.
34.18 ____ Amount of Benefits.
34.19 ____ SSI: Based on Financial Need.
34.20 ____ SSDIB: Based on FICA Withholding.
34.21 ____ Eligibility for Both SSI and SSDIB.
34.22 ____ Retroactivity of Benefits.
34.23 Administrative Procedure.
34.24 ____ Application.
34.25 ____ Reconsideration.
34.26 ____ Termination of Benefits.
34.27 ____ Administrative Hearing.
34.28 ____ Appeals Council.
34.29 ____ Federal District Court.
34.30 ____ Court of Appeals, Second Circuit.
34.31 Handling the Case—Generally.
34.32 ____ Initial Interview.
34.33 ____ Retainer Agreements.
34.34 ____ Social Security Administration's Records.

TABLE OF CONTENTS

Sec.
34.35 ____ ____ Medical Evidence.
34.36 ____ ____ Hospital Records.
34.37 ____ ____ Reports from Treating Physicians.
34.38 ____ Other Evidence.
34.39 ____ ____ Former Co-workers and Employers.
34.40 ____ ____ Family Members.
34.41 ____ Preparing for the Hearing.
34.42 ____ ____ Preparing the Claimant.
34.43 ____ ____ Other Witnesses or Documents.
34.44 ____ Conducting the Hearing.
34.45 ____ ____ Testimony of the Claimant.
34.46 ____ ____ Medical Advisors.
34.47 ____ ____ Vocational Experts.
34.48 ____ Post-hearing Evidence and Memoranda.
34.49 Implementing Favorable Decisions.
34.50 ____ Collecting SSDIB Benefits.
34.51 ____ Collecting SSI Benefits.
34.52 ____ Collecting Fees.
34.53 ____ ____ Fee Applications.
34.54 ____ ____ Fee Agreements.
34.55 Appealing Unfavorable Decisions.
34.56 ____ Strategic Considerations Regarding Unfavorable Decisions.
34.57 ____ Strategic Considerations Regarding Partially Favorable Decisions.
34.58 Reopening Prior Applications.
34.59 ____ Reopening SSDIB.
34.60 ____ Reopening SSI.
34.61 ____ Review of Grants of Reopening.
34.62 ____ Review of Denials of Reopening.
34.63 ____ Court Decisions Requiring Reopening.
34.64 ____ Statutes and Regulations Requiring Reopening.
34.65 Procedural Checklist.
34.66 Checklists of Allegations—Medical Claims.
34.67 ____ Psychiatric Claims.
34.68 Forms—Claimant Questionnaire. 💾
34.69 ____ Retainer Agreement. 💾
34.70 ____ Retainer Agreement: Concurrent Benefits. 💾
34.71 ____ Fee Agreement: Maximum Fee. 💾
34.72 ____ Request for Medical Records. 💾
34.73 ____ Medical Release. 💾
34.74 ____ Medical Questionnaire for Treating Physician. 💾
34.75 ____ Psychiatric Questionnaire. 💾
34.76 ____ Cover Letter to Treating Physician. 💾
34.77 ____ Thank-you Letter to Treating Physician. 💾
34.78 ____ Request for Appeals Council Review. 💾

CHAPTER 35. INCOME TAX

35.1 Scope Note.
35.2 Strategy.

XCII

TABLE OF CONTENTS

Sec.
- 35.3 ____ Checklist.
- 35.4 Personal Income Tax.
- 35.5 ____ Computing Federal Adjusted Gross Income.
- 35.6 ____ Computing Federal Taxable Income.
- 35.7 ____ Definition of New York Taxable Income.
- 35.8 ____ Computing New York Adjusted Gross Income.
- 35.9 ____ Computing New York Taxable Income.
- 35.10 ____ New York Personal Exemptions.
- 35.11 ____ Itemized Deductions for Married Couple.
- 35.12 ____ Exclusion of Pension and Disability Distributions From New York Income.
- 35.13 ____ New York Minimum Tax.
- 35.14 ____ Definition of Residency.
- 35.15 ____ Burden of Proving Non-residency.
- 35.16 ____ Domicile and Change of Domicile.
- 35.17 ____ New York Income Tax on Non-resident Individuals.
- 35.18 ____ Checklist.
- 35.19 New York Corporate Franchise Tax.
- 35.20 ____ Comparison With Federal Taxation.
- 35.21 ____ Initial Tax on Corporate Capital Structure.
- 35.22 ____ Foreign Corporations.
- 35.23 ____ Corporations Subject to Tax.
- 35.24 ____ Corporations Exempt From Tax.
- 35.25 ____ Necessary Level of Activity.
- 35.26 ____ Calculation.
- 35.27 ____ Tax on Net Income Base.
- 35.28 ____ ____ Subtractions From Federal Taxable Income.
- 35.29 ____ Items From Subsidiaries.
- 35.30 ____ Tax on Capital Base.
- 35.31 ____ ____ Definition of Capital Base.
- 35.32 ____ ____ Exemption for Small Businesses.
- 35.33 ____ Minimum Taxable Income Base.
- 35.34 ____ Fixed Dollar Minimum Tax.
- 35.35 ____ Apportionment of Tax Bases to New York.
- 35.36 ____ ____ Business Allocation Percentage.
- 35.37 ____ ____ Investment Allocation Percentage.
- 35.38 ____ Definition of Subsidiary Capital.
- 35.39 ____ Franchise Tax Checklist.
- 35.40 Department of Taxation and Finance.
- 35.41 ____ Role of Office of the Counsel.
- 35.42 ____ Taxpayer Services Division.
- 35.43 ____ Office of Revenue and Information Management.
- 35.44 ____ Office of Tax Operations.
- 35.45 ____ ____ Audit Division.
- 35.46 ____ ____ Tax Compliance Division.
- 35.47 ____ ____ Revenue Opportunity Division.
- 35.48 ____ ____ Office of Tax Enforcement.
- 35.49 ____ ____ Division of Tax Appeals.
- 35.50 ____ Summary.
- 35.51 Filing Returns.

TABLE OF CONTENTS

Sec.

35.52	——	Where to File.
35.53	——	Keeping Records of Returns.
35.54	——	Extensions of Time for Filing.
35.55	——	Obtaining New York Tax Forms.
35.56	——	Filing Claims for Refund.
35.57	——	Time Limitations.
35.58	——	Where to File.
35.59	——	Special Refund Authority.
35.60	——	Claim Based on Federal Changes.
35.61	——	Petitions for Refund.
35.62	——	Judicial Review of Denied Refund Claims.
35.63	——	Checklist.
35.64		Statutes of Limitation.
35.65	——	General Statutes for Income Tax Assessment.
35.66	——	Effect.
35.67	——	Exceptions.
35.68	——	Request for Prompt Assessment.
35.69	——	Waiver.
35.70		Penalties.
35.71	——	Late Filing.
35.72	——	Late Payment.
35.73	——	Reasonable Cause.
35.74	——	Negligence.
35.75	——	Substantial Understatement.
35.76	——	Underpayment of Estimated Taxes.
35.77	—— ——	Exceptions.
35.78	——	Fraud.
35.79	—— ——	Elements.
35.80	—— ——	Specific Determination Methods.
35.81	—— ——	Common Cases.
35.82	—— ——	Creative Methods of Proof.
35.83	——	Interest on Underpayment or Overpayment.
35.84	——	Checklist.
35.85		Audits and Appeals.
35.86	——	Audit Methods.
35.87	——	Taxpayer Bill of Rights.
35.88	——	Representation of Taxpayer.
35.89	——	Audit Results.
35.90	——	Bureau of Conciliation and Mediation Services.
35.91	—— ——	Requesting a Conciliation Conference.
35.92	—— ——	Conferences.
35.93	—— ——	Conference Orders.
35.94	——	Petition to Division of Tax Appeals.
35.95	—— ——	Referral to Bureau of Conciliation and Mediation Services.
35.96	—— ——	Small Claims Hearings.
35.97	——	Summary.
35.98	——	Checklist.
35.99		Judicial Actions.
35.100	——	Appeal by Article 78 Proceeding.

TABLE OF CONTENTS

Sec.
35.3 ____ Checklist.
35.4 Personal Income Tax.
35.5 ____ Computing Federal Adjusted Gross Income.
35.6 ____ Computing Federal Taxable Income.
35.7 ____ Definition of New York Taxable Income.
35.8 ____ Computing New York Adjusted Gross Income.
35.9 ____ Computing New York Taxable Income.
35.10 ____ New York Personal Exemptions.
35.11 ____ Itemized Deductions for Married Couple.
35.12 ____ Exclusion of Pension and Disability Distributions From New York Income.
35.13 ____ New York Minimum Tax.
35.14 ____ Definition of Residency.
35.15 ____ Burden of Proving Non-residency.
35.16 ____ Domicile and Change of Domicile.
35.17 ____ New York Income Tax on Non-resident Individuals.
35.18 ____ Checklist.
35.19 New York Corporate Franchise Tax.
35.20 ____ Comparison With Federal Taxation.
35.21 ____ Initial Tax on Corporate Capital Structure.
35.22 ____ Foreign Corporations.
35.23 ____ Corporations Subject to Tax.
35.24 ____ Corporations Exempt From Tax.
35.25 ____ Necessary Level of Activity.
35.26 ____ Calculation.
35.27 ____ Tax on Net Income Base.
35.28 ____ ____ Subtractions From Federal Taxable Income.
35.29 ____ Items From Subsidiaries.
35.30 ____ Tax on Capital Base.
35.31 ____ ____ Definition of Capital Base.
35.32 ____ ____ Exemption for Small Businesses.
35.33 ____ Minimum Taxable Income Base.
35.34 ____ Fixed Dollar Minimum Tax.
35.35 ____ Apportionment of Tax Bases to New York.
35.36 ____ ____ Business Allocation Percentage.
35.37 ____ ____ Investment Allocation Percentage.
35.38 ____ Definition of Subsidiary Capital.
35.39 ____ Franchise Tax Checklist.
35.40 Department of Taxation and Finance.
35.41 ____ Role of Office of the Counsel.
35.42 ____ Taxpayer Services Division.
35.43 ____ Office of Revenue and Information Management.
35.44 ____ Office of Tax Operations.
35.45 ____ ____ Audit Division.
35.46 ____ ____ Tax Compliance Division.
35.47 ____ ____ Revenue Opportunity Division.
35.48 ____ ____ Office of Tax Enforcement.
35.49 ____ ____ Division of Tax Appeals.
35.50 ____ Summary.
35.51 Filing Returns.

TABLE OF CONTENTS

Sec.

35.52	____	Where to File.
35.53	____	Keeping Records of Returns.
35.54	____	Extensions of Time for Filing.
35.55	____	Obtaining New York Tax Forms.
35.56	____	Filing Claims for Refund.
35.57	____	Time Limitations.
35.58	____	Where to File.
35.59	____	Special Refund Authority.
35.60	____	Claim Based on Federal Changes.
35.61	____	Petitions for Refund.
35.62	____	Judicial Review of Denied Refund Claims.
35.63	____	Checklist.
35.64		Statutes of Limitation.
35.65	____	General Statutes for Income Tax Assessment.
35.66	____	Effect.
35.67	____	Exceptions.
35.68	____	Request for Prompt Assessment.
35.69	____	Waiver.
35.70		Penalties.
35.71	____	Late Filing.
35.72	____	Late Payment.
35.73	____	Reasonable Cause.
35.74	____	Negligence.
35.75	____	Substantial Understatement.
35.76	____	Underpayment of Estimated Taxes.
35.77	____ ____	Exceptions.
35.78	____	Fraud.
35.79	____ ____	Elements.
35.80	____ ____	Specific Determination Methods.
35.81	____ ____	Common Cases.
35.82	____ ____	Creative Methods of Proof.
35.83	____	Interest on Underpayment or Overpayment.
35.84	____	Checklist.
35.85		Audits and Appeals.
35.86	____	Audit Methods.
35.87	____	Taxpayer Bill of Rights.
35.88	____	Representation of Taxpayer.
35.89	____	Audit Results.
35.90	____	Bureau of Conciliation and Mediation Services.
35.91	____ ____	Requesting a Conciliation Conference.
35.92	____ ____	Conferences.
35.93	____ ____	Conference Orders.
35.94	____	Petition to Division of Tax Appeals.
35.95	____ ____	Referral to Bureau of Conciliation and Mediation Services.
35.96	____ ____	Small Claims Hearings.
35.97	____	Summary.
35.98	____	Checklist.
35.99		Judicial Actions.
35.100	____	Appeal by Article 78 Proceeding.

XCIV

TABLE OF CONTENTS

Sec.
35.101 ___ ___ Payment of Taxes.
35.102 ___ ___ Initiation.
35.103 ___ ___ Burden of Proof.
35.104 ___ Declaratory Judgment Actions.
35.105 ___ Appeal to New York Court of Appeals.
35.106 ___ Summary.
35.107 ___ Checklist.
35.108 Assessment and Collection of Tax.
35.109 ___ Summary Assessment.
35.110 ___ Deficiency Assessment.
35.111 ___ Statute of Limitations.
35.112 ___ Jeopardy Assessment.
35.113 ___ Collection of Tax.
35.114 ___ ___ Lien.
35.115 ___ ___ Duration of Lien.
35.116 ___ Collection by Levy or Warrant.
35.117 ___ Installment Payment Agreements.
35.118 ___ Offer in Compromise.
35.119 ___ Bankruptcy as an Option.
35.120 ___ Checklist.
35.121 Criminal Tax Provisions.
35.122 ___ Failure to File Return.
35.123 ___ False or Fraudulent Return.
35.124 ___ Aiding or Assisting in False Return or Statement.
35.125 ___ Failure to Pay Tax.
35.126 ___ Failure to Properly Withhold Taxes.
35.127 Forms.
35.128 ___ Power of Attorney to Represent an Individual.
35.129 ___ Application for Automatic Extension of Time for Filing Return.
35.130 ___ Application For Additional Extension of Time to File for Individuals.
35.131 ___ Notice of Exception to Tax Tribunal.
35.132 ___ Petition to Division of Tax Appeals.
35.133 ___ Petition for Advisory Opinion.
35.134 ___ Statement of Financial Condition.
35.135 ___ Petition for Declaratory Ruling.
35.136 ___ Request for Conciliation Conference.
35.137 ___ Offer in Compromise.

CHAPTER 36. ALCOHOLIC BEVERAGE CONTROL LAW

36.1 Scope Note.
36.2 Strategy.
36.3 ___ Checklist.
36.4 Historical Background of State and Federal Regulations.
36.5 Jurisdiction.
36.6 New York State Liquor Authority.
36.7 Licenses.
36.8 ___ Retail Licenses.

TABLE OF CONTENTS

Sec.
36.9 ____ ____ On-Premises Licenses.
36.10 ____ ____ Off-Premises Licenses.
36.11 ____ Wholesale Licenses.
36.12 ____ Manufacturing Licenses.
36.13 ____ General Application Requirements.
36.14 ____ Special Qualifications for Licensees.
36.15 Permits.
36.16 ____ Temporary Permits.
36.17 ____ Other Permits.
36.18 Brand and/or Label Registration.
36.19 Penal and Tax Bonds.
36.20 Application Form (Retail) Reviewed.
36.21 ____ Lease Information.
36.22 ____ Applicant Information.
36.23 ____ Information Regarding Premises.
36.24 ____ Financial Information and Criminal Background.
36.25 ____ Community Notification.
36.26 ____ Landlord Information.
36.27 ____ Additional Requirements for On–Premises Consumption Licenses.
36.28 ____ ____ Neighborhood.
36.29 ____ ____ Premises Exterior.
36.30 ____ ____ Premises Interior.
36.31 ____ ____ Bars.
36.32 ____ ____ Kitchen.
36.33 ____ ____ Permits.
36.34 ____ ____ Hotel.
36.35 ____ Proposed Method of Operation.
36.36 ____ Additional Requirements for Off–Premises Liquor Store Applicants.
36.37 ____ Additional Requirements for Grocery Store Applicants.
36.38 ____ Liquidators Permit.
36.39 ____ Affidavit Requirements.
36.40 ____ Personal Questionnaire.
36.41 ____ On-Premises Liquor Applications 500 Foot Verification.
36.42 ____ Miscellaneous Requirements.
36.43 ____ Checklist.
36.44 Record–Keeping Requirements.
36.45 Reporting Changes.
36.46 ____ Application for Endorsement Certificate.
36.47 ____ Application for Approval of Corporate Change.
36.48 ____ Alteration of Premises.
36.49 ____ Removal of Premises.
36.50 ____ Financing and Method of Operation.
36.51 Renewals.
36.52 Trade Practices.
36.53 Enforcement.
36.54 Penalties.
36.55 ____ Revocation Order.
36.56 ____ Cancellation Order.

XCVI

TABLE OF CONTENTS

Sec.
36.57 ____ Suspension Order.
36.58 ____ ____ Forthwith.
36.59 ____ ____ Deferred.
36.60 ____ ____ Combined Forthwith and Deferred Suspension.
36.61 ____ Letters of Warning.
36.62 ____ Suspension Proceedings.
36.63 ____ Revocation Notice of Pleading.
36.64 Pleadings and Procedure.
36.65 ____ Hearings.
36.66 ____ Judicial Review.
36.67 Forms.
36.68 ____ Application for Alcoholic Beverage Control Retail License.
36.69 ____ Application for Endorsement Certificate.
36.70 ____ Application for Approval of Corporate Change.
36.71 ____ Application for Permission to Make Alterations.
36.72 ____ Application for Wholesale License.
36.73 ____ Retail License and Filing Fee Schedule.

CHAPTER 37. CIVIL APPELLATE PRACTICE BEFORE THE APPELLATE DIVISION AND OTHER INTERMEDIATE APPELLATE COURTS

37.1 Scope Note.
37.2 Strategy.
37.3 Judiciary Structure.
37.4 Administration of the Appellate Division.
37.5 Administrative Powers of the Appellate Division.
37.6 ____ Admission, Removal and Disciplinary Jurisdiction.
37.7 ____ Administration of the Courts.
37.8 ____ Law Guardian Program.
37.9 ____ Mental Hygiene Legal Service Oversight.
37.10 ____ Assigned Counsel.
37.11 ____ Powers Relating to Appellate Term.
37.12 ____ Marshals.
37.13 An Overview of the Statutory Framework of the Appellate System and the Rules of the Court.
37.14 Appeals to the Appellate Division.
37.15 ____ Courts of Original Jurisdiction From Which Appeals Lie.
37.16 ____ ____ Supreme Court and County Court.
37.17 ____ ____ Court of Claims.
37.18 ____ ____ Surrogate's Court.
37.19 ____ ____ Family Court.
37.20 ____ Appeals From Other Appellate Courts.
37.21 ____ Who May Appeal.
37.22 ____ ____ Aggrieved Parties.
37.23 ____ ____ ____ Defaulters; Orders or Judgments on Consent.
37.24 ____ ____ ____ Intervenors.
37.25 ____ ____ ____ Substitution of Parties.
37.26 ____ ____ ____ Third Party Defendants.
37.27 ____ Scope of Review.

TABLE OF CONTENTS

Sec.
37.28	____ ____	Questions of Law.
37.29	____ ____	Questions of Fact and the Exercise of Discretion.
37.30	____ ____	Limitations in Notice of Appeal or Brief.
37.31	____ ____	Mootness.
37.32	____ ____	Change in Law While Case Is Pending.
37.33	____	Appeals as of Right.
37.34	____ ____	Appeals From Final and Interlocutory Judgments.
37.35	____ ____	Appeals From Orders.
37.36	____	Appeals by Permission.
37.37	____	Non-appealable Matters.
37.38	____	Appealable Paper.
37.39	____	Time for Taking the Appeal.
37.40	____ ____	Appeal as of Right.
37.41	____ ____	Appeal by Permission.
37.42	____ ____	Cross-Appeal.
37.43	____ ____	Extensions; Omissions.
37.44	____ ____	Other Statutory Provisions.
37.45	____	Notice of Appeal—Form and Content.
37.46	____ ____	Service and Filing Requirements.
37.47	____	Reargument; Subsequent Orders.
37.48	____	Assignment of Counsel.
37.49	____	Perfecting the Appeal.
37.50	____ ____	Time.
37.51	____ ____	Methods of Perfection.
37.52	____ ____	Briefs.
37.53	____ ____	Consolidation.
37.54	____	What to File; Number of Copies.
37.55	____ ____	First Department.
37.56	____ ____	Second Department.
37.57	____ ____	Third Department.
37.58	____ ____	Fourth Department.
37.59	____	Location; Transfer Plan.
37.60	____	Calendars.
37.61	____	Preferences.
37.62	____	Oral Arguments.
37.63	____	Disposition of the Appeal.
37.64	____ ____	Affirmance.
37.65	____ ____	Reversal or Modification.
37.66	____ ____	Dismissal.
37.67	____ ____	Costs and Disbursements; Attorneys' Fees.
37.68	____	Post-disposition Proceedings.
37.69	____ ____	Reargument.
37.70	____ ____	Leave to Appeal to the Court of Appeals.
37.71	____ ____	Enforcement.
37.72	____ ____	Resettlement or Clarification.
37.73	____ ____	*Certiorari* to the U.S. Supreme Court.
37.74	____	Motion Practice—Generally.
37.75	____ ____	First Department.
37.76	____ ____	Second Department.
37.77	____ ____	Third Department.

TABLE OF CONTENTS

Sec.
37.78	—— ——	Fourth Department.
37.79	—— ——	Interim Relief.
37.80	—— ——	Stays.
37.81	—— ——	*Amicus Curiae.*
37.82	—— ——	Miscellaneous Motions.
37.83	——	Sanctions.
37.84	——	Preargument Conferences.
37.85	——	Unperfected Appeals.
37.86		Other Proceedings in the Appellate Division.
37.87	——	CPLR Article 78 Proceedings.
37.88	——	Writs of *Habeas Corpus.*
37.89	——	CPLR 5704 *Ex Parte* Order Review.
37.90	——	Miscellaneous Proceedings.
37.91		Appeals to Other Intermediate Courts.
37.92	——	Appeals from Justice Courts.
37.93	—— ——	Courts to Which Appeals Are Taken.
37.94	—— ——	Applicability of CPLR Article 55.
37.95	—— ——	Appeals as of Right and by Permission.
37.96	—— ——	Taking the Appeal: Settlement of Case and Return on Appeal.
37.97	—— ——	Perfection of Appeal.
37.98	—— ——	Costs on Appeal.
37.99	—— ——	Small Claims Review.
37.100	—— ——	Rule Governance by Administrative Board.
37.101	——	Appeals From City Courts.
37.102	—— ——	Courts to Which Appeals Are Taken.
37.103	—— ——	Applicability of CPLR Article 55.
37.104	—— ——	Appeals as of Right and by Permission.
37.105	—— ——	Taking the Appeal: Settlement of Case and Return on Appeal; Variations from CPLR.
37.106	—— ——	Perfection of Appeal.
37.107	—— ——	Costs on Appeal.
37.108	—— ——	Small Claims Review.
37.109	——	Appeals From District Courts.
37.110	—— ——	Court to Which Appeals Are Taken.
37.111	—— ——	Applicability of CPLR Article 55.
37.112	—— ——	Appeals as of Right and by Permission.
37.113	—— ——	Taking the Appeal: Settlement of Case and Return on Appeal.
37.114	—— ——	Perfecting the Appeal.
37.115	—— ——	Costs on Appeal.
37.116	—— ——	Small Claims Review.
37.117	——	Appeals from the Civil Court of the City of New York.
37.118	—— ——	Courts to Which Appeals Are Taken.
37.119	—— ——	Applicability of CPLR Article 55.
37.120	—— ——	Appeals as of Right and by Permission.
37.121	—— ——	Appeals to the Court of Appeals.
37.122	—— ——	Taking the Appeal: Settlement of Case and Return on Appeal; Variations From CPLR.
37.123	—— ——	Perfecting the Appeal.

TABLE OF CONTENTS

Sec.
37.124 ___ ___ Costs on Appeal.
37.125 ___ ___ Small Claims Review.
37.126 ___ Appeals from County Courts.
37.127 Procedural Checklist.
37.128 Forms.
37.129 ___ Notice of Appeal. 💾
37.130 ___ Notice of Motion for a Stay of Proceedings. 💾
37.131 ___ Order to Show Cause for a Stay of Proceedings. 💾
37.132 ___ Affirmation in Support of Motion or Order To Show Cause for a Stay of Proceedings. 💾
37.133 ___ Notice of Motion for a Preference to Expedite the Appeal. 💾
37.134 ___ Affirmation in Support of Motion for a Preference to Expedite the Appeal. 💾
37.135 ___ Notice of Motion to Enlarge Time for (Appellant to Perfect Appeal)(Respondent To File Brief). 💾
37.136 ___ Affirmation in Support of Motion to Enlarge Time for (Appellant to Perfect Appeal) (Respondent to File Brief). 💾
37.137 ___ Notice of Motion to Strike Matter *Dehors* the Record (Appendix)(Brief). 💾
37.138 ___ Affirmation in Support of Motion to Strike Matter *Dehors* the Record(Appendix)(Brief). 💾
37.139 ___ Notice of Motion for Reargument or Leave to Appeal to the Court of Appeals. 💾
37.140 ___ Affirmation in Support of Motion for Reargument or Leave to Appeal to the Court of Appeals. 💾

Volume 25

CHAPTER 38. CRIMINAL APPELLATE PRACTICE BEFORE THE APPELLATE DIVISION AND OTHER INTERMEDIATE APPELLATE COURTS

38.1 Scope Note.
38.2 Strategy.
38.3 Appeals to the Appellate Division—General Principles.
38.4 ___ Courts of Original Jurisdiction From Which Appeals Lie.
38.5 ___ Who May Appeal.
38.6 ___ ___ Status as Aggrieved by "Adverse" Determination.
38.7 ___ ___ Appeals by the Defendant From Superior Courts.
38.8 ___ ___ ___ As of Right.
38.9 ___ ___ ___ Appeals by Permission.
38.10 ___ ___ Appeals by the People.
38.11 ___ ___ Appeals from Orders Accepting or Sealing Grand Jury Reports; Appeals by Prosecutors; Appeals by Public Servants.
38.12 ___ Appeal Process—Appeals as of Right.
38.13 ___ ___ Appeals by Permission: Certificate Granting Leave.
38.14 ___ ___ Extensions of Time.
38.15 ___ ___ Stay of Judgment or Order.
38.16 ___ ___ Poor Person Relief and Assignment of Counsel.

TABLE OF CONTENTS

Sec.
38.17 ___ ___ Perfecting and Calendaring the Appeal.
38.18 ___ Scope of Review.
38.19 ___ ___ Questions of Law.
38.20 ___ ___ Questions of Fact; Weight of Evidence.
38.21 ___ ___ Interest of Justice/Discretion.
38.22 ___ ___ Change in Law While Case Pending.
38.23 ___ Disposition of Appeal.
38.24 ___ ___ Affirmance.
38.25 ___ ___ Modification.
38.26 ___ ___ Reversal.
38.27 ___ ___ Character of Order of Reversal or Modification: On the Law, On the Facts, in the Interest of Justice.
38.28 ___ ___ Corrective Action.
38.29 ___ Post-disposition Proceedings.
38.30 ___ ___ Responsibilities of Counsel.
38.31 ___ ___ Reargument.
38.32 ___ ___ Leave to Appeal.
38.33 ___ ___ *Certiorari* to U.S. Supreme Court.
38.34 ___ ___ *Coram Nobis*—Ineffective Assistance of Appellate Counsel.
38.35 ___ ___ Clarification/Resettlement.
38.36 ___ Motions in Connection With Appeals—Generally.
38.37 ___ ___ *Pro Se* Supplemental Brief.
38.38 ___ ___ *Anders* Brief.
38.39 ___ ___ Dismissal.
38.40 ___ ___ Reconstruction Hearing; Summary Reversal.
38.41 ___ ___ Death or Absence of a Defendant.
38.42 ___ ___ Assignment of New Counsel.
38.43 ___ ___ Expanding the Judgment Roll.
38.44 ___ ___ Briefs.
38.45 ___ ___ Withdrawal of Appeal.
38.46 Appeals to Intermediate Appellate Courts Other Than the Appellate Division.
38.47 ___ Appeals From Village Courts, Town Courts, City Courts and District Courts.
38.48 ___ Appeals From Criminal Court of the City of New York.
38.49 ___ ___ New York and Bronx County Branches.
38.50 ___ ___ Kings, Queens, Richmond County Branches.
38.51 ___ Orders, Sentences and Judgments Appealable.
38.52 ___ Taking the Appeal—Appeal as of Right.
38.53 ___ ___ Appeals by Permission.
38.54 ___ Stays Pending Appeal.
38.55 ___ Perfecting the Appeal.
38.56 ___ Determination of the Appeal.
38.57 Governance of the Appellate Term.
38.58 Original Application to County Court for Change of Venue.
38.59 Procedural Checklist for Appeals to Appellate Division.
38.60 Forms—Notice of Motion for a Stay of Execution of Judgment. 💾

TABLE OF CONTENTS

Sec.
38.61 ____ Affirmation in Support of Motion for a Stay of Execution of Judgment. 💾
38.62 ____ Notice of Motion for an Extension of Time to Take an Appeal. 💾
38.63 ____ Affirmation in Support of Motion for an Extension of Time to Take an Appeal. 💾
38.64 Chart.

CHAPTER 39. CIVIL AND CRIMINAL APPEALS TO THE COURT OF APPEALS

39.1 Scope Note.
39.2 Strategy.
39.3 Civil Appeals.
39.4 ____ Finality.
39.5 ____ Non-appealable Orders.
39.6 ____ Appealable Paper.
39.7 ____ Scope of Review.
39.8 ____ Appeal as of Right.
39.9 ____ ____ Appellate Division Orders or Judgments.
39.10 ____ ____ Final Judgment of Court of Original Instance.
39.11 ____ ____ Judgment of Court of Original Instance to Review Prior Non-final Determination of the Appellate Division.
39.12 ____ Appeals by Permission of the Appellate Division or the Court of Appeals.
39.13 ____ ____ Judgment of Court of Original Instance to Review Prior Non-final Determination of the Appellate Division.
39.14 ____ ____ Final Order of the Appellate Division Determining the Action.
39.15 ____ ____ Non-final Appellate Division Orders in Proceedings by or Against Public Officers or Others.
39.16 ____ Appeals by Permission of the Appellate Division.
39.17 ____ Form, Content and Service of Motions for Leave to Appeal.
39.18 ____ ____ Motions Filed in the Appellate Division.
39.19 ____ ____ Motions Filed in the Court of Appeals.
39.20 ____ Time for Taking the Appeal or Moving for Leave to Appeal—Appeals as of Right.
39.21 ____ ____ Motions for Leave to Appeal.
39.22 ____ ____ Cross Appeals.
39.23 ____ ____ Extensions of Time.
39.24 ____ ____ Omissions.
39.25 ____ Notice of Appeal—Form and Content.
39.26 ____ The Jurisdictional Statement.
39.27 ____ Jurisdictional Inquiry.
39.28 ____ Perfecting and Readying the Appeal.
39.29 ____ ____ Full Briefing and Oral Argument.
39.30 ____ ____ *Sua Sponte* Merits Consideration ("SSM").
39.31 ____ Determination of the Appeal—*Remittitur*.
39.32 ____ Motion Practice.
39.33 ____ ____ Motion for a Stay.

TABLE OF CONTENTS

Sec.
39.34 ___ ___ Motion to File an *Amicus* Brief.
39.35 ___ ___ Motion for Poor Person Relief.
39.36 ___ ___ Motion for Reconsideration.
39.37 Criminal Appeals.
39.38 ___ Definition of Criminal Case.
39.39 ___ Orders and Judgments From Which Appeals May Be Taken.
39.40 ___ By the Defendant in Death Penalty Cases.
39.41 ___ By the Prosecution in Death Penalty Cases.
39.42 ___ Intermediate Appellate Courts.
39.43 ___ Additional Limitations on Appealability.
39.44 ___ Appeals by Permission.
39.45 ___ ___ Obligation of Intermediate Appellate Court Counsel.
39.46 ___ ___ Who May Grant Leave to Appeal.
39.47 ___ ___ Criminal Leave Application ("CLA") Practice.
39.48 ___ ___ Stays and Continuation of Bail.
39.49 ___ Appeals Practice.
39.50 ___ Scope of Review.
39.51 ___ Disposition of Appeal.
39.52 ___ Motion Practice.
39.53 ___ ___ Poor Person Relief and Assignment of Counsel.
39.54 ___ ___ Extension of Time to Seek Leave to Appeal.
39.55 ___ ___ Dismissal of Appeal.
39.56 ___ ___ Withdrawal of Appeal.
39.57 ___ ___ Reargument.
39.58 Other Proceedings in the Court of Appeals.
39.59 ___ Review of Determinations of the Commission on Judicial Conduct.
39.60 ___ Certified Questions From Other Courts.
39.61 ___ Matters Regarding Admission of Attorneys and Licensing of Foreign Legal Consultants.
39.62 *Certiorari* to the Supreme Court of the United States.
39.63 Procedural Checklists.
39.64 ___ Civil Appeals as of Right.
39.65 ___ Civil Appeals by Permission of Court of Appeals.
39.66 ___ Criminal Appeals by Leave of a Court of Appeals Judge.
39.67 ___ Civil Appeals by Leave of the Appellate Division and Criminal Appeals by Leave of an Appellate Division Justice.
39.68 ___ Appeals Selected for Expedited Review Pursuant to Rule 500.4
39.69 ___ Appeals Tracked to Full Briefing and Oral Argument.
39.70 Drafting Checklists.
39.71 ___ Notice of Appeal.
39.72 ___ Rule 500.2 Jurisdictional Statement.
39.73 ___ Motion for Leave to Appeal to Court of Appeals Filed in Court of Appeals.
39.74 ___ Application for Leave to Appeal in Criminal Case Filed in Court of Appeals.
39.75 ___ Appellant's Brief on the Merits.
39.76 ___ Respondent's Brief on the Merits.

TABLE OF CONTENTS

Sec.
39.77 Forms—Notice of Appeal to Court of Appeals From Order of Appellate Division Finally Determining Action With Two Dissents on Question of Law. 🖫
39.78 ⎯⎯ Notice of Appeal to Court of Appeals From Order of Appellate Division Finally Determining Action Where Construction of Constitution is Directly Involved. 🖫
39.79 ⎯⎯ Notice of Appeal to Court of Appeals From Judgment of Supreme Court Where Constitutionality of Statute is Directly Involved. 🖫
39.80 ⎯⎯ Notice of Appeal to Court of Appeals From Appellate Division Order of Reversal Granting New Trial With Stipulation for Judgment Absolute. 🖫
39.81 ⎯⎯ Notice of Appeal to Court of Appeals From Judgment of Supreme Court to Review Prior Non-final Determination of Appellate Division. 🖫
39.82 ⎯⎯ Rule 500.2 Jurisdictional Statement. 🖫
39.83 ⎯⎯ Notice of Motion in Court of Appeals for Leave to Appeal to Court of Appeals From Order of Appellate Division. 🖫
39.84 ⎯⎯ Affidavit in Support of Motion in Court of Appeals for Leave to Appeal to Court of Appeals From Order of Appellate Division. 🖫
39.85 ⎯⎯ Notice of Motion in Court of Appeals for Reargument of Motion for Leave to Appeal. 🖫
39.86 ⎯⎯ Notice of Motion in Court of Appeals for Leave to Appear *Amicus Curiae*. 🖫
39.87 ⎯⎯ Notice of Motion to Dismiss Appeal as Untimely Taken. 🖫
39.88 ⎯⎯ Affidavit in Support of Motion to Dismiss Appeal as Untimely Taken. 🖫
39.89 ⎯⎯ CPLR 5531 Statement. 🖫
39.90 ⎯⎯ Letter Seeking Leave to Appeal in Criminal Case. 🖫

	Page
Table of Jury Instructions	235
Table of Forms	236
Table of Statutes	iii
Table of Rules	iii
Table of Cases	iii
Index	iii

WEST'S NEW YORK PRACTICE SERIES

GENERAL PRACTICE IN NEW YORK

Volume 23

Chapter 21

DOMESTIC RELATIONS

by
Myrna Felder

Table of Sections

21.1	Scope Note.
21.2	Strategy.
21.3	Jurisdiction.
21.4	___ Residence Requirements.
21.5	___ Uniform Child Custody Jurisdiction Act.
21.6	Competency of the Court to Grant Relief.
21.7	___ Equitable Distribution.
21.8	___ Support.
21.9	___ Custody and Visitation.
21.10	Jurisdiction Over the Defendant's Person or Property.
21.11	___ Personal Jurisdiction.
21.12	___ Long Arm Jurisdiction.
21.13	___ *In Rem* Jurisdiction.
21.14	*Quasi in Rem* Jurisdiction.
21.15	Venue.
21.16	___ Changing Venue.
21.17	Joinder, Consolidation and Joint Trials.
21.18	Grounds for Divorce.
21.19	___ No Official No–Fault Ground.
21.20	___ Cruel and Inhuman Treatment.
21.21	___ ___ Defenses.
21.22	___ Abandonment.
21.23	___ ___ Defenses.
21.24	___ ___ Effect of Separation Agreement.
21.25	___ Imprisonment.
21.26	___ Adultery.
21.27	___ ___ Defenses.
21.28	___ ___ Effect of Separation Agreement.
21.29	___ Divorce Action Based Upon Living Apart Pursuant to Separation Decree or Judgment.
21.30	___ Divorce Action Based Upon Living Apart Pursuant to Separation Agreement.
21.31	___ Dual Divorce.
21.32	Effect of Sister State Divorce Judgment.
21.33	Equitable Distribution.
21.34	___ When Available.

Ch. 21 DOMESTIC RELATIONS

21.35 —— Identification of Property.
21.36 —— Characterization of Property.
21.37 —— —— Marital Property.
21.38 —— —— —— Pensions.
21.39 —— —— —— Professional Practices, Licenses, Degrees and Careers.
21.40 —— —— Separate Property.
21.41 —— —— —— Increase in Value of Separate Property.
21.42 —— Valuation Dates.
21.43 —— Valuation Methods.
21.44 —— Distribution Factors.
21.45 —— Tax Considerations.
21.46 Maintenance.
21.47 —— Legislative Factors.
21.48 —— Effect of Fault.
21.49 —— Current Trends.
21.50 —— Payments Fixed by Agreement.
21.51 —— Tax Consequences.
21.52 Child Support.
21.53 —— Child Support Standards Act.
21.54 —— —— Where Statutory Percentages Are Unfair or Inappropriate.
21.55 —— —— Recent Trends.
21.56 —— Effect of Agreement or Stipulation.
21.57 Health and Life Insurance.
21.58 Custody.
21.59 —— Visitation.
21.60 —— Relocation of Custodial Parent With the Child.
21.61 —— Joint Custody.
21.62 —— Proceedings in Which Custody Dispositions Are Available.
21.63 Financial Disclosure.
21.64 Disclosure on Matters Going to the Merits of the Case.
21.65 Net Worth Statement.
21.66 Statement of Proposed Disposition.
21.67 Findings of Fact and Conclusions of Law; Judgments.
21.68 Modification.
21.69 —— Maintenance.
21.70 —— Child Support.
21.71 —— Custody.
21.72 Enforcement.
21.73 —— Plenary Action to Enforce Agreement.
21.74 —— Defenses.
21.75 Practice Considerations.
21.76 —— Procedure for Attorneys in Domestic Relations Matters.
21.77 —— Disciplinary Rules.
21.78 —— Fee Arbitration Rules.
21.79 —— Rules Regarding Case Management.
21.80 Procedural Checklist—Calendar Control.
21.81 Drafting Checklist—Retainer Agreements.
21.82 —— Complaint in Action for Divorce.
21.83 —— Statement of Proposed Disposition.
21.84 Forms.
21.85 —— Retainer Agreement. 💾

§ 21.1 DOMESTIC RELATIONS Ch. 21

21.86 ____ Complaint for Divorce.
21.87 ____ Statement of Net Worth.
21.88 ____ Statement of Proposed Disposition.
21.89 ____ Findings of Fact and Conclusions of Law.
21.90 ____ Matrimonial Judgments.
21.91 ____ Referee's Report on Findings of Fact and Conclusions of Law.
21.92 ____ Matrimonial Judgment Entered Upon Referee's Report.

WESTLAW Electronic Research
See WESTLAW Electronic Research Guide preceding the Summary of Contents.

§ 21.1 Scope Note

This chapter begins with an analysis of who may use our courts to obtain relief in matrimonial actions[1] and custody proceedings.[2] Next, the competency of our courts to grant relief is reviewed.[3] Jurisdiction over a party is then discussed,[4] including personal jurisdiction over the defendant or respondent and how it is obtained,[5] long-arm jurisdiction,[6] *in rem* jurisdiction,[7] and *quasi in rem* jurisdiction.[8] Venue is the next subject addressed.[9]

Before a substantive discussion of the rights and responsibilities of the parties upon the dissolution of a marriage can begin, the basis for the dissolution of the marriage must be examined. There are six grounds for divorce in New York. Each specific ground is discussed in Sections 21.20 through 21.30. Where New York stands on no-fault divorce is explored in Section 21.19 and the effect of a divorce judgment from another state is examined briefly in Section 21.32.

The economic rights and responsibilities of the parties upon dissolution of the family unit comprise a main part of this chapter. The law governing the division of property upon dissolution of marriage, is examined in Sections 21.33 through 21.45. First, property must be identified.[10] Next, the property must be characterized as marital or separate.[11] This includes whether pensions[12] or professional practices, licenses, degrees and careers[13] qualify as property under the statute. Whether the increase in the value of separate property constitutes marital property is analyzed in Section 21.41. Once property has been characterized as marital, it must be valued. The dates used for valuation

§ 21.1

1. See infra, § 21.4.
2. See infra, § 21.5.
3. See infra, §§ 21.6–21.9.
4. See infra, § 21.10.
5. See infra, § 21.11.
6. See infra, § 21.12.
7. See infra, § 21.13.
8. See infra, § 21.14.
9. See infra, §§ 21.15–21.16.
10. See infra, § 21.35.
11. See infra, §§ 21.37–21.41.
12. See infra, § 21.38.
13. See infra, § 21.39.

of an asset are explored in Section 21.41 and the methods of valuation are discussed in Section 21.42. A court is mandated to consider certain factors when determining an equitable distribution of marital assets. Each of these factors are presented in Section 21.44. Finally, the tax considerations involved in a marital property division are explored in Section 21.45.

The chapter continues with a discussion of maintenance,[14] exploring the legislative factors[15] that are to be considered by a court, as well as how recent cases are interpreting the statutory mandates.[16]

Next, the chapter addresses the issue of child support.[17] The chapter explains the complex statute, which provides the guidelines for determining the child support obligations of the parents, in Sections 21.53 and 21.54. Recent trends addressed in a seminal court decision, which analyzes the requirements of the statute, are discussed in Section 21.55.

The discussion of the economic relief available concludes with coverage of the provisions requiring a party to maintain health or life insurance, discussed in Section 21.57.

The chapter next addresses custody,[18] with discussion of the standards used to make a custody determination.[19] A detailed discussion of the new standard that applies when a custodial parent seeks to relocate with a child is presented in Section 21.60 and the option of joint custody is explored in Section 21.61.

The discovery issues that are pertinent to a domestic relations case are addressed in Sections 21.63 and 21.64. Section 21.65 presents a discussion of the net worth statement.

Once there is a judgment or an agreement, the issues of modification and enforcement take on importance. The rules regarding modification are examined in Sections 21.68 through 21.71. A brief discussion of enforcement is presented in Sections 21.72 through 21.74.

No chapter on domestic relations would be complete without an examination of the significant changes in the practice rules dealing with both the attorney-client relationship and the management of matrimonial cases. This chapter discusses the rules relating to the procedures for attorneys in domestic relations matters,[20] disciplinary rules,[21] fee arbitration rules,[22] and rules regarding case management.[23]

The chapter concludes with checklists and forms in Sections 21.80 through 21.92.

14. See infra, §§ 21.46–21.51.
15. See infra, § 21.47.
16. See infra, § 21.49.
17. See infra, §§ 21.52–21.56.
18. See infra, §§ 21.58–21.62.
19. See infra, § 21.58.
20. See infra, § 21.76.
21. See infra, § 21.77.
22. See infra, § 21.78.
23. See infra, § 21.79.

§ 21.2 Strategy

Handling a matrimonial case presents counsel with numerous challenges. First, counsel must understand the legal requirements and implications of the Domestic Relations Law ("DRL"), the Family Court Act and the Civil Practice Laws and Rules ("CPLR"). Next, counsel must be familiar with contract,[1] real estate[2] and relevant tax law.[3]

The matrimonial attorney, perhaps more than any other attorney, must have good interpersonal skills. The matrimonial client is in the midst of a traumatic event and counsel must be able to deal with the client competently and sensitively. The attorney's skills will be put to the test at the start of the attorney-client relationship, where it is essential that counsel obtain necessary information and details and communicate options to the client.

Initially, counsel will need the answers to the following questions:

a. Are the parties validly married?[4]

b. Does a New York court have jurisdiction over the case?[5]

c. Can personal jurisdiction be obtained?[6]

d. Does the court have authority to grant the relief sought?[7]

e. Does the client have grounds for divorce?[8]

f. Have the parties executed any prior agreements?[9]

g. Who controls and has access to the financial holdings and records of the family?[10]

h. What is the extent of the client's financial reliance on the other spouse?[11]

---

§ 21.2

1. *See* Chapter 5 "Commercial Sales Contracts," *supra*.

2. *See* Chapter 12 "Purchase and Sale of Real Estate," *supra*.

3. *See* Chapter 35 "State Income Tax," *infra*.

4. The fact of the marriage must be pleaded in the complaint. *See infra*, § 21.82, for a drafting checklist for a complaint in a matrimonial action.

5. *See infra*, § 21.4.

6. *See infra*, § 21.11.

7. *See infra*, §§ 21.7–21.8.

8. *See infra*, §§ 21.18–21.30.

9. The court may not provide for a property distribution when the parties have settled the matter between themselves pursuant to DRL § 236(B)(3). *See infra*, § 21.34.

Parties can also agree to maintenance, *see infra*, § 21.50, child support, *see infra*, § 21.56 and custody, *see infra*, § 21.61.

10. **PRACTICE POINTER:** One of counsel's most important tasks is to analyze the financial information. The client will have to provide financial information for counsel and the initial interview is a good time to discuss that information and whether the client has easy access to it. Some of the financial information includes: income tax returns; bank accounts and records; securities and investments; safe deposit boxes; debts and obligations; real property instruments; business interests; insurance; credit cards; social security, pension and retirement benefits; and personal property, furniture and furnishings.

11. If the client is a dependent spouse, counsel will have to address the issue of maintenance. *See infra*, §§ 21.46–21.51.

i. What is the length of the parties' marriage?[12]
j. Is the timing of an agreement in the client's best interest at this point in time?[13]
k. Were the parties married in a religious or civil ceremony?[14]
l. If custody is an issue, what is the scope of both parents' relationship with the child or children of the marriage.[15]

One of the early decisions to be made involves determining whether to proceed as the plaintiff, or to wait for the other spouse to file the action. If the other spouse has already commenced the action, counsel must determine if it is prudent to oppose the action or to assert a counterclaim.

If no action has been taken by any party when counsel first sees the client, counsel has the time to review the pros and cons of proceeding as the plaintiff in an action. One factor that weighs in favor of proceeding as a plaintiff is the desire to stop the continued acquisition of marital property. Commencement of the action prevents property or interests in property that are acquired after commencement of the action from being included in marital property.[16] The convenience of the client may be another reason for proceeding as the plaintiff. The parties may be separated and living in different counties, both of which may be suitable for purposes of venue.[17] Commencing the action in the county where the client resides may be convenient to the client and perhaps also to counsel and to experts.

Where the client's grounds are not strong, counsel might be well advised to have such a client, particularly one who is financially dependent, wait and let the other spouse make the initial move.

If the client's spouse has initiated divorce proceedings, there are also some initial considerations. First and foremost, counsel must ascertain if

---

12. **PRACTICE POINTER:** The duration of the parties' marriage affects many issues. First, the length of the marriage may be a factor in determining whether a divorce on the ground of cruel and inhuman treatment will be granted. See infra, § 21.20. Additionally, the duration of the marriage is a factor that courts consider in both equitable distribution and maintenance. See infra, §§ 21.44, 21.47.

Further, if the parties have been married for ten years or more, the Social Security Administration permits one spouse to collect on the other's Social Security account. It may be more advantageous for the client to collect social security under the spouse's account, rather than collect on his or her own account. Indeed, where there has been no work history the client may not even have such an account.

13. See infra, §§ 21.37–21.42.

14. **PRACTICE POINTER:** Such information is crucial if the client is Jewish and will require a "get" from the other spouse in order to remarry. In equitable distribution, a barrier to remarriage is to be considered as a factor which may influence the statutory factors. See infra, § 21.44. Where the marriage was solemnized by clergy, in drafting the divorce complaint, there must be an allegation that all steps have been taken to remove any barrier to the defendant's remarriage. See infra, § 21.82.

15. See infra, §§ 21.58–21.62.

16. See infra, § 21.37.

17. See infra, § 21.15.

§ 21.2

the client wants to challenge the termination of the marriage. This involves analyzing the plaintiff's grounds to determine if there are facts supporting the defendant's position.[18] Obviously, if the plaintiff has proof of abandonment,[19] adultery[20] or imprisonment,[21] then resistance to the divorce may be futile. Chances are better when the basis for divorce is cruel and inhuman treatment,[22] particularly when the marriage is one of long duration.

Another response by a defendant in a matrimonial action may be to counterclaim for divorce. If both parties establish grounds for divorce (except in actions where both parties allege either adultery or abandonment), the court may grant a dual divorce.[23] Generally, marital fault will not be considered in the equitable distribution of property and the determination of maintenance, except in egregious cases; economic fault can be considered on both these issues.[24]

In nearly all instances, the best strategy, for both plaintiff and defendant, is to negotiate and settle matrimonial actions and custody proceedings. The uncertainty of the result, unavoidable delays and the inherent escalation of hostilities usually makes litigation the choice of last resort.

However, there are many matters which cannot be settled unless each party understands that the other is ready willing and able to litigate to conclusion, if necessary, armed with the ability to obtain the relief from a court if the other party does not agree. The alternative is to assume the posture of a beggar: asking for only what the other spouse is willing to offer with virtually no bargaining power.

§ 21.3 Jurisdiction

In contrast to most other areas of law, there is virtually no common law basis for matrimonial and family law. All of it derives from statute. At the time when the colonies adopted the common law of England, marriage and divorce was governed by the Church of England. As a result, all authority in family law matters is derived from statute.[1] This becomes particularly relevant when we consider jurisdiction.

Library References:

West's Key No. Digests, Divorce ⟸289; Infants ⟸18; Parent and Child ⟸2(5).

18. See infra, §§ 21.18–21.30.
19. See infra, §§ 21.22–21.24.
20. See infra, §§ 21.26–21.28.
21. See infra, § 21.25.
22. See infra, §§ 21.20–21.21.
23. See infra, § 21.31.

24. See infra, §§ 21.44, § 21.48.

§ 21.3

1. Caldwell v. Caldwell, 298 N.Y. 146, 81 N.E.2d 60 (1948); Seitz v. Drogheo, 21 N.Y.2d 181, 287 N.Y.S.2d 29, 234 N.E.2d 209 (1967).

§ 21.4 Jurisdiction—Residence Requirements

In matrimonial actions, Domestic Relations Law § 230 governs statutory residence requirements.[1] The statute requires that at least one of the parties have deep enough ties to New York or that sufficient conduct occurred in New York to warrant the exercise of jurisdiction by New York courts. There are five standards set out in the statute. The statute is complied with if both the parties are residents of the state on the day the action is commenced. Where only one party is a resident, that party has to have been a resident for two years unless the parties were married in this state, resided here as husband and wife, or the cause of action arose in this state, in which case the party who is a resident has to have been a resident for one year. This statute applies whether the action is one for divorce, separation or annulment.[2]

The early cases construing this statute held that compliance with its residency requirements conferred "subject matter jurisdiction" on the court. However, in 1975, the Court of Appeals held in *Lacks v. Lacks*[3] that the residence requirements of Section 230 were one element of the matrimonial cause of action and not a limitation on the subject matter jurisdiction of the courts.

Since compliance with DRL § 230 is necessary whatever it is called, one may wonder what difference it makes. The answer lies in the fact that a defect in subject matter jurisdiction is not waivable and may be raised at any time, even post-judgment. Whether a cause of action has been proven is a question resolved in a final judgment. As the Court of Appeals explained in *Lacks v. Lacks*:

> Hence, a divorce judgment granted in the absence of one of the specified connections with the State, even if erroneously determined as a matter of law or fact, is not subject to vacatur under CPLR 5015 (subd. [a], par. 4).[4]

§ 21.4

1. DRL § 230 provides that an action to annul a marriage, or to declare the nullity of a void marriage, or for divorce or separation may be maintained only when:

   1. The parties were married in the state and either party thereof is a resident when the action is commenced and has been a resident for a continuous period of one year immediately preceding, or

   2. The parties have resided in this state as husband and wife and either party is a resident thereof when the action is commenced and has been a resident for a continuous period of one year immediately preceding, or

   3. The cause occurred in the state and either party has been a resident thereof for a continuous period of at least one year immediately preceding the commencement of the action, or

   4. The cause occurred in the state and both parties are residents thereof at the time of the commencement of the action, or

   5. Either party has been a resident of the state for a continuous period of at least two years immediately preceding the commencement of the action.

2. DRL § 230.

3. 41 N.Y.2d 71, 390 N.Y.S.2d 875, 359 N.E.2d 384 (1976).

4. *Id.*

§ 21.4

DRL § 230 is entitled "Required Residence of Parties." Case law has established that proof of either domicile or residency will suffice to show compliance.[5]

Library References:

West's Key No. Digests, Divorce ⚯289; Infants ⚯18; Parent and Child ⚯2(5).

§ 21.5 Jurisdiction—Uniform Child Custody Jurisdiction Act

To determine whether the court may entertain a proceeding for custody, whether brought separately or as part of a matrimonial action, one needs to consult New York State's version on The Uniform Child Custody Jurisdiction Act (DRL Article 75) which governs jurisdiction in matters of child custody. The relevant section is DRL § 75–d, which provides that a court of this state which is competent to decide child custody matters has jurisdiction to make a child custody determination by initial or modification decree only when:

(a) this state (i) is the home state of the child at the time of commencement of the custody proceeding, or (ii) had been the child's home state within six months before commencement of such proceeding and the child is absent from this state because of his removal or retention by a person claiming his custody or for other reasons, and a parent or person acting as parent continues to live in this state; or

(b) it is in the best interest of the child that a court of this state assume jurisdiction because (i) the child and his parents, or the child and at least one contestant, have a significant connection with this state, and (ii) there is within the jurisdiction of the court substantial evidence concerning the child's present or future care, protection, training, and personal relationships; or

(c) the child is physically present in this state and (i) the child has been abandoned or (ii) it is necessary in an emergency to protect the child; or

(d) (i) it appears that no other state would have jurisdiction under prerequisites substantially in accordance with paragraph (a), (b), or (c), or another state has declined to exercise jurisdiction on the ground that this state is the more appropriate forum to determine the custody of the child, and (ii) it is in the best interest of the child that this court assume jurisdiction.[1]

---

5. Capdevilla v. Capdevilla, 149 A.D.2d 312, 539 N.Y.S.2d 365 (1st Dep't 1989); Unanue v. Unanue, 141 A.D.2d, 31, 532 N.Y.S.2d 769 (2d Dep't 1988).

§ 21.5
1. DRL § 75–d(1).

Except under paragraphs (c) and (d) of subdivision one of DRL § 75–d, the physical presence in this state of the child, or of the child and one of the contestants, is not alone sufficient to confer jurisdiction on a court of this state to make a child custody determination.[2] The physical presence of the child, while desirable, is not a prerequisite for jurisdiction to determine his or her custody.[3]

There are instances where a New York court has jurisdiction to proceed in the matrimonial action between the parties, but lacks jurisdiction to adjudicate the child custody aspect of the case. Soon after New York's enactment of the statute, the New York Court of Appeals gave significant guidance on how to deal with competing claims of jurisdiction in *Vanneck v. Vanneck*,[4] including the practical advice that, where there is a conflict, the judges from the two states should confer. As a result, these matters are often resolved by a telephone call between judges.

A court which has jurisdiction to make a decree may decline to exercise its jurisdiction if it finds that it is an inconvenient forum to make a custody determination under the circumstances of the case and that a court of another state is a more appropriate forum.[5] If the petitioner for a decree has wrongfully taken the child from another state or has engaged in some other misconduct, the court has the discretion to decline to exercise jurisdiction.[6]

Library References:

West's Key No. Digests, Divorce ⚖️289; Infants ⚖️18; Parent and Child ⚖️2(5).

§ 21.6 Competency of the Court to Grant Relief

Once it is determined that a New York court would be able to entertain a client's matrimonial action or custody proceeding, the next step is to analyze whether the relief sought is available from the court.[1] As New York family law is purely statutory, one must look to the statutes to analyze the competency of the court to grant the requested relief.

Library References:

West's Key No. Digests, Divorce ⚖️289; Infants ⚖️18; Parent and Child ⚖️2(5).

2. DRL § 75–d(2).
3. DRL § 75–d(3).
4. 49 N.Y.2d 602, 427 N.Y.S.2d 735, 404 N.E.2d 1278 (1980).
5. DRL § 75–h(1).
6. DRL § 75–i(1).

§ 21.6

1. **PRACTICE POINTER:** Since family law is purely statutory, you must have statutory authority for any relief you seek. If the statute doesn't provide for it, a court cannot grant it.

§ 21.7 Competency of the Court to Grant Relief—Equitable Distribution

DRL § 236(B)(5) authorizes the supreme court to determine the respective rights of the parties in their separate or marital property in an action wherein all or a part of the relief granted is divorce, or the dissolution, annulment or declaration of the nullity of a marriage, and in proceedings to obtain a distribution of marital property following a foreign judgment of divorce.[1]

Notice that a court can *only* make equitable distribution where a divorce is granted, an annulment or declaration of the nullity of a marriage is granted, or in a proceeding to obtain distribution of marital property following a foreign judgment of divorce. Thus, there can be no equitable distribution if a party fails to establish grounds for divorce or annulment; or if only a separation is sought or granted; or if there was a foreign annulment without equitable distribution rather than a foreign divorce.[2] If the complaint in an action for divorce is dismissed, the court has the authority to grant maintenance and/or child support; however, the court cannot distribute the property.

There is no grant of authority in the Family Court Act for equitable distribution. Thus, since the family court is a court of limited jurisdiction, the family court has no original jurisdiction to make or enforce equitable distribution orders.[3]

Library References:

West's Key No. Digests, Divorce ⚖=200.

§ 21.8 Competency of the Court to Grant Relief—Support

Spousal support, which is denoted maintenance in New York State, can be part of the relief granted in a matrimonial action.[1] Child support can be awarded as part of a matrimonial action or custody proceeding.[2]

Either maintenance and/or child support can be awarded in supreme court or family court in what lawyers describe as a "bare support proceeding," a support application which is not part of a matrimonial

---

§ 21.7

1. *See infra*, §§ 21.33–21.45.
2. Brawer v. Pinkins, N.Y.L.J., 6/12/95, p.3, col.1.
3. Pearson v. Pearson, 108 A.D.2d 402, 489 N.Y.S.2d 332 (2d Dep't 1985), appeal dismissed 66 N.Y.2d 915, 498 N.Y.S.2d 1027, 489 N.E.2d 773, appeal granted 68 N.Y.2d 609, 508 N.Y.S.2d 1026, 501 N.E.2d 36, aff'd, 69 N.Y.2d 919, 516 N.Y.S.2d 629, 509 N.E.2d 324 (1987); Kolar v. Kolar, 133 Misc.2d 995, 509 N.Y.S.2d 245 (Fam.Ct., Onondaga County, 1986); Theresa S. v. Karel S., 120 Misc.2d 395, 466 N.Y.S.2d 216 (Fam.Ct., N.Y. County, 1983).

§ 21.8

1. *See infra*, §§ 21.46–21.51.
2. *See infra*, §§ 21.52–21.56.

action or child custody proceeding. Jurisdiction derives from the Family Court Act.[3]

Family Court Act § 412 provides that a married person is chargeable with the support of his or her spouse and may be required to pay a fair and, reasonable sum, as the court may determine, having due regard for the circumstances of the respective parties.[4]

The statutory authority for child support proceedings is in Family Court Act § 413,[5] which then goes on to set forth the Child Support Guidelines. Note that Family Court Act § 413 contains the identical language as that found in Domestic Relations Law 240(1–b).[6]

A court has no authority to grant support for a child after the age of 21.[7] Many settlement agreements provide that support will cease upon the child's completion of four years of college, but in no event past the age of 22 (or 23). In negotiating for child support counsel must be aware that an extension of child support past the age of 21 cannot be obtained from a court. The statute controls absolutely. Unless granted authority by statute, the court has no authority, absent agreement of the parties.

Library References:
West's Key No. Digests, Divorce ⚖︎200.

§ 21.9 Competency of the Court to Grant Relief—Custody and Visitation

An adjudication as to custody and/or visitation may be part of the relief granted in a matrimonial action.[1] The issue may also be litigated as a separate proceeding commenced in either the supreme court or the family court. If commenced in the supreme court, the custody and visitation issues may be referred by that supreme court to the family court.[2] In either case, the court will issue its order or judgment setting forth custody and visitation arrangements for the parties' minor children.

Library References:
West's Key No. Digests, Divorce ⚖︎289.

3. Family Court Act §§ 412, 413.

4. Family Court Act § 412.

5. Family Court Act § 413 provides:

1.(a) Except as provided in subdivision two of this section, the parents of a child under the age of twenty-one years are chargeable with the support of such child and, if possessed of sufficient means or able to earn such means, shall be required to pay for child support a fair and reasonable sum as the court may determine. The court shall make its award for child support pursuant to the provisions of this subdivision. The court may vary from the amount of the basic child support obligation determined pursuant to paragraph (c) of this subdivision only in accordance with paragraph (f) of this subdivision.

6. See infra, §§ 21.52–21.54.

7. Hirsch v. Hirsch, 142 A.D.2d 138, 534 N.Y.S.2d 681 (2d Dep't 1988).

§ 21.9

1. See infra, §§ 21.58–21.62.

2. Family Court Act § 467(a).

§ 21.10 Jurisdiction Over the Defendant's Person or Property

Thus far we have seen who can be a plaintiff or petitioner in our courts, and what relief they can obtain; all as prescribed and limited by statute. Similarly circumscribed by statute is how jurisdiction over the person of the defendant or respondent is obtained or, if personal jurisdiction is not obtainable, how to obtain jurisdiction over the property of the defendant or respondent from which financial relief can be granted. Finally, if jurisdiction is obtainable over neither the person nor the property of the defendant or respondent, there is a form of *quasi in rem* jurisdiction which allows the court to alter just the status of the parties.

Library References:
West's Key No. Digests, Divorce ⚖=57–65.

§ 21.11 Jurisdiction Over the Defendant's Person or Property—Personal Jurisdiction

Matrimonial actions are commenced by the filing of a summons, with the notice designated in DRL § 232, or a summons and verified complaint as provided in CPLR 304, with the clerk of the court in which the action is to be brought.[1] Once the summons (with either the complaint or notice) has been filed, the defendant must be served.

As in all areas of the law, personal service within the State of New York will result in *in personam* jurisdiction. However, in contrast to all other areas, the basic service statute does *not* allow substituted service without a court order.

CPLR 308(1) provides that personal service upon a natural person shall be made by delivering the summons within the state to the person to be served. Subdivision (2) provides for delivery to a person of suitable age and discretion at the actual place of business, dwelling place or usual place of abode. Subdivision (3) provides for delivery to the agent for service upon the person to be served as designated under CPLR 318. Where service cannot be made under paragraph (1) and (2) with due diligence, subdivision (4) provides for service by "nailing and mailing." Subdivisions (2), (3) and (4) *each* contain the following exclusionary clause regarding matrimonial actions:

> ... except in matrimonial actions where service hereunder may be made pursuant to an order made in accordance with the provisions of subdivision a of section two hundred thirty-two of the domestic relations law.[2]

§ 21.11
1. DRL § 211.
2. CPLR 308. DRL § 232 provides:

§ 232. Notice of nature of matrimonial action; proof of service.
a. In an action to annul a marriage or for divorce or separation, if the complaint

CPLR 308(5), which sets forth the last method of service, provides for service "in such manner as the court, upon motion without notice, directs, if service is impracticable under paragraphs one, two and four of this section."

DRL § 232 provides for service on the defendant pursuant to an order directing the method of service of the summons in accordance with the provisions of CPLR 308 or 315.[3] A court, upon a motion, may permit service of a summons by publication[4] if service cannot be made by another prescribed method with due diligence.[5] Before service by publication will be authorized, a plaintiff must show that service under CPLR 308(1), (2) and (4) cannot be made. Further, the plaintiff must provide the court with any information regarding the possible means of expedient service under CPLR 308(5).[6]

DRL § 232 provides that the summons and complaint or summons with notice is to be served upon the defendant by personal delivery.[7] Any other method of service may be permitted only by court order.[8] Note then, that the *only* method of obtaining jurisdiction of the defendant or respondent by service within the State of New York without a court order is by personal delivery within the state.

Library References:
West's Key No. Digests, Divorce ⚖=57–65.

§ 21.12 Jurisdiction Over the Defendant's Person or Property—Long Arm Jurisdiction

If the defendant or respondent is not a resident or domiciliary of the State of New York, CPLR 302(b) sets forth the *only* instances where is not personally served with the summons, the summons shall have legibly written or printed upon the face thereof: "Action to annul a marriage," "Action to declare the nullity of a void marriage," "Action for a divorce," or "Action for a separation," as the case may be, and shall specify the nature of any ancillary relief demanded. A judgment shall not be rendered in favor of the plaintiff upon the defendant's default in appearing or pleading, unless either (1) the summons and a copy of the complaint were personally delivered to the defendant or (2) the copy of the summons (a) personally delivered to the defendant, or (b) served on the defendant pursuant to an order directing the method of service of the summons in accordance with the provisions of section three hundred eight or three hundred fifteen of the civil practice law and rules, shall contain such notice.

b. An affidavit or certificate proving service shall state affirmatively in the body thereof that the required notice was written or printed on the face of the copy of the summons delivered to the defendant and what knowledge the affiant or officer who executed the certificate had that he was the defendant named and how he acquired such knowledge. The court may require the affiant or officer who executed the affidavit or certificate to appear in court and be examined in respect thereto.

3. DRL § 232(a)(2)(b).
4. CPLR 314.
5. CPLR 315.
6. *See* Iroff v. Iroff, 125 A.D.2d 197, 509 N.Y.S.2d 316 (1st Dep't 1986) (default judgment obtained upon publication; service vacated on appeal; plaintiff knew but did not disclose information which would have allowed court to fashion a method of expedient service).
7. DRL §§ 232(a)(1), (a)(2)(a).
8. DRL § 232(a)(2)(b).

New York will exercise personal jurisdiction.[1] There are three instances where personal jurisdiction will be exercised:

1. this state was the matrimonial domicile of the parties before their separation,[2]
2. defendant abandoned the plaintiff in this state,[3] or
3. the claim for support, alimony, maintenance, distributive awards, or special relief in matrimonial actions accrued under the laws of this state or under an agreement executed in this state.[4]

Library References:
West's Key No. Digests, Divorce ⟺57–65.

§ 21.13 Jurisdiction Over the Defendant's Person or Property—*In Rem* Jurisdiction

There are instances where, while jurisdiction over the person of the defendant or respondent cannot be obtained, there is property located in New York which can serve as a jurisdictional predicate. DRL § 233 specifically makes provision for obtaining jurisdiction limited to the property being sequestered as a jurisdictional basis.[1] Where sequestra-

§ 21.12

1. CPLR 302(b) provides:

(b) Personal jurisdiction over non-resident defendant in matrimonial actions or family court proceedings.

A court in any matrimonial action or family court proceeding involving a demand for support, alimony, maintenance, distributive awards or special relief in matrimonial actions may exercise personal jurisdiction over the respondent or defendant notwithstanding the fact that he or she no longer is a resident or domiciliary of this state, or over his or her executor or administrator, if the party seeking support is a resident of or domiciled in this state at the time such demand is made, provided that this state was the matrimonial domicile of the parties before their separation, or the defendant abandoned the plaintiff in this state, or the claim for support, alimony, maintenance, distributive awards or special relief in matrimonial actions accrued under the laws of this state or under an agreement executed in this state. The family court may exercise personal jurisdiction over a non-resident respondent to the extent provided in sections one hundred fifty-four and one thousand thirty-six of the family court act.

2. CPLR 302(b). Considerable case law has arisen over how long before the parties' separation New York was the state of matrimonial domicile. *Cf.* Lieb v. Lieb, 53 A.D.2d 67, 385 N.Y.S.2d 569 (2d Dep't 1976); Paparella v. Paparella, 74 A.D.2d 106, 426 N.Y.S.2d 610 (4th Dep't 1980); Klette v. Klette, 167 A.D.2d 197, 561 N.Y.S.2d 580 (1st Dep't 1990); Levy v. Levy, 185 A.D.2d 15, 592 N.Y.S.2d 480 (3d Dep't 1993).

3. CPLR 302(b).

4. CPLR 302(b).

§ 21.13

1. DRL § 233 provides:

§ 233. Sequestration of defendant's property in action for divorce, separation or annulment where defendant cannot be personally served.

Where in an action for divorce, separation, annulment or declaration of nullity of a void marriage it appears to the court that the defendant is not within the state, or cannot be found therein, or is concealing himself or herself therein, so that process cannot be personally served upon the defendant, the court may at any time and from time to time make any order or orders without notice directing the se-tion is permitted, property is taken from one spouse and controlled by a receiver and utilized to satisfy court imposed obligations owing to the other spouse or to the children of the parties.

Library References:

West's Key No. Digests, Divorce ⚖︎57–65.

§ 21.14 *Quasi in Rem* Jurisdiction

Provided that the plaintiff in the matrimonial action has complied with DRL § 230 and, thus, is a proper plaintiff, if there is no way to exercise jurisdiction over the person or over the property of the defendant, the court may still grant relief directed solely to the status of the marriage itself.

The concept is that when one of the parties enters the courtroom, that party brings the status of the marriage with him or her so that the court is empowered to change that status, upon the proper proof, by granting a divorce. Note that this will be *ex parte* relief.

After the granting of a divorce in this fashion, the parties may still litigate the custodial and financial aspects of their dissolution in a state, territory, or county where there is full personal jurisdiction over both parties. First confirmed in this state in *Vanderbilt v. Vanderbilt*[1] and commonly referred to as "divisible divorce," the power to do this was expressly incorporated into the Domestic Relations Law.[2]

questration of his or her property, both real and personal and whether tangible or intangible, within the state, and may appoint a receiver thereof, or by injunction or otherwise take the same into its possession and control. The property thus sequestered and the income therefrom may be applied in whole or in part and from time to time, under the direction of the court and as justice may require, to the payment of such sum or sums as the court may deem it proper to award, by order or judgment as the case may be, and during the pendency of the action or at the termination thereof, for the education or maintenance of any of the children of marriage, or for the support of a spouse, or for his or her expenses in bringing and carrying on said action and the proceedings incidental thereto or connected therewith; and if the rents and profits of the real estate, together with the other property so sequestered, be insufficient to pay the sums of money required, the court, upon such terms and conditions as it may prescribe, may direct the mortgage or sale of sufficient of said real estate to pay such sums. The court may appoint the plaintiff spouse receiver or sequestrator in such cases. The court may authorize such spouse to use and occupy, free of any liability for rent or use and occupation or otherwise, any house or other suitable property of the defendant spouse as a dwelling for himself or herself with or without the children of the marriage, and may likewise turn over to the plaintiff spouse for the use of such spouse with or without the children of the marriage any chattel or chattels of the defendant spouse. The relief herein provided for is in addition to any and every other remedy to which a spouse may be entitled under the law.

§ 21.14

1. 1 N.Y.2d 342, 153 N.Y.S.2d 1, 135 N.E.2d 553 (1956). *Cf.* Estin v. Estin, 334 U.S. 541, 68 S.Ct. 1213, 92 L.Ed. 1561 (1948), aff'g 296 N.Y. 308, 73 N.E.2d 113 (1947).

2. DRL § 236(B)(5).

§ 21.14 DOMESTIC RELATIONS Ch. 21

Library References:

West's Key No. Digests, Divorce ⚿57–65.

§ 21.15 Venue

In matrimonial actions, like civil actions generally, venue is based upon residence. The place of trial, or venue, of a matrimonial action must be in the county in which one of the parties resides at the time the action is commenced.[1] A party who is resident in more than one county is considered, for venue purposes, a resident of each county.[2] Although a person may have more than one residence for venue purposes, to consider a place as such, he or she must stay there for some time and have a *bona fide* intent to retain the place of residence for some length of time and with some degree of permanency. If neither party resides in the state, the plaintiff may designate any county as the place of trial.[3] However, if neither party is a resident of the state, it is not likely that any matrimonial relief may be granted since jurisdiction over the marital *res* may not have been acquired and the durational residence tests applicable in divorce, separation, and annulment actions may not be satisfied. CPLR 507 provides that, where the judgment demanded in the action would affect the title to, or the possession, use or enjoyment of real property, the action is to be venued in the county where any part of the realty is located.[4]

Library References:

West's Key No. Digests, Divorce ⚿57–65.

§ 21.16 Venue—Changing Venue

The grounds for changing venue allowed by CPLR 510 are: (a) the county in which venue was placed was not a proper venue county; (b) there is reason to believe that an impartial trial cannot be had in the venue county; and (c) the convenience of material witnesses and the ends of justice would be promoted by a change in venue.[1]

Library References:

West's Key No. Digests, Divorce ⚿57–65.

§ 21.15
1. CPLR 503(a).
2. CPLR 503(a).
3. CPLR 503(a).
4. CPLR 507.

§ 21.16
1. CPLR 510. *See* Amann v. Caccese, 223 A.D.2d 663, 637 N.Y.S.2d 217 (2d Dep't 1996) (change of venue was required to protect court from even appearance of impropriety, since wife was daughter of resident county court of claims justice and acting supreme court justice, who also served county in state assembly).

§ 21.17 Joinder, Consolidation and Joint Trials

CPLR 601 addresses joinder of claims and allows the plaintiff in a complaint to join as many claims as he or she may have against an adverse party. Thus, a divorce action can be joined with such other causes of action as an action to set aside a separation agreement.[1]

CPLR 602 provides for joint trial or consolidation. When actions involving common questions of law or fact are pending before a court, the court, upon motion, may order a joint trial of any or all of the matters in issue, may order the actions consolidated, and may make such other orders concerning proceedings therein as may tend to avoid costs or delay.[2]

Library References:
West's Key No. Digests, Divorce ⟊146.

§ 21.18 Grounds for Divorce

A divorce, as the term is used in the statutes of this state, is an absolute divorce. It severs the bonds of the marital relationship. Prior to September 1, 1967, New York recognized only adultery as a ground for divorce. Effective September 1, 1967, DRL § 170 was amended to increase the grounds for divorce to six: (1) cruel and inhuman treatment such that the conduct of the defendant so endangers the physical or mental well being of the plaintiff as renders it unsafe or improper to cohabit; (2) abandonment for a period of 1 or more years; (3) confinement in prison for a period of 3 or more consecutive years after the marriage; (4) adultery, which has been defined as the voluntary commission of an act of sexual or deviate sexual intercourse with a person other than the plaintiff after the marriage; (5) living apart pursuant to a decree or judgment of separation for a period of 1 or more years; and (6) living apart pursuant to a written separation agreement for a period of 1 or more years.

Library References:
West's Key No. Digests, Divorce ⟊11.

§ 21.19 Grounds for Divorce—No Official No-Fault Ground

New York does not have no-fault divorce. The two grounds which are based on a separation agreement or decree are the closest New York comes to grounds for divorce which do not allege fault.

§ 21.17

1. De Oteris v. Mario, 185 Misc. 1029, 60 N.Y.S.2d 674 (Sup.Ct., Kings County, 1945), aff'd 270 App.Div. 820, 60 N.Y.S.2d 297 (2d Dep't 1946).

2. CPLR 602(a). See Karasik v. Karasik, 172 A.D.2d 294, 568 N.Y.S.2d 384 (1st Dep't 1991) (supreme court acted within its discretion in consolidating matrimonial action with plenary action, based on existence of common questions of law and fact and to prevent unnecessary duplication and possible injustice resulting from divergent decisions).

§ 21.19   DOMESTIC RELATIONS   Ch. 21

The ground of living apart pursuant to a separation judgment or decree is sometimes referred to as a "no-fault" ground for divorce. However, since fault must be established to obtain a New York separation judgment in the first instance, fault still plays a role in establishing this ground.[1] Once there is a separation decree, either party may pursue the statutory ground for divorce after one year; even the "guilty" party from the separation action can use the separation judgment as a basis for obtaining a divorce.[2]

The ground of living apart pursuant to a separation agreement is sometimes described as a "no-fault" ground for divorce. This is because it is the only ground upon which a judgment of divorce may be maintained with no required showing of fault at any stage of any litigation between the parties.[3] However, it can only be used where both parties have come to an agreement. The essence of a no-fault ground is that one party can get a divorce without the cooperation or agreement of the other party, and even over the objection of the other party.

Both grounds require that the parties live separate and apart for one or more years after the granting of a decree or judgment or the execution of the agreement. The terms and conditions of the separation decree or separation agreement must have been substantially complied with.

Library References:

West's Key No. Digests, Divorce ⚖12.

§ 21.20 Grounds for Divorce—Cruel and Inhuman Treatment

An action for divorce may be maintained upon the ground of the cruel and inhuman treatment of the plaintiff by the defendant such that the conduct of the defendant so endangers the physical or mental well being of the plaintiff as renders it unsafe or improper for the plaintiff to cohabit with the defendant.[1] Corroboration is not required in order to establish a divorce based on cruel and inhuman treatment.[2]

The statutory provision does not permit the dissolution of every marriage simply because the parties are not compatible. The Legislature, in amending DRL § 170, did not provide a ground for divorce where a marriage is "dead" or the parties are incompatible. To constitute cruel and inhuman treatment, more than mere incompatibility must be

---

§ 21.19

1. See DRL § 200.

2. See infra, § 21.29 for discussion of this ground.

3. See infra, § 21.30 for discussion of this ground.

§ 21.20

1. DRL § 170(1). See infra, § 21.82 for essential allegations when drafting a complaint and § 21.86 for a sample complaint.

2. See Pascarella v. Pascarella, 210 A.D.2d 915, 621 N.Y.S.2d 821 (4th Dep't 1994).

shown.[3] Courts must therefore examine the conduct of the defendant to determine if such conduct constitutes cruel and inhuman treatment.

In *Hessen v. Hessen*,[4] the Court of Appeals set forth the considerations to be weighed by courts in determining whether particular conduct constitutes cruel and inhuman treatment. While the court noted that conduct endangering a party's physical or mental well being warrants divorce if the conduct makes cohabitation improper, or unsafe, the statute does not permit divorce simply because the marital relationship appears to have been destroyed. The Court of Appeals concluded that whether to grant a divorce on the ground of cruel and inhuman treatment is within the broad discretion of the court. This discretion is to be exercised by considering several important factors, including the degree, scope, and probable effect of the misconduct between the spouses. Objective proof of physical or mental injury is not a prerequisite, however, it may be a decisive basis for granting a divorce.

The *Hessen* court stressed that it is appropriate to consider the respective ages of the husband and wife and the duration of the marriage.[5] An appearance of misconduct, which in a matured marriage might not justify a finding of substantial misconduct, may justify an inference of substantial misconduct in a newer marriage. Similarly, the effects of the aging process on the physical and mental disposition of spouses may create problems in an otherwise stable marriage. The *Hessen* court noted that the adage, "for better or worse," may apply to such situations.

The high standard of proof required to end a marriage of long duration is demonstrated by *Palin v. Palin*.[6] There, even though the wife showed that she had been verbally abused on occasion, had been threatened, and had been physically assaulted, the appellate division held that this was not enough to suggest cruel and inhuman treatment.[7] The court was influenced by the fact that the wife continued to cohabit with the

---

3. *See* Haydock v. Haydock, 222 A.D.2d 554, 634 N.Y.S.2d 766 (2d Dep't 1995) (action of spouse in having extramarital affair with knowledge of other spouse can be cruel and inhuman treatment); Fuchs v. Fuchs, 216 A.D.2d 648, 628 N.Y.S.2d 193 (3d Dep't 1995) (evidence supported granting of divorce on grounds of cruel and inhuman treatment; husband had smoked four cigarettes a day, despite the wife's asthma, repeatedly threatened to kill her, stalked her and one time engaged in a dangerous high speed car chase, following within a few feet of the vehicle in which the wife was a passenger).

4. 33 N.Y.2d 406, 353 N.Y.S.2d 421, 308 N.E.2d 891 (1974).

5. *See* Preston v. Preston, 165 Misc.2d 151, 627 N.Y.S.2d 518 (Sup.Ct., Otsego County, 1995) (mere showing of dead marriage or irreconcilable differences is insufficient, particularly in marriage of long duration; plaintiff need not establish instances of physical abuse; course of conduct involving verbal abuse, intimidation and harassment may be sufficient); Soto v. Soto, 216 A.D.2d 455, 628 N.Y.S.2d 391 (2d Dep't 1995) (evidence that in marriage of short duration, wife verbally abused husband in both public and private and physically harassed him was sufficient to support divorce on grounds of cruel and inhuman treatment).

6. 213 A.D.2d 707, 624 N.Y.S.2d 630 (2d Dep't 1995).

7. Note, however, the court's alternative finding that the evidence supported the granting of a divorce to the wife based on adultery.

husband for more than a year after she commenced the action for divorce. It has been suggested, however, that courts should be sensitive to the fact that there often are valid reasons why spouses, despite fear and despite good faith belief that cohabitation is improper, remain in the marital residence.[8] One reason may be that the spouse lacks funds to relocate and may not be able to obtain those funds by *pendente lite* motion. Another reason maybe the parties' minor children. Relocating with the children could be faulted by the court; relocating without the children may adversely impact upon the issue of custody. The fact that a spouse moves out of the marital residence does not, by itself, mean that he or she has a valid cause of action for divorce based upon cruel and inhuman treatment. That a spouse remains in the home, while a factor in assessing whether there is legitimate concern of fear or inappropriate behavior, must be looked at in the context of other issues, such as financial and custodial concerns.[9]

Another important factor from *Hessen* regards the consequences that the granting of a divorce would have upon the issue of support. Under DRL § 236 Part A, and its predecessor, fault was an absolute bar to any alimony payments for the benefit of the guilty spouse. At the time *Hessen* was decided, alimony could be awarded only to wives. The court noted that it may be inappropriate to deprive a dependent older woman of support, through the granting of a divorce to her husband, absent proof of grievous forms of misconduct.

The Court of Appeals, in *Brady v. Brady*,[10] reconsidered *Hessen* in light of the changes brought about by the Equitable Distribution Law and held that the duration of the marriage as a relevant consideration continues to be applicable. The court noted that the fundamental reason for such a rule was, and remains, the notion that the conduct which the plaintiff alleges as the basis for a course of action must be viewed in the context of the entire marriage, including its duration, in deciding whether the particular actions can be labeled cruel and inhuman.

Library References:
West's Key No. Digests, Divorce ⚖27.

§ 21.21 Grounds for Divorce—Cruel and Inhuman Treatment—Defenses

No action for divorce upon the ground of cruel and inhuman treatment may be maintained where the ground arose more than five

---

8. *See* Scheinkman, *Practice Commentaries*, DRL § 170, C:170:2.
9. *Id.*
10. 64 N.Y.2d 339, 486 N.Y.S.2d 891, 476 N.E.2d 290 (1985).

In Brady, the husband also argued that Hessen created an unconstitutional double standard if the evidentiary requirements applicable to long-term marriages were applied only to husbands who seek a divorce. The Court of Appeals held that Hessen is applicable whether the person seeking the divorce is the husband or the wife.

years before the date of the commencement of the action.[1] Since Section 210 of the Domestic Relations Law is treated as a Statute of Limitations, it is an affirmative defense that must be pleaded and proven by the defendant. A cruel and inhuman treatment claim usually consists of a number of incidents occurring over a significant period of time, a "continuous course of conduct", which taken together are alleged to constitute cruel and inhuman treatment sufficient to warrant divorce. The Statute of Limitations begins to run when the ground arose. It may be difficult to pinpoint exactly when the ground arose, especially where the acts complained of occurred over an extended period of time and constituted a course of conduct.

Aside from the Statute of Limitations, the Domestic Relations Law does not provide for any other defenses in divorce actions based upon cruel and inhuman treatment. The defenses set forth in DRL § 171 have been specifically held not to apply to causes of action based upon cruel and inhuman treatment.[2] Although not a true defense, case law indicates that provocation can be considered in determining whether the defendant's wrongful acts were incited by the plaintiff.[3] Of course, any appropriate defense allowed by CPLR 3211(a) could be asserted in a divorce action based on cruel and inhuman treatment, such as *res judicata*, the pendency of another action, or lack of subject matter jurisdiction.

Library References:

West's Key No. Digests, Divorce ⟜111.

§ 21.22 Grounds for Divorce—Abandonment

The Domestic Relations Law provides that an action for a divorce may be maintained upon the ground of the abandonment of the plaintiff by the defendant for a period of one or more years.[1] The essence of abandonment is a refusal on the part of one spouse to fulfill basic obligations springing from the marriage contract.

§ 21.21

1. DRL § 210.
2. Volkell v. Volkell, 102 A.D.2d 889, 477 N.Y.S.2d 60 (2d Dep't 1984); Fritz v. Fritz, 88 A.D.2d 778, 451 N.Y.S.2d 519 (4th Dep't 1982); Woicik v. Woicik, 66 Misc.2d 357, 321 N.Y.S.2d 5 (Sup.Ct., N.Y. County, 1971); Ray v. Ray, 62 Misc.2d 652, 309 N.Y.S.2d 53 (Sup.Ct., Bronx County, 1970).
3. *See, e.g.*, Mante v. Mante, 34 A.D.2d 134, 309 N.Y.S.2d 944 (2d Dep't 1970).

§ 21.22

1. DRL § 170(2). *See* Emanuele v. Emanuele, 218 A.D.2d 726, 630 N.Y.S.2d 558 (2d Dep't 1995) (husband was not entitled to divorce on ground of constructive abandonment; though he alleged that wife refused to have sexual relations with him after February 14, 1991, he admitted that he resided with his mother from November 26, 1990 to June 24, 1991; alleged constructive abandonment by wife lasted less than minimum one year period).

See infra, § 21.82 for the essential allegations when drafting a complaint for divorce and § 21.86 for a sample complaint.

An abandonment may take the form of an actual physical departure from the marital residence. The requisite elements of a claim based upon an actual physical abandonment are an unjustified, voluntary separation or departure, with an intention on the part of the separating or departing spouse not to return, to which the other spouse has not consented.[2] Where the plaintiff has committed conduct that would give the defendant grounds for divorce, the defendant's subsequent absence from the marital residence cannot give rise to a cause of action for divorce based on abandonment. Since one of the elements of such a cause of action is the unjustified nature of the departure, the existence of grounds for divorce in favor of the defendant prevents the plaintiff from proving that the defendant's absence was unjustified.[3]

Where one spouse has left the marital residence but the absence is temporary, a good faith offer by the absent spouse to return must be accepted. The critical question is whether the offer to return is made in good faith. For an offer to qualify as a good faith offer, the absent spouse must offer to resume the marital relationship.[4]

Another form of abandonment, which is termed a constructive abandonment, is where one spouse unjustifiably excludes the other from the marital residence without consent. The exclusion must be total and cannot have been justified.[5]

The doctrine of constructive abandonment also recognizes the unjustified failure or refusal of one spouse to engage in sexual relations with the other spouse, although capable of doing so, as a sufficient abrogation of marital responsibilities to constitute an abandonment.[6] In *Diemer v. Diemer*,[7] the Court of Appeals stated that sexual relations between a man and a woman are given a socially and legally sanctioned status when they take place in marriage. The court held that a refusal to engage in such relations undermines the essential structure of marriage and constitutes abandonment.

2. Bazant v. Bazant, 80 A.D.2d 310, 439 N.Y.S.2d 521 (4th Dep't 1981).

3. *See* Johnson v. Johnson, 167 A.D.2d 954, 561 N.Y.S.2d 1018 (4th Dep't 1990).

4. Merely asking to return, in order to better manage marital assets or because of problems with the absent spouse's landlord, does not qualify as a good faith offer. *See* Gleckman v. Kaplan, 215 A.D.2d 527, 626 N.Y.S.2d 549 (2d Dep't 1995).

5. *See, e.g.,* Schine v. Schine, 31 N.Y.2d 113, 335 N.Y.S.2d 58, 286 N.E.2d 449 (1972); Lind v. Lind, 89 A.D.2d 518, 452 N.Y.S.2d 204 (1st Dep't 1982), aff'd 58 N.Y.2d 965, 460 N.Y.S.2d 524, 447 N.E.2d 72 (1983); Yaron v. Yaron, 84 Misc.2d 644, 378 N.Y.S.2d 285 (Sup.Ct., N.Y. County, 1975).

6. Donohue v. Donohue, 222 A.D.2d 646, 636 N.Y.S.2d 104 (2d Dep't 1995) (evidence of wife's constructive abandonment of husband entitled husband to grant of application for divorce; husband and wife had not had sexual relations for years, husband had not acquiesced to lifestyle of sexual abstention, and husband had made multiple good-faith requests for resumption of sexual relations which wife allegedly had consistently and without justification refused).

7. 8 N.Y.2d 206, 203 N.Y.S.2d 829, 168 N.E.2d 654 (1960).

In *Pascarella v. Pascarella*,[8] the Fourth Department set forth a statement as to what constitutes constructive abandonment. *Pascarella* holds that to make out a *prima facie* case of constructive abandonment it must be shown that there was a failure and refusal on the part of the defendant to engage in marital relations for at least a year prior to commencement of the action. Once that is established, the divorce will be granted unless the defendant pleads and proves justification.

Library References:

West's Key No. Digests, Divorce ☞37.

§ 21.23 Grounds for Divorce—Abandonment—Defenses

DRL § 210 excepts the abandonment divorce ground from the coverage of the Statute of Limitations.[1] An abandoned spouse cannot be deprived of a divorce because of limitations even if that spouse refrains from commencing an action for more than five years. It has been said that the inapplicability of limitations to abandonment is consistent with the nature of the wrong and with public policy considerations.[2] Abandonment is a continuing wrong. A spouse who has been abandoned is not compelled to seek a divorce within a certain time period on pain of forever losing the right to obtain one. An abandoned spouse may well have reasons for withholding a divorce action, including hopes for reconciliation or religious beliefs.[3]

The Domestic Relations Law does not provide for any special defenses in divorce actions based upon abandonment. However, it has been held that justification for the conduct alleged to constitute an abandonment may be asserted as an affirmative defense to an abandonment cause of action.[4] Once the plaintiff makes out a *prima facie* case of abandonment, judgment will be granted unless the defendant pleads and proves justification.[5] Further, any appropriate defense allowed by CPLR 3211(a) could be asserted in a divorce action based on abandonment, such as *res judicata*, the pendency of another action, or lack of subject matter jurisdiction.

Library References:

West's Key No. Digests, Divorce ☞111.

8. 210 A.D.2d 915, 621 N.Y.S.2d 821 (4th Dep't 1994).

§ 21.23

1. DRL § 210(a).

2. Scheinkman, 9 West McKinney's Forms, MFL, § 12.35.

3. *Id.*

4. Del Galdo v. Del Galdo, 51 A.D.2d 741, 379 N.Y.S.2d 479 (2d Dep't 1976).

5. Maryon v. Maryon, 60 A.D.2d 623, 400 N.Y.S.2d 160 (2d Dep't 1977); Pascarella v. Pascarella, 210 A.D.2d 915, 621 N.Y.S.2d 821 (4th Dep't 1994) (the court followed Maryon to hold that justification is to be pleaded and proven by the defendant).

§ 21.24 Grounds for Divorce—Abandonment—Effect of Separation Agreement

To constitute an abandonment, it must be shown that the separation is against the will and without the consent of the complaining spouse.[1] Therefore, the separation of a husband and wife pursuant to a separation agreement constitutes consent and neither party will be deemed to have abandoned the other.[2] Similarly, where a judicial separation has been granted, the decree sanctions the separation of the spouses and while the decree is in effect neither party will be guilty of abandonment by living apart.[3]

Library References:
West's Key No. Digests, Divorce ⚖36.

§ 21.25 Grounds for Divorce—Imprisonment

An action for divorce may be maintained on the ground of the confinement of the defendant in prison for a period of 3 or more consecutive years after the marriage of the plaintiff and the defendant.[1] The legislative history of the statute makes it clear that actual physical imprisonment is required.[2] Any consecutive period of confinement of at least three years duration will suffice. If a judgment of conviction is entered, the three year test is measured from time of confinement, not the date of conviction. Thus, if defendant was out on bail during the pendency of the criminal proceedings, the three year period should not begin to run until the defendant has first actually been confined.

The imprisonment ground arises once the defendant spouse has been incarcerated for three years. DRL § 210 provides that no action for divorce upon the ground of imprisonment may be maintained where the ground arose more than five years before the date of the commencement of the action. Therefore, if the divorce action has not been commenced by the time the defendant has been imprisoned for eight years (three years plus the five years limitations period) the defense of limitations may be asserted, and the divorce action will be time barred. Although the requirement of three years' consecutive imprisonment is a condition

---

§ 21.24

1. DRL § 170(2).

2. Tagliasacchi v. Tagliasacchi, 83 A.D.2d 963, 443 N.Y.S.2d 17 (2d Dep't 1981) (where the parties entered into a separation agreement, the separation of the parties was consensual from the date of the execution of the agreement forward and the separation could not form a basis for divorce on abandonment grounds, even if the separation agreement was not valid).

PRACTICE POINTER: If the parties have not yet signed a separation agreement and want to use the abandonment ground in an uncontested divorce they can (1) file the summons for divorce on the ground of abandonment and serve the summons; (2) delete from the agreement its description as a separation agreement and the provision that the parties are agreeing to separate; and (3) execute the agreement as an agreement or stipulation resolving all of the issues in the pending action on the ground of abandonment.

3. Rosenbaum v. Rosenbaum, 56 Misc.2d 221, 288 N.Y.S.2d 285 (Sup.Ct., N.Y. County, 1968).

§ 21.25

1. DRL § 170(3). See infra, § 21.82 for the essential allegations in a complaint for divorce and § 21.86 for a sample complaint.

2. See McKinney's 1968 Session Laws of New York, p. 2308.

precedent to the action, the five year period contained in Section 210 is a Statute of Limitations and can be waived.

Aside from the Statute of Limitations, the Domestic Relations Law does not provide for any other special defenses in divorce actions based upon imprisonment. Any appropriate defense allowed by CPLR 3211(a) could be asserted in a divorce action based on imprisonment, such as *res judicata*, the pendency of another action, or lack of subject matter jurisdiction.

Library References:
West's Key No. Digests, Divorce ⇔19.1.

§ 21.26 Grounds for Divorce—Adultery

An action for divorce may be maintained on the ground of the commission of an act of adultery. Adultery is defined as the commission of an act of sexual or deviate sexual intercourse, voluntarily performed by the defendant, with a person other than the plaintiff after the marriage of plaintiff and defendant. Deviate sexual intercourse includes, but is not limited to, sexual conduct as defined in Penal Law §§ 130.00(2) and 130.20(3).[1]

The adultery must occur after the marriage.[2] Even a single act of adultery is sufficient to sustain a cause of action.[3] The separation of the married parties, even if by separation agreement or judgment, is not a defense to adultery.[4] However, where all of the financial issues have been disposed of by a separation agreement, litigation on the ground of adultery may serve no useful function.

The courts have traditionally refused to view intercourse engaged in by a married person while insane as adultery.[5] The basis for this rule is that adultery is a voluntary act. If a mentally ill person cannot appreciate the nature and effect of his or her act, then the act is not voluntary. Where a spouse is raped by a third person, the lack of voluntariness would also preclude viewing the intercourse as adulterous. A husband's rape of his wife is not adultery,[6] although spousal rape is a criminal act.

Adultery can be difficult to establish and may be costly to prove (such as the cost of hiring detectives). Adultery can be established in a variety of ways. Confessions of adultery are admissible in evidence, if

---

§ 21.26

1. DRL § 170(4). *See infra*, § 21.82 for the essential allegations in a complaint for divorce and § 21.86 for a sample complaint. *See also*, Greenberg, Marcus, *et al., New York Criminal Law* (West 1996) §§ 30.2, 34.11.

2. DRL § 170(4).

3. Salomon v. Salomon, 102 Misc.2d 427, 423 N.Y.S.2d 605 (Sup.Ct., Suffolk County, 1979).

4. *See* Schlachet v. Schlachet, 84 Misc.2d 782, 378 N.Y.S.2d 308 (Sup.Ct., Kings County, 1976).

5. Anonymous v. Anonymous, 166 Misc. 861, 2 N.Y.S.2d 663 (Sup.Ct., Erie County, 1938).

6. *See* People v. Hall, 49 N.Y.S.2d 309 (County Ct., Otsego County, 1944). *See* Greenberg, Marcus, *et al., New York Criminal Law* (West 1996) § 8.11.

proved through the testimony of third persons or of the admitting spouse. However, a divorce may not be granted on the basis of adultery solely on a confession; there must be corroborating evidence.[7] One spouse cannot testify against the other on the ground of adultery because adultery is still a crime in New York, and the CPLR specifically provides for incompetency where the issue is adultery.[8]

Adultery can be established through the testimony of eyewitnesses. Witnesses may include a co-respondent or a private detective. However, the testimony of such witnesses must be carefully weighed. While it has sometimes been said that the testimony of a private detective must be corroborated, that is not a rule of evidence.

In order to grant a divorce on the ground of adultery, the court need not be convinced beyond a reasonable doubt as to the fact of adultery but the evidence must be more consistent with guilt than with innocence.[9] If the facts and circumstances are equally capable of both an innocent and guilty interpretation, the court will give them an innocent construction. The evidence must be clear and convincing.[10]

In 1985 the Legislature amended DRL § 210, the general limitations section, so as to make it inapplicable to divorce actions based on adultery. DRL § 171(3) then became the sole and exclusive limitations provision applicable to adultery claims asserted in divorce actions commenced on or after July 28, 1985. DRL § 171(3) provides that an adultery divorce is to be denied, even if the adultery was proved, if the action was not commenced within five years after the discovery by the plaintiff of the offense, notwithstanding the absence of express forgiveness or voluntary cohabitation. The five year limitations period provided in DRL § 171(3) is not measured from the commission of the adultery but from the discovery by the plaintiff of the offense.

Library References:
West's Key No. Digests, Divorce ⚷26.

§ 21.27 Grounds for Divorce—Adultery—Defenses

Unlike the other grounds for divorce, there are statutory defenses to an action for divorce based on adultery. These defenses, if proven, will result in the denial of a divorce, even if adultery has been proven:

7. See Palin v. Palin, 213 A.D.2d 707, 624 N.Y.S.2d 630 (2d Dep't 1995) (husband admitted to his son that he had a child with another woman; the other evidence that supported the finding of adultery was the husband's invocation of the privilege against self-incrimination when asked about that child and the other woman).

8. CPLR 4502(a). See also, Barker and Alexander, *Evidence in New York State and Federal Courts* (West 1996) § 503.2.

9. Fleck v. Fleck, 6 Misc.2d 202, 163 N.Y.S.2d 218 (Sup.Ct., Monroe County, 1957).

10. Maroth v. Maroth, 64 N.Y.S.2d 260 (Sup.Ct., N.Y. County, 1946); Nottingham v. Nottingham, 209 App.Div. 459, 204 N.Y.S. 750 (4th Dep't 1924).

PRACTICE POINTER: Adultery is a difficult ground to prove. Many practitioners reallege the acts of adultery as cruel and inhuman treatment, since the level of proof is easier to meet.

1. Where the offense was committed by the procurement or with the connivance of the plaintiff;
2. Where the offense charged has been forgiven by the plaintiff. The forgiveness may be proven, either affirmatively, or by the voluntary cohabitation of the parties with the knowledge of the fact;
3. Where, even if there was no express forgiveness and no voluntary cohabitation of the parties, but the action was not commenced within five years after the discovery by the plaintiff of the offense charged;
4. Where the plaintiff has also been guilty of adultery under such circumstances that the defendant would have been entitled, if innocent, to a divorce.[1]

Mental illness has traditionally been held to constitute a defense to an accusation of adultery. Adultery is defined as a voluntary act. If the mentally ill person cannot appreciate the nature and effect of his acts, then the act is not regarded as voluntary and is not adulterous.[2]

Library References:
West's Key No. Digests, Divorce ⋘111.

§ 21.28 Grounds for Divorce—Adultery—Effect of Separation Agreement

The separation of the married parties, even if by separation agreement or judgment, is not a defense to adultery.[1] In one divorce action predicated on the wife's adultery, the husband alleged that the separation agreement of the parties permitted them to live with others, so that no breach of faith or infidelity was possible thereafter. The agreement contained a clause wherein the parties agreed to "live separate and apart ... free from interference ... direct or indirect, from the other, as fully as if he or she were single and unmarried ..." The court struck the defense and took the position that the agreement did not state, nor could the defendant construe its language to sanction, a new concept of legalized adultery and that it would not give judicial approval to that which the Legislature has declared illegal and violative of the Penal Law.[2] However, as a practical matter, where there is an agreement, a contested divorce action on the ground of adultery is seldom brought; it is usually more expeditious to bring an uncontested divorce when the agreement has been in effect for one year.

§ 21.27
1. DRL § 171.
2. Anonymous v. Anonymous, 166 Misc. 861, 2 N.Y.S.2d 663 (Sup.Ct., Erie County, 1938).

§ 21.28
1. *See* Schlachet v. Schlachet, 84 Misc.2d 782, 378 N.Y.S.2d 308 (Sup.Ct., Kings County, 1976).
2. *Id.*

§ 21.29 Grounds for Divorce—Divorce Action Based Upon Living Apart Pursuant to Separation Decree or Judgment

A divorce action may be maintained upon the ground that the husband and wife have lived apart pursuant to a decree or judgment of separation for a period of one or more years after the granting of such decree or judgment, and satisfactory proof has been submitted by the party who seeks the divorce that he or she has substantially performed all the terms and conditions of the separation decree or judgment.[1] The ground permits the existence of, and compliance with, a prior separation judgment or decree to be used as a predicate for a divorce action; a separation decree or judgment is not automatically converted into a divorce judgment or decree. A new action, based upon the ground, must be commenced. Should the action succeed, an entirely separate and new divorce judgment is entered and economic questions, such as equitable distribution, spousal support, child support, and other matters must be addressed *de novo* in the divorce action.

Even though proof of marital fault is required to obtain a separation judgment in New York,[2] the judgment, once issued, can be used by either party as a basis for obtaining a divorce based upon it.[3]

The first question posed by the statute is whether there is a decree or judgment of separation. A separation judgment granted by a New York court, in an action brought pursuant to Section 200 of the Domestic Relations Law, clearly qualifies as a separation judgment or decree for divorce purposes.[4] It has been held that nothing less than a judicial separation judgment qualifies as the predicate for a divorce judgment.[5] Some forms of decrees and judgments have qualified, however, they must be sufficiently affirmative with respect to the direction of a formal separation of the parties and the terms and conditions of such separation.[6]

Once it is established that a judgment or decree of separation was previously entered, it must be demonstrated that the parties have actually lived apart, pursuant to the judgment or decree for a period of one or more years. Showing that the parties maintained separate homes, and separate lives, during the requisite period satisfies this requirement. The fact that the parties may have engaged in sexual intercourse during

---

§ 21.29
1. DRL § 170(5).
2. DRL § 200.
3. Gleason v. Gleason, 26 N.Y.2d 28, 308 N.Y.S.2d 347, 256 N.E.2d 513 (1970).
4. *Id.*
5. *See* Wechter v. Wechter, 50 A.D.2d 826, 376 N.Y.S.2d 180 (2d Dep't 1975).
6. *See* Wang v. Wang, 87 Misc.2d 980, 386 N.Y.S.2d 922 (Sup.Ct., N.Y. County, 1976).

the term of separation will not, in and of itself, defeat the divorce action.[7] Pursuant to DRL § 203, a New York separation judgment is revocable only by court order, obtained upon the joint application of the parties.

Lastly, the party who is seeking the divorce must establish that he or she has substantially performed all the terms and conditions of the decree or judgment. The statute does not require perfect performance of the judgment or decree, only that there has been substantial performance.[8]

There is no statutory limitation applicable to actions on this ground. Once the parties have lived apart for more than one year pursuant to a separation judgment or decree which has been complied with, there is no time limit within which the parties must seek a divorce. The divorce action can be brought after one year; ten years; or not at all.

If the parties have lived apart, defenses to an action for divorce upon the ground of living apart pursuant to a separation judgment or decree are quite limited.[9] If the separation judgment is successfully collaterally attacked, such as for excusable default, fraud, or lack of jurisdiction,[10] a divorce action can no longer be maintained based upon the vacated judgment. In addition, any appropriate defense allowed by CPLR 3211(a) could be asserted in a divorce action based on the ground of living apart pursuant to a separation judgment or decree.

Library References:

West's Key No. Digests, Divorce ⚖═36.

§ 21.30 Grounds for Divorce—Divorce Action Based Upon Living Apart Pursuant to Separation Agreement

A divorce action may be maintained upon the ground that the husband and wife have lived apart pursuant to a written, subscribed, and acknowledged or proven agreement of separation for a period of one or more years after the execution of such agreement, and the party who seeks the divorce has substantially performed all the terms and conditions of the separation agreement.[1]

This ground is often referred to as a conversion ground for divorce, although the ground does not literally convert a separation agreement, which is a private contract, into a divorce judgment. A new divorce

---

7. *See* Wilkins v. Wilkins, 85 Misc.2d 985, 382 N.Y.S.2d 240 (Sup.Ct., Kings County, 1976).

8. Davidoff v. Davidoff, 93 A.D.2d 805, 460 N.Y.S.2d 603 (2d Dep't 1983).

9. Harris v. Harris, 35 A.D.2d 894, 315 N.Y.S.2d 773 (3d Dep't 1970).

10. *See* CPLR 5015.

§ 21.30

1. DRL § 170(6).

action must be filed and a new divorce judgment is entered should the action succeed, incorporating the terms of the agreement.[2]

Only an agreement of separation in compliance with DRL § 236(B)(3) may form the basis for a conversion divorce under DRL § 170(6).[3] Section 170(6) of the Domestic Relations Law sets forth the formalities which must accompany a separation agreement if such an agreement is to be utilized as predicate for a conversion divorce based upon living separate and apart pursuant to such an agreement. It must be in writing, subscribed by the parties, and acknowledged or proven in the form required to entitle a deed to be recorded.[4] Furthermore, either the agreement or a memorandum thereof, must be filed in the office of the Clerk of the County wherein either party resides, before the divorce action based upon the agreement is commenced.

In *Zelnik v. Zelnik*,[5] the court took a liberal view as to the type of agreement that constituted a formal agreement. There, the parties entered into a tersely written, short agreement in which they acknowledged that they were living apart. Although the agreement did not contain any provision for actually distributing marital property and other common subjects of separation agreements, it did provide for the parties to live apart and did make explicit provision for such major issues as custody, child support, and spousal maintenance. As a result, the agreement qualified as a "separation agreement" sufficient to serve as the predicate for a conversion divorce.

In order to obtain a conversion divorce, after establishing that a duly executed separation agreement is in place, it must be shown that the parties have actually lived apart, pursuant to it, for a period of one or more years. Demonstrating that the parties maintained separate homes, and separate lives, during the requisite period satisfies this requirement. However, it is important to note that a separation agreement may be voided by a reconciliation of the parties.[6] Occasional cohabitation by the parties during the period of separation is, by itself, insufficient to rescind the agreement and defeat the divorce claim.[7] The

---

2. See DRL § 236(B)(3).

3. Sagan v. Sagan, 53 N.Y.2d 635, 438 N.Y.S.2d 782, 420 N.E.2d 974 (1981) (a signed hand-written document entitled "Preliminary Agreement, Marriage Settlement," the terms of which differed from a later unsigned proposed formal agreement, was held to be too incomplete and preliminary to constitute a separation agreement).

4. See Rose v. Rose, 167 Misc.2d 562, 637 N.Y.S.2d 1002 (Sup.Ct., N.Y. County, 1995) (in a case of first impression, the court was faced with the question of whether a shareholder's agreement entered into by the parties constitutes sufficient evidence of a written agreement of separation to support a divorce under DRL § 170(6); the agreement could not be the foundation for the conversion divorce where it was not properly acknowledged).

5. 169 A.D.2d 317, 573 N.Y.S.2d 261 (1st Dep't 1991).

6. See Pasquale v. Pasquale, 210 A.D.2d 387, 620 N.Y.S.2d 95 (2d Dep't 1994); Berger v. Estate of Berger, 203 A.D.2d 502, 611 N.Y.S.2d 246 (2d Dep't 1994).

7. Zelnik v. Zelnik, 169 A.D.2d 317, 573 N.Y.S.2d 261 (1st Dep't 1991) (the husband's return to the marital residence for one week in a reconciliation attempt, shortly after the agreement was made and years

question becomes whether the reconciliation of the parties evidences an intention to abandon the agreement.[8]

The party who is seeking the divorce on this ground must also establish that he or she has substantially performed all the terms and conditions of the separation agreement. The statute does not require perfect or flawless performance of the agreement, only that there has been substantial performance.[9]

There is no statutory limitation applicable to actions on this ground.[10] Once the parties have lived apart for more than one year pursuant to a separation agreement, there is no time limit within which the parties must seek a divorce. Defenses to an action for divorce upon the ground of living apart pursuant to a separation agreement are usually limited to showing a lack of compliance with its terms.[11] Where an agreement is invalid as a result of fraud, duress or incapacity, the agreement is void *ab initio* and may not be used as the predicate for a conversion divorce.[12] In addition, any appropriate defense allowed by

before the action was brought, was not a resumption of the marriage sufficient to demonstrate an abandonment of the agreement); Lippman v. Lippman, 192 A.D.2d 1060, 596 N.Y.S.2d 241 (4th Dep't 1993) (sporadic cohabitation and the intermittent resumption of sexual relations did not vitiate a 17 year old separation agreement and did not prevent the granting of a divorce judgment; the parties, for the most part, maintained separate residences and continued to abide by the financial terms of the agreement).

8. *See* Buckley v. Buckley, 142 Misc.2d 560, 537 N.Y.S.2d 943 (Sup.Ct., Saratoga County, 1988) (the court denied a divorce based on living separate and apart pursuant to a separation agreement where the parties reconciled during the one year period; if the parties had simply resumed living together, without having abandoned the agreement, the one year period could recommence when they separated; however, once they abandoned the agreement by reconciliation, the one year period would not start running unless and until they executed a new agreement and physically separated pursuant to the new agreement).

9. *See, e.g.*, Fairley v. Fairley, 75 A.D.2d 975, 428 N.Y.S.2d 530 (3d Dep't 1980), aff'd for reasons stated in appellate division opinion 53 N.Y.2d 726, 439 N.Y.S.2d 354, 421 N.E.2d 846 (1981); Zambito v. Zambito, 171 A.D.2d 918, 566 N.Y.S.2d 789 (3d Dep't 1991) (the wife's denial of visitation to the husband during a three month period was not such a material breach of the agreement as to warrant denying the wife a conversion divorce; the three judges in the majority described the denial of visitation as temporary, with the wife having provided visitation both before and after the period during which visitation was denied and given her circumstances and emotional state at the time, the majority concluded that the wife's conduct should not result in the denial of the divorce; a two judge dissent found that the wife's denial of visitation was irrational and argued that it constituted a "material and manifest repudiation of the agreement").

10. DRL § 210(a) excepts this ground from the Statute of Limitations.

11. Harris v. Harris, 35 A.D.2d 894, 315 N.Y.S.2d 773 (3d Dep't 1970).

12. Angeloff v. Angeloff, 56 N.Y.2d 982, 453 N.Y.S.2d 630, 439 N.E.2d 346 (1982). *See* Towner v. Towner, 225 A.D.2d 614, 639 N.Y.S.2d 133 (2d Dep't 1996) (evidence that parties had lived apart pursuant to written separation agreement for more than one year and that husband had substantially performed all terms and conditions of agreement was sufficient to make *prima facie* showing on part of husband that he was entitled to divorce as matter of law; wife failed to submit any affidavits to establish that she had received treatment for alcoholism to support her contention that she suffered from severe and chronic alcoholism at time she entered agreement and set forth no facts which would indicate lack of capacity to enter contract).

§ 21.30   DOMESTIC RELATIONS   Ch. 21

CPLR 3211(a) could be asserted in a divorce action based on the ground of living apart pursuant to a separation agreement.

Library References:

West's Key No. Digests, Divorce ⚖═36.

§ 21.31   Grounds for Divorce—Dual Divorce

In divorce actions, except where both parties are suing on the ground of adultery or abandonment, if the court finds that both parties have established grounds for divorce, the court may grant a dual divorce—each party is entitled to a judgment of divorce. Where both parties have committed such marital misconduct, the result is the grant of a dual decree.[1]

Under DRL §§ 170(5) and (6), each party must have lived separate from the other for the requisite period. If both parties have complied with the separation agreement or judgment, both are theoretically entitled to a divorce.[2]

Dual divorce is not permissible in the abandonment situation. It is not conceptually possible, or legally permissible, for there to be dual decrees, or a mutual divorce, on the ground of abandonment. Since one party has already been abandoned, he or she could not abandon the other party who has already evinced a refusal to abide by the marriage contract.[3]

Dual divorce is also not permissible in the adultery situation. According to the doctrine of recrimination, if both parties are guilty of adultery, then neither party is entitled to a divorce.[4]

§ 21.32   Effect of Sister State Divorce Judgment

Since other states have more liberal divorce laws than New York, what is the effect of a divorce decree obtained from another state? Pursuant to Article 4 of the U.S. Constitution, full faith and credit must be given in each state to the public acts, records and judicial proceedings of every other state. A decree of divorce, which is granted within the United States by a court having jurisdiction to do so is entitled to full

---

§ 21.31

1. *See, e.g.*, De Marinis v. De Marinis, 74 A.D.2d 815, 425 N.Y.S.2d 361 (2d Dep't 1980); John W.S. v. Jeanne F.S., 48 A.D.2d 30, 367 N.Y.S.2d 814 (2d Dep't 1975); Jay v. Jay, 67 Misc.2d 371, 323 N.Y.S.2d 387 (Sup. Ct., Niagara County, 1971).

2. Blauner v. Blauner, 60 A.D.2d 215, 400 N.Y.S.2d 335 (1st Dep't 1977).

3. Belandres v. Belandres, 58 A.D.2d 63, 395 N.Y.S.2d 458 (1st Dep't 1977).

4. *See supra*, § 21.27. It is possible for a dual decree to be awarded, where one party is awarded a divorce on adultery grounds and the other receives the divorce for cruel and inhuman treatment. *See* Anonymous v. Anonymous, 57 A.D.2d 938, 395 N.Y.S.2d 103 (2d Dep't 1977).

faith and credit.[1] In order for a court to have jurisdiction, domicile must be established, which normally requires actual residence in the divorce jurisdiction, coupled with an intention to remain there and to abandon the former domicile. If residence in the sister state was solely for the purpose of obtaining a divorce, full faith and credit need not be given.[2]

A divorce decree based on a finding of domicile and entered in a proceeding in which the nonresident defendant appears and participates or is personally served in the jurisdiction where the divorce is granted is entitled to full faith and credit and cannot be impeached in another jurisdiction on the ground that there was no jurisdiction for lack of the requisite domicile of the parties unless it can also be impeached in the state in which it was rendered.[3]

The judicial power to grant a divorce is based on domicile. Where the defendant has neither been personally served nor entered an appearance, the domicile of the plaintiff in the forum state is essential for the court to have jurisdiction to entitle the divorce decree to be recognized.[4] Where the form and nature of substituted service meet the requirements of due process and the domicile requirement is met, an *ex parte* divorce judgment will be recognized.[5]

Pursuant to the divisible divorce doctrine, although a sister state divorce may be entitled to full faith and credit with regard to the termination of the marital status of the parties, the decree may not be entitled to full faith and credit as regards the parties' subsidiary property rights, spousal or child support, or custody of children.[6]

While a court may have had jurisdiction to grant a divorce by a constructive service of process against a nonresident, and such divorce would be entitled to full faith and credit with regard to the marital status of the parties, the court must have personal jurisdiction over the

§ 21.32
1. *See, e.g.*, Kahn v. Kahn, 801 F.Supp. 1237 (S.D.N.Y.1992).

Whether a foreign country divorce decree will be recognized is to be determined by the doctrine of comity. *See* Greschler v. Greschler, 51 N.Y.2d 368, 434 N.Y.S.2d 194, 414 N.E.2d 694 (1980). New York courts will generally recognize bilateral divorce judgments of foreign nations under the doctrine of comity, unless there is some defect in jurisdiction which is against the public policy of the state. *See* In re Estate of Lovick, 201 A.D.2d 736, 608 N.Y.S.2d 310 (2d Dep't 1994).

2. *See, e.g.*, Pneuman v. Pneuman, 33 A.D.2d 646, 305 N.Y.S.2d 272 (4th Dep't 1969), aff'd 27 N.Y.2d 982, 318 N.Y.S.2d 742, 267 N.E.2d 478 (1970).

3. *See* Sherrer v. Sherrer, 334 U.S. 343, 68 S.Ct. 1087, 92 L.Ed. 1429 (1948).

4. Williams v. North Carolina, 317 U.S. 287, 63 S.Ct. 207, 87 L.Ed. 279 (1942).

5. *See* Chenu v. Board of Trustees, 12 A.D.2d 422, 212 N.Y.S.2d 818 (1st Dep't 1961), aff'd 11 N.Y.2d 688, 225 N.Y.S.2d 760, 180 N.E.2d 913 (1962).

6. *See, e.g.*, Estate of Nicholson, 180 A.D.2d 685, 580 N.Y.S.2d 65 (2d Dep't 1992) (a decree of divorce granted in another state without personal jurisdiction of one of the parties has no effect on properties held by the parties outside the jurisdiction of the state issuing the judgment); Mahoney v. Mahoney, 131 A.D.2d 822, 517 N.Y.S.2d 184 (2d Dep't 1987) (a spouse is not barred from seeking maintenance after a sister state divorce decree where maintenance was not resolved in the decree).

§ 21.33 Equitable Distribution

Chapter 281 of the Laws of 1980, referred to as the Equitable Distribution Law, completely changed New York law with respect to the economic aspects of a dissolution.

The Equitable Distribution Law changed the standards which govern the division of property upon dissolution of marriage.[1] Prior to the enactment of the statute, property was generally divided between spouses on the basis of legal title. Thus, a spouse who was a joint tenant with respect to a property item was entitled to one half of the value of the property. A spouse who held sole legal title was entitled to the entire property and the non-titled spouse would receive nothing. Under the enactment of the Equitable Distribution Law, the marriage relationship is to be viewed as an economic partnership. Upon its dissolution, property accumulated during the marriage should be distributed in a manner which is equitable to the parties regardless of the form in which title is held.[2]

Library References:
West's Key No. Digests, Divorce ⚖═249.1.

§ 21.34 Equitable Distribution—When Available

Subdivision 2 of Part B of DRL § 236 sets forth the actions and proceedings to which Part B has general application.[1] Subdivision 5(a) of

---

[7.] See Lansford v. Lansford, 96 A.D.2d 832, 465 N.Y.S.2d 583 (2d Dep't 1983).

§ 21.33

1. The Equitable Distribution Law also eliminated the concept of alimony and replaced it with a system of maintenance, which permits the court to tailor spousal support to address the needs and circumstances of particular parties. See infra, §§ 21.46–21.51. Other major changes include alterations in the considerations to be taken into account in determining the issue of child support (see infra, §§ 21.52–21.56) and expanded authority for the court to direct that provision be made for life and health insurance for dependents (see infra, § 21.57).

The Equitable Distribution Law provisions with respect to property distribution, maintenance, child support, spousal agreements, and other matters appear in Part B of DRL § 236. The statute is divided into two parts: Part A, which retains the former alimony provisions for application to cases commenced prior to July 19, 1980, the effective date of the Equitable Distribution Law, and Part B which applies to cases commenced on or after July 19, 1980.

See generally, Scheinkman, 9B West McKinney's Forms, MFL, § 17.01.

2. See Governor's Memorandum of Approval, McKinney's 1980 Session Laws, p. 1863.

§ 21.34

1. DRL § 236(B)(2) provides:

Matrimonial actions. Except as provided in subdivision five of this part, the provisions of this part shall be applicable to actions for an annulment or dissolution

Part B of DRL § 236 identifies the circumstances when the court has authority to determine the rights of the parties to property distribution.[2]

Pursuant to DRL § 236(B)(5), the court may not provide for a property distribution where the parties have settled the matter between themselves in an agreement made pursuant to subdivision 3 of Part B. Subdivision 3 expressly provides that the parties to an antenuptial, postnuptial or separation agreement may make provision in their agreement for the ownership, division or distribution of separate and marital property. Court-ordered property division is not authorized if the parties have settled the matter pursuant to subdivision 3 and the agreement provides "for the disposition of their property"[3] Note that an agreement which does not dispose of all the property does not preclude equitable distribution of property which is not covered by the express terms of the agreement.

A property distribution is authorized only when the court grants matrimonial relief which has the effect of terminating or dissolving the marriage or after a foreign judgment of divorce.[4] The statute states that the action must be one in which "all or part of the relief granted is divorce, or the dissolution, annulment or declaration of the nullity of a marriage."[5] Note that there is no authority for a property distribution in an action for a separation or after a foreign judgment of annulment.

Library References:
West's Key No. Digests, Divorce ⚖→249.1.

§ 21.35 Equitable Distribution—Identification of Property

The first step in any equitable distribution case is to identify all the types of property that may exist. The traditional view of property limits

of a marriage, for a divorce, for a separation, for a declaration of the nullity of a void marriage, for a declaration of the validity or nullity of a foreign judgment of divorce, for a declaration of the validity or nullity of a marriage, and to proceedings to obtain maintenance or a distribution of marital property following a foreign judgment of divorce, commenced on and after the effective date of this part.

2. DRL § 236(B)(5)(a) provides:

Except where the parties have provided in an agreement for the disposition of their property pursuant to subdivision three of this part, the court, in an action wherein all or part of the relief granted is divorce, or the dissolution, annulment or declaration of the nullity of a marriage, and in proceedings to obtain a distribution of marital property following a foreign judgment of divorce, shall determine the respective rights of the parties in their separate or marital property, and shall provide for the disposition thereof in the final judgment.

3. *See* Mancini v. Mancini, 216 A.D.2d 535, 628 N.Y.S.2d 803 (2d Dep't 1995) (former husband was not entitled to one-half the rental value of marital residence upon former wife's remarriage where parties' separation agreement indicated parties' intent that they were to be equally obligated to pay monthly expenses related to residence until it was sold).

4. **PRACTICE POINTER:** Counsel must be aware that the statutory language is absolutely controlling. Therefore, before a property distribution will be authorized, the court must terminate or dissolve the marriage. There will be no equitable distribution if the divorce action is unsuccessful.

5. DRL § 236(B)(5)(a).

§ 21.35

the concept to that which has an exchange value on the open market and is capable of sale, assignment or transfer.[1]

The Equitable Distribution Law put the emphasis on whether property is marital[2]—it does not specify that the property have such characteristics as salability, assignability or transferability or be an item that has exchange value. Thus, after enactment of the Equitable Distribution Law, New York began to demonstrate flexibility in identifying property that was subject to distribution. In *Majauskas v. Majauskas*,[3] the Court of Appeals held that vested or matured rights in a pension plan are subject to equitable distribution.[4] In *Litman v. Litman*,[5] it was held that a professional practice, acquired during marriage is subject to equitable distribution. However, until the decision in *O'Brien v. O'Brien*,[6] courts held that the concept of property did not embrace professional education, degrees or licenses.[7] In the landmark case of *O'Brien v. O'Brien*,[8] the Court of Appeals held that marital property is not limited to traditional property concepts; instead, the court stated that the Equitable Distribution Law recognizes equitable claims in "things of value" arising out of the marital relationship. *O'Brien* recognized that the enhanced earning capacity of a license-holder was a property interest capable of valuation when it held that a medical license was subject to equitable distribution.[9]

Library References:

West's Key No. Digests, Divorce ⟲252.3–252.5.

§ 21.36 Equitable Distribution—Characterization of Property

DRL § 236, Part B, subdivision 1(c), provides that "marital property" is all property acquired by either or both spouses during the marriage and before the execution of a separation agreement or the commencement of a matrimonial action. Marital property does not include "separate property" as defined in Part B, subd. 1(d)(1–4).

The form in which title to any property is held is immaterial. Prior to the enactment of the Equitable Distribution Law, New York was a

---

§ 21.35

1. O'Brien v. O'Brien, 66 N.Y.2d 576, 498 N.Y.S.2d 743, 489 N.E.2d 712 (1985).

2. *See infra*, §§ 21.37–21.39 for discussion of marital property.

3. 61 N.Y.2d 481, 474 N.Y.S.2d 699, 463 N.E.2d 15 (1984).

4. For discussion of the characterization of pensions as marital property, *see infra*, § 21.38.

5. 93 A.D.2d 695, 463 N.Y.S.2d 24 (2d Dep't 1983), aff'd 61 N.Y.2d 918, 474 N.Y.S.2d 718, 463 N.E.2d 34 (1984).

6. 66 N.Y.2d 576, 498 N.Y.S.2d 743, 489 N.E.2d 712 (1985).

7. Lesman v. Lesman, 88 A.D.2d 153, 452 N.Y.S.2d 935 (4th Dep't 1982), appeal dismissed 57 N.Y.2d 956 (N.Y.1982).

8. 66 N.Y.2d 576, 498 N.Y.S.2d 743, 489 N.E.2d 712 (1985).

9. For discussion of the characterization of professional practices, licenses, degrees and careers as marital property, *see infra*, § 21.39.

"title" state, with property distributed to the title-holding spouse.[1]

Classification of property as either marital or separate is of great import. Marital property is subject to equitable distribution, while separate property is not.

Library References:

West's Key No. Digests, Divorce ⚖︎252.3–252.5.

§ 21.37 Equitable Distribution—Characterization of Property—Marital Property

To constitute "marital property," the property must be acquired during the marriage.[1] Property acquired before the marriage is defined as separate property.[2] Property is not treated as "marital property" if acquired after a separation agreement has been signed or after a matrimonial action has been commenced unless it can be shown to have derived from, or have been in exchange for, marital property.[3] Thus, property acquired after either event is not "marital property" even though the parties remain married.

A separation agreement should be effective to terminate accrual of marital property only when both parties have executed it. An oral agreement to physically separate is not, by itself, a terminating event.[4] However, a stipulation made in family court confirming that the parties have separated has been viewed as sufficient.[5]

Property acquired after a matrimonial action is commenced is not "marital property." A matrimonial action is commenced by the filing and service of a summons with notice or a summons with verified complaint.[6] Thus, the filing and service of a summons in a matrimonial action cuts off the acquisition of marital property.[7]

The burden of establishing that property is not marital property is on the party seeking to exclude the property from equitable distribution.

§ 21.36

1. See supra, § 21.33.

§ 21.37

1. DRL § 236, Part B(1)(c).
2. DRL § 236, Part B(1)(d)(1–4).
3. DRL § 236, Part B(1)(c).
4. Davis v. Davis, 128 A.D.2d 470, 513 N.Y.S.2d 405 (1st Dep't 1987).
5. Clerk v. Clerk, 132 A.D.2d 456, 517 N.Y.S.2d 512 (1st Dep't 1987).
6. DRL § 211.
7. **CAVEAT:** There is an important caveat to this rule. This issue is not determined strictly by looking at the date of acquisition of the property and comparing it to the commencement date. The real question is when did the right to the property or funds in question accrue. See Antoian v. Antoian, 215 A.D.2d 421, 626 N.Y.S.2d 535 (2d Dep't 1995) (wife's IRA was her separate property because she established that she acquired the funds in the account after the commencement of the action); Hartog v. Hartog, 85 N.Y.2d 36, 623 N.Y.S.2d 537, 647 N.E.2d 749 (1995) (a bonus received after the commencement date is marital property if earned by pre-commencement employment).

§ 21.37   DOMESTIC RELATIONS   Ch. 21

There is a case law presumption that property acquired during the marriage is marital.[8] To overcome this presumption, the property must either be traced to separate property or it must be shown that separate property was the only possible source.[9]

Banking Law § 675, subdivision b, creates a rebuttable presumption that when a joint bank account is created, the funds on deposit belong to those whose names appear on the account.[10] If a spouse places his or her separate property into joint names, a presumption of gift arises which, unless rebutted, results in the conclusion that the property is to be treated as marital property.[11] If successfully rebutted, the asset will be treated as separate property.[12]

Although property acquired after the physical separation of the parties but before the execution of a separation agreement or commencement of a matrimonial action is marital, it does not mean that the property will necessarily be equally divided or even that the non-titled spouse will receive any distribution of the property at all. It only means that the property is subject to equitable distribution. How the property should be distributed will depend upon the court's exercise of discretion, which depends on the application of the relevant factors to the particular facts involved.[13]

Library References:

West's Key No. Digests, Divorce ⇨252.3(1).

8. Lord v. Lord, 124 A.D.2d 930, 508 N.Y.S.2d 676 (3d Dep't 1986); Lischynsky v. Lischynsky, 120 A.D.2d 824, 501 N.Y.S.2d 938 (3d Dep't 1986).

9. Sarafian v. Sarafian, 140 A.D.2d 801, 528 N.Y.S.2d 192 (3d Dep't 1988).

10. Dugue v. Dugue, 172 A.D.2d 974, 568 N.Y.S.2d 244 (3d Dep't 1991) (the statutory presumption was given effect in a case in which the husband claimed that the proceeds of a $30,000 loan from his mother should be treated as separate property; the husband asserted that he invested the loan proceeds to start a business and he should receive credit for the $30,000 prior to any equitable distribution of the balance of the worth of the business; his claim was rejected by the court, which pointed out that the husband had deposited the $30,000 into a joint account and only later took the funds out to invest in the business; the court reasoned that, given the presumption that the parties are equally entitled to deposits made into a joint account and the husband's failure to successfully rebut the presumption, the loan proceeds were converted into marital property). See Dunn v. Dunn, 224 A.D.2d 888, 638 N.Y.S.2d 238 (3d Dep't 1996).

11. Lischynsky v. Lischynsky, 120 A.D.2d 824, 501 N.Y.S.2d 938 (3d Dep't 1986).

12. McGarrity v. McGarrity, 211 A.D.2d 669, 622 N.Y.S.2d 521 (2d Dep't 1995) (inherited funds placed in a joint bank account were treated as entirely separate property upon a showing that the husband (whose inheritance it was) simply deposited the money into whatever bank account was most convenient; the court also looked to the parties' circumstances at the time, concluding that, because the parties were living apart at the time when most of the money was received and deposited, it was unlikely that the husband intended to make the wife a gift of his separate property); Gundlach v. Gundlach, 223 A.D.2d 942, 636 N.Y.S.2d 914 (3d Dep't 1996).

13. See infra, § 21.44 for a discussion of the factors.

§ 21.38 Equitable Distribution—Classification of Property—Marital Property—Pensions

In 1984, in *Majauskas v. Majauskas*,[1] the Court of Appeals held that vested or matured rights in a pension plan, whether the plan is contributory or not, are marital property, to the extent that the rights result from employment time after the marriage and to the date of the commencement of a matrimonial action. To determine what portion of a pension is marital property a fraction is used: The numerator is the number of months the parties were married; the denominator is the total number of months of employment covered by the pension. The rationale underlying the rule is that pension rights which accrue during the marriage are a form of deferred compensation, taken in lieu of compensation which would have increased marital assets.

The appellate divisions have held that a spouse's interest in a pension or retirement plan, even if not vested, is subject to equitable distribution.[2] In 1994, in *Burns v. Burns*,[3] the Court of Appeals agreed, and held that the absence of vesting does not preclude the equitable distribution of a pension or retirement account.

In *Parrish v. Parrish*,[4] the court held that the burden of proof is on the party claiming that the pension is separate property. In *Parrish*, the parties each presented experts and the court found that neither expert was credible. The court held that since there was no reliable evidence of what was the separate property component, the entire pension would be viewed as marital.[5]

Treated similarly to pensions, and regarded as marital property if accrued during the marriage and before commencement of the matrimonial action, are Individual Retirement Accounts,[6] Social Security benefits,[7] the employee spouse's interest in an employment savings and investment plan,[8] and the employee spouse's vested interest in a profit-sharing plan.[9]

---

§ 21.38

1. 61 N.Y.2d 481, 474 N.Y.S.2d 699, 463 N.E.2d 15 (1984).

2. *See* Cavaretta v. Cavaretta, 127 A.D.2d 1002, 512 N.Y.S.2d 945 (4th Dep't 1987); Damiano v. Damiano, 94 A.D.2d 132, 463 N.Y.S.2d 477 (2d Dep't 1983).

3. 84 N.Y.2d 369, 618 N.Y.S.2d 761, 643 N.E.2d 80 (1994).

4. 213 A.D.2d 928, 623 N.Y.S.2d 955 (3d Dep't 1995).

5. The non-employee spouse who claims an interest in a pension must establish that there is a pension plan and what the marital portion of the plan is. *See* Grenier v. Grenier, 210 A.D.2d 557, 620 N.Y.S.2d 139 (3d Dep't 1994). Parrish is consistent with this rule. Once the non-employee spouse shows that there is a pension plan and establishes the portion generated by marital employment, the burden of proof has been met. If the employee spouse wishes to avoid equitable distribution of the pension rights earned during marriage, the burden is on the employee spouse to show that the pension is separate property.

6. *See* Carney v. Carney, 202 A.D.2d 907, 609 N.Y.S.2d 425 (3d Dep't 1994).

7. Wiercinski v. Wiercinski, 116 A.D.2d 789, 497 N.Y.S.2d 179 (3d Dep't 1986).

CAVEAT: Note that any portion of the benefits that represent compensation for personal injuries are separate property. *See infra*, § 21.40.

8. *See* Dawson v. Dawson, 152 A.D.2d 717, 544 N.Y.S.2d 172 (2d Dep't 1989).

9. *See* Glasberg v. Glasberg, 162 A.D.2d 586, 556 N.Y.S.2d 772 (2d Dep't 1990).

In *Olivo v. Olivo*,[10] the Court of Appeals held that post-divorce retirement incentives are not marital, except to the extent that such incentives enhance pension benefits attributable to the pre-divorce marital period.

Library References:

West's Key No. Digests, Divorce ⚷252.3(4).

§ 21.39 Equitable Distribution—Classification of Property—Marital Property—Professional Practices, Licenses, Degrees and Careers

A spouse's professional practice, if established during the marriage and prior to the commencement of a matrimonial action or the execution of a separation agreement, is subject to equitable distribution.[1] In *O'Brien v. O'Brien*, the Court of Appeals held that a spouse's license to practice a profession, if acquired during the marriage and prior to the commencement of a matrimonial action or the execution of a separation agreement, is subject to equitable distribution.[2]

Until recently, the concept of merger was utilized to hold that a professional license should not be assigned an independent value where the licensee had maintained a professional practice for a substantial period. The license lost its status as an independently valuable marital asset and merged with the practice itself; only the practice was a distributable asset.[3] In *McSparron v. McSparron*,[4] the Court of Appeals reexamined the merger doctrine and held that the holding in *O'Brien* is best served by eliminating the concept of "merger" from the inquiry. The merger doctrine should be discarded, stated the court, in favor of a common sense approach that recognizes the ongoing independent vitality that a professional license may have and focuses solely on the problem of valuing that asset in a way that avoids duplicative awards.[5] As a result, a

---

10. 82 N.Y.2d 202, 604 N.Y.S.2d 23, 624 N.E.2d 151 (1993).

§ 21.39

1. *See* Arvantides v. Arvantides, 64 N.Y.2d 1033, 489 N.Y.S.2d 58, 478 N.E.2d 199 (1985).

2. 66 N.Y.2d 576, 498 N.Y.S.2d 743, 489 N.E.2d 712 (1985).

A professional license acquired during the marriage is marital property even if the holder of the license is not engaged in private practice. *See* Cronin v. Cronin, 131 Misc.2d 879, 502 N.Y.S.2d 368 (Sup.Ct., Nassau County, 1986).

A professional license may be classified as marital property even if acquired after commencement of a matrimonial action, where the parties contributed toward achieving the license during the marriage. *See* Freyer v. Freyer, 138 Misc.2d 158, 524 N.Y.S.2d 147 (Sup.Ct., Suffolk County, 1987).

3. White v. White, 204 A.D.2d 825, 611 N.Y.S.2d 951 (3d Dep't 1994); Marcus v. Marcus, 135 A.D.2d 216, 525 N.Y.S.2d 238 (2d Dep't 1988).

4. 87 N.Y.2d 275, 639 N.Y.S.2d 265, 662 N.E.2d 745 (1995).

5. *See infra*, § 21.43 for further discussion of McSparron and valuation.

court will value both a professional license and the professional practice utilizing that license.

Prior to the *O'Brien* decision, it was held that an educational degree was not an asset that could be equitably distributed.[6] However, in *O'Brien*, the Court of Appeals stated that the Equitable Distribution Law recognizes equitable claims in "things of value" arising out of the marital relationship.[7] In *McGowan v. McGowan*,[8] the appellate division held that if an educational degree can be shown to have value and was acquired during the marriage, then it, too, may be considered marital property subject to equitable distribution. *McGowan* held that there was no basis for drawing a distinction between the equitable distribution treatment of a professional license and that of an academic degree.[9]

Courts have relied upon the *O'Brien* decision in a number of cases. *Procario v. Procario*,[10] involved a husband who was a physician and who had completed a general surgical residency during the marriage. While the wife argued that the value of the husband's degree had been enhanced by this specialty training, the husband maintained that completion of the residency merely made him eligible to take the test for board certification and that "eligibility" is valueless since he is able to work as a general surgeon without the certification. The court accepted the wife's argument by drawing upon *O'Brien*, which established that whether an item constitutes marital property depends upon whether there is an enhanced earning ability. Without the specialty training, the husband would have been only a general practitioner. If, with the training, the husband had a useable specialty that would generate more income, that is a "thing of value" and, if acquired during marriage, a marital asset.[11]

---

6. *See* Conner v. Conner, 97 A.D.2d 88, 468 N.Y.S.2d 482 (2d Dep't 1983).

7. 66 N.Y.2d 576, 498 N.Y.S.2d 743, 489 N.E.2d 712 (1985).

8. 142 A.D.2d 355, 535 N.Y.S.2d 990 (2d Dep't 1988) (a master's degree acquired by the wife was marital property; in addition to the master's degree, the wife also had acquired a teaching certificate, a certificate issued two weeks after the marriage; while the certificate was formally awarded after marriage, it was uncontradicted that the wife had fulfilled all of the requirements for the certificate prior to the marriage; the court declined to treat the certificate as marital property, holding that the real interest in the certificate, the wife's knowledge and ability, was acquired before the marriage).

9. Following McGowan, a number of decisions have held various types of certificates to be marital property, where acquired during marriage. *See* Morimando v. Morimando, 145 A.D.2d 609, 536 N.Y.S.2d 701 (2d Dep't 1988) (license as physician's assistant); McAlpine v. McAlpine, 143 Misc.2d 30, 539 N.Y.S.2d 680 (Sup.Ct., Suffolk County, 1989) (fellowship in society of actuaries). *Cf.* Kyle v. Kyle, 156 A.D.2d 508, 548 N.Y.S.2d 781 (2d Dep't 1989), appeal after remand 202 A.D.2d 643, 610 N.Y.S.2d 839 (1994) (uncompleted studies that might lead to a license are not to be treated as marital property).

10. 164 Misc.2d 79, 623 N.Y.S.2d 971 (Sup.Ct., Westchester County, 1994).

11. The absence of a formal diploma or certification is not determinative; it is the skill and learning acquired in the speciality that constitute the asset. *Cf.* West v. West, 213 A.D.2d 1025, 625 N.Y.S.2d 116 (4th Dep't 1995) (wife was not entitled to an award based upon the value of her husband's banking career; the court pointed to the wife's failure to prove that the husband's college degree was essential for his

§ 21.39 DOMESTIC RELATIONS Ch. 21

In cases in which spouses have no specialized degrees or licenses, courts have held that the value in a spouse's "career" may still be a distributable asset if there is a high capacity to earn associated with it. In *Golub v. Golub*,[12] the court held that an increase in value in the acting and modeling career of the wife was marital property.[13] In *Elkus v. Elkus*,[14] the appellate division held that a spouse's interest in a career with celebrity status, even though not documented by a license or degree, is a cognizable property right which is subject to equitable distribution.

Library References:

West's Key No. Digests, Divorce ⚖=252.3(1).

§ 21.40 Equitable Distribution—Characterization of Property—Separate Property

DRL § 236, Part B, subdivision 1(d) provides a list of certain specific types of property which must be considered the "separate property" of the titleholding spouse: (1) property acquired before marriage or property acquired by bequest, devise, or descent, or gift from a party other than the spouse; (2) compensation for personal injuries; (3) property acquired in exchange for or the increase in value of separate property, except to the extent that such appreciation is due in part to the contributions or efforts of the other spouse; (4) property described as separate property by written agreement of the parties.

Property acquired before the marriage is separate property, as is property acquired by inheritance or by gift from a party other than the other spouse. In essence, property which is not the product of the matrimonial partnership is not regarded as partnership property. Certain types of property, acquired before the marriage but in contemplation thereof, may be "marital" and not separate property. With respect to "gifts," it is necessary for the party who claims that the property is "separate" to show that the property was intended for him or her alone.[1] The nature of the gift and the use made of it may be important facts.

---

significant advancement; there was no indication that a career in banking has any inherent value).

12. 139 Misc.2d 440, 527 N.Y.S.2d 946 (Sup.Ct., N.Y. County, 1988).

13. The husband's interest was limited to appreciation in value because the wife had commenced her career prior to the marriage.

14. 169 A.D.2d 134, 572 N.Y.S.2d 901 (1st Dep't 1991) (plaintiff was an opera singer; during the course of the marriage, her career progressed, her income increased, and she became an internationally renowned celebrity; defendant was plaintiff's voice teacher and coach and he claimed that he assisted plaintiff in her career endeavors).

§ 21.40

1. Nehorayoff v. Nehorayoff, 108 Misc.2d 311, 437 N.Y.S.2d 584, 588 (Sup. Ct., Nassau County, 1981) (wedding gifts are marital or joint property, despite the source, unless the gift was something that could be used only by one spouse or was specifically earmarked as exclusively intended for one spouse).

Gifts exchanged between the spouses during the marriage are marital property.

Property which is acquired prior to the marriage is separate property, even where the parties have an established relationship. Thus, in *Nell v. Nell*,[2] the court held that a cooperative apartment, acquired by the husband prior to marriage, was his separate property, even though he was romantically involved with the wife at the time and intended the apartment to be the marital home. A different result was reached in *Ryan v. Ryan*,[3] where the parties acquired a house shortly before the marriage and renovated it, with both parties contributing towards the purchase price. However, title to the house was held in the husband's name alone because the wife's employment kept her from attending the closing. The court held that the entire amount of the property, not just the appreciation in value, should be considered marital property.[4]

Compensation received for personal injuries for pain and suffering, is regarded as separate property.[5] The definition of what constitutes "personal injury" is found in General Construction Law § 37–a.[6] Lost earnings as a result of an injury are not separate property.

The statute provides that property acquired in exchange for separate property continues to be separate property, as does income earned from separate property.[7] The increase in the value of the separate property acquired during the marriage may be marital property depending on if the appreciation is due in part to the contributions of the other spouse.[8] Where property acquired during the marriage is paid for entirely with the separate funds of a spouse and there is no showing of appreciation in value, it remains that spouse's separate property.[9] Where part of the consideration for the acquisition is separate property, then the portion of

---

2. 166 A.D.2d 154, 560 N.Y.S.2d 426 (1st Dep't 1990).

3. 123 A.D.2d 679, 506 N.Y.S.2d 977 (2d Dep't 1986).

4. Note that in Ryan, both parties contributed to the purchase price; technically, though the house was acquired by the husband alone prior to the marriage. Ryan has been limited to its facts. See Zelnik v. Zelnik, 169 A.D.2d 317, 573 N.Y.S.2d 261 (1st Dep't 1991) (the court treated a townhouse, acquired by the husband with his separate funds shortly before the marriage, as the husband's separate property, though it was acquired to serve as the marital residence).

5. An equitable distribution case from 1984 held that, where a party recovers a personal injury award, it is the portion that represents an award for pain and suffering that is separate property; a recovery for economic loss should be marital. See Rich v. Rich, 126 Misc.2d 536, 483 N.Y.S.2d 150 (Sup.Ct., Ontario County, 1984). That view was rejected as not authorized by the statutory language. See Fleitz v. Fleitz, 200 A.D.2d 874, 606 N.Y.S.2d 825 (3d Dep't 1994) (the fact that the compensation (disability payments) was due to policies paid for with marital funds did not strip the payments of the statutory exemption).

6. See generally, Bensel, Frank, McKeon, et al., *Personal Injury Practice in New York* (West 1997).

7. See Glazer v. Glazer, 190 A.D.2d 951, 593 N.Y.S.2d 905 (3d Dep't 1993); Sauer v. Sauer, 91 A.D.2d 1166, 459 N.Y.S.2d 131 (4th Dep't 1983).

8. See infra, § 21.41.

9. See Cappiello v. Cappiello, 66 N.Y.2d 107, 495 N.Y.S.2d 318, 485 N.E.2d 983 (1985).

the property so purchased is separate property.[10] The separate property distinction may be lost if it is commingled with marital assets.[11]

The parties may agree to describe certain property as "separate property" in a written antenuptial or separation agreement, entered into pursuant to DRL § 236, Part B, subdivision 3. The parties are afforded a great deal of flexibility in adjusting their own property rights and interests.

Library References:

West's Key No. Digests, Divorce ⚖=252.3(3).

§ 21.41 Equitable Distribution—Characterization of Property—Increase in Value of Separate Property

DRL § 236 Part B, subd. 1(d)(3) provides that any increase in the value of separate property remains separate property, except to the extent that "such appreciation" is due in part to the contributions or efforts of the other spouse. Therefore, if the titled spouse was aided by the non-titled spouse, then the appreciation is the product of the marital partnership. For example, if the husband had a business before the marriage and after the marriage the wife worked in the office and helped manage the books and records, such contributions to the value of the practice are recognized.

In *Price v. Price*,[1] the Court of Appeals held that spousal contributions as a spouse, parent or homemaker may be considered. It held that where the separate property of one spouse has appreciated in value due to the efforts of the titled spouse and where those efforts were aided directly or indirectly by the non-titled spouse, including by homemaker services, the appreciation is the product of the marital partnership and is subject to equitable distribution. The Court stated that the question as to indirect contributions of the nontitled spouse as parent and homemaker is whether there was an appreciation of separate property as a result of the efforts of the titled spouse during the period when it is shown that those efforts were being aided or facilitated in some way by these indirect contributions.

The *Price* Court contrasted an active asset, such as a business, with passive property whose "appreciation is not due, in any part, to the efforts of the titled spouse but to the efforts of others or to unrelated factors including inflation or other market factors, as in the case of a mutual fund, an investment in unimproved land, or in a work of

---

10. Jolis v. Jolis, 111 Misc.2d 965, 446 N.Y.S.2d 138, aff'd 98 A.D.2d 692, 470 N.Y.S.2d 584 (1st Dep't 1983).

11. *See supra*, § 21.37.

§ 21.41

1. 69 N.Y.2d 8, 511 N.Y.S.2d 219, 503 N.E.2d 684 (1986).

art.... "[2] The non-titled spouse must establish that the appreciation was caused by efforts of the parties, as distinguished from appreciation resulting from market factors or other circumstances beyond the control of the parties.

It has been noted that requiring a party to put a dollar value on market and non-market appreciation imposes an extraordinary burden.[3] While experts may be able to provide opinion testimony as to the value of property, often an attempt to explain why values have changed over time may be nothing more than speculation. For example, where a spouse has worked in the business, it may be difficult to establish what appreciation resulted from his or her efforts, what resulted from the efforts of others, and what resulted from market factors. Likewise, where the parties have improved and renovated a house, it may be difficult to pinpoint what portion of the appreciation is attributable to renovations and what portion is due to market factors.[4]

Hartog v. Hartog,[5] examined the issue where the titled spouse's involvement with separate property is both limited and active, and the property itself is active in nature. It may be difficult to link such limited specific efforts to quantifiable, tangible results.[6] To rule that all of the appreciation in active property should be retained by the titled spouse, ruled the court, would allow the titled spouse a windfall by nullifying the contributions of the non-titled spouse, at least insofar as that property is concerned.[7] But the non-titled spouse is entitled to share in the fruits of his or her labor, even if the connection between the activity and the appreciation cannot be established with precision. The court held that where an asset, like an ongoing business, is, by its very nature, active and the titled spouse is engaged in active efforts towards that asset, even to a small degree, then the appreciation in that asset is, to a proportionate degree, marital property.[8]

2. 69 N.Y.2d at 18, 511 N.Y.S.2d at 225.
3. *See* Scheinkman, 9B West McKinney's Forms, MFL, § 17.10.
4. *Id.*
5. 85 N.Y.2d 36, 623 N.Y.S.2d 537, 647 N.E.2d 749 (1995).
6. In Hartog, the husband was primarily involved in the family jewelry business, but was also a shareholder and director of two other family businesses. The husband's brother or others had primary responsibility for the day to day management of these two other concerns. The husband was listed as a part-time employee, had check writing authority, attended regular corporate meetings, and participated in the corporate profit-sharing plans. The husband's separate-property interest in the jewelry concern had appreciated in value during marriage and that, because of the wife's contributions to the husband's direct efforts in that business, the appreciation was treated as being entirely marital property. The dispute involved the appreciation in the value of the other two businesses. The husband argued that he was heavily involved in the jewelry business, that his efforts in relation to the other two companies were minimal, and that the wife had not shown that his efforts had any bearing on the appreciation. The wife asserted that the husband's efforts, however minimal, were active, that the existence of active efforts rendered the entire appreciation marital, and that the appreciation should be divided equally, as the other marital assets were divided equally.
7. 85 N.Y.2d at 47, 623 N.Y.S.2d at 543.
8. 85 N.Y.2d at 48, 623 N.Y.S.2d at 544.

§ 21.42 Equitable Distribution—Valuation Dates

A critical equitable distribution question is the date as of which marital property is to be valued. While marital property ceases, by definition, to be acquired once a matrimonial action is commenced, the statute does not mandate that property be valued as of the time of the commencement of the action.

Paragraph b to subdivision 4 of Part B of DRL § 236 provides that, as soon as practicable after the commencement of a matrimonial action, the court must set the date or dates the parties are to use for valuation of each asset. The valuation date or dates may be anytime from the date of the commencement of the action to the date of trial. Thus, the statute confirms that the court may select any valuation date as long as the date chosen is no sooner than the date the action was commenced and is not later than the date the trial commenced.[1] The same date need not be applied to all assets; different dates may be applied to different assets.

Pension rights are almost always determined as of the date of commencement of the action, since rights earned subsequently cannot be considered marital property.[2] As to other property, the selection of a valuation date is a matter within the discretion of the court, with the choice of date being dependent upon the circumstances presented.

The courts have disagreed as to the question of valuation dates. The Appellate Division, Second Department, has held that the selection of a date for valuation is a matter within the discretion of the court. The trial court also has the ability to change the date after it is set. Where the marital residence is concerned, the Appellate Division, Second Department, has stated that the trend has been to employ the date of trial as the valuation date.[3] On the other hand, the Appellate Division, Third Department, has held that valuation of marital property is to be determined as of the date of commencement of the action, unless doing so would be "patently inequitable."[4]

Several cases have adopted a general rule based upon whether the

---

§ 21.42

1. Fleitz v. Fleitz, 223 A.D.2d 946, 636 N.Y.S.2d 911 (3d Dep't 1996) (in the absence of unusual events, post–trial changes in value of marital assets are generally irrelevant for purposes of marital property division).

2. Majauskas v. Majauskas, 61 N.Y.2d 481, 474 N.Y.S.2d 699, 463 N.E.2d 15 (1984); Willis v. Willis, 107 A.D.2d 867, 484 N.Y.S.2d 309 (3d Dep't 1985).

3. Wegman v. Wegman, 123 A.D.2d 220, 509 N.Y.S.2d 342 (2d Dep't 1986), remittitur amended 512 N.Y.S.2d 410 (2d Dep't 1987) (the appellate division also directed that the valuation of the husband's business interests be as of a date as close to the date of trial as possible).

4. Lord v. Lord, 124 A.D.2d 930, 508 N.Y.S.2d 676 (3d Dep't 1986).

property is an "active" or "passive" asset.[5] Valuation of an active asset, according to the rule, should be as of the time of the commencement of the action; any appreciation or depreciation in value which occurs thereafter is no longer a product of the economic partnership. In contrast, valuation of a passive asset should be as of the time of trial; any increase or decrease in value will occur regardless of the conduct of the parties and neither party should receive a windfall or be penalized because of valuation changes brought about by outside forces.[6]

In *McSparron v. McSparron*,[7] the Court of Appeals noted the general rule and stated that such formulations may prove too rigid to be useful in particular cases. They should be regarded only as helpful guideposts and not as immutable rules of law.

Library References:

West's Key No. Digests, Divorce ⚖═253(3).

§ 21.43 Equitable Distribution—Valuation Methods

Valuation is an exercise within the fact-finding power of the trial court, guided by expert testimony. The court may determine that one expert is more credible than the other when competing theories are proposed by the parties.[1] However, expert testimony is not always vital if there is some other evidence to support the valuation. Thus, in one case, the valuation of a marital residence was based on the testimony of one of the spouses concerning the sale of a neighbor's home which was similar to the marital residence.[2] The parties are free to stipulate to the value of marital property or stipulate to have the marital property valued by an agreed-upon expert or court appointed expert.

The largest asset of the parties is often the marital home. An appraisal of marital real property will usually include consideration of three standard approaches to value: (1) market or sales comparison approach; (2) capitalization of income approach and (3) cost approach.[3] The market approach is usually used for the appraisal of an owner-occupied one-family home. Investment properties, such as apartments or office buildings are usually valued by the income approach. The cost approach is most often used to value new or fairly newly built improvements; it may also be used as a check on the other methods.

---

5. *See* Greenwald v. Greenwald, 164 A.D.2d 706, 565 N.Y.S.2d 494 (1st Dep't 1991); Zelnik v. Zelnik, 169 A.D.2d 317, 573 N.Y.S.2d 261 (1st Dep't 1991); Kallins v. Kallins, 170 A.D.2d 436, 565 N.Y.S.2d 227 (2d Dep't 1991).

6. *See* Smerling v. Smerling, 177 A.D.2d 429, 576 N.Y.S.2d 271 (1st Dep't 1991).

7. 87 N.Y.2d 275, 639 N.Y.S.2d 265, 662 N.E.2d 745 (1995).

§ 21.43

1. Lesch v. Lesch, 201 A.D.2d 900, 608 N.Y.S.2d 39 (4th Dep't 1994).

2. Del Vecchio v. Del Vecchio, 131 A.D.2d 536, 516 N.Y.S.2d 700 (2d Dep't 1987).

3. *See* The Appraisal of Real Property (9th ed., American Institute of Real Estate Appraisers).

§ 21.43 DOMESTIC RELATIONS Ch. 21

In valuing pension rights for equitable distribution, the courts must divide the number of years the pensioned spouse worked for the pension provider during the parties' marriage and before commencement of the matrimonial action, by the total number of years the spouse worked for the provider and apply this percentage to the pension entitlement, reduced by the taxes payable upon realization of the pension.[4] The pension entitlement is subject to the requirement that if the nonpensioned spouse is to receive a lump-sum distributive award, it must be reduced to current value.[5]

Burns v. Burns,[6] offers two approaches to the valuation and distribution of a nonvested pension. The first approach is to calculate the present cash value of the pension, with a discount where appropriate for lack of vesting. The second approach is to allocate a portion of each future payment to the nontitled spouse.[7]

Generally, a partnership agreement establishes the value of a partner's interest in the partnership for purposes of equitable distribution, however such agreements are not necessarily conclusive. In *Amodio v. Amodio*,[8] the Court of Appeals ruled that, while buy-sell agreements should be considered in valuation, such agreements are not conclusive. This decision did not settle the issue as to law firm partnerships, as the Fourth Department had held to the view that the value of a law firm was fixed by the terms of the partnership agreement and no other method of valuation could be employed.[9] In *Burns v. Burns*,[10] the Court of Appeals settled the issue when it held that, even as to law firm partnerships, agreements between the members are not conclusive on valuation.[11]

A valuation method commonly used to value businesses or professional practices is the capitalization of earnings approach. This method takes into consideration the nature and history of the business, its particular economic outlook and that of its industry generally, the book value of the stock and financial condition of the business, the company's earning capacity, its dividend paying capacity, its goodwill and other intangible assets, other sales of the stock of the corporation and the

---

4. *See* Dawson v. Dawson, 152 A.D.2d 717, 544 N.Y.S.2d 172 (2d Dep't 1989).

5. *See* Majauskas v. Majauskas, 61 N.Y.2d 481, 474 N.Y.S.2d 699, 463 N.E.2d 15 (1984).

6. 84 N.Y.2d 369, 618 N.Y.S.2d 761, 643 N.E.2d 80 (1994).

7. *Id.* **PRACTICE POINTER:** It may also be appropriate to use the pay-out approach where there is not enough cash, or other assets, which the employee spouse can use to pay the non-titled spouse for his or her share of the pension. Qualified Domestic Relations Orders (QDROs) transfer a specific portion of a pension to the non–participant spouse.

8. 70 N.Y.2d 5, 516 N.Y.S.2d 923, 509 N.E.2d 936 (1987).

9. *See* Dignan v. Dignan, 156 A.D.2d 995, 549 N.Y.S.2d 539 (4th Dep't 1989), appeal dismissed 75 N.Y.2d 915, 554 N.Y.S.2d 832, 553 N.E.2d 1342 (1990).

10. 84 N.Y.2d 369, 618 N.Y.S.2d 761, 643 N.E.2d 80 (1994).

11. The law firm partnership limited the partners, upon withdrawal, to the value of their capital accounts. But that value is not determinative of the value of the partnership interest upon divorce since the attorney spouse would continue to be a productive partner in an ongoing enterprise.

market price of the stock of comparable companies.[12] The court must consider company sales over the most recent 5-year period, however, the court must take care to exclude abnormally high (or low) years.[13] The court must also take into account the marketability, or lack thereof, of the particular business.[14]

The capitalization of earnings approach is an approach used to value practices, not licenses. A license is valued by: (a) calculating the difference between the average total lifetime income of a person without the license and the average lifetime income that a person in the relevant licensed profession would expect; and (b) reducing that amount to present value.[15]

In *McSparron v. McSparron*,[16] the court addressed the issue of whether a license that has been exploited by the licensee to establish and maintain a career may be deemed to have merged with the career and thereby lost its character as a separate distributable asset. The Court of Appeals held that the appellate division erred in treating defendant's law license as having merged with defendant's career. The merger principle on which the appellate division's decision was based was derived from the Second Department's ruling in *Marcus v. Marcus*,[17] in which it was held that a professional license should not be assigned an independent value where the licensee has maintained a professional practice for a substantial period. In that situation, the *Marcus* court stated, the license should be deemed to have merged with and been subsumed by the practice itself. The rationale of the merger doctrine is that the equitable considerations that motivated the *O'Brien* court are fundamentally different where the license has been utilized for a substantial period to establish a career or professional practice and to generate tangible assets for the family.

---

12. *See* IRS Revenue Ruling 59-60.

13. Sommer v. Sommer, 176 A.D.2d 1022, 575 N.Y.S.2d 178 (3d Dep't 1991).

14. *Id.*

15. O'Brien v. O'Brien, 66 N.Y.2d 576, 498 N.Y.S.2d 743, 489 N.E.2d 712 (1985) (the expert calculated the value of the medical license at issue by using the average income of a general surgeon (the medical specialty of the license holder) over a working lifetime).

See Kessler v. Kessler 212 A.D.2d 1038, 623 N.Y.S.2d 435 (4th Dep't 1995) (involving valuation of the enhanced earnings capacity of a post-graduate degree earned by a professional teacher; in the ordinary course of things, the enhanced earnings calculation consists of a comparison between the average earnings of a college graduate as compared to the average earnings of a person holding the advance degree in question; where teachers are concerned, school districts provide a formula for increasing the pay of teachers who have earned advance degrees; the appellate division held that it is the formula of the local school district which employs the teacher-spouse that should provide the valuation methodology— all it takes is calculating the difference between the salary the teacher-spouse earns with the degree and the salary that was earned without the degree; use of this methodology resulted in a significant reduction in the valuation of the advanced degree, a Master's degree in special education).

16. 87 N.Y.2d 275, 639 N.Y.S.2d 265, 662 N.E.2d 745 (1995).

17. 137 A.D.2d 131, 525 N.Y.S.2d 238 (2d Dep't 1988).

§ 21.43　　　DOMESTIC RELATIONS　　　Ch. 21

In the years after the merger theory was first articulated, lower courts had applied it with varying results; the courts had also made significant modifications to address the numerous situations in which the problem of matured professional licenses arise.[18] In an approach to the problems created by professional mobility, the lower courts had held that a license which has previously merged with a professional career or practice might reemerge as a significant and separately distributable asset if the licensed spouse experienced a significant career change.[19] Other cases acknowledged the applicability of the merger principle but treated the enhanced earning power associated with a spouse's professional license as a marital asset anyway.[20] Although the Court of Appeals in *McSparron* noted that such a concept had merit, it held that such an approach was ultimately flawed because of its continued reference to the concept of merger.

The court's first objection to the concept of merger was that the concept rests on the belief that an unrevoked professional license can somehow lose its character as a component of marital property solely because of its use in advancing its holder's career. If, as was held in *O'Brien*, a currently valid professional license is a distributable item of economic value, it should logically retain that quality throughout its existence. A second objection to the merger theory was that it is difficult to apply. For example, there can be no clear yardstick for measuring when the licensee's practice or career has matured to the point where it has "subsumed" the license. Finally, the court believed that the merger doctrine was flawed because its practical effect was to limit the *O'Brien* rule's application to recently acquired licenses: application of the merger doctrine favors the nonlicensed spouse in a shorter marriage over the nonlicensed spouse who is faced with rebuilding his or her economic life after the breakup of a long-term marriage.

Therefore, the *McSparron* court held that the merger doctrine should be discarded in favor of a common sense approach that recognizes the ongoing independent vitality that a professional license may have and focuses solely on the problem of valuing that asset in a way that

18. *See* Shoenfeld v. Shoenfeld, 168 A.D.2d 674, 563 N.Y.S.2d 500 (2d Dep't 1990) (a two-year-old practice was too new to have subsumed the underlying professional license); Phelps v. Phelps, 199 A.D.2d 608, 609, 604 N.Y.S.2d 339, 341 (3d Dep't 1993) (not error to assign separate distributable value to a medical license that had been in use for seven years because the licensee had made several changes in the form of his practice and his earnings had not yet "stabilized sufficiently to permit a valuation of his practice which would truly reflect the increased earning capacity [attributable to his] license"); Aborn v. Aborn, 196 A.D.2d 561, 601 N.Y.S.2d 339 (2d Dep't 1993) (Second Department declined to apply the merger rule to a spouse's professional license where the licensee had dissolved what had once been a profitable professional partnership and had relocated his practice several times).

19. *See* Behrens v. Behrens, 143 A.D.2d 617, 532 N.Y.S.2d 893 (2d Dep't 1988).

20. *See* Finocchio v. Finocchio, 162 A.D.2d 1044, 556 N.Y.S.2d 1007 (4th Dep't 1990).

avoids duplicative awards.[21] It held that *O'Brien* permits the court to include in the marital estate the present value of any increased earning capacity attributable to a professional license earned during the marriage.[22] That increased earning capacity continues to exist, to a greater or lesser degree, throughout the life of the license. Even after the licensee has had the time and opportunity to exploit the license and to realize a portion of the enhanced earning potential it affords, and establish a professional practice, the license itself retains some residual economic value. That value can be measured and distributed in the same way as a newly acquired license is valued.[23]

The Court of Appeals recognized that the valuation inquiry is made more complicated by the passage of time and the licensee's harvesting of some portion of the enhanced earning capacity that accompanies the license.[24] Where there is a newly earned license, it may be measured by simply comparing the average lifetime income of a person without the license and the average lifetime earnings of a person holding such a license and reducing the difference to its present value. In contrast, where the licensee has already embarked on his or her career and has acquired a history of actual earnings, an analysis based on the particular licensee's remaining professional earning potential must be utilized.

Library References:
West's Key No. Digests, Divorce ⟐253(3).

§ 21.44 Equitable Distribution—Distribution Factors

Courts are not mandated to distribute marital property on an equal basis; marital property is distributed in light of the circumstances of the parties.[1] Subdivision 5(d) of Part B of DRL § 236 sets forth 13 specific factors which the court must consider in determining an equitable distribution.[2] The Legislature intended to require the court to consider all the factors but left the relative weight to be accorded each factor in a particular case to the determination of the court.

1. *The income and property of each party at the time of marriage, and at the time of the commencement of the action*: The court must look at the earning power and property each spouse brought into the mar-

---

21. 87 N.Y.2d 275, 285, 639 N.Y.S.2d 265, 270, 662 N.E.2d 745, 750 (1995).

22. 87 N.Y.2d at 285, 639 N.Y.S.2d at 270, 662 N.E.2d at 750.

23. Id.

24. 87 N.Y.2d at 286, 639 N.Y.S.2d at 271, 662 N.E.2d at 751. The court also noted that care will have to be taken to ensure that the monetary value assigned to the license does not overlap with the value assigned to other marital assets that are derived from the license, such as the licensed spouse's professional practice. The courts will also have to guard against duplication in the form of maintenance awards that are premised on earnings derived from professional licenses.

§ 21.44

1. *See, e.g.*, Strang v. Strang, 222 A.D.2d 975, 635 N.Y.S.2d 786 (3d Dep't 1995).

2. For detailed discussion of each of the factors, *see* Scheinkman, 9B West McKinney's Forms, MFL, § 17.13.

riage and the earning power and property of each at the time dissolution proceedings were commenced.

2. *The duration of the marriage and the age and health of both parties*: This factor recognizes that in a longer marriage, the parties' financial positions have been affected by the marital relationship. The age and health of the parties are also considerations under this factor. These factors are relevant to consideration of the future financial prospects of the parties, as age or ill health may preclude a spouse from the pursuit of a full-time career. Even where a spouse is not considered elderly, his or her age may make it more difficult to enter the job market for the first time or to re-enter after many years.

3. *The need of a custodial parent to occupy or own the marital residence and to use or own its household effects*: This factor requires the court to consider whether it is appropriate to physically break up the marital residence at the time of the divorce or whether the interests of children and their custodial parent require that the home and its furnishings remain intact. The court has authority to provide that one of the spouses be given the exclusive occupancy of the marital residence.[3] Such authority is exercised in order to minimize the disruption of the lives of minor children, and preserve their home environment. Where an exclusive occupancy award is appropriate, Factor 3 gives the court two options.[4] It may order the spouse holding title to the marital residence and its furnishings to convey title immediately to the custodial spouse or it may delay a disposition of the marital residence until the children are grown.[5] The court also could determine that, under the circumstances, it would be appropriate to order an immediate sale of the property and require both the spouses and the children to relocate.[6]

---

3. DRL §§ 234, 236(B)(5)(f). *See* Nolan v. Nolan, 215 A.D.2d 795, 626 N.Y.S.2d 568 (3d Dep't 1995) (restates the judicial preference for permitting a custodial parent to remain in the marital home until the youngest child attains age 18).

4. *See* Scheinkman, 9B West McKinney's Forms, MFL, §§ 17.13, 17.49A.

5. The non-custodial spouse may object to the first alternative where the marital home and its furnishings constitute the bulk of the marital assets, since the custodial spouse will most likely be unable to transfer property which would equitably recompense the non-custodial spouse for his or her equitable share of the residence and its personal property. The non-custodial spouse may similarly object to the second alternative since it deprives the non-custodial spouse of the use or transferability of his or her interest in the property. *See* Scheinkman, 9B West McKinney's Forms, MFL, §§ 17.13, 17.49A.

6. The inability of the parents to afford the house can occur when a parent has lost a job or suffered a decrease in pay, or it may be due to increased expenses, such as the expenses of running two households. The question becomes whether the needs of the custodial parent and children to remain in the house are outweighed by either parent's need for immediate access to funds. Unless the parties are burdened with heavy debt or expenses which can be met only by using the equity in the house, it is rare for the need for immediate funds to outweigh the need for children, particularly younger children, to remain in their present home. *See, e.g.*, Mitzner v. Mitzner, 209 A.D.2d 487, 619 N.Y.S.2d 51 (2d Dep't 1994).

4. *The loss of inheritance and pension rights upon dissolution of the marriage as of the date of dissolution*: Factor 4 permits the court to take the loss of inheritance rights directly into account. The inclusion of the loss of "pension rights" as a factor has been relied upon to assert that the Legislature intended to include pension or retirement benefits as marital property. The value of such benefits may be difficult to compute, particularly where the pension has not yet vested,[7] however the nonemployee spouse, under equitable distribution, could be assigned half of the employee spouse's pension or retirement interest.

5. *An award of maintenance*: The court is to consider whether an award of maintenance has been made to one of the spouses. If an award has been made, the court should consider the amount and duration of the award. The major purpose of Factor 5 is to insure that the court can integrate all the elements of a comprehensive financial determination.

6. *Any equitable claim to, interest in, or direct or indirect contribution made to the acquisition of such marital property by the party not having title, including joint efforts or expenditures and contributions and services as a spouse, parent, wage earner and homemaker, and to the career or career potential of the other party*: Pursuant to Factor 6, the nontitled spouse is entitled to have non-monetary contributions to a marital partnership taken into account when marital property is divided. Factor 6 identifies certain types of contributions which may give rise to an equitable claim to a share of marital property to which title is held by the other spouse. Factor 6 also recognizes the role of the spouse who contributes to the career or career potential of the other spouse. This covers the spouse who entertains the other spouse's employer, clients, customers and business associates. It also includes the spouse who makes it possible for the other spouse to improve his or her career potential through the pursuit of advanced education or training.[8]

7. *The liquid or non-liquid character of all marital property*: This factor requires the court to consider whether various items of marital property consist of cash or can be readily converted into cash. There may be property which cannot be sold or which could only be sold at a significant loss. This factor may influence whether the court orders a distributive award or orders an allocation for marital property by physical exchange.

8. *The probable future financial circumstances of each party*: Pursuant to Factor 8, courts must consider how each spouse will fare financially in the future. Factor 2 considerations—duration of the marriage and the age and the health of the parties—also come into play.

---

7. *See supra*, § 21.43.

8. *See* Scheinkman, 9B West McKinney's Forms, MFL, § 17.13.

9. *The impossibility or difficulty of evaluating any component asset or any interest in a business, corporation or profession, and the economic desirability of retaining such asset or interest intact and free from any claim or interference by the other party*: Factor 9 recognizes the difficulty of evaluating any component asset or any interest in a business, corporation or profession. Marital property includes all property acquired during the marriage, including interest in a professional practice or closely held business. However, it may not always be possible to precisely value a business or professional practice. Additionally, there may be ethical or legal prohibitions against assigning an interest in a professional practice or license to a spouse who does not have the necessary training and experience. Factor 9 must be read together with Part B, subdivision 5(e), which authorizes the court to make a distributive award in lieu of an actual allocation of a share in a business, corporation or profession.

10. *The tax consequences to each party*: The court is to consider the tax consequences to each party.[9]

11. *The wasteful dissipation of assets by either spouse*: Prior to a 1986 amendment this factor was considered by the courts on a discretionary basis. Using assets for gambling or in furtherance of an extra marital affair are common examples of wasteful dissipation of assets.

12. *Any transfer or encumbrance made in contemplation of a matrimonial action without fair consideration*: This factor deals with the problem of a party who seeks to place assets out of his or her control in contemplation of an action in which equitable distribution will be made. This statutory factor allows the court to award a greater share of any remaining property to the other spouse who has been victimized.

13. *Any other factor which the court shall expressly find to be just and proper*: The court is given discretion to consider other factors. The court is not expressly empowered to consider the effect of award of child support. If need be, the court may include the effect of a child support award by resort to Factor 13.

In 1992, the Legislature added a new paragraph (h) to subdivision 5 of Part B of Section 236 which requires the court to consider, where appropriate, the effect that a barrier to remarriage would have on the various legislative factors, thus interpolating the provisions of DRL § 253 into the court's considerations.

The seminal case dealing with the consideration of fault in equitable distribution of property is *Blickstein v. Blickstein*.[10] Except in "egregious

---

9. See infra, § 21.45.

10. 99 A.D.2d 287, 472 N.Y.S.2d 110 (2d Dep't 1984), appeal dismissed 62 N.Y.2d 802 (1984).

cases which shock the conscience of the court," marital fault is not to be considered in the equitable distribution of marital property.[11] To consider marital fault, said the Court of Appeals, in *O'Brien v. O'Brien*,[12] would be inconsistent with the view that marriage is an economic partnership and that the partners, upon dissolution, are entitled to a fair share of the marital estate. Additionally, fault would usually be difficult to assign and consideration of fault would involve the courts in time-consuming procedural maneuvers relating to collateral issues.[13] While marital fault is not to be considered, economic fault as evidenced by Factors 11 and 12, may be considered in distributing marital property.[14]

Library References:
West's Key No. Digests, Divorce ⇔253(3).

§ 21.45 Equitable Distribution—Tax Considerations

Where, as part of a marital property distribution, one spouse transfers to the other spouse property which has appreciated in value since it was originally acquired by the transferor spouse, there are tax issues that must be taken into consideration. Major changes in this area have been brought about by the Domestic Relations Tax Reform Act of 1984.[1]

Under the Domestic Relations Tax Reform Act, no gain or loss is recognized on a transfer from an individual to, or in trust for the benefit of, a spouse. Similarly, no gain or loss is recognized on a transfer from an individual to, or in trust for the benefit of, a former spouse, provided that the transfer is incident to a divorce.[2] Transfers by one spouse to another, or by one former spouse to another former spouse made as incident to a divorce, are treated, for tax purposes, as a gift[3] and the transferor spouse realizes no gain or loss and the transferee spouse takes the transferred property at the transferor's basis.[4] Where the property transferred appreciates in value from the time of its acquisition, the tax burden, which arises when the transferee spouse sells the property, is imposed on the transferee spouse.

Where the transfer is from one former spouse to another, the transfer, to qualify for the statutory treatment, must be incident to

---

11. O'Brien v. O'Brien, 66 N.Y.2d 576, 498 N.Y.S.2d 743, 489 N.E.2d 712 (1985), approving Blickstein v. Blickstein, 99 A.D.2d 287, 472 N.Y.S.2d 110 (2d Dep't 1984).

12. 66 N.Y.2d 576, 498 N.Y.S.2d 743, 489 N.E.2d 712 (1985).

13. Id.

14. *See* Kozlowski v. Kozlowski, 221 A.D.2d 322, 633 N.Y.S.2d 523 (2d Dep't 1995) (distribution of 100% of parties' interest in marital residence was properly distributed to wife given that bulk of funds used in purchasing house were wife's separate property, husband had history of dissipating assets by gambling, and husband made only minimal contribution to maintenance of home).

§ 21.45

1. P.L. 98–369, Title IV, Subtitle B, enacted July 18, 1984.
2. 26 U.S.C.A. § 1041(a).
3. 26 U.S.C.A. § 1041(b)(1).
4. 26 U.S.C.A. § 1041(b)(2).

divorce.[5] The transfer is incident to a divorce if it takes place within 1 year after the date that the marriage ceases. Declarations of nullity and annulments are considered by the Internal Revenue Service to be divorces for the purposes of the statute.[6] Accordingly, a transfer which takes place within 1 year of cessation of marriage by reason of a declaration of nullity or annulment decree is deemed incident to a divorce for purposes of tax treatment of property transfers between former spouses.

Even if the transfer does not take place within 1 year of the cessation of the marriage, it qualifies under the statute if the transfer is related to the cessation of the marriage.[7] A transfer is related to the cessation of the marriage if the transfer is made pursuant to a divorce or separation instrument and the transfer occurs not more than 6 years after the date that the marriage ceases. A transfer which is not made pursuant to a divorce or separation instrument or which occurs more than 6 years after the date that the marriage ceases is presumed not to be related to the cessation of the marriage. Showing that the transfer was made to effect the division of property owned by the former spouses at the time of the cessation of the marriage can successfully rebut the presumption.

Library References:
West's Key No. Digests, Divorce ⚖=253(3).

§ 21.46 Maintenance

In 1986, the Legislature extensively amended the provisions concerning maintenance awards. The Legislature expressed the view that the maintenance provisions of the Equitable Distribution Law had been "incorrectly interpreted" by the courts so as to "deny indefinite (permanent) maintenance to divorced women who come away from long term marriages" or from "short term marriages where there are young children to be cared for." Such interpretations, it was said, contribute to the "feminization of poverty."[1] On the basis of these legislative findings, DRL § 236, Part B, subd. 6 was revised so as to delete the prior stress on maintenance for the purpose of meeting "reasonable needs." The emphasis has shifted so that the court is to award the amount that justice requires, having regard for the standard of living of the parties established during the marriage. While the court must still consider the

---

5. 26 U.S.C.A. § 1041(c). The statute holds that a property transfer between former spouses is incident to divorce if the transfer takes place within 1 year after the date on which the marriage ceases or is related to the cessation of the marriage.

6. See Temp.Regs., 26 C.F.R. § 1.1041–1T, T.D. 7973, published in 49 Fed.Register No. 171, August 31, 1984, Q–8, A–8.

7. Id.

§ 21.46

1. Assembly Memorandum In Support of Assembly Bill 10567–A. See Scheinkman, 9B West McKinney's Forms, MFL, § 17.41.

"reasonable needs" of the parties, what is reasonable should be viewed within the context of the parties' established living standard.[2] This change took effect on August 2, 1986 and applies to all actions commenced on or after August 2, 1986 and to all actions pending as of that date in which a trial has not been commenced.[3]

Under DRL § 236, Part B, subdivision 6(a), the court has discretion to determine whether maintenance should be awarded, and if so, how much and for how long.[4] The Legislature has provided a more comprehensive list of factors to be considered than was available under the prior statute.[5] The court is required to set forth the factors considered and the reasons for the conclusion in its decision.[6]

Unless the court provides for a definite period of maintenance, payments are due until either party dies, the supported spouse remarries, or the court modifies the award.[7]

§ 21.47 Maintenance—Legislative Factors

Subdivision 6 of Part B of DRL § 236 contains the substantive provisions with respect to maintenance. The Legislature has identified 11 specific factors for consideration in determining the amount and duration of maintenance.[1]

1. *The income and property of the respective parties including marital property distributed pursuant to subdivision five*: The court is expressly permitted to consider the marital property distributed to each party under equitable distribution to assure that the court has the ability to fully integrate a complete financial resolution. In addition to income, the court should consider the extent of the separate property of each party and the extent of property acquired by either party after the commencement of the action. Increases in property or income which occur between the commencement of the action and the time of trial are not excluded from consideration when determining maintenance.

2. *The duration of the marriage and the age and health of both parties*: As with property distribution,[2] the age and health of the parties and the duration of the marriage are factors for the court to consider.

---

2. *See* Scheinkman, 9B West McKinney's Forms, MFL, § 17.41.

3. L. 1986, Ch. 884, §§ 4, 5.

4. *See* Damato v. Damato, 215 A.D.2d 348, 626 N.Y.S.2d 221 (2d Dep't 1995).

5. *See infra*, § 21.47.

6. DRL § 236(B)(6)(b). *See* Kim v. Kim, 215 A.D.2d 356, 626 N.Y.S.2d 217 (2d Dep't 1995) (requirement that trial court adequately set forth factors considered and reasons for its determination cannot be waived by either party).

7. DRL § 236(B)(1)(a).

§ 21.47

1. DRL § 236(B)(6)(a). For detailed discussion of each of the factors, *see* Scheinkman, 9B West McKinney's Forms, MFL, § 17.44.

2. *See supra*, § 21.44.

3. *The present and future earning capacity of both parties*: Under prior law, Factor 3 provided for consideration of the present and future capacity of the needy spouse to be self-supporting. Factor 3 now considers the present and future earning capacities of both parties.

4. *The ability of the party seeking maintenance to become self-supporting and, if applicable, the period of time and training necessary therefor*: Factor 4, under prior law, asked the court to consider the period of time and training that the needy spouse would require in order to become self-supporting. It was assumed that the needy spouse could become self-supporting; the only question was when that would happen. By amending Factor 4, the Legislature recognized that it may not always be possible for a homemaker spouse, after a long term marriage, or with young children present in the home, to be capable of self-support. Factor 4 has now been broken down into two parts: (1) the court must look to whether the party seeking maintenance has the ability to become self-supporting and (2) if such an ability is found, the court must consider the period of time and training necessary for the spouse to become self-supporting. Note that the parties' standard of living is considered when determining the issue of the spouse's ability to become self-supporting.[3]

5. *Reduced or lost lifetime earning capacity of the party seeking maintenance as a result of having foregone or delayed education, training, employment, or career opportunities during the marriage*: Where a spouse passed up, or delayed, career opportunities during the marriage, Factor 5 provides that the reduced or lost lifetime earning capacity of the spouse be considered in awarding maintenance.

6. *The presence of children of the marriage in the respective homes of the parties*: This factor recognizes that a spouse's ability to enter the job market and be self-supporting may be affected by the presence of children in the home. In some cases it may be appropriate for a custodial parent to remain at home with the children.

7. *The tax consequences to each party*: The court is to consider the tax consequences that a maintenance award would have on each party.[4]

8. *Contributions and services of the party seeking maintenance as a spouse, parent, wage earner and homemaker, and to the career or career potential of the other party*: This factor is intended to ensure that the contributions of a spouse, even non-economic ones, are taken into account when that spouse seeks a support award.

9. *The wasteful dissipation of marital property by either spouse*: Under prior law, the court could consider the wasteful dissipation of "family assets." Factor 9 now limits the consideration to wasteful dissipa-

---

3. See infra, § 21.49.   4. See infra, § 21.51.

tion of "marital property." The revision precludes the court from considering, under Factor 9, the wasteful dissipation of separate property. However, note that a wasteful dissipation of separate property may still impact on maintenance; it may be considered under Factor 11, which allows the court to consider such additional factors as it finds appropriate.

10. *Any transfer or encumbrance made in contemplation of a matrimonial action without fair consideration*: This factor addresses the problem that arises when a party places assets out of his or her control in contemplation of a matrimonial action. Where a transfer cannot be undone, this factor allows the court to award additional maintenance to the victimized spouse.

11. *Any other factor which the court shall expressly find to be just and proper*: The court is given discretion to consider other factors.

§ 21.48 Maintenance—Effect of Fault

It has been argued that fault should be a consideration in awarding maintenance—the guilty party in a fault divorce should not be allowed to profit by relying on the former marital status to obtain support from a former spouse. Under DRL § 236, Part A, and its predecessor, fault was an absolute bar to any alimony payments for the benefit of the guilty spouse. No such prohibition appears in DRL § 236(B)(6). The seminal case dealing with the consideration of fault in equitable distribution of property is *Blickstein v. Blickstein*.[1] *Blickstein* did not reach the question of the effect of fault in regard to maintenance. Subsequent cases have discussed the impact of fault on maintenance.[2]

Library References:
West's Key No. Digests, Divorce ⚖︎238.

§ 21.49 Maintenance—Current Trends

In *Hartog v. Hartog*,[1] the Court of Appeals stressed that the predivorce standard of living is entitled to be treated as an essential component in the decision as to maintenance. The court reviewed the history of the 1986 amendment to DRL § 236, Part B, which moved the predivorce standard of living from mere inclusion in a list of factors into the

§ 21.48

1. 99 A.D.2d 287, 472 N.Y.S.2d 110 (2d Dep't 1984), appeal dismissed 62 N.Y.2d 802 (1984).

2. *See* Wilson v. Wilson, 101 A.D.2d 536, 476 N.Y.S.2d 120, 125 (1st Dep't 1984), appeal dismissed 63 N.Y.2d 768, 481 N.Y.S.2d 688, 471 N.E.2d 460 (1984) (the court ruled that fault is generally not a factor in maintenance as well as in property distribution); Nolan v. Nolan, 107 A.D.2d 190, 486 N.Y.S.2d 415 (3d Dep't 1985) (marital fault is a proper consideration in awarding maintenance); Pacifico v. Pacifico, 101 A.D.2d 709, 475 N.Y.S.2d 952 (4th Dep't 1984) (marital fault a proper consideration).

§ 21.49

1. 85 N.Y.2d 36, 623 N.Y.S.2d 537, 647 N.E.2d 749 (1995).

§ 21.49 DOMESTIC RELATIONS Ch. 21

statutory mandate itself. The purpose of the amendment was to require the courts to consider the marital standard of living in making maintenance awards. In *Hartog*, the Court of Appeals held that lifetime maintenance was appropriate.[2] Even though the wife had the ability to be self-supporting by some standard of living, that did not mean that she was self-supporting in the context of the marital standard of living.

The holding in *Hartog* does not require lifetime maintenance in every case, even in cases involving a luxurious lifestyle. That the needy spouse has some ability to earn does not eliminate the possibility of lifetime support; a luxurious lifestyle does not guarantee entitlement to a lifetime of support. What is required is that the court consider the parties' predivorce standard of living in the context of the other statutory factors.[3] In *Fleitz v. Fleitz*,[4] the Third Department held that the supreme court abused its discretion in determining both the amount and the duration of maintenance and agreed with the plaintiff that, her age (42); her lack of earning capacity, having withdrawn from the workplace to be a wife, mother and homemaker; the foregone educational opportunities occasioned by her withdrawal from school to accompany defendant to California where he sat for the dentistry boards: defendant's tax-free income; and the parties' preseparation standard of living, all militated in favor of an award of permanent maintenance.

The courts have focused on what lifetime support means. Where there are enough retirement benefits available, one party should not be compelled to work longer than was contemplated during marriage in order to support the other.[5] Protection must be provided to the other spouse to assure that any retirement is undertaken at an appropriate age and in good faith.[6]

2. At issue in Hartog was the length of the award, not the amount. The issue was of limited significance in the context of the case itself. The trial court directed lifetime support; the appellate division reduced the period to five years, noting the wife's ability to be self-supporting. Neither period ultimately mattered since it was clear that the husband, stricken with a fatal illness, would not live very long anyway. Indeed, he died shortly after the Court of Appeals decision was handed down. The issue, in the context of the case, was important in terms of the amount of life insurance, or estate lien, that the wife sought to secure to protect her upon his death. See *infra*, § 21.57.

3. See Summer v. Summer, 85 N.Y.2d 1014, 630 N.Y.S.2d 970, 654 N.E.2d 1218 (1995); O'Keefe v. O'Keefe, 216 A.D.2d 549, 628 N.Y.S.2d 766 (2d Dep't 1995).

4. 223 A.D.2d 946, 636 N.Y.S.2d 911 (3d Dep't 1996) (keeping in mind the redistribution of the marital assets by supreme court and the investment income that can be generated, the court concluded that plaintiff should receive maintenance in the amount of $1,500 per month until defendant reaches the age of 65, at which time maintenance should be reduced to $1,000 per month in recognition of the reduction in defendant's disability payments, or until plaintiff's death or remarriage).

5. See Scheinkman, *Practice Commentaries*, DRL § 236, C236B:35.

6. See McGarrity v. McGarrity, 211 A.D.2d 669, 622 N.Y.S.2d 521 (2d Dep't 1995) (maintenance would be paid until the husband's retirement, but with payments required until at least his 65th birthday; the determination was made in the light of the wife's current employment, the substantial distributions expected by both parties from the husband's profit-sharing plan, and the other equitable distribution provisions); McLane v. McLane, 209 A.D.2d 1001, 619 N.Y.S.2d 899 (4th Dep't), appeal

§ 21.50 Maintenance—Payments Fixed by Agreement

Where the parties contract with respect to maintenance, the termination events are those that the parties list in their agreement. Where the parties list several terminating events, their list is generally construed by the courts as being exclusive, even if the omitted events would otherwise be available by operation of law. The parties are free to expand the list of terminating events; they are also free to contract the list.[1] For example, there are situations where the parties may bargain to have maintenance payments continue despite remarriage, notwithstanding the fact that under the statute maintenance ceases on remarriage.[2]

Library References:

West's Key No. Digests, Husband and Wife ⟐278(1).

§ 21.51 Maintenance—Tax Consequences

Payments made for spousal support are generally tax deductible by the payor and taxable to the payee so long as they are made in cash, the spouses are divorced or legally separated under a separation decree (except for *pendente lite* awards), the payments end on the payee's death, and they are not attributable to child support.[1] However, the Internal Revenue Code permits the parties by agreement, or the court in an order, to designate the payments as not deductible by the payor and not taxable to the payee.[2] Whether to make the payments deductible or not

---

dismissed 85 N.Y.2d 924, 627 N.Y.S.2d 324, 650 N.E.2d 1326 (1995) (maintenance was ordered until the wife began to receive pension benefits from the husband's prior employer); *cf.* Grenier v. Grenier, 210 A.D.2d 557, 620 N.Y.S.2d 139 (3d Dep't 1994) (support was continued past age 70, though reduced, mindful that there was no pension distribution).

§ 21.50

1. Slagsvol v. Schneck, 213 A.D.2d 537, 624 N.Y.S.2d 182 (2d Dep't), appeal dismissed 85 N.Y.2d 968, 629 N.Y.S.2d 726, 653 N.E.2d 622 (1995).

2. Quaranta v. Quaranta, 212 A.D.2d 683, 622 N.Y.S.2d 778 (2d Dep't 1995) (the wife relinquished all claims to her husband's pension in exchange for lifetime maintenance payments; the only terminating events listed in the agreement were the deaths of the parties; it was also stipulated that, if the husband's pension payments increased, the wife's maintenance would also be increased; when the wife remarried, the husband sought to be relieved of the maintenance payments, noting that the agreement did not explicitly require him to continue them; the court denied the husband's application, without hearing, holding that the tenor of the agreement reflected an intent of both parties to continue the maintenance payments regardless of the marital status of the wife).

PRACTICE POINTER: It is good practice to list the terminating events in the agreement. If particular events are not put on the list, the payor spouse may properly be held to have waived or abandoned any attempt to use non-listed events as a basis for terminating.

§ 21.51

1. *See* 26 U.S.C.A. § 71(a). The rules governing the tax treatment of spousal support payments were significantly revised by reason of the Domestic Relations Tax Reform Acts of 1984 and 1986. For additional discussion of these issues *see* Scheinkman, et al., *New York Law of Domestic Relations* (West 1996) Ch. 17, "Tax Considerations."

2. *See* 26 U.S.C.A. § 71(b)(1)(B).

deductible is up to the sound discretion of the court.[3] In a sense, this may be a distinction without a difference.[4] If the court makes the payments deductible by the payor and income to the payee, the court must consider that the payments will not cost the payor as much because of the deductibility, and conversely that the net to the payee will be less than the gross. On the other hand, if the court eliminates deductibility, it must recognize that the cost to the payor has been increased and the net to the payee has also been increased. Courts typically adjust the amount of the award depending on whether it is made deductible or nondeductible.

Library References:

West's Key No. Digests, Divorce ⚞306–309; Parent and Child ⚞3.

§ 21.52   Child Support

In any matrimonial action or custody proceeding the court must verify the status of any child with respect to custody and support.[1] The court is required to enter orders for support and custody as, in its discretion, justice requires. Under DRL § 240(1), the court must verify whether there is a support order, whether support is being paid and by whom, and whether the amount paid is appropriate. Once the court has verified the status of the child, it may defer entering an order if the circumstances warrant such a deferral. The statute mandates, however, that once the court decides to make a child support order, child support be determined in accordance with the provisions of the Child Support Standards Act. In resolving the issue of child support, the trial court must apply the provisions of the Child Support Standards Act, must set forth the basis for its calculations, and provide a justification for any deviation from the child support guidelines.[2]

Library References:

West's Key No. Digests, Divorce ⚞306–309; Parent and Child ⚞3.

§ 21.53   Child Support—Child Support Standards Act

In 1989, the Legislature introduced new procedures for the determination of awards of child support through the enactment of the Child

---

3. See Lowe v. Lowe, 211 A.D.2d 595, 622 N.Y.S.2d 26 (1st Dep't 1995).

PRACTICE POINTER: Counsel must alert the court to the parties' potential use of available deductions and exemptions. If the payee spouse can deduct home mortgage interest and real estate taxes, and has little earned income, it would be a waste of the parties' resources to make maintenance nondeductible since the tax burden on the payor has been needlessly increased.

4. See Scheinkman, *Practice Commentaries*, DRL § 236, C236B:41.

§ 21.52

1. DRL § 240(1). Note that the Domestic Relations Law pertaining to custody and child support does not apply to children of unmarried parents. See Brentrup v. Culkin, 167 Misc.2d 211, 639 N.Y.S.2d 247 (Sup.Ct., N.Y. County, 1996).

2. Dean v. Dean, 214 A.D.2d 786, 624 N.Y.S.2d 666 (3d Dep't 1995). See generally, Scheinkman, *Practice Commentaries*, DRL § 240, C:240:27.

Support Standards Act.[1] The legislation amended Section 240 of the Domestic Relations Law to require that an award of child support be made in accordance with the provisions of subdivision 1–b of that section. The legislation also amended Section 236, Part B, subdivision 7, of the Equitable Distribution Law by eliminating all of the former criteria for determining child support. Instead, the court is instructed to use the new guidelines imposed in Section 240, subdivision 1–b.

The procedure required by the guidelines is for the court to determine the combined parental income, *i.e.*, the income of both parents, and multiply that income, up to $80,000, by a child support percentage, which varies depending upon the number of children involved. The resulting figure is then apportioned between the parents "in the same proportion as each parent's income is to the combined parental income."[2] The two final figures then represent the "basic" child support obligation of the parents.[3]

To determine the incomes of the parents, the first place to look is the amount reported by each parent as his or her gross income on the most recent federal income tax return.[4] If the parties file joint income tax returns, each party must prepare a form, sworn to under penalty of perjury, disclosing his or her gross individual income.

In addition to the amount reported on the income tax return, the court is required to add amounts not included which represent net investment income (investment income as reduced by sums expended in connection with such investment);[5] workers' compensation benefits; disability benefits; unemployment insurance benefits; social security benefits; veterans benefits; pension and retirement benefits; fellowships and stipends; and annuity payments.[6] The court has discretion to add to the income figure values attributable to: non-income producing assets; em-

---

§ 21.53

1. L. 1989, Ch. 567, which generally took effect on September 18, 1989.

2. DRL § 240(1–b)(c)(2).

3. DRL § 240(1–b)(b)(2) defines child support as a sum to be paid pursuant to court order or decree by either or both parents or pursuant to a valid agreement between the parties for care, maintenance and education of any unemancipated child under the age of twenty-one years.

PRACTICE POINTER: Most attorneys use "Child Support Worksheets" printed by Julius Blumberg, Inc. The form tracks DRL § 240(1–b) and provides eleven steps for determining child support.

4. DRL § 240(1–b)(b)(5)(i). *See* Murphy–Artale v. Artale, 219 A.D.2d 587, 632 N.Y.S.2d 19 (2d Dep't 1995) (supreme court was not bound by husband's actual reported income in applying formula for determining child support and instead should have used husband's actual earning capacity as determined, for example, by averaging his reported income for five years immediately preceding the suspect tax return, where husband's reported income in 1992 tax return was found not to be credible).

5. DRL § 240(1–b)(b)(5)(ii). *See* McFarland v. McFarland, 221 A.D.2d 983, 634 N.Y.S.2d 290 (4th Dep't 1995) (trial court erred in excluding former husband's capital gains from husband's income in determining husband's child support obligation under Child Support Standards Act ("CSSA") where defendant did not work but supported himself almost entirely from dividends and capital gains earned in connection with large stock portfolio, and no showing was made that application of CSSA formula would be unjust or inappropriate).

6. DRL § 240(1–b)(b)(5)(iii).

ployment expense payments for meals, lodging, memberships, automobiles or other perquisites to the extent that such payments cover personal expenses or confer personal benefits; other employment fringe benefits; and "money, goods, or services provided by relatives or friends."[7] The court must also add an amount imputed as income based on the parent's former resources or income, if the court determines that a parent has reduced resources or income in order to reduce or avoid child support obligations.[8] The court must add, as well, amounts for any excess depreciation deductions taken on tax returns for determining business income or investment credits and amounts for travel and entertainment allowances deducted from business income, to the extent that such allowances reduce personal expenditures.[9]

Where a parent is or may be entitled to receive non-recurring payments from extraordinary sources not otherwise considered as income, including but not limited to: (1) life insurance policies; (2) discharges of indebtedness; (3) recovery of bad debts and delinquency amounts; (4) gifts and inheritances; and (5) lottery winnings, the court may allocate a proportion of the same to child support, and such amount shall be paid in a manner determined by the court.[10]

On the other hand, the court is required to make certain reductions from income, *i.e.*: the amounts for (a) unreimbursed employee business expenses (except to the extent that such expenses reduce personal expenses); (b) alimony or maintenance actually paid to a prior spouse; (c) alimony or maintenance actually paid to the other party to the action, provided that there will be an adjustment in child support when the alimony or maintenance terminates; (d) child support actually paid on behalf of children other than those involved in the pending action; (e) public assistance; (f) supplemental security income; (g) New York City or Yonkers income or earning taxes actually paid; and Federal Insurance Contributions Act ("FICA") taxes actually paid.[11]

When each parent's income has been calculated, the two income figures are added to come up with the combined parental income. Once combined parental income has been ascertained, a percentage is applied to calculate the amount of basic child support. That percentage is: 17%

---

7. DRL § 240(1–b)(b)(5)(iv).

8. DRL § 240(1–b)(b)(5)(v). *See* McBride v. McBride, 222 A.D.2d 563, 635 N.Y.S.2d 298 (2d Dep't 1995) (trial court improperly increased father's share of child support obligation beyond his share of basic obligation, absent evidence that father was able to increase his current compensation level to former level, and given finding that father did not intentionally diminish his resources or income to avoid his legal obligations).

9. DRL § 240(1–b)(b)(5)(vi).

10. DRL § 240(1–b)(e).

11. DRL § 240(1–b)(b)(5)(vii). *See* LaBombardi v. LaBombardi, 220 A.D.2d 642, 632 N.Y.S.2d 829 (2d Dep't 1995) (remand was necessary for recalculation of former spouses' child support obligations, where trial court failed to deduct city taxes paid by husband in calculating child support and imputed amounts for consulting fees and other income, which were unsupported by record and speculative, to husband's annual income).

for one child; 25% for two children; 29% for three children; 31% for four children; and at least 35% for five or more children.[12]

The basic child support obligation, as computed in accordance with the foregoing procedure, may be supplemented in a number of ways. Where the custodial parent is working, or is receiving training or education that will lead to employment, and incurs child care expenses as a result, the court is required to ascertain the reasonable amount of such expenses and apportion responsibility for such expenses between the parties "in the same proportion as each parent's income is to the combined parental income." This amount is to be separately stated and added to the basic support obligation.[13] Where the custodial parent is seeking work and incurs child care expenses as a result, the court may determine reasonable child care expenses and apportion the same between the custodial and non-custodial parent. The non-custodial parent's share of such expenses is to be separately stated and paid in a manner determined by the court.[14] The court must prorate each parent's share of future reasonable health care expenses of the child, not covered by insurance, in accordance with the proportion that each parent's income bears to the combined parental income.[15] The non-custodial parent's share is to be paid in a manner to be determined by the court; it may include direct payments to the health care provider. Where the court determines that the child requires educational expenses, such as for college or private school or for special or enriched education, the court may award educational expenses. The non-custodial parent may be required to pay those expenses as the court directs, including direct payment to the education provider.[16]

The statute recognizes the prospect that the annual amount of the basic child support obligation may reduce a non-custodial parent's income below the federal poverty level. Where that happens, the basic child support obligation is $25 per month or the difference between the non-custodial parent's income and the federal self-support reserve, if greater. If the non-custodial parent's income would be reduced below the self-support reserve, but not below the poverty level, then the basic child support obligation is to be $50 per month or the difference between the non-custodial parent's income and the self-support reserve, whichever is greater.[17]

Use of the guidelines is mandatory only up to $80,000 in combined parental income. As to any portion of combined parental income over

12. DRL § 240(1–b)(b)(3).
13. DRL § 240(1–b)(c)(4).
14. DRL § 240(1–b)(c)(6).
15. DRL § 240(1–b)(c)(5). See LaBombardi v. LaBombardi, 220 A.D.2d 642, 632 N.Y.S.2d 829 (2d Dep't 1995) (provision of judgment entered in divorce action which directed husband to pay all unreimbursed medical expenses for couple's child violated section of the domestic relations law which provided for pro-rata sharing of such expenses).
16. DRL § 240(1–b)(c)(7).
17. DRL § 240(1–b)(d).

$80,000, the court may apply the guidelines and/or may apply the factors enumerated in subdivision (f) to complete the assessment of child support obligations.[18]

Library References:

West's Key No. Digests, Divorce ⚖306–309; Parent and Child ⚖3.

§ 21.54 Child Support—Child Support Standards Act—Where Statutory Percentages Are Unfair or Inappropriate

Pursuant to the Act, child support payments are made by the non-custodial parent to the custodial parent. If the court concludes that the non-custodial parent's share of the basic child support obligation is "unjust or inappropriate," the court may vary the amount to be paid, either upward or downward.[1] However, before finding that the amount is "unjust or inappropriate," the court must consider nine statutory factors, as well as any other factor it finds appropriate to consider. As is the case generally in the Equitable Distribution Law, the court's consideration of the statutory factors is mandatory (where guidelines are not to be followed) and must be set forth in a written order, together with the reasons for the level of support fixed by the court.[2] This requirement may not be waived. The nine statutory factors are: (1) the financial resources of the custodial and non-custodial parent and of the child; (2) the physical and emotional health of the child and his or her special needs and aptitudes; (3) the standard of living the child would have enjoyed but for the dissolution of the household; (4) the tax consequences; (5) the non-monetary contributions that the parents will make toward the child; (6) the educational needs of either parent; (7) a determination that the gross income of one parent is substantially less than the other parent's gross income; (8) the needs of other children that the non-custodial parent is supporting, if not already taken into account, and the financial resources of any person also obligated to support such other children, provided that the resources available to support such other children are less than those available to the children for whom support is now being considered; and (9) provided that the child is not on public assistance, extraordinary visitation expenses of the non-custodial parent or expenses incurred by the non-custodial parent during extended visitation that reduce the expenses of the custodial parent.[3]

18. DRL § 240(1–b)(c)(3). See infra, § 21.54 for discussion of DRL § 240(1–b)(f).

§ 21.54

1. DRL § 240(1–b)(f).

2. LaPorta v. LaPorta, 216 A.D.2d 365, 628 N.Y.S.2d 364 (2d Dep't 1995) (remittal to trial court for new determination of maintenance, child support, equitable distribution of marital property and counsel fees, based on statutory factors and articulable findings, required where determination of those issues was, for the most part, devoid of court's reasons where the factors court considered, and determinations made did not appear to be supported by the record).

3. DRL § 240(1–b)(f).

In no event may the court order child support of less than $25 per month. Where the non-custodial parent's income is less than or equal to the poverty income level, unpaid child support arrears in excess of $500 shall not accrue.[4] In determining whether the application of the child support standards would be unjust or inappropriate, the court is prohibited from making such a finding on the basis that the share of child support liability thus derived exceeds the amount of a public assistance grant attributable to the children.[5]

Library References:
West's Key No. Digests, Divorce ⚖306–309; Parent and Child ⚖3.

§ 21.55 Child Support—Child Support Standards Act— Recent Trends

In cases addressing combined parental income of less than $80,000, courts rarely deviate from the strict application of the statutory formula.[1] In those circumstances in which the courts will permit a deviation from the statutory formula with respect to income levels below $80,000 per annum, it is more likely than not that the deviation will result in an upward adjustment of support.[2]

In *Cassano v. Cassano*,[3] the Court of Appeals addressed the considerations involved where combined parental income is in excess of $80,-

---

4. DRL § 240(1–b)(g).

5. DRL § 240(1–b)(g). The rationale behind the legislation is the fact that the amount of assistance that the government provides for children should not be used as a benchmark for measuring the fairness, or lack of fairness, of the support to be provided the children by their parents.

§ 21.55

1. See Rochler v. Rochler, 215 A.D.2d 831, 626 N.Y.S.2d 312 (3d Dep't 1995) (the court found that the children's actual needs were less than the amount of support dictated by application of the statutory formula; the non-custodial parent argued that, because the children's needs were less than what he would have to pay under the formula, that fact alone made use of the formula unjust or inappropriate; the appellate division rejected this contention, holding that such a disparity is a factor to be considered, but does not by itself warrant a deviation).

2. See Santy v. Santy, 207 A.D.2d 535, 616 N.Y.S.2d 92 (2d Dep't 1994) (the non-custodial parent could not retain his position due to his employer's financial problems and opted for early retirement and, as a result, he would not be receiving any regular income for some two years until his pension benefits would kick in; notwithstanding the suggestion that the early retirement was occasioned by events outside the husband's control, the appellate division viewed the husband's reduction in earnings as self-created and declined to base support on the statutory formula).

3. 85 N.Y.2d 649, 628 N.Y.S.2d 10, 651 N.E.2d 878 (1995). The lower courts applied the statutory formula to combined parental income of $99,944, nearly $20,000 over the $80,000 figure. The non-custodial parent maintained that the courts should not apply the statutory formula to the advanced level of income without providing reasons which relate to the child's needs. A number of cases from each of the Departments hold that the statutory formula should not be applied to income over $80,000 absent findings as to the child's actual needs. See, e.g., Harmon v. Harmon, 173 A.D.2d 98, 578 N.Y.S.2d 897 (1st Dep't 1992); Slankard v. Chahinian, 204 A.D.2d 529, 611 N.Y.S.2d 300 (2d Dep't 1994); Chasin v. Chasin, 182 A.D.2d 862, 582 N.Y.S.2d 512 (3d Dep't 1992); Panossian v. Panossian, 201 A.D.2d 983, 607 N.Y.S.2d 840 (4th Dep't 1994). See generally, Scheinkman, *Practice Commentaries*, DRL § 236, C240:27.

000 per year. The focus of the appeal was the critical statutory language providing that "the court shall determine the amount of child support for the amount of the combined parental income in excess of such dollar amount through consideration of the factors set forth in paragraph (f) of this subdivision and/or the child support percentage."[4] The court concluded that the "and/or" language in the statute gives the courts discretion regarding when to apply the statutory formula to income over $80,000 or to determine support in accordance with the support factors listed in paragraph (f). *Cassano* holds that, in making the choice as to which approach to take, the court is not required to make findings as to the children's actual needs. The court stated that:

> some record articulation of the reasons for the court's choice to apply the percentage is necessary to facilitate ... review ... [T]he stated basis for an exercise of discretion to apply the formula to income over $80,000 should, in sum and substance, reflect both that the court has carefully considered the parties' circumstances and that it has found no reason why there should be a departure from the prescribed percentage.[5]

Cassano also holds that the requirement that the non-custodial parent pay a *pro rata* share of unreimbursed medical expenses does not constitute an impermissible open-ended obligation.[6] Since medical expenses are often difficult to predict, the court may require the payment of a *pro rata* share of future, reasonable medical expenses.[7] Prior to the CSSA, if a parent wanted to compel the other parent to contribute to "extraordinary" medical expenses, an application to force such a payment would have to be made. Now, instead of the custodial parent having to come into court to establish a right to reimbursement for the costs of "extraordinary" medical expenses, the non-custodial parent is ordered, in advance, to pay his or her share of reasonable medical expenses. If the matter is contested, it is the non-custodial parent who must bring the application and who, to avoid liability, would have to show that the medical expense in question was not reasonable.[8]

---

4. Cassano, 85 N.Y.2d at 653, 628 N.Y.S.2d at 13.

5. *Id.*, 85 N.Y.2d at 655, 628 N.Y.S.2d at 14. *See* Manno v. Manno, 224 A.D.2d 395, 637 N.Y.S.2d 743 (2d Dep't 1996) (boilerplate language that court considered factors set forth in Domestic Relations Law, particularly financial resources of defendant and children's previous standard of living, was insufficient to satisfy statutory requirement that court set forth basis for applying child support percentage to parental income in excess of $80,000 as court was obligated to set forth ultimate facts that supported its conclusions and court had merely recited standard it was applying and failed to set forth ultimate facts).

6. LaPorta v. LaPorta, 216 A.D.2d 365, 628 N.Y.S.2d 364 (2d Dep't 1995) (award in divorce proceeding of prospective open-ended, unreimbursed medical expenses for parties' child was proper); Landau v. Landau, 214 A.D.2d 541, 625 N.Y.S.2d 239 (2d Dep't 1995).

7. *See* Ames v. Ames, 212 A.D.2d 653, 622 N.Y.S.2d 774 (2d Dep't 1995).

8. CAVEAT: With respect to orthodontic expenses, the Third Department suggests that a prior court order authorizing such expenses must be obtained. Urbach v. Krouner, 213 A.D.2d 833, 623 N.Y.S.2d 380 (3d Dep't 1995) (also holding that medical insurance premiums are not medical expenses within the ambit of the statute).

Where a child care expense is known, and is reasonable, the non-custodial parent can be ordered to pay a particular amount of the known expense.[9] If the child care expense changes, an application to modify the award may be made.

The Second Department's decision in *Cassano* recognized that the CSSA changed the criteria for evaluating whether a parent should be ordered to pay for a private school education. One of the crucial factors to be considered is whether, and to what extent, there exists a real difference in quality between the education furnished by the public schools, and that which is available at the private school which the child in question attends or plans to attend.[10]

Library References:

West's Key No. Digests, Divorce ⟬306–309; Parent and Child ⟬3.

§ 21.56 Child Support—Effect of Agreement or Stipulation

The Act provides that a validly executed agreement or stipulation entered into by the parties after the effective date of the statute, which is presented to the court for incorporation in an order of judgment, must include a provision stating that the parties have been advised of the provision of the statute and that the basic child support obligation provided for in the statute would presumptively result in the correct amount of child support.[1] The statute also provides that where an agreement or stipulation deviates from the basic support obligation, it must specify the amount that the basic support obligation would have been and the reason or reasons that the agreement or stipulation does not provide for payment of that amount. These requirements cannot be waived.[2]

Library References:

West's Key No. Digests, Divorce ⟬306–309; Parent and Child ⟬3.

§ 21.57 Health and Life Insurance

In any matrimonial action, the court may order a party to purchase, maintain or assign a policy of insurance providing benefits for health and hospital care and related services for either a spouse or children of the

---

[9]. See Nolan v. Nolan, 215 A.D.2d 795, 626 N.Y.S.2d 568 (3d Dep't 1995).

[10]. Cassano v. Cassano, 203 A.D.2d 563, 612 N.Y.S.2d 160 (2d Dep't 1994). This aspect of Cassano was not reviewed by the Court of Appeals.

§ 21.56

[1]. DRL § 240(1–b)(h). See Bill v. Bill, 214 A.D.2d 84, 631 N.Y.S.2d 699 (2d Dep't 1995) (child support provisions of stipulation of settlement which does not award custodial parent child care expenses may not be enforced where it does not indicate that the parents were aware of the provisions of the Child Support Standards Act ("CSSA"), or that they were knowingly waiving them).

[2]. DRL § 240(1–b)(h).

marriage, not to exceed the period of time that the party is obligated to provide maintenance, child support or make payments of a distributive award.[1]

DRL § 240(1), governing child support, specifies that where either parent has health insurance available through an employer or organization that may be extended to cover the child, and the employer or organization will pay a substantial portion of the premium on such extension of coverage, the court must direct such parent to exercise the option for additional coverage. Where a parent fails to provide required coverage, that parent is penalized by being made presumptively liable for medical expenses incurred after the order was made. Since the liability is only presumptive, the defaulting party is permitted to try to avoid liability by furnishing an acceptable excuse. The statute does not provide any guidance as to what may constitute a sufficient excuse to overcome the presumption of liability.

DRL § 236 (b)(8)(a) permits a court to order a party to purchase, maintain or assign a policy of insurance on the life of either spouse, and to designate either the spouse or children as irrevocable beneficiaries during a period of time fixed by the court, with the interest of the beneficiary ceasing upon the termination of such party's obligation to provide maintenance, child support or make payments of a distributive award, or when the beneficiary remarries or predeceases the insured.

In *Hartog v. Hartog*,[2] the Court of Appeals discussed the statutory language concerning the court's power to order a spouse to maintain life insurance for the protection of the other spouse. The statute, while empowering the courts to require a party to maintain life insurance, contains a proviso that the beneficiary's interest "shall cease upon the termination" of the payor spouse's obligation to pay support. In *Hartog*, the husband argued that, upon his death, his obligation to pay maintenance would end as a matter of law, and therefore, the court could not order him to provide life insurance to cover any payments that would be due after his death. While this argument was consistent with the literal wording of the statute and was accepted by the appellate division, the Court of Appeals reversed on this issue and held that life insurance may be ordered to substitute for maintenance.[3] "Despite the fact that responsibility of maintenance payments cease upon the payor's death, the statute authorizes discretionary security type financial protection in the form of life insurance."[4]

Another issue discussed in *Hartog* involves the effect of a failure to maintain life insurance. The record in *Hartog* did not indicate that the husband had any insurance, and because he was seriously ill, he was

---

§ 21.57
1. DRL § 236(B)(8)(a).
2. 85 N.Y.2d 36, 623 N.Y.S.2d 537, 647 N.E.2d 749 (1995).
3. 85 N.Y.2d at 50, 623 N.Y.S.2d at 545.
4. *Id.*

uninsurable. The trial court held that if the husband died without having the requisite insurance, the wife would be entitled to a lien on his estate in the amount of the insurance that should have been provided. The Court of Appeals agreed with the appellate division that the courts do not have the authority to create a lien on the estate of the payor spouse as a remedy for the failure to maintain life insurance.[5]

§ 21.58 Custody

In the first half of the century, New York courts followed the "tender years" presumption that in a custody dispute, in the absence of a showing of unfitness, the custody of a young child should be awarded to the mother. In 1963, the Domestic Relations Law abrogated the presumption and provides that there is no *prima facie* right to the custody of a child in either parent.[1] The issue now revolves around the determination of what is in the best interest of the child. Although joint or shared custody is permissible, most often custody is awarded to one of the parties, with the other parent having visitation rights. Many factors are examined by the courts in determining what is in the best interests of the child when it comes to fashioning a custody arrangement. However no single factor is dispositive, since each case has individual aspects that interact uniquely.

Among the factors considered are: the relative fitness of the parents; the need to maintain stability in the child's life; which parent has been the child's primary caretaker or care provider; which parent has the greater amount of time to care for the child; the parental guidance given to the child in the past; which parent can best provide for and guide the child's emotional and intellectual development; the quality of the home environment; race; religion; ability of parent to foster child's relationship with other parent; interference in the other parent's access to the child; child's preference; keeping siblings together; and the financial position of each of the parties.[2] In 1996, the Legislature amended DRL § 240(1) to establish domestic violence as a factor for the court to consider in child custody and visitation proceedings, regardless of whether the child has

---

5. PRACTICE POINTER: Since courts do not have the power to create a lien on an estate for a payor spouse's failure to maintain life insurance, where life insurance is directed, the spouse who is to be protected must keep a watchful eye to assure that the policy is procured and maintained.

§ 21.58

1. DRL § 240(1).
2. *See, e.g.*, Eschbach v. Eschbach, 56 N.Y.2d 167, 451 N.Y.S.2d 658, 436 N.E.2d 1260 (1982); In re Custody of Rebecca B., 204 A.D.2d 57, 611 N.Y.S.2d 831 (1st Dep't), app. denied 84 N.Y.2d 808, 621 N.Y.S.2d 517, 645 N.E.2d 1217 (1994); Acevedo v. Acevedo, 200 A.D.2d 567, 606 N.Y.S.2d 307 (2d Dep't 1994); Fialkowski v. Gilroy, 200 A.D.2d 668, 607 N.Y.S.2d 50 (2d Dep't 1994); Kazmi v. Kazmi, 201 A.D.2d 857, 608 N.Y.S.2d 535 (3d Dep't 1994); Melancon v. Melancon, 204 A.D.2d 1061, 613 N.Y.S.2d 65 (4th Dep't 1994); Garvin v. Garvin, 176 A.D.2d 318, 574 N.Y.S.2d 760 (2d Dep't), app. denied 79 N.Y.2d 752, 580 N.Y.S.2d 199, 588 N.E.2d 97 (1992); Farmer v. Farmer, 109 Misc.2d 137, 439 N.Y.S.2d 584 (Sup.Ct., Nassau County, 1981).

witnessed or has been a direct victim of the violence.[3] The legislature recognized the wealth of research demonstrating the effects of domestic violence upon children, even when the children have not been physically abused themselves or witnessed the violence.

Library References:

West's Key No. Digests, Divorce ☞289–305; Parent and Child ☞2.

§ 21.59 Custody—Visitation

Where custody of a child is given to one parent, the court usually provides for visitation by the non-custodial parent.[1] The right to visitation will only be denied where it presents a risk of physical or emotional harm to the child.[2] Visitation arrangements are often left for the parties to agree upon. Section 240 of the Domestic Relations Law specifically provides that the court may provide for reasonable visitation rights to the maternal and/or paternal grandparents of any child of the parties.[3] Discretion is left to the court and such visitation may be denied if it would be harmful to the child.[4]

Library References:

West's Key No. Digests, Divorce ☞289–305; Parent and Child ☞2.

§ 21.60 Custody—Relocation of Custodial Parent With the Child

A major issue has arisen in regard to the rights of the non-custodial parent if the custodial parent seeks to geographically relocate with the child. Such a relocation could have the practical effect of terminating or substantially diminishing the non-custodial parent's access to the child. Until recently, custodial parents who wanted to move had to meet several strict standards. In 1981, the Court of Appeals held that absent

---

3. The added language provides: Where either party to an action concerning custody of or a right to visitation with a child alleges in a sworn petition or complaint or sworn answer, cross-petition, counterclaim or other sworn responsive pleading that the other party has committed an act of domestic violence against the party making the allegation or a family or household member of either party, as such family or household member is defined in article eight of the family court act, and such allegations are proven by a preponderance of the evidence, the court must consider the effect of such domestic violence upon the best interests of the child, together with such other facts and circumstances as the court deems relevant in making a direction pursuant to this section.

§ 21.59

1. *See* Weiss v. Weiss, 52 N.Y.2d 170, 436 N.Y.S.2d 862, 418 N.E.2d 377 (1981).

2. *Id.*

3. DRL § 240(1).

4. *See* Barry v. Chefales, 185 A.D.2d 842, 586 N.Y.S.2d 989 (2d Dep't), app. denied 80 N.Y.2d 761, 592 N.Y.S.2d 670, 607 N.E.2d 817 (1992). *See generally* Scheinkman, *et al., New York Law of Domestic Relations* (West 1996) Ch. 21.

exceptional circumstances, defined as employment, health, education or marital reasons, relocation would not be allowed.[1] The lower courts evolved a series of formulae and presumptions to aid them in making their decisions in difficult relocation cases. The most commonly used formula involved a three-step analysis that looked first to whether the proposed relocation would deprive the non-custodial parent of "regular and meaningful access to the child."[2] Where a disruption of "regular and meaningful access" was not shown, the inquiry was truncated, and the courts generally did not go on to assess the merits and strength of the custodial parents' motive for moving. On the other hand, where such a disruption was established, a presumption that the move was not in the child's best interest was invoked and the custodial parent seeking to relocate had demonstrate "exceptional circumstances" to justify the move. Once that hurdle was overcome, the court considered the child's best interests.

In 1996, the Court of Appeals examined the issue and completely revised the law governing relocation of custodial parents.[3] The court recognized that cases in which a custodial parent's desire to relocate conflicts with the desire of a non-custodial parent to maximize visitation opportunities are simply too complex to be satisfactorily handled by a mechanical, tiered analysis that does not allow a simultaneous weighing and comparative analysis of all of the relevant facts and circumstances. Although the court recognized the need of the child and the right of the non-custodial parent to have regular and meaningful contact, it stated that no single factor should be treated as dispositive or given such disproportionate weight as to predetermine the outcome.[4]

Rather than endorsing the three-step meaningful access-exceptional circumstance analysis, the Court of Appeals held that each relocation request must be considered on its own merits with due consideration of all the relevant facts and circumstances and with predominant emphasis being placed on what outcome is most likely to serve the bests interests of the child. The Court of Appeals held that, in all cases, the courts should be free to consider and give appropriate weight to all of the

§ 21.60

1. Weiss v. Weiss, 52 N.Y.2d 170, 436 N.Y.S.2d 862, 418 N.E.2d 377 (1981).

2. *See, e.g.*, Lavane v. Lavane, 201 A.D.2d 623, 608 N.Y.S.2d 475 (2d Dep't 1994); Lake v. Lake, 192 A.D.2d 751, 596 N.Y.S.2d 171 (3d Dep't 1993); Zaleski v. Zaleski, 128 A.D.2d 865, 513 N.Y.S.2d 784 (2d Dep't 1987).

3. Tropea v. Tropea & Browner v. Kenward, 87 N.Y.2d 727, 642 N.Y.S.2d 575, 665 N.E.2d 145 (1996).

4. The court noted that there are undoubtedly circumstances in which the loss of mid-week or every-weekend visits necessitated by a distant move may be devastating to the relationship between the non-custodial parent and the child. However, there are undoubtedly also many cases where less frequent but more extended visits over summers and school vacations would be equally conducive, or perhaps even more conducive, to the maintenance of a close parent-child relationship, since such extended visits give the parties the opportu-

factors that may be relevant to the determination.[5] These factors include, but are not limited to: each parent's reasons for seeking or opposing the move, the quality of the relationships between the child and the custodial and non-custodial parents, the impact of the move on the quantity and quality of the child's future contact with the non-custodial parent, the degree to which the custodial parent's and child's life may be enhanced economically, emotionally and educationally by the move, and the feasibility of preserving the relationship between the non-custodial parent and child through suitable visitation arrangements.

Courts will have to determine, based on all of the proof, whether it has been established by a preponderance of the evidence that a proposed relocation would serve the child's best interests.

Library References:

West's Key No. Digests, Divorce ⚖︎289–305; Parent and Child ⚖︎2.

§ 21.61 Custody—Joint Custody

Joint custody, sometimes referred to as shared custody, gives both parents a shared responsibility for, and control of, a child's upbringing. Joint custody may reduce the trauma of divorce by providing the child with access to both parents. However, particularly where the joint custody involves alternating physical custody, it can result in insecurity and may deepen the trauma of the divorce.

Parents are free to agree upon joint custody in the event of the termination of their marriage relationship. The agreement of the parents can run the gamut, from merely recognizing the entitlement of the visiting parent to have some input in major decisions affecting the children and providing for primary custody in one parent and visitation rights for the other, to equal custody. Agreements have been prepared which involve rotating the physical custody of the children between the separate homes of parents. In a few instances, parents have agreed to maintain the children in one home and to have the parents alternate periods of residence with the children.[1]

nity to interact in a normalized domestic setting.

5. 87 N.Y.2d at 738, 642 N.Y.S.2d at 580, 665 N.E.2d at 150.

§ 21.61

1. *See* Scheinkman, 10 West McKinney's Forms, MFL, § 20.73, discussing the chances for success for joint custody arrangements. In these sorts of equal custody settings, the success of the arrangement depends virtually entirely upon the good will and faith of the parents and their belief that, despite differences between the parents, the arrangement is best preserved for the children. While the language of equal custody agreements can provide guidelines, judicial enforcement is largely impracticable and the shared custody arrangement will collapse if either parent refuses to comply with either the letter or the spirit of the agreement. The joint custody arrangement can be easily disrupted even where the parents act in the best of faith. For example, a relocation by one parent to a more distant location, prompted by a remarriage or by employment requirements, will inevitably require drastic changes in, if not cancellation of, the joint custody arrangement.

While the parties may agree upon shared custody, the courts have been reluctant to impose any form of joint custody where either parent objects. The major Court of Appeals decision on the subject of joint custody came in *Braiman v. Braiman*.[2] The court held that while joint custody is encouraged as a voluntary alternative for relatively stable amicable parents behaving in a mature and civilized fashion, it can only enhance family chaos as "a court-ordered arrangement imposed upon already embattled and embittered parents, accusing one another of serious vices and wrongs...."[3]

In the years since *Braiman*, courts seem more disposed to imposing joint custody in situations where the parties have exhibited "the type of mature and civilized behavior that makes an award of joint custody appropriate."[4] On the other hand, courts will not impose joint custody where it is apparent that intense acrimony exists between the parties.[5]

Library References:

West's Key No. Digests, Divorce ⟐289–305; Parent and Child ⟐2.

§ 21.62 Custody—Proceedings in Which Custody Dispositions Are Available

General jurisdiction to determine the custody of a child, as an incident to a matrimonial action, is vested in the supreme court, although by statute the matter may be referred to the family court.[1]

DRL § 240 requires that the court verify the status of any child with respect to custody and support. DRL § 240(1) provides that in any action or proceeding brought (1) to annul a marriage or to declare the nullity of a void marriage, or (2) for a separation, or (3) for a divorce, or (4) to obtain, by a writ of *habeas corpus* or by petition and order to show cause, the custody of or right to visitation with any child of a marriage, the court shall require verification of the status of any child of the marriage with respect to such child's custody and support, including any prior orders, and shall enter orders for custody and support as, in the court's discretion, justice requires, having regard to the circumstances of the case and of the respective parties and to the best interests of the child.

Library References:

West's Key No. Digests, Divorce ⟐289–305; Parent and Child ⟐2.

2. 44 N.Y.2d 584, 407 N.Y.S.2d 449, 378 N.E.2d 1019 (1978).
3. 44 N.Y.2d at 589–590, 407 N.Y.S.2d at 451.
4. Guarnier v. Guarnier, 155 A.D.2d 744, 547 N.Y.S.2d 455 (3d Dep't 1989). See Palmer v. Palmer, 223 A.D.2d 944, 637 N.Y.S.2d 225 (3d Dep't 1996) ("although plaintiff and defendant possess different parenting styles, each has the children's best interests at heart and has been able to work together towards that end").

5. Lenczycki v. Lenczycki, 152 A.D.2d 621, 543 N.Y.S.2d 724 (2d Dep't 1989).

§ 21.62

1. Family Court Act § 467(a).

§ 21.63 Financial Disclosure

The right to pre-trial disclosure is statutory and the disclosure devices of the CPLR are available to obtain financial information in a matrimonial action.[1] CPLR 3101 provides that there shall be full disclosure of all evidence material and necessary in the prosecution or defense of an action regardless of the burden of proof.

The courts recognize that equal access to financial information is key to an effective and fair equitable distribution determination. Each party is entitled to discover the extent of marital property, the extent of separate property, to uncover hidden assets and waste and to develop information that may bear on the determination of the financial issues.[2]

Under Section 202.16 of the new Uniform Trial Court Rules, a court presiding over a matrimonial action is to order a preliminary conference.[3] At the conference, the court is to consider establishing a timetable for the completion of all disclosure proceedings. The rules further provide that all disclosure proceedings must be completed within 6 months of the time that the case was assigned to the judge, unless the court extends or shortens the time.[4] When the court acts to shorten the time allowed for disclosure proceedings, the court must be sure that the time allowed is reasonably sufficient for proceedings to be completed.[5]

Under the court rules governing matrimonial matters, each expert that a party expects to call at trial must submit a written report.[6] The written reports are to be exchanged and submitted to the court no later than 60 days before the date set for trial. Reply reports, if any, are to be exchanged and submitted no later than 30 days before the date set for trial. Failure to comply may result in preclusion. Late retention of experts and consequently late reports will be permitted only upon a showing of good cause under the statutory formulation set forth in CPLR 3101(d)(1)(i). Under the court rules, the court has discretion to allow the expert report to serve as a substitute for direct examination.[7]

Sanctions will be imposed on those who deliberately refuse to comply with court discovery orders.[8]

§ 21.63

1. CPLR 3101.

2. *See* Snow v. Snow, 209 A.D.2d 399, 618 N.Y.S.2d 442 (2d Dep't 1994) (emphasizes the continuing nature of matrimonial disclosure).

3. *See infra*, § 21.79 for a thorough discussion of 22 NYCRR § 202.16.

4. 22 NYCRR § 202.16(f)(2).

5. *See* Trach v. Trach, 162 A.D.2d 678, 557 N.Y.S.2d 112 (2d Dep't 1990) (the appellate division ordered a new trial on the financial issues between the parties because the wife had not been afforded a reasonable opportunity to complete discovery and to obtain appraisals and valuations).

6. 22 NYCRR § 202.16(g).

7. *Id.*

8. Fucci v. Fucci, 166 A.D.2d 551, 560 N.Y.S.2d 833 (2d Dep't 1990) (defendant's answer stricken due to deliberate, repeated refusal to furnish documents); Demis v. Demis, 168 A.D.2d 840, 564 N.Y.S.2d 515 (3d Dep't 1990) ($3,500 sanction imposed, rather than preclusion order).

§ 21.64 Disclosure on Matters Going to the Merits of a Case

The rule varies on disclosure on the "merits" of the parties' matrimonial cause of action: The First and Second Departments do not allow such disclosure,[1] while the Third and Fourth Departments permit it.[2]

Library References:
West's Key No. Digests, Divorce ⚖85.

§ 21.65 Net Worth Statement

In all matrimonial actions and proceedings in which alimony, maintenance or support is in issue, there is to be compulsory disclosure by both parties of their respective financial states.[1] No showing of special circumstances is required before such disclosure is ordered. A sworn statement of net worth[2] is to be provided upon receipt of a notice in writing demanding the same, within twenty days after the receipt thereof. In the event such a statement is not demanded, it is to be filed with the clerk of the court by each party, within ten days after joinder of issue, in the court in which the proceeding is pending.

The term "net worth" means the amount by which total assets, including income, exceed total liabilities, including fixed financial obligations. It includes all income and assets of any kind and nature and wherever situated and includes a list of all assets transferred in any manner during the preceding three years, or the length of the marriage, whichever is shorter. However, transfers in the routine course of busi-

---

§ 21.64

1. McMahan v. McMahan, 100 A.D.2d 826, 474 N.Y.S.2d 974 (1st Dep't 1984) (in view of Blickstein v. Blickstein, 99 A.D.2d 287, 472 N.Y.S.2d 110 (2d Dep't 1984), appeal dismissed 62 N.Y.2d 802 (1984), which held that marital fault is generally not an equitable distribution factor, and the tendency of discovery on the merits to exacerbate an already acrimonious relationship, merits discovery should not generally be allowed; the court left the door open for merits discovery in "exceptional" or "compelling circumstances"); Van Ess v. Van Ess, 100 A.D.2d 848, 474 N.Y.S.2d 90 (2d Dep't 1984) (the court also rejected the sought-after disclosure in view of the failure of the discovering party to show that such disclosure was needed to establish her cause of action for divorce; this leaves open the possibility that, in those instances when disclosure is needed to establish the cause of action, it might be obtained); Corsel v. Corsel, 133 A.D.2d 604, 519 N.Y.S.2d 710 (2d Dep't 1987) (disclosure is not permitted with respect to the merits of the underlying matrimonial causes of action).

2. Maxwell v. Maxwell, 88 Misc.2d 535, 389 N.Y.S.2d 84 (Sup.Ct., Albany County, 1976); Lemke v. Lemke, 100 A.D.2d 735, 473 N.Y.S.2d 646 (4th Dep't 1984) (in view of many recent Domestic Relations Law changes, no rational reason why less than full disclosure should be the rule in matrimonial actions); Vaccaro v. Vaccaro, 98 Misc.2d 406, 413 N.Y.S.2d 875 (Sup.Ct., Erie County, 1979).

§ 21.65

1. DRL § 236(B)(4).

2. *See infra*, § 21.87 for statement of net worth.

§ 21.65

ness which resulted in an exchange of assets of substantially equivalent value need not be specifically disclosed where such assets are otherwise identified in the statement of net worth.[3]

All sworn statements of net worth must be accompanied by a current and representative paycheck stub and the most recently filed state and federal income tax returns.

As part of the amendments to the court rules provisions concerning matrimonial actions, it is now required that any papers filed with the court which contain factual claims, including net worth statements, must be accompanied by a certification by counsel that counsel has no knowledge that the substance of the papers is inaccurate. The statement is to appear without qualification on any paper which is submitted. The certification of counsel is made under penalties of perjury.[4]

In actions in supreme court, the new rules also require that a signed copy of the retainer agreement between the client and counsel accompany the net worth statement filed with the court. The court is mandated to review the agreement to assure that it complies with applicable rules.[5]

Noncompliance is punishable by any or all of the penalties prescribed in CPLR 3126 in examination before or during trial.[6]

Library References:
West's Key No. Digests, Divorce ⊜85.

§ 21.66 Statement of Proposed Disposition

Each party is required to exchange a statement of proposed disposition.[1] A copy of any written agreement entered into by the parties relating to financial arrangements or custody or visitation must be annexed to the statement. The statement, with proof of service upon the other party, is to be filed with the note of issue. The other party, if he or she has not already done so, must file a statement of proposed disposition within 20 days of such service.

§ 21.67 Findings of Fact and Conclusions of Law; Judgments

In a contested or uncontested divorce action, a judgment has to be submitted for signature to the judge. A judgment must refer to, and state

---

3. DRL § 236(B)(4).
4. 22 NYCRR § 202.16(e).
5. 22 NYCRR § 1400.3; 22 NYCRR § 202.16(c)(1). *See infra,* § 21.81 for a drafting checklist for retainer agreements and § 21.85 for a sample retainer agreement.
6. DRL § 236(B)(4).

§ 21.66

1. 22 NYCRR § 202.16(h). *See infra,* §§ 21.83, 21.88.

PRACTICE POINTER: This form is often overlooked and can be a useful tool for settling the case or advocating a particular proposed disposition.

the results of the verdict or decision, or recite the default on which it is based.[1]

The paragraphs in Appendix B of the Uniform Trial Court Rules, modified or deleted as may be required to conform to the law and the facts of a particular action, are to be used in preparing the papers.[2] The Uniform Trial Court Rules require that findings and conclusions be in a separate paper from the judgment.[3] The papers are to be labeled "Findings of Fact and Conclusions of Law"[4] and "Judgment,"[5] respectively. In an undefended action, which has been referred to a referee, they are to be labeled "Referee's Report of Findings of Fact and Conclusions of Law"[6] and "Judgment,"[7] respectively.

The Office of Court Administration requires that Form USC–113 be filled out by counsel or litigants to obtain entry of a divorce judgment.[8] The form requires the provision of information as to background matters, such as the names and birth dates of children, and financial information. The form collects information regarding the incomes of the parties, the basic terms of the child support provisions, whether the amount of child support deviated from the Child Support Standards Act amount and, if so, why, and the essential terms of the provisions for spousal maintenance, equitable distribution and other awards. The form collects information for statistical purposes only and is not retained in the case file.

§ 21.68 Modification

Subdivision 9(b) of Part B of DRL § 236 sets forth the governing principles in respect of modification of judgments, orders and decrees. The statute makes no mention of modification of an award of equitable distribution or even a distributive award. The rationale is that those aspects are one-time property divisions not subject to later modification.[1]

§ 21.67

1. CPLR 5011.

PRACTICE POINTER: Certain forms and decisions are required by the clerk's office in certain counties. The practitioner would do well to check with the clerk's office in the particular county.

2. 22 NYCRR § 202.50. See infra, §§ 21.89–21.92.

3. 22 NYCRR § 202.50.

4. See infra, § 21.89.

5. See infra, § 21.90.

6. See infra, § 21.91.

7. See infra, § 21.92.

8. See McKinney's Forms, MFL, § 12:147A.

§ 21.68

1. Greenwald v. Greenwald, 164 A.D.2d 706, 565 N.Y.S.2d 494 (1st Dep't), app. denied 78 N.Y.2d 855, 573 N.Y.S.2d 645, 578 N.E.2d 443 (1991) (the court reaffirmed the principle that an equitable distribution determination is not modifiable based on post-judgment economic changes; the husband moved to reargue the trial court's determination and re-open the trial because two of his major assets had declined in value; the appellate division termed the post-trial changes irrelevant since, by statutory limitation, the last valuation date the court can use is the "date of trial"; moreover, to allow post-trial changes in value to become a basis for modifying a property distribution would undermine the finality of judgments in matrimonial actions).

§ 21.69 Modification—Maintenance

The court may annul or modify any prior order or judgment as to maintenance upon a showing of the recipient's inability to be self-supporting or a substantial change in circumstances, including financial hardship.[1] The determination of whether there has been a substantial change in circumstances warranting modification is left to the discretion of the trial court and the court's determination will depend upon the particular facts of each case.[2]

The court may not reduce or annul maintenance arrears which have been reduced to judgment pursuant to DRL § 244.[3] Arrears in maintenance, which have not been reduced to judgment, may be annulled or modified only if the defaulting party shows good cause for failing to make an application for relief from the judgment or order requiring the payments prior to the accrual of arrears. If the court finds that good cause for not making a prior application was shown, it must set forth the facts and circumstances it finds to be good cause, in a written decision.[4]

The statutory provisions contemplate downward modification. Maintenance cannot generally be adjusted upward. The only situation where upward maintenance is permissible is under the standard set forth in *McMains v. McMains*,[5] where the Court of Appeals held that modification of a judgment to increase alimony is proper if the former spouse is actually unable to support himself or herself on the amount allowed and is in actual danger of becoming a public charge.

Where an agreement of the parties has merged into a matrimonial decree, it has no independent existence apart from the decree,[6] and the decree may be modified pursuant to the normal statutory standards,[7] notwithstanding the fact that it incorporates the terms of the agreement merged therein. Merger will be found unless the parties expressly stipulate that the separation agreement is to survive the judgment of divorce.[8]

However, a valid separation agreement will not be viewed as terminating with the grant of a divorce decree where either the agreement itself or the decree provides that the agreement is intended to survive

---

§ 21.69

1. DRL § 236(B)(9)(b). *See* Manno v. Manno, 224 A.D.2d 395, 637 N.Y.S.2d 743 (2d Dep't 1996) (in determining whether there has been substantial change in circumstances for request for annulment or modification of prior order or judgment as to maintenance or child support, court must consider not only alleged change in circumstances of petitioning party, but also whether there has been substantial change in circumstances of respondent).

2. *See* Stempler v. Stempler, 200 A.D.2d 733, 607 N.Y.S.2d 111 (2d Dep't 1994), appeal after remand 233 A.D.2d 435, 650 N.Y.S.2d 600 (2d Dep't 1996).

3. DRL § 236(B)(9)(b).

4. DRL § 244.

5. 15 N.Y.2d 283, 258 N.Y.S.2d 93, 206 N.E.2d 185 (1965).

6. *See* Rainbow v. Swisher, 72 N.Y.2d 106, 531 N.Y.S.2d 775, 527 N.E.2d 258 (1988).

7. DRL § 236(B)(9)(b).

8. *See* Minarovich v. Sobala, 121 A.D.2d 701, 504 N.Y.S.2d 143 (2d Dep't 1986).

the divorce judgment.[9] Where a separation agreement remains in force "no modification of a prior order or judgment incorporating the terms of the agreement shall be made as to maintenance without a showing of extreme hardship on either party, in which event the judgment or order as modified shall supersede the terms of the prior agreement and judgment for such period of time and under such circumstances as the court determines."[10]

Library References:

West's Key No. Digests, Divorce ⚖=245.

§ 21.70 Modification—Child Support

The Equitable Distribution Law provides that the court may annul or modify any prior order or judgment as to child support upon a showing of the recipient's inability to be self-supporting or a substantial change in circumstances, including financial hardship.[1] The determination of whether there has been a substantial change in circumstances warranting modification is left to the discretion of the trial court and the court's determination will depend upon the particular facts of each case.[2] The statute also provides that no modification or annulment shall reduce or annul any arrears of child support which have accrued prior to the date of application to annul or modify any prior order or judgment as to child support.

Section 240 of the Domestic Relations Law provides that where a direction for child support is made by order or final judgment, the court may annul or modify any such direction.[3]

The Child Support Standards Act provides that in any action or proceeding for modification of an order of child support existing prior to the effective date of a 1990 amendment, the child support standards set forth in the Act do not constitute a change of circumstances warranting modification of such support order; provided, however, that where the circumstances warrant modification of such order, or where an adjustment of a child support order is sought by the support collection unit or either of the parties pursuant to subdivision 12 of Section 111–h of the Social Services Law, or subdivision 3 of Section 413 of the Family Court

---

9. See Rainbow v. Swisher, 72 N.Y.2d 106, 531 N.Y.S.2d 775, 527 N.E.2d 258 (1988).

10. DRL § 236(B)(9)(b).

§ 21.70

1. DRL § 236(B)(9)(b).

2. See Stempler v. Stempler, 200 A.D.2d 733, 607 N.Y.S.2d 111 (2d Dep't 1994), appel after remand 233 A.D.2d 435, 650 N.Y.S.2d 600 (2d Dep't 1996).

3. DRL § 240(1) provides in pertinent part:

Upon the application of either parent, or of any other person or party having the care, custody and control of such child pursuant to such judgment or order, after such notice to the other party, parties or persons having such care, custody and control and given in such manner as the court shall direct, the court may annul or modify any such direction, whether made by order or final judgment.

Act or subdivision 4 of Section 240 of the Domestic Relations Law such standards shall apply.[4] In applying such standards, when the order to be modified incorporates by reference or merges with a validly executed separation agreement or stipulation of settlement, the court may consider, in addition to the factors set forth in paragraph (f) of Section 240, the provisions of such agreement or stipulation concerning property distribution, distributive award and/or maintenance in determining whether the amount calculated by using the standards would be unjust or inappropriate.[5]

In case no direction for child support was made in the final judgment the court may amend the judgment by inserting such direction. Therefore, a divorce judgment that did not provide for child support can be amended to insert such a provision, even in the absence of a showing of changed circumstances.[6]

Any order of support issued on behalf of a child in receipt of public assistance or child support services pursuant to Section 111–g of the Social Services Law is subject to review and adjustment by the support collection unit pursuant to subdivision 12 of Section 111–h of the Social Services Law.[7] Such review and adjustment is in addition to any other activities undertaken by the support collection unit relating to the establishment, modification, and enforcement of support orders payable to such unit. All court orders directing the payment of child support through the support collection unit must contain, on their face, in conspicuous type, specific language alerting the parties to a right to request review of the order for compliance with the Child Support Standards Act 36 months after the issuance of the order.[8] A new, revised order must be entered when it is shown that the correct amount of support, as calculated under the CSSA, deviates from the current order by at least ten (10%) percent or where it is shown that the current order does not provide for the child's health care needs, either by insurance or otherwise.[9]

The statute also directs that where a child support order is made or modified after September 15, 1989, and the original order did not apply the guidelines because it was found that doing so would be unjust or inappropriate, the court and the support collection unit must consider whether the factors that caused that result still exist.[10]

Library References:
West's Key No. Digests, Divorce ⟜309; Parent and Child ⟜3.3(8).

4. DRL § 240(1–b)(*l*).
5. Id.
6. DRL § 240(1).
7. DRL § 240(2)(c).
8. DRL § 240(4).
9. Id.
10. Id.

§ 21.71 Modification—Custody

Jurisdiction over the parties and the subject matter of the matrimonial action continues after the entry of judgment. Where the court in a matrimonial action makes provision by order or in the final judgment for the care, custody and control of any child of the marriage, Section 240 of the Domestic Relations Law provides that "upon the application of either parent, or of any other person or party having the care, custody and control of such child pursuant to such judgment or order, after such notice to the other party, parties or persons having such care, custody and control and given in such manner as the court shall direct, the court may annul or modify any such direction."[1]

Section 467, subdivision (a), of the Family Court Act provides that the supreme court may refer to the family court the determination of applications to modify judgments or orders of custody. Upon such a referral, the family court may modify the judgment or order upon a showing that there has been a subsequent change of circumstances and that modification is required. Pursuant to Section 467, subdivision (b), of the Family Court Act, the family court, even in the absence of a referral from supreme court, may determine any application to enforce or modify an order or judgment awarding custody or visitation. However, the family court is precluded from exercising jurisdiction where the supreme court provided in the order or judgment to be enforced or modified that enforcement or modification may be obtained only in supreme court.

The best interest of the child, the standard test used to determine custody in the first place, is also utilized in resolving applications to modify preexisting custody awards or arrangements between parents.[2]

While an agreement between the parties as to custody will generally be approved, no agreement will bind a court to a custody disposition that is not in the best interest of the child. Of some import is whether the prior custody disposition resulted from a full hearing by the trial court or was merely incorporated in the court's judgment pursuant to an

---

§ 21.71

1. DRL § 240(1).

2. *See, e.g.,* La Bow v. La Bow, 59 N.Y.2d 956, 466 N.Y.S.2d 304, 453 N.E.2d 533 (1983); In re Custody of Rebecca B., 204 A.D.2d 57, 611 N.Y.S.2d 831 (1st Dep't), app. denied 84 N.Y.2d 808, 621 N.Y.S.2d 517, 645 N.E.2d 1217 (1994); Salvati v. Salvati, 221 A.D.2d 541, 633 N.Y.S.2d 819 (2d Dep't 1995), appeal dismissed 87 N.Y.2d 954, 641 N.Y.S.2d 827, 664 N.E.2d 893 (1996) (change of custody should be made only if totality of circumstances warrants change that is in best interests of child; among factors to be considered are quality of home environment and parental guidance that custodial parent provides child, ability of each parent to provide for child's emotional and intellectual development, financial status and ability of each parent to provide for child, relative fitness of respective parents, and length of time that present custody arrangement has been in effect; priority in custody disputes should usually be given to parent who was first awarded custody by court or by voluntary agreement); Drummond v. Drummond, 205 A.D.2d 847, 613 N.Y.S.2d 717 (3d Dep't 1994) (must be showing of a sufficient change in circumstances to establish real need to effect change to ensure best interests).

§ 21.71 DOMESTIC RELATIONS Ch. 21

uncontested stipulation. The agreement would be accorded less weight under the latter scenario.

Library References:

West's Key No. Digests, Divorce ⚖=303; Parent and Child ⚖=2(18).

§ 21.72 Enforcement

Section 236 of the Domestic Relations Law provides that orders and judgments entered in matrimonial actions are enforceable pursuant to the provisions of the CPLR or in any other manner provided by law.[1] These methods include income execution,[2] income deduction order,[3] contempt,[4] security,[5] and sequestration.[6] In 1995, the Legislature added two more enforcement weapons: suspension of driver's licenses[7] and suspension of professional or occupational license.[8]

Section 240 of the Domestic Relations Law provides that an order directing payment of money for child support is enforceable pursuant to Section 5241 or 5242 of the CPLR or in any other manner provided by law.[9] Such orders or judgments for child support and maintenance are also enforceable pursuant to Article 52 of the CPLR upon a debtor's default as such term is defined in paragraph seven of subdivision (a) of Section 5241 of the CPLR. The establishment of a default is subject to

§ 21.72

1. DRL § 236(B)(9)(a) provides:

All orders or judgments entered in matrimonial actions shall be enforceable pursuant to section fifty-two hundred forty-one or fifty-two hundred forty-two of the civil practice law and rules, or in any other manner provided by law. Orders or judgments for child support, alimony and maintenance shall also be enforceable pursuant to article fifty-two of the civil practice law and rules upon a debtor's default as such term is defined in paragraph seven of subdivision (a) of section fifty-two hundred forty-one of the civil practice law and rules. The establishment of a default shall be subject to the procedures established for the determination of a mistake of fact for income executions pursuant to subdivision (e) of section fifty-two hundred forty-one of the civil practice law and rules. For the purposes of enforcement of child support orders or combined spousal and child support orders pursuant to section five thousand two hundred forty-one of the civil practice law and rules, a "default" shall be deemed to include amounts arising from retroactive support. The court may, and if a party shall fail or refuse to pay maintenance, distributive award or child support the court shall, upon notice and an opportunity to the defaulting party to be heard, require the party to furnish a surety, or the sequestering and sale of assets for the purpose of enforcing any award for maintenance, distributive award or child support and for the payment of reasonable and necessary attorney's fees and disbursements.

2. CPLR 5241.

3. CPLR 5242.

4. DRL § 245.

5. DRL § 243.

6. *Id. See* Manno v. Manno, 224 A.D.2d 395, 637 N.Y.S.2d 743 (2d Dep't 1996) (Domestic Relations Law permits sequestering of property where obligated spouse fails to make any payment required by terms of matrimonial judgment or order; however, remedy of sequestration is drastic and is invoked only when record establishes that such remedy is necessary and appropriate, such as where obligated person repeatedly fails to pay and refuses to comply with court orders).

7. DRL § 244–b.

8. DRL § 244–c.

9. DRL § 240(2).

the procedures established for the determination of a mistake of fact for income executions pursuant to subdivision (e) of Section 5241 of the CPLR. For the purposes of enforcement of child support orders or combined spousal and child support orders pursuant to Section 5241 of the CPLR, a "default" includes amounts arising from retroactive support.[10]

The Department of Social Services and social service districts are required to make services relating to the enforcement of support obligations available to persons not receiving Aid to Dependent Children upon the application of such persons.[11]

Payments of child support or combined child and spousal support ordered by the court are to be directed to be made to the support collection unit where such payments are to be collected on behalf of persons who are in receipt of public assistance or who are in receipt of child support (establishment or enforcement) services pursuant to Section 111-g of the Social Services Law.[12] Moreover, unless the court finds in writing that there is good cause not to do so or when a child is not in receipt of public assistance and a written agreement providing an alternative arrangement has been made, the support collection unit must issue an income execution immediately for child support or combined spousal and child support. Such written agreement includes an oral stipulation made on the record which culminates in a written order. Good cause means substantial harm to the debtor, but neither the absence of arrears nor the mere execution of an income execution constitutes good cause. Where the statutory exceptions to the issuance of an immediate income execution are met, the court must provide expressly in the order of support that the support collection unit shall not issue an immediate income execution. The statute also authorizes the support collection unit, in a case involving either support for a child on public assistance or a case brought at the behest of a person who is receiving child support enforcement services by request made under Social Services Law § 111-g, to enter an execution for medical support enforcement.[13]

In any proceeding for enforcement of a sum of money required by judgment or order, the party seeking enforcement may amend the papers in support of the application for enforcement to include any additional arrears which have accrued since the commencement of such enforcement proceeding at the time of a hearing upon or submission of the matter, provided that written notice of the intention to so amend has been given eight days previously.[14] This provides a procedure whereby a party who has brought an enforcement proceeding may bring the total of

10. DRL § 240(2)(a); DRL § 236(B)(9)(a).
11. See DRL § 240(1).
12. DRL § 240(2)(b).
13. DRL § 240(2)(b).
14. DRL § 244-a.

arrears up to date prior to the hearing or submission of the enforcement application.

Library References:
West's Key No. Digests, Divorce ⚖︎305, 311.

§ 21.73 Enforcement—Plenary Action to Enforce Agreement

An agreement that is not merged into a judgment of divorce survives as a basis for suit, independent of other available procedures for enforcing the divorce judgment.[1] Either of the parties may bring a separate plenary action after a divorce judgment to enforce the terms of a stipulation which is incorporated but not merged into the judgment. The doctrines of *res judicata* and collateral estoppel do not apply to bar such actions.[2]

Library References:
West's Key No. Digests, Husband and Wife ⚖︎281.

§ 21.74 Enforcement—Defenses

The court must enter a judgment with respect to arrears in maintenance if the defaulting party does not show good cause for failing to apply for relief from the matrimonial judgment or order prior to the accrual of arrears.[1] Good cause is not a defense where the arrears relate to child support.[2]

A mistake of fact defense is made when it is alleged that there is an error in the amount of current support or arrears or in the identity of the debtor, or that the order of support does not exist or has been vacated.[3] When an income execution for support enforcement has been issued by the support collection unit, the debtor may assert a mistake of fact and is given an opportunity to make a submission in support of the objection.[4]

Library References:
West's Key No. Digests, Husband and Wife ⚖︎281.

§ 21.75 Practice Considerations

Matrimonial actions, and the conduct of attorneys in handling matrimonial cases, have been the subject of intense scrutiny. There have

§ 21.73

1. *See* Rainbow v. Swisher, 72 N.Y.2d 106, 531 N.Y.S.2d 775, 527 N.E.2d 258 (1988).

2. *See* Siegel v. Siegel, 197 A.D.2d 569, 602 N.Y.S.2d 421 (2d Dep't 1993).

§ 21.74

1. DRL § 244.
2. DRL § 244.
3. CPLR 5241(a)(8).
4. CPLR 5241(e).

been complaints that the legal system exacerbates the problems that arise in a divorce, as well as serious charges that attorneys have taken unfair advantage of the system, and of their clients, to generate and collect inappropriate fees. These complaints were examined by a committee of judges and attorneys, chaired by Hon. E. Leo Milonas, with the committee delivering its report to Chief Judge Judith S. Kaye in May, 1993. The report of the Milonas Committee recommended significant reforms dealing with both the attorney-client relationship and the management of matrimonial cases.[1] Since their enactment, the rules have been amended numerous times.

The rules were recently challenged in *Corletta v. Oliveri*.[2] The judge held that the requirement for written retainer agreements mandating fee arbitration violates the constitutional right to contract.[3] The court held that "to the extent the Presiding Justices of the Appellate Divisions, or the Chief Administrative Judge of the Courts direct matrimonial attorneys to abstain from implied contracts under threat of disciplinary proceedings, they invade a common law right to contract and transgress the providence of the Legislature as specified in Judiciary Law § 474." There may well be further litigation on this issue.

§ 21.76 Practice Considerations—Procedure for Attorneys in Domestic Relations Matters

New York Rules of Court, appellate division, provide a comprehensive procedure for attorneys in domestic relations matters.[1] These rules

---

§ 21.75

1. The appellate division added a new Part 1400 to Title 22 of the Official Compilation of Codes Rules and Regulations of the State of New York (22 NYCRR), titled Procedure for Attorneys in Domestic Relations Matters. The Chief Judge of the State of New York amended the Disciplinary Rules of the Lawyers Code of Professional Responsibility by amending §§ 1200.3 and 1200.11 of Part 1200 of 22 NYCRR and added new § 1200.10–a. The Chief Administrative Judge of the Courts adopted a new Part 136 of the Rules of the Chief Administrator, relating to mandatory "Fee Arbitration in Matrimonial Cases." Finally, the Chief Administrative Judge of the Courts amended § 202.16 of the Uniform Trial Court Rules, in relation to calendar control of disclosure in matrimonial cases.

2. 169 Misc.2d 1, 641 N.Y.S.2d 498 (Sup.Ct., Monroe County, 1996). Attorney Corletta was initially telephoned by the Respondent on December 1, 1993 to ask if he would undertake representation. The case was a pending matrimonial action with extensive history. The file was delivered to Petitioner and he began reviewing it the next day. Over a ten day period, Petitioner spent two and a half (2.5) hours reviewing the documents. He further spent time in preliminary research, discussions and evaluation.

3. Note that in a letter to the editor of the New York Law Journal, the counsel to the State Office of Court Administration asserted that the decision did not hold that the mandatory fee arbitration process itself is unconstitutional or in any way illegal. What it addresses, he argued, in resolving a proceeding between private parties to vacate an arbitration award with respect to an attorney's fee, is one court's view of the legality of the requirement for a written retainer agreement when applied to a fee arrangement between an attorney and client covering the period of time before the attorney agreed to undertake representation of the client in a domestic relations matter. N.Y.L.J., 3/13/96, p.2, col.6.

§ 21.76

1. 22 NYCRR Pt. 1400.

§ 21.76 DOMESTIC RELATIONS Ch. 21

are vitally important to any attorney who is handling a domestic relations matter.

Part 1400 applies to all attorneys who, on or after November 30, 1993, undertake to represent a client in a claim, action or proceeding, or preliminary to the filing of a claim, action or proceeding, in either supreme court or family court, or in any court of appellate jurisdiction, for divorce, separation, annulment, custody, visitation, maintenance, child support, or alimony, or to enforce or modify a judgment or order in connection with any such claims, actions or proceedings.[2]

Excluded from the application of the rules are attorneys representing clients without compensation, although such attorneys still are obligated to provide their clients with a redacted version of the Statement of Client's Rights and Responsibilities.

Part 1400 requires an attorney to deliver to a prospective client a Statement of Client's Rights and Responsibilities at the initial conference and prior to the signing of a written retainer agreement.[3] The attorney must obtain a signed acknowledgment of receipt from the client, stating that he or she has received the statement. If the attorney is not being paid a fee, those provisions relating to fees may be deleted. Section 1400.2 specifically provides that the Statement of Client's Rights and Responsibilities must be in the form prescribed by the appellate division.[4]

An attorney who undertakes to represent a party and enters into an arrangement for, charges or collects any fee from a client must execute a written agreement with the client setting forth in plain language the terms of compensation and the nature of services to be rendered.[5] The agreement, and any amendment thereto, must be signed by both the client and the attorney. In actions in the supreme court, a copy of the signed agreement must be filed with the statement of net worth. Where substitution of counsel occurs after the filing of the net worth statement, a signed copy of the attorney's retainer agreement must be filed with the court within 10 days of its execution. A copy of a signed amendment must be filed within 15 days of signing. A duplicate copy of the filed agreement and any amendment is to be provided to the client.

An attorney is prohibited from entering into an arrangement for, charging or collecting a nonrefundable retainer fee from a client. An attorney may enter into a "minimum fee" arrangement with a client

---

2. 22 NYCRR § 1400.1.

PRACTICE POINTER: Counsel should note the facial conflict between 22 NYCRR Part 1400, which is applicable to retainer agreements entered into after November 30, 1993, and 22 NYCRR § 202.16, which is applicable to actions and proceedings commenced on or after November 30, 1993.

3. 22 NYCRR § 1400.2.

4. *See infra*, § 21.85 for the Statement of Client's Rights and Responsibilities which is appended to the sample retainer agreement.

5. 22 NYCRR § 1400.3. *See infra*, § 21.81 for the terms that must be included in a retainer agreement and § 21.85 for a sample retainer agreement.

that provides for the payment of a specific amount below which the fee will not fall based upon the handling of the case to its conclusion.[6]

An attorney is allowed to obtain a confession of judgment or promissory note, take a lien on real property, or otherwise obtain a security interest to secure his or her fee only where: (1) the retainer agreement provides that a security interest may be sought; (2) notice of an application for a security interest has been given to the other spouse; and, (3) the court grants approval for the security interest after submission of an application for counsel fees.[7] An attorney may not foreclose on a mortgage placed on the marital residence while the spouse who consents to the mortgage remains the titleholder and the residence remains the spouse's primary residence.

A closing statement must be filed with the clerk of the court in connection with every claim, action or proceeding in which a written retainer agreement is filed.[8] The statement must be filed within 15 days of entry of the judgment or other act concluding the case or terminating the retainer agreement and must include: (1) the caption of the claim, action or proceeding; (2) the name and present address of the client; (3) the date the claim, action or proceeding was commenced and the date it was settled, default entered or order or judgment entered; (4) the terms of the settlement, order or judgment; (5) the amount of fees paid and dates of payment; (6) whether a security interest was obtained, the amount thereof, the date of court approval, and the address, if any, of the secured property; (7) the amount of fees outstanding, terms of or payment schedule, if appropriate; (8) the date on which a copy of the closing statement was forwarded to the client; and (9) the date, attorney's name, address, telephone number and signature.[9]

Finally, in the event of a fee dispute between the attorney and the client, the client may seek to resolve the dispute by arbitration, which is to be binding upon both attorney and client and subject to review under CPLR Article 75.[10] The attorney does not have the reciprocal right to resolve the matter by arbitration.

§ 21.77 Practice Considerations—Disciplinary Rules

The Disciplinary Rules were amended in conjunction with the enactment of 22 NYCRR Part 1400.[1] It is a violation of the rules[2] for an

---

6. 22 NYCRR § 1400.4.
7. 22 NYCRR § 1400.5.
8. 22 NYCRR § 1400.6.

PRACTICE POINTER: Since the supreme court is the only place where the retainer agreement must be filed, this would appear to limit the requirement of filing a closing statement to supreme court proceedings.

9. 22 NYCRR § 1400.6.

10. 22 NYCRR § 1400.7.

§ 21.77
1. The Chief Judge of the State of New York amended the Disciplinary Rules of the Lawyers Code of Professional Responsibility by amending §§ 1200.3 and 1200.11 of Part 1200 of 22 NYCRR and adding new § 1200.10–a.
2. 22 NYCRR § 1200.11 was amended, adding new sections (c)(2)(B), (c)(2)(C) and (e).

§ 21.77 DOMESTIC RELATIONS Ch. 21

attorney to fail to comply with 22 NYCRR Part 1400, Sections 1400.4, 1400.5, 1400.7 and the first part of 1400.3.

The rules provide in part:

(c) A lawyer shall not enter into an arrangement for, charge or collect:

* * *

(2) Any fee in a domestic relations matter ...

(B) Unless a written retainer agreement is signed by the lawyer and client setting forth in plain language the nature of the relationship and the details of the fee arrangement. A lawyer shall not include in the written retainer agreement a nonrefundable fee clause;

(C) Based upon a security interest, confession of judgment or other lien, without prior notice to the client in a signed retainer agreement and approval from the Court after notice to the adversary. A lawyer shall not foreclose on a mortgage placed on the marital residence while the spouse who consents to the mortgage remains the titleholder and the residence remains the spouse's primary residence.

* * *

(e) In domestic relations matters to which Part 1400 of the joint rules of the Appellate Divisions is applicable, a lawyer shall resolve fee disputes by arbitration at the election of the client.[3]

The rules also provide that a lawyer may not, in a domestic relations matter, begin a sexual relationship with a client during the course of the lawyer's representation of the client.[4]

§ 21.78 Practice Considerations—Fee Arbitration Rules

New Part 136 was effective on November 30, 1993.[1] It dictates the circumstances where mandatory fee arbitration is required. The rules apply, where representation has commenced on or after November 30, 1993, to all attorneys who undertake to represent a client in a claim, action or proceeding, or preliminary to the filing of a claim, action or proceeding, in either supreme court or family court, or in any court of appellate jurisdiction, for divorce, separation, annulment, custody, visitation, maintenance, child support, alimony, or to enforce or modify a

3. 22 NYCRR § 1200.11.
4. 22 NYCRR § 1200.3.

§ 21.78
1. The Rules of the Chief Administrator, 22 NYCRR Pt. 136.

judgment or order in connection with any such claims, actions or proceedings.[2]

In the event of a fee dispute between an attorney and client, whether or not the attorney already has received the fee in dispute, the client may seek to resolve the dispute by arbitration, which is binding upon both attorney and client.[3]

Disputes involving a sum less than $3,000 are to be submitted to one attorney arbitrator and disputes involving a sum of $3,000 or more are to be submitted to a panel of three arbitrators, consisting of one attorney, one layperson, and a third panel member who is selected at random from a pool of arbitrators comprised of both attorneys and laypersons.[4] The arbitration program may not hear any fee dispute in which the amount in dispute is in excess of $100,000.[5]

Where the attorney and client cannot agree as to the attorney's fee, the attorney must inform the client in writing by certified mail or by personal service that he or she has 30 days from receipt of the notice in which to elect to resolve the dispute by arbitration, the result of which is binding upon both attorney and client.[6] The attorney must include standard instructions developed by the Chief Administrator regarding the arbitration procedure, and a copy of a request for arbitration. If the client does not file the request for arbitration within the 30-day period, the attorney may commence an action to recover the fee and the client no longer has the right to request arbitration.[7]

A 1995 article in the New York Law Journal examined the result of fee disputes since the enactment of the new rules.[8] According to the author, matrimonial attorneys are prevailing by comfortable margins in most cases of disputed fees.[9] Lawyers who have gone through the arbitration process indicate that they believe they are getting "a fair shake"; a member of the court system panel appointed to monitor implementation of the rules reported that most lawyers have found the program to be "a speedy and satisfactory process."[10]

Throughout the state, there are 13 arbitration programs, one in each judicial district, except the Twelfth District, which has separate programs in Nassau and Suffolk Counties. According to statistics com-

2. 22 NYCRR § 136.1.
3. 22 NYCRR § 136.2.
4. 22 NYCRR § 136.3.
5. 22 NYCRR § 136.4.
6. 22 NYCRR § 136.5.

A State Supreme Court justice in Westchester County dismissed a matrimonial lawyer's lawsuit to recover attorney's fees because he failed to comply with a requirement of the matrimonial rules. Justice Aldo A. Nastasi dismissed lawyer Paul J. Miklus's lawsuit for $5,900 because he failed to state that he had informed his former client, Ann D. Massoti, both that she had a right to take his fee claim to arbitration and that she had 30 days within which to do so, as allowed by the matrimonial rules. N.Y.L.J., 2/1/96, p.1, col.1.

7. 22 NYCRR § 136.5.

8. D. Wise, *Divorce Lawyers Win Most Fee Disputes*, N.Y.L.J., 12/14/95, p.1, col.3.

9. Id.

10. Id.

§ 21.78   DOMESTIC RELATIONS   Ch. 21

piled by the Office of Court Administration, usage has varied: usage has generally been highest on Long Island and the Eighth District (Erie and neighboring counties), and low in New York City.[11]

§ 21.79 Practice Considerations—Rules Regarding Case Management

The case management rules, effective October 1, 1993, are found in Section 202.16 of the Uniform Trial Court Rules.[1] The rules are designed to assure the prompt processing of matrimonial actions through pre-trial proceedings to trial.[2]

The rules are applicable to all contested actions and proceedings in the supreme court in which statements of net worth are required by Section 236 of the Domestic Relations Law to be filed and in which a judicial determination may be made with respect to alimony, counsel fees *pendente lite*, maintenance, custody and visitation, child support, or the equitable distribution of property, including those referred to family court by the supreme court pursuant to Section 464 of the Family Court Act.[3]

The rules provide that sworn statements of net worth, exchanged and filed pursuant to Section 236 of the Domestic Relations Law, must be in substantial compliance with the official Statement of Net Worth form.[4] A signed copy of the attorney's retainer agreement with the client must accompany the statement of net worth filed with the court, and the court must examine the agreement to assure that it conforms to appellate division attorney conduct and disciplinary rules.[5] In case of substitution of counsel after the net worth statement has been filed, a signed copy of the retainer agreement between the client and the substituted counsel is to be filed within ten days of its execution. An attorney seeking to obtain an interest in any property of his or her client to secure payment of the attorney's fee must make an application to the court for approval of the interest, on notice to the client and to his or her adversary. Such an application may be granted only after the court reviews the finances of the parties and an application for attorney's fees.[6]

---

11. *Id.*

§ 21.79

1. 22 NYCRR § 202.16. The pre-November 30, 1993 rules continue to apply to all actions and proceedings commenced on or before Nov. 29, 1993. Since subdivision (a) of the new rules states that it is applicable only to contested actions and proceedings, it does not apply when the case is uncontested.

2. PRACTICE POINTER: Efforts are being made by the Office of Court Administration to promote consistent and widespread implementation of the case management rules. Without judicial adherence to the rules it will be difficult to contain costs or expedite the process of a divorce. Additionally, it is very difficult for counsel to anticipate the course of a case with the uncertainty of whether the court will be adhering to the rules.

3. 22 NYCRR § 202.16(a).

4. 22 NYCRR § 202.16(b). *See infra*, § 21.87 for the net worth form.

5. 22 NYCRR § 202.16(c)(1).

6. 22 NYCRR § 202.16(c)(2).

Each attorney must file a closing statement with the clerk of the court within 15 days of entry of judgment, or other act concluding the case or terminating the retainer agreement.[7]

The rules are designed to assure the prompt processing of matrimonial actions through pre-trial proceedings to trial. A request for judicial intervention must be filed by the plaintiff no later than 45 days from the date of service of the summons and complaint or summons and notice upon the defendant, unless both parties file a notice of no necessity with the court, in which event the request for judicial intervention may be filed no later than 120 days from the date of service of the summons and complaint or summons and notice upon the defendant.[8] The rules do not set any preconditions to the filing of a notice of no necessity. Counsel is given the freedom to agree that the parties and counsel do not have to attend a conference which is not needed; the court avoids having to schedule and attend an unnecessary conference.

As far as counsel is concerned, the most important provision of the rules requires that any paper submitted to the court by a party represented by counsel, which contains statements or allegations of fact, including the statement of net worth, is to be accompanied by a certification directed to the court, under penalties of perjury by counsel as an officer of the court, that counsel has no knowledge that the substance of the submission is false.[9] The statement is to appear without qualification on any papers submitted.[10]

The filing of a request for judicial intervention triggers the holding of a preliminary conference at which a timetable is to be established for the completion of all pre-trial proceedings.

A preliminary conference is to be ordered by the court to be held within 30 days after the action has been assigned.[11] The order must set the time and date for the conference and specify the papers, including statements of net worth that, if not yet filed, must be filed with the court at such time before the conference, but the court must require the statement of net worth to be filed no later than ten days prior to the

---

7. 22 NYCRR § 202.16(c)(3).
8. 22 NYCRR § 202.16(d).
9. 22 NYCRR § 202.16(e). *See* Rosen v. Rosen, 161 Misc.2d 795, 614 N.Y.S.2d 1018 (Sup.Ct., Queens County, 1994) (initial omission of wife's attorney's certification that attorney had no knowledge of false allegations of fact in original submission in matrimonial proceeding could be excused, and late certification could be accepted nunc pro tunc).
10. **PRACTICE POINTER:** Effective May 1, 1996, subsection (e) was amended to add: "The statement is to appear without qualification on any papers submitted." The amendment was in response to the actions of practitioners who were submitting the certification with qualifying language. The amendment makes clear counsel's obligation to ensure that their clients provide accurate information.
11. 22 NYCRR § 202.16(f)(1).

PRACTICE POINTER: If a conference is not scheduled by the court, counsel can initiate the scheduling of the conference by filing a Request For A Conference form with the clerk of the court.

preliminary conference.[12] Both parties personally must be present in court at the time of the conference.[13]

The matters to be considered at the conference may include, among other things: (i) applications for *pendente lite* relief, including interim counsel fees; (ii) compliance with the requirement of compulsory financial disclosure, including the exchange and filing of a supplemental statement of net worth indicating material changes in any previously exchanged and filed statement of net worth; (iii) simplification and limitation of issues; (iv) the establishment of a timetable for the completion of all disclosure proceedings, provided that all such procedures must be completed within six months of the assignment of the action to the judge, unless otherwise shortened or extended by the court depending upon the circumstances of the case; (v) and any other matters which the court deems appropriate.[14]

Motions for alimony, maintenance, counsel fees (other than a motion made pursuant to Section 237(c) or Section 238 of the Domestic Relations Law for counsel fees for services rendered by an attorney to secure the enforcement of a previously granted order or decree) or child support or any modification of an award thereof are to be made before or at the preliminary conference, if practicable.[15]

---

12. 22 NYCRR § 202.16(f)(1).

13. 22 NYCRR § 202.16(f)(1).
PRACTICE POINTER: In the past, parties were discouraged from attending court conferences. The new rule makes the presence of the parties mandatory, however, it is doubtful that it will be rigidly enforced. If both parties are present, it may be possible to engage in settlement discussions. Counsel will have to review each judge's individual rules of practice in advance of the conference. The rules do not provide for a sanction in the event a party does not personally appear, though a nonappearance may not be to the party's tactical advantage if the appearance is requested by the court. There is also no mechanism which compels a court to hold all of the conference in the presence of both parties.

14. 22 NYCRR § 202.16(f)(2).

15. 22 NYCRR § 202.16(k)(1). No motion for alimony, maintenance, counsel fees or child support or any modification of an award thereof will be heard unless the moving papers include a statement of net worth. 22 NYCRR § 202.16(k)(2). No motion for counsel fees will be heard unless the moving papers also include the affidavit of the movant's attorney stating the moneys, if any, received on account of such attorney's fee from the movant or any other person on behalf of the movant, and the moneys such attorney has been promised by, or the agreement made with, the movant or other persons on behalf of the movant, concerning or in payment of the fee. 22 NYCRR § 202.16(k)(3). The party opposing any motion will be deemed to have admitted, for the purpose of the motion but not otherwise, such facts set forth in the moving party's statement of net worth as are not controverted in: a statement of net worth, completed and sworn to by the opposing party, and made a part of the answering papers, or other sworn statements or affidavits with respect to any fact which is not feasible to controvert in the opposing party's statement of net worth. 22 NYCRR § 202.16(k)(4). Failure to comply with the provisions of the subdivision will constitute good cause, in the discretion of the judge presiding, either: to draw an inference favorable to the adverse party with respect to any disputed fact or issue affected by such failure; or to deny the motion without prejudice to renewal upon compliance with the provisions of the section. 22 NYCRR § 202.16(k)(5). The notice of motion submitted with any motion for or related to interim maintenance or child support must contain a notation indicating the nature of the motion. Any such motion must be determined within 30 days after the motion is submitted for decision. 22 NYCRR § 202.16(k)(6). Upon any application for an

At the close of the conference, the court must direct the parties to stipulate, in writing or on the record, as to all resolved issues, which the court then shall "so order," and as to all issues with respect to fault, custody and finance that remain unresolved.[16] Any issues with respect to fault, custody and finance that are not specifically described in writing or on the record at that time may not be raised in the action unless good cause is shown.[17]

The court must fix a schedule for discovery as to all unresolved issues and, in a noncomplex case, schedules a date for trial not later than six months from the date of the conference.[18] The court may appoint a law guardian for the infant children, or may direct the parties to submit to the court, within 20 days of the conference, a list of suitable law guardians for selection by the court.[19] The court also may direct that a list of expert witnesses be filed within 20 days of the conference from which the court may select a neutral expert to assist the court.[20] The court may also schedule a compliance conference, and the parties personally must be present in court at the time of the conference.[21]

Each expert witness whom a party expects to call at the trial is to submit a written report, which will be exchanged and submitted to the court no later than 60 days before the date set for trial, and reply reports, if any, are to be exchanged and submitted no later than 30 days before such date.[22] Failure to submit a report in conformance with these requirements may, in the court's discretion, preclude the use of the expert. Late retention of experts and consequent late submission of reports is permitted only upon a showing of good cause as authorized by CPLR 3101(d)(1)(i). In the discretion of the court, written reports may be used to substitute for direct testimony at the trial, but the reports must be submitted by the expert under oath, and the expert is to be present and available for cross-examination. In the discretion of the

---

award of counsel fees or appraisal/accounting fees made prior to the conclusion of the trial of the action, the court must set forth in specific detail, in writing or on the record, the factors it considered and the reasons for its decision. 22 NYCRR § 202.16(k)(7).

16. 22 NYCRR § 202.16(f)(3).
17. 22 NYCRR § 202.16(f)(3).
18. *Id.*

PRACTICE POINTER: Although the rules give no guidance as to what is or is not a complex case, a "noncomplex" case is ordinarily one where the parties are W-2 income earners, the assets are capable of ready valuation (bank account, family residence), and there is no need for lengthy disclosure or detailed expert testimony.

19. 22 NYCRR § 202.16(f)(3).
20. 22 NYCRR § 202.16(f)(3).

PRACTICE POINTER: At this point in the litigation counsel may not yet have engaged experts. The expense of retaining an expert may be unnecessary if the matter is settled and counsel may not even know what the issues are that require expert testimony. Even if an expert has been retained, counsel may not as yet have determined whether or not the expert will testify. Therefore, although the court is given discretion to require the list of experts, it may refrain from the requirement.

21. 22 NYCRR § 202.16(f)(3).
22. 22 NYCRR § 202.16(g).

court, in a proper case, parties may be bound by the expert's report in their direct case.[23]

The rules also provide that each party is to exchange a statement of proposed disposition;[24] that no action or proceeding to which the rules are applicable will be deemed ready for trial unless there is compliance with the rules by the party filing the note of issue and certificate of readiness;[25] that in all actions or proceedings to which the rules apply and which are referred to family court by the supreme court pursuant to Section 464 of the Family Court Act, all statements, including supplemental statements, exchanged and filed by the parties pursuant to the rules shall be transmitted to the family court with the order of referral.[26] To the extent feasible, trial should proceed from day to day to conclusion.[27]

§ 21.80 Procedural Checklist—Calendar Control

This checklist summarizes the court rules with respect to calendar control of cases. The case management rules, effective October 1, 1993, are found in Section 202.16 of the Uniform Trial Court Rules (*see* § 21.79).

1. Net Worth Statement.

    - Upon receipt of a notice in writing demanding a sworn statement of net worth, provided within 20 days after receipt of demand.[1] (*See* § 21.65)

    - Where no statement demanded, the statement is filed with the clerk of the court within 10 days after joinder of issue, in the court in which the proceeding is pending.[2] (*See* § 21.65)

    - If the statement is not yet filed when preliminary conference ordered, it must be filed no later than 10 days prior to preliminary conference.[3] (*See* § 21.79)

2. Retainer Agreement.

    - The agreement is filed with statement of net worth.[4] (*See* §§ 21.76, 21.79)

    - In case of substitution of counsel, the agreement is filed within 10 days of execution.[5] (*See* §§ 21.76, 21.79)

23. 22 NYCRR § 202.16(g).
24. 22 NYCRR § 202.16(h).
25. 22 NYCRR § 202.16(i).
26. 22 NYCRR § 202.16(j).
27. 22 NYCRR § 202.16(*l*).

§ 21.80
1. DRL § 236(B)(4).
2. DRL § 236(B)(4).
3. 22 NYCRR § 202.16(f)(1).
4. 22 NYCRR §§ 202.16(c)(1), 1400.3.
5. 22 NYCRR §§ 202.16(c)(1), 1400.3.

- Copy of a signed amendment to the agreement must be filed within 15 days of signing.[6] (*See* § 21.76)

3. Closing Statement.
   - The statement must be filed with clerk of court within 15 days of entry of judgment or other act concluding the case or terminating the retainer agreement.[7] (*See* §§ 21.76, 21.79)

4. Request for Judicial Intervention ("RJI").
   - Must be filed no later than 45 days from the date of service of the summons and complaint or summons and notice upon the defendant.[8] (*See* § 21.79)
   - Where both parties file with the court a "notice of no necessity," the RJI must be filed by the plaintiff no later than 120 days from the date of service of the summons and complaint or summons and notice upon the defendant.[9] (*See* § 21.79)

5. Preliminary Conference.
   - Held within 30 days after the action has been assigned.[10] (*See* § 21.79)

6. Disclosure.
   - The timetable established at preliminary conference, provided all disclosure to be completed within six months of the assignment of the action to the judge, unless shortened or extended by the court.[11] (*See* §§ 21.63, 21.79)

7. Trial Scheduled in Non Complex Case.
   - The trial date must be no later than six months from the date of the conference.[12] (*See* § 21.79)

8. Expert Witnesses.
   - Court may require list of expert witnesses to be filed within 20 days of the conference.[13] (*See* § 21.79)
   - Written reports of expert witnesses expected to be called at trial must be exchanged and submitted to the court no later than 60 days before date set for trial.[14] (*See* §§ 21.63, 21.79)

6. 22 NYCRR § 1400.3.
7. 22 NYCRR §§ 202.16(c)(3), 1400.6.
8. 22 NYCRR § 202.16(d).
9. 22 NYCRR § 202.16(d).
10. 22 NYCRR § 202.16(f)(1).
11. 22 NYCRR § 202.16(f)(2).
12. 22 NYCRR § 202.16(f)(3).
13. 22 NYCRR § 202.16(f)(3).
14. 22 NYCRR § 202.16(g).

§ 21.80　　　　　DOMESTIC RELATIONS　　　　　Ch. 21

Reply reports must be exchanged and submitted no later than 30 days before date set for trial.[15] (*See* §§ 21.63, 21.79)

9. Statement of Proposed Disposition.
   - With proof of service upon the other party, filed with the note of issue.[16] (*See* §§ 21.66, 21.79)
   - The other party, if he or she has not already done so, must file a statement of proposed disposition within 20 days of such service.[17] (*See* §§ 21.66, 21.79)

§ 21.81　Drafting Checklist—Retainer Agreements

As prescribed by 22 NYCRR § 1400.3, the retainer agreement must provide:[1]

1. Names and addresses of the parties entering into the agreement;
2. Nature of the services to be rendered;
3. Amount of the advance retainer, if any, and what it is intended to cover;
4. Circumstances under which any portion of the advance retainer may be refunded. Should the attorney withdraw from the case or be discharged prior to the depletion of the advance retainer, the written retainer agreement shall provide how the attorney's fees and expenses are to be determined, and the remainder of the advance retainer shall be refunded to the client;
5. Client's right to cancel the agreement at any time; how the attorney's fee will be determined and paid should the client discharge the attorney at any time during the course of the representation;
6. How the attorney will be paid through the conclusion of the case after the retainer is depleted; whether the client may be asked to pay another lump sum;
7. Hourly rate of each person whose time may be charged to the client; any out-of-pocket disbursements for which the client will be required to reimburse the attorney. Any changes in such rates or fees shall be incorporated into a written agreement constituting an amendment to the original agreement, which must be signed by the client before it may take effect;
8. Any clause providing for a fee in addition to the agreed-upon rate, such as a reasonable minimum fee clause, must be defined

---

15. 22 NYCRR § 202.16(g).
16. 22 NYCRR § 202.16(h).
17. 22 NYCRR § 202.16(h).

§ 21.81

1. *See infra,* § 21.85 for sample retainer agreement

Ch. 21   STATEMENT OF PROPOSED DISPOSITION   § 21.83

in plain language and set forth the circumstances under which such fee may be incurred and how it will be calculated.

9. Frequency of itemized billing, which shall be at least every 60 days; the client may not be charged for time spent in discussion of the bills received;

10. Client's right to be provided with copies of correspondence and documents relating to the case, and to be kept apprised of the status of the case;

11. Whether and under what circumstances the attorney might seek a security interest from the client, which can be obtained only upon court approval and on notice to the adversary;

12. Under what circumstances the attorney might seek to withdraw from the case for nonpayment of fees, and the attorney's right to seek a charging lien from the court.

13. Should a dispute arise concerning the attorney's fee, the client may seek arbitration, which is binding upon both attorney and client; the attorney shall provide information concerning fee arbitration in the event of such dispute or upon the client's request.

§ 21.82 Drafting Checklist—Complaint in Action for Divorce

A complaint for divorce must contain the following:

1. Residential allegations. (*See* §§ 21.4, 21.86, #1)
2. Allegations setting forth the marriage. (*See* § 21.86, #2)
3. Allegations setting forth the grounds for divorce. (*See* §§ 21.18–21.30, 21.86, ##7, 8, 9, 11, 13, 15, 16)
4. Allegation that all steps within the party's power have been taken, or will be taken, prior to entry of final judgment, to remove any barrier to the defendant's remarriage following the divorce, or, in the alternative that defendant has waived in writing the requirements of subdivision 2 of Section 253 of the Domestic Relations Law. *This applies only to marriages solemnized by a person pursuant to DRL § 11(1).* (*See* § 21.86, #5)

§ 21.83 Drafting Checklist for Statement of Proposed Disposition

As prescribed by 22 NYCRR § 202.16(h), the statement of proposed disposition[1] must include:

1. The assets claimed to be marital property. (*See* §§ 21.37–21.39, 21.88(a))

§ 21.83   1. See *infra*, § 21.88.

§ 21.83 DOMESTIC RELATIONS Ch. 21

2. The assets claimed to be separate property. (*See* §§ 21.40–21.41, 21.88(b))

3. An allocation of debts or liabilities to specific marital or separate assets, where appropriate. (*See* § 21.88(c))

4. The amount requested for maintenance, indicating and elaborating upon the statutory factors forming the basis for the maintenance requests. (*See* §§ 21.46–21.51, 21.88(d))

5. The proposal for equitable distribution, where appropriate, indicating and elaborating upon the statutory factors forming the basis for the proposed distribution. (*See* §§ 21.33–21.45, 21.88(e))

6. The proposal for a distributive award, if requested, including a showing of the need for a distributive award. (*See* §§ 21.44, ##7, 9; *see also,* 21.88(f))

7. The proposed plan for child support, indicating and elaborating upon the statutory factors upon which the proposal is based. (*See* §§ 21.52–21.56, 21.88(g))

8. The proposed plan for custody and visitation of any children involved in the proceeding, setting forth the reasons therefor. (*See* §§ 21.58–21.62, 21.88(h))

§ 21.84 Forms

The retainer agreement (Section 21.85) and complaint (Section 21.86) that follow are presented for illustrative purposes only and can be adapted for use by counsel. The statement of net worth (Section 21.87) that is provided was revised effective May 1, 1996. It is an official form and can be found in Appendix A of the Uniform Trial Court Rules. The statement of proposed disposition (Section 21.88) which follows should be filled in by counsel to reflect the facts of the particular case. The findings of fact and conclusions of law and judgments (Sections 21.89–21.92) can be found in Appendix B of the Uniform Trial Court Rules.

§ 21.85 Forms—Retainer Agreement

THIS AGREEMENT FOR LEGAL SERVICES by and between _____, _____, New York (Law Firm) and _____, residing at _____, New York (Client) entered into the _____ day of _____, 1998. This agreement constitutes a binding legal contract and should be reviewed carefully.

This Agreement confirms that you have retained this firm as your attorney to render services in connection with your matrimonial situation.

In order for us to begin our representation you have agreed to pay us and we have agreed to accept a retainer payment of $_____. This retainer payment does not necessarily represent the amount of the overall fee which you may incur by virtue of our services. The amount of the eventual fee will be based upon our regular schedule of established hourly time charges at the rate of $_____ per hour, along with any out-of-pocket disbursements (such as court costs, messenger services, transcripts of proceedings, long distance telephone calls, telefaxes, process service fees, mileage, deposition and court transcripts, and excess postage) which are incurred in your behalf.

You understand that the hourly rates applies to all time expended relative to your matter, including but not limited to, office meetings and conferences, telephone calls and conferences, either placed by or placed to you, or otherwise made on your behalf or related to your matter, preparation, review and revision of correspondence, pleadings, motions, disclosure demands and responses, affidavits and affirmations, or any other documents, memoranda, or papers relative to your matter, legal research, court appearances, conferences, file review, preparation time, travel time, and any other time expended on behalf of or in connection with your matter.

If your matter is concluded, whether by settlement (*e.g.*, a separation agreement or stipulation of settlement) or by a judicial determination, with the expenditure of fewer hours by the Law Firm than you have paid as a retainer, the unearned balance will be returned to you.

You have the absolute right to cancel this Retainer Agreement at any time. Should you exercise this right, you will be charged only the fee expenses (time charges and disbursements) incurred within that period, and the fair and reasonable fee would be determined in accordance with legally accepted standards, with the unearned balance of the retainer fee, if any, being promptly refunded to you. Presently, the legally recognized elements of a reasonable fee, as set forth in the Code of Professional Responsibility, are as follows:

- The time and labor required, the novelty and difficulty of the questions involved and the skill requisite to perform the legal services properly.

- The likelihood, if apparent or made known to the client, that the acceptance of the particular employment will preclude other employment by the lawyer. (You should know that the Law Firm, by accepting retention as your attorney, is clearly precluded from representing the opposing party against you.)

- The fee customarily charged in the locality for similar legal services.

- The amount involved and the results obtained.

- The time limitations imposed by the client or by circumstances.

- The nature and length of the professional relationship with the client.
- The experience, reputation and ability of the lawyer or lawyers performing the services.
- Whether the fee is fixed or contingent. (You should know that the Code of Professional Responsibility provides: "A lawyers shall not enter into an arrangement for, charge or collect ... [a]ny fee in a domestic relations matter, the payment or amount of which is contingent upon the securing of a divorce or upon the amount of maintenance, support, equitable distribution, or property settlement ....").

You agree to pay us such additional fees earned and to reimburse us for our advances on your behalf that may be due from time to time not later than ten (10) days from the date that we shall submit a bill to you for same. If an amount due to us is not paid within ten (10) days after our statement to you of the amount due, interest at the prevailing statutory rate as set forth in the Civil Practice Law and Rules shall be added to the balance due us.

The retainer fee shall be credited toward an hourly rate of $___ per hour. In addition to the foregoing, your responsibility will include direct payment or reimbursement of this firm for disbursements advanced on your behalf, the same to include, but not necessarily be limited to, court filing fees, recording fees, charges of process servers, travel expenses, copying costs, messenger services, necessary secretarial overtime, transcripts and the customary fees of stenographers referable to examinations before trial in the event such examinations are utilized. If the services of an "outside" stenographer for examinations and/or depositions are necessary, we require $500 deposit for scheduled half day examinations, and $1,000 for the full day. It is specifically understood and agreed that such payment shall be made prior to commencing such examination and will be placed in our escrow account. The same shall apply to all court filing fees. The foregoing are all your responsibility.

You will be billed periodically, generally each month but in no event less frequently than every 60 days. Included in the billing will be a detailed explanation of the services rendered, and the disbursements incurred by our firm in connection with your matter. Upon receipt of our bill, you are expected to review the bill and promptly bring to our attention any objections you may have to the bill. While we strive to keep perfectly accurate time records, we recognize the possibility of human error, and we shall discuss with you any objections you raise to our bill. You will not be charged for time expended in discussing with us any aspect of the bill rendered to you.

We shall keep you informed of the status of your case, and agree to explain the laws pertinent to your situation, the available course of action, and the attendant risks. We shall notify you promptly of any developments in your case, including court appearances, and will be available for meetings and telephone conversations with you at mutually convenient times. We do insist that appointments be made for personal visits to our offices. Copies of all papers will be supplied to you as they are prepared (unless you request to the contrary), and you will be billed a reasonable photocopy charge (at present, $.10 cents per page) for these materials which will be included in your periodic billing.

It is *not* and *has not* been our practice to seek security interests from clients. However, you are advised that the law requires, if we did seek same, that a security interest take the form of a confession of judgment, promissory note, or mortgage upon specified property. In either event, a lien would attach to your property. In the case of your marital residence, any such security interest would be nonforeclosable, *i.e.,* we would not force a sale of your home but would be paid at the time you sell the premises. You are advised that any such security interest can be granted to us only with the permission of the justice assigned to your case upon an application on notice to the opposing party, and after an application has been made for your spouse to pay the outstanding fees. However, we want to reiterate, it is *not* and has not been our practice to seek security interests from clients.

In the event such application for payment of counsel fees by your spouse and a security interest for the fees due this firm is made to the Court, you agree to cooperate in connection with such application and to consent to the relief being requested from the Court. Failure on your part to so cooperate and consent shall be deemed as a basis for withdrawal by the Law Firm from your representation.

In the event that any bill from the Law Firm remains unpaid beyond a thirty (30) day period, you agree that the Law Firm may withdraw its representation, at the option of the firm. In the event that an action is pending, and absent your consent, an application must be made to the Court for such withdrawal. Where the fee is unpaid for the period set forth above, you acknowledge that in connection with any such withdrawal application, that the account delinquency shall be good cause for withdrawal.

While we seek to avoid any fee disputes with our clients, and rarely have such disputes, in the event such a dispute does arise, you are advised that you have the right, at your election, to seek arbitration to resolve the fee dispute. In such event, we shall advise you in writing by certified mail that you have 30 days from receipt of such notice in which to elect to resolve the dispute by arbitration, as we shall enclose a copy of the arbitration rules and a form for requesting arbitration. The decision resulting from arbitration is binding upon both you and this firm.

You have been advised that in order for us to properly protect your interests, it may be necessary to retain outside experts such as appraisers, actuaries and accountants. You will be responsible for the costs

§ 21.85 DOMESTIC RELATIONS Ch. 21

incurred for any such service which in some cases may have to be paid in advance depending upon the requirements of the particular expert. No expert or appraiser shall be retained without your prior approval. If necessary and applicable, an application will be made to the court to have your spouse pay all or part of the aforementioned fees for our experts.

You acknowledge that you have read this agreement in its entirety, have had full opportunity to consider its terms, and have had full and satisfactory explanation of same, and fully understand its terms and agree to such terms.

You fully understand and acknowledge that there are no additional or different terms or agreements other than those expressly set forth in this written agreement.

You acknowledge that you were provided with and read the Statement of Client's Rights and Responsibilities, a copy of which is attached to your Retainer Agreement.

We have informed you that pursuant to Court Rule, we are required, as your attorneys, to certify Court papers submitted by you which contain statements of fact, and specifically to certify that we have no knowledge that the substance of the submission is false. Accordingly, you agree to provide us with complete and accurate information which forms the basis of Court papers and to certify in writing to us, prior to the time the papers are actually submitted to the Court, the accuracy of the Court submissions which we prepare on your behalf, and which you shall review and sign.

You are aware of the hazards of litigation and acknowledge that we have made no guarantees in the disposition of any phase of the matter for which you have retained this office. If this fee arrangement meets with your approval, kindly sign your name where indicated on the copy of this letter and return same to me in the envelope enclosed for your convenience. You acknowledge that pursuant to Court Rule, a copy of this Retainer Agreement is required to be filed with the Court in which your action is pending.

Very truly yours,

[Lawyer]

I HAVE READ AND UNDERSTAND THE
ABOVE LETTER, HAVE RECEIVED A
COPY AND ACCEPT ALL OF ITS TERMS:

_____
(Client)

STATEMENT OF CLIENT'S RIGHTS AND RESPONSIBILITIES

Your attorney is providing you with this document to inform you of what you, as a client, are entitled to by law or by custom. To help prevent any misunderstanding between you and your attorney please read this document carefully.

If you ever have any questions about these rights, or about the way your case is being handled, do not hesitate to ask your attorney. He or she should be readily available to represent your best interests and keep you informed about your case.

An attorney may not refuse to represent you on the basis of race, creed, color, sex, sexual orientation, age, national origin or disability.

You are entitled to an attorney who will be capable of handling your case; show you courtesy and consideration at all times; represent you zealously; and preserve your confidences and secrets that are revealed in the course of the relationship.

You are entitled to a written retainer agreement which must set forth, in plain language, the nature of the relationship and the details of the fee arrangement. At your request, and before you sign the agreement, you are entitled to have your attorney clarify in writing any of its terms, or include additional provisions.

You are entitled to fully understand the proposed rates and retainer fee before you sign a retainer agreement, as in any other contract.

You may refuse to enter into any fee arrangement that you find unsatisfactory.

Your attorney may not request a fee that is contingent on the securing of a divorce or on the amount of money or property that may be obtained.

Your attorney may not request a retainer fee that is nonrefundable. That is, should you discharge your attorney, or should your attorney withdraw from the case, before the retainer is used up, he or she is entitled to be paid commensurate with the work performed on your case and any expenses, but must return the balance of the retainer to you. However, your attorney may enter into a minimum fee arrangement with you that provides for the payment of a specific amount below which the fee will not fall based upon the handling of the case to its conclusion.

You are entitled to know the approximate number of attorneys and other legal staff members who will be working on your case at any given time and what you will be charged for the services of each.

You are entitled to know in advance how you will be asked to pay legal fees and expenses, and how the retainer, if any, will be spent.

At your request, and after your attorney has had a reasonable opportunity to investigate your case, you are entitled to be given an estimate of approximate future costs of your case, which estimate shall be made in good faith but may be subject to change due to facts and circumstances affecting the case.

You are entitled to receive a written, itemized bill on a regular basis, at least every 60 days.

You are expected to review the itemized bills sent by counsel, and to raise any objections or errors in a timely manner. Time spent in discussion or explanation of bills will not be charged to you.

You are expected to be truthful in all discussions with your attorney, and to provide all relevant information and documentation to enable him or her to competently prepare your case.

You are entitled to be kept informed of the status of your case, and to be provided with copies of correspondence and documents prepared on your behalf or received from the court or your adversary.

You have the right to be present in court at the time that conferences are held.

You are entitled to make the ultimate decision on the objectives to be pursued in your case, and to make the final decision regarding the settlement of your case.

Your attorney's written retainer agreement must specify under what circumstances he or she might seek to withdraw as your attorney for nonpayment of legal fees. If an action or proceeding is pending, the court may give your attorney a "charging lien," which entitles your attorney to payment for services already rendered at the end of the case out of the proceeds of the final order or judgment.

You are under no legal obligation to sign a confession of judgment or promissory note, or to agree to a lien or mortgage on your home to cover legal fees. Your attorney's written retainer agreement must specify whether, and under what circumstances, such security may be requested. In no event may such security interest be obtained by your attorney without prior court approval and notice to your adversary. An attorney's security interest in the marital residence cannot be foreclosed against you.

You are entitled to have your attorney's best efforts exerted on your behalf, but no particular results can be guaranteed.

If you entrust money with an attorney for an escrow deposit in your case, the attorney must safeguard the escrow in a special bank account. You are entitled to a written escrow agreement, a written receipt, and a complete record concerning the escrow. When the terms of the escrow agreement have been performed, the attorney must promptly make payment of the escrow to all persons who are entitled to it.

In the event of a fee dispute, you may have the right to seek arbitration. Your attorney will provide you with the necessary information regarding arbitration in the event of a fee dispute, or upon your request.

Receipt Acknowledged:

_____

Attorney's signature

_____

Client's signature

_____

Date

§ 21.86 Forms—Complaint for Divorce

SUPREME COURT OF THE STATE OF NEW YORK
COUNTY OF _____

```
_____ )
                        )
_____,)
             Plaintiff, )
                        ) COMPLAINT
        -against-       )
                        ) Index No.: _____
_____,)
                        )
            Defendant.  )
_____ )
```

Plaintiff, by her attorney, _____, Esq., complaining of the defendant herein, alleges:

1. That plaintiff has been a resident of the State of New York for more than one year.

2. That the plaintiff and the defendant were married on the _____ day of _____, 19__.

3. That there are two children born of this marriage, to wit: _____, born _____, 19__ and _____, born _____, 19__.

4. That no judgment of divorce, separation or annulment of this marriage has heretofore been granted to the plaintiff or the defendant by the Courts of this State, any other State or foreign country.

5. All steps have been taken, or will be taken, prior to entry of final judgment, to remove any barrier to the defendant's remarriage following the divorce.

CAUSE OF ACTION FOR CRUEL AND INHUMAN TREATMENT

6. Repeats and realleges each and every allegation contained in paragraphs "1"through "5" as if stated with particularity herein.

7. The defendant has been guilty of cruel and inhuman treatment towards the plaintiff and of such conduct toward the plaintiff as to endanger the physical or mental well-being of the plaintiff so as to render it unsafe or improper for the plaintiff to cohabit with the defendant as herein alleged.

8. The acts of cruel and inhuman treatment of the defendant towards the plaintiff consisted of at least the following:

    a. The defendant has neglected or refused to provide for the plaintiff and for the support and maintenance of the issue of the marriage for a continuous period of more than three (3) years last past.

    b. The defendant told the plaintiff that he cannot and will not live with her any more which he stated on _____, 19__.

    c. The defendant did, on various occasions including _____, 19__, use profane and obscene language to her all without justification.

    d. The defendant did on various occasions including _____, 19__, and prior thereto, [*employ gross, vulgar, coarse and deeply offensive language to the plaintiff including the use of such words as "bastard, bitch, cheat, liar" and other similar language, all without justification*].

    e. The defendant accused and charged the plaintiff on various occasions of [*infidelity and having extra-marital sexual affairs and charged her with having a boyfriend,*] all of which was untrue.

    f. The defendant on various occasions including _____, 19__, without provocation threatened the plaintiff with [*bodily harm and put her in fear of her life and went into a tantrum, threw various things and objects in the vicinity of the plaintiff and on adjacent walls*].

    g. The defendant at various times at and during social events became [*intoxicated to the point where he then became unmanageable*].

9. The aforesaid course of cruel and inhuman treatment has been committed by the defendant with neither cause nor justification.

CAUSE OF ACTION FOR ABANDONMENT

10. Repeats and realleges each and every allegation contained in paragraphs "1" through "5" and "7" through "9" as if stated with particularity herein.

11. Heretofore and on _____, 19__, the defendant abandoned the plaintiff and the infant issue herein with intent not to return and without any cause or justification and without the plaintiff's consent and

has continuously absented himself and abandoned them since the said date, _____, 19__, to the present time for a period of one or more years.

CAUSE OF ACTION FOR IMPRISONMENT

12. Repeats and realleges each and every allegation contained in paragraphs "1" through "5," "7" through "9" and "11" as if stated with particularity herein.

13. The defendant, _____, has been continuously and consecutively confined in _____, at _____, pursuant to said sentence which remains in full force and effect, from _____, 19__ to the present date, which period of confinement exceeds three years (3) years.

CAUSE OF ACTION FOR ADULTERY

14. Repeats and realleges each and every allegation contained in paragraphs "1" through "5," "7" through "9," "11" and "13" as if stated with particularity herein.

15. On numerous occasions within the past [*4 months*] defendant has committed adultery at various places including [*Street*], _____, New York.

16. The adultery hereinbefore mentioned was not condoned by the plaintiff nor done with the plaintiff's connivance.

WHEREFORE, plaintiff demands judgment divorcing said plaintiff and defendant and dissolving said marriage; custody of the children of the marriage; child support in the amount of $_____ per week per child; maintenance in the amount of $_____ per week; equitable distribution of the marital property; attorney's fees in the amount of $_____; exclusive possession of the marital home until the youngest child reaches the age of eighteen; declaration of interest in husband's pension and/or profit sharing plan reflecting [*fifteen*] years of marriage; all stock and other property in husband's name; for plaintiff to be made irrevocable beneficiary of life insurance with the face value of at least $_____; all household furnishings; and such other and further relief as the court may deem just and proper.

Dated: _____, New York
_____, 19__

                                            Yours, etc.,

                                            _____, Esq.
                                            Attorney for Plaintiff
                                            [*P.O. Address:*
                                            Tel. No.:]

[*Verification*]

§ 21.87 Forms—Statement of Net Worth[1]

_____ COURT: STATE OF NEW YORK
COUNTY OF _____   Index No. _____

```
_____
                   )
         Plaintiff,) STATEMENT OF
                   ) NET WORTH
      -against-    )
                   ) (DRL § 236)
         Defendant.)
                   )
_____
```

Date of commencement of action _____

(Complete all items, marking "NONE," "INAPPLICABLE" and "UNKNOWN," if appropriate)

STATE OF _____)
) ss.:
COUNTY OF _____)

_____, the (Petitioner) (Respondent) (Plaintiff) (Defendant) herein, being duly sworn, deposes and says that the following is an accurate statement as of _____, of my net worth (assets of whatsoever kind and nature and wherever situated minus liabilities), statement of income from all sources and statement of assets transferred of whatsoever kind and nature and wherever situated:

I. FAMILY DATA:
   (a) Husband's age _____
   (b) Wife's age _____
   (c) Date married _____
   (d) Date (separated) (divorced) _____
   (e) Number of dependent children under 21 years _____
   (f) Names and ages of children
      _____
      _____
      _____
   (g) Custody of children _____ Husband _____ Wife
   (h) Minor children of prior marriage: _____ Husband _____ Wife
   (i) (Husband) (Wife) (paying) (receiving) $_____ as alimony (maintenance) and/or $_____ child support in connection with prior marriage

§ 21.87   effective 5/01/96.
1. Uniform Trial Court Rules, Appendix A. This a revised Statement of Net Worth,

Ch. 21   STATEMENT OF NET WORTH   § 21.87

(j) Custody of children of prior marriage:
   Name _____
   Address _____
(k) Is marital residence occupied by Husband _____ Wife _____ Both _____
(l) Husband's present address _____
   _____
   Wife's present address _____
   _____
(m) Occupation of Husband _____ Occupation of Wife _____
(n) Husband's employer
   _____
(o) Wife's employer
   _____
(p) Education, training and skills [Include dates of attainment of degrees, etc.]
   Husband _____
   Wife _____
(q) Husband's health _____
(r) Wife's health _____
(s) Children's health _____

II. EXPENSES: (You may elect to list all expenses on a weekly basis or all expenses on a monthly basis, however, you must be consistent. If any items are paid on a monthly basis, divide by 4.3 to obtain weekly payments; if any items are paid on a weekly basis, multiply by 4.3 to obtain monthly payment. Attach additional sheet, if needed. Items included under "Other" should be listed separately with separate dollar amounts.)

Expenses listed   [ ] weekly   [ ] monthly

(a) Housing
   1. Rent   _____
   2. Mortgage and amortization   _____
   3. Real estate taxes   _____
   4. Condominium charges   _____
   5. Cooperative apartment mainte-
      nance   _____
                    Total: Housing $_____
(b) Utilities
   1. Fuel oil   _____
   2. Gas   _____
   3. Electricity   _____
   4. Telephone   _____
   5. Water   _____
                    Total: Utilities $_____
(c) Food
   1. Groceries   _____
   2. School lunches   _____
   3. Lunches at work   _____
   4. Dining out   _____

§ 21.87   DOMESTIC RELATIONS   Ch. 21

        5. Liquor/alcohol   _____
        6. Home entertainment   _____
        7. Other   _____
                      Total: Food $_____

(d) Clothing
        1. Husband   _____
        2. Wife   _____
        3. Children   _____
        4. Other   _____
                      Total: Clothing $_____

(e) Laundry
        1. Laundry at home   _____
        2. Dry cleaning   _____
        3. Other _____ _____
                      Total: Laundry $_____

(f) Insurance
        1. Life   _____
        2. Homeowner's/tenant's   _____
        3. Fire, theft and liability   _____
        4. Automotive   _____
        5. Umbrella policy   _____
        6. Medical plan   _____
        7. Dental plan   _____
        8. Optical plan   _____
        9. Disability   _____
       10. Worker's Compensation   _____
       11. Other _____ _____
                      Total: Insurance $_____

(g) Unreimbursed medical
        1. Medical   _____
        2. Dental   _____
        3. Optical   _____
        4. Pharmaceutical   _____
        5. Surgical, nursing, hospital   _____
        6. Other _____ _____
                      Total: Unreimbursed medical $_____

(h) Household maintenance
        1. Repairs   _____
        2. Furniture, furnishings housewares   _____
        3. Cleaning supplies   _____
        4. Appliances, including maintenance   _____
        5. Painting   _____
        6. Sanitation/carting   _____
        7. Gardening/landscaping   _____
        8. Snow removal   _____
        9. Extermination   _____
       10. Other _____ _____
                      Total: Household maintenance $_____

(i) Household help
   1. Babysitter _____
   2. Domestic (housekeeper, maid, etc.) _____
   3. Other _____ _____
                  Total: Household help $_____

(j) Automotive
   Year: _____ Make: _____ Personal: _____
   Business: _____
   Year: _____ Make: _____ Personal: _____
   Business: _____
   Year: _____ Make: _____ Personal: _____
   Business: _____
   1. Payments _____
   2. Gas and oil _____
   3. Repairs _____
   4. Car wash _____
   5. Registration and license _____
   6. Parking and tolls _____
   7. Other _____ _____
                  Total: Automotive $_____

(k) Educational
   1. Nursery and pre-school _____
   2. Primary and secondary _____
   3. College _____
   4. Post-graduate _____
   5. Religious instruction _____
   6. School transportation _____
   7. School supplies/books _____
   8. Tutoring _____
   9. School events _____
   10. Other _____ _____
                  Total: Educational $_____

(l) Recreational
   1. Summer camp _____
   2. Vacations _____
   3. Movies _____
   4. Theatre, ballet, etc. _____
   5. Video rentals _____
   6. Tapes, CDs, etc. _____
   7. Cable television _____
   8. Team sports _____
   9. Country club/pool club _____
   10. Health club _____
   11. Sporting goods _____
   12. Hobbies _____
   13. Music/dance lessons _____
   14. Sports lessons _____
   15. Birthday parties _____
   16. Other _____ _____

§ 21.87 DOMESTIC RELATIONS Ch. 21

       Total: Recreational $_____

(m) Income Taxes
  1. Federal
  2. State
  3. City
  4. Social Security and Medicare
      Total: Income taxes $_____

(n) Miscellaneous
  1. Beauty parlor/barber
  2. Beauty aids/cosmetics, drug items
  3. Cigarettes/tobacco
  4. Books, magazines, newspapers
  5. Children's allowances
  6. Gifts
  7. Charitable contributions
  8. Religious organization dues
  9. Union and organization dues
  10. Commutation and transportation
  11. Veterinarian/pet expenses
  12. Child support payments (prior marriage)
  13. Alimony and maintenance payments (prior marriage)
  14. Loan payments
  15. Unreimbursed business expenses
      Total: Miscellaneous $_____

(o) Other
  1. _____
  2. _____
  3. _____
  4. _____
      Total: Other $_____
      TOTAL EXPENSES: $_____

III. GROSS INCOME: (State source of income and annual amount. Attach additional sheet, if needed.)

(a) Salary or wages: (State whether income has changed during the year preceding date of this affidavit _____. If so, set forth name and address of all employers during preceding year and average weekly wage paid by each. Indicate overtime earnings separately.
Attach previous year's W–2 or income tax return.)

_____
_____

(b) Weekly deductions:
  1. Federal tax ....
  2. New York State tax ....
  3. Local tax ....

Ch. 21 STATEMENT OF NET WORTH § 21.87

      4. Social Security .... _____
      5. Medicare .... _____
      6. Other payroll deductions (specify) .... _____
- (c) Social Security number _____
- (d) Number and names of dependents claimed: _____
- (e) Bonus, commissions, fringe benefits (use of auto, memberships, etc.) .... _____
- (f) Partnership, royalties, sale of assets (income and installment payments) .... _____
- (g) Dividends and interest (state whether taxable or not) ..... _____
- (h) Real estate (income only) ...... _____
- (i) Trust, profit sharing and annuities (principal distribution and income) .... _____
- (j) Pension (income only) .... _____
- (k) Awards, prizes, grants (state whether taxable)............ _____
- (l) Bequests, legacies and gifts .... _____
- (m) Income from all other sources .. (including alimony, maintenance or child support from prior marriage) _____
- (n) Tax preferences items:
    1. Long term capital gain deduction .... _____
    2. Depreciation, amortization or depletion.............. _____
    3. Stock options—excess of fair market value over amount paid .... _____
- (o) If any child or other member of your household is employed, set forth name and that person's annual income .... _____
- (p) Social Security................ _____
- (q) Disability benefits .... _____
- (r) Public assistance.............. _____
- (s) Other....................... _____

                              TOTAL INCOME: _____

IV. ASSETS: (If any asset is held jointly with spouse or another, so state, and set forth your respective shares, Attach additional sheets, if needed.)
    A. Cash Accounts
       Cash
       1.1 a. Location _____

§ 21.87 DOMESTIC RELATIONS Ch. 21

    b. Source of funds _____
    c. Amount _____ $_____
       Total: Cash $_____

Checking Accounts
2.1 a. Financial institution _____
    b. Account number _____
    c. Title holder _____
    d. Date opened _____
    e. Source of funds _____
    f. Balance _____ $_____

2.2 a. Financial institution _____
    b. Account number _____
    c. Title holder _____
    d. Date opened _____
    e. Source of funds _____
    f. Balance _____ $_____
       Total: Checking $_____

Savings accounts (including individual, joint, totten trust, certificates of deposit, treasury notes)
3.1 a. Financial institution _____
    b. Account number _____
    c. Title holder _____
    d. Type of account _____
    e. Date opened _____
    f. Source of funds _____
    g. Balance _____ $_____

3.2 a. Financial institution _____
    b. Account number _____
    c. Title holder _____
    d. Type of account _____
    e. Date opened _____
    f. Source of funds _____
    g. Balance _____ $_____
       Total: Savings $_____

Security deposits, earnest money, etc.
4.1 a. Location _____
    b. Title owner _____
    c. Type of deposit _____
    d. Source of funds _____
    e. Date of deposit _____
    f. Amount _____ $_____
       Total: Security Deposits, etc. $_____

Other
5.1 a. Location _____
    b. Title owner _____
    c. Type of account _____
    d. Source of funds _____

Ch. 21   STATEMENT OF NET WORTH   § 21.87

       e. Date of deposit _____
       f. Amount _____ $_____
            Total: Other $_____
            Total: Cash Accounts $_____
   B. Securities
     Bonds, notes, mortgages
      1.1   a. Description of security _____

          b. Title holder _____
          c. Location _____
          d. Date of acquisition _____
          e. Original price or value _____

          f. Source of funds to acquire

          g. Current value _____ $_____
             Total: Bonds, notes,
               etc. $_____
     Stocks, options and commodity contracts
      2.1   a. Description of security _____

          b. Title holder _____
          c. Location _____
          d. Date of acquisition _____
          e. Original price or value _____
          f. Source of funds to acquire

          g. Current value _____ $_____
      2.2   a. Description of security _____

          b. Title holder _____
          c. Location _____
          d. Date of acquisition _____
          e. Original price or value _____

          f. Source of funds to acquire

          g. Current value _____ $_____
      2.3   a. Description of security _____

          b. Title holder _____
          c. Location _____
          d. Date of acquisition _____
          e. Original price or value _____

          f. Source of funds to acquire

          g. Current value _____ $_____
             Total: Stocks, options, etc. $_____
     Broker margin accounts
      3.1   a. Name and address of broker _____
          b. Title holder _____

  c. Date account opened _____
  d. Original value of account _____

  e. Source of funds _____
  f. Current value _____ $_____
    Total: Margin accounts $_____
    Total value of securities: $_____

C. Loans to others and accounts receivable
 1.1 a. Debtor's name and address _____

  b. Original amount of loan or debt _____
  c. Source of funds from which loan made or origin of debt _____
  d. Date payment(s) due _____
  e. Current amount due _____ $_____

 1.2 a. Debtor's name and address _____

  b. Original amount of loan or debt _____
  c. Source of funds from which loan made or origin of debt _____
  d. Date payment(s) due _____
  e. Current amount due _____ $_____
    Total: Loans and accounts receivable $_____

D. Value of interest in any business
 1.1 a. Name and address of business _____
  b. Type of business (corporate, partnership, sole proprietorship or other) _____

  c. Your capital contribution _____

  d. Your percentage of interest _____

  e. Date of acquisition _____
  f. Original price or value _____

  g. Source of funds to acquire _____

  h. Method of valuation _____
  i. Other relevant information _____

  j. Current net worth of business _____ $_____

Total: Value of business interest $____

E. Cash surrender value of life insurance
    1.1 a. Insurer's name and address ____
           b. Name of insured ____
           c. Policy number ____
           d. Face amount of policy ____
           e. Policy owner ____
           f. Date of acquisition ____
           g. Source of funding to acquire ____
           h. Current cash surrender value ____ $____
              Total: Value of life insurance $____

F. Vehicles (automobile, boat, plane, truck, camper, etc.)
    1.1 a. Description ____
           b. Title owner ____
           c. Date of acquisition ____
           d. Original price ____
           e. Source of funds to acquire ____
           f. Amount of current lien unpaid ____
           g. Current fair market value ____ $____
    1.2 a. Description ____
           b. Title owner ____
           c. Date of acquisition ____
           d. Original price ____
           e. Source of funds to acquire ____
           f. Amount of current lien unpaid ____
           g. Current fair market value ____ $____
              Total: Value of Vehicles $____

G. Real estate (including real property, leaseholds, life estates, etc. at market value—do not deduct any mortgage)
    1.1 a. Description ____
           b. Title owner ____
           c. Date of acquisition ____
           d. Original price ____
           e. Source of funds to acquire ____

§ 21.87 DOMESTIC RELATIONS Ch. 21

  f. Amount of mortgage or lien unpaid _____
  g. Estimated current market value _____ $_____

 1.2 a. Description _____
  b. Title owner _____
  c. Date of acquisition _____
  d. Original price _____
  e. Source of funds to acquire _____
  f. Amount of mortgage or lien unpaid _____
  g. Estimated current market value _____ $_____

 1.3 a. Description _____
  b. Title owner _____
  c. Date of acquisition _____
  d. Original price _____
  e. Source of funds to acquire _____
  f. Amount of mortgage or lien unpaid _____
  g. Estimated current market value _____ $_____

   Total: Value of real estate $_____

H. Vested interests in trusts (pension, profit sharing, legacies, deferred compensation and others)

 1.1 a. Description of trust _____
  b. Location of assets _____
  c. Title owner _____
  d. Date of acquisition _____
  e. Original investment _____
  f. Source of funds _____
  g. Amount of unpaid liens _____
  h. Current value _____ $_____

 1.2 a. Description of trust _____
  b. Location of assets _____
  c. Title owner _____
  d. Date of acquisition _____
  e. Original investment _____
  f. Source of funds _____
  g. Amount of unpaid liens _____
  h. Current value _____ $_____

   Total: Vested interest in trusts $_____

I. Contingent interests (stock options, interests subject to life estates, prospective inheritances, etc.)
   1.1 a. Description _____
       b. Location _____
       c. Date of vesting _____
       d. Title owner _____
       e. Date of acquisition _____
       f. Original price or value _____
       g. Source of funds to acquire _____
       h. Method of valuation _____
       i. Current value _____ $_____
          Total: Contingent interests $_____

J. Household furnishings
   1.1 a. Description _____
       b. Location _____
       c. Title owner _____
       d. Original price _____
       e. Source of funds to acquire _____
       f. Amount of lien unpaid _____
       g. Current value _____ $_____
          Total: Household furnishings $_____

K. Jewelry, art, antiques, precious objects, gold and precious metals (only if valued at more than $500)
   1.1 a. Description _____
       b. Title owner _____
       c. Location _____
       d. Original price or value _____
       e. Source of funds to acquire _____
       f. Amount of lien unpaid _____
       g. Current value _____ $_____
   1.2 a. Description _____
       b. Title owner _____
       c. Location _____
       d. Original price or value _____
       e. Source of funds to acquire _____
       f. Amount of lien unpaid _____
       g. Current value _____ $_____
          Total: Jewelry, art, etc.: $_____

L. Other (*e.g.,* tax shelter investments, collections, judgments, causes of action, patents, trademarks, copy-

§ 21.87   DOMESTIC RELATIONS   Ch. 21

    rights, and any other asset not hereinabove itemized)
    1.1 a. Description _____
           b. Title owner _____
           c. Location _____
           d. Original price or value _____
           e. Source of funds to acquire _____
           f. Amount of lien unpaid _____
           g. Current value _____ $_____
    1.2 a. Description _____
           b. Title owner _____
           c. Location _____
           d. Original price or value _____
           e. Source of funds to acquire _____
           f. Amount of lien unpaid _____
           g. Current value _____ $_____
              Total: Other $_____
              TOTAL: ASSETS $_____

V. LIABILITIES
  A. Accounts payable
    1.1 a. Name and address of creditor _____
           b. Debtor _____
           c. Amount of original debt _____
           d. Date of incurring debt _____
           e. Purpose _____
           f. Monthly or other periodic payment _____
           g. Amount of current debt _____ $_____
    1.2 a. Name and address of creditor _____
           b. Debtor _____
           c. Amount of original debt _____
           d. Date of incurring debt _____
           e. Purpose _____
           f. Monthly or other periodic payment _____
           g. Amount of current debt _____ $_____
    1.3 a. Name and address of creditor _____
           b. Debtor _____
           c. Amount of original debt _____
           d. Date of incurring debt _____
           e. Purpose _____
           f. Monthly or other periodic payment _____
           g. Amount of current debt _____ $_____

Ch. 21   STATEMENT OF NET WORTH   § 21.87

    1.4 a. Name and address of creditor _____
            b. Debtor _____
            c. Amount of original debt ___
            d. Date of incurring debt ___
            e. Purpose _____
            f. Monthly or other periodic payment _____
            g. Amount of current debt ___ $_____
    1.5 a. Name and address of creditor _____
            b. Debtor _____
            c. Amount of original debt ___
            d. Date of incurring debt ___
            e. Purpose _____
            f. Monthly or other periodic payment _____
            g. Amount of current debt ___ $_____
               Total: Accounts payable _____ $_____
B. Notes payable
    1.1 a. Name and address of noteholder _____
            b. Debtor _____
            c. Amount of original debt ___
            d. Date of incurring debt ___
            e. Purpose _____
            f. Monthly or other periodic payment _____
            g. Amount of current debt ___ $_____
    1.2 a. Name and address of note holder _____
            b. Debtor _____
            c. Amount of original debt ___
            d. Date of incurring debt ___
            e. Purpose _____
            f. Monthly or other periodic payment _____
            g. Amount of current debt ___ $_____
               Total: Notes payable $_____
C. Installment accounts payable (security agreements, chattel mortgages)
    1.1 a. Name and address of creditor _____
            b. Debtor _____
            c. Amount of original debt ___
            d. Date of incurring debt ___
            e. Purpose _____

§ 21.87   DOMESTIC RELATIONS   Ch. 21

           f. Monthly or other periodic payment _____
           g. Amount of current debt ___ $_____
     1.2 a. Name and address of creditor _____
           b. Debtor _____
           c. Amount of original debt _____
           d. Date of incurring debt ___
           e. Purpose _____
           f. Monthly or other periodic payment _____
           g. Amount of current debt ___ $_____
               Total: Installment accounts $_____
D. Brokers' margin accounts
     1.1 a. Name and address of broker _____
           b. Amount of original debt _____
           c. Date of incurring debt ___
           d. Purpose _____
           e. Monthly or other periodic payment _____
           f. Amount of current debt ___ $_____
               Total: Brokers' margin accounts $_____
E. Mortgages payable on real estate
     1.1 a. Name and address of mortgagee _____
           b. Address of property mortgaged _____
           c. Mortgagor(s) _____
           d. Original debt _____
           e. Date of incurring debt ___
           f. Monthly or other periodic payment _____
           g. Maturity Date _____
           h. Amount of current debt ___ $_____
     1.2 a. Name and address of mortgagee _____
           b. Address of property mortgaged _____
           c. Mortgagor(s) _____
           d. Original debt _____
           e. Date of incurring debt ___
           f. Monthly or other periodic payment _____
           g. Maturity Date _____
           h. Amount of current debt ___ $_____
               Total: Mortgages payable $_____

Ch. 21 STATEMENT OF NET WORTH § 21.87

 F. Taxes payable
   1.1 a. Description of tax _____
     b. Amount of tax _____
     c. Date due _____
       Total: Taxes payable $_____
 G. Loans on life insurance policies
   1.1 a. Name and address of insurer _____
     b. Amount of loan _____
     c. Date incurred _____
     d. Purpose _____
     e. Name of borrower _____
     f. Monthly or other periodic payment _____
     g. Amount of current debt __ $_____
       Total: Life insurance loans $_____
 H. Other liabilities
   1.1 a. Description _____
     b. Name and address of creditor _____
     c. Debtor _____
     d. Original amount of debt __
     e. Date incurred _____
     f. Purpose _____
     g. Monthly or other periodic payment _____
     h. Amount of current debt __ $_____

   1.2 a. Description _____
     b. Name and address of creditor _____
     c. Debtor _____
     d. Original amount of debt __
     e. Date incurred _____
     f. Purpose _____
     g. Monthly or other periodic payment _____
     h. Amount of current debt __ $_____
       Total: Other liabilities $_____
       TOTAL LIABILITIES: $_____

NET WORTH

TOTAL ASSETS: $_____
TOTAL LIABILITIES: (minus) ($_____)
NET WORTH: $_____
 VI. ASSETS TRANSFERRED: (List all assets transferred in any manner during the preceding three years, or length of the

§ 21.87   DOMESTIC RELATIONS   Ch. 21

marriage, whichever is shorter [transfers in the routine course of business which resulted in an exchange of assets of substantially equivalent value need not be specifically disclosed where such assets are otherwise identified in the statement of net worth.])

Description of Property	To Whom Transferred and Relationship to Transferee	Date of Transfer	Value
_____	_____	_____	_____
_____	_____	_____	_____
_____	_____	_____	_____

VII. SUPPORT REQUIREMENTS:
   (a) Deponent is at present (paying) (receiving) $_____ per (week) (month), and prior to separation (paid) (received) $_____ per (week) (month) to cover expenses for _____

These payments are being made (voluntarily) (pursuant to court order or judgment) (pursuant to separation agreement), and there are (no) arrears outstanding (in the sum of $_____ to date).
   (b) Deponent requests for support of each child $_____ per (week) (month).
      Total for child(ren) $_____.
   (c) Deponent requests for support of self $_____ per (week) (month).
   (d) The day of the (week) (month) on which payment should be made is _____.

VIII. COUNSEL FEE REQUIREMENTS:
   (a) Deponent requests for counsel fee and disbursements the sum of $_____.
   (b) Deponent has paid counsel the sum of $_____ and has agreed with counsel concerning fees as follows:
      _____
      _____
   (c) There is (not) a retainer agreement or written agreement relating to payment of legal fees. (A copy of any such agreement must be annexed.)

IX. ACCOUNTANT AND APPRAISAL FEES REQUIREMENTS
   (a) Deponent requests for accountants' fees and disbursements the sum of $_____.
      (Include basis for fee, e.g. hourly rate, flat rate)
   (b) Deponent requests for appraisal fees and disbursements the sum of $_____.
      (Include basis for fee, e.g. hourly rate, flat rate)
   (c) Deponent requires the services of an accountant for the following reasons:
      _____

Ch. 21   STATEMENT OF PROPOSED DISPOSITION   § 21.88

(d) Deponent requires the services of an appraiser for the following reasons: _____

X. Other data concerning the financial circumstances of the parties that should be brought to the attention of the Court are:
_____
_____
_____
_____

The foregoing statements and a rider consisting of _____ page(s) annexed hereto and made part hereof, have been carefully read by the undersigned who states that they are true and correct.

_____
(Petitioner)   (Respondent)
(Plaintiff)   (Defendant)

Sworn to before me this day of _____, 19__

CERTIFICATION OF ATTORNEY

I hereby certify under penalty of perjury and as an officer of the court that I have no knowledge that the substance of any of the factual submissions contained in this document is false.

_____
[The name signed must be printed beneath]

Dated:

§ 21.88 Forms—Statement of Proposed Disposition

SUPREME COURT OF THE STATE OF NEW YORK
COUNTY OF _____

_____,)
)
)
)
                       Plaintiff,)
) STATEMENT OF PROPOSED
           -against-   ) DISPOSITION
)
) Index No.: _____
_____,)
)
)
                      Defendant.)
)

(Petitioner) (Respondent) (Plaintiff) (Defendant) herein, states the following as required by Section 202.16 of the Rules of the Chief Administrator of the Courts (22 NYCRR § 202.16(h)).

(a) The following assets are marital property and are subject to equitable distribution. *[List assets].*

(b) The following assets are separate property and, as such, are not subject to equitable distribution. *[List assets].*

(c) There are outstanding debts or liabilities as to the following marital or separate assets. *[Allocate debts or liabilities as to specific marital or separate assets, where appropriate].*

(d) The following amount is requested for maintenance. *[State requested amount, detailing the statutory factors forming the basis for such request].*

(e) The following proposal is made for equitable distribution. *[State proposal, where appropriate, detailing the statutory factors forming the basis for such distribution].*

(f) The following proposal is made for a distributive award (if requested). *[State proposal, including a showing of the need for such award].*

(g) The following plan is proposed for child support. *[State proposal & detail the statutory factors upon which such proposal is based].*

(h) The following plan is proposed for custody and visitation of the children involved in this proceeding (if applicable). *[State proposal for custody and visitation, setting forth the reasons therefor].*

[Signature]

_____

[Type Name]

§ 21.89 Forms—Findings of Fact and Conclusions of Law

FINDINGS OF FACT AND CONCLUSIONS OF LAW[1]

Title

The issues of this action having duly come on for hearing before me as one of the Justices of this Court at Part _____ hereof, held in

---

§ 21.89
1. Appendix B, Uniform Trial Court Rules. These provisions are to be modified or deleted as may be necessary to conform to the law and facts in a particular action.

and for the County of _____, on the _____ day(s) of _____, 19__, and having heard the allegations and proofs of the respective parties, and due deliberation having been had thereon

NOW, after hearing _____, Esq., attorney for the plaintiff, and _____, Esq., attorney for the defendant, I do hereby make the following findings of essential facts which I deem established by the evidence and reach the following conclusions of law.

Age of Parties—No Guardian Needed

FIRST: That plaintiff and defendant were both over the age of 18 when this action was commenced.

Age of Parties—Under Age Party

FIRST: That (plaintiff) (defendant) was over the age of 18 years when this action commenced and (defendant) (plaintiff) was then and now is under 18, to wit: _____ years of age and appears herein by _____, (parent and natural guardian) (duly appointed as guardian by order dated _____, 19__).

Residence—One Year

SECOND: That at the time of the commencement of this action and for a continuous period of at least one year immediately preceding such commencement (plaintiff) (defendant) resided in this State and (the parties were married in the State) (the parties have resided in this State as husband and wife) (the cause occurred in this State).

Residence—Two Years

SECOND: That for a continuous period of at least two years immediately preceding commencement of this action (plaintiff) (defendant) resided in this State.

Residence—No Required Time

SECOND: That at the time of the commencement of this action both plaintiff and defendant resided in this State and the cause occurred in this State.

Marriage

THIRD: That plaintiff and defendant were married on _____, 19__ in

No Children

FOURTH: That there is no issue of this marriage.

Parenthesized portions indicate alternative provisions. 22 NYCRR § 202.50.

Children

> FOURTH: That there are ___ children (born of) (adopted by) the parties to this marriage, whose names and dates of birth are as follows:

Cruelty

> FIFTH: That at the following times, none of which is earlier than five years before the date of commencement of this action, defendant committed the following acts which endangered the plaintiff's (physical) (mental) (physical and mental well-being) and rendered it (unsafe) (improper) (unsafe and improper) for plaintiff to continue to reside with defendant.
>
> (Spell out in letter subparagraphs, the acts or omissions to act for which there is proof in the minutes).

Abandonment

> FIFTH: That the defendant without cause or justification and without plaintiff's consent on the ___ day of _____ 19__ abandoned plaintiff with intent not to return and has been wilfully and continuously absent from the home of the parties since (in divorce actions add: for a period of one year prior to the commencement of this action).

Confinement to Prison

> FIFTH: (a) That after the marriage of plaintiff and defendant, defendant was confined in prison for a period of three or more consecutive years, to wit: that defendant was confined in _____ prison on the ___ day of _____ 19__ and remained confined until the ___ day of _____ 19__; and
>
> (b) not more than five years elapsed between the date the cause of action arose and the date of commencement of this action.

Adultery

> FIFTH: (a) That on the ___ day of _____ 19__ at premises _____ the defendant committed adultery with _____; and
>
> (b) not more than five years elapsed between the date of said adultery and the date of commencement of this action.

Neglect to Support

> FIFTH: (a) That defendant has (neglected) (refused) to provide for the support of plaintiff since the ___ day of _____ 19__; and
>
> (b) not more than five years elapsed between the date the cause of action arose and the date of commencement of this action.

FINDINGS OF FACT/CONCLUSIONS OF LAW § 21.89

Living Apart Under Separation Decree

FIFTH: (a) That a judgment separating the parties was entered on the ___ day of _____ 19__ by the _____ Court of the State of _____; and

(b) that the parties have lived apart pursuant to said judgment for a period of one year after the granting of such judgment; and

(c) that the plaintiff has substantially performed all the terms and conditions of such judgment.

Living Apart Under Separation Agreement

FIFTH: (a) That the plaintiff and defendant entered into a written agreement of separation, which they subscribed and acknowledged on the ___ day of _____ 19__ in the form required to entitle a deed to be recorded; and

(b) that the (agreement) (a memorandum of said agreement) was filed in the office of the Clerk of the County of _____, wherein (plaintiff) (defendant) resided on the ___ day of _____ 19__; and

(c) that the parties have lived separate and apart for a period of one year after the execution of said agreement; and

(d) that the plaintiff has substantially performed all the terms and conditions of such agreement.

Annulment for Fraud

FIFTH: (a) That prior to the marriage of the parties the defendant represented to plaintiff that _____ (state representation); and

(b) that said representation was false; and

(c) that said representation was made to induce plaintiff to enter into the marriage; and

(d) that plaintiff believed and relied upon said representation, and would not have entered into the marriage had the representation not been made or had plaintiff known that defendant did not intend to _____ [refer to representation]; and

(e) that defendant after the marriage refused to _____ [refer to representation]; and

(f) that plaintiff has not cohabited with defendant since discovery of the falsity of the representation; and

(g) that three years have not elapsed since discovery of the facts constituting the fraud.

[for other grounds see § 140 DRL].

§ 21.89   DOMESTIC RELATIONS   Ch. 21

Declaration of Nullity of Void Marriage

FIFTH: (a) That prior to his marriage to plaintiff and on the ___ day of _____ 19__, defendant married _____ [name] in _____ [place]; and

(b) that on the date of the marriage of plaintiff and defendant the marriage between defendant and _____ [name] had not been terminated by the judgment of any court; and

(c) on the date of the marriage of plaintiff and defendant, defendant's prior spouse was alive and the prior marriage of defendant was valid and subsisting.

Arrears Due Under Temporary Order

SIXTH: (a) That by order of this court (or by order of the Family Court, _____ County) dated the ___ day of _____ 19__, defendant was required to pay to plaintiff as and for maintenance and child support, the sum of $_____ per week and as counsel fee, the sum of $_____; and

(b) that there became due under said order through the week of _____ 19__, the total sum of $_____, no part of which has been paid except $_____; and

(c) that defendant is in arrears under said order in the total sum of $_____ for said period.

Separate and Marital Property

SEVENTH: (a) That the following is separate property owned by plaintiff:

                                                ; and

(b) that the following is separate property owned by defendant:

                                                ; and _____

(c) that the following is marital property to be disposed of equitably pursuant to DRL § 236B(5):

[List findings required under DRL § 236B(5)(d)(1–10)]

Custody

EIGHTH: That the children of the marriage now reside with (plaintiff) (defendant).

Visitation

NINTH: That the (plaintiff) (defendant) is entitled to visitation with the infant child(ren) away from the custodial residence.

134

Ch. 21   FINDINGS OF FACT/CONCLUSIONS OF LAW § 21.89

Exclusive Occupancy

TENTH: That the parties hereto are the owners of premises known as _____

_____ (P.O. address).

Maintenance (pursuant to DRL § 236B(6))

ELEVENTH: (a) That plaintiff is (not) employed and is earning $*(net)* per week; and

(b) that defendant is (not) employed and is earning $*(net)* per week; and

(c) that (plaintiff) (defendant) now receives $_____ per _____ pursuant to an outstanding _____ Court order;

(d) that (plaintiff) (defendant) now requires $_____ per week for maintenance; and

(List findings required under DRL § 236B(6)(a)(1–10)); and

(e) that the parties have entered into (a stipulation) (or/and agreement) dated _____ wherein (plaintiff) (defendant) agrees to accept and (plaintiff) (defendant) agrees to pay $_____ per week as maintenance (and $_____ per week per child as and for child support, which (stipulation) (agreement) includes a provision stating that the parties have been advised of the provisions of DRL § 240(1-b)(h).) That the terms of the agreement were fair and reasonable at the time of the making of the agreement and are not unconscionable at the time of the entry of judgment herein.

(f) neither of the parties seeks equitable distribution of the marital property.

Child Support

TWELFTH: (a) The award of child support in accordance with DRL § 240(1-b) is based on the following findings:

   (i) the children of the marriage entitled to receive parental support are: [*state names and dates of birth*];

   (ii) the income of the plaintiff, who is the (custodial) (non-custodial) parent, is $_____ per year;

   (iii) the income of the defendant, who is the (custodial) (non-custodial) parent, is $_____ per year;

   (iv) the applicable child support percentage is ____%;

   (v) the basic child support obligation is $_____ per (week) (month) [*plus, if applicable, expenses for child care, health care not covered by insurance, and educational or other extraordinary expenses*]

(vi) the non-custodial parent's pro rata share of the basic child support obligation is calculated as follows:

    A. $_____ per (week) (month) representing _____% of the combined parental income under $80,000 per year; plus

    B. $_____ per (week) (month), representing _____% of the combined parental income, if any, over $80,000 per year;

    C. __% of future reasonable health care expenses not covered by insurance; [*delete if inapplicable*]

    D. __% of the reasonable child care expenses; [*delete if inapplicable*]

    E. __% of educational or other extraordinary expenses; [*delete if inapplicable*]

[2](b) The non-custodial parent's pro rata share of the basic child support obligation is neither unjust nor inappropriate.

OR

[3](b) Upon consideration of the following factors specified in Section 140(1–b)(f) of the Domestic Relations Law:

the non-custodial parent's pro rata share of the basic child support obligation is unjust or inappropriate in that:

OR

[4](b) The parties have entered into a (stipulation) (agreement) dated _____ wherein (plaintiff) (defendant) agrees to pay $__ per (week) (month) for child support, such (stipulation) (agreement) reciting, in compliance with DRL § 240(1–b)(h), that:

The parties have been advised of the provisions of Section 240(1–b) of the Domestic Relations Law;

The unrepresented party, if any, has received a copy of the child support standards chart promulgated by the commissioner of Social Services pursuant to Social Services Law § 111–i;

2. Only one of the three alternative subparagraphs (b) will be appropriate; delete the inapplicable provisions.

3. Only one of the three alternative subparagraphs (b) will be appropriate; delete the inapplicable provisions.

4. Only one of the three alternative subparagraphs (b) will be appropriate; delete the inapplicable provisions.

The basic child support obligation as defined in DRL Section 240(1–b) presumptively results in the correct amount of child support to be awarded;

The basic child support obligation in this case is $_____ per ___; [plus, if applicable, expenses for child care, health care not covered by insurance, and educational or other extraordinary expenses]; and

[5](c) The amount of child support agreed to therein conforms to the basic child support obligation.

OR

[6](c) The amount of child support agreed to therein deviates from the basic child support obligation, and the parties' reasons for not providing that amount are

_____ ;

And the court having found the parties' agreement to deviate from the basic child support obligation is approved for the following reasons: [*Set forth reasons; see DRL § 240(1–b)(f)*]

(d) that the amount of combined parental income in excess of $80,000 is $_____. The amount of child support based upon parental income exceeding $80,000 is $_____.

(e) that the custodial parent is (working) (seeking work) (receiving (elementary) (secondary) (higher) (vocational) education which will lead to employment) and incurring child care expenses as a result thereof. The following are the reasonable child care expenses to be prorated in the same proportion as each parent's income is to the combined parental income:

(f) that the following are the future reasonable health care expenses of the child not covered by insurance to be prorated in the same proportion as each parent's income is to the combined parental income:

(g) that under the circumstances of the case and of the respective parties and in the best interests of the child, and as justice requires, the (present) (future) provision of (post-secondary) (private) (special) (enriched) education for the child(ren) is appropriate.

(h) that the parties have entered into (a stipulation) (or/and agreement) dated _____ wherein (plaintiff) (defendant) agrees to pay $_____ per week per child for child support and now receives $_____ per week pursuant to an outstanding court order, which (stipulation) (agreement) includes a provision stating that the parties have been advised of the provisions of DRL § 240(1–b)(h).

---

5. Only one of the two alternative subparagraphs (c) will be appropriate; delete the inapplicable provisions.

6. Only one of the two alternative subparagraphs (c) will be appropriate; delete the inapplicable provisions.

§ 21.89

Counsel Fees

THIRTEENTH: That the attorney for the (plaintiff) (defendant) is entitled to counsel fees.

Jurisdiction Obtained

FOURTEENTH: That jurisdiction as required by Section 230 of the Domestic Relations Law has been obtained.

Removal of Barriers to Remarriage

FIFTEENTH: That plaintiff has filed a verified statement that (he) (she) has taken all steps solely within (his) (her) power to remove all barriers to defendant's remarriage following the (annulment) (divorce).

Plaintiff Entitled to Judgment

SIXTEENTH: That plaintiff is entitled to judgment (of divorce) (of separation) (of annulment) (declaring the nullity of the marriage) and granting the incidental relief awarded (herein) (in the JUDGMENT signed this date).

Dated:

_____
Justice Supreme Court

§ 21.90 Forms—Matrimonial Judgments

MATRIMONIAL JUDGMENTS[1]

Title

Nature of Action—Divorce

The plaintiff having brought this action for a judgment of absolute divorce by reason of

[*Insert one or more of the following grounds:*]

- the cruel and inhuman treatment of the plaintiff by the defendant
- the abandonment of the plaintiff by the defendant for a period of one or more years
- the confinement of defendant in prison for a period of three or more consecutive years after the marriage of plaintiff and defendant

---

§ 21.90

1. Appendix B, Uniform Trial Court Rules. These provisions are to be modified or deleted as may be necessary to conform to the law and facts in a particular action. Parenthesized portions indicate alternative provisions. 22 NYCRR § 202.50.

- the commission by the defendant of adultery
- the plaintiff and defendant having lived apart after the granting of a judgment of separation for a period of one or more years
- the plaintiff and defendant having lived separate and apart pursuant to a written agreement for a period of one or more years

Nature of Action—Separation

The plaintiff having brought this action for a judgment of separation by reason of

[*Insert one or more of the following grounds*:]

- the cruel and inhuman treatment of the plaintiff by the defendant
- the abandonment of the plaintiff by the defendant
- the neglect or refusal of defendant to provide for plaintiff
- the commission by defendant of adultery
- the confinement of defendant in prison for a period of three or more consecutive years after the marriage of plaintiff and defendant

Nature of Action—Annulment

The plaintiff having brought this action for a judgment of annulment by reason of the fraud of the defendant in inducing the marriage

[*or other grounds, see § 140 DRL*]

Nature of Action—Declaration of the Nullity of a Void Marriage

The plaintiff having brought this action for a judgment declaring the nullity of (his) (her) marriage to the defendant by reason of the prior subsisting marriage of the defendant

Service of Process

and the summons bearing the notation ("Action for a Divorce") ("Action for a Separation") ("Action to Annul a Marriage") ("Action to Declare the Nullity of a Void Marriage") and a statement of any ancillary relief demanded having been duly served upon the defendant (personally within this State) (personally without this State by publication)

Defendant's Non-appearance

and the defendant not having appeared within the time prescribed therefor by statute, and it appearing from (non-military affidavit)

§ 21.90   DOMESTIC RELATIONS   Ch. 21

(testimony given in open court) that the defendant is not in the military service of the United States

Defendant's Appearance and Non-answer

and the defendant having appeared by _____, Esq. and plaintiff's verified complaint having been duly served upon the attorney for defendant and the defendant not having answered although the time to do so has fully expired

Defendant's Appearance, Answer and Withdrawal of Answer

and the defendant having appeared by _____, Esq. and plaintiff's verified complaint having been duly served upon the attorney for defendant and the defendant having answered the complaint and having thereafter (by written stipulation) (in open court) withdrawn (his) (her) answer

Defendant's Appearance and Answer—Contested Action

and the defendant having appeared by _____, Esq. and plaintiff's verified complaint having been duly served upon the attorney for defendant and defendant having answered the complaint

Inquest Held

and the plaintiff having applied (if defendant has appeared insert: on due notice to defendant's attorney) to the court for judgment for the relief demanded in the complaint and the matter having been set down for trial on the ___ day of _____ 19__, and the plaintiff having on that day appeared before me and presented written and oral proof of service and in support of the essential allegations of the complaint, and such proof having been heard and considered by me, I decide and find as stated in the separate FINDINGS OF FACT AND CONCLUSIONS OF LAW of even date herewith

Contested Trial—Non-jury

and the matter having come on for trial before me on the following days _____ and the parties having appeared before me and presented their written and oral proof, and the court having made and filed its memorandum decision dated

Contested Trial—Jury

and the matter having come on before the undersigned and a jury on the following days

_____ and the parties having presented their written and oral proof before the court and jury, and the jury having been instructed to answer each of the following questions "Yes" or "No"

1.

2.

and having after due deliberation, made written answers to said questions as follows:

Question 1 _____; Question 2 _____

NOW, on motion of _____, Esq. attorney for the (plaintiff) (defendant) it is

Adjudged that the marriage between _____, plaintiff, and _____, defendant, is dissolved by reason of (State ground or grounds in the language set forth above); and it is further

Separation

Adjudged that _____, plaintiff be and (s)he hereby is separated from the bed and board of _____, defendant by reason of _____ (State ground or grounds in the language set forth above); and it is further

Annulment

Adjudged that the marriage contract heretofore existing between _____, plaintiff, and _____, defendant, is annulled because of the fraud of the defendant; and it is further

Declaration of Nullity of Void Marriage

Adjudged that the marriage entered into between _____, plaintiff, and _____, defendant, on the ___ day of _____ 19__ is declared null and void because of the prior subsisting marriage of the defendant; and it is further

Custody of Children

Adjudged that (plaintiff) (defendant) is awarded custody of the infant issue of the marriage to wit:

    born _____ -19__

    born _____ -19__

    born _____ -19__;

and it is further

Visitation

Ordered and Adjudged that (plaintiff) (defendant) may have visitation with the _____ (number) infant children away from the custodial residence during the following periods:

§ 21.90　　　　　DOMESTIC RELATIONS　　　　　Ch. 21

(a) on Saturday or Sunday of each week between the hours of __ a.m. and __ p.m., provided (defendant) (plaintiff) shall notify (defendant) (plaintiff) not later than Wednesday of each week of the day selected;

(b) on the following holiday days, between the hours of __ a.m. and __ p.m., in odd numbered years (specify holidays);

(c) on the following holiday days between the hours of __ a.m. and __ p.m., in even numbered years (specify holidays); and

(d) for a period of __ consecutive calendar weeks during the summer recess from school beginning on Sunday of the first week selected, provided (defendant) (plaintiff) shall notify (plaintiff) (defendant) not later than June 10th in each year of the particular weeks selected; and it is further

Family Court Order Continued

Ordered and Adjudged that the order made the _____ day of _____ 19__ by the Family Court of the State of New York, County of _____ in the proceeding bearing Docket number _____ is continued, and a copy of this judgment shall be served by plaintiff's attorney upon the Clerk of said Court within 10 days after the date hereof; and it is further

Findings as to Pro Rata Share

and it is further Adjudged that:

(a) The basic child support obligation in this case is $____ per _____; [*plus, if applicable, expenses for child care, health care not covered by insurance, and educational or other extraordinary expenses*]; and

[2](b) The non-custodial parent's pro rata share of the basic child support obligation is neither unjust nor inappropriate.

OR

[3](b) Upon consideration of the following factors specified in § 240(1-b)(f):

　　　　　　　　　　　　　　　　　　　　　　　　　　　　；

the non-custodial parent's pro rata share of the basic child support obligation is unjust or inappropriate in that:

　　　　　　　　　　　　　　　　　　　　　　　　　　　　；

2. Only one of the three alternative subparagraphs (b) will be appropriate in each case; delete the inapplicable paragraphs.

3. Only one of the three alternative subparagraphs (b) will be appropriate in each case; delete the inapplicable paragraphs.

OR

⁴(b) The parties have voluntarily agreed to child support for the child(ren) *[names]* payable by _____ to _____ in the amount of $____ per _____, such stipulation reciting, in compliance with DRL § 240(1–b):

The parties have been advised of the provisions of DRL § 240(1–b);

The unrepresented party, if any, has received a copy of the child support standards chart promulgated by the commissioner of Social Services pursuant to Social Services Law § 111–i;

The basic child support obligation as defined in DRL § 240(1–b) presumptively results in the correct amount of child support to be awarded;

The basic child support obligation in this case is $____ per _____ *[plus, if applicable, expenses for child care, health care not covered by insurance, and educational or other extraordinary expenses]*; and

⁵(c) The amount of child support agreed to therein conforms to the basic child support obligation.

OR

⁶(c) The amount of child support agreed to therein deviates from the basic child support obligation, for the following reasons:

_____;

And the Court having found the parties' agreement to deviate from the basic child support obligation is approved for the following reasons: *[provide reasons, see DRL § 240(1–b)(f)]*

and it is further

Maintenance Payable to (Plaintiff) (Defendant)

Ordered and Adjudged that the (defendant) (plaintiff) shall pay to the (plaintiff) (defendant) (third party _____) by check or money order drawn to (his) (her) order and forwarded on _____ (day) of each week commencing with _____ (date) 19__, the first _____ (day) after the date of this judgment, to the (defendant) (plaintiff) (third party _____) at (his) (her) residence or at such other place as (he) (she) may designate in writing, the sum of $_____ per week

---

4. Only one of the three alternative sub-paragraphs (b) will be appropriate in each case; delete the inapplicable paragraphs.

5. Only one of the two sub-paragraphs (c) will be appropriate to the agreement or stipulation; delete the inapplicable provisions.

6. Only one of the two sub-paragraphs (c) will be appropriate to the agreement or stipulation; delete the inapplicable provisions.

as maintenance, which sum is inclusive of all obligations of (defendant) (plaintiff) for the maintenance of (plaintiff) (defendant) except extraordinary medical or dental expense (if exclusive possession of marital premises is awarded, add: and extraordinary repairs of marital premises; consider requirement for purchase of insurance policy); and it is further

Child Support Payable to (Plaintiff) (Defendant)

Ordered and Adjudged that (defendant) (plaintiff) shall pay to (defendant) (plaintiff) (third party _____) by check or money order drawn to (his) (her) order and forwarded on _____ (day) of each week commencing with _____ (date) 19__, the first _____ (day) after the date of this judgment, to (defendant) (plaintiff) (third party _____) at (his) (her) residence or at such other place as (he) (she) may designate in writing, the sum of $_____ per week per child for the support of the child(ren), making a total sum of $_____ per week; and it is further

Ordered and Adjudged that (defendant) (plaintiff) shall pay to (defendant) (plaintiff) (third party _____) as and for child care expenses the sum of $_____ by check or money order drawn to (his) (her) order as follows:

; and it is further

Ordered and Adjudged that (defendant) (plaintiff) shall pay to (defendant) (plaintiff) (third party _____) the sum of $_____, as and for future reasonable health care expenses not covered by insurance as follows:

; and it is further

Ordered and Adjudged that (defendant) (plaintiff) shall pay to (defendant) (plaintiff) (third party _____) the sum of $_____, as and for (present) (future) (post-secondary) (private) (special) (enriched) education for the child(ren) as follows:

Exclusive Possession of Real Property

Ordered and Adjudged that (plaintiff) (defendant) is awarded exclusive possession of the marital premises to wit:

(set forth either street address, or if there is no street number, the metes and bounds description)

until the youngest child is 21, or sooner emancipated and (plaintiff) (defendant) shall within _____ days after service upon (him) (her) of a copy of this judgment with notice of entry remove (himself) (herself) therefrom and upon proof by affidavit of (plaintiff) (defendant) and (his) (her) attorney of (defendant's) (plaintiff's) failure to remove from said premises within the time herein provided, a writ of assistance shall issue without further notice to (defendant) (plaintiff); and it is further

Equitable Distribution

Ordered and Adjudged that the marital property shall be distributed as follows: (include disposition of property upon termination of exclusive possession of real property, if any.); and it is further

Counsel Fee

Ordered and Adjudged that the defendant shall pay to the plaintiff, by check or money order, forwarded to (him) (her) at (his) (her) (residence) (the office of (his) (her) attorney) within ___ days after service upon him of a copy of this judgment with notice of entry, as and for counsel fee and expenses, the sum of $_____; and it is further

Separation Agreement or Stipulation

Ordered and Adjudged that the (separation agreement) (stipulation) entered into between the parties on the _____ day of _____ 19__, a copy of which is attached to and incorporated in this judgment by reference, shall (not survive and shall be merged) (survive and shall not be merged) in this judgment, and the parties hereby are directed to comply with every legally enforceable term and provision of such (separation agreement) (stipulation) including any provision to submit an appropriate issue to arbitration before a single arbitrator, as if such term or provision were set forth in its entirety herein, and the court retains jurisdiction of the matter concurrently with the Family Court for the purpose of specifically enforcing such of the provisions of that (separation agreement) (stipulation) as are capable of specific enforcement, to the extent permitted by law, and of making such further judgment with respect to maintenance, support, custody or visitation as it finds appropriate under the circumstances existing at the time application for that purpose is made to it, or both; and it is further

Permission to Resume Prior Surname

Ordered and Adjudged that (plaintiff) (defendant) is authorized to resume the use of her maiden name or other former surname, to wit _____; and it is further

Money Judgment for Arrears

Ordered and Adjudged that plaintiff, _____, residing at _____ recover from _____ residing at _____ the sum of $_____, as arrears due under the order of this court, (Family Court, _____ County) dated _____ 19__ and that plaintiff have execution therefor.

§ 21.90   DOMESTIC RELATIONS   Ch. 21

Signature

ENTER (IN _____ COUNTY)
Justice Supreme Court

§ 21.91 Forms—Referee's Report on Findings of Fact and Conclusions of Law

REFEREE'S REPORT—FINDINGS OF FACT AND CONCLUSIONS OF LAW[1]

SUPREME COURT OF THE
STATE OF NEW YORK
COUNTY OF
TITLE OF ACTION
Cal. No.
Index No.

Nature of Action—Divorce

The plaintiff having brought this action for a judgment of absolute divorce by reason of

(Insert one or more of the following grounds:)

- the cruel and inhuman treatment of the plaintiff by the defendant
- the abandonment of the plaintiff by the defendant for a period of one or more years
- the confinement of defendant in prison for a period of three or more consecutive years after the marriage of plaintiff and defendant
- the commission by the defendant of adultery
- the plaintiff and defendant having lived apart after the granting of a judgment of separation for a period of one or more years
- the plaintiff and defendant having lived separate and apart pursuant to a written agreement for a period of one or more years

Nature of Action—Separation

The plaintiff having brought this action for a judgment of separation by reason of

§ 21.91
1. Appendix B, Uniform Trial Court Rules. These provisions are to be modified or deleted as may be necessary to conform to the law and facts in a particular action. Bracketed portions indicate alternative provisions. 22 NYCRR § 202.50.

[*Insert one or more of the following grounds:*]
- the cruel and inhuman treatment of the plaintiff by the defendant
- the abandonment of the plaintiff by the defendant
- the neglect or refusal of defendant to provide for plaintiff
- the commission by defendant of adultery
- the confinement of defendant in prison for a period of three or more consecutive years after the marriage of plaintiff and defendant

Nature of Action—Annulment

The plaintiff having brought this action for a judgment of annulment by reason of the fraud of the defendant in inducing the marriage [*or other grounds, see § 140 DRL*]

Nature of Action—Declaration of the Nullity of a Void Marriage

The plaintiff having brought this action for a judgment declaring the nullity of (his) (her) marriage to the defendant by reason of the prior subsisting marriage of the defendant

Service of Process

and the summons bearing the notation ("Action for a Divorce") ("Action for a Separation") ("Action to Annul a Marriage") ("Action to Declare the Nullity of a Void Marriage") and a statement of any ancillary relief demanded having been duly served upon the defendant (personally within this State) (personally without this State by publication)

Defendant's Non-appearance

and the defendant not having appeared within the time prescribed therefor by statute, and it appearing from (non-military affidavit) (testimony given in open court) that the defendant is not in the military service of the United States

Defendant's Appearance and Non-answer

and the defendant having appeared by _____, Esq. and plaintiff's verified complaint having been duly served upon the attorney for defendant and the defendant not having answered although the time to do so has fully expired

Defendant's Appearance, Answer and Withdrawal of Answer

and the defendant having appeared by _____, Esq. and plaintiff's verified complaint having been duly served upon the attorney for defendant and the defendant having answered the complaint and

§ 21.91 DOMESTIC RELATIONS Ch. 21

having thereafter (by written stipulation) (in open court) withdrawn (his) (her) answer

Defendant's Appearance and Answer—Contested Action

and the defendant having appeared by _____, Esq. and plaintiff's verified complaint having been duly served upon the attorney for defendant and defendant having answered the complaint

Inquest Held

and the plaintiff having applied (if defendant has appeared insert: on due notice to defendant's attorney)

to the court for judgment for the relief demanded in the complaint and the matter having been set down for trial on the __ day of _____ 19__, and the plaintiff having on that day appeared before me and presented written and oral proof of service and in support of the essential allegations of the complaint, and such proof having been heard and considered by me, I decide and find as follows:

Contested Trial—Non-jury

and the matter having come on for trial before me on the following days _____ and the parties having appeared before me and presented their written and oral proof, and the court having made and filed its memorandum decision dated

Contested Trial—Jury

and the matter having come on before the undersigned and a jury on the following days _____ and the parties having presented their written and oral proof before the court and jury, and the jury having been instructed to answer each of the following questions "Yes" or "No"

1.
2.

and having after due deliberation, made written answers to said questions as follows:

Question 1 _____; Question 2 _____

Age of Parties—No Guardian Needed

FIRST: That plaintiff and defendant were both over the age of 18 when this action was commenced.

Age of Parties—Under Age Party

FIRST: That (plaintiff) (defendant) was over the age of 18 years when this action commenced and (defendant) (plaintiff) was then and now is under 18, to wit: __ years of age and appears herein by

_____, (parent and natural guardian) (duly appointed as guardian by order dated _____ 19__).

Residence—One Year

SECOND: That at the time of the commencement of this action and for a continuous period of at least one year immediately preceding such commencement (plaintiff) (defendant) resided in this State and (the parties were married in the State) (the parties have resided in this State as husband and wife) (the cause occurred in this State).

Residence—Two Years

SECOND: That for a continuous period of at least two years immediately preceding commencement of this action (plaintiff) (defendant) resided in this State.

Residence—No Required Time

SECOND: That at the time of the commencement of this action both plaintiff and defendant resided in this State and the cause occurred in this State.

Marriage

THIRD: That plaintiff and defendant were married on _____, 19__ in

No Children

FOURTH: That there is no issue of this marriage.

Children

FOURTH: That there are __ children (born of) (adopted by) the parties to this marriage, whose names and dates of birth are as follows:

Cruelty

FIFTH: That at the following times, none of which is earlier than five years before the date of commencement of this action, defendant committed the following acts which endangered the plaintiff's (physical) (mental) (physical and mental well-being) and rendered it (unsafe) (improper) (unsafe and improper) for plaintiff to continue to reside with defendant.

(Spell out in letter subparagraphs, the acts or omissions to act for which there is proof in the minutes).

Abandonment

FIFTH: That the defendant without cause or justification and without plaintiff's consent on the __ day of _____ 19__ abandoned plaintiff with intent not to return and has been wilfully and continuously absent from the home of the parties since (in divorce actions add: for a period of one year prior to the commencement of this action).

Confinement to Prison

FIFTH: (a) That after the marriage of plaintiff and defendant, defendant was confined in prison for a period of three or more consecutive years, to wit: that defendant was confined in _____ prison on the __ day of _____ 19__ and remained confined until the __ day of _____ 19__; and

(b) not more than five years elapsed between the date the cause of action arose and the date of commencement of this action.

Adultery

FIFTH: (a) That on the __ day of _____ 19__ at premises _____ the defendant committed adultery with _____; and

(b) not more than five years elapsed between the date of said adultery and the date of commencement of this action.

Neglect to Support

FIFTH: (a) That defendant has (neglected) (refused) to provide for the support of plaintiff since the __ day of _____ 19__, and has not done so; and

(b) not more than five years elapsed between the date the cause of action arose and the date of commencement of this action.

Living Apart Under Separation Decree

FIFTH: (a) That a judgment separating the parties was entered on the __ day of _____ 19__ by the _____ Court of the State of _____; and

(b) that the parties have lived apart pursuant to said judgment for a period of one year after the granting of such judgment; and

(c) that the plaintiff has substantially performed all the terms and conditions of such judgment.

Living Apart Under Separation Agreement

FIFTH: (a) That the plaintiff and defendant entered into a written agreement of separation, which they subscribed and acknowledged on the __ day of _____ 19__ in the form required to entitle a deed to be recorded; and

(b) that the (agreement) (a memorandum of said agreement) was filed in the office of the Clerk of the County of _____, wherein (plaintiff) (defendant) resides on the __ day of _____ 19__; and

(c) that the parties have lived separate and apart for a period of one year after the execution of said agreement; and

(d) that the plaintiff has substantially performed all the terms and conditions of such agreement.

Annulment for Fraud

FIFTH: (a) That prior to the marriage of the parties the defendant represented to plaintiff that _____ (state representation); and

(b) that said representation was false; and

(c) that said representation was made to induce plaintiff to enter into the marriage; and

(d) that plaintiff believed and relied upon said representation, and would not have entered into the marriage had the representation not been made or had plaintiff known that defendant did not intend to _____ (refer to representation); and

(e) that defendant after the marriage refused to (refer to representation); and

(f) that plaintiff has not cohabited with defendant since discovery of the falsity of the representation; and

(g) that three years have not elapsed since discovery of the facts constituting the fraud.

[*for other grounds see § 140 DRL*].

Declaration of Nullity of Void Marriage

FIFTH: (a) That prior to the marriage to plaintiff and on the __ day of _____ 19__, defendant married _____ (name) in _____ (place); and

(b) that on the date of the marriage of plaintiff and defendant the marriage between defendant and _____ (name) had not been terminated by the judgment of any court; and

(c) on the date of the marriage of plaintiff and defendant, defendant's prior spouse was alive and the prior marriage of defendant was valid and subsisting.

Arrears Due Under Temporary Order

SIXTH: (a) That by order of this court (or by order of the Family Court, _____ County) dated the __ day of _____ 19__, defendant was required to pay to plaintiff as and for maintenance and child support, the sum of $_____ per week and as counsel fee, the sum of $_____; and

§ 21.91   DOMESTIC RELATIONS   Ch. 21

(b) that there became due under said order through the week of _____ 19__, the total sum of $_____, no part of which has been paid except $_____; and

(c) that defendant is in arrears under said order in the total sum of $_____ for said period.

Separate and Marital Property

SEVENTH: (a) That the following is separate property owned by plaintiff:

(b) that the following is separate property owned by defendant:

; and

(c) that the following is marital property to be disposed of equitably pursuant to DRL § 236B(5):

(List findings required under DRL § 236(5)(d)(1–10))

Custody

EIGHTH: That the children of the marriage now reside with (plaintiff) (defendant).

Visitation

NINTH: That the (plaintiff) (defendant) is entitled to visitation with the infant child(ren) away from the custodial residence.

Exclusive Occupancy

TENTH: That the parties hereto are the owners of premises known as _____ (P.O. address).

Maintenance (pursuant to DRL § 236B(6))

ELEVENTH: (a) That plaintiff is (not) employed and is earning $*(net)* per week; and

(b) that defendant is (not) employed and is earning $*(net)* per week; and

(c) that (plaintiff) (defendant) now receives $_____ per _____ pursuant to an outstanding _____ Court order; and

(d) that (plaintiff) (defendant) now requires $_____ per week for maintenance; and

(List findings required under DRL § 236B(6)(a)(1–10)); and

(e) that the parties have entered into (a stipulation) (or/and agreement) dated _____ wherein (plaintiff) (defendant) agrees to accept and (plaintiff) (defendant) agrees to pay $_____ per week as maintenance (and $_____ per week per child as and for child support, which (stipulation) (agreement) includes a provision stating

Ch. 21 **REFEREE'S REPORT** **§ 21.91**

that the parties have been advised of the provisions of DRL § 240(1–b)(h).) That the terms of the agreement were fair and reasonable at the time of the making of the agreement and are not unconscionable at the time of the entry of judgment herein.

(f) Neither of the parties seeks equitable distribution of the marital property.

Child Support

TWELFTH: (a) The award of child support in accordance with DRL § 240(1–b) is based on the following findings:

    (i) the children of the marriage entitled to receive parental support are: [*state names and dates of birth*];

    (ii) the income of the plaintiff, who is the (custodial) (non-custodial) parent, is $___ per year;

    (iii) the income of the defendant, who is the (custodial) (non-custodial) parent, is $___ per year;

    (iv) the applicable child support percentage is ___%;

    (v) the basic child support obligation is $___ per (week) (month) [*plus, if applicable, expenses for child care, health care not covered by insurance, and educational or other extraordinary expenses*]

    (vi) the non-custodial parent's pro rata share of the basic child support obligation is calculated as follows:

        A. $___ per (week) (month) representing ___% of the combined parental income under $80,000 per year; plus

        B. $___ per (week) (month), representing ___% of the combined parental income, if any, over $80,000 per year;

        C. ___% of future reasonable health care expenses not covered by insurance; [*delete if inapplicable*]

        D. ___% of the reasonable child care expenses; [*delete if inapplicable*]

        E. ___% of educational or other extraordinary expenses; [*delete if inapplicable*]

[2](b) The non-custodial parent's pro rata share of the basic child support obligation is neither unjust nor inappropriate.

---

2. Only one of the three alternative subparagraphs (b) will be appropriate; delete the inapplicable provisions.

§ 21.91 DOMESTIC RELATIONS Ch. 21

OR

[3](b) Upon consideration of the following factors specified in Section 140(1–b)(f) of the Domestic Relations Law:

the non-custodial parent's pro rata share of the basic child support obligation is unjust or inappropriate in that:

;

OR

[4](b) The parties have entered into a (stipulation) (agreement) dated _____ wherein (plaintiff) (defendant) agrees to pay $____ per (week) (month) for child support, such (stipulation) (agreement) reciting, in compliance with DRL § 240(1–b)(h), that:

The parties have been advised of the provisions of Section 240(1–b) of the Domestic Relations Law;

The unrepresented party, if any, has received a copy of the child support standards chart promulgated by the commissioner of Social Services pursuant to Social Services Law § 111–i;

The basic child support obligation as defined in DRL Section 240(1–b) presumptively results in the correct amount of child support to be awarded;

The basic child support obligation in this case is $____ per _____; [*plus, if applicable, expenses for child care, health care not covered by insurance, and educational or other extraordinary expenses*]; and

[5](c) The amount of child support agreed to therein conforms to the basic child support obligation.

OR

[6](c) The amount of child support agreed to therein deviates from the basic child support obligation, and the parties' reasons for not providing that amount are

;

And the court having found the parties' agreement to deviate from the basic child support obligation is approved for the following reasons: [*State reasons, see DRL § 240(1–b)(f)*]

3. Only one of the three alternative subparagraphs (b) will be appropriate; delete the inapplicable provisions.

4. Only one of the three alternative subparagraphs (b) will be appropriate; delete the inapplicable provisions.

5. Only one of the two alternative subparagraphs (c) will be appropriate; delete the inapplicable provisions.

6. Only one of the two alternative subparagraphs (c) will be appropriate; delete the inapplicable provisions.

(d) that the amount of combined parental income in excess of $80,000 is $_____. The amount of child support based upon parental income exceeding $80,000 is $_____.

(e) that the custodial parent is (working) (seeking work) (receiving (elementary) (secondary) (higher) (vocational) education which will lead to employment) and incurring child care expenses as a result thereof. The following are the reasonable child care expenses to be prorated in the same proportion as each parent's income is to the combined parental income:

(f) that the following are the future reasonable health care expenses of the child not covered by insurance to be prorated in the same proportion as each parent's income is to the combined parental income:

(g) that under the circumstances of the case and of the respective parties and in the best interests of the child, and as justice requires, the (present) (future) provision of (post-secondary) (private) (special) (enriched) education for the child(ren) is appropriate.

(h) that the parties have entered into (a stipulation) (or/and agreement) dated _____ wherein (plaintiff) (defendant) agrees to pay $_____ per week per child for child support and now receives $_____ per week pursuant to an outstanding court order, which (stipulation) (agreement) includes a provision stating that the parties have been advised of the provisions of DRL § 240(1-b)(h).

Counsel Fees

THIRTEENTH: That the attorney for the (plaintiff) (defendant) is entitled to counsel fees.

Jurisdiction Obtained

FOURTEENTH: That jurisdiction as required by Section 230 of the Domestic Relations Law has been obtained.

FIFTEENTH: That plaintiff has filed a verified statement that (he) (she) has taken all steps solely within (his) (her) power to remove all barriers to defendant's remarriage following the (annulment) (divorce).

Plaintiff Entitled to Judgment

SIXTEENTH: That plaintiff is entitled to judgment (of divorce) (of separation) (of annulment) (declaring the nullity of the marriage) and granting the incidental relief awarded (herein) (in the JUDGMENT signed this date).

Dated: New York, New York _____ day of _____, 19__.

§ 21.91   DOMESTIC RELATIONS   Ch. 21

_____
_____ Referee

§ 21.92   Forms—Matrimonial Judgment Entered Upon Referee's Report

MATRIMONIAL JUDGMENT ENTERED UPON REFEREE'S REPORT[1]

At the Supreme Court, _____ County,
held at the courthouse at _____,
New York, on the _____ day of
_____,
19__.

PRESENT:
HON. (Justice Supreme Court)
TITLE OF ACTION

The issues in this action having been referred to a referee to hear and report, and the referee having submitted his report,

NOW, on motion of _____, Esq., attorney for the (plaintiff) (defendant), it is

ORDERED, that the Referee's Report is confirmed; and it is further

Adjudged that the marriage between _____, plaintiff, and _____, defendant, is dissolved by reason of _____ (State ground or grounds in the language set forth above); and it is further

Separation

Adjudged that _____, plaintiff be and (s)he hereby is separated from the bed and board of _____, defendant by reason of _____ (State ground or grounds in the language set forth above); and it is further

Annulment

Adjudged that the marriage contract heretofore existing between _____, plaintiff, and _____, defendant, is annulled because of the fraud of the defendant; and it is further

§ 21.92
1. Appendix B, Uniform Trial Court Rules. These provisions are to be modified or deleted as may be necessary to conform to the law and facts in a particular action. Parenthesized portions indicate alternative provisions. 22 NYCRR § 202.50.

Declaration of Nullity of Void Marriage

Adjudged that the marriage entered into between _____, plaintiff, and _____, defendant, on the __ day of _____ 19__ is declared null and void because of the prior subsisting marriage of the defendant; and it is further

Custody of Children

Adjudged that (plaintiff) (defendant) is awarded custody of the infant issue of the marriage to wit:

                                                                    born _____ 19__

                                                                    born _____ 19__

                                                                    born _____ 19__

and it is further

Visitation

Ordered and Adjudged that (plaintiff) (defendant) may have visitation with the _____ (number) infant children away from the custodial residence during the following periods:

(a) on Saturday or Sunday of each week between the hours of __ a.m. and __ p.m., provided (defendant) (plaintiff) shall notify (defendant) (plaintiff) not later than Wednesday of each week of the day selected;

(b) on the following holiday days, between the hours of __ a.m. and __ p.m., in odd numbered years (specify holidays);

(c) on the following holiday days between the hours of __ a.m. and __ p.m. in even numbered years (specify holidays); and

(d) for a period of __ consecutive calendar weeks during the summer recess from school beginning on Sunday of the first week selected, provided (defendant) (plaintiff) shall notify (plaintiff) (defendant) not later than June 10th in each year of the particular weeks selected; and it is further

Family Court Order Continued

Ordered and Adjudged that the order made the __ day of _____ 19__ by the Family Court of the State of New York, County of _____ in the proceeding bearing Docket number _____ is continued, and a copy of this judgment shall be served by plaintiff's attorney upon the Clerk of said Court within 10 days after the date hereof; and it is further

Findings as to Pro Rata Share

and it is further Adjudged that:

§ 21.92   DOMESTIC RELATIONS   Ch. 21

(a) The basic child support obligation in this case is $___ per _____; [plus, if applicable, expenses for child care, health care not covered by insurance, and educational or other extraordinary expenses]; and

[2](b) The non-custodial parent's pro rata share of the basic child support obligation is neither unjust nor inappropriate.

OR

[3](b) Upon consideration of the following factors specified in Section 140(1–b)(f) of the Domestic Relations Law:

the non-custodial parent's pro rata share of the basic child support obligation is unjust or inappropriate in that:

;

OR

[4](b) The parties have voluntarily agreed to child support for the child(ren) *[names]* payable by _____ to _____ in the amount of $___ per _____, such stipulation reciting, in compliance with DRL § 240(1–b):

The parties have been advised of the provisions of D.R.L. § 240(1–b);

The unrepresented party, if any, has received a copy of the child support standards chart promulgated by the Commissioner of Social Services pursuant to Social Services Law § 111–i;

The basic child support obligation in this case is $___ per _____; and

The basic child support obligation as defined in DRL § 240(1–b) presumptively results in the correct amount of child support to be awarded;

The basic child support obligation in this case is $___ per _____ [plus, if applicable, expenses for child care, health care not covered by insurance, and educational or other extraordinary expenses]; and

[5](c) The amount of child support agreed to therein conforms to the basic child support obligation.

   2. Only one of the three alternative sub-paragraphs (b) will be appropriate, in each case; delete the inapplicable provisions.

   3. Only one of the three alternative sub-paragraphs (b) will be appropriate, in each case; delete the inapplicable provisions.

   4. Only one of the three alternative sub-paragraphs (b) will be appropriate, in each case; delete the inapplicable provisions.

   5. Only one of the two sub-paragraphs (c) will be appropriate to the agreement or stipulation; delete the inapplicable provisions.

Ch. 21   JUDGMENT UPON REFEREE'S REPORT   § 21.92

OR

⁶(c) The amount of child support agreed to therein deviates from the basic child support obligation, for the following reasons:

And the Court having found the parties' agreement to deviate from the basic child support obligation is approved for the following reasons: [State reasons, see DRL § 240(1–b)(f)]

and it is further

Maintenance Payable to (Plaintiff) (Defendant)

Ordered and Adjudged that the (defendant) (plaintiff) shall pay to the (plaintiff) (defendant) (third party _____) by check or money order drawn to (his) (her) order and forwarded on _____ (day) of each week commencing with _____ (date) 19__, the first _____ (day) after the date of this judgment, to the (defendant) (plaintiff) (third party _____) at (his) (her) residence or at such other place as (he) (she) may designate in writing, the sum of $_____ per week as maintenance, which sum is inclusive of all obligations of (defendant) (plaintiff) for the maintenance of (plaintiff) (defendant) except extraordinary medical or dental expense

(if exclusive possession of marital premises is awarded add: and extraordinary repairs of marital premises; consider requirement for purchase of insurance policy); and it is further

Child Support Payable to (Plaintiff) (Defendant)

Ordered and Adjudged that (defendant) (plaintiff) shall pay to (defendant) (plaintiff) (third party _____) by check or money order drawn to (his) (her) order and forwarded on _____ (day) of each week commencing with _____ (date) 19__, the first _____ (day) after the date of this judgment, to (defendant) (plaintiff) (third party _____) at (his) (her) residence or at such other place as (he) (she) may designate in writing, the sum of $_____ per week per child for the support of the child(ren) making a total sum of $_____ per week; and it is further

Ordered and Adjudged that (defendant) (plaintiff) shall pay to (defendant) (plaintiff) (third party _____) as and for child care expenses the sum of $_____ by check or money order drawn to (his) (her) order as follows:

; and it is further

Ordered and Adjudged that (defendant) (plaintiff) shall pay to (defendant) (plaintiff) (third party _____) the sum of $_____, as and for future reasonable health care expenses not covered by insurance as follows:

6. Only one of the two sub-paragraphs (c) will be appropriate to the agreement or stipulation; delete the inapplicable provisions.

; and it is further

Ordered and Adjudged that (defendant) (plaintiff) shall pay to (defendant) (plaintiff) (third party _____) the sum of $_____, as and for (present) (future) (post-secondary) (private) (special) (enriched) education for the child(ren) as follows:

Exclusive Possession of Real Property

Ordered and Adjudged that (plaintiff) (defendant) is awarded exclusive possession of the marital premises to wit:

(set forth either street address, or if there is no street number, the metes and bounds description)

until the youngest child is 21, or sooner emancipated and (plaintiff) (defendant) shall within __ days after service upon (him) (her) of a copy of this judgment with notice of entry remove (himself) (herself) therefrom and upon proof by affidavit of (plaintiff) (defendant) and (his) (her) attorney of (defendant's) (plaintiff's) failure to remove from said premises within the time herein provided, a writ of assistance shall issue without further notice to (defendant) (plaintiff); and it is further

Equitable Distribution

Ordered and Adjudged that the marital property shall be distributed as follows:

(include disposition of property upon termination of exclusive possession of real property, if any); and it is further

Counsel Fee

Ordered and Adjudged that the defendant shall pay to the plaintiff, by check or money order, forwarded to (him) (her) at (his) (her) (residence) (the office of (his) (her) attorney) within __ days after service upon him of a copy of this judgment with notice of entry, as and for counsel fee and expenses, the sum of $_____; and it is further

Separation Agreement or Stipulation

Ordered and Adjudged that the (separation agreement) (stipulation) entered into between the parties on the _____ day of _____, 19__, a copy of which is attached to and incorporated in this judgment by reference, shall (not survive and shall be merged) (survive and shall not be merged) in this judgment, and the parties hereby are directed to comply with every legally enforceable term and provision of such (separation agreement) (stipulation) including any provision to submit an appropriate issue to arbitration before a single arbitrator, as if such term or provision were set forth in its entirety herein, and the court retains jurisdiction of the matter concurrently with the Family Court for the purpose of specifically enforcing such of the provisions of that (separation agreement) (stipulation) as are capable of specific enforcement, to the extent permitted by law, and of making such further judgment with respect to maintenance, support, custody or visitation as it finds appropriate under the circumstances existing at the time application for that purpose is made to it, or both; and it is further

Permission to Resume Prior Surname

Ordered and Adjudged that (plaintiff) (defendant) is authorized to resume the use of her maiden name or other former surname, to wit _____; and it is further

Money Judgment for Arrears

Ordered and Adjudged that plaintiff, _____, residing at _____ recover from _____ residing at _____, the sum of $_____, as arrears due under the order of this court, (Family Court, _____ County) dated _____ 19__ and that plaintiff have execution therefor.

Signature

            ENTER (IN _____ COUNTY)
            Justice Supreme Court

Chapter 22

GUARDIANSHIP

by
Miriam R. Adelman

Table of Sections

22.1	Scope Note.
22.2	Strategy.
22.3	Checklists.
22.4	Prior Law—Generally.
22.5	___ Role of Committees and Conservators.
22.6	___ Problems Encountered.
22.7	___ Impact of *Matter of Grinker (Rose)*.
22.8	Legislative Purpose of Mental Hygiene Law Article 81.
22.9	Definitions.
22.10	Summary.
22.11	Power to Appoint Guardian—Generally.
22.12	___ Elements.
22.13	___ Incapacity.
22.14	___ Primary Considerations.
22.15	___ Jurisdiction.
22.16	___ Venue.
22.17	___ Standing to Commence Proceeding.
22.18	___ Summary.
22.19	Proceeding to Appoint Guardian.
22.20	___ Time and Method of Service of Notice.
22.21	___ Persons Entitled to Notice.
22.22	___ Notice Requirements.
22.23	___ Petition.
22.24	___ Summary.
22.25	Court Evaluator—Persons Eligible for Appointment.
22.26	___ Duties.
22.27	___ Compensation.
22.28	___ Appointment of Counsel for the Alleged Incapacitated Person.
22.29	___ Summary.
22.30	Hearing and Order—An Overview.
22.31	___ Procedure.
22.32	___ Presence of Person Alleged to be Incapacitated.
22.33	___ Evidence.
22.34	___ Findings of the Court.
22.35	___ ___ Voluntary Appointment.
22.36	___ ___ Personal Needs.
22.37	___ ___ Property Management.
22.38	___ Dispositional Alternatives.
22.39	___ Award of Counsel Fees to Petitioner.

Ch. 22   **GUARDIANSHIP**

22.40 ____ Person to be Appointed Guardian.
22.41 ____ Priority and Criteria for Appointment.
22.42 ____ Requirement of Bond.
22.43 ____ Designation of Clerk and Issuance of Commission.
22.44 ____ Summary.
22.45 Role of Guardian—Overview.
22.46 ____ Duties.
22.47 ____ Powers; Property Management.
22.48 ____ Substituted Judgment.
22.49 ____ Petition for Authorization to Transfer Property.
22.50 ____ ____ Notice of Application.
22.51 ____ ____ Considerations of Court.
22.52 ____ ____ Granting Petition.
22.53 ____ Powers; Personal Needs.
22.54 ____ Effect of Appointment on Incapacitated Person.
22.55 ____ Summary.
22.56 Provisional Remedies.
22.57 ____ Temporary Guardian.
22.58 ____ Injunction and Temporary Restraining Orders.
22.59 ____ Notice of Pendency.
22.60 ____ Summary.
22.61 Compensation of Guardian.
22.62 Reports by Guardian.
22.63 ____ Initial Report.
22.64 ____ Annual Report.
22.65 ____ Examination; Court Examiners.
22.66 ____ Intermediate and Final Reports.
22.67 ____ Decree Upon Approving Accounts.
22.68 ____ Summary.
22.69 Removal, Discharge and Resignation of Guardian—Removal.
22.70 ____ Discharge or Modification of Powers.
22.71 ____ Resignation or Suspension of Powers.
22.72 ____ Vacancy in Office; Appointment of Interim and Successor Guardians.
22.73 ____ Standby Guardian.
22.74 ____ Summary.
22.75 Education Requirements—Generally.
22.76 ____ Guardian Training.
22.77 ____ Court Evaluator Training.
22.78 ____ Court Examiner Training.
22.79 ____ Compliance.
22.80 ____ Summary.
22.81 Proceedings to Discover Property Withheld.
22.82 ____ Petition and Supporting Papers.
22.83 ____ Grounds For Inquiry.
22.84 ____ Answer.
22.85 ____ Trial.
22.86 ____ Decree.
22.87 ____ Summary.
22.88 Drafting Checklists.
22.89 ____ Order to Show Cause.

22.90	____ Petition.
22.91	____ Court Evaluator's Report.
22.92	____ Order and Judgment.
22.93	____ Initial Report of the Guardian.
22.94	____ Annual Report.
22.95	____ Decree Approving Accounts.
22.96	____ Petition on Proceeding to Discover Property Withheld.
22.97	Forms.
22.98	____ Order to Show Cause. 🖫
22.99	____ Petition. 🖫
22.100	____ Court Evaluator's Report. 🖫
22.101	____ Order and Judgment Appointing Guardian of the Person and Property. 🖫
22.102	____ Oath and Designation of Guardian. 🖫
22.103	____ Commission of Guardian. 🖫
22.104	____ Initial Report of Guardian. 🖫
22.105	____ Annual Report and Inventory of Guardian. 🖫
22.106	____ Decree Upon Approving Accounts. 🖫
22.107	____ Petition on Proceeding to Discover Property Withheld. 🖫

WESTLAW Electronic Research

See WESTLAW Electronic Research Guide preceding the Summary of Contents.

§ 22.1 Scope Note

The problems with implementation of the former statutes[1] governing the appointment of committees and conservators, and the limitations on the use of a conservator as a consequence of the decision in *Matter of Grinker (Rose)*,[2] led to the repeal of Mental Hygiene Law Articles 77 and 78 and the enactment of Mental Hygiene Law Article 81.[3] The purpose of Article 81 is to create a guardianship system with the necessary flexibility to meet the personal and/or property needs of the incapacitated person, so as to foster the least restrictive form of intervention consistent with an individual's self-determination.

This chapter discusses the purpose and philosophy underlying Mental Hygiene Law Article 81 and describes the procedures for the appointment of a guardian pursuant to the statute. Mental Hygiene Law Article 81 applies only to the appointment of a guardian for an incapacitated adult, as defined by the statute.[4]

§ 22.1

1. Former Mental Hygiene Law Arts. 77, Conservators, and 78, Committee of Incompetent or Patient.

2. 77 N.Y.2d 703, 570 N.Y.S.2d 448, 573 N.E.2d 536 (1991).

3. L. 1992, Ch. 698, eff. April 1, 1993.

4. Mental Hygiene Law § 81.15; *see infra*, § 22.34.

The chapter begins, in Sections 22.4 through 22.7, with a discussion of the prior law relating to the appointment of committees and conservators and the problems encountered under former Mental Hygiene Law Articles 77 and 78. Section 22.8 sets forth the legislative purpose of Mental Hygiene Law Article 81 and Section 22.9 contains the definitions of the terms used in Article 81.

Sections 22.11 through 22.14 discuss the power to appoint a guardian and the elements and primary considerations which are required to reach the determination that a person is incapacitated and requires the appointment of a guardian. The jurisdiction of the various courts to entertain a proceeding to appoint a guardian and the proper venue for such proceedings are discussed in Sections 22.15 and 22.16. Standing to bring a proceeding is dealt with in Section 22.17.

The procedure for appointing a guardian, including the time and place of service of notice, the persons entitled to notice, the requirements of the notice which must be given in all guardianship proceedings and the detailed contents of the petition to appoint a guardian are covered by Sections 22.19 through 22.23.

A key element of the guardianship proceeding, the appointment of a court evaluator, who acts as a fact finder for the court, is discussed in Sections 22.25 through 22.27. These sections include a description of the persons eligible to serve as court evaluator, the duties of the court evaluator and his or her compensation. The appointment of counsel to represent the interests of the alleged incapacitated person in the proceeding is discussed in Section 22.28.

The procedure on the hearing to appoint a guardian is set forth in Sections 22.30 through 22.38. These sections outline the necessity for the presence of the alleged incapacitated person at the hearing, the required evidence and burden of proof. In particular, Sections 22.34 through 22.37 set forth the necessary findings of fact which the court must make to support a determination that a person is incapacitated and requires the appointment of a guardian. The court is also provided with various dispositional alternatives to consider in devising an order which imposes the least restrictive form of intervention. These alternatives are discussed in Section 22.38.

The chapter, following the statutory sequence, then discusses the procedure for the appointment of a guardian where such appointment is deemed appropriate. Sections 22.40 and 22.41 deal with the proper person to appoint as guardian; Section 22.42 discusses the requirement of a bond; and the designation of the clerk as agent for service and the issuance of the commission to the guardian are covered by Section 22.43.

The heart of the chapter, the powers of the guardian, is covered in Sections 22.45 through 22.53. The court may grant to a guardian only those powers which are tailored to the needs of the incapacitated person with respect to personal care, property management or both so as to

§ 22.1 GUARDIANSHIP Ch. 22

result in the least restrictive form of intervention, leaving the incapacitated person with all other powers and rights.[5] The common law doctrine of substituted judgment is recognized and implemented by Mental Hygiene Law Article 81.[6] The guardian is granted the power to transfer the property of the incapacitated person and Sections 22.49 through 22.52 discuss the procedure for obtaining authorization for such transfer.

To protect the alleged incapacitated person or his or her property, Mental Hygiene Law Article 81 authorizes the use of certain provisional remedies, including the appointment of a temporary guardian,[7] the issuance of an injunction or temporary restraining orders,[8] and the filing of a notice of pendency.[9]

Section 22.61 discusses the compensation of the guardian. The guardian is required to make certain reports during the course of the guardianship. The initial report must be made within 90 days after issuance of the guardian's commission.[10] Section 22.63 discusses the requirements of the initial report. The guardian is also required to file annual reports[11] and the contents of these reports are discussed in Section 22.64. These reports are examined by the court examiner and the procedure for such examination is described in Section 22.65. The procedures for obtaining permission to file an intermediate report and the circumstances necessitating the filing of a final report are discussed in Section 22.66. Section 22.67 describes the decree approving the various reports.

The procedures for the removal, discharge or resignation of a guardian are covered in Sections 22.69 through 22.71. The appointment of an interim and successor guardian when there is a vacancy is discussed in Section 22.72 and the appointment of a standby guardian in Section 22.73.

Mental Hygiene Law Article 81 establishes specified education requirements for guardians,[12] court evaluators,[13] and court examiners.[14] These requirements are discussed in Sections 22.75 through 22.78.

Sections 22.81 through 22.86 discuss the proceedings which the guardian may bring to discover property which belongs to the incapacitated person.

The chapter concludes with a series of illustrative forms for use pursuant to Mental Hygiene Law Article 81. Drafting Checklists for the forms appear in Sections 22.88 through 22.96. The forms include: the

5. Mental Hygiene Law § 81.29(a); see infra, § 22.54.
6. Mental Hygiene Law § 81.21(a); see infra, § 22.48.
7. Mental Hygiene Law § 81.23(a); see infra, § 22.57.
8. Mental Hygiene Law § 81.23(b); see infra, § 22.58.
9. Mental Hygiene Law § 81.24; see infra, § 22.59.
10. Mental Hygiene Law § 81.30.
11. Mental Hygiene Law § 81.31.
12. Mental Hygiene Law § 81.39.
13. Mental Hygiene Law § 81.40.
14. Mental Hygiene Law § 81.41.

notice and petition in a proceeding to appoint a guardian;[15] the court evaluator's report;[16] the order and judgment appointing a guardian and the documents necessary for the guardian to qualify;[17] the initial and annual reports of the guardian;[18] the decree approving the accounts;[19] and the petition on a proceeding to discover property withheld.[20]

§ 22.2 Strategy

In bringing a proceeding pursuant to Mental Hygiene Law Article 81, the attorney must be guided by the philosophy of the article to provide powers to the guardian which are tailored to the individual needs of the incapacitated person so as to result in the least restrictive form of intervention. The attorney must determine the functional limitations of the person alleged to be incapacitated and must determine whether there are any other resources available to assist the person alleged to be incapacitated. Since the appointment of a guardian is considered only as a last resort, if other resources are available, such as a duly executed durable power of attorney or community services which can provide care to the person alleged to be incapacitated, the court will be reluctant to appoint a guardian.

To overcome the reluctance of the courts to appoint a guardian unless absolutely necessary and to assure that if a guardian is appointed, the powers are only those necessary in the particular circumstances of the individual, there must be strict compliance with the statutory requirements for commencing a proceeding for the appointment of a guardian. Failure to comply with the statutory requirements and set forth allegations meeting the statutory criteria can result in refusal of the court to sign the order to show cause to commence the proceeding.[1]

The person bringing the application to appoint a guardian must provide the court with an assessment of the alleged incapacitated person's (1) management of activities of daily living, (2) understanding and appreciation of the nature and consequences of any inability to manage activities of daily living, (3) preferences, wishes, and values with regard to managing activities of daily living, (4) nature and extent of the person's property and financial affairs and his or her ability to manage them.[2] The court must also be advised of (1) the extent of demands placed on the alleged incapacitated person by that person's personal needs and by the nature and extent of that person's property and financial affairs, (2) any physical illness and prognosis of such illness, (3)

---

15. *See infra*, §§ 22.98, 22.99.
16. *See infra*, § 22.100.
17. *See infra*, §§ 22.101–22.103.
18. *See infra*, §§ 22.104–22.105.
19. *See infra*, § 22.106.
20. *See infra*, § 22.107.

§ 22.2

1. Matter of Leiva, 170 Misc.2d 361, 650 N.Y.S.2d 949 (Sup.Ct., Bronx County, 1996).

2. *See infra*, § 22.14.

any mental disability, alcoholism or substance dependence, and prognosis of such disability, alcoholism or substance dependence, and (4) any medications with which the person is being treated and their effect on such person's behavior, cognition and judgment.[3] The petition[4] should, therefore, include the following categories of information: 1) an explanation of the functional level of the person alleged to be incapacitated; 2) the reasons for the guardianship; 3) the available alternative resources that have been explored; 4) the particular powers sought and their relationship to the functional level of the person; 5) the proposed guardian and the reasons why the proposed guardian is suitable; 6) any conflicts of interest between the petitioner and the person alleged to be incapacitated, and any conflicts of interest between the person alleged to be incapacitated and any proposed guardian. If any provisional relief[5] is sought this fact must be set forth in the petition. However, absent the consent of the alleged incapacitated person, the inclusion of medical affidavits with the petition is a violation of the physician-patient privilege.[6] Moreover, such inclusion also defeats the statute's intent to reduce the reliance upon medical testimony.

The court will appoint a court evaluator[7] to assist it in determining whether a guardian should be appointed. The court evaluator is intended to act as an independent investigator to gather information to aid the court in reaching a determination about the person's capacity, the availability and reliability of alternative resources, assigning the proper powers to the guardian, and selecting the guardian. The court evaluator does not represent the alleged incapacitated person and if the alleged incapacitated person wishes representation, or under specified circumstances, the court is obliged to appoint counsel to represent him or her.[8] The court evaluator must interview the alleged incapacitated person, if such interview is possible. The court evaluator must file a report and recommendations which shall include the court evaluator's personal observations as to the person alleged to be incapacitated and his or her condition, affairs and situation. The court evaluator may apply to the court for permission to inspect the records of medical, psychological and/or psychiatric examinations of the person alleged to be incapacitated. Except as otherwise provided by federal or state law, if the court determines that such records are likely to contain information which will assist the court evaluator in completing his or her report to the court, the court may order disclosure of such records to the court evaluator, notwithstanding the physician-patient privilege. The availability of medical records has raised many questions concerning the physician-patient privilege and the need for a medical affidavit to support the petition for appointment of a guardian. As the law currently stands, such affidavit

3. Id.
4. See infra, §§ 22.23, 22.99.
5. See infra, §§ 22.56–22.59.
6. See infra, §§ 22.26, 22.33 for discussion of physician-patient privilege.
7. See infra, §§ 22.25—22.27.
8. See infra, § 22.28.

and any medical records should not be attached[9] but if such information is deemed necessary, the court evaluator should apply to the court for such records.[10]

Since the appointment of a guardian depends upon a functional evaluation of the abilities of the alleged incapacitated person, the petition and the investigation of the court evaluator must focus on how such person carries out the activities of daily living and what resources are available. This information should include the items set forth in the Functional Evaluation Checklist.[11]

The attorney must take into consideration available resources, whether private or public. If the alleged incapacitated person is unable to carry on certain daily activities or cannot take care of his or her property, such may be an indication of the need for a guardian. However, if these needs are being taken care of, or can be provided through, agents, such as one appointed by the alleged incapacitated person in a durable power of attorney, health care proxy or similar delegation, and there are community resources, such as, visiting nurses, social workers, meals on wheels, or family members, the court will be reluctant to appoint a guardian. It is only where such resources are not available, or are being inadequately or improperly provided, that the guardianship proceeding should be brought. Improperly bringing a guardianship proceeding could result in the imposition of sanctions.[12]

Once the court determines that the person is incapacitated and appoints a guardian, the guardian becomes responsible for the personal needs and/or property management of the incapacitated person and must act within the scope of the powers granted in the appointing order. The guardian stands in a unique relationship to the incapacitated person. Prior to undertaking his or her duties as guardian, the guardian must complete a training program[13] approved by the chief administrator which covers (1) the legal duties and responsibilities of guardian; (2) the rights of the incapacitated person; (3) the available resources to aid the incapacitated person; (4) an orientation to medical terminology, particularly that related to the diagnostic and assessment procedures used to characterize the extent and reversibility of any impairment; and (5) the preparation of annual reports, including financial accounting for the property and financial resources of the incapacitated person.

Decision making is a fundamental part of the guardian's role. In order to carry out this responsibility in the most careful and diligent

9. Matter of Higgins (England), N.Y.L.J., 10/6/95, p.27, col.2 (Sup.Ct., N.Y. County). *See also* Matter of Tara X, N.Y.L.J., 9/18/96, p. 27, col. 1 (Sup.Ct., Suffolk County); Matter of Goldfarb, 160 Misc.2d 1036, 612 N.Y.S.2d 788 (Sup.Ct., Suffolk County, 1994). *See infra*, §§ 22.26, 22.33.

10. Mental Hygiene Law § 81.09(d); *see infra*, § 22.26.

11. *See infra*, § 22.3(a).

12. *See, e.g.,* Petition of Rocco, 161 Misc.2d 760, 615 N.Y.S.2d 260 (Sup.Ct., Suffolk County, 1994); *see infra*, § 22.39.

13. *See infra*, § 22.76.

manner, the guardian should develop a personal relationship with the ward, in the event one does not exist, so that the guardian can understand the impact of any decision from the perspective of the incapacitated person and can involve the incapacitated person in the decisions to the greatest extent possible. This can be done through an interview with the incapacitated person and through discussions with family and friends to ascertain the preferences of the incapacitated person. In order to develop and maintain the necessary relationship with the incapacitated person, the guardian must visit the incapacitated person not less than four times per year or more frequently as specified in the court order.[14]

No later than 90 days after issuance of the commission to the guardian, the guardian must file with the court an initial report[15] in the form prescribed by the court stating what steps the guardian has taken to fulfill his or her responsibilities. The initial report fulfills several purposes. First, it clarifies the guardian's responsibilities and the course of action to be taken. Second, it gives the guardian an opportunity to assess the circumstances of the incapacitated person and whether any changes need to be made in the guardian's powers. Third, the plan provides a tool for evaluating the guardian's performance. If the guardian has been granted powers with respect to property management, the initial report must contain 1) a verified and complete inventory of the property and financial resources over which the guardian has control, 2) the location of any will executed by the incapacitated person, 3) the guardian's plan, consistent with the court's order of appointment, for management of such property and financial resources, and 4) the need for any change in the powers authorized by the court. If the guardian has been granted powers regarding personal needs, the initial report must contain 1) a report of guardian's personal visits with the incapacitated person, 2) the steps the guardian has taken, consistent with the court's order, to provide for the personal needs of that person, 3) the guardian's plan, consistent with the court's order of appointment, for providing for the personal needs of the incapacitated person, 4) a copy of any directives, including a Do Not Resuscitate (DNR) Order, a health care proxy, any living will and any other advance directive, and 5) any necessary change in the powers authorized by court.

In the month of May or at any other time on motion or order of the court, every guardian must file an annual report.[16] The information required to be contained in the annual report concerns the personal status of the incapacitated person, and/or the condition of the person's finances and property, to the extent of the guardian's authority. It is critical that the court regularly receive and review basic information about the well-being of the incapacitated person. Article 81, therefore, imposes specific informational requirements on the guardian in complet-

---

14. See infra, § 22.46.
15. See infra, § 22.63; see also infra, § 22.3(i) for Checklist.
16. See infra, § 22.64; see also, infra, § 22.3(j) for Checklist.

ing his or her annual report. The use of uniform report forms allowing for narrative responses will educate the guardian as to what information the court expects and assist the guardian in evaluating his or her performance.

Mental Hygiene Law Article 81 imposes sanctions for failure of the guardian to file the initial or any annual report. It is, therefore, essential that the guardian comply with the statute and file the necessary reports.[17]

§ 22.3 Checklists

These Checklists are intended to highlight the statutory requirements at various stages of a proceeding pursuant to Mental Hygiene Law Article 81, from the commencement of the proceeding through the ongoing oversight by the court of the guardian in carrying out his or her duties. They are intended as guides to the information which the parties to the proceeding must obtain and provide the court at each stage of the proceeding.

(a) Functional Evaluation of Abilities of Alleged Incapacitated Person[1]

A functional evaluation assesses the extent to which the person carries out the activities of daily living effectively and provides information about a person's basic needs and how they are met. The information which should be obtained includes:

(1) income adequacy and spending patterns, such as, physical ability to write checks and manage currency and whether pension checks and disability payments arrive on time;

(2) adequacy of food, clothing and shelter, such as, ability to buy and prepare food, ability to eat and choice of diet, ability to dress and undress, adequacy of laundry facilities, upkeep of shelter, warmth and ventilation, cleanliness of environment, safety of home;

(3) physical functioning, such as, ability to walk, climb stairs, reach, get in and out of chair and tub; sensory functioning, such as, ability to see, hear, feel, react in ways that do not endanger health or safety;

(4) access to helpful resources such as friends, relatives, physicians, emergency facilities, transportation;

(5) satisfaction with present circumstances, desire for change and specific assistance the person wishes;

(6) emotional factors, such as, loneliness and anxiety; and

---

17. See infra, §§ 22.69–22.72.

§ 22.3
1. See infra, § 22.14.

(7) mental status including orientation to reality, memory functioning, reasoning ability.

(b) Petition; Required Allegations[2]

The petition must be verified under oath and must include the following:

(1) the name, age, address, and telephone number of the person alleged to be incapacitated;

(2) the name, address, and telephone number of the person or persons with whom the person alleged to be incapacitated resides, if any;

(3) a description of the alleged incapacitated person's functional level including that person's ability to manage activities of daily living, behavior, and understanding and appreciation of the nature and consequences of any inability to manage the activities of daily living;

(4) if powers are sought with respect to the personal needs[3] of the alleged incapacitated person, specific factual allegations as to personal actions or other actual occurrences involving the person alleged to be incapacitated which are claimed to demonstrate that the person is likely to suffer harm because he or she cannot adequately understand and appreciate the nature and consequences of his or her inability to provide for personal needs;

(5) if powers are sought with respect to property management[4] for the alleged incapacitated person, specific factual allegations as to financial transactions or other actual occurrences involving the person alleged to be incapacitated which are claimed to demonstrate that the person is likely to suffer harm because he or she cannot adequately understand and appreciate the nature and consequences of his or her inability to provide for property management;

(6) the particular powers being sought and their relationship to the functional level and the needs of the person alleged to be incapacitated;

(7) the duration of the powers being sought;

(8) the approximate value and description of the financial resources of the person alleged to be incapacitated and whether, to the best of petitioner's knowledge, the person is a recipient of public assistance;

---

2. *See infra,* § 22.23.

3. *See* Mental Hygiene Law § 81.22, discussed *infra* at § 22.53.

4. *See* Mental Hygiene Law § 81.21, discussed *infra* at § 22.47.

(9) the nature and amount of any claim, debt, or obligation of the person alleged to be incapacitated, to the best of petitioner's knowledge;

(10) the names, addresses, and telephone numbers of presumptive distributees of the person alleged to be incapacitated unless they are unknown and cannot be reasonably ascertained;

(11) the name, address, and telephone number of the petitioner;

(12) the name, address, and telephone number of the person or persons, if any, proposed as guardian and standby guardian, the relationship of the proposed guardian or standby guardian to the person alleged to be incapacitated, and the reasons why the proposed guardian or standby guardian is suitable to exercise powers necessary to assist the person alleged to be incapacitated;

(13) any relief sought under Mental Hygiene Law Section 81.23;[5]

(14) available resources, if any, that have been considered by the petitioner and the petitioner's opinion as to their sufficiency and reliability;

(15) any other information which in the petitioner's opinion will assist the court evaluator in completing his or her investigation and report.

(c) *Duties of Court Evaluator*[6]

To provide the court with the information necessary to assist it in determining whether to appoint a guardian, the duties of the court evaluator include the following:

(1) meeting, interviewing, and consulting with the person alleged to be incapacitated regarding the proceeding;

(2) explaining to the person alleged to be incapacitated, in a manner which such person can reasonably be expected to understand, the nature and possible consequences of the proceeding, the general powers and duties of the guardian, available resources, and rights to which the person is entitled, including the right to counsel;

(3) determining whether the person alleged to be incapacitated wishes legal counsel to be appointed and otherwise evaluating whether legal counsel should be appointed;

(4) interviewing the petitioner, or, if the petitioner is a facility or government agency, the person within the facility or the agency

---

5. Mental Hygiene Law § 81.23 relates to provisional remedies, which are discussed *infra* at §§ 22.56–22.59.

6. *See infra*, § 22.26.

fully familiar with the alleged incapacitated person's condition, affairs and situation;[7] and

(5) investigating and a making written report and recommendations to the court.

(d) Criteria for Selecting Guardian[8]

In order to determine whether, and who, to appoint as guardian, the court must have the following information, which should be included in the Petition:

(1) any appointment or delegation made by the person alleged to be incapacitated in a general power of attorney, Do Not Resuscitate (DNR) Order, health care proxy, or living will;

(2) the social relationship between the incapacitated person and the person, if any, proposed as guardian, and the social relationship between the incapacitated person and other persons concerned with the welfare of the incapacitated person;

(3) the care and services being provided to the incapacitated person at the time of the proceeding;

(4) the powers which the guardian will exercise;

(5) the educational, professional and business experience relevant to the nature of the services sought to be provided;

(6) the nature of the financial resources involved;

(7) the unique requirements of the incapacitated person; and

(8) any conflicts of interest between the person proposed as guardian and the incapacitated person.

(e) Duties of Guardian: Property Management[9]

The guardian who is granted powers with respect to property management has the following duties:

(1) afford the incapacitated person the greatest amount of independence and self-determination with respect to property management in light of that person's functional level, understanding and appreciation of his or her functional limitations, and personal wishes, preferences and desires with regard to managing the activities of daily living;

(2) preserve, protect, and account for such property and financial resources faithfully;

---

7. *See supra,* Functional Evaluation Checklist, which is also information which it is necessary for the court evaluator to obtain.

8. *See infra,* § 22.41.

9. Mental Hygiene Law § 81.20; *see infra,* § 22.46.

(3) determine whether the incapacitated person has executed a will, determine the location of any will, and of the appropriate persons to be notified in the event of the death of the incapacitated person and, in the event of the death of the incapacitated person, notify those persons;

(4) use the property and financial resources and income available from such property to maintain and support the incapacitated person, and to maintain and support those persons dependent on the incapacitated person;

(5) at the termination of the appointment, deliver such property to the person legally entitled to it;

(6) file with the recording officer of the county in which the incapacitated person is possessed of real property, an acknowledged statement to be recorded and indexed under the name of the incapacitated person identifying real property possessed by the incapacitated person, and the tax map numbers of such property, and stating the date of adjudication of incapacity of the person regarding property management, and the name, address, and telephone number of the guardian and the guardian's surety; and

(7) perform all other duties required by law.

(f) Duties of Guardian: Personal Needs[10]

The guardian who is granted powers with respect to personal needs has the following duties:

Afford the incapacitated person the greatest amount of independence and self-determination with respect to personal needs in light of that person's functional level, understanding and appreciation of that person's functional limitations, and personal wishes, preferences and desires with regard to managing the activities of daily living.

(g) Powers of Guardian: Property Management[11]

The court may grant the guardian the following powers with regard to property management:

(1) make gifts;

(2) provide support for persons dependent on the incapacitated person for support, whether or not the incapacitated person is legally obligated to provide that support;

---

10. *Id.*

11. Mental Hygiene Law § 81.21; *see infra*, §§ 22.47–22.52.

(3) convey or release contingent and expectant interests in property, including marital property rights and any right of survivorship incidental to joint tenancy or tenancy by entirety;

(4) exercise or release powers held by the incapacitated person as trustee, personal representative, guardian for a minor, guardian, or donee of a power of appointment;

(5) enter into contracts;

(6) create revocable or irrevocable trusts of the property of the estate which may extend beyond the incapacity or life of the incapacitated person;

(7) exercise options of the incapacitated person to purchase securities or other property;

(8) exercise rights to elect options and change beneficiaries under insurance and annuity policies and to surrender the policies for their cash value;

(9) exercise any right to an elective share in the estate of the incapacitated person's deceased spouse;

(10) renounce or disclaim any interest by testate or intestate succession or by *inter vivos* transfer consistent with EPTL Section 2-1.11;

(11) authorize access to or release of confidential records; and

(12) apply for government and private benefits.

(h) Powers of Guardian: Personal Needs[12]

The court may grant the guardian the following powers with regard to personal needs:

(1) determine who provides personal care or assistance;

(2) make decisions regarding the social environment and other social aspects of the life of the incapacitated person;

(3) determine whether the incapacitated person should travel;

(4) determine whether the incapacitated person should possess a license to drive;

(5) authorize access to or release of confidential records;

(6) make decisions regarding education;

(7) apply for government and private benefits;

(8) consent to or refuse generally accepted routine or major medical or dental treatment. The guardian must make treatment decisions consistent with the findings under Mental Hygiene Law Section 81.15 and in accordance with the patient's wishes,

---

12. Mental Hygiene Law § 81.22; *see* infra, § 22.53.

including the patient's religious and moral beliefs, or if the patient's wishes are not known and cannot be ascertained with reasonable diligence, in accordance with the person's best interests, including consideration of the dignity and uniqueness of every person, the possibility and extent of preserving the person's life, preservation, improvement or restoration of the person's health or functioning, relief of the person's suffering, adverse side effects associated with the treatment, any less intrusive alternative treatments, and such other concerns and values as a reasonable person in the incapacitated person's circumstances would wish to consider; and

(9) choose the place of abode.

(i) Initial Report: Requirements[13]

Proof of completion of the guardian education requirements must be filed with the initial report.[14]

To the extent that the guardian has been granted powers with respect to property management, the initial report must contain:

(1) a verified and complete inventory of the property and financial resources over which the guardian has control;

(2) the location of any will executed by the incapacitated person;

(3) the guardian's plan, consistent with the court's order of appointment, for management of such property and financial resources; and

(4) the need for any change in the powers authorized by the court.

To the extent that the guardian has been granted powers regarding personal needs, the initial report must contain:

(1) a report of the guardian's personal visits with the incapacitated person;

(2) the steps the guardian has taken, consistent with the court's order, to provide for the personal needs of that person;

(3) the guardian's plan, consistent with the court's order of appointment, for providing for the personal needs of the incapacitated person;

(4) a copy of any directives, including a Do Not Resuscitate (DNR) Order, a health care proxy, any living will and any other advance directive; and

(5) any necessary change in the powers authorized by court.

The plan for providing for the personal needs of the incapacitated person must include the following information:

13. Mental Hygiene Law § 81.30; see infra, § 22.63.

14. Id.; see also, infra, § 22.76.

(1) the medical, dental, mental health, or related services that are to be provided for the welfare of the incapacitated person;

(2) the social and personal services that are to be provided for the welfare of the incapacitated person;

(3) any physical, dental, and mental health examinations necessary to determine the medical, dental, and mental health treatment needs; and

(4) the application of health and accident insurance and any other private or government benefits to which the incapacitated person may be entitled to meet any part of the costs of medical, dental, mental health, or related services provided to the incapacitated person.

(j) Annual Report: Requirements[15]

The annual report of guardian must be in a form prescribed by the court and shall include the following information:

(1) the present address and telephone number of the guardian;

(2) the present address, and telephone number of the incapacitated person; if the place of residence of the incapacitated person is not his or her personal home, the name, address, and telephone number of the facility or place at which the person resides and the name of the chief executive officer of the facility or person otherwise responsible for the person's care;

(3) any major changes in the physical or mental condition of the incapacitated person and any substantial change in medication;

(4) the date that the incapacitated person was last examined or otherwise seen by a physician and the purpose of that visit;

(5) a statement by a physician, psychologist, nurse clinician, or social worker, or other person who has evaluated or examined the incapacitated person within the three months prior to the filing of the report regarding an evaluation of the incapacitated person's condition and the current functional level of the incapacitated person;

(6) to the extent the guardian is charged with providing for the personal needs of the incapacitated person:

    (i) a statement of whether the current residential setting is best suited to the current needs of the incapacitated person;

    (ii) a resume of any professional medical treatment given to the ward in the preceding year;

---

15. Mental Hygiene Law § 81.31; *see infra,* § 22.64.

(iii) the plan for medical, dental, and mental health treatment, and related services in the coming year;

(iv) information concerning the social condition of the incapacitated person, including: the social and personal services currently utilized by the incapacitated person; the social skills of the incapacitated person; and the social needs of the incapacitated person;

(7) to the extent the guardian is charged with property management, information required by the provisions of the SCPA Section 1719 prescribing the form of papers to be filed upon the annual accounting of a general guardian of an infant's property; this information includes:[16]

(i) a statement and description of each item of personal property of the incapacitated person received by the guardian since his or her appointment or since the filing of the last annual account; the value of each item so received; a list of the items remaining in the guardian's hands; a statement of the manner in which all property no longer remaining in the guardian's hands has been disposed of; and a description of the amount and nature of each investment of money made by the guardian;

(ii) an account in the form of debtor and creditor of all the guardian's receipts and disbursements of money during the preceding year; charging him or herself with any balance remaining in the last account rendered and stating the balance remaining at the conclusion of the year to be charged to the guardian in the next year's account;

(iii) the names and addresses of the sureties on the guardian's bond; if natural persons whether they are living and whether the security of the bond has become impaired;

(8) where the guardian has used or employed the services of the incapacitated person or where moneys have been earned by or received on behalf of such incapacitated person an accounting of any moneys earned or derived from such services;

(9) a resume of any other activities performed by the guardian on behalf of the incapacitated person;

(10) facts indicating the need to terminate the appointment of the guardian, or for any alteration in the powers of the guardian and what specific authority is requested or what specific authority of the guardian will be affected;

(11) any other information which the guardian may be required to file by the order of appointment.

16. *See infra,* § 22.105.

§ 22.4 Prior Law—Generally

Persons who are unable to manage themselves or their own affairs have long been subject to the *parens patriae* power of the state.[1] Until April 1, 1993,[2] Articles 77 and 78 of the Mental Hygiene Law comprised New York's legislative scheme regarding the appointment of a surrogate decisionmaker for a person who was no longer capable of handling his or her personal and financial affairs.[3]

Prior to 1972, the sole statutory authority for dealing with such issues was found in Mental Hygiene Law Article 78, Committee of Incompetent or Patient,[4] which provided for the appointment of a committee of the person or property or both of a person who had been judicially determined to be incompetent.[5] The statute was a codification of the state's inherent jurisdiction over persons of unsound mind within its territorial limits.[6] The appointment of a committee was dependent upon a finding of complete incompetence,[7] with a loss of civil rights which accompanied such a finding, such as loss of the right to vote.[8]

In 1972, because of the stigma attached to the finding of incompetence and the loss of civil rights,[9] a less restrictive alternative was enacted,[10] providing for the appointment of a conservator of the property.[11] The conservatorship proceeding was made available for persons who had not been declared incompetent and did not require a committee, but who, by reason of advanced age, illness, infirmity, mental weakness,

---

§ 22.4

1. In re Fisher, 147 Misc.2d 329, 552 N.Y.S.2d 807 (Sup.Ct., N.Y. County, 1989); Hughes by Hughes v. Physicians Hospital, 149 Misc.2d 661, 566 N.Y.S.2d 496 (Sup.Ct., Queens County, 1991).

2. *See infra*, § 22.8, for discussion of enactment of Mental Hygiene Law Art. 81, Proceedings for Appointment of a Guardian for Personal Needs or Property Management.

3. R.M. Bailly, *Guardianship Reform for Older Adults in New York*, 2 Elder Law Attorney (N.Y.S.B.A.) 28 (Spring/Summer 1992).

4. Former Mental Hygiene Law Art. 78, §§ 78.01 *et seq. See generally*, 1966 Report of the Law Revision Commission, Recommendations and Study Relating to Conservators of the Property of Persons Unable to Manage Their Own Affairs.

5. In re Fisher, 147 Misc.2d 329, 552 N.Y.S.2d 807 (Sup.Ct., N.Y. County, 1989). *See generally*, R.M. Bailly, *Guardianship Reform for Older Adults in New York*, 2 Elder Law Attorney (N.Y.S.B.A.) 28 (Spring/Summer 1992).

6. Sporza v. German Sav. Bank, 192 N.Y. 8, 84 N.E. 406 (1908); In re Seronde, 99 Misc.2d 485, 416 N.Y.S.2d 716 (Sup.Ct., Westchester County, 1979).

7. Hughes by Hughes v. Physicians Hospital, 149 Misc.2d 661, 566 N.Y.S.2d 496 (Sup.Ct., Queens County, 1991); In re Fisher, 147 Misc.2d 329, 552 N.Y.S.2d 807 (Sup.Ct., N.Y. County, 1989). *See generally*, G.O. Koppell & K.J. Munnelly, *The New Guardian Statute: Article 81 of the Mental Hygiene Law*, 65 N.Y.S.B.J. 16 (February 1993).

8. In re Fisher, 147 Misc.2d 329, 552 N.Y.S.2d 807 (Sup.Ct., N.Y. County, 1989). *See generally*, G.O. Koppell & K.J. Munnelly, *The New Guardian Statute: Article 81 of the Mental Hygiene Law*, 65 N.Y.S.B.J. 16 (February 1993). See Chapter 18 "New York Civil Rights Law," *supra*.

9. G.O. Koppell & K.J. Munnelly, *The New Guardian Statute: Article 81 of the Mental Hygiene Law*, 65 N.Y.S.B.J. 16 (February 1993).

10. L. 1972, Ch. 251; *see* Memorandum of State Executive Department to L. 1974, Ch. 297.

11. Former Mental Hygiene Law Art. 77, Conservators, §§ 77.01, *et seq.*

alcohol abuse, addiction to drugs or other cause had suffered substantial impairment of his or her ability to care for his or her property and had become unable to provide for him or herself or others dependent upon him or her for support.[12] The appointment of a conservator did not require a finding of incompetence,[13] nor did it deprive the conservatee of any of the civil rights or other individual choices which might be lost as a result of the declaration of incompetency and appointment of a committee.[14] There was a perception that the enactment of the conservatorship procedure was intended to substitute for the committee procedure,[15] and this perception contained the potential for blurring the roles of the committee and conservator and for the ultimate abandonment of the committee statute.[16]

The conservatorship statute was intended to deal solely with the property and finances of the conservatee,[17] and the conservator's powers were limited by the court's approval of a plan for preservation, maintenance and care of the conservatee's income and assets.[18]

Former Article 77 of the Mental Hygiene Law was enacted to benefit older impaired persons to provide them with necessary services, and enable them to have their income applied to the expenses of maintaining and treating them in the community for as long as possible,[19] and was generally gauged for persons with small and moderate estates, to protect them against excessive costs of administration.[20]

In 1974, the statutes were amended to expand the role of the conservator, and as a consequence, further support the perception that the conservatorship procedure was intended to replace the committee procedure.[21] The first of these amendments established a statutory preference in both Article 77 and Article 78 for the appointment of a conservator.[22] The second amendment allowed the conservator to assume

---

12. *Id.*
13. In re Fisher, 147 Misc.2d 329, 552 N.Y.S.2d 807 (Sup.Ct., N.Y. County, 1989). *See generally,* G.O. Koppell & K.J. Munnelly, *The New Guardian Statute: Article 81 of the Mental Hygiene Law,* 65 N.Y.S.B.J. 16 (February 1993).
14. Former Mental Hygiene Law § 77.25(a); In re Fisher, 147 Misc.2d 329, 552 N.Y.S.2d 807 (Sup.Ct., N.Y. County, 1989).
15. R.M. Bailly, *Guardianship Reform for Older Adults in New York,* 2 Elder Law Attorney (N.Y.S.B.A.) 28, 29 (Spring/Summer 1992).
16. *Id.*
17. Former Mental Hygiene Law § 77.19; In re Fisher, 147 Misc.2d 329, 552 N.Y.S.2d 807 (Sup.Ct., N.Y. County, 1989).
18. Former Mental Hygiene Law § 77.19.

See generally, R.M. Bailly, *Guardianship Reform for Older Adults in New York,* 2 Elder Law Attorney (N.Y.S.B.A.) 28 (Spring/Summer 1992); G.O. Koppell & K.J. Munnelly, *The New Guardian Statute: Article 81 of the Mental Hygiene Law,* 65 N.Y.S.B.J. 16 (February 1993).

19. In re Estate of Bauer, 96 Misc.2d 40, 408 N.Y.S.2d 649 (Sup.Ct., N.Y. County, 1978).
20. *Id.*
21. G.O. Koppell & K.J. Munnelly, *The New Guardian Statute: Article 81 of the Mental Hygiene Law,* 65 N.Y.S.B.J. 16 (February 1993).
22. L. 1974, Ch. 297; codified at former Mental Hygiene Law §§ 77.04, 78.02.

a limited role in protecting the well-being of the conservatee.[23]

§ 22.5 Prior Law—Role of Committees and Conservators

A committee was a fiduciary who had powers over a person who had been adjudicated incompetent to manage him or herself or his or her affairs by reason of age, alcohol abuse, mental illness, or other cause, or was a patient in a state mental facility, who was unable to conduct his or her personal and business affairs.[1] The duties of a committee of the property, as described in the statute[2] involved managing the financial affairs of the incompetent.[3] The statute contained no provision regarding the powers of the committee over the person. However, case law had established that the committee of the person was charged with the responsibility of taking care of the physical needs of the incompetent, protecting his person, furnishing him or her with such medical and other care and treatment as was required and looking into the incompetent's health and general welfare.[4] A committee was required to account annually to the court regarding the care of the incompetent's financial affairs.[5]

The authority of a conservator of the property of an individual included the control, charge and management of the estate, real and personal, of the conservatee and the powers and duties granted to or imposed upon a committee of the property of an incompetent.[6] The conservator's powers were limited by the court's approval of a plan for the preservation, maintenance and care of the conservatee's income, assets and personal well-being.[7] The powers conferred upon the conservator could be increased or restricted during the term of the conservatorship by the court.[8] The conservator was required to annually account for the care of the conservatee's financial affairs in the same manner as a

---

23. L. 1974, Ch. 623; codified at former Mental Hygiene Law § 77.19. *See infra*, § 22.6, discussing the problems created by the blurring of the roles of the conservator and committee and § 22.7, discussing the impact of Matter of Grinker (Rose), 77 N.Y.2d 703, 570 N.Y.S.2d 448, 573 N.E.2d 536 (1991).

§ 22.5

1. Former Mental Hygiene Law § 78.01.

2. Former Mental Hygiene Law § 78.15.

3. Former Mental Hygiene Law § 78.15. Under the prior statute, the powers of the committee were narrowly drawn and, except in limited circumstances, the committee had no power to act in respect of the incompetent's property without court authority. Former Mental Hygiene Law § 78.15(a).

4. In re Webber's Will, 187 Misc. 674, 64 N.Y.S.2d 281 (Surr.Ct., Kings County, 1946).

5. Former Mental Hygiene Law § 78.23.

6. Former Mental Hygiene Law § 77.19.

7. Former Mental Hygiene Law § 77.19; In re Kurnyk, 109 Misc.2d 1019, 441 N.Y.S.2d 328 (Sup.Ct., Queens County, 1981). *See infra*, § 22.6, discussing problems concerning the power of a conservator to provide for the personal well-being of the conservatee.

8. Former Mental Hygiene Law § 77.19; In re Kurnyk, 109 Misc.2d 1019, 441 N.Y.S.2d 328 (Sup.Ct., Queens County, 1981).

committee was required to account under Mental Hygiene Law Article 78.[9] In addition, the conservator was required to report on the current status of the conservatee, the conservator's plan for continued care and the need for the continuation of the conservatorship.[10]

Under prior law, because a conservatorship did not involve control over the person of the conservatee, nor the adjudication of incompetency, the appointment of a conservator was preferred.[11] The statute provided that the court could not make a finding of incompetency unless it first determined that it was not in the person's best interest to appoint a conservator.[12] If the court found the appointment of a conservator appropriate, it could treat a petition for appointment of a committee as a petition for the appointment of a conservator.[13]

§ 22.6 Prior Law—Problems Encountered

The Conservator and Committee statutes[1] were all or nothing type statutes,[2] allowing no flexibility to meet the individual needs of the person alleged to be incapacitated. However, the commentators noted that there was a spectrum of degrees of disability and functional difficulties.[3] Conservatorship, involving protection only of the property, was frequently inadequate to meet the needs of the incapacitated person, whereas, a committee was often an excessive remedy requiring demonstration of psychopathology of such magnitude as to justify the loss of all decision-making powers. The statutory distinctions were said not to reflect the real world.[4]

Another problem was that the 1974 amendments[5] tended to blur the distinction between a committee and a conservator by establishing a preference for the appointment of a conservator and allowing a conservator to assume a limited role in protecting the personal well-being of the conservatee and requiring greater court control by providing that the court approve a plan with respect to both the maintenance and care of the assets and the "personal well-being" of the conservatee.[6] However,

---

9. Former Mental Hygiene Law § 77.29.
10. Former Mental Hygiene Law § 77.29.
11. In re Morrison, 147 Misc.2d 657, 559 N.Y.S.2d 448 (Sup.Ct., Bronx County, 1990).
12. Former Mental Hygiene Law § 78.02.
13. Former Mental Hygiene Law § 77.04.

§ 22.6
1. Former Mental Hygiene Law Arts. 77, Conservators, and 78, Committee of Incompetent or Patient.
2. W.L. Leinheardt, *The New Mental Hygiene Law: Article 81—Proceedings for Appointment of a Guardian for Personal Needs or Property Management*, 25 Newsletter, Trusts and Estates Law Section (N.Y.S.B.A.) 7 (Fall 1992).

3. R.M. Bailly, *Guardianship Reform for Older Adults in New York*, 2 Elder Law Attorney (N.Y.S.B.A.) 28, 29 (Spring/Summer 1992), citing Memorandum of Eugene Kerr, M.D., Office of Psychiatry, New York City Department of Human Resources 1.

4. Id.

5. See supra, § 22.4, discussing the 1974 amendments.

6. L. 1974, Ch. 623, codified in former Mental Hygiene Law § 77.19.

§ 22.6　　　　　　　　　　GUARDIANSHIP　　　　　　　　　　Ch. 22

the legislation did not include any definition of the term "personal well-being" or any clear limitation on the ability of the conservator to force a decision about personal well-being on the conservatee against his or her will.[7] As a consequence, there were conflicting views among the courts about the extent of a conservator's authority over the person of the conservatee.[8] The courts were trying to avoid the stigma of a finding of incompetence and at the same time were attempting to fashion remedies to provide assistance for persons whose needs did not fit the statutory scheme.[9] One issue which arose was whether the statutory authority to assume a limited role in protecting the personal well-being of the conservatee included power in the conservator to commit the conservatee to a nursing home.[10] However, the Court of Appeals answered this question in the negative in *Matter of Grinker (Rose)*.[11]

§ 22.7　Prior Law—Impact of *Matter of Grinker (Rose)*[1]

On April 30, 1991, the Court of Appeals decided *Matter of Grinker (Rose)*.[2] The court held that the limited power over a conservatee's person granted by former Mental Hygiene Law Article 77 incidentally related to the primary power over property[3] and did not authorize the "potent personal transformation of involuntary commitment of a conservatee to a nursing home."[4] The court ruled that the "availability of such a significant involuntary displacement of personal liberty should be confined to a [former] Mental Hygiene Law article 78 incompetency proceeding, with its full panoply of procedural due process safeguards."[5]

---

7. In re Fisher, 147 Misc.2d 329, 552 N.Y.S.2d 807 (Sup.Ct., N.Y. County, 1989). See generally R.M. Bailly, *Guardianship Reform for Older Adults in New York*, 2 Elder Law Attorney (N.Y.S.B.A.) 28 (Spring/Summer 1992).

8. See, e.g., Matter of Detzel, 134 A.D.2d 205, 521 N.Y.S.2d 6 (1st Dep't 1987) (authorizing the conservator to involuntarily commit the conservatee to a nursing home could only follow a plenary hearing pursuant to Article 78); Matter of Evelyn P., 135 A.D.2d 716, 522 N.Y.S.2d 617 (2d Dep't 1987) (provision in the order appointing a conservator which required the conservator to provide home care for the conservatee was within the court's authority under Mental Hygiene Law § 77.10); Matter of Fisher, 147 Misc.2d 329, 552 N.Y.S.2d 807 (Sup.Ct., N.Y. County, 1989) (Article 77 only permitted appointment of a conservator upon a clear and convincing showing of the conservatee's impairment in her ability to manage her assets, and such conservator has only those powers necessary to manage the assets of the conservatee for her benefit).

9. R.M. Bailly, *Guardianship Reform for Older Adults in New York*, 2 Elder Law Attorney (N.Y.S.B.A.) 28, 30 (Spring/Summer 1992).

10. See, e.g., Matter of Detzel, 134 A.D.2d 205, 521 N.Y.S.2d 6 (1st Dep't 1987); Matter of Evelyn P., 135 A.D.2d 716, 522 N.Y.S.2d 617 (2d Dep't 1987), discussed *supra* note 8.

11. 77 N.Y.2d 703, 570 N.Y.S.2d 448, 573 N.E.2d 536 (1991); see *infra*, § 22.7 for a discussion of this case.

§ 22.7

1. See also *infra*, § 22.13, discussing *Matter of Grinker (Rose)* with regard to determination of capacity.

2. 77 N.Y.2d 703, 570 N.Y.S.2d 448, 573 N.E.2d 536 (1991).

3. Former Mental Hygiene Law § 77.19.

4. 77 N.Y.2d at 710, 570 N.Y.S.2d at 451.

5. 77 N.Y.2d at 710, 570 N.Y.S.2d at 451.

The case settled the debate regarding whether former Mental Hygiene Law Article 77 allowed the grant of power to a conservator to make decisions concerning the person of the conservatee.[6] By so holding the court clarified the distinction between the two statutes. However, by doing so, *Grinker* highlighted the very problem that the courts had been grappling with: the absence of any remedy for persons who required some assistance but who did not require the drastic remedy of either a conservator or a committee.[7] As a consequence of the problems surrounding the application of former Mental Hygiene Law Articles 77 and 78, the New York State Law Revision Commission recommended the enactment of a single statute with a standard of appointment which focused on the needs of the individual and permitted the appointment of a guardian who could make decisions regarding either the person or the property of the person, or both if appropriate.[8]

§ 22.8 Legislative Purpose of Mental Hygiene Law Article 81

In response to the deficiencies in former Mental Hygiene Law Articles 77 and 78 and a desire to specifically tailor legal remedies to an incapacitated person's individual assistance needs,[1] the Legislature, in 1992, enacted Mental Hygiene Law Article 81.[2] The stated purpose of Article 81 is to create a guardianship system with the necessary flexibility to meet the personal and/or property needs of the incapacitated person, so as to foster the *least restrictive form of intervention*[3] consistent with an individual's self-determination.[4]

---

6. See supra, § 22.6, regarding the problems arising under former Mental Hygiene Law Arts. 77 and 78, with particular regard to the authority of a conservator to place a conservatee in a nursing home.

7. See supra, § 22.6.

8. See infra, §§ 22.8, et seq. for discussion of Mental Hygiene Law Art. 81. See generally, R.M. Bailly, *Guardianship Reform for Older Adults in New York*, 2 Elder Law Attorney (N.Y.S.B.A.) 28 (Spring/Summer 1992); A.G. Krams & R. O'Halloran, *Matter of Grinker (Rose): A Legal Analysis*, 2 Elder Law Attorney No. 1 (N.Y.S.B.A.) 21 (Spring/Summer 1992); L. Beane, *The Adult Guardian—Mental Hygiene Law, Article 81*, 3 Elder Law Attorney No. 1 (N.Y.S.B.A.) 27 (Spring 1993); W.L. Leinheardt, *The New Mental Hygiene Law: Article 81—Proceedings for Appointment of a Guardian for Personal Needs or Property Management*, 25 Newsletter, Trusts and Estates Law Section (N.Y.S.B.A.) 7 (Fall 1992).

§ 22.8

1. Matter of Hammons (Ehmke), 164 Misc.2d 609, 625 N.Y.S.2d 408 (Sup.Ct., Queens County, 1995); Matter of Presbyterian Hospital in the City of New York (Helen Early), N.Y.L.J., 7/2/93, p.22, col.2 (Sup. Ct., N.Y. County).

2. L. 1992, Ch. 698, eff. April 1, 1993.

3. See infra, § 22.9, for definition.

4. Mental Hygiene Law § 81.01; Matter of Maher, 207 A.D.2d 133, 621 N.Y.S.2d 617 (2d Dep't 1994); Matter of Sulzberger, 159 Misc.2d 236, 603 N.Y.S.2d 656 (Sup.Ct., N.Y. County, 1993); Matter of Presbyterian Hospital in the City of New York (Helen Early), N.Y.L.J., 7/2/93, p.22, col.2 (Sup.Ct., N.Y. County). See generally R.M. Bailly, *Guardianship Reform for Older Adults in New York*, 2 Elder Law Attorney (N.Y.S.B.A.) 28 (Spring/Summer 1992); L. Beane, *The Adult Guardian—Mental Hygiene Law, Article 81*, 3 Elder Law Attorney No. 1 (N.Y.S.B.A.) 27 (Spring 1993); W.L. Leinheardt, *The New Mental Hygiene Law: Article 81—Proceedings for Appointment of a Guardian for Personal Needs or Property Management*, 25 Newsletter, Trusts and Estates Law Section (N.Y.S.B.A.) 7 (Fall

The definition of "least restrictive form of intervention" emphasizes the goal of the statute which is that the guardian should have only those powers necessary to assist the incapacitated person to compensate for limitations and to allow the person the greatest amount of independence and self-determination in light of the person's ability to appreciate and understand his or her functional limitations.[5] In appointing a guardian, the court should be guided by the concept of the least restrictive form of intervention. That goal is reflected particularly in the provisions governing the power of the court to appoint a guardian[6] and the provision governing dispositional alternatives.[7]

The guardianship system takes into account the personal wishes, preferences and desires of the person,[8] and affords the person the greatest amount of independence and self-determination and participation in all decisions affecting such person's life.[9]

The Legislature specifically set forth its findings and purpose in Section 81.01 of the Mental Hygiene Law as follows:

> The legislature hereby finds that the needs of persons with incapacities are as diverse and complex as they are unique to the individual. The current system of conservatorship and committee does not provide the necessary flexibility to meet these needs. Conservatorship which traditionally compromises a person's rights only with respect to property frequently is insufficient to provide necessary relief. On the other hand, a committee, with its judicial finding of incompetence and the accompanying stigma and loss of

---

1992); G.O. Koppell & K.J. Munnelly, *The New Guardian Statute: Article 81 of the Mental Hygiene Law*, 65 N.Y.S.B.J. 16 (February 1993).

Although the impetus for enactment of Article 81 was to create a guardianship law to meet the needs of elderly persons, nothing in the statute precludes its use for the young. A guardian may be appointed for anyone, of whatever age, who is functionally disabled to make a decision affecting his or her life. Matter of Marmol (Pineda), 168 Misc.2d 845, 640 N.Y.S.2d 969 (Sup.Ct., N.Y. County, 1996). *But see* Matter of Lavecchia, 170 Misc.2d 211, 650 N.Y.S.2d 955 (Sup.Ct., Rockland County, 1996) (The court held that the purpose of Mental Hygiene Law Article 81 was to address the decision-making needs of disabled older adults and to replace the existing statutes governing conservators of property and committees under former Articles 77 and 78. It was not intended as an alternative to the existing statutes governing infants and mentally retarded and developmentally disabled persons under SCPA Articles 17 and 17–A. In the case of an infant who is physically disabled, an Article 17 guardianship proceeding is the more appropriate proceeding to appoint a guardian than an Article 81 Mental Hygiene Law guardianship proceeding.).

5. Matter of Maher, 207 A.D.2d 133, 621 N.Y.S.2d 617 (2d Dep't 1994).

6. Mental Hygiene Law § 81.02; *see infra*, §§ 22.11, *et seq.*

7. Mental Hygiene Law § 81.16; *see infra*, § 22.38.

8. *But see* Matter of Kustka, 163 Misc.2d 694, 622 N.Y.S.2d 208 (Sup.Ct., Queens County, 1994)(the court departed from this principle in the selection of a guardian. The court found that the proposed guardian selected by the alleged incapacitated person, his wife, had an interest adverse to that of the alleged incapacitated person, and her appointment could cause harm to his assets).

9. Matter of Heumann, N.Y.L.J., 11/17/93, p.29, col.6 (Sup.Ct., Kings County). *See generally*, L. Beane, *The Adult Guardian—Mental Hygiene Law, Article 81*, 3 Elder Law Attorney No. 1 (N.Y.S.B.A.) 27 (Spring 1993).

civil rights, traditionally involves a deprivation that is often excessive and unnecessary. Moreover, certain persons require some form of assistance in meeting their personal and property management needs but do not require either of these drastic remedies. The legislature finds that it is desirable for and beneficial to persons with incapacities to make available to them the least restrictive form of intervention which assists them in meeting their needs but, at the same time, permits them to exercise the independence and self-determination of which they are capable. The legislature declares that it is the purpose of this act to promote the public welfare by establishing a guardianship system which is appropriate to satisfy either personal or property management needs of an incapacitated person in a manner tailored to the individual needs of that person, which takes in account the personal wishes, preferences and desires of the person, and which affords the person the greatest amount of independence and self-determination and participation in all the decisions affecting such person's life.[10]

The Legislature, while repealing both Articles 77 and 78 of the Mental Hygiene Law, effective April 1, 1993, also included provisions for the continuation of previously appointed conservators and committees and for the continuation of proceedings commenced under Articles 77 and 78. These specifically provide that after April 1, 1993, unless the court deems it impracticable, all proceedings relating to persons with incapacities shall be governed by Mental Hygiene Law Article 81.[11]

Library References:
West's Key No. Digests, Mental Health ⚖111.

§ 22.9 Definitions

Mental Hygiene Law Section 81.03 sets forth the definitions of certain terms as used in Article 81. These definitions are as follows:

10. L. 1992, Ch. 698, § 3, eff. April 1, 1993.

11. L. 1992, Ch. 698, § 4, provides as follows:

§ 4. (a) Continuation of conservators and committees. Except as otherwise provided in this section, any orders, determinations or decisions of the appointing or a subsequent court order under articles 77 and 78 of the mental hygiene law, shall continue in force and effect until duly modified or abrogated by a judge pursuant to article 81 of the mental hygiene law as added by section three of this Act. Any conservator or committee appointed prior to April 1, 1993 shall be governed by the reporting requirements of sections 81.31 and 81.32 of the mental hygiene law, as of May 1, 1994.

(b) Prior proceedings. In all proceedings commenced under article 77 or 78 of the mental hygiene law prior to April 1, 1993 for which a conservator or a committee has not been appointed on April 1, 1993, the court shall make the findings required by section 81.15 of the mental hygiene law and dispose of the matter in accordance with the dispositional alternatives of section 81.16 of the mental hygiene law. Unless the court deems it impracticable, such proceedings shall otherwise be governed by all other provisions of article 81 of the mental hygiene law. Wherever a statute uses the terms conservators or committees, such statute shall be construed to include the term guardian notwithstanding the provisions of such article unless the context otherwise requires.

§ 22.9 GUARDIANSHIP Ch. 22

(a) *Guardian* means a person who is eighteen years of age or older, a corporation, or a public agency, including a local department of social services, appointed in accordance with terms of Mental Hygiene Law Article 81 by the supreme court, the surrogate's court, or the county court to act on behalf of an incapacitated person in providing for personal needs and/or for property management.

(b) *Functional level* means the ability to provide for personal needs and/or the ability with respect to property management.

(c) *Functional limitations* means behavior or conditions of a person which impair the ability to provide for personal needs and/or property management.

(d) *Least restrictive form of intervention* means that the powers granted by the court to the guardian with respect to the incapacitated person represent only those powers which are necessary to provide for that person's personal needs and/or property management and which are consistent with affording that person the greatest amount of independence and self-determination in light of that person's understanding and appreciation of the nature and consequences of his or her functional limitations.

(e) *Available resources* means resources such as, but not limited to, visiting nurses, homemakers, home health aides, adult day care and multipurpose senior citizen centers, powers of attorney, trusts, representative and protective payees, and residential care facilities.

(f) *Personal needs* means needs such as, but not limited to, food, clothing, shelter, health care, and safety.

(g) *Property management* means taking actions to obtain, administer, protect, and dispose of real and personal property, intangible property, business property, benefits, and income and to deal with financial affairs.

(h) *Activities of daily living* means activities such as, but not limited to, mobility, eating, toileting, dressing, grooming, housekeeping, cooking, shopping, money management, banking, driving or using public transportation, and other activities related to personal needs and to property management.

(i) *Major medical or dental treatment* means a medical, surgical or diagnostic intervention or procedure where a general anesthetic is used or which involves any significant risk or any significant invasion of bodily integrity requiring an incision or producing substantial pain, discomfort, debilitation, or having a significant recovery period, or which involves the administration of psychotropic medication or electroconvulsive therapy. It does not include any routine diagnosis or treatment such as the administration of medications other than chemotherapy for nonpsychiatric conditions or nutrition or the extraction of bodily fluids for analysis; or dental care performed with a local anesthetic. Nor does it include any procedures which are provided under emergency circumstances, pursuant to Public Health Law Section 2504.

§ 22.10 Summary

The problems with implementation of the former statutes[1] governing the appointment of committees and conservators, and the limitations on the use of a conservator as a consequence of the decision in *Matter of Grinker (Rose)*,[2] led to the repeal of Mental Hygiene Law Articles 77 and 78 and the enactment of Mental Hygiene Law Article 81.[3] The purpose of Article 81 is to create a guardianship system with the necessary flexibility to meet the personal and/or property needs of the incapacitated person, so as to foster the least restrictive form of intervention consistent with an individual's self-determination.

§ 22.11 Power to Appoint Guardian—Generally

The cornerstone of Mental Hygiene Law Article 81 is the concept of appointing a guardian whose powers are tailored specifically to the particular needs of a person with respect to personal care, property management, or both.[1] Mental Hygiene Law Section 81.02 sets forth the concept of a specifically tailored appointment based on a functional assessment of the person and sets the tone for the remaining provisions.

The Section has three parts. The first part describes the power of the court to appoint a guardian.[2] The second part describes the criteria by which the court determines whether a person is incapacitated.[3] The third part presents the concept of tailoring the guardian's powers so that the guardian has only those powers which meet the specific needs of the person and which represent the least restrictive alternative.[4]

Library References:

West's Key No. Digests, Guardian and Ward ⚹9.5; Mental Health ⚹104.

§ 22.12 Power to Appoint Guardian—Elements

In order for the court to appoint a guardian for a person, there must be a two-prong determination: 1) that the appointment is necessary to meet personal care or property management needs of the person; and 2)

§ 22.10

1. Former Mental Hygiene Law Arts. 77, Conservators, and 78, Committee of Incompetent or Patient.

2. 77 N.Y.2d 703, 570 N.Y.S.2d 448, 573 N.E.2d 536 (1991).

3. L. 1992, Ch. 698, eff. April 1, 1993.

§ 22.11

1. *See* Mental Hygiene Law § 81.02.

2. *See* Mental Hygiene Law § 81.02(a) discussed *infra* in § 22.12. *See* Matter of Claiman, 169 Misc.2d 881, 646 N.Y.S.2d 940 (Sup.Ct., Queens County, 1996) (it is the function of the court, not a jury, to determine who will be appointed a guardian and the powers of the guardian).

3. *See* Mental Hygiene Law § 81.02(b), discussed *infra* in § 22.13.

4. *See* Mental Hygiene Law §§ 81.02(c), (d), discussed *infra* in § 22.14.

that the person agrees to the appointment or is incapacitated, as the term is defined in the statute.[1]

Under the first prong of the test, the appointment of a guardian must be found to be necessary to provide for personal needs of that person, including food, clothing, shelter, health care, or safety and/or to manage property and financial affairs of that person.[2] Unlike the dual structure of former Mental Hygiene Law Articles 77, Conservators, and 78, Committee of Incompetent or Patient, Article 81 provides a single structure governing both property management and personal care. In deciding whether the appointment of a guardian is necessary, the court must consider all the evidence including the information and independent observations provided by the court evaluator's report[3] as to the person's condition, affairs and situation, and the sufficiency and reliability of available resources[4] such as visiting nurses, homemakers, home health aides, adult day care, powers of attorney, trusts and representative and protective payees. The court should regard guardianship as a last resort and should assess the advantages and disadvantages of alternatives to guardianship, deciding on guardianship only when it clearly benefits the person who is the subject of the proceeding and when the alternatives are not sufficient and reliable to meet the needs of the person.[5]

The second prong of the test requires that the person either agree to the appointment or be found by the court to be incapacitated.[6] Providing for an appointment of a guardian where the person agrees to it permits the court to fashion relief for individuals who are unable to meet their personal or property management needs because of a physical disability and welcome the appointment of someone to act on their behalf.[7]

§ 22.12

1. Matter of Maher, 207 A.D.2d 133, 621 N.Y.S.2d 617 (2d Dep't 1994); Matter of Hammons (Ehmke), 164 Misc.2d 609, 625 N.Y.S.2d 408 (Sup.Ct., Queens County, 1995); Matter of Kustka, 163 Misc.2d 694, 622 N.Y.S.2d 208 (Sup.Ct., Queens County, 1994). See infra, § 22.13, for discussion of the statutory definition of incapacity.

2. Mental Hygiene Law § 81.02(a).

3. See infra, §§ 22.25–22.27 discussing the court evaluator.

4. See supra, § 22.9, for definition of "available resources" contained in Mental Hygiene Law § 81.03(e).

Where Protective Services for Adults would provide house cleaning services and assist in arranging for medical care for alleged incompetent persons, the appointment of a guardian was denied. Matter of Hammons (Perreau), N.Y.L.J., 7/7/95, p.29, col.3 (Sup.Ct., N.Y. County).

5. Matter of Maher, 207 A.D.2d 133, 621 N.Y.S.2d 617 (2d Dep't 1994). See Law Revision Commission Commentary to Mental Hygiene Law § 81.02; G.O. Koppell & K.J. Munnelly, *The New Guardian Statute: Article 81 of the Mental Hygiene Law*, 65 N.Y.S.B.J. 16 (February 1993).

6. *See infra*, § 22.13, for discussion of the statutory definition of incapacity. See Matter of Peterson, N.Y.L.J., 1/15/97, p. 26, col. 4 (Sup.Ct., N.Y. County) (proceeding for appointment of guardian dismissed where the court found that the appointment of a guardian was not necessary in the face of the opposition to such appointment by the alleged incapacitated person and the finding that the petitioner had failed to establish that the respondent was incapacitated).

7. *See* In re Saunderson, N.Y.L.J., 4/12/94, p.26, col.6 (Sup.Ct., Suffolk County). Where the record did not establish that the respondent was an incapacitated person, the appointment of a guardian was

In all other situations, *i.e.*, when the appointment is not voluntary, the court must find that the person is incapacitated as that term is defined in Mental Hygiene Law Section 81.02(b) before an appointment can be made.

Library References:
West's Key No. Digests, Guardian and Ward ⟐9.5; Mental Health ⟐104.

§ 22.13 Power to Appoint Guardian—Incapacity

Determination of incapacity must be based on clear and convincing evidence[1] and must consist of a determination that the person is likely to suffer harm because: (1) the person is unable to provide for personal needs and/or property management, and (2) the person cannot adequately understand and appreciate the nature and consequences of such inability.[2] This standard does away with the labels of incompetency and substantial impairment in former Articles 77 and 78 of the Mental Hygiene Law and their requirement of some underlying illness or condition.[3] This functional approach has been endorsed by the New York Court of Appeals, which has recognized that the presence of a particular condition does not necessarily preclude a person from functioning effectively.[4] In *Rivers v. Katz*,[5] the Court held that an involuntarily committed mental patient had the right to refuse to consent to the administration of antipsychotic drugs absent "a judicial determination that the patient lacked the capacity to make a reasoned decision with respect to the proposed treatment."[6]

This concept was confirmed in *Matter of Grinker (Rose)*,[7] where the Court of Appeals noted that under former Mental Hygiene Law Article 77, the mental illness of a proposed conservatee was relevant only to the extent the illness caused substantial impairment of ability to care for property and provide for financial needs and held that the standard for

dependent upon his consent thereto. The respondent could withhold his consent to the appointment of a guardian and, as in this case, execute a health care proxy pursuant to Public Health Law Art. 29–C, a procedure which required no court approval.

§ 22.13

1. Matter of Maher, 207 A.D.2d 133, 621 N.Y.S.2d 617 (2d Dep't 1994). *See infra*, §§ 22.30, *et seq.*, discussing the hearing and proof required to establish incapacity.

2. Mental Hygiene Law § 81.02(b).

3. Matter of Application of Rochester General Hospital (Levin), 158 Misc.2d 522, 601 N.Y.S.2d 375 (Sup.Ct., Monroe County, 1993) (based upon the rationale behind the enactment of Article 81, the terms "disability" or "incompetence" may no longer have relevance with regard to the appointment of a guardian under Article 81). *See* Law Revision Commission Commentary to Mental Hygiene Law § 81.02.

4. Matter of Grinker (Rose), 77 N.Y.2d 703, 570 N.Y.S.2d 448, 573 N.E.2d 536 (1991); Rivers v. Katz, 67 N.Y.2d 485, 504 N.Y.S.2d 74, 495 N.E.2d 337 (1986).

5. 67 N.Y.2d 485, 504 N.Y.S.2d 74, 495 N.E.2d 337 (1986).

6. *See, e.g.*, Matter of Gordon, 162 Misc.2d 697, 619 N.Y.S.2d 235 (Sup.Ct., Rockland County, 1994).

7. 77 N.Y.2d 703, 570 N.Y.S.2d 448, 573 N.E.2d 536 (1991). *See supra*, § 22.7 for discussion of the impact of *Matter of Grinker (Rose)* concerning the grant of power to a conservator.

appointment was not satisfied where no causal connection was established between the mental condition of the person alleged to be incapacitated and his or her alleged impairment. Accordingly, the court must look at the person's behavior and whether this behavior manifests itself as an inability to care for himself or herself and a lack of understanding and appreciation of problems associated with such limitations.[8]

Library References:

West's Key No. Digests, Guardian and Ward ⚖9.5; Mental Health ⚖104.

§ 22.14 Power to Appoint Guardian—Primary Considerations

In reaching its determination of incapacity, Mental Hygiene Law Section 81.02(c) requires the court to give primary consideration to the functional level and functional limitations of the person. Such consideration must include assessment of that person's (1) management of activities of daily living, (2) understanding and appreciation of the nature and consequences of any inability to manage activities of daily living, (3) preferences, wishes, and values with regard to managing activities of daily living, and (4) nature and extent of the person's property and financial affairs and his or her ability to manage them. The court must also include assessment of (1) the extent of demands placed on the person by that person's personal needs and by the nature and extent of that person's property and financial affairs, (2) any physical illness and prognosis of such illness, (3) any mental disability, alcoholism or substance dependence, and prognosis of such disability, alcoholism or substance dependence, and (4) any medications with which the person is being treated and their effect on such person's behavior, cognition and judgment.

In addition, in making determination of incapacity, the court must consider all other relevant facts and circumstances regarding the person's (1) functional level and (2) understanding and appreciation of the nature and consequences of his or her functional limitations.[1]

---

8. The record of the trial court in Matter of Grinker (Rose) was found to contain no proof to satisfy the standard for appointing a conservator under former Mental Hygiene Law Art. 77—substantial impairment of the ability of the person alleged to be incompetent to manage her finances. The trial court was found to have relied heavily on evidence of the nature of the respondent's "alleged mental condition, how it manifested itself in her artwork, and what the proper treatment for the condition should be." As the Court of Appeals noted, however, it was information regarding a person's functional abilities, namely a person's "spending patterns, ability to budget and allocate concededly limited resources, or knowledge of existing accounts payable, their balances, and income" that is critical to a determination of whether a surrogate decisionmaker with power over the financial affairs should be appointed. 77 N.Y.2d 703, 570 N.Y.S.2d 448, 573 N.E.2d 536 (1991). See also Matter of Maher, 207 A.D.2d 133, 621 N.Y.S.2d 617 (2d Dep't 1994).

§ 22.14

1. Mental Hygiene Law § 81.02(d).

The words "primary consideration" are used to reinforce the underlying intent of the statute that the court not assign undue weight to any medical diagnosis but rather should consider such diagnosis in light of information about the behavior and functional limitations of the person.[2] To the extent a physical or mental condition is present, information concerning the medication and the prognosis with respect to the condition should be closely scrutinized.[3] The prognosis of any medical condition is especially useful to the court in tailoring the powers of the guardian and the duration of the guardianship.

A functional evaluation assesses the extent to which the person carries out the activities of daily living effectively and provides information about a person's basic needs and how they are met: income adequacy and spending patterns, such as, physical ability to write checks and manage currency and whether pension checks and disability payments arrive on time; adequacy of food, clothing and shelter, such as, ability to buy and prepare food, ability to eat and choice of diet, ability to dress and undress, adequacy of laundry facilities, upkeep of shelter, warmth and ventilation, cleanliness of environment, safety of home; physical functioning, such as, ability to walk, climb stairs, reach, get in and out of chair and tub; sensory functioning, such as, ability to see, hear, feel, react in ways that do not endanger health or safety; access to helpful resources such as friends, relatives, physicians, emergency facilities, transportation; satisfaction with present circumstances, desire for change and specific assistance the person wishes; emotional factors, such as, loneliness and anxiety; and mental status including orientation to reality, memory functioning, reasoning ability.[4]

Mental Hygiene Law Section 81.02 emphasizes that even if all the elements of incapacity are present, a guardian should be appointed only as a last resort and should not be imposed if available resources or other alternatives will adequately protect the person.[5] If the court determines that the appointment of a guardian is necessary, the guardian should be granted only those powers that are necessary to provide for the person's needs in a manner consistent with the principle of employing the least restrictive alternative, *i.e.*, the appointment of a guardian is appropriate to the individual and affords the person the greatest amount of self-

---

2. Matter of Loury (Loury), N.Y.L.J., 9/23/93, p.26, col.2 (Sup.Ct., Kings County), aff'd 210 A.D.2d 227, 619 N.Y.S.2d 351 (2d Dep't 1994). *See* Law Revision Commission Commentary to Mental Hygiene Law § 81.02.

3. *See*, for example, the analysis used in Matter of Maher, N.Y.L.J., 9/7/93, p.24, col.6 (Sup.Ct., Kings County), aff'd 207 A.D.2d 133, 621 N.Y.S.2d 617 (2d Dep't 1994), and Matter of Presbyterian Hospital in the City of New York (Helen Early), N.Y.L.J., 7/2/93, p.22, col.2 (Sup.Ct., N.Y. County).

4. Law Revision Commission Commentary to Mental Hygiene Law § 81.02.

5. Matter of Maher, 207 A.D.2d 133, 621 N.Y.S.2d 617 (2d Dep't 1994). *See* Matter of O'Hear (Rodriguez), 219 A.D.2d 720, 631 N.Y.S.2d 743 (2d Dep't 1995); *see also* Law Revision Commission Commentary to Mental Hygiene Law § 81.02.

§ 22.14 GUARDIANSHIP Ch. 22

determination and independence in light of his or her understanding and appreciation of his or functional limitations.[6]

Library References:

West's Key No. Digests, Guardian and Ward ⇐9.5; Mental Health ⇐104.

§ 22.15 Power to Appoint Guardian—Jurisdiction

Pursuant to Section 81.04 of the Mental Hygiene Law, the supreme court and county courts outside of New York City have jurisdiction over proceedings to appoint a guardian for personal needs or property management of a person alleged to be incapacitated.[1] These courts have power to provide relief for (1) a resident of New York, (2) a nonresident of New York present in the state, and (3) a nonresident of New York under Mental Hygiene Law Section 81.18.[2]

The surrogate's court has limited concurrent jurisdiction to appoint a guardian with property management powers.[3] Mental Hygiene Law Section 81.04(b) provides that,

> when it appears in any proceeding[4] in the surrogate's court that a person interested in an estate is entitled to money or property as a beneficiary of the estate, or entitled to the proceeds of any action as provided in section 5–4.1[5] of the estates, powers and trusts law, or to the proceeds of a settlement of a cause of action brought on behalf of an infant for personal injuries, and that the interested person is a resident of, or is physically present in, the county in which the proceeding is pending[6] and is allegedly incapacitated with respect to

---

6. *See infra*, §§ 22.47–22.53 discussing the powers which may be granted to a guardian consistent with the principle of least restrictive intervention.

§ 22.15

1. Mental Hygiene Law § 81.04 is drawn from the jurisdictional provisions in former Articles 77 and 78 of the Mental Hygiene Law. *See* Law Revision Commission Commentary to Mental Hygiene Law § 81.04. The court of claims does not possess jurisdiction to entertain such a proceeding. Fales v. State, 108 Misc.2d 636, 438 N.Y.S.2d 449 (Ct.Cl.1981).

2. *See, e.g.*, Matter of Le, 168 Misc.2d 384, 637 N.Y.S.2d 614 (Sup.Ct., Queens County, 1995) (court had jurisdiction where alleged incapacitated person was present in the state at the time the proceeding to appoint a guardian was commenced); In re Seronde, 99 Misc.2d 485, 416 N.Y.S.2d 716 (Sup.Ct., Westchester County, 1979) (Appointment proper where virtually all of the alleged incapacitated person's property is located in the state).

See infra, § 22.40, for discussion of appointment of foreign guardian.

3. Mental Hygiene Law § 81.04(b).

4. *See* In re Condon, 118 Misc.2d 544, 461 N.Y.S.2d 181 (Surr.Ct., Bronx County, 1983), holding, under former Mental Hygiene Law Art. 77, that there need not be an already pending proceeding in surrogate's court to make an application for a conservator but that the application could be brought to protect a distributee's right to commence a proceeding in surrogate's court.

5. EPTL §§ 5–4.1, *et seq.*, deals with actions for wrongful death.

6. Matter of Anonymous, R.A., N.Y.L.J., 9/28/93, p.27, col.2 (Surr.Ct., Nassau County); Matter of Lisle, N.Y.L.J., 8/9/94, p.27, col.4 (Surr.Ct., Nassau County) (the court in each case found it had jurisdiction to hear and determine the need for the appointment of a guardian for property management based upon the residence within the county of the alleged incompetent per-

194

property management under the provisions of this article, and the surrogate's court is satisfied after a hearing or trial in accordance with the provisions of this article that the interested person is incapacitated with respect to property management, the surrogate's court shall have the power to order relief for that person with respect to property management in accordance with the provisions of this article [81].[7]

Library References:
West's Key No. Digests, Guardian and Ward ⬤—13(1); Mental Health ⬤—108.

§ 22.16 Power to Appoint Guardian—Venue

A proceeding under Mental Hygiene Law Article 81 must be brought in the supreme court within the judicial district, or in the county court of the county in which the person alleged to be incapacitated resides,[1] or is physically present, or in the surrogate's court having jurisdiction as provided in Mental Hygiene Law Section 81.04(b).[2] If the person alleged to be incapacitated is being cared for as a resident in a facility, hospital, or school, or alcoholism facility in New York,[3] a substance abuse program,[4] an adult care facility,[5] or a residential health care facility or general hospital,[6] the residence of that person is deemed to be in the county where the facility is located and the proceeding must be brought in that county.[7] However, an interested party can apply for a change in venue to another county because of the inconvenience of parties or witnesses or the condition of the person alleged to be incapacitated.[8] If the person alleged to be incapacitated is not present in New York, or the residence of such person cannot be ascertained, residence is deemed to

son and the court's jurisdiction over the estate of the deceased spouse of the alleged incompetent person). *Cf.*, Matter of Guardianship of Bowers, 164 Misc.2d 298, 624 N.Y.S.2d 750 (Surr.Ct., N.Y. County, 1995), where the alleged incompetent person did not reside in New York but was the sole beneficiary of a deceased New York domiciliary. The surrogate's court held that it had jurisdiction to appoint a guardian of the incapacitated person, in this instance, the guardian previously appointed by the court in the state where the incapacitated person resided. The court noted that while it appeared that the statute did not grant jurisdiction, such jurisdiction was found by reading Mental Hygiene Law § 81.04(b) together with Mental Hygiene Law § 81.05, and in the general jurisdiction of the surrogate's court over the affairs of decedents.

7. **CAVEAT**: The surrogate's court has jurisdiction only to appoint a guardian for property management and if a guardian for personal needs is necessary, a separate proceeding must be brought in a court of competent jurisdiction. Matter of Lisle, N.Y.L.J., 8/9/94, p.27, col.4 (Surr.Ct., Nassau County). This limitation was requested by the Surrogate's Association of New York. *See* Matter of Guardianship of Bowers, 164 Misc.2d 298, 624 N.Y.S.2d 750 (Surr.Ct., N.Y. County, 1995).

§ 22.16

1. In re Avery, 93 A.D.2d 886, 461 N.Y.S.2d 734 (2d Dep't 1983).

2. Mental Hygiene Law § 81.05(a). *See supra*, § 22.15, for discussion of jurisdiction of surrogate's court.

3. *See* Mental Hygiene Law § 1.03.

4. *See* Mental Hygiene Law § 19.03.

5. *See* Social Services Law § 2.

6. *See* Public Health Law § 2801.

7. Mental Hygiene Law § 81.05(a).

8. *Id.*

be in the county in which all or some of such person's property is situated.[9]

After appointment of a temporary guardian,[10] special guardian, standby guardian, or alternate standby guardians,[11] any proceeding to modify a prior order must be brought in the supreme court, county court, or surrogate's court which granted the prior order.[12] If, at the time the application to modify the prior order is made, the incapacitated person is being cared for as a resident in a facility, hospital, or school, or alcoholism facility in New York, a substance abuse program, an adult care facility, or a residential health care facility or general hospital, the proceeding must be brought in the county where the facility is located, subject to an application by an interested party for a change of venue to the court which granted the prior order because of the inconvenience of parties or witnesses or the condition of the incapacitated person.[13]

Library References:
West's Key No. Digests, Mental Health ⇔108.

§ 22.17 Power to Appoint Guardian—Standing to Commence Proceeding

The following persons can commence a proceeding under Mental Hygiene Law Article 81 for the appointment of a guardian by the filing of a petition[1] with the court:[2]

(1) the person alleged to be incapacitated;

(2) a presumptive distributee of the person alleged to be incapacitated;

(3) the executor or administrator of an estate when the alleged incapacitated person is or may be a beneficiary of that estate;

(4) a trustee of a trust when the alleged incapacitated person is or may be the grantor or beneficiary of that trust;

(5) a person with whom the person alleged to be incapacitated resides;

(6) a person otherwise concerned with the welfare of the person alleged to be incapacitated. For the purposes of this section a person otherwise concerned with the welfare of the person alleged to be incapacitated[3] may include a corporation, or public

9. *Id.*
10. *See infra,* § 22.57.
11. *See infra,* § 22.73.
12. Mental Hygiene Law § 81.05(b).
13. *Id.*

§ 22.17
1. *See infra,* § 22.23 for discussion of the requirements of the petition.
2. Mental Hygiene Law § 81.06(a).
3. Under prior law it was held that an "interested person" must be interested in the well being or best interest of the person alleged to be incapacitated and this defini-

agency, including the department of social services[4] in the county where person alleged to be incapacitated resides regardless of whether the person alleged to be incapacitated is a recipient of public assistance; or

(7) the chief executive officer[5] of a facility, hospital, school, or alcoholism facility in New York,[6] a substance abuse program,[7] an adult care facility,[8] or a residential health care facility or general hospital,[9] in which person alleged to be incapacitated is patient or resident.

Library References:
West's Key No. Digests, Guardian and Ward ⚖13(3); Mental Health ⚖124.

§ 22.18 Proceeding to Appoint Guardian—Summary

Article 81 of the Mental Hygiene Law provides for the appointment of a guardian whose powers are tailored specifically to the particular needs of a person with respect to personal care, property management, or both.[1] In order for the court to appoint a guardian for a person, there must be a two-prong determination: 1) that the appointment is necessary to meet personal care or property management needs of the person; and 2) that the person agrees to the appointment or is incapacitated, as defined in the statute.[2] In reaching its determination of incapacity the court must give primary consideration to the functional level and functional limitations of the person.[3] The proceeding for the appointment of a guardian may be brought in the supreme court, the county court[4] and, for property management only, in the surrogate's court,[5] in the county where the person alleged to be incapacitated resides.[6] The statute speci-

tion did not include a person or corporation which had a conflict of interest with such person or was an opposing party in litigation against such person or was seeking to protect his or her own well being rather than that of the person alleged to be incapacitated. *See, e.g.,* Klotz v. Klotz, 176 A.D.2d 661, 575 N.Y.S.2d 663 (1st Dep't 1991), appeal dismissed 79 N.Y.2d 915, 581 N.Y.S.2d 667, 590 N.E.2d 252 (1992), appeal dismissed 80 N.Y.2d 923, 589 N.Y.S.2d 310, 602 N.E.2d 1126 (1992); In re Wais, 119 Misc.2d 911, 464 N.Y.S.2d 634 (Sup.Ct., Albany County, 1983).

4. In re Kaufman, 114 Misc.2d 1078, 453 N.Y.S.2d 304 (Sup.Ct., Bronx County, 1982).

5. Although the petition was verified by the vice president of administration of the hospital, the court upheld the proceeding on the ground that a proceeding may be commenced by a person otherwise concerned with the welfare of the person alleged to be incapacitated under Mental Hygiene Law § 81.06(a)(6), and concluded that the proceeding had been brought by someone authorized to commence such proceeding. Matter of Application of Rochester General Hospital (Levin), 158 Misc.2d 522, 601 N.Y.S.2d 375 (Sup.Ct., Monroe County, 1993).

6. *See* Mental Hygiene Law § 1.03.
7. *See* Mental Hygiene Law § 19.03.
8. *See* Social Services Law § 2.
9. *See* Public Health Law § 2801.

§ 22.18

1. *See supra,* § 22.11.
2. *See supra,* §§ 22.11, 22.12.
3. *See supra,* § 22.14.
4. *See supra,* § 22.15.
5. *Id.*
6. *See supra,* § 22.16.

fies the persons who may bring the proceeding,[7] who may generally be described as persons having some relationship to or some interest in the personal welfare or property of the person alleged to be incapacitated, including the person alleged to be incapacitated.

§ 22.19 Proceeding to Appoint Guardian

A proceeding for the appointment of a guardian for the personal needs or property management of a person alleged to be incapacitated is commenced by the filing of a petition.[1] The form of the notice,[2] the order to show cause,[3] and the persons to be notified of a guardianship proceeding[4] are specified in detail by the statute. Mental Hygiene Law Section 81.07 mandates the form of notice including a warning in large bold face type,[5] the manner of service[6] and the time in which it must be accomplished.[7]

§ 22.20 Proceeding to Appoint Guardian—Time and Method of Service of Notice

The time periods established in the statute for serving the notice, the petition, and any supporting papers are designed to encourage the prompt resolution of a guardianship proceeding while at the same time allowing sufficient time for the petitioner's attorney to accomplish service within reasonable time constraints.[1]

On the filing of the petition, the court must set a date no more than 28 days from the date of filing of the petition on which the order to show cause is returnable. The court may for good cause shown set the date less than 28 days from the date of the filing of the petition.[2]

The order to show cause must fix as the hearing date the same date on which the order to show cause is returnable. The date of the hearing may be adjourned only for good cause shown.[3]

Mental Hygiene Law Section 81.07(d)(2) provides that the order to show cause and a copy of the petition must be personally delivered to the person alleged to be incapacitated not less than 14 days prior to the return date of the order to show cause. However, the court may direct

---

7. *See supra*, § 22.17.

§ 22.19

1. Mental Hygiene Law § 81.08; *see infra*, §§ 22.20, *et seq*. Service of a cross-petition in a pending proceeding has been approved. Matter of Staiano, 160 Misc.2d 494, 609 N.Y.S.2d 1021 (Sup.Ct., Suffolk County, 1994).

2. Mental Hygiene Law § 81.07(c); *see infra*, § 22.22.

3. Mental Hygiene Law § 81.07(a), (b); *see infra*, § 22.22.

4. Mental Hygiene Law § 81.07(d); *see infra*, § 22.21.

5. *See infra*, §§ 22.22, 22.98.

6. *See infra*, § 22.20.

7. *Id*.

§ 22.20

1. *See* Law Revision Commission Commentary to Mental Hygiene Law § 81.07.

2. Mental Hygiene Law § 81.07(a).

3. *Id*.

that the order to show cause and the copy of the petition be served on the person alleged to be incapacitated in a manner other than personal delivery.[4] The petitioner must demonstrate to the court's satisfaction that the person alleged to be incapacitated has refused to accept service.[5] A copy of the order to show cause and petition also must be left with a person of suitable age and discretion at the residence of the person alleged to be incapacitated if he or she is not served there.[6]

The order to show cause and a copy of the petition must be served by mail or by delivery to the office of the court evaluator[7] and the court appointed attorney, if there is one,[8] within seven days following appointment of the court evaluator and attorney.[9]

The order to show cause and a copy of the petition must be served personally or by mail on the other persons entitled to notice pursuant to Mental Hygiene Law Section 81.07(d)(1)[10] not less than 14 days prior to return date of order to show cause.[11]

The court may direct that the order to show cause be served within a time period less than the required period for good cause shown.[12]

---

4. *See* Matter of Nixon (Corey), N.Y.L.J., 6/4/96, p. 36, col. 6 (Sup.Ct., Suffolk County) (where petitioner was unable to locate and serve the alleged incapacitated person, the court fashioned a remedy by combining the Mental Hygiene Law Article 81 proceeding with a *habeas corpus* proceeding to allow an inquiry whether the alleged incapacitated person was being unlawfully restrained, detained or confined; service upon the alleged incapacitated person would be pursuant to the provisions of the *habeas corpus* statute (CPLR Article 70) and papers served in the *habeas corpus* proceeding would include the order to show cause and supporting papers in the Mental Hygiene Law Article 81 proceeding).

Under prior law it was held that the notice of petition to appoint conservator was properly served under CPLR 308(2) where papers were taken to home in which conservatee resided and were given to the wife of the person who owned the home, and papers were also sent by certified mail to same address. In re Foley, 140 A.D.2d 892, 528 N.Y.S.2d 709 (3d Dep't 1988), appeal dismissed 150 A.D.2d 884, 541 N.Y.S.2d 141 (3d Dep't 1989).

5. Mental Hygiene Law § 81.07(d)(2)(i). *See* Matter of Hammons (McCarthy), 168 Misc.2d 874, 645 N.Y.S.2d 392 (Sup.Ct., Queens County, 1996) (application to fashion alternate method of service on alleged incapacitated person was denied where petitioner failed to demonstrate that the alleged incapacitated person had refused to accept service or had evaded service; the situation in the case was that the alleged incapacitated person could not be located and, therefore, had not explicitly refused service).

6. *Id.*

7. *See infra,* §§ 22.25–22.27, for discussion of the court evaluator.

8. *See infra,* § 22.28 for discussion of the appointment of an attorney for the person alleged to be incapacitated. Where counsel has been appointed for the alleged incapacitated person and such counsel has appeared and participated in the proceedings, a cross petition may be served by mail on the alleged incapacitated person's counsel. Matter of Staiano, 160 Misc.2d 494, 609 N.Y.S.2d 1021 (Sup.Ct., Suffolk County, 1994).

9. Mental Hygiene Law § 81.07(d)(2)(ii).

10. *See infra,* § 22.21 for discussion of persons entitled to notice.

11. Mental Hygiene Law § 81.07(d)(2)(iii).

12. Mental Hygiene Law § 81.07(e). *See* Law Revision Commission Commentary to Mental Hygiene Law § 81.07, which states:

The order to show cause must set the date for the hearing on the same date the order to show cause is returnable and the hearing date may be adjourned only for good cause shown. This provision is also designed to encourage prompt resolution of the proceeding. The section further pro-

§ 22.20 GUARDIANSHIP Ch. 22

Library References:

West's Key No. Digests, Guardian and Ward ⚖13(3); Mental Health ⚖127.

§ 22.21 Proceeding to Appoint Guardian—Persons Entitled to Notice

Mental Hygiene Law Section 81.07(d)(1) specifies a broad group of persons upon whom service is required in a proceeding for the appointment of a guardian, many of whom were not entitled to service under prior law, in order to involve persons who may be able to shed some light on the situation. For example, someone who had been living with the proposed incapacitated person for a long period of time prior to the person's admission to a hospital or nursing home, yet lacked the legal status of spouse or presumptive distributee, was not entitled to notice of the proceeding under former Mental Hygiene Law Articles 77 or 78, while relatives who lived a great distance from the person and who may not have been interested, would have been entitled to receive notice under those former statutes.[1] However, as the language of the current section makes clear, in most situations, notice need be given only to those persons in each category who are known or whose existence and address can be ascertained with reasonably diligent efforts by the petitioner.

Persons entitled to service include:[2]

(1) the person alleged to be incapacitated;

(2) the following persons, other than the petitioner, who are known to the petitioner or whose existence and address can be ascertained by the petitioner with reasonably diligent efforts: (a) the spouse of the person alleged to be incapacitated, if any, (b) the parents of the person alleged to be incapacitated, if living, (c) the adult children of person alleged to be incapacitated, if any,[3] (d) the adult siblings of the person alleged to be incapacitated, if any, (e) the person or persons with whom the person alleged to be incapacitated resides;

(3) in the event no person listed in (2) above is given notice, notice must be given to at least one and not more than 3 living relatives of the person alleged to be incapacitated in nearest degree of kinship who are known to the petitioner or whose

vides in subdivisions (a) and (e) that the court may shorten time periods for service and for the holding of the hearing for good cause shown in order to respond to the needs of the allegedly incapacitated person.

§ 22.21

1. *See* Law Revision Commission Commentary to Mental Hygiene Law § 81.07.

2. Mental Hygiene Law § 81.07(d)(1).

3. Notice requirements were met where the papers before the court established that the address of the alleged incapacitated person's son could not be ascertained after reasonably diligent efforts. Matter of Rupp (Stollmeyer), N.Y.L.J., 1/14/94, p.28, col.3 (Sup.Ct., Suffolk County).

existence and address can be ascertained by the petitioner with reasonably diligent efforts;

(4) any person or persons designated by the alleged incapacitated person with authority under a power of attorney pursuant to General Obligations Law Sections 5–1501, 5–1601, and 5–1602,[4] or a Do Not Resuscitate (DNR) Order pursuant to Public Health Law Section 2905 or a health care proxy pursuant to Public Health Law Section 2981, if known to the petitioner;

(5) if known to the petitioner, any person, whether or not a relative of the person alleged to be incapacitated, or an organization that has demonstrated a genuine interest in promoting the best interests of the person alleged to be incapacitated such as by having a personal relationship with the person, regularly visiting the person, or regularly communicating with the person;

(6) the attorney for the person alleged to be incapacitated, if known to the petitioner;

(7) the court evaluator;[5]

(8) if it is known to the petitioner that the person alleged to be incapacitated receives public assistance or protective services under Social Services Law Article 9–B, the local department of social services;[6]

(9) if the person alleged to be incapacitated resides in a facility, hospital, school, or alcoholism facility in New York,[7] a substance abuse program,[8] an adult care facility,[9] or a residential health care facility or general hospital,[10] the chief executive officer in charge of the facility,[11] and the Mental Hygiene Legal Service ("MHLS") of the judicial department in which such residence is located;[12] and

(10) such other persons as the court may direct based on the recommendation of the court evaluator.

---

4. Pursuant to L. 1994, Ch. 419, effective October 1, 1994, the General Obligations Law was amended to repeal Sections 5–1601 and 5–1602; these provisions were reenacted as General Obligations Law §§ 5–1505 and 5–1506, respectively. Mental Hygiene Law § 81.07 has not been amended to reflect that change.

5. *See infra*, §§ 22.25–22.27 for discussion of the court evaluator.

6. *See* Matter of Baird, 167 Misc.2d 526, 634 N.Y.S.2d 971 (Sup.Ct., Suffolk County, 1995) (the NYS Department of Social Services is not entitled to notice).

7. *See* Mental Hygiene Law § 1.03.

8. *See* Mental Hygiene Law § 19.03.

9. *See* Social Services Law § 2.

10. *See* Public Health Law § 2801.

11. *See* Uniform Rules for the supreme court and the county court, 22 NYCRR § 202.54, Proceedings Relating to Appointments of Guardians With Respect to Patients in Facilities Defined in the Mental Hygiene Law.

12. *See infra*, § 22.28 for discussion of the role of the MHLS.

§ 22.22 Proceeding to Appoint Guardian—Notice Requirements

Mental Hygiene Law Section 81.07 establishes the form of the order to show cause and the information that must be included in the notice given to the alleged incapacitated person and others entitled to notice.[1] In addition to the return date,[2] the order to show cause must include the name, address, and telephone number of the person appointed as court evaluator,[3] and must be served together with a copy of the petition and any supporting papers on the persons identified in Mental Hygiene Law Section 81.07(d)[4] and in the prescribed form and manner.[5]

Mental Hygiene Law Section 81.07(b) provides that the order to show cause must be written in large type, in plain language, and in language other than English if necessary to inform the person alleged to be incapacitated of his or her rights, in a manner that he or she can easily understand, and must include following information:

(1) the date, time, and place of hearing of petition;

(2) a clear and easily readable statement of the rights of the person alleged to be incapacitated;[6]

(3) the name, address, and telephone number of the person appointed as court evaluator;[7]

(4) the name, address, and telephone number of the attorney, if one has been appointed, for the person alleged to be incapacitated;[8] and

(5) a list of the powers which the guardian would have authority to exercise on behalf of the person alleged to be incapacitated if the relief sought in petition is granted.[9]

Mental Hygiene Law Section 81.07(c) provides that the order to show cause must also include on its face a legend addressed to the person alleged to be incapacitated, with specified text[10] explaining, *inter*

---

§ 22.22

1. *See supra*, § 22.21 for discussion of the persons entitled to notice.

2. *See supra*, § 22.20 for discussion of the time limits established by Mental Hygiene Law § 81.07.

3. *See infra*, §§ 22.25–22.27 for discussion of the court evaluator.

4. *See supra*, § 22.21 for discussion of the persons entitled to notice.

5. Mental Hygiene Law § 81.07(a).

6. *See infra*, § 22.32 for discussion of the rights of the alleged incapacitated person at the hearing.

7. *See infra*, §§ 22.25–22.27 for discussion of the court evaluator.

8. *See infra*, § 22.28 for discussion of the appointment of an attorney for the alleged incapacitated person.

9. *See infra*, §§ 22.45–22.53 for discussion of the powers of the guardian.

10. *See infra*, § 22.98 for a form of order to show cause including the specified language.

alia, such person's right to a hearing, trial by jury and representation.[11] The legend describes the nature and seriousness of the proceeding, and the person's right to due process.[12] The legend also advises the person alleged to be incapacitated that a court evaluator will be appointed to conduct an investigation of the claims made in the petition,[13] and that the person has the right to object to the court evaluator's inspection of his or her medical and psychiatric records.[14]

Library References:
West's Key No. Digests, Guardian and Ward ⚿13(3); Mental Health ⚿127.

§ 22.23 Proceeding to Appoint Guardian—Petition

Mental Hygiene Law Section 81.08(a) sets forth the information that must be included in the petition for the appointment of a guardian. The petition must be verified under oath and must include following:

(1) the name, age, address, and telephone number of the person alleged to be incapacitated;

(2) the name, address, and telephone number of the person or persons with whom the person alleged to be incapacitated resides, if any;

(3) a description of the alleged incapacitated person's functional level including that person's ability to manage activities of daily living, behavior, and understanding and appreciation of the nature and consequences of any inability to manage the activities of daily living;

(4) if powers are sought with respect to the personal needs[1] of the alleged incapacitated person, specific factual allegations as to personal actions or other actual occurrences involving the person alleged to be incapacitated which are claimed to demonstrate that the person is likely to suffer harm because he or she cannot adequately understand and appreciate the nature and consequences of his or her inability to provide for personal needs;

(5) if powers are sought with respect to property management[2] for the alleged incapacitated person, specific factual allegations as to financial transactions or other actual occurrences involving

---

11. See *infra*, §§ 22.30–33 for a discussion of the conduct of the hearing for the appointment of a guardian.

12. See Law Revision Commission Commentary to Mental Hygiene Law § 81.07.

13. See *infra*, §§ 22.25–22.27 for discussion of the court evaluator.

14. Matter of Goldfarb, 160 Misc.2d 1036, 612 N.Y.S.2d 788 (Sup.Ct., Suffolk County, 1994). See *infra*, § 22.26 for discussion of the physician/patient privilege in a guardianship hearing.

§ 22.23

1. See Mental Hygiene Law § 81.22, discussed *infra* at § 22.53.

2. See Mental Hygiene Law § 81.21, discussed *infra* at §§ 22.47–52.

the person alleged to be incapacitated which are claimed to demonstrate that the person is likely to suffer harm because he or she cannot adequately understand and appreciate the nature and consequences of his or her inability to provide for property management;

(6) the particular powers being sought and their relationship to the functional level and the needs of the person alleged to be incapacitated;[3]

(7) the duration of the powers being sought;

(8) the approximate value and description of the financial resources of the person alleged to be incapacitated and whether, to the best of petitioner's knowledge, the person is a recipient of public assistance;

(9) the nature and amount of any claim, debt, or obligation of the person alleged to be incapacitated, to the best of petitioner's knowledge;

(10) the names, addresses, and telephone numbers of presumptive distributees[4] of the person alleged to be incapacitated unless they are unknown and cannot be reasonably ascertained;

(11) the name, address, and telephone number of the petitioner;

(12) the name, address, and telephone number of the person or persons, if any, proposed as guardian and standby guardian,[5] the relationship of the proposed guardian or standby guardian to the person alleged to be incapacitated, and the reasons why the proposed guardian or standby guardian is suitable to exercise powers necessary to assist the person alleged to be incapacitated;

(13) any relief sought under Mental Hygiene Law Section 81.23;[6]

(14) available resources, if any, that have been considered by the petitioner and the petitioner's opinion as to their sufficiency and reliability;

(15) any other information which in the petitioner's opinion will assist the court evaluator[7] in completing his or her investigation and report.

Six general categories of information are to be included in the petition. They are: 1) an explanation of the functional level of the person

---

3. See supra, § 22.14, for discussion of the need to tailor the powers of the guardian to the needs of the alleged incapacitated person.

4. See EPTL § 4-1.1, descent and distribution of a decedent's estate, for determination of distributees.

5. See infra, §§ 22.40, 22.73, for discussion of who may be appointed guardian and standby guardian.

6. See infra, §§ 22.56–22.59, for discussion of provisional remedies, including appointment of a temporary guardian.

7. See infra, §§ 22.25–22.27, for discussion of the court evaluator.

alleged to be incapacitated; 2) the reasons for the guardianship; 3) the available alternative resources that have been explored; 4) the particular powers sought and their relationship to the functional level of the person; 5) the proposed guardian and the reasons why the proposed guardian is suitable; 6) any conflicts of interest between the petitioner and the person alleged to be incapacitated, and any conflicts of interest between the person alleged to be incapacitated and any proposed guardian. In addition, any provisional relief that is sought pursuant to Mental Hygiene Law Section 81.23 must be set forth in the petition.[8]

Library References:
West's Key No. Digests, Mental Health ⚖126.

§ 22.24 Proceeding to Appoint Guardian—Summary

A proceeding for the appointment of a guardian for the personal needs or property management of a person alleged to be incapacitated is commenced by the filing of a petition.[1] The form of the notice,[2] the order to show cause,[3] and the persons to be notified of a guardianship proceeding[4] are specified in detail by the statute. Mental Hygiene Law Section 81.07 mandates the form of notice including a warning in large bold face type,[5] the manner of service[6] and the time in which it must be accomplished.[7]

§ 22.25 Court Evaluator—Persons Eligible for Appointment

At the time the order to show cause[1] is issued, the court must appoint a court evaluator.[2] The appointment of a court evaluator is mandatory in every case, with one exception. The court may dispense with or suspend the appointment of the court evaluator, although it need not do so, only when the court appoints counsel[3] under Mental Hygiene Law Section 81.10.[4] The court may appoint as court evaluator any person

---

8. Law Revision Commission Commentary to Mental Hygiene Law § 81.08.

§ 22.24

1. Mental Hygiene Law § 81.08; see supra, §§ 22.19, et seq.; see also, infra, § 22.99.

2. Mental Hygiene Law § 81.07(c); see supra, § 22.22; see also, infra, § 22.98.

3. Id.

4. Mental Hygiene Law § 81.07(d); see supra, § 22.21.

5. See infra, § 22.98.

6. See supra, § 22.20.

7. Id.

§ 22.25

1. See supra, § 22.22.

2. Mental Hygiene Law § 81.09(a). See also, 22 NYCRR Pt. 36, Appointment of Fiduciaries.

3. See infra, § 22.28 for discussion of the appointment of counsel.

4. Appointment of court evaluator was dispensed with where the Mental Hygiene Legal Service was appointed counsel and could perform essentially the same services as a court evaluator. Matter of Application of Rochester General Hospital (Levin) 158 Misc.2d 522, 601 N.Y.S.2d 375 (Sup.Ct., Monroe County, 1993). Appointment of a court evaluator was dispensed with and

drawn from a list maintained by the Office of Court Administration.[5] Such person shall have knowledge of property management, personal care skills, problems associated with disabilities, and private and public resources available for the type of limitations the person alleged to be incapacitated is alleged to have.[6] The court evaluator replaces the guardian *ad litem* under prior law and need not be an attorney.[7] The person appointed may be, but is not limited to, an attorney-at-law, physician, psychologist, accountant, social worker, or nurse.[8]

If the person alleged to be incapacitated resides in a facility, hospital, or school, or alcoholism facility,[9] a substance abuse program,[10] an adult care facility,[11] or a residential health care facility or general hospital,[12] the Mental Hygiene Legal Service in the judicial department where the person resides may be appointed court evaluator.[13] Mental Hygiene Law Section 81.09(b)(3), provides that, if the court appoints the Mental Hygiene Legal Service as court evaluator and on investigation it appears to the Service that it represents the person alleged to be incapacitated as counsel, or that counsel should otherwise be appointed for the person alleged to be incapacitated, the Service must so report to court. The Service must be relieved of its appointment as court evaluator whenever the Service represents the person alleged to be incapacitated as counsel, or is assigned to represent such person as counsel.

The court evaluator is intended to act as an independent investigator to gather information to aid the court in reaching a determination about the person's capacity, the availability and reliability of alternative resources, assigning the proper powers to the guardian, and selecting the guardian.[14]

counsel appointed where the alleged incapacitated person resided in France and the issues to be investigated were predominantly legal questions. Matter of Sulzberger, 159 Misc.2d 236, 603 N.Y.S.2d 656 (Sup.Ct., N.Y. County, 1993).

But see Matter of Whitehead, N.Y.L.J., 5/30/95, p. 34, col. 1 (Sup.Ct., Suffolk County) (Where alleged incapacitated person was a Canadian citizen residing in Arizona, the court found that the appointment of a court evaluator should not be dispensed with; the petition was devoid of a description or proof of the alleged incapacitated person's mental or physical condition; moreover, it appeared that the value of the alleged incapacitated person's property was substantial and far in excess of the cost which might be incurred by the court evaluator traveling to either Canada or Arizona to meet with the alleged incapacitated person).

5. 22 NYCRR Pt. 36, Appointment of Fiduciaries, § 36.2, Lists of Available Applicants.

6. Mental Hygiene Law § 81.09(b)(1).

7. G.O. Koppell & K.J. Munnelly, *The New Guardian Statute: Article 81 of the Mental Hygiene Law*, 65 N.Y.S.B.J. 16, 18 (February 1993).

8. Mental Hygiene Law § 81.09(b)(1).

9. *See* Mental Hygiene Law § 1.03.

10. *See* Mental Hygiene Law § 19.03.

11. *See* Social Services Law § 2.

12. *See* Public Health Law § 2801.

13. Mental Hygiene Law § 81.09(b)(2).

14. Law Revision Commission Commentary to Mental Hygiene Law § 81.09. *See infra*, § 22.28, discussing the role of counsel.

§ 22.26 Court Evaluator—Duties

The duties of the court evaluator are detailed in Mental Hygiene Law Section 81.09(c). The description of these duties is designed to provide guidance and direction to the court evaluator in fulfilling his or her role in the proceeding.[1] The duties of court evaluator shall include the following:[2]

(1) meeting, interviewing, and consulting with the person alleged to be incapacitated regarding the proceeding;

(2) explaining to the person alleged to be incapacitated, in a manner which such person can reasonably be expected to understand, the nature and possible consequences of the proceeding, the general powers and duties of the guardian, available resources, and rights to which the person is entitled, including the right to counsel;

(3) determining whether the person alleged to be incapacitated wishes legal counsel to be appointed and otherwise evaluating whether legal counsel should be appointed;

(4) interviewing the petitioner, or, if the petitioner is a facility or government agency, the person within the facility or the agency fully familiar with the alleged incapacitated person's condition, affairs and situation; and

(5) investigating and a making written report and recommendations to the court.[3]

The report and recommendations shall include the court evaluator's personal observations as to the person alleged to be incapacitated and his or her condition, affairs and situation,[4] as well as information in response to the following questions:

(a) does the person alleged to be incapacitated agree to the appointment of the proposed guardian and to the powers proposed for the guardian;

---

§ 22.26

1. Law Revision Commission Commentary to Mental Hygiene Law § 81.09.

2. The enumerated powers of the court evaluator do not include the power to consent to a discontinuance. Matter of Chachkers (Shirley W.), 159 Misc.2d 912, 606 N.Y.S.2d 959 (Sup.Ct., N.Y. County, 1993).

3. See infra, § 22.100, for a form of the court evaluator's report.

4. This language is included to demonstrate that the report of the court evaluator should not be "a rubber stamp" of how others view the person but rather a meaningful independent exploration of all aspects of the life of the allegedly incapacitated person. This concept of an independent evaluation is re-enforced by the requirement that the court evaluator's description of the person's functional level "shall be based on the evaluator's own assessment of the person alleged to be incapacitated to the extent possible" as well as examinations of third parties. Law Revision Commission Commentary to Mental Hygiene Law § 81.09.

(b) does the person wish legal counsel to be appointed or is the appointment of counsel in accordance with Mental Hygiene Law Section 81.10 otherwise appropriate;

(c) can the person alleged to be incapacitated come to the courthouse for the hearing;

(d) if the person alleged to be incapacitated cannot come to the courthouse, is the person completely unable to participate in the hearing;

(e) if the person alleged to be incapacitated cannot come to the courthouse, would any meaningful participation result from the person's presence at the hearing;

(f) are available resources sufficient and reliable to provide for personal needs or property management without the appointment of a guardian;

(g) how is the person alleged to be incapacitated functioning with respect to the activities of daily living and what is the prognosis and reversibility of any physical and mental disabilities, alcoholism or substance dependence? The response to this question shall be based on the evaluator's own assessment of the person alleged to be incapacitated to the extent possible, and where necessary, on the examination of assessments by third parties, including records of medical, psychological and/or psychiatric examinations obtained pursuant to Mental Hygiene Law Section 81.09(d). As part of this review, the court evaluator shall consider the diagnostic and assessment procedures used to determine the prognosis and reversibility of any disability and the necessity, efficacy, and dose of each prescribed medication;

(h) what is the person's understanding and appreciation of the nature and consequences of any inability to manage the activities of daily living;

(i) what is the approximate value and nature of the financial resources of the person alleged to be incapacitated;

(j) what are the alleged incapacitated person's preferences, wishes, and values with regard to managing the activities of daily living;[5]

(k) has the person alleged to be incapacitated made any appointment or delegation pursuant to a power of attorney,[6] a Do Not Resuscitate (DNR) Order,[7] a health care proxy,[8] or a living will;

---

5. See supra, § 22.14, for discussion of consideration of the preferences, wishes and values of the alleged incapacitated person.

6. General Obligations Law §§ 5–1501, et seq.

7. Public Health Law § 2965.

8. Public Health Law § 2981.

(*l*) what would be the least restrictive form of intervention consistent with the person's functional level and the powers proposed for the guardian;[9]

(m) what assistance is necessary for those who are financially dependent upon the person alleged to be incapacitated;

(n) is the choice of proposed guardian appropriate, including a guardian nominated by the allegedly incapacitated person pursuant to Mental Hygiene Law Section 81.17 or Mental Hygiene Law Section 81.19(c);[10] and what steps has the proposed guardian taken or does the proposed guardian intend to take to identify and meet the current and emerging needs of the person alleged to be incapacitated unless that information has been provided to the court by the local department of social services when the proposed guardian is a community guardian program operating pursuant to the provisions of title three of article nine-B of the Social Services Law;

(o) what potential conflicts of interest, if any, exist between or among family members and/or other interested parties regarding the proposed guardian or the proposed relief;

(p) what potential conflicts of interest, if any, exist involving the person alleged to be incapacitated, the petitioner, and the proposed guardian;[11] and

(q) are there any additional persons who should be given notice and an opportunity to be heard.[12] The report and recommendations shall also include any information required under Mental Hygiene Law Section 81.09(e)[13] and any additional information required by the court.

(6) interviewing or consulting with professionals having specialized knowledge in the area of the person's alleged incapacity including but not limited to mental retardation, developmental disabilities, alcohol and substance abuse, and geriatrics;

(7) retaining an independent medical expert where the court finds it is appropriate, the cost of which is to be charged to the estate of the allegedly incapacitated person unless the person is indigent;[14]

(8) conducting any other investigations or making recommendations with respect to other subjects as the court deems appropriate; and

---

9. *See supra*, § 22.14 for discussion of the least restrictive form of intervention.

10. *See infra*, § 22.40 for discussion of who may be appointed guardian.

11. *Id.*

12. *See supra*, § 22.21 for discussion of persons entitled to notice.

13. *See* discussion later in this section, in text accompanying note 19.

14. Matter of Cherniakova (Kolischer), N.Y.L.J., 7/10/92, p.21, col.4 (Sup.Ct., N.Y. County).

(9) attending all court proceedings and conferences.

The court evaluator may apply to the court for permission to inspect the records of medical, psychological and/or psychiatric examinations of the person alleged to be incapacitated. Except as otherwise provided by federal or state law, if the court determines that such records are likely to contain information which will assist the court evaluator in completing his or her report to the court, the court may order disclosure of such records to the court evaluator, notwithstanding the physician-patient privilege.[15] If the court orders that such records be disclosed to the court evaluator, the court may, on the court's own motion, at the request of the court evaluator, or on application of counsel for the person alleged to be incapacitated, or the petitioner, also direct such further disclosure of such records as the court deems proper.[16] Moreover, it has been found that Mental Hygiene Law Article 81 appears to offer no definitive rules governing the admission of medical, psychological or psychiatric evidence which would be subject to the physician-patient privilege if not specifically permitted in a proceeding for the appointment of a guardian. While the physician-patient privilege was found to apply to guardianship proceedings, the privilege can be waived or overcome by a judge's order permitting a court evaluator to inspect the medical records of the alleged incapacitated person.[17] However, absent such court order or the consent of the alleged incapacitated person, the inclusion of medical affidavits on a petition for the appointment of a guardian has been held to be a violation of the physician-patient privilege.[18]

The court evaluator also has authority to take any steps necessary to preserve the property of the person alleged to be incapacitated pending the hearing in the event the property is in danger of waste, misappropriation, or loss. If the court evaluator exercises such authority, the court

---

15. Matter of Tara X, N.Y.L.J., 9/18/96, p. 27, col. 1 (Sup.Ct., Suffolk County); Matter of Goldfarb, 160 Misc.2d 1036, 612 N.Y.S.2d 788 (Sup.Ct., Suffolk County, 1994).

16. Mental Hygiene Law § 81.09(d).

CAVEAT: Medical, psychological and psychiatric records of the allegedly incapacitated person are protected by the physician-privilege. While some courts have held that medical affidavits should not be attached to the petition for appointment of a guardian, see, e.g., Matter of Higgins (England), N.Y.L.J., 10/6/95, p.27, col.2 (Sup.Ct., N.Y. County), other courts require the inclusion of such medical affidavits and records. The court evaluator may examine such records only with the permission of the person alleged to be incapacitated or upon a finding by the court that the records are likely to contain information that will assist the court evaluator in completing the report to the court. The allegedly incapacitated person has the right to object to such inspection and is notified of this right in the notice of the proceeding. See Law Revision Commission Commentary to Mental Hygiene Law § 81.09. See supra, § 22.22, discussing the information that must be given in the order to show cause.

17. Matter of Tara X, N.Y.L.J., 9/18/96, p. 27, col. 1 (Sup.Ct., Suffolk County); Matter of Goldfarb, 160 Misc.2d 1036, 612 N.Y.S.2d 788 (Sup.Ct., Suffolk County, 1994).

18. Matter of Higgins (England), N.Y.L.J., 10/6/95, p.27, col.2 (Sup.Ct., N.Y. County).

CAVEAT: See discussion supra at note 16.

evaluator must include an explanation of the actions he or she has taken and the reasons for such action in his or her report to court.[19]

§ 22.27 Court Evaluator—Compensation

Mental Hygiene Law Section 81.09(f) provides that when the judgment grants the petition to appoint a guardian, the court may award a reasonable allowance to the court evaluator, including the Mental Hygiene Legal Service, payable by the estate of the allegedly incapacitated person. When the judgment denies or dismisses the petition, the court may award a reasonable allowance to the court evaluator, including the Mental Hygiene Legal Service, payable by the petitioner or by the person alleged to be incapacitated, or both, in such proportions as the court may deem just.[1] When the person alleged to be incapacitated dies before a determination is made in the proceeding, the court may award a reasonable allowance to the court evaluator, payable by the petitioner or by the estate of the decedent, or by both, in such proportions as the court may deem just.[2]

Although Mental Hygiene Law Article 81 does not set forth the basis for determination of reasonable compensation, the factors were outlined under prior law for determination of the reasonable compensation of a guardian *ad litem* in an Article 77 conservatorship proceeding, as follows:[3]

(1) the time and labor required, the difficulty of the questions involved and the skill required to handle the problems presented;

(2) the experience, ability and reputation of the guardian [court evaluator];

(3) the amount involved and the benefit flowing to the alleged incapacitated person as a result of the services rendered;

(4) the fees awarded in similar cases;

(5) the contingency or certainty of compensation;

(6) the results obtained; and

---

19. Mental Hygiene Law § 81.09(e).

§ 22.27

1. Matter of Gelezewski, N.Y.L.J., 11/17/93, p.30, col.2 (Sup.Ct., Nassau County) (compensation awarded to court evaluator where petition dismissed). *See also* Matter of Chachkers (Shirley W.), 159 Misc.2d 912, 606 N.Y.S.2d 959 (Sup.Ct., N.Y. County, 1993) (where proceeding discontinued, court awarded compensation to court evaluator, to be paid by the alleged incapacitated person).

Matter of Krishnasastry, N.Y.L.J., 8/25/95, p. 31, col. 1 (Sup.Ct., Nassau County) (upon petitioner's request to discontinue Article 81 proceeding, fees of court evaluator and appointed counsel for alleged incapacitated person were apportioned between petitioner and respondent). *See also* Matter of Pollack, N.Y.L.J., 9/27/96, p. 31, col. 1 (Sup.Ct., Nassau County).

See generally, 22 NYCRR Pt. 36, Appointment of Fiduciaries, § 36.4, Compensation.

2. Mental Hygiene Law § 81.09(f).

3. Matter of Stark, 174 A.D.2d 746, 571 N.Y.S.2d 772 (2d Dep't 1991).

§ 22.28 Court Evaluator—Appointment of Counsel for the Alleged Incapacitated Person

(7) the responsibility involved.[4]

Under former Articles 77 and 78 of the Mental Hygiene Law, it was often unclear whether the guardian *ad litem* was acting as an advocate for the person who was the subject of the proceeding or as a neutral evaluator for the court. To reduce this confusion, Mental Hygiene Law Article 81 distinguishes between the roles of counsel and guardian *ad litem*, now known as the court evaluator, and creates separate roles for each.[1] The role of court evaluator is to provide an independent assessment of the allegedly incapacitated person. The role of counsel, as governed by Mental Hygiene Law Section 81.10, is to represent the person alleged to be incapacitated and ensure that the point of view of the person alleged to be incapacitated is presented to the court. Although the statute provides no guidelines with regard to the specific role of counsel at the hearing,[2] at a minimum, that representation should include conducting personal interviews with the alleged incapacitated person; explaining to the person his or her rights and counseling the person regarding the nature and consequences of the proceeding; securing and presenting evidence and testimony; providing vigorous cross-examination; and offering arguments to protect the rights of the allegedly incapacitated person.[3]

Any person for whom relief under Article 81 is sought has the right to be represented by legal counsel of that person's choice.[4] If the person alleged to be incapacitated is not represented by counsel at the time the order to show cause is issued, the court evaluator must assist the court in determining whether counsel should be appointed.[5]

Although the appointment of counsel is, in some instances, discretionary with the court, such appointment is required under certain circumstances specified by the statute.[6] Mental Hygiene Law Section

---

4. *See also* 22 NYCRR Pt. 36, Appointment of Fiduciaries, § 36.4, Compensation, which provides:

(a) Fees to appointees pursuant to this rule shall not exceed the fair value of the services rendered.

(b) Each award of fees of $2,500 or more to appointees pursuant to this section shall be accompanied by an explanation, in writing, of the reasons therefor by the judge making the award.

(c) No fees shall be awarded unless the appointee has filed the notice of appointment and certification of compliance required by section 36.3(a) of this Part.

§ 22.28

1. Law Revision Commission Commentary to Mental Hygiene Law § 81.10. *See supra*, §§ 22.25–22.27, discussing the court evaluator.

2. Matter of Sulzberger, 159 Misc.2d 236, 603 N.Y.S.2d 656 (Sup.Ct., N.Y. County, 1993).

3. Law Revision Commission Commentary to Mental Hygiene Law § 81.10.

4. Mental Hygiene Law § 81.10(a).

5. Mental Hygiene Law § 81.10(b).

6. Matter of Application of Rochester General Hospital (Levin), 158 Misc.2d 522, 601 N.Y.S.2d 375 (Sup.Ct., Monroe County,

81.10(c) provides that court must appoint counsel in any of following circumstances:

(1) the person alleged to be incapacitated requests counsel;

(2) the person alleged to be incapacitated wishes to contest the petition;

(3) the person alleged to be incapacitated does not consent to the authority requested in the petition to move the person alleged to be incapacitated from where that person presently resides to a nursing home or other residential facility,[7] or other similar facility;

(4) if the petition alleges that the person is in need of major medical or dental treatment and the person alleged to be incapacitated does not consent;[8]

(5) the petition requests temporary powers under Mental Hygiene Law Section 81.23;[9]

(6) the court determines that a possible conflict of interest may exist between the court evaluator's role and the advocacy needs of the person alleged to be incapacitated;[10] or

(7) if at any time the court determines that the appointment of counsel would be helpful to a resolution of the matter.

The appointment of counsel has been held to be constitutionally mandated where the petition under Article 81 seeks powers for a guardian of the person to either place the alleged incapacitated person in a nursing home or other institutional facility, or to make major medical decisions.[11] The Court of Appeals has held that by requiring the assignment of counsel for indigents pursuant to the provisions of Article 81, the Legislature intended to authorize the court to compensate such

---

1993); Matter of Sulzberger, 159 Misc.2d 236, 603 N.Y.S.2d 656 (Sup.Ct., N.Y. County, 1993); Matter of St. Luke's-Roosevelt Hospital Center (Marie H.), 159 Misc.2d 932, 607 N.Y.S.2d 574 (Sup.Ct., N.Y. County, 1993), modified on other grounds and remanded, 215 A.D.2d 337, 627 N.Y.S.2d 357 (1st Dep't 1995); on remand it was held that the responsibility for paying for assigned counsel appointed for indigents pursuant to Mental Hygiene Law § 81.10 shall be upon the county or the City of New York pursuant to County Law Article 18–B. Matter of St. Luke's-Roosevelt Hospital Center (Marie H.), 89 N.Y.2d 889, 653 N.Y.S.2d 257, 675 N.E.2d 1209 (1996) (see discussion below).

7. See Public Health Law § 2801.

See Matter of Lichtenstein (Wogelt), 223 A.D.2d 309, 646 N.Y.S.2d 94 (1st Dep't 1996).

8. See Matter of Beritely (Luberoff), N.Y.L.J., 12/8/95, p. 37, col. 3 (Sup.Ct., Suffolk County) (there was no requirement that an attorney be appointed where nothing in the record reflected that the alleged incapacitated person was an involuntary participant in a drug administration regimen).

9. See infra, §§ 22.56–22.59 for discussion of provisional remedies.

10. Estate of Wargold, 152 Misc.2d 172, 575 N.Y.S.2d 230 (Surr.Ct., N.Y. County, 1991).

11. Matter of St. Luke's-Roosevelt Hospital Center (Marie H.), 159 Misc.2d 932, 607 N.Y.S.2d 574 (Sup.Ct., N.Y. County, 1993), modified on other grounds and remanded 215 A.D.2d 337, 627 N.Y.S.2d 357 (1st Dept. 1995). See discussion below.

§ 22.28 GUARDIANSHIP Ch. 22

counsel. The responsibility for paying for assigned counsel appointed pursuant to Mental Hygiene Law § 81.10 shall be upon the county or the City of New York pursuant to County Law Article 18–B.[12]

If the person alleged to be incapacitated refuses the assistance of counsel, the court may, nevertheless, appoint counsel if the court is not satisfied that the person is capable of making an informed decision regarding the appointment of counsel.[13]

Mental Hygiene Law Section 81.10(e) provides that if the person alleged to be incapacitated resides in a facility, hospital, or school, or alcoholism facility,[14] a substance abuse program,[15] an adult care facility,[16] or a residential health care facility or general hospital,[17] the court may appoint as counsel the Mental Hygiene Legal Service in the judicial department where the residence is located.

Mental Hygiene Law Section 81.10(f) provides that the court must determine reasonable compensation for the Mental Hygiene Legal Service or any attorney appointed under the section.[18] The person alleged to be incapacitated is liable for such compensation unless court is satisfied that such person is indigent.[19] If the petition is dismissed, the court may, in its discretion, direct that the petitioner pay such compensation for the person alleged to be incapacitated.[20] When the person alleged to be incapacitated dies before a determination is made in the proceeding, the court may award reasonable compensation to the Mental Hygiene Legal Service or any appointed attorney, payable by the petitioner or the estate of the decedent or by both in such proportions as court may deem just.[21]

---

12. Matter of St. Luke's-Roosevelt Hospital Center (Marie H.), 89 N.Y.2d 889, 653 N.Y.S.2d 257, 675 N.E.2d 1209 (1996).

13. Mental Hygiene Law § 81.10(d).

14. See Mental Hygiene Law § 1.03.

15. See Mental Hygiene Law § 19.03.

16. See Social Services Law § 2.

17. See Public Health Law § 2801.

18. Matter of Gelezewski, N.Y.L.J., 11/17/93, p.30, col.2 (Sup.Ct., Nassau County).

See 22 NYCRR Pt. 36, Appointment of Fiduciaries, § 36.4, Compensation, which provides:

(a) Fees to appointees pursuant to this rule shall not exceed the fair value of the services rendered.

(b) Each award of fees of $2,500 or more to appointees pursuant to this section shall be accompanied by an explanation, in writing, of the reasons therefor by the judge making the award.

(c) No fees shall be awarded unless the appointee has filed the notice of appointment and certification of compliance required by section 36.3(a) of this Part.

But see Petition of Rocco, 161 Misc.2d 760, 615 N.Y.S.2d 260 (Sup.Ct., Suffolk County, 1994), where the court concluded that Mental Hygiene Law § 81.10(f) has no application when the alleged incapacitated person has retained his or her own attorney; the court urged the Legislature to consider amendment of the section.

19. Where the appointment of counsel is constitutionally mandated, payment of such compensation shall be the responsibility of the county or the City of New York pursuant to County Law Article 18–B. Matter of St. Luke's-Roosevelt Hospital Center (Marie H.), 89 N.Y.2d 889, 653 N.Y.S.2d 257, 675 N.E.2d 1209 (1996).

20. Mental Hygiene Law § 81.10(f). Matter of Krishnasastry, N.Y.L.J., 8/25/95, p. 31, col. 1 (Sup.Ct., Nassau County).

21. Id.

If the court appoints counsel, the court may dispense with the appointment of a court evaluator or may vacate or suspend the appointment of previously appointed court evaluator.[22]

§ 22.29 Court Evaluator—Summary

The court must appoint a court evaluator from a list of persons maintained by the Office of Court Administration,[1] who shall have knowledge of property management, personal care skills, problems associated with disabilities, and private and public resources available for the person alleged to be incapacitated.[2] The court evaluator may be an attorney, physician, psychologist, accountant, social worker, or nurse.[3] The court evaluator is intended to act as an independent investigator to gather information to aid the court in reaching a determination about the person's capacity, the availability and reliability of alternative resources, assigning the proper powers to the guardian, and selecting the guardian.[4] The report and recommendations of the court evaluator shall include the court evaluator's personal observations as to the person alleged to be incapacitated and his or her condition, affairs and situation.[5] The court evaluator has authority to take any steps necessary to preserve the property of the person alleged to be incapacitated pending the hearing.[6] The court may award a reasonable allowance to the court evaluator.[7]

The role of counsel is to represent the person alleged to be incapacitated and ensure that the point of view of the person alleged to be incapacitated is presented to the court.[8] If the person alleged to be incapacitated is not represented by counsel the court evaluator must

---

22. Mental Hygiene Law § 81.10(g). See supra, §§ 22.25–22.27, for a discussion of the court evaluator and the circumstances when such appointment may be dispensed with. See Matter of Application of Rochester General Hospital (Levin), 158 Misc.2d 522, 601 N.Y.S.2d 375 (Sup.Ct., Monroe County, 1993) (appointment of court evaluator dispensed with where the Mental Hygiene Legal Service was appointed counsel and could perform essentially the same services as a court evaluator); Matter of Sulzberger, 159 Misc.2d 236, 603 N.Y.S.2d 656 (Sup.Ct., N.Y. County, 1993) (appointment of a court evaluator was dispensed with and counsel appointed where the alleged incapacitated person resided in France and the issues to be investigated were predominantly legal questions).

CAVEAT: Mental Hygiene Law Art. 81 is silent as to the duties and responsibilities of the counsel to the alleged incapacitated person where such person is unable to meaningfully participate in his or her case and provide instruction to counsel. It has been suggested that either an ethics opinion be published to clarify the role of counsel for an alleged incapacitated person in a guardianship proceeding or that the statute be modified to allow judges the option to appoint counsel where the judge is convinced that the alleged incapacitated person can neither direct counsel nor meaningfully participate in his or her case. See R. Abrams, E.L. Flowers & J. Newman, *Article 81: One Year Later*, 4 Elder Law Attorney No 1 (N.Y.S.B.J.) 10, 12 (Summer 1994).

§ 22.29

1. See supra, § 22.25.
2. Id.
3. Id.
4. See supra, § 22.26.
5. See infra, § 22.100 for form of court evaluator's report.
6. See supra, § 22.26.
7. See supra, § 22.27.
8. See supra, § 22.28.

§ 22.29

assist the court in determining whether counsel should be appointed. Although the appointment of counsel is, in some instances, discretionary, such appointment is required under certain circumstances specified by the statute.[9] The court must determine reasonable compensation for the Mental Hygiene Legal Service or any attorney appointed as counsel.[10]

§ 22.30 Hearing and Order—An Overview

The determination of whether the appointment of a guardian is necessary for the person alleged to be incapacitated may be made only after a hearing, at which any party to the proceeding has a right to (1) present evidence, (2) call witnesses, including expert witnesses, (3) cross examine witnesses, including witnesses called by the court, and (4) be represented by counsel of his or her choice.[1] The proceeding under Mental Hygiene Law Article 81 is entitled to a preference over all other causes in the court.[2] The hearing must be conducted in the presence of the person alleged to be incapacitated, either at the courthouse or where the person alleged to be incapacitated resides, if the person alleged to be incapacitated physically cannot come or be brought to the courthouse.[3] If the person alleged to be incapacitated is not represented by counsel, the court must explain to that person the purpose and possible consequences of the proceeding, the right to be represented by counsel and the fact that the court will appoint an attorney to represent the person alleged to be incapacitated if such person wishes to be represented by counsel.[4] The determination that the person is incapacitated must be based on clear and convincing evidence.[5] The burden of proof is on petitioner.[6] The rules of evidence apply to a proceeding to appoint a guardian unless the court, for good cause shown, waives such rules.[7]

If the court appoints a guardian, certain findings must be made on the record which track the standards for the three types of appointment: voluntary appointment; an appointment to provide for personal needs; and an appointment to provide for property management.[8] Various dispositional alternatives available to the court emphasize the underlying goal of promoting the least restrictive alternative and allow the court to fashion remedies which may include protective arrangements or single transactions which assure security, service or care to meet the foreseeable needs of the incapacitated person but do not deprive the person of

9. Id.
10. Id.

§ 22.30
1. See infra, §§ 22.31–22.38.
2. Mental Hygiene Law § 81.13.
3. Mental Hygiene Law § 81.11(c); see infra, § 22.32.
4. Mental Hygiene Law § 81.11(e); see infra, § 22.32.

5. Mental Hygiene Law § 81.12(a); see infra, § 22.33.
6. Id.
7. Mental Hygiene Law § 81.12(b); see infra, § 22.33.
8. Mental Hygiene Law § 81.15; see infra, §§ 22.34–22.37.

independence and autonomy.[9] The order appointing a guardian must specify the exact scope of the guardian's authority.[10] When the petition is granted, or where the court otherwise deems it appropriate the court may award reasonable compensation for the attorney for the petitioner.[11]

The person alleged to be incapacitated may nominate a guardian in the petition, or in a duly executed written instrument.[12] The minimum requirements necessary for a person to be appointed guardian are that the individual be over 18 years of age, or any parent under 18 years of age, found suitable to exercise the powers necessary to assist the incapacitated person.[13] The criteria that the court should consider in selecting the guardian address the relationship between the proposed guardian and the incapacitated person, the needs of the incapacitated person, and the experience of the proposed guardian.[14] The court may require or dispense with the filing of a bond by a guardian, temporary guardian, or special guardian.[15]

No commission may issue until the guardian has executed, acknowledged, and filed an instrument with the clerk of the court designating the clerk as a person on whom service of any process may be made whenever the guardian cannot, with due diligence, be served within state.[16] Within five days after the guardian has filed the designation and has filed a bond, if required, the clerk of the court must issue a commission to the guardian.[17]

Library References:

West's Key No. Digests, Guardian and Ward ⚖13(7); Mental Health ⚖146.

§ 22.31 Hearing and Order—Procedure

A hearing is a required part of a proceeding under Mental Hygiene Law Article 81. The determination of whether the appointment of a guardian is necessary for the person alleged to be incapacitated may be made only after a hearing.[1] Where all the factors suggest that no

---

9. Mental Hygiene Law § 81.16; see infra, § 22.38.

10. Mental Hygiene Law § 81.16(c); see infra, § 22.101 for form of order appointing guardian.

11. Mental Hygiene Law § 81.16(f); see infra, § 22.39.

12. Mental Hygiene Law § 81.17; see infra, § 22.40.

13. Mental Hygiene Law § 81.19(a); see infra, § 22.40.

14. Mental Hygiene Law § 81.19(d); see infra, § 22.40.

15. Mental Hygiene Law § 81.25; see infra, § 22.42.

16. Mental Hygiene Law § 81.26; see infra, § 22.43.

17. Mental Hygiene Law § 81.27; see infra, § 22.43.

§ 22.31

1. Mental Hygiene Law § 81.11(a). Law Revision Commission Commentary to Mental Hygiene Law § 81.11. This was also required under prior law. For cases requiring a hearing, see, e.g., Matter of Bonesteel, 175 A.D.2d 361, 571 N.Y.S.2d 961 (3d Dep't 1991); Matter of Von Bulow, 122 Misc.2d 129, 470 N.Y.S.2d 72 (Sup.Ct., N.Y. County, 1983).

§ 22.31 GUARDIANSHIP Ch. 22

guardian is needed, and the parties all agree, it has been held that a proceeding under Article 81 may be discontinued without a hearing.[2] Any party to the proceeding brought under Mental Hygiene Law Article 81, has a right to (1) present evidence, (2) call witnesses, including expert witnesses, (3) cross examine witnesses, including witnesses called by the court, and (4) be represented by counsel of his or her choice.[3]

If, on or before the return date designated in the order to show cause,[4] any party to the proceeding raises issues of fact regarding the need for the appointment of a guardian under Mental Hygiene Law Article 81 and demands a jury trial of such issues, the court must order a trial by jury. The failure to make such demand is deemed a waiver of the right to trial by jury.[5]

Unless the court, for good cause shown, orders otherwise, the proceeding under Mental Hygiene Law Article 81 is entitled to a preference over all other causes in the court.[6] Moreover, unless the court, for good cause shown, orders otherwise, the hearing or trial must be conducted within time set forth in Mental Hygiene Law Section 81.07(a).[7] The decision determining whether a guardian should be appointed must be rendered within 45 days of the date of signing the order to show cause, unless for good cause shown the court extends the time period for rendering the decision.[8] In the event the time period is extended, the court must set forth the factual basis for such extension. The commission[9] must be issued to the guardian within 15 days after the court's decision is rendered.[10]

A record of the proceedings must be made in all cases.[11] A court may not enter an order sealing court records in a proceeding under Mental Hygiene Law Article 81, either in whole or in part, except on a written finding of good cause, which must specify the grounds thereof.[12] In

---

2. Matter of Chachkers (Shirley W.), 159 Misc.2d 912, 606 N.Y.S.2d 959 (Sup.Ct., N.Y. County, 1993); see also Rau v. Rau, 78 A.D.2d 617, 434 N.Y.S.2d 336 (1st Dep't 1980), decided under prior law.

3. Mental Hygiene Law § 81.11(b).

4. See supra, § 22.20, for discussion of statutory time limits within which the hearing must be conducted.

5. Mental Hygiene Law § 81.11(f). Where there was no issue of fact regarding the need for the appointment of a guardian, the court denied petitioner's demand for a trial by jury. Matter of Claiman, 169 Misc.2d 881, 646 N.Y.S.2d 940 (Sup.Ct., Queens County, 1996).

6. Mental Hygiene Law § 81.13.

7. See supra, § 22.20, for discussion of statutory time limits within which the hearing must be conducted.

8. Mental Hygiene Law § 81.13.

9. See Mental Hygiene Law § 81.27, discussed infra at § 22.43.

10. Mental Hygiene Law § 81.13.

CAVEAT: The above time limits have sometimes proven difficult to adhere to and it has been recommended that Mental Hygiene Law Art. 81 be reviewed and modified, if necessary, to ensure that the time limits be reasonable and that they be complied with. See R. Abrams, E.L. Flowers & J. Newman, Article 81: One Year Later, 4 Elder Law Attorney No 1 (N.Y.S.B.A.) 10, 11 (Summer 1994).

11. Mental Hygiene Law § 81.14(a).

12. 22 NYCRR Pt. 216, Sealing of Court Records in Civil Actions in the Trial Courts, § 216.1, Sealing of Court Records, which provides in pertinent part:

(a) Except where otherwise provided by statute or rule, a court shall not enter

determining whether good cause has been shown, the court must consider the interest of the public, the orderly and sound administration of justice, the nature of the proceedings, and the privacy of the person alleged to be incapacitated.[13] Where it appears necessary or desirable, the court may prescribe appropriate notice and opportunity to be heard. Court records include all documents and records of any nature filed with the clerk in connection with the proceeding. Documents obtained through disclosure and not filed with the clerk must remain subject to protective orders under the Civil Practice Law and Rules.[14] Mental Hygiene Law Section 81.14(c) provides that the court may not exclude any person or persons or the general public from a proceeding under Mental Hygiene Law Article 81 except on written findings of good cause shown. In determining whether good cause has been shown, the court must consider the interest of the public, the orderly and sound administration of justice, the nature of the proceedings, and the privacy of the person alleged to be incapacitated. At the time the hearing commences, the court must inform the alleged incapacitated person of his or her right to request for good cause that the court records be sealed and that any person, persons, or the general public be excluded from the hearing.[15]

Library References:

West's Key No. Digests, Guardian and Ward ⚖13(7); Mental Health ⚖146.

§ 22.32 Hearing and Order—Presence of Person Alleged to Be Incapacitated

Mental Hygiene Law Section 81.11 demonstrates how seriously Article 81 regards the deprivation of a person's rights that may occur with the appointment of a guardian and the importance of having the person whose rights may be affected by the proceeding present at the

an order in any action or proceeding sealing the court records, whether in whole or in part, except upon a written finding of good cause, which shall specify the grounds thereof. In determining whether good cause has been shown, the court shall consider the interests of the public as well as of the parties. Where it appears necessary or desirable, the court may prescribe appropriate notice and an opportunity to be heard.

See also Law Revision Commission Commentary to Mental Hygiene Law § 81.14. See, e.g., Matter of Brownstone, 191 A.D.2d 167, 594 N.Y.S.2d 31 (1st Dep't 1993) (An order sealing the court records was reversed where the court failed to specify, in writing, the reason for its order sealing the records and no legitimate basis had been stated which warranted the sealing of the documents in the case).

13. See, e.g., Matter of Evelyn P., 135 A.D.2d 716, 522 N.Y.S.2d 617 (2d Dep't 1987). The order appointing a conservator, based on the parties' stipulation, should have included a provision requiring that records of the proceeding be sealed, which was one ground for the conservatee's consent to the appointment of the conservator.

14. Mental Hygiene Law § 81.14(b). See generally, CPLR Art. 31, Disclosure, for descriptions of disclosure devices.

15. Mental Hygiene Law § 81.14(d).

§ 22.32   GUARDIANSHIP   Ch. 22

hearing.¹ To effect this purpose, Mental Hygiene Law Section 81.11(c) provides that the hearing must be conducted in the presence of the person alleged to be incapacitated, either at the courthouse or where the person alleged to be incapacitated resides, so as to permit the court to obtain its own impression of the person's capacity.

Requiring the presence of the person at the hearing satisfies many important goals. It allows the judge to make first hand observations and draw first hand impressions of the alleged incapacitated person. The alleged incapacitated person's presence also permits the person to be part of the decision making process, thereby recognizing, respecting and preserving the person's dignity. The presence of the alleged incapacitated person may allow that person to accept the appointment of a guardian more readily than someone who has been excluded from the process. Moreover, by seeing the person, the court is able to draw an order which takes into account the person's dignity, autonomy, and abilities because the judge has had the opportunity to learn more about the person as an individual rather than a case description in a report.[2]

The importance of the presence of the person alleged to be incapacitated has been demonstrated in several cases. In *Matter of Gelezewski*,[3] the person alleged to be incapacitated took the stand and testified. As a consequence of the court's ability to observe him and listen to his testimony, the court concluded that the person alleged to be incapacitated, while exhibiting some signs of his age, did not require the appointment of a guardian. The alleged incapacitated person was found to understand his medical condition and need for medication and also to be aware of his assets and the need to husband them.

In *Matter of Maher*,[4] the person alleged to be incapacitated was present throughout the hearing. Based upon a careful observation of his demeanor, facial expressions and gestures, the court was convinced that he knew the appropriate responses to the questions, but was unable to express them verbally. While the evidence demonstrated that he had certain functional limitations, the court concluded that the appointment of a guardian was not necessary.[5]

The general expectation underlying the statute is that the hearing will usually be conducted at the courthouse and the person alleged to be incapacitated will be present regardless of his or her ability to participate.[6] However, in *In re Steinberg*,[7] decided under prior law, it was held that the trial judge "showed a lack of discretion and compassion" toward

---

§ 22.32

1. Law Revision Commission Commentary to Mental Hygiene Law § 81.11.
2. See id.
3. N.Y.L.J., 11/17/93, p.30, col.2 (Sup. Ct., Nassau County).
4. 207 A.D.2d 133, 621 N.Y.S.2d 617 (2d Dep't 1994).
5. Id.
6. Law Revision Commission Commentary to Mental Hygiene Law § 81.11.
7. 121 A.D.2d 872, 503 N.Y.S.2d 795 (1st Dep't 1986).

the infirm conservatee at the conservatorship hearing when she required the conservatee to attend the hearing despite the conservatee's advanced age, inability to walk more than short distance, and deteriorated mental condition.[8] Under Mental Hygiene Law Article 81, the court would be able, under such circumstances, to hold the hearing at the residence of the alleged incapacitated person. If the person alleged to be incapacitated physically cannot come or be brought to the courthouse, Mental Hygiene Law Section 81.11(c) provides that the hearing must be conducted where the person alleged to be incapacitated resides.[9]

Mental Hygiene Law Section 81.11(c) provides two exceptions to the requirement that the hearing be held at the residence of the person alleged to be incapacitated:

(1) the person is not present in New York;[10] or

(2) all the information before the court clearly establishes that (a) the person alleged to be incapacitated is completely unable to participate in the hearing or (b) no meaningful participation will result from the person's presence at the hearing.[11]

These two exceptions are neither intended, nor should they be construed, to deprive the person of an opportunity to be part of the proceeding. Rather, the exceptions will only apply when such application would not compromise the integrity and fairness of the court's decision. Even if the allegedly incapacitated person cannot communicate verbally[12] his or her appearance and demeanor can convey information to the judge which will help the judge assess, among other things, his or her ability to manage activities of daily living, the consequences to the person resulting from the inability to manage daily activities, whether the present place of abode is best suited to the needs of the individual, and the

---

8. *Id.*

9. *See, e.g.*, Matter of Richman, 164 Misc.2d 403, 625 N.Y.S.2d 443 (Sup.Ct., Queens County, 1995), aff'd 224 A.D.2d 625, 639 N.Y.S.2d 390 (2d Dep't 1996). The alleged incapacitated person, a patient in a hospital, was 37 years old and extremely obese, weighing between 400 and 500 pounds. Although it was determined that the courthouse and courtroom could accommodate her and the hospital agreed to provide transportation to and from the courthouse, the alleged incapacitated person refused to come to the hearing at the courthouse. The court therefore conducted the hearing at the hospital. *See also*, Matter of Heumann, N.Y.L.J., 11/17/93, p.29, col.6 (Sup.Ct., Kings County) (hearing conducted at nursing home where person alleged to be incapacitated resided).

10. If the person lives out of state and cannot come to the courthouse, requiring the judge to travel out of the jurisdiction is not feasible. Law Revision Commission Commentary to Mental Hygiene Law § 81.11.

11. Matter of Lisle, N.Y.L.J., 8/9/94, p.27, col.4 (Surr.Ct., Nassau County) (court evaluator's report and medical evidence established that the respondent was unable to understand or meaningfully participate in the proceedings); Matter of Application of Rochester General Hospital (Levin), 158 Misc.2d 522, 601 N.Y.S.2d 375 (Sup.Ct., Monroe County, 1993) (after hearing commenced at hospital where alleged incapacitated person was a patient, the court concluded, based on its own observations, that the respondent was completely unable to participate in the hearing and that no meaningful participation would result from his continued presence).

12. *See* Matter of Maher, 207 A.D.2d 133, 621 N.Y.S.2d 617 (2d Dep't 1994).

§ 22.32   GUARDIANSHIP   Ch. 22

appropriate scope of the guardian's authority. Additionally, having the judge hold the hearing at the person's residence may also convey information to the person which would facilitate the person's acceptance of an appointment of a guardian.[13]

If the hearing is conducted without the presence of the person alleged to be incapacitated and the court appoints a guardian, the order of appointment must set forth the factual basis for conducting the hearing without the presence of the person for whom the appointment is made.[14]

If the hearing is conducted in the presence of the person alleged to be incapacitated and the person is not represented by counsel,[15] the court must explain to that person, on the record, the purpose and possible consequences of the proceeding, the right to be represented by counsel and the fact that the court will appoint an attorney to represent the person alleged to be incapacitated if such person wishes to be represented by counsel. The court must inquire of the alleged incapacitated person whether he or she wishes to have an attorney appointed. If the person refuses the assistance of counsel, the court may nevertheless appoint counsel if the court is not satisfied that the person alleged to be incapacitated is capable of making an informed decision regarding the appointment of counsel.[16]

Library References:

West's Key No. Digests, Guardian and Ward ⟐13(7); Mental Health ⟐146.

§ 22.33   Hearing and Order—Evidence

Given the gravity of the liberty and property interests at stake, the Legislature decided that the determination that the person is incapacitated must be based on clear and convincing evidence. The burden of proof is on petitioner.[1]

The rules of evidence apply to a proceeding to appoint a guardian.[2] However, it has been held that Mental Hygiene Law Article 81 appears to offer no definitive rules governing the admission of medical, psychological or psychiatric evidence which would be subject to the physician-patient privilege if not specifically permitted in a proceeding for the

---

13. Law Revision Commission Commentary to Mental Hygiene Law § 81.11.

14. Mental Hygiene Law § 81.11(d).

15. See supra, § 22.28 for a discussion of the appointment and role of counsel in a proceeding to appoint a guardian.

16. Mental Hygiene Law § 81.11(e).

§ 22.33

1. Mental Hygiene Law § 81.12(a). See, e.g., Matter of Maher, 207 A.D.2d 133, 621 N.Y.S.2d 617 (2d Dep't 1994); In re Waxman, 96 A.D.2d 906, 466 N.Y.S.2d 85 (2d Dep't 1983), later proceeding 110 A.D.2d 644, 487 N.Y.S.2d 381 (2d Dep't 1985); Estate of Wargold, 152 Misc.2d 172, 575 N.Y.S.2d 230 (Surr.Ct., N.Y. County, 1991); In re Fisher, 147 Misc.2d 329, 552 N.Y.S.2d 807 (Sup.Ct., N.Y. County, 1989).

2. Law Revision Commission Commentary to Mental Hygiene Law § 81.12. See generally, Barker and Alexander, *Evidence in New York State and Federal Courts* (West 1996) §§ 502.1(d), (e).

Ch. 22   HEARING AND ORDER—EVIDENCE   § 22.33

appointment of a guardian. While the physician-patient privilege was found to apply to guardianship proceedings, the privilege can be waived or overcome by a judge's order permitting a court evaluator to inspect the medical records of the alleged incapacitated person.[3]

There is nothing in Article 81 that mandates medical testimony in a guardianship hearing. The test is one of determining the functional limitations of the alleged incapacitated person in order to tailor the guardianship to the person's needs and medical testimony may not be needed for such a determination.[4]

The court may, for good cause shown, waive the rules of evidence.[5] The function of the "good cause" exception is to facilitate the court's determination in uncontested proceedings and in cases where there are no substantial issues of fact provided that the reliability of the evidence sought to be admitted is established and the integrity of the proceeding is not impaired by the waiver of the particular rule of evidence.[6]

Admission of the court evaluator's report[7] is subject to separate requirements. Recognizing that much of the information in the report will be based upon hearsay statements which would otherwise be inadmissible under the rules of evidence, Mental Hygiene Law Section 81.12(b) provides that the report may be admitted in evidence if the court evaluator testifies and is subject to cross examination. However, if the court determines that the information contained in the report is, in

---

3. Matter of Tara X, N.Y.L.J., 9/18/96, p. 27, col. 1 (Sup.Ct., Suffolk County); Matter of Goldfarb, 160 Misc.2d 1036, 612 N.Y.S.2d 788 (Sup.Ct., Suffolk County, 1994). See supra, § 22.26, for discussion of physician-patient privilege.

4. Matter of Harriet R., 224 A.D.2d 625, 639 N.Y.S.2d 390 (2d Dep't 1996); Matter of Kustka, 163 Misc.2d 694, 622 N.Y.S.2d 208 (Sup.Ct., Queens County, 1994). See also Matter of Higgins (England), N.Y.L.J., 10/6/95, p.27, col.2 (Sup.Ct., N.Y. County) (absent consent of the alleged incapacitated person, the inclusion of medical affidavits with the petition seeking appointment of a guardian is a violation of the physician-patient privilege; such inclusion also defeats the statute's intent to reduce the reliance upon medical testimony).

CAVEAT: Medical, psychological and psychiatric records of the allegedly incapacitated person are protected by the physician-privilege. While some courts have held that medical affidavits should not be attached to the petition for appointment of a guardian, see, e.g., Matter of Higgins (England), N.Y.L.J., 10/6/95, p.27, col.2 (Sup.Ct., N.Y. County), other courts require the inclusion of such medical affidavits and records. The court evaluator may examine such records only with the permission of the person alleged to be incapacitated or upon a finding by the court that the records are likely to contain information that will assist the court evaluator in completing the report to the court. The allegedly incapacitated person has the right to object to such inspection and is notified of this right in the notice of the proceeding. See Matter of Tara X, N.Y.L.J., 9/18/96, p. 27, col. 1 (Sup.Ct., Suffolk County); Matter of Goldfarb, 160 Misc.2d 1036, 612 N.Y.S.2d 788 (Sup.Ct., Suffolk County, 1994). See also Law Revision Commission Commentary to Mental Hygiene Law § 81.09. See supra, § 22.22 discussing the information that must be given in the order to show cause.

5. Mental Hygiene Law § 81.12(b).

6. Law Revision Commission Commentary to Mental Hygiene Law § 81.12. See Matter of Tara X, N.Y.L.J., 9/18/96, p. 27, col. 1 (Sup.Ct., Suffolk County) (court's authority to waive rules of evidence applies only to uncontested proceedings and only to those in which the integrity of the proceeding was not impaired by such waiver).

7. See supra, § 22.26; see infra, § 22.100 for form of court evaluator's report.

the particular circumstances of the case, not sufficiently reliable, the court must require that the person who provided the information testify and be subject to cross examination.[8]

Library References:

West's Key No. Digests, Guardian and Ward ⚿13(7); Mental Health ⚿146.

§ 22.34 Hearing and Order—Findings of the Court

Mental Hygiene Law Section 81.15 mandates that certain findings must be made on the record if the court appoints a guardian.[1] These findings track the standards for appointment.[2] The three subdivisions of the section set forth the necessary findings for three types of appointment:[3] the first is a voluntary appointment;[4] the second is an appointment to provide for personal needs;[5] and the third is an appointment to provide for property management.[6] In order to enable the court to give thorough consideration to all the issues in determining whether the appointment of a guardian is necessary, particularly when close or complicated questions require special scrutiny of the testimony, the court may direct that the parties provide it with such portions of the transcript as are necessary to its deliberations and may direct that any one or all of the parties bear the cost of such transcript.[7]

Library References:

West's Key No. Digests, Guardian and Ward ⚿13(7); Mental Health ⚿146.

§ 22.35 Hearing and Order—Findings of the Court— Voluntary Appointment

Where the court determines that the person agrees to the appointment and that the appointment is necessary, the court must make the following findings on the record:[1]

(1) the person's agreement to the appointment;

(2) the person's functional limitations which impair the person's ability to provide for personal needs or property management;

8. Mental Hygiene Law § 81.12(b).

§ 22.34

1. See infra, § 22.84 for the form of order appointing a guardian.

2. For examples of the format of a court's findings and conclusions, see, e.g., Matter of Bailin (Geiger), N.Y.L.J., 5/19/95, p.36, col.4 (Sup.Ct., Rockland County); Matter of Zarriello, N.Y.L.J., 1/25/95, p.32, col.5 (Sup.Ct., Rockland County).

3. Law Revision Commission Commentary to Mental Hygiene Law § 81.15.

4. See infra, § 22.35.

5. See infra, § 22.36.

6. See infra, § 22.37.

7. Matter of Staiano, N.Y.L.J., 5/13/94 p.36, col.4 (Sup.Ct., Suffolk County) (Although the court found no statute specifically addressing the authority of the court to direct the parties to pay the expense of the transcript, it held that the court could fashion a remedy which directed the parties to share the cost of the transcript.).

§ 22.35

1. Mental Hygiene Law § 81.15(a).

(3) the necessity of the appointment of a guardian as a means of providing for the personal needs and/or property management for the person;

(4) the specific powers of the guardian which constitute the least restrictive form of intervention[2] consistent with the person's functional limitations; and

(5) the duration of the appointment.

Library References:
West's Key No. Digests, Guardian and Ward ⚖13(7); Mental Health ⚖146.

§ 22.36 Hearing and Order—Findings of the Court—Personal Needs

Where the petition requests the appointment of a guardian to provide for the personal needs for a person alleged to be incapacitated, and the court determines that such person is incapacitated and that the appointment is necessary, the court must make the following findings on the record:[1]

(1) the person's functional limitations which impair the person's ability to provide for personal needs;

(2) the person's lack of understanding and appreciation of the nature and consequences of his or her functional limitations;

(3) the likelihood that the person will suffer harm because of the person's functional limitations and inability to adequately understand and appreciate the nature and consequences of such functional limitations;

(4) the necessity of the appointment of a guardian to prevent such harm;

(5) the specific powers of the guardian which constitute the least restrictive form of intervention[2] consistent with such findings; and

(6) the duration of the appointment.

Library References:
West's Key No. Digests, Guardian and Ward ⚖13(7); Mental Health ⚖146.

§ 22.37 Hearing and Order—Findings of the Court—Property Management

Where the petition requests the appointment of a guardian for property management for the person alleged to be incapacitated, and the court determines that the person is incapacitated and that the appoint-

---

2. *See supra,* § 22.14 for discussion of the concept of least restrictive form of intervention.

§ 22.36
1. Mental Hygiene Law § 81.15(b).

2. *See supra,* § 22.14 for discussion of the concept of least restrictive form of intervention.

ment of a guardian is necessary, the court must make the following findings on the record:[1]

(1) the type and amount of property and financial resources of the person alleged to be incapacitated;

(2) the person's functional limitations which impair the person's ability with respect to property management;

(3) the person's lack of understanding and appreciation of the nature and consequences of his or her functional limitations;

(4) the likelihood that the person will suffer harm because of such person's functional limitations and inability to adequately understand and appreciate the nature and consequences of such functional limitations;

(5) any additional findings that are required under Mental Hygiene Law Section 81.21;[2]

(6) the necessity of the appointment of a guardian to prevent such harm;

(7) if so, the specific powers of the guardian which constitute the least restrictive form of intervention[3] consistent with the person's functional limitations and the likelihood of harm because of the person's inability to adequately understand and appreciate the nature and consequences of such functional limitations; and

(8) the duration of the appointment.

Library References:

West's Key No. Digests, Guardian and Ward ⚖13(7); Mental Health ⚖146.

§ 22.38 Hearing and Order—Dispositional Alternatives

Mental Hygiene Law Section 81.16 sets forth the various dispositional alternatives that are available to the court. The list emphasizes the statute's underlying goal of promoting the least restrictive alternative.[1] The most significant part of this section is the provision governing protective arrangements and single transactions. With this section, Article 81 fills a gap in New York's law identified by the Court of Appeals in

§ 22.37
1. Mental Hygiene Law § 81.15(c).
2. *See infra*, § 22.47 for discussion of the powers of a guardian for property management.
3. *See supra*, § 22.14 for discussion of the concept of least restrictive form of intervention.

§ 22.38
1. *See supra*, § 22.14 for discussion of the concept of least restrictive form of intervention.

Matter of Grinker (Rose),[2] namely, where a person may require assistance but does not require the appointment of a guardian. Article 81 allows the court to fashion remedies which may include protective arrangements or single transactions which assure security, service or care to meet the foreseeable needs of the incapacitated person but do not deprive the person of independence and autonomy.[3]

If the person alleged to be incapacitated is found not to be incapacitated, the court must dismiss petition.[4]

Mental Hygiene Law Section 81.16(b) provides that if the person alleged to be incapacitated is found to be incapacitated, the court, without appointing a guardian, may authorize, direct, or ratify any transaction or series of transactions necessary to achieve any security, service, or care arrangement meeting foreseeable needs of the incapacitated person, or may authorize, direct, or ratify any contract, trust, or other transaction relating to the incapacitated person's property and financial affairs if the court determines that the transaction is necessary as a means of providing for the personal needs and/or property management for the alleged incapacitated person.[5] Before approving any protective arrangement or other transaction, the court must consider the interests of dependents and creditors of the incapacitated person, and in view of the person's functional level, whether the person needs the continuing protection of a guardian.

The court may appoint a special guardian to assist in the accomplishment of any protective arrangement or other transaction so authorized. The special guardian has authority conferred by the order of appointment, must report to the court on all matters done pursuant to the order of appointment, and must serve until discharged by an order of the court. The court may approve reasonable compensation for the special guardian. However, if the court finds that the special guardian has failed to discharge his or her duties satisfactorily in any respect, the court may deny or reduce the amount of compensation or remove the

---

2. 77 N.Y.2d 703, 570 N.Y.S.2d 448, 573 N.E.2d 536 (1991).

3. Law Revision Commission Commentary to Mental Hygiene Law § 81.16.

4. Mental Hygiene Law § 81.16(a). *See* Matter of Maher, 207 A.D.2d 133, 621 N.Y.S.2d 617 (2d Dep't 1994); Matter of Heumann, N.Y.L.J., 11/17/93, p.29, col.6 (Sup.Ct., Kings County); *see also*, Matter of Anonymous, R.A., N.Y.L.J., 9/28/93, p.27, col.2 (Surr.Ct., Nassau County) (where the court found that the alleged incapacitated person owned real and personal property which required active management but which such person was unable to personally attend to but also found that she was capable of determining who she desired to see to her financial needs and had executed a durable power of attorney for that purpose, the court dismissed the petition seeking the appointment of a guardian).

5. **PRACTICE POINTER**: The provisions relating to single transactions are frequently used in situations relating to Medicaid spend-down where the purpose is to spend-down the assets of the alleged incapacitated person, usually where they are less than $50,000, so the alleged incapacitated person may qualify for Medicaid. The provisions of Mental Hygiene Law § 81.16(b) may also be used in other situations.

special guardian.[6]

If the court determines that the appointment of a guardian is necessary, the court must tailor the order by limiting the powers of the guardian to those which are necessary to assist the incapacitated person.[7] The order appointing a guardian should delineate the exact scope of the guardian's authority because it will be the reference document for those with whom the guardian will interact on behalf of the incapacitated person.[8]

If the person alleged to be incapacitated is found to have agreed to the appointment of a guardian and the court determines that appointment of a guardian is necessary,[9] the order of the court must be designed to accomplish the least restrictive form of intervention[10] by appointing a guardian with powers[11] limited to those which the court has found necessary to assist the person in providing for his or her personal needs and/or property management.[12]

If the person alleged to be incapacitated is found to be incapacitated and the court determines that the appointment of guardian is necessary,[13] the order of the court must be designed to accomplish least restrictive form of intervention[14] by appointing a guardian with powers[15] limited to those which the court has found necessary to assist the incapacitated person in providing for his or her personal needs and/or property management.[16]

Mental Hygiene Law Section 81.16(c)(3) provides that the order of appointment shall identify all persons entitled to notice of all further

---

6. Mental Hygiene Law § 81.16(b). *See, e.g.,* Matter of Wingate (Mascolone), 169 Misc.2d 701, 647 N.Y.S.2d 433 (Sup.Ct., Queens County, 1996) (special guardian appointed solely for purpose of selling the shares of the alleged incapacitated person's co-op apartment so she could become Medicaid eligible); Matter of Janczak (Jacobs), 167 Misc.2d 766, 634 N.Y.S.2d 1020 (Sup. Ct., Ontario County, 1995) (special guardian appointed for limited purpose of providing adult protective services in the form of arranging for visiting nurse or other home health care services and arranging regular medical examinations of alleged incapacitated person).

7. Where the court found that a guardian was not necessary to care for the personal needs of the alleged incapacitated person but concluded that there was clear and convincing evidence that the alleged incapacitated person was unable to provide for property management, the court appointed a guardian solely for property management. Matter of Kustka, 163 Misc.2d 694, 622 N.Y.S.2d 208 (Sup.Ct., Queens County, 1994).

8. Law Revision Commission Commentary to Mental Hygiene Law § 81.16. *See infra,* § 22.101 for a form of order appointing a guardian.

9. *See supra,* §§ 22.34–22.37, for discussion of the findings of the court.

10. *See supra,* § 22.14 for discussion of the concept of least restrictive form of intervention.

11. *See infra,* §§ 22.42, et seq., for discussion of the powers of a guardian.

12. Mental Hygiene Law § 81.16(c)(1).

13. *See supra,* §§ 22.34–22.37 for discussion of the findings of the court.

14. *See supra,* § 22.14 for discussion of the concept of least restrictive form of intervention.

15. *See infra,* §§ 22.42, et seq., for discussion of the powers of a guardian.

16. Mental Hygiene Law § 81.16(c)(2).

proceedings.[17]

The court shall direct that judgment be entered determining rights of parties.[18] A copy of the order and judgment must be personally served on and read to the person who is the subject of the proceedings by the court evaluator[19] or by counsel[20] for the person.[21]

Library References:
West's Key No. Digests, Guardian and Ward ⚖13(7); Mental Health ⚖146.

§ 22.39 Hearing and Order—Award of Counsel Fees to Petitioner

When the petition is granted, or where the court otherwise deems it appropriate, Mental Hygiene Law Section 81.16(f) provides that the court may award reasonable compensation for the attorney for the petitioner,[1] including the attorney general[2] and the attorney for the local department of social services.

---

17. *See supra,* § 22.22 for discussion of persons entitled to notice. *But see* Matter of Kator (Elefant), 164 Misc.2d 265, 624 N.Y.S.2d 348 (Sup.Ct., N.Y. County 1995), where the court discussed a problem which may arise where there is a pre-Article 81 order of appointment. While Article 81 orders appointing a guardian are required to identify the persons entitled to notice of further proceedings (Mental Hygiene Law § 81.16(c)(3)), pre-Article 81 orders contain no such provision. Therefore, in such instances, compliance with the notice provisions of Article 81 may be impracticable and the courts may have to look to prior law.

18. Mental Hygiene Law § 81.16(d).

19. *See supra,* §§ 22.25–22.27 for discussion of the court evaluator.

20. *See supra,* § 22.28 for discussion of counsel for the person alleged to be incapacitated.

21. Mental Hygiene Law § 81.16(e).

§ 22.39

1. Where the court believed that the services rendered by the petitioners' numerous attorneys did not call for special skills or major talents and could have been handled with equal dispatch and diligence by any attorney who had taken the widely offered course provided by all local bar associations and found that many of the hours billed by several partners and associates were unnecessary, duplicative and not the responsibility of the alleged incapacitated person, the court allowed only a fee based upon the court's experience and analysis of the time reasonably involved in preparing, processing and presenting the petition to the court. Matter of Spingarn, 164 Misc.2d 891, 626 N.Y.S.2d 650 (Sup.Ct., N.Y. County, 1995).

The terms of a privately negotiated retainer agreement between a petitioner in a Mental Hygiene Law Article 81 proceeding and counsel retained by such petitioner are not binding on the court and are not necessarily determinative of "reasonable compensation" within the meaning of Mental Hygiene Law § 81.16(f). The determination of reasonable compensation is for the court and involves more than reference to a fee earned pursuant to the contractual terms of a retainer agreement. Matter of Roy (Lepkowski), 164 Misc.2d 146, 623 N.Y.S.2d 995 (Sup.Ct., Suffolk County, 1995).

In a proceeding involving the local assets of an alleged incapacitated person who was Canadian citizen, it was for the New York court in which the proceeding was brought and heard to fix reasonable counsel fees. The New York court should not defer to a determination made by a foreign court as to a counsel fee payable by an incapacitated person. The fee should be supervised by the court to insure that no more than a reasonable fee is paid out of the incapacitated person's assets which are subject to the New York court's jurisdiction, pursuant to the standards of Mental Hygiene Law § 81.16(f). Matter of Whitehead, 169 Misc.2d 554, 642 N.Y.S.2d 979 (Sup.Ct., Suffolk County, 1996).

This provision has been held to authorize an award to a cross-petitioner. Matter of DeVita, N.Y.L.J., 2/17/95, p.33, col.5 (Sup.Ct., Suffolk County).

2. See Note 2 on p. 230.

§ 22.39   GUARDIANSHIP   Ch. 22

The award must be reasonable in light of the value of the incapacitated person's assets as well as the value of the services rendered,[3] and the submission in support of an award should describe specifically what was done, when, why, and by whom. To assist the court in making an appropriate award of counsel fees, the petitioner's attorney should submit an affirmation by the attorney in charge of the matter setting forth the following:[4]

(1) a general description of the services rendered and difficulties, if any, presented by the particular proceeding;

(2) identify each person affiliated with the firm who performed any services; contemporaneous time records might replace the narrative, depending on their detail;

(3) describe the tasks performed and the time expended by each;

(4) the hourly billing rate for such person;

(5) state what agreement or understanding exists between counsel of record and the petitioner;

(6) whether any fee has been paid by any third party;

(7) whether anyone other than the firm of record will share in the fee; and

(8) the amount sought as an award.

Under Article 81 the petitioner's attorney's fees may be borne by the person alleged to be incapacitated if the court deems it appropriate. However, where the matter has been discontinued or dismissed, that the

---

2. This appears to reverse prior law. See In re James "AA", 188 A.D.2d 60, 594 N.Y.S.2d 430 (3d Dep't 1993) (Attorney General was not entitled to counsel fees under former Mental Hygiene Law § 77.07(d) for his representation of director of state developmental center who had petitioned for appointment of conservator for patient, since only when interest of state is implicated may Attorney General properly represent director of state facility in conservatorship proceeding, such representation is exercise of governmental function, and public expenditures made in performance of governmental function are not recoverable).

But see Matter of Kern, 165 Misc.2d 108, 627 N.Y.S.2d 257, 264, note 1 (Sup.Ct., Suffolk County, 1995), where the court noted that although the statutory authority exists to award reasonable compensation for the legal services rendered by the county attorney, such authority does not mean that awards of reasonable compensation for the services of county attorneys should be made routinely. The court noted that the offices of county attorneys and the N.Y.S. Attorney General were publicly funded with taxpayers' dollars and to award compensation for such services constituted double taxation of the alleged incapacitated person. The court construed Mental Hygiene Law § 81.16(f) as authority to impose the cost of reasonable compensation of the county attorney or N.Y.S. Attorney General only in those instances when some unusual or compelling circumstance warrants such imposition.

3. See Matter of Spingarn, 164 Misc.2d 891, 626 N.Y.S.2d 650 (Sup.Ct., N.Y. County, 1995), discussed in note 1, supra.

4. See Matter of Roy (Lepkowski), 164 Misc.2d 146, 623 N.Y.S.2d 995 (Sup.Ct., Suffolk County, 1995); Matter of Grady, N.Y.L.J., 4/21/95, p.25, col.5 (Sup.Ct., N.Y. County).

proceeding was brought in good faith was found not sufficient[5] and a showing of special circumstances would be necessary to shift the burden to the alleged incapacitated person.[6]

§ 22.40 Hearing and Order—Person to Be Appointed Guardian

The person alleged to be incapacitated may nominate a guardian in the petition, or in a written instrument duly executed, acknowledged and filed in the proceeding before the appointment of a guardian.[1]

Where the person alleged to be incapacitated is not present in New York and a guardian, by whatever name designated, has been duly appointed under the laws of any other state, territory, or country where the person alleged to be incapacitated resides to assist such person in property management, the court, in its discretion, may make an order appointing the foreign guardian as guardian under Mental Hygiene Law Article 81 with powers with respect to property management[2] within New York on the foreign guardian's giving such security as the court deems proper.[3] And although the court has authority, in its discretion, to

---

5. *See, e.g.,* Petition of Rocco, 161 Misc.2d 760, 615 N.Y.S.2d 260 (Sup.Ct., Suffolk County, 1994) (the parties were given an opportunity to be heard on the issue of whether sanctions should be imposed upon the petitioner and her attorney; the focus of the court's inquiry in such circumstances was whether the proceeding had been brought by the petitioner to advance a personal vendetta against the respondent (person alleged to be incapacitated) rather than as a means of seeking, in good faith, a determination as to whether the respondent was an incapacitated person in need of the appointment of a guardian).

6. Matter of Chachkers (Shirley W.), 159 Misc.2d 912, 606 N.Y.S.2d 959 (Sup.Ct., N.Y. County, 1993).

§ 22.40

1. Mental Hygiene Law § 81.17. *See, e.g.,* Matter of Loccisano, N.Y.L.J., 8/28/96, p. 27, col. 6 (Sup.Ct., Suffolk County) (Where such nomination is properly made and the appointment of a guardian shown to be necessary, the court must appoint such person unless it determines such nominee is unfit or the person making the nomination no longer wishes the nominee appointed; court found nominee met the minimal eligibility requirements and was suitable to serve as personal needs guardian; however, due to an apparent conflict of interest resulting from a possible debtor-creditor relationship between the incapacitated person and the nominee, the court appointed an independent guardian of the property); Matter of Pasner (Tenenbaum), N.Y.L.J., 7/14/95, p.29, col.1 (Sup.Ct., Kings County).

2. Matter of Buckner (Buckner), 157 Misc.2d 23, 595 N.Y.S.2d 862 (Surr.Ct., N.Y. County, 1993).

3. Mental Hygiene Law § 81.18. *See, e.g.* Application of Witten, 78 Misc.2d 162, 355 N.Y.S.2d 533 (Sup.Ct., N.Y. County, 1974) (decided under prior law).

CAVEAT: Early decisions under Mental Hygiene Law Art. 81 have expressed some reservations about the application of the power to appoint a foreign guardian. One court has stated that the section serves only to regulate who may apply for ancillary guardianship and does not require the appointment of the foreign guardian as a guardian in New York. *See* Matter of Sulzberger, 159 Misc.2d 236, 603 N.Y.S.2d 656 (Sup.Ct., N.Y. County, 1993).

Cf., Matter of Whitehead, N.Y.L.J., 5/30/95, p. 34, col. 1 (Sup.Ct., Suffolk County) (there is no requirement that the court give full faith and credit to a decision of a court of another state or country that an alleged incapacitated person requires the appointment of a guardian). *See also* decision in Matter of Whitehead, 169 Misc.2d 554, 642 N.Y.S.2d 979 (Sup.Ct., Suffolk County, 1996) (discussion of determination of reasonable counsel fees for foreign co-committees).

§ 22.40 GUARDIANSHIP Ch. 22

grant powers to a foreign guardian with respect to the ward's New York property, one court has expressed doubt whether New York courts should exercise such discretion where the appointing court is clearly better situated to decide whether such powers are appropriate.[4]

Mental Hygiene Law Section 81.19 sets forth the eligibility to serve as a guardian. The section includes three parts: 1) the minimum requirements for appointment as a guardian; 2) the order of priority of appointment;[5] and 3) the criteria that the court should consider in appointing the guardian.[6]

The minimum requirements are set forth in Mental Hygiene Law Section 81.19(a)(1), which provides that any individual over 18 years of age, or any parent under 18 years of age, who is found by the court to be suitable to exercise the powers necessary to assist the incapacitated person may be appointed as guardian, including but not limited to a spouse, adult child, parent, or sibling.[7]

A not-for-profit corporation organized to act in such capacity, a social services official, or a public agency authorized to act in such capacity which has a concern for the incapacitated person, and any community guardian program operating under Social Services Law Article 9–B, Title 3, which is found by the court to be suitable to perform the duties necessary to assist the incapacitated person may be appointed as guardian, provided that the community guardian program shall be appointed only where a special proceeding for the appointment of a guardian has been commenced by a social services official with whom such program was contracted.[8] A corporation may be appointed as guardian except that no corporation (other than as provided in Mental Hygiene Law Section 81.19(a)(2)) may be authorized to exercise powers necessary to assist the incapacitated person with personal needs.[9]

Library References:

West's Key No. Digests, Guardian and Ward ⚖10; Mental Health ⚖116.

4. Matter of Buckner (Buckner), 157 Misc.2d 23, 595 N.Y.S.2d 862 (Surr.Ct., N.Y. County, 1993).

5. See infra, § 22.41.

6. Law Revision Commission Commentary to Mental Hygiene Law § 81.19.

7. While it is the usual practice to appoint the next of kin, close blood relatives or their nominees as fiduciaries, Matter of Pasner (Tenenbaum), N.Y.L.J., 7/14/95, p.29, col.1 (Sup.Ct., Kings County), the court is authorized to depart from this principle where such relative or nominee has an interest adverse to the interest of the ward; Matter of Loury (Loury), N.Y.L.J., 9/23/93, p.26, col.2 (Sup.Ct., Kings County), aff'd 210 A.D.2d 227, 619 N.Y.S.2d 351 (2d Dep't 1994), or where the relative is unsuitable to act as guardian, Matter of Zdeb, 215 A.D.2d 803, 626 N.Y.S.2d 298 (3d Dep't 1995). See also, Matter of Klein, 145 A.D.2d 145, 538 N.Y.S.2d 274 (2d Dep't 1989) (strangers will not be appointed unless it is impossible to find within the family circle, or their nominees, one who is qualified to serve).

8. Mental Hygiene Law § 81.19(a)(2).

9. Mental Hygiene Law § 81.19(a)(3).

§ 22.41 Hearing and Order—Person to Be Appointed Guardian—Priority and Criteria for Appointment

In appointing a guardian, the court shall observe the following *priority*:[1]

(1) The court shall appoint the person nominated as guardian in accordance with Mental Hygiene Law Section 81.17,[2] unless the court determines that the nominee is unfit or the alleged incapacitated person indicates that he or she no longer wishes the nominee to be appointed.[3]

(2) In the absence of a nomination in accordance with Mental Hygiene Law Section 81.17, the court must appoint the person nominated by the person alleged to be incapacitated orally or by conduct during the hearing or trial unless the court determines for good cause that such appointment is not appropriate.[4]

The *criteria* that the court should consider in selecting the guardian address the relationship between the proposed guardian and the incapacitated person,[5] the needs of the incapacitated person, and the experience of the proposed guardian.[6] Mental Hygiene Law Section 81.19(d) provides that, in making any appointment under Article 81, the court shall consider:

(1) any appointment or delegation made by the person alleged to be incapacitated in a general power of attorney,[7] Do Not Resuscitate (DNR) Order,[8] health care proxy,[9] or living will;[10]

(2) the social relationship between the incapacitated person and the person, if any, proposed as guardian, and the social relationship between the incapacitated person and other persons concerned with the welfare of the incapacitated person;[11]

§ 22.41

1. *See generally,* P.G. Guthrie, Annotation, *Priority and Preference in Appointment of Conservator or Guardian For an Incompetent,* 65 A.L.R.3d 991 (1975).

2. *See* Matter of Pasner (Tenenbaum), N.Y.L.J., 7/14/95, p.29, col.1 (Sup.Ct., Kings County).

3. Mental Hygiene Law § 81.19(b).

4. Mental Hygiene Law § 81.19(c).

5. Matter of Pasner (Tenenbaum), N.Y.L.J., 7/14/95, p.29, col.1 (Sup.Ct., Kings County).

6. Law Revision Commission Commentary to Mental Hygiene Law § 81.19.

7. General Obligations Law §§ 5–1501, et seq. *But see* Matter of Kern, 165 Misc.2d 108, 627 N.Y.S.2d 257 (Sup.Ct., Suffolk County, 1995), where the court refused to appoint the agent as guardian where such appointment would create a situation in which there was the appearance of and potential for actual impropriety.

8. Public Health Law § 2965.

9. Public Health Law § 2981.

10. *See generally,* Chapter 23 "Elder Law," for discussion of advance health care directives.

11. *See, e.g.,* Younker v. Younker, 42 A.D.2d 534, 344 N.Y.S.2d 758 (1st Dep't 1973) (Where all the persons intimately concerned with the welfare of the incompetent person had endorsed the appointment of a specified person as co-committee, it was an improvident exercise of discretion not to accede to the wishes and concerns of those

(3) the care and services being provided to the incapacitated person at the time of the proceeding;

(4) the powers which the guardian will exercise;[12]

(5) the educational, professional and business experience relevant to the nature of the services sought to be provided;

(6) the nature of the financial resources involved;

(7) the unique requirements of the incapacitated person; and

(8) any conflicts of interest between the person proposed as guardian and the incapacitated person.[13]

most closely affiliated with the incompetent.).

12. See infra, §§ 22.47–22.53 for discussion of powers of guardian.

13. The court appointed as guardian the nephew of the alleged incapacitated person where it found that the incapacitated person had nominated this nephew as his guardian and for many years the nephew had been the primary caregiver for the incapacitated person and there existed a trusting personal and financial relationship between the two. The court found no conflict of interest, although there was some testimony that there had been a disagreement many years ago; nor did the fact that the guardian was a potential inheritor under the incapacitated person's will or a trust agreement disqualify him from serving as guardian. The court noted that it appointed family members as guardians on a daily basis, the preference being to appoint relatives, with full knowledge that such family members will most likely inherit from their wards. Matter of Pasner (Tenenbaum), N.Y.L.J., 7/14/95, p.29, col.1 (Sup.Ct., Kings County). But see Matter of Commissioner of Cayuga County (Bessie C.), 225 A.D.2d 1027, 639 N.Y.S.2d 234 (4th Dep't 1996) (it was error to appoint son of incapacitated person as guardian of her property where son was executor and beneficiary of the estate of incapacitated person's predeceased husband; there was no bar to his appointment as guardian of her person).

The court refused to appoint as guardian the person named as the alleged incapacitated person's attorney-in-fact where such appointment would create a situation in which there was the appearance of and potential for actual impropriety. Matter of Kern, 165 Misc.2d 108, 627 N.Y.S.2d 257 (Sup.Ct., Suffolk County, 1995).

The court would not appoint either the brother or nephew as co-guardians where the court found that both had an interest adverse to that of the alleged incapacitated person where both had indicated in their testimony a strong desire to see that the money claimed by the incapacitated person's father (and father and grandfather of the proposed co-guardians) be repaid. Matter of Loury (Loury), N.Y.L.J., 9/23/93, p.26, col.2 (Sup.Ct., Kings County), aff'd 210 A.D.2d 227, 619 N.Y.S.2d 351 (2d Dep't 1994).

Where the incapacitated person was in a nursing home and the cost of her care was borne by Medicaid, the Commissioner of Social Services would be a preferred creditor to recoup payments or resources from the recipient of public assistance, the Commissioner had a conflict of interest with the incapacitated person and should not have been appointed the guardian of her property; a neutral, disinterested person should have been appointed; it was also error, under the circumstances, to appoint the Commissioner special guardian for the purpose of exercising the incapacitated person's right of election against the estate of her husband; the neutral, disinterested person appointed guardian of her property should apply to the court for such authority. Matter of Commissioner of Cayuga County (Bessie C.), 225 A.D.2d 1027, 639 N.Y.S.2d 234 (4th Dep't 1996). See also Matter of Lula XX, 224 A.D.2d 742, 637 N.Y.S.2d 234 (3d Dep't 1996) (in view of respondent's deep personal resentment toward the Department of Social Services and the fact that the Department acted as an adversary to respondent in this proceeding, appointment of the Commissioner of Social Services presented a conflict of interest; either respondent's counsel or a community

Unless the court finds that no other person or corporation is available or willing to act as guardian, or to provide the needed services for the incapacitated person, the following persons or corporations may not serve as guardian: (1) one whose only interest in the person alleged to be incapacitated is that of a creditor, and (2) one, other than a relative, who is a provider, or employee of a provider, of health care, day care, educational, or residential services to the incapacitated person, whether direct or indirect.[14] The Mental Hygiene Legal Service may not serve as guardian.[15]

Library References:
West's Key No. Digests, Guardian and Ward ⚖10; Mental Health ⚖116.

§ 22.42 Hearing and Order—Requirement of Bond

The court may require or dispense with the filing of a bond before a guardian, or special guardian enters upon the execution of the guardian's duties.[1] The court may require or dispense with the filing of a bond by a temporary guardian.[2] If the temporary guardian is required to file a bond, such bond must be filed within 10 days after issuance of the temporary guardian's commission.[3]

If the court requires the filing of a bond, the guardian or special or temporary guardian must file with the clerk of the court which appointed the guardian, a bond that he or she will faithfully discharge the powers[4] granted by the court to the guardian, obey all directions of the court in regard to such powers, and make and render a true account[5] of all properties received by him or her and the application thereof and a true report of his or her acts in the administration of his or her powers, whenever so required to do by the court.

The amount of the bond must be fixed by the court.[6] If the guardian received after-acquired property not covered by the bond, the guardian must immediately have such acquisition approved by the court and file a further bond.[7]

Notwithstanding any other provision of the section, any community guardian program, appointed as guardian may file with the clerk of the court before a specified date each year a consolidated undertaking up to a specified amount, in lieu of filing individual undertakings for each

guardian program could properly have been appointed respondent's guardian).

14. Mental Hygiene Law § 81.19(e).

15. Mental Hygiene Law § 81.19(f). See supra, § 22.24 for discussion of the role of the MHLS as court evaluator, and § 22.28 for discussion of the role of MHLS as counsel to the alleged incapacitated person.

§ 22.42

1. Mental Hygiene Law § 81.25(a).

2. See infra, § 22.57, for discussion of temporary guardian.

3. Mental Hygiene Law § 81.25(b).

4. See infra, §§ 22.47–22.53 for discussion of the powers of the guardian.

5. See infra, §§ 22.62–22.67 for discussion of the reports required of the guardian.

6. In re Salz, 80 A.D.2d 769, 436 N.Y.S.2d 713 (1st Dep't 1981).

7. Mental Hygiene Law § 81.25(d).

incapacitated person for whom it serves as guardian. To the extent of the aggregate value of such consolidated undertaking, the community guardian program will certify to the clerk of the court the faithful discharge of the trust imposed on it, to obey all directions of the court in regard to the trust, and to make and render a true account of all properties received by it and the application thereof and of its acts in the administration of its trust whenever required to do so by the court. At such time as the aggregate amount of the individual bonds, fixed by the court for persons for whom the community guardian program is appointed guardian, exceeds the consolidated bond filed by such program, the program must, before entering on execution of its duties, file with the clerk of the court individual undertakings, in amounts fixed by the court, that it will faithfully discharge the trust imposed on it.[8]

Library References:

West's Key No. Digests, Guardian and Ward ⇐10; Mental Health ⇐116.

§ 22.43 Hearing and Order—Designation of Clerk and Issuance of Commission

Pursuant to Mental Hygiene Law Section 81.26, no commission may issue nor may any order which in itself constitutes a commission become effective until an instrument executed and acknowledged by the guardian has been filed with the clerk of the court designating the clerk and the clerk's successor in office as a person on whom service of any process may be made in like manner and with like effect as if it were served personally on the guardian, whenever the guardian cannot, with due diligence, be served within state.[1]

Within five days after the guardian has filed the designation under Mental Hygiene Law Section 81.26, and has filed a bond, unless the court has waived the filing of a bond[2] and unless guardian's appointment is under Mental Hygiene Law Section 81.23,[3] the clerk of the court must issue a commission which states (1) the title of the proceeding and the name, address, and telephone number of the incapacitated person, and (2) the name, address, and telephone number of the guardian and the specific powers of such guardian,[4] and (3) the date when the appointment of the guardian was ordered by the court, and (4) the date on which the appointment terminates if one has been ordered by the court.[5]

8. Mental Hygiene Law § 81.25(c).

§ 22.43

1. *See infra,* § 22.102 for form of oath and designation of a guardian.

2. Mental Hygiene Law § 81.25(a). *See supra,* § 22.42 for discussion of requirement of bond.

3. *See infra,* § 22.57 for discussion of appointment of temporary guardian.

4. *See infra,* §§ 22.47–22.53 for discussion of powers of guardian.

5. Mental Hygiene Law § 81.27. *See infra,* § 22.103 for form of commission.

§ 22.44 Hearing and Order—Summary

The determination of whether the appointment of a guardian is necessary for the person alleged to be incapacitated may be made only after a hearing. The hearing must be conducted in the presence of the person alleged to be incapacitated, either at the courthouse or where the person alleged to be incapacitated resides, if the person alleged to be incapacitated physically cannot come or be brought to the courthouse.[1] The person alleged to be incapacitated is entitled to be represented by counsel.[2] The determination that the person is incapacitated must be based on clear and convincing evidence.[3] The burden of proof is on petitioner.[4] The rules of evidence apply to a proceeding to appoint a guardian unless the court, for good cause shown, waives such rules.[5]

The order appointing a guardian must contain certain findings based upon whether the appointment is voluntary; to provide for personal needs; or to provide for property management.[6] Various dispositional alternatives available to the court emphasize the underlying goal of promoting the least restrictive alternative and allow the court to fashion remedies which may include protective arrangements or single transactions which assure security, service or care to meet the foreseeable needs of the incapacitated person but do not deprive the person of independence and autonomy.[7] The order appointing a guardian must specify the exact scope of the guardian's authority.[8] The court may award reasonable compensation for the attorney for the petitioner.[9]

The court may appoint as guardian a person nominated by the alleged incapacitated person[10] or a person meeting certain minimum statutory qualifications, found suitable to exercise the powers necessary to assist the incapacitated person.[11] The criteria that the court should consider in selecting the guardian address the relationship between the proposed guardian and the incapacitated person, the needs of the incapacitated person, and the experience of the proposed guardian.[12] The court may require or dispense with the filing of a bond by a guardian, temporary guardian, or special guardian.[13]

§ 22.44

1. See supra, §§ 22.30, et seq.
2. Mental Hygiene Law § 81.11(e); see supra, § 22.32.
3. Mental Hygiene Law § 81.12(a); see supra, § 22.33.
4. Id; see supra, § 22.33.
5. Mental Hygiene Law § 81.12(b); see supra, § 22.33.
6. Mental Hygiene Law § 81.15; see supra, §§ 22.34–22.37.
7. Mental Hygiene Law § 81.16; see supra, § 22.38.
8. Mental Hygiene Law § 81.16(c); see infra, § 22.101 for form of order appointing guardian.
9. Mental Hygiene Law § 81.16(f); see supra, § 22.39.
10. Mental Hygiene Law § 81.17; see supra, § 22.40.
11. Mental Hygiene Law § 81.19(a); see supra, § 22.40.
12. Mental Hygiene Law § 81.19(d); see supra, § 22.41.
13. Mental Hygiene Law § 81.25; see supra, § 22.42.

§ 22.45 Role of Guardian—Overview

The guardian's relationship to the incapacitated person is that of a fiduciary.[1] In order to carry out this responsibility in the most careful and diligent manner, the guardian should develop a personal relationship to the ward, in the event one does not exist, so that the guardian can understand the impact of any decision from the perspective of the incapacitated person and can involve the incapacitated person in the decisions to the greatest extent possible.[2]

The guardian may exercise only those powers relating to property management or personal needs that are authorized by the court order.[3] The common law doctrine of substituted judgment[4] is recognized and implemented by Article 81, pursuant to which the court may authorize the transfer of an incapacitated person's property where there is clear and convincing evidence satisfying either of the following two standards: (1) the incapacitated person, if capable, would actually have made the proposed transfer, or (2) the incapacitated person as a reasonably prudent person would make the proposed transfer. The transfer must not jeopardize the welfare of the incapacitated person and sufficient assets must remain to satisfy his or her present and future needs. An objective standard is established for determining whether to approve the application to transfer the property of the incapacitated person.[5]

The powers of the guardian set out in the statute are meant to be illustrative rather than exclusive. The incapacitated person for whom a guardian has been appointed retains all powers and rights except those powers and rights which have been granted to the guardian.[6] The appointment of a guardian is not conclusive evidence that the person lacks capacity for any other purpose, including the capacity to dispose of property by will.[7] The title to all property of the incapacitated person remains in such person, subject to the possession of the guardian.[8]

Library References:

West's Key No. Digests, Guardian and Ward ⟐111; Mental Health ⟐211–275.

§ 22.46 Role of Guardian—Duties

The guardian's relationship to the incapacitated person is that of a

§ 22.45
1. See infra, § 22.46.
2. Id.
3. Mental Hygiene Law § 81.16; see infra, §§ 22.47–22.53 for discussion of the duties and powers of a guardian.
4. See infra, § 22.48.
5. See infra, §§ 22.47–22.52.
6. Mental Hygiene Law § 81.29(a); see infra, § 22.54.
7. Mental Hygiene Law § 81.29(b); see infra, § 22.54.
8. Mental Hygiene Law § 81.29(c); see infra, § 22.54.

fiduciary.[1] The guardian must exercise the utmost care and diligence when acting on behalf of the incapacitated person.[2] The guardian must exhibit the utmost degree of trust, loyalty and fidelity in relation to the incapacitated person.[3]

Mental Hygiene Law Section 81.20 emphasizes the guardian's unique relationship to the incapacitated person. Decision making is a fundamental part of the guardian's role. In order to carry out this responsibility in the most careful and diligent manner, the guardian should develop a personal relationship to the ward, in the event one does not exist, so that the guardian can understand the impact of any decision from the perspective of the incapacitated person and can involve the incapacitated person in the decisions to the greatest extent possible.[4] This can be done through an interview with the incapacitated person and through discussions with family and friends to ascertain the preferences of the incapacitated person. In order to develop and maintain the necessary relationship with the incapacitated person, the guardian must visit the incapacitated person not less than four times per year or more frequently as specified in the court order.[5] In situations where there is no indication of the prior preferences of the incapacitated person, the guardian must make decisions in accordance with the best interests of the ward.[6]

To effectuate these purposes, Mental Hygiene Law Section 81.20 establishes the duties of the guardian. First and foremost, the guardian may exercise only those powers that the guardian is authorized to exercise by the court order.[7]

The guardian must file initial and annual reports in accordance with Mental Hygiene Law Sections 81.30 and 81.31.[8]

The guardian who is given authority with respect to property

§ 22.46

1. Law Revision Commission Commentary to Mental Hygiene Law § 81.20.

2. Mental Hygiene Law § 81.20(a)(2).

3. Mental Hygiene Law § 81.20(a)(3).

4. Law Revision Commission Commentary to Mental Hygiene Law § 81.20.

5. Mental Hygiene Law § 81.20(a)(5). But see Matter of Jospe (Grala), N.Y.L.J., 1/30/95, p.30, col.2 (Sup.Ct., Nassau County) where the court ruled that it was unreasonable and unrealistic to assume that any guardian appointed pursuant to Article 81, except a close family member living with or close to the incapacitated person, could serve as required backup to home care aides and make daily visits. In Jospe, the incapacitated person strongly desired to return home; however, such arrangement would have required home aides financed by the county department of social services and a person to serve as backup, who would have to check daily to determine if the aide had arrived. The court noted that such a role was not one intended by the Legislature for a Mental Hygiene Law Art. 81 guardian.

6. Law Revision Commission Commentary to Mental Hygiene Law § 81.20.

7. Mental Hygiene Law § 81.20(a)(1). See infra, §§ 22.47–22.53.

The guardian should always act within the scope of the order of appointment. Law Revision Commission Commentary to Mental Hygiene Law § 81.20.

8. Mental Hygiene Law § 81.20(a)(4). See infra, §§ 22.62–22.67, for discussion of the reports required by the guardian.

management for the incapacitated person must:[9]

(1) afford the incapacitated person the greatest amount of independence and self-determination with respect to property management in light of that person's functional level, understanding and appreciation of his or her functional limitations, and personal wishes, preferences and desires with regard to managing the activities of daily living;

(2) preserve, protect, and account for such property and financial resources faithfully;[10]

(3) determine whether the incapacitated person has executed a will, determine the location of any will, and of the appropriate persons to be notified in the event of the death of the incapacitated person and, in the event of the death of the incapacitated person, notify those persons;

(4) use the property and financial resources and income available from such property to maintain and support the incapacitated person, and to maintain and support those persons dependent on the incapacitated person;[11]

(5) at the termination of the appointment, deliver such property to the person legally entitled to it;

(6) file with the recording officer of the county in which the incapacitated person is possessed of real property, an acknowledged statement to be recorded and indexed under the name of the incapacitated person identifying real property possessed by the incapacitated person, and the tax map numbers of such property, and stating the date of adjudication of incapacity of the person regarding property management, and the name, address, and telephone number of the guardian and the guardian's surety; and

(7) perform all other duties required by law.

The guardian who is given authority relating to the personal needs of the incapacitated person must afford the incapacitated person the greatest amount of independence and self-determination with respect to personal needs in light of that person's functional level, understanding and appreciation of that person's functional limitations, and personal wishes, preferences and desires with regard to managing the activities of daily living.[12]

9. Mental Hygiene Law § 81.20(a)(6) sets forth the duties listed below.

10. *See, e.g.*, In re Le Bovici, 135 A.D.2d 635, 522 N.Y.S.2d 214 (2d Dep't 1987). Sale by conservator of conservatee's stock holdings, and placement of proceeds therefrom into insured bank investments, without prior court approval, was not improper where conservator exercised requisite prudence in making investment since conservator has power to invest conservatee's funds without prior court authorization.

11. Matter of Klapper, N.Y.L.J., 8/9/94, p.26, col.1 (Sup.Ct., Kings County).

12. Mental Hygiene Law § 81.20(a)(7).

§ 22.47 Role of Guardian—Powers; Property Management

Mental Hygiene Law Section 81.21 sets forth the powers that the court may authorize the guardian to exercise with respect to property management, including the power to transfer a part of the incapacitated person's assets to or for the benefit of another person on the ground that the person would have made the transfer if he or she had the capacity to act.[1] The statutory list of powers is intended to be illustrative rather than exclusive.[2]

Mental Hygiene Law Section 81.21(a) provides that, consistent with functional limitations of the incapacitated person, that person's understanding and appreciation of the harm that he or she is likely to suffer as a result of the inability to manage property and financial affairs,[3] and that person's personal wishes, preferences, and desires with regard to managing the activities of daily living, and the least restrictive form of intervention,[4] the court may authorize the guardian:

(1) to exercise those powers necessary and sufficient to manage the property and financial affairs of the incapacitated person;

(2) to provide for the maintenance and support of the incapacitated person, and those persons depending on the incapacitated person; and

(3) to transfer part of the incapacitated person's assets to or for the benefit of another person under specified circumstances.[5]

Any transfers made pursuant to Mental Hygiene Law Article 81 may be in any form that the incapacitated person could have employed if he or

---

§ 22.47

1. *See infra,* § 22.48 for discussion of the doctrine of substituted judgment.

2. **PRACTICE POINTER**: Because the court will grant only those powers which are necessary to the needs and functional capabilities of the incapacitated person, the person seeking the appointment of a guardian must ascertain these needs and must apprise the court of those powers which are necessary. The court will not grant unnecessary powers.

3. Matter of Kustka, 163 Misc.2d 694, 622 N.Y.S.2d 208 (Sup.Ct., Queens County, 1994).

4. The fundamental policy underlying Mental Hygiene Law Art. 81 is to assist the incapacitated person to compensate for limitations and to provide the least restrictive alternative for him or her. In order to effectuate this policy, an incapacitated person should be permitted to have the same options available to him or her with respect to transfers of his or her property that are available to competent individuals. Matter of Klapper, N.Y.L.J., 8/9/94, p.26, col.1 (Sup.Ct., Kings County). *See also* Matter of Loury (Loury), N.Y.L.J., 9/23/93, p.26, col.2 (Sup.Ct., Kings County), aff'd 210 A.D.2d 227, 619 N.Y.S.2d 351 (2d Dep't 1994).

See supra, § 22.14 for discussion of the doctrine of the least restrictive form of intervention.

5. *See infra,* § 22.48 for discussion of the doctrine of substituted judgment.

§ 22.47 GUARDIANSHIP Ch. 22

she had requisite capacity, except in the form of a will or codicil.[6] Those powers which may be granted to the guardian include, but are not limited to, the power to:[7]

(1) make gifts;[8]

(2) provide support for persons dependent on the incapacitated person for support, whether or not the incapacitated person is legally obligated to provide that support;[9]

(3) convey or release contingent and expectant interests in property, including marital property rights and any right of survivorship incidental to joint tenancy or tenancy by entirety;[10]

(4) exercise or release powers held by the incapacitated person as trustee, personal representative, guardian for a minor, guardian, or donee of a power of appointment;

(5) enter into contracts;[11]

(6) create revocable or irrevocable trusts of the property of the estate which may extend beyond the incapacity or life of the incapacitated person;[12]

---

6. Mental Hygiene Law § 81.21(a). See Matter of Livreri, N.Y.L.J., 2/23/96, p. 30, col. 3 (Sup.Ct., Suffolk County) (the guardian may never be given authority to transfer property by means of a will or codicil).

7. Id.

8. The powers to be granted to the property management guardian may include authority to make annual gifts of $10,000 utilizing the annual exclusion for the tax year. Matter of Lisle, N.Y.L.J., 8/9/94, p.27, col.4 (Surr.Ct., Nassau County). *But see* Matter of Schulze, N.Y.L.J., 9/3/96, p. 30, col. 1 (Surr.Ct., N.Y. County) (power to make substantial gifts to family members denied; possibility of tax savings to heirs held insufficient ground to justify approval of gift).

9. Although incapacitated person was not legally obligated to provide for her son and his family, it was evident that she did provide such support and that they were dependent upon her for such support; based upon her regularly providing such support, if she had the capacity to act, she would have continued to provide such support; the power to continue such support was ordered. Matter of Klapper, N.Y.L.J., 8/9/94, p.26, col.1 (Sup.Ct., Kings County).

10. *Cf.* Matter of Daniels, N.Y.L.J., 11/7/94, p.34, col.4 (Sup.Ct., Suffolk County).

11. *Compare* In re Cook, 133 A.D.2d 823, 520 N.Y.S.2d 400 (2d Dep't 1987), appeal denied 71 N.Y.2d 802, 527 N.Y.S.2d 768, 522 N.E.2d 1066 (1988) (court would void contract for sale of conservatee's property where conservator, who drafted agreement, failed to exercise agreed-upon option to cancel when it appeared that title would not be cleared imminently and waited nearly two years before instituting proceeding to clear title, during which time, and for two years which had elapsed until judgment clearing title was issued, value of property increased dramatically; conservatee, by virtue of conservator's actions, was thus precluded from validly disaffirming contract and was also barred from entering into new contract which more accurately reflected appreciated value of property).

12. Absent any contrary intention shown in the governing instrument, a conservator may exercise the conservatee's power to withdraw principal or even terminate a trust, but such power may be exercised only with the approval of the court which appointed the conservator, which is in best position to determine whether the withdrawal is in the best interests of the conservatee; such interpretation is supported by Mental Hygiene Law Art. 81, which authorizes the supreme court to grant broader powers to newly created guardians for mentally incapacitated person than were available to conservators and committees under prior law. Matter of Buckner (Buckner), 157 Misc.2d 23, 595 N.Y.S.2d 862 (Surr.Ct., N.Y. County, 1993).

(7) exercise options of the incapacitated person to purchase securities or other property;

(8) exercise rights to elect options and change beneficiaries under insurance and annuity policies and to surrender the policies for their cash value;

(9) exercise any right to an elective share in the estate of the incapacitated person's deceased spouse;[13]

(10) renounce or disclaim any interest by testate or intestate succession or by *inter vivos* transfer consistent with Estates, Powers and Trusts Law Section 2–1.11;[14]

(11) authorize access to or release of confidential records; and

(12) apply for government and private benefits.[15]

Library References:

West's Key No. Digests, Guardian and Ward ⚖111; Mental Health ⚖211–275.

§ 22.48 Role of Guardian—Substituted Judgment

Mental Hygiene Law Section 81.21 gives statutory recognition to the common law doctrine of substituted judgment recognized by the courts of New York.[1] The statute also provides assurance that the prior compe-

Application by conservator for authority to establish irrevocable *inter vivos* trust for lifetime benefit of conservatee, containing provisions for continuation of trust on her death to provide for supplemental needs of her mentally retarded adult son who received governmental assistance benefits, would be granted. In re Conservatorship of Garbow, 155 Misc.2d 1001, 591 N.Y.S.2d 754 (Surr.Ct., Kings County, 1992). See Preminger, *et al., New York Trusts and Estates Practice* (West 1997).

13. See EPTL §§ 5–1.1 and 5–1.1–A for determination of elective share. Matter of Mattei, 169 Misc.2d 989, 647 N.Y.S.2d 415 (Sup.Ct., Nassau County, 1996) (discussion of effect of exercise of right of election upon eligibility for Medicaid); *but see* Matter of Furrer, N.Y.L.J., 2/22/96, p. 35, col. 2 (Sup. Ct., Suffolk County) (guardian denied power to exercise right of election where guardian *ad litem* had been appointed by surrogate's court and, under the circumstances, the extent of the incapacitated person's right of election had to be determined, an issue which was best reserved for the special expertise of the surrogate).

14. Matter of Lisle, N.Y.L.J., 8/9/94, p.27, col.4 (Surr.Ct., Nassau County); Matter of Scheiber (Zahodnick), N.Y.L.J., 10/18/93, p.38, col.5 (Sup.Ct., Nassau County); Matter of Driscoll, N.Y.L.J., 10/22/93, p.30, col.4 (Sup.Ct., Nassau County).

15. Order appointing a conservator and requiring New York City Commissioner of Social Services "to provide social services to the conservatee to the same extent as were provided before the appointment of a conservator" would be reversed, and it would be ordered that appointment of the conservator did not relieve commissioner from any obligation to provide social services and continuous supervision of the conservatee through its caseworkers, supervisors and other staff members "to the extent that the Commissioner deems appropriate," and that the commissioner should also communicate and cooperate with the conservator so that their joint actions would result in best serving interests of the conservatee. In re Gross (Kushner), 127 A.D.2d 658, 511 N.Y.S.2d 885 (2d Dep't 1987). *See also* In re Gross (Elkins), 127 A.D.2d 658, 511 N.Y.S.2d 1018 (2d Dep't 1987).

§ 22.48

1. Law Revision Commission Commentary to Mental Hygiene Law § 81.21. See, *e.g.*, Matter of Daniels, 162 Misc.2d 840,

tent choices of the person will be given effect.[2] The section details the matters which the court must consider in approving property transfers and other property arrangements. Under the doctrine of substituted judgment the courts will authorize the transfer of an incapacitated person's property where either of the following two standards are satisfied: (1) the incapacitated person, if capable, would actually have made the proposed transfer, or (2) the incapacitated person as a reasonably prudent person would make the proposed transfer.[3] The first standard involves an assessment of the expressed desires of the incapacitated person before the onset of his or her incapacity.[4] The second standard requires the court to assess how a reasonably prudent person would act under the circumstances presented.[5] Crucial to either assessment is a finding that the transfer would not jeopardize the welfare of the incapacitated person and that sufficient assets remain to satisfy his or her present and future needs.[6] If the person has manifested a prior intent inconsistent with the act for which approval is sought, it must be shown that the person is likely to have changed such intention under the circumstances existing at the time of the petition to transfer part of the incapacitated person's assets to or for benefit of another person under specified circumstances.[7] However, the absence of proof of any prior pattern or plan need not be taken as conclusive proof that the proposed plan must be rejected.[8] Under such circumstances, what must be proved by clear and convincing evidence is the likelihood of performance of the acts by a competent, reasonable individual in the position of the incapac-

618 N.Y.S.2d 499 (Sup.Ct., Suffolk County, 1994); Matter of Moretti, 159 Misc.2d 654, 606 N.Y.S.2d 543 (Sup.Ct., Kings County, 1993); Matter of Driscoll, N.Y.L.J., 10/22/93, p.30, col.4 (Sup.Ct., Nassau County); In re Florence, 140 Misc.2d 393, 530 N.Y.S.2d 981 (Surr.Ct., Nassau County, 1988); In re Estate of Fairbairn, 56 A.D.2d 259, 392 N.Y.S.2d 152 (4th Dep't 1977).

2. *See, e.g.,* In re Kurnyk, 109 Misc.2d 1019, 441 N.Y.S.2d 328 (Sup.Ct., Queens County, 1981) (Application withdrawn where there was substantial proof that conservatee was capable of making decisions with respect to the disposition of her property and her own financial needs).

3. In re Conservatorship of Garbow, 155 Misc.2d 1001, 591 N.Y.S.2d 754 (Surr.Ct., Kings County, 1992); In re Florence, 140 Misc.2d 393, 530 N.Y.S.2d 981 (Surr.Ct., Nassau County, 1988).

4. In re Salz, 80 A.D.2d 769, 436 N.Y.S.2d 713 (1st Dep't 1981); Matter of Klapper, N.Y.L.J., 8/9/94, p.26, col.1 (Sup. Ct., Kings County); In re Conservatorship of Garbow, 155 Misc.2d 1001, 591 N.Y.S.2d 754 (Surr.Ct., Kings County, 1992).

5. Matter of Scheiber (Zahodnick), N.Y.L.J., 10/18/93, p.38, col.5 (Sup.Ct., Nassau County); In re Conservatorship of Garbow, 155 Misc.2d 1001, 591 N.Y.S.2d 754 (Surr.Ct., Kings County, 1992).

6. Matter of Daniels, N.Y.L.J., 11/7/94, p.34, col.4 (Sup.Ct., Suffolk County); Matter of Scheiber (Zahodnick), N.Y.L.J., 10/18/93, p.38, col.5 (Sup.Ct., Nassau County); In re Conservatorship of Garbow, 155 Misc.2d 1001, 591 N.Y.S.2d 754 (Surr.Ct., Kings County, 1992).

7. Law Revision Commission Commentary to Mental Hygiene Law § 81.21. *See* Matter of Daniels, N.Y.L.J., 11/7/94, p.34, col.4 (Sup.Ct., Suffolk County); Matter of Scheiber (Zahodnick), N.Y.L.J., 10/18/93, p.38, col.5 (Sup.Ct., Nassau County).

8. Matter of Heller (Ratner), N.Y.L.J., 7/28/95, p.24, col.5 (Sup.Ct., Kings County); Matter of Scheiber (Zahodnick), N.Y.L.J., 10/18/93, p.38, col.5 (Sup.Ct., Nassau County).

itated person.[9]

The doctrine of substituted judgment has been exercised in the following situations, assuming that the needs of the incapacitated person will be met:

(1) transfers for the purposes of estate planning to minimize taxes;[10]
(2) transfers for the purposes of Medicaid planning;[11]
(3) renounce an inheritance;[12]
(4) establish a supplemental needs trust.[13]

9. Id. See also Matter of Daniels, N.Y.L.J., 11/7/94, p.34, col.4 (Sup.Ct., Suffolk County).

10. Matter of Heller (Ratner), N.Y.L.J., 7/28/95, p.24, col.5 (Sup.Ct., Kings County); Matter of Scheiber (Zahodnick), N.Y.L.J., 10/18/93, p.38, col.5 (Sup.Ct., Nassau County); Matter of Klapper, N.Y.L.J., 8/9/94, p.26, col.1 (Sup.Ct., Kings County).

11. Medicaid planning is a proper objective of a proposed disposition of an incapacitated persons property. See, e.g., Matter of John "XX", 226 A.D.2d 79, 652 N.Y.S.2d 329 (3d Dep't 1996); Matter of Mattei, 169 Misc.2d 989, 647 N.Y.S.2d 415 (Sup.Ct., Nassau County, 1996); Matter of Baird, 167 Misc.2d 526, 634 N.Y.S.2d 971 (Sup.Ct., Suffolk County, 1995) (discussion of the public policy allowing renunciation of a portion of a bequest to permit incapacitated person to continue receiving Medicaid for nursing home care); Matter of DaRonco, 167 Misc.2d 140, 638 N.Y.S.2d 275 (Sup.Ct., Westchester County, 1995); Matter of Heller (Ratner), N.Y.L.J., 7/28/95, p.24, col.5 (Sup.Ct., Kings County); Matter of Parnes, N.Y.L.J., 11/2/94, p.32, col.2 (Sup.Ct., Kings County); see also, N.Y.L.J., 4/7/95, p.33, col.5 (Sup.Ct., Kings County); Matter of Daniels, 162 Misc.2d 840, 618 N.Y.S.2d 499 (Sup.Ct., Suffolk County, 1994); see also, N.Y.L.J., 11/7/94, p.34, col.4 (Sup.Ct., Suffolk County); Matter of Klapper, N.Y.L.J., 8/9/94, p.26, col.1 (Sup.Ct., Kings County); Matter of Driscoll, N.Y.L.J., 10/22/93, p.30, col.4 (Sup.Ct., Nassau County); In re De Luca, N.Y.L.J., 12/14/93, p.27, col.3 (Sup. Ct., Nassau County).

See Matter of Pugliese (Nicolais), N.Y.L.J., 7/28/97, p. 30, col. 5 (Sup.Ct., Queens County) (discussion of impact of Section 217 of the Health Insurance Accountability and Portability Act of 1996, which makes it a crime to transfer assets in order to qualify for Medicaid under certain circumstances).

12. See, e.g., Matter of Mattei, 169 Misc.2d 989, 647 N.Y.S.2d 415 (Sup.Ct., Nassau County, 1996); Matter of Baird, 167 Misc.2d 526, 634 N.Y.S.2d 971 (Sup.Ct., Suffolk County, 1995) (discussion of the public policy allowing renunciation of a portion of a bequest to permit incapacitated person to continue receiving Medicaid for nursing home care); Matter of Driscoll, N.Y.L.J., 10/22/93, p.30, col.4 (Sup.Ct., Nassau County); cf. Matter of Daniels, N.Y.L.J., 11/7/94, p.34, col.4 (Sup.Ct., Suffolk County).

13. Matter of Moretti, 159 Misc.2d 654, 606 N.Y.S.2d 543 (Sup.Ct., Kings County, 1993) (Conservator granted power to transfer property of incapacitated person to a supplemental needs trust for benefit of the incapacitated person on ground that if the incapacitated person had the capacity to act, he would create the trust fund naming himself as the beneficiary which would supplement and not supplant governmental entitlements, thereby enabling him to enjoy an enhanced quality of life; while Mental Hygiene Law § 81.21(a)(6), in describing the guardian's powers to make transfers on behalf of the incapacitated person, refers to such transfers as those made for the benefit of another person, under federal law, the disabled person's assets may be transferred to a supplemental needs trust for his or her own benefit.).

In re Conservatorship of Garbow, 155 Misc.2d 1001, 591 N.Y.S.2d 754 (Surr.Ct., Kings County, 1992) (Application by conservator for authority to establish irrevocable inter vivos trust for lifetime benefit of conservatee, containing provisions for continuation of trust on her death to provide for supplemental needs of her mentally retarded adult son who received governmental assistance benefits, would be granted pursuant to "substituted judgment" doctrine, which permits court to authorize transfer of ward's property where ward, if competent,

§ 22.48 GUARDIANSHIP Ch. 22

Library References:

West's Key No. Digests, Guardian and Ward ⚖111; Mental Health ⚖211–275.

§ 22.49 Role of Guardian—Petition for Authorization to Transfer Property

Mental Hygiene Law Section 81.21(b) provides that, if the petitioner or guardian seeks authority to exercise a power which involves the transfer of a part of the incapacitated person's assets to or for the benefit of another person,[1] including the petitioner or the guardian, the petition on such application must include the following information:

(1) whether any prior proceeding has at any time been commenced by any person seeking such power with respect to the property of the incapacitated person and, if so, a description of the nature of such application and the disposition made of such application;

(2) the amount and nature of the financial obligations of the incapacitated person including the funds presently and prospectively required to provide for the incapacitated person's own maintenance, support and well-being and to provide for other persons dependent on the incapacitated person for support, whether or not the incapacitated person is legally obligated to provide that support;[2] a copy of any court order or written agreement setting forth the support obligations of the incapacitated person must be attached to the petition if available to the petitioner or guardian;

(3) the property of the incapacitated person that is the subject of the present application;

would actually have made proposed transfer since (1) reasonably prudent person would make proposed transfer, (2) creation of trust was in best interests of conservatee, and (3) terms and purpose of trust were in conformity with conservatee's past conduct and declarations indicating intent to preserve her son's government entitlements.).

Cf., Matter of DeVita, N.Y.L.J., 2/17/95, p.33, col.5 (Sup.Ct., Suffolk County). (An order establishing a supplemental needs trust could not be signed in the form submitted where clauses in the trust created a potential conflict of interest. The application was denied without prejudice to a new submission.).

See also Matter of McMullen, 166 Misc.2d 117, 632 N.Y.S.2d 401 (Sup.Ct., Suffolk County, 1995) (discussion of impact of eligibility for Medicaid on establishment of supplemental needs trust); Matter of Morales (Morales), N.Y.L.J., 7/28/95, p. 25, col. 1 (Sup.Ct., Kings County) (requirements of EPTL 7–1.12 with regard to supplemental needs trusts); Matter of Kacer (Osohowsky), N.Y.L.J., 11/1/94, p.33, col.1 (Sup.Ct., Suffolk County).

§ 22.49

1. Conservator granted power to transfer property of incapacitated person to a supplemental needs trust for benefit of the incapacitated person; while Mental Hygiene Law § 81.21(a)(6), in describing the guardian's powers to make transfers on behalf of the incapacitated person, refers to such transfers as those made for the benefit of another person, under federal law, the disabled person's assets may be transferred to a supplemental needs trust for his or her own benefit. Matter of Moretti, 159 Misc.2d 654, 606 N.Y.S.2d 543 (Sup.Ct., Kings County, 1993).

2. Matter of Klapper, N.Y.L.J., 8/9/94, p.26, col.1 (Sup.Ct., Kings County).

(4) the proposed disposition of such property and the reasons why such disposition should be made;

(5) whether the incapacitated person has sufficient capacity to make the proposed disposition;[3] if the incapacitated person has such capacity, his or her written consent must be attached to the petition;

(6) whether the incapacitated person has previously executed a will or similar instrument and, if so, the terms of the most recently executed will together with a statement as to how the terms of will the became known to the petitioner or guardian.[4] Additional provisions specify how the will should be located and attached:

(i) if the petitioner or guardian can, with reasonable diligence, obtain a copy, a copy of the most recently executed will or similar instrument shall be attached to the petition; in such case, the petition shall contain a statement as to how the copy was secured and the basis for the petitioner or guardian's belief that such copy is a copy of the incapacitated person's most recently executed will or similar instrument;

(ii) if the petitioner or guardian is unable to obtain a copy of the most recently executed will or similar instrument, or if the petitioner or guardian is unable to determine whether the incapacitated person has previously executed a will or similar instrument, what efforts were made by the petitioner or guardian to ascertain such information;

(iii) if a copy of the most recently executed will or similar instrument is not otherwise available, the court may direct an attorney or other person who has the original will or similar instrument in his or her possession to turn a photocopy over to the court for its examination, in camera. A photocopy of the will or similar instrument shall then be turned over by the court to the parties in such proceeding unless the court finds that to do so would be contrary to the best interests of the incapacitated person;

(7) a description of any significant gifts or patterns of gifts made by the incapacitated person;[5]

3. Application withdrawn where there was substantial proof that conservatee was capable of making decisions with respect to the disposition of her property and her own financial needs. In re Kurnyk, 109 Misc.2d 1019, 441 N.Y.S.2d 328 (Sup.Ct., Queens County, 1981).

4. The term "will" has the meaning specified in EPTL § 1-2.19; the term "similar instrument" includes a revocable or irrevocable trust. *Cf.* Matter of Heller (Ratner), N.Y.L.J., 7/28/95, p.24, col.5 (Sup.Ct., Kings County) (Totten trusts). *See* Chapter 24 "Estate Planning," *infra. See also,* Preminger, *et al., Trusts and Estates Practice in New York* (West 1997).

5. Matter of Klapper, N.Y.L.J., 8/9/94, p.26, col.1 (Sup.Ct., Kings County). However, the absence of proof of any prior pattern or testamentary plan need not be taken as conclusive proof that the proposed plan must be rejected. Matter of Scheiber (Za-

§ 22.49

(8) names, post-office addresses and relationships of presumptive distributees of the incapacitated person and beneficiaries under the most recent will or similar instrument executed by the incapacitated person.

Nothing in Mental Hygiene Law Article 81 imposes any duty on the guardian to commence a special proceeding under the article seeking to transfer part of the assets of the incapacitated person to or for the benefit of another person and the guardian is not liable or accountable to any person for having failed to commence a special proceeding under the article seeking to transfer part of assets of incapacitated person to or for the benefit of another person.[6]

Library References:

West's Key No. Digests, Guardian and Ward ⚖111; Mental Health ⚖211–275.

§ 22.50 Role of Guardian—Petition for Authorization to Transfer Property—Notice of Application

Notice of the petition seeking the transfer of property of the incapacitated person must be served on (1) the persons entitled to notice in accordance with Mental Hygiene Law Section 81.07(d)(1);[1] (2) if known to the petitioner or guardian, the presumptive distributees of the incapacitated person unless the court dispenses with such notice; and (3) if known to the petitioner or guardian, any person designated in the most recent will or similar instrument of the incapacitated person as beneficiary whose rights or interests would be adversely affected by the relief requested in the petition unless the court dispenses with such notice.[2]

Library References:

West's Key No. Digests, Guardian and Ward ⚖111; Mental Health ⚖211–275.

§ 22.51 Role of Guardian—Petition for Authorization to Transfer Property—Considerations of Court

Mental Hygiene Law Section 81.21(d) establishes an objective stan-

---

hodnick), N.Y.L.J., 10/18/93, p.38, col.5 (Sup.Ct., Nassau County).

6. Mental Hygiene Law § 81.21(f).

§ 22.50

1. See supra, § 22.21 for discussion of the persons entitled to notice of the application to declare a person incapacitated.

2. Mental Hygiene Law § 81.21(c). For estate and gift tax ramifications of transfer-

dard[1] for determining whether to approve the application for transfer of the property of the incapacitated person, and provides that the court must consider the following factors:

(1) whether the incapacitated person has sufficient capacity to make the proposed disposition himself or herself, and, if so, whether he or she has consented to proposed disposition;[2]

(2) whether the disability of the incapacitated person is likely to be of sufficiently short duration such that he or she should make the determination with respect to the proposed disposition when no longer disabled;[3]

(3) whether the needs of the incapacitated person and his or her dependents or other persons depending on the incapacitated person for support can be met from the remainder of the assets of the incapacitated person after the transfer is made;[4]

(4) whether the donees or beneficiaries of the proposed disposition are the natural objects of the bounty of the incapacitated person and whether the proposed disposition is consistent with any known testamentary plan or pattern of gifts he or she has made;[5]

(5) whether the proposed disposition will produce estate, gift, income or other tax savings which will significantly benefit the incapacitated person or his or her dependents or other persons for whom the incapacitated person would be concerned;[6] and

(6) such other factors as the court deems relevant.

Library References:

West's Key No. Digests, Guardian and Ward ⟜111; Mental Health ⟜211–275.

---

ring the incapacitated person's assets, see infra, Chapter 24, "Estate Planning," infra.

§ 22.51

1. Matter of Scheiber (Zahodnick), N.Y.L.J., 10/18/93, p.38, col.5 (Sup.Ct., Nassau County).

2. In re Kurnyk, 109 Misc.2d 1019, 441 N.Y.S.2d 328 (Sup.Ct., Queens County, 1981).

3. In considering these factors the court noted that given the incapacitated person's medical condition and prognosis, she lacked sufficient mental capacity to make the proposed dispositions and was not likely to regain such capacity. Matter of Klapper, N.Y.L.J., 8/9/94, p.26, col.1 (Sup.Ct., Kings County). See also Matter of Heller (Ratner), N.Y.L.J., 7/28/95, p.24, col.5 (Sup.Ct., Kings County).

4. Matter of Daniels, N.Y.L.J., 11/7/94, p.34, col.4 (Sup.Ct., Suffolk County); Matter of Scheiber (Zahodnick), N.Y.L.J., 10/18/93, p.38, col.5 (Sup.Ct., Nassau County).

5. Matter of Klapper, N.Y.L.J., 8/9/94, p.26, col.1 (Sup.Ct., Kings County). However, the absence of proof of any prior pattern or testamentary plan need not be taken as conclusive proof that the proposed plan must be rejected. Matter of Scheiber (Zahodnick), N.Y.L.J., 10/18/93, p.38, col.5 (Sup.Ct., Nassau County).

6. Matter of Heller (Ratner), N.Y.L.J., 7/28/95, p.24, col.5 (Sup.Ct., Kings County); Matter of Scheiber (Zahodnick), N.Y.L.J., 10/18/93, p.38, col.5 (Sup.Ct., Nassau County). For estate and gift tax ramifications of transferring the incapacitated person's assets, see Chapter 24 "Estate Planning," infra.

§ 22.52 Role of Guardian—Petition for Authorization to Transfer Property—Granting Petition

The court may grant the application for transfer of property of the incapacitated person if there is clear and convincing evidence of the following and must make a record of such findings:[1]

(1) the incapacitated person lacks the requisite mental capacity to perform the act or acts for which approval has been sought and is not likely to regain such capacity within a reasonable period of time or, if the incapacitated person has requisite capacity, that he or she consents to the proposed dispositions;[2]

(2) a competent, reasonable individual in the position of the incapacitated person would be likely to perform such act or acts under the same circumstances;[3] and

(3) the incapacitated person has not manifested an intention inconsistent with the performance of the act or acts for which approval has been sought at some earlier time when he or she had the requisite capacity or, if such intention was manifested, the particular person would be likely to have changed such intention under the circumstances existing at time of filing of petition.[4]

Library References:

West's Key No. Digests, Guardian and Ward ⟜111; Mental Health ⟜211–275.

§ 22.53 Role of Guardian—Powers; Personal Needs

Mental Hygiene Law Section 81.22 identifies the types of powers that the court may authorize the guardian to exercise with respect to meeting the personal needs of the incapacitated person. The list set out in Section 81.22 is meant to be illustrative rather than exclusive.[1] Mental Hygiene Law Section 81.22(a) provides that, consistent with the functional limitations of the incapacitated person, such person's understanding and appreciation of the harm that he or she is likely to suffer as a result of the inability to provide for his or her personal needs, and such person's personal wishes, preferences, and desires with regard to managing the activities of daily living, and the least restrictive form of intervention,[2] the court may grant to the guardian powers necessary and sufficient to provide for the personal needs of the incapacitated person.

§ 22.52

1. Mental Hygiene Law § 81.21(e).

2. Matter of Heller (Ratner), N.Y.L.J., 7/28/95, p.24, col.5 (Sup.Ct., Kings County); Matter of Klapper, N.Y.L.J., 8/9/94, p.26, col.1 (Sup.Ct., Kings County).

3. Matter of Heller (Ratner), N.Y.L.J., 7/28/95, p.24, col.5 (Sup.Ct., Kings County); Matter of Klapper, N.Y.L.J., 8/9/94, p.26, col.1 (Sup.Ct., Kings County).

4. However, the absence of proof of any prior pattern or testamentary plan need not be taken as conclusive proof that the proposed plan must be rejected. Matter of Scheiber (Zahodnick), N.Y.L.J., 10/18/93, p.38, col.5 (Sup.Ct., Nassau County).

§ 22.53

1. See Law Revision Commission Commentary to Mental Hygiene Law § 81.22.

2. Matter of Loury (Loury), N.Y.L.J., 9/23/93, p.26, col.2 (Sup.Ct., Kings County), aff'd 210 A.D.2d 227, 619 N.Y.S.2d 351 (2d Dep't 1994).

See supra, § 22.14, for discussion of the doctrine of the least restrictive form of intervention.

Those powers which may be granted include, but are not limited to, the power to:[3]

(1) determine who provides personal care or assistance;

(2) make decisions regarding the social environment and other social aspects of the life of the incapacitated person;

(3) determine whether the incapacitated person should travel;

(4) determine whether the incapacitated person should possess a license to drive;

(5) authorize access to or release of confidential records;

(6) make decisions regarding education;

(7) apply for government and private benefits;

(8) consent to or refuse generally accepted routine or major medical or dental treatment. The guardian must make treatment decisions consistent with the findings under Mental Hygiene Law Section 81.15[4] and in accordance with the patient's wishes, including the patient's religious and moral beliefs, or if the patient's wishes are not known and cannot be ascertained with reasonable diligence, in accordance with the person's best interests, including consideration of the dignity and uniqueness of every person, the possibility and extent of preserving the person's life, preservation, improvement or restoration of the person's health or functioning, relief of the person's suffering, adverse side effects associated with the treatment, any less intrusive alternative treatments, and such other concerns and values as a reasonable person in the incapacitated person's circumstances would wish to consider;[5] and

---

3. Mental Hygiene Law § 81.22.

4. *See supra,* §§ 22.34–22.37 for discussion of the findings required by the court.

5. These determinations should be consistent with the decision of the New York Court of Appeals in Rivers v. Katz, 67 N.Y.2d 485, 504 N.Y.S.2d 74, 495 N.E.2d 337 (1986) (the Court of Appeals held that an involuntarily committed mental patient had the right to refuse to consent to the administration of antipsychotic drugs absent "a judicial determination that the patient lacked the capacity to make a reasoned decision with respect to the proposed treatment."); *see also* Law Revision Commission Commentary to Mental Hygiene Law § 81.22.

The court denied appointment of a guardian where the only powers requested were to compel the alleged incapacitated person to receive psychiatric treatment and the administration of antipsychotic drugs without the person's consent. Nothing in Mental Hygiene Law Art. 81 implies that the court has the authority to grant such powers, in denial of the person's fundamentally protected liberties. The proper remedy would be an application pursuant to Mental Hygiene Law Art. 9 for an involuntary commitment and an application for administration of medication. Matter of Gordon, N.Y.L.J., 11/22/94, p.33, col.4 (Sup.Ct., Rockland County). *See also* Matter of Beth Israel Medical Center (Farbstein), 163 Misc.2d 26, 619 N.Y.S.2d 239 (Sup.Ct., N.Y. County, 1994).

It may not be necessary to bring a guardianship proceeding for the purpose of making medical decisions as such is not the only method of empowering a person to make medical decisions for another. *See* Matter of Gaskell, N.Y.L.J., 3/1/94, p.27, col.2 (Sup. Ct., Suffolk County) (the court ruled that it would impose the cost of attorney's fees and

§ 22.53 GUARDIANSHIP Ch. 22

(9) choose the place of abode.[6]

The power of the guardian to choose an abode for the incapacitated person, under the guidelines stated in Mental Hygiene Law Section 81.22(a)(9), overrules the decision in *Matter of Grinker (Rose)*.[7] The choice of abode must be consistent with the findings under Mental Hygiene Law Section 81.15,[8] the existence of and availability of family, friends and social services in the community, the care, comfort and maintenance, and where appropriate, rehabilitation of the incapacitated person, the needs of those with whom the incapacitated person resides. Placement of the incapacitated person in a nursing home or residential care facility[9] or other similar facility shall not be authorized without the consent of the incapacitated person so long as it is reasonable under the circumstances to maintain the incapacitated person in the community, preferably in the home of the incapacitated person.[10]

Pursuant to Mental Hygiene Law Section 81.22(b), no guardian may (1) consent to the voluntary formal or informal admission of the incapacitated person to a mental hygiene facility[11] or to an alcoholism facility,[12] or (2) revoke any appointment or delegation made by the incapacitated person in a durable power or springing durable power of attorney,[13] a Do

the court evaluator upon the nursing home if it needlessly put a patient's family through a guardianship proceeding).

PRACTICE POINTER: The existence of a health care proxy appointing an agent to make health care decisions may preclude powers to a guardian to make health care decisions and may, if appropriate, preclude appointment of a guardian. *See* Mental Hygiene Law § 81.22(b)(2). The application for appointment of a guardian must show that such powers are necessary.

6. Application by conservator to transfer conservatee from nursing home in Bronx County to facility in Maine should have been granted since move would not be medically harmful, conservatee would receive comparable care, many surviving members of conservatee's family resided near Maine facility, and conservatee's property, as well as conservatorship itself, would remain under jurisdiction of New York courts. In re Harrington, 127 A.D.2d 468, 511 N.Y.S.2d 26 (1st Dep't 1987).

7. 77 N.Y.2d 703, 570 N.Y.S.2d 448, 573 N.E.2d 536 (1991) (former Mental Hygiene Law § 77.19 did not authorize involuntary commitment of conservatee to nursing home; availability of such significant involuntary displacement of personal liberty should be confined to incompetency proceeding under former Mental Hygiene Law Art. 78). *See supra,* discussion in § 22.7. *See also* Matter of Application of Rochester General Hospital (Levin), 158 Misc.2d 522, 601 N.Y.S.2d 375 (Sup.Ct., Monroe County, 1993).

8. *See supra,* §§ 22.34–22.37, for discussion of the findings required by the court.

9. *See* Public Health Law § 2801.

10. Matter of Jospe (Grala), N.Y.L.J., 1/30/95, p.30, col.2 (Sup.Ct., Nassau County).

11. Mental Hygiene Law Arts. 9 and 15. *See* Matter of Gordon, 162 Misc.2d 697, 619 N.Y.S.2d 235 (Sup.Ct., Rockland County, 1994); Matter of Beth Israel Medical Center (Farbstein), 163 Misc.2d 26, 619 N.Y.S.2d 239 (Sup.Ct., N.Y. County, 1994).

12. Mental Hygiene Law Art. 21.

13. General Obligations Law §§ 5–1501, *et seq.* **CAVEAT**: The reasons for enactment of Mental Hygiene Law Art. 81, including the legislative and judicial history, may call into question the continued viability of certain aspects of General Obligations Law § 5–1601 [now General Obligations Law § 5–1505], and in particular, the authority of a guardian to revoke a power of attorney, without a court order. *See* Matter of Application of Rochester General Hospital (Levin), 158 Misc.2d 522, 601 N.Y.S.2d 375 (Sup.Ct., Monroe County, 1993).

See Matter of Kern, 165 Misc.2d 108, 627 N.Y.S.2d 257 (Sup.Ct., Suffolk County,

Not Resuscitate (DNR) Order,[14] a health care proxy,[15] or any living will.

Library References:

West's Key No. Digests, Guardian and Ward ⚖111; Mental Health ⚖211–275.

§ 22.54 Role of Guardian—Effect of Appointment on Incapacitated Person

Mental Hygiene Law Section 81.29 emphasizes the concept of tailoring the guardian's powers. The incapacitated person for whom a guardian has been appointed retains all powers and rights except those powers and rights which have been granted to the guardian.[1] Moreover, the appointment of a guardian is not conclusive evidence that the person lacks capacity for any other purpose, including the capacity to dispose of property by will.[2] The title to all property of the incapacitated person remains in such person and is not in the guardian. The property is subject to the possession of the guardian and to the control of the court for the purposes of administration, sale or other disposition only to the extent directed by the court order appointing the guardian.[3]

If the court determines that the person is incapacitated and appoints a guardian, the court may modify, amend, or revoke any previously executed appointment, power, or delegation,[4] or any contract, conveyance, or disposition during lifetime or to take effect on death, made by the incapacitated person prior to the appointment of the guardian if the court finds that the previously executed appointment, power, delegation, contract, conveyance, or disposition during lifetime or to take effect on

---

1995), discussing the power of the court to revoke a non-durable power of attorney. *See also* Matter of Bailin (Geiger), N.Y.L.J., 5/19/95, p.36, col.4 (Sup.Ct., Rockland County) revoking the appointment of an attorney in fact.

See infra, § 22.54, for discussion of the effect of the appointment of a guardian on incapacitated persons.

14. Public Health Law § 2965.

15. Public Health Law § 2981.

§ 22.54

1. Mental Hygiene Law § 81.29(a).

2. Mental Hygiene Law § 81.29(b). Matter of Livreri, N.Y.L.J., 2/23/96, p. 30, col. 3 (Sup.Ct., Suffolk County) (testamentary capacity is not an issue before the court on an application to appoint a guardian).

See Mental Hygiene Law § 81.21(a), discussed *supra* at § 22.47, which provides that transfers made pursuant Mental Hygiene Law Art. 81 may be in any form that the incapacitated person could have employed if he or she had the requisite capacity, except in the form of a will or codicil.

3. Mental Hygiene Law § 81.29(c).

4. *See* General Obligations Law §§ 5–1501, *et seq.*; Public Health Law §§ 2965, 2981; *see also supra,* § 22.53, for discussion of Mental Hygiene Law § 81.22(b)(2) which provides that guardian may not revoke powers of attorney, Do Not Resuscitate Orders, health care proxies, or living wills.

The court held that it could revoke a power of attorney where it found that the attorney-in-fact had breached her fiduciary duty to the alleged incapacitated person. Under such circumstances it was not necessary for the court to make a finding that the alleged incapacitated person was incapacitated at the time she executed the power of attorney. Matter of Wingate (Mascolone), 169 Misc.2d 701, 647 N.Y.S.2d 433 (Sup.Ct., Queens County, 1996).

death, was made while the person was incapacitated.[5]

Nothing in Mental Hygiene Law Article 81 may be construed either to prohibit a court from granting, or to authorize a court to grant, to any person the power to give consent for withholding or withdrawal of life sustaining treatment, including artificial nutrition and hydration.[6] When used in Article 81, "life sustaining treatment" means medical treatment which is sustaining life functions and without which, according to reasonable medical judgment, that patient will die within a relatively short time period.[7]

This section makes clear that Article 81 does not change the current law in New York regarding whether a guardian has the authority to make decisions with respect to the withholding or withdrawal of life sustaining treatment nor does it impede the development of the law in this area. Under current New York law, the right to decline treatment is a personal one whose exercise has been denied to a third party when the patient is unable to do so unless a health care proxy or Do Not Resuscitate Order is in place or there is otherwise clear and convincing evidence of the patient's wishes regarding such treatment expressed while the patient was competent.[8]

Library References:

West's Key No. Digests, Guardian and Ward ⚖111; Mental Health ⚖211–275.

§ 22.55 Role of Guardian—Summary

The guardian's relationship to the incapacitated person is that of a

5. Mental Hygiene Law § 81.29(d). See Matter of Johnson and Smith (Dot E.W.), N.Y.L.J., 3/26/97, p. 32, col. 6 (Sup.Ct., Suffolk County) (the court annulled the marriage of the alleged incapacitated person entered into after the petition to appoint a guardian had been brought, finding marriage a civil contract subject to revocation by the court in an Article 81 proceeding, without the necessity of bringing a matrimonial action).

6. Application of Barsky, 165 Misc.2d 175, 627 N.Y.S.2d 903 (Sup.Ct., Suffolk County, 1995).

7. Mental Hygiene Law § 81.29(e).

8. See Application of Barsky, 165 Misc.2d 175, 627 N.Y.S.2d 903 (Sup.Ct., Suffolk County, 1995); Law Revision Commission Commentary to Mental Hygiene Law § 81.29. With regard to the law concerning the authority to make decisions about the withholding or withdrawing of life sustaining treatment, see Grace Plaza of Great Neck, Inc. v. Elbaum, 82 N.Y.2d 10, 603 N.Y.S.2d 386, 623 N.E.2d 513 (1993); In the Matter of Westchester County Medical Center (O'Connor), 72 N.Y.2d 517, 534 N.Y.S.2d 886, 531 N.E.2d 607 (1988); Matter of Storar (Eichner), 52 N.Y.2d 363, 438 N.Y.S.2d 266, 420 N.E.2d 64 (1981), cert. denied 454 U.S. 858, 102 S.Ct. 309, 70 L.Ed.2d 153 (1981); Elbaum v. Grace Plaza of Great Neck, Inc., 148 A.D.2d 244, 544 N.Y.S.2d 840 (2d Dep't 1989); Delio v. Westchester County Medical Center, 129 A.D.2d 1, 516 N.Y.S.2d 677 (2d Dep't 1987).

The court denied an application to expand the authority of the temporary guardian to include the issuance of do not resuscitate and do not intubate orders where the petitioner failed to show by clear and convincing evidence that such orders would have been the patient's choice. Matter of Maxwell Z, N.Y.L.J., 10/1/96, p. 27, col. 3 (Sup.Ct., Suffolk County).

fiduciary.[1] In order to carry out this responsibility in the most careful and diligent manner, the guardian should develop a personal relationship to the ward, in the event one does not exist, so that the guardian can understand the impact of any decision from the perspective of the incapacitated person and can involve the incapacitated person in the decisions to the greatest extent possible.[2]

The guardian may exercise only those powers relating to property management or personal needs that are authorized by the court order.[3] The common law doctrine of substituted judgment[4] is recognized and implemented by Article 81.[5]

The powers of the guardian set out in the statute are meant to be illustrative rather than exclusive. The incapacitated person for whom a guardian has been appointed retains all powers and rights except those powers and rights which have been granted to the guardian.[6] The appointment of a guardian is not conclusive evidence that the person lacks capacity for any other purpose, including the capacity to dispose of property by will.[7] The title to all property of the incapacitated person remains in such person, subject to the possession of the guardian.[8]

Library References:

West's Key No. Digests, Guardian and Ward ⇔111; Mental Health ⇔211–275.

§ 22.56 Provisional Remedies

Mental Hygiene Law Article 81 specifies the availability of two provisional remedies: 1) the appointment of a temporary guardian with limited powers;[1] and 2) the issuance of an injunction.[2]

Mental Hygiene Law Section 81.24 provides for the filing of a notice of pendency.[3]

Library References:

West's Key No. Digests, Guardian and Ward ⇔111; Mental Health ⇔211–275.

§ 22.55

1. See supra, § 22.45.
2. See supra, § 22.46.
3. Mental Hygiene Law § 81.16; see supra, §§ 22.46–22.53, for discussion of the duties and powers of a guardian.
4. See supra, § 22.48.
5. See supra, §§ 22.49–22.52.
6. Mental Hygiene Law § 81.29(a); see supra, § 22.54.
7. Mental Hygiene Law § 81.29(b); see supra, § 22.54.
8. Mental Hygiene Law § 81.29(c); see supra, § 22.54.

§ 22.56

1. Mental Hygiene Law § 81.23(a); see infra, § 22.57.
2. Mental Hygiene Law § 81.23(b); see infra, § 22.58.
3. See infra, § 22.59.

§ 22.57 Provisional Remedies—Temporary Guardian

Mental Hygiene Law Section 81.23(a) provides for the appointment of a temporary guardian. At the commencement of the proceeding or at any subsequent stage of the proceeding prior to the appointment of a guardian, the court may, on the showing of danger in the reasonably foreseeable future to the health and well being of the alleged incapacitated person, or danger of waste, misappropriation, or loss of the property of the alleged incapacitated person, appoint a temporary guardian for a period not to extend beyond the date of issuance of the commission[1] to the guardian appointed under Mental Hygiene Law Article 81. The powers and duties of the temporary guardian must be specifically enumerated in the order of appointment and are limited in same manner as are the powers of a guardian.[2] Prior to expiration of the term of appointment, the temporary guardian must report to the court all actions taken pursuant to the order of appointment. The court may approve reasonable compensation for the temporary guardian.[3] However, if the court finds that the temporary guardian has failed to discharge his or her duties satisfactorily in any respect, the court may deny or reduce the amount of compensation or remove the temporary guardian.[4]

Notice of the appointment of a temporary guardian must be given to the person alleged to be incapacitated and to any person having custody or control over the person or property of the person alleged to be incapacitated in such manner as the court may prescribe.[5]

The authority and responsibility of the temporary guardian begins on issuance of the commission of temporary guardianship.[6]

The court may require the temporary guardian to file a bond in accordance with Mental Hygiene Law Section 81.25.[7]

Library References:

West's Key No. Digests, Guardian and Ward ⟐111; Mental Health ⟐211–275.

§ 22.58 Provisional Remedies—Injunction and Temporary Restraining Orders

Mental Hygiene Law Section 81.23(b) authorizes the issuance of an injunction as well as temporary restraining orders. The court may, with

---

§ 22.57

1. See supra, § 22.43 for discussion of the issuance of a commission to the guardian.

2. See supra, §§ 22.47–22.52 for discussion of the powers of a guardian; see also infra, § 22.101 for form of order appointing guardian.

3. See infra, § 22.61 for discussion of compensation of a guardian.

4. Mental Hygiene Law § 81.23(a)(1).

5. Mental Hygiene Law § 81.23(a)(2). See supra, § 22.21 for discussion of the required notice in a proceeding for the appointment of a guardian.

6. Mental Hygiene Law § 81.23(a)(3). See supra, § 22.43 for discussion of the issuance of a commission to the guardian.

7. Mental Hygiene Law § 81.23(a)(4). See supra, § 22.42 for discussion of the filing of a bond by a guardian.

or without security, enjoin any person, other than the incapacitated person or the person alleged to be incapacitated, from selling, assigning, or disposing of property or confessing judgment which may become a lien on property or receiving or arranging for another person to receive property from the incapacitated person or the person alleged to be incapacitated or doing or suffering to be done any act or omission endangering the welfare of the incapacitated person or the person alleged to be incapacitated. Such injunction may be issued when an application under Mental Hygiene Law Article 81 seeks such an injunction and it satisfactorily appears from the application, the affidavits, and other proofs that a person has done, has suffered to be done or omitted to do, or threatens to do or is about to do an act that endangers the welfare of the incapacitated person or the person alleged to be incapacitated or has acquired or is about to acquire any property from the incapacitated person or the person alleged to be incapacitated during the time of that person's incapacity or alleged incapacity without adequate consideration.

Such order shall be made upon an order to show cause or upon the initiative of the court and may, in the discretion of the court, on the application for the appointment of a guardian, be continued for 10 days after the appointment of an adult guardian.[1]

Notice of any injunction must be given to any person enjoined, to the incapacitated person or the person alleged to be incapacitated, and to any person having custody or control over the person or property of the incapacitated person or person alleged to be incapacitated in such manner as the court may prescribe.[2]

The court may grant a temporary restraining order, with or without security, when an application seeks an injunction and where the court is satisfied that, in the absence of such restraining order, the property of the incapacitated person or the person alleged to be incapacitated would be dissipated to that person's detriment or that the welfare of the incapacitated person or person alleged to be incapacitated would be endangered.[3]

Notice of the temporary restraining order must be given to any person restrained, to the incapacitated person or the person alleged to be incapacitated, and to any person having custody or control over the person or property of the incapacitated person or the person alleged to be incapacitated in such manner as the court may prescribe. Such temporary restraining order shall neither be vacated nor modified except on notice to the petitioner and to each person required to receive notice of the petition under Mental Hygiene Law Section 81.07(d)(1).[4]

§ 22.58
1. Mental Hygiene Law § 81.23(b)(1).
2. Id.
3. Mental Hygiene Law § 81.23(b)(2).
4. Mental Hygiene Law § 81.23(b)(2). See supra, § 22.21 for discussion of persons

§ 22.58 GUARDIANSHIP Ch. 22

When the court is satisfied that the interest of the incapacitated person or the person alleged to be incapacitated would be appropriately served, the court may provide in a temporary restraining order that such order shall have the effect of (1) a restraining notice when served in the manner and on such persons as the court in its discretion deems appropriate; and (2) conferring information subpoena power upon the attorney for the petitioner when the court in its discretion deems it appropriate.[5]

Where such temporary restraining order provides for a restraining notice, the person having custody or control over the person or property of the incapacitated person or the person alleged to be incapacitated is forbidden to make or suffer any sale, assignment, transfer or interference with any property of the incapacitated person or the person alleged to be incapacitated except pursuant to an order of the court.[6] Where such temporary restraining order provides the petitioner's attorney with information subpoena power, service of a copy of the order together with an information subpoena requires any person so subpoenaed to provide the petitioner's attorney with any information concerning the financial affairs of the incapacitated person or the person alleged to be incapacitated.[7]

Library References:
West's Key No. Digests, Guardian and Ward ⟐111; Mental Health ⟐211–275.

§ 22.59 Provisional Remedies—Notice of Pendency

Prior to judgment, the petitioner shall file a notice of pendency if real property or any interest therein is or may be affected by the proceeding for the appointment of a guardian under Mental Hygiene Law Article 81.[1]

This section continues the requirement under former Mental Hygiene Law Articles 77 and 78 of requiring the filing of a notice of pendency if any real property will be affected by the proceeding. The protection that is afforded by this section is consistent with Mental Hygiene Law Section 81.20(a)(6)(vi)[2] which requires a guardian with powers for property management to file an acknowledged statement of his or her appointment in any county where the incapacitated person has real property.[3]

who must be notified of a proceeding for the appointment of a guardian.
  5. Mental Hygiene Law § 81.23(b)(3).
  6. Mental Hygiene Law § 81.23(b)(4).
  7. Mental Hygiene Law § 81.23(b)(5).

  2. *See supra*, § 22.47.
  3. *See* Law Revision Commission Commentary to Mental Hygiene Law § 81.24.

§ 22.59
  1. Mental Hygiene Law § 81.24. *See generally supra*, § 12.46 for discussion of notice of pendency.

Library References:

West's Key No. Digests, Guardian and Ward ⚖111; Mental Health ⚖211–275.

§ 22.60 Provisional Remedies—Summary

Prior to the appointment of a guardian, the court may, on the showing of danger in the reasonably foreseeable future to the health and well being of the alleged incapacitated person, or danger of waste, misappropriation, or loss of the property of the alleged incapacitated person, appoint a temporary guardian for a period not to extend beyond the date of issuance of the commission to the guardian.[1] The powers and duties of the temporary guardian must be specifically enumerated in the order of appointment.[2] The court may enjoin any person from selling, assigning, or disposing of property or confessing judgment which may become a lien on property or receiving or arranging for another person to receive property from the incapacitated person or the person alleged to be incapacitated or doing or suffering to be done any act or omission endangering the welfare of the incapacitated person or the person alleged to be incapacitated.[3] The court may grant a temporary restraining order when an application seeks an injunction and where the court is satisfied that, in the absence of such restraining order, the property of the incapacitated person or the person alleged to be incapacitated would be dissipated to that person's detriment or that the welfare of the incapacitated person or person alleged to be incapacitated would be endangered.[4] The petitioner shall file a notice of pendency if real property or any interest therein is or may be affected by the proceeding for the appointment of a guardian.[5]

Library References:

West's Key No. Digests, Guardian and Ward ⚖111; Mental Health ⚖211–275.

§ 22.61 Compensation of Guardian

The court must establish, and from time to time modify, a plan for reasonable compensation of the guardian. Such a plan may be similar to the compensation of a trustee under Surrogate's Court Procedure Act Section 2309.[1] However, the plan must take into account the specific

---

§ 22.60

1. Mental Hygiene Law § 81.23(a); see supra, § 22.57.
2. Id.
3. See supra, § 22.58.
4. Mental Hygiene Law § 81.23(b). See supra, § 22.58.
5. Mental Hygiene Law § 81.24; see supra, § 22.59.

§ 22.61

1. Mental Hygiene Law § 81.28(a). See SCPA § 2309, Commissions of trustees under wills of persons dying, or lifetime trusts established, after August 31, 1956. See also, 22 NYCRR Pt. 36, Appointment of Fiduciaries, § 36.4, Compensation, which provides:

(a) Fees to appointees pursuant to this rule shall not exceed the fair value of the services rendered.

authority of the guardian to provide for the personal needs[2] and/or property management for the incapacitated person.[3] As those responsibilities change, the plan established by the court for the guardian's compensation should be modified to reflect those changes.[4]

In developing the plan for compensation, the court may consider structuring the compensation to the extent it reflects fiscal management in a manner similar to the compensation schedule for a trustee under Surrogate's Court Procedure Act Section 2309. A trustee, unlike a typical executor or administrator of an estate, is involved in ongoing money and property management and to the extent a guardian is authorized to exercise powers of property management, the plan for his or her compensation may reflect a similar manner of compensation. However, the court is not, and should not consider itself, bound by that scheme in all cases, particularly where the primary responsibilities of the guardian involve personal care.[5]

Under former Mental Hygiene Law Articles 77 and 78, the rule was that a committee or conservator was entitled to commissions only on property which he or she received and paid out.[6]

(b) Each award of fees of $2,500 or more to appointees pursuant to this section shall be accompanied by an explanation, in writing, of the reasons therefor by the judge making the award.

(c) No fees shall be awarded unless the appointee has filed the notice of appointment and certification of compliance required by section 36.3(a) of this Part.

CAVEAT: Practice has shown that the compensation provided by SCPA § 2309 may not be adequate compensation for guardians. Suggestions have been made to remedy this problem. See, e.g., Matter of Pineda, N.Y.L.J., 5/28/97, p. 26, col. 3 (Sup. Ct., N.Y. County) (finding application of SCPA 2307 and 2309 not to be mandatory, the court held that a fixed hourly rate was a better approach to compensating Article 81 guardians, who are required to provide personal care services not contemplated by the SCPA sections).

See also Matter of Sehr, 169 Misc.2d 543, 646 N.Y.S.2d 937 (Sup.Ct., N.Y. County, 1996) (court has discretion to devise any compensation plan it deems reasonable).

The court may direct the petitioner to compensate the guardian where the funds of the incapacitated person are insufficient. Matter of Skinner, 171 Misc.2d 551, 655 N.Y.S.2d 311 (Sup.Ct., N.Y. County, 1997).

2. See supra, § 22.53. See In re Rosecrans, 144 A.D.2d 214, 534 N.Y.S.2d 528 (3d Dep't 1988). Order appointing parents as conservators of son, who contracted spinal meningitis and was in state of unawareness and unresponsiveness, but denying their request for $1,500 per month compensation based upon their moving to Massachusetts to be able to make daily visits to their son, would be remitted for determination of some appropriate compensation for services properly rendered as conservators; however, decision to move to Massachusetts reflected devotion of loving parents and was well beyond duty owed by conservator and was, therefore, noncompensable, especially where conservatee's estate was expected to be insufficient to provide for him for remainder of his life.

3. Mental Hygiene Law § 81.28(a). See supra, §§ 22.47, et seq.

4. Law Revision Commission Commentary to Mental Hygiene Law § 81.28.

5. Id.

6. In a proceeding seeking approval of final account of conservator of deceased conservatee, no money representing insurance death benefits was commissionable since, on conservatee's death, conservator ceased having power to reduce that property to his possession, and proceeds of individual retirement account, which conservator did not have to invade for conservatee's benefit, was not commissionable since that asset was never received by conservator;

Library References:
> West's Key No. Digests, Guardian and Ward ⚖111; Mental Health ⚖211–275.

§ 22.60 Provisional Remedies—Summary

Prior to the appointment of a guardian, the court may, on the showing of danger in the reasonably foreseeable future to the health and well being of the alleged incapacitated person, or danger of waste, misappropriation, or loss of the property of the alleged incapacitated person, appoint a temporary guardian for a period not to extend beyond the date of issuance of the commission to the guardian.[1] The powers and duties of the temporary guardian must be specifically enumerated in the order of appointment.[2] The court may enjoin any person from selling, assigning, or disposing of property or confessing judgment which may become a lien on property or receiving or arranging for another person to receive property from the incapacitated person or the person alleged to be incapacitated or doing or suffering to be done any act or omission endangering the welfare of the incapacitated person or the person alleged to be incapacitated.[3] The court may grant a temporary restraining order when an application seeks an injunction and where the court is satisfied that, in the absence of such restraining order, the property of the incapacitated person or the person alleged to be incapacitated would be dissipated to that person's detriment or that the welfare of the incapacitated person or person alleged to be incapacitated would be endangered.[4] The petitioner shall file a notice of pendency if real property or any interest therein is or may be affected by the proceeding for the appointment of a guardian.[5]

Library References:
> West's Key No. Digests, Guardian and Ward ⚖111; Mental Health ⚖211–275.

§ 22.61 Compensation of Guardian

The court must establish, and from time to time modify, a plan for reasonable compensation of the guardian. Such a plan may be similar to the compensation of a trustee under Surrogate's Court Procedure Act Section 2309.[1] However, the plan must take into account the specific

---

§ 22.60

1. Mental Hygiene Law § 81.23(a); see supra, § 22.57.
2. Id.
3. See supra, § 22.58.
4. Mental Hygiene Law § 81.23(b). See supra, § 22.58.
5. Mental Hygiene Law § 81.24; see supra, § 22.59.

§ 22.61

1. Mental Hygiene Law § 81.28(a). See SCPA § 2309, Commissions of trustees under wills of persons dying, or lifetime trusts established, after August 31, 1956. See also, 22 NYCRR Pt. 36, Appointment of Fiduciaries, § 36.4, Compensation, which provides:

   (a) Fees to appointees pursuant to this rule shall not exceed the fair value of the services rendered.

authority of the guardian to provide for the personal needs[2] and/or property management for the incapacitated person.[3] As those responsibilities change, the plan established by the court for the guardian's compensation should be modified to reflect those changes.[4]

In developing the plan for compensation, the court may consider structuring the compensation to the extent it reflects fiscal management in a manner similar to the compensation schedule for a trustee under Surrogate's Court Procedure Act Section 2309. A trustee, unlike a typical executor or administrator of an estate, is involved in ongoing money and property management and to the extent a guardian is authorized to exercise powers of property management, the plan for his or her compensation may reflect a similar manner of compensation. However, the court is not, and should not consider itself, bound by that scheme in all cases, particularly where the primary responsibilities of the guardian involve personal care.[5]

Under former Mental Hygiene Law Articles 77 and 78, the rule was that a committee or conservator was entitled to commissions only on property which he or she received and paid out.[6]

(b) Each award of fees of $2,500 or more to appointees pursuant to this section shall be accompanied by an explanation, in writing, of the reasons therefor by the judge making the award.

(c) No fees shall be awarded unless the appointee has filed the notice of appointment and certification of compliance required by section 36.3(a) of this Part.

CAVEAT: Practice has shown that the compensation provided by SCPA § 2309 may not be adequate compensation for guardians. Suggestions have been made to remedy this problem. See, e.g., Matter of Pineda, N.Y.L.J., 5/28/97, p. 26, col. 3 (Sup. Ct., N.Y. County) (finding application of SCPA 2307 and 2309 not to be mandatory, the court held that a fixed hourly rate was a better approach to compensating Article 81 guardians, who are required to provide personal care services not contemplated by the SCPA sections).

See also Matter of Sehr, 169 Misc.2d 543, 646 N.Y.S.2d 937 (Sup.Ct., N.Y. County, 1996) (court has discretion to devise any compensation plan it deems reasonable).

The court may direct the petitioner to compensate the guardian where the funds of the incapacitated person are insufficient. Matter of Skinner, 171 Misc.2d 551, 655 N.Y.S.2d 311 (Sup.Ct., N.Y. County, 1997).

2. See supra, § 22.53. See In re Rosecrans, 144 A.D.2d 214, 534 N.Y.S.2d 528 (3d Dep't 1988). Order appointing parents as conservators of son, who contracted spinal meningitis and was in state of unawareness and unresponsiveness, but denying their request for $1,500 per month compensation based upon their moving to Massachusetts to be able to make daily visits to their son, would be remitted for determination of some appropriate compensation for services properly rendered as conservators; however, decision to move to Massachusetts reflected devotion of loving parents and was well beyond duty owed by conservator and was, therefore, noncompensable, especially where conservatee's estate was expected to be insufficient to provide for him for remainder of his life.

3. Mental Hygiene Law § 81.28(a). See supra, §§ 22.47, et seq.

4. Law Revision Commission Commentary to Mental Hygiene Law § 81.28.

5. Id.

6. In a proceeding seeking approval of final account of conservator of deceased conservatee, no money representing insurance death benefits was commissionable since, on conservatee's death, conservator ceased having power to reduce that property to his possession, and proceeds of individual retirement account, which conservator did not have to invade for conservatee's benefit, was not commissionable since that asset was never received by conservator;

If the court finds that the guardian has failed to discharge his or her duties satisfactorily in any respect, the court may deny or reduce compensation which would otherwise be allowed.[7]

Library References:
> West's Key No. Digests, Guardian and Ward ⟜111; Mental Health ⟜211–275.

§ 22.62 Reports by Guardian

It is the duty of a guardian to file initial and annual reports as required by Mental Hygiene Law Sections 81.30 and 81.31.[1]

Library References:
> West's Key No. Digests, Guardian and Ward ⟜111; Mental Health ⟜211–275.

§ 22.63 Reports by Guardian—Initial Report

No later than 90 days after issuance of the commission[1] to the guardian, the guardian must file with the court a report in the form[2] prescribed by the court stating what steps the guardian has taken to fulfill his or her responsibilities.[3]

The initial report is intended to fulfill several purposes. First, it clarifies the guardian's responsibilities and the course of action to be taken. Second, it gives the guardian an opportunity to assess the circumstances of the incapacitated person and whether any changes need to be made in the guardian's powers. Third, the plan provides a tool for evaluating the guardian's performance.[4]

Proof of completion of the guardian education requirements[5] must be filed with the initial report.[6]

however, commissionable disbursements would include amounts turned over to executor since conservatee enjoyed benefit of having his assets passed on to beneficiaries or heirs at law, and to deny conservator commission where conservatee had died would unfairly diminish commissions simply because conservatee did not recover from his incapacity. Petition of Levine, 137 A.D.2d 394, 529 N.Y.S.2d 301 (1st Dep't 1988).

Where it never became necessary for conservator to invade a Totten Trust account to provide for the needs of his ward, such funds were never "received" within the purview of the operative statute governing the allowance of commissions. In re Reich, 94 Misc.2d 319, 404 N.Y.S.2d 781 (Sup.Ct., N.Y. County, 1978).

7. Mental Hygiene Law § 81.28(b).

§ 22.62

1. Mental Hygiene Law § 81.20(a)(4). See supra, § 22.46 for discussion of the duties of a guardian. See infra, §§ 22.63 22.64, for discussion of the initial and annual reports. See infra, § 22.104 for form of initial report; § 22.105 for form of annual report.

§ 22.63

1. See supra, § 22.43 for discussion of commission to guardian.
2. See infra, § 22.104 for form of initial report.
3. Mental Hygiene Law § 81.30(a).
4. Law Revision Commission Commentary to Mental Hygiene Law § 81.30.
5. See infra, § 22.76.
6. Mental Hygiene Law § 81.30(a).

To the extent that the guardian has been granted powers with respect to property management,[7] the initial report must contain a verified and complete inventory of the property and financial resources over which the guardian has control, the location of any will executed by the incapacitated person, the guardian's plan, consistent with the court's order of appointment, for management of such property and financial resources, and the need for any change in the powers authorized by the court.[8]

To the extent that the guardian has been granted powers regarding personal needs,[9] the initial report must contain a report of guardian's personal visits[10] with the incapacitated person, and the steps the guardian has taken, consistent with the court's order, to provide for the personal needs of that person, the guardian's plan, consistent with the court's order of appointment, for providing for the personal needs of the incapacitated person, a copy of any directives, including a Do Not Resuscitate ("DNR") Order,[11] a health care proxy,[12] any living will and any other advance directive, and any necessary change in the powers authorized by court.[13] The plan for providing for the personal needs of the incapacitated person must include the following information:[14]

(1) the medical, dental, mental health, or related services that are to be provided for the welfare of the incapacitated person;

(2) the social and personal services that are to be provided for the welfare of the incapacitated person;

(3) any physical, dental, and mental health examinations necessary to determine the medical, dental, and mental health treatment needs; and

(4) the application of health and accident insurance and any other private or government benefits to which the incapacitated person may be entitled to meet any part of the costs of medical, dental, mental health, or related services provided to the incapacitated person.

If the initial report sets forth any reasons for change in the powers authorized by the court, the guardian must make application within ten days of filing of the report on notice to the persons entitled to such

---

7. See supra, §§ 22.47–22.52 for discussion of powers with respect to property management.

8. Mental Hygiene Law § 81.30(b). See generally I. Salzman, *The Obligation of Guardians Under Article 81 of the Mental Hygiene Law to Apply to Have Their Powers Modified*, 3 Elder Law Attorney No. 2 (N.Y.S.B.A.) 11 (Fall/Winter 1993).

9. See supra, § 22.53 for discussion of the guardian's powers with respect to personal needs.

10. See supra, § 22.46 for discussion of the guardian's duty to visit the incapacitated person.

11. Public Health Law § 2965.

12. Public Health Law § 2981.

13. Mental Hygiene Law § 81.30(c).

14. *Id.*

notice in accordance with Mental Hygiene Law Section 81.07(d)(1)[15] for such relief. If the initial report sets forth any reasons for change in the powers authorized by the court and the guardian fails to act, any person entitled to commence a proceeding under Mental Hygiene Law Article 81[16] may petition the court for a change in such powers on notice to the guardian and the persons entitled to such notice for such relief.[17]

Library References:

West's Key No. Digests, Guardian and Ward ⚖111; Mental Health ⚖211–275.

§ 22.64 Reports by Guardian—Annual Report

In the month of May or at any other time on motion or order of the court, every guardian must file an annual report.[1] The information required to be contained in the annual report concerns the personal status of the incapacitated person, and/or the condition of the person's finances and property, to the extent of the guardian's authority. Given the loss of liberties involved in the guardianship process and the vulnerability of persons under guardianship, it is critical that the court regularly receive and review basic information about the well-being of the incapacitated person.[2]

Although Article 81 contains many of the requirements of former Mental Hygiene Law Articles 77 and 78, dealing with the filing of annual reports by conservators and committees respectively, Article 81 imposes specific informational requirements on the guardian in completing his or her annual report which perform a significant monitoring function. These additional requirements benefit the guardianship process in several ways. First, these requirements will aid the court in determining whether the incapacitated person is maintained in the least restrictive environment.[3] Second, the imposition of more detailed reporting requirements will focus the guardian on the fulfillment of his or her duties to the incapacitated person. Third, regular and detailed reporting requirements will effectively aid the courts in ensuring that the guardianship system is functioning properly.[4]

The annual report of guardian must be in a form[5] prescribed by the

---

15. *See supra,* § 22.21 for discussion of persons entitled to notice. *See generally,* I. Salzman, *The Obligation of Guardians Under Article 81 of the Mental Hygiene Law to Apply to Have Their Powers Modified,* 3 Elder Law Attorney No. 2 (N.Y.S.B.A.) 11 (Fall/Winter 1993).

16. *See supra,* § 22.17 for discussion of persons entitled to commence proceeding.

17. Mental Hygiene Law § 81.30(d).

§ 22.64

1. Mental Hygiene Law § 81.31(a).

2. Law Revision Commission Commentary to Mental Hygiene Law § 81.31.

3. *See supra,* § 22.14 for discussion of least restrictive form of intervention.

4. Law Revision Commission Commentary to Mental Hygiene Law § 81.31.

5. *See infra,* § 22.105 for form of annual report.

court and shall include the following information:[6]

(1) the present address and telephone number of the guardian;

(2) the present address, and telephone number of the incapacitated person; if the place of residence of the incapacitated person is not his or her personal home, the name, address, and telephone number of the facility or place at which the person resides and the name of the chief executive officer of the facility or person otherwise responsible for the person's care;

(3) any major changes in the physical or mental condition of the incapacitated person and any substantial change in medication;

(4) the date that the incapacitated person was last examined or otherwise seen by a physician and the purpose of that visit;

(5) a statement by a physician, psychologist, nurse clinician, or social worker, or other person who has evaluated or examined the incapacitated person within the three months prior to the filing of the report regarding an evaluation of the incapacitated person's condition and the current functional level of the incapacitated person;

(6) to the extent the guardian is charged with providing for the personal needs[7] of the incapacitated person:

  (i) a statement of whether the current residential setting is best suited to the current needs of the incapacitated person;

  (ii) a resume of any professional medical treatment given to the ward in the preceding year;

  (iii) the plan for medical, dental, and mental health treatment, and related services in the coming year;

  (iv) information concerning the social condition of the incapacitated person, including: the social and personal services currently utilized by the incapacitated person; the social skills of the incapacitated person; and the social needs of the incapacitated person;

(7) to the extent the guardian is charged with property management,[8] information required by the provisions of the Surrogate's Court Procedure Act prescribing the form of papers to be filed upon the annual accounting of a general guardian of an infant's property;[9]

---

6. Mental Hygiene Law § 81.31(b).
7. See supra, § 22.53.
8. See supra, §§ 22.47–22.52.
9. See SCPA § 1719, Annual account. The statutory requirements of SCPA § 1719 are included in the form of Annual Report set forth infra in § 22.105.

(8) where the guardian has used or employed the services of the incapacitated person or where moneys have been earned by or received on behalf of such incapacitated person an accounting of any moneys earned or derived from such services;

(9) a resume of any other activities performed by the guardian on behalf of the incapacitated person;

(10) facts indicating the need to terminate the appointment of the guardian, or for any alteration in the powers of the guardian and what specific authority is requested or what specific authority of the guardian will be affected;[10]

(11) any other information which the guardian may be required to file by the order of appointment.

The use of uniform report forms allowing for narrative responses will educate the guardian as to what information the court expects, assist the guardian in evaluating his or her performance, and should alleviate any concerns that the reporting requirements will unduly burden the guardianship system.[11]

The guardian must send a copy of the annual report to the incapacitated person by mail and must file[12] a copy of the annual report.[13] If the incapacitated person resides in a facility, hospital, school, or alcoholism treatment facility in New York,[14] a substance abuse program,[15] an adult care facility,[16] a residential health care facility, or general hospital,[17] the guardian must send a duplicate of such report to the chief executive officer of that facility and the Mental Hygiene Legal Service of the judicial department in which the residence is located.[18]

The annual report of the guardian must be filed in the office of the clerk of the county in which the incapacitated person last resided before appointment of the guardian if he or she was at such time resident of New York City. If the incapacitated person was not then a resident of New York City, the report must be filed in office of the clerk of the court which appointed the guardian.[19]

If the annual report sets forth any reasons for change in the powers authorized by the court,[20] Mental Hygiene Law Section 81.31(e) requires the guardian to make an application within ten days of the filing of the

---

10. *See generally*, I. Salzman, *The Obligation of Guardians Under Article 81 of the Mental Hygiene Law to Apply to Have Their Powers Modified*, 3 Elder Law Attorney No. 2 (N.Y.S.B.A.) 11 (Fall/Winter 1993).

11. Law Revision Commission Commentary to Mental Hygiene Law § 81.31.

12. *See* Mental Hygiene Law § 81.31(d), discussed below.

13. Mental Hygiene Law § 81.31(c).

14. Mental Hygiene Law § 1.03.

15. Mental Hygiene Law § 19.03.

16. Social Services Law § 2.

17. Public Health Law § 2801.

18. Mental Hygiene Law § 81.31(c).

19. Mental Hygiene Law § 81.31(d).

20. *See supra*, §§ 22.47, *et seq.*, for discussion of the duties and powers of a guardian. *See generally*, I. Salzman, *The Obligation of Guardians Under Article 81 of the Mental Hygiene Law to Apply to Have Their Powers Modified*, 3 Elder Law Attorney No. 2 (N.Y.S.B.A.) 11 (Fall/Winter 1993).

report on notice to the persons entitled to such notice in accordance with Mental Hygiene Law Section 81.16(c)(3) for such relief.[21] If the annual report sets forth any reasons for change in the powers authorized by the court, and the guardian fails to apply for such change in powers, any person entitled to commence a proceeding under Mental Hygiene Law Article 81[22] may petition the court for a change in such powers on notice to the guardian and the persons entitled to such notice for such relief.[23]

Library References:
West's Key No. Digests, Guardian and Ward ⚖111; Mental Health ⚖211-275.

§ 22.65 Reports by Guardian—Examination; Court Examiners

The initial report filed by the guardian must be examined within 30 days of its filing.[1] Within 30 days after the filing of the annual report of the preceding year, the annual reports filed by guardians under Article 81 must be examined to determine the condition and care of the incapacitated person, the finances of the incapacitated person, and the manner in which the guardian has carried out his or her duties and exercised his or her powers.[2]

Mental Hygiene Law Article 81 provides for monitoring of the initial and annual reports through the establishment of a position of court examiner. Mental Hygiene Law Section 81.32(b) provides that the presiding justice of the appellate division in each department, or a justice of the supreme court or a special referee designated by the majority of justices of the Appellate Division in each department, at the request of the presiding justice, must examine, or cause to be examined by persons designated by the presiding justice or justices as examiners, all such reports.

Moreover, Article 81 contains sanctions for noncompliance with the filing requirements for guardians. The sanctions available under Article 81 are more forceful than those that were available under former Mental Hygiene Law Articles 77 and 78 and they are intended to re-enforce the serious nature of the guardian's obligation to report to the court on the affairs of the incapacitated person.[3] If the guardian fails to file his or her initial or annual report, the person authorized to examine the report shall demand that the guardian file the report within 15 days after service of the demand on him or her. A copy of the demand shall be

21. See supra, § 22.21 for discussion of persons entitled to notice.

22. See supra, § 22.17 for discussion of who may bring proceeding.

23. Mental Hygiene Law § 81.31(e). See generally, I. Salzman, *The Obligation of Guardians Under Article 81 of the Mental Hygiene Law to Apply to Have Their Powers Modified*, 3 Elder Law Attorney No. 2 (N.Y.S.B.A.) 11 (Fall/Winter 1993).

§ 22.65

1. Mental Hygiene Law § 81.32(a)(1).

2. Mental Hygiene Law § 81.32(a)(2).

3. Law Revision Commission Commentary to Mental Hygiene Law § 81.32.

served on the guardian or his or her resident agent[4] by certified mail.[5] Upon the guardian's failure to comply with the demand for filing the report, the court may, upon motion of the court examiner, enter an order requiring compliance with the demand and may deny or reduce the amount of the compensation of guardian,[6] or remove the guardian,[7] absent a showing that the guardian has acted in good faith.[8]

If the person authorized to examine the report is of the opinion that a more complete or satisfactory report should be filed, the court examiner shall demand that the guardian file a revised report or proof of any item in the report. A copy of the demand shall be served on the guardian or his or her resident agent[9] by certified mail.[10] Upon failure of the guardian to comply with the demand for a more complete or satisfactory report, the court may, on motion of the court examiner, enter an order requiring compliance with the demand and may deny or reduce amount of compensation of guardian,[11] or remove the guardian,[12] absent a showing that guardian has acted in good faith.[13]

The person examining the report may examine the guardian and other witnesses under oath and reduce their testimony to writing. The person examining the report shall, on five days' notice to the guardian, file a report in the form and manner prescribed by order appointing the examiner.[14]

The expenses of the examination are payable out of the estate of the incapacitated person examined if the estate amounts to $5,000 or more, or, if the estate amounts to less than such sum, by the county treasurer of the county, or, within New York City, by the comptroller of New York City, out of any court funds in his or her hands.[15]

Library References:

West's Key No. Digests, Guardian and Ward ⚖111; Mental Health ⚖211–275.

§ 22.66 Reports by Guardian—Intermediate and Final Reports

Mental Hygiene Law Article 81 continues the requirements of former Mental Hygiene Law Articles 77 and 78 for the filing of interme-

4. See Mental Hygiene Law § 81.26 and see supra, § 22.43 regarding the requirement that the guardian designate the clerk of the court as agent for service.

5. Mental Hygiene Law § 81.32(c)(1).

6. See supra, § 22.61 for discussion of compensation of the guardian.

7. See infra, § 22.69 for discussion of removal of a guardian.

8. Mental Hygiene Law § 81.32(c)(2).

9. See Mental Hygiene Law § 81.26 and see supra, § 22.43 regarding the requirement that the guardian designate the clerk of the court as agent for service.

10. Mental Hygiene Law § 81.32(d)(1).

11. See supra, § 22.61 for discussion of compensation of the guardian.

12. See infra, § 22.69 for discussion of removal of a guardian.

13. Mental Hygiene Law § 81.32(d)(2).

14. Mental Hygiene Law § 81.32(e).

15. Mental Hygiene Law § 81.32(f).

§ 22.66

diate and final reports by the guardian.[1]

The guardian may move in the court of his or her appointment for an order permitting him or her to render an intermediate report to the date of the filing thereof in a form prescribed by the court which includes the same information required for the annual report.[2] The court may order the report to be filed with the clerk of the court on or before a fixed date.[3]

When a guardian dies or is removed, suspended, discharged, or allowed to resign,[4] the court shall order a final report in a form prescribed by the court, which must include the same information as is required for annual report. When such report has been made in the course of a proceeding to remove the guardian, the court may dispense with a further report.[5]

The notice of the filing of an intermediate or final report must be served on the persons entitled to notice under Mental Hygiene Law Section 81.16(c)(3).[6] If the incapacitated person is deceased, notice must also be served on his or her executor or administrator, if any.[7]

The court may appoint counsel for the incapacitated person,[8] if living, for the protection of such person's rights and interests with regard to such intermediate or final report. The court may appoint a referee to hear the matter and report to the court.[9] Upon motion for confirmation of the report of the referee, or if the report is made before the court, upon the court's determination, the report must be judicially approved and filed. The compensation of the referee and of counsel, if appointed, shall be fixed by the court and is payable out of the estate of the incapacitated person unless it is determined that the incapacitated person is indigent.[10]

If the incapacitated person resides in a facility, hospital, school, or alcoholism facility,[11] a substance abuse program,[12] an adult care facility,[13] or a residential health care facility or a general hospital,[14] a copy of the report must be served on the chief executive officer in charge of that

§ 22.66

1. Law Revision Commission Commentary to Mental Hygiene Law § 81.33.

2. *See supra,* § 22.64 for discussion of the requirements of an annual report; see *infra,* § 22.105 for form of annual report.

3. Mental Hygiene Law § 81.33(a).

4. *See infra,* §§ 22.69, *et seq.*, for discussion of removal, suspension, discharge and resignation of guardian.

5. Mental Hygiene Law § 81.33(b).

6. *See supra,* § 22.21 for discussion of persons entitled to notice.

7. Mental Hygiene Law § 81.33(c).

8. *See supra,* § 22.28 for discussion of the appointment of counsel for the incapacitated person in a guardianship proceeding.

9. Mental Hygiene Law § 81.33(d).

10. Mental Hygiene Law § 81.33(e).

11. *See* Mental Hygiene Law § 1.03.

12. *See* Mental Hygiene Law § 19.03.

13. *See* Social Services Law § 2.

14. *See* Public Health Law § 2801.

facility and on the Mental Hygiene Legal Service of the judicial department in which the residence is located.[15]

Library References:
> West's Key No. Digests, Guardian and Ward ⇌111; Mental Health ⇌211–275.

§ 22.67 Reports by Guardian—Decree Upon Approving Accounts

Where the incapacitated person has died or the guardian has died, or has been removed, suspended, or discharged, or allowed to resign,[1] the guardian or the personal representative of the guardian may file a petition with the court showing the names and addresses of all persons entitled to receive notice under Mental Hygiene Law Section 81.16(c)(3)[2] and showing that, to the extent the guardian is responsible for the property of the incapacitated person, all taxes have been paid or that no taxes are due and that the petitioner has fully reported and has made full disclosure in writing of all the guardian's actions affecting the property of the incapacitated person to all persons interested and seeking a decree judicially settling his or her final account and releasing and discharging the petitioner.[3]

The petitioner shall also file with the petition acknowledged instruments executed by all persons interested or, in the case of an infant, or incapacitated person whose claim has been paid, by the guardian, or guardian receiving payment, approving the report of the petitioner and releasing and discharging the petitioner.[4]

Upon the filing of such petition and instruments, the court may make a decree releasing and discharging the petitioner and the sureties on his or her bond,[5] if any, from any further liability to the persons interested.[6]

Library References:
> West's Key No. Digests, Guardian and Ward ⇌111; Mental Health ⇌211–275.

§ 22.68 Reports by Guardian—Summary

The court must establish a plan for reasonable compensation of the guardian, which must take into account the specific authority of the

---

15. Mental Hygiene Law § 81.33(f). See 22 NYCRR § 202.54, Proceedings Relating to Appointments of Guardians With Respect to Patients in Facilities Defined in the Mental Hygiene Law.

§ 22.67

1. Mental Hygiene Law § 81.34(b). See infra, § 22.69, et seq., for discussion of removal, suspension, discharge or resignation of a guardian.

2. See supra, § 22.21 for discussion of persons entitled to notice.

3. Mental Hygiene Law § 81.34(a).

4. Mental Hygiene Law § 81.34(c).

5. See supra, § 22.42 for discussion of requirement of bond.

6. Mental Hygiene Law § 81.34(d).

guardian to provide for the personal needs and/or property management for the incapacitated person. If the court finds that the guardian has failed to discharge his or her duties satisfactorily in any respect, the court may deny or reduce compensation which would otherwise be allowed.[1]

The guardian must file initial[2] and annual[3] reports. The initial report states what steps the guardian has taken to fulfill his or her responsibilities with respect to property management and the personal needs of the incapacitated person.[4]

In the month of May or at any other time on motion or order of the court, every guardian must file an annual report.[5] The annual report of guardian must be in a form prescribed by the court and must include the certain specified information.[6] The information required in the annual report concerns the personal status of the incapacitated person, and/or the condition of the person's finances and property, to the extent of the guardian's authority. Article 81 imposes specific informational requirements on the guardian in completing his or her annual report which perform a significant monitoring function. The guardian must send a copy of the annual report to the incapacitated person by mail and must file a copy of the annual report.[7]

The initial and annual reports filed by the guardian must be examined by a court examiner,[8] to determine the condition and care of the incapacitated person, the finances of the incapacitated person, and the manner in which the guardian has carried out his or her duties and exercised his or her powers.[9] The statute provides sanctions for noncompliance with the filing requirements.[10] The guardian may be required to file a more complete or revised report if required by the court examiner.[11]

The guardian may move in the court of his or her appointment for an order permitting him or her to render an intermediate report[12] and when a guardian dies or is removed, suspended, discharged, or allowed to

§ 22.68

1. Mental Hygiene Law § 81.28; see supra, § 22.61.
2. Mental Hygiene Law § 81.30; see supra, § 22.63.
3. Mental Hygiene Law § 81.31; see supra, § 22.64.
4. Mental Hygiene Law § 81.30(a), (b). See infra, § 22.104 for form of initial report of guardian.
5. Mental Hygiene Law § 81.31(a). See supra, § 22.64; see infra, § 22.105 for form of annual report of guardian.
6. Mental Hygiene Law § 81.31(b); see infra, § 22.105 for form of annual report of guardian.
7. Mental Hygiene Law § 81.31(c). See supra, § 22.64.
8. Mental Hygiene Law § 81.32(b). See supra, § 22.65.
9. Mental Hygiene Law § 81.32(a). See supra, § 22.65.
10. Mental Hygiene Law § 81.32(c). See supra, § 22.65.
11. Mental Hygiene Law § 81.32(d). See supra, § 22.65.
12. Mental Hygiene Law § 81.33(a); see supra, § 22.66.

resign, the court shall order a final report which must include the same information as is required for annual report and must be judicially approved and filed.[13] Where the incapacitated person has died or the guardian has died, or has been removed, suspended, or discharged, or allowed to resign, the guardian or the personal representative of the guardian may file a petition seeking a decree judicially settling his or her final account and releasing and discharging the petitioner.[14]

Library References:

West's Key No. Digests, Guardian and Ward ⚖111; Mental Health ⚖211–275.

§ 22.69 Removal, Discharge and Resignation of Guardian—Removal

Mental Hygiene Law Section 81.35 continues the standard for removal of a conservator under former Mental Hygiene Law Article 77.[1] Upon motion, the court appointing the guardian may remove the guardian when the guardian fails to comply with an order,[2] is guilty of misconduct,[3] or for any other cause which to the court appears just.[4] Notice of the motion to remove the guardian must be served on the guardian and persons entitled to receive notice under Mental Hygiene Law Section 81.16(c)(3).[5] The motion may be made by the person

---

13. Mental Hygiene Law § 81.33(b); *see supra*, § 22.66.

14. Mental Hygiene Law § 81.34; *see supra*, § 22.67; *see infra*, § 22.106 for form of decree approving accounts.

§ 22.69

1. *See generally*, S.R. Shapiro, Annotation, *Resignation or Removal of Executor, Administrator, Guardian, or Trustee, Before Final Administration or Before Termination of Trust as Affecting His Compensation*, 96 A.L.R.3d 1102 §§ 8, 9, 10 (1979).

2. *See, e.g.*, Mental Hygiene Law § 81.32(c), concerning the failure to file the initial or annual report, discussed *supra* at §§ 22.62, *et seq.*

3. *See, e.g.*, In re Brownell, 112 Misc.2d 719, 447 N.Y.S.2d 591 (Delaware Co.Ct. 1981), decided under prior law. On an application to remove a conservator, where the issues raised involved whether there had been self-dealing by the conservator, the court did not remove the conservator, but dealt instead with whether the conservator should be surcharged and held that although there had some questionable actions by the conservator, since all the parties to the proceeding were members of the same family and the services had been rendered to their mother during difficult times, the mistakes were negligent, not malicious, the interest of justice would be served by not surcharging the respondents or allowing them commissions.

4. *See, e.g.*, In re Schunk, 136 A.D.2d 904, 524 N.Y.S.2d 925 (4th Dep't 1988), decided under prior law. An application to remove the conservator was properly denied where the court found that his management of the conservatee's property had been beneficial to conservatorship, the conservatee was receiving proper medical care, and, despite minor errors of judgment, charges of misconduct were unfounded.

See also, In re Cook, 133 A.D.2d 823, 520 N.Y.S.2d 400 (2d Dep't 1987), appeal denied 71 N.Y.2d 802, 527 N.Y.S.2d 768, 522 N.E.2d 1066 (1988). Under prior law, where conservator did not act in the best interests of his ward or did not properly execute his duties, court could nullify actions taken on behalf of the conservatee and restore to the conservatee rights which might otherwise have been asserted.

5. *See supra*, § 22.21 for discussion of persons entitled to notice.

§ 22.69 GUARDIANSHIP Ch. 22

examining the initial and annual reports,[6] or by any person entitled to commence proceeding under Mental Hygiene Law Article 81,[7] including the incapacitated person. The court may fix the compensation of the attorney or person prosecuting the motion.[8] The court may compel the guardian to pay personally the costs of the motion if it is granted.[9]

Library References:

West's Key No. Digests, Guardian and Ward ⚖111; Mental Health ⚖211–275.

§ 22.70 Removal, Discharge and Resignation of Guardian—Discharge or Modification of Powers

Mental Hygiene Law Section 81.36 provides a means for determining whether the powers of the guardian are still consistent with the incapacitated person's needs. The court appointing the guardian shall discharge the guardian, or modify the powers of the guardian where appropriate, if it appears to the satisfaction of the court that (1) the incapacitated person has become able to exercise some or all of the powers necessary to provide for personal needs or property management which the guardian is authorized to exercise,[1] (2) the incapacitated person has become unable to exercise powers necessary to provide for personal needs or property management which the guardian is not authorized to exercise, (3) the incapacitated person dies,[2] or (4) for some

---

6. See supra, §§ 22.59, et seq., for discussion of initial and annual reports.

7. See supra, § 22.17 for discussion of persons entitled to commence proceeding.

Where petitioner brought proceeding to amend the conservatorship as "friend" of the incapacitated person, the court held that it lacked standing to obtain such relief; its remedy was limited to seeking to remove the conservators for failure to execute a plan to insure the preservation, maintenance, and care of the proposed conservatee's income, assets, and personal well-being, and appointment of a new conservator. In re Petition of Association for Retarded Citizens, 94 A.D.2d 958, 464 N.Y.S.2d 84 (4th Dep't 1983).

8. Mental Hygiene Law § 81.35. See, e.g., In re Silverstein, 121 A.D.2d 728, 504 N.Y.S.2d 62 (2d Dep't 1986). In a proceeding to remove the conservator for alleged falsification of estate records, after examination by a referee it was determined that the conservator should not be removed where it was found that most of the charges were based upon supposition and suspicion; however, the court denied the application to charge the referee's fee to the petitioner; the court held that the conservator is under a statutory duty to have a court-appointed referee review the accounts of the conservatee's estate, and although many of the charges appeared frivolous, the expense of the annual examination of accounts shall be payable out of the conservatee's estate.

9. Mental Hygiene Law § 81.35. But see, In re Silverstein, 121 A.D.2d 728, 504 N.Y.S.2d 62 (2d Dep't 1986), discussed in note 8, supra.

§ 22.70

1. See, e.g., Matter of Warshawsky, N.Y.L.J., 1/9/95, p.30, col.4 (Sup.Ct., Kings County) (where the clear and convincing evidence satisfied the court that the formerly incapacitated person was able to exercise all of the powers necessary to provide for personal needs and property management, the guardian was directed to file a final account and upon judicial settlement would be discharged).

2. Upon the death of the conservatee, the conservator is simply authorized to "wind up" the conservatee's estate and arrange for the conservatee's burial; the death of the conservatee causes the authority of the conservator to end and requires the conservator's discharge. Matter of Glen–

other reason, the appointment of the guardian is no longer necessary for the incapacitated person, or the powers of the guardian should be modified based upon changes in the circumstances of the incapacitated person.[3]

An application for discharge or modification of a guardian's powers may be made by the guardian,[4] the incapacitated person, or any person entitled to commence a proceeding under Mental Hygiene Law Article 81.[5] On an application for discharge or modification of a guardian's powers, there must be a hearing on notice to the persons entitled to notice under Mental Hygiene Law Section 81.16(c)(3).[6] If any party to the proceeding raises an issue of fact as to the ability of the incapacitated person to provide for his or her personal needs or property management and demands a jury trial of such issue, the court must order a jury trial.[7]

To the extent that discharge or modification of a guardian's powers would terminate the guardianship or restore certain powers to the incapacitated person, the burden of proof is on the person objecting to such relief.[8] To the extent that discharge or modification would further limit the powers of the incapacitated person, the burden is on person seeking such relief.[9]

If the guardian is discharged because the incapacitated person becomes fully able to care for his or her property, the court must order that the property remaining in the hands of the guardian be restored to such person.[10] If the incapacitated person dies, the guardian must provide for such person's burial or other disposition, the cost of which is to be borne by the estate of the incapacitated person.[11]

---

er, 202 A.D.2d 503, 609 N.Y.S.2d 26 (2d Dep't 1994). *See also* Matter of Kator (Elefant), 164 Misc.2d 265, 624 N.Y.S.2d 348 (Sup.Ct., N.Y. County, 1995); In re Tepperman (Bloom), N.Y.L.J., 9/12/95, p. 30, col. 2 (Sup.Ct., Nassau County).

The special guardianship was continued after the death of the incapacitated person to allow continued cooperation with law enforcement officials in effort to recover a valuable stolen violin. Matter of Saphier (Siracusano), 167 Misc.2d 130, 637 N.Y.S.2d 630 (Sup.Ct., N.Y. County, 1995).

3. Mental Hygiene Law § 81.36(a).

4. *See generally*, I. Salzman, *The Obligation of Guardians Under Article 81 of the Mental Hygiene Law to Apply to Have Their Powers Modified*, 3 Elder Law Attorney No. 2 (N.Y.S.B.A.) 11 (Fall/Winter 1993).

5. Mental Hygiene Law § 81.36(b). *See supra*, § 22.17 for discussion of who may bring an Article 81 proceeding.

6. *See supra*, § 22.21. *But see* Matter of Kator (Elefant), 164 Misc.2d 265, 624 N.Y.S.2d 348 (Sup.Ct., N.Y. County, 1995), where the court discussed a problem which may arise where there is a pre-Article 81 order of appointment. While Article 81 orders appointing a guardian are required to identify the persons entitled to notice of further proceedings (Mental Hygiene Law § 81.16(c)(3)), pre-Article 81 orders contain no such provision. Therefore, in such instances, compliance with the notice provisions of Article 81 may be impracticable and the courts may have to look to prior law.

7. Mental Hygiene Law § 81.36(c). *See supra*, § 22.31 for discussion of the right to a jury trial on a proceeding to appoint a guardian.

8. *See supra*, § 22.33 for discussion of burden of proof and quantum of evidence.

9. Mental Hygiene Law § 81.36(d).

10. *Cf.*, Matter of Warshawsky, N.Y.L.J., 1/9/95, p.30, col.4 (Sup.Ct., Kings County).

11. Mental Hygiene Law § 81.36(e).

§ 22.70   GUARDIANSHIP   Ch. 22

Library References:

West's Key No. Digests, Guardian and Ward ⊂111; Mental Health ⊂211–275.

§ 22.71 Removal, Discharge and Resignation of Guardian—Resignation or Suspension of Powers

Mental Hygiene Law Section 81.37 continues the conditions for resignation and suspension provided for in former Mental Hygiene Law Article 77.[1] The court appointing the guardian may allow the guardian to resign or may suspend the powers of the guardian.[2] The statute provides no guidelines for allowing a guardian to resign. Permission to resign shall be granted in the exercise of the court's good judgment and discretion.[3]

Where the guardian is engaged in war service, the court, on motion by the guardian or any other person and on such notice as the court may direct, may suspend the powers of the guardian until further order of court. If the suspension will leave no other person acting as guardian, the motion must seek appointment of a successor. When the suspended guardian becomes able to serve, he or she may be reinstated by the court on motion and such notice as the court may direct. If the suspended guardian is reinstated, the court must thereupon discharge his or her successor, who may be required to account, and make any other order as justice requires.[4]

Library References:

West's Key No. Digests, Guardian and Ward ⊂111; Mental Health ⊂211–275.

§ 22.72 Removal, Discharge and Resignation of Guardian—Vacancy in Office; Appointment of Interim and Successor Guardians

A vacancy created by the death, removal, discharge, resignation, or suspension of a guardian shall be filled by the court.[1] On the application of any person entitled to commence a proceeding under Mental Hygiene Law Art 81,[2] the court shall appoint an interim guardian who shall serve for a period of 90 days or until a final accounting[3] is filed and a successor

---

§ 22.71

1. *See* Law Revision Commission Commentary to Mental Hygiene Law § 81.37.

2. Mental Hygiene Law § 81.37(a). *See* In re Kaufman, 114 Misc.2d 1078, 453 N.Y.S.2d 304 (Sup.Ct., Bronx County, 1982) (determination allowing conservator to resign).

3. Matter of Beritely (Luberoff), N.Y.L.J., 12/8/95, p. 37, col. 3 (Sup.Ct., Suffolk County).

4. Mental Hygiene Law § 81.37(b).

§ 22.72

1. Mental Hygiene Law § 81.38(a).

2. *See supra*, § 22.17 for discussion of who may commence proceeding.

3. *See supra*, § 22.66 for discussion of final accounting.

guardian is appointed by the court. The order of appointment shall enumerate the powers and duties of the interim guardian.[4] The court may require service of the order to show cause seeking appointment of an interim guardian on any persons it deems appropriate.[5]

Library References:

West's Key No. Digests, Guardian and Ward ⚖111; Mental Health ⚖211–275.

§ 22.73 Removal, Discharge and Resignation of Guardian—Standby Guardian

Mental Hygiene Law Section 81.38(b) authorizes the court to appoint standby guardians as well as alternate and/or successive guardians to the standby guardian to act in the event the standby guardian resigns, dies, is removed, discharged or suspended, or becomes incapacitated. The section follows the format of a similar provision in Surrogate's Court Procedure Act Article 17–A.[1] At the time of the appointment of the guardian, the court may, in its discretion, appoint a standby guardian to act in the event that the guardian resigns, dies, is removed, is discharged, is suspended, or becomes incapacitated. The court may also appoint an alternate and/or successive alternates to the standby guardian, to act if the standby guardian resigns, dies, is removed, is discharged, is suspended, or becomes incapacitated. Such standby guardian, or alternate, is, without further proceedings, empowered to immediately assume duties of office immediately upon the resignation, death, removal, discharge, suspension or adjudication of incapacity, of the guardian or the standby guardian as set forth in the order of appointment, subject only to confirmation of the appointment by the court 60 days following assumption of the duties of office. Before confirming the appointment of a standby guardian, the court may conduct a hearing in accordance with Mental Hygiene Law Section 81.11[2] on the petition of any person entitled to commence a proceeding under Mental Hygiene Law Article 81.[3]

Library References:

West's Key No. Digests, Guardian and Ward ⚖111; Mental Health ⚖211–275.

§ 22.74 Removal, Discharge and Resignation of Guardian—Summary

The court appointing the guardian may allow the guardian to resign

---

4. *See supra*, §§ 22.45, *et seq.*, for discussion of powers and duties of a guardian.

5. Mental Hygiene Law § 81.38(a).

§ 22.73

1. Law Revision Commission Commentary to Mental Hygiene Law § 81.38. See SCPA Art. 17–A, Guardians of Mentally Retarded and Mentally Disabled Persons.

2. *See supra*, §§ 22.30, *et seq.*

3. *See supra*, § 22.17 for discussion of who may commence proceeding.

or may suspend the powers of the guardian.[1]

At the time of the appointment of the guardian, the court may appoint standby and alternate standby guardians to act in the event that the guardian resigns, dies, is removed, is discharged, suspended, or becomes incapacitated, who are empowered to immediately assume duties of office of guardian subject to confirmation within 60 days following assumption of office.[2]

The court appointing the guardian may remove the guardian when the guardian fails to comply with an order, is guilty of misconduct, or for any other cause which to the court appears just.[3] The court appointing the guardian shall discharge the guardian, or modify the powers of the guardian where appropriate.[4] The court that appointed the guardian may also allow a guardian to resign or it may suspend the powers of the guardian.[5] Where a vacancy has been created in the office of guardian, the court may appoint an interim guardian.[6] At the time the court appoints a guardian, it may also appoint a standby guardian who can immediately assume the powers of the guardian should a vacancy occur in the office guardian,[7] provided the standby guardian moves within 60 days to confirm such assumption of powers.[8]

Library References:

West's Key No. Digests, Guardian and Ward ⚖111; Mental Health ⚖211–275.

§ 22.75 Education Requirements—Generally

Mental Hygiene Law Sections 81.39, 81.40 and 81.41 underscore the recognition by Article 81 that the complexity of guardianship issues require thorough understanding by all persons playing a role in the guardianship proceeding by establishing education requirements for guardians, court evaluators and court examiners.[1] Waiver of the training requirements should only occur if the person to be appointed to such

§ 22.74

1. Mental Hygiene Law § 81.35; see supra, § 22.69.

2. Mental Hygiene Law § 81.38(b); see supra, § 22.73.

3. Mental Hygiene Law § 81.35; see supra, § 22.69.

4. Mental Hygiene Law § 81.36; see supra, § 22.70.

5. Mental Hygiene Law § 81.37; see supra, § 22.71.

6. Mental Hygiene Law § 81.38(a); see supra, § 22.72.

7. Mental Hygiene Law § 81.38(b); see supra, § 22.73.

8. Id.

§ 22.75

1. See infra, §§ 22.76–22.78, for discussion of the specific education requirements for guardians, court evaluators and court examiners.

See 22 NYCRR Pt. 36, Appointment of Fiduciaries, § 36.5, Education and Training, which provides:

> The Chief Administrator or the appointing judge may require that applicants for appointment complete designated courses or training curricula prior to receiving an appointment.

position has the education and experience in the required training areas.[2]

Library References:
> West's Key No. Digests, Guardian and Ward ⚖111; Mental Health ⚖211-275.

§ 22.76 Education Requirements—Guardian Training

Each incapacitated person is entitled to a guardian whom the court finds to be sufficiently capable of performing the duties and exercising the powers of a guardian necessary to protect the incapacitated person.[1]

Guardians should be trained so that they understand what is expected of them and how to best serve the incapacitated person. Training will improve guardianship performance and accountability. In addition to understanding the legal duties and responsibilities of a guardian, the guardian should be trained regarding medical and mental health terminology, the process of aging, and community services and programs.[2]

Each person appointed by the court to be a guardian must complete a training program approved by the chief administrator which covers (1) the legal duties and responsibilities of guardian;[3] (2) the rights of the incapacitated person;[4] (3) the available resources to aid the incapacitated person; (4) an orientation to medical terminology, particularly that related to the diagnostic and assessment procedures used to characterize the extent and reversibility of any impairment; and (5) the preparation of annual reports,[5] including financial accounting for the property and financial resources of the incapacitated person.[6]

The court may, in its discretion, waive some or all of the requirements regarding the training of a guardian or impose additional requirements. In doing so, the court must consider the experience and education of the guardian with respect to the training requirements, duties and powers assigned to the guardian, and the needs of the incapacitated person.[7]

---

2. Mental Hygiene Law §§ 81.39(c), 81.40(c), 81.41(c). *See, e.g.,* Matter of Lisle, N.Y.L.J., 8/9/94, p.27, col.4 (Surr.Ct., Nassau County), which held that although the nominated guardian had some college training, his life experiences did not suggest any basis to dispense with the training requirements set forth in Mental Hygiene Law § 81.39.

§ 22.76

1. Mental Hygiene Law § 81.39(a).

2. Law Revision Commission Commentary to Mental Hygiene Law § 81.39.

3. *See supra,* § 22.45, *et seq.*, for discussion of duties and responsibilities of guardian.

4. *See supra,* § 22.54 for discussion of impact of appointment of guardian on incapacitated persons.

5. *See supra,* § 22.64 for discussion of requirements of annual report.

6. Mental Hygiene Law § 81.39(b).

7. Mental Hygiene Law § 81.39(c). *See, e.g.,* Matter of Lisle, N.Y.L.J., 8/9/94, p.27, col.4 (Surr.Ct., Nassau County) (although nominated guardian had some college training, his life experiences did not suggest any basis to dispense with the training requirements set forth in Mental Hygiene Law § 81.39).

Library References:

West's Key No. Digests, Guardian and Ward ⚖111; Mental Health ⚖211–275.

§ 22.77 Education Requirements—Court Evaluator Training

Each incapacitated person is entitled to a court evaluator whom the court finds to be sufficiently capable of performing the duties of a court evaluator necessary to ensure that all the relevant information regarding the petition for appointment of a guardian comes before the court and to assist the court in reaching a decision regarding the appointment of a guardian.[1]

The court evaluator should have thorough knowledge of both the evaluator's responsibilities and medical and mental health terminology, particularly relating to diagnostic and assessment procedures, the side effects of medications, the myths and the process of aging, and community services and programs. Waiver of the training requirement should only occur if the person appointed court evaluator has education and experience in the training areas required under Mental Hygiene Law Section 81.40.[2]

Each person appointed by the court to be a court evaluator shall complete a training program approved by the chief administrator which covers: (1) the legal duties and responsibilities of a court evaluator;[3] (2) the rights of the incapacitated person with emphasis on the due process rights to aid the court evaluator in determining his or her recommendation regarding the appointment of counsel and the conduct of the hearing;[4] (3) the available resources to aid the incapacitated person; (4) an orientation to medical terminology, particularly that related to diagnostic and assessment procedures used to characterize the extent and reversibility of any impairment; (5) entitlements; and (6) psychological and social concerns relating to disabled and frail older adults.[5]

The court may, in its discretion, waive some or all of the requirements regarding training of court evaluators or impose additional requirements. In doing so, the court must consider the experience and

---

§ 22.77

1. Mental Hygiene Law § 81.40(a). *See* Matter of Sulzberger, 159 Misc.2d 236, 603 N.Y.S.2d 656 (Sup.Ct., N.Y. County, 1993).

2. Law Revision Commission Commentary to Mental Hygiene Law § 81.40. *Cf.*, Matter of Lisle, N.Y.L.J., 8/9/94, p.27, col.4 (Surr.Ct., Nassau County).

3. *See supra,* § 22.26 for discussion of duties and responsibilities of court evaluator.

4. *See supra,* §§ 22.30, *et seq.*, for discussion of the rights of the alleged incapacitated person at the hearing.

5. Mental Hygiene Law § 81.40(b). *See generally,* R.M. Bailly, *Guardianship Reform for Older Adults in New York*, 2 Elder Law Attorney (N.Y.S.B.A.) 28 (Spring/Summer 1992).

education of the court evaluator with respect to the training requirements.[6]

Library References:

West's Key No. Digests, Guardian and Ward ⚖111; Mental Health ⚖211–275.

§ 22.78 Education Requirements—Court Examiner Training

Each incapacitated person is entitled to a thorough examination of all the reports required to be filed by guardian.[1] Each person appointed as a court examiner pursuant to Mental Hygiene Law Section 81.32 must complete a training program approved by the chief administrator which covers the legal duties and responsibilities of the examiner and of the guardians.[2]

Accountability of guardians is critical to ensuring the protection of the incapacitated person and the effectiveness of the guardianship system in general.[3] The court examiner training requirements are designed to ensure that the annual review of guardian reports is an effective tool for evaluating the performance of the guardian and assessing the need for the continuation of the guardianship. Waiver of the training requirement should only occur if the person appointed court examiner has education and experience in the training areas required under this section.[4]

The court may, in its discretion, waive some or all of the requirements regarding training of court examiners or impose additional requirements. In so doing, the court must consider the experience and education of the court examiner with respect to the training requirements.[5]

Library References:

West's Key No. Digests, Guardian and Ward ⚖111; Mental Health ⚖211–275.

6. Mental Hygiene Law § 81.40(c). *Cf.*, Matter of Lisle, N.Y.L.J., 8/9/94, p.27, col.4 (Surr.Ct., Nassau County).

§ 22.78

1. Mental Hygiene Law § 81.41(a). *See supra*, §§ 22.62, *et seq.*, for discussion of the reports required to be filed by guardian.

2. Mental Hygiene Law § 81.41(b). *See supra*, § 22.65 for discussion of the appointment of a court examiner.

3. *Cf.*, Matter of Roy (Lepkowski), N.Y.L.J., 10/31/94, p.34, col.3 (Sup.Ct., Suffolk County), directing the person who had been managing incapacitated person's property without formal court appointment to account and appointing a property management guardian.

4. Law Revision Commission Commentary to Mental Hygiene Law § 81.41. *Cf.*, Matter of Lisle, N.Y.L.J., 8/9/94, p.27, col.4 (Surr.Ct., Nassau County).

5. Mental Hygiene Law § 81.41(c). *Cf.*, Matter of Lisle, N.Y.L.J., 8/9/94, p.27, col.4 (Surr.Ct., Nassau County).

§ 22.79 Education Requirements—Compliance

Mental Hygiene Law Section 81.42 makes it clear that technical mistakes, deficiencies, and omissions that do not result in actual prejudice that affects the integrity of the guardianship proceeding cannot be the basis for dismissal of a proceeding under Article 81. The guardian who acts pursuant to an order of the court is held harmless for any actions taken pursuant to the order unless the order was obtained through fraud, conspiracy, or misrepresentation.[1]

A motion to dismiss based on the alleged failure to comply with any of the provisions of Mental Hygiene Law Article 81, other than the requirement of service upon the person alleged to be incapacitated,[2] must be determined without regard to technical mistakes, deficiencies, and omissions that do not result in actual prejudice that affects the integrity of the proceeding.[3]

A judgment or order made pursuant to Mental Hygiene Law Article 81, unless reversed on appeal, releases the guardian and the sureties from all claims of the incapacitated person and/or any person affected thereby based on any act or omission directly authorized, approved or confirmed in the judgment or order. This section does not apply where the judgment or order is obtained by fraud or conspiracy or by misrepresentation contained in the notice, petition, account, or in the judgment or order as to any material fact. For purposes of this subdivision, misrepresentation of a material fact includes but is not limited to the omission of a material fact.[4]

Library References:

West's Key No. Digests, Guardian and Ward ⟜111; Mental Health ⟜211–275.

§ 22.80 Education Requirements—Summary

Article 81 establishes specified education requirements for guardians,[1] court evaluators[2] and court examiners.[3] Waiver of the training requirements should only occur if the person to be appointed to such position has the education and experience in the required training areas.[4] Technical mistakes, deficiencies, and omissions that do not result in actual prejudice that affects the integrity of the proceeding cannot be

§ 22.79

1. Law Revision Commission Commentary to Mental Hygiene Law § 81.42.

2. Mental Hygiene Law § 81.07(d)(1)(i). See supra, § 22.21 for discussion of persons entitled to notice of the proceeding to appoint a guardian.

3. Mental Hygiene Law § 81.42(a).

4. Mental Hygiene Law § 81.42(b).

§ 22.80

1. Mental Hygiene Law § 81.39; see supra, § 22.76.

2. Mental Hygiene Law § 81.40; see supra, § 22.77.

3. Mental Hygiene Law § 81.41; see supra, § 22.78.

4. Mental Hygiene Law §§ 81.39(c), 81.40(c), 81.41(c). See supra, §§ 22.75, et seq.

the basis for dismissal of a proceeding under Article 81.[5] The guardian who acts pursuant to an order of the court is held harmless for any actions taken pursuant to the order unless the order was obtained through fraud, conspiracy, or misrepresentation.[6]

Library References:
> West's Key No. Digests, Guardian and Ward ⚖111; Mental Health ⚖211-275.

§ 22.81 Proceedings to Discover Property Withheld

To the extent that it is consistent with the authority otherwise granted by the court,[1] the guardian may commence a proceeding, in the court which appointed the guardian, to discover property withheld.[2]

Library References:
> West's Key No. Digests, Guardian and Ward ⚖111; Mental Health ⚖211-275.

§ 22.82 Proceedings to Discover Property Withheld—Petition and Supporting Papers

The petition in a proceeding to discover property withheld must set forth on knowledge, or information and belief, any facts tending to show that any interest in real property, money or other personal property, or the proceeds or value thereof, which should be delivered and paid to the guardian, is in the possession, under the control, or within the knowledge or information of the respondent who withholds the property from the guardian, whether such possession or control was obtained before or after the appointment of the guardian, or that the respondent refuses to disclose knowledge or information which such person may have concerning such property or which will aid the guardian in making discovery of such property. The petition must request that the respondent be ordered to attend the inquiry and be examined accordingly and deliver the property of the incapacitated person if it is within his or her control. The petition may be accompanied by an affidavit or other written evidence, tending to support the allegations of the petition.[1]

Library References:
> West's Key No. Digests, Guardian and Ward ⚖111; Mental Health ⚖211-275.

§ 22.83 Proceedings to Discover Property Withheld—Grounds for Inquiry

If the court is satisfied on the papers so presented that there are reasonable grounds for the inquiry, it must make an order accordingly,

---

5. Mental Hygiene Law § 81.42(a); see supra, § 22.79.

6. Mental Hygiene Law § 81.42(b); see supra, § 22.79.

§ 22.81

1. See supra, §§ 22.42, et seq., for discussion of powers of guardian.

2. Mental Hygiene Law § 81.44(a).

See, e.g., Matter of Albenda (Gonzalez), N.Y.L.J., 1/3/92, p.27, col.5 (Sup.Ct., Kings County).

§ 22.82

1. Mental Hygiene Law § 81.44(a).

§ 22.83

which may be returnable forthwith, or at a future time fixed by the court, and may be served at any time before the hearing.[1]

If it appears from the petition or from the answer interposed thereto, or in the course of the inquiry made pursuant to such order that a person other than the respondent in the proceeding claims an interest in the property or the proceeds or value thereof, the court may by original order or by supplemental order, direct such additional party to attend and be examined in the proceeding in respect of his or her adverse claim, and deliver the property if it is in his or her control or the proceeds or value thereof. Service of such order must be made by delivery of a certified copy thereof to the person or persons named therein and payment or tender to each of the sum required by law to be paid or tendered to a witness who is subpoenaed to attend a trial in court.[2]

Library References:
West's Key No. Digests, Guardian and Ward ⚖111; Mental Health ⚖211-275.

§ 22.84 Proceedings to Discover Property Withheld—Answer

If the person directed to appear submits an answer denying any knowledge concerning or possession of any property which belongs to the incapacitated person or should be delivered to the guardian, or defaults in answering the petition, he or she must be sworn to answer truly all questions put to him or her regarding the inquiry requested in the petition.[1] Any claim of title to or right to possession of any property of the incapacitated person must be made by a verified answer in writing.

Library References:
West's Key No. Digests, Guardian and Ward ⚖111; Mental Health ⚖211-275.

§ 22.85 Proceedings to Discover Property Withheld—Trial

If such answer is interposed, the issues raised thereby must be tried according to the usual practice of the court as a litigated issue. However, interposition of such answer shall not limit the right of the guardian to proceed with the inquiry in respect of property not so claimed by the verified answer. If possession of the property is denied, proof on that issue may be presented to the court by either party. In an appropriate case, the court may make interim decrees directing delivery of property

§ 22.83
1. Mental Hygiene Law § 81.44(a).
2. Mental Hygiene Law § 81.44(a).

§ 22.84
1. Mental Hygiene Law § 81.44(b).

not claimed by the verified answer and may continue the proceeding for determination of any litigated issue.[1]

Library References:

West's Key No. Digests, Guardian and Ward ⚖111; Mental Health ⚖211–275.

§ 22.86 Proceedings to Discover Property Withheld—Decree

If it appears that the guardian is entitled to possession of the property, the decree shall direct delivery thereof to the guardian or, if the property has been diverted or disposed of, the decree may direct payment of the proceeds or the value of the property or may impress a trust on the proceeds or make any determination which a court of equity might decree in following trust property funds.[1] In any case in which a verified answer is served and the court after trial or hearing determines the issue, the court may in its discretion award costs not exceeding $50 and disbursements to be paid by the unsuccessful party.[2]

Library References:

West's Key No. Digests, Guardian and Ward ⚖111; Mental Health ⚖211–275.

§ 22.87 Proceedings to Discover Property Withheld—Summary

The guardian may commence a proceeding, in the court which appointed the guardian, to discover property withheld.[1] If it appears that the guardian is entitled to possession of the property, the court shall direct delivery thereof to the guardian or, if the property has been diverted or disposed of, the court may direct payment of the proceeds or the value of the property or may impress a trust on the proceeds or make any determination which a court of equity might decree in following trust property funds.[2]

§ 22.85

1. Mental Hygiene Law § 81.44(b).

§ 22.86

1. *See, e.g.*, Matter of Albenda (Gonzalez), N.Y.L.J., 1/3/92, p.27, col.5 (Sup.Ct., Kings County) (Where funds were held jointly, each joint tenant had the right to a moiety or less for his or her own use, and where one joint tenant drew an amount in excess of his or her moiety, the other tenant has an absolute right during the lifetime of both, to recover such excess; where the joint tenant had redeemed the entire amount of jointly held savings bonds, the conservatee was entitled to have a trust impressed upon one-half of the proceeds realized from the disposition of such bonds.) *See* Preminger, *et al., Trusts and Estates Practice in New York* (West 1997).

2. Mental Hygiene Law § 81.44(b).

§ 22.87

1. Mental Hygiene Law § 81.44; *see supra,* § 22.81.

2. Mental Hygiene Law § 81.44(b). *See supra,* § 22.86.

Library References:

West's Key No. Digests, Guardian and Ward ⚖111; Mental Health ⚖211-275.

§ 22.88 Drafting Checklists

The forms used in a proceeding pursuant to Mental Hygiene Law Article 81 must comply with the general drafting requirements applicable to all forms, as well as with the specific requirements of Article 81. The following sections set forth guidelines for drafting the specific forms included in this chapter.

In drafting these forms it is essential that the attorney or the guardian strictly comply with the statutory requirements for such form imposed by Mental Hygiene Law Article 81. The court must be provided with all the information specified in the statute. In particular, on the proceeding to appoint the guardian, it is essential that the order to show cause and the petition set forth in detail the condition of the alleged incapacitated person and specify all the powers sought. Failure to provide such information to the court may result in denial of the appointment of a guardian or granting insufficient powers to the guardian which do not permit the guardian to act on behalf of the incapacitated person when necessary.

§ 22.89 Drafting Checklists—Order to Show Cause

The requirements of the order to show cause are established by Mental Hygiene Law Section 81.07 (*see* § 22.22):

1. Must be written in large type, in plain language, and in a language other than English if necessary to inform the person alleged to be incapacitated of his or her rights.

2. Must include the following information:

    - Date, time, and place of the hearing of the petition, which shall be no more than 28 days from the date of the filing of the petition and order to show cause; the hearing date shall be the same date on which the order to show cause is returnable;

    - A clear and easily readable statement of the rights of the person alleged to be incapacitated that are set forth Mental Hygiene Law Section 81.11;

    - The name, address, and telephone number of the person appointed as court evaluator;

    - The name, address, and telephone number of the attorney if one has been appointed for the person alleged to be incapacitated; and

- A list of the powers which the guardian would have the authority to exercise on behalf of the person alleged to be incapacitated if the relief sought in the petition is granted.

3. Must include on its face the legend set forth in Mental Hygiene Law Section 81.07(c) in twelve point or larger bold face double spaced type.

§ 22.90 Drafting Checklists—Petition

The requirements of a petition are established by Mental Hygiene Law Section 81.08.

1. The petition must contain, to the best of the petitioner's knowledge, the following information (see § 22.23):

   - The name, age, address, and telephone number of the person alleged to be incapacitated;
   - The name, address, and telephone number of the person or persons with whom the person alleged to be incapacitated resides, if any;
   - A description of the alleged incapacitated person's functional level including that person's ability to manage the activities of daily living, behavior, and understanding and appreciation of the nature and consequences of any inability to manage the activities of daily living;
   - If powers are sought with respect to the personal needs of the alleged incapacitated person, specific factual allegations as to the personal actions or other actual occurrences involving the person alleged to be incapacitated which are claimed to demonstrate that the person is likely to suffer harm because he or she cannot adequately understand and appreciate the nature and consequences of his or her inability to provide for personal needs (see § 22.53);
   - If powers are sought with respect to property management for the alleged incapacitated person, specific factual allegations as to the financial transactions or other actual occurrences involving the person alleged to be incapacitated which are claimed to demonstrate that the person is likely to suffer harm because he or she cannot adequately understand and appreciate the nature and consequences of his or her inability to provide for property management (see §§ 22.47–22.52);
   - The particular powers being sought and their relationship to the functional level and needs of the person alleged to be incapacitated (see § 22.14);
   - The duration of the powers being sought;

- The approximate value and description of the financial resources of the person alleged to be incapacitated and whether the person is a recipient of public assistance;
    (i) The nature and amount of any claim, debt, or obligations of the person alleged to be incapacitated;
- The names, addresses, and telephone numbers of presumptive distributees of the person alleged to be incapacitated as that term is defined in Surrogate's Court Procedure Act Section 103(42), unless they are unknown and cannot be reasonably ascertained;
- The name, address, and telephone number of the petitioner;
- The name, address, and telephone number of the person or persons, if any, proposed as guardian and standby guardian, the relationship of the proposed guardian or standby guardian to the person alleged to be incapacitated, and the reasons why the proposed guardian or standby guardian is suitable to exercise the powers necessary to assist the person alleged to be incapacitated (see §§ 22.40, 22.41, 22.73);
- Any provisional relief sought pursuant to Mental Hygiene Law Section 81.23 (see §§ 22.56–22.59);
- The available resources, if any, that have been considered by the petitioner and the petitioner's opinion as to their sufficiency and reliability;
- any other information which in the petitioner's opinion will assist the court evaluator in completing his or her investigation and report. (See §§ 22.25–22.27)

2. The petition shall be verified under oath.

§ 22.91 Drafting Checklists—Court Evaluator's Report

The court evaluator's written report and recommendations must comply with Mental Hygiene Law Section 81.09.

1. The report and recommendations shall include (see § 22.26):
    - The court evaluator's personal observations as to the person alleged to be incapacitated and his or her condition, affairs and situation. (See § 22.26)
    - Information in response to the following questions:
        (i) Does the person alleged to be incapacitated agree to the appointment of the proposed guardian and to the powers proposed for the guardian? (See § 22.35)
        (ii) Does the person wish legal counsel to be appointed or is the appointment of counsel otherwise appropriate? (See § 22.28)

(iii) Can the person alleged to be incapacitated come to the courthouse for the hearing? (*See* § 22.32)

(iv) If the person alleged to be incapacitated cannot come to the courthouse, is the person completely unable to participate in the hearing? (*See* § 22.32)

(v) If the person alleged to be incapacitated cannot come to the courthouse, would any meaningful participation result from the person's presence at the hearing? (*See* § 22.35)

(vi) Are available resources sufficient and reliable to provide for personal needs or property management without the appointment of a guardian? (*See* §§ 22.12, 22.14)

(vii) How is the person alleged to be incapacitated functioning with respect to the activities of daily living and what is the prognosis and reversibility of any physical and mental disabilities, alcoholism or substance dependence?

(viii) What is the person's understanding and appreciation of the nature and consequences of any inability to manage the activities of daily living?

(ix) What is the approximate value and nature of the financial resources of the person alleged to be incapacitated?

(x) What are the person's preferences, wishes, and values with regard to managing the activities of daily living? (*See* § 22.14)

(xi) Has the person alleged to be incapacitated made any appointment or delegation pursuant to a durable power of attorney, Do Not Resuscitate Order, health care proxy or a living will?

(xii) What would be the least restrictive form of intervention consistent with the person's functional level and the powers proposed for the guardian? (*See* § 22.14)

(xiii) What assistance is necessary for those who are financially dependent upon the person alleged to be incapacitated?

(xiv) Is the choice of proposed guardian appropriate, including a guardian nominated by the allegedly incapacitated person? (*See* § 22.40)

(xv) What steps has the proposed guardian taken or does the proposed guardian intend to take to identify and meet the current and emerging needs of the person alleged to be incapacitated? (*See* §§ 22.45–22.53)

§ 22.91 GUARDIANSHIP Ch. 22

(xvi) What potential conflicts of interest, if any, exist between or among family members and/or other interested parties regarding the proposed guardian or the proposed relief? (*See* §§ 22.40, 22.41)

(xvii) What potential conflicts of interest, if any, exist involving the person alleged to be incapacitated, the petitioner, and the proposed guardian? and

(xviii) Are there any additional persons who should be given notice and an opportunity to be heard? (*See* § 22.21)

- If the court evaluator took any steps to preserve the property of the person alleged to be incapacitated pending, the hearing the court evaluator's report shall include an explanation of the actions taken and the reasons for such actions.

§ 22.92 Drafting Checklists—Order and Judgment

The order and judgment in a proceeding to appoint an Article 81 guardian must reflect the disposition and findings of the court, as provided in Mental Hygiene Law Sections 81.15 and 81.16.

1. Finding of capacity: the order shall dismiss the petition. (*See* § 22.38)

2. Finding of incapacity without appointing a guardian (*see* § 22.38):

    - Authorize, direct, or ratify any transaction or series of transactions necessary to achieve any security, service, or care arrangement meeting the foreseeable needs of the incapacitated person; or

    - Did the court authorize, direct, or ratify any contract, trust, or other transaction relating to the incapacitated person's property and financial affairs?

3. Appointment of a special guardian. (*See* § 22.38) The order shall state:

    - The authority conferred upon the special guardian;

    - That the special guardian shall report to the court on all matters done pursuant to the order of appointment; and

    - That the special guardian shall serve until discharged by order of the court.

4. Appointment of a guardian:

    - If the person alleged to be incapacitated is found to have agreed to the appointment of a guardian, the order shall include the following findings (*see* § 22.35):

        (i) The person's agreement to the appointment;

(ii) The person's functional limitations which impair his or her ability to provide for personal needs or property management;

(iii) The necessity of the appointment of a guardian as a means of providing for personal needs and/or property management for the person;

(iv) The specific powers of the guardian, designed to accomplish the least restrictive form of intervention, which may include those powers specified in Mental Hygiene Law Sections 81.21 and 81.22 (*See* §§ 22.14, 22.47–22.53); and

(v) The duration of the appointment.

- If the person is found to be incapacitated, the order shall include the following findings (*see* § 22.38):

    (i) A determination that the appointment of a guardian is necessary;

    (ii) The powers granted to the guardian designed to accomplish the least restrictive form of intervention, which may include those powers specified in Mental Hygiene Law Sections 81.21 and 81.22 (*see* §§ 22.14, 22.47–22.53);

    (iii) Powers limited to those which the court has found necessary to assist the incapacitated person in providing for personal needs and/or property management;

    (iv) Where the guardian is appointed for personal needs, the order shall include the following (*see* § 22.53):

    1) The person's functional limitations which impair his or her ability to provide for personal needs;

    2) The person's lack of understanding and appreciation of the nature and consequences of his or her functional limitations;

    3) The likelihood that the person will suffer harm because of his or her functional limitations and inability to adequately understand and appreciate the nature and consequences of such functional limitations;

    4) The necessity of the appointment of a guardian to prevent such harm;

5) The specific powers of the guardian which constitute the least restrictive form of intervention; and

6) The duration of the appointment.

(v) Where the guardian is appointed for property management, the order shall include the following (*see* § 22.47):

1) The type and amount of the property and financial resources of the person alleged to be incapacitated;

2) The person's functional limitations which impair his or her ability with respect to property management;

3) The person's lack of understanding and appreciation of the nature and consequences of his or her functional limitations;

4) The likelihood that the person will suffer harm because of his or her functional limitations and inability to adequately understand and appreciate the nature and consequences of such functional limitations;

5) Any additional findings that are required under Mental Hygiene Law Section 81.21, Powers of guardian, property management;

6) The necessity of the appointment of a guardian to prevent such harm;

7) The specific powers of the guardian which constitute the least restrictive form of intervention; and

8) The duration of the appointment.

5. State the name, address and telephone number of the guardian.

6. Identify all persons entitled to notice of all further proceedings. (*See* § 22.21)

7. Provide for the compensation of the attorney for the petitioner. (*See* § 22.39)

8. Provide for payment of any fees for the court evaluator, witnesses, etc. (*See* § 22.27)

9. Provide for the amount of the bond to be filed by the guardian. (*See* § 22.42)

10. Direct that a judgment be entered determining the rights of the parties.

§ 22.93 Drafting Checklists—Initial Report of the Guardian

The requirements of the guardian's initial report are governed by Mental Hygiene Law Section 81.30 (see § 22.63):

1. Must be filed no later than 90 days after the issuance of the commission to the guardian.

2. Must state what steps the guardian has taken to fulfill his or her responsibilities.

3. Must include proof of completion of the guardian education requirements. (See § 22.76)

4. To the extent that the guardian has been granted powers with respect to property management, the initial report shall contain (see §§ 22.47–22.52):

    - A verified and complete inventory of the property and financial resources over which the guardian has control;

    - The location of any will executed by the incapacitated person;

    - The guardian's plan, consistent with the court's order of appointment, for the management of such property and financial resources, and any need for any change in the powers authorized by the court.

5. To the extent that the guardian has been granted powers regarding personal needs, the initial report shall contain, consistent with the court's order (see § 22.53):

    - A report of the guardian's personal visits with the incapacitated person;

    - The steps the guardian has taken to provide for the personal needs of that person;

    - The guardian's plan for providing for the personal needs of the incapacitated person;

    - A copy of any directives in accordance with any Do Not Resuscitate Order, health care proxy, living will, or any other advance directive; and

    - Any necessary change in the powers authorized by the court.

6. The guardian's plan for providing for the personal needs of the incapacitated person shall include the following information (see § 22.53):

    - The medical, dental, mental health, or related services that are to be provided for the welfare of the incapacitated person;

    - The social and personal services that are to be provided for the welfare of the incapacitated person;

§ 22.93   GUARDIANSHIP   Ch. 22

- Any physical, dental, and mental health examinations necessary to determine the medical, dental, and mental health treatment needs; and
- The application of health and accident insurance and any other private or government benefits to which the incapacitated person may be entitled to meet any part of the costs of medical, dental, mental health, or related services provided to the incapacitated person.

§ 22.94   Drafting Checklists—Annual Report

The requirements of the guardian's annual report are governed by Mental Hygiene Law Section 81.31 (*see* § 22.64):

1. Shall be filed annually in the month of May, or at any other time upon motion or order of the court.
2. Shall include the following information:
   - The present address and telephone number of the guardian;
   - The present address, and telephone number of the incapacitated person; if the incapacitated person does not reside in his or her personal home, the name, address, and telephone number of the facility or place at which the person resides and the name of the chief executive officer of the facility or person otherwise responsible for the person's care;
   - Any major changes in the physical or mental condition of the incapacitated person and any substantial change in medication;
   - The date that the incapacitated person was last examined or otherwise seen by a physician and the purpose of that visit;
   - A statement by a physician, psychologist, nurse clinician, or social worker, or other person that has evaluated or examined the incapacitated person within the three months prior to the filing of the report, regarding an evaluation of the incapacitated person's condition and his or her current functional level;
   - To the extent the guardian is charged with providing for the personal needs of the incapacitated person, the annual report shall include the following (*see* § 22.53):

     (i) A statement of whether the current residential setting is best suited to the current needs of the incapacitated person;

     (ii) A resume of any professional medical treatment given to the incapacitated person in the preceding year;

(iii) The plan for medical, dental, and mental health treatment, and related services in the coming year;

(iv) Information concerning the social condition of the incapacitated person, including: the social and personal services currently utilized; his or her social skills; and his or her social needs.

- To the extent the guardian is charged with property management, information required by the provisions of SCPA Section 1719 prescribing the form of papers to be filed upon the annual accounting of a general guardian of an infant's property (*see* §§ 22.47–22.52);
- Where the guardian has used or employed the services of the incapacitated person or where moneys have been earned by or received on behalf of such incapacitated person an accounting of any moneys earned or derived from such services;
- A resume of any other activities performed by the guardian on behalf of the incapacitated person;
- Facts indicating the need to terminate the appointment of the guardian, or for any alteration in the powers of the guardian and what specific authority is requested or what specific authority of the guardian will be affected; and
- Any other information which the guardian may be required to file by the order of appointment.

§ 22.95 Drafting Checklists—Decree Approving Accounts

The requirements of a decree approving accounts is governed by Mental Hygiene Law Section 81.34. (*See* § 22.67) The decree shall:

1. Indicate whether the incapacitated person has died or the guardian has died, or has been removed, suspended, or discharged, or allowed to resign.
2. Set forth all pleadings and other documents upon which the order is based.
3. Include a summary statement of the amounts with which the guardian is charged and credited.
4. Set forth the commissions of the guardian. (*See* § 22.61)
5. Set forth the compensation and expenses to be paid to the attorney for the guardian.
6. If the incapacitated person has died, a direction that the balance of any property of the incapacitated person be transferred to his or her personal representative.

§ 22.95 GUARDIANSHIP Ch. 22

7. If the guardian has died, or has been removed, suspended, or discharged, or allowed to resign, and a successor guardian appointed, a direction that the property of the incapacitated person be transferred to the successor guardian. (*See* §§ 22.69–22.73)

8. A direction that upon proof of service of a copy of the order with notice of entry upon all parties who have appeared, and upon satisfying the court by receipts, and an affidavit that the payments directed have been made and the terms of the order have been fully complied with, that an order may be entered discharging the guardian and canceling the bond and discharging the surety from all liability thereunder as to all matters embraced in the Final Account.

Library References:

West's Key No. Digests, Guardian and Ward ⚖111; Mental Health ⚖211–275, 291–313.

§ 22.96 Drafting Checklists—Petition on Proceeding to Discover Property Withheld

Mental Hygiene Law Section 81.44 governs proceedings to discover property withheld. (*See* §§ 22.81–22.86)

1. The guardian may commence a proceeding to discover property withheld if it is within the authority granted by the court. It is necessary, therefore, to ascertain the guardian's powers and set forth the authority to commence the proceeding.

2. The petition shall contain knowledge, or information and belief, of the following (*see* § 22.82):

   - Any facts tending to show that any interest in real property or money or other personal property, or the proceeds or value thereof, which should be delivered and paid to the guardian, is in the possession, under the control, or within the knowledge or information of the respondent, who is withholding the property from the guardian;

   - Whether such possession or control was obtained before or after the appointment of the guardian;

   - Whether the respondent refuses to disclose knowledge or information which such person may have concerning the property or which will aid the guardian in discovery of such property; and

   - Request that respondent be ordered to attend an inquiry and be examined, and deliver property of the incapacitated person if it is within his or her control.

3. The petition may be accompanied by an affidavit or other written evidence, in support of the allegations of the petition.

§ 22.97 Forms

The sections which follow include the essential forms for commencing a proceeding to appoint a guardian pursuant to Mental Hygiene Law Article 81, the forms required of the guardian to qualify for such position, and the reports which the guardian must file during the course of the guardianship. Each form sets forth the general requirements and necessary allegations applicable to such a proceeding. The practitioner must adapt the forms to the particular facts in the specific guardianship proceeding.

Library References:

West's Key No. Digests, Guardian and Ward ⚖111; Mental Health ⚖211–275, 291–313.

§ 22.98 Forms—Order to Show Cause[1]

At a _____ Part _____ of the Supreme Court of the State of New York, held in and for the County of _____, at the Courthouse, located at _____, New York on the _____ day of _____, 19__.

PRESENT:
    HON. _____, JUSTICE

_____

In the Matter of the Application of)
_____,)
                                    Petitioner,)

For the Appointment of a Guardian) Order to Show Cause
for the Personal Needs and Property)
Management of) Index. No. _____
_____,)
)
A Person Alleged to be Incapacitated,)
)
                                    Respondent.)
_____

§ 22.98

1. See supra, § 22.22 for discussion of the notice requirements applicable to a proceeding to appoint a guardian.

§ 22.98 GUARDIANSHIP Ch. 22

IMPORTANT[2]

AN APPLICATION HAS BEEN FILED IN COURT BY _____ WHO BELIEVES YOU MAY BE UNABLE TO TAKE CARE OF YOUR PERSONAL NEEDS OR FINANCIAL AFFAIRS. _____ IS ASKING THAT SOMEONE BE APPOINTED TO MAKE DECISIONS FOR YOU. WITH THIS PAPER IS A COPY OF THE APPLICATION TO THE COURT SHOWING WHY _____ BELIEVES YOU MAY BE UNABLE TO TAKE CARE OF YOUR PERSONAL NEEDS OR FINANCIAL AFFAIRS. BEFORE THE COURT MAKES THE APPOINTMENT OF SOMEONE TO MAKE DECISIONS FOR YOU THE COURT HOLDS A HEARING AT WHICH YOU ARE ENTITLED TO BE PRESENT AND TO TELL THE JUDGE IF YOU DO NOT WANT ANYONE APPOINTED. THIS PAPER TELLS YOU WHEN THE COURT HEARING WILL TAKE PLACE. IF YOU DO NOT APPEAR IN COURT, YOUR RIGHTS MAY BE SERIOUSLY AFFECTED.

YOU HAVE THE RIGHT TO DEMAND A TRIAL BY JURY. YOU MUST TELL THE COURT IF YOU WISH TO HAVE A TRIAL BY JURY. IF YOU DO NOT TELL THE COURT, THE HEARING WILL BE CONDUCTED WITHOUT A JURY. THE NAME AND ADDRESS, AND TELEPHONE NUMBER OF THE CLERK OF THE COURT ARE: _____.

THE COURT HAS APPOINTED A COURT EVALUATOR TO EXPLAIN THIS PROCEEDING TO YOU AND TO INVESTIGATE THE CLAIMS MADE IN THE APPLICATION. THE COURT MAY GIVE THE COURT EVALUATOR PERMISSION TO INSPECT YOUR MEDICAL, PSYCHOLOGICAL, OR PSYCHIATRIC RECORDS. YOU HAVE THE RIGHT TO TELL THE JUDGE IF YOU DO NOT WANT THE COURT EVALUATOR TO BE GIVEN THAT PERMISSION. THE COURT EVALUATOR'S NAME, ADDRESS, AND TELEPHONE NUMBER ARE: _____.

YOU ARE ENTITLED TO HAVE A LAWYER OF YOUR CHOICE REPRESENT YOU. IF YOU WANT THE COURT TO APPOINT A LAWYER TO HELP YOU AND REPRESENT YOU, THE COURT WILL APPOINT A LAWYER FOR YOU. YOU WILL BE REQUIRED TO PAY THAT LAWYER UNLESS YOU DO NOT HAVE THE MONEY TO DO SO.

On reading and filing the annexed petition of _____, duly verified the ___ day of _____, 19__, and the affirmation of _____, dated _____, 19__, and the affirmation of _____ dated _____, 19__, and the exhibits annexed hereto, from which it appears that _____, the

---

2. This legend must appear on the face of the order to show cause and must be in twelve point or larger bold face double spaced type. Mental Hygiene Law § 81.07(c). See supra, § 22.22.

alleged incapacitated person herein, resides at _____, is a domiciliary of the County of _____, New York, is unable to provide for his [her] personal needs and [or] to manage his [her] property and financial affairs, it is

ORDERED, that _____, the alleged incapacitated person, _____, the Court Evaluator, and the attorney for the alleged incapacitated person, hereinafter named, show cause at Part _____, Room _____ of this Court, to be held at the Courthouse located at _____, New York, on the _____ day of _____, 19__, at ___ A.M. [P.M.] or as soon thereafter as counsel can be heard, why an Order should not be entered:

1. Appointing a Guardian for personal needs and [or] property management of the alleged incapacitated person who shall have the power to: manage the alleged incapacitated person's financial affairs and property matters, provide the alleged incapacitated person with home care services, place the alleged incapacitated person into a nursing home, arrange for medical care and treatment, prepare and execute a trust agreement, reimburse the Medicaid program for money expended on behalf of the alleged incapacitated person to provide heavy duty cleaning of his [her] apartment [*Set forth any other powers which the petitioner seeks for the guardian*];[3]

2. Appointing a temporary guardian for the personal needs or property management of the alleged incapacitated person who shall have the power to: [*Set forth powers sought for the temporary guardian*][4]

3. Awarding reasonable counsel fees to the petitioner herein;[5]

4. Granting such other, further or different relief as may be just and proper; and it is further

ORDERED, that _____, at _____, New York, telephone number _____, upon filing his [her] consent and affidavit of responsibility be and hereby is appointed Court Evaluator for the above-named alleged incapacitated person to appear for and protect his [her] interests in this proceeding, upon duly qualifying and consenting according to law, complying with Part 36 of the rules of the Chief Judge and filing the certificate required by Section 36.1(d) and the notice of appointment required by Section 36.3 of the Rules of the Chief Judge;[6]

and it is further

ORDERED, that _____, at _____, New York, telephone number _____, upon filing his [her] notice of appearance be and hereby is appointed attorney for the above-named alleged incapacitated person to

---

3. See supra, §§ 22.46, et seq., for discussion of duties and powers of guardian.

4. See supra, § 22.57.

5. See supra, § 22.39.

6. See Rules of the Chief Judge, 22 NYCRR Pt. 36, Appointment of Guardians, Guardians Ad Litem, Court Evaluators, Attorneys for Incapacitated Persons, Receivers, Persons Designated to Perform Services for a Receiver, and Referees. See supra, § 22.25 for discussion of court evaluator.

appear for and represent the alleged incapacitated person in this proceeding;[7] and it is further

ORDERED, that _____, at _____, New York, telephone number _____, upon issuance of the commission of temporary guardianship be and hereby is appointed temporary guardian for the above-named alleged incapacitated person with the following powers and duties: [*Set forth powers granted to temporary guardian*]

STATEMENT OF ALLEGED INCAPACITATED PERSON'S RIGHTS

In a proceeding brought pursuant to this article any party to the proceeding shall have the right to:[8]

1. present evidence;
2. call witnesses, including expert witnesses;
3. cross examine witnesses, including witnesses called by the court;
4. be represented by counsel of his or her choice.

The hearing must be conducted in the presence of the person alleged to be incapacitated,[9] either at the courthouse or where the person alleged to be incapacitated resides, so as to permit the court to obtain its own impression of the person's capacity. If the person alleged to be incapacitated physically cannot come or be brought to the courthouse, the hearing must be conducted where the person alleged to be incapacitated resides unless:

1. the person is not present in the state; or
2. all the information before the court clearly establishes that (i) the person alleged to be incapacitated is completely unable to participate in the hearing or (ii) no meaningful participation will result from the person's presence at the hearing.

If the hearing is conducted without the presence of the person alleged to be incapacitated and the court appoints a guardian, the order of appointment shall set forth the factual basis for conducting the hearing without the presence of the person for whom the appointment is made.

If the hearing is conducted in the presence of the person alleged to be incapacitated and the person is not represented by counsel, the court shall explain to that person, on the record, the purpose and possible consequences of the proceeding, the right to be represented by counsel, and the fact that the court will appoint an attorney to represent the person alleged to be incapacitated if the person wishes to be represented by counsel, and shall inquire of the person whether he or she wishes to

---

7. *See supra*, § 22.28 for discussion of appointment of counsel for alleged incapacitated person.

8. *See supra*, §§ 22.30, *et seq.*, for discussion of hearing on proceeding to appoint a guardian.

9. *See supra*, § 22.32.

have an attorney appointed. If the person refuses the assistance of counsel, the court may nevertheless appoint counsel if the court is not satisfied that the person is capable of making an informed decision regarding the appointment of counsel.

If any party to the proceeding on or before the return date designated in the order to show cause raises issues of fact regarding the need for an appointment under this Article 81 and demands a jury trial of such issues, the court shall order a trial by jury thereof. Failure to make such a demand shall be deemed a waiver of the right to trial by jury.

SUFFICIENT CAUSE APPEARING THEREFOR,

LET fourteen (14) days service by personal delivery of a copy of this Order to Show Cause and petition upon the alleged incapacitated person, be deemed good and sufficient and let service of a copy of this Order to Show Cause and petition by regular mail or delivery to the office of the Court Evaluator, _____, and Court Appointed Attorney, _____, and temporary guardian, _____, on or before the ___ day of _____, 19__, be deemed good and sufficient.

ENTER

_____
Justice of the Supreme Court

Library References:

West's Key No. Digests, Guardian and Ward ⚖111; Mental Health ⚖211–275, 291–313.

§ 22.99 Forms—Petition[1]

SUPREME COURT OF THE STATE OF NEW YORK
COUNTY OF _____

In the Matter of the Application of _____, Petitioner,	))))))
For the Appointment of a Guardian for the Personal Needs and Property Management of _____,	) Petition)) Index. No. _____))
A Person Alleged to be Incapacitated, Respondent.	))))

§ 22.99

1. See supra, § 22.23.

TO THE SUPREME COURT OF THE STATE OF NEW YORK: COUNTY OF _____.

The petition of _____ respectfully states and alleges:

1. _____ is an alleged incapacitated person who is ___ years of age and resides at _____ Street, _____, New York. Such person's telephone number is _____.

2. The alleged incapacitated person resides with the following person(s): [*Enter Name(s)*] _____ at [*Enter Address(es)*] _____. Such person(s) telephone number(s) is [*are*] _____.

3. [*Set forth a description of the alleged incapacitated person's functional level including that person's ability to manage the activities of daily living, behavior, and understanding and appreciation of the nature and consequences of any inability to manage the activities of daily living.*]

4. Petitioner seeks the following powers with respect to the personal needs of the alleged incapacitated person: [*If powers are sought with respect to the PERSONAL NEEDS*[2] *of the alleged incapacitated person, set forth specific allegations as to the personal actions or other actual occurrences involving the person alleged to be incapacitated which are claimed to demonstrate that the person is likely to suffer harm because he or she cannot adequately understand and appreciate the nature and consequences of his or her inability to provide for personal needs.*]

5. Petitioner seeks the following powers with respect to property management for the alleged incapacitated person: [*If powers are sought with respect to PROPERTY MANAGEMENT*[3] *for the alleged incapacitated person, set forth specific factual allegations as to the financial transactions or other actual occurrences involving the person alleged to be incapacitated which are claimed to demonstrate that the person is likely to suffer harm because he or she cannot adequately understand and appreciate the nature and consequences of his or her inability to provide for property management.*]

6. [*Set forth the particular powers being sought and their relationship to the functional level and needs of the person alleged to be incapacitated.*][4]

7. The duration of the powers being sought shall be until [*set forth*].

8. The approximate value and description of the financial resources of _____, the person alleged to be incapacitated, are, to the best of Petitioner's information, as follows: [*set forth*]. To the best of the

---

2. *See* Mental Hygiene Law § 81.22 discussed *supra* at § 22.53.

3. *See* Mental Hygiene Law § 81.21, discussed *supra* at § 22.47.

4. *See supra*, §§ 22.46–22.53 for discussion of duties and powers of guardian.

Petitioner's knowledge, _____, the person is [*is not*] a recipient of public assistance.

9. To the best of Petitioner's knowledge, the nature and amount of all claims, debts, or obligations of _____, the person alleged to be incapacitated, are as follows: [*set forth*].

10. The names, addresses, and telephone numbers of the presumptive distributees of _____, the person alleged to be incapacitated, as that term is defined in Surrogate's Court Procedure Act section 103(42) are as follows: [*set forth*]. [*State if any are unknown or cannot be reasonably ascertained.*]

11. The name, address and telephone number of petitioner are as follows: [*Enter name*] [*Enter address*] [*Enter telephone number*].

12. The name, address and telephone number of the person or persons proposed as guardian and standby guardian are [*Enter name*] [*Enter address*] [*Enter telephone number*] [*If none, so state*]. The relationship of the proposed guardian or standby guardian to the person alleged to be incapacitated is as follows: [*Enter relationship; if none, so state*]. The reasons why the proposed guardian or standby guardian is suitable to exercise the powers necessary to assist the person alleged to be incapacitated are as follows: [*Set forth reasons*].

13. [*Set forth any relief sought pursuant to Mental Hygiene Law Section 81.23 (provisional remedies such as temporary guardian, injunction and temporary restraining order).*][5]

14. [*Set forth the available resources,*[6] *if any, that have been considered by the petitioner and the petitioner's opinion as to their sufficiency and reliability.*]

15. [*Set forth any other information which in the petitioner's opinion will assist the court evaluator in completing the investigation and report in accordance with Mental Hygiene Law Section 81.09.*][7]

16. No previous application has been made to any other court or judge for the relief requested herein. [*If there has been, recite the history.*]

WHEREFORE, Petitioner respectfully requests that the court sign the order to show cause[8] annexed hereto requiring [*Enter name of alleged incapacitated person, the named court evaluator and anyone else entitled to notice*] to show cause why a guardian should not be appointed pursuant to Article 81 of the Mental Hygiene Law of the State of New York for the above reasons and with the powers requested herein, and

---

5. *See supra*, § 22.56, *et seq.*

6. *See supra*, § 22.9 for definition of available resources.

7. *See supra*, § 22.26; *see infra*, § 22.100 for form of court evaluator's report.

8. *See supra*, § 22.98.

§ 22.99 GUARDIANSHIP Ch. 22

for such other and further relief as to the court may seem just and proper.

Dated this _____ day of _____, 19__.

[Signed] _____

[Typed Name]

PETITIONER

_____

Attorney for Petitioner
[Address]
[Telephone]

VERIFICATION

STATE OF NEW YORK)
) ss.:
COUNTY OF _____)

[Enter name of petitioner] [being duly sworn] [affirms] that I am the petitioner herein, that I have read the foregoing petition and that the same is true to the best of my knowledge and belief.

[Signed] _____

[Typed Name]

PETITIONER

Sworn [Affirmed] to before me this ___ day of _____, 19__

_____

NOTARY PUBLIC

Library References:

West's Key No. Digests, Guardian and Ward ⚖111; Mental Health ⚖211–275, 291–313.

§ 22.100 Forms—Court Evaluator's Report

SUPREME COURT OF THE STATE OF NEW YORK
COUNTY OF _____

_____
In the Matter of the Application of)
_____,   )
)
                      Petitioner,   )
)
For the Appointment of a Guardian   ) Report of Court Evaluator
for the Personal Needs and Property)
Management of   ) Index. No. _____
)
_____,   )
)
A Person Alleged to be Incapacitated,)
)
                      Respondent.   )
_____

TO THE SUPREME COURT OF THE STATE OF NEW YORK: COUNTY OF _____

I, _____, [set forth whether attorney-at-law, physician, psychologist, accountant, social worker, or nurse, or other position], having been appointed as Court Evaluator[1] in this proceeding, respectfully reports to the Court as follows:

1. I was duly appointed as Court Evaluator by Order of the Hon. _____, on _____, 19__.

2. I duly filed the Certification of Compliance[2] and Statement of Appointment.[3]

3. I was served with and received a complete copy of the Order of Hon. _____, and the papers upon which the Order was based. I ascertained that I had no adverse interest or conflict with the alleged incapacitated person, _____, (AIP) nor was I related to, nor connected in business with any party in this proceeding, or the attorney for any party in the proceeding, nor was I entitled to share in the Estate and property in which the AIP has any interest.[4]

4. I duly qualified as Court Evaluator to protect the rights and interests of the AIP, by executing, serving, and filing my Consent and Affidavit of Responsibility with the Court.

---

§ 22.100
1. See supra, §§ 22.25–22.27 for discussion of court evaluator.
2. Office of Court Administration Form UCS 830.3, filed pursuant to 22 NYCRR Pt. 36, § 36.3(a), Reporting of Appointments.
3. Office of Court Administration Form UCS 830.2, filed pursuant to 22 NYCRR Pt. 36, § 36.3(a), Reporting of Appointments.
4. 22 NYCRR Pt. 36, Appointment of Fiduciaries, § 36.1, Appointments.

5. On [*date of visit*], I met with _____, the AIP, at his [*her*] home at [*address*]. [*Set forth the details of the visit with the AIP, describing the setting, i.e., whether the AIP's home, or a nursing home, hospital, or other circumstances; the nature of the discussion; the AIP's responses; the living arrangements; the AIP's alertness; whether the AIP understood the nature of the proceedings and the questions asked; whether the AIP knew the names of the relatives listed in the Petition, his [her] date of birth, where he [she] was living, the extent of his [her] assets; etc.*]

[*If the AIP was in a nursing home or hospital, describe the type of facility and the surroundings; the room the AIP occupied; etc.*]

[*If at home and there was a home care person present, indicate any discussions regarding such person's background, length of service for the AIP, days and hours of work, any visitors to the AIP, activities of the AIP, etc.*]

[*Set forth any discussions with any social worker at the hospital or other facility; nurses; hospital staff; inquiries regarding whether any relatives or friends visited the AIP; who seemed involved with the care of the AIP; etc.*]

6. I contacted and spoke with the following relatives: [*provide information and details, family tree, relationship with the AIP and when such person(s) last visited; if there are no close relatives, describe the relationship with the proposed Guardian; was the AIP ever married; did he [she] have any children; etc.*]

7. [*Describe discussions with the AIP's doctors; provide information concerning medical condition; medication being taken by AIP; therapy; prognosis.*][5]

8. I met with _____, the Proposed Guardian on _____, 19__. [*Provide details including the relationship between the proposed guardian and the AIP; education and financial background of the proposed guardian; proposed plan and the duties and responsibilities of the guardian; etc.*].

9. I have independently investigated and confirmed the assets of the AIP to be as follows:

(a) The AIP receives Social Security in the sum of $_____ per month which is automatically deposited to his [*her*] account in _____ Bank.

(b) The AIP is entitled to a pension in the sum of $_____ per month from _____ Co.

---

5. *But see supra*, §§ 22.26, 22.33, discussing the application of the physician-patient privilege and the need for a court order allowing the court evaluator to review the alleged incapacitated person's medical records.

(c) The AIP has assets in the following banks: [*set forth names and addresses of bank; account numbers; balances in accounts*].

(d) The AIP has a stock portfolio and securities with _____ Co. which includes the following securities: [*set forth the number of shares in each holding; approximate value, and annual dividends; set forth any bonds and their approximate value; etc.*].

(e) The AIP also holds the following investments individually: [*set forth the number of shares in each holding; the approximate value; annual dividends; whether any dividends are subject to an automatic reinvestment plan*].

(f) [*Set forth if the AIP is the beneficiary of any insurance policies which are currently available; set forth the value of the insurance proceeds available to the AIP and the steps necessary to obtain the proceeds for the AIP.*]

(g) [*Set forth if the AIP is the beneficiary of any currently pending estate proceeding; set forth the approximate value of the estate and the steps taken and those which are necessary to obtain the AIP's share.*]

(h) [*Set forth whether there are any jointly held assets, including any bank accounts, and the value of the AIP's share.*]

(i) [*Set forth if there are any Totten trust accounts; the identity of the beneficiary; the value of the accounts; location of the accounts; whether the accounts should be turned over to a guardian if one is appointed.*]

(j) [*State whether the AIP has a safe deposit box; its location; whether anyone other than the AIP has access to the box; whether a key is available; whether an inventory of the contents of the safe deposit box should be ordered by the court.*]

10. I have reviewed the proposed plan with the nominated Guardian, the AIP's family and the AIP's physician(s). The AIP is currently in the _____ Nursing Home and is receiving good care. However, based upon the medical information, the AIP should be able to return to his [*her*] home within the next few months provided adequate home care is provided. [*Set forth any available details of a home care plan for the AIP, including the nature of the care necessary; the amount of daily hours it should be available; etc.*]

11. [*Set forth the identity of any experts that were contacted with the court's permission and attach any reports from such experts.*]

12. I obtained access to the AIP's apartment with the permission of the landlord and have inventoried the contents of the apartment. Present at the time of the inventory was _____, the social worker. Attached

§ 22.100 GUARDIANSHIP Ch. 22

is a copy of the inventory. [*Set forth the value of any cash or other property found in the apartment and the actions taken to preserve such property, i.e., depositing cash in a bank account; placing jewelry in a safe deposit box; etc.*] In addition, to secure the property remaining in the apartment, I had the lock changed and arranged with the landlord that the keys would be provided to the Guardian to be appointed.

13. I reviewed the mail that had accumulated at the AIP's apartment and based on the information obtained from the mail, I contacted various banks and financial institutions to ascertain whether the AIP has other assets. [*Set forth the details of any financial information obtained.*]

14. In my opinion, _____, the alleged incapacitated person does need a Guardian as he [she] is not able to properly manage his [her] own affairs and personal needs. A Guardian should be appointed as soon as possible, with the powers outlined below.

15. [*Set forth whether the petitioner is a proper Guardian and the reasons why such person should, or should not, be appointed as Guardian of the AIP.*]

16. [*Set forth whether the AIP has previously designated a person as a nominated guardian and the identity of such person and the reasons why such person should, or should not, be appointed the Guardian of the AIP.*]

17. [*Set forth the powers which are deemed necessary for a Guardian, in consideration of the principle of granting only those powers which are necessary to provide for the personal needs and [or] property management of the incapacitated person in such manner as appropriate to the individual and which constitute the least restrictive form of intervention.*][6]

Respectfully submitted this _____ day of _____, 19__

[Signed] _____

[Typed Name]

Court Evaluator

Library References:

West's Key No. Digests, Guardian and Ward ⟐111; Mental Health ⟐211–275, 291–313.

6. *See supra*, §§ 22.47, *et seq.*, for discussion of powers of guardian. *See also supra*, § 22.14 for discussion of least restrictive form of intervention.

§ 22.101 Forms—Order and Judgment Appointing Guardian of the Person and Property[1]

At an IAS Part _____ of the Supreme Court of the State of New York, held in and for the County of _____ at the Courthouse, located at _____, New York on the _____ day of _____, 19__

PRESENT:

    HON. _____, JUSTICE

In the Matter of the Application of

_____,

              Petitioner,

For the Appointment of a Guardian for the Personal Needs and Property Management of

_____,

A Person Alleged to be Incapacitated,

              Respondent.

Judgment and Order

Index. No. _____

A Petition, verified by _____, on _____, 19__, having been presented to this Court, alleging that _____, is so mentally and physically incapacitated as to require the appointment of a Guardian for Personal Needs and Property Management; and

An Order to Show Cause containing the required Notice having been signed by this Court on _____, 19__, directing _____ [*set forth parties whose appearance was directed*][2] to show cause why a Guardian for the Personal Needs and Property Management should not be appointed for _____, and granting other relief and _____, having been appointed as Court Evaluator[3] and having duly appeared as such, and _____, Esq.,

---

§ 22.101

1. *See, e.g.*, Matter of Bailin (Geiger), N.Y.L.J., 5/19/95, p.36, col.4 (Sup.Ct., Rockland County) and Matter of Zarriello, N.Y.L.J., 1/25/95, p.32, col.5 (Sup.Ct., Rockland County), for decisions showing required findings and conclusions of law for appointment of guardian.

2. *See supra*, § 22.21 for persons entitled to notice.

3. *See supra*, §§ 22.25–22.27 for discussion of court evaluator.

§ 22.101

having been appointed as attorney[4] for the alleged incapacitated person and having appeared on behalf of the alleged incapacitated person, and _____, Esq., having appeared for the Petitioner, and this matter having regularly come on for hearing on _____, 19__, and

This Court having taken testimony in court [*having visited and taken the testimony*] of the Respondent, _____, the person alleged to be incapacitated, on _____, 19__, and having read the Court Evaluator's report[5] and heard testimony and argument from the Petitioner, [*his medical expert,* _____, *M.D.*],[6] _____, the Court Evaluator, and [_____, *the Respondent's internist-geriatrician,*][7] as well as expert testimony on home care programs from the Court Evaluator's witness, _____, and upon all the pleadings and proceedings heretofore had herein, and due deliberation having been had, it is found and determined that:

1. _____ has suffered a series of mini-strokes which have impeded him [*her*] ability to be fully ambulatory without assistance and have caused him [*her*] to suffer minimal paralysis to his [*her*] left arm and hand, and some degree of memory impairment;

2. _____ can ambulate with assistance in his [*her*] home and has, by clear and convincing evidence, rejected the services of a nursing facility and expressed a desire to remain in his [*her*] home;

3. _____ recognizes that he [*she*] requires some assistance with personal care and money management in order to remain in his [*her*] home, and does not object to the provision of such assistance;

4. _____ does not currently have a trust or other protective arrangement in place, and is unable to designate a third party whom he [*she*] wants or trusts to assist him [*her*] with his [*her*] personal and financial needs;

5. _____'s personal and financial needs include assistance with housekeeping; nutrition; physical therapy; visits to physicians and [*or*] obtaining a homecare physician and podiatrist; bathing, dressing, cooking, toileting, and recreational visits outside his [*her*] home; shopping; paying rent, utilities, insurance premiums and other bills; reconciling bank statements and making deposits; submitting and collecting Medicare and other insurance claims; filing tax returns; renewing his [*her*] apartment lease and vacating a pending eviction proceeding; collecting social security and pension payments; [*set forth any other needs of the respondent as found by the court*]; and

4. See supra, § 22.28 for discussion of appointment of counsel for alleged incapacitated person.

5. See supra, § 22.100.

6. See supra, §§ 22.26, 22.33, discussing the application of the physician-patient privilege and the propriety of allowing medical testimony.

7. Id.

Ch. 22 JUDGMENT APPOINTING GUARDIAN § 22.101

6. Without the assistance of home attendants and someone to help procure and supervise such care, obtain other necessary medical-related equipment, ambulation assistance, as well as meet monthly bills and resolve the other matters set forth above, _____ is likely to suffer serious physical and financial harm and lose the opportunity to remain in his [her] home;

NOW on motion of _____, Esq., attorney for the petitioner, it is hereby

ORDERED that _____ be and hereby is determined to be a person requiring the appointment of a Guardian for Personal Needs and Property Management as the court has found that said incapacitated person is likely to suffer harm because of the inability to provide for personal needs and property management and is unable to adequately understand and appreciate the nature and consequences of such inability; and it is further

ORDERED that _____, Esq., whose address and telephone number is _____ Street, _____, New York, _____, be and he [she] hereby is appointed _____ 's Guardian for Personal Needs and Property Management with the usual powers incident thereto and the following specific powers set forth herein, upon his [her] filing with this Court a Bond[8] in the sum of $_____, and such other papers as are necessary to qualify as such Guardian, including the designation required under Mental Hygiene Law Section 81.26[9] and Forms 830.1 and 830.2 required by the Office of Court Administration, upon condition that he [she] will in all things faithfully discharge the trust imposed upon him [her] and obey all directions of this Court in regard to such trust, will make and render an initial report[10] on his [her] activities on behalf of _____ and his [her] property within ninety (90) days of issuance of his [her] Guardian Commission,[11] with proof that he [she] has completed those requirements of the Guardian education training[12] not otherwise dispensed with in this Order, and will otherwise make and render a just and true account to this Court of all monies and [or] other property received by him [her] as Guardian annually in May of each year in compliance with Mental Hygiene Law Section 81.31(a)[13] and at such other and further times as she may be required to do so by this Court, together with his [her] annual report concerning the status and progress of _____ in compliance with the requirements of Mental Hygiene Law Section 81.31(b); and it is further

8. See supra, § 22.42 for discussion of requirement of bond.

9. See supra, § 22.43; see infra, § 22.102 for form of designation and oath of guardian.

10. See supra, § 22.63; see infra, § 22.104 for form of initial report of guardian.

11. See supra, § 22.43; see infra, § 22.103 for form of commission.

12. See supra, § 22.76.

13. See supra, § 22.64; see infra, § 22.105 for form of annual report of guardian.

§ 22.101 GUARDIANSHIP Ch. 22

ORDERED that upon filing such bond and designation as required by statute, a Commission in due form shall be issued to the Guardian by the Clerk of the County of _____ ; and it is further

ORDERED that the duration of the appointment of the Guardian hereunder shall be for an indefinite time, subject to the reporting requirements herein set forth and the requirements of Mental Hygiene Law Section 81.31(b)(10); and it is further

ORDERED that the authority of the Guardian shall extend to all of the property, assets and income of _____ both real and personal, in whatever form, including government benefits, entitlements, and foreign pensions, as well as the contents of any safe deposit box or vault in which _____ may have an interest; and it is further

ORDERED that all persons, including banking and other financial entities, are hereby directed and commanded to deliver forthwith to the Guardian upon his [her] personal demand and presentation of a certified copy of his [her] Guardian Commission, without more, all of the property of _____ of every kind and nature; and it is further

ORDERED that upon qualifying the Guardian shall marshall _____ 's assets and shall invest and reinvest them as would a prudent investor of discretion and intelligence in such matters seeking reasonable income and shall apply so much of the income and principal as is necessary for the comfort, support, maintenance, well-being, expenses and recreation of _____, retaining for _____ such assets and property as shall be considered exempt or non-countable in the event _____ shall become eligible for government entitlements, the eligibility for which is keyed to resource and income limitations, and to obtain the same for him [her] as, if, and when he [she] becomes eligible therefor, in the Guardian's discretion; and it is further

ORDERED, that the application for placement of _____ in a nursing facility is denied; and it is further

ORDERED that absent an emergency, _____ may not be moved to a nursing home facility without an Order of this Court procured by the Guardian and, in the event of an emergency requiring transfer of _____ to such facility, the Guardian shall notify this Court within forty-eight (48) hours of such transfer and shall comply with any further order of this Court made at such time; and it is further

ORDERED that the Guardian shall do whatever is necessary to renovate _____ 's apartment and maintain it in a reasonably safe and habitable condition providing _____ with services of one or more aides to cook, clean, shop, and otherwise assist _____ to bathe, dress, and attend to his [her] personal needs and social and recreational activities, and shall also arrange appropriate visits from the Visiting Nurse Service including monitoring by a registered or practical nurse, plus physical therapy, and physician services, all such services to be coordinated by a licensed and qualified internist with certification of special knowledge of geriatric medicine; and it is further

ORDERED that the Guardian shall make all necessary arrangements with the physician and visiting nurse to obtain for _____, use of appropriate medical equipment, such as a hospital bed, a wheelchair, a walker, [*set forth all such equipment needed by the incapacitated person*], so as to assist _____, both in and out of his [*her*] home; and it is further

ORDERED that the Guardian shall arrange for _____ 's taxes and returns to be brought current, and to vacate the pending eviction proceeding, as well as make claims with the Social Security Administration to replace any and all social security checks alleged to be missing and the Guardian shall apply to become _____ 's representative payee for all future social security checks; and it is further

ORDERED that the Guardian shall arrange for transportation to the _____ Senior Citizen Center through _____ or other similar non-profit transportation company for disabled individuals; and it is further

ORDERED that the Guardian shall visit _____ at least four (4) times per year;[14] and it is further

ORDERED that the Guardian shall not impose additional services to those set forth in this Order over the opposition of _____ without further order of this Court; and it is further

ORDERED that the guardian shall permit _____ to participate in decisions concerning his [*her*] activities of daily living to the extent he [*she*] is currently and [*or*] shall in the future be able to do so, shall honor the expressed medical decisions of _____, and shall employ the least restrictive alternative for _____ in carrying out the orders of this Court; and it is further

ORDERED that the following property of _____ shall be placed under Guardianship, together with any other property that may be traced by the Guardian from time to time:

[*Set forth all known property of the incapacitated person and the location of such property, such as, bank accounts in whatever form held; certificates of deposit; uncashed checks; social security benefits; pension benefits; other real and personal property; as the Court directs to be held by the Guardian*]; and it is further

ORDERED that the compensation of the Guardian for Property Management services shall be as set forth for trustees in SCPA Section 2309, with leave to the Guardian to apply to this Court for additional compensation based on an appropriate affirmation setting forth the

---

14. Mental Hygiene Law § 81.20(a)(5); *see supra*, § 22.46.

§ 22.101 GUARDIANSHIP Ch. 22

extent of the personal needs services provided by the Guardian to _____ or for his [*her*] benefit;[15] and it is further

ORDERED that upon presentation by the Guardian of a certified copy of his [*her*] Commission the restraining order previously issued on _____ 's bank accounts and property shall be deemed terminated and of no further force and effect; and it is further

ORDERED that the Guardian shall pay from _____ 's assets to _____, the Court Evaluator, the sum of $_____, in full payment for his [*her*] services to this Court;[16] and it is further

ORDERED that the Guardian shall pay from _____ 's assets to _____, the attorney for _____, the incapacitated person, the sum of $_____, in full payment for his [*her*] legal services rendered herein, and a further sum of $_____, in full payment for his [*her*] costs and disbursements;[17] and it is further

ORDERED that the Guardian shall pay from _____'s assets to _____, the Petitioner's attorney, the sum of $_____, in full payment for his [*her*] legal services rendered herein, and a further sum of $_____, in full payment for his [*her*] costs and disbursements;[18] and it is further

ORDERED that the Guardian pay to _____, M.D., _____, M.D., _____,[19] [*and any other witnesses who testified at the hearing*], the following sums in payment of their fees and other costs and disbursements: [*set forth*]; and it is further

ORDERED that the Guardian shall give _____ a monthly allowance of $_____, which shall not be accountable except to show delivery thereof by the Guardian or, in lieu of such sum, and in the discretion of the Guardian, he [*she*] shall maintain an interest bearing checking account with a refillable balance of $_____, at a bank close to _____ 's residence, upon which _____ may draw funds for his [*her*] personal and social spending requirements; and it is further

ORDERED that pursuant to Mental Hygiene Law Section 81.16(e) notice of all further proceedings with regard to this matter shall be given to _____;[20] and it is further

ORDERED that pursuant to Mental Hygiene Law Section 81.16(e) a copy of this order and judgment shall be personally served upon and read to the incapacitated person by _____ [*enter either the name of the court evaluator or the name of counsel for the incapacitated person*];[21] and it is further

15. *See supra*, § 22.61 for discussion of compensation of guardian.
16. *See supra*, § 22.27.
17. *See supra*, § 22.28.
18. *See supra*, § 22.39.
19. *See supra*, §§ 22.26, 22.33 discussing the application of the physician-patient privilege and the propriety of allowing medical testimony.
20. *See supra* § 22.38.
21. *Id.*

ORDERED that pursuant to Mental Hygiene Law Section 81.38 _____ is hereby appointed Standby Guardian for the Personal Needs and Property Management of the incapacitated person and, upon qualification, the Standby Guardian shall have all the duties, powers and responsibilities of the original Guardian for the Personal Needs and Property Management appointed herein;[22] and it is further

ORDERED the upon the filing with the court by the Standby Guardian for the Personal Needs and Property Management of a bond[23] and designation of the Clerk of the Court[24] as agent for service of process in the same form as required by the Guardian for the Personal Needs and Property Management originally appointed herein, and in addition upon the filing of an acknowledged statement of resignation signed by the original Guardian for the Personal Needs and Property Management appointed herein, a certified death certificate of said Guardian, or a certified copy of a judicial order indicating that said Guardian has been removed, discharged, suspended or become incapacitated, the Clerk of the Court shall issue a commission[25] in the due form of law which shall state that it is valid for sixty days from its issuance; and it is further

ORDERED [*set forth any other directions of the Court to the Guardian and any other powers granted to the Guardian*].

ENTER

_____

J.S.C.

Library References:

West's Key No. Digests, Guardian and Ward ⚖111; Mental Health ⚖211–275, 291–313.

22. See supra § 22.73.
23. See supra § 22.42.
24. See supra § 22.43.
25. Id.

§ 22.102 Forms—Oath and Designation of Guardian[1]

SUPREME COURT OF THE STATE OF NEW YORK
COUNTY OF _____
_____

In the Matter of the Application of)
_____,)
)
Petitioner,)
)
For the Appointment of a Guardian) Oath and Designation
for the Personal Needs and Property)
Management of) Index. No. _____
_____,)
)
A Person Alleged to be Incapacitated,)
)
Respondent.)
_____

STATE OF NEW YORK)
COUNTY OF _____)

_____, being duly sworn, deposes and says:

(1) *OATH OF GUARDIAN*: I am a citizen of the United States and over the age of eighteen (18) years [*I am under the age of eighteen (18) years and the parent of the incapacitated person*]. I will well, faithfully and honestly discharge the trust reposed in me as the Guardian for Personal Needs and [*or*] Property Management of _____, whom this Court has found to be incapacitated. I will obey all lawful directions of any court of competent jurisdiction, and I will render an initial report and a just and true account of all monies and other property received by me and of my application of the same whenever required to do so by a court of competent jurisdiction and pursuant to the Order of this Court made _____, 19__.

(2) *DESIGNATION OF CLERK FOR SERVICE OF PROCESS*: I have been appointed Guardian for Personal Needs and [*or*] Property Management of _____, who resides at _____ Street, _____, New York. I hereby designate the Clerk of the Supreme [*or County*] Court, _____ County, and his [*her*] successor in office as the person on whom service of any process issuing from said Court in this proceeding, or in any other proceeding, which shall affect the estate or personal affairs of _____, the incapacitated person, in like manner and with like effect as if it were served personally upon me whenever I cannot be found and

§ 22.102
1. *See supra*, § 22.43.

served within the State of New York after due diligence is used. I further advise the Clerk that I am a resident of the State of New York and reside at:

[*State complete address*]

[*Signed*] _____

[*Typed Name*]

GUARDIAN

ACKNOWLEDGMENT

STATE OF NEW YORK)
COUNTY OF _____)

On the _____ day of _____, 19__, before me personally appeared _____, to me known and known to me to be the individual described in and who executed the foregoing Combined Oath and Designation of Guardian, and he [*she*] personally acknowledged to me that he [*she*] executed the same.

_____
Notary Public

Library References:

West's Key No. Digests, Guardian and Ward ⚖111; Mental Health ⚖211–275, 291–313.

§ 22.103 Forms—Commission of Guardian[1]

SUPREME COURT OF THE STATE OF NEW YORK
COUNTY OF _____

_____
In the Matter of the Application of   )
_____,   )
)
                               Petitioner,   )
)
For the Appointment of a Guardian   ) Commission of Guardian
for the Personal Needs and Property)
Management of   ) Index. No. _____
)
_____,   )
)
A Person Alleged to be Incapacitated,)
)
                               Respondent.)
_____

THE PEOPLE OF THE STATE OF NEW YORK,

TO ALL TO WHOM THESE PRESENTS SHALL COME,

GREETING,

WHEREAS, by Order duly made on _____, 19__, and entered in the Office of the Clerk of the County of _____, on _____, 19__, in the above entitled proceeding in the Supreme [*County*] Court for the appointment of a Guardian of the Personal Needs and [*or*] Property Management of _____, residing at _____ Street, _____, New York, Telephone No. _____, wherein it was found that _____, was an incapacitated person; and

WHEREAS, by the above Order, _____, who resides at _____ Street, _____, New York, Telephone No. _____, was appointed the Guardian of the Personal Needs and [*or*] Property Management of _____ [*and was directed to file in the Clerk's Office of _____ County a bond for the security required by law in the sum of $_____ conditioned that the Guardian will in all things faithfully discharge the duties and obey all lawful directions of any Court or officer of competent jurisdiction pertaining to said trust and render a just and true account of all monies received and disbursed whenever required to do so by a court of competent jurisdiction*]; and

WHEREAS, the designation of the Clerk of this Court has been duly executed and filed in this office;[2] and

§ 22.103
1. *See supra*, § 22.43.

2. *See supra*, § 22.102.

[WHEREAS, the Bond required by the Order has been duly executed, and filed in the Clerk's Office;]³ and

WHEREAS, the Guardian has been granted the following powers:

[set forth specific powers granted]⁴

and

WHEREAS, the appointment as Guardian shall be indefinite [shall terminate on _____, 19__].

NOW, THEREFORE, KNOW YE, that we have granted, given and committed, and by these presents do give, grant and commit to the Guardian, the possession, care and management of the person and [or] property of _____, the incapacitated person.

WITNESS the Honorable _____, one of the Justices [Judges] of the Supreme [County] Court of the State of New York, at the Courthouse, in the County of _____, this _____ day of _____, 19__.

BY THE COURT

[Signed] _____

Clerk of the County of _____

Library References:

West's Key No. Digests, Guardian and Ward ⚖111; Mental Health ⚖211–275, 291–313.

3. See supra, § 22.42.

4. See supra, §§ 22.47, et seq., for discussion of powers of guardian.

§ 22.104　　　　　　　　GUARDIANSHIP　　　　　　　　Ch. 22

§ 22.104　Forms—Initial Report of Guardian[1]

SUPREME COURT OF THE STATE OF NEW YORK
COUNTY OF _____

```
_____
                                )
In the Matter of                )
_____,            )
                                )
                 Guardian,      )
                                ) Initial Report
For the Personal Needs and Property )
Management of                   ) Index. No. _____
                                )
_____,            )
                                )
An Incapacitated Person,        )
                                )
                 Respondent.    )
_____)
```

I, _____, of _____ Street, _____, New York, Guardian of _____, the incapacitated person, hereby render the following as my initial report, as required by Mental Hygiene Law Section 81.30.

1. I was duly appointed Guardian of _____, the incapacitated person, by Order[2] of the Hon. _____, dated _____, 19__. I duly qualified by filing the bond required by the order, in the sum of $_____, with _____, as Surety and duly filed my designation of the Clerk of this Court as my agent for service.[3] A Commission[4] was duly granted by the Clerk of the Court on _____, 19__, and I entered into my duties as Guardian.

2. Attached to this Report is proof of my completion of the guardian education requirements pursuant to Mental Hygiene Law Section 81.39.[5]

3. As Guardian with respect to the management of the property[6] of the incapacitated person, I prepared an inventory of the property of the incapacitated person. Attached to this report is a verified and complete inventory of the property and financial resources of the incapacitated person, over which I have control as Guardian.

4. Attached to this Report is my plan for the management of such property.

§ 22.104
1. See supra, § 22.63.
2. See supra, § 22.101 for form of order.
3. See supra, § 22.43; see also supra, § 22.103 for form of oath and designation.
4. See supra, § 22.43; see also supra, § 22.103 for form of commission.
5. See supra, § 22.76.
6. See supra, § 22.47.

5. After due consideration of the powers granted to me as Guardian of the property and financial resources of the incapacitated person, it is my determination that the powers granted to me [do] [do not] need to be changed. [*If the allegation is that a change in the powers is necessary, the report should set forth the requested changes of such powers and the grounds for such changes.*]

6. As Guardian with respect to the personal needs[7] of the incapacitated person, I visited the incapacitated person on _____, 19__, at his [*her*] residence at _____ Street, _____, New York. [*Set forth a description of the circumstances of the incapacitated person, as observed by the visit[s] and all other information obtained as a result of the personal visit[s].*]

7. [*Set forth the steps taken by the Guardian, consistent with the Court's order, to provide for the personal needs of the incapacitated person; and whether there is any advance directive such as a DNR order, health care proxy, or living will, and if such directive exists, set forth a copy of same.*]

8. Consistent with the Order of the Court, I have developed the following plan for the personal needs of the incapacitated person: [*Set forth the plan, which shall include the following information:*

   (1) the medical, dental, mental health, or related services that are to be provided for the welfare of the incapacitated person;

   (2) the social and personal services that are to be provided for the welfare of the incapacitated person;

   (3) any physical, dental, and mental health examinations necessary to determine the medical, dental, and mental health treatment needs; and

   (4) the application of health and accident insurance and any other private or government benefits to which the incapacitated person may be entitled to meet any part of the costs of medical, dental, mental health, or related services provided to the incapacitated person.]

9. After due consideration of the powers granted to me as Guardian of the personal needs of the incapacitated person, it is my determination that the powers granted to me [do] [do not] need to be changed. [*If the allegation is that a change in the powers is necessary, the report should set forth the requested changes of such powers and the grounds for such changes.*]

[Signed] _____

[Typed Name]

GUARDIAN

---

7. *See supra,* § 22.53.

§ 22.104　　　　　　　　GUARDIANSHIP　　　　　　　　Ch. 22

VERIFICATION

STATE OF NEW YORK　）
　　　　　　　　　　　）ss.:
COUNTY OF _____　）

[Name of Guardian] [being duly sworn] [affirms] that I am the Guardian for _____, the incapacitated person, that I have read the foregoing report and that the same is true to the best of my knowledge and belief.

[Signed] _____

[Typed Name]

GUARDIAN

Sworn [Affirmed] to before me
this ____ day of _____, 19__

_____
NOTARY PUBLIC

Library References:
West's Key No. Digests, Guardian and Ward ⚖111; Mental Health ⚖211-275, 291-313.

§ 22.105 Forms—Annual Report and Inventory of Guardian[1]

SUPREME COURT OF THE STATE OF NEW YORK
COUNTY OF _____

_____
In the Matter of　　　　　　　　　）
　　　　　　　　　　　　　　　　）
_____,　　　）
　　　　　　　　　　　　　　　　）
　　　　　　　　　　　Guardian,　）
　　　　　　　　　　　　　　　　）　Annual Report and Inventory
For the Personal Needs and Property　）
Management of　　　　　　　　　）　Index. No. _____
　　　　　　　　　　　　　　　　）
_____,　　　）
　　　　　　　　　　　　　　　　）
An Incapacitated Person,　　　　　）
　　　　　　　　　　　　　　　　）
　　　　　　　　　　Respondent.　）
_____

_____, Guardian of _____, the incapacitated person, hereby renders the following as my Annual Report and Inventory, as required by Mental Hygiene Law Section 81.31.

§ 22.105
1. See supra, § 22.64.

320

Ch. 22   ANNUAL REPORT OF GUARDIAN   § 22.105

INVENTORY AND ACCOUNT

On _____, 19__, I was duly appointed Guardian of _____, above named, by order of the Supreme Court of _____ County and have continued to act as such fiduciary since that date, giving a bond in the original sum of $_____, now in the sum of $_____, pursuant to subsequent orders, which is still in force and effect with _____, as Surety. There has been no change in the Surety thereon, and the Surety is in good financial standing as when the bond was given.

The following is a true and full account of all receipts and disbursements for the year 19__:

SUMMARY

Schedule "A"—Principal on hand at date of appointment or last accounting	$_____
Schedule "B"—Changes in principal	$_____
Schedule "C"—Income received	$_____
Schedule "D"—Paid disbursements	$_____
Schedule "E–1"—Balance of cash and securities to be charged to next year's account	$_____
Schedule "E–2"—Real estate	$_____
Schedule "E–3"—All other personal property	$_____
Total Estate	$_____

[*Set forth all appropriate Schedules*]

ANNUAL REPORT

1. My present address and telephone number are as follows: _____ Street, _____, New York, _____.

2. The present address and telephone number of _____, the incapacitated person, are as follows: _____ Street, _____, New York, _____. [*If the incapacitated person does not reside in his or her personal residence, set forth the name, address, and telephone number of the facility or place at which the person resides and the name of the chief executive officer of the facility or the person otherwise responsible for the person's care.*]

3. During the past year there have been the following changes in the physical and mental condition of _____, the incapacitated person: [*set forth*].

As a consequence of these changes, the following changes have been made with respect to _____'s medication: [*set forth*].

4. _____ was last visited by Dr. _____ on _____, 19__. A copy of Dr. _____'s statement is annexed to this report. [*The statement shall be by a physician, psychologist, nurse clinician, or social worker, or*

other person who has evaluated or examined the incapacitated person within the three months prior to the filing of the report and shall contain an evaluation of the incapacitated person's condition and the current functional level of the incapacitated person].

5. *[To the extent the guardian is charged with providing for the personal needs[2] of the incapacitated person, the report should set forth the following:*

(i) a statement of whether the current residential setting is best suited to the current needs of the incapacitated person;

(ii) a resume of any professional medical treatment given to the ward in the preceding year;

(iii) the plan for medical, dental, and mental health treatment, and related services in the coming year;

(iv) information concerning the social condition of the incapacitated person, including: the social and personal services currently utilized by the incapacitated person; the social skills of the incapacitated person; and the social needs of the incapacitated person].

6. *[To the extent the guardian is charged with property management,[3] the report shall include the information required by the provisions of the Surrogate's Court Procedure Act Section 1719 prescribing the form of papers to be filed upon the annual accounting of a general guardian of an infant's property; this information shall include:*

(i) a statement and description of each item of personal property of the incapacitated person received by the guardian since his or her appointment or since the filing of the last annual account; the value of each item so received; a list of the items remaining in the guardian's hands; a statement of the manner in which all property no longer remaining in the guardian's hands has been disposed of; and a description of the amount and nature of each investment of money made by the guardian;

(ii) an account in the form of debtor and creditor of all the guardian's receipts and disbursements of money during the preceding year; charging him or herself with any balance remaining in the last account rendered and stating the balance remaining at the conclusion of the year to be charged to the guardian in the next year's account;

(iii) the names and addresses of the sureties on the guardian's bond; if natural persons whether they are living and whether the security of the bond has become impaired].

2. *See supra,* § 22.53.

3. *See supra,* § 22.47.

7. I have [*not*] employed the services of _____, the incapacitated person [*or the incapacitated person has earned or I have received moneys on behalf of the incapacitated person*] as follows: [*set forth*].

8. [*Set forth a description of all other activities performed by the guardian on behalf of the incapacitated person.*]

9. After due consideration of the powers granted to me as Guardian of _____, the incapacitated person, it is my determination that [*the guardianship should be terminated*] [*the powers granted to me [do] [do not] need to be changed*]. [*If the allegation is that a change in the powers is necessary, the report should set forth the specific authority requested or what specific authority of the guardian will be affected.*]

10. [*Set forth any other information which the guardian has been required to provide by the order of appointment.*]

[*Signed*] _____

[*Typed Name*]

GUARDIAN

VERIFICATION

STATE OF NEW YORK)
) ss.:
COUNTY OF _____)

[*Name of Guardian*] [*being duly sworn*] [*affirms*] that I am the Guardian for _____, the incapacitated person. The foregoing account and inventory contains, to the best of my knowledge and belief, a full and true statement of all my receipts and disbursements on account of the incapacitated person; and of all money and other personal property of said person which have come to my hands or have been received by any other persons by my order or authority since my appointment or since filing my last annual account and inventory, and of the value of all such property, together with a full and true statement and account of the manner in which I have disposed of the same and of all property remaining in my hands at the time of filing this account and inventory; also a full and true description of the amount and nature of each investment made by me since my appointment or since the filing of my last account and inventory. I do not know of any error or omission in the account and inventory to the prejudice of the incapacitated person.

I have read the foregoing Annual Report and the same is true to the best of my knowledge and belief.

[*Signed*] _____
[*Typed Name*]

GUARDIAN

§ 22.105 GUARDIANSHIP Ch. 22

Sworn [*Affirmed*] to before me
this ____ day of _____, 19__
NOTARY PUBLIC

   Library References:
     West's Key No. Digests, Guardian and Ward ⚖111; Mental Health ⚖211–275, 291–313.

§ 22.106 Forms—Decree Upon Approving Accounts[1]

At an IAS Part _____ of the Supreme Court of the State of New York, held in and for the County of _____ at the Courthouse, located at _____, New York on the _____ day of _____, 19__.

PRESENT:

    HON. _____, JUSTICE

_____

In the Matter of the Final Accounting)
of _____,)
                               Petitioner,) Decree Approving Account
as Guardian For the Personal Needs)
and Property Management of) Index. No. _____
_____,)
)
An Incapacitated Person,)
                                 Respondent.)

   _____, Guardian of _____, the incapacitated person, having petitioned this Court for an Order judicially settling the Final Account herein and for other relief, and the proceeding having come on to be heard on _____, 19__, and there being no objection filed thereto,

   NOW on reading the Notice of Petition and Petition, verified _____, 19__, in support of the application, the Final Account, the Affidavit of Service of the Petition and supporting documents, sworn to

§ 22.106   1. *See supra,* § 22.67.

Ch. 22   DECREE UPON APPROVING ACCOUNTS   § 22.106

_____, 19__, the Initial Report[2] filed by the Guardian on _____, 19__, the Annual Reports filed by the Guardian since his [*her*] appointment, the death certificate filed as proof of the death of _____ , the incapacitated person, [*set forth all other papers filed on the proceeding for the Final Accounting*]; and due deliberation having been had,

NOW, on motion of _____, attorney for the Guardian, it is

ORDERED, that the Final Accounting be and the same is judicially settled and allowed as follows:

The Guardian is charged with the amount shown in Total Schedule A of the Summary Statement: $_____

The Guardian is credited with the amount shown in total Schedule B of the Summary Statement: $_____

Leaving a balance with which the Guardian is charged of: $_____

consisting of the property itemized in the annexed Schedule C, the balance on hand, of the Final Account; and it is further

ORDERED, that the Guardian retain the sum of $_____, being the commissions due to the Guardian;[3] and it is further

ORDERED, that the Guardian pay to _____, attorney for the Guardian, the sum of $_____, for services rendered as attorney for the Guardian, and the sum of $_____, for expenses incurred in connection with this proceeding, and the attorney is a creditor of the estate of the deceased incapacitated person in proceedings before the Surrogate of _____ County; and it is further

ORDERED that the Guardian pay the balance then remaining to _____, the Executrix of the Estate of _____, the incapacitated person; and it is further

ORDERED that upon proof of service of a copy of this Order with notice of entry upon all parties who have appeared herein, and upon satisfying the Court by receipts, and an affidavit that the payments herein directed to be made have been duly made and the terms of this Order have been fully complied with, an Order may be entered discharging _____, as Guardian of _____, the incapacitated person, and canceling the bond and discharging the Surety from all liability thereunder as to all matters embraced in the Final Account herein.

                                        ENTER

                                        [*Signed*]

                                        JUSTICE OF THE SUPREME COURT

---

2. See supra, § 22.63; see also supra, § 22.104 for form of initial report.

3. See supra, § 22.61.

§ 22.107 **Forms—Petition on Proceeding to Discover Property Withheld**[1]

SUPREME COURT OF THE STATE OF NEW YORK
COUNTY OF _____

_____)
)
In the Matter of the Application of   )
_____,   )
)
                        Petitioner,   )
)
As Guardian for the Property   )   Petition
Management of _____, an   )
Incapacitated Person, to Recover   )   Index. No. _____
Property of the Incapacitated Person)
Withheld by _____,   )
)
                      Respondent.)
_____)

TO THE SUPREME COURT OF THE STATE OF NEW YORK : COUNTY OF _____

The petition of _____ respectfully states and alleges:

1. I was duly appointed Property Management Guardian of _____, the incapacitated person, by Order of the Hon. _____, dated _____, 19__. I duly qualified by filing the bond[2] required by said order, in the sum of $_____, with _____, as Surety and duly filed my designation[3] of the Clerk of this Court as my agent for service. A Commission[4] was duly granted by the Clerk of the Court on _____, 19__, and I entered into my duties as Guardian.

2. In the course of my duties as Guardian, I caused to have an inventory made of the property of the incapacitated person. During such inventory, I discovered that the incapacitated person had deposited funds into two bank accounts, in _____ Bank, _____ Street, _____, New York. These accounts were established at the bank as convenience joint accounts with _____ as the named joint tenant.

3. Upon information and belief, _____, the named joint tenant, has in his [her] possession the check books, statements, and other documents relevant to these accounts.

§ 22.107
1. See supra, § 22.82.
2. See supra, § 22.42.
3. See supra, § 22.43; see also supra, § 22.102 for form of oath and designation.
4. See supra, § 22.43; see also supra, § 22.103 for form of commission.

4. _____ has failed and refused to provide Petitioner, as Property Management Guardian of _____, the incapacitated person, with any information concerning the amounts remaining in such accounts and has refused to turn over to Petitioner the check books, statements, and other documents relevant to these accounts.

5. These bank accounts were, upon information and belief, established as convenience joint accounts and as such are the property of _____, the incapacitated person.

6. Petitioner requests that this Court order _____ to appear before this Court and be examined with regard to these bank accounts and be directed to deliver the check books, statements, and other documents relevant to these accounts to Petitioner.

WHEREFORE, it is respectfully requested that this Court grant an order directing _____ to appear before this Court and be examined with regard to these bank accounts and be directed to deliver the check books, statements, and other documents relevant to these accounts to Petitioner, together with such other and further relief as this Court deems just and proper.

[Signed] _____

[Typed Name]

GUARDIAN

VERIFICATION

STATE OF NEW YORK)
) ss.:
COUNTY OF _____)

[Name of Guardian] [being duly sworn] [affirms] that I am the Guardian for _____, the incapacitated person, that I have read the foregoing petition and that the same is true to the best of my knowledge and belief.

[Signed] _____

[Typed Name]

GUARDIAN

Sworn [Affirmed] to before me this ____ day of _____, 19__

_____
NOTARY PUBLIC

§ 22.107 GUARDIANSHIP Ch. 22

Library References:
West's Key No. Digests, Guardian and Ward ⚖111; Mental Health ⚖211-275, 291-313.

Chapter 23

ELDER LAW

by
Robert M. Freedman
and
Frances M. Pantaleo*

Table of Sections

23.1	Scope Note.
23.2	Strategy.
23.3	Ethical Considerations.
23.4	____ Identifying the Client.
23.5	____ Confidentiality.
23.6	____ Diminished Capacity.
23.7	Social Security Benefits.
23.8	____ Quarters of Coverage.
23.9	____ Insured Status.
23.10	____ Calculation of Benefits.
23.11	____ Retirement Benefits.
23.12	____ Benefits for Spouses, Survivors and Dependents.
23.13	____ Reduction in Benefits Due to Earned Income.
23.14	____ Overpayments and Underpayments.
23.15	____ Administrative and Judicial Appeals.
23.16	____ Representation by Attorneys.
23.17	Supplemental Security Income for the Elderly.
23.18	____ Categorical Eligibility.
23.19	____ Financial Eligibility.
23.20	____ Benefit Calculation.
23.21	____ Underpayments and Overpayments.
23.22	____ Administrative and Judicial Appeals.
23.23	____ Representation by Attorneys.
23.24	Retirement Income from Qualified Plans.
23.25	____ Eligibility, Vesting and Accrual.
23.26	____ Contribution Limitations.
23.27	____ Payment of Benefits.
23.28	____ Alienation and Assignment.
23.29	____ Spousal Rights.
23.30	____ Qualified Domestic Relations Orders.
23.31	____ Waiver of Spousal Rights.
23.32	____ Taxation of Contributions.
23.33	____ Distributions.

* The authors would like to gratefully acknowledge the assistance of Todd Krichmar, an associate at the firm of Freedman and Fish, New York City, and Kathleen Lois Brandt, a student at Pace Law School, in the preparation of this material.

23.34	____ Termination or Merger.
23.35	____ Appeals.
23.36	Railroad Retirement Benefits.
23.37	Benefits for Federal Employees.
23.38	____ Federal Employees Retirement System ("FERS").
23.39	____ Civil Service Retirement Act ("CSRA").
23.40	____ Appeals.
23.41	Veterans' Benefits.
23.42	Medicare.
23.43	____ Eligibility and Enrollment.
23.44	____ Part A Benefits.
23.45	____ ____ Hospital Services.
23.46	____ ____ Skilled Nursing Facilities.
23.47	____ ____ Home Health Care.
23.48	____ ____ Hospice Care.
23.49	____ Part B Supplementary Medical Insurance.
23.50	____ ____ Deductibles and Coinsurance.
23.51	____ ____ Assignment of Claims/Participating Physicians.
23.52	____ ____ Limitations on Balance Billing.
23.53	____ Administrative and Judicial Appeals.
23.54	____ ____ Eligibility for Benefits.
23.55	____ ____ Part A Fiscal Intermediary Decisions.
23.56	____ ____ Part A Peer Review Organization Decisions.
23.57	____ ____ Part B Determinations.
23.58	Supplemental Medical Insurance (Medigap Plans).
23.59	____ Gaps in Medicare Coverage.
23.60	____ Federal and State Regulation of the Industry.
23.61	____ Ten Standard Plans.
23.62	____ Criteria for Choosing the Right Plan.
23.63	Long Term Care Insurance.
23.64	____ Regulation Under New York Law.
23.65	____ Relationship to Medicaid Eligibility.
23.66	____ The Partnership For Long Term Care/Robert Wood Johnson Program.
23.67	____ Choosing a Policy.
23.68	____ Tax Issues.
23.69	Medicaid.
23.70	____ Covered Services.
23.71	____ Basic Eligibility Requirements.
23.72	____ Surplus Income Program for the "Medically Needy."
23.73	____ Income.
23.74	____ Resources.
23.75	____ Exempt Resources.
23.76	____ Transfer of Resources.
23.77	____ Treatment of Trusts.
23.78	____ ____ Self Settled Trusts.
23.79	____ ____ Third Party Trusts.
23.80	____ Spousal Budgeting: Protection of Resources and Income for the Community Spouse.
23.81	____ Recoveries Against Estates.
23.82	____ Liens.

Ch. 23   **ELDER LAW**

23.83   ____ Administrative and Judicial Appeals.
23.84   Home Care Coverage.
23.85   ____ Medicare.
23.86   ____ Medicaid.
23.87   ____ Expanded In–Home Services for the Elderly Program ("EISEP").
23.88   ____ Private Insurance.
23.89   Hospital Patients Rights.
23.90   ____ Bill of Rights.
23.91   ____ Discharge Planning.
23.92   Nursing Home Resident Rights.
23.93   ____ Admission to a Facility.
23.94   ____ Bill of Rights.
23.95   ____ Financial Rights.
23.96   ____ Transfer and Discharge.
23.97   ____ Bed Hold Policy.
23.98   ____ Remedies for Violation of Rights or Improper Treatment.
23.99   Housing Issues.
23.100   ____ Real Property Tax Exemption.
23.101   ____ Real Property Tax Credit.
23.102   ____ Tax Assistance Loans.
23.103   ____ Home Repair Assistance.
23.104   ____ Reverse Mortgages and Home Equity Loans.
23.105   ____ Home Energy Assistance Program ("HEAP").
23.106   ____ Tenant Protections.
23.107   ____ Life Care Retirement Communities.
23.108   ____ Community Based Services.
23.109   Health Care Decision Making.
23.110   ____ Health Care Proxy.
23.111   ____ The Living Will.
23.112   ____ Do Not Resuscitate Orders.
23.113   ____ Physician Assisted Suicide.
23.114   Tax Issues.
23.115   ____ Additional Standard Deduction for the Aged and Blind.
23.116   ____ Incapacity.
23.117   ____ Sale of a Principal Residence.
23.118   ____ Medical Deductions.
23.119   Miscellaneous Programs.
23.120   ____ Elderly Pharmaceutical Insurance Coverage ("EPIC").
23.121   ____ Life Line Telephone Service.
23.122   Forms.
23.123   ____ Documentation Letter. 💾
23.124   ____ Consultation Letter. 💾
23.125   ____ Health Care Proxy Statutory Form. 💾
23.126   ____ Sample Living Will. 💾

WESTLAW Electronic Research

See WESTLAW Electronic Research Guide preceding the Summary of Contents.

§ 23.1 Scope Note

This chapter will provide an overview of major legal issues and government benefit programs which affect elderly[1] New Yorkers. The explosion of interest in the field has been driven by a combination of demographic and economic realities. Our society is aging. In 1900, people over the age of 65 comprised only 3% of the total population. Today, approximately 13% of the population is over 65.[2] The number of elderly will grow to 20% of the population by the year 2030.[3] The greatest growth among elderly population is among the "frail elderly;" those who are over the age of 85. Currently, these individuals comprise approximately 1% of the total population.[4] However, by the year 2030, the percentage will grow to approximately 3%.[5] Most senior citizens can expect to enjoy many years of healthy, active life. However, by age 75, the chance of developing chronic disabling conditions such as Alzheimer's Disease increases dramatically.[6] Many of these individuals require extensive personal assistance, supervision and medical care at great emotional and financial expense to themselves and their families.

Although lawyers have always provided services to older clients, the term "elder law" has come into use within the past twenty years.[7] Despite frequent use of the term and recent approval of certification in elder law by the American Bar Association,[8] there is no easy answer to

---

§ 23.1

1. The definition of the term "elderly" is subject to debate. For the purpose of most benefit programs, a senior citizen is defined as a person over the age of 65, although some benefits may be obtained at age 60.

2. U.S. Bureau of the Census, United States Population Estimates, by Age, Sex, Race, and Hispanic Origin, 1990–1995 (projections based on 1990 census data).

3. U.S. Bureau of the Census, Projections of the Population, by Age, Sex, Race and Hispanic Origin for the United States: 1993 to 2050, Middle Series (projections based on 1990 census data).

4. U.S. Bureau of the Census, United States Population Estimates, by Age, Sex, Race, and Hispanic Origin, 1990–1995.

5. U.S. Bureau of the Census, Projections of the Population, by Age, Sex, Race and Hispanic Origin for the United States: 1993 to 2050, Middle Series.

6. Approximately 3% of individuals between ages 65 to 74 have Alzheimer's Disease. However, the rate increases to over 18% of those 75 to 84 and is a staggering 47% of the population over age 85. D.A. Evans and J.J. Funkenstein, *Prevalence of Alzheimer's Disease in a Community of Older Persons: Higher Than Previously Reported*, J.A.M.A. 11/10/89.

7. The American Bar Association's Commission on Legal Problems of the Elderly was established in 1978. The Commission was instrumental in bringing together individual practitioners from across the country with practices concentrating in the representation of elderly individuals. From these informal meetings, a core group of about thirty-five lawyers formed the National Association of Elder Law Attorneys ("NAELA") in 1988. For information about membership contact NAELA at 1604 N. Country Club Road, Tucson, Arizona 85716. Telephone (520) 881–4005.

The New York State Bar Association formed a Special Committee on Seniors in 1986. A permanent Elder Law Section was established in 1991. For information about membership contact the New York State Bar Association, One Elk Street, Albany, New York 12207. (518) 463–3200.

8. For information about certification contact NAELA. **CAVEAT:** Currently, New York recognizes no specialties except patent law and admiralty. Attorneys practicing in any other areas of the law may not claim a specialty. See New York Code of Professional Responsibility, DR2–105(A), (B). State

§ 23.2 ELDER LAW Ch. 23

option for many poor and middle-class clients and should be considered even for clients with more substantial assets.[13]

The practitioner's first step toward advising the client and assembling the proper estate plan is to gather complete information. This information should be obtained from the client prior to or during the initial consultation. A sample letter to send to the client prior to the consultation, with a list of necessary documents, is included at the end of the chapter.[14] Necessary information includes, but may not be limited to the following:

1. Copies of existing powers of attorney;
2. Copies of existing health care proxies and living wills;
3. Medicare card;
4. Private health insurance card;
5. Amount of monthly Social Security check;
6. Amount of pension check;
7. Current last will and testament;
8. Deed, if any real property is owned;
9. Life insurance—identification of ownership and beneficiary—face value and cash surrender value;
10. List of all bank accounts, including title of accounts, designated beneficiary and value;
11. List of all brokerage accounts, including title of accounts and value;
12. List of all stocks and bonds, including title of the accounts and value;
13. List of any other substantial assets (over $10,000);
14. List of any IRAs or qualified plans;
15. List of any assets transferred in the last thirty-six (36) months; and
16. Last income tax return.

The practitioner may feel comfortable providing advice to the clients at the initial consultation. It is strongly recommended that following the consultation, the practitioner provide the client with a written summary of the information gathered at the consultation and the advice or options given. A sample form letter covering a typical elder law consultation is provided at the end of the chapter.[15]

13. See infra, §§ 23.69—23.83.
14. See infra, § 23.123.
15. See infra, § 23.124.

the question, "What is elder law?" Most elder law attorneys in private practice spend about half of their time engaged in estate planning, financial planning and probate administration. However, these issues are covered in depth in Chapter 24 "Estate Planning," Chapter 25 "Probate and Estate Administration" and Chapter 35 "Income Tax" and will not be discussed in this chapter. Guardianship is also a substantial portion of elder law practice but is covered in depth in Chapter 22. This chapter will focus on coverage of government benefit programs which affect the elderly, with particular concentration on legal programs which provide or regulate pensions and health related services.

The chapter begins, in Sections 23.3 through 23.6, with a discussion of common ethical problems which arise during representation of elderly individuals and their families. The next sections address the basic sources of retirement income for elderly individuals. Sections 23.7 through 23.16 cover Social Security retirement benefits, including eligibility and calculation of benefits, administrative appeals and rules governing representation by attorneys. Sections 23.17 through 23.23 cover benefits provided by the Supplemental Security Income program, including financial and categorical eligibility requirements, benefit calculation, administrative appeals and rules governing representation by attorneys. Sections 23.24 through 23.35 concern retirement income from private pension plans with an emphasis on ERISA requirements for qualified plans. Section 23.36 provides an overview of Railroad Retirement benefits. Sections 23.37 through 23.40 discuss retirement benefits provided to federal employees. Section 23.41 discusses Veterans benefits.

The next sections address private and public sources of health insurance for elderly individuals. Sections 23.42 through 23.57 address the Medicare program, including eligibility and enrollment, Part A and Part B coverage and the administrative appeals process. Sections 23.58 through 23.62 discuss Supplemental Medical Insurance, or Medigap plans, which provide additional coverage to Medicare beneficiaries. Sections 23.63 through 23.68 discuss interest in long term care insurance, including regulation of the industry, the relationship of long term care insurance to Medicaid eligibility and tips for deciding whether to purchase a policy. Sections 23.69 through 23.83 provide an overview of the rules governing the Medicaid program, including eligibility requirements, treatment of transfers of assets and trusts, protection of income and resources for a community spouse, recoveries, liens, and the administrative appeals process.

Coverage of home care services under Medicare, Medicaid and New York's EISEP program receive separate coverage in Sections 23.84 through 23.88. The rights of hospital patients and nursing home residents follow in Sections 23.89 through 23.98. Sections 23.99 through

Bar Association has not authorized new attorneys to claim to specialize in any area of law. *See* New York Code of Professional Responsibility, DR 2–105(A), (B).

23.108 provide an overview of housing issues of particular concern to elderly individuals, including mortgage, tax payment and home repair assistance programs, special protections for elderly renters and the newly emerging market of life care retirement communities.

Sections 23.109 through 23.113 cover health care decision making, including New York's health care proxy statute, living wills, Do Not Resuscitate Orders and court decisions concerning physician assisted suicide. Sections 23.114 through 23.118 highlight special tax considerations of interest to the elderly, including the additional standard deduction for the aged and blind, tax treatment of the sale of a principal residence and medical deductions. The chapter concludes, in Sections 23.119 through 23.121, with a discussion of miscellaneous programs, including the EPIC pharmaceutical reimbursement program and Life Line telephone service. The chapter includes forms for letters requesting documentation from a client, an elder law consultation letter, a health care proxy and a sample living will in Sections 23.122 through 23.126.

§ 23.2 Strategy

At the core of the elder law practice is the development of an estate plan for the elderly client. The elder law estate plan will cover the following topics:

Health Care Decision Making. Every client should be advised to have a current health care proxy[1] and living will.[2] The attorney should determine whether or not the client has already executed these documents and, if not, should provide advice concerning the need for them followed by preparation and execution of the documents.

Substitute Management of the Financial Estate. Every client should be advised to consider a plan for management of his or her finances and property in the event of future incapacity. This includes discussion of the possibility of preparation and execution of a power of attorney and/or living trust.[3]

Distribution of the Estate Upon Death. The practitioner should discuss with every client the value of having a current valid will and the appropriate use of testamentary substitutes for distribution of the estate, including joint and survivorship assets and revocable trusts.[4]

IRAs, Qualified Plans and Pensions. The practitioner should review the client's IRAs, qualified plans and pensions. For most elderly clients, the focus will be upon the distribution of these assets. The

---

§ 23.2

1. See infra, § 23.110 for a discussion of health care proxies. See infra, § 23.125 for the statutory form.

2. For a discussion of living wills, see infra, § 23.111. See infra, § 23.126 for a sample form for a living will.

3. A discussion of these issues is contained in Chapter 24 "Estate Planning," infra. See infra, § 24.79 on revocable trusts. See infra, § 24.87 on powers of attorney.

4. These issues are discussed in Chapter 24 "Estate Planning," infra.

attorney must therefore review the distribution scheme and discuss the taxation of distributions.[5]

Gift and Estate Tax Planning. The gift and estate tax implications of any estate plan should be discussed with the client.[6] This is particularly necessary if the estate is in excess of $600,000 and thus subject to federal estate and gift taxes. However, it should be done with all clients where there is a New York State gift or estate tax, generally for all clients with assets in excess of $115,000.

Income Tax Planning. The client should be advised as to the income tax ramifications of the estate plan. The practitioner should discuss whether or not the plan will shift income and income tax liability from the client to someone else. Attention should be paid to an estate plan which has substantial income tax ramifications, particularly distributions from qualified plans and transfers of assets which affect the capital gains tax.[7]

Health Insurance and Payment of Health Care Costs. The client's health insurance should be reviewed to determine whether coverage is adequate and whether the policies are appropriate for the client's needs. It should be determined whether the client receives Medicare, and if not, whether the client is eligible for Medicare benefits.[8] The attorney should also determine whether the client has Supplemental ("Medigap") Medical Insurance. If so, the plan should be reviewed and advice provided regarding whether to retain or replace the policy.[9]

Long Term Care Insurance and Payment of Long Term Care Costs. It should be determined whether the client can qualify for long term care insurance and whether or not it is appropriate to recommend purchase of such insurance.[10] The client should also be advised regarding Medicare coverage of long term care costs.[11] The attorney should also review and discuss with the client whether Medigap insurance will cover any long term care costs.[12] In addition to insurance, it should be determined whether the client is eligible for Medicaid coverage or whether the client should take steps which would qualify him or her for future Medicaid coverage of long term care costs. Medicaid may be

---

5. See §§ 23.24, et seq., for a discussion of IRAs and qualified plans, particularly § 23.33, which discusses taxation of distributions. See also, §§ 23.7—23.16 for a discussion of Social Security benefits, § 23.36 on Railroad Retirement Benefits, and §§ 23.37—23.40 on federal pensions.

6. Chapter 24 "Estate Planning," infra, contains a discussion of gift and estate tax planning.

7. See infra, § 23.33 for a discussion of the taxation of distributions from qualified plans. Chapter 24 "Estate Planning", infra, contains a discussion of income tax and capital gains.

8. See infra, §§ 23.41—23.51 for cussion of the Medicare program.

9. See infra, §§ 23.58—23.61 cussion of Medigap insurance poli

10. See infra, §§ 23.63—23.

11. See infra, § 23.46 for Medicare coverage of nursi § 23.48 for a discussion of age of hospice care, and cussion of Medicare cove

12. See infra, §§ 23

335

§ 23.3 Ethical Considerations

Ethical considerations pervade every interaction between client and attorney.[1] Attorneys who represent elderly individuals and their families must be particularly sensitive to potential ethical dilemmas.[2] The need for heightened awareness stems from several sources. First, the incidence of medical and psychological conditions which may affect competency is increased among the elderly population. These conditions may also affect the ability to communicate. Frail elderly individuals may be vulnerable to over-reaching by family members and care providers on whom they are dependent for support. Financial and medical considerations may threaten their autonomy and ability to live independently. Frequently, the first contact with the attorney is made by family members who seek advice concerning divestment of the elderly person's assets. The conscientious attorney will be alert to these ethical minefields and assure that his or her conduct adheres to the highest professional standards.

The ethical standards governing the conduct of attorneys in New York State are contained in the Lawyer's Code of Professional Responsibility ("Code"), as adopted by the New York State Bar Association and the Administrative Board of Courts in 1970, as amended in 1990. Where relevant, references will be made to the American Bar Association's Model Rules of Professional Conduct ("Model Rules") which were adopted in 1983[3] and also provide guidance concerning the ethical dilemmas confronted by attorneys representing the elderly. Both the Code and Model Rules have been criticized for failing to provide sufficient guidance to attorneys who work with the elderly.[4]

§ 23.4 Ethical Considerations—Identifying the Client

The most basic ethical question that an attorney must answer is, "Who is the client?" The answer may not be immediately apparent. Frequently, the elderly individual is accompanied to the office by family members, friends or social workers. The attorney must take steps to clearly identify which of these individuals is the client and to memorial-

---

§ 23.3

1. For in-depth coverage of professional responsibility standards for lawyers see, C.W. Wolfram, *Modern Legal Ethics* (1986).

2. In recognition of the growing concern about ethical issues that arise during representation of the elderly, Fordham Law School convened a Conference on Ethical Issues in Representing Older Clients. The conference papers and recommendations are contained in the Fordham Law Review, Vol. 62, No. 5 (1994). *See also*, J. Sangerman, *Ethical Issues in Elder Law*, N.Y.S.B.J., Vol. 65, No. 3, 9/93, p.35.

3. The Model Rules have been adopted by 35 other states.

4. *See* B.A. Green and N. Coleman, *Foreward to Special Issue: Ethical Issues in Representing Older Clients*, 65 Fordham L. Rev. 967 (1994); American College of Trusts and Estates Counsel, *ACTEC Commentaries on the Model Rules of Professional Conduct* (October 1993). The ACTEC Commentaries provide guidance concerning appropriate conduct in the trust and estate planning context. The Fordham Conference and ACTEC Commentaries recognize that both the Code and Model Rules emphasize rules governing conduct in adversarial settings and litigation. Much representation by elder law attorneys is non-adversarial.

§ 23.4

ize this decision in the retainer agreement. The attorney's duty of loyalty is to the client[1] and must not be compromised by influences of third parties.[2] Normally, the person who pays the lawyer's fee will be the client.[3] However, the Code permits a third party to pay the fee provided that the client consents after full disclosure. The lawyer must not permit a person who pays the fee to direct or regulate the professional services rendered to the client.[4]

In many instances, it may be possible for the attorney to represent multiple parties. Multiple representation is perilous due to the possibility that conflicting interests of the parties will impede the lawyer's loyalty to each client.[5] The lawyer must carefully analyze the potential for conflicts and should resolve any doubts about the propriety of multiple representation by refusing joint representation.[6] Slight differences in the interests of the parties may be acceptable.[7] However, if these differences result in irreconcilable conflicts in the course of representation, the lawyer must withdraw from representation of all parties.[8] The lawyer may only represent multiple parties if the possibility of conflict is discussed with all parties and each consents to multiple representation.[9]

There is a particular potential for conflict of interest in the Medicaid planning area when friends or family members seek an attorney's advice and assistance in divesting the assets of the elderly person. While the elderly individual may indeed support the divestiture plan, the attorney must be alert to the possibility of over-reaching by family members. The attorney must take steps to assure that he or she is not assisting the clients in perpetrating a fraud or other illegal act upon the elderly

---

§ 23.4

1. The duty of loyalty is commensurate with the obligation to represent a client zealously within the bounds of the law. Canon 7 of the Lawyer's Code of Professional Responsibility ("Code"). DR 7–101 provides that an attorney may be disciplined for failing to seek the lawful objectives of the client. The duty of loyalty is also discussed in the Comment to Model Rule 1.7.

2. *See* Canon 5: A Lawyer Should Exercise Independent Professional Judgement On Behalf Of A Client. EC 5–1 elaborates that "(t)he professional judgment of a lawyer should be exercised ... solely for the benefit of the client and free of compromising influences and loyalties. Neither the lawyer's personal interests, nor the interests of other clients, nor the desires of third persons should be permitted to dilute the lawyer's loyalty to the client." *See also,* EC 5–21 which cautions that a lawyer must be alert to pressures by non-clients and should disclose their existence to the client. If the lawyer or the client believes that the effectiveness of the lawyer's representation is impaired by these influences, the lawyer should withdraw from representation of the client.

3. EC 5–22 cautions that receipt of compensation from a non-client may lead the attorney to feel a sense of responsibility to the non-client. Similarly, EC 5–23 provides that a lawyer who accepts third party compensation must be on constant guard against compromising influences.

4. DR 5–107(A), (B). Similarly, *see* Model Rules 1.7, 1.8(f).

5. *See* EC 5–14.

6. EC 5–15; DR 5–105(A), (B).

7. EC 5–17.

8. *Id*. The lawyer must defer to the opinion of the client that a conflict exists. EC 5–19. The Comment to Model Rule 1.7 discusses factors to be considered in determining whether a conflict may arise.

9. EC 5–16; DR 5–105(C). For a discussion of multiple representation by the Model Rules, *see* Model Rule 1.7.

individual.[10] Many attorneys refuse to provide divestment advice unless they have personally met or spoken with the elderly individual. Others provide general information about Medicaid transfer penalties and eligibility rules, but will not take affirmative action to accomplish the divestment[11] unless they have obtained the consent of the elderly individual.[12] An attorney may not give legal advice to an individual who is not a client, except to advise the person to retain a lawyer.[13]

§ 23.5 Ethical Considerations—Confidentiality

A lawyer may not generally disclose to a third party information received from a client without the client's consent.[1] Attorneys who represent older clients who suffer from diminished capacity may be tempted to ignore the confidentiality requirement. Interested family members, friends, social workers, government benefits officers and medical providers may contact the attorney seeking information about the client. Many of these individuals may sincerely believe that the information is necessary for the best interests of the client. The attorney must not assume that the client would consent to disclosure of confidential information. When in doubt, the client must be consulted to obtain approval for disclosure of the information.[2]

§ 23.6 Ethical Considerations—Diminished Capacity

Neither the Code nor the Model Rules contain disciplinary rules governing representation of clients with diminished mental capacity.

---

10. DR 7–101(B)(2); DR 7–102(A)(7).

11. For example, preparation of powers of attorney, stock transfers, deeds etc.

12. For further discussion of ethics in Medicaid and estate planning, see E.M. Crosby and I.M. Leff, *Ethical Considerations in Medicaid Estate Planning: An Analysis of the ABA Model Rules of Professional Conduct*, 62 Fordham L. Rev. 1503 (1994) and S.H. Hobbs and F. Wilson Hobbs, *The Ethical Management of Assets for Elder Clients: A Context, Role and Law Approach*, 62 Fordham L. Rev. 1411 (1994).

13. EC 7–18.

§ 23.5

1. Canon 4: A Lawyer Shall Preserve The Confidences And Secrets Of A Client; EC 4–1 through 4–7. The Code provides limited exceptions when disclosure is 1) required by law or a court, 2) necessary to prevent the client from committing a crime, 3) necessary for the lawyer to collect a fee or defend the lawyer against an accusation of improper conduct, or 4) required in order for the lawyer to withdraw an opinion or advice to a third party which was based upon materially inaccurate information or is being used to perpetrate a crime or fraud. DR 4–101(C)(2)-(5). *See also*, DR 7–102(B); Model Rule 1.6.

2. The Fordham Conference on Ethical Issues in Representing Older Clients issued a recommendation that the Comments to Model Rules 1.6 and 1.14 reflect the following:

> Where a lawyer reasonably believes that a client's diminished capacity renders the client unable to appreciate the client's risk of harm, the lawyer may disclose confidential information ... without client consent with the goal of protecting the client from harm....

See Proceedings of the Conference on Ethical Issues in Representing Older Clients, 62 Fordham L. Rev. 989, 992–993. To date, this recommendation has not been adopted by the ABA, the New York State Bar Association or the Administrative Board. Accordingly, attorneys who violate confidentiality, even in an effort to protect the client from harm, run the risk of violating professional standards.

However, both provide limited guidance regarding an attorney's duties to a client with diminished capacity.[1] A client with a mental or physical condition that interferes with his or her decision making ability may thrust additional responsibilities upon the attorney. The attorney may make some decisions for the client, but must attempt to include the client in the decision making process.[2] If the individual has a legally appointed representative such as a guardian, the lawyer should accept direction from the representative.[3]

A client with diminished mental capacity may not be capable of forming the requisite intent to retain the services of an attorney. Alternately, the individual may refuse to follow the attorney's advice due to an impairment of the reasoning process.[4] The Code is silent concerning whether the attorney may take any action to protect the legal interests of the individual in these circumstances.[5]

§ 23.6

1. *See* EC 7–11, 7–12; Model Rule 1.14.

2. EC 7–12. Similarly, Model Rule 1.14 provides that the lawyer shall strive to maintain a normal client-lawyer relationship with a client with diminished capacity. The lawyer shall seek the appointment of a guardian or take other protective action only when the lawyer reasonably believes that the client cannot adequately act in the client's own interest. The comment recognizes that disclosure of the client's disability may adversely affect the client's interests, such as a resulting referral for involuntary commitment. The lawyer may seek guidance from a diagnostician.

3. EC 7–12. **CAVEAT:** Whether an attorney can accept direction from an individual who holds a power of attorney without verifying the validity of the appointment is subject to debate. The attorney who assists the agent to divest the assets of the elderly individual should be particularly cautious.

4. For example, the client may refuse representation in an eviction or foreclosure proceeding in the mistaken belief that legal action is not necessary. For a discussion of representation of clients with diminished mental capacity, *see* P. Margulies, *Access, Connection and Voice: A Contextual Approach to Representing Senior Citizens of Questionable Capacity*, 62 Fordham L. Rev. 1073 (1994); J.E. Rein, *Clients With Destructive and Socially Harmful Choices—What's an Attorney To Do?: Within and Beyond the Competency Construct*, 62 Fordham L. Rev. 1101 (1994).

5. Model Rule 1.14(b) makes cryptic reference to the lawyer's ability to take "protective action" when the lawyer believes that the client cannot adequately act in the client's own interest. The Fordham Conference on Ethical Issues in Representing Older Clients issued a recommendation that Model Rule 1.14(d) be amended to clarify that in the absence of a contractual agreement or pre-existing relationship, an attorney may not act on behalf of a client. However, the Conference recommended that an attorney be permitted to act on behalf of a "purported client" even without the client's agreement for the purpose of taking actions necessary to maintain the status quo or to avoid irreversible harm. The following conditions must be satisfied: 1) an emergency situation exists in which the purported client's substantial health, safety, financial or liability interests are at stake; 2) the lawyer has a good faith belief that the purported client lacks the capacity to make considered judgments about the action due to an impairment of decision-making capacity; 3) time is of the essence; and 4) the lawyer reasonably believes in good faith that no other lawyer is available or willing to act on behalf of the purported client. No professional discipline could be invoked if a lawyer's action or inaction has a reasonable basis. *Recommendations of the Conference*, 62 Fordham Law Review at 990–990. Steps are in progress to have the recommendations of the Conference adopted by the ABA. However, to date there remains no clarification of what "protective action" may be taken by an attorney under Model Rule 1.14(b).

§ 23.7 Social Security Benefits

The Old Age, Survivors, and Disability Program ("OASDI") was enacted in 1935 and is more commonly known as the Social Security Act.[1] The Act provides cash benefits to retired and disabled workers, their dependents and survivors. The program is administered by the Social Security Administration ("SSA").[2] Benefits are financed by taxes that are contributed by workers and employees through the Federal Insurance Compensation Act ("FICA").[3] The following sections will discuss the requirements to receive retirement and survivor's benefits under the Act. The requirements to receive disability benefits are discussed in Chapter 34 "Social Security Disability Cases," *infra*.

§ 23.8 Social Security Benefits—Quarters of Coverage

In order to be eligible to receive Social Security benefits, an individual must have worked in employment which is "covered" by the program.[1] Each year of employment is divided into four equal calendar quarters beginning on January 1, April 1, July 1 and October 1. A worker is credited for each quarter in which he or she meets the minimum earnings requirement.[2] Since 1977, quarters of coverage may be based on annual income regardless of the actual earnings in each quarter: the total income earned in the year is divided by the minimum earnings required for a quarter of coverage.[3]

§ 23.7

1. The Social Security Act is found at 42 U.S.C.A. §§ 401, *et seq*. The regulations governing the program are at 20 C.F.R. §§ 404 *et seq*.

2. **PRACTICE POINTER:** Applications for benefits are filed at local Social Security offices. For information about any aspect of the Social Security program, or to obtain the address and telephone number of a local SSA office, call 1-800-772-1213. New York State is part of Region II of the SSA. The Region II office is located at 26 Federal Plaza, New York, N.Y. 10278.

The SSA publishes the multi-volume Program Operations Manual System ("POMS") as a guideline to local offices on the day to day administration of the program. The POMS do not have the force of law but are widely relied upon by local SSA offices. The complete POMS may be inspected and photocopied at any local SSA office. In addition, the SSA issues Social Security Rulings containing statements of official policies, court decisions, and other interpretations of the law and regulations. Social Security Rulings are published in the Federal Register and may be obtained at SSA regional offices. They are also reported in West's Social Security Reporting Service.

Attorneys who seek additional information concerning Social Security law should consult McCormick, *Social Security Claims and Procedures* (4th ed. 1991); Krauskopf *et al.*, *Elderlaw: Advocacy for the Aging* (2d ed. 1993) Chapter 15 and the Commerce Clearing House Unemployment Insurance Reporter.

3. 42 U.S.C.A. § 401. FICA taxes are also used to finance the Medicare program.

§ 23.8

1. 42 U.S.C.A. § 410. Nearly all work is "covered" by the Act with the most notable exceptions being federal civilian employees hired before 1984, employees of state or local governments not covered by a federal-state agreement, and certain agricultural and domestic workers. *Id.*

2. 42 U.S.C.A. § 413.(d)(1); 20 C.F.R. § 404.143. In 1997, the minimum earnings per quarter were $670. 61 Federal Register 55346. The amount is adjusted each year for inflation.

3. 42 U.S.C.A. § 413(a)(2)(A)(ii); 20 C.F.R. § 404.143(a).

§ 23.9 Social Security Benefits—Insured Status

In order to receive retirement, survivors or dependent benefits, a worker must be "fully insured."[1] Workers are fully insured if they have 40 quarters of coverage, or at least one quarter of coverage, for each year after 1950 (or the year the worker became 21) until the year the worker reached age 62, became disabled or died.[2]

§ 23.10 Social Security Benefits—Calculation of Benefits

The amount of benefits that a retiree, survivor or dependent receives is based on the amount of wages earned while the worker was paying taxes into the system as well as the number of years that the individual worked. The SSA determines the worker's Primary Insurance Amount ("PIA")[1] based upon the worker's earnings record.[2]

Library References:

West's Key No. Digests, Social Security and Public Welfare ⚖140.1.

§ 23.11 Social Security Benefits—Retirement Benefits

A worker is entitled to full retirement benefits at age 65.[1] After December 31, 1999, normal retirement age will increase annually by two month intervals until it reaches age 67 by the year 2022.[2] Workers may file for early retirement at age 62 but the amount of the benefit will be reduced.[3] Workers who delay retirement past age 65 are credited with an

§ 23.9

1. 42 U.S.C.A. § 402(a)(1).

2. 42 U.S.C.A. § 414(a); 20 C.F.R. § 404.110(b).

§ 23.10

1. Calculation of the PIA is a complicated process which is based on indexing a worker's annual earnings to account for inflation. The 35 years of highest earnings are used in determining the PIA. 42 U.S.C.A. § 415; 20 C.F.R. §§ 404.204, et seq.

2. **PRACTICE POINTER:** Anyone may request a copy of his or her earnings record from the local Social Security office. It is a good idea to review the earnings record on a periodic basis to assure that the information is correct. Generally, the earnings record information is correct. However, occasionally the record may be wrong due to the use of incorrect social security numbers or an employer's failure to report wages to the SSA. Information on the earnings record is generally conclusive unless the record is challenged within three years, three months and fifteen days of the end of the year in which the earnings were received. However, the record may be amended at a later time if any of a large number of exceptions are met. See 42 U.S.C.A. § 405(c); 20 C.F.R. §§ 404.802 et seq.

§ 23.11

1. 42 U.S.C.A. § 416(*l*)(1).

2. *Id.*; 20 C.F.R. § 404.313(a)(2).

3. 42 U.S.C.A. § 402(q); 20 C.F.R. §§ 404.312, 404.410–404.413. The amount of the reduction is 5/9ths of 1 per cent for each month before the worker turns 65. Currently the maximum reduction for a worker who elects benefits at age 62 is 20%. When normal retirement age reaches 67, workers who choose early retirement at age

increase in their PIA until age 70.[4]

§ 23.12 Social Security Benefits—Benefits for Spouses, Survivors and Dependents

The spouse, divorced spouse, widow and dependent children of a retired worker may be eligible to receive benefits on the worker's earnings record. A spouse must be at least 62 years of age or be responsible for the care of a child of the insured who is under age 16 or disabled.[1] A spouse of a retired worker receives a benefit equal to one half of the insured's PIA[2] if he or she applies after age 65.[3]

A divorced spouse may receive benefits on the earnings record of a former spouse who is at least 62 years of age or disabled if the marriage lasted at least 10 years and the divorce has been final for at least two years.[4] The divorced spouse must be at least 62 years of age and may not be remarried or entitled to a greater benefit on his or her own earnings record.[5] A divorced spouse receives a benefit equal to one half of the insured's PIA.[6]

A widow or widower is entitled to receive benefits on the account of the deceased fully insured worker.[7] Widows' or widowers' benefits are generally equal to the full PIA of the deceased worker.[8] A widow or widower may apply for benefits at age 60, or as early as age 50 if he or

---

62 will suffer a 30% reduction in monthly benefits.

4. 42 U.S.C.A. § 402(w); 20 C.F.R. § 404.313. The amount of the percentage increase in the PIA for delayed retirement depends on the person's age and the year in which he or she actually applies for retirement benefits. Individuals who delay retirement may still apply for Medicare at age 65. 42 U.S.C.A. § 426.

§ 23.12

1. 42 U.S.C.A. § 416(h)(1); 20 C.F.R. §§ 404.345–404.436. The marriage must have lasted at least one year unless the insured and the spouse have a child together. The marriage must be valid under state law or meet SSA requirements for a "deemed marriage." A "deemed marriage" will be established upon proof that the spouse had a good faith belief that the marriage ceremony was valid and that the marriage would have been valid except for a legal impediment such as an unterminated previous marriage or defect in the marriage procedure.

2. See supra, § 23.10.

3. 42 U.S.C.A. § 402(b)(2); 20 C.F.R. § 404.333. As with a retired worker, a spouse who elects to retire before age 65 will receive reduced benefits. Spousal benefits will not be awarded if the spouse is entitled to greater benefits on his or her own earnings record.

4. 42 U.S.C.A. §§ 402(b)(1)(G),(H), (J), 416(d); 20 C.F.R. § 404.331. Although a spouse may only receive benefits if the insured is collecting benefits, a divorced spouse may receive benefits on the account of a former spouse who is still working. 20 C.F.R. § 404.331. See also, discussion of divorce strategy considerations in Chapter 21 "Domestic Relations," § 21.2, note 9, supra.

5. Id.

6. 42 U.S.C.A. §§ 402(b)(2), (c)(2). However, if the divorced spouse elects to apply for benefits before age 65, the amount of the benefit will be reduced.

7. 42 U.S.C.A. §§ 412(e), (f); 20 C.F.R. § 404.335.

8. 42 U.S.C.A. § 402(e)(2)(A). The benefit amount will be reduced if the widow or widower applies before age 65.

§ 23.12 ELDER LAW Ch. 23

she is disabled.[9] A widow or widower who remarries after age 60 will continue to be eligible for benefits after remarriage.[10]

Qualified children are entitled to receive benefits on the account of an insured retired, disabled or deceased worker.[11] Benefits may also be paid to a dependent parent of an insured worker.[12] Upon the death of an insured worker, the SSA will make a lump sum death payment of $255 or three times the worker's PIA, whichever is smaller.[13]

Library References:

West's Key No. Digests, Social Security and Public Welfare ⇔135.1.

§ 23.13 Social Security Benefits—Reduction in Benefits Due to Earned Income

Social Security retirement benefits may be reduced if an individual continues to work up until age 70. In 1997, individuals under age 65 were allowed to earn up to $8,640 without affecting their Social Security retirement benefit. However, after this exempt amount was exceeded, the amount of the benefit was reduced by $1 for each $3 in excess of the exempt amount. Individuals age 65 through 69 were allowed to earn up to $13,500. After this amount, their benefit was reduced by $1 for each $3 over the exempt amount.[1]

§ 23.14 Social Security Benefits—Overpayments and Underpayments

The Social Security Administration is required to make adjustments to benefit payments in the event that a beneficiary receives either more

---

9. 42 U.S.C.A. §§ 402(e)(1)(B), 402(f)(1)(B); 20 C.F.R. § 404.335(c). A disabled widow or widower will receive only 50% of the insured's PIA if he or she applies at age 50.

10. 42 U.S.C.A. §§ 402(e)(3), (f)(4); 20 C.F.R. § 404.335(e). A disabled spouse may remarry after age 50 and retain eligibility for benefits on the account of the former spouse. However, if the widow or widower would be entitled to greater benefits on the account of the new spouse, the benefits on the account of the former spouse will cease.

11. 42 U.S.C.A. §§ 402(d), 416(e); 20 C.F.R. §§ 404.350 *et seq*. The term "child" includes adopted children, stepchildren and grandchildren under some circumstances.

12. 42 U.S.C.A. § 402(h); 20 C.F.R. §§ 404.370 *et seq*.

13. 42 U.S.C.A. § 402(i); 20 C.F.R. § 404.390.

§ 23.13

1. 42 U.S.C.A. §§ 403(b), 403(f)(3); 20 C.F.R. §§ 404.415, 404.434. The 1997 figures are published in 61 Federal Register 55346. The amount exempt from consideration is revised annually to reflect increases in the cost of living index.

CAVEAT: Individuals are advised to report their earnings to the SSA so that the amount of their benefit will reflect any reductions due to earned income. Unreported income is likely to be identified by the SSA through matching of computerized earnings records. An overpayment of benefits may lead to termination of benefits until the amount of the overpayment is recovered. 42 U.S.C.A. § 404(a)(1)(A); 20 C.F.R. § 404.502. *See infra*, for further discussion of overpayments and underpayments.

or less than is correct.[1] Notification to the beneficiary of the underpayment or overpayment is made in an initial determination.[2] An underpayment is corrected by a lump sum adjustment to future payments.[3] An overpayment may be repaid in full by the beneficiary or, more usually, is corrected by a reduction in future benefit payments.[4] A beneficiary who believes that an overpayment determination is erroneous may request reconsideration through the appeals process.[5] Additionally, the beneficiary may seek a reduction in the amount of the overpayment which is deducted from the monthly benefit check or request a waiver of the amount of the overpayment.[6]

Library References:

West's Key No. Digests, Social Security and Public Welfare ⇔140.3.

§ 23.15 Social Security Benefits—Administrative and Judicial Appeals[1]

An initial determination concerning an aspect of eligibility for Social Security benefits may be appealed by filing a request for reconsideration.[2] A reconsideration request must be filed within 60 days of the initial determination.[3] Generally, reconsideration is a paper review of the file by a person who did not take part in the initial determination.[4] The reconsideration decision will be in writing[5] and may be appealed by filing a request for a hearing before an Administrative Law Judge ("ALJ")[6] within 60 days of the reconsideration decision.[7] The claimant may appear personally or by a representative, present evidence, make oral and

§ 23.14

1. 42 U.S.C.A. § 404(a)(1).
2. 20 C.F.R. §§ 404.902(j), (k)(1).
3. 42 U.S.C.A. § 404(a)(1)(B).
4. 42 U.S.C.A. § 404(a)(1)(A); 20 C.F.R. § 404.502. Note that if the beneficiary fails to correct the overpayment, the Social Security Administration is permitted to collect the overpayment by a reduction in a future tax refund after notice to the Secretary of the Treasury. Id.
5. 20 C.F.R. § 404.902. See infra, § 23.15 for a description of the appeals process.
6. 42 U.S.C.A. § 404(b); 20 C.F.R. §§ 404.506—404.512. Waiver of recovery will be granted if the beneficiary establishes that he or she was without fault in causing the overpayment and that recovery of the overpayment would defeat the purposes of the Act or be against equity and good conscience. 20 C.F.R. § 404.506. There is no time limit for a request for a waiver.

§ 23.15

1. For a more detailed discussion of the appeals process before the SSA, see Chapter 34 "Social Security Disability Cases," §§ 34.25–34.30, 34.41–34.64, infra. The statute sets forth a general outline of the appeals process at 42 U.S.C.A. § 405. The regulations at 20 C.F.R. §§ 404.907 et seq. contain more specific provisions governing the administrative process.
2. 20 C.F.R. § 404.907.
3. 20 C.F.R. § 404.909.
4. 20 C.F.R. § 404.913.
5. 20 C.F.R. § 404.922.
6. 20 C.F.R. §§ 404.929, 404.930.
7. 20 C.F.R. §§ 404.930, 404.933. For the addresses and telephone numbers of Offices of Hearings and Appeals, see Chapter 34 "Social Security Disability Cases," § 34.34, infra.

§ 23.15 ELDER LAW Ch. 23

written legal arguments, subpoena documents and witnesses, and examine and cross-examine witnesses.[8]

The ALJ's decision may be appealed by requesting review by the SSA Appeals Council within 60 days of the decision of the ALJ.[9] The Appeals Council may also review an ALJ decision on its own motion.[10] The Appeals Council may review a claim on the following grounds: abuse of discretion by the ALJ, an error of law, that the decision is not supported by substantial evidence, or that there are policy or procedural issues which affect the public interest.[11] The Appeals Council has discretion to accept or deny a request for review.[12]

The claimant may file a judicial action in federal district court appealing a final decision of the SSA.[13] The federal court action must be filed within 60 days of the Appeals Council's final decision or denial of review.[14]

Library References:
West's Key No. Digests, Social Security and Public Welfare ⚖142.5.

§ 23.16 Social Security Benefits—Representation by Attorneys

A claimant may be represented by counsel in any dealings with the SSA.[1] The claimant should file an Appointment of Representative Form so the representative may obtain information about the claim, review documents and act on behalf of the claimant.[2] Attorney's fees are subject to review by the agency.[3] The SSA may make direct payments to an attorney[4] from an award of retroactive benefits in an amount which is the smaller of 25% of the past-due benefits, the fee awarded by the

---

8. 20 C.F.R. §§ 404.929, 404.950.

9. 20 C.F.R. §§ 404.967, 404.968. For a sample form for requesting Appeals Council review, see Chapter 34 "Social Security Disability Cases," § 34.75, infra.

10. 20 C.F.R. § 404.969.

11. 20 C.F.R. § 404.970.

12. 20 C.F.R. § 404.967.

13. 42 U.S.C.A. § 405(g); 20 C.F.R. § 404.981.

14. Id.

§ 23.16

1. 42 U.S.C.A. § 406(a)(1); 20 C.F.R. § 404.1705. Non-attorney agents may also represent claimants before the SSA if they establish that they are of good character and are competent to provide representation.

2. 20 C.F.R. §§ 404.1707, 404.1710. Appointment of Representative Forms are available from any local SSA office.

3. 42 U.S.C.A. § 406(a)(1); 20 C.F.R. § 404.1720. For more information concerning approval of fees by the SSA, see Chapter 34 "Social Security Disability Cases," §§ 34.33, 34.52–34.54, infra. For sample retainer agreement forms for representation of clients in Social Security and SSI disability cases, see Chapter 34 "Social Security Disability Cases," infra §§ 34.67, 34.68.

4. Non-attorney claimants may collect a fee for their representation if the fee is approved by the SSA. However, the agency will not make direct payments out of an award of past-due benefits to a non-attor-

agency, or the amount agreed upon by the claimant and the attorney.[5] The SSA will automatically approve a fee agreement if the agreed upon fee does not exceed the lesser of 25% of a past-due award of benefits or $4,000.[6] The SSA may award a fee even if no retroactive benefits are payable.[7] Alternately, an attorney may be entitled to an award of fees paid by the SSA under the Equal Access to Judgment Act.[8]

§ 23.17 Supplemental Security Income for the Elderly

The Supplemental Security Income ("SSI") program provides cash benefits to financially needy aged, blind and disabled individuals. The eligibility requirements for the program are governed by federal law and regulations.[1] The program is administered by the SSA.[2] The federal government provides a basic income grant to eligible individuals which is supplemented by New York State.

The following sections will cover the basic eligibility requirements for SSI payments to needy elderly individuals.[3] The requirements to receive benefits based on blindness and disability are covered in Chapter 34 "Social Security Disability Cases," *infra*.

Library References:

West's Key No. Digests, Social Security and Public Welfare ⚖175.5.

---

ney. 20 C.F.R. §§ 404.1720(b)(4), 404.1730(b)(2).

5. 42 U.S.C.A. § 406(b); 20 C.F.R. § 404.1730(b).

6. 42 U.S.C.A. § 406(a)(2).

7. 20 C.F.R. § 404.1725(b)(2).

CAVEAT: Attorneys should be warned that the SSA is not generous in awarding fees in the absence of an award of past-due benefits.

8. 5 U.S.C.A. § 504; 28 U.S.C.A. § 2412. The most common argument used to justify an award of fees against the SSA is that the attorney represented a prevailing party in an adversary proceeding, the government's position was not substantially justified, and that there are no circumstances which make an award of fees against the government unjust. 28 U.S.C.A. § 2412(d)(1)(A).

§ 23.17

1. 42 U.S.C.A. §§ 1381–1385; 20 C.F.R. Pt. 416.

2. **PRACTICE POINTER:** Applications for benefits are filed at local Social Security offices. For information about any aspect of the SSI program and to obtain the address and telephone number of a local Social Security office, call 1-800-772-1213. New York State is part of Region II of the SSA. The Region II office is located at 26 Federal Plaza, New York, N.Y. 10278.

The SSA publishes the multi-volume Program Operations Manual System ("POMS") as a guideline to local offices on the day to day administration of the SSI program. The POMS do not have the force of law but are widely relied upon by local SSA offices. The complete POMS may be inspected and photocopied at any local SSA office. In addition, the SSA issues Social Security Rulings containing statements of official policies, court decisions and other interpretations of law and regulations governing the SSI program. Social Security Rulings are published in the Federal Register and can be obtained at the Region II office. They are also reported in West's Social Security Reporting Service.

Attorneys who seek additional information concerning the SSI program should consult West's Social Security Reporting Service and Krauskopf et al., *Elderlaw: Advocacy for the Aging* (2d ed. 1993) Chapter 17.

3. **CAVEAT:** The eligibility requirements and procedural aspects of the SSI program are extremely complex. This chapter will provide only a basic outline of the program. Attorneys are cautioned to refer

§ 23.18 Supplemental Security Income for the Elderly—Categorical Eligibility

In order to be categorically eligible to receive SSI benefits, an individual must be aged, blind or disabled.[1] An aged individual is 65 years or older.[2] The claimant must also establish that he or she is 1) a resident of the United States and 2) either a citizen or an alien lawfully admitted for permanent residence or otherwise permanently residing in the United States under color of law.[3]

§ 23.19 Supplemental Security Income for the Elderly—Financial Eligibility

In addition to establishing categorical eligibility for SSI benefits, a claimant's countable income and resources must not exceed limits established by the program.[1] Excluded resources include but are not limited to the following: the home (including related land) so long as the individual continues to use it as a principal residence;[2] household goods and personal effects;[3] an automobile;[4] a burial space, or an agreement representing the purchase of a burial space, for the use of the claimant or his or her immediate family;[5] up to $1,500, plus accumulated interest, which is separately identifiable and has been set aside to meet the burial and related expenses of the claimant or spouse;[6] property essential to self-

to primary sources when representing a client before the SSA.

§ 23.18

1. 42 U.S.C.A. § 1382c(a)(1)(A); 20 C.F.R. § 416.202(a).

2. *Id.* **PRACTICE POINTER:** Proof of age is generally a simple matter which can be established by birth and baptism certificates. However, the regulations contain examples of other ways in which age can be established in the absence of such preferred documentation. *See* C.F.R. §§ 416.801–806.

3. 42 U.S.C.A. § 1382c(a)(1)(B)(1); 20 C.F.R. §§ 416.202(b), 416.1600 *et seq.*

§ 23.19

1. 42 U.S.C.A. § 1382(a)(1); 20 C.F.R. § 416.202.

2. 42 U.S.C.A. § 1382b(a)(1); 20 C.F.R. § 416.1212. The home of an individual who resides in an institution such as a nursing home will retain its exempt status as long as the individual intends to return to the home or the home continues to be occupied by a spouse or dependent relative. 20 C.F.R. § 416.1212(c).

3. 42 U.S.C.A. § 1382a(a)(2)(A); 20 C.F.R. § 416.1216(b). The maximum value of excluded household goods and personal effects is $2,000. However, the SSA will generally assume that this value has not been exceeded unless it is alerted to the possibility that the claimant possesses unusual or valuable items.

4. 42 U.S.C.A. § 1382b(a)(2)(A); 20 C.F.R. § 416.1218. The regulations provide that the value of the automobile must not exceed $4,500 unless the automobile is necessary for employment, medical treatment, essential daily activities, or is for the use of a handicapped individual.

5. 42 U.S.C.A. § 1382b(a)(2)(B); 20 C.F.R. § 416.1231(a).

6. 42 U.S.C.A. § 1382b(d); 20 C.F.R. § 416.1231(b). The amount that may be retained in the burial fund will be reduced by the cash surrender value of any life insurance policies or irrevocable trusts available to meet burial expenses of the claimant or his or her spouse. *Id.*

CAVEAT: The SSA may determine that the entire amount of a burial fund is an available resource if the individual fails to keep the account separate from other funds and/or uses any of the funds. For this reason, clients should be cautioned to keep the burial funds totally separate from other funds. Withdrawals must never be made

support;[7] life insurance policies with a cash surrender value under $1,500;[8] and retroactive awards of Social Security or SSI benefits for six months following receipt.[9]

The maximum value of non-excluded resources which may be retained by an individual is $2,000.[10] A couple may retain combined resources of $3,000.[11] A claimant who meets the income requirements, but whose resources exceed the limits, may transfer or dispose of the excess resources and immediately establish eligibility for benefits.[12]

In determining the claimant's income, the SSA includes both earned[13] and unearned[14] income. In-kind income includes non-cash assistance with food, clothing and shelter.[15] The first $20 of both earned and unearned income is excluded per month.[16] In addition, the first $65 per month of earned income plus one half of the remainder is excluded.[17] Up to $20 per month of infrequent earned income[18] and $10 per month of

from the account, even to remove accumulated interest.

7. 42 U.S.C.A. § 1382b(a)(3); 20 C.F.R. §§ 416.1220 et seq.

8. 42 U.S.C.A. § 1382b(a); 20 C.F.R. § 416.1230. Note that the combined cash value of life insurance policies and the burial fund may not exceed $1,500.

9. 42 U.S.C.A. § 1382b(a)(7); 20 C.F.R. § 416.1233.

10. 42 U.S.C.A. §§ 1382(a)(1)(B), 1382(a)(3)(B); 20 C.F.R. § 404.1205.

11. 42 U.S.C.A. §§ 1382(a)(2)(B), 1382(a)(3)(A); 20 C.F.R. § 404.1205.

12. 42 U.S.C.A. § 1382b(b)(1); 20 C.F.R. § 416.1246. Prior to July 1, 1988, such transfers resulted in a period of ineligibility for benefits.

CAVEAT: Although there is no longer any penalty for transferring assets under the SSI program, such transfers will result in a period of ineligibility for Medicaid and possibly subject the attorney to criminal penalties. See infra, § 23.76. Individuals who dispose of resources in order to obtain SSI benefits should document how these resources were disposed of in order to convince SSA authorities that the resources are no longer available to them.

13. 42 U.S.C.A. § 1382a(a)(1); 20 C.F.R. § 416.1110. Earned income includes wages, net earnings from self-employment, refunds of federal income taxes, royalties, honorariums and earnings from services in a sheltered workshop.

14. 42 U.S.C.A. § 1382a(a)(2); 20 C.F.R. §§ 416.1120, 416.1121. All income which is not earned is unearned. This includes annuities, pensions, retirement or disability payments, worker's compensation, veteran's benefits, social security and unemployment benefits, alimony and support payments, prizes, awards, rents, interests, royalties, dividends, inheritances and gifts.

15. 42 U.S.C.A. § 1382a(a)(2)(A); 20 C.F.R. §§ 416.1121(h), 416.1130 et seq. In-kind income may be either earned or unearned and is valued at the current market value. In-kind shelter includes third party payment of rent, mortgage payments, property taxes, heating, fuel, gas, electricity, water, sewer and garbage fees. In-kind payments made by a non-profit organization or heating company are excluded from income. 42 U.S.C.A. § 1382a(b)(13); 20 C.F.R. § 416.1157.

PRACTICE POINTER: In-kind assistance which cannot be used for food, clothing or shelter is not counted. Examples of uncounted in-kind income include payment of telephone or cable television fees, medical payments, transportation and trips. The in-kind assistance must be paid directly by a third party. A claimant who lives in the household of another and receives both food and shelter from that person will be presumed to receive 1/3 of the federal benefit rate as in-kind income. 42 U.S.C.A. § 1382a(a)(2)(A)(i); 20 C.F.R. §§ 416.1131, 416.1132.

16. 42 U.S.C.A. § 1382a(b)(2)(A); 20 C.F.R. § 416.1124(c)(12).

17. 42 U.S.C.A. § 1382a(b)(4); 20 C.F.R. §§ 416.1112(c)(5), (7).

18. 42 U.S.C.A. § 1382a(b)(3)(A); 20 C.F.R. § 416.1124(c)(6).

§ 23.19 ELDER LAW Ch. 23

infrequent unearned income[19] are also excluded.

The SSA will "deem" the income and resources of a spouse who resides with the claimant, the parent of a claimant who is under 18 years of age, or the sponsor of an alien to be available to the claimant.[20]

§ 23.20 Supplemental Security Income for the Elderly—Benefit Calculation

SSI benefits will be paid to individuals whose other countable income does not exceed the maximum income level set for the program.[1] This maximum varies in each state and is adjusted annually to reflect increases in the cost of living.[2] Claimants receive SSI payments which bring their income up to the maximum permitted for their household size and living arrangement. In 1997, New York provides the following monthly benefit levels: $570 for an individual or $828.50 for a couple who live alone; $507 for an individual or $771 for a couple who live with others;[3] $345.67 for an individual or $529 for a couple who live in the household of another.[4] Individuals who reside in congregate care facilities and nursing homes receive minimal payments to cover their personal needs.[5]

§ 23.21 Supplemental Security Income for the Elderly—Underpayments and Overpayments

SSI beneficiaries are required to report changes in their eligibility status to the SSA.[1] The program's complex financial eligibility rules lead to frequent determinations that the amount of the benefit check that the individual received was erroneous. Beneficiaries may receive notice that they have been either underpaid or overpaid. Underpayments are cor-

---

19. 42 U.S.C.A. § 1382a(b)(3)(B); 20 C.F.R. § 416.1112(c)(2).

20. 42 U.S.C.A. § 1382c(f); 20 C.F.R. §§ 416.1202–416.1204. *See generally,* Chapter 19 "Immigration Law," *supra.*

§ 23.20

1. SSI benefits are intended to supplement other sources of income. Thus an individual who receives Social Security retirement, veterans' benefits or other pension may receive an additional SSI payment if the total income from other sources is less than the maximum countable income permitted by the program.

2. 42 U.S.C.A. §§ 1382a(a)(1)(A), 1382a(a)(2)(A), 1382f.

PRACTICE POINTER: The maximum monthly income level is a combination of the federal benefit level and state supplementation. The adjusted federal rate is published each year in the Federal Register. The New York State Department of Social Services publishes a chart of the SSI combined state and federal benefit levels each year. Figures for years after 1997 may be obtained by calling the local office of the Department of Social Services.

3. This rate applies where the couple or individual lives with others and shares food with at least one other person.

4. This rate applies when the SSA has determined that the household receives in-kind support subject to the one-third reduction rule discussed *supra.*

5. The personal needs allowance for an individual who resides in a nursing home which is paid for by Medicaid is $55 per month.

§ 23.21

1. 20 C.F.R. § 416.708.

rected by adjustments in future payments.[2] Overpayments are usually collected by reductions in the amounts of future benefit checks.[3] The SSA generally reduces future benefits by 10% per month unless the overpayment was the result of fraud or misrepresentation.[4] The beneficiary may also elect to make a lump sum repayment of the amount of the overpayment. Beneficiaries who believe that the overpayment decision is erroneous may appeal by requesting reconsideration through the regular appeals process.[5] Additionally, the beneficiary may seek a reduction in the amount of the overpayment which is deducted from the monthly benefit check[6] or request a waiver of the overpayment.[7]

§ 23.22 Supplemental Security Income for the Elderly—Administrative and Judicial Appeals[1]

The process to appeal SSI decisions is generally the same as the process for appealing Social Security retirement benefits.[2] An initial determination by the SSA is appealed by filing a request for reconsideration within 60 days.[3] If the beneficiary requests reconsideration within 10 days of an initial termination, the SSA may not reduce, suspend or terminate benefits until the reconsideration decision has been made.[4] The reconsideration decision may be appealed to an ALJ by filing a request for a hearing within 60 days.[5] The decision of the ALJ may be appealed within 60 days to the Appeals Council.[6] A final determination of

2. 42 U.S.C.A. § 1383(b)(1)(A); 20 C.F.R. §§ 416.535, 416.536, 416.538–416.543.

3. 42 U.S.C.A. § 1383(b)(1)(A); 20 C.F.R. §§ 416.535, 416.537, 416.438, 416.570.

4. 42 U.S.C.A. § 1383(b)(1)(B)(ii); 20 C.F.R. § 416.571.

5. See infra, § 23.21.

6. 42 U.S.C.A. § 1383(b)(1)(B); 20 C.F.R. § 416.571.

PRACTICE POINTER: A beneficiary who seeks to lower the amount of the monthly reduction of the benefit check should establish proof that he or she needs a higher amount in order to meet monthly living expenses, but that the overpayment can still be repaid in a reasonable period of time.

7. 20 C.F.R. §§ 416.550–416.556. Waiver of recovery will be granted if the beneficiary establishes that he or she was without fault in causing the overpayment and that recovery of the overpayment would either defeat the purposes of the program, be against equity and good conscience, or impede the efficient administration of the program due to the small amount of the overpayment. There is no time limit for a request for waiver. However, if the waiver request is made within 30 days of the overpayment notice, the SSA will not collect the overpayment until a decision is made on the request for the waiver.

§ 23.22

1. For a more detailed discussion of the appeals process before the SSA, see Chapter 34 "Social Security Disability Cases," §§ 34.25–34.30 infra.

2. The statutory provisions governing the appeals process for SSI determinations are found at 42 U.S.C.A. § 1383(c). For a discussion of the appellate process in Social Security cases, see supra, § 23.15.

3. 20 C.F.R. § 416.1409. Reconsideration may take the form of a case review, informal conference or formal conference depending on the nature of the case and the type of evidence which the beneficiary seeks to introduce. 20 C.F.R. § 416.1413.

4. 20 C.F.R. § 416.1336(b).

5. 20 C.F.R. §§ 416.1429, et seq., 416.1433.

6. 20 C.F.R. §§ 416.1467–416.1468.

§ 23.22   ELDER LAW   Ch. 23

the Appeals Council may be appealed to federal district court within 60 days.[7]

§ 23.23   Supplemental Security Income for the Elderly—Representation by Attorneys

The rules governing representation of claimants in SSI cases are the same as for representing claimants for Social Security benefits.[1] Representation by attorneys and qualified non-attorney representatives is permitted.[2] Attorneys fees must be approved by the SSA.[3] In addition, successful parties may be eligible for an award of fees against the SSA under the Equal Access to Justice Act.[4]

§ 23.24   Retirement Income From Qualified Plans

Approximately half of all workers are employed at jobs which will pay a pension upon the retirement of the worker. Most of these private pensions are subject to regulation by the Employee Retirement Income Security Act of 1974 ("ERISA").[1] The Tax Code provides numerous incentives for employers to establish pensions plans.

Qualified plans are pension plans which meet ERISA tax requirements. These plans result in tax benefits to the employee as well as the employer. Generally, qualified plans are one of three types.

(1) A *defined benefit plan* establishes a definite payment amount for each employee, such as five dollars per month for every year of service. Contributions are fixed at whatever amount is needed to produce that benefit.

(2) A variation of the defined benefit plan is a *target benefit plan* which aims for a defined benefit and calculates the contribution necessary to produce that amount. However, the benefit is not guaranteed and will be adjusted to whatever the contributions produce.

(3) The *defined contribution plan*, now the most common plan, establishes a certain contribution amount per employee and pays whatever that contribution generates.

§ 23.25   Retirement Income From Qualified Plans—Eligibility, Vesting and Accrual

An employee has the right to join the pension plan upon obtaining

---

7. 42 U.S.C.A. § 1383(c)(3); 20 C.F.R. §§ 416.1481, *et seq.*

§ 23.23

1. For more information, *see supra,* § 23.16. *See also* Chapter 34 "Social Security Disability Cases," §§ 34.33, 33.52–33.54, *infra.*

2. 42 U.S.C.A. § 1383(d)(2)(A); 20 C.F.R. §§ 416.1520, *et seq.*

3. 20 C.F.R. §§ 416.1520, 416.1525.

4. 5 U.S.C.A. § 504; 28 U.S.C.A. § 2412.

§ 23.24

1. 26 U.S.C.A. §§ 401, *et seq.*; 29 U.S.C.A. §§ 1001 *et seq.*

age 21 or completing one year of service.[1] Credit must be given for each year in which 1,000 hours of service are completed. Annual service of less than 500 hours may cause a break in service. Annual service of 500 to 1,000 hours may be added to other periods. Since 1988, employers may not exclude employees from participating due to their age.[2] Prior to 1988, employees past age 65 could be excluded.

After an employee qualifies to join the pension plan, the next issue is when the pension right vests. An employee whose rights have vested has the right to receive retirement benefits even if he or she changes jobs or terminates employment. Qualified plans may use various vesting schedules. However, they must provide either that the employee has a nonforfeitable right to 100% of accrued benefits from employer contributions after five years of service or that the vested right be graded over three to seven years beginning with 20% at year 3 until 100% is vested after seven years.[3] Vesting rights vary. Thus, each plan must be reviewed to determine the specific vesting schedule.

"Accrued benefits" is the term used for the amount of benefits a person is entitled to receive in a defined contribution plan, *i.e.*, the balance in the plan at a particular time.[4]

Library References:

West's Key No. Digests, Pensions ⊙=61, 62.

§ 23.26 Retirement Income From Qualified Plans— Contribution Limitations

ERISA sets limits on the amounts which may be contributed to qualified plans. Compensation included in determining the amount of non-taxable contributions cannot exceed $150,000, plus cost of living adjustments, for plans after December 31, 1993.[1] Employee contributions were limited to $9,500 in 1997.

Library References:

West's Key No. Digests, Pensions ⊙=101.

§ 23.27 Retirement Income From Qualified Plans— Payment of Benefits

Pension plans may pay benefits according to fixed benefit or unit formulas. *Fixed plans* pay a certain amount per month. A *unit plan* pays

§ 23.25
1. 29 U.S.C.A. § 1052(a)(1)(A).
2. 29 C.F.R. § 860.120(f)(1)(iv)(B)(1)-(7).
3. 29 U.S.C.A. § 1053.
4. 29 U.S.C.A. § 1054(b).

§ 23.26
1. Internal Revenue Code ("I.R.C.") § 402(q)(1).

a certain percentage of the plan balance per month.[1]

Benefits may be paid out in the following manners:

(1) A *straight life annuity* pays for the life of the retiree;

(2) A *joint and survivor annuity* pays for the lifetime of the retiree and one other beneficiary, usually the spouse;

(3) A *straight life annuity with the period certain* pays for the retiree's life and for a guaranteed period of time, for example, 20 years. If the retiree dies before the end of the time period, the beneficiary receives the same sum for the balance of the period;

(4) A *fixed amount fixed period benefit* is paid in a number of installments. For example, $50,000 in 60 equal monthly payments and if the retiree dies before the period expires, the beneficiary receives the remaining payments; and

(5) Certain plans pay benefits which are coordinated with Social Security and adjusted to provide a level income, depending on when Social Security payments begin.

Library References:

West's Key No. Digests, Pensions ⟸138.

§ 23.28 Retirement Income From Qualified Plans—Alienation and Assignment

Generally, employees may not assign or alienate more than 10% of their pension benefits.[1] This protects them from creditors.[2]

Library References:

West's Key No. Digests, Pensions ⟸138.

§ 23.29 Retirement Income From Qualified Plans—Spousal Rights

Defined benefit and defined contribution plans must provide for survivorship benefits unless they are waived by the spouse.[1] Usually, survivor benefits are paid as a joint and survivor annuity with the payment to the surviving spouse of not less than 50% of the amount payable during the joint lives of the participant and the spouse. If the participant dies before retirement, payment to the surviving spouse must still be the actuarial equivalent of 50% of the balance of the participant's

---

§ 23.27

1. I.R.C. § 401(a)(9).

§ 23.28

1. I.R.C. § 414; 29 U.S.C.A. § 1056. See generally, Scheinkman, et al., *New York Law of Domestic Relations* (West 1996) Ch. 18 "Private and Public Retirement Plans."

2. *See* Borges, et al., *Enforcing Judgments and Collecting Debts in New York* (West 1996) ¶¶ 7:269–7:273.

§ 23.29

1. 29 U.S.C.A. § 1055.

account at death.[2] These rules do not apply if the marriage lasts less than a year.[3]

§ 23.30 Retirement Income From Qualified Plans—Qualified Domestic Relations Orders

A Qualified Domestic Relations Order ("QDRO") is issued in family court or supreme court in marital disputes. It can provide for the distribution of the present value of a joint and survivor annuity to a spouse. The QDRO can order an immediate distribution of the plan proceeds if the value of the order does not exceed $3,500. A QDRO may also provide that a divorced spouse is entitled to be treated as a surviving spouse.[1]

§ 23.31 Retirement Income From Qualified Plans—Waiver of Spousal Rights

A spouse may waive his or her rights in a qualified plan. The waived consent must be witnessed by a plan representative or a notary public.[1] If the spouse is legally incompetent, a legal guardian may give consent.[2]

§ 23.32 Retirement Income From Qualified Plans—Taxation of Contributions

Employers' contributions are not taxable to the employee until the pension is distributed.[1] Employees may take deductions from gross income for their contributions to qualified retirement plans or to an IRA.[2]

§ 23.33 Retirement Income From Qualified Plans—Distributions

Distributions from qualified plans are generally taxable when distributed.[1] Therefore, it is important to carefully plan the distribution.

2. 29 U.S.C.A. § 1055(e)(2).
3. 29 U.S.C.A. § 1055(f)(1).

§ 23.30

1. 29 U.S.C.A. § 1056(d)(3). *See generally*, Scheinkman, *et al.*, *New York Law of Domestic Relations* (West 1996) Ch. 18, § 18.20.

§ 23.31

1. 29 U.S.C.A. § 1055(c)(2)(A). **CAVEAT:** An antenuptial agreement waiving all rights to property of a future spouse does not constitute a valid consent to the waiver of the spouse's right to survivorship annuity since the signer of the ante-nuptial agreement was not a spouse at the time the agreement was signed. Hurwitz v. Sher, 982 F.2d 778 (2d Cir.1992), cert. denied 508 U.S. 912, 113 S.Ct. 2345, 124 L.Ed.2d 255 (1993). Therefore, parties to a prenuptial agreement who desire to design an effective waiver should include an agreement obligating each party to execute the waiver after the marriage has taken place.

2. 26 C.F.R. § 1.401(a)–20(Q27).

§ 23.32

1. I.R.C. § 402(a)(1).
2. I.R.C. § 219(a).

§ 23.33

1. I.R.C. §§ 402(a)(1), 408.

§ 23.33 ELDER LAW Ch. 23

For a discussion of strategy in planning distributions, *see infra*, Chapter 24 "Estate Planning," § 24.37.

§ 23.34 Retirement Income From Qualified Plans—Termination or Merger

An employer may terminate a pension plan. ERISA regulates the allocation priority of plan assets among participants in the event of plan termination.[1] Defined benefit plans which become insolvent may be protected by the Pension Benefit Guarantee Corporation.[2] Consolidation of a plan must provide rights equal to those included prior to merger.

§ 23.35 Retirement Income From Qualified Plans—Appeals

ERISA requires every qualified plan to establish claim procedures providing adequate information regarding plan claims and appeals.[1] Federal and state courts have jurisdiction over disputes concerning qualified plans.[2] Note that the federal courts are authorized to award attorneys' fees to a prevailing party.[3]

§ 23.36 Railroad Retirement Benefits

The Railroad Retirement program provides benefits very similar to Social Security for employees covered under the Railroad Retirement Act.[1] The program is administered by the Railroad Retirement Board ("RRB"), an independent agency. Its office is located in Chicago and it has regional field offices throughout the country. The RRB also distributes Social Security benefits to people who are eligible for both Railroad Retirement and Social Security benefits.

The Railroad Retirement Act is found at 45 U.S.C.A. Pts. 231, *et seq.* Regulations are found at 20 C.F.R. Pts. 200 through 266. The Railroad Retirement Board issues a Retirement Claims Manual, Retirement Claims Manual Circulars, Policy Decisions and a Field Operating Manual. It also publishes decisions and rulings of the Railroad Retirement Board at 20 C.F.R. § 200.3.

Railroad Retirement benefits include retirement benefits, spousal benefits and disability benefits. To be eligible for full pension benefits, a retiree must be either 60 years of age with 30 years of service or 65 years of age with 10 years of service. A reduced pension will be paid to

§ 23.34
1. 29 U.S.C.A. § 1344; 26 C.F.R. § 1.401–6.
2. 29 U.S.C.A. §§ 1321(b), 1322, 1322a, 1431.

§ 23.35
1. 29 U.S.C.A. § 1133.

2. 29 U.S.C.A. § 1132.
3. 29 U.S.C.A. § 1132(g).

§ 23.36
1. 45 U.S.C.A. § 231.

participants who retire at age 62 with 10 to 30 years of service. Surviving spouses and dependent children may also be eligible for benefits on the account of a participant.[2] A worker who becomes disabled may be eligible for disability benefits. If a person lacks capacity to receive benefits, a representative payee may be appointed.[3]

If a claim for Railroad Retirement benefits is denied, the applicant may seek reconsideration.[4] Additional information may be submitted upon reconsideration. If the reconsideration is denied, a hearing officer's hearing may be requested.[5] Appeal from the hearing officer's decision is to the Railroad Retirement Board. Appeal from the Railroad Retirement Board is to the U.S. Court of Appeals for the circuit in which the claimant resides, to the U.S. Court of Appeals for the Seventh Circuit, or to the U.S. Court of Appeals for the District of Columbia.[6] An award of retroactive benefits may be paid only to the claimant and will not include an assessment of attorneys fees.[7] Accordingly, attorney fee arrangements must be made with the client in advance.

Library References:
West's Key No. Digests, Social Security and Public Welfare ⚖166.1.

§ 23.37 Benefits for Federal Employees

Federal employees are covered under two retirement systems. Federal employees hired before 1984 are generally covered under the Civil Service Retirement System.[1] Federal employees hired after January 1, 1987 are generally covered under the Federal Employee Retirement System ("FERS").[2] Federal Civil Service employees hired between January 1, 1984 and December 31, 1986 were entitled to elect FERS coverage.

Library References:
West's Key No. Digests, United States ⚖39(15).

§ 23.38 Benefits for Federal Employees—Federal Employees Retirement System ("FERS")

Participants in FERS receive a combination of Social Security and supplemental retirement benefits. Employees may also participate in a tax deferred savings plan.[1] The federal government contributes a percentage of the participant's base pay. The percentage depends on the

2. 45 U.S.C.A. § 231(a)(c); 20 C.F.R. § 216.20.

3. 45 U.S.C.A. § 231k. See 20 C.F.R. Pt. 266 for full discussion of the process for appointing a representative payee.

4. 20 C.F.R. § 260.3.

5. 20 C.F.R. § 260.5.

6. 45 U.S.C.A. § 231g.

7. 20 C.F.R. § 262.12.

§ 23.37

1. 5 U.S.C.A. §§ 8331, et seq.; 5 C.F.R. Pts. 831 et seq.

2. 5 U.S.C.A. §§ 8401, et seq.; 5 C.F.R. Pts. 841–843.

§ 23.38

1. 5 U.S.C.A. §§ 8403, 8423, 8461.

§ 23.38 ELDER LAW Ch. 23

type of employment. Most employees receive a contribution of seven percent of their base pay.[2]

Most FERS participants receive their distributions in the form of an annuity. If the participant is married, the annuity must be payable for the joint lives of the retiree and the spouse unless the spouse consents to another payment option.[3] Federal employees who leave government service are entitled to receive the contributions or to roll them over into another qualified plan.[4]

In addition to retirement benefits, FERS provides survivor's benefits for spouses, certain former spouses, and dependent and/or disabled children of deceased workers[5]. Employees who are unable to provide "useful and efficient service" due to a disease or injury may qualify for disability benefits.[6] FERS also provides for continuation of health benefits upon leaving service.[7]

§ 23.39 Benefits for Federal Employees—Civil Service Retirement Act ("CSRA")

Federal employees hired prior to 1984 are still governed under the Civil Service Retirement Benefit Program.[1] Program information is contained in the Federal Personnel Manual ("FPM") published by the Office of Personnel Management and available at their offices. There is also a handbook for the system which is available at employee offices or personnel management offices.

The CSRA provides immediate and deferred pensions to qualified federal employees. Immediate pensions are available for federal employees who retire voluntarily at age 55 with thirty years of service, age 60 with 20 years of service, or age 62 with five years of service.[2] Deferred retirement is payable at age 62 to any person who accumulated five years of government service.[3] CSRA also provides survivorship benefits unless they are waived by the spouse.[4] Disability pensions are also provided.[5]

CSRA participants who leave government service are entitled to withdraw accrued benefits in lieu of a pension. Withdrawals are subject

---

2. 5 C.F.R. § 841.503.

3. 5 C.F.R. §§ 842.601–842.615. See generally, Scheinkman, et al., New York Law of Domestic Relations (West 1996) Ch. 18 "Private and Public Retirement Plans."

4. 5 C.F.R. §§ 843.201, 843.202.

5. 5 C.F.R. §§ 843.301—843.312.

6. 5 C.F.R. §§ 843.401—843.411, §§ 843.501—843.504.

7. 5 U.S.C.A. §§ 8901, et seq.; 5 C.F.R. §§ 890.101, et seq.

§ 23.39

1. 5 U.S.C.A. §§ 8331, et seq.; 5 C.F.R. Pts. 831 et seq.

2. 5 U.S.C.A. § 8336(d); 5 C.F.R. § 831.504.

3. 5 U.S.C.A. § 8338(a); 5 C.F.R. § 831.701(c).

4. 5 U.S.C.A. § 8341; 5 C.F.R. § 831.604.

5. 5 U.S.C.A. § 8337(a); 5 C.F.R. § 831.502.

to income tax unless rolled over within 60 days to another qualified plan, preferably an IRA.[6]

§ 23.40 Benefits for Federal Employees—Appeals

If there is an adverse decision in a claim for federal pension benefits, the claimant may request a reconsideration within 30 days of the decision.[1] If reconsideration is unsuccessful, a request is made for an administrative hearing before the Merit Systems Protection Board ("MSPB").[2] The agency has forms and procedures which can be obtained directly from the MSPB. Note that the MSPB may order the agency to pay reasonable attorneys fees if the employee is a prevailing party and the payment is in the interest of justice.[3] Appeal from the MSPB is made to the U.S. Court of Appeals for the Federal Circuit.[4]

§ 23.41 Veterans' Benefits

A large percentage of the male population over age 65 is comprised of veterans. Many are eligible for or receive a variety of veterans' benefits.[1] These benefits include compensation for service-connected disability or death, pensions for non-service-connected disability or death, health care benefits (including hospitalization, nursing home and home care), life insurance, burial benefits and benefits for surviving family members.[2] For the purpose of establishing eligibility for veterans' benefits, a veteran must not have been dishonorably discharged from military service.[3]

To be eligible for service-connected disability compensation, the veteran must be disabled due to an injury or disease incurred or aggravated by military service. The disability must not be a result of

---

6. PRACTICE POINTER: A participant who believes that he or she can invest and outperform the return of the pension would be better off rolling it into an IRA. Rolling it into a non-qualified plan is usually not advisable because of immediate tax liability.

It is possible, and often advisable, to make contributions for prior years of service when contributions were not previously made. This is typically done for years of prior military service.

§ 23.40
1. 5 C.F.R. § 831.109.
2. 5 U.S.C.A. § 8347(d)(2).
3. 5 U.S.C.A. § 7701(g)(1).
4. 5 U.S.C.A. § 7703(b)(1).

§ 23.41
1. A full description of the range of benefits provided to veterans is beyond the scope of this chapter. The following discussion will provide only a brief outline of the major categories of assistance.
2. The statutes governing veterans' benefits are 38 U.S.C.A. §§ 101, et seq. and 38 U.S.C.A. §§ 1101, et seq. Regulations for the program are found at 38 C.F.R. §§ 3.1, et seq. The Department of Veterans' Affairs publishes a booklet entitled Federal Benefits for Veterans and Dependents which contains eligibility requirements for the various benefit programs and other helpful information. It can be ordered through the Department of Veterans' Affairs by calling 1-800-827-1000.
3. 38 U.S.C.A. § 101(2); 38 C.F.R. 3.1(d).

§ 23.41   ELDER LAW   Ch. 23

willful misconduct or abuse of alcohol or drugs.[4] Once a disability is determined to be service connected, the Department of Veterans' Affairs rates the percentage of decrease in earning capacity that is caused by the particular disability.[5] The amount of compensation is based on the percentage of disability and is adjusted for inflation each November.[6] These benefits are not means-tested, *i.e.*, they are paid regardless of the veteran's income and resources from other sources. The surviving spouse, minor children and adult disabled children of a veteran who dies from a service-connected disability may receive monthly benefits.[7]

Pensions are also available for veterans who have non-service-connected disabilities. The veteran must have been engaged in active service for 90 or more days during a period of war and be permanently and totally disabled from a non-service-connected injury or illness. This program is means-tested: the veteran's income and net worth may not exceed the limits established for the program.[8] The amount of the pension takes into consideration the veteran's marital status, number of dependents, annual income from other sources and need for aid and attendance.[9] The surviving widow or widower of a veteran who served for at least 90 days during a period of war may be eligible for a survivor's pension if his or her income is below the pension limit.[10]

The Department of Veterans' Affairs operates hospitals which provide mandatory medical care to veterans with service-connected disabilities, or who receive Medicaid or a veteran's pension.[11] Veterans with non-service-connected disabilities are eligible for care in a veteran's hospital if their income is below a threshold established by the Department.[12] If

4. 38 U.S.C.A. § 1110; 38 C.F.R. § 3.4.

5. 38 U.S.C.A. § 1114, 1155. The ratings tables are organized according to impaired organs and body systems. The tables can be found at 38 C.F.R. Pt. IV.

6. 38 U.S.C.A. § 114. In 1997, the benefit payment ranges were from $94 per month for 10% disability to $1,924 per month for 100% disability. 62 Federal Register 10112.

7. 38 U.S.C.A. §§ 1310–1315. In 1997, benefits for a surviving spouse started at $833 per month. 62 Federal Register 10112.

8. 38 U.S.C.A. §§ 1501, 1502, 1521,-1522. There is no specific dollar limit on the total resources that a veteran may have. However, benefits may be denied if the veteran's total income and resources make it reasonable to assume that some portion of the veteran's estate should be used for his or her support. Each case is determined on its own merits. In practice, a claim will rarely be denied if the veteran's net worth is less than $50,000. 38 C.F.R. §§ 3.274, 3.275.

9. 38 U.S.C.A. § 1521. The maximum annual rates are adjusted for inflation annually and are published in the Federal Register. In 1997, a single veteran with no dependents received $8,486 per year. *See* 62 Federal Register 2442 for a complete list of 1997 benefit rates for all categories of assistance.

10. 38 U.S.C.A. § 1541. The amount of the survivors benefit is adjusted for inflation each year and published in the Federal Register. In 1997, benefit rates for a surviving spouse started at $5,688. *See* 62 Federal Register 2442 for a complete list of 1997 benefit rates for surviving spouses. Like the benefits for veterans, the payment to a surviving spouse will be increased if the spouse needs aid or assistance or is responsible for dependent children.

11. 38 U.S.C.A. § 1710; 38 C.F.R. §§ 17.47 (a)(1)-(5).

12. 38 U.S.C.A. § 1710(a)(2)(F); 38 C.F.R. §§ 17.47, 17.48.

beds are available, veterans with non-service-connected disabilities may be eligible for discretionary care for which they will be charged.[13] Eligible veterans may receive out-patient care, prescription drugs, dental care and prosthetic devices. Care in a private or Department operated nursing home may also be available.[14] Veterans with a service-connected disability are entitled to first preference for nursing home care. Generally, nursing home care is limited to six months unless the veteran has a service-connected disability.[15]

Veterans and their dependents are entitled to burial in one of the 114 national veterans' cemeteries. Up to $1,500 for burial costs is paid if death is service-connected. A $300 burial allowance plus $150 for a burial plot will be paid for a veteran who received disability benefits or died while in a facility operated by the Department of Veterans' Affairs.[16]

Veterans apply for benefits by filing claims with their local Department of Veterans' Affairs office.[17] Traditionally, advocates for veterans have been non-attorney organizations recognized by the Department of Veterans' Affairs.[18] However, attorneys are also authorized to represent veterans.[19] Veterans may appeal any adverse decision by filing a notice of disagreement within one year of the decision.[20] The decision will be reviewed by the regional office. If the initial determination is upheld, the

---

13. 38 C.F.R. § 17.48(e)(1).

14. The veteran may be charged $5 per day plus an amount equal to the Medicare nursing home stay deductible for each 90 day stay. 38 C.F.R. § 17.48(e)(1).

15. 38 C.F.R. § 17.51. Approval for more than six months of care may be obtained if the veteran is awaiting payment from Medicaid or another source, or is terminally ill and expected to die within six months. *Id.*

16. 38 C.F.R. § 38.1600.

17. There are two regional offices in New York State. The New York City office processes claims from New York City, Westchester, Nassau, Suffolk, Albany, Clinton, Columbia, Delaware, Dutchess, Essex, Franklin, Fulton, Greene, Hamilton, Orange, Otsego, Putnam, Rensselaer, Richmond, Rockland, Saratoga, Schenectady, Schoharie, Sullivan, Ulster, Warren and Washington counties. It is located at 252 Seventh Avenue, New York, N.Y. Telephone (212) 620–6901. The Buffalo office handles all other locations. It is located at 111 West Huron Street, Buffalo, N.Y. Telephone (716) 846–5191. For toll free information call 1–800–827–1000.

18. The New York State Division of Veterans' Affairs can assist veterans with establishing eligibility for benefits. Call 1–800–635–6534 to obtain a referral to a local counselor. Local telephone directories will also contain names of county and local veterans' service offices.

19. 38 C.F.R. § 14.629. Attorneys who seek assistance in representing veterans may contact the non-profit National Veterans' Legal Services Program ("NVLSP"), 2001 S Street, Washington, D.C. 20009. (202) 265–8305. Manuals, guides and other publications are available.

PRACTICE POINTER: Attorneys and other representatives may only charge a fee for services rendered after a final decision has been rendered by the Board of Veterans' Appeals. The fee agreement must be filed with the Department of Veterans' Affairs. The fee is subject to review and may be reduced if it is determined to be unreasonable or excessive. 38 U.S.C.A. § 5904. Contingency agreements in which the representative's compensation will be paid out of a future award of benefits are limited to 20% of any retroactive award. 38 U.S.C.A. § 7263. Attorneys may also be eligible for awards of fees under the Equal Access to Justice Act, 28 U.S.C.A. § 2412 for representation before the Court of Veterans' Appeals.

20. 38 C.F.R. § 20.302.

§ 23.41   ELDER LAW   Ch. 23

veteran will be sent a "statement of the case" summarizing the decision and the facts and law upon which it is based.[21] The veteran may file a "substantive appeal" to the Board of Veterans' Appeals within 60 days from receipt of the statement of the case or the remainder of the one year period from the date of the initial determination.[22] The claimant may request a hearing at which he or she may present evidence, testimony and obtain subpoenas for the production of witnesses.[23] The veteran may request reconsideration of the decision of the Board of Veterans' Appeals if new and material evidence arises, or if he or she claims there has been an error of fact or law. There is no deadline for filing a request for reconsideration.[24] Alternately, a claimant may appeal a final Board of Veterans' Appeals decision to the Court of Veterans' Appeals within 120 days of the date of the decision.

Library References:

West's Key No. Digests, Armed Services ⇒101.

§ 23.42 Medicare

The Medicare program was established as part of the Social Security Amendments of 1965.[1] It is a national health insurance program for the elderly and some disabled individuals. Unlike the Medicaid program, eligibility for Medicare benefits is not based upon financial need.[2] The program is administered by the Department of Health and Human Services ("HHS") through the Health Care Financing Administration ("HCFA"), and the Social Security Administration ("SSA"). HCFA contracts with fiscal intermediaries, usually private insurance companies, to administer aspects of the program, including processing the claims of beneficiaries.[3]

The Medicare program is comprised of two parts, Part A and Part B. Part A provides basic coverage of care in a hospital, skilled nursing facility or hospice as well as some health care provided in the home.[4] Part B is a voluntary, supplementary program which covers outpatient services by physicians, other health services, outpatient rehabilitation,

---

21. 38 C.F.R. §§ 19.26–19.29.
22. 38 C.F.R. § 20.302(b).
23. The hearing procedures are set forth at 38 C.F.R. § 20.700.
24. 38 C.F.R. § 20.1000.

§ 23.42

1. Title VIII of the Social Security Act, 42 U.S.C.A. §§ 1395, *et seq.* The regulations are at 42 C.F.R. Pts. 405—424. HCFA also publishes the Health Insurance Manual ("HIM") containing detailed policy pronouncements concerning the program.

2. For a discussion of the eligibility requirements for the Medicare program, *see infra,* § 23.43.

3. For additional resource material concerning the Medicare program, *see* McCormick, *Medicare and Medicaid Claims and Procedures* (2d ed. 1986); V. Russo and M. Rachlin, *New York Elder Law Practice,* (West 1997) Ch. 6 "Medicare"; Krauskopf, Brown, Tokarz and Bogutz, *Elderlaw: Advocacy for the Aging* (2d ed. 1993); and the Commerce Clearing House Medicare and Medicaid Guide.

4. 42 U.S.C.A. §§ 1395c, 1395d.

medical supplies and equipment.[5]

Library References:
West's Key No. Digests, Social Security and Public Welfare ⚖241.15.

§ 23.43 Medicare—Eligibility and Enrollment

An individual who is 65 years old and receives monthly Social Security or Railroad Retirement benefits is eligible for Part A and Part B Medicare benefits.[1] Spouses, widows and widowers of such eligible individuals are also entitled to coverage upon reaching age 65.[2]

A person under age 65 who has received or been entitled to Social Security or Railroad Retirement Disability benefits for at least 24 months may qualify for Part A benefits in the 25th month.[3] Part A coverage is also available for government employees who are not eligible for Social Security benefits but have paid hospital insurance premiums,[4] and for individuals who are suffering from end-stage renal disease.[5]

Application for Social Security or Railroad Retirement benefits operates as automatic application for Part A and Part B Medicare benefits.[6] Individuals who are not automatically enrolled in Part A of the Medicare program can apply for benefits at any Social Security office. Individuals who are entitled to Railroad Retirement benefits should contact the Railroad Retirement Board to enroll.

An individual is eligible for Part A coverage on the first day of the month that he or she turns 65.[7] Coverage will be retroactive to the first month of eligibility if the application is filed within six months of the date that the person became eligible.[8] If the application is not filed within six months of commencement of eligibility, coverage will be retroactive to six months before the application is filed.[9]

The "initial enrollment period" for individuals who are not automatically enrolled in Part B is the seven month period commencing

---

5. 42 U.S.C.A. §§ 1395j, 1395k; 42 C.F.R. §§ 410.1–410.105.

§ 23.43

1. 42 U.S.C.A. § 1395c; 42 C.F.R. §§ 406.5(a), 407.17(a).

2. Id.

3. 42 U.S.C.A. § 426(b), 42 C.F.R. § 406.12(a)(1).

4. 42 U.S.C.A. § 418(n); 42 C.F.R. § 406.15.

5. 42 U.S.C.A. § 426–l(a)(2); 42 C.F.R. § 406.13. To be eligible for Medicare Part A under these provisions, an individual must require hemodialysis or a renal transplant due to irreversible and permanent kidney damage. 42 C.F.R. § 406.13(b). The spouse and children of the eligible individual may also receive benefits. Id. Eligibility begins on the earliest of the following dates; the third month after the condition is diagnosed, the month in which self-dialysis begins, or the month in which a kidney transplant is received. 42 C.F.R. § 406.13(e).

6. 42 U.S.C.A. § 426(a); 42 C.F.R. §§ 406.6(a), 406.10(a). However, since enrollment in Part B is voluntary, an individual may decline Part B coverage.

7. 42 C.F.R. § 406.10(b)(1).

8. 42 U.S.C.A. § 426(a); 42 C.F.R. § 406.6(d)(4).

9. Id.

three months before the individual's 65th birthday.[10] If the application is made before the birthday month, enrollment will begin in the month of the 65th birthday.[11] If application is made during or up to three months after the birthday month, coverage will begin in the month after the application.[12] If the individual fails to enroll during this initial enrollment period, he or she must wait until the next "general enrollment period" which occurs in the first three months of every year.[13] Individuals who enroll in the general enrollment period do not become eligible for coverage until July 1 of that year.[14]

Individuals who are not automatically enrolled in Part A pay a monthly premium.[15] The Part A premium is adjusted annually.[16] All individuals pay a premium for Part B Medicare coverage.[17] Individuals who are eligible for New York State Medicaid benefits have their Medicare premiums paid by the New York State Medicaid program under a voluntary buy-in agreement between the state and HCFA.[18]

§ 23.44 Medicare—Part A Benefits

Part A of the Medicare program is known as Hospital Insurance, although Part A provides coverage for care provided not only by a hospital, but by skilled nursing facilities, home health care agencies and hospices.[1] Services must be rendered by a participating Medicare provider.[2] Descriptions of the conditions and limits upon Medicare coverage for these services are described in the following sections.

Library References:

West's Key No. Digests, Social Security and Public Welfare ⚖=241.21.

§ 23.45 Medicare—Part A Benefits—Hospital Services

The Medicare program provides coverage of reasonable and necessary medical care provided in a hospital.[1] The patient is responsible for a

10. 42 C.F.R. § 407.14(a)(1).

11. 42 C.F.R. § 407.25(a)(1).

12. 42 C.F.R. § 407.25(a)(2)—(5).

13. 42 U.S.C.A. §§ 1395p(e); 42 C.F.R. § 406.21(c)(1).

14. 42 U.S.C.A. § 1395a(a)(2)(E); 42 C.F.R. §§ 406.21(c)(3), 407.25(b)(1).

15. 42 U.S.C.A. § 1395i–2(a); 42 C.F.R. §§ 406.5(b), 406.20.

16. 42 C.F.R. § 406.32. In 1997, the monthly Part A premium was $311 for individuals with 0 to 29 quarters of Social Security coverage or $187 for individuals with 30–39 quarters of coverage.

17. 42 U.S.C.A. § 1395(e)(1)(A); 42 C.F.R. §§ 408.4(a)(1) and 408.20(c). In 1997, the Part B Medicare premium was $43.80 per month.

18. 42 U.S.C.A. §§ 1396a(a)(10)(E), 1396d(p); 42 C.F.R. § 407.40; 18 NYCRR §§ 360–7.7 and 360–7.8.

§ 23.44

1. 42 U.S.C.A. § 1395c.

2. 42 U.S.C.A. §§ 1395f(a), 1395cc(a)(1).

§ 23.45

1. Covered hospital services include semi-private room and board, miscellaneous services and supplies, special diets, nursing care, special care units, drugs, laboratory tests, diagnostic x-rays, medical supplies, operating and recovery room, anesthesia and rehabilitation services. 42 U.S.C.A. § 1395x(b); 42 C.F.R. §§ 409.10–409.16.

deductible for each *spell of illness*.[2] The amount of the deductible is adjusted for inflation each year.[3]

In addition to the deductible, the patient is responsible to pay coinsurance after the first 60 days of hospitalization in each spell of illness.[4] For days 61 through 90 of a spell of illness, the daily coinsurance rate is one quarter of the hospital deductible.[5] Each beneficiary has a *lifetime reserve* of 60 days of Medicare insurance for hospitalizations that exceed 90 days.[6] The Medicare beneficiary is responsible to pay coinsurance equal to one half of the hospital deductible for each *lifetime reserve day*.[7]

§ 23.46 Medicare—Part A Benefits—Skilled Nursing Facilities

Medicare provides very limited coverage for care in a skilled nursing facility ("SNF").[1] The patient must: (1) have been hospitalized for medically necessary hospital care for at least three consecutive calendar days for the same condition that is to be treated in the SNF; (2) be admitted to the SNF within 30 calendar days after the hospital discharge; and (3) require and receive skilled care on a daily basis.[2] Custodial care is not covered.[3] Nursing or skilled rehabilitation services are the most common qualifying services. Personal care services which do not require the skills of professional personnel are not covered.[4]

Note that not all charges incurred during a hospital stay will be covered under Part A. In particular, charges for physicians, private duty-nurses and personal convenience items such as telephones and televisions are not covered. 42 U.S.C.A. §§ 1395x(b)(4), (5).

2. The term *benefit period* is sometimes used in the Medicare regulations. A spell of illness is defined as beginning on the first day that a patient is hospitalized and ending 60 days after the patient is discharged from the hospital. If the patient is re-hospitalized before 60 days have elapsed, the subsequent hospitalization is part of the same spell of illness regardless of whether or not the reason for the second hospitalization is related to the prior hospital stay. 42 U.S.C.A. § 1395x(a); 42 C.F.R. § 409.60(a).

3. The amount of the deductible in 1997 was $760.

4. 42 U.S.C.A. § 1395e(a)(1).

5. 42 U.S.C.A. § 1395e(a)(1)(A). $190 per day in 1997.

6. The 60 lifetime reserve days may be used only once in a lifetime. Lifetime reserve days will be used automatically if a hospital stay is more than 90 days unless the patient provides written notice that this coverage is not wanted. 42 C.F.R. § 409.61(a)(2).

7. 42 U.S.C.A. § 1395e(a)(1)(B). $380 per day in 1997.

§ 23.46

1. A skilled nursing facility is a facility which is primarily engaged in the provision of skilled nursing and rehabilitative services. 42 U.S.C.A. § 1395r.

2. 42 U.S.C.A. § 1395x(I); 42 C.F.R. §§ 409.30—409.33. *See also,* HCFA Medicare Intermediary Manual §§ 4130, *et seq.* Skilled nursing and rehabilitation care requires the skills of technical or professional personnel such as registered nurses, licensed practical nurses, physical therapists, occupational therapists or speech pathologists. The services must be furnished directly by or under the supervision of the skilled personnel. 42 C.F.R. § 409.31.

3. 42 U.S.C.A. § 1395y(a)(9).

4. *Id.* 42 C.F.R. § 409.33(d) lists examples of non-covered personal care services including, but not limited to, administration of medication, routine catheter care, changes of dressings, routine skin care, incontinence care, assistance with dressing,

§ 23.46 ELDER LAW Ch. 23

A maximum of 100 days of coverage in an SNF[5] will be covered per *spell of illness*.[6] Medicare provides full payment for days one through 20 of nursing facility placement and payment for all but a daily coinsurance amount for days 21 through 100.[7]

§ 23.47 Medicare—Part A Benefits—Home Health Care

In theory, a Medicare beneficiary may receive unlimited home health care[1] visits provided that he or she meets the following conditions: (1) the beneficiary is homebound;[2] (2) he or she requires either skilled nursing services on a part-time[3] or intermittent basis,[4] or physical, occupational or speech therapy; and (3) a physician certifies the need for home health care.[5] An unlimited number of home health care visits are covered.[6] Prior hospitalization is not required and services are provided without deductible or coinsurance payments.[7]

eating and going to the toilet, periodic turning and positioning in bed. A condition which does not usually require skilled care may require them due to special medical complications. 42 C.F.R. § 409.32(b).

5. 42 U.S.C.A. § 1395d(a)(2)(A); 42 C.F.R. § 409.61(b).

6. For discussion of the Medicare program's definition of a "spell of illness" see *supra*, § 23.45.

7. 42 U.S.C.A. § 1395e; 42 C.F.R. § 409.61(b). Co-insurance was $92 per day in 1996.

PRACTICE POINTER: Some Medicare Supplemental Insurance policies may cover the coinsurance. See *infra*, §§ 23.57—23.61 for a discussion of Medicare Supplemental Insurance policies. Clients should also be advised that federal law prohibits a SNF from demanding advance deposits or fees from Medicare beneficiaries. 42 U.S.C.A. § 1395cc(a)(1)(A); 42 C.F.R. §§ 489.20—489.34.

§ 23.47

1. Home health services are provided by a home health care agency under a plan of services which is established and periodically reviewed by a physician. The services are provided on a visiting basis at the individual's home. 42 U.S.C.A. § 1395x(m).

2. 42 U.S.C.A. § 1395f(a)(2)(C); 42 C.F.R. § 409.42. A person is homebound if the assistance of an individual or supportive device is required to leave the home or if leaving is contraindicated due to medical conditions. The patient need not be bedridden. Brief or infrequent absences are permitted, especially for the purpose of receiving medical care. 42 U.S.C.A. §§ 1395f(a)(8), 1395n(a)(2)(F).

3. Services should be considered "part-time" if provided less than eight hours per day or less than seven days per week. Duggan v. Bowen, 691 F.Supp. 1487 (D.D.C. 1988).

4. Services will be considered "intermittent" if provided at least once in 60 days and less than seven days per week. HCFA Medicare Intermediary Manual § 3118.1.C.

5. 42 U.S.C.A. § 1395f(a)(2)(C); 42 C.F.R. § 409.42.

6. **PRACTICE POINTER:** Home health care services are frequently denied because the patient may need an extended period of assistance. Such denials should be appealed. The law provides no limit on the length of time that home health care can be provided as long as the beneficiary meets the other conditions for eligibility. 42 C.F.R. § 409.61(d).

7. 42 C.F.R. § 409.61(d).

§ 23.48 Medicare—Part A Benefits—Hospice Care

Terminally ill[1] patients may receive hospice[2] care for two 90 day periods and one subsequent 30 day period for total coverage of 210 days.[3] The patient may receive additional coverage upon recertification of terminal illness.[4] To apply for hospice benefits, the patient must file an election of hospice coverage with a particular hospice.[5] The election statement identifies the hospice which will provide services, acknowledges that services will be primarily palliative rather than curative in nature and waives the patient's right to receive other Medicare benefits except for physician services and services provided by the hospice.[6] Outpatient drugs furnished by the hospice are subject to a coinsurance payment approximating 5% of the cost of the drug.[7] Coinsurance payments are also required for respite services.[8]

§ 23.49 Medicare—Part B Supplementary Medical Insurance

Part B of the Medicare program provides additional coverage beyond the basic package of services covered under Part A.[1] Part B covers physicians' services, laboratory tests, medical equipment and supplies, rehabilitation and therapy, outpatient services and home health care.[2] Enrollment in Part B is voluntary but an individual who is automatically enrolled in Part A will also be enrolled in Part B unless Part B coverage is declined.[3] Beneficiaries are required to pay a monthly premium for

§ 23.48

1. Terminal illness is defined as having been diagnosed as having six or fewer months to live. 42 U.S.C.A. § 1395x(dd)(3)(A).

2. A hospice is a public agency or private organization that is primarily engaged in providing care to terminally ill individuals. 42 C.F.R. § 418.3. Hospice care includes nursing care, therapy, social services, counseling, medical supplies and physician services provided to terminally ill patients. 42 U.S.C.A. § 1395x(dd)(1). Hospice care may be provided in the individual's home or on an inpatient basis. 42 U.S.C.A. § 1395x(dd)(2)(A)(ii).

3. 42 U.S.C.A. § 1395d(d)(1); 42 C.F.R. 418.21(a).

4. Id.

5. 42 C.F.R. § 418.24(a).

6. 42 U.S.C.A. §§ 1395d(a)(4), 1395d(d); 42 C.F.R. § 418.24(b)(2). The patient agrees to forego treatment for the terminal condition but Medicare coverage for other conditions is retained. 42 C.F.R. § 418.24(d)(2). The patient may cancel hospice coverage and reinstate regular Medicare coverage before the expiration of the hospice period. 42 C.F.R. § 418.28.

7. 42 C.F.R. § 418.400(a).

8. 42 C.F.R. § 418.400(b). Respite coinsurance is equal to 5% of the Medicare payment for a respite care day. Id. Respite care is occasional inpatient care for five days or less when necessary to relieve the family members or other persons caring for the terminally ill individual. 42 C.F.R. § 418.204(b).

§ 23.49

1. Certain medical expenses are excluded from coverage under both Part A and Part B of the Medicare program. The most common include routine check-ups, self-administered pharmaceuticals, eyeglasses and eye examinations, hearing aids, dental care, routine foot care, orthopedic care, the first three pints of blood, cosmetic surgery, most immunizations and personal comfort items. 42 U.S.C.A. § 1395y(a); 42 C.F.R. § 411.15.

2. 42 U.S.C.A. § 1395k.

3. 42 C.F.R. § 407.17.

§ 23.49 ELDER LAW Ch. 23

coverage.[4]

§ 23.50 Medicare—Part B Supplementary Medical Insurance—Deductibles and Coinsurance

Part B benefits are subject to a deductible of $100 for each calendar year.[1] After satisfaction of the deductible, Part B will pay for 80% of the Medicare-approved charge. Beneficiaries are responsible for the remaining 20% as coinsurance.[2] The Medicare approved charge is based on the reasonable charge as determined by the insurance carrier which administers the Part B program in the patient's locality.[3]

§ 23.51 Medicare—Part B Supplementary Medical Insurance—Assignment of Claims/Participating Physicians

Generally, Medicare Part B payments are made directly to the beneficiary.[1] However, if the provider agrees, the beneficiary may elect to assign the claim to be paid directly to the medical provider.[2] Physicians and other medical suppliers may agree to become *Participating Providers* who agree to accept assignment of all claims by Medicare beneficiaries and to accept the Medicare approved charge[3] as payment in full.[4] In such case, the beneficiary may only be billed for the deductible, if applicable, and the remaining 20% coinsurance.

§ 23.52 Medicare—Part B Supplementary Medical Insurance—Limitations on Balance Billing

A provider who does not accept assignment may charge a patient more than Medicare's approved charge. This practice is known as *balance billing*. However, federal law prohibits providers from charging fees to Medicare beneficiaries which exceed Medicare's *limiting charge, i.e.*,

4. $43.80 per month in 1997.

§ 23.50

1. 42 U.S.C.A. § 1395*l*(b); 42 C.F.R. § 410.160(f).

2. 42 U.S.C.A. § 1395*l*; 42 C.F.R. § 410.152(b)(1).

CAVEAT: The beneficiary will be responsible for paying any difference between the Medicare approved charge and the actual charge.

3. Since 1992, all physician services are paid pursuant to a national fee schedule which is adjusted to reflect regional differences in costs. 42 U.S.C.A. § 1395w–4.

§ 23.51

1. 42 U.S.C.A. § 1395u(h); 42 C.F.R. § 424.55.

2. There is no requirement that physicians accept an assignment of any Medicare claim. If the physician does not accept assignment of the claim, he or she may insist that the patient pay the bill and submit the claim to Medicare for reimbursement. However, physicians are required to file the Medicare reimbursement claim for the patient. 42 U.S.C.A. § 1395w–4(g)(4).

3. *See supra*, § 23.44 for a discussion of the Medicare-approved charge.

4. 42 U.S.C.A. § 1395u; 42 C.F.R. § 424.55.

an amount which is 115% of the Medicare approved charge.[1] New York provides additional protection to Medicare beneficiaries by limiting balance billing for most services to 5% over the Medicare approved charge.[2]

§ 23.53 Medicare—Administrative and Judicial Appeals

The Medicare claims process is complicated and often results in denials of coverage to beneficiaries. The following sections contain descriptions of the appeals process for different types of Medicare claims.

Library References:

West's Key No. Digests, Social Security and Public Welfare ⇔241.30, 241.41.

§ 23.54 Medicare—Administrative and Judicial Appeals—Eligibility for Benefits

Decisions about eligibility for enrollment in the Medicare program[1] are made by the Social Security Administration and appealed in the same manner as social security benefit appeals.[2]

§ 23.55 Medicare—Administrative and Judicial Appeals—Part A Fiscal Intermediary Decisions

When a patient receives services under Medicare Part A, he or she signs an assignment of benefits form requesting that the provider of services be paid directly by the Medicare program.[1] The provider submits a claim for Part A coverage to the "fiscal intermediary" which administers Part A benefits in the provider's locality.[2] The fiscal intermediary

---

§ 23.52

1. 42 U.S.C.A. § 1395w–4; 42 C.F.R. § 414.48(b).

2. Public Health Law § 19. This statute was upheld in Medical Society of the State of New York v. Cuomo, 777 F.Supp. 1157 (S.D.N.Y.1991), aff'd 976 F.2d 812 (2d Cir. 1992) and Medical Society of the State of New York v. New York State Health Dep't, 189 A.D.2d 453, 596 N.Y.S.2d 477 (3d Dep't 1993), aff'd 83 N.Y.2d 447, 611 N.Y.S.2d 114, 633 N.E.2d 468 (1994).

PRACTICE POINTER: The limitations on balance billing apply to all licensed physicians who provide services to Medicare beneficiaries. Violations are subject to fines, as well as refunds of the amount overcharged. Beneficiaries who believe that a physician has violated the balance billing limits should be advised to request a refund or revision of their bill. If the problem persists, a complaint may be filed with the New York State Department of Health. Beneficiaries may also file an appeal under the Part B claims process. See infra, § 23.57.

§ 23.54

1. See supra, § 23.43 for a discussion of eligibility and enrollment in the Medicare program.

2. 42 U.S.C.A. § 1395ff(b); 20 C.F.R. § 404.701(a). See supra, § 23.15 for a discussion of the Social Security appeals process.

§ 23.55

1. 42 U.S.C.A. § 1395f(a)(1); 42 C.F.R. § 424.51.

2. 42 U.S.C.A. § 1395h. Fiscal intermediaries are entities which enter into agreements with HCFA to administer benefit claims, monitor program quality and regulate provision of services to Medicare bene-

§ 23.55 ELDER LAW Ch. 23

issues an "initial determination" concerning coverage for the services.[3] The beneficiary can appeal any initial determination by filing a request for reconsideration within 60 days of receipt of the Notice of Denial, unless good cause for failure to make a timely appeal can be shown.[4] The decision upon reconsideration is based upon a paper review of the evidence by the fiscal intermediary.[5]

A decisions upon reconsideration may be appealed to an ALJ by filing a Request for Hearing[6] with the Social Security Administration within 60 days of receipt of the reconsideration determination.[7] In order to file an appeal, the amount in controversy must be at least $100.[8] Claims may be aggregated to meet the $100 limitation.[9] The beneficiary may present evidence and subpoena witnesses at the hearing.[10]

A request for review by the Social Security Appeals Council must be filed within 60 days after receipt of an unfavorable hearing decision.[11] The review decision is based upon a paper review of the records.[12] The right to subsequent judicial review is limited to claims in which the amount in controversy is $1,000 or more.[13]

§ 23.56 Medicare—Administrative and Judicial Appeals—Part A Peer Review Organization Decisions

Peer Review Organizations ("PRO") are entities empowered by federal law to review services covered by Medicare, to determine whether such services are medically necessary and whether the level of care is

ficiaries. *Id.* Generally, the fiscal intermediaries are private insurance companies.

3. 42 C.F.R. § 405.702. The initial determination is provided to both the beneficiary and the provider of services. *Id.*

4. 42 U.S.C.A. § 1395ff; 42 C.F.R. §§ 405.711, 405.712.

CAVEAT: Appeal may only be taken from an official Medicare initial determination. Unofficial statements by physicians or other providers that Medicare will not cover a specific procedure or item are not appealable since they are not Medicare initial determinations. The beneficiary should insist that the provider submit the claim to Medicare. If an initial determination denying the claim is received, this denial may then be appealed.

5. 42 C.F.R. § 405.715.

6. Form HA 501.1.

7. 42 U.S.C.A. § 1395ff(b); 42 C.F.R. §§ 405.720, 405.722.

8. 42 U.S.C.A. § 1395ff(b)(2)(A); 42 C.F.R. § 405.720(d).

9. 42 U.S.C.A. § 1395ff(b)(2)(B); 42 C.F.R. § 405.740(a)(3).

10. PRACTICE POINTER: Attorneys should advise beneficiaries not to be reluctant to request hearings. More than 50% of all hearing decisions are favorable to beneficiaries.

11. 42 C.F.R. § 405.724; 20 C.F.R. § 404.968. The Social Security Administration will presume that a reconsideration decision is received five days after the date of issuance of the decision, unless the beneficiary can reasonably show otherwise. 42 C.F.R. § 405.722.

12. However, note that the beneficiary may request an appearance. The Appeals Council has the discretion to permit oral argument for important questions of law or policy. 20 C.F.R. § 404.976(c).

13. 42 U.S.C.A. § 1395ff(b)(2); 42 C.F.R. § 405.730.

appropriate.[1] PROs make determinations concerning hospital and nursing home stays, including continued stay decisions for hospitalized patients.[2]

If a PRO makes a determination that hospitalization is no longer reasonable and medically necessary for a Medicare patient, it must issue a "continued stay denial notice" indicating that the hospital care will no longer be covered by Medicare.[3] The notice must be served upon the patient, the patient's physician and the hospital.[4] The patient cannot be billed for care until three days after the continued stay denial notice has been served.[5] Such notice to a hospitalized patient must be served within one day of the PRO determination or three days if the patient is no longer hospitalized. The patient may contest the determination by filing a request for reconsideration with the PRO or the Social Security Administration[6] within three days after receipt of the continued stay denial notice.[7] Patients have 60 days to request reconsideration of other PRO decisions.[8] Reconsideration decisions must be made within three days of receipt of the request for reconsideration if the patient is contesting a continued stay denial, within ten days if the reconsideration concerns inpatient services in a skilled nursing facility, or within thirty days for all other requests.[9]

If the amount in controversy is $200 or more, the beneficiary may appeal the reconsideration decision to an ALJ.[10] If the amount in controversy is $2,000 or more, the ALJ decision may be appealed to the Social Security Appeals Council and then to federal court.[11]

§ 23.57 Medicare—Administrative and Judicial Appeals—Part B Determinations

Initial determinations of coverage under Part B are made by the insurance carriers who administer Part B benefits.[1] The carrier must give the beneficiary written notice of the carrier's denial or partial

§ 23.56

1. 42 U.S.C.A. §§ 1320c, et seq.; 42 C.F.R. §§ 466.70, et seq.

2. 42 U.S.C.A. § 1320c–3; 42 C.F.R. § 466.70.

3. 42 U.S.C.A. § 1320c–3(a)(3)(A); 42 C.F.R. § 466.94. The continued stay denial notice is an "initial determination" of Medicare benefits. 42 C.F.R. § 466.83. For further discussion of the rights of hospitalized patients, see infra, §§ 23.88—23.90.

4. 42 C.F.R. § 466.94(a)(1).

5. 42 C.F.R. § 466.78(b)(4).

6. 42 U.S.C.A. § 1320c–4; 42 C.F.R. § 473.18.

7. 42 C.F.R. § 473.20(c).

8. PROs also issue determinations concerning the medical necessity of services and the appropriate level of care for treatment of particular patients, such as whether services should be provided in a skilled nursing facility or a hospital.

9. 42 C.F.R. § 473.32.

10. 42 C.F.R. § 473.12(a)(2). See supra, § 23.15 for a discussion of the appeals process before the Social Security Administration, including Administrative Law Judge and Appeals Council review.

11. 42 C.F.R. § 473.12(a)(3).

§ 23.57

1. 42 C.F.R. § 405.803.

§ 23.57

payment of a claim.[2] This written notice constitutes an "initial determination" concerning the Part B claim. The beneficiary may file a request for the carrier to review its decision within six months of issuance of the initial determination.[3] The beneficiary may request a hearing before the carrier within six months after receipt of its review decision if the amount in controversy is at least $100.[4] The hearing examiner will be selected by the carrier and will conduct the hearing in an informal manner.[5] There is no authority for the hearing examiner to issue subpoenas or documents.

If the hearing examiner's decision is unsatisfactory, the beneficiary may request a hearing before an ALJ if the amount in controversy of aggregated claims is at least $500.[6] The request for an ALJ hearing must be filed within 60 days of receipt of the hearing examiner's decision.[7] The ALJ decision may be appealed to the Social Security Administration Appeals Council within 60 days if the amount in controversy is at least $500. Judicial review is available if the amount in controversy after the decision of the Appeals Council is at least $1,000.[8]

§ 23.58 Supplemental Medical Insurance (Medigap Plans)

Most elderly individuals should be advised to purchase a private medical insurance policy to supplement the coverage provided by Medicare. Medicare was designed to provide a basic floor of coverage for out-of-pocket medical expenses. However, health care costs which are not covered by Medicare may be substantial. The following sections discuss the gaps in Medicare coverage which necessitate the purchase of supplemental medical insurance (often referred to as Medigap plans) and provide guidance in choosing a supplemental insurance policy.

§ 23.59 Supplemental Medical Insurance (Medigap Plans)—Gaps in Medicare Coverage

Individuals with Medicare coverage may face substantial out-of-pocket expenses if they do not hold additional insurance coverage. The following expenses are not covered by Medicare Part A:

2. 42 U.S.C.A. § 1395u(b)(3)(C); 42 C.F.R. § 405.804.

3. 42 C.F.R. § 405.807(c). Initial determinations of Part B benefits are generally contained on a form entitled "Explanation of Medicare Benefits."

4. 42 C.F.R. § 405.815. A request for review may take the form of any writing filed with the carrier, the Social Security Administration or HCFA. 42 C.F.R. § 405.807(b). The carrier may extend the six month period for filing a request for review for good cause. 42 C.F.R. § 405.821.

5. 42 C.F.R. § 405.823.

6. *Id. See supra,* § 23.15 for a discussion of the appeals process before the Social Security Administration, including hearings before Administrative Law Judges, appeals to the Appeals Council and judicial review.

7. *Id.*

8. *Id.*

- hospital deductible per spell of illness;[1]
- hospital coinsurance;[2]
- hospital stays after utilization of the lifetime reserve;[3]
- nursing home coinsurance and deductibles;[4]
- nursing home stays over 100 days;[5]
- home care services which do not meet the Medicare program's requirements for coverage;[6]
- private duty nurses.[7]

The following expenses are not covered by Medicare Part B:

- Part B deductible;[8]
- Coinsurance;[9]
- Amounts in excess of the Medicare approved charge;[10]
- Prescriptions;[11] and
- Non–Medicare approved procedures and services.[12]

§ 23.60 Supplemental Medical Insurance (Medigap Plans)—Federal and State Regulation of the Industry

In 1990, Congress passed legislation standardizing Medicare supplemental insurance policies to reduce abuses in marketing and sales of

§ 23.59

1. $760 in 1997. See supra, § 23.45.
2. Medicare covers the first 60 days in full, except for the hospital deductible. However, the patient is responsible for a daily deductible equal to one quarter of the hospital deductible for days 61–90 ($190 in 1997) and one half of the hospital deductible for the lifetime reserve days 91–150 ($380 in 1997). See supra, § 23.45.
3. Id.
4. Medicare pays for the first 20 days. After this expires, the patient is responsible for daily coinsurance for days 21–100. See supra, § 23.46.
5. Medicare will only pay for 100 days in a nursing home. See supra, § 23.46.
6. Medicare only pays for part-time or intermittent skilled home care services. See supra, § 23.47. This stringent definition excludes from coverage all full-time home care assistance. Moreover, Medicare does not cover unskilled homemaking services.
7. 42 C.F.R. § 409.12(b).
8. Annual Part B deductible was $100 in 1997. See supra, § 23.50.

9. Medicare only pays 80% of the Medicare approved charge for medical services. The patient remains responsible for the remaining 20% as coinsurance. See supra, § 23.50.

10. If the physician does not accept assignment, the patient will be responsible for paying the physician the balance over the Medicare approved charge. However, New York law limits most physician's charges to 5% over the Medicare approved charge. See supra, § 23.52.

11. Medicare does not pay for most outpatient pharmaceuticals.

12. Medicare will provide some coverage for most medically necessary care. However, there are many services which are generally not covered. A partial list of these uncovered services includes acupuncture, chiropractic, cosmetic surgery, dental care, eyeglasses and routine eye care, routine foot care and orthopedic shoes, health care provided in a foreign country, hearing aids and examinations, most immunizations, and routine physical examinations and tests.

§ 23.60   ELDER LAW   Ch. 23

these plans to elderly individuals.[1] These reforms have also been implemented in regulations issued by the New York State Insurance Department.[2] The state and federal protections include the following:

Standardization of Plans. The regulations are designed to make it easier for consumers to compare plans offered by different insurers. No more than ten kinds of supplemental insurance plans may be sold in any state.[3] Each insurer must offer a basic core package and provide an explanation summarizing coverage under each plan.[4]

Guaranteed Renewal. Insurers may only cancel or refuse to renew a plan if the insured fails to pay premiums or makes a material misrepresentation of fact on the initial application.[5] The insurer may not refuse to renew a policy due to the claims experience or health status of the insured.[6]

Pre-existing Condition Exclusions. Insurers' ability to deny coverage due to pre-existing conditions is extremely limited during the applicant's first six months of Medicare eligibility or if the applicant is seeking to replace a prior Medigap plan. However, individuals who are not subject to such protections may be disqualified for any coverage due to pre-existing conditions.[7]

Loss Ratio[8] Standard. For individual plans, the loss ratio must be at least 65 per cent. For group plans, the minimum loss ratio must be at least 75 per cent.[9]

Duplicate Sales Protection. The insurer must obtain a signed statement stating whether the purchaser has other supplemental insurance coverage or Medicaid. Sale of a plan which duplicates an existing supplemental insurance plan is prohibited although the purchaser may elect to replace an existing policy.[10]

State law also requires that insurance companies offer open enrollment for Medigap plans with acceptance of individuals at all times

§ 23.60

1. This legislation was included in the Omnibus Budget Reconciliation Act of 1990 and can be found at 42 U.S.C.A. §§ 1395ss et seq.

2. 11 NYCRR §§ 52.1, 52.11, 52.16, 52.17, 52.18, 52.22, 52.63.

3. 42 U.S.C.A. § 1395ss(p)(2); 11 NYCRR § 52.22(d).

4. 42 U.S.C.A. § 1395ss(p)(9); 11 NYCRR § 52.22(d).

PRACTICE POINTER: Note that consumers who purchased Supplemental Insurance coverage before adoption of the new federal standards in 1990 may have Medigap plans which are different from the ten standard plans now offered. These plans are still valid but may no longer be sold to new purchasers.

5. 42 U.S.C.A. § 1395ss(q); 11 NYCRR §§ 52.22(b)(1), (c)(1).

6. Id.

7. 42 U.S.C.A. § 1395dd(s); 11 NYCRR § 52.22(b)(3).

8. The loss ratio standard defines the percentage of premium payments which must be returned in payment of benefits to all policy holders. In essence, it regulates the amount of profit which may be made by the insurance company.

9. 42 U.S.C.A. § 1395ss(r).

10. 42 U.S.C.A. § 1395ss(d)(3); 11 NYCRR § 52.22(f)(5).

throughout the year.[11] Insurance companies must also "community rate" Medigap policies.[12] Community rating means that premiums must be based on the experience rating of the risk pool and not on an individual's age, sex or health status.[13]

§ 23.61 Supplemental Medical Insurance (Medigap Plans)—Ten Standard Plans

Federal law permits a maximum of ten different supplemental insurance plans to be offered in each state.[1] The National Association of Insurance Commissioners has adopted ten standard policies which are available nationally and are designated Plans A through J. This standardization of policies was designed to make it easier for consumers to comparison shop for supplemental insurance coverage. New York allows all ten plans to be marketed.[2]

Plan A is the basic or core plan which contains a minimal level of benefits. All the other plans include the basic coverage of Plan A, plus additional benefits. Plan A covers Part A hospital co-insurance for days 61–90, lifetime reserve coinsurance for days 91–150, a lifetime maximum of 365 days of hospital coverage beyond the lifetime reserve days, three pints of blood excluded as Part A and Part B deductibles and Part B coinsurance of 20 per cent of the Medicare approved charge.[3]

Plans B through J offer additional benefits in differing combinations. These additional benefits include payment of the Part A hospital deductible, Part A skilled nursing facility coinsurance, Part B deductible, Part B coverage for amounts above the Medicare approved charge, emergency foreign medical care, outpatient prescription drugs, and preventive care and home care services not covered by Medicare. The following table shows the specific benefits included in each of the ten basic plans.[4]

A	B	C	D	E	F	G	H	I	J
Basic Benefits	Basic Benefits	Basic Benefits	Basic Benefits	Basic Benefits	Basic Benefits	Basic Benefits	Basic Benefits	Basic Benefits	Basic Benefits
		Skilled Nursing Co-ins.	Skilled Nursing Co-ins.	Skilled Nursing Co-ins.	Skilled Nursing Co-ins.	Skilled Nursing Co-ins.	Skilled Nursing Co-ins.	Skilled Nursing Co-ins.	Skilled Nursing Co-ins.
	Part A Deductible	Part A Deductible	Part A Deductible	Part A Deductible	Part A Deductible	Part A Deductible	Part A Deductible	Part A Deductible	Part A Deductible

11. Insurance Law § 3231.

12. Id.

13. The insurer may establish different risk pools for individuals and family groups and for different geographical regions. Insurance Law §§ 3231(b), (c); 11 NYCRR § 360.4.

§ 23.61

1. 42 U.S.C.A. § 1395ss(p)(2).

2. 11 NYCRR § 52.22.

3. **PRACTICE POINTER:** Note that Plan A does **not** cover the Part A hospital deductible ($760 in 1997).

4. The table is reprinted from 11 NYCRR § 52.63.

§ 23.61 ELDER LAW Ch. 23

				Part B Deductible			Part B Deductible			Part B Deductible
				Part B Excess (100%)	Part B Excess (100%)		Part B Excess (100%)	Part B Excess (100%)
	Foreign Travel Emergency	Foreign Travel Emergency	Foreign Travel Emergency	Foreign Travel Emergency	Foreign Travel Emergency	Foreign Travel Emergency	Foreign Travel Emergency	Foreign Travel Emergency
		At-Home Recovery			At-Home Recovery		At-Home Recovery	At-Home Recovery
					Basic Drugs ($1,250 Limit)	Basic Drugs ($1,250 Limit)	Basic Drugs ($1,250 Limit)
		Preventive Care					Preventive Care

No supplemental medical insurance plan covers the following expenses: eye care, dental care, hearing aids, non-medically necessary care or long term skilled nursing or custodial care.

§ 23.62 Supplemental Medical Insurance (Medigap Plans)—Criteria For Choosing the Right Plan

The coverage included in each of the ten basic supplemental insurance plans varies greatly, as does the cost. Obviously, the plans offering the greatest number of options are the most expensive. Moreover, each insurer may not offer all of the ten available plans.

Clients should be advised to purchase the most coverage they can afford, emphasizing the items which are most important to their situations. Plan A is the least expensive plan, offering the least protection. Plans B, C and D meet the needs of most seniors. Plans H, I and J are the most comprehensive and expensive but may provide unnecessary protection.[1]

In some cases, the client may need to pay for a benefit which is not needed in order to obtain coverage for another important benefit.[2] Moreover, the client should evaluate whether some expenses would be better off paid out-of-pocket in order to keep the cost of the policy down or to purchase coverage for a more significant benefit.[3]

§ 23.62

1. Plans H and I cover prescription drugs up to $1,250 per year. However, the additional premium to purchase this benefit may be almost as high as the coverage provided.

2. For example, all plans except A and B cover foreign travel emergencies.

3. For example, the Part B deductible of $100 per year is covered by Plans C, F and J. Most people can probably afford to handle this expense out-of-pocket.

Additionally, Plans D and E are identical except that Plan D covers $1,600 per year in at-home recovery costs such as home care assistance, while Plan E covers $120 per year in preventive care. Even if the $120 benefit was used every year for ten years, it is not worth as much as the home care benefit of $1,600 if used only once.

Supplemental insurance policies only provide limited coverage for long term care in an institutional setting or at home. Plans A and B provide no coverage for skilled nursing facility services.

Although the number of plans which can be offered in each state has been standardized, the rates which can be charged have not. Insurers may charge vastly different premiums for the same plan. Moreover, insurers may try to steer consumers to plans which offer the highest profitability for the company.[4] Clients should be advised to comparison shop for rates but also pay attention to the financial solvency of the insurer and whether the company's agent will provide assistance in filing claims.[5]

Some Part B Medicare recipients may have elected to join a Health Maintenance Organization ("HMO"). Most individuals who are served by a HMO have no need for Supplemental Medical Insurance.[6] The Taxpayer Relief Act of 1997 § 4006(c) provides the option of a medical savings account, effective with taxable years beginning after December 31, 1998.

§ 23.63 Long Term Care Insurance

The high cost of nursing home placement can quickly deplete the resources of all but the most wealthy families.[1] Medicare provides only limited coverage for nursing home placement. Moreover, Medicare's strict eligibility requirements disqualify most placements.[2] The Medicaid

---

Plan F offers coverage for amounts in excess of Medicare's approved charge. If most of the consumers' physicians accept assignment, the value of this coverage will be reduced. Moreover, since New York limits balance billing for most services to 5 per cent above the Medicare approved charge, this benefit is not as valuable as it was in the past. *See supra,* § 23.52.

4. For an excellent discussion of how to shop for supplemental medical insurance see *Filling the Gaps in Medicare,* Consumer Reports, 8/94, pp.523-32. The report indicates that most companies steer consumers toward purchase of Plans C and F which are identical, except that Plan F covers charges in excess of the Medicare approved rate. Plan F was rated by Consumer Reports as providing less value than some other plans.

5. **PRACTICE POINTER:** Attorneys should advise clients that Area Offices for the Aging and the New York State Insurance Department often offer assistance to consumers in evaluating supplemental medical insurance plans. Call the Department for the Aging Hotline at 1–800–342–9871.

6. **PRACTICE POINTER:** Review the HMO benefits statement to determine whether the coverage meets or exceeds the coverage available in a supplemental insurance policy.

§ 23.63

1. Private pay rates for nursing home placements in New York State average about $65,000 per year or more. New York State Insurance Department, *Insurance Policies Covering Long Term Care Services in New York State* (1994 ed.) p.4. In the greater New York City area, costs can easily exceed $100,000 per year, especially in the better facilities.

The Department of Health and Human Services has estimated that 20 to 45% of all individuals will enter a nursing home during their lifetimes. About 75% of those who enter a nursing home will remain there for 2½ years. *Id.*

2. The Medicare program covers only 100 days of care in a SNF. The patient must have been hospitalized prior to the institutionalization and must require skilled care on a daily basis. *See supra,*

program pays for long term care in a skilled nursing facility but has stringent financial eligibility rules designed to restrict the program to individuals with limited income and resources.[3] Moreover, traditional Medicaid planning techniques may become less effective in the wake of recent legislation to criminalize certain Medicaid asset transfers. Supplemental Medical Insurance policies (Medigap plans) cover Medicare's deductibles and coinsurance for skilled nursing care but do not provide for extended nursing home stays.[4] For all of these reasons, individuals who are concerned about the future need for long term institutional care are increasingly considering the purchase of Long Term Care insurance policies.

Long Term Care insurance policies pay for skilled, and sometimes custodial, care in a nursing home. Some cover home care services as well. Long Term Care insurance policies are a very recent phenomenon and may not be appropriate for all clients. Policy provisions vary widely, as do costs. All plans should be carefully examined by qualified professionals.[5]

§ 23.64 Long Term Care Insurance—Regulation Under New York Law

Long Term Care insurance policies sold in New York State must meet minimum standards established by the New York State Insurance Department.[1] Policies must cover at least twenty four months of long term care services.[2] The regulations set forth three optional plans which provide for a minimum rate of payment in a nursing facility and coverage for home care services.[3] Policies which do not meet the stan-

§ 23.46 for a more detailed discussion of Medicare coverage for skilled nursing facilities.

3. *See infra,* §§ 23.71—23.80 for a discussion of the financial eligibility requirements of the Medicaid program.

4. *See supra,* §§ 23.58—23.62 for a discussion of Supplemental Medical Insurance policies.

5. **PRACTICE POINTER**: Attorneys may want to work with Certified Financial Planners in evaluating whether a given client's financial situation justifies the purchase of Long Term Care insurance. Insurance professionals may also assist in researching the various Long Term Care insurance products available in the market.

§ 23.64

1. The major regulations concerning sale of long term care insurance are published at 11 NYCRR §§ 52.12, 52.13, 52.16, 52.17, 52.18, 52.25, 52.29, 52.65.

2. 11 NYCRR § 52.12(a).

3. Option I covers all levels of care in a nursing home of at least $100 per day in New York City, Nassau, Rockland, Suffolk, and Westchester Counties and $70 per day in other locations and coverage of home care at 50% of the nursing home amount. 11 NYCRR § 52.12 (a)(1)(i), (ii).

Option II covers all levels of care in a nursing home and home care services at no less than 60% of the reasonable charges. 11 NYCRR § 52.12 (a)(2)(i), (ii).

Option III covers all levels of care in a nursing home which has contracted with the insurer at no less than 75% of the negotiated rate. For non-contracting homes, payment may be no less than 50% of the reasonable charge or $55 per day. Home care services by a provider under contract with the insurer must be paid at no less than 75% of the negotiated rate. For non-contract providers, payment must be no less than 50% of the reasonable charge or $30

dards contained in the regulations may not be labeled Long Term Care insurance policies.[4]

Long Term Care insurance policies may not exclude benefits for Alzheimer's Disease or organic brain syndrome.[5] Exclusion of coverage for a preexisting condition is limited to six months after the effective date of the policy.[6] Prior hospitalization may not be required.[7] The policy may not require the individual to utilize home care services before coverage in a nursing home will be provided.[8] Policies may not restrict coverage to services that are provided only by registered or licensed practical nurses.[9] As long as the policy holder continues to pay premiums, policies must be guaranteed renewable.[10] Insurers must offer options of inflation protection in the amount of benefits provided[11] and non-forfeiture of a portion of premiums[12] in the event the policy lapses. However, both of these options may substantially increase the cost of the policy.

§ 23.65 Long Term Care Insurance—Relationship to Medicaid Eligibility

The Medicaid program requires that individuals utilize all available resources before resorting to public benefits for payment of their health care costs.[1] Long Term Care insurance benefits must be exhausted before an individual will be certified as eligible for Medicaid payment of long term care. If a Long Term Care insurance policy does not provide for the full cost of a covered service, and the individual meets Medicaid eligibility requirements, the remaining costs may be covered by Medicaid provided that they do not exceed the amount that Medicaid would pay for the service.

Certain Long Term Care insurance policies may qualify as Partnership policies. Individuals who purchase Partnership policies may qualify for Medicaid benefits after benefits under the Partnership policy have been exhausted, without meeting normal Medicaid eligibility rules.[2]

per day, whichever is less. 11 NYCRR § 52.12 (a)(3)(i), (ii).

4. 11 NYCRR § 52.12 (b), 52.16 (j). However, note that such policies may qualify to be labeled as nursing home insurance only, home care insurance only or nursing home and home care insurance. The regulations for such policies are found at 11 NYCRR § 52.13.

5. 11 NYCRR § 52.25 (b)(2)(ii).

6. 11 NYCRR § 52.25 (b)(2)(i). A preexisting condition is a condition for which medical advice or treatment was given or sought during the six months prior to the effective date of the insurance policy. *Id.*

7. 11 NYCRR § 52.25 (c)(1)(i).

8. 11 NYCRR § 52.25 (c)(1)(ii).

9. 11 NYCRR § 52.25 (c)(1)(iii).

10. 11 NYCRR § 52.25 (b)(1).

11. 11 NYCRR § 52.25(c)(3).

12. 11 NYCRR § 52.25(c)(7).

§ 23.65

1. 42 U.S.C.A. § 1396a(a)(17).

2. *See infra*, § 23.66 for a discussion of the Partnership program.

§ 23.66 Long Term Care Insurance—The Partnership for Long Term Care/Robert Wood Johnson Program

The New York State Partnership for Long Term Care ("Partnership Program") was established to encourage the purchase of Long Term Care insurance.[1] Individuals who purchase Long Term Care insurance policies approved by the Partnership program ("Partnership policies") may qualify for Medicaid upon expiration of the insurance coverage without spending down their assets. However normal Medicaid income rules will be applied.[2]

In order to qualify for approval as a Partnership policy, insurance policies must contain at least the following benefits:

(1) Coverage for at least 36 months of nursing home[3] care at a rate of $122 per day in 1997, and increasing by 5% in subsequent years;[4]

(2) Coverage for 72 months of home care services[5] payable at half the rate of nursing home care;[6]

(3) Permit the insured to combine or substitute nursing home and home care services with two days of home care services counting as one day of nursing home care;[7]

(4) Respite care of 14 days per year payable at the nursing home daily benefit amount.[8] The policy may require that respite care be available only after the insured has been eligible for nursing home or home care benefits for six months and only if the policy's elimination period has been met;[9]

---

§ 23.66

1. The New York State Insurance Department booklet, *Insurance Policies Covering Long Term Care In New York State*, published annually by the New York State Insurance Department, contains a listing of approved Partnership insurance policies, including information about benefit amounts, rates, waiting periods and exclusions. Copies may be requested by calling (518) 474-4557 or by writing to Publications Unit, 5th Floor, New York State Insurance Department, Agency Building One, Empire State Plaza, Albany, New York 12257.

2. The statutes governing the Partnership program are found at 52A Social Services Law § 367-f and Insurance Law § 3229. Regulations concerning the program can be found at 11 NYCRR Pt. 39.

3. Covered care in a nursing home includes skilled, intermediate and custodial care. 11 NYCRR § 39.3(b)(1).

4. 11 NYCRR § 39.3(b)(1) contains a list of the minimum daily benefits rates through the year 2002.

5. 11 NYCRR § 39.3(b)(2)(ii). Home care services may include skilled nursing care, services of home health aids, personal attendants and assisted living care. 11 NYCRR § 39.3 (b)(2)(i). Home care services must be provided in the insured's home, in a group setting such as an adult day care center or where "human assistance" is needed to aid the adult in necessary travel, such as to a doctor's office. 11 NYCRR § 39.3(b)(2).

6. 11 NYCRR § 39.3(b)(2)(iii).

7. 11 NYCRR § 39.3(b)(2)(ii).

8. 11 NYCRR § 39.3(b)(3). Respite care is a service that provides family members with a rest from their care giving responsibilities. It can be provided in a variety of settings including an individual's home or short term nursing home placement.

9. *Id.*

(5) Coverage of alternate levels of care when the insured is in a hospital awaiting nursing home or home care services. These benefits are payable at the nursing home daily rate;[10]

(6) Inflation protection at a rate of at least 5% per year unless the policy is purchased after age 80;[11]

(7) Elimination or waiting periods that do not exceed 100 days.[12]

Individuals who consider purchasing a Partnership insurance policy should consider that the minimum payment rate for nursing home or home care coverage under these policies is very low and may not be sufficient to cover the actual cost of nursing home or home care services. Thus, the individual may need to utilize substantial income and resources to meet the cost of care, or pay higher insurance costs to provide coverage of a larger percentage of actual costs. Additionally, if the insured moves outside of New York State, the policy will still provide nursing care benefits; however the individual will not be exempted from the Medicaid financial eligibility rules in the new state of residence.

§ 23.67 Long Term Care Insurance—Choosing a Policy

Before choosing a Long Term Care insurance product, the following factors should be considered.

Is the daily benefit high enough to pay all or most of the cost of care? The average daily cost of quality nursing homes and home care providers in the area should be determined. An inflation protection option should be purchased. The policy holder should have sufficient resources to cover privately any charges which will not be covered by the policy.

Is the policy affordable? The cost of premiums should be predictable and affordable. Premiums are most affordable for younger individuals.[1] Premiums should be level and not subject to annual redetermination. There should be a provision which provides for a waiver of premiums once benefits have been paid for a set period of time.

Is the client insurable? Clients with chronic medical conditions which increase the risk of nursing home placement are unlikely to be approved for Long Term Care insurance.[2]

---

10. 11 NYCRR § 39.39(b)(4).
11. 11 NYCRR § 39.3(b)(5).
12. 11 NYCRR § 39.3(b)(9).

§ 23.67

1. An individual who purchases Long Term Care insurance at age 50 may be able to obtain a policy for about $500 per year. However, the rate would typically rise to $1,500 to $2,000 by age 65; $5,000 by age 75 and about $9,000 by age 85. Moreover, the older client may now have medical problems which make him or her uninsurable.

2. Insurers can be expected to refuse approval of a policy to an individual who is discovered to have any of the following conditions at the time of application: Alzheimer's or Parkinson's Disease, Organic Brain Syndrome or other illnesses causing dementia, history of prior strokes, severe arthritis, Multiple Sclerosis, or Lou Gehrig's Disease.

§ 23.67

What are the requirements for the payments under the policy? Policies generally contain elimination periods which require that a nursing home stay exceed a specified number of days before payments will be made under the policy. Common elimination periods range from 0 to 100 days with policies containing the shorter periods commanding the greatest costs. Similarly, the duration of coverage may be limited to two, three or four years or be unlimited.

Carefully examine the policy's criteria for determining that the patient is in need of long term care. Will the opinion of the patient's doctor be enough? Is a second opinion required? What is the appeals process for disputes concerning coverage?

Policies which contain any of the following provisions should be excluded from consideration:

Prior hospitalization;

Exclusions of coverage for custodial care or home care services;

No guaranteed renewal for life; or

Redetermination of premiums from year to year.

§ 23.68 Long Term Care Insurance—Tax Issues

A 1995 amendment to the New York State Tax Law provides for a deduction against New York State taxes for the payment of premiums for certain Long Term Care insurance policies.[1] The taxpayer must be at least 55 years of age and the amount of the deduction is subject to limitations which increase for older taxpayers.[2] This deduction is also available to New York City taxpayers.[3] In order to qualify for the deduction, the insurance policy must be approved by the Superintendent of Insurance and include certain minimum benefit requirements.[4]

The insured's medical condition may justify the insurer's refusal of coverage. Moreover, the insurer may apply a preexisting coverage exclusion of up to six months. 11 NYCRR § 52.25 (b)(2)(i). Once the policy has been approved and subject to any preexisting condition exclusion, the insurer may not exclude coverage for Alzheimer's Disease, senile dementia or organic brain disease. 11 NYCRR § 52.25 (b)(2)(ii). However, an insurer may validly refuse to cover long term care services which are necessitated by mental illness, intentionally self-inflicted injuries, alcoholism or drug addiction. 11 NYCRR § 52.25 (b)(2)(ii),(iii), (iv).

§ 23.68

1. Chapter 81 of the Laws of 1995, amending Tax Law § 612(c)(31).

2. For taxpayers between the ages of 55 and 60, the limitation is $750; between the ages of 60 and 70, the limitation is $2,000; over age 70, the limitation is $2,500. Tax Law § 612(c)(31).

3. New York City Administrative Code § 11–1712(c)(31).

4. Insurance Law § 1117(g)(1). Approved policies must provide coverage for a minimum of three years. Policies must also include case management to prevent inappropriate utilization of long term care services. No minimum stay in a hospital or other institutional setting may be required. Group policies must permit individuals to convert to individual coverage. All Long Term Care insurance policies offered for sale in New York State must indicate whether they meet the tax deductibility requirements of the law.

Currently, no policies offered for sale in New York State qualify for the deduction permitted under the statute.

The Health Insurance Portability and Accountability Act of 1996, commonly known as The Kennedy/Kassebaum Health Reform Act, enacted August 21, 1996, attempts to clarify the tax treatment of long term care and long term care insurance.[5]

The statute provides that a qualified long-term care insurance contact should be treated as an accident and health insurance contract.[6] And the statute also allows a partial deduction for payment of long term care insurance premiums.[7]

The statute provides that amounts received under a long term care insurance contract, regardless of whether the contract reimburses expenses or pays benefits on a periodic basis, are treated for tax purposes as reimbursement for expenses which are actually incurred for long term care.[8]

This favorable tax treatment is provided for certain existing policies and the statute allows for a tax-free exchange of existing long term care contracts.[9]

These provisions became effective January 1, 1997.[10]

§ 23.69 Medicaid

Congress established the Medical Assistance ("Medicaid") program under the 1965 amendments to the Social Security Act.[1] Medicaid is a joint federal-state third party payment system which provides comprehensive coverage of health-related services for needy individuals. The Health Care Financing Administration ("HCFA") of the United States Department of Health and Human Services promulgates national program standards and requirements to which each state Medicaid program must conform in order to receive federal financial participation. Pursuant to the state Social Services Law, the New York State Department of Social Services ("DSS") administers the program, and issues regulations[2] and promulgates administrative directives ("ADMs") and Informational Letters ("INFs").[3] The New York State Medicaid program is directly

---

CAVEAT: At the time this chapter was written, several bills to amend the Insurance Law provisions regarding long term care insurance were under consideration. Therefore, the practitioner is cautioned to research the current status of this statute.

5. CAVEAT: At the time this chapter was written, numerous technical amendments to the statute were being considered. Therefore, the practitioner is cautioned to research and investigate the current status of this state.

6. I.R.C. § 7702B
7. I.R.C. § 213(d)(i).
8. I.R.C. § 7702B.
9. I.R.C. § 7702B(g)(3).

10. I.R.C. § 7702B(g).

§ 23.69

1. 42 U.S.C.A. §§ 1396 et seq.
2. Social Services Law § 363–a; 18 NYCRR Pt. 360.
3. **PRACTICE POINTER:** ADMs and INFs may be obtained from the New York State Department of Social Services, Office of Local District Policy Communications, 40 North Pearl Street, Albany, New York 12243. Telephone (518) 473–6369. Another useful, though not legally binding, resource is the Medical Assistance Reference Guide ("MARG"). The MARG is a desk reference published for the use of Medicaid intake personnel during the application process.

§ 23.69 ELDER LAW Ch. 23

administered by each local county Department of Social Services and by the New York City Human Resources Administration.

The federal Medicaid statute sets forth minimum requirements for the Medicaid program. States have much discretion concerning the specific benefits which they elect to provide. The discussion in this chapter will be limited to the benefits provided in New York's Medicaid program.

§ 23.70 Medicaid—Covered Services

The Medicaid program covers a broad range of health services within the following three categories: (1) community medical services, (2) home care, and (3) institutional (generally nursing home) care.[1] Community medical services include a wide range of physician, hospital, and dental services, outpatient and clinic services, rehabilitative services, and medical supplies. Home care services include at-home personal care, nursing and rehabilitative care.

Library References:

West's Key No. Digests, Social Security and Public Welfare ⚖=241.91.

§ 23.71 Medicaid—Basic Eligibility Requirements

Individuals who receive means-tested public benefits such as Supplemental Security Income ("SSI"), Aid to Families with Dependent Children or home relief are "categorically eligible" for Medicaid.[1] Medicaid coverage also is available to New York State residents who are at least age 65, disabled, or blind, and whose net available income and resources are insufficient to cover the cost of their necessary medical care.[2] Such individuals are classified as "medically needy." In order to qualify as "medically needy," the applicant's income and resources must not exceed certain limits, and this information must be fully documented in the Medicaid application.[3] During 1997, the resource limit was $3,450 for an individual and $5,000 for a Medicaid-covered couple.[4] The 1997 monthly income limit for individuals who reside in the community was $575 per month for an individual or $834, for a Medicaid-covered couple.[5] A Medicaid recipient who resides in a nursing home is entitled to retain a

§ 23.70

1. See 18 NYCRR §§ 505–510 for a complete listing of Medicaid-covered services.

§ 23.71

1. See Social Services Law § 366(1)(a)(1)-(4); 18 NYCRR § 360–3.3(a).

2. Social Services Law § 366(1)(a)(5); 18 NYCRR § 360–3.3(b).

3. 18 NYCRR § 360–2.3(c).

4. General Information System Memorandum to Local District Commissioners #GIS 96 MA/037 (November 14, 1996). Contact Sharon Burgess at 800–343–8859, ext.3–5531 for information for years after 1997. See also, Social Services Law § 366(2); 18 NYCRR § 360–4.2(b).

5. Id.

"personal needs allowance" of $50 per month.[6]

Library References:

West's Key No. Digests, Social Security and Public Welfare ⇒241.76.

§ 23.72 Medicaid—Surplus Income Program for the "Medically Needy"

Under the "surplus income" or "spend down" program, an individual may receive Medicaid coverage even if his or her monthly income exceeds the applicable monthly income allowance, as long as all other eligibility criteria have been met.[1] Any monthly income which exceeds the applicable monthly income limit—*i.e.*, $574 in the community setting or $50 in the institutional setting,[2] is considered to be "surplus" or "excess" income. Medicaid will provide coverage where the recipient can show that he or she incurred medical expenses in that month which exceed the excess income amount. These include expenses for: health insurance premiums, deductibles and co-insurance charges; and "necessary and remedial services that are recognized under State law", whether or not covered by Medicaid.[3]

The Medicaid recipient need only have *incurred* the medical expense; it is *not* necessary that any excess income actually have been paid out toward that expense. Both paid and unpaid bills (including those of the recipient's spouse) may be used to meet the spend down requirement. Bills may be credited prospectively for up to six months, so that Medicaid coverage will be provided if it can be shown that the Medicaid recipient has incurred medical expenses which equal or exceed six months of the surplus income amount.[4]

In the community services context, the recipient (or representative) must present documentation of the incurred medical expenses to the local Medicaid office. In the home care context, the home care agency bills the Medicaid recipient directly for the excess income amount. The nursing home bills the recipient (or representative) for the excess income amount, commonly referred to as NAMI ("net available monthly income"), subject to the "spousal protection" provisions.[5]

6. Social Services Law § 366(2)(a)(10)(ii)(A); 18 NYCRR §§ 360–4.9(a)(1), 360–4.10(b)(4)(i).

§ 23.72

1. Social Services Law § 366(2)(b)(3); 18 NYCRR § 360–4.8(c).

2. PRACTICE POINTER: As a practical matter, most every recipient of Medicaid nursing home benefits will have a spend down requirement, since most individuals have a monthly income greater than $50. In the non-institutional setting, there will be no monthly spend down if the individual's monthly income does not exceed the income limit (including any applicable income exemptions).

3. 18 NYCRR § 360–4.8(c)(1).

4. 18 NYCRR § 360–4.8(c)(4).

5. *See infra*, § 23.80 for a discussion of spousal protection provisions.

§ 23.73 Medicaid—Income

The Department of Social Services defines "income" to "include any payment from any source," including payments of money, goods, or services on a one-time basis or on a recurring basis.[1] Payments are counted as income only in the month received; if retained beyond the month of receipt, then that payment becomes a "resource."[2] Net rental income—gross rental payment minus the monthly cost of property-related taxes, mortgage interest, depreciation, repairs and maintenance—is includible income.[3]

However, not all "income" payments are deemed to be actually "available" for the cost of a Medicaid recipient's care, as the Social Services Law carves out numerous "income disregards."[4] The following are some of the most common "income disregards" for elderly, blind, and disabled Medicaid recipients: (1) the first $20 per month of unearned income per household (*e.g.*, Social Security);[5] (2) privately-paid health insurance premiums;[6] (3) interest earned on excluded burial funds;[7] (4) certain retroactive SSI payments;[8] (5) German and Austrian reparation payments;[9] and (6) Japanese–American restitution payments.[10] In addition, payment of "in-kind" income or support (*i.e.*, direct payments to a provider of goods, services, or shelter) on behalf of an elderly Medicaid recipient by a non-spouse of that individual is not considered "available income" to that individual for Medicaid purposes.[11]

§ 23.74 Medicaid—Resources

The Department of Social Services defines "resources" to include "property of all kinds, including real property and personal property".[1] A Medicaid applicant's "available resources" include: all liquid or easily liquidated resources in the control of the applicant or a party acting on the applicant's behalf, such as a guardian;[2] a portion of the equity value of certain income-producing property (such as a family farm); and the resources of a "legally responsible relative" (generally, the applicant's

---

§ 23.73

1. 18 NYCRR § 360–4.3(b).
2. 18 NYCRR § 360–4.3(b).
3. 18 NYCRR § 360–4.3(d).
4. Social Services Law § 366(2)(b)(1); 18 NYCRR §§ 360–4.1(b), 360–4.6(a).
5. 18 NYCRR § 360–4.6(a)(2)(iii).
6. 18 NYCRR § 360–4.6(a)(2)(vii).
7. 18 NYCRR § 360–4.6(a)(2)(xvii).
8. 18 NYCRR § 360–4.6(a)(2)(xix). These are retroactive SSI benefits paid pursuant to 42 U.S.C.A. §§ 1382(e)(1)(E) or 1382(e)(1)(G). *See* 42 U.S.C.A. § 1396a(*o*). Retroactive SSI and Social Security benefits retained beyond the month of receipt are exempt resources for a period of six months from receipt. 18 NYCRR § 360–4.6(b)(2)(v).
9. 18 NYCRR §§ 360–4.6(a)(2)(ii), (xxii). *See also*, 42 U.S.C.A. § 1396a(r)(1).
10. 18 NYCRR § 360–4.6(a)(1)(xxi).
11. 18 NYCRR § 360–4.3(e).

§ 23.74

1. 18 NYCRR § 360–4.4(a)(1).
2. Social Services Law §§ 366(2)(b), 366(5)(d)(1)(i), (v).

spouse in the elder law context).[3]

Library References:
West's Key No. Digests, Social Security and Public Welfare ⚖︎241.80.

§ 23.75 Medicaid—Exempt Resources

All "available resources" must be applied toward the cost of the applicant's care before Medicaid coverage may be obtained.[1] However, as with income, not all "resources" are considered to be "available." A Medicaid recipient may keep up to the prevailing Medicaid resource allowance, which was $3,450 during 1997.[2] A Medicaid recipient also may retain a "burial fund" of up to $1,500,[3] or may enter into a pre-need funeral agreement with a funeral firm, funeral director, undertaker or cemetery provided that all funds pursuant to the agreement are placed in an irrevocable burial trust.[4] Perhaps most importantly, the value of the Medicaid recipient's personal residence, or "homestead," including all "contiguous" property is exempt.[5] Even where a Medicaid recipient resides in a nursing home, as long as he or she can evidence a subjective intent to return home at the medically appropriate time, the home will retain its exempt status.[6] If the home loses its exempt status, then DSS

---

3. 18 NYCRR § 360–4.4(b). Under Social Services Law, a "legally responsible relative" is a person who is legally responsible for the support of one or more relatives. Generally, this refers to the obligation of spouses to each other and the obligation of a parent to a child under age 21. Social Services Law §§ 101, 366(3)(b)(iii); 18 NYCRR § 360–1.4(h).

§ 23.75

1. 42 U.S.C.A. § 1396p(a)(17).

2. General Information System Memorandum to Local District Commissioners #GIS 96 MA/037 (November 14, 1996). Contact Sharon Burgess at 800–343–8859, ext.3–5531, for information for years after 1997. *See also*, Social Services Law § 366(2); 18 NYCRR § 360–4.2(b).

PRACTICE POINTER: The exempt amounts are generally kept in a non-interest bearing checking account. This account must be monitored so that the balance does not exceed the resource limit; otherwise problems could arise on the Medicaid recipient's annual "recertification."

3. Social Services Law § 366(2)(a)(3); 18 NYCRR § 360–4.6(b)(1).

PRACTICE POINTER: The "burial fund" usually is a savings account designated as such, with an opening deposit of $1,500. Interest may accrue on this account, but there may be no further deposits into or withdrawals from the account until the funds are needed for the Medicaid recipient's funeral expenses. Instead of a bank account, a life insurance policy with a face value of up to $1,500 may be considered to be the "burial fund." 18 NYCRR § 360–4.6(b)(ii).

4. Chapter 660 of the Laws of 1996 amending Social Services Law § 209(6)(a).

PRACTICE POINTER: The new law eliminates the prior distinction between "burial space" items which could be pre-paid in any amount and "non-burial space" items which could previously be pre-paid only up to $1,500. There is now no limit to the amount or type of services which can be pre-paid in the burial trust. However, any funds left over after funeral and burial expenses have been paid must be remitted by the funeral director to the Department of Social Services. Social Services Law § 141(6).

5. Social Services Law § 366(2)(a)(1); 18 NYCRR §§ 360–1.4(f), 360–4.6(b)(2), 360–4.7(a)(1).

6. Anna W. v. Bane, 863 F.Supp. 125 (W.D.N.Y.1993).

PRACTICE POINTER: Although the Medicaid-covered nursing home resident may retain title to the homestead, practical problems may arise if no family member is residing there. In that event, the home could be rented out to cover maintenance, tax, and mortgage costs; any rental profit

may attach a lien to it to the extent of Medicaid benefits paid.[7] Other common "resource disregards" include: (1) accumulated German or Austrian Holocaust reparation payments, provided that these accumulated payments remain identifiable as such;[8] (2) all Japanese–American restitution payments;[9] and (3) retroactive SSI or Social Security payments retained for up to six months from receipt.[10]

§ 23.76 Medicaid—Transfer of Resources

When an institutionalized applicant or applicant's spouse makes a gift of an excess (*i.e.*, non-exempt) resource, or the applicant's or spouse's interest in the exempt homestead, within the 36 months prior to the date of the Medicaid application, a period of ineligibility for Medicaid coverage of nursing home services is imposed.[1] The number of months of the "penalty period" is determined by dividing the total amount of the uncompensated transfer by the average cost of private pay nursing home care in the region where the Medicaid applicant is institutionalized.[2] The penalty period begins on the first day of the month following the month of the transfer.[3]

> **Example:** A resident of a New York City nursing home gave $50,000 to a friend on January 17, 1996. Three months later, the individual applies for Medicaid nursing home coverage. The DSS determined average regional private-pay rate is $6,521 per month. To calculate the amount of the transfer penalty take the amount transferred (in this case $50,000) and divide by the DSS determined regional private pay rate (in this case $6,521). The resulting sum is the penalty period. Any partial month penalty will be counted as would be owed to the nursing home as part of the Medicaid recipient's monthly contribution of income to the nursing home.

7. 42 U.S.C.A. § 1396p(a)(1)(B); Social Services Law § 369(2)(a)(ii); 18 NYCRR 360–7.11. *See infra*, § 23.81.

8. 18 NYCRR §§ 360–4.6(b)(2)(iv), (viii).

9. 18 NYCRR § 360–4.6(b)(6).

10. 18 NYCRR § 360–4.6(b)(2)(v).

§ 23.76

1. 42 U.S.C.A. § 1396p(c); Social Services Law § 366(5)(d)(3); 18 NYCRR § 360–4.4(c). The Department of Social Services has issued Administrative Directive, 96 ADM–8 (March 29, 1996) describing the manner in which the transfer penalty is applied.

2. 42 U.S.C.A. § 1396p(c)(1)(E)(i); Social Services Law § 366(5)(d)(4); 18 NYCRR § 360–4.4(c)(2)(iv). Note that the federal statute provides that states may use either the average private cost of nursing home care in the state, or the region when calculating the penalty period. New York has elected to use regional rates.

PRACTICE POINTER: The Department of Social services issues Administrative Directives ("ADMs") containing current rates. However, these ADMs are often issued many months after local offices begin to apply new rates. For example, 96 ADM–17 containing 1996 rates was not issued until September 1996. The ADM contains the following 1996 regional rates: Central-$4,536; Long Island-$6,790; New York City-$6,521; Northeastern-$4,810; Northern Metropolitan-$5,930; Rochester-$4,852; Western-$4,380. Attorneys should contact the Department of Social Services at 1–800–343–8859 to obtain subsequent regional rates.

3. 42 U.S.C.A. § 1396p(c)(1)(D); Social Services Law § 366(5)(d)(4); 18 NYCRR § 350–4.4(c)(2)(iv)(b); DSS Administrative Directive 96 ADM–8, p.15.

part of the Net Available Monthly Income ("NAMI") in the first month of eligibility. (In this case, 7 months plus $4,353). The transfer penalty will begin with the first day of the month after the transfer (in this case February 1, 1996). This individual is ineligible for Medicaid nursing home coverage until September 1, 1996 and will be responsible for a NAMI contribution of $4,353 in this first month of eligibility.

The Taxpayer Relief Act of 1997 amended 42 U.S.C.A. § 1320a–7b(a) by providing criminal penalties for whoever "for a fee knowingly and willfully counsels or assists an individual to dispose of assets (including by any transfer in trust) in order for the individual to become eligible for medical assistance under an estate plan under title XIX, if disposing of the assets results in the imposition of a period of ineligibility" under 42 U.S.C.A. § 1396p(c). This law amends Section 217 of the Health Insurance Portability and Accountability Act of 1996 and limits the criminalization to individuals who knowingly and willfully counsel or assist in this conduct for a fee, presumably attorneys.[4] The statute applies to acts after August 5, 1997. This statute does not apply to counseling or assisting with transfers of assets which do not "impose a period of ineligibility" for Medicaid. Therefore it would not apply to transfer of assets which occurred prior to the look-back period used to determine Medicaid eligibility (generally 36 months prior to the application for Medicaid, but 60 months in the case of transfers to certain trusts) or if the application for Medicaid is made after the period of ineligibility is exhausted.[5] It also does not apply to transfers of assets to spouses, disabled children, or transfers of a homestead to a caretaker child or sibling with an equity interest in the homestead.

The federal Medicaid statute mandates that states apply the transfer of assets penalty to "institutionalized" Medicaid applicants. States have the option of applying the penalty to "noninstitutionalized" individuals.[6] New York State only applies the transfer of asset prohibitions to individuals who receive institutional care.[7] An institutionalized individual receives care as an inpatient in a nursing home or intermediate care facility for the mentally retarded or receives "nursing facility services" such as those provided in an alternate level of care in a hospital, or the "Lombardi—Nursing Home Without Walls" home care program.[8] The

---

4. **CAVEAT:** At the time this book was going to press, technical amendments to the statute and litigation contesting the statute were being considered. Therefore, the practitioner is cautioned to research and investigate the current status of this statute.

5. Peebler v. Reno, 965 F.Supp. 28 (D.Or.1997).

6. 42 U.S.C.A. § 1396p(c)(1)(A).

7. Social Services Law § 366(5)(d)(3); 18 NYCRR § 360–4.4(c)(2)(ii).

CAVEAT: Legislation to extend the transfer penalties to individuals who receive non-institutional Medicaid services has been proposed.

8. 42 U.S.C.A. § 1396p(c)(1)(C)(i); Social Services Law § 366(5)(d)(1)(vii-x); 18 NYCRR § 360–4.4(c)(2)(i)(b).

transfer prohibitions do not apply to Medicaid coverage of hospital, community or other home care services.[9]

There are some significant exceptions to the transfer-of-asset rules. First, no penalty is imposed if the asset is transferred to the applicant's spouse, blind or disabled child, or to a trust established "solely" for the benefit of a disabled individual under age 65.[10] Second, the applicant's homestead may be freely transferred to the applicant's: (a) spouse; (b) minor, disabled, or blind child; (c) sibling with an "equity interest" in the home who resided there for at least a year prior to the applicant's nursing home admission; or (d) adult "caretaker child" who resided there for at least two years prior to the applicant's nursing home admission.[11] Third, a Medicaid applicant may transfer "exempt resources" other than the homestead, such as identifiable Holocaust reparations payments, to anyone without incurring a penalty period.[12] Finally, no penalty will be imposed if it can be shown that the asset was intended to be transferred for fair market value or other valuable consideration, if the gift was made exclusively for a purpose other than to qualify for Medicaid coverage, or if the gift is returned to the applicant or spouse.[13]

A Medicaid application must include all financial records of the applicant and applicant's spouse for the 36 months prior to the date of application.[14] Medicaid may request information about all transactions made during this time period in order to determine if any penalty period applies.

The timing of submission of the Medicaid application is crucial since premature submission may result in an excessive penalty period. Since 1993, there has been no limit to the length of the penalty period.[15] However, the "look back" period for identifying transfers subject to the penalty is limited to the thirty six months prior to the Medicaid application. The thirty six month look-back period operates, in effect, as a Statute of Limitations. Thus, in 1996, a transfer of $600,000 within the

---

9. Social Services Law § 366(5)(d)(3); 18 NYCRR § 360–4.4(c)(2)(ii).

10. 42 U.S.C.A. § 1396p(c)(2)(B); Social Services Law § 366(5)(d)(3)(ii); 18 NYCRR § 360–4.4(c)(2)(iii)(c).

11. 42 U.S.C.A. § 1396p(c)(2)(A); Social Services Law § 366(5)(c)(3)(i); 18 NYCRR § 360–4.4(c)(2)(iii)(b). A "caretaker child" must show that he or she provided direct or indirect care which delayed the parent's institutionalization. *See* 18 NYCRR § 311.4(a)(1).

PRACTICE POINTER: Generally, it should be easy for an adult child who has resided with the parent for at least two years to qualify as a "caretaker child." There is no need to show that the child provided all care, or even primary care. For example, the child could have assisted in meal preparation, dispensation of medication, or overseeing of a home attendant. *See* Matter of DeLuca, N.Y.L.J., 12/14/93, p.27, col.3 (Sup.Ct., Nassau County).

12. 18 NYCRR § 360–4.4(c)(2)(iii)(a).

13. 42 U.S.C.A. § 1396p(c)(2)(C); Social Services Law § 366(5)(d)(3)(iii); 18 NYCRR § 360–4.4(c)(2)(iii)(d).

14. Social Services Law §§ 366(5)(d)(1)(vi), 366(5)(d)(3); 18 NYCRR §§ 360–4.4(c)(2)(i)(c), 360–4.4(c)(2)(ii).

15. Prior to August 11, 1993, there was a 30–month cap on Medicaid penalty periods. Former 42 U.S.C.A. § 1396p(c)(1)(A); 18 NYCRR § 360–4.4(c)(1).

36-month look-back period could create a 92 month penalty for a New York City nursing home resident ($600,000 ÷ $6,521= 92 months). However, if the individual does not file the Medicaid application until 37 months from the completion of the transfer, the $600,000 transfer will not be penalized. Within that 36-month "window," however, any nursing home care would have to be paid for privately.[16] If the applicant funds an irrevocable "income-only" trust on his behalf, then a 60-month look-back period would apply.[17]

Before assisting the clients with a transfer of assets the attorney must be confident of the competency of any individual whose assets will be divested.[18] If the individual lacks capacity to retain counsel and/or consent to the transfer of assets, the attorney should consider filing a petition for a guardian under Article 81 of the Mental Hygiene Law.[19] The court may authorize a transfer of assets from an alleged incapacitated person for the purpose of Medicaid planning.[20]

Jointly-owned assets require a brief discussion. Since 1993, any withdrawal from a joint account by a non-Medicaid applicant owner (unless a spouse or disabled or blind child) has been subject to a transfer penalty, absent a showing that the non-applicant owner contributed these funds to the account.[21] The applicant does not make an impermissible transfer merely by placing his assets into joint ownership with another. As long as the applicant still has the right to withdraw funds unilaterally (such as in a joint bank account), the asset still belongs to the individual for Medicaid purposes.[22] However, when the placement of assets into a joint account actually limits the applicant's control of the assets (such as a brokerage account requiring dual signatures for withdrawals), an impermissible transfer has occurred. In addition, the with-

---

16. PRACTICE POINTER: As a practical matter, a nursing home will not admit an individual who is not Medicaid-eligible unless sufficient funds remain accessible to the individual (or his legal representative) which can be paid to the nursing home until the penalty period ends and the individual financially qualifies for Medicaid.

17. 42 U.S.C.A. § 1396p(c)(1)(B); Social Services Law § 366(5)(d)(1)(vi); 18 NYCRR § 360-4.4(c)(2)(i)(c). For a discussion of Medicaid treatment of trusts, see infra, § 23.77.

18. See supra, §§ 23.3—23.6 for a discussion of ethical considerations in elder law practice. In particular, the attorney who participates in a transfer of assets plan must clearly identify the client, take precautions against conflicts of interest in any joint representation and be confident that the elderly individual whose assets are transferred has the requisite mental capacity to understand and consent to any divestment.

19. For a full discussion of New York's Guardianship statute, See Chapter 22 "Guardianship," supra.

20. Matter of Heller (Ratner), N.Y.L.J., 7/28/95, p.24, col.5 (Sup.Ct., Kings County); Matter of Parnes, N.Y.L.J., 11/2/94, p.32, col.2 (Sup.Ct., Kings County); see also N.Y.L.J., 4/7/95, p.33, col.5 (Sup.Ct., Kings County); Matter of Daniels, 162 Misc.2d 840, 618 N.Y.S.2d 499 (Sup.Ct., Suffolk County, 1994); Matter of Klapper, N.Y.L.J., 8/9/94, p.26, col.1 (Sup.Ct., Kings County); Matter of Driscoll, N.Y.L.J., 10/22/92, p.30, col.4 (Sup.Ct., Nassau County); In re De Luca, N.Y.L.J., 12/14/93, p.27, col.3 (Sup. Ct., Nassau County).

21. 42 U.S.C.A. § 1396p(c)(3); HCFA Transmittal No. 64, § 3258.7 (Nov. 1994); Social Services Law § 366(5)(d)(5); 18 NYCRR § 360-4.4(d).

22. Id.

drawal of funds from a jointly-owned account by the non-applicant joint owner is presumed to constitute a transfer of the full amount of the withdrawal, unless it can be established that the transferred portion actually belonged to the non-applicant joint owner.[23]

§ 23.77 Medicaid—Treatment of Trusts

Medicaid's treatment of trusts distinguishes between third party trusts in which the assets in the trusts were not the assets of the Medicaid recipient or the recipient's spouse, and self settled trusts in which the Medicaid recipient or the recipient's spouse contributed the assets.[1]

§ 23.78 Medicaid—Treatment of Trusts—Self Settled Trusts

Corpus and income generated by a revocable trust are considered available to the Medicaid recipient.[1] Irrevocable trusts cause issues of eligibility. There are innumerable variations of irrevocable trusts. This section will address the most common Medicaid trusts.

The most common trust for many individuals who wish to create Medicaid eligibility for themselves or their spouses is an irrevocable "income only" trust in which the grantor retains the income of the trust for life, but there can be no payments from the principal to or for the benefit of the grantor.[2] This shelters the principal of the trust and allows the grantor of the trust to qualify for Medicaid following the expiration of the penalty period of ineligibility for institutional Medicaid. The period of ineligibility is calculated by dividing the uncompensated portion of the transfer to the trust by the average monthly cost of a nursing home.[3] In an income only trust, the principal would not be counted as an available asset for the grantor. The net annual income would be paid to the grantor and counted as income for the purposes of determining the grantor's Medicaid eligibility. This trust is the most common Medicaid Trust and is still an effective planning tool. However, 1993 amendments

---

23. *Id.* **PRACTICE POINTER**: Under this analysis, the addition of a joint tenant or tenant-in-common on a deed will constitute a transfer resulting in a penalty period.

§ 23.77

1. An individual will be considered to have established a trust (and hence be subject to the trust look back period) if assets of the individual were used to form all or part of the corpus of the trust, and if the trust was established by the individual's spouse or a person, court or administrative body acting with legal authority or upon the direction of the individual or his or her spouse. 42 U.S.C.A. § 1396p(d)(2)(A).

§ 23.78

1. 42 U.S.C.A. § 1396p(d)(3)(A)(i); 18 NYCRR § 360–4.5(b)(2)(i).

2. PRACTICE POINTER: Effective April 2, 1992, a trust provision which in any way diverts the beneficial interest of a trust away from the grantor of grantor's spouse in the event that medical care is required or a Medicaid application is submitted is void as against public policy. EPTL § 7–3.1; 18 NYCRR § 360–4.5(d).

3. For a discussion of Medicaid transfer of asset rules, *see supra*, § 23.76.

to federal Medicaid statute ("OBRA 93") have made such trusts a less attractive option by increasing the penalty periods for transfers into trusts.

For a trust created on or after April 11, 1993, the "look-back period" for determining transfers subject to a penalty period of ineligibility for institutional Medicaid was extended to sixty months prior to the Medicaid application rather than the usual 36 months. The extended look-back period creates potential for a greatly increased penalty period. For example, if Mr. Smith were to transfer $1 million outright to other individuals (putting aside for the moment any tax planning considerations), he would have to wait at least 37 months to apply for Medicaid.[4] However, if Mr. Smith were to transfer $1 million to an irrevocable trust, he would have to wait 61 months.

Self settled trusts in which the trustee has the discretion to make distributions to the grantor or grantor's spouse are considered available to the extent of the trustee's discretion.[5] OBRA 93 created new Medicaid planning opportunities for self settled trusts for disabled individuals under age 65. A Medicaid recipient under age 65 may transfer assets into a qualified OBRA 93 "payback" or "pooled" trust and there is no penalty period of ineligibility for Medicaid, nor is the trust considered available in determining the recipient's Medicaid eligibility.[6]

In order to qualify as a "payback" trust, the trust must be created by the beneficiary's parent, grandparent, legal guardian or court. The trust agreement must provide a "payback" provision whereby, after the beneficiary's death, all of the amounts remaining in the trust, up to the amount of the Medicaid benefits paid, would be paid back to the Department of Social Services.[7]

In order to qualify as a "pooled" trust, the trust must be established and managed by a not-for-profit organization which maintains separate accounts under the trust for other disabled individuals. The accounts are pooled for management investment purposes only. Funds in each individual's account are used exclusively for that individual. Upon the individu-

4. 42 U.S.C.A. § 1396p(c)(1)(B); Social Services Law § 366(5)(d)(1)(vi); 18 NYCRR § 360–4.4(c)(2)(i)(c).

5. 42 U.S.C.A. § 1396p(d)(3)(B); Social Services Law § 366(2)(b)(2)(i); 18 NYCRR § 360–4.5(b)(1)(ii).

6. 42 U.S.C.A. §§ 1396p(c)(2)(B)(iv), 1396p(d)(4); Social Services Law §§ 366(2)(b)(2)(iii), 366(5)(d)(3)(ii)(D); 18 NYCRR §§ 360–4.4(c)(2)(iii)(c)(1)(iv), 360–4.5(b).

7. 42 U.S.C.A. §§ 1396p(d)(4)(A); Social Services Law § 366(5)(d)(3)(ii)(D); 18 NYCRR § 360–4.5(b)(5)(i)(a).

PRACTICE POINTER: The trustee of a "payback" trust is required to report to the local social services district regarding the creation and funding of the trust and the death of the beneficiary. The trustee generally must provide proof of bonding in trusts exceeding $1,000,000, and obtain prior approval from the local social services district before making certain large transactions or transfers for less than fair market value. DSS or the local social services district may commence a proceeding against a trustee who fails to comply with these requirements or otherwise violates his or her fiduciary duty to the beneficiary. Social Services Law § 366(2)(b)(2) (iv), (v); 18 NYCRR § 360–4.5(b)(5)(iii).

al's death, the amounts remaining in the individual's account must remain in the trust or be repaid to New York State up to the amount of Medicaid benefits paid.[8]

Self settled trusts which do not qualify as "payback" or "pooled" trusts will result in a period of ineligibility to the extent that uncompensated assets are transferred into the trust.

§ 23.79 Medicaid—Treatment of Trusts—Third Party Trusts

Third party trusts must be analyzed for their effect upon the Medicaid eligibility of the grantor and upon the beneficiary of the trust.

No penalty period of ineligibility is incurred by the transfer of assets to a trust which is established solely for the benefit of a disabled individual under age 65, or established solely for the benefit of an applicant's child who is blind or disabled. The trust must be solely for the benefit of the disabled individual and no other party can have a vested interest in the trust.[1]

A Medicaid applicant or recipient who is a beneficiary of a trust will be considered to have available any income or principal which is mandated by the trustees to be paid for the beneficiary. To the extent that the trustee has the discretion to make payments from principal to the beneficiary, under the *Escher* doctrine, the trustee can not be compelled to exercise this discretion.[2] However, the Department of Social Services does have a right to commence proceedings against the trustee to compel

---

8. 42 U.S.C.A. § 1396p(d)(4)(C); Social Services Law § 366(5)(d)(3)(ii)(D); 18 NYCRR § 360–4.5(b)(5)(i)(b). At this time, the only known OBRA '93 "pooled trust" is the UJA–Federation Community Trust II. Contact: United Jewish Appeal–Federation of Jewish Philanthropies, Department of Planned Giving and Endowments, 130 East 59th Street, Suite 737, New York, New York 10022. Telephone (212) 836–1811.

§ 23.79

1. 42 U.S.C.A. § 1396p(c)(2)(B)(iv); Social Services Law § 366(5)(d)(3)(ii)(D); 18 NYCRR § 360–4.4(c)(2)(iii)(c)(iv).

2. Matter of Escher established the principle that a trust created by a third party (*i.e.*, not the applicant for government benefits or the applicant's spouse) is not considered a countable resource or income for the purpose of determining Medicaid eligibility even where the trustee has the discretion to use the income and/or principal of the trust. Matter of Escher, 94 Misc.2d 952, 407 N.Y.S.2d 106 (Surr.Ct., Bronx County, 1978), aff'd 75 A.D.2d 531, 426 N.Y.S.2d 1008 (1st Dep't 1980), aff'd 52 N.Y.2d 1006, 438 N.Y.S.2d 293, 420 N.E.2d 91 (1981). Escher, and cases which follow it make it clear that properly drafted third party trusts are not an "available resource" for the purposes of Medicaid eligibility. *See also*, Hoelzer v. Blum, 93 A.D.2d 605, 462 N.Y.S.2d 684 (2d Dep't 1983); Wick v. Gozigian, 85 A.D.2d 805, 445 N.Y.S.2d 643 (3d Dep't 1981); Maul v. Fitzgerald, 78 A.D.2d 706, 432 N.Y.S.2d 282 (3d Dep't 1980).

PRACTICE POINTER: New York State codified Escher by enacting EPTL § 7–1.12 to encourage testamentary and *inter vivos* Supplemental Needs Trusts and to provide language which would be statutorily approved. The "supplemental need" language in EPTL § 7–1.12 is more restrictive than the holding in Escher, but the holding in Escher that the trust assets and/or income are not available where the trustee has the discretion to make distributions remains good law.

payment if the beneficiary would have that right.[3]

§ 23.80 Medicaid—Spousal Budgeting: Protection of Resources and Income for Community Spouse

When both spouses apply for Medicaid, the income and resource rules for a couple will apply.[1] If only one spouse applies for Medicaid, the Department of Social Services will presume that the income and resources of the non-applicant spouse are available to the Medicaid applicant.[2] Medicaid benefits must be furnished even where a spouse with "sufficient" income and resources refuses to make any contribution toward the cost of the Medicaid spouse's care.[3] However, the furnishing of Medicaid creates an "implied contract" between the "refusing spouse" and the local social services district for recovery of the Medicaid benefits paid.[4]

Special income and resource rules apply when an applicant for Medicaid receives institutional care and has a spouse who remains in the community.[5] The "community spouse" may retain a "community spouse resource allowance" ("CSRA")[6] and a "community spouse monthly income allowance" ("CSMIA").

DSS must provide an assessment of the total value of the resources available to a couple and assess the CSRA and CSMIA upon receipt of a Medicaid application, or if requested by an institutionalized individual or community spouse.[7] In calculating the CSRA, DSS will total all resources, regardless of the manner in which title is held. The "spousal share" of the community spouse will be one half of the value of the total

---

3. Social Services Law § 369(3); 18 NYCRR § 360–7.11(b)(4).

§ 23.80

1. In fact, the Department of Social Services will presume that the Medicaid household contains any "legally responsible" relative who lives with the Medicaid applicant. 18 NYCRR § 360–4.2(a).

2. 42 U.S.C.A. § 1396a(a)(17); 18 NYCRR §§ 360–4.3(a)(3), 360–4.3(f)(1).

3. Social Services Law § 366(3)(a); 18 NYCRR § 360–4.3(f)(1). **PRACTICE POINTER:** If the spouse refuses to contribute income and support, the income and resource limits for a one person household will be applied. As part of the Medicaid application, the non-applicant spouse should complete a form, supplied by DSS, which states that he or she refuses to make his or her income and resources available to the Medicaid applicant. In turn, the applicant will execute an assignment of his or her right to support on another DSS form. If the applicant is unable to sign due to a physical or mental impairment, then the applicant's physician must submit a statement to this effect.

4. Commissioner v. Spellman, N.Y.L.J., 2/11/97, p.26, col.3 (Sup.Ct., New York County).

5. 42 U.S.C.A. § 1396r–5; Social Services Law § 366–c; 18 NYCRR § 360–4.10.

6. 42 U.S.C.A. § 1396r–5(f)(1); Social Services Law § 366–c(5)(a); 18 NYCRR § 360–4.10(c)(2).

7. 42 U.S.C.A. § 1396r–5 (c)(1)(B); Social Services Law § 366–c(7); 18 NYCRR § 360–4.10(c)(1). DSS may charge a fee of $25 for providing the assessment if it is requested in advance of submission of a Medicaid application. 18 NYCRR § 360–4.10(c)(1)(i).

§ 23.80   ELDER LAW   Ch. 23

resources.[8] DSS will consider the portion of the "spousal share" which exceeds the CSRA to be available to the institutionalized spouse.[9]

The CSRA is the greatest of the following amounts: 1) $74,820 (known as the **Minimum CSRA**); 2) the amount of the spousal share, not to exceed the **maximum CSRA** ($79,020 in 1997 and adjusted annually to reflect changes in the Consumer Price Index); 3) the amount established for support of the community spouse pursuant to a fair hearing; or 4) the amount established for the support of the community spouse pursuant to a court order.[10] DSS must provide the community spouse with notice of the right to a fair hearing to seek an enhanced CSRA or CSMIA.[11] If the community spouse's income is below the MMMNA, an enhanced CSRA may be awarded at an amount sufficient to generate income up to the MMMNA.[12] The spouse has the right to insist on an enhanced CSRA to generate the MMMNA and need not agree that the income be provided from the institutionalized spouse's income.[13] In addition to calculating the CSRA, DSS will calculate the Community Spouse Monthly Income Allowance ("CSMIA") which may be retained by the community spouse. The CSMIA is the amount of the institutionalized spouse's income which is needed to bring the community spouse's income up to the "minimum monthly maintenance needs

---

8. 42 U.S.C.A. § 1396r–5(c)(1)(A); Social Services Law § 366–c(2)(c).

9. 42 U.S.C.A. § 1396r–5(c)(2); Social Services Law § 366–c(5)(a); 18 NYCRR § 360–4.10(c)(2).

PRACTICE POINTER: A spouse whose resources exceed the CSRA may refuse to contribute the excess resources to the Medicaid applicant spouse. In this case, DSS may no longer consider the resources to be available and must provide Medicaid if the institutionalized spouse is eligible. However, DSS may pursue a support action against the refusing spouse. For a discussion of spousal refusal, see supra, § 23.80 note 3. See Matter of Parnes, N.Y.L.J., 11/2/94, p.32, col.2, motion to vacate denied N.Y.L.J., 4/7/95, p.33, col.5 (Sup.Ct., Kings County).

10. 42 U.S.C.A. § 1396r–5(f)(2); Social Services Law § 366–c(2)(d); 18 NYCRR § 360–4.10(a)(4).

PRACTICE POINTER: Even prior to the 1988–89 legislative enactment of the federal and state community spouse protections, New York case law recognized a community spouse's entitlement to support from an institutionalized spouse receiving Medicaid benefits. See Septuagenarian v. Septuagenarian, 126 Misc.2d 699, 483 N.Y.S.2d 932 (Fam.Ct., Queens County, 1984) ("[T]o deprive women (whose husbands are confined to nursing homes), and particularly women of petitioner's generation who, in many cases, were denied an equal opportunity to fulfill their potential in the employment market and are, therefore, dependent on their husbands for support, access to their husband's pension and assets in their later years effectively sentences many of them to tremendous hardship and a complete disruption of their lives at a time when they are extremely vulnerable.").

11. 42 U.S.C.A. § 1396r–5(e)(1); Social Services Law § 366–c(7)(c); 18 NYCRR § 360–4.10(c)(1)(iii).

12. 42 U.S.C.A. § 1396r–5(e)(2)(C); Social Services Law § 366–c(8)(c); 18 NYCRR § 360–4.10(c)(7).

PRACTICE POINTER: Caseworkers generally permit the community spouse to retain resources above the CSRA, without requiring a fair hearing decision or support order, where it is clear that the community spouse requires these resources to generate income that will approach or equal the MMMNA. The attorney should submit a letter with the Medicaid application specifically explaining why a higher CSRA should be awarded.

13. Social Services Law § 366–c(8)(c); 18 NYCRR § 360–4.10(c)(7); Golf v. Department of Social Services, 221 A.D.2d 997, 634 N.Y.S.2d 581 (4th Dep't 1995).

allowance" ("MMMNA"), unless a larger amount is established pursuant to a fair hearing or court order for the support of the community spouse.[14] In 1997, the MMMNA was $1,976 per month.[15] In order to obtain income beyond the MMMNA pursuant to a fair hearing or support order, the community spouse must demonstrate such that enhancement is required "due to exceptional circumstances resulting in significant financial duress."[16] The community spouse must show more than a mere threat to his or her accustomed standard of living.[17]

None of the community spouse's income may be counted in determining the institutionalized spouse's "net available monthly income" payable to the nursing home, even where the community spouse retains her own income in excess of the MMMNA.[18]

Under state regulations, the local Social Services district will request a contribution from the community spouse of 25% of his or her income in excess of the MMMNA, but the institutionalized spouse must receive Medicaid even if the community spouse refuses or fails to comply with such a request.[19] However, even if the community spouse makes the requested contribution, the local Social Services district may seek from the community spouse any further support or recovery permitted under the Social Services Law.[20]

Upon the state's determination of the institutionalized spouse's Medicaid eligibility and the CSRA, the state must notify both spouses of their right to a fair hearing to challenge the determinations of the CSRA and/or CSMIA.[21]

§ 23.81 Medicaid—Recoveries Against Estates

The federal Medicaid Act places no limitations upon states' efforts to

---

14. 42 U.S.C.A. § 1396r–5(d)(2); Social Services Law § 366–c(2)(g); 18 NYCRR § 360–4.10(a)(3).

15. Social Services Law § 366–c(2)(h); 18 NYCRR § 360–4.10(a)(8). General Information System Memorandum to Local District Commissioners #GIS 96 MA/037 contains the community spouse resource and income figures for 1997. The amount is revised annually to reflect increases in the Consumer Price Index.

16. 42 U.S.C.A. § 1396r–5(e)(2)(B); Social Services Law § 366–c(8)(b); 18 NYCRR § 360–4.10(b)(6).

PRACTICE POINTER: The regulations define significant financial distress as exceptional expenses which the community spouse cannot be expected to meet from the MMNA or from resources. These expenses may be of a recurring nature or one-time costs. Examples include, but are not limited to, noncovered medical expenses, major household repairs and amounts necessary to preserve an income producing asset. 18 NYCRR § 360–4.10(a)(10).

17. Schachner v. Perales, 85 N.Y.2d 316, 624 N.Y.S.2d 558, 648 N.E.2d 1321 (1995); Gomprecht v. Gomprecht, 86 N.Y.2d 47, 629 N.Y.S.2d 190, 652 N.E.2d 936 (1995) (Family Court support awards must incorporate the community spouse resource and income standards of the Social Services Law).

18. 42 U.S.C.A. § 1396r–5(b)(1); Social Services Law § 366–c(3)(b); 18 NYCRR § 360–4.10(b)(2)(i), (ii).

19. 18 NYCRR § 360–4.10(b)(5).

20. Id.

21. 42 U.S.C.A. § 1396r–5(e); Social Services Law § 366–c(7)(c); 18 NYCRR § 360–4.10(c)(iii). See infra, § 23.82.

seek recovery of Medicaid benefits which have been incorrectly paid.[1] However, the federal statute strictly limits the circumstances under which states may seek recovery of correctly paid benefits.[2] The pressure to balance budgets and trim the Medicaid program has led Congress to mandate that states seek recovery of correctly paid medical assistance benefits from estates of deceased Medicaid recipients and to expand the options available to states for such recoveries.[3]

Pursuant to New York State Social Services Law, estate recovery is mandated for Medicaid benefits paid since the recipient's 55th birthday.[4] "Estate" is defined as the probate estate: "all real and personal property and other assets included within the individual's estate and passing under the terms of a valid will or by intestacy."[5]

Generally the Medicaid recipient's homestead is the major source of estate recovery.[6] However, recovery against the estate may be made only after the death of the surviving spouse[7] and if there is no surviving minor (under age 21), blind, or disabled child.[8] In addition, there may be no recovery against a homestead which is subject to a Medicaid lien[9] for as long as the recipient's sibling or adult "caretaker child" continues to lawfully reside on the property.[10] The sibling must have resided in the home for at least a year before the recipient's institutionalization. The "caretaker child" must have resided in the home for at least two years

§ 23.81

1. 42 U.S.C.A. § 1396p(b).

2. *Id.* For a discussion of recovery against incorrectly paid benefits, *see infra*, §§ 23.81.

3. 42 U.S.C.A. § 1396p(b).

4. Social Services Law § 369(2)(b)(i)(B).

CAVEAT: Note that prior to October 1993, the age at which Medicaid benefits became recoverable from the estate was 65. This former "age 65" provision survived constitutional equal protection challenges. *See* Estate of Davis, 57 N.Y.2d 382, 456 N.Y.S.2d 716, 442 N.E.2d 1227 (1982).

5. Social Services Law § 369(6).

6. The home is generally an exempt resource while the Medicaid recipient or certain family members reside there, or if an institutionalized Medicaid recipient intends to return to the home. *See* Social Services Law § 366(2)(a)(1); 18 NYCRR § 360-4.7(a)(1).

7. **PRACTICE POINTER:** A surviving spouse need not have resided with the decedent in order for DSS to be barred from recovery. Estate of Rundell, 41 A.D.2d 995, 344 N.Y.S.2d 6 (3d Dep't 1973). Moreover, DSS may not recover where there is a surviving spouse even when the surviving spouse is not a named beneficiary of the decedent's estate. Estate of McLane, 90 Misc.2d 1067, 398 N.Y.S.2d 460 (Surr.Ct., Ontario County, 1976), aff'd 54 A.D.2d 1133, 389 N.Y.S.2d 79 (4th Dep't 1976), aff'd 42 N.Y.2d 1057, 399 N.Y.S.2d 215, 369 N.E.2d 772 (1977).

8. Social Services Law § 369(2)(b)(ii); 18 NYCRR § 360-7.11(b)(2).

PRACTICE POINTER: The Second Department has held that DSS may recover against the estate of a deceased recipient survived by a disabled child if the child was not a dependent of the decedent and is not a named beneficiary of the decedent's estate. Matter of Samuelson, 110 A.D.2d 187, 493 N.Y.S.2d 784 (2d Dep't 1985). However, the New York County Surrogate has declined to follow this rationale and barred recovery although an adult disabled child had not been dependent upon the decedent. In that case, Surrogate Preminger noted that the Second Department's holding appeared to limit the protection of the surviving disabled child by adding requirements that do not appear in the statute. Matter of Burstein, 160 Misc.2d 900, 611 N.Y.S.2d 739 (Surr.Ct., N.Y. County, 1994).

9. For a discussion of Medicaid liens, *see infra,* § 23.82.

10. Social Services Law § 369(2)(b)(iii); 18 NYCRR § 360-7.11(b)(3).

prior to the recipient's institutionalization and have provided care which delayed the institutionalization.[11]

Although an executor or administrator generally is not chargeable for claims not presented on or before the date cited in publication or seven months from the date upon which letters testamentary or letters of administration are issued,[12] this will not bar a Medicaid estate recovery claim. The seven-month rule protects the fiduciary only where distributions have been made in good faith. When the fiduciary knew or should have known about the claim, the fiduciary will be personally liable. Thus, the decedent's hospitalization or nursing home placement should constitute adequate notice of the possibility of a DSS right of recovery.[13]

§ 23.82 Medicaid—Liens

A lien may be placed against a Medicaid recipient's property under only three circumstances: (1) where a court has determined that benefits have been incorrectly paid;[1] (2) where the Medicaid recipient has received a personal injury judgment or settlement to the extent of benefits paid since the injury;[2] and (3) where the lien is placed against the homestead of a recipient of Medicaid nursing home benefits.[3]

In the case of a personal injury lien, the local social services district must serve proper written notice of lien upon the parties to the personal

---

11. *Id.* **PRACTICE POINTER:** In order to qualify as a caretaker child, it is not necessary that the child have been a primary or formal care giver. For example, assistance with meals and housekeeping, paying of bills, dispensation of medication, oversight of a home attendant, and companionship all are types of care that prolong an individual's ability to remain in the community. *See* Matter of DeLuca, N.Y.L.J., 12/14/93, p.27, col.3 (Sup.Ct., Nassau County).

12. SCPA § 1802.

13. *See* Estate of Brickel, N.Y.L.J., 1/13/94, p.26, col.5 (Surr.Ct., N.Y. County); Estate of Greene, N.Y.L.J., 3/1/93, p.29, col.4 (Surr.Ct., Bronx County); Estate of Bailey, 147 Misc.2d 46, 554 N.Y.S.2d 791 (Surr.Ct., Bronx County, 1990).

PRACTICE POINTER: If an estate is potentially subject to Medicaid recovery, the personal representative must either resolve the claim or keep the estate open and undistributed for six years from the date of death. *See* CPLR 210(b), 213(1). Otherwise the personal representative may be held personally liable for the DSS claim. If the claim is not resolved, then DSS or the personal representative could petition for a proceeding pursuant to SCPA § 1809 to determine the validity of the claim, or for a compulsory accounting pursuant to SCPA § 2205. *See* Preminger, *et al., New York Trusts and Estates Practice* (West 1997).

§ 23.82

1. 42 U.S.C.A. § 1396p(a)(1)(A); Social Services Law § 369(2)(a)(i); 18 NYCRR § 360-7.11(a)(1). **PRACTICE POINTER:** Incorrectly paid Medicaid benefits are always recoverable, even during the recipient's lifetime. Matter of Rhodes, 148 Misc.2d 744, 561 N.Y.S.2d 344 (Surr.Ct., N.Y. County, 1990). However, in order to establish that benefits have been incorrectly paid, DSS generally must demonstrate that the recipient has engaged in fraud or misrepresentation on the initial application. Matter of Akullian, 167 A.D.2d 596, 563 N.Y.S.2d 223 (3d Dep't 1990).

2. Social Services Law § 369(2)(c); 18 NYCRR § 360-7.11(a)(2). Cricchio v. Pennisi, 90 N.Y.2d 296, amended, slip copy (7/1/97); Link v. Town of Smithtown, amended, slip copy, (N.Y.Ct.App. 7/1/97).

3. 42 U.S.C.A. § 1396p(a)(1)(B); Social Services Law § 369(2)(a)(ii); 18 NYCRR § 360-7.11(a)(3).

§ 23.82   ELDER LAW   Ch. 23

injury lawsuit, their attorneys, and any insurance carrier; a copy also must be filed with the county clerk.[4] The local social services district may recover from any personal injury insurance settlement which includes an amount for medical bills, the amount of Medicaid coverage provided for treatment of the subject injuries.[5]

A lien against an institutionalized individual's homestead may be imposed only if it is not "reasonably expected" that the individual will return home; however any such lien must dissolve upon the individual's return home.[6] Moreover, no lien may be imposed if any of the following relatives of the individual lawfully resides in the home: (1) spouse; (2) minor, blind, or disabled child; or (3) sibling with an "equity interest" in the home.[7] The sibling must have resided with the individual for at least one year prior to the individual's institutionalization.[8] The "equity interest" requirement does not require that the sibling have title to the property; it is enough that the sibling either invested money in the property (for example by contributing to capital improvements) or has a right of use.[9]

Recovery against the real property lien may be made only upon sale of the property, or from the Medicaid recipient's estate subject to certain limitations.[10]

§ 23.83 Medicaid—Administrative and Judicial Appeals

The local social services district must issue a written determination when a decision is reached regarding a Medicaid application, or before reducing or terminating Medicaid eligibility or services, and must offer the applicant/recipient the opportunity to appeal this decision.[1] An applicant/recipient has a right to a "local conference" with a Medicaid caseworker or other local social services official in order to seek an informal review of the decision.[2] An applicant/recipient also has a right to request a New York State DSS administrative fair hearing within 60 days of the notice date.[3] Even after a fair hearing is requested, an

---

4. Social Services Law § 104–b. See also, Bensel, et al., New York Personal Practice (West 1997).

5. 18 NYCRR §§ 350–7.2, 360–7.11(5).

6. 42 U.S.C.A. §§ 1396p(a)(1)(B)(ii), 1396p(a)(3); Social Services Law § 369(2)(a)(ii); 18 NYCRR § 360–7.11(a)(3)(i).

7. 42 U.S.C.A. § 1396p(a)(2); Social Services Law § 369(2)(a)(ii); 18 NYCRR § 360–7.11(a)(3)(ii).

8. 42 U.S.C.A. § 1396p(a)(2)(C); Social Services Law § 369(2)(a)(ii)(C); 18 NYCRR § 360–7.11(a)(3)(ii).

9. DSS Administrative Directive 92 ADM–53 (Dec. 15, 1992) at 3.

10. 42 U.S.C.A. § 1396p(b)(1)(A); Social Services Law § 369(2)(b)(i)(A); 18 NYCRR § 360–7.11(b)(1)(ii). See supra, § 23.80 for a description of the limitations.

§ 23.83

1. 42 U.S.C.A. § 1396a(a)(3); Social Services Law § 22; 18 NYCRR §§ 358–3.1, 358–3.3(a), 360–2.5, 360–2.7.

2. 18 NYCRR § 360–2.8.

3. 18 NYCRR § 360–2.9.

PRACTICE POINTER: Fair hearing requests may be made by calling the Department of Social Services at (518) 474–8781, or by writing to the DSS Fair Hearings Section, 40 North Pearl Street, Albany, New York 12243. The local Social Services office may also take the request for a fair

"agency conference" may still be requested in order to resolve the matter.[4] The deadlines for requesting appeals on initial applications must be adhered to in order to preserve the original "pick-up" date—the requested commencement date of coverage.

When existing Medicaid benefits or services are threatened to be reduced or terminated, the recipient has the right to continue to receive unchanged benefits or services ("aid continuing") until the fair hearing decision is issued if the request for a fair hearing and continuing benefits is made within ten days of the notice of the proposed action.[5]

The applicant/recipient may be represented at the hearing by an attorney or other representative.[6] The appellant or representative has the right to review the entire case record prior to the hearing, and to receive copies of the documents that the local district intends to submit in support of its proposed action.[7] The hearing officer may grant adjournments of the assigned hearing date for good cause.[8] The hearing is conducted before a hearing officer who is employed by the Department of Social Services.[9] The hearing officer may compel the attendance of witnesses and the production of books and records at the hearing.[10] Technical rules of evidence do not apply.[11] However, the decision must be based on substantial evidence.[12] The hearing examiner submits a written report and recommendation to the state DSS Fair Hearings Section. The formal decision is issued by the Commissioner, usually within four weeks of the hearing.[13]

While fair hearing decisions do not have formal precedential value, when a decision finds that the local agency has misapplied relevant law, the Commissioner may direct the local agency to review other cases with

---

hearing. All communications, especially those requesting "aid continuing status" should be confirmed in writing. Mail and delivery slips should be retained.

4. 18 NYCRR §§ 358–2.4, 358–3.8.

PRACTICE POINTER: When an initial application is denied for insufficient documentation, the missing documentation should be supplied with a "request for reconsideration" within 90 days of the notice date. However, in order to avoid the closing of a case, the reconsideration should be requested before the 60–day deadline for requesting a fair hearing. Generally, it is easier and faster to satisfy the caseworker's documentation request than to go to a fair hearing.

5. 18 NYCRR § 358–3.6(a)(3). Note that in circumstances where "timely notice" is required, "aid continuing" status will be granted if a fair hearing is requested before the effective date of the planned action. 18 NYCRR § 358–3.6(a)(1). The notice will specify the effective date of the planned action and how many days in which the fair hearing must be requested in order to obtain aid continuing status.

6. 18 NYCRR § 358–3.4(e). Where possible, the appellant applicant/representative should execute a written authorization for the fair hearing representative, if the representative is not an attorney or the employee of an attorney. 18 NYCRR § 358–3.9.

7. 18 NYCRR § 360–3.7.

8. 18 NYCRR § 358–5.3.

9. 18 NYCRR §§ 358–2.13, 358–5.6.

10. 18 NYCRR §§ 360–5.6(b)(8), 360–5.7(d).

11. 18 NYCRR § 358–5.9(c).

12. 18 NYCRR § 358–5.9(b).

13. 18 NYCRR § 358–6.1.

similar facts for conformity with the decision.[14]

Since a written fair hearing decision is a final determination by the New York State Department of Social Services, it may be challenged in an Article 78 proceeding. In order to prevail in court, the appellant generally must demonstrate that the final determination "was made in violation of lawful procedure, was affected by an error of law or was arbitrary and capricious or an abuse of discretion", or that the hearing decision is not supported by "substantial evidence."[15] An Article 78 proceeding must be initiated in New York State supreme court within four months of the hearing decision.[16]

§ 23.84 Home Care Coverage

Clients and attorneys who seek to locate appropriate home care services for elderly individuals must be familiar with the broad range of home care services available in New York State and the sources of funding for these services. Services may be covered by Medicare, Medicaid, New York's Expanded In Home Services for the Elderly program ("EISEP") or private insurance. Whether the services will be funded will depend on a careful examination of the nature of the care that is needed.

Services which must be performed by a skilled nurse or therapist are most readily covered. It is far more difficult to obtain coverage for unskilled "personal care" services.[1] Activities of daily living are sometimes referred to as ADL's. Many individuals have a primary need for housekeeping services such as cleaning, shopping, laundry, errands and transportation assistance. Housekeeper services are not covered by Medicare or private health insurance plans, although they may be covered under Medicaid and the EISEP program.

Government and insurance funded home care services must generally be provided by agencies which are certified to provide this care. Referrals to appropriate certified home care providers can be obtained from local area Offices for the Aging, senior centers, geriatric care managers and hospital discharge planners. Care provided through a certified agency is generally more expensive than services provided by an individual.[2]

---

14. 18 NYCRR § 358–6.3.
15. CPLR 7803.
16. CPLR 217(1). *See* Chapter 4 "Administrative Law," *supra*.

§ 23.84

1. Personal care services include assistance with any of the following activities of daily living: bathing, dressing, grooming, feeding, toileting, walking, transferring, skin care, assistance with self-administered medications and medical equipment and supplies.

2. **PRACTICE POINTER:** Families that pay privately for care may seek to reduce the cost by hiring an individual who is not affiliated with an agency. These private arrangements may work satisfactorily. However, the family must take responsibility for payment of appropriate taxes. Contingency plans must be prepared in the event that the worker is ill or unavailable. The employment of unaffiliated workers tends to work best when family members are readily available to supervise the quality of the care. Counsel may advise the prepara-

The following sections will discuss the general requirements for coverage of home care services under Medicare, Medicaid, the EISEP program and private insurance policies.

Library References:
West's Key No. Digests, Social Security and Public Welfare ⇔241.25, 241.91.

§ 23.85 Home Care Coverage—Medicare

The Medicare program provides an unlimited number of home health care visits to beneficiaries who meet the following conditions: (1) the beneficiary is homebound;[1] (2) he or she requires either skilled nursing services on a part-time[2] or intermittent basis,[3] or physical, occupational or speech therapy; and (3) a physician certifies the need for home health care.[4] No prior institutional care is required. An unlimited number of home health care visits are covered.[5] There is no deductible or coinsurance requirement.

§ 23.86 Home Care Coverage—Medicaid

New York State has elected to provide extensive Medicaid coverage for services provided in the home.[1] Covered services include home health services, skilled nursing, skilled therapy, personal care, and housekeeping services.[2] In order to apply for home care services under Medicaid, tion of a contract with the home care provider setting forth the specific expectations for service.

§ 23.85

1. 42 U.S.C.A. § 1395f(a)(2)(C); 42 C.F.R. § 409.42. A person is homebound if the assistance of an individual or supportive device is required to leave the home or if leaving is contraindicated due to medical conditions. The patient need not be bedridden. Brief or infrequent absences are permitted, especially for the purpose of receiving medical care. 42 U.S.C.A. §§ 1395f(a)(8), 1395n(a)(2)(F).

2. Services should be considered "part-time" if provided less than eight hours per day or less than seven days per week. Duggan v. Bowen, 691 F.Supp. 1487 (D.D.C. 1988).

3. Services will be considered "intermittent" if provided at least once in 60 days and less than seven days per week. HCFA Medicare Intermediary Manual § 3118.1.C.

4. 42 U.S.C.A. § 1395f(a)(2)(C); 42 C.F.R. § 409.42.

5. **PRACTICE POINTER**: Home health care services may not be denied simply because the patient may need assistance for an extended period of time. There is no limit on the length of time that home health care can be provided as long as the beneficiary meets the other conditions for eligibility. 42 C.F.R. § 409.61(d).

§ 23.86

1. *See supra*, §§ 23.69—23.83 for further discussion of the Medicaid program.

2. Social Services Law § 365–a; 18 NYCRR § 505.14. An individual qualifies for personal care services if he or she requires some or total assistance with personal hygiene, dressing and feeding; nutritional and environmental support functions; and health-related tasks. 18 NYCRR § 505.14(a)(1). Level I services are limited to nutritional and environmental support such as cleaning, shopping, laundry services and meal preparation. 18 NYCRR § 505.14(a)(6)(i)(a). Level II personal care services include some or total assistance with bathing, dressing, grooming, toileting, walking, transferring, preparation of meals in accordance with modified diets, feeding, assistance with self administered medication, routine skin care, use of medical supplies and equipment and changing of simple dressings. 18 NYCRR § 505.14(a)(6)(ii)(a). Level III services include all of the above, plus health related

the patient's physician must complete a form which describes the patient's medical condition and need for assistance.[3] There is no limit on the number of hours of care that the patient may receive, provided that he or she meets the requirements set forth in the regulations.[4] Continuous 24-hour personal care (often referred to as split shift care) is available for a patient who, because of his or her medical condition and disabilities, requires total assistance with toileting and/or walking and/or transferring and/or feeding at unscheduled times during the day or night.[5]

§ 23.87 Home Care Coverage—Expanded In-Home Services for the Elderly Program ("EISEP")

New York State established the Expanded In-Home Services for the Elderly Program ("EISEP") in 1986.[1] The program is administered through local area Offices for the Aging which accept applications and determine eligibility for the program. In order to be eligible for EISEP services, an individual must be at least 60 years of age;[2] functionally impaired;[3] have unmet needs for such assistance;[4] not be eligible for

tasks such as specialized skin care, preparation of foods under special diets, exercise programs, changing of dressings, ostomy care.

3. In 1993, the Department of Social Services promulgated regulations which eliminated the requirement that the physician order form include a recommendation as to the number of hours of care that the patient requires. The new regulations specify that the physician may not make such a recommendation. 18 NYCRR § 505.14(b)(3)(i)(a)(3). Plaintiffs in the ongoing class action, Kuppersmith v. Perales, 145 A.D.2d 1005, 535 N.Y.S.2d 510 (1st Dep't 1988), amended their complaint and moved for summary judgment to invalidate the regulations. The state has agreed not to implement the regulations until the motions for summary judgment have been decided by the court.

4. Initial authorization for services under Level I is limited to eight hours per week. Initial authorization for levels II or III is limited to four hours per day or 28 hours per week. However, an individual may be authorized for additional services, up to twenty four hours per day if he or she requires total assistance with toileting and/or walking, and/or transferring, and/or feeding. 18 NYCRR § 505.14(a)(6)(ii)(b)(1), 505.14(a)(6)(iii)(c)(1).

The statute and regulations require that a fiscal assessment be performed if personal care services are expected to exceed 60 days or if the individual requires home health care services. Social Services Law §§ 367-j, 367-k, 367-l; 18 NYCRR § 505.14(b)(3)(vi). If the assessment indicates that personal care services are more expensive than 90% of the average cost of nursing home care, the patient may be discontinued from the home care program upon the availability of an appropriate long term care placement, unless the patient meets one of the exception criteria set forth in the regulations. Id.

At the time of publication, the fiscal assessment regulations were not being widely implemented by local social services offices.

5. 18 NYCRR § 505.14(a)(3). The assessment must indicate that there are no alternative means for providing the necessary care. 18 NYCRR § 505.14(b)(4)(i)(c).

§ 23.87

1. 18 Executive Law §§ 541(2)(e)—(h); 9 NYCRR §§ 6654.1 et seq.

2. 9 NYCRR § 6654.15(a)(1).

3. Functional impairment is shown by a need for the assistance of another person in at least one activity of daily living, such as bathing, dressing, toileting, transferring, eating or incontinence of urine and/or feces, or by the need for assistance with two instrumental activities of daily living which are defined as including housekeeping, shopping, preparation of meals, managing money, laundry, using transportation, telephoning and leaving the home. 9 NYCRR § 6654.15(a)(2).

4. 9 NYCRR § 6654.15(a)(3).

these services under Medicaid, Medicare or other governmental programs.[5] Services available through the EISEP program include housekeeping and personal care,[6] case management,[7] respite care,[8] meals,[9] and ancillary services.[10] Financial eligibility is determined by calculation of income only. Resources are disregarded. Clients are expected to share the cost of services if their income exceeds the threshold established by the Department for the Aging.[11] The amount of cost sharing is determined by a sliding fee scale based on adjusted monthly income.[12] If income exceeds 250% of the poverty level, the client must pay for the full cost of services.[13]

Funding for the EISEP program has never kept pace with the demand for services. Thus, individuals who meet the eligibility requirements for the program can expect to be placed on long waiting lists before services will be provided.[14] There is no statutory or regulatory right to a hearing if an individual has been denied EISEP services. However, the New York State Department for the Aging has established a hearing process for individuals who appeal a decision as to medical eligibility, the amount of cost share, or dismissal from the program.[15]

§ 23.88 Home Care Coverage—Private Insurance

Most private health insurance policies provide only limited, short term coverage for home care services. Many policies will only provide

---

5. 9 NYCRR § 6654.15(a)(4).

6. 9 NYCRR § 6654.17(e), (f).

7. 9 NYCRR § 6654.16.

8. 9 NYCRR § 6654.18.

9. 9 NYCRR § 6654.11.

10. 9 NYCRR § 6654.19. Ancillary services include removal of architectural barriers, purchase, maintenance and repair of appliances and durable medical equipment such as commodes, walkers and wheelchairs, and modification of the client's living environment. *Id.*

11. The threshold amounts are established by the New York State Department for the Aging and subject to annual cost of living adjustments. 9 NYCRR § 6654.6(b)(2)(ii). In 1997, the threshold was $1,333 for couples and $996 for individuals.

12. 9 NYCRR § 6654.6(a). The sliding scale of cost sharing percentages is contained at 9 NYCRR § 6654.6(c)(2). The scale is based on adjusted monthly income, which is defined as monthly income minus the threshold and a housing adjustment. 9 NYCRR § 6654.6(b)(2). Applicants are eligible for the housing adjustment if their monthly housing expenses exceed 40% of the income threshold. 9 NYCRR § 6654.6(b)(2)(iii). The sliding fee cost sharing schedule is revised annually to reflect changes in the consumer price index. In 1997, full cost sharing was required if adjusted monthly income exceeded $888 for couples, or $664 for individuals.

13. 9 NYCRR § 6654.6(a)(2).

14. **PRACTICE POINTER:** Unlike the Medicaid and Medicare programs, individuals who meet the financial and other requirements for the EISEP program have no entitlement to receive services. Clients should be counseled to apply for EISEP services at the first sign of need. Once the individual moves to the top of the waiting list, a current needs assessment will be done.

15. Current information concerning cost sharing methodology and hearing procedures can be obtained by requesting a copy of "EISEP Hearings and Cost Collection Standards" from the director of the EISEP program at the State Department for the Aging. Call (518) 474-5444.

§ 23.88 ELDER LAW Ch. 23

coverage for skilled nursing services and will exclude coverage for personal care services.

Some Supplemental Medical Insurance policies[1] (Medigap plans) provide coverage for "At–Home Recovery" services not covered by Medicare. Coverage is provided for short term assistance with activities of daily living for those recovering from an illness, injury or surgery.[2] The individual must be receiving services under a Medicare approved home care plan of treatment.[3] The Medigap plan will cover a maximum of $1,600 per calendar year at a rate of up to $40 per visit[4] for a maximum of eight weeks after the Medicare home care services are completed.

Some long term care insurance policies provide coverage for home care services.[5] These policies vary widely. The specific policy terms must be carefully examined to determine whether the client will be eligible for services under the plan.

§ 23.89 Hospital Patient Rights

Medicare and Medicaid law guarantee many rights for hospital patients whose treatment is covered by these programs.[1] The New York State Department of Health has promulgated regulations which provide additional rights for all hospitalized patients, regardless of the source of payment. The following sections will examine the Bill of Rights for hospitalized patients[2] and the requirements for appropriate discharge planning.[3]

§ 23.90 Hospital Patient Rights—Bill of Rights

Patients or their representatives must be given of a copy of their rights at the time of admission.[1] A copy of these rights shall also be posted throughout the hospital.[2] The hospital shall provide staff to explain these rights to each inpatient and answer questions from those who receive outpatient and emergency services.[3] Translations and interpreter services must be available for non-English speaking groups which

---

§ 23.88

1. Only Plans D, G, I and J provide coverage for "at home recovery." *See supra*, §§ 23.58—23.62 for further discussion of Supplemental Medical Insurance policies.

2. 10 NYCRR § 52.22(d)(6)(x).

3. Typically, the individual would receive skilled nursing services, physical or occupational therapy.

4. There is no limit on the length of a visit. However, each consecutive four hour period constitutes one visit. 10 NYCRR § 52.22(d)(6)(x)(4).

5. *See supra*, §§ 23.63—23.68 for a discussion of long term care insurance policies.

§ 23.89

1. *See supra*, §§ 23.42—23.57 (Medicare) and §§ 23.69—23.83 (Medicaid).

2. 10 NYCRR § 405.7.

3. 10 NYCRR § 405.9.

§ 23.90

1. 10 NYCRR §§ 405.7(a)(1), (2). A patient who receives any services at the hospital is entitled to be afforded these rights. This includes inpatient, outpatient and emergency room services. *Id.*

2. 10 NYCRR § 405.7(a)(3).

3. 10 NYCRR §§ 405.7(a)(5), (6).

comprise more than one percent of the hospital population and for those with vision and hearing impairments.[4]

Hospitals must utilize the form for the Patients' Bill of Rights which is issued by the New York State Department of Health.[5] The form contains the following rights:

(1) Assistance in understanding and using rights. This includes provision of interpreter services as described above;[6]

(2) Treatment without discrimination as to race, color, religion, sex, national origin, disability, sexual orientation, or source of payment;[7]

(3) Consideration and respectful care in a clean and safe environment free of unnecessary restraints;[8]

(4) Emergency care, if needed;[9]

(5) The name and position of the doctor who will be in charge of the patient's care in the hospital;[10]

(6) The names, positions, and functions of any hospital staff involved in the patient's care and the right to refuse their treatment, examination or observation;[11]

(7) A no smoking room;[12]

(8) Receive complete information about the diagnosis, treatment and prognosis;[13]

(9) Receive all information needed to give informed consent for any proposed procedure or treatment, including the possible risks and benefits of the procedure or treatment;[14]

(10) Receive all the information needed to give informed consent for an order not to resuscitate. The patient may also designate an individual to give this consent if the patient is too ill to do so;[15]

(11) Refuse treatment and be told what effect this may have on the patient's health;[16]

---

4. 10 NYCRR § 405.7(a)(7).
5. 10 NYCRR § 405.7(c).
6. 10 NYCRR §§ 405.7(a)(5)—(7), 405.7(b)(1).
7. 10 NYCRR §§ 405.7(b)(2), 405.9(b)(2).
8. 10 NYCRR §§ 405.7(b)(3), (5). Physical restraints must be ordered by a physician for a limited period of time to protect the patient from injury to himself or others. In an emergency, a registered professional nurse may order the restraints pending the arrival of a physician who shall be immediately summoned. 10 NYCRR § 405.7(b)(5).
9. 10 NYCRR § 405.7(b)(6).
10. Id.
11. 10 NYCRR §§ 405.7(b)(7), (10).
12. 10 NYCRR § 405.7(b)(21).
13. 10 NYCRR § 405.7(b)(8).
14. 10 NYCRR § 405.7(b)(9).
15. 10 NYCRR § 405.7(b)(11). *See infra*, § 23.112 for a full discussion of the requirements for issuance of Do Not Resuscitate Orders.
16. 10 NYCRR § 405.7(b)(10).

(12) Refuse to take part in research;[17]

(13) Privacy while in the hospital and confidentiality regarding all information and regards;[18]

(14) Participate in all decisions about treatment and discharge from the hospital. This includes the right to a written discharge plan and a written description of how to appeal a discharge;[19]

(15) Review your medical record without charge and obtain a copy upon payment of a reasonable fee. However, copies cannot be denied solely because of inability to pay;[20]

(16) Receive an itemized bill and explanation of all charges;[21] and

(17) Make complaints without fear of reprisal. The patient is entitled to a written response, if requested. If not satisfied with the hospital's response, the hospital must inform the patient of the right to file a further complaint with the New York State Health Department and provide the telephone number of the local area Health Department office.[22]

Library References:

West's Key No. Digests, Hospitals ⟸5.

§ 23.91 Hospital Patient Rights—Discharge Planning

Cost control efforts by private and government health insurance programs have limited the sole discretion of physicians to decide how long a patient should remain in the hospital.[1] Some critics have claimed that this has resulted in a trend toward "Quicker and Sicker" discharges of patients.[2] New York State Health Department regulations require hospitals to develop appropriate discharge plans[3] for all patients and to

17. 10 NYCRR § 405.7(b)(18).
18. 10 NYCRR §§ 405.7(b)(12), (13).
19. 10 NYCRR §§ 405.7(b)(15), (16).
20. 10 NYCRR § 405.7(b)(24).
21. 10 NYCRR § 405.7(b)(19).
22. 10 NYCRR § 405.7(b)(23).

§ 23.91

1. Since 1983, the Medicare program has reimbursed hospitals a pre-determined amount for each patient based on an evaluation of the patient's Diagnosis Related Group ("DRG"), as determined on admission. 42 U.S.C.A. § 1395ww(d), (e). The hospital's Medicare payment is based on an estimate of the length of the necessary hospital stay and the amount of services to be provided to the average patient in the DRG category. Medicaid payments and most private insurance payments are now based on a similar methodology.

2. J. Kosecoff, et al., *Prospective Payment System and Impairment at Discharge: The 'Quicker and Sicker' Story Revisited*, 264 J.A.M.A. 1980, 1982 (1990) (reporting a 22% increase in the number of Medicare patients discharged from the hospital in an unstable condition after implementation of the Medicare prospective payment system). Similar results were reported by V.R. Fuchs, *The Health Economy*, pp.154–65 (1986) (significant increase in hospital mortality rates after implementation of Medicare's prospective payment system) and *Quicker and Sicker: Substandard Treatment of Medicare Patients*: H.R. Report No. 101–387 (1989).

3. 10 NYCRR § 405.9(f)(1).

notify patients of their right to appropriate discharge planning.[4] Separate forms are available for Medicare and non-Medicare patients.[5]

Medicare patients must receive an admissions notice[6] informing them of their right to a written discharge plan describing any health care that is needed after discharge and specifying that the patient may not be discharged until the services required are secured or determined to be reasonably available. The notice must state that patients who are not satisfied with the discharge plan or believe the services are not reasonably available may complain by calling the Health Department.[7]

Medicare regulations require that participating hospitals develop a discharge plan for Medicare patients who have been identified as likely to suffer adverse consequences if discharged without adequate planning, or upon request by the patient's physician.[8] The discharge planning process evaluates the need for health care services after discharge and the availability of such services.[9]

Non-medicare patients must receive an admissions notice which informs them of their right to receive a written discharge notice and discharge plan.[10] The notice must state that the patient's discharge date should be determined only by the patient's health care needs, not by insurance payment or Medicaid reimbursement category. The discharge plan for a Medicaid patient must be prepared within five days of the patient's admission to the hospital.[11]

Regardless of payment status, the hospital staff and patient's physician must permit the patient or his or her representative to participate in developing the discharge plan.[12] No patient may be discharged unless necessary health services identified by the plan are secured or reasonably available.[13]

---

4. Patients receive two notices concerning their rights upon discharge. The first notice is received at the time of admission to the hospital. 10 NYCRR § 405.9(b)(14). Upon an actual determination that the patient is to be discharged, a discharge notice must be issued. 10 NYCRR § 405.9(g)(9)(i).

5. The admissions notice for Medicare patients may be found at 10 NYCRR § 405.9(b)(14)(i). All other patients receive the admissions notice found at 10 NYCRR § 405.9(b)(14)(ii). Forms for the discharge notice for non-Medicare patients are found at 10 NYCRR §§ 405.9(g)(9)(i), (ii). The requirements for the discharge notice for Medicare beneficiaries are found at 42 C.F.R. § 466.94.

6. The admissions notice for Medicare patients is found at 10 NYCRR § 405.9(b)(14)(i). The patient must also receive a notice entitled "An Important Notice from Medicare." *Id.*; 42 U.S.C.A. § 1395cc(a)(1)(M); 42 C.F.R. § 466.78(b)(3).

7. *Id.*

8. 42 C.F.R. § 482.43(c).

9. 42 C.F.R. § 482.43(b)(3).

PRACTICE POINTER: The Medicare program establishes additional requirements for notification and appeal of a determination that a hospital stay will no longer be covered by Medicare. For a discussion of these requirements, *see supra*, § 23.56.

10. The admissions notice for non-Medicare patients is set forth at 10 NYCRR § 405.9(b)(14)(ii). The discharge planning requirements for all patients are set forth at 10 NYCRR § 405.9(f).

11. 10 NYCRR § 85.6.

12. 10 NYCRR § 405.9(f)(3)(viii).

13. 10 NYCRR § 405.9(f)(1).

§ 23.91   ELDER LAW   Ch. 23

If the hospital and attending physician agree that a non-Medicare patient is no longer in need of inpatient care, the hospital must provide the patient with an appropriate discharge plan and discharge notice.[14] The notice may be appealed by requesting a review by the independent professional review organization specified on the notice.[15] If an inpatient appeals the discharge by noon of the first working day after receipt of the notice, the determination by the review agent must be made no later than one full working day after receipt of the request for review.[16] The patient may not be billed for hospital services before noon of the day after the patient receives the determination by the review agent.[17]

If the patient is no longer hospitalized, the request for review must be made within 30 days after receipt of the Discharge Notice or within seven days of receipt of a complete bill for hospital services.[18] The determination by the review agent must be made within three working days after receipt of the request for review and the records necessary for the review.[19]

A hospital may continue to receive Medicaid payments for a patient who is determined to no longer require hospital care if placement in a skilled nursing facility is medically necessary but no bed is available.[20] Such patients are placed in "Alternate Level of Care" ("ALC") status. The hospital must act promptly to effect placement arrangements for such patients.[21] Each week, hospitals are required to maintain admissions contracts with at least three nursing homes in a fifty mile radius of the hospital.[22] Within twenty-four hours of the certification that a Medicaid patient is in ALC status, the hospital must submit the patient's admission information to at least five nursing homes in the area.[23] If the

---

14. 10 NYCRR § 405.9(g)(3)(i).

PRACTICE POINTER: The discharge notice and appeals process discussed herein apply only to non-Medicare patients. For a discussion of the Medicare program requirements for discharge and continued stay denial notices, see supra, § 23.56.

15. Ordinarily, the hospital and the patient's attending physician will agree that the patient no longer requires hospital care. If the attending physician disagrees with the hospital's discharge plan, the hospital must request a telephone review by the independent professional review organization before the patient may receive a discharge notice and plan. 10 NYCRR § 405.9(g)(3)(ii). The review organization must render a decision within one working day. If the review organization agrees that the patient may be discharged, the patient may then receive a discharge notice indicating that the patient shall be financially responsible for any continued stay.

16. 10 NYCRR § 405.9(g)(4)(ii).

17. 10 NYCRR § 405.9(g)(6). Of course, the patient may still be held financially liable for any deductibles, copayments or other charges which would not ordinarily be paid by third party reimbursement. Id.

18. 10 NYCRR § 405.9(g)(4)(i).

19. Id.

20. 18 NYCRR § 505.20(b)(1).

21. 18 NYCRR § 505.20(b)(3)(i).

22. 18 NYCRR § 505.20(b)(3)(iii).

23. Id. An exception may be made if the patient is awaiting priority admission to a facility in which the patient previously resided prior to the hospitalization. Id.

PRACTICE POINTER: The hospital discharge planning staff will generally ask the patient and/or his or her family to provide the names of the five nursing facilities to which admission will be sought. The patient and family should be counseled to comply with this request while making efforts to secure admission to the facility of their first choice.

patient refuses to accept a placement in a skilled nursing facility, the patient's Medicaid payments for the hospital stay will be discontinued.[24]

Library References:
West's Key No. Digests, Hospitals ⚖5.

§ 23.92 Nursing Home Resident Rights

In the past, the poor quality of care in some nursing homes often resulted in shocking maltreatment and neglect of residents. The exposures of scandalous conditions in New York nursing homes in the 1970's resulted in extensive regulation of the industry by the New York State Department of Health.[1] In 1987, Congress enacted revisions to the federal system of nursing home regulation by passage of the Nursing Home Reform Act.[2] The requirements of the Act apply to all nursing homes which accept Medicare or Medicaid payments. These federal and state rules assure that the standards of care for New York nursing home residents are among the highest in the nation.

These nursing home regulations govern initial admission to a facility, personal and financial rights of residents and transfer and discharge procedures. The full range of these regulations is beyond the scope of this chapter. However, the major provisions affecting residents are highlighted in the following sections.

§ 23.93 Nursing Home Resident Rights—Admission to a Facility

Gaining admission to a nursing home can be a difficult process. The need for nursing home placement is frequently triggered by an emergency medical or social problem or a notice that a hospital placement will no longer be covered by Medicare or Medicaid.[1] Elderly individuals and their family may be forced to locate a suitable facility within a very short

---

24. 18 NYCRR § 505.20(b)(6). The patient may appeal this notice through the Medicaid appeals process. *See supra*, § 23.83.

§ 23.92

1. Public Health Law § 2803-c requires that every nursing home post a statement of the rights and responsibilities of nursing home residents. Certain basic rights are enumerated in the statute. Further elaboration of the rights of nursing home residents are contained in New York Health Department regulations at 10 NYCRR Pts. 415, *et seq.*

2. The Nursing Home Reform Act was enacted by Congress as part of the Omnibus Budget Reconciliation Act of 1987, Pub. L. No. 100–203. The Medicare provisions can be found at 42 U.S.C.A. § 1395i–3(c). The provisions governing Medicaid facilities are at 42 U.S.C.A. § 1396r(c). The federal regulations implementing the Nursing Home Reform Act are at 42 C.F.R. Pt. 483.

§ 23.93

1. PRACTICE POINTER: Most nursing home residents gain admission directly after discharge from a hospital, with many homes giving preference to hospital discharges. Individuals who seek to be placed from the community should make placement plans as far in advance as possible.

period of time.[2] Despite these pressures, family members should be counseled to carefully inspect the facility and the admissions contract before entering into a nursing home placement.[3]

Daily nursing home rates for private pay patients generally exceed the rates paid by Medicare and Medicaid. As a consequence, individuals who can afford to pay privately for a period of time are the most attractive to nursing home operators.[4] Nursing homes may not request pre-payment by more than three months of charges from private pay patients.[5] Admissions contracts may not require that a resident pay privately for a period of time before applying for Medicare or Medicaid coverage.[6] Guarantee of private payment by a third party also is prohibited.[7] Facilities are prohibited from soliciting or accepting gifts or donations from Medicaid eligible individuals as a pre-condition of admission, expedited admission or continued stay in a facility.[8]

2. If the patient's stay in a hospital is determined to no longer be medically necessary, the patient may be in danger of losing Medicare or insurance reimbursement for the hospital stay. *See supra*, § 23.56 for a discussion of Medicare Continued Stay Denial Notices. State regulations require that hospital discharge planners provide patients who no longer require acute care in a hospital setting with assistance in locating residential facilities. 10 NYCRR § 505.9(f). *See supra*, § 23.91 for hospital discharge planning requirements.

3. PRACTICE POINTER: The following organizations provide information and assistance concerning the nursing home admissions process:

1. Local Area Office for the Aging. Contact the State Department for the Aging at 1–800–342–9871 for a referral to the local area office.

2. Friends and Relatives of Institutionalized Aged ("FRIA"), 11 John St., Suite 601, New York, N.Y. 10038, (212) 732–4455 (Non-profit consumer organization working for nursing home reform which operates hotline which provides information about nursing home selection, evaluation and care.)

3. The Greater New York Chapter of the National Association of Professional Geriatric Care Managers, 1–b Quaker Ridge Road, New Rochelle, N.Y. 10804, (212) 222–9163. (Provides referrals to professional geriatric care managers who can assist in locating and evaluating potential nursing home placements.)

4. Discrimination on the basis of source of payment is prohibited by both federal and New York law. 42 U.S.C.A. § 1395i–3(c)(4); 42 U.S.C.A. § 1396r(c)(4)(A); 10 NYCRR §§ 415.3(h)(5), 415.3(b)(5). However, courts have not applied these regulations to prohibit discrimination in admissions against Medicaid recipients given the disparity between Medicaid and private pay rates. Kaye v. Whalen, 56 A.D.2d 111, 391 N.Y.S.2d 712 (3d Dep't 1977), aff'd 44 N.Y.2d 754, 405 N.Y.S.2d 682, 376 N.E.2d 1327 (1978), app. dismissed 439 U.S. 922, 99 S.Ct. 303, 58 L.Ed.2d 315 (1978); Blue v. Whalen, 57 A.D.2d 240, 394 N.Y.S.2d 290 (3d Dep't 1977).

5. 10 NYCRR § 415.26(i)(1)(v).

6. 42 U.S.C.A. § 1395i–3(c)(5)(A)(i); 42 U.S.C.A. § 1396r(c)(5)(A)(i); 42 C.F.R. §§ 483.12(d)(1)(i), (ii); 10 NYCRR §§ 415.3(b)(3), (4).

7. 42 U.S.C.A. § 1395i–3(c)(5)(A)(ii); 42 U.S.C.A. § 1396r(c)(5)(A)(ii); 42 C.F.R. § 483.12(d)(2); 10 NYCRR § 415.3 (b)(1). However, note that a facility may require an individual who has legal access to a resident's income or resources, such as an attorney in fact or trustee, to sign a contract agreeing to make payments to the facility without incurring personal financial liability for these payments. 42 C.F.R. § 483.12(d)(2); 10 NYCRR § 415.3(b)(6).

8. 42 U.S.C.A. § 1396r(c)(5)(A)(iii); 42 C.F.R. § 483.13(d)(3); 10 NYCRR § 415.3(b)(2). However, the facility may accept a voluntary donation if it is not a condition of admission, expedited admission or continued stay. *Id.*

Generally, nursing homes will admit only those individuals who are certain to have sufficient private funds or be eligible for Medicaid coverage.[9] When transfers of assets to qualify for Medicaid coverage are contemplated,[10] many nursing homes will require that the family retain an attorney to advise on the transfers. The home may request that the attorney certify that the individual will be eligible for Medicaid coverage, any waiting period which will elapse due to the transfers and that sufficient funds will remain available until Medicaid eligibility is obtained.

The nursing home must have a written statement of its admissions policies and procedures.[11] This statement must be made available to interested parties upon request.[12] Medicaid certified facilities are required to perform initial screening and annual assessments[13] of individuals who suffer from mental illness[14] or mental retardation in order to assure that these individuals receive appropriate care. As a result, these individuals may find it more difficult to gain admission to a facility.

Nursing homes may only admit individuals who have been certified by a physician or Social Services official as requiring care in a nursing home.[15] A pre-admission interview with the prospective resident or his or her designee and his or her physician is required.[16] The facility must complete assessment documents which assure that the individual is in need of nursing home care.[17]

Library References:

West's Key No. Digests, Asylums ⊜5.

9. **PRACTICE POINTER:** Nursing homes generally prefer private pay patients, since they receive higher payment than from Medicare or Medicaid. However, the home may be concerned about the inability or failure of the private pay resident to make future payments due to incapacity or lack of funds. Although Medicaid pays a lower rate, the payment is guaranteed. Homes will generally not be persuaded to accept a resident for a long term stay based on Medicare payment alone since Medicare only pays for short term nursing home stays. See supra, § 23.46 for a discussion of Medicare payments for nursing home stays.

10. See supra, § 23.76 for a discussion of Medicaid transfer of asset requirements and strategy.

11. 10 NYCRR § 415.26(i)(1)(x).

12. 10 NYCRR § 415.26(i)(1)(xi).

13. The requirements for the Patient Assessment and Annual Resident Review ("PASARR") are found at 42 U.S.C.A. § 1396r(b)(3)(F); 42 C.F.R. § 483.102(a); 10 NYCRR § 415.11(e).

14. The federal regulations specify that individuals with a primary diagnosis of dementia or Alzheimer's Disease are not to be considered mentally ill. 42 C.F.R. § 482.102(b)(1).

15. 10 NYCRR § 415.26(i)(1)(i).

16. 10 NYCRR § 415.26(i)(1)(iii).

17. **PRACTICE POINTER:** The requirements for these documents, known as the PRI and SCREEN are contained at 10 NYCRR §§ 400.12, 400.13. On the basis of the PRI, the individual is assigned to a Resource Utilization Group ("RUG"). The nursing home's Medicaid reimbursement rate is based on the average RUG scores of the residents. Individuals with high RUG scores, but who are judged as not too difficult to manage, are the most attractive to nursing home admission officers. The SCREEN is used to determine whether or not the person can be cared for in the community or an adult home, rather than in a skilled nursing facility. It is also used to screen out individuals with mental illness.

§ 23.94 Nursing Home Resident Rights—Bill of Rights

The Nursing Home Reform Act[1] and corresponding New York State law[2] require that all facilities respect certain basic civil rights of residents. These are often referred to as the Residents' Bill of Rights. Facilities must inform residents of their rights, both orally and in writing.[3]

These rights include:

Free Choice. Residents are entitled to choose their own physician.[4] They have the right to advance notice concerning their care and treatment.[5] Unless they have been adjudicated incompetent, they may participate in planning their care and treatment.[6]

A change in roommate assignment shall be acceptable, where possible, to all affected residents.[7] Residents have the right to share a room with a spouse, partner or relative who resides at the facility and agrees to the arrangement.[8]

Privacy and Confidentiality. Residents are entitled to privacy in regard to their accommodations, medical treatment, written and telephone communication, visits with friends, family members, attorneys, and other residents.[9] A private room need not be provided for each resident. However, the resident shall have the right to have locked storage space in the room.[10]

Residents and their legal representatives are entitled to access to their clinical and personal records within twenty-four hours of a request.[11] The resident's approval is required for the release of records to any individual outside of the facility except when the individual is transferred or the release is otherwise required by law.[12]

Freedom from Abuse and Restraints. Residents have the right to be free from physical or mental abuse, corporal punishment, involuntary

---

§ 23.94

1. 42 U.S.C.A. §§ 1395i–3(c), 1396r(c); 42 C.F.R. § 483.10.

2. Public Health Law § 2803–c(3); 10 NYCRR § 415.3.

3. 42 U.S.C.A. § 1395i–3(c)(1)(B); 42 U.S.C.A. § 1396r(c)(1)(B); 42 C.F.R. § 483.10(b)(1). 10 NYCRR § 415.3(a)(2) additionally requires that the facility post an easily understood large print summary of these rights in the facility.

4. 42 U.S.C.A. § 1395i–3(c)(1)(A)(i); 42 U.S.C.A. § 1396r(c)(1)(A)(i); 10 NYCRR § 415.3(e)(1)(iii).

5. 42 U.S.C.A. § 1395i–3(c)(1)(A)(i); 42 U.S.C.A. § 1396r(c)(1)(A)(i); 10 NYCRR §§ 415.3(e)(1)(i), (iv), (v).

6. *Id.*

7. 10 NYCRR § 415.3(c)(2)(b).

8. 10 NYCRR § 415.3(f)(3).

9. 42 U.S.C.A. § 1395i–3(c)(1)(A)(iii); 42 U.S.C.A. § 1396r(c)(1)(A)(iii); 42 C.F.R. § 483.10(e); Public Health Law §§ 2803c(3)(b), (f), 10 NYCRR § 415.3(d).

10. 10 NYCRR § 415.3(f)(2).

11. 42 U.S.C.A. § 1395i–3(c)(1)(A)(iv); 42 U.S.C.A. § 1396r(c)(1)(A)(iv); 42 C.F.R. §§ 483.10(b)(2)(i), (e).

12. 42 U.S.C.A. § 1395i–3(c)(1)(A)(iv); 42 U.S.C.A. § 1396r(c)(1)(A)(iv); 42 C.F.R. § 483.10(e); 10 NYCRR § 415.3(d).

seclusion, or chemical or physical restraints imposed for the purposes of discipline or convenience.[13]

Restraints must be required for the treatment of medical symptoms and to ensure the physical safety of the resident, or other residents.[14] Except in an emergency, a physician must issue a written order governing the duration and circumstances under which the restraints are to be used.[15] Restraints may be used only in unusual circumstances and only after all reasonable less restrictive alternatives have been rejected.[16] Physical restraints must be carefully monitored.[17] The resident must be released at least every two hours, except when sleeping. The individual's care plan must indicate the type of restraint, release schedules, type of exercise, necessary skin care and ambulation.[18] The need for the restraint shall be periodically reevaluated.[19]

Grievances. Residents have the right to voice grievances about their treatment or care without fear of discrimination or reprisal. Facilities must undertake prompt efforts to resolve resident grievances, including those that relate to the behavior of other residents.[20] Responses to grievances must generally be provided within 21 days.[21]

Participation in Group Activities. Residents have the right to organize and participate in resident groups.[22] Resident and family groups must be permitted to meet privately in the facility.[23] Facility staff or guests may attend only upon invitation of the group.[24]

Library References:

West's Key No. Digests, Asylums ⚖═5.

§ 23.95 Nursing Home Resident Rights—Financial Rights

Every resident is entitled to manage his or her own financial affairs.[1] Nursing facilities may not require residents to deposit their

---

13. 42 U.S.C.A. § 1395i–3(c)(1)(A)(ii); 42 U.S.C.A. § 1396r(c)(1)(A)(ii); 42 C.F.R. §§ 483.13(a), (b);Public Health Law § 2803–c(3)(h); 10 NYCRR § 415.4.

14. *Id.*

15. *Id.* An emergency situation must be approved by the medical director, attending physician or nursing director. A physician consultation must be obtained within twenty-four hours. 10 NYCRR § 415.4(a)(6).

16. 10 NYCRR § 415.4(a)(2)(iii).

17. 10 NYCRR § 415.4(a)(3)(ii).

18. 10 NYCRR § 415.4(a)(2)(ii).

19. 10 NYCRR § 415.4(a)(3)(iii).

20. 42 U.S.C.A. § 1395i–3(c)(1)(A)(vi); 42 U.S.C.A. § 1396r(c)(1)(A)(vi); 42 C.F.R. § 483.10(f); 10 NYCRR §§ 415.3(c)(1)(ii), 415.26(b)(6).

21. 10 NYCRR § 415.26(b)(6)(iii).

22. 42 U.S.C.A. § 1395i–3(c)(1)(A)(vii); 42 U.S.C.A. § 1396r(c)(1)(A)(vii); 42 C.F.R. § 483.15(c); 10 NYCRR § 415.5(c).

23. *Id.*

24. 42 C.F.R. §§ 483.15(c)(3), (4); 10 NYCRR §§ 415.5(c)(3), (4).

§ 23.95

1. Public Health Law § 2803–c(1)(d); 10 NYCRR § 415.3(g)(1).

§ 23.95   ELDER LAW   Ch. 23

personal funds with the facility.[2] Upon written authorization of the resident, the facility must deposit personal funds in excess of $50 in an interest bearing account which is kept separate from the facility's operating expenses.[3]

Residents are entitled to notice of the charges for items and services available at the facility, including those charges which are not covered by third party sources such as Medicare or in the facility's basic daily rate.[4] Upon admission, Medicaid recipients are entitled to receive notice of the items and services which are covered by Medicaid and the specific charges for items and services which are not covered by Medicaid.[5] Facilities may not charge a resident for services which are paid for by Medicaid or Medicare.[6] Any charges for items not included in the facility's basic daily rate require the written approval of the resident, next of kin or resident's physician.[7]

Library References:

West's Key No. Digests, Asylums ⚖5.

§ 23.96 Nursing Home Resident Rights—Transfer and Discharge

Residents may not be transferred or discharged from a facility[1] unless the transfer or discharge is necessary to the resident's welfare and the resident's welfare cannot be met in the facility, the resident's health has improved sufficiently so that the resident no longer needs the services of the facility, the health or safety of others in the facility is

---

2. 42 U.S.C.A. § 1395i–3(c)(6); 42 U.S.C.A. § 1396r(c)(6); 42 C.F.R. § 483.10(c).

3. 42 U.S.C.A. § 1395i–3(c)(6)(B); 42 U.S.C.A. § 1396r(c)(6)(B); 42 C.F.R. § 483.10(c); 10 NYCRR § 415.26(h)(5). Funds less than $50 may be kept in a non-interest bearing account or petty cash fund. Id.

4. 42 U.S.C.A. § 1395i–3(c)(1)(B)(iii); 42 U.S.C.A. § 1396r(c)(1)(B)(iv); 42 C.F.R. § 483.10(b)(6); 10 NYCRR § 415.3(g)(2)(iii).

5. 42 U.S.C.A. § 1396r(c)(1)(B)(iii); 42 C.F.R. § 485.10(b)(5); 10 NYCRR § 415.3(g)(2)(i).

6. 42 C.F.R. § 483.10(c)(8); 10 NYCRR § 415.26(h)(5)(vi).

PRACTICE POINTER: Items included in the Medicaid and Medicare rate include nursing, rehabilitation and dietary services, an activities program, maintenance of bed and room, routine personal hygiene items and services including soap, razors, toothbrushes and toothpaste, deodorant, incontinence supplies, towels, washcloths, bathing and basic personal laundry. Upon the authorization of the resident, charges may be made for the following items or services which are not covered by Medicare or Medicaid; private telephone or radio, smoking materials, notions, candy, novelties, cosmetic and grooming services, clothing, reading material, gifts, flowers and plants, off-premise social events, private duty nurses, and special food services. Id.

7. 10 NYCRR § 415.26(i)(1)(vi).

§ 23.96

1. PRACTICE POINTER: Transfer or discharge from a facility includes movement to a bed outside the certified facility, even if that bed is in the same physical plant. It does not include movement to a bed within the same certified facility. 42 C.F.R. § 483.12(a)(1); 10 NYCRR § 415.3(h). However, residents are entitled to be consulted about and receive 30 days notice of a room change unless the change is requested by the resident, a sooner change is required by the resident's medical condition or an emergency situation develops. 10 NYCRR § 415.3(c)(2)(ii)(a).

416

endangered, the resident has failed to pay the facility's charges or the facility ceases to operate.[2] The resident is entitled to receive advance written notice of the reasons for the transfer or discharge.[3] The notice shall be made at least 30 days in advance, unless the transfer or discharge is necessary for the resident's welfare, the health or safety of others in the facility is endangered, the resident's health has improved sufficiently to permit a more immediate transfer or discharge, an immediate transfer or discharge is required by the resident's urgent medical needs, or the transfer or discharge has been requested by the resident.[4]

The resident may appeal the transfer or discharge to the State Department of Health.[5] The resident has the right to an on site hearing and may remain in the facility pending the appeal determination if the appeal is made within 15 days of the notice, except in cases involving imminent danger to others.[6] The nursing home has the burden of proof to show that the discharge or transfer is necessary.[7] The decision on appeal must be rendered within 15 days.[8] If the resident prevails on the appeal but has already been discharged, the facility must readmit the resident prior to admitting any other person.[9]

Library References:

West's Key No. Digests, Asylums ⚖5.

§ 23.97 Nursing Home Resident Rights—Bed Hold Policy

Regardless of payment status, all nursing home residents are entitled to verbal and written information concerning the duration of the facility's bed hold policy in the event that the resident needs to leave the facility for hospital or therapeutic care.[1] Medicaid recipients[2] who have

2. 42 U.S.C.A. § 1395i–3(c)(2)(A); 42 U.S.C.A. § 1396r(c)(2)(A); 42 C.F.R. § 483.12(a)(2); 10 NYCRR § 415.3(h)(1).

3. 42 U.S.C.A. § 1395i–3(c)(2)(B)(i)(I), 42 U.S.C.A. § 1396r(c)(2)(B)(i)(I); 42 C.F.R. § 483.12(a)(4); 10 NYCRR § 415.3(h)(1)(iii).

4. 42 U.S.C.A.§ 1395i–3(c)(2)(B)(ii); 42 U.S.C.A. § 1396r(c)(2)(B)(ii); 42 C.F.R. § 483.12(a)(5); 10 NYCRR § 415.3(h)(1)(iv).

5. 42 C.F.R. § 483.12(a)(6)(iv); 10 NYCRR §§ 415.3(h)(1)(v)(a), 415.3(h)(1), (2).

6. 10 NYCRR § 415.3(h)(2)(i).

7. 10 NYCRR § 415.3(h)(2)(iii).

8. 10 NYCRR § 415.3(h)(2)(v).

9. 10 NYCRR § 415.3(h)(3).

§ 23.97

1. 42 U.S.C.A. § 1395i–3(c)(2)(D) (Medicare); 42 U.S.C.A. § 1396r(c)(2)(D); 42 C.F.R. § 483.12(b)(1)(i) (Medicare and Medicaid); 10 NYCRR § 415.3(h)(4)(i) (all residents).

Therapeutic leave is defined as an overnight absence to visit friends or relatives or to participate in medically acceptable therapy or rehabilitation. Therapeutic leave is limited to 18 days per 12 month period and must be included in the resident's plan of care. *Id.*

2. **PRACTICE POINTER:** Residents with pending Medicaid applications are not entitled to a guarantee of bed reservation. However, if the resident has resided in the facility for at least 30 days and the Medicaid application is subsequently approved, the reimbursement may be retroactive to include a period covered under a bed hold period. Thus, a facility may require that the resident sign a contract agreeing to be responsible for private payment if the Medicaid application is denied.

§ 23.97 ELDER LAW Ch. 23

resided in the facility for 30 days are entitled to a bed reservation for a period of 15 days.[3] This bed reservation can be extended to 20 days under certain circumstances.[4] Unless medically contraindicated, the facility must reserve the same bed and room that the resident occupied before leaving the facility.[5] If the Medicaid recipient's leave exceeds the bed hold period, the resident must be readmitted to the first available bed.[6]

Library References:

West's Key No. Digests, Asylums ⇌5.

§ 23.98 Nursing Home Resident Rights—Remedies for Violations of Rights or Improper Treatment

The Public Health Law contains a powerful but rarely utilized[1] tool for enforcement of the rights of nursing home residents. Public Health Law § 2801–d establishes a private right of action for deprivation of any right or benefit created or established for the well-being of a nursing home patient under the terms of any contract, federal or state statute, code, rule or regulation.[2] The statute provides for compensatory as well as punitive damages.[3] Minimal compensatory damages shall be no less than twenty-five percent of the facility's daily per patient rate of payment.[4] Any damages recovered by the resident are exempt from Medicaid.[5] Injunctive and declaratory relief are also available.[6] Individual or class action litigation may be commenced without the need to exhaust administrative remedies.[7] Attorney's fees may also be awarded.[8]

3. Regulations concerning the Medicaid bed hold policy are found at 18 NYCRR § 505.9(d). Department of Social Services bed hold policies are also set forth in Administrative Directive, 96 ADM–1: Payment for Reserved Beds in Medical Institutions: Clarification of Policy. In order to qualify for a bed reservation, the facility's vacancy rate must not exceed five per cent.

4. 18 NYCRR § 505.9(d)(5)(i)(b).

5. Id.

6. 42 U.S.C.A. § 1396r(c)(2)(D)(iii); 42 C.F.R. § 483.12(b)(3); 10 NYCRR § 415.3(h)(4)(iii), 18 NYCRR § 505.9(d).

§ 23.98

1. PRACTICE POINTER: Despite the availability of compensatory and punitive damages and attorney's fees, very few cases have been brought under the statute, which was enacted in 1975. Many attorneys are reluctant to commence tort actions on behalf of elderly clients due to difficulties in establishing causation and valuation of damages. J.T. O'Reilly, *The Lawyer's Guide to Elder Injury And Accident Compensation*, pp.20–22 (Lawyer's Division of The A.B.A. 1995) (*See* Chapter 17 regarding nursing home responsibility for injuries suffered by residents.)

The authors are hopeful that increased awareness of the remedies available under Section 2801–d will result in more aggressive protection of the rights of nursing home residents.

2. Public Health Law § 2801–d(1).

3. Public Health Law § 2801–d(2). An award of punitive damages requires a finding that the deprivation of the right or benefit was willful or in reckless disregard of the lawful rights of the patient. *Id.*

4. Id.

5. Public Health Law § 2801–d(5).

6. Public Health Law § 2801–d(3).

7. Public Health Law § 2801–d(4). Patients who believe their rights have been violated have the option of filing a com-

8. See Note 8 on p. 419.

Complaints concerning abuse or neglect of nursing home residents, as well as deprivation of rights guaranteed under federal or state law, may also be filed with the Department of Health[9] or the Long Term Care Ombudsman Program.[10]

Library References:

West's Key No. Digests, Asylums ⊙5, 7, 8.

§ 23.99 Housing Issues

Housing has tremendous importance to most elderly individuals. The home is frequently an appreciated asset at a time when other financial resources may be dwindling. The home represents financial security, a source of inheritance expectations, and a sense of personal history. Most elderly individuals place a high priority on the ability to remain in their homes. Yet high costs of maintenance and repairs, physical barriers and social isolation cause many seniors to consider relocation. Elderly renters may face difficulties in maintaining their apartments as their rental costs rise more rapidly than their retirement income.[1]

Attorneys who work with the elderly should be prepared to provide guidance concerning the numerous sources of housing assistance which are available from both governmental and private sources. The full range of housing assistance programs is beyond the scope of this chapter. The following sections will highlight New York State's Real Property Tax Exemption and Real Property Tax Credit, home repair, home energy and mortgage assistance programs, reverse mortgages and home equity loans, tenant protections, rental assistance and life care retirement communities.

§ 23.100 Housing Issues—Real Property Tax Exemption

New York Real Property Tax Law § 467 permits local governments to provide an exemption from property taxes for senior property owners.

---

plaint with the Commissioner of Health. If the Commissioner finds the complaint to have merit, he shall conduct a hearing upon the charges. Public Health Law § 2801-d(10)(b).

8. Public Health Law § 2801-d(6).

9. Public Health Law § 2803-d requires the Department of Health to investigate complaints of abuse and neglect of nursing home residents. Individuals found guilty of acts of abuse and neglect may be fined. Referrals may also be made to the district attorney's office for criminal prosecution and to disciplinary boards for revocation of professional licenses.

10. The Long Term Care Ombudsman Program assists residents of nursing homes and adult care facilities and their families. The State Department for the Aging administers the Ombudsman Program. To locate a local office call the Department for the Aging hotline at 1-800-342-9871.

§ 23.99

1. Many elderly renters pay up to 50% of their incomes on housing. L.A. Frolik and A. Patrucco Barnes, *Elderlaw Cases and Materials* (1992) p.669.

§ 23.100   ELDER LAW   Ch. 23

To be eligible for the exemption, the property owner must be 65 years of age or older.[1] The property must be used exclusively for residential purposes[2] and be the legal residence of the owner.[3] Title must have been vested in the owner for at least twelve months prior to application for the exemption.[4] An otherwise eligible individual will retain eligibility for the exemption if the property is held in a trust solely for his or her benefit.[5] The ownership requirement is satisfied if the individual holds a life estate to the property.[6] Localities are permitted to set their own income eligibility standards within limits established under the statute. Recent amendments permit maximum annual income of $25,900.[7] Eligible individuals may be granted an exemption of up to fifty percent of the assessed valuation of the property, dependent on their income.[8]

Municipalities are required to include a notice concerning the availability of the exemption with the tax bill. The annual deadline for acceptance of applications must be stated in the notice, along with the name, telephone number and address of the person or department responsible for administering the program.[9] Applications for the exemption must be refiled each year.[10] Local tax assessor offices administer the program in each locality.[11]

§ 23.101   Housing Issues—Real Property Tax Credit

New York State provides an income tax credit, known as the "Circuit Breaker" credit to homeowners or renters who pay a disproportionate amount of their income for real property taxes.[1] Annual household income must not exceed $18,000.[2] Other eligibility requirements

§ 23.100

1. Real Property Tax Law § 467(1)(a). All owners of jointly held property must be 65 or older. However, if the property is held by husband and wife or by siblings, one must be 65 or older. Id.

2. Real Property Tax Law § 467(3)(c).

3. Real Property Tax Law § 467(3)(d). The owner may be an inpatient in a residential health care facility and retain the right to the exemption. Id.

4. Real Property Tax Law § 467 (3)(b). When a residence within the state is sold and replaced with another residence in the state, the period of ownership for both residences may be combined. Id.

5. Real Property Tax Law § 467(9).

6. 9 Op.Counsel S.B.E.A. 92-52; 9 Op. Counsel S.B.E.A. 92-49; 1 Op. Counsel S.B.E.A. No. 34.

7. Real Property Tax Law §§ 467(1)(b), (3)(a).

8. Real Property Tax Law § 467(1) sets forth a sliding scale of exemption percentages based upon the extent to which the applicant's income exceeds the floor established by the locality.

9. Real Property Tax Law § 467(4).

10. Real Property Tax Law § 467(6)(a). In cities with population over one million, applications may be refiled every two years. After five years, exemptions may be granted automatically if the owner submits with the tax payment a sworn affidavit that he or she continues to be eligible for the exemption. Real Property Tax Law §§ 467(6)(b), (c).

11. Contact the Office for the Aging hotline at 1–800–342–9871 for the address and telephone number of the local assessment office. Applicants need proof of income, birth date, residency and ownership of the property.

§ 23.101

1. Tax Law § 606(e).

2. Tax Law § 606(e)(7)(A).

include one year of New York State residency[3] and occupancy of the residence for at least six months.[4] For homeowners, the value of the home must not exceed $85,000.[5] Tenants may also be eligible for the credit if their adjusted rent[6] is no more than $450 per month.[7]

To obtain the credit, the taxpayer must file form IT-214 with the New York State Tax Department.[8] Eligible individuals will receive a credit against taxes due or a rebate if no taxes are payable. Retroactive applications for credits or rebates may be submitted up to three years after the tax filing date.[9]

§ 23.102 Housing Issues—Tax Assistance Loans

New York Banking Law § 6-a permits banking institutions to make loans to individuals over age 65 in an amount up to the aggregate of all real property taxes, special *ad valorem* levies, and special assessments paid or owing by the borrower for a principal residence. The loan is secured by a first or second mortgage on the property and is not payable until the sale or other disposition of the property, although the borrower may voluntarily discharge the debt at any time. Banks which offer such loans make direct payments of the taxes which are owed.

§ 23.103 Housing Issues—Home Repair Assistance

Many older homeowners find themselves unable to afford the repairs and maintenance required to keep their homes in good condition. Federal and state programs provide grants and low interest loans which make necessary repairs and maintenance more affordable.[1]

The Farmer's Home Administration ("FMHA") of the U.S. Department of Agriculture provides loans and grants to remove safety and health hazards. Persons over 62 years of age may qualify for grants of up to $5,000. Loans of up to $15,000 are also available.[2] The New York State Department of Housing and Community Renewal and the New York State Office for the Aging operate the RESTORE program which provides low income homeowners over age 60 with loans or grants of up

---

3. Tax Law § 606(e)(7)(G).
4. Tax Law § 606(e)(1)(A).
5. Tax Law § 606(e)(7)(C).
6. Adjusted rent excludes charges for heat, gas, electricity, furnishings or board. Tax Law § 606(e)(1)(G).
7. Tax Law § 606(e)(7)(D).
8. Free assistance with filing and completing form IT-214 is provided by New York State District Tax offices. Further information concerning the Circuit Breaker credit can be obtained by calling the New York State Department for the Aging hotline at 1-800-342-9871.
9. Tax Law § 606(e)(9).

§ 23.103

1. To find out which programs are available in a specific area, contact the local area Office for the Aging. To find out the number of the office in your area, contact the Office for the Aging hotline at 1-800-342-9871.
2. Contact the FMHA at (315) 423-5290.

§ 23.103   ELDER LAW   Ch. 23

to $5,000 for home repairs necessary to correct emergency situations which pose a threat to the life or safety of elderly residents.[3]

§ 23.104 Housing Issues—Reverse Mortgages and Home Equity Loans

It has been estimated that over 75% of seniors over the age of 65 own their homes mortgage-free.[1] When combined with the tremendous rise in property values during the 1970's and early 1980's, many older individuals find that their homes are their most substantial asset. Reverse mortgage and home equity loans permit homeowners to tap into the value of their homes to supplement retirement income and improve their quality of life.[2] Extensive regulation of this industry is intended to assure that unwary seniors do not take undue financial risks when entering into these loans.

New York Real Property Law §§ 280 and 280–a regulate reverse mortgages for persons over age 60 and 70, respectively.[3] A reverse mortgage is defined as a loan which is secured by a first mortgage on a one to four family residence or condominium.[4] The proceeds of the loan may be advanced in equal installments, through a line of credit, in a lump sum or in a combination of these.[5] No payments need be made until expiration of a fixed term or upon the sale of the residence or death of the borrower.[6] However, the outstanding balance may be repaid at any time without penalty.[7]

---

3. Contact the New York State Division of Housing and Community Renewal ("DHCR") at (518) 486–3305, or the Office for the Aging hotline at 1–800–342–9871 for more information or to apply.

§ 23.104

1. The National Consumer Law Center, *Reverse Mortgages: Mandatory Counseling and Other Protections for the Elderly Homeowner*, Clearinghouse Review, 10/93 p.622 (reporting on a study conducted by the American Association of Retired Persons).

2. The American Association for Retired Persons ("AARP") has published extensive materials concerning reverse mortgages and home equity loans. Contact the AARP Home Equity Information Center at 601 E. Street, N.W., Washington, D.C. 20049 to request Ken Scholen, Home–Made Money: Consumer's Guide to Home Equity Conversion (Stock #D12894) (4th ed. 1993) and Reverse Mortgage Lenders List (Stock #D13253) (containing names, addresses, telephone numbers and contact persons for reverse mortgage lending institutions and counseling programs, listed by state and updated periodically.) *See also* E.A. Radow, *Reverse Mortgages in New York State: A Federal and State Law Analysis*, One on One, Vol.15, No.3 (Fall 1994) (newsletter of the General Practice Section of the New York State Bar Association).

3. RPL § 280 regulates reverse mortgages to individuals age 60 and older. RPL § 280–a provides special rules for reverse mortgages for borrowers over age 70 whose income does not exceed 80% of the median income in the county of their residence. Additional protections are required for loans to these older middle income borrowers including mandatory loan insurance and establishment of escrow accounts for payment of real property taxes, insurance premiums or other fees and expenses.

4. Unlike conventional mortgages, the income of the home owner is generally not relevant to the issuance of a reverse mortgage.

5. RPL §§ 280(1)(a), 280–a(1)(a).

6. RPL §§ 280(1)(b), (c), 280–a(1)(b), (c).

7. Upon expiration of a fixed term loan, the borrower may elect to refinance the loan or extend the maturation date, if the home is reappraised and has increased in

Financial institutions must provide the borrower with extensive information about the nature of the loan and may not issue the loan unless the borrower presents a statement that the terms of the loan have been explained by an attorney or authorized mortgage counselor or the borrower signs an affidavit indicating he or she is aware of but refuses these services.[8] Closing costs, origination fees, insurance, legal and counseling fees and other costs may be added to value of the loan.[9] The loan will terminate upon the sale or transfer of the home.[10]

The Department of Housing and Urban Development ("HUD") of the federal government also offers federally insured reverse mortgage loans through the Home Equity Conversion Mortgage Program ("HECM"). Lenders who offer HECM mortgages must be approved by HUD.[11] Individuals who receive HUD–HECM mortgages must be 62 years of age and either own the home free and clear or with a very minimal remaining mortgage. The residence must be a single family home or approved condominium. Mandatory counseling is required.[12]

§ 23.105 Housing Issues—Home Energy Assistance Program ("HEAP")

The Home Energy Assistance Program ("HEAP") provides financial assistance to low income New Yorkers of any age who need help paying heating costs.[1] Households must pay for heat directly or pay rent which includes heating costs. Households receiving Supplemental Security Income, Aid to Dependent Children ("ADC"), Home Relief, or food stamps are categorically eligible to receive HEAP benefits. All others must meet the income limits for the program.[2] Since HEAP grants are intended to assist low income individuals to meet heating costs, individuals with the following living arrangements are ineligible for benefits: tenants of

value and the total amount borrowed will not exceed the loan to value ratio determined by the Banking Board. RPL §§ 280(8), 280–a(8).

8. RPL §§ 280(2)(g), 280–a(2)(j).
9. RPL §§ 280(3)(a), 280–a(3)(b).
10. RPL §§ 280(7), 280–a(7).
11. To obtain the names and numbers of the lending institutions currently offering HUD–HECM mortgages in New York State contact the Department of Housing and Urban Development. The New York field office is at 26 Federal Plaza, New York, N.Y. 10278. Telephone (212) 264–8068. The Buffalo field office is at Lafayette Court, 5th floor, 465 Main Street, Buffalo, N.Y. 14203. Telephone (716) 551–5755.
12. For more information about HUD–HECM mortgages see, Money From Home: A Consumer's Guide to Home Equity Conversion Mortgages, available from the FannieMae Customer Education Group, 3900 Wisconsin Ave, N.W. Washington, D.C. 20016–2899.

§ 23.105

1. The regulations governing the HEAP program can be found at 18 NYCRR §§ 393.1—393.5.
2. There are different eligibility levels for Tier I and Tier II benefits. In 1997, maximum monthly income for Tier I was $839 for an individual or $1,122 for a couple. For Tier II benefits, maximum income was $968 for an individual or $1,295 for a couple. Additional income is permitted for households of larger size.

§ 23.105   ELDER LAW   Ch. 23

government subsidized housing who have heating costs included in their rent, individuals paying room and board in non-commercial establishments and residents of congregate care facilities.[3]

HEAP funds are provided by a block grant from the federal government[4] and are extremely limited. Eligible individuals must apply annually to their local social services office between November 15 and March 30th of each year, except that the application period may be extended if sufficient funds are available.[5] Some local offices provide home visits for elderly and disabled individuals who cannot travel.

Regular HEAP benefits[6] are provided in the form of a cash payment to the eligible individual or the home energy supplier, by two party check, or by the establishment of a line of credit. Individuals who are denied HEAP benefits are entitled to a fair hearing to appeal the denial.[7]

In addition to regular benefits, the HEAP program also provides emergency assistance to individuals who are without heating fuel or within seven days of depleting their fuel, have had heat-related utility service disconnected or scheduled for disconnection, need repair of inoperable or unsafe heating equipment or experience other heat-related emergencies. Individuals who receive emergency assistance must not have access to funds or alternate accommodations to ameliorate the problem.[8]

The Weatherization Referral and Packaging Program ("WRAP") supplements HEAP in some counties. The program provides weather stripping, caulking, insulation, replacement of storm doors and windows, cleaning or minor repairs to heating equipment and other energy saving improvements at no charge. Eligibility standards are the same as for the HEAP program.[9]

Assistance with the cost of home energy improvements may also be obtained from the Energy Conservation Bank program which is funded by the New York State energy office, in cooperation with utilities

---

3. 18 NYCRR § 393.4(3).

4. 42 U.S.C.A. §§ 8621, et seq.

5. Information about the location of the local social services office can be obtained by calling the Office for the Aging hotline at 1–800–342–9871. The Public Utilities Law Project ("PULP") is the best source for information concerning the HEAP program. To receive current information call PULP at (518) 449–3375.

6. Calculation of the amount of the regular HEAP benefit is based on assignment of points to the application based on 1) the income of the household (Tier I gets 2 points, Tier II gets 1 point), 2) the presence of vulnerable populations (children under age 6, seniors over age 60 or disabled individuals), 3) the energy burden ratio (the home energy expenditures divided by the income of the household.)

7. The appeals process is set forth at 18 NYCRR § 393.5. An appeal may be taken if the application is denied, not acted upon within 30 days or to challenge the amount of the grant. Appeals must be filed within 60 days after the notice is sent and no more than 105 days after the close of the application date for the year.

8. 18 NYCRR § 393.4(d).

9. To find out if the WRAP program is available in your locality, call the Office for the Aging hotline at 1–800–486–3298.

throughout the state.[10]

§ 23.106 Housing Issues—Tenant Protections

Senior Citizen Rent Increase Exemption ("SCRIE"). Senior citizen tenants who live in apartments which are regulated under local rent control or rent stabilization laws pursuant to the Emergency Tenant Protection Act may be eligible for a Senior Citizen Rent Increase Exemption ("SCRIE"). The SCRIE program provides protection against rent increases if the head of the household is 62 years or older, household income meets the threshold established by the locality, and the rent exceeds one third of net household income.[1] Eligible tenants must apply for the exemption every two years. The landlord receives a property tax abatement equal to the amount of the rent exemption.

Eviction Protections. Tenants who are over 62 years of age and who have lived in apartments subject to local rent control or rent stabilization laws for 20 years, or who are disabled, may not be evicted on the grounds that the landlord desires the apartment for his or her own use or the use of an immediate family member.[2]

Tenants who are 62 years of age or disabled are also protected against eviction in the event that their dwelling undergoes conversion to condominium or cooperative ownership. The senior citizen or disabled tenant may elect to purchase the apartment but may not be evicted if he or she chooses not to purchase, even if the conversion is pursuant to an eviction plan.

§ 23.107 Housing Issues—Life Care Retirement Communities

Article 46 of the Public Health Law regulates life care retirement communities.[1] A life care retirement community is a facility which enters into a life care contract in which the facility agrees to provide an independent living unit and board, a range of health and social services, including physician services, prescription drugs, rehabilitation, home health and nursing care and the services of an on site or affiliated skilled

---

10. Call the Energy Hotline at 1–800–342–3722 or the Office for the Aging hotline at 1–800–486–3298 for more information.

§ 23.106

1. Real Property Tax Law § 467–b. Consult local rent stabilization and rent control programs for information concerning the operation of the SCRIE program in a specific locality. For a referral to the local SCRIE program administrator call the Office for the Aging hotline at 1–800–342–9871, or the New York State Division of Housing and Community Renewal at (212) 519–5700.

2. Unconsolidated Laws §§ 8585(2)(a)(rent control), 8630(a) (rent stabilization). *See also,* Finkelstein and Ferrara, *New York Landlord and Tenant Practice* (West 1997).

§ 23.107

1. Public Health Law §§ 4601, *et seq.* Regulations governing life care communities are found at 10 NYCRR Pt. 900.

§ 23.107　　　　　　　　ELDER LAW　　　　　　　　Ch. 23

nursing facility for the life time of the resident.[2] The resident typically pays an up front entrance fee plus an additional monthly fee which guarantees all services under the contract and the right to occupy a specific independent living unit. The high cost of nursing home care and the strict asset and income restrictions of the Medicaid program have contributed to the growth of life care communities.[3] However, strict regulation of the industry has discouraged the development of these communities in New York State. The statute and regulations regulate the financing required to obtain a certificate of authorization to develop a facility, the initial disclosure to potential purchasers, the terms of the life care contract, the refund provisions, the escrow provisions for deposits received before completion of a facility, and they require facilities to maintain minimum reserves. Recent amendments to the Public Health Law[4] are intended to encourage the development of more of these facilities.

§ 23.108　Housing Issues—Community Based Services

New York State encourages older individuals to "age in place", *i.e.*, remain for as long as possible in their current homes and apartments. Accordingly, local Offices for the Aging[1] can provide information about and make referrals to a large variety of housing alternatives for seniors including enriched housing and assisted living programs, adult day care, caregiver support classes, short term care giver respite, home-sharing match-up assistance, shared living residences, elder cottages, accessory apartments, single room occupancy apartments, congregate housing facilities and adult homes.

§ 23.109　Health Care Decision Making

The rights of patients to make health care decisions have evolved tremendously in New York State and the nation in the past twenty years. In the past, health care decisions for incompetent and dying patients were nearly always made by physicians. Moreover, available interventions were limited and consisted mostly of pain relief or largely ineffectual remedies. Advances in medical technology have resulted in greatly increased life expectancies. However, these advances may be

---

2. Public Health Law § 4601(8), (9).

3. **PRACTICE POINTER**: High entrance and maintenance costs make life care communities a feasible option for only a very small percentage of seniors. Potential purchasers should be advised to examine a facility extremely carefully since much, if not all, of the entrance fee may not be refundable after expiration of an initial cancellation period. Individuals with high assets and income who lack nearby family supports are most likely to consider the life care community option.

4. These amendments permit life care contracts to provide for the payment of nursing home or home health care through the purchase of long term care insurance or by Medicaid, through the long term care security program. Public Health Law § 4601(8).

§ 23.108

1. Call the Office for the Aging hotline at 1–800–342–9871 for referral to the local office in your locality.

accompanied by significant pain, lack of independence, depression, financial deprivation and loss of individual autonomy. Some patients opt to prolong life, regardless of these personal and financial costs. Others prefer to expedite death and to alleviate their suffering.

New York law recognizes the right of a *competent*[1] individual to give informed consent for all medical decisions.[2] This right to personal autonomy extends even to decisions to decline life-sustaining treatment.[3] However, "clear and convincing" evidence that an *incompetent* patient had a prior firm and settled conviction to permit termination of life supports under circumstances like those presented is required.[4] This stringent evidentiary standard was upheld by the United States Supreme Court in *Cruzan v. Director, Missouri Dep't of Health*.[5]

It is not necessary for an individual to have executed written instructions for the clear and convincing evidentiary standard to be satisfied.[6]

§ 23.110 Health Care Decision Making—Health Care Proxy

New York State enacted Article 29–C of the Public Health Law[1] in 1991. This statute authorizes the creation of the Health Care Proxy, a springing durable power of attorney in which an individual authorizes an agent to make health care decisions.[2]

Any competent adult may appoint an agent to make health care decisions.[3] Competency is presumed unless the individual has been

§ 23.109

1. A guardian appointed under Article 81 of the Mental Hygiene Law may be granted authority to consent to or refuse generally accepted routine or major medical or dental treatment. Mental Hygiene Law § 81.22. For further discussion of the standard that must be applied by the guardian in making medical decisions, see Chapter 22 "Guardianship," *supra* at § 22.53.

2. Matter of Schloendorff v. Society of New York Hospital, 211 N.Y. 125, 105 N.E. 92 (1914).

3. Fosmire v. Nicoleau, 75 N.Y.2d 218, 551 N.Y.S.2d 876, 551 N.E.2d 77 (1990); Matter of Storar, 52 N.Y.2d 363, 438 N.Y.S.2d 266, 420 N.E.2d 64 (1981), cert. denied 454 U.S. 858, 102 S.Ct. 309, 70 L.Ed.2d 153 (1981).

4. In re Westchester County Medical Center (O'Connor), 72 N.Y.2d 517, 534 N.Y.S.2d 886, 531 N.E.2d 607 (1988). (The trier of fact must be convinced that the strength of the patient's beliefs and the durability of the patient's commitment to those beliefs make a recent change of heart unlikely).

5. 497 U.S. 261, 110 S.Ct. 2841, 111 L.Ed.2d 224 (1990).

6. Elbaum v. Grace Plaza of Great Neck, Inc., 148 A.D.2d 244, 544 N.Y.S.2d 840 (2d Dep't 1989).

PRACTICE POINTER: The absence of written instructions may increase the likelihood that an individual's decisions will be rejected by medical providers or become the subject of costly and sluggish administrative or judicial proceedings. For this reason, the preparation of a health care proxy should be an essential element of any consultation with an elder law practitioner. See *infra*, § 23.110.

§ 23.110

1. Public Health Law §§ 2980–2994.

2. *See infra*, § 23.125 for the form for a health care proxy contained in the Public Health law.

3. Public Health Law § 2981.1(a).

adjudicated incompetent.[4] The principal must sign the document and may not serve as the agent. Another person may sign and date the proxy as the principal's agent if the principal is unable to do so.[5] Individuals are generally prohibited from serving as agents for more than ten principals.[6] Health care providers are generally prohibited from serving as agents for patients under their care.[7]

The agent's authority commences upon the entry of a written statement inserted into the medical record by an attending physician that the patient lacks the ability to make medical decisions.[8] For a decision to withdraw life sustaining treatment, a second physician must concur that the patient lacks capacity.[9] Notice of a decision that a patient lacks capacity must be served on the principal and the agent.[10] If the principal objects to the determination, the agent's authority will not commence unless a court adjudicates the patient to be incapable of making medical decisions.[11] The agent's authority will cease if the attending physician determines that the principal has regained capacity to make medical decisions[12] or if the principal has revoked the agent's authority.[13]

The agent may make any and all medical decisions that the patient could make.[14] After consulting with medical personnel, the agent should make health care decisions in accordance with the principal's wishes, including religious and moral beliefs. If the individual's wishes are not known and cannot be ascertained, the agent may make decisions in accordance with the principal's best interests. However, the agent may not make decisions concerning the provision of artificial nutrition or hydration unless the principal's wishes concerning these treatments are known.[15]

The agent has the right to receive medical information, to consult with the principal's physicians and to review all medical records.[16] Decisions of the appointed proxy have priority over the wishes of other

4. Public Health Law § 2981.1(b).
5. Public Health Law § 2981.2(a).
6. Public Health Law § 2981.3(d). An exception is made for the spouse, child, parent, brother, sister or grandparent of the principal, or a person who is the issue of or married to one of the foregoing. Id.
7. Public Health Law §§ 2981.3(a)-(c). Exception is made for an operator, administrator or employee of a hospital who is related to the principal by blood, marriage or adoption. Public Health Law § 2981(3)(a).
8. Public Health Law § 2983.1.
9. Id.
10. Public Health Law § 2983.3.
11. Public Health Law § 2983.5.
12. Public Health Law § 2983.7.
13. Public Health Law § 2985. The statute specifies that revocation may be oral, in writing, by execution of a subsequent proxy or by any act evidencing an intent to revoke. Appointment of a spouse is revoked upon divorce or legal separation unless the principal specifies otherwise.
14. Public Health Law § 2982.1.
15. Public Health Law § 2982.2.
16. Public Health Law § 2982.3.

individuals[17] and are binding upon health care providers.[18] Providers and agents who use good faith in exercising health care decisions are immune from civil and criminal liability.[19]

New York recognizes proxies validly executed in other states.[20] Most states will recognize a proxy validly executed in New York. However, practitioners must check the provisions of the state in question.

Library References:

West's Key No. Digests, Physicians and Surgeons ⚖=42, 44.

§ 23.111 Health Care Decision Making—The Living Will

A living will, or advance directive, is a written document which contains specific instructions concerning an individual's wishes about future health care.[1] Like the health care proxy, the living will is only utilized in the event that the individual becomes incompetent to make medical decisions. The document typically states that life sustaining medical treatment shall not be continued in the event that the individual should become terminally ill, permanently unconscious, in a persistent vegetative state, or conscious with irreversible brain damage with no possibility of regaining the ability to make medical decisions.[2]

New York is one of the few states that does not specifically recognize or regulate the validity of living wills by statute. However, a properly drafted living will may satisfy New York's common law requirement that an individual's wishes concerning withdrawal of life-sustaining treatment be proven by "clear and convincing" evidence.[3]

The living will should contain general instructions concerning the continuation or termination of medical treatment. Definite preferences concerning specific treatments such as cardiac resuscitation, artificial

---

17. Public Health Law § 2982.4.
18. Public Health Law § 2984.2. However, note that providers who object to decisions on moral or religious grounds may transfer the patient to another physician or facility after notification to the agent. Public Health Law §§ 2984.3, 2984.4.
19. Public Health Law § 2986.
20. Public Health Law § 2990.

§ 23.111

1. *See infra*, § 23.126 for a sample form for a living will.
2. **PRACTICE POINTER**: The living will is not limited to wishes to discontinue life-sustaining treatment. Some individuals may want the document to express a desire that life-supports be continued under all permissible circumstances. The living will may contain provisions that medical treatment should be guided by specific religious or moral guidelines. Some religious organizations have prepared specific forms to be used by their followers.

3. In re Westchester County Medical Center (O'Connor), 72 N.Y.2d 517, 534 N.Y.S.2d 886, 531 N.E.2d 607 (1988). The Court of Appeals indicated that "the ideal situation is one in which the patient's wishes were expressed in some form of a writing, perhaps a 'living will', while he or she was still competent. The existence of a writing suggests the author's seriousness of purpose and ensures that the court is not being asked to make a life-or-death decision based upon casual remarks." *Id.* at 531.

respiration, artificial nutrition and hydration, antibiotics, pain medication, or any other specific intervention should also be included.[4]

Library References:

West's Key No. Digests, Physicians and Surgeons ⊕45.

§ 23.112 Health Care Decision Making—Do Not Resuscitate Orders

Article 29–B of the New York Public Health Law was enacted in 1987 to clarify the rights and obligations of health care providers and patients concerning cardiopulmonary resuscitation ("CPR").[1] The statute specifies that hospital patients shall be presumed to desire CPR unless consent to issuance of a Do Not Resuscitate ("DNR") order has been granted.[2] All adults are presumed capable of making decisions concerning CPR unless determined otherwise by a court or an attending physician who obtains the concurrence of another physician.[3] Hospital patients may consent to the issuance of a DNR order orally in the presence of at least two witnesses, one of whom is a physician affiliated with the hospital.[4] Written consent orders may be prepared during or prior to hospitalization and must be dated and signed by at least two witnesses.[5] Attending physicians must record the DNR decision in the patient's chart. Physicians who object to issuance of the order must either arrange to transfer the patient to another physician or submit the dispute to mediation.[6]

An agent appointed by a health care proxy may make a decision to consent to issuance of a DNR order for an incompetent patient.[7] In the absence of an appointed agent, the statute sets forth a priority list of individuals who can consent to issuance of the order.[8]

The surrogate must make a decision regarding CPR on the basis of the patient's wishes, including consideration of the patient's religious

---

4. **CAVEAT**: Although individuals execute living wills in order to provide clear and convincing evidence concerning their wishes for medical treatment, the document may not provide sufficient guidance when the need arises. Many commonly used terms such as "terminal illness," "imminent death" and "when the burdens of treatment outweigh the benefits," are subjective and may result in differences of interpretation by health care providers or family members. Moreover, documents which address only end of life decision making provide no guidance as to the desirability of other treatments for incompetent but non-terminal patients. The living will cannot advocate with the force of an appointed agent.

§ 23.112

1. Public Health Law §§ 2960–2979.
2. Public Health Law § 2962.
3. Public Health Law § 2963.
4. Public Health Law § 2964.2(a).
5. Public Health Law § 2964.2(b).
6. Public Health Law § 2964.2(c).
7. Public Health Law § 2965.1(a).

8. In order of preference, they are a committee of the person under Article 17–A of the SCPA, a spouse, a son or daughter over 18 years of age, a parent, a brother or sister over 18 years of age, or a close friend. The individual chosen to be surrogate should be identified in the medical chart. Public Health Law § 2965.2.

and moral beliefs, or in the event such wishes are unknown, according to the patient's best interests.[9] The surrogate[10] may consent to a DNR order only if two physicians certify that the patient has a terminal condition, is permanently unconscious, that resuscitation would be futile, or that resuscitation would impose an extraordinary burden on the patient in light of the patient's condition and the expected outcome of the CPR.[11] A surrogate's decision to consent to a DNR order will be overruled if the patient objects, even if the patient has been determined to lack capacity to make medical decisions.[12] Patients and surrogates may revoke consent to a DNR order at any time, either orally or in writing.[13] The statute sets forth procedures for review of DNR orders by attending physicians.[14]

DNR orders may be issued for persons who are not patients in a hospital.[15] Standard forms and identity bracelets have been developed by the Commissioner of Health. Such forms shall be honored by emergency medical personnel unless they have a good faith belief that consent to the order has been revoked or if family members or others on the scene object and physical confrontation appears likely. The order may also be disregarded if there are "other significant and exceptional medical circumstances."[16]

Library References:
West's Key No. Digests, Physicians and Surgeons ⚖=45.

§ 23.113 Health Care Decision Making—Physician Assisted Suicide

While it is not illegal for an individual to attempt or succeed in taking his or her own life, the Penal Law provides that a person who assists another to commit or attempt to commit a suicide is guilty of a felony.[1] Physicians who provide assistance to terminally ill patients who wish to hasten their deaths have feared criminal prosecution under these provisions of the Penal Law. Physicians who wished to provide assistance to terminally ill patients who desired to hasten their deaths challenged New York's prohibition of physician-assisted suicide in *Vacco*

---

9. Public Health Law § 2965.3(a).
10. Public Health Law § 2965.3(c).
11. In the event no surrogate decision maker is available, an attending physician may issue a DNR order upon a finding that resuscitation would be medically futile and upon the concurrence of a second physician. Public Health Law § 2966. A physician may also commence a special proceeding for a court order directing issuance of a DNR order where the patient has a terminal condition, is permanently unconscious, or resuscitation would impose an extraordinary burden on the patient and issuance of the order is consistent with the patient's religious beliefs, or is in the patient's best interests. Public Health Law § 2976.
12. Public Health Law § 2965.5.
13. Public Health Law § 2969.
14. Public Health Law § 2970.
15. Public Health Law § 2977.
16. Public Health Law § 2977.10.

§ 23.113

1. Penal Law §§ 120.30, 125.15(3). Assisted suicide may also be prosecuted under Penal Law § 120.15(1) as reckless manslaughter.

§ 23.113 ELDER LAW Ch. 23

v. *Quill*.[2] In *Washington v. Glucksberg*,[3] a similar challenge was raised by physicians in the State of Washington. The Supreme Court rejected the physicians' arguments in both cases. In *Washington v. Glucksberg*, the court held that mentally competent, terminally ill adults do not possess a fundamental liberty interest to commit physician-assisted suicide which is protected by the Due Process Clause. In *Vacco v. Quill*, the court held that New York's ban on physician-assisted suicide did not violate the Equal Protection Clause.[4]

Library References:

West's Key No. Digests, Physicians and Surgeons ⊂⇒43.

§ 23.114 Tax Issues

The following sections will highlight the major federal income tax provisions which affect elderly individuals. For a full discussion of New York income tax law, *see* Chapter 35 "Income Tax," *infra*. Individuals who are over 65 years of age must file income tax returns if their gross income, not counting Social Security benefits exceeds federally specified minimum income levels.[1]

§ 23.115 Tax Issues—Additional Standard Deduction for the Aged and Blind

In addition to the personal exemption[1] and basic standard deduction,[2] individuals who are aged or blind are entitled to an additional standard deduction.[3] The amount of the additional standard deduction for the aged and blind is $1,000 (in 1996) for an unmarried individual (other than a qualifying surviving spouse) or head of household, or $800 (in 1996) for a married individual or qualifying surviving spouse.[4] Taxpayers who are elderly *and* blind may claim two additional deductions, *i.e.*, $1,600 if married or a qualifying surviving spouse, or $2,000 if single

---

2. ___ U.S. ___, 117 S.Ct. 2293, 138 L.Ed.2d 834 (1997).

3. ___ U.S. ___, 117 S.Ct. 2258, 138 L.Ed.2d 772 (1997).

4. The physicians had argued that similarly situated terminally ill individuals were not treated alike under New York law in that those who are on life-support systems are allowed to hasten their deaths by directing removal but other terminally ill individuals are not permitted to receive assistance in dying from their physicians.

§ 23.114

1. I.R.C. § 6012(a). In 1996, a single individual 65 years or older was required to file a return if income was more than $7,550. A couple filing a joint return when both are 65 years or older was required to file if gross income exceeded $13,400.

§ 23.115

1. I.R.C. § 151.

2. I.R.C. § 63(b).

3. I.R.C. §§ 63(c)(3), 63(f). An "aged" individual must have attained age 65 before the close of the taxable year. I.R.C. § 63(f)(1). An individual is defined as "blind" if vision is no better than 20/200 in the better eye, with corrective lenses or if the field of vision is impaired. I.R.C. § 63(f)(4).

4. *Id.*

(in 1996). The amount of the additional deduction is adjusted each year for inflation.[5]

If an elderly or blind taxpayer is claimed as a dependent on another's return, the basic standard deduction for the elderly or disabled person is the greater of $650 (in 1996) or the dependent taxpayer's earned income up to the basic standard deduction amount.[6] Moreover, the dependent elderly or blind taxpayer may not claim a personal exemption, but may claim the additional standard deduction of $800 if married or a qualifying surviving spouse, or $1,000 if single.[7]

§ 23.116 Tax Issues—Incapacity

If the taxpayer is unable to sign the return, a filing spouse can sign the disabled spouse's name and add "by husband" or "by wife" and attach a statement of explanation. Individual returns must be filed and signed by a duly authorized agent such as a guardian or attorney-in-fact. IRS Form 284a (Power of Attorney and Declaration of Representative) should be used.

§ 23.117 Tax Issues—Sale of Principal Residence

The Taxpayer Relief Act of 1997 amends I.R.C. § 121 to provide an exclusion from gross income of the gain from the sale or exchange of property which has been used as the taxpayer's principal residence for periods totalling two years or more within the five year period ending on the date of the sale or exchange. The amount of gain excluded from gross income can not exceed $500,000 if a husband and wife file jointly for the tax year of the sale or exchange. This exclusion is limited to one sale or exchange every two years.[1]

The capital gains rollover may be used if the house is held in a trust, provided that the trust is a grantor-type trust for purposes of income and principal.[2] Drafting techniques to qualify the trust as a grantor-type trust would be to give the grantor the right to remove and replace trustees and/or have the grantor retain a power of appointment.[3]

§ 23.118 Tax Issues—Medical Deductions

All taxpayers may deduct the cost of medical care for themselves, their spouse and their dependents in excess of 7.5% of adjusted gross

---

5. I.R.C. § 63(c)(4).
6. I.R.C. § 63(c)(5).
7. *Id.*

§ 23.117
1. I.R.C. § 121(b)(3).
2. I.R.C. § 121(a); Revenue Ruling 85-45.

3. I.R.C. § 674(a).

CAVEAT: The grantor should not retain only use and occupancy. This is insufficient under I.R.C. § 121. Also note that the retained powers of the grantor may effect the grantor's eligibility for Medicaid and/or Medicaid's rights of recovery for benefits paid.

§ 23.118   ELDER LAW   Ch. 23

income.[1] The following medical expenses are of particular interest to elderly clients.

Payment of nursing home costs are deductible if medical care is "a principal reason" for the nursing home confinement.[2] Since New York State limits admission to skilled nursing facilities to residents who require medical care, the cost of a skilled nursing facility should be deductible. Payment of an intermediate health care facility or an adult home for which medical care was not a principal reason for admission could still be partially deductible to the extent that a portion of the cost could be allocated to medical care.[3]

The deductibility of home care is more problematic. To the extent that home care services are necessitated by a physical or medical condition, the care is deductible.[4] To the extent that the care is personal rather than medical, it is not deductible. However, the deduction may be taken for the portion of the care which can be allocated to the medical or physical need.[5]

The Health Insurance Portability and Accountability Act of 1996, commonly known as The Kennedy/Kassebaum Health Reform Act, enacted August 21, 1996 addresses the deductibility of long term care insurance.[6] The statute treats payment of qualified long term care services and long term care insurance premiums as medical expenses under I.R.C. § 213 except if paid to a relative.[7] Qualified long term care services are defined in I.R.C. § 7702B as necessary diagnostic, preventa-

§ 23.118

1. I.R.C. § 213.

2. *See* Treasury Regulation § 1.213–1(e)(1)(v). *See also,* Dodge v. The Commissioner, T.C. Memo. 1961–346, 20 T.C.M. (CCH) 1811 (1961); and Counts v. The Commissioner, 42 T.C. 755 (1964).

3. Estate of Smith, 79 T.C. 313 (1982).
PRACTICE POINTER: Use the deductions to offset income created by withdrawals from qualified plans and to offset capital gain income from the sale of appreciated property.

If the person in need of long term care can not utilize the medical deduction due to insufficient income, his or her children could pay for the care. If the parent is a U.S. citizen and the child pays for more than one-half of the parent's support for the calendar year, the parent would be a dependent under I.R.C. § 152, and the child could take the deduction under § 151. The payment of medical care for the parent is not a gift under I.R.C. § 2503(e)(2)(b) provided that the child pays the provider directly.

If a number of children get together to support their parent by paying the long term care costs, one child can deduct the care pursuant to a multiple support agreement. I.R.C. § 152(c).

CAVEAT: Is long term care insurance "medical insurance" as defined in I.R.C. § 213, and does it qualify as a medical deduction? Premiums are deductible for health insurance if the expenses covered would be deductible if paid directly. I.R.C. § 213(a)(1)(C). Are the expenses covered by the policy deductible as medical expenses? Despite repeated requests, the I.R.S. has refused to clarify this issue.

4. Dodge v. The Commissioner, T.C. Memo. 1961–346.

5. *Id.*

6. **CAVEAT:** At the time this chapter was written, numerous technical amendments of the statute were being considered. The effect of this statute upon prior statutes, regulations and case law is unclear. Therefore, the practitioner is cautioned to research and investigate the current status of this state.

7. I.R.C. § 7702B(e)(10).

tive, therapeutic, curing, treating, mitigating and rehabilitative services, and maintenance or personal care services which are required by a chronically ill individual and are provided pursuant to a plan of care prescribed by a licensed health care practitioner. A chronically ill individual is defined as an individual who has been certified by a licensed health care practitioner as being unable to perform (without substantial assistance from another individual) at least 2 activities of daily living for a period of at least 90 days due to loss of functional capacity, or having a small level of disability determined by the secretary. A licensed health care practitioner is any physician or registered professional nurse, licensed social worker, or any other individual who meets requirements as prescribed by the secretary.

§ 23.119 Miscellaneous Programs

The following sections discuss additional benefit programs of interest to older New Yorkers.

§ 23.120 Miscellaneous Programs—Elderly Pharmaceutical Insurance Coverage ("EPIC")

The Elderly Pharmaceutical Insurance Coverage Program ("EPIC") provides financial assistance in purchasing prescription medications to elderly New Yorkers.[1] Eligible individuals must be 65 years of age, residents of New York State and meet the income requirements of the program.[2] Individuals who are in receipt of Medicaid or private insurance which provides equivalent or superior drug coverage are excluded from the program.[3] As of April 1, 1996, the financial rules governing the EPIC program were substantially revised. The program now provides two tiers of coverage dependent on household size and income. In 1996, individuals with incomes up to $10,000 and couples with incomes up to $13,000[4] paid an application fee of $10.[5] Thereafter, they were responsible for a co-payment for each pharmaceutical they purchased. The co-payment was $6 (or the actual cost, if lower) for items under $30 or $15 for items over $30.[6] Annual out of pocket expenses were capped.[7] Individuals and couples with higher incomes[8] could have received coverage subject to the

---

§ 23.120

1. The statute governing the EPIC program is set forth at Executive Law §§ 547, et seq. The regulations governing the program can be found at 9 NYCRR Pt. 9600.

2. Executive Law §§ 547–b(1), (2).

3. Executive Law § 547–b(3).

4. Executive Law § 547–b(1). In 1997, an individual may have income up to $12,000, a couple up to $15,000. Id.

5. Executive Law § 547–g(2).

6. Executive Law § 547–g(3).

7. Limitations on co-payments are governed by a sliding scale dependent on household size and income. For individuals with income of $5,000 or less, the maximum co-payment is $400. For couples with incomes of $15,000, co-payments meet the cap at $900. Executive Law § 547–g(4) contains a table with the specific limits on co-payments for households of different size and income.

8. In 1996, this second tier of eligibility applies to individuals with incomes between $10,000 and $16,000 and couples with incomes between $13,000 and $21,000. In

§ 23.120   ELDER LAW   Ch. 23

same co-payments described above once each had satisfied an annual deductible of $150.[9] Total out of pocket expenditures are capped dependent on household size and income.[10] The program covers the purchase of prescription drugs, insulin and insulin syringes and needles[11] from registered providers.[12] Individuals who are accepted for the program receive an identification card which they must present when purchasing prescription medications. The program is run by private agencies which contract with the state.[13] Individuals who are not satisfied with determinations by the contractor may request reconsideration. Reconsideration decisions must be made within 30 days.[14] Individuals who are dissatisfied with decisions after reconsideration may request a fair hearing.[15]

§ 23.121   Miscellaneous Programs—Life Line Telephone Service

Individuals who receive food stamps, Medicaid, HEAP, SSI, Home Relief, AFDC, Veterans disability or Veterans surviving spouse pensions may be eligible for NYNEX Life Line Telephone Service.[1] Under the Basic Life Line service plan, individuals pay only $1.00 per month for basic service and pay for each outgoing call. The Flat Rate service plan saves $8.10 per month on basic monthly charges and includes unlimited calls within the local calling area.[2] In addition, installation charges for Life Line customers are only $10.

NYNEX also provides "special protections" for individuals who notify them that they are over age 62, disabled or have a serious medical condition. NYNEX will take steps to work out special payment plans for individuals recorded as eligible for "special protections" and who are in danger of service disconnection due to failure to pay their bills. Seniors over age 62 may also qualify for quarterly payment options if their annual bills are less than $150, and for a change in bill payment date to coordinate with the receipt of their monthly income. Customers with visual, hearing or speech disabilities may lease or purchase special

---

1997, individuals must have income between $12,000 and $18,000; couples' income must be between $15,000 and $23,000. Executive Law § 547–b(2)(a), (b).

9. Executive Law § 547–h(2).

10. For an individual with income of $10,000 or less the maximum is $575. For a couple with income of $23,000, the maximum is $992. Executive Law § 547–h(4) contains a table containing the specific limits on co-payments for households of different size and income.

11. Executive Law § 547–a(1).

12. Executive Law § 547–a(2).

13. To locate the local contracting agency call the EPIC program at 1–800–332–3742, or write to EPIC at P.O. Box 15018, Albany, N.Y. 12214–5527.

14. 9 NYCRR § 9630.1.

15. The fair hearing process is set forth at 9 NYCRR §§ 9720, *et seq.*

§ 23.121

1. To obtain more information or to apply for Life Line service call NYNEX at 1–800–555–5000.

2. Flat Rate Service is not available in all areas.

telecommunications equipment through the Communications Center for People with Disabilities.[3]

§ 23.122 Forms

The sections which follow include basic forms for handling an elder law case. There are a form letter to send the client prior to the consultation, including a list of necessary documents, a consultation letter, a statutory form of health care proxy and a sample living will. Each form sets forth the general requirements. The practitioner must adapt the forms to the particular facts in the specific Elder Law matter.

§ 23.123 Forms—Documentation Letter—[Text § 23.2]

[Mrs. A. Smith
555 Anystreet
Brooklyn, N.Y. 11200]

Dear [Mrs. Smith]:

Thank you for your interest in our firm. Enclosed is a list of documents which would be helpful at the consultation. I would appreciate it if you could send these documents before the consultation. If you are not able to get copies of all of these documents, we can still meet and you can send them in later.

Copies of the documents are sufficient. I do not need originals.

The consultation fee is $_____. It covers our first meeting, a detailed letter and a follow up meeting. The consultation fee is payable at the initial consultation.

I look forward to meeting with you on [January 12th].

Sincerely,

[John Elder Law], Esq.

ITEMS TO BRING TO CONSULTATION

1. Current Power of Attorney.
2. Health care proxy and/or living will.
3. Medicare card.

---

3. The Center may be contacted at 1-800-482-9020, or 1-800-342-4181 (TDD users) or by writing to the Communications Center, 204 Second Avenue, New York, N.Y. 10009. Special equipment available through the Center includes enlarged and raised number inserts, free operator assistance, braille and large-print bills, electronic artificial larynx devices, volume increase handsets, telecommunications devices for the deaf ("TDD"), impaired hearing handsets, loud tone ringers and light signaling devices.

§ 23.123 ELDER LAW Ch. 23

4. Private health insurance card.
5. Amount of Social Security check.
6. Current Last Will and Testament.
7. Deed to any property owned.
8. Life insurance—proof of ownership and "cash surrender value".
9. List of savings, checking and brokerage accounts.
10. List of assets transferred in the past thirty six (36) months.
11. Most recent tax returns.

Date: _____

DOCUMENTS REQUIRED FOR MEDICAID APPLICATION
APPLICANT NAME: _____

____ A. **Proof of Identity and Family Relationship**
    ____ Union card
    ____ Social Security card
    ____ Medicare card
    ____ One of the following:
    ____ Birth certificate *or* census records *or* baptismal certificate *or* certificate of naturalization *or* passport *or* visa *or* driver's license
    ____ Military discharge papers
    ____ Marriage certificate or divorce/separation papers
    ____ Death certificate of spouse
    ____ Private health insurance card and premium stub
    ____ Other: _____

____ B. **Residency and Living Arrangement**
    ____ Rent receipt and/or lease
    ____ Most current utility and telephone bills
    ____ Other

____ C. **Income**
    ____ Pension or pay stubs
    ____ Support payments-divorce or separation papers
    ____ Award letter for the following benefits:
        ( ) Social Security (Call 1–800–772–1213)
        ( ) Military or Veterans Pension
        ( ) Pension
        ( ) Railroad Retirement
        ( ) Insurance Endowment
        ( ) Annuity
        ( ) New York State Disability
        ( ) Worker's Compensation
    ____ Business records, if self employed
    ____ 1993, 1994, and 1995 income tax returns, with 1099 forms (as available)
    ____ Other: _____

D. Resources

___ All bank account statements, IRA account statements, mutual fund statements and investment account statements for the past three years, including closed accounts.*

___ All passbook bank accounts for the past 3 years, including closed accounts.*

___ All checking account statements for the past 3 years with all checks (front and back) in the amount of $500 and over.*

___ Life insurance policies and current cash value

___ Stock and bond certificates

___ Real estate deeds or co-op shares

___ Closing papers on property sales

___ Information about any pending law suits

___ Other: _____

* All financial documentation must be accompanied by an explanation for deposits and withdrawals over $500. For example, if an account is closed, you must provide the bank name and account number that the funds were transferred to, and proof of receipt by that account.

§ 23.124 Forms—Consultation Letter[1]

[Mrs. A. Smith
555 Anystreet
Brooklyn, N.Y. 11200]

Dear [Mrs. Smith]:

BACKGROUND

You came to this office regarding Medicaid eligibility for your husband, Mr. Smith, following his hospitalization. Your husband is 68 years old and suffers from a right hemiparesis, diabetes and aphasia. At this time, he requires total assistance with all acts of daily living. You are 56 years old and in good health.

FAMILY TREE

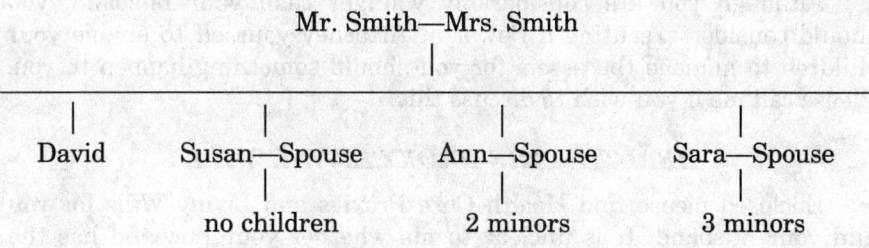

Both of you have executed Wills, dated October 1, 1982. These Wills provide the surviving spouse will receive the entire estate and upon the

---

§ 23.124

1. See supra, § 23.2.

death of the survivor, the assets will pass equally to all four children, in equal shares, per stirpes. These Wills do not contain Self–Proving Affidavits. This means that the witnesses will have to be located prior to probate of the Wills so that depositions may be taken from them. This may unduly delay the probate process.

I recommend that you execute a new Will disinheriting your husband and leaving your estate to your children. If your husband should inherit from you, it will cause him to lose his eligibility for Medicaid and the Department of Social Services will have a right of recovery against his estate. In addition, there is an issue as to whether or not a guardian would need to be appointed to manage his finances. If you die before your husband and your will does not leave him anything, he has a right to "elect", *i.e.*, take one third of your estate. The Department of Social Services may make him exercise this right of election. There is no way of preventing this since he does not appear to have the capacity to waive his right of election at this time. Your husband's will is fine.

POWER OF ATTORNEY

Your husband executed a Power of Attorney prior to his stroke for the sale of a business. This Power of Attorney is a general Power of Attorney and is "durable" meaning that it will survive this subsequent disability and will not be revoked by his current incapacity.

The Power of Attorney gives you (called the "attorney-in-fact") the power to assist your husband with financial and legal matters which normally only he could do. Because the Power of Attorney is "durable", it allows you, as attorney-in-fact, to continue acting for him even though he now appears to be mentally incompetent.

Some banks, brokerage houses and other transfer agents prefer to honor their own Power of Attorney forms. You may have difficulty using the Power of Attorney at certain financial institutions. It so, please contact me and I will assist you in this matter.

Although you are considerably younger than your husband, you should consider executing a Power of Attorney yourself to enable your children to manage the assets for you should something happen to you. Please call me if you wish to discuss this.

HEALTH CARE PROXY/LIVING WILL

Enclosed please find Health Care Proxies and Living Wills for you and your husband. It is unclear to me whether your husband has the capacity to execute these documents, *i.e.*, capacity to understand that he is authorizing you to make medical decisions for him and instructing you as to his wishes. He should execute these documents if he has the capacity to understand them. You should execute both documents for yourself. These documents permit you to do advance medical care

HEALTH INSURANCE

Mr. Smith is covered by Medicare and an AARP Medigap Policy "J". These policies will cover most of his hospital stay unless he is hospitalized for a very long time. They will cover his nursing home care or home care only if he is receiving a skilled level of care in the nursing home (for example, rehabilitation will qualify him for Medicare and Medigap coverage for the nursing home for up to 100 days so long as he continues to receive the rehabilitation).

You have fairly complete coverage for yourself through your employer. You will not be eligible for Medicare until age 65.

ASSETS AND INCOME

You have disclosed to me the following assets which you and your husband hold:

Real Property
Located at 555 Anystreet, Brooklyn
Held in the name of Mrs. Smith only.
Original cost basis—$25,000
Current market value .... $ 250,000

Anchor Bank for Savings
Mrs. Smith only.
Current value .... $ 800

Anchor Bank for Savings
Mrs. Smith only.
Current value .... $ 32,497

Putnam High Income Government Trust
Joint Mr. and Mrs. Smith.
Current value .... $ 58,925

Putnam Option II
Joint Mr. and Mrs. Smith.
Current value .... $ 22,852

Shearson Lehman, MLS Multi Market Trust
Joint Mr. and Mrs. Smith.
Current Value... $ 15,000

Total: **$380,074**

Mr. Smith receives $446.00 per month in Social Security income. You receive approximately $800.00 per month in salary.

ESTATE TAXES

At this time the taxes on the combined estate at the time of the death of the survivor of the two of you would be subject to New York State Estate taxes on the value of the assets, other than the home, in excess of $115,000. The home would be subject to estate taxes to the extent its value exceeds $250,000. There would be no federal estate tax

planning and are crucial in the event that you suffer an incapacitating disability.

The Health Care Proxy should be used to designate someone to be your health care agent. Your husband may designate you; you should designate one of your children. A health care agent is allowed to make all decisions concerning your medical treatment when your doctor has determined that you can no longer make those decisions yourself. When it is determined that you are unable to direct your own medical treatment, your agent will then have the power to make medical decisions for you including, but not limited to, the refusal of life sustaining treatment. However, if you do not want to receive artificial nutrition and hydration (food and water), you must tell your agent, preferably in writing on the Proxy form. If there are other decisions regarding your medical care which you do not wish the agent to make, please so indicate by specifying on the Proxy form. An alternate agent should be designated in the event that your first choice for agent cannot act on your behalf.

The Health Care Proxy form that we have enclosed is being distributed by the New York State Department of Health. We believe that physician, hospital and nursing home personnel will be most familiar with this form. Attached to this Proxy is further information which you should carefully review. The Proxy must be signed before two (2) witnesses. Your designated health care agent may not act as a witness to the signing of the Proxy.

The Living Will is a document which expresses one's wishes as to medical treatment when he or she can no longer communicate these wishes. We suggest that you sign a Living Will to support your Health Care Proxy. This document may be needed if, for any reason, the agent and alternate agent cannot serve on your behalf, or if you are being treated outside of New York State.

You should only sign the Living Will if it reflects your wishes. Our Living Will form is very broad. It proscribes treatment when your doctor has determined that you have suffered a disability which prevents you from making medical decisions and from communicating with others in a meaningful way, *and* there is no reasonable hope of recovery. Our form also prohibits the use of artificial nutrition and hydration under these circumstances. This document may also be used to ensure that you receive or continue certain treatment under certain circumstances. We can modify this form to suit your own desires.

You should fully discuss your Health Care Proxy and Living Will with your family and physician and seek their full cooperation in carrying out your wishes.

If you have any further questions or desire any changes to your Health Care Proxy or Living Will, please call me.

because the estate does not exceed the amount which is sheltered by the federal estate tax credit ($600,000).

MEDICAID

As we discussed, Medicaid will pay for long term custodial care in an institutional setting or at home, provided that the applicant qualifies financially and medically.

Medicaid is a "means tested" combined federal and state program designed to provide medical assistance. In order to receive Medicaid, your husband will have to qualify financially. At the present time, applicants for Medicaid in New York State can have no more than $3,350 personal savings and can protect an additional $1,500 if placed in a burial fund.

Individuals who apply for Medicaid must submit bank and other financial records for the 36 months prior to their application. Medicaid reviews all of these documents, looking for large withdrawals. If they see large withdrawals (above $500.00, generally), they request information regarding the withdrawal. If the withdrawal was a gratuitous transfer of assets to someone *other than the applicant's spouse*, the individual will be ineligible for Medicaid *institutional* benefits from the date of the transfer until the end of the period of ineligibility. There is period of ineligibility for transfers between spouses.

The period of ineligibility for Medicaid institutional benefits in New York City is one month for every $6,531 transferred. In New York the period of ineligibility only applies to Medicaid *institutional* benefits. It does not apply to applications for Medicaid *home care* benefits in New York.

Recipients of Medicaid institutional benefits may retain $50.00 each month as a personal allowance while the remainder of their income is paid to the nursing home. If your husband receives Medicaid home care benefits he will be allowed to retain his entire Social Security check for his monthly expenses because it is below the $559.00 monthly income cap for Medicaid home care eligibility. If he had income in excess of this amount, he would still be eligible for Medicaid home care. However, he would be required to spend the excess income on the cost of his care.

LONG TERM CARE PLANNING

At this time, I recommend that you remove Mr. Smith's name from all of the joint accounts. While this will be considered to be a transfer of assets, it will not make Mr. Smith ineligible for Medicaid because transfers between spouses do not effect eligibility. This transfer will, however, give you more than the $74,820 in resources which Medicaid regulations say that the community spouse of an institutionalized Medicaid recipient may have. This means that you will have to refuse, in writing, to support Mr. Smith before Medicaid will accept him. Medicaid

§ 23.124 ELDER LAW Ch. 23

must then provide coverage for him. Their recourse against you for holding onto the additional funds is to sue you in court.

You have some valid defenses against a suit because your income is below the income allowance which the Medicaid regulations state that the community spouse of an institutionalized Medicaid recipient should have. You are entitled to retain sufficient resources to produce the additional income required to bring your income up to the Medicaid income allowance of $1,919.

DISCLAIMER

Please note that you are my client and not your husband or children: He is free to accept my advice, reject it, or to seek his own attorney.

ATTORNEY FEES

You have paid a consultation fee which includes the consultation and this letter. All additional services will be billed hourly. My current billing rate is $200.00 per hour.

If you have any questions, do not hesitate to contact me.

Sincerely yours,

John Elder Law, Esq.

§ 23.125 Forms—Health Care Proxy Statutory Form[1]

The Public Health Law contains the following statutory form[2] for appointment of a health care proxy.[3] *Id.*

I [*name of principal*] hereby appoint [*name, address and telephone number of agent*] as my health care agent to make any and all health care decisions for me, except to the extent I state otherwise.

This health care proxy shall take effect in the event I become unable to make my own health care decisions.

NOTE: Although not necessary, and neither encouraged nor discouraged, you may wish to state instructions or wishes, and limit your agent's authority. Unless your agent knows your wishes about artificial nutrition and hydration, your agent will not have authority to decide about artificial nutrition and hydration. If you choose to state instructions, wishes or limits, please do so below:[4]

§ 23.125
1. *See supra,* § 23.2.
2. Public Health Law § 2981.5(d).
3. **PRACTICE POINTER**: Use of the statutory form is not required, but is highly recommended since it will be most familiar to providers and is unlikely to result in challenges to the agent's authority.
4. **PRACTICE POINTER**: The agent may not make decisions concerning artificial nutrition and hydration unless the principal's wishes concerning these treat-

Ch. 23   HEALTH CARE PROXY STATUTORY FORM § 23.125

I direct my agent to make health care decisions in accordance with my wishes and instructions as stated above or as otherwise known to him or her. I also direct my agent to abide by any limitations on his or her authority as stated above or as otherwise known to him or her.

In the event the person I appoint above is unable, unwilling or unavailable to act as my health care agent, I hereby appoint [*name, address and telephone number of alternate agent*] as my health care agent.[5] Pub He § 2981.6[6]

I understand that unless I revoke it, this proxy will remain in effect indefinitely or until the date or occurrence of the condition I have stated below:

[*Please complete the following if you do NOT want this health care proxy to be in effect indefinitely*]:

This proxy shall expire: [*Specify date or condition*][7]

Signature: _____

Address: _____

Date: _____

I declare that the person who signed or asked another to sign this document is personally known to me and appears to be of sound mind and acting willingly and free from duress. He or she signed [*or asked another to sign for him or her*] this document in my presence and that person signed in my presence. I am not the person appointed as agent by this document.

Witness: _____

Address: _____

Witness: _____

Address: _____

ments are known. Thus, it is recommended that the following language be inserted into the statutory form:

"My agent has been informed of my wishes concerning artificial nutrition and hydration and has been authorized to make decisions concerning these treatments."

Experienced Elder Law practitioners differ on the question of whether the form should contain other specific limitations or instructions concerning medical care. Specific instructions may provide moral support and guidance to the principal and are more likely to be honored by medical providers. However, they may result in medical providers second guessing the agent's interpretations of the wishes of the principal.

5. The principal may appoint alternate or successor agents. However, there is no provision for appointment of joint agents.

6. Public Health Law § 2981.6.

7. In the absence of such a provision, the proxy shall remain in effect until revoked. Public Health Law § 2981.5(c).

Library References:

West's Key No. Digests, Physicians and Surgeons ⊙=42, 44.

§ 23.126 Forms—Sample Living Will[1]

I, _____, of the County of _____, State of New York, have made the following decisions with respect to my medical care and treatment in the event I am unable for any reason to make known my wishes at the time medical decisions must be made.

   1. *Directive not to use or to discontinue life-prolonging medical treatment when recovery is unlikely.*

In the event I suffer from an injury, disease, illness or other physical or mental condition which renders me unable to make medical decisions on my own behalf, which leaves me unable to communicate meaningfully with others, and from which there is no reasonable prospect of recovery to a cognitive and sentient life, I direct that no medical treatments or procedures be utilized in my care, or if begun, that they be discontinued.

   2. *Definition of medical treatment*

By "medical treatments or procedures", I mean interventions by medical doctors, nurses, paramedics, or any other health care provider (including a nursing home) in the care of my body and mind, and including all medical and surgical procedures(mechanical or otherwise), treatments and therapies (including drugs and hormones) which may substitute for, replace, supplant, enhance or assist any bodily function. This specifically includes maintenance of respiration, nutrition and hydration by artificial means. With respect to all medical treatments or procedures, I include both existing technology and any methods or techniques which may hereafter be developed and perfected.

   3. *Provision for pain control.*

I ask that medical treatment to alleviate pain, to provide comfort and to mitigate suffering be provided even if it may hasten my death.

   4. *Determination of prognosis.*

This declaration is intended to serve as a guide to assist my duly appointed health care agent in making medical decisions on my behalf. However, it is not intended to limit my health care agent's sole discretion to interpret this document and to make medical decisions in good faith after full consideration of my medical condition and prognosis. If my health care agent is unable to serve for any reason, any other person shall comply with my directions upon certification by two physicians that my condition is as described in Section 1, above.

   5. *Acknowledgement of effects of this Living Will.*

§ 23.126   1. *See supra,* § 23.2.

I make and execute this Living Will knowing that, if complied with, my death may occur sooner than it would were all available and appropriate medical treatments considered and used. I accept this as a necessary result of a decision to avoid dependence and pain. I make this decision now, after careful consideration, to assure that I will have the level of medical care that I want, and to relieve others of the burden of decision.

IN WITNESS WHEREOF, I have hereunto set my hand and seal this _____ day of _____, 199__.

ACKNOWLEDGEMENT

_____, the declarant named in the foregoing instrument, signed this instrument consisting of three typewritten pages (including this attestation page) on the _____ day of _____, 199__ . At that time, (s)he declared that the instrument reflects his/her will and intent with respect to his/her medical care and treatment. At her request, in his/her presence and in the presence of each other, each of us believing him/her to be of sound mind, emotionally and mentally competent, we have signed our names as witnesses.

_____ residing at _____

_____ residing at _____

Library References:

West's Key No. Digests, Physicians and Surgeons ⚖=45.

Chapter 24

ESTATE PLANNING

by
Gideon Rothschild

Table of Sections

24.1 Scope Note.
24.2 Strategy.
24.3 Wills.
24.4 ____ Execution Requirements.
24.5 ____ ____ Signature.
24.6 ____ ____ Publication.
24.7 ____ ____ Witnesses.
24.8 ____ ____ Self Proving Affidavit.
24.9 ____ Provisions—Personal Property Dispositions.
24.10 ____ ____ Debts and Taxes.
24.11 ____ ____ Real Property.
24.12 ____ ____ Residuary Estate.
24.13 ____ ____ Dispositions in Trust.
24.14 ____ ____ Guardianships.
24.15 ____ ____ Appointment of Executors and Trustees.
24.16 ____ ____ Fiduciary Powers.
24.17 ____ ____ Miscellaneous.
24.18 Federal Estate and Gift Taxes.
24.19 ____ Rates.
24.20 New York State Estate and Gift Tax.
24.21 Estate Tax Planning—Utilizing the Unified Credit.
24.22 ____ Utilizing the Marital Deduction.
24.23 ____ Formula Clauses.
24.24 Generation Skipping Transfer Tax.
24.25 ____ Taxable Termination.
24.26 ____ Direct Skip.
24.27 ____ Taxable Distribution.
24.28 ____ Generation Assignment.
24.29 ____ Multiple Skips.
24.30 ____ Exemption.
24.31 ____ "Reverse QTIP."
24.32 Charitable Bequests.
24.33 Planning With Certain Assets.
24.34 ____ Life Insurance.
24.35 ____ ____ Life Insurance Trusts.
24.36 ____ ____ ____ "Crummey Powers."

Ch. 24 ESTATE PLANNING

24.37 ____ Retirement Benefits.
24.38 ____ Closely Held Business Interests.
24.39 ____ ____ Buy-Sell Agreements.
24.40 ____ ____ Liquidity Issues.
24.41 ____ ____ Minority Discounts.
24.42 ____ Farms and Business Real Property.
24.43 ____ Installment Obligations.
24.44 Lifetime Planning.
24.45 ____ Valuation of Gifts.
24.46 ____ ____ Grantor Retained Trusts.
24.47 ____ ____ Residence Trusts.
24.48 ____ ____ ____ Income Tax Considerations.
24.49 ____ Annual Gift Tax Exclusion.
24.50 ____ ____ Section 2503(c) Trusts.
24.51 ____ ____ Uniform Transfers to Minor's Act Accounts.
24.52 ____ ____ Crummey Trusts.
24.53 ____ ____ Family Limited Partnerships.
24.54 ____ Charitable Remainder Trusts.
24.55 ____ Charitable Lead Trusts.
24.56 Planning in Special Situations—Terminally Ill.
24.57 ____ ____ Self-Canceling Installment Notes.
24.58 ____ Non-citizen Spouses.
24.59 ____ Multiple Marriages.
24.60 ____ ____ Spousal Rights.
24.61 ____ ____ ____ Joint Wills and Contracts to Make Wills.
24.62 ____ ____ Long Term Care.
24.63 ____ Separation.
24.64 ____ Divorce.
24.65 ____ ____ Death During Divorce Proceeding.
24.66 ____ Unmarried Couples.
24.67 Postmortem Planning.
24.68 ____ Disclaimers.
24.69 ____ ____ Disclaimer Trusts.
24.70 ____ ____ Creditor Avoidance.
24.71 ____ ____ New York Statutory Requirements.
24.72 ____ Partial QTIP Election.
24.73 ____ Electing Alternate Valuation Date.
24.74 ____ Allocation of Income and Expenses.
24.75 ____ ____ U.S. Savings Bonds.
24.76 ____ ____ Expenses.
24.77 ____ Choosing the Fiscal Year of the Estate.
24.78 ____ Electing to File Joint Return with Decedent's Spouse.
24.79 ____ Waiving Commissions.
24.80 Probate Avoidance.
24.81 ____ Revocable Trusts.
24.82 ____ Totten Trusts.
24.83 ____ Jointly Held Assets.
24.84 Asset Protection.
24.85 ____ Statutory Exemptions.
24.86 ____ Family Partnerships.
24.87 ____ Domestic Trusts.

24.88 ___ Foreign Trusts.
24.89 Powers of Attorney.
24.90 Advance Directives.
24.91 ___ Health Care Proxy.
24.92 ___ Living Will.
24.93 Ethical Considerations in Estate Planning.
24.94 ___ Multiple Clients.
24.95 ___ Attorney/Draftsman as Fiduciary or Beneficiary.
24.96 Forms
24.97 ___ Estate Planner's Checklist. 💾
24.98 ___ Sample Information Request Letter. 💾
24.99 ___ Client Questionnaire. 💾
24.100 ___ "Durable" Power of Attorney Form. 💾
24.101 ___ Crummey Notice. 💾
24.102 ___ Spousal Conflicts Letter. 💾

WESTLAW Electronic Research

See WESTLAW Electronic Research Guide preceding the Summary of Contents.

§ 24.1 Scope Note

This chapter provides an overview of issues which a New York practitioner must consider when assisting clients in planning transfers of their wealth, both during their lifetime and upon their death. In addition to discussing formal requirements of a will, we discuss estate, gift and generation skipping transfer tax regimes and methods of minimizing such taxes. We also reflect on the myriad of special situations which the practitioner may encounter, such as planning for terminally ill persons or for persons who have been married more than once.[1]

The requirements for a valid will, or for a trust or other nontestamentary instrument, are determined by state law. The substantive statutory requirements for a will or trust are found in the New York Estates, Powers and Trusts Law ("EPTL"). The discussion of the nature of a will, the requirements for a valid New York will, and suggested will provisions are found in sections 24.4 through 24.17.

To a large measure, estate planning involves the ultimate preservation and transfer of assets to intended beneficiaries, either during a person's lifetime or upon their death. In order to properly prepare an estate plan, the practitioner must be cognizant of the consequences of the relevant federal and state transfer taxes. The substantive law regarding the federal estate, gift, and generation skipping transfer taxes is found in chapters 11 through 13 of the Internal Revenue Code of 1986

§ 24.1

1. See Preminger, et al., Trusts and Es- tates Practice in New York (West 1997).

("I.R.C."), as amended,[2] in the Treasury regulations thereunder, in caselaw, and in administrative interpretations. Similarly, New York State also imposes estate and gift taxes, pursuant to New York tax law,[3] regulations, and caselaw. The discussion of the transfer tax system, and planning suggestions to minimize these taxes, is found in sections 24.18 through 24.58.

In order to make this subject more readily understandable to practitioners, the discussion is divided into several major categories:

- Estate tax planning is covered in sections 24.21 to 24.23;
- Generation skipping transfer tax planning, involving the tax on transfers to persons two generations removed from the transferor, such as grandchildren, is covered in sections 24.24 to 24.31;
- Charitable bequests is covered in section 24.32;
- Planning with certain assets, namely assets which require special considerations, such as life insurance, closely held businesses, and installment obligations, is covered in sections 24.33 to 24.43;
- Lifetime planning involving the plan for lifetime dispositions in order to minimize transfer taxes and to accomplish specific client goals, is covered in sections 24.44 to 24.55;
- Planning in special situations, such as for terminally ill persons, persons who have been married more than once, non-citizen spouses, and unmarried couples, is covered in sections 24.56 to 24.66; and
- Postmortem planning is covered in sections 24.67 through 24.79.

Estate planners today are often called upon to minimize, to the extent possible, the time and non-tax costs involved in transferring assets at death to an intended beneficiary. Thus, an estate planner must be familiar with the means by which probate[4] can be avoided, and this issue is covered in sections 24.80 through 24.83.

Due to the highly litigious nature of our society, as well as the ordinary business risks that people face daily, some clients may be at substantial risk of losing most or all of their assets during their lifetime. Thus, comprehensive estate planning must also take into account the need to protect assets *before* creditor problems arise. The issues and techniques involved in protecting assets from creditors are discussed in section 24.84 to 24.88.

Sections 24.89 through 24.92 discuss certain ancillary issues related to estate planning, namely planning for incapacity. These issues have become an increasingly large concern for clients who, while living, may

---

2. 26 U.S.C.A. §§ 1 *et seq.*

3. For gifts made on or after January 1, 2000, the gift tax is repealed. L.1997, Ch. 389.

4. *See* Chapter 25 "Probate and Estate Administration," *infra.*

become incapable of managing their financial affairs or of making medical decisions.[5]

No discussion on estate planning would be complete without a consideration of ethical issues. In particular, sections 24.93 through 24.95 discuss whether there are conflicts of interest when representing a married couple, and other related issues.

The final sections of this chapter contain a checklist, an introductory letter to clients, a client questionnaire and a conflict letter to be used when representing both husband and wife. A table, referencing chapter sections to appropriate West's McKinney's Forms concludes the chapter.

§ 24.2 Strategy

Prior to meeting with a client for the first time, the client should be provided a questionnaire which will provide all the information necessary to create an estate plan. Besides the obvious personal information that must be obtained such as name, address, and phone numbers, the practitioner needs to determine the client's age, citizenship, marital status (single, divorced, or widowed), age and citizenship of spouse or significant other, number and ages of children and grandchildren, and whether the children are from a prior marriage. If the client has minor children, the estate planner needs to ascertain who the client would want to take care of the children in the event that he dies before the children reach majority.

The estate planner also needs to know whether there are any special circumstances which might affect the design of an appropriate estate plan, such as mental or physical disabilities of any intended beneficiary. Further, the estate planner must determine whether any of the beneficiaries, or the client, has existing or potential creditor problems.

Finally, but perhaps most important, is the need to ascertain the estate's liquidity. The attorney must identify the cash needed to pay debts, funeral expenses, administrative expenses and estate taxes. Obviously, the use of life insurance may provide the necessary liquidity. Married clients may wish to consider the popular second-to-die policies offered by most companies for just this purpose since the estate taxes are not due until the second death, assuming the optimum marital deduction is utilized. However, the client should not be the owner of such insurance.[1] Other ways to overcome liquidity problems include reducing the taxable estate by lifetime gifts; using a buy-sell agreement, and where the client owns a closely held business, taking advantage of provisions

---

5. A related subject to both estate planning and issues regarding incapacity involves "Medicaid planning," which involves planning for the preservation of assets in the event that long term care, i.e., institutionalization or home care, is required. This related subject is discussed in detail elsewhere and will therefore not be included herein. See Chapter 22 "Guardianship," supra and Chapter 23 "Elder Law," supra.

§ 24.2

1. See infra, § 24.34.

allowing installment payments of taxes and redemption of closely held stock.[2]

Needless to say, an accurate financial snapshot is crucial in determining the appropriate method for planning an estate. The practitioner needs to examine not only the aggregate net worth of the client, but also what constitutes a client's net worth. Does the client own a home? Does the client have any individual retirement accounts ("IRAs"), Keogh accounts, or other retirement assets? Does the client own a business? Does the client have life insurance, and if so, is it adequate? Does the client own installment obligations? Are the assets held jointly with the spouse or children, or separately?

The planner must identify the client's goals, and must inquire if there are goals other than to minimize taxes. How generously does the client want to provide for his spouse? Does he want assets for a spouse or children to be held in trust or paid outright? Does he want to put aside funds for educational purposes? Does he want to provide for grandchildren? Is the client charitably inclined?

Clients must also consider who might be named as appropriate trustees and executors. Should family members be appointed, or should professional advisors, such as accountants, lawyers, and financial advisors be appointed? Should a professional fiduciary, such as a bank, be appointed?[3] The client should consider the possibility for conflicts or adverse interests between trustees and beneficiaries.

The advisor also needs information regarding prior transfers of wealth by the client, and whether the client is receptive to making future gifts. A balanced approach should be utilized—one that recognizes the clients' own needs for financial security balanced with the tax savings goals.

A client questionnaire can help both the client and the estate planner consider the myriad of needs that must be addressed.[4]

§ 24.3 Wills

A will is a declaration of a person's wishes as to the disposition of his property, including, in some circumstances, his body.[1] In addition, a

2. See infra, § 24.40.

3. While the client might initially have some ideas regarding beneficiaries, fiduciaries, and goals, a knowledgeable estate planner must provide the client with information that the client might not have known when formulating his initial ideas, such as tax considerations or the advisability of using a corporate, as opposed to an individual, fiduciary. The final decisions must be made by the client, but it is the estate planner's duty to ensure that the decisions made by a client are informed ones.

4. See infra, §§ 24.98–24.99 for a sample of an information request letter and a sample client questionnaire.

§ 24.3

1. PRACTICE POINTER: While a will can direct the funeral and burial wishes, it is generally advisable to provide such directions in a separate writing since

will sets forth the source of any payments of taxes, debts and expenses of administering the estate, and appoints the executors, trustees and guardians for minors.

Failure to dispose of assets either by will, or by other testamentary substitutes, such as life insurance, joint accounts, trusts and retirement plan designations, results in intestacy. Property passing through intestacy becomes distributable to the decedent's heirs as determined by the New York statute of descent and distribution.[2] If there are no living heirs, then such property "escheats" to the state.[3]

Even if property does not escheat to the state, intestacy often results in dispositions that the decedent might not have expected or desired. For example, where a person dies intestate with a spouse and two children, the first $50,000 plus ½ of the remaining estate assets will pass to the spouse, and the remainder is distributed to the children.[4] Real property, however, passes by intestacy pursuant to the law of the jurisdiction where the property is situated.

A will also offers estate tax planning opportunities, as well as the ability to use testamentary trusts to control the timing and method of distributions benefiting a decedent's spouse or descendants. While many of these goals can be met through the establishment of *inter vivos* vehicles, such as the popular "probate avoidance" device known as the revocable "living" trust, assets not transferred to the trust will still possibly pass by intestacy if a will is not executed.[5]

§ 24.4 Wills—Execution Requirements

The requirements for the execution of a valid will under New York law, other than a nuncupative or holographic will,[1] are as follows:

(1) Subscription, meaning the signature of the testator at the end of the document;

(2) Publication; and

(3) Witnesses.[2]

---

the will is often not read until after the funeral and burial arrangements are made.

2. EPTL Art. 4.

3. *See* Abandoned Property Law § 103(b)(i); In re Melrose Ave. in Borough of the Bronx, 234 N.Y. 48, 136 N.E. 235 (1922); In re Hammond's Estate, 2 A.D.2d 160, 154 N.Y.S.2d 820 (2d Dep't 1956), aff'd 3 N.Y.2d 567, 170 N.Y.S.2d 505, 147 N.E.2d 777 (1958).

4. EPTL § 4–1.1.

5. *See infra*, § 24.81 for a discussion of the advantages and disadvantages of revocable trusts.

§ 24.4

1. A nuncupative will is an oral will made in front of two witnesses, and a holographic will is one written entirely in the testator's handwriting, but without any of the regular formalities. Holographic and nuncupative wills are only valid under certain circumstances for mariners while at sea or members of the armed services. EPTL § 3–2.2.

2. EPTL § 3–2.1. A fourth procedure, which is to have the witnesses sign an affidavit attesting to the execution of the will, is not required for the will to be admitted to probate, but is highly desirable. *See infra*, § 24.8.

§ 24.5 Wills—Execution Requirements—Signature

The testator must sign the will at the end of the instrument, but above the witnesses' attestation clause.[1] If someone is signing for the testator, he must sign the testator's name in the testator's presence and, at the testator's direction, must sign his own name and affix his own address to the will.[2] West's McKinney's Forms, appropriate to this section, are available.[3]

Library References:

West's Key No. Digests, Wills ⟜111.

§ 24.6 Wills—Execution Requirements—Publication

The testator must declare to the attesting witnesses that the document he has signed or is about to sign is his last will and testament.[1] Generally, this is satisfied by having the attorney conducting the will execution ceremony ask the testator, in the witnesses' presence, "Is this your will?" and by the testator responding affirmatively.

Library References:

West's Key No. Digests, Wills ⟜119.

§ 24.7 Wills—Execution Requirements—Witnesses

In order for a will to be valid in New York, there must be at least two attesting witnesses. The witnesses do not actually have to see the testator sign the will. The will can either be signed in the presence of the witnesses, or the testator can acknowledge in their presence that he signed the will.[1] The witnesses must, at the request of the testator, sign the will and affix their addresses.[2] The two witnesses must both attest to either witnessing the testator sign his will or both attest that he acknowledged that he signed the will, within 30 days of each other.[3]

§ 24.5

1. Provisions of a will below the testator's signature have no effect. EPTL § 3–2.1(a)(1)(B).

2. EPTL § 3–2.1(a)(1). Failure to add the address of the person executing the will for the testator, however, does not invalidate the will. EPTL § 3–2.1(a)(1)(C).

CAVEAT: A person who signs the will for the testator cannot be counted as one of the witnesses to the will. EPTL § 3–2.1(a)(1)(C).

3. *See* West's McKinney's Forms—Estate and Surrogate's Practice §§ 7:71–7:72 (testimonium clause).

§ 24.6

1. EPTL § 3–2.1(a)(3).

§ 24.7

1. EPTL § 3–2.1(a)(2).

2. EPTL § 3–2.1(a)(4).

3. EPTL §§ 3–2.1(a)(3), (4). Failure to affix the address, however, does not invalidate the will. EPTL § 3–2.1(a)(4).

A beneficiary should not act as a witness to the will. While a will is not automatically invalid if a beneficiary acts as a witness, if there are not two other disinterested witnesses, any disposition to the beneficiary-witness is void.[4] This does not mean that the beneficiary is *precluded* from receiving the bequest, because if the invalidity of the bequest results in an intestacy and the beneficiary-witness would be the intestate taker, then the beneficiary would receive the bequest.[5] West's McKinney's Forms, appropriate to this section, are available.[6]

Library References:
West's Key No. Digests, Wills ⇐113.

§ 24.8 Wills—Execution Requirements—Self-Proving Affidavit

A self-proving affidavit signed by the witnesses indicates that the testator had testamentary capacity and that the will was executed in accordance with the statutory requirements. While neither the EPTL nor the Surrogate Court Procedure Act ("SCPA") requires that one be signed at the will execution, good practice dictates including one. This will avoid having to locate the witnesses many years later when the testator dies.[1]

West's McKinney's Forms, appropriate to this section, are available.[2]

§ 24.9 Wills—Provisions—Personal Property Dispositions

Most wills have a provision calling for the disposition of tangible personal property to one or more beneficiaries. This provision can either be extremely specific, *e.g.*, "my pear shaped 3 karat diamond engagement ring to my daughter, Ellen, if she survives me," or can provide for all tangible personal property to be distributed to one or more beneficiaries. The provision can also be drafted to give the executor discretion in dividing assets among a class of beneficiaries, in deciding which property should be preserved for in-kind distributions to minor beneficiaries, or to permit the sale of property for the benefit of the residuary beneficiaries.[1]

---

4. EPTL § 3–3.2(a).
5. EPTL § 3–3.2(a)(3).
6. *See* West's McKinney's Forms—Estate and Surrogate's Practice §§ 7:76–7:78 (attestation clause).

§ 24.8
1. **PRACTICE POINTER:** The law requires generally that witness affidavits be submitted with a probate petition, or otherwise requires the testimony of the witnesses to the will execution. SCPA § 1404. If the witnesses cannot be located, then the will cannot be admitted to probate, unless the witness' signatures can be authenticated to the satisfaction of the Surrogate. SCPA § 1405. The self-proving affidavit avoids delays, litigation, and the potential that the testator's desires will be frustrated.

2. *See* West's McKinney's Forms—Estate and Surrogate's Practice §§ 7:85–7:86 (self-proving affidavit).

§ 24.9
1. *See infra*, § 24.12.

The personal property clause should also reflect the testator's desire with respect to expenses relating to storing, packing, shipping, or insuring the property. For example, since the beneficiaries of tangible personal property might not have been bequeathed liquid assets, the testator might be advised to specifically declare such expenses to be administration expenses payable by the estate.[2]

A well drafted tangible personal property clause will also state whether art and other collectibles, such as coin collections, are included as tangible personal property for the purposes of the disposition.[3]

West's McKinney's Forms, appropriate to this section, are available.[4]

§ 24.10 Wills—Provisions—Debts and Taxes

Although not necessary, a will generally has a provision directing the executor to pay the testator's funeral expenses, existing debts, expenses of administering the estate, and estate taxes. Under the law such debts and expenses are payable by the estate, and only if the estate is insufficient then such expenses and debts of the decedent and taxes are to be paid by the beneficiaries in the following order of priority:

(1) Distributees;

(2) Residuary beneficiaries;[1]

(3) General beneficiaries, meaning beneficiaries receiving a gift that is not of a particular thing or from a particular fund;[2]

(4) Specific beneficiaries, meaning beneficiaries receiving a specified or identified item of the testator's property;[3] and

---

2. Note that unless otherwise indicated, expenses relating to specifically bequeathed property are not properly chargeable to the estate as administration expenses. *See* In re Boerner's Will, 58 Misc.2d 144, 294 N.Y.S.2d 725 (Surr.Ct., Yates County, 1968); In re Morawetz' Will, 35 Misc.2d 762, 231 N.Y.S.2d 1000 (Surr.Ct., Albany County, 1962).

3. *See* In re Estate of Rothko, 77 Misc.2d 168, 352 N.Y.S.2d 574 (Surr.Ct., N.Y. County, 1974) (dispute over bequest of household contents included art collection); In re Frohmann's Will, 205 Misc. 913, 133 N.Y.S.2d 239 (Surr.Ct., N.Y. County, 1954) ("personal effects" did not include a stamp collection).

CAVEAT: A separate letter or memorandum of instruction telling the executor to give pieces of tangible personal property to specific persons that is not executed with the formalities of a will is not a codicil, and is not binding on the executor, even if the will makes specific reference to such letter. Thus, any reference to such letter or memorandum should be precatory in nature, since the executor will have no legal duty to obey the separate letter.

EXAMPLE: "My Executor shall distribute my tangible personal property to such persons as he shall determine in his sole and absolute discretion. It is my wish, however, that my Executor will distribute such tangible personal property in accordance with a memorandum of instruction that is located in my safe deposit box at X Bank."

4. *See* West's McKinney's Forms—Estate and Surrogate's Practice §§ 7:135–7:138 (personal property dispositions).

§ 24.10

1. *See infra*, § 24.12.

2. EPTL § 1–2.8; Crawford v. McCarthy, 159 N.Y. 514, 54 N.E. 277 (1899), reh'g denied 160 N.Y. 668, 55 N.E. 1094 (1899).

3. EPTL § 1–2.16; Crawford v. McCarthy, *supra* note 2.

(5) A surviving spouse to whom a disposition qualifying for the estate tax marital deduction has been made.[4]

Such debts and expenses, without allocation by the testator in his will, are apportioned *pro rata* among the class of beneficiaries.[5]

In the absence of a will provision apportioning estate and death tax burdens, estate and death taxes are generally apportioned among all beneficiaries of the decedent's gross estate, including beneficiaries of nontestamentary provisions such as insurance and assets held in revocable *inter vivos* trusts, with exemptions allocated to charitable bequests and marital bequests qualifying for the marital deduction,[6] and for insurance proceeds inuring to a charity or a spouse.[7]

The testator may provide that taxes be charged against the residuary estate,[8] so that pre-residuary bequests and nontestamentary dispositions will not be liable for the taxes. However, if federal estate tax liability is incurred due to bequests or non-testamentary dispositions which do not qualify for the marital deduction and exceed the unified credit, the tax allocation clause must be drafted with caution.[9]

Where the marital deduction is obtained in the estate of the first spouse to die, the marital property remaining at the second spouse's death is subject to estate tax. Unless the surviving spouse specifically directs otherwise, I.R.C. § 2207A and EPTL § 2–1.12 provide for the right to recover the *increased* tax which results from such inclusion from the persons receiving such property. A direction in the surviving spouse's will (or revocable trust) to the contrary must specifically indicate an intent to waive any right of recovery with respect to such QTIP property.[10]

West's McKinney's Forms, appropriate to this section, are available.[11]

§ 24.11   Wills—Provisions—Real Property

Generally, when the testator owns real property, other than investment property, a separate clause disposing of such property is advisable.

---

4. EPTL § 12–1.2; *see also*, EPTL § 12–1.3 (same order of priority for insolvent estate).

5. EPTL § 12–1.3.

6. *See infra*, § 24.22.

7. EPTL § 2–1.8.

8. *See infra*, § 24.12.

9. CAVEAT: Too often practitioners allocate all expenses and death taxes to the residuary without considering whether nontestamentary dispositions have left the residuary with insufficient assets to provide anything to the residuary beneficiaries after expenses, or whether estate taxes may result in apportionment to non-taxable residuary beneficiaries, such as charities or a surviving spouse. If taxes are apportioned to such non-taxable beneficiaries there will be an overall tax increase since the marital or charitable tax deduction must be reduced by the amount of tax allocated thereto, requiring an interrelated calculation.

10. Qualified terminable interest property. *See infra*, § 24.22.

11. *See* West's McKinney's Forms—Estate and Surrogate's Practice §§ 7:412–7:416 (apportionment of taxes); § 7:423 (payment of expenses clause); § 7:232 (payment of expenses clause—real estate).

Such a provision is important because a specifically devised asset will not carry out any of the estate's distributable net income ("DNI"). In other words, the beneficiary who receives the property specifically devised will not be charged with receiving income earned by the estate during its administration.[1]

West's McKinney's Forms, appropriate to this section, are available.[2]

§ 24.12 Wills—Provisions—Residuary Estate

Any properly drafted will has a "catchall" provision providing for the disposition of the "rest, residue and remainder" of the testator's property, *i.e.*, all probate property that was not otherwise disposed of by the will. This is known as the "residuary clause." Having a residuary clause in the will is crucial, because without it, the testator would have to separately list all property in order to avoid a potential intestacy.[1] The residuary clause can dispose of assets outright, in trust, pour over assets into an *inter vivos* trust, or provide for some combination of the above. The value of assets allocated to the residuary estate can also be established by formula to maximize use of the unified credit exemption equivalent and marital deduction.[2]

West's McKinney's Forms, appropriate to this section, are available.[3]

§ 24.13 Wills—Provisions—Dispositions in Trust

The testator can provide that bequests be held in trust rather than paid outright to the beneficiary. Testamentary trusts can be established to provide for one or more persons during their lifetime(s) with the remainder going to other beneficiaries. For example, a trust can provide lifetime benefits to a surviving spouse, and remainder to children. Trusts can also be used to postpone distributions of large amounts to relatively young beneficiaries, instead spreading out payments of principal over time.

Retaining estate assets in trust may also be advantageous if the beneficiary is at risk of losing any outright dispositions to creditors or soon-to-be ex-spouses. Similarly, placing money in trust for a beneficiary who is either a minor, a spendthrift, a substance abuser, or simply

---

§ 24.11

1. Rev. Rul. 68-49, 1968-1 C.B. 304; I.R.C. § 663(a).

CAVEAT: However, if an estate is not large enough to fund a Credit Shelter Trust with other property, in order to use the applicable exemption, a specific bequest of real property may result in underutilization of the exemption. *See infra*, § 24.21.

2. *See* West's McKinney's Forms—Estate and Surrogate's Practice §§ 7:218-7:229 (real estate dispositions).

§ 24.12

1. EPTL § 3-3.4; Estate of Markus, 188 A.D.2d 361, 591 N.Y.S.2d 35 (1st Dep't 1992).

2. *See infra*, §§ 24.21-24.22.

3. *See* West's McKinney's Forms—Estate and Surrogate's Practice §§ 7:348-7:355, 7:357 (residuary provisions).

incapable of properly handling money is clearly more desirable than an outright bequest.

Planners often recommend trusts to:

(1) Take advantage of the federal estate tax unified credit while adequately providing for a surviving spouse by using "credit shelter trusts,"[1]

(2) Take advantage of generation skipping transfers,[2] and

(3) Provide for the supplemental (or "luxury") needs of a recipient of governmental assistance without disqualifying the beneficiary from receiving his or her benefits.[3]

§ 24.14 Wills—Provisions—Guardianships

If the testator has minor children, then the will should name guardians in the event that both parents die during the children's minority. The role of guardian may be bifurcated between a guardian of the person and a guardian of the property.[1]

In the event that one of the parents is still living, a provision in the will naming someone other than the surviving parent as a guardian (even a parent who was not awarded custody in a divorce action) will not be effective as to the guardianship of the person,[2] but such a clause has been construed to identify the named guardian as the donee of a power in trust as to any property passing to the minor child under the deceased parent's will.[3] Giving the donee a power in trust, in effect, results in a constructive trust for the minor's benefit.

West's McKinney's Forms, appropriate to this section, are available.[4]

§ 24.15 Wills—Provisions—Appointment of Executors and Trustees

The will should provide for appointment of one or more persons to serve as executor and trustee of any testamentary trusts established, as well as successor executors or trustees in case one or more of the chosen

---

§ 24.13

1. See infra, § 24.21. These are also commonly referred to as "by-pass" or "exempt" trusts.

2. See infra, §§ 24.24, et seq.

3. Discussion of Medicaid planning is beyond the scope of this chapter. It is discussed in detail in Chapter 23 "Elder Law," supra.

§ 24.14

1. DRL § 81. See also, Chapter 22 "Guardianship", supra.

2. Matter of Thorne, 240 N.Y. 444, 148 N.E. 630 (1925); Will of Tunney, 101 Misc.2d 1058, 422 N.Y.S.2d 622 (Surr.Ct., Nassau County, 1979); Armstrong v. Grimes, 70 Misc.2d 549, 334 N.Y.S.2d 558 (Fam.Ct., N.Y. County, 1972).

3. See e.g., In re Roy's Will, 9 Misc.2d 991, 174 N.Y.S.2d 119 (Surr.Ct., Nassau County, 1957).

4. See West's McKinney's Forms—Estate and Surrogate's Practice §§ 7:379–7:382 (guardianship clause).

fiduciaries cannot serve, resigns, or becomes incapable of doing so.[1] Individuals or corporations authorized by law may serve as executors or trustees except for the following persons who are disqualified from serving:

(1) An infant;

(2) An incompetent;

(3) A nondomiciliary alien, except for a natural person who is either the spouse, grandparent or descendent of the testator's grandparent, grandparent or descendent of the testator's spouse, or the spouse of any such person, provided that such nondomiciliary alien must serve with one or more co-fiduciaries, one of whom is a New York resident;

(4) A felon; or

(5) A person who is incompetent due to drunkenness, dishonesty, improvidence or want of understanding.[2]

The testator should indicate whether his fiduciaries will be entitled to statutory commissions, pursuant to SCPA § 2307 for executors and § 2309 for trustees, or be entitled to corporate fiduciary fee schedules, and whether the testator waives a fiduciary bond.[3]

§ 24.16 Wills—Provisions—Fiduciary Powers

EPTL § 11–1.1 provides for a broad range of powers for fiduciaries, which may be broadened or limited by the testator's will. Among the powers that the draftsperson should consider including in a will, which are not included in EPTL § 11–1.1, are the following:

(1) The power to make all necessary tax elections for the estate, regardless of its effect on any one beneficiary;

§ 24.15

1. **CAVEAT:** For a discussion regarding the ethical considerations and statutory requirements involved in naming the attorney-draftsperson as a fiduciary, *see infra*, § 24.95.

2. SCPA § 707(1). A surrogate may also exercise his or her discretion to declare other persons ineligible, including a person unable to read or write English. SCPA § 707(2).

3. **PRACTICE POINTER:** In determining whether to permit family fiduciaries to be paid commissions, the practitioner and testator must bear in mind that such commissions reduce the overall estate, and therefore the estate taxes, but is taxable income to the fiduciary. Thus, the practitioner should determine whether the beneficiaries will be better off receiving funds as an inheritance or as a commission. If the testator does not specifically waive a bond, the surrogate may require one to be obtained. *See* SCPA § 806 (requiring bond where executor is required to hold, manage or invest personal or real property for benefit of another unless bond waived by will).

CAVEAT: While a testator may want to waive a bond in order to reduce expenses, if an individual fiduciary either absconds with or otherwise loses estate assets, the individual, but not a corporate fiduciary, may be "judgment proof." Under these circumstances, the cost of a fiduciary bond might be outweighed by the protection it affords the estate beneficiaries.

§ 24.16 ESTATE PLANNING Ch. 24

(2) The power to continue a business owned by the testator during administration of the estate;

(3) The power to retain assets owned by the testator at his death, regardless of risk or lack of diversification;

(4) The power to allocate between income and principal where such allocation is not clear under applicable law;

(5) The power to permit the executor or testamentary trustee to hold back dispositions in further trust;

(6) The power to permit the fiduciaries to engage in self-dealing[1] or to lend money to a beneficiary;[2] and

West's McKinney's Forms, appropriate to this section, are available.[3]

§ 24.17 Wills—Provisions—Miscellaneous

There are numerous other provisions that generally appear in a well-drafted will. Some of these are discussed below.

Minors Provision. A minor is under a legal disability to administer property, and, in any event, it would not be advisable to make outright gifts to minors. On the other hand, the executor may not want to hold property until the child reaches majority. A minor's provision can detail the various options that a fiduciary has when disposition to a minor is called for, including making payments to a custodian for a minor,[1] establishing a trust for the minor, giving the property to the minor's parents, if the gift is $5,000 or less,[2] or giving the property to the minor's guardian.

"Wipeout Clause." A provision supplementing the residuary clause, which provides for takers of last resort in the event no residuary beneficiaries survive. The purpose of this clause is to avoid potential escheat.

Power of Appointment. This clause indicates whether the testator is exercising any power of appointment, whether created by someone else's last will or *inter vivos* trust. This also causes the testator to consider *whether* he has a power of appointment, and whether he wants to exercise it.

§ 24.16

1. CAVEAT: The purpose of the general prohibition against self-dealing is to prevent a conflict between individual and fiduciary considerations. Generally, where family members are involved, and especially where the fiduciary is also the primary beneficiary, this is not a substantial risk. However, even where a will permits a fiduciary to engage in self-dealing, the fiduciary is still required to act honestly and in good faith. *See, e.g.,* O'Hayer v. De St. Aubin, 30 A.D.2d 419, 293 N.Y.S.2d 147 (2d Dep't 1968).

2. *See id.*

3. *See* West's McKinney's Forms—Estate and Surrogate's Practice §§ 7:375, 7:391–7:399 (executor and trustee powers).

§ 24.17

1. EPTL § 7-4.8.
2. SCPA § 2220; EPTL § 11-1.1(b)(9).

Simultaneous Death. This provides what will be presumed if it cannot be determined which of two persons died first. If no provision is made, EPTL § 2–1.6 provides, generally, that the testator survived.[3]

Alternate or Successor Fiduciaries. This provision permits the fiduciaries to name co-executors or co-trustees, and to name successors in the event that the will has not already provided for successors. In particular, it is useful to permit the fiduciaries to name co-executors or co-trustees in the event that an independent fiduciary is desirable, or necessary for tax reasons, in order to approve a distribution to a beneficiary-fiduciary. It may also be desirable to have a "trust protector" appointed with the power to discharge and appoint successor trustees.

Accountings. The testator can specify the extent that fiduciary accountings be rendered to beneficiaries.

Maximum Duration of Trusts. This is a savings provision to ensure that any trusts created by the will do not run afoul of the Rule Against Perpetuities or rules against accumulations.

West's McKinney's Forms, appropriate to this section, are available.[4]

§ 24.18 Federal Estate and Gift Taxes

The federal government, as well as many states, including New York, impose taxes on the transfer of wealth from one person to another. A gift made during a person's lifetime is subject to the gift tax. A transfer made upon a person's death is subject to the estate tax. In 1976, the federal estate and gift taxes were "unified," that is, the tax rates for lifetime gifts and bequests at death became uniform[1] and the exemption amount is applied to the aggregate gifts made during lifetime and transfers at death.[2] The computation of the estate tax now takes into account not only the decedent's taxable estate, namely all assets included for computing estate taxes, whether probate or nonprobate assets, less certain deductions, but also "adjusted taxable gifts" made during the decedent's lifetime, namely gifts subject to tax, less applicable deduc-

---

3. PRACTICE POINTER: Generally, for married testators, it is advisable for the will of the wealthier spouse to presume that the less-wealthy spouse is the survivor, and for such spouse's will to presume that the wealthier spouse predeceased the poorer spouse. This is done to ensure that (a) each spouse's unified credit is fully used, and (b) the lower estate tax rate imposed on the smaller estate is used.

4. *See* West's McKinney's Forms—Estate and Surrogate's Practice §§ 7:334–7:336, 7:339–7:340 (minors provisions); §§ 7:348, last four lines (wipeout clause); §§ 7:343–7:3344 (nonexercise of power of appointment); §§ 7:251–7:255 (simultaneous death clause); § 7:371 (successor fiduciaries clause); § 10.607 (maximum duration of trusts clause). **CAVEAT:** Although a beneficiary can be given the power to remove and appoint trustees, such power should be limited to appointing someone who is not related or subservient. See Rev. Rul. 95.58.

§ 24.18

1. I.R.C. §§ 2001, 2502.

2. I.R.C. §§ 2010, 2505. *See infra*, § 24.21 for a discussion of the unified credit.

§ 24.18   ESTATE PLANNING   Ch. 24

tions.[3] Since the estate and gift taxes are progressive taxes, that is, the more assets transferred, the higher the rate of taxation, the inclusion of taxable gifts in the estate tax computation ensures that the rate of taxation will be the same whether assets are transferred during lifetime or at death.[4]

The primary reduction of the federal estate and gift tax is the "unified credit." Essentially, the tax is computed by adding adjusted taxable gifts, that is, gifts subject to taxation less deductions, to the taxable estate. The taxable estate is the gross estate, less permitted deductions, including debts, administration expenses and the marital and charitable deductions. After the tax is computed, the transferor is entitled to the unified credit, against the amount of tax payable[5] and a credit for gift taxes previously paid.

EXAMPLE: In 1997, Gus Donor makes a taxable gift of $600,000 to his friend, Roberta Donee. Assuming that Gus has made no other taxable gifts during his lifetime, he would incur a federal gift tax of $192,800. However, Gus would not have to pay any federal gift tax, because he would apply his available $192,800 credit against the tax.

For gifts made or decedents dying on or before December 31, 1997 the exemption amount is $600,000. The Taxpayer Relief Act of 1997 increased the unified credit beginning in 1998. The exemption equivalent (referred to as the "applicable exclusion" amount) is determined as follows:

In the case of estates of decedents dying, and gifts made, during:	Applicable Exclusion Amount
1998	$625,000
1999	$650,000
2000 and 2001	$675,000
2002 and 2003	$700,000
2004	$850,000
2005	$950,000
2006	$1,000,000

§ 24.19   Federal Estate and Gift Taxes—Rates

The following are the rates imposed on taxable gifts or estates:[1]

3. I.R.C. § 2001(b).

4. **PRACTICE POINTER:** Note, however, that gifts made during lifetime are taxed on a tax-exclusive basis whereas the tax on transfers at death is calculated on a tax-inclusive basis. The effect of this is that lifetime gifts result in one-third less taxes being paid, provided the donor does not die within three years of the date of the gift. See infra, § 24.44.

5. I.R.C. §§ 2010(a), 2505(a).

§ 24.19

1. I.R.C. §§ 2001, 2502. These rates are applied prior to the application of the unified credit. See infra, § 24.21.

Ch. 24   RATES   § 24.19

If the amount with respect to which the tentative tax to be computed is:	The tentative tax is:
Not over $10,000	18 percent of such amount.
Over $10,000 but not over $20,000	$1,800, plus 20 percent of the excess of such amount over $10,000.
Over $20,000 but not over $40,000	$3,800, plus 22 percent of the excess of such amount over $20,000.
Over $40,000 but not over $60,000	$8,200, plus 24 percent of the excess of such amount over $40,000.
Over $60,000 but not over $80,000	$13,000, plus 26 percent of the excess of such amount over $60,000.
Over $80,000 but not over $100,000	$18,200, plus 28 percent of the excess of such amount over $80,000.
Over $100,000 but not over $150,000	$23,800, plus 30 percent of the excess of such amount over $100,000.
Over $150,000 but not over $250,000	$38,800, plus 32 percent of the excess of such amount over $150,000.
Over $250,000 but not over $500,000	$70,800, plus 34 percent of the excess of such amount over $250,000.
Over $500,000 but not over $750,000	$155,800, plus 37 percent of the excess of such amount over $500,000.
Over $750,000 but not over $1,000,000	$248,300, plus 39 percent of the excess of such amount over $750,000.
Over $1,000,000 but not over $1,250,000	$345,800, plus 41 percent of the excess of such amount over $1,000,000.
Over $1,250,000 but not over $1,500,000	$448,300, plus 43 percent of the excess of such amount over $1,250,000.

§ 24.19 ESTATE PLANNING Ch. 24

If the amount with respect to which the tentative tax to be computed is:	The tentative tax is:
Over $1,500,000 but not over $2,000,000	$555,800, plus 45 percent of the excess of such amount over $1,500,000.
Over $2,000,000 but not over $2,500,000	$780,800, plus 49 percent of the excess of such amount over $2,000,000.
Over $2,500,000 but not over $3,000,000	$1,025,800, plus 53% of the excess of such amount over $2,500,000.
Over $3,000,000	$1,290,800, plus 55% of the excess of such amount over $3,000,000.

For truly large estates, to the extent that the *tax* exceeds $10,000,000 but is below the amount at which the average tax rate is 55 percent, an additional 5 percent is added to such amount.[2]

Besides the unified credit, an estate is entitled to a credit for state death taxes. This credit is based upon the "adjusted taxable estate," namely the taxable estate less $60,000. The credit is progressive.[3] Many states use a so-called "sponge tax," which is an estate tax that equals the maximum federal credit for death taxes. The effect of such a sponge tax is that the total tax paid would be the same whether or not a state imposed such a tax, since the state death tax credit is only available to the extent it is paid to the state. New York, however, is one of the four states which taxes estates at a higher rate than the state death tax credit.[4]

Library References:

West's Key No. Digests, Internal Revenue ⟿4140, 4203.20.

§ 24.20 New York State Estate and Gift Tax

New York imposes a tax on the estates of domiciliaries and of non-domiciliaries with real or tangible personal property located within the state. The tax on domiciliaries is on the decedent's intangible assets wherever located and on real and personal property located in New York.[1]

---

2. I.R.C. § 2001(c)(2). The purpose of this 5% surcharge is to eliminate the graduated rates for large estates and to eliminate the unified credit. For years before January 1, 1998, the phaseout adjustment applies to estates up to $21,040,000.

3. I.R.C. § 2011. The state tax credit cannot exceed the amount of the federal estate tax less the unified credit.

4. *But see* § 24.20, *infra*.

§ 24.20

1. Tax Law §§ 952, 954, 956.

Ch. 24 NEW YORK STATE ESTATE AND GIFT TAX § 24.20

Nondomiciliaries are taxed on real and tangible property with a New York situs. The tax on the entire estate is apportioned by the ratio of New York situs property to all property which would be subject to tax had the person died a New York resident.[2] The key distinction between the taxation of the estate of a New York domiciliary and a non-New York domiciliary is that a non-New York domiciliary's *intangible* property, *e.g.*, stocks, bonds, and bank accounts, is *not* considered New York situs property for this computation.

For estates of decedents dying on or after February 1, 2000, the New York estate tax is equal to the maximum amount allowable as a credit against the federal estate tax.[3] For gifts made on or after January 1, 2000, the gift tax is repealed.[4] For estates of decedents dying before February 1, 2000 and for gifts made before January 1, 2000, the tax rate Schedule for the New York estate and gift tax is as follows:

Taxable Amount Over	Taxable Amount Not Over	Tax is
$ 0	50,000	2% of such amount
50,000	150,000	$1,000 + 3% of excess over $50,000
150,000	300,000	4,000 + 4% of excess over 150,000
300,000	500,000	10,000 + 5% of excess over 300,000
500,000	700,000	20,000 + 6% of excess over 500,000
700,000	900,000	32,000 + 7% of excess over 700,000
900,000	1,100,000	46,000 + 8% of excess over 900,000
1,100,000	1,600,000	62,000 + 9% of excess over 1,100,000
1,600,000	2,100,000	107,000 + 10% of excess over 1,600,000
2,100,000	2,600,000	157,000 + 11% of excess over 2,100,000
2,600,000	3,100,000	212,000 + 12% of excess over 2,600,000
3,100,000	3,600,000	272,000 + 13% of excess over 3,100,000
3,600,000	4,100,000	337,000 + 14% of excess over 3,600,000
4,100,000	5,100,000	407,000 + 15% of excess over 4,100,000
5,100,000	6,100,000	557,000 + 16% of excess over 5,100,000
6,100,000	7,100,000	717,000 + 17% of excess over 6,100,000
7,100,000	8,100,000	887,000 + 18% of excess over 7,100,000
8,100,000	9,100,000	1,067,000 + 19% of excess over 8,100,000
9,100,000	10,100,000	1,257,000 + 20% of excess over 9,100,000
10,100,000		1,457,000 + 21% of excess over 10,100,000

2. Tax Law § 960.
3. Tax Law § 952, as amended by L.1997, Ch.389.
4. **PRACTICE POINTER:** For gifts made on or after January 1, 1999 the gift tax exemption is equivalent to $300,000. Since the gift tax is repealed entirely after December 31, 1999 it may be advisable to postpone making taxable gifts until then.

§ 24.20 ESTATE PLANNING Ch. 24

A unified credit is allowed for estates of decedents dying before October 1, 1998 and for gifts made before January 1, 1999 as follows:

If Tentative Tax is Over:	But Not Over:	Credit is:
$ –0–	$2,950	Up to $2,950 (amount of tax)
2,950	5,399	Difference between $5,900 and tax
5,399		$500

For estates of decedents dying on or after October 1, 1998, but prior to February 1, 2000 and for gifts made on or after January 1, 1999, the unified credit is computed as follows:

If Tentative Tax is Over:	But Not Over:	Credit is:
$ 0	$10,000	Amount of Tax
$10,000	$19,499	Difference between $20,000 and tax
$19,499		$500

For estates of decedents dying before February 1, 2000 up to $250,000 in value of the decedent's principal residence is excluded from the gross estate.[5]

Library References:

West's Key No. Digests, Taxation ⇐856–906.22.

§ 24.21 Estate Tax Planning—Utilizing the Unified Credit

Each person may effectively transfer during his life or at death an aggregate amount which is equivalent to the unified credit amount, otherwise referred to as the applicable exclusion amount.[1] This, combined with the marital deduction[2] provides for numerous opportunities to reduce, or defer estate taxes imposed on a family.

First, if the combined estates of a husband and wife are less than the applicable exclusion amount no federal estate or gift tax will ever be imposed. Where the combined value of both estates is greater than such exclusion amount, it is generally advisable for the wealthier spouse to transfer, at a minimum, enough property to the poorer spouse to ensure that the poorer spouse has sufficient assets to use up his or her unified credit upon death.[3]

---

5. Tax Law § 952, as amended by L.1997, Ch. 389.

PRACTICE POINTER: For gifts made on or after January 1, 1999 the gift tax exemption is equivalent to $300,000. Since the gift tax is repealed entirely after December 31, 1999 it may be advisable to postpone making taxable gifts until then.

§ 24.21

1. I.R.C. §§ 2010, 2505. *See supra* § 24.18.

2. *See infra*, § 24.22 for a more in-depth discussion of marital bequests.

3. PRACTICE POINTER: Frequently, spouses own all property jointly or all in one name. The problem is that though there is no tax at the first spouse's death due to the unlimited marital deduction, the surviving spouse loses the ability to utilize

Ch. 24   UTILIZING THE MARITAL DEDUCTION   § 24.22

Library References:
West's Key No. Digests, Internal Revenue ⇔4182.30.

§ 24.22 Estate Tax Planning—Utilizing the Marital Deduction

The federal estate and gift tax both provide for an unlimited deduction for interspousal gifts,[1] provided that the spouse is a U.S. citizen.[2] In order for such gifts or bequests to qualify for the marital deduction, the gift cannot be a "terminable interest" unless such property is "qualified terminable interest property" ("QTIP").[3] A "terminable interest" is one in which:

(1) The spouse's interest terminates on the lapse of time, on the occurrence of an event or contingency, or a failure of an event or contingency to occur;

(2) An interest is given to someone other than the surviving spouse; *and*

(3) The third party must be able to possess or enjoy any part of the property after termination of the spouse's interest.[4]

Thus, property left to the surviving spouse for life, with remainder to other persons, is a terminable interest, which, unless it meets one of the enumerated exceptions, would not qualify for the marital deduction.

The most commonly used device to avoid making outright gifts to a spouse while qualifying for the marital deduction is the QTIP trust. In order to qualify as a QTIP, the surviving spouse must be entitled to all the income from the trust payable at least annually for life, no power must be held by any person to appoint property to anyone other than the

more than one exemption. It is not enough, however, to simply have each spouse own at least the applicable exclusion amount in his or her own name. The client should be advised to use a trust arrangement designed to give the surviving spouse liberal access. These trust arrangements are sometimes referred to as "credit shelter" or "bypass" trusts. Typically, the trust pays all income to the spouse and allows the trustee discretion to distribute principal to the spouse. Alternatively, the trust may give "sprinkling" powers to the trustee to make distributions among the spouse and descendants. The spouse may also be given limited withdrawal powers. For example, the power to withdraw an amount of not more than 5% or $5,000 per year, whichever is greater, or a power limited by an ascertainable standard. This is known as a limited power of appointment. I.R.C. § 2041. Since the spouse only has a life interest which terminates at death, the trust is not includable in the surviving spouse's estate. *Cf.* I.R.C. § 2036(a) (property transferred *by decedent* in which decedent retains life estate is included in gross estate).

§ 24.22

1. I.R.C. §§ 2056(d), 2523(i).

2. *See infra,* § 24.58 for a discussion on planning for non-U.S. citizen spouses.

3. I.R.C. §§ 2056(a), (b). **CAVEAT:** Although a disposition is made to a spouse, it may not entirely qualify for the marital deduction if such amount does not actually pass to the spouse. For example, if the tax apportionment clause requires taxes to be paid from the residue, and assuming the marital bequest is a residuary bequest, the amount of such taxes will reduce the marital deduction and cause additional estate tax to be due.

4. I.R.C. § 2056(b).

§ 24.22 ESTATE PLANNING Ch. 24

surviving spouse, and the executor, or the donor spouse in the case of lifetime gifts, must elect QTIP treatment.[5]

In order to meet the QTIP requirement of the spouse's right to income, the QTIP trust must either contain income producing property or the surviving spouse must have the right to require the trustee to make trust property productive, that is, income generating.[6] Also, upon the termination of a QTIP trust, all accrued and unpaid income must be paid to the surviving spouse's estate.[7]

Exceptions to the terminable interest rule include certain life insurance arrangements,[8] power of appointment trusts, a survivorship clause in a will meeting certain criteria,[9] and an "estate trust." An example of a power of appointment trust is a trust where the surviving spouse is entitled to income for life payable at least annually, the spouse may appoint the property to herself or her estate in all events, and no portion may be appointed to any person other than the surviving spouse.[10] An estate trust is a trust in which income is accumulated during the surviving spouse's lifetime, but at death is distributed to the spouse's estate and is thus includible in such survivor's estate for estate tax purposes.[11]

Since a marital bequest only defers the payment of tax, it may be advantageous not to utilize the maximum marital deduction and pay some estate tax at the first spouse's death. This would allow both estates to "ride the tax brackets." In other words, because the transfer tax rates are progressive, that is, the more you transfer, the higher the rate of taxation,[12] the married couple can *twice* take advantage of the lower transfer tax rates by having each one incur the tax. In most situations, however, clients will not desire to pay an "up-front" tax and you will have to illustrate the benefits of different planning strategies.[13]

---

5. I.R.C. § 2056(b)(7).

PRACTICE POINTER: The executor may elect to have all or a portion of a QTIP trust qualify for the marital deduction. A partial election may allow for post-mortem planning if it is desirable to incur some tax at the first death. *See infra*, § 24.72. In order to make a qualified election, Treas. Reg. § 20.2056(b)–7(b)(4) requires it to be made on a timely filed gift or estate tax return.

6. Treas. Reg. § 20.2056(b)–5(f).

7. Treas. Reg. § 20.2056(b)–5(f)(5).

CAVEAT: A testator who only leaves his spouse with interests in trust might have his testamentary scheme upset by a spouse, who exercises her "right of election" for an outright one-third of the deceased spouse's estate. EPTL § 5–1.1–A.; *see infra*, § 24.60.

8. I.R.C. § 2056(b)(6).

9. The exception provides that the termination of the spouse's interest can only occur within a period that does not exceed six months of the decedent's death or as a result of common disaster, assuming that the surviving spouse actually lives long enough to inherit the property. I.R.C. § 2056(b)(3). This exception is useful where one wishes to condition a marital bequest on the spouse surviving a period of time not to exceed six months. This will allow for post-mortem planning to equalize both estates.

10. I.R.C. § 2056(b)(5); Treas. Reg. § 20.2056(b)–5(a).

11. Rev. Rul. 68–554, 1968–2 C.B. 412; Rev. Rul. 72–333, 1972–2 C.B. 530; Rev. Rul. 75–128, 1975–1 C.B. 308.

12. *See supra*, § 24.19.

13. PRACTICE POINTER: Incurring the tax up front makes particular sense where the life expectancy of the surviving

EXAMPLE: Assume H and W each have a $3 million estate ($6 million total). If they utilize the optimum marital deduction ($600,000, in 1997, transferred to use up the unified credit, the next $2.4 million transferred to the surviving spouse, thus incurring no federal estate tax upon the first to die), the estate tax upon the death of the second to die is $2,748,000. If, upon the first spouse's death, the estate did not elect to use the marital deduction, the estate tax on each $3 million (net of the exemption) would be $1,098,000 for a total tax on both estates of $2,196,000, or a net savings of $552,000.

West's McKinney's Forms, appropriate to this section, are available.[14]

Library References:

West's Key No. Digests, Internal Revenue ⚖4169.

§ 24.23 Estate Tax Planning—Formula Clauses

Since the amount of the available exemption cannot be determined until death, credit shelter and marital bequest clauses are often drafted by means of a formula designed to define the maximum federal estate tax-free amount, taking into account the effect of other dispositions, both during lifetime and at death. Such formula bequests can be drafted as either fractional or pecuniary bequests.

A pecuniary bequest is a fixed amount, which means it is not affected by appreciation or depreciation of the assets during administration. A fractional share bequest, on the other hand, is a formula which seeks to establish a fraction representing that proportion of the taxable estate that would be entitled to the marital deduction, which thereby shares in the rise and fall of values during administration.

If the credit shelter trust is a pecuniary bequest, the marital share will receive all appreciation or depreciation. If assets are expected to appreciate it may be advantageous to draft the marital share as a pecuniary, pre-residuary bequest so that the credit shelter trust is allocated the appreciation thereby keeping the appreciation out of the surviving spouse's estate.[1]

---

spouse is short. In other words, the present value of the tax savings will assuredly be greater than the interest that can be earned on the deferred tax over the life of the second spouse to die. In addition, the surviving spouse's estate may be eligible for the previously tax paid credit under I.R.C. § 2013. The practitioner must be sensitive, however, to the lifestyle and income needs of both spouses. The payment of transfer taxes upon the first death may frighten the survivor and/or threaten his or her ability to live comfortably.

14. See West's McKinney's Forms—Estate and Surrogate's Practice § 7:273 (power of appointment trust); § 7:277 (QTIP trust).

§ 24.23

1. For a sample Marital Deduction pecuniary formula bequest, see § 7:275A of McKinney's Forms—Estates and Surrogate Practice.

CAVEAT: Where the pecuniary bequest is satisfied by delivery in kind at the date of distribution value, there is recognized, for

§ 24.23 ESTATE PLANNING

The marital bequest can also be drafted as a fractional share of the residuary estate, thereby sharing in any appreciation or depreciation in value. In general fractional formulas are more difficult to administer since each time assets are distributed they have to be revalued. Furthermore, any non-*pro-rata* distribution will cause a change in the fraction. Each type of clause has its advantages and disadvantages and must be tailored to the client's particular situation since selecting the wrong clause may result in disputes between the surviving spouse and residuary beneficiaries.

A West's McKinney's Form, appropriate to this section, is available.[2]

§ 24.24 Generation Skipping Transfer Tax

The generation skipping transfer ("GST") tax is designed to ensure taxation of wealth transfer from each generation. The problem that Congress perceived was that a decedent could bequeath money to grandchildren or more remote descendants without any transfer tax at the child's death. Since a well-advised decedent could establish trusts which would benefit his children without being subject to estate taxation upon their death, the GST tax is imposed to make up for the lost transfer tax upon the death of the succeeding generation(s).[1]

The GST tax is confiscatory in nature. It is imposed at the highest marginal federal estate tax rate[2] of 55% on top of the decedent's estate tax. It is imposed on "generation skipping transfers" to a person who is assigned, by statute, to a generation two or more below that of the decedent.[3]

A "generation skipping transfer" can occur in one of three ways:

(1) A taxable termination;

(2) A direct skip; or

(3) A taxable distribution.

income tax purposes, a gain or loss measured by the difference between the value of the property at the date of distribution and the estate tax value.

PRACTICE POINTER: In drafting the formula provision for New York State residents, where the state inheritance tax will exceed the I.R.C. § 2011 credit for state death taxes, a modification of the formula language, to take into account state death tax credits, will increase the amount that can be sheltered in the credit shelter trust to $642,424. However, when the New York estate tax equals the state death tax credit (for decedents dying after 1999), no modification should be made. That is, the formula clause should only take into account the state death tax credit to the extent it does not increase the tax.

2. *See* West's McKinney's Forms—Estate and Surrogate's Practice § 7:275A (marital deduction pecuniary bequest).

§ 24.24

1. Staff of Joint Committee on Taxation, *General Explanation of the Tax Reform Act of 1976*, 565. (The GST enacted in 1976 was replaced with a "simpler" GST by the Tax Reform Act of 1986, P.L. 99–514, § 1433(c)).

2. I.R.C. § 2641(a)(1).

3. I.R.C. §§ 2611, 2612, 2613, 2642(c). For a complete discussion of generation assignment, *see infra*, § 24.28.

§ 24.25 Generation Skipping Transfer Tax—Taxable Termination

Suppose that a "non-skip person," *i.e.*, a person to whom a transfer does *not* trigger the GST tax,[1] has a life interest in a trust established by decedent, with the remainder payable to the non-skip person's child. Upon the death of the non-skip person, there is a taxable termination that is a taxable generation skipping transfer. The tax is paid by the trustee of the trust in which the skip person obtains an interest.[2]

A taxable termination occurs when, as a result of death, lapse of time, release of a power, or otherwise, a "non-skip person's" interest in property held in trust terminates unless either:

(1) Immediately after the termination, another non-skip person has an interest in the property, or

(2) At no time after a termination may a distribution be made from the trust to a skip person.[3]

A termination is not subject to the GST tax if the termination itself is subject to federal gift or estate tax.[4] For example, if a transferor establishes a trust with income to his child for life, and upon the child's death the remainder is payable (a) as the child appoints pursuant to a testamentary general power of appointment, or (b) to the grandchild in the absence of such exercise, there will not be GST tax upon the death of the child because the property is subject to estate tax as part of the child's estate.[5]

In order for a non-skip person to be treated as having an interest in the property the non-skip person must have a present right to receive income or principal, be a current permissible recipient of income or corpus, or must be an organization to which a gift or bequest would qualify for a charitable deduction for property in a "charitable remainder annuity trust," "charitable remainder unitrust" or "pooled income

---

§ 24.25

1. "Skip person" is defined as (1) a natural person assigned to a generation which is two or more generations below the transferor's generation, (2) a trust if all of the interests are held by skip persons and (3) a trust where *no person* is holding an interest and no distribution may be made to a non-skip person. I.R.C. § 2613(a). A non-skip person is a person who is not a skip person. I.R.C. § 2613(b).

2. I.R.C. § 2603(a)(2).
3. I.R.C. § 2612(a)(1).
4. Treas. Reg. § 26.2612–1(b)(1)(i).
5. Property over which decedent has a general power of appointment is includible in his estate. *See* I.R.C. § 2041 (definition of "general power of appointment"); Treas. Reg. § 26.2652–1(a)(1) ("the individual with respect to whom property was most recently subject to federal estate or gift tax is the transferor of that property for purposes of [the GST tax].") If the testator wishes to avoid GST tax, but limit the child's appointees to descendants, the power may be limited to the child's creditors or creditors of the child's estate (which is unlikely to be exercised, yet still cause the trust to be subject to estate tax). Alternatively, the trustee could have the power to grant a general power of appointment where it is desirable to avoid the GST tax.

fund."[6]

Library References:

West's Key No. Digests, Internal Revenue ⇔4220–4228.

§ 24.26 Generation Skipping Transfer Tax—Direct Skip

A direct skip is an immediate transfer of an interest in property to a "skip person," that is subject to estate or gift tax.[1] For example, both an outright transfer to a grandchild as well as the establishment of an irrevocable trust solely for the grandchild's benefit that is a completed gift qualify as direct skips. Note that a direct skip results in both gift or estate tax *and* GST tax. A gift solely of a remainder interest to a skip person does not count as an "interest" taxable as a direct skip because future interests are not currently taxable.[2] Because direct skips are taxed on a tax-exclusive basis, *i.e.*, the tax is paid by the transferor, direct skips are more efficient than other generation skipping transfers.[3]

Library References:

West's Key No. Digests, Internal Revenue ⇔4220–4228.

§ 24.27 Generation Skipping Transfer Tax—Taxable Distribution

A taxable distribution is a distribution, other than a taxable termination or direct skip, to a skip person.[1]

For example, if a grantor established a trust which pays income to his child for life and one-half of the principal to his grandchild when the grandchild attains age 35, the payment to the grandchild constitutes a taxable distribution.[2] The GST tax on a taxable distribution is payable by the transferee.[3]

Library References:

West's Key No. Digests, Internal Revenue ⇔4220–4228.

§ 24.28 Generation Skipping Transfer Tax—Generation Assignment

The key to whether the GST tax applies is the generation to which a person is assigned for purposes of the tax. The GST tax is not merely

6. I.R.C. § 2652(c). For a discussion of charitable remainder annuity trusts, charitable remainder unitrusts and pooled income funds, *see infra*, § 24.54.

§ 24.26
1. I.R.C. § 2612(c).
2. I.R.C. § 2652(c) (definition of "interest" in property held in trust).
3. I.R.C. § 2603(a)(3).

§ 24.27
1. I.R.C. § 2612(b).
2. Treas. Reg. § 26.2613–1(f)(Ex. 12).
3. I.R.C. § 2603(a)(1).

applicable to a transfer which skips a generation in a family as a bequest to a younger unrelated person can also be subject to the GST tax.

For family members, the transferee's generation is determined by consanguinity. Specifically, all lineal descendants of the transferee's grandparents are assigned to a generation regardless of age. For example, a child, nephew or niece is in the first generation, a grandchild in the second generation, and a first cousin is in the same generation as the transferor.[1]

A spouse of either the transferor or of the transferor's relative is deemed to be in the same generation as the person to whom he or she is, or was previously married, regardless of age.[2]

EXAMPLE: If an 86 year old man marries his 25 year old housekeeper, she is deemed to be in his generation for GST tax purposes. Similarly, if the 86 year old man's 55 year old son marries a 25 year old woman, the son's wife is considered to be in the first generation below the 86 year old father-in-law. Thus, if the 86 year old man makes a transfer to either of the 25 year old women, such transfer is not a generation skipping transfer.

Note, that if a transferor's child has predeceased the transferor, and, after the child's death, the transferor makes a gift or testamentary bequest to that child's issue, *i.e.*, his grandchild, such a gift is *not* considered to be a direct skip.[3]

For the purposes of the GST tax, nonrelated transferors are assigned to generations, based upon age differentials. Each generation is 25 years in length, and the transferor is in the middle of his generation.[4] Thus, a person within 12½ years of age of the transferor is in the same generation as the transferor, while a person more than 12½ years but no more than 37½ years younger than the transferor is in the first generation below the transferor. A person more than 37½ years younger than the transferor, but less than 62½ years younger (*i.e.*, 25 years) is treated as being in the second generation below the transferor.[5] Note that there is no equivalent rule in the case of spouses of nonrelatives which would assign a younger spouse to a higher generation for GST tax purposes.

EXAMPLE: If the 86 year old man transferred property to his 55 year old friend and the friend's 25 year old wife, the transfer to his friend would not be a generation skipping transfer because the age differential (31 years) places the friend in the first generation below

§ 24.28
1. I.R.C. § 2651(b).
2. I.R.C. § 2651(c).
3. I.R.C. § 2612(c).

CAVEAT: This exception, referred to as the "step-up" rule, applies to all direct skips and those taxable terminations and taxable distributions where the parent of the particular beneficiary was deceased at the earliest time that the transfer (from which the beneficiary's interest was created) is subject to estate or gift tax. I.R.C. § 2651(e).

4. I.R.C. § 2651(d).
5. *Id.*

§ 24.28 ESTATE PLANNING Ch. 24

the transferor, making him a non-skip person. The transfer to his friend's 25 year old wife, however, is subject to the GST tax because the age differential, 61 years, places her two generations below the transferor for GST tax purposes.

Library References:

West's Key No. Digests, Internal Revenue ⚖4220–4228.

§ 24.29 Generation Skipping Transfer Tax—Multiple Skips

A generation skipping transfer in trust will continue to be subject to the GST tax. However, in determining whether subsequent transfers incur the GST tax, the transferor is deemed to have moved down on the generational ladder to the generation above the highest generation of anyone having an interest in the property after the transfer.[1]

Library References:

West's Key No. Digests, Internal Revenue ⚖4220–4228.

§ 24.30 Generation Skipping Transfer Tax—Exemption

Each individual is entitled to make generation skipping transfers of up to an aggregate of $1 million free[1] of GST tax.[2] This exemption may be allocated by the transferor to lifetime gifts on his or her federal gift tax return, or may be allocated in whole or in part by the person's executor.[3] Each person is entitled to a $1 million exemption or, for lifetime transfers, may elect to "split" lifetime gifts with a spouse, thus obtaining the GST tax exemption of $2 million.[4]

Where the transferor's available exemption is allocated to the value of a transfer, no GST tax will be due whether the transfer is a direct skip, a termination or distribution. That is, distributions from a trust

---

§ 24.29
1. I.R.C. § 2653.

§ 24.30
1. This amount is indexed for inflation for individuals who die after 1998. I.R.C. § 2631(c).
2. I.R.C. § 2631(a).
3. I.R.C. § 2632; Treas. Reg. § 26.2632–1(a). **PRACTICE POINTER:** The value of the property for allocation purposes for *inter vivos* generation skipping transfers depends upon when the allocation is made. If the allocation is made on a timely filed gift tax return, then the value of the property is determined as of the date of transfer. I.R.C. § 2642(b). If the allocation is made, however, on a gift tax return that is not timely filed, the valuation is made as of the date of the late filing. I.R.C. § 2642(b). This presents a planning opportunity for generation skipping transfers other than direct skips. If the property has depreciated since the making of a gift, the allocation can be intentionally made late, and thus more of the $1 million exemption will be available for later use. This may often be the case with term life insurance if the premium due date is set before April 15.

CAVEAT: A risk with making a late allocation where life insurance is involved is that the insured may die before the late allocation is made.

4. I.R.C. § 2652(a)(2).

which has the transferor's exemption allocated to the entire amount of the transfer in trust will always be exempt.

A partial allocation, on the other hand, of the transferor's million dollar exemption will result in a tax determined by a formula, which is the maximum federal estate tax rate, currently 55%, multiplied by the "inclusion ratio."[5] The "inclusion ratio" is one minus the "applicable fraction," the numerator of which is the GST tax exemption allocated to the property transferred and the denominator is the value of the property transferred.[6]

EXAMPLE: G gives his granddaughter $1 million dollars outright, and on his federal gift tax return allocates $750,000 of his one million dollar lifetime GST tax exemption (assuming he has previously allocated $250,000). The applicable tax rate for this gift is determined as follows:

Maximum Federal Estate Tax Rate x Inclusion Ratio:

= 55% × (1−($750,000 Exemption/$1M Value of Property))

= 55% × (1−.75)

= 13.75%

Thus, the GST tax on G's transfer of $1 million to his granddaughter is 13.75% of $1 million, or $137,500.[7]

---

5. I.R.C. § 2641(a).
6. I.R.C. § 2642(a).
7. **PRACTICE POINTER:** In allocating the million dollar exemption, a planner's goal is to ensure that all trusts are assigned an inclusion ratio of either zero or one; that is, either wholly exempt or taxable. A fractional inclusion ratio results in the "wasting" of the GST tax exemption and extra taxation.

EXAMPLE: Joe Testator establishes a testamentary trust with $3 million in corpus, which provides income plus discretionary principal distributions to his son, Junior, and upon Junior's death, the remainder is payable to his grandson, Joe Testator III. The executor allocates the entire $1 million exemption to this trust, creating an inclusion ratio of 2/3 ($1 million/ $3 million). During Junior's lifetime, the trustee distributes $1 million in trust corpus to Junior. Such a distribution is tax free since Junior is a non-skip person. Upon Junior's death the remaining $2 million, and any appreciation, is subject to the GST tax at a rate of 36.33% (2/3 of 55%), for a tax of $733,333.

Had Joe Testator's will provided for the creation of two trusts, one with an inclusion ratio of zero and the other with an inclusion ratio of one, the effect of the GST tax would have been as follows: The executor would create one trust with $1 million which would have the entire exemption allocated to it, resulting in an inclusion ratio of zero. Since all future distributions from this trust would be exempt from GST tax, the trustee is directed to make distributions to Junior from the non-exempt trust first. The non-exempt trust would have an inclusion ratio of one. If $1 million was distributed to Junior from the non-exempt trust, the remaining $1 million, plus any appreciation thereon, distributed on Junior's death, from the non-exempt trust, would be subject to tax at 55% (inclusion ratio of 1 x 55%) resulting in a tax of $550,000. The $1 million, plus any appreciation, distributed from the exempt trust would be exempt entirely (inclusion ratio of 0 x 55%), thereby saving $233,333 in GST tax.

PRACTICE POINTER: Although explicitly provided for in EPTL § 7-1.13, the draftsperson could include a provision in the fiduciary power clause to allow the executor or trustee to establish separate trusts with an inclusion ratio of one or zero.

§ 24.30　　　　ESTATE PLANNING　　　　Ch. 24

West's McKinney's Forms, appropriate to this section, are available.[8]

Library References:

West's Key No. Digests, Internal Revenue ⇒4220–4228.

§ 24.31　Generation Skipping Transfer Tax—"Reverse QTIP"

As a technical matter, when a QTIP election is made, the spouse, rather than the testator, is deemed the transferor of the property for GST tax purposes. However, a "reverse QTIP" election may be made.[1] This permits the testator to be deemed the transferor for GST tax purposes, and thus able to allocate some or all of the $1 million exemption to the QTIP trust, while being able to take advantage of the marital deduction.[2]

EXAMPLE: Assuming no prior taxable gifts have been made, upon a client's death, the executor would allocate the applicable exclusion amount of the GST exemption to the bypass trust. If the will directs the balance to a trust qualifying for the marital deduction, the executor should elect to create a separate marital trust, to be allocated and funded for the remainder of the GST tax exemption, which would be referred to as an exempt marital trust. The remainder would be the non-exempt marital trust or can be distributed to the spouse outright. The executor would elect reverse QTIP treatment for the exempt trust.

A West's McKinney's Form, appropriate to this section, is available.[3]

Library References:

West's Key No. Digests, Internal Revenue ⇒4220–4228.

§ 24.32　Charitable Bequests

In the past, New York, like many states, limited the amount that a decedent could leave to charitable organizations. Since July 7, 1981,

---

8. See West's McKinney's Forms—Estate and Surrogate's Practice §§ 10:804–10:805 (generation skipping trust).

§ 24.31

1. I.R.C. § 2652(a)(3).
2. **PRACTICE POINTER:** Where generation skipping transfers are planned using a testamentary marital trust, the will should provide for a nonexempt and exempt QTIP, i.e., a reverse QTIP, in case the marital share exceeds the testator's remaining $1 million exemption. Further, if the QTIP is to pour over into another trust upon the spouse's death, e.g., a credit shelter trust, the will should provide that the exempt QTIP will only pourover into the credit shelter trust if it has an inclusion ratio of zero, otherwise it should continue to be held separately. Even if held separately, however, the exempt QTIP property can be administered in accordance with the terms of the other trust, i.e., using the same dispositive scheme.

3. See West's McKinney's Forms—Estate and Surrogate's Practice § 10:806 (reverse QTIP language).

however, New York no longer limits a testator from making such gifts.[1]

In order for the bequest to qualify for a charitable deduction, it must satisfy the conditions of I.R.C. § 2055. A bequest that qualifies for the estate tax charitable deduction must be sufficiently clear and definite in amount rather than merely giving "authority" to the fiduciary to make charitable gifts.[2] Generally, a contribution to an organization for which an income tax charitable deduction may be obtained will also result in an estate tax deduction.[3]

In addition to outright bequests, a client may wish to utilize charitable trusts or bequests to pooled funds.[4]

Note that if a charitable contribution is made to a qualifying charity during a person's lifetime, current income taxes are reduced,[5] and no federal gift tax is payable thereon.[6]

West's McKinney's Forms, appropriate to this section, are available.[7]

§ 24.33 Planning With Certain Assets

In developing an estate plan, the attorney must be alert to the tax consequences or planning opportunities which certain types of assets create. Special consideration should be given to life insurance, retirement plan benefits, and assets which create income in respect of decedent.

§ 24.34 Planning With Certain Assets—Life Insurance

Insurance on the decedent's life, which he has incidents of ownership over, is includible in the decedent's gross estate for estate tax purposes.[1] Furthermore, if the decedent transferred such life insurance policies within three years of his death, the insurance proceeds will be includible in his estate.[2]

In order to avoid the inclusion of insurance proceeds from one's estate, the insured must rid himself of any "incidents of ownership" over the policy, whether exercisable alone or in conjunction with any other person. In other words, he cannot keep any form of control over the economic benefits of the policy.[3]

---

§ 24.32

1. Ch. 461, L. 1981, which repealed EPTL § 5-3.3.
2. Rev. Rul. 55-335, 1955-1 C.B. 455; Delbridge v. United States, 89 F.Supp. 845 (E.D.Mich.1950); see also, Paris v. United States, 381 F.Supp. 597 (N.D.Ohio 1974).
3. Cf. I.R.C. §§ 170(c), 2055(a).
4. For a more complete discussion on charitable trusts see infra, §§ 24.54, et seq.
5. I.R.C. § 170(f)(2)(A). The amount that may be deducted depends, in part, on the type of property transferred.
6. I.R.C. § 2572.
7. See West's McKinney's Forms—Estate and Surrogate's Practice §§ 7:316–7:332 (charitable bequest).

§ 24.34

1. I.R.C. § 2042; Treas. Reg. § 20.2042-1(a).
2. I.R.C. § 2035(d)(2).
3. Treas. Reg. § 20.2042-1(c)(2).

§ 24.34 ESTATE PLANNING Ch. 24

Among the types of "incidents of ownership" that must be ceded in order to avoid inclusion are the following powers or interests to:

(1) Change beneficiaries;

(2) Assign the policy;

(3) Revoke an assignment;

(4) Pledge the policy for a loan;

(5) Obtain from the insurer a loan against the cash or surrender value of the policy;

(6) Retain a reversionary interest in the policy or its proceeds if the value of the reversionary interest immediately before the decedent's death exceeds 5% of the policy's value; and

(7) Retain an insurance policy in trust, if under the trust terms, the decedent, as trustee or otherwise, can change beneficial ownership in the policy or its proceeds, or the time or manner of enjoyment thereof.

Although the transfer of ownership of a policy constitutes a taxable gift equal to the policy's interpolated terminal reserve value, the potential for gift tax on such value is much smaller than the ultimate burden that an estate would bear on the policy proceeds. In addition, through judicious use of gift tax annual exclusions and "Crummey powers"[4] most, if not all, of the gift tax consequences associated with transferring a policy can be eliminated.[5]

§ 24.35 Planning With Certain Assets—Life Insurance—Life Insurance Trusts

A popular method of keeping insurance proceeds out of the estates of both the insured and his spouse is to have the life insurance policy owned or assigned to a properly drafted irrevocable life insurance trust ("ILIT"). The grantor should not be given any powers amounting to "incidents of ownership" over the policies.[1] In order to avoid inclusion in the estate, the transfer of policies to the trust must be made at least three years prior to the insured's death.[2] This contingency can be avoided by having the policy purchased by the trust in the first instance.

The ILIT, rather than the insured or any intended beneficiary, should be designated as both the owner and beneficiary of the policy. In addition, premiums should not be paid directly by the grantor. Rather,

4. See infra, § 24.52.
5. See infra, § 24.35.

§ 24.35
1. PRACTICE POINTER: The grantor should never be made the trustee of the ILIT, because the Internal Revenue Service might argue that one or more fiduciary powers constitutes an "incident of ownership."

2. I.R.C. § 2035(d)(2).

the funds should be gifted to the trust for payment of the premium by the trustee.

A married insured can use an ILIT to both provide for his spouse while keeping the policy proceeds out of the spouse's gross estate for estate tax purposes. The ILIT can provide for distributions of income and principal to the spouse at the trustee's discretion. As long as the spouse cannot control the trust and does not have a "general power of appointment"[3] over the principal, the proceeds will not be includible in her estate.[4]

If the proceeds are intended to benefit adult children, rather than the insured's spouse, a transfer of the ownership and beneficiary designation to the child or children will accomplish the same tax-free results as a trust.[5]

West's McKinney's Forms, appropriate to this section, are available.[6]

§ 24.36 Planning With Certain Assets—Life Insurance—Life Insurance Trusts—"Crummey Powers"

A person can make use of the $10,000 annual exclusion (or $20,000 for married couples)[1] for "present interest" gifts to transfer insurance policies and make gifts to an ILIT largely free of gift tax consequences. In order for the gift to a trust to qualify as a present interest, the beneficiary must be entitled to withdraw the lesser of the annual gift tax exclusion or the complete amount of the gift. Generally, the grantor will not, in fact, want the beneficiary to exercise this withdrawal power, because such withdrawal would cause the trust to be unable to pay the insurance premium. Thus, the ILIT should instead provide each beneficiary a "Crummey power."[2] The trustee must be obligated to inform

---

3. A "general power of appointment" is the power to appoint the property to herself, her estate, her creditors, or the creditors of her estate. I.R.C. § 2041(b).

4. **PRACTICE POINTER:** The surviving spouse may be given a "limited power of appointment," to determine which of the grantor's descendants shall receive trust principal upon her death, in what proportions, and whether outright or in further trust. This effectively gives the grantor, through the surviving spouse, a post-mortem "second look" at the needs of potential beneficiaries. The power should be drafted narrowly to permit such gifts only to a particular class of beneficiaries in order to:

(1) Avoid characterization of this power as a general power, or

(2) Avoid the spouse being able to contravene the decedent's wishes by appointing to, for example, a second husband.

The spouse can also be given the limited power to invade principal for her health, welfare and maintenance or the greater of $5,000 or 5% of the principal each year.

5. **CAVEAT:** The client may still be well advised to consider a trust to avoid the possibility that a child's death or divorce might frustrate the insured's intentions.

6. *See* West's McKinney's Forms—Estate and Surrogate's Practice §§ 10:420A–10:420A–3 (life insurance trust).

§ 24.36

1. I.R.C. § 2503(b). *See infra*, § 24.49.

2. This is known as a "Crummey power" from the Tax Court case Vega v. C.I.R., T.C. Memo. 1966-144, 71 T.C.M. (CCH)

§ 24.36   ESTATE PLANNING   Ch. 24

each beneficiary of a withdrawal power, in writing, that assets have been contributed to the trust by providing a "Crummey notice,"[3] and that the ILIT only permits a withdrawal to occur within a limited period of time, *i.e.*, 30 days. By meeting these minimum standards, the criteria under *Crummey v. Commissioner*,[4] are satisfied, and up to $10,000 per beneficiary, or $20,000 for a married donor, may be contributed without gift tax consequences.

The Crummey notices should be given by the trustee to each beneficiary every time an additional gift is made to the trust. The beneficiary, or his guardian, should acknowledge receipt of such notices and copies thereof should be maintained by the trustee.

In order to avoid adverse gift tax consequences which arise if a withdrawal power in excess of $5,000 (or 5% of principal if greater) is allowed to lapse by a beneficiary, the trust should limit such withdrawal powers to $5,000 per beneficiary in any one year. Any excess amount contributed to the trust should be permitted to be withdrawn in a later year when less than $5,000 is contributed per beneficiary. This provision in the trust instrument is often referred to as a "hanging" power.

§ 24.37 Planning With Certain Assets—Retirement Benefits

Other than their home, the most substantial assets owned by a couple are often their retirement assets, including IRAs, Keogh plans, and "qualified plans."[1] However, because of the complex income, estate, and excise tax rules relating to these plans, inadequate, or nonexistent, planning often leads to the loss of large portions, even the *majority*, of such benefits to taxing authorities.

IRAs and qualified plans are distributable upon death based upon the decedent's designation with the plan administrator. Like other assets, IRAs and qualified plan account balances are includible in the decedent's gross estate for estate tax purposes. In addition, post-mortem payments from qualified plans or IRAs are "income with respect of a decedent" ("IRD"), under I.R.C. § 691 to the extent that, had the decedent received the payments directly, the decedent would have been treated as receiving gross income subject to taxation. In other words, the recipient of qualified plans or IRAs is subject to income taxation as well as estate taxation. However, the imposition of income taxation on such retirement benefits is tempered by a deduction from gross income for

---

2534 (U.S.Tax Ct.1966), aff'd 397 F.2d 82 (9th Cir.1968).

3. *See infra*, § 24.101 for a sample Crummey notice.

4. *Id.*

§ 24.37

1. "Qualified plans" refers to retirement plans which receive favorable tax treatment because they satisfy requirements of I.R.C. §§ 401 *et seq.*

estate taxes imposed on such items.[2]

Between the estate tax and the income tax, more than 75% of retirement benefits can be lost to federal and state taxation. One method of reducing the tax burden is to name the surviving spouse as the "designated beneficiary" of IRAs and qualified plans. This would permit the spouse to roll-over such retirement assets into an IRA free of current income taxation,[3] and would qualify for the estate tax marital deduction.[4]

In the event that the IRA owner or plan participant does not wish to leave the benefits outright, *e.g.*, where there is a second marriage scenario with children from a prior marriage, he may designate a QTIP trust as the beneficiary in order for the asset to qualify for the marital deduction while deferring income recognition. The IRA itself must be treated as a QTIP,[5] and may be structured to pay to the marital trust either:

(1) all income earned by the IRA annually *plus* annual installments of the IRA principal,[6] or

(2) the greater of all IRA income and the "minimum distribution" amounts.[7]

Remember that in order to qualify as a QTIP, all income must be distributed to the surviving spouse at least annually.[8]

---

2. I.R.C. § 691(c). The deduction is the excess of the actual federal estate tax liability over the hypothetical federal estate tax which would have been imposed in the absence of IRD items and their related deductions.

3. I.R.C. § 408(d)(3).

4. I.R.C. § 2056(a).

5. See Private Letter Ruling 9544038, Private Letter Ruling 9537005, Private Letter Ruling 931035.

6. Rev. Rul. 89-89, 1989-2 C.B. 231.

7. See Private Letter Ruling 9704029, Private Letter Ruling 9544038, Private Letter Ruling 9321035 "Minimum distributions" would be based upon the life expectancy of the surviving spouse. Failure to make minimum distributions could lead to a 50% excise tax. I.R.C. § 4974(a).

8. I.R.C. §§ 2056(b)(7)(B)(i)(II), (ii)(I). Note that in order for a trust beneficiary to be treated as a designated beneficiary of an IRA, the trust must:

(1) Be valid under state law or would be if it had a corpus,

(2) Be irrevocable,

(3) Have beneficiaries identifiable under the terms of the trust, and

(4) A copy of the trust document must be provided to the plan or IRA institution.

Prop. Treas. Reg. § 1.401(a)(9)-1, Q & A D-5.

PRACTICE POINTER: The QTIP trust should provide that the trustees must allocate to income the portion of each payment from the plan or IRA equal to the income earned by the plan or IRA during the annual period, so that this amount will be distributed to the spouse, meeting the QTIP rules, and that the trustees should have the power to demand sufficient distributions so that at least all current income is payable to the QTIP. The QTIP trust should also provide that any expenses attributable to principal distributions of an IRA are not allocated to income distributions from the IRA. Finally, the QTIP trust should provide that the trustees shall take whatever actions are necessary to qualify the surviving spouse as the "designated beneficiary" of any plan and to allow such plan benefits to qualify for the marital deduction. The distribution provisions should also be included with the IRA designation.

CAVEAT: In order to designate a QTIP trust or someone other than a spouse as a beneficiary of a qualified plan, the spouse

§ 24.37 ESTATE PLANNING Ch. 24

Generally, option #2 is preferable because it avoids unnecessary income recognition by the marital trust upon distribution of IRA principal.

In some cases, it might be more advantageous from a tax perspective to name someone other than the spouse as the "designated beneficiary" of an IRA or a qualified plan. Since the minimum distribution requirement can be based upon the life expectancy of the designated beneficiary,[9] having a far younger beneficiary may result in substantial income tax deferral, or savings where the person is in a lower tax bracket than the spouse. This should not be done, however, unless there are sufficient liquid assets available to provide for the needs of the surviving spouse and other assets available to pay the estate taxes, if any, on such IRA amounts.[10]

For practitioners with charitably-inclined clients, retirement assets may be the best assets to bequeath to a qualifying charity since the noncharitable beneficiaries would receive much less of such assets on an after tax basis then they would of other assets. Not only are such amounts deductible from the gross estate in determining estate tax, but the charity is not subject to income tax on the IRD.[11]

§ 24.38 Planning With Certain Assets—Closely Held Business Interests

Typically, owners of closely held businesses have unique concerns when planning their estates. One of these concerns, of course, is to minimize the amount of transfer taxes imposed on their estates. Particular attention, however, is required to provide for the orderly transition of management and control from one generation to another. A second objective is to prevent the sale or inheritance of an interest in the business which would force the remaining owner(s) to engage in business with someone not of their choosing. Finally, estate liquidity is another aspect that owners of closely-held businesses must consider.

Qualified Family-Owned Business Interest Exclusion. The Taxpayer Relief Act of 1997 allows an estate tax exclusion for qualified family-owned business interests for estates of decedents dying after 1997.[1] The amount of the exclusion is the difference between $1.3 million and the applicable exemption amount (*e.g.,.* $625,000 in 1998). When the exclusion is fully phased in 2006 it will decrease to $300,000.

must sign a waiver which must be filed with the plan administrator.
9. I.R.C. § 401(a)(9)(B)(iii); Prop. Treas. Reg. § 1.401(a)(9)-1, Q & A F.
10. CAVEAT: The tax allocation clause must be carefully drafted so as not to cause estate tax to be paid by the marital share. If, however, there are insufficient resources available to the IRA beneficiary to pay the tax allocated to the IRA, he would need to use some of the IRA funds to pay the tax which frustrates the ability to deferr such withdrawals.
11. Private Letter Ruling 9237020.

§ 24.38
1. I.R.C. § 2033A.

Example: A decedent's estate consists of a qualified family owned business interest with a value of $1,000,000 and other property valued at $600,000. If the decedent died in 1998, the exclusion for the business interest is $675,000 and the unified credit would exclude $625,000 for a total of $1,300,000 exclusion.

In order to qualify for the exclusion the decedent (or family members) must have materially participated in the business five of the eight years preceding death and the business interest must comprise more than half the "adjusted gross estate" and must have its principal place of business in the United States.

A business qualifies as family-owned if one family owns at least 50% of the entity, two families own at least 70% or three families own at least 90%.

The estate only qualifies for the exclusion if the decedent was a U.S. citizen or resident at his death. The executor must elect to have the exclusion apply and file an agreement signed by each person who has an interest in the property consenting to the recapture rules if a sale of the business interest occurs within 10 years of the decedent's death.

§ 24.39 Planning With Certain Assets—Closely Held Business Interests—Buy–Sell Agreements

A particularly effective method of planning for the eventual retirement or death of a closely held business owner is to have a "buy-sell" agreement in place. A buy-sell agreement can take the form of an agreement between the business itself and the individual owners, an agreement between individual owners, an agreement between the individual owners and one or more non-owners, or some combination. The exact form of the agreement will depend on the type of entity the business operates under. For example, if the entity is a corporation, then either a stock redemption plan or a cross-purchase plan may be used. For partnerships, in lieu of a stock redemption plan, a partnership liquidation plan can be used, in which the partnership, in effect, purchases the withdrawing partner's interest by distributing assets to liquidate that partner's interest.

Buy-sell agreements are often funded by the purchase of life insurance on the lives of the business owners. If a stock redemption is planned, the corporation, rather than the individual shareholders or partners, will own the policy and pay the premiums. On the other hand, in a cross-purchase each shareholder, or partner will own the policy on the life of the other and pay the premiums.

Buy-sell agreements entered into before October 9, 1990, on an arm's length basis, which also restrict a shareholder's ability to dispose of his interest in the business during his lifetime with a *bona fide* business reason for the arrangement, such as the common purpose of maintaining control within an ownership group and maintaining continuity of management, or maintaining family control, would fix the value of the business interest for estate tax purposes.[1]

For agreements entered into after October 8, 1990, or which were "substantially modified" after that date,[2] a buy-sell agreement must conform to the more stringent requirements of I.R.C. § 2703. Specifically, in order for an agreement to be honored for the purpose of establishing the valuation of the business interest for estate tax purposes, the agreement must:

(1) Be a *bona fide* business arrangement;

(2) Not be a device to transfer the interest to family members for less than full and adequate consideration; and

(3) The terms of the agreement must be comparable to similar arrangements entered into in an arm's length transaction.

If the agreement does not meet this statutory criteria, appraisals may have to be obtained in order to substantiate the value of the interests for estate tax purposes. An agreement for which more than 50% of the value of the business is owned by non-family members is deemed to meet statutory requirements.[3]

§ 24.40 Planning With Certain Assets—Closely Held Business Interests—Liquidity Issues

An estate consisting in large part of an interest in a closely held business might not be able to easily liquidate sufficient assets to pay estate taxes, or would have to liquidate a going business at "fire sale" price. Fortunately Congress provided some relief to estates which satisfy certain requirements. Specifically, the executor can elect to pay a portion of the estate tax in two to ten equal annual installments if 35% or more of the adjusted gross estate consists of an interest in a closely held business.[1] The portion that can be paid on an installment basis is the percentage of the estate tax that is equal to the following ratio:

Value of Closely Held Business Interest/Adjusted Gross Estate[2]

The first installment need not be made until five years after the ordinary date on which the estate tax is due, *i.e.*, the ninth month after

§ 24.39

1. Treas. Reg. § 20.2031–2(h); Rev. Rul. 59–60, 1959–1 C.B. 237; Estate of Bischoff v. Commissioner of Internal Revenue, 69 T.C. 32 (U.S.Tax Ct.1977); *cf.* St. Louis County Bank v. United States, 674 F.2d 1207 (8th Cir.1982) (existence of *bona fide* business purpose does not preclude inquiry as to whether agreement constitutes tax avoidance testamentary device).

2. P.L. 101–508, § 11602(e)(1)(A)(ii), 101st Cong., 2d Sess. (Nov. 5, 1990).

3. Treas. Reg. § 25.2703–1(b)(3).

§ 24.40

1. I.R.C. § 6166(a)(1). "Adjusted gross estate" means the decedent's gross estate, less certain allowable deductions. I.R.C. § 6166(b)(6).

2. I.R.C. § 6166(a)(2).

the decedent's death. During that period, only interest need be paid.[3] Interest is charged on the unpaid portion of the tax that is being paid under this installment payment election, a portion of which can be paid at a favorable rate of 2%. The portion that will only be charged at a 2% rate is the estate tax attributable to the first $1 million in taxable value of the business interest[4] (indexed for inflation after 1998).[5] In effect, for 1998 the reduced interest rate applies to $458,000 of deferred tax.

If it is anticipated that the estate will not qualify for this election, the client should consider purchasing sufficient life insurance to ensure liquidity for the estate.[6]

If the value of a closely-held corporation exceeds 35% of the value of the excess of the decedent's gross estate over the permissible deductions in determining the taxable estate, redemptions of stock by the estate which do not exceed the estate taxes, funeral and administrative expenses are treated as an exchange of stock rather than as a dividend.[7] Since the "tax basis" of the stock is stepped up to fair market value at decedent's death,[8] or alternate valuation date,[9] an exchange, as opposed to a dividend, will not trigger additional *income* tax for the estate. Thus, under those circumstances, distributions from a closely-held corporation, with sufficient liquidity, can be used for the payment of estate taxes and administration expenses.

§ 24.41 Planning With Certain Assets—Closely Held Business Interests—Minority Discounts

The owner of a closely held business can reduce the overall transfer taxes that his estate will incur by making *inter vivos* transfers of minority interests in the business.[1] The transferred interests will be valued on a discounted basis depending upon the types of restrictions on the transfers of such interests and the limitations on control, from either being in a minority position or from owning an interest, such as a limited partnership interest, that grants the transferee limited or no control of the business. Typical methods of transferring discounted interests in closely held businesses include transferring limited partnership interests with transfer restrictions, minority common stock inter-

---

3. I.R.C. §§ 6166(a)(3), 6601(j).

4. For estates of decedents dying before January 1, 1998 the interest rate was 4% on the lesser of (1) $345,800 less the allowable unified credit, or the amount of estate tax extended under this election. The interest paid was deductible as an administration expense.

5. I.R.C. § 6601(j)(2).

6. **CAVEAT:** If the decedent owns the policy upon death, the proceeds will also be included in the gross estate. Thus, the amount of insurance necessary to cover estate taxes will have to be "grossed up" to cover the additional estate taxes that will be incurred from the ownership of the policy. *See supra,* §§ 24.34–24.36 for discussions on planning with life insurance.

7. I.R.C. §§ 303(a), (b).

8. I.R.C. § 1014.

9. I.R.C. § 1034(a)(2). *See infra,* § 24.73.

§ 24.41

1. Rev. Rul. 93–12, 1993–1 C.B. 202.

ests subject to transfer restrictions, or recapitalization where the shareholder retains voting stock and gives common stock to the children. Use of these forms of transfers has enabled taxpayers to argue successfully for discounts for lack of marketability and minority interests ranging from 10% to more than 50%.[2]

By reducing one's interest in a closely held business to that of a minority interest, the taxpayer's estate will also be able to take advantage of valuation discounts when valuing the interests remaining in the decedent's estate.

§ 24.42 Planning With Certain Assets—Farms and Business Real Property

If certain conditions are met the executor may elect to use the special valuation rules for real property used for farming or in a closely held business to reduce the value for estate tax purposes.[1] The maximum reduction under such provision, however, is $750,000.

In order to qualify for such reduced valuation the following requirements must be met:

(1) The property must be used for a "qualified use" by the decedent or a member of his family;[2]

(2) The value of the property in the decedent's estate must be at least 50% of the decedent's gross estate (less debts);

(3) At least 25% of the gross estate (less debts) must consist of qualified property;

(4) Such property must pass to "qualified heirs;"[3]

(5) The property must have been held and used as a farm or in a closely held business for five of the last eight years by the decedent or a member of his family, during which time such

---

2. Propstra v. United States, 680 F.2d 1248 (9th Cir.1982) (15% discount in real estate); Lefrak v. C.I.R., TC Memo 1993–526, 66 T.C.M. (CCH) 1297 (U.S.Tax Ct.1993) (30% discount permitted for minority transfers in apartment buildings and commercial realty); Moore v. C.I.R., TC Memo 1991–546, 62 T.C.M. (CCH) 1128 (U.S.Tax Ct.1991) (35% discount for transfers of partnership interests to family members); Estate of O'Keefe v. C.I.R., TC Memo 1992–210, 63 T.C.M. (CCH) 2699 (U.S.Tax Ct.1992) (discounts from 25% to 75% for lack of marketability of artwork); Estate of Wildman v. C.I.R., TC Memo 1989–667, 58 T.C.M. (CCH) 1006 (U.S.Tax Ct.1989) (40% discount); Estate of Katz v. C.I.R., TC Memo 1968–171, 27 T.C.M. (CCH) 825 (U.S.Tax Ct.1968) (45.5% discount).

PRACTICE POINTER: An appraisal of the interests transferred should be obtained and attached to the taxpayer's gift tax returns to substantiate the taxpayer's position.

CAVEAT: Practitioners must also be aware of I.R.C. § 2701, which imposes restrictions on the types of transfers to family members which can be used to reduce transfer taxes, I.R.C. § 2703, discussed *supra* at § 24.39, and I.R.C. § 2704, which requires certain "applicable restrictions" and lapses of rights to be ignored for valuation purposes.

§ 24.42
1. I.R.C. § 2032A.
2. I.R.C. § 2032A(b)(2).
3. I.R.C. § 2032A(e).

person must have materially participated in the operation thereof;[4] and

(6) If the farm or business qualifies, then an additional estate tax will be due if, within 10 years after the decedent's death and before the death of the qualified heir, the qualified heir disposes of any interest in the property, other than to a family member, or ceases to use such property in the manner in which its use was qualified for.

§ 24.43 Planning With Certain Assets—Installment Obligations

If a decedent dies owning an installment obligation, generally an obligation to make payments over more than one taxable year,[1] then the amount of unrecognized gain from the property sale constitutes a source of IRD.[2] Collection or cancellation of the installment obligation by the estate will result in IRD for the estate, or for a specific or residuary beneficiary entitled to such obligation.[3] In addition, *the estate*, rather than a specific or residuary beneficiary, will recognize the IRD if the beneficiary is the obligor.[4] This means, for example, that if a client wishes to forgive the remaining principal owed on the installment obligation, the client can instead specifically bequeath the installment obligation to someone else in a lower tax bracket, and leave the obligor a bequest sufficient to satisfy the remaining obligation. In this manner, the IRD income is taxed at a lower rate.

§ 24.44 Lifetime Planning

Estate planning does not end with the drafting of a last will and testament. In fact, depending upon the size of an estate and the person's circumstances, such as whether the person owns a closely held business,[1] making lifetime transfers may significantly reduce the amount of transfer taxes that will eventually be incurred.

One significant advantage to making lifetime gifts is that a gift made during lifetime is tax exclusive, *i.e.* the tax paid is on the net gift, whereas the estate tax is tax inclusive, *i.e.* the tax paid is on the gross estate. For example, suppose a person makes a taxable gift which incurs, after application of the unified credit and all other available credits and deductions, a gift tax of $300,000. Since the person had to pay the

---

4. I.R.C. § 2032A(b)(1)(C).

§ 24.43

1. I.R.C. § 453.
2. *See supra*, § 24.37.
3. I.R.C. § 691; Treas. Reg. § 1.691(a)–4. **CAVEAT:** If the installment obligation is allocated to the residuary marital share, a fractional share marital formula should be used, rather than a pecuniary formula, to avoid immediate IRD to the estate. *See supra*, § 24.23, regarding the distinction between pecuniary and fractional share bequests.

4. I.R.C. §§ 691(a)(2), (5).

§ 24.44

1. *See supra*, § 24.38.

$300,000 gift tax, the estate is dissipated by that amount, and there is no tax on that $300,000.[2] If, however, the $300,000 tax had not been paid during lifetime, the estate would be taxed on, not only the amount that the beneficiaries of the estate receive, but on the $300,000 as well. Thus, it may always be more advantageous to make lifetime gifts even at the cost of paying tax currently.[3] Another advantage of making lifetime gifts is that all future appreciation is transferred out of the estate.

§ 24.45   Lifetime Planning—Valuation of Gifts

As discussed above, fractional gifts of closely held businesses or other assets can result in the interest being conveyed to be valued at a discount.[1] For example, a 30% interest in a wholly owned business worth $1,000,000 is conveyed from father to son, and, due to the minority interest discount and a discount for lack of marketability, the fair market value of that interest, as determined by an appraiser, is reduced by 30%.[2] Thus, for gift tax purposes, the amount gifted is worth $210,000, rather than $300,000 (30% of $1 million = $300,000; 30% discount on $300,000 = $90,000; $300,000—$90,000 = $210,000).

Investment assets may also be conveyed during lifetime to take advantage of such valuation discounts. A common method used to obtain discounts is to establish a family limited partnership. In a family limited partnership, parents place assets, such as real estate, stocks, and bonds, into a partnership, and make gifts of the limited partnership interests to their children while retaining control as general partners. Pursuant to the partnership agreement, the children have no control over the partnership's assets, and cannot transfer their interests without the approval of the general partners. Such restrictions may result in discounts for the limited partnership interests.[3]

2. CAVEAT: This advantage is lost if the transferor dies within three years of the gift since all gift taxes paid for gifts made during the preceding three years must be added back to the estate. I.R.C. § 2035(c).

3. CAVEAT: The advantage of making lifetime gifts, however, must be weighed against the loss of step-up in basis, which is unavailable to lifetime transfers. Therefore, it is recommended that high basis assets be used for such gifts, where possible. Other disadvantages include the loss of the use of the funds paid in gift tax and the lack of a credit against federal gift tax for the state gift tax paid. *Cf.* I.R.C. § 2011 which provides a federal estate tax credit for state death tax paid.

2. Note that the IRS recently reversed its long-standing position that inter-family gifts do not warrant minority discounts or discounts for lack of marketability. *See supra,* Rev. Rul. 93–12; *see also supra,* § 24.41, discussing Rev. Rul. 93–12.

3. CAVEAT: In Private Letter Ruling 9436005, the Internal Revenue Service took the position that giving a "swing vote" to a transferee would offset some of the discounts.

CAVEAT: Recently, the Internal Revenue Service has challenged the use of such discounts for family partnerships formed to hold primarily marketable securities. *See* Private Letter Rulings 9735003 and 9719006.

§ 24.45
1. *See supra,* § 24.41.

§ 24.46 Lifetime Planning—Valuation of Gifts—Grantor Retained Trusts

Generally, gifts of remainder interests in property are valued using the residual method. That is, the value of the gifted remainder equals the value of the underlying asset less the actuarial value of any interest retained by the grantor.[1] The actuarial value of the interest is determined using 120% of the federal mid-term rate then in effect under I.R.C. § 1274(d)(1).[2]

Gifts of remainder interests to family members, however, are valued using special valuation rules, which assign a value of zero to the retained interest unless the interest retained qualifies under one of the exceptions.[3]

For assets other than a residence, there are generally only two types of trusts that fall within the exceptions: a grantor retained annuity trust ("GRAT"), and a grantor retained unitrust ("GRUT"). For a GRAT, the grantor must be entitled to a fixed amount, regardless of the income earned by the trust, payable at least annually. The amount must be either a fixed dollar amount or a fixed percentage of the initial fair market value of the trust corpus.[4] In order to avoid having the trust corpus included in the grantor's estate, and thus defeating the purpose of establishing the GRAT, the fixed payments must be made for a term of years, and the grantor must, in fact, outlive the term.[5] The value of the retained interest in the GRAT is determined using actuarial tables and a rate of interest determined under I.R.C. § 7520.[6]

§ 24.46

1. Treas. Reg. § 25.2512-5.
2. I.R.C. § 7520.
3. I.R.C. § 2702(a)(i). Family members are defined as the grantor's spouse, ancestor, or lineal descendent of the grantor or the grantor's spouse, or a sibling of the grantor. Any spouse of a family member is also a family member. I.R.C. §§ 2702(a)(1), 2702(c)(2), 2702(e), 2704(c)(2).

PRACTICE POINTER: Note that the valuation rules of I.R.C. § 2702 only apply to family members. Therefore, if a client wishes to benefit nieces or nephews or more distant relatives, or friends, the general valuation rules under I.R.C. § 2512 apply.

4. The actual amount of payment may vary from year to year, but each payment will be considered a qualified payment only to the extent it does not exceed the preceding year's payment by more than 120%. Treas. Reg. § 25.2702-3(b).

5. **PRACTICE POINTER:** The most desirable structure for a GRAT is one where the remainder interest is "zeroed out." This can be accomplished by selecting a combination of high annuity rate and a short term, or a lower annuity rate combined with a long term. Since the grantor must outlive the term, it is better to use a short term, e.g., two years, and a high rate. For example, assuming an I.R.C. § 7520 rate of 8%, a 60 year old person establishing a two year trust, with a contingent reversion, will cause a zero gift value by retaining a 56.854% annuity. The payment of such an annuity would generally require the use of principal. However, since the trust is a grantor trust there is no income recognized on such transfer to the grantor. I.R.C. § 671.

CAVEAT: Treas. Reg. § 25.2702-3(e) Example 5 indicates that a zero value is not possible. *See* Rev. Rul. 77-454, 1977-2 C.B. 351. Most commentators believe the IRS position is incorrect.

6. Treas. Reg. § 25.2702-2(b)(2). **CAVEAT:** If the trust income is insufficient to pay the annuity, principal must be invaded to do so, which, in turn, reduces the gift to the remainderman. In order for a GRAT to

§ 24.46

A GRAT is a most useful technique for passing wealth to the next generation. As long as the property transferred to the trust earns a higher rate of return, including appreciation than the I.R.C. § 7520 rate, there is a distinct gift tax advantage. Clients with assets generating above-average returns or assets having substantial appreciation potential are ideal candidates for a GRAT.

A GRUT is similar to a GRAT in that the grantor must be entitled to fixed payments calculated as a fixed percentage of the fair market value of the trust corpus, but such value is redetermined annually. Also like the GRAT, the payments must be made for a term of years, and the grantor must actually survive the term in order to avoid having the corpus included in the grantor's estate. However, a GRUT is rarely utilized since it cannot be zeroed-out in value, eliminating one of the major planning benefits available.[7]

A West's McKinney's Form, appropriate to this section, is available.[8]

§ 24.47 Lifetime Planning—Valuation of Gifts—Residence Trusts

There are two types of trusts that may be established to transfer a future interest in a residence: a personal residence trust ("PRT") and a qualified personal residence trust ("QPRT").[1] The QPRT allows for greater flexibility and is therefore most often used. The principal difference between a PRT and a QPRT is that a QPRT is permitted to hold a limited amount of cash for repairs, payment of a mortgage, or other expenses, or for the purchase of an initial or replacement residence.[2] Unlike a PRT, a QPRT is also permitted to sell the residence. If the residence is sold, a new residence must be purchased within two years or else the trust will cease to be qualified and the proceeds will have to be distributed to either the grantor or converted to a GRAT. The distribution must occur within 30 days of the date that the trust ceases to be a QPRT. A QPRT must also require distribution of the trust income not less frequently than annually.[3]

Like the GRAT and GRUT, the grantor must outlive the trust term in order to avoid having the residence included in his estate. Also, the PRT or QPRT may include a reversionary interest for the Grantor, which will further lower the value of the gift of the remainder interest.

---

provide a benefit to the remainderman, the GRAT must outperform the I.R.C. § 7520 interest rate. It is therefore, more effective to use a GRAT where the asset is expected to appreciate by substantially more than the I.R.C. § 7520 rate.

7. Treas. Reg. § 25.2702–2(b)(2).

8. *See* West's McKinney's Forms—Estate and Surrogate's Practice § 10:214 (grantor retained annuity trust).

§ 24.47

1. Treas. Reg. § 25.2702–5(a).
2. Treas. Reg. § 25.2702–5(c)(5)(ii).
3. Treas. Reg. § 25.2702–5(c)(8).

As with a GRAT, the value of the remainder interest is determined using actuarial tables and interest rates under I.R.C. § 7520. In other words, higher interest rates and a longer term will result in the smallest possible gift, but making the term particularly long carries with it the risk that the grantor will not survive the trust term and will thus lose the entire savings on transfer taxes.

EXAMPLE: A 50 year old man transfers his home to a QPRT, when the I.R.C. § 7520 rate is 7% for a term of 10 years. If he dies during the term, the house reverts to his estate. The fair market value of the house is $400,000, the gift tax value of such transfer is $186,000.[4]

A person may establish up to two residence trusts during his lifetime. Such trusts may be established with either the person's "principal residence," as defined by I.R.C. § 1034, one "other residence," as defined by I.R.C. § 280A,[5] or a fractional interest in either.[6] If a person creates two personal residence trusts, one must be for the grantor's principal residence.

A West's McKinney's Form, appropriate to this section, is available.[7]

§ 24.48 Lifetime Planning—Valuation of Gifts—Residence Trusts—Income Tax Considerations

PRTs and QPRTs are considered to be "grantor trusts" for income tax purposes,[1] meaning that the income and deductions of the trust are attributable to the grantor for income tax purposes. Moreover, if the grantor retains a reversionary interest in the trust, the grantor will be taxed on any gain on the sale of the property. This is desirable, since it permits the grantor to take advantage of the $250,000 ($500.000 if married) capital gains exclusion for the sale of a residence.[2] In the past, since the trust would be characterized as a grantor trust, a grantor could retain the power to repurchase the residence from the trust at fair market value before the end of the trust term without any tax consequence.[3] For example, if the grantor had originally purchased the home for $10,000 and the house was sold by the remaindermen at the end of the trust term for $300,000, the remaindermen would have to recognize capital gains of $290,000 ($300,000—$10,000). Instead, if the grantor repurchased the residence from the trust and died owning the property,

---

4. These amounts are derived from Publication 1457 (U.S. Treasury) Table H(7.0). There are several computer programs available to make these computations.

5. I.R.C. § 280A requires that the property must be used for personal purposes, or if the unit is rented, the unit is used for personal purposes for the greater of 14 days or 10% of the number of days that it is rented.

6. Treas. Reg. § 25.2702-5(c).

7. *See* West's McKinney's Forms—Estate and Surrogate's Practice § 10:212 (qualified personal residence trust).

§ 24.48

1. I.R.C. §§ 671–677.
2. I.R.C. § 121.
3. *See* Private Letter Ruling 9026036.

the persons inheriting the property would have obtained a stepped up "tax basis" in the property equal to the fair market value of the residence,[4] meaning that there would be no capital gains taxes if the property was sold shortly after the decedent's death (assuming no post-mortem appreciation). At the same time, the heirs would have received, at the end of the trust term, the assets used to pay for the repurchase of the residence, free of further gift tax consequences.

Prop. Treas. Reg. § 25.2702–5(b)(1) and (c)(9), however, precludes such repurchase of the residence by the grantor (or related party) and requires residence trust agreements to specifically prohibit such sales.

In determining whether to place a residence into either a PRT or a QPRT, the estate planner must determine whether the transfer tax savings outweigh the loss of the stepped-up tax basis, and thus the capital gains savings.[5]

§ 24.49 Lifetime Planning—Annual Gift Tax Exclusion

The term "$10,000 gift" has obtained a talismanic significance to senior citizens in particular and to their families. As almost every senior citizen knows, an annual gift of up to $10,000 ($20,000 for married couples who elect to "split the gift") per donee is exempt from federal gift taxes.[1] This presents the opportunity for persons having estates that exceed the applicable exclusion amount to reduce their estates below that figure during lifetime without incurring any transfer taxes.

> **EXAMPLE:** W, a widow, has assets worth $650,000. W has five children. She can give each child $10,000, reducing her estate to $600,000. If she dies the next day, her estate will owe no federal estate taxes (assuming that she has not made any taxable gifts during her lifetime) because of the unified credit.

Various aspects of how this annual exclusion works, however, have not become universal mantras, and therefore lead to certain misperceptions. First, the annual exclusion is only available for gifts of present interests in property. In other words, property placed in trust or any trust-like arrangement by which the commencement of "use, possession, or enjoyment" of the property is limited until "some future date or

---

4. I.R.C. § 1223(11). The valuation is either at the date of death or at the "alternate valuation date," which is nine months after death, if that date is elected by the executor for the purpose of computing estate taxes.

5. **PRACTICE POINTER:** It may be possible to sell the house to the remainder-persons during the trust term and utilize the § 121 exclusion while providing a new basis to the remainder person.

§ 24.49

1. I.R.C. §§ 2503(b), 2513(a). The gift-splitting exemption only applies if both spouses are either U.S. citizens or residents. The election must be made on a federal gift tax return (Form 709), which is filed by April 15th in the following calendar year. Treas. Reg. § 25.2513–2. The annual exclusion will be adjusted for inflation after 1998. I.R.C. § 2503(b)(2).

time" does not qualify for the annual exclusion.[2] Second, while there is no marital deduction for gifts made to non-citizen spouses, the annual exclusion for gifts made to a non-citizen spouse is $100,000, rather than $10,000.[3]

In addition to annual exclusion gifts, I.R.C. § 2503(e) provides an exclusion for tuition payments made to educational institutions described in I.R.C. § 170(b)(1)(A)(ii) for the donee's education and payments to medical care providers, as defined in I.R.C. § 213(d) for the donee's medical care. To qualify for such exclusions, the payments must be made directly to the institution or service providers.[4]

Library References:
West's Key No. Digests, Internal Revenue ⚖4206.10.

§ 24.50 Lifetime Planning—Annual Gift Tax Exclusion—Section 2503(c) Trusts

An exception to the general rule about transfers of future interests qualifying for the annual exclusion is a transfer in trust for the benefit of minors that satisfies certain requirements—a so-called "Section 2503(c) Trust." A Section 2503(c) trust allows the grantor to exercise extensive control over the trust property and the minor's access to it because, in order to qualify for the annual exclusion, the trust must simply provide that the trust corpus and income "may be expended by, or for the benefit of, the donee before attaining the age of 21 years."[1] To the extent that funds are not expended, the funds pass to the donee when he attains age 21, or if the donee dies before attaining age 21, the money must be payable to his estate or as the donee appoints under a general power of appointment.[2]

Section 2503(c) trusts are particularly popular devices for funding college education, because the grantor may exercise complete control as to when and for what purposes distributions are made. In addition, the grantor even has the opportunity to use these trusts to shift some income to children, who presumably are in a lower tax bracket than the parents. Generally, children under the age of 14 are taxed on unearned income exceeding $1,300 (in 1997), indexed at the parent's marginal tax rate.[3] However, the grantor/trustee can simply elect not to make any distributions over $1,300 per year to a child under 14, and the income will instead be taxed at the marginal rate for trusts which might be less that the parent's rate.[4]

2. Treas. Reg. § 25.2503–3(a).
3. I.R.C. § 2523(i).
4. Treas. Reg. § 25.2503–6(b)(3).

§ 24.50
1. I.R.C. § 2503(c)(1).
2. I.R.C. § 2503(c)(2).

3. I.R.C. § 1(g).
4. **PRACTICE POINTER:** A way to maximize the use of lower trust marginal rates for children under 14 is to establish multiple trusts for their benefit. Each parent can establish a trust for a child, take advantage of the annual exclusion, and dou-

§ 24.50   ESTATE PLANNING   Ch. 24

A serious drawback to these trusts is that the property must be distributed to the beneficiary at age 21, regardless of how responsible or irresponsible he is.[5]

West's McKinney's Forms, appropriate to this section, are available.[6]

Library References:
West's Key No. Digests, Internal Revenue ⚖4206.10.

§ 24.51 Lifetime Planning—Annual Gift Tax Exclusion—Uniform Transfers to Minor's Act Accounts

Effective for transfers made on or after January 1, 1997, New York has adopted the Uniform Transfers to Minor's Act ("UTMA"), which is codified at EPTL Sections 7–6.1 through 7–6.24. Under the UTMA, a parent or other adult may establish an account for the benefit of a minor.[1] This will qualify for the annual gift tax exclusion, because the assets must be distributed to the child when he reaches age 21.[2]

Like the Section 2503(c) trust, however, the primary drawback is that the assets must be distributed to the beneficiary no later than when he attains age 21, no matter how mature or immature the beneficiary is.

Library References:
West's Key No. Digests, Internal Revenue ⚖4206.10.

§ 24.52 Lifetime Planning—Annual Gift Tax Exclusion—Crummey Trusts

A trust can be drafted giving a "Crummey power" to minor beneficiaries which permits them to withdraw the contribution for a limited period of time, generally 30 days, thereby qualifying the transfer as a present interest eligible for the gift tax annual exclusion.[1] Such a trust must comply with the "Crummey" notice requirements. This is a particularly useful type of trust which can be used to provide for beneficiaries

---

ble the income that will be taxed at lower trust rates.

5. **PRACTICE POINTER:** One way to avoid terminating the trust when the child reaches age 21 is to give the child a withdrawal right at age 21, limited for a period (*i.e.*, 30 days) after which the trust continues until the child reaches a later specified age.

6. *See* West's McKinney's Forms—Estate and Surrogate's Practice §§ 10:171–10:171A, 10:470B (Section 2503(c) trust).

§ 24.51
1. **CAVEAT:** The donor parent should not be named as custodian since if he dies while the child is a minor, the account will be included in the parent's estate.

2. EPTL § 7–6.11 permits the donor to designate age 18, rather than age 21, as the age at which the property must be distributed to the beneficiary. In the absence of such an affirmative designation, the property is distributable to the beneficiary when he attains age 21. EPTL §§ 7–6.20(a).

§ 24.52
1. *See supra*, § 24.36.

496

beyond age 21 while retaining control of the assets. The one drawback to this type of trust is that the beneficiary could decide to take advantage of the right to withdraw the contribution to the trust.

West's McKinney's Forms, appropriate to this section, are available.[2]

Library References:

West's Key No. Digests, Internal Revenue ⟐4206.10.

§ 24.53 Lifetime Planning—Annual Gift Tax Exclusion—Family Limited Partnerships

One of the major concerns clients have about making gifts is that of giving up control. A popular planning technique which allows the transferror to retain control is that of the family limited partnership. The partnership can initially be formed by having the parents contribute property in consideration of the general and limited partnership interests.[1] The parents can then make gifts of the limited partnership interests to their children, taking appropriate discounts for minority interests and lack of marketability. As general partners, the parents retain control over the timing and amount of distributions, even after the children reach majority. Since gifts of limited partnership interests qualify as present interest gifts, they can be used to take advantage of the annual gift tax exclusion.[2] In addition, since valuation discounts may be available with respect to such gifts, greater leverage of the exemption amount is possible.[3]

Library References:

West's Key No. Digests, Internal Revenue ⟐4206.10.

§ 24.54 Lifetime Planning—Charitable Remainder Trusts

A charitably-inclined individual with appreciated assets, *i.e.*, assets that have appreciated in value since they were acquired, can establish a charitable remainder trust which will not only provide an income tax deduction for the donor, but can be used to provide an income stream for the donor without the need to recognize any taxable gain when the assets are sold. Moreover, since the gift will qualify for a charitable deduction, the gift or estate tax can be reduced.

Specifically, there are three types of charitable remainder trusts:

2. See West's McKinney's Forms—Estate and Surrogate's Practice § 10:470A (Trust with "Crummey Power").

§ 24.53

1. *See also*, Chapter 2 "Non-corporate Entities: Limited Liability Companies and Partnerships," *supra*.

2. Private Letter Ruling 9415007.

3. **CAVEAT:** The partnership agreement must be carefully drafted in order to obtain valuation discounts. *See supra* §§ 24.41, 24.45.

1. a charitable remainder annuity trust ("CRAT"),
2. a charitable remainder unitrust ("CRUT"), and
3. a pooled income fund.

A CRAT is similar to a GRAT.[1] The trust must provide a fixed annual annuity to the grantor or other noncharitable beneficiary, although for a CRAT, it must not be less than 5% nor more than 50% of the net fair market value of the assets when placed into the trust.[2] The major dissimilarity between a GRAT and CRAT is that the grantor's interest in the GRAT must terminate at some point prior to death, whereas the grantor's interest in the CRAT can be a life interest.

The parallels between a CRUT and a GRUT[3] are similar to those between a CRAT and GRAT. A CRUT must provide a fixed percentage of the fair market value of the trust corpus, redetermined annually, to the non-charitable beneficiary and, such amount cannot be less than 5%,[4] nor more than 50% of the annually redetermined value of trust assets[5] and the interest of the grantor may be a life interest.

A pooled income fund is a fund maintained by a charitable organization, which commingles the contributions of the various donors, and pays the income beneficiaries based upon the fund's rate of return.[6] Like the CRAT and CRUT, the remainder becomes the property of the charity.

Aside from the charitable deductions obtained from establishing a charitable remainder trust, a donor can use a charitable remainder trust to convert appreciated property into income producing property without recognition of capital gain.

EXAMPLE: If a Donor who owns stock, which pays no dividends and cost $10 per share, but is now worth $100 per share, transfers that stock to a CRAT, he must receive an annuity of at least 5% per year. If the CRAT then sells the stock and invests in U.S. Treasury notes to provide annuity payments to Donor, neither Donor nor the trust recognizes capital gain on the sale, and Donor's income stream is increased because the trust can reinvest the gross pre-tax proceeds.[7]

---

§ 24.54
1. A grantor retained annuity trust. *See supra,* § 24.46.
2. I.R.C. § 664(d)(1)(A).
3. *See supra,* § 24.46.
4. I.R.C. § 664(d)(2)(A).
5. **CAVEAT:** Under the 1997 Act, a trust will not qualify for a tax deduction and will be void from its inception unless the value of the charitable remainder with respect to any transfer is at least 10% of the fair market value of the property transferred. Such requirement may be difficult to meet for a testamentary trust due to the variable factors that are not determinable until death.
6. I.R.C. § 642(c)(2).
7. **PRACTICE POINTER:** Use of a charitable remainder trust can be combined with an insurance trust to replace the amount that descendants would have otherwise received. The insurance trust purchases enough insurance on the life of the donor to replace the assets contributed to the charitable remainder trust, using income, and the income tax savings, from the charitable remainder trust to pay the premium.

An asset that is well suited to being contributed to a testamentary charitable remainder trust is an IRA. By naming a charitable remainder trust as the beneficiary, the IRA proceeds payable at the owner's death will not be subject to income tax.[8] This means that, while a life beneficiary, such as a child, will have to pay tax on actual income distributions from the trust, the amount which the trust will be investing will be greater since it would not have been reduced by income taxes.

A West's McKinney's Form, appropriate to this section, is available.[9]

§ 24.55 Lifetime Planning—Charitable Lead Trusts

Another technique available to the charitably inclined who have sufficient income during their lifetimes but want to ensure that assets will eventually be passed to their descendants is the charitable lead trust. A charitable lead annuity trust or unitrust provides an annuity to the charity, with the remainder going to the named beneficiary (or to the grantor) at the end of the trust term.[1] If the lead trust is a grantor trust, the donor will be entitled to an income tax deduction for the value of the income (or lead) interest,[2] and will be treated as the owner of the income and be taxed on it each year under the grantor trust rules.[3] On the other hand, a testamentary lead trust can provide an estate tax deduction for the value of the lead interest.

§ 24.56 Planning in Special Situations—Terminally Ill

One of the most sensitive situations that an attorney is called on to handle is estate planning for a terminally ill individual. Besides having to cope with the emotional turmoil involved with the person's imminent demise, use of many estate planning tools that could otherwise have been used with a healthy person is precluded. For example, gifts of certain interests, such as insurance,[1] made within three years of death that are includible in the taxable estate, will not reduce estate taxes. Furthermore, any gift tax paid on gifts made within three years of death is added back to the estate.[2] The ill client also is unable to make use of any trusts that require the person to outlive the trust term, such as a

---

8. Private Letter Ruling 9237020.

9. *See* West's McKinney's Forms—Estate and Surrogate's Practice §§ 10:111B, 10:113M, 10:113N (charitable remainder annuity trust); §§ 10:113A–10:113E, 10:113H–10:113J (charitable remainder unitrust).

§ 24.55

1. I.R.C. §§ 170(f)(2)(B), 2055(e)(2)(B), 2522(c)(2)(B).

2. I.R.C. § 170(f)(2)(B).

3. I.R.C. § 671. **CAVEAT:** The donor of the lead interest can be subject to recapture of the previously allowed deduction if the taxpayer is no longer taxed on the yearly income of the trust. I.R.C. § 170 (f)(2)(B). For example, if the individual contributes the lead interest for five years but dies in the third year, his income for the year of death would include the excess deduction that he took when the trust was established, *i.e.*, an amount to take into account the additional two years of income that the charity did not receive.

§ 24.56

1. I.R.C. § 2035(d).
2. I.R.C. § 2035(C).

§ 24.56 ESTATE PLANNING Ch. 24

GRAT or a GRUT.[3] One device, however, that is still effective, is the ability to make annual $10,000 gifts to any number of donees. To avoid non-utilization of capital losses, the sale of capital gain property should be co-ordinated before the client's death. Another device especially useful in such situations is the self-canceling installment note ("SCIN"). Other planning options may include forming a family partnership or transferring closely held business interests to take advantage of minority interest discounts.[4] Besides the estate planning concerns, the attorney should inquire whether a durable power of attorney and health care proxy has been executed.[5] In addition, the attorney should obtain a current list of all assets, how they are held, liabilities (including contingent) and a list of family members with their addresses.

§ 24.57 Planning in Special Situations—Terminally Ill—Self-Canceling Installment Notes

One of the few techniques available to reduce an estate of an ill individual whose life expectancy can still be measured in years rather than months[1] is the use of a SCIN[2] as consideration for the sale of property to intended beneficiaries. The SCIN, which is also sometimes referred to as a "death-terminating installment note" is a debt obligation that, by its terms, extinguishes upon the seller's death, with the remaining balance being automatically canceled.

In order to ensure that the Internal Revenue Service will recognize the *bona fides* of this transaction, the note must provide some form of premium to the seller, either in the form of an above market interest rate or a higher selling price. The note must have a principal payment schedule rather than a balloon payment at the end of the note term, and the term cannot exceed the life expectancy of the seller. By following these guidelines, neither the note nor the property sold is includible in

---

3. *See supra*, § 24.46.

4. *See supra*, § 24.41. **CAVEAT:** A deathbed transfer of an .0008% interest in a closely-held business to reduce the decedent's estate's interest to below 50%, and thereby eliminating the control premium, did not entitle an estate's interest to a minority discount. Estate of Murphy v. C.I.R., TC Memo 1990–472, 60 T.C.M. (CCH) 645 (U.S.Tax Ct.1990). *Cf.* Estate of Bright v. United States, 658 F.2d 999 (5th Cir.1981) (no control premium attributed to spouse where husband and wife owned 55% of stock; upon decedent's death, community property rights ceased so that decedent and surviving spouse only treated as each owning 27 1/2% of stock); Estate of Anthony J. Frank Sr., 69 T.C.M. (CCH) 2255 (U.S Tax Ct.1995).

5. *See infra*, §§ 24.89 and 24.91.

§ 24.57

1. Treas. Reg. §§ 1.7520–3(b)(3), 20.7520–3(b)(3), 25.7520–3(b)(3), which prohibit the use of the actuarial tables if the person who is the "measuring life" for valuation purposes is known to have an incurable illness or other deteriorating condition and the odds are greater than 50% that the person will die within one year. *Concur* McLendon Estate v. C.I.R., TC Memo 1993–459, 66 T.C.M. (CCH) 946 (U.S.Tax Ct.1993) (standard actuarial tables inappropriate for valuation of private annuity where actual life expectancy was less than one year).

2. *See supra*, § 24.56.

the decedent's estate.[3]

The seller will recognize any gain on the sale for income tax purposes, but generally the gain will be recognized over the term of the note, because the seller can recognize the gain, plus interest, on the installment basis.[4] The buyer will be entitled to deductions on the note interest.[5] The IRS has taken the position that the gain that is not recognized at the decedent's death is IRD[6] that must be recognized by the estate.[7]

§ 24.58 Planning in Special Situations—Non-citizen Spouses

Generally gifts between spouses, either *inter vivos* or upon death, qualify for the marital deduction.[1] However, if the recipient spouse is not a U.S. citizen, special rules apply. Generally, lifetime gifts to a noncitizen spouse are not eligible for the marital deduction, although a gift of up to $100,000 per year, rather than the usual $10,000, to the noncitizen spouse qualifies for the annual exclusion from gift tax.[2] Similarly, outright bequests to the noncitizen spouse generally do not qualify for the marital deduction.[3]

Bequests for the benefit of a noncitizen spouse left in a "qualified domestic trust" ("QDOT") will, however, qualify for the marital deduction if the bequest would otherwise qualify for the marital deduction. For example, the QDOT must also satisfy the requirements of a QTIP trust.[4] A QDOT must meet the following criteria:

---

3. Estate of Moss v. Commissioner of Internal Revenue, 74 T.C. 1239 (U.S.Tax Ct.1980); G.C.M. 39503 (May 7, 1986). See Rev. Rul. 86–72, 1986–1 C.B. 2 and T.A.M. 8906002.

4. *See* I.R.C. § 453.

5. I.R.C. § 163.

6. *See supra*, § 24.37.

7. Rev. Rul. 86–72, 1986–1 C.B. 253. In a reviewed decision, all 19 judges of the Tax Court rejected this approach in Estate of Frane v. C.I.R., 98 T.C. 341 (U.S.Tax Ct.1992), but were reversed by the Eighth Circuit. 998 F.2d 567 (8th Cir.1993).

PRACTICE POINTER: Fiduciaries of estates located outside of the Eighth Circuit can, with confidence, take the position that the IRS and the Eighth Circuit are in error, because the Tax Court is free to limit its adherence to the appellate decision in Frane to cases arising from that circuit. Golsen v. Commissioner of Internal Revenue, 54 T.C. 742, 756–757 (U.S.Tax Ct.1970). The important distinction here is whether the gain not recognized should be reported by the estate or the decedent's final income tax return. If it is reportable on the decedent's final return, the tax liability arising therefrom will be a deduction from the decedent's gross estate.

§ 24.58

1. *See supra*, § 24.22. *See* Preminger, *et al., Trusts and Estates Practice in New York* (West 1997).

2. I.R.C. § 2523(i).

3. I.R.C. § 2056(d). This rule is imposed to ensure that the estate of at least one of the spouses is subject to estate tax, *i.e.*, that an estate passing to a non-citizen spouse does not escape estate taxation due to expatriation. Thus, I.R.C. § 2056(d) also provides that the surviving spouse's estate will receive a credit for taxes imposed on property passing to the non-citizen spouse which did not qualify for the marital deduction.

4. I.R.C. § 2056(d)(2). *See supra*, § 24.22.

(1) At least one trustee must be a "U.S. Trustee," that is, a U.S. citizen or a domestic corporation;

(2) No distribution of corpus may be made unless a U.S. Trustee has the right to withhold the tax imposed on the distribution;

(3) The executor must elect to treat the trust as a QDOT; and

(4) The trust must satisfy Treasury regulations prescribed to ensure collection of the tax.[5]

Principal distributions to the surviving spouse, as well as amounts remaining in the QDOT upon the death of the noncitizen spouse are taxed as additional amounts of the *first* deceased spouse's estate.[6] An exception to the imposition of estate taxes exists for "hardship" distributions to the spouse.[7]

The noncitizen spouse can avoid tax upon distributions from the trust by becoming a U.S. citizen prior to the due date of the estate tax return, or after the trust is established if:

(1) The surviving spouse was a U.S. resident from the date of the deceased spouse's death through the date he becomes a U.S. citizen, or

(2) Either no taxable distributions were made before the spouse becomes a U.S citizen or if the spouse elects to have prior distributions treated as taxable gifts *by the surviving spouse*.[8]

---

5. I.R.C. § 2056A(a). Final and Temporary regulations add five other requirements for a trust to be treated as a QDOT:

(1) if the fair market value of the assets passing to a QDOT exceeds $2 million, (i) at least one U.S. Trustee must be a bank, or (ii) the U.S. Trustee must furnish a bond or letter of credit equal to 65% of the value of the corpus passing to the trust, based on date of death values;

(2) if the fair market value is $2 million or less, the trust must either (i) fulfill the foregoing requirements regarding a bank or a bond, or (ii) require that no more than 35% of the value of the trust consist of non-U.S. situs realty;

(3) the trust must be administered and be subject to U.S. jurisdiction;

(4) if the U.S. Trustee is an individual, the individual must maintain a "tax home" in the United States, within the meaning of I.R.C. § 911(d)(3); and

(5) the trust would have to meet certain reporting requirements, including an annual list of trust assets and valuations.

Treas. Reg. §§ 20.2056A–2(a), 20.2056A–2T(d).

6. I.R.C. § 2056A(b).

7. I.R.C. § 2056A(b)(3). The regulations define hardship to mean a "distribution in response to an immediate and substantial financial need relating to the spouse's health, maintenance or support," and specifically excludes from hardship a situation in which the spouse personally owns publicly traded stock or a certificate of deposit which can be liquidated. Treas. Reg. § 20.2056A–5(c)(1).

8. I.R.C. § 2056A(b)(12). **PRACTICE POINTER:** Given the extensive restrictions that are imposed upon making tax-deferred bequests to noncitizen spouses, if the spouse has no intention of becoming a U.S. citizen, the citizen-spouse should be advised to make lifetime gifts of up to $100,000 per year to the spouse to build up the non-citizen spouse's estate. In this manner, if the non-citizen spouse dies first, the credit shelter trust and unlimited marital deduction are available.

A West's McKinney's Form, appropriate to this section, is available.[9]

§ 24.59 Planning in Special Situations—Multiple Marriages

Estate planning considerations may differ for couples where one or both of the spouses have been married previously. For example, there may be children from the prior marriage. In such a case, it is common for that parent to want to ensure that these children are provided for upon death, and may not want to leave such children at the mercy of a stepparent. Under those circumstances, the parent might want to only provide assets in trust, such as a QTIP trust, for the current spouse while ensuring that assets will ultimately pass to the children from the prior marriage. Alternatively, one may not want to leave any assets to the current spouse at all, especially where there may be wide age differences. However, providing limited benefits to a second spouse necessarily becomes a subject of negotiation and compromise rather than a simple assertion of "will." (Pun intended).[1]

§ 24.60 Planning in Special Situations—Multiple Marriages—Spousal Rights

In New York, one cannot simply disinherit a spouse, or limit their inheritance to amounts in trust. EPTL § 5–1.1–A provides that a spouse has six months from the time letters testamentary or administration are issued, but in any event no later than two years from the decedent's death, to exercise his or her "right of election" against the will. The spouse of a New York decedent is entitled to elect to take the greater of:

(1) $50,000, or

(2) one-third of the "net estate."

The net estate not only includes the probate estate, but all other "testamentary substitutes," such as Totten trusts, property held jointly with the right of survivorship, remainder interests in trusts established by the decedent where the decedent held a life estate or a power to consume, invade, alter or revoke the disposition,[1] gifts within one year of death, and qualified plans. Life insurance is not a testamentary substi-

---

[9] *See* West's McKinney's Forms—Estate and Surrogate's Practice § 7:280C (qualified domestic trust).

§ 24.59
[1] *See infra*, § 24.60.

§ 24.60
[1] *Cf.* Matter of Estate of Reynolds, 214 A.D.2d 944, 626 N.Y.S.2d 603 (4th Dep't 1995) which held that a trust providing income was not a testamentary substitute because the trust terminated, as did the grantor's right to change beneficiaries, "the day before [her] death." This case appears to be wrongly decided.

tute includible in the decedent's net estate for the purposes of computing the surviving spouse's elective share.[2]

A spouse who elects against a will is treated as having predeceased the testator for all other purposes of the will. For example, if the testator established a QTIP trust for his spouse and the spouse exercises the right of election to receive one-third outright, the spouse is deemed to have predeceased, and the remaining property is disposed of accordingly.[3]

Aside from an elective share, EPTL § 5–3.1 provides that $15,000, plus certain personal property, vests in a surviving spouse and is not considered to be part of the probate estate.

In order to effectively "disinherit" a spouse, the spouse must waive his or her right of election,[4] although such a waiver will not prevent the spouse from receiving the family allowance.[5] The spouse can execute such a waiver either before or after the marriage, which may be either a unilateral waiver or may be a waiver of election executed by both spouses.[6] The waiver does not have to be supported by consideration,[7] and may be either absolute or conditional.[8] A spouse may also waive the right of election as against a particular will, against any last will, against the estate at any time, or merely as against a particular testamentary substitute.[9]

An effective waiver of the right of election must be in writing and acknowledged in the manner required for the conveyance of realty.[10]

In order to disinherit a spouse from pension plan proceeds, the spouse must agree to a waiver of her rights *after* the marriage has taken place—in other words, a prenuptial agreement will not suffice.[11]

2. Will of Boyd, 161 Misc.2d 191, 613 N.Y.S.2d 330 (Surr.Ct., Nassau County, 1994).

CAVEAT: It is possible that a decedent, within a relatively brief time before death, can convert most of his or her assets into life insurance through the purchase of single premium policies, thus depriving the surviving spouse of a meaningful elective share. However, a client should be warned that such conversion of assets might not withstand judicial scrutiny on the theory that a single premium policy is not legitimately life insurance for this purpose.

3. **PRACTICE POINTER:** EPTL § 5–1.1–A is only available to the surviving spouse if the deceased spouse was a New York domiciliary at death or elected to have New York law apply to the disposition of New York situs property. In Matter of Estate of Rhoades, 160 Misc.2d 262, 607 N.Y.S.2d 893 (Sup.Ct., Rensselaer County, 1994), the decedent was a Florida domiciliary who owned New York realty which he had devised to his former spouse pursuant to his marriage settlement agreement. The Florida elective share claim did not affect New York realty, and since the decedent did not elect to have New York law apply to the disposition of his New York property, the surviving spouse could not elect against the property.

4. EPTL § 5–1.1–A(e)(1).

5. "Family exemption" property is not considered to be part of the estate. EPTL § 5–3.1(a).

6. EPTL §§ 5–1.1–A(e)(3)(A), (C).

7. EPTL § 5–1.1–A(e)(3)(D).

8. EPTL § 5–1.1–A(e)(3)(E).

9. EPTL § 5–1.1–A(e)(1).

10. EPTL § 5–1.1–A(e)(2).

11. Hurwitz v. Sher, 789 F.Supp. 134 (S.D.N.Y.1992), aff'd 982 F.2d 778 (2d Cir. 1992), cert. denied 508 U.S. 912, 113 S.Ct. 2345, 124 L.Ed.2d 255 (1993). *Contra* In re Estate of Hopkins, 214 Ill.App.3d 427, 158 Ill.Dec. 436, 574 N.E.2d 230 (Ill.App.Ct., 2d

Aside from disinheriting a spouse, pre-and postnuptial agreements are useful, court-sanctioned devices for providing for the financial arrangements during a marriage, *e.g.*, who makes mortgage payments, who pays for utilities, for the amounts that will be bequeathed to the surviving spouse or the spouse's children from a prior marriage, and for the property settlement in lieu of equitable distribution in the event of a divorce.[12]

West's McKinney's Forms, appropriate to this section, are available.[13]

§ 24.61 Planning in Special Situations—Multiple Marriages—Spousal Rights—Joint Wills and Contracts to Make Wills

The prenuptial or postnuptial agreement may contain contractual provisions relating to the wills of the parties. Specifically, the agreement may provide that existing wills cannot be revoked, or that wills be drafted disposing of property in a particular manner.[1]

A joint will is a will executed by both parties which provides the dispositive plan for the property of both parties. Mutual wills are separate wills with reciprocal provisions. Neither a joint will nor mutual wills precludes a party from revoking the will or otherwise disposing of their property unless the parties have a contractual obligation expressed either in the will or in a separate writing. Whether joint wills in particular have imposed this contractual obligation on the parties has been the subject of substantial litigation, along with whether the surviving person may dispose of the property.[2]

Generally, the survivor of persons who have drafted joint or mutual wills subject to a contractual obligation not to revoke cannot dispose of

---

Dist., 1991), appeal denied 141 Ill.2d 542, 162 Ill.Dec. 489, 580 N.E.2d 115 (1991). Treas. Reg. § 1.401(a)-20, Q & A 28 also provides that consent in a prenuptial agreement does not satisfy the consent requirements to name a beneficiary other than a spouse for a qualified plan.

PRACTICE POINTER: Any prenuptial agreement dealing with pension benefits should require the soon-to-be spouse to execute after the marriage any and all documents necessary to waive the right to be the beneficiary of a joint and survivor annuity, and should provide for the forfeiture of other property and/or payment of attorney's fees for failure to do so.

12. *See also*, Scheinkman, *et al.*, *New York Law of Domestic Relations* (West 1996) Ch. 6 "Antenuptial Agreements" and Appendix A.

13. *See* West's McKinney's Forms—Estate and Surrogate's Practice §§ 7:312–7:313, substituting "5–1.1A" for "5–1.1" wherever it appears (waiver of right of election); § 7:309 substituting "5–1.1A" for "5–1.1" (waiver of right of election—antenuptial).

§ 24.61

1. *See* Preminger, *et al.*, *Trusts and Estates Practice in New York* (West 1997).

2. *See e.g.*, Matter of Wierzbieniec's Estate, 93 A.D.2d 978, 461 N.Y.S.2d 653 (4th Dep't 1983); In re Silverman's Estate, 43 Misc.2d 909, 252 N.Y.S.2d 587 (Surr.Ct., Westchester County, 1964).

specifically bequeathed property during their lifetimes, and may only make gifts that are within the realm of good faith and do not defeat the purpose of the agreement.[3]

A West's McKinney's Form, appropriate to this section, is available.[4]

§ 24.62 Planning in Special Situations—Multiple Marriages—Long Term Care

New York law requires each spouse to provide for the support of the other, and this obligation cannot be waived by agreement.[1] In the event that one spouse requires nursing home care, the well spouse will either have to pay for the nursing home in New York at a rate of $5,000 to $12,000 per month, or have Medicaid pay the costs by signing a "spousal refusal."[2] However, if the well spouse has significant assets, not including the family home, or income, Medicaid can assert the institutionalized spouse's right of support and sue for the excess.[3] In effect, estates that would otherwise have likely passed to the well spouse's children will instead be used to pay for the nursing home costs of the second spouse.

A husband and wife might require, in a pre-or postnuptial agreement, each other to obtain and pay for an adequate long-term care insurance policy. While these policies can be fairly expensive, a younger couple with significant income and assets should be able to afford these policies and lock in preferable premiums. In this manner, the inheritance of children from a first marriage can be protected from the parent's obligation to support an institutionalized second spouse.

§ 24.63 Planning in Special Situations—Separation

The rights of a surviving spouse after a separation will depend upon the manner in which the separation was obtained. If the deceased spouse obtained a final court-decreed separation from the surviving spouse, rather than merely executing a separation agreement, the surviving

---

3. *See e.g.*, Schwartz v. Horn, 31 N.Y.2d 275, 338 N.Y.S.2d 613, 290 N.E.2d 816 (1972); Rich v. Mottek, 11 N.Y.2d 90, 226 N.Y.S.2d 428, 181 N.E.2d 445 (1962); Margulis v. Teichman, 125 Misc.2d 729, 479 N.Y.S.2d 953 (Surr.Ct., Nassau County, 1984), reh'g denied 127 Misc.2d 168, 485 N.Y.S.2d 930. *See* Chapter 23 "Elder Law," *supra*.

CAVEAT: In the case of both contracts to make wills and joint and mutual wills subject to contractual obligations, there is the potential for gift tax consequences. If the surviving spouse's right to enjoy his or her property is limited by an ascertainable standard, the contract may have gift tax implications. *See* Treas. Reg. § 25.2511-2(c); Hambleton v. Commissioner of Internal Revenue, 60 T.C. 558 (U.S.Tax Ct.1973), acq. in result only 1974–1 C.B. 2; Pyle by Straub v. United States, 766 F.2d 1141 (7th Cir.1985), cert. denied 475 U.S. 1015, 106 S.Ct. 1197, 89 L.Ed.2d 311 (1986).

4. *See* West's McKinney's Forms—Estate and Surrogate's Practice § 7:19 (agreement to execute mutual wills).

§ 24.62

1. DRL § 32.
2. Social Services Law § 366–c(3).
3. Social Services Law § 366–c(5)(b).

spouse's right of election, right to the family allowance, or right to an intestate share of the estate are automatically terminated.[1] New York makes a further distinction regarding separations according to whether the deceased spouse had obtained a separation decree against the surviving spouse. The forfeiture of the right to elect, right to inherit through intestacy, and the right to the family allowance only applies if the separation decree or judgment was obtained *against* the surviving spouse. If the decree was obtained by the surviving spouse against the decedent, then none of the marital rights will be extinguished.[2]

While the right to elect against a will, to inherit intestate or to the family allowance will be extinguished upon the issuance of a final decree of separation against the surviving spouse, the separation decree *does not* terminate the spouse's right to inherit under the decedent's will. Thus, if the decedent who obtains a separation decree has not revoked a will leaving property to the spouse, the surviving spouse still inherits under the will.[3]

A separation agreement executed by the married couple does not extinguish any marital rights unless the document so provides. Typically, however, a well drafted separation agreement will address the question of marital rights of inheritance. For example, a separation agreement between parties of equal financial footing will typically provide that each person waives all rights of election, and agrees to renounce any inheritance[4] or insurance proceeds obtained upon the death of the other.[5]

§ 24.64 Planning in Special Situations—Divorce

Once a couple is divorced, all dispositions under a will executed prior to the divorce will be revoked by operation of law, unless the will

§ 24.63

1. EPTL § 5–1.2.

2. *See* In re Smith's Estate, 243 App. Div. 348, 276 N.Y.S. 646 (4th Dep't 1935).

3. *Compare* EPTL § 5–1.4 (applies only to divorce, annulment or dissolution) to EPTL § 5–1.2 (disqualification as "spouse" for elective share, intestate share and family allowance applies to separation decree); *see also*, EPTL § 3–4.1 (no revocations of wills except as provided by statute).

4. **CAVEAT:** Such a renunciation must be specific, as ambiguity might render such intended renunciation a nullity. *See* Matter of Will of Chmiel, 164 Misc.2d 854, 626 N.Y.S.2d 681 (Surr.Ct., Broome County, 1995) (waiver of "any statutory or intestate interest or right" did not revoke bequests in prior will to estranged wife).

5. **CAVEAT:** The surviving spouse could challenge the effectiveness of the agreement on the basis of a reconciliation. *See* In re Whiteford's Estate, 61 Misc.2d 402, 306 N.Y.S.2d 32 (Surr.Ct., Broome County, 1969), aff'd 35 A.D.2d 751, 314 N.Y.S.2d 811 (3d Dep't 1970). In order to prevent costly litigation and the potential threat that the separation agreement might not be honored, wills should be redrafted, beneficiaries under insurance policies should be changed, and joint tenancies should be severed. Thus, as a practical matter, a spouse separated pursuant to agreement should also specifically disinherit his spouse, although disinheritance will not itself affect rights of election or the family allowance.

specifically provides otherwise.[1] Any property inherited by the former spouse will no longer be eligible for the marital deduction.

A divorce will not, in itself, result in the automatic disinheritance of the former spouse where the wills were executed pursuant to reciprocal agreement.[2] In such a case, the further steps of executing mutual releases, followed by rewriting wills, is advisable. Note that mutual releases alone from a will executed pursuant to reciprocal agreement does not act as a revocation of the underlying will, although EPTL § 5-1.4 will automatically revoke all dispositions to the former spouse.[3] Thus, if the testator left property to the former spouse's children from a prior marriage pursuant to a reciprocal agreement, the testator who intends to disinherit such children must not only obtain a release from his or her former spouse, but must affirmatively revoke the prior will.

A former spouse will remain a beneficiary of a life insurance policy unless a new beneficiary designation is filed.[4] Property held as tenants by the entireties in New York automatically reverts to a tenancy in common upon divorce.[5]

§ 24.65 Planning in Special Situations—Divorce—Death During Divorce Proceeding

Generally, an action for divorce is pre-eminently one of a personal character which abates with the death of either party to it.[1] Under certain circumstances, however, the divorce may be finalized even after the decedent's death, with the resulting termination of marital rights.

If the divorce would affect the rights of third parties, and the trial has been completed and the court has already found that a divorce should be granted prior to the spouses' death except for the entry of a formal judgment, a judgment of divorce may be entered.[2] Also, where the court has signed the judgment in a divorce action but a party dies before the judgment is filed with the county clerk, the parties are effectively

---

§ 24.64

1. EPTL § 5-1.4. See Preminger, et al., Trusts and Estates Practice in New York (West 1997); Scheinkman, et al., New York Law of Domestic Relations (West 1996) § 2.18.

2. Matter of Coffed's Estate, 88 Misc.2d 610, 388 N.Y.S.2d 552 (Surr.Ct., Erie County, 1976), rev'd on other grounds 59 A.D.2d 297, 399 N.Y.S.2d 548 (4th Dep't 1977), aff'd 46 N.Y.2d 514, 414 N.Y.S.2d 893, 387 N.E.2d 1209 (1979).

3. Id.

4. See e.g., Teachers Ins. and Annuity Ass'n. of America v. Rogers, 41 A.D.2d 1020, 343 N.Y.S.2d 956 (4th Dep't 1973); Davis v. Travelers Ins. Companies, 105 Misc.2d 582, 432 N.Y.S.2d 592 (Sup.Ct., Broome County, 1980); Stanford v. Union Labor Life Ins. Co., 74 Misc.2d 781, 345 N.Y.S.2d 928 (Sup.Ct., Monroe County, 1973).

5. See Kahn v. Kahn, 43 N.Y.2d 203, 401 N.Y.S.2d 47, 371 N.E.2d 809 (1977).

§ 24.65

1. In re Crandall's Estate, 196 N.Y. 127, 89 N.E. 578, overruled on other grounds by Cornell v. Cornell, 7 N.Y.2d 164, 196 N.Y.S.2d 98, 164 N.E.2d 395 (1959). See Sheinkman, et al., New York Law of Domestic Relations (West 1996) § 1.33.

2. Jayson v. Jayson, 54 A.D.2d 687, 387 N.Y.S.2d 274 (2d Dep't 1976).

divorced, even though the judgment provides that it will take effect upon filing with the county clerk.[3] A judgment may be entered *nunc pro tunc* in a divorce action after the death of one of the parties, if such party was entitled to have the judgment entered while both parties were living.[4]

Obviously, when a client is separated or in the middle of a divorce, a client should be advised to review his will and nontestamentary dispositions, such as who is named as the beneficiary of life insurance, and joint assets, with an eye towards affirmatively disinheriting a soon-to-be former spouse.

§ 24.66 Planning in Special Situations—Unmarried Couples

Arrangements that are less conventional than the typical husband-wife living arrangement create increasingly common estate planning issues. First, unmarried couples are not entitled to a right of election, a family allowance, and have no entitlement to an intestate share of the decedent's estate. Further, no marital deduction is permitted for the surviving domestic partner. New York does not recognize common law marriage,[1] *i.e.*, where a man and woman cohabited and hold themselves out to others as married, but may recognize a common law marriage that is valid in another jurisdiction.[2]

An obvious expedient where feasible is for the couple to marry, including deathbed marriages, to preserve tax benefits and marital rights for the domestic partner. If the partners are determined not to marry, or the marriage is not recognized for estate purposes, such as same sex marriages, the planner must consider other options. The partners could draft wills leaving property, up to the amount of the decedent's unused unified credit, to a bypass trust[3] and thereby avoid estate tax on such amount at both partners' death.

One problem with using wills as the method to convey property to a domestic partner is that, because distributees must be notified upon the

---

3. Handzel v. Handzel, 59 A.D.2d 810, 399 N.Y.S.2d 79 (3d Dep't 1977).

4. Cornell v. Cornell, 7 N.Y.2d 164, 196 N.Y.S.2d 98, 164 N.E.2d 395 (1959).

§ 24.66

1. L. 1933, Ch. 606.

2. *See, e.g.*, Matter of Will of Garr, 192 A.D.2d 396, 596 N.Y.S.2d 53 (1st Dep't 1993); Cross v. Cross, 146 A.D.2d 302, 541 N.Y.S.2d 202 (1st Dep't 1989); Peart v. T.D. Bross Line Const. Co., 45 A.D.2d 801, 357 N.Y.S.2d 53 (3d Dep't 1974).

PRACTICE POINTER: Since New York does recognize common law marriages valid in other jurisdictions, this provides an opportunity for postmortem planning for the benefit of the surviving partner. Specifically, if the surviving partner can prove that she spent time with the decedent in a jurisdiction that recognized common law marriage and satisfied that state's requirements, then the survivor could be treated as a surviving spouse.

CAVEAT: Postmortem proof of a common law marriage may be a difficult, if not impossible task, particularly if the couple did not live in the jurisdiction.

3. *See supra*, § 24.21.

§ 24.66   ESTATE PLANNING   Ch. 24

filing of a will for probate,[4] a family member might be tempted to challenge the will.[5] A better solution in these situations may be to establish an *inter vivos* trust naming the domestic partner as the primary beneficiary. Consideration may also be given to lifetime gifts, or using other nontestamentary devices, such as the placement of property into joint tenancies with right of survivorship. Such transfers will take place by operation of law at the decedent's death without notice to potential contestants and generally without the scrutiny of the courts.[6]

§ 24.67   Postmortem Planning

Generally, estate planning ends at the time of death. However, there are several postmortem options available to the executor and beneficiaries to minimize taxes. Specifically, consideration should be given to whether a beneficiary should disclaim property,[1] whether an "alternate valuation date" should be used for estate tax purposes,[2] and whether certain other tax elections should be made.[3]

§ 24.68   Postmortem Planning—Disclaimers

Couples sometimes are reticent about utilizing a bypass trust to make full use of the unified credit because they are fearful that they will not have sufficient assets outside of the trust at their disposal. In such a case, the ability of the spouse to make a "qualified disclaimer" of property allows the surviving spouse flexibility to make such division on a postmortem basis.

By renouncing property in the manner that satisfies the requirements of a "qualified disclaimer" under I.R.C. § 2518(b), the assets are treated as never having been transferred to the person making the renunciation.[1] In other words, the renouncing person is treated as predeceasing the person making the transfer, the result of which is that the original transferor, rather than the renouncing beneficiary, is considered to transfer the property to the ultimate beneficiary. The renouncing beneficiary is not considered to be making a gift, and his gross estate does not include such property.[2]

---

4. SCPA § 1403(1).

5. A will bequeathing all of the testator's property to a cohabitant may be subject to challenge on the grounds of undue influence. While the will could be drafted with an *in terrorem* clause, *i.e.*, a no contest clause, and with significant bequests to potential litigants, the litigants can initiate proceedings such as examining witnesses without risk of forfeiture. EPTL § 3–3.5. Thus, even an *in terrorem* clause, coupled with significant bequests, might not preclude harassment, delay, and the ultimate need for the domestic partner to settle for less than what the will provided. *See also*,

Preminger, *et al.,Trusts and Estates Practice in New York* (West 1997).

6. *See infra*, §§ 24.80 *et seq.*, regarding avoidance of probate.

§ 24.67

1. *See infra*, §§ 24.68, *et seq.*
2. *See infra*, § 24.73.
3. *See infra*, §§ 24.74–24.79.

§ 24.68

1. I.R.C. § 2518(a).
2. Treas. Reg. § 25.2518–1(b), (d).

In order for a renunciation to be a qualified disclaimer, it must meet the following criteria:

(1) The refusal must be in writing;

(2) The refusal must be received by the transferor of the property interest, or in the case of an estate, the executor or administrator, no later than nine months after the date on which the transfer creating the interest is made, *i.e.*, date of death in the case of an inheritance; or nine months after the disclaimant's 21st birthday, if later;

(3) The disclaimant has not accepted the interest or any benefit therefrom; and

(4) As a result of the refusal, the interest passes, without any direction on the part of the disclaimant, to *either* the decedent's spouse or a person other than the disclaimant.[3]

The disclaimer may cover all of an interest in property passing at death, or of an undivided portion of the interest.[4]

West's McKinney's Forms, appropriate to this section, are available.[5]

§ 24.69 Postmortem Planning—Disclaimers—Disclaimer Trusts

Because a qualified disclaimer can include a renunciation by a spouse which passes, in another form, for the benefit of the disclaiming spouse, the decedent can establish a "disclaimer trust" in his will. By including a disclaimer trust, the surviving spouse is given the option, within nine months of the decedent's death, to disclaim some or all assets and take advantage of the unified credit without fully sacrificing the benefit of these assets during her life.[1] In other words, the will can provide that all property is left to the surviving spouse, either outright or in a marital trust, and that if the spouse disclaims any property, the property will be held in trust for the benefit of the spouse, with income

---

[3]. I.R.C. § 2518(b).

[4]. I.R.C. § 2518(c). *But see* Proposed Treasury Regulation § 25.2518-2 for guidance in determining when the nine month period to disclaim begins with respect to joint property.

[5]. *See* West's McKinney's Forms—Estate and Surrogate's Practice §§ 7:418–7:424 (disclaimers).

§ 24.69

1. **CAVEAT:** As a practical matter, it may sometimes be difficult to get a spouse to disclaim with nine months of death at a time when he or she is still insecure about their future needs. Therefore, such disclaimer provisions should be relied upon only after its purpose is spelled out to the clients.

PRACTICE POINTER: This device may be most useful where the couple's assets are between $600,000 and $1,200,000 (or between one and two times the applicable exclusion amount) and they would rather not fully fund a bypass trust. For example, if the husband has $600,000 in assets and the wife has only $300,000, rather than directing in the husband's will that the credit shelter trust be funded for the maximum amount ($600,000) the disclaimer trust can be used so that the wife can disclaim $300,000 only and receive $300,000 outright.

§ 24.69   ESTATE PLANNING   Ch. 24

payable to her for life and payments of principal permitted in the trustee's discretion. As long as the surviving spouse does not retain the right to direct beneficial enjoyment of the disclaimed property, except for the right to withdraw pursuant to an "ascertainable standard," *e.g.*, health education, support, and maintenance,[2] the decedent, rather than the surviving spouse, will be treated as having transferred the property.[3]

§ 24.70   Postmortem Planning—Disclaimers—Creditor Avoidance

Aside from tax considerations, disclaimers of interests in property can also be used to defeat creditors. For example, if the beneficiary of a will has creditor problems, he can renounce his bequest. New York courts have ruled that a renunciation that meets statutory requirements[1] is treated as having never been owned by the debtor/beneficiary, and is not subject to his creditor's claims.[2]

§ 24.71   Postmortem Planning—Disclaimers—New York Statutory Requirements

In order for a disclaimer to qualify as such, the requirements of the New York statute on renunciations, EPTL § 2–1.11, must be satisfied. EPTL § 2–1.11 repeats the requirements of I.R.C. § 2518 for a qualified disclaimer: the renunciation must be in writing, must be within nine months of the creation of the interest,[1] the transferor may not renounce an interest in property that the person has already accepted, and only the spouse may renounce an interest and yet, as a result of the renunciation, continue to have an interest therein. However, additional statutory requirements which must be satisfied are:

(1) The writing must be acknowledged in the same manner as is required for a deed;

(2) The renunciation must be filed with the clerk of the court that has jurisdiction over the will, trust or administration, or if there is no probate or administration, the court which would have jurisdiction over the probate or administration;

---

2. I.R.C. § 2514(c).

3. Treas. Reg. § 25.2518–2(e)(2). **CAVEAT:** This means that, in the disclaimer trust, the spouse cannot be given a "limited power of appointment" to divide the trust corpus, upon her death, between the decedent's descendants or other class of beneficiaries.

§ 24.70

1. *See infra*, § 24.71.

2. *See* Estate of Schiffman, 105 Misc.2d 1029, 430 N.Y.S.2d 229 (Surr.Ct., N.Y. County, 1980).

§ 24.71

1. EPTL § 2–1.11(b)(2) permits the court to extend the time for filing a renunciation—however, while such a renunciation would be effective for the purposes of effectuating the transfer to a contingent beneficiary, it would not be a qualified disclaimer under I.R.C. § 2518.

(3) The renunciation must be accompanied by an affidavit stating that the disclaimant did not receive, and is not to receive, consideration for the renunciation; and

(4) Notice must be served *personally,* or in any other manner permitted by the court, on the transferor of the interest, or the fiduciary in the case of a trust or estate, and also must be served by mail on all persons whose property interests are accelerated. [2]

Renunciations on behalf of infants, incompetents, or the deceased must be made by a guardian or personal representative.[3]

§ 24.72 Postmortem Planning—Partial QTIP Election

A decedent can leave property to a QTIP trust which will qualify for the marital deduction.[1] In order for the property to qualify for the deduction, however, the decedent's executor must make a QTIP election on the decedent's estate tax return.[2] The executor, however, is not constrained to making an all or nothing decision relating to a QTIP election. The executor could, instead, make an election for only part of the property, provided that the election be made with respect to a fractional or percentage share of the property.[3] In other words, the QTIP can be divided into two trusts, one for which the election will be made, and another which will not qualify for the marital deduction.[4]

The ability to make a partial QTIP election provides considerable flexibility to remedy unexpected consequences of the decedent's testamentary scheme.

EXAMPLE: Suppose a testator with an estate worth $3 million left the maximum amount exempt from federal estate tax in a credit shelter trust and the rest to a QTIP trust. Also suppose that the surviving spouse had only $600,000 in assets. If the full QTIP election were made, the surviving spouse would have an estate of $3 million upon her death which would incur a federal estate tax of $1,098,000. Instead, if a partial QTIP election were made for $1,200,000, the decedent would incur a federal estate tax of $498,000, and upon the surviving spouse's death, she would have a taxable estate of $1.8 million, which would also incur a tax of $498,000, for a total federal estate tax of $996,000 or a savings of $102,000.[5]

As illustrated, because each estate is taking advantage of the lower estate tax rates, the combined tax is significantly lower than if a QTIP election is made for the entire marital bequest.

2. EPTL § 2–1.11(b)(2).
3. EPTL § 2–1.11(c).

§ 24.72
1. *See supra,* § 24.22.
2. I.R.C. § 2056(b).

3. Treas. Reg. § 20.2056(b)–7(b).
4. Treas. Reg. § 20.2056(b)–7(b)(2)(ii); EPTL § 7–1.13.
5. The example assumes 1997 unified credit amounts.

§ 24.73 Postmortem Planning—Electing Alternate Valuation Date

Another postmortem option available to the executor is the choice of valuation date. The ability to determine when the assets are valued could have a substantial impact on the taxes incurred by both the estate and the beneficiaries, depending upon fluctuations in their values.

Generally, for estate tax purposes, assets are valued as of the date of death.[1] However, the executor may make an alternate valuation election. By doing so, the executor elects to value all property that is distributed, sold, exchanged or otherwise disposed of as of the date of disposition, and otherwise, all remaining property is valued as of the six month anniversary of the decedent's death.[2] This election, however, can only be made if the effect of such an election will (a) reduce the value of the gross estate, and (b) reduce the federal estate and generation skipping transfer tax imposed on the decedent's gross estate.[3]

Note that this election is an all or nothing election. The executor cannot choose to value some property on the alternate valuation date and other property on a date of death basis.

Electing to value property on the alternate valuation date, rather than on the decedent's date of death, may not always be worthwhile, however, depending upon the asset mix and the amount of estate and generation skipping tax it will reduce. The reason for this is because the beneficiaries obtain a "step-up" in tax basis to fair market value at either valuation date.[4] Thus, electing an alternate valuation which reduces estate and generation skipping taxes may increase the tax the beneficiaries will realize on capital gains when they sell assets.

EXAMPLE: Wanda Widow dies on January 1st, 1997 owning only one asset: 100,000 shares of Gizmos, Inc. common stock. Wanda purchased her 100,000 shares at $5 per share. The per share value of Wanda's Gizmos, Inc. stock is $9 per share on the date of her death. Suppose that the per share value decreases to $6 per share on July 1st, the six month anniversary of Wanda's death, but most experts expect that the shares will trade at $9 per share in another year when Wanda's sole beneficiary is planning on selling the stock. Wanda's beneficiary is in the highest tax bracket for income tax purposes, so his capital gains will be taxed at 28%.

In this case, the executor should elect to value the estate as of the alternate valuation date. If the estate were valued as of the date of death, it would be valued at $900,000 (100,000 shares at $9 per share), which, after the unified credit were applied, would incur a federal estate tax of $114,000. Wanda's beneficiary would obtain a

---

§ 24.73
1. I.R.C. § 2031.
2. I.R.C. § 2032(a).
3. I.R.C. § 2032(c).
4. I.R.C. § 1014.

tax basis in the stock of $9 per share, and upon sale at $9 per share, would have no capital gains. Thus, date of death valuation would lead to a total tax of $114,000. If alternate valuation date is used, there will be no federal estate tax (due to the unified credit), and the beneficiary will obtain a basis of $6 per share. Upon a later sale at $9 per share, the beneficiary would recognize a $300,000 capital gain ($900,000 amount realized less tax basis of $600,000) and incur a capital gains tax of $84,000. Thus, using the alternate valuation would lead to a total tax of $84,000, for a savings of $30,000 to the beneficiary.[5]

§ 24.74 Postmortem Planning—Allocation of Income and Expenses

Aside from an estate tax return, a final return for the decedent must be filed, and generally, fiduciary income tax returns for the estate must be filed. In this regard, a determination as to whether certain items should be included on the estate tax return or an income tax return must be made.

In order to understand when an item should be reported on the federal estate tax return, rather than the federal income tax return, the practitioner needs to understand how an estate's income is taxed. Essentially, an estate is taxed on its gross income, including "income with respect of a decedent" ("IRD"), namely, income to which the decedent is entitled but is not properly includible in his final return or any prior return,[1] less deductions. From this amount, an estate is entitled to a deduction equal to the distributions to beneficiaries to the extent that such distributions do not exceed "distributable net income" ("DNI").[2] The maximum income tax rate on an estate is 39.6%, which applies to estates with taxable income exceeding $7,500.00 in 1997.[3] Beneficiaries, except for specific legatees, are generally taxable on distributions to the extent that they do not exceed DNI.

---

5. **CAVEAT:** This example was relatively simple because there was only one beneficiary, one asset, and an assumption about the future value of the asset. In most cases, there are usually multiple assets which often must be divided among numerous beneficiaries. In addition, depending upon how the estate taxes are apportioned under the terms of the will, the burden of higher estate taxes may fall on a beneficiary who will not receive the benefit of any reduction in capital gains taxes. *See supra,* § 24.10.

§ 24.74

1. I.R.C. § 691(a). Note that items of IRD are includible in the estate's gross income only if the estate itself is entitled to receive the IRD and the estate has not distributed the right to such payment to a beneficiary. Treas. Reg. § 1.691(a)–2(a).

2. DNI is, in turn, essentially taxable income computed with certain adjustments. I.R.C. § 643.

3. I.R.C. § 1(e), as adjusted for inflation. The amount is indexed with inflation and needs to be checked annually.

§ 24.75 Postmortem Planning—Allocation of Income and Expenses—U.S. Savings Bonds

An individual with discounted U.S. Treasury securities that are commonly referred to as "U.S. Savings Bonds," "E Bonds" or "EE Bonds" generally does not recognize the interest income,[1] and therefore, his estate may have significant IRD. The executor may, however, elect to either report all accrued income on the decedent's final income tax return,[2] or to include such income on the estate's income tax return.

§ 24.76 Postmortem Planning—Allocation of Income and Expenses—Expenses

Medical expenses of the decedent which are paid by the estate within one year of death may be taken as a deduction against either the decedent's final income tax return or against the gross estate for estate tax purposes,[1] subject, however, that if taken on the income tax return, to the limitation that such expenses are only deductible to the extent they exceed 7.5% of the decedent's adjusted gross income.

Administration expenses and losses during administration of an estate may be deducted on either the fiduciary income tax return in the year that the expenses are incurred, or on the estate tax return.[2]

§ 24.77 Postmortem Planning—Choosing the Fiscal Year of the Estate

Another method of deferring, or possibly reducing income taxes for beneficiaries of an estate involves the choice of a fiscal year for the estate for fiduciary income tax purposes. In other words, instead of determining taxes based upon a year ending on December 31, a calendar year, the estate may elect to pay taxes based upon a year that ends no later than twelve months from the anniversary of the death of the decedent.[1] The

---

§ 24.75

1. I.R.C. § 454(a). Unless the decedent elected to recognize the income during lifetime, the accrued income is only recognized when the bonds are either disposed of or transferred.

2. Rev. Rul. 68–145, 1968–1 C.B. 203. **PRACTICE POINTER:** To the extent that this increases the decedent's income tax liability, the increased income tax will reduce the decedent's net estate, as an allocable deduction, in computing federal estate tax.

§ 24.76

1. I.R.C. § 213(c); Treas. Reg. § 1.213–1(d).

2. I.R.C. § 642(g). An election to deduct administration expenses on the income tax return must be attached to the return. Note, however, that if the executor elects to deduct ordinary administration expenses on the fiduciary income tax return rather than on the estate tax return, the executor must add to principal from income the amount of estate tax which would have been saved on the estate tax return had the expenses been taken as a deduction thereon. In re Warms' Estate, 140 N.Y.S.2d 169 (Surr.Ct., N.Y. County, 1955); codified by EPTL § 11–1.2(a).

§ 24.77

1. I.R.C. § 441(f).

primary benefit of choosing a fiscal year is that if distributions are made to a beneficiary, the distributions are taxable to the beneficiary in the taxable year in which the fiscal year of the estate ends. For example, if the estate has an August 31st fiscal year and a distribution is made to a beneficiary on September 1, the beneficiary does not include that distribution as income until the *next* calendar year.[2]

§ 24.78 Postmortem Planning—Electing to File Joint Return With Decedent's Spouse

The decedent's fiduciary may elect whether to file the decedent's final income tax return jointly with the surviving spouse.[1] The advantages of filing a joint return are the ability to take advantage of lower marginal tax rates and to take advantage of certain deductions and capital loss carry forwards which might otherwise be lost.

§ 24.79 Postmortem Planning—Waiving Commissions

If the named executor of a will is also one of its primary beneficiaries, it might make sense for the executor to take his statutory commissions. The reason for this is that, although the executor must report the commissions for income tax purposes,[1] the commissions are deductible for estate tax purposes.[2] The decision will depend on whether the estate will be subject to federal estate tax, and the marginal income tax rates of both the estate and the fiduciary. If there is no taxable estate, the executor should consider waiving commissions.

§ 24.80 Probate Avoidance

Probate is a public proceeding which requires notification of certain parties, not all of whom may be amenable to the contemplated disposition of a decedent's estate.[1] Probate also involves numerous administration costs, such as court filing fees, including a fee for the *privilege* of filing the estate tax return with the surrogate's court, which can cost as much as $1,000,[2] as well as the potential for significant delays in distributing the estate. Such delays may arise where the decedent dies leaving his assets to friends because no close family members survived

2. PRACTICE POINTER: Consider spreading distributions over fiscal years to avoid "bunching" of income for either the estate or beneficiaries in order to take advantage of lower marginal tax brackets of the beneficiary.

CAVEAT: Because the income tax rates on estates reach 39.6% for relatively small amounts of gross income, this type of planning may be difficult to implement.

§ 24.78
1. I.R.C. §§ 6012(b)(1), 6013.

§ 24.79
1. I.R.C. § 61.
2. I.R.C. § 2053(a)(2); Treas. Reg. § 20.2053-3(b).

§ 24.80
1. *See supra*, § 24.66.
2. SCPA § 2402.

him. The proposed fiduciary will then have to satisfy publication requirements and "due diligence" to find any living relatives who could contest the will. In addition, the Public Administrator's office and the Attorney General's office will be involved with the proceeding.[3] There are numerous methods that can be used to avoid probate, including the establishment of revocable trusts, Totten trusts, and holding assets jointly.[4]

§ 24.81 Probate Avoidance—Revocable Trusts

Perhaps the most common method used to avoid probate is to establish a revocable trust. The settlor of the trust may name himself, as the trustee of the trust,[1] retaining the right to all income and principal. The settlor also retains the right to revoke or amend the trust in whole or part,[2] and the trust provides that upon the settlor's death, the property is distributed either outright or in further trust. In this manner, the trust acts as a testamentary substitute.

For tax purposes, the settlor of a revocable trust is treated as the owner of the trust in the same manner as if he still owned the assets outright,[3] and the assets remain includible in the settlor's estate.[4]

A separate federal income tax return is not even required for a revocable trust, provided that the settlor is a trustee and beneficiary, until, under the terms of the trust agreement, a triggering event occurs, such as the settlor's death, which makes the trust irrevocable.[5]

A revocable trust is particularly useful for a person who owns realty located outside of New York. By transferring title of the property to the trust, ancillary non-New York probate proceedings are also avoided.[6]

In addition, a revocable trust provides a convenient method of managing a person's financial affairs in the event of incapacity. The other trustee(s) can manage the settlor's assets without the necessity for court intervention.[7]

---

3. *See* Chapter 25 "Probate and Estate Administration," *infra*.

4. PRACTICE POINTER: Clients often confuse probate with taxation. That is, they believe that avoiding probate may reduce their estate tax burden. It should be pointed out that estate taxes apply equally to probate and non-probate assets as long as the decedent maintained any incidents of ownership or retained any rights to income or principal which are not otherwise excluded by the Internal Revenue Code.

§ 24.81
1. EPTL § 7–1.1.
2. The trust can be revoked or amended by an express direction in the settlor's will. EPTL § 7–1.17.

3. I.R.C. §§ 674, 676, 677. A tax identification number for the trust is not required until it becomes irrevocable.

4. I.R.C. §§ 2036, 2038.

5. Treas. Reg. §§ 1.6012–3(a)(9); 1.671–4(b)(1).

6. *See* Chapter 25 "Probate and Estate Administration," *infra*.

7. PRACTICE POINTER: Although durable powers of attorney are also useful to manage one's affairs during incapacity, many financial institutions do not, as a practical matter, recognize such instruments as readily as a trust.

The primary disadvantage of a revocable trust involves the time and expense incurred in:

(1) creating the trust itself, and

(2) funding the trust.

Too often, clients believe that, by simply signing a trust instrument, their assets are automatically held in trust. However, the assets must, in fact, be conveyed to the *trustees* under the trust agreement.[8] Bank accounts, brokerage accounts, stocks and bonds must be duly retitled, and new deeds must be executed for realty. For those with either substantial assets or numerous forms of holdings, *i.e.*, a number of smaller accounts, this is not an insignificant nuisance, especially since failure to effectively place the assets into the trust will, perhaps, defeat the trust's primary purpose of avoiding probate.[9]

A West's McKinney's Form, appropriate to this section, is available.[10]

§ 24.82 Probate Avoidance—Totten Trusts

Another method of passing assets to an intended beneficiary while retaining complete control during the owner's lifetime is the establishment of so-called "Totten trusts."[1] These are bank accounts deposited in the name of the donor "in trust for" a designated beneficiary. Until the donor dies, the donor retains complete control over the funds in the account, and the beneficiary has no ownership rights therein. Upon death, however, any funds remaining in that account pass to the named beneficiary outside of probate.[2]

§ 24.83 Probate Avoidance—Jointly Held Assets

People often hold assets jointly for convenience. If the account is established as joint tenants with right of survivorship, such account will

---

8. EPTL § 7-1.18.

9. **PRACTICE POINTER:** In order to avoid intestacy if an asset "slips through the cracks" and is not effectively placed in trust, a "pourover" will, *i.e.*, one that bequeaths all assets to the *inter vivos* trust, should also be executed. If probate is necessary, the surrogate's court will require the filing of the trust agreement, thereby giving up any confidentiality.

10. See West's McKinney's Forms—Estate and Surrogate's Practice §§ 10.552-10.553 (revocable trust).

§ 24.82

1. These types of bank accounts are referred to as "Totten trusts" after the In re Totten, 179 N.Y. 112, 71 N.E. 748 (1904).

2. **CAVEAT:** A Totten trust may be revoked by a will specifically referring to the account. EPTL § 7-5.2. However, if there is any discrepancy between the account listed in the purported revocation and the actual account description, for example, as a result of a bank merger, or because the testator "rolled over" the account from one certificate of deposit account to another, a court may hold the testamentary revocation to be invalid. The better course of action is to simply remove the monies from the Totten trust account to effect the revocation.

pass to the surviving co-owner(s) outside of probate. If a bank account or other property is placed into the name of two or more people, other than spouses in the case of real property, without specifically designating the account as a joint tenancy, each individual owns his or her interest as a tenant in common,[1] which means that the goal of probate avoidance is not achieved. That is, the property will then pass pursuant to such person's will.

In the case of a bank account, the creation of a joint tenancy is deemed to be a completed gift of one half of the account value under New York State Banking Law.[2] This could create gift tax consequences if such accounts are established between non-spouses, *e.g.*, a parent and child.[3] While effectively placing assets into a joint tenancy will avoid probate, the entire value of such assets are includible in the donor's estate, unless the survivor can prove his or her contribution thereto or, in the case of spouses, one-half of jointly held assets are includible in the decedent's estate.[4]

Real property, including shares in a cooperative housing corporation conveyed on or after January 1, 1996,[5] owned jointly between spouses is held as tenants by the entireties,[6] unless the dispositive document specifically states that they hold the asset as tenants in common. Holding assets as tenants by the entireties also avoids probate. The distinction between joint tenancies and tenancies by the entireties are that:

(1) Only married persons can hold property as tenants by the entireties, and, in New York, they can only hold real property, including co-op apartments, in that manner, and

(2) Whereas joint tenancies are severable by either owner, both husband and wife must consent to the dissolution of a tenancy by the entirety.[7]

§ 24.84 Asset Protection

Asset protection planning can be broadly defined to include planning

---

§ 24.83
1. EPTL § 6-2.2(a); Banking Law § 675.
2. Banking Law § 675.
3. Treas. Reg. § 25.2511-1(h)(1).

CAVEAT: If the bank account is located in another state, a taxable gift may not occur until the joint tenant actually withdraws funds from the account.

4. I.R.C. § 2040.

PRACTICE POINTER: Since only one-half is included in the estate of the first spouse to die, only one-half the value will receive the step-up in basis. Since there would be no estate tax consequences in any event, assuming an optimum marital deduction, it may be advisable to transfer ownership of highly appreciated assets to an ill spouse's sole name to obtain a complete step-up in basis for income tax purposes. Such transfer, however, is only effective if completed more than one year before death. I.R.C. § 1014(e).

5. EPTL § 6-2.2(c).
6. EPTL § 6-2.2(b).

7. See infra, § 24.85 for a discussion of the use of tenancies by the entireties for asset protection.

to minimize income and estate taxes, planning for Medicaid eligibility[1] and planning to protect accumulated wealth from future creditors and potential litigants. Most high net worth clients should be advised to consider some asset protection strategies. In particular, candidates for such planning include professionals, business owners, real property owners and developers, and others for whom adequate and complete insurance coverage may not be available at a reasonable cost. Proper advance planning may also increase a client's ability to negotiate a favorable settlement with a future creditor.

Before engaging in such planning, the attorney must ascertain that the client is not intending to engage in a fraudulent conveyance. A fraudulent conveyance is a transfer or concealment of property from certain protected creditors.[2] As long as there are no protected creditors, an owner is free to dispose of property even if the reason for doing so is to protect assets should a problem later develop.[3]

Asset protection techniques spread across a continuum ranging from the familiar—funding retirement plans and transferring assets to a spouse—to the more complex, such as creating a foreign trust.

§ 24.85 Asset Protection—Statutory Exemptions

For certain assets, state and federal laws offer a few "built-in" protection aspects. For example, the federal Bankruptcy Code lists exempt property in 11 U.S.C.A. § 522(d). Under the Employee Retirement Income Security Act of 1974 ("ERISA"),[1] contributions to a qualified plan are exempt from creditors. Furthermore, in New York, IRA's and Keogh plans are exempt from creditors.[2]

Property owned jointly as tenants by the entireties also enjoys some asset protection if one of the owners becomes subject to a creditor's lien. Since tenancy by the entirety can only be severed by both owners or upon an owner's death, a creditor can generally only obtain a lien on the debtor's interest.[3] Such lien will be extinguished if the debtor spouse dies first. Of course, if the non-debtor spouse dies first, or if the owners wish

---

§ 24.84

1. *But see* Chapter 23 "Elder Law," *supra* § 23.76 for a discussion of criminal penalties under the Tax Payer Relief Act of 1997 for attorneys who counsel or assist clients in the disposal of assets under certain circumstances.

2. *See* Debtor and Creditor Law §§ 270–281 (the Uniform Fraudulent Conveyance Act as adopted by New York).

3. *See e.g.* Klein v. Klein, 112 N.Y.S.2d 546 (Sup.Ct., Cattaraugus County, 1952).

§ 24.85

1. 29 U.S.C.A. §§ 1001, *et seq.*

2. Debtor and Creditor Law § 282; EPTL § 9–1.7; CPLR 5205(c)(2), (d).

3. *See* In re Persky, 893 F.2d 15, 20 (2d Cir.1989) for an analysis of 11 U.S.C.A. § 363(h), which sets forth the considerations to be weighed regarding the sale of jointly owned interests. On remand, the bankruptcy court ruled that 11 U.S.C.A. § 363(h) could not, as a matter of Constitutional law, be applied to sever tenancies by the entireties. 134 B.R. 81 (Bankr.E.D.N.Y. 1991).

to sell the property or get divorced, the creditor's lien can be executed thereon.

§ 24.86 Asset Protection—Family Partnerships

Limited partnerships allow the general partner to retain control, while imposing certain restrictions on the limited partners.[1] The law generally restricts a creditor's remedy to that of a charging order against the debtor/partner's interest.[2] Such charging order merely gives a creditor the right to receive the debtor's share of income. Since such distributions are in the general partner's discretion, the creditor may be limited in its ability to collect on the judgment.

§ 24.87 Asset Protection—Domestic Trusts

It is well established that a settlor cannot create a trust to avoid his own creditors while retaining certain interests therefrom.[1] However, domestic trusts can serve as effective asset protection devices to protect other beneficiaries from their creditors, including existing creditors, provided a spendthrift trust provision is included in the trust agreement.[2] Domestic trusts can also be used to obtain generation skipping tax benefits while protecting beneficiaries from their creditors. Other situations where domestic trusts are useful include the use of special needs trusts to minimize the resources of disabled persons for Medicaid or other governmental program eligibility purposes, while providing for certain "luxury" items or supplemental care.[3]

§ 24.88 Asset Protection—Foreign Trusts

Perhaps the most effective asset protection technique is that of the foreign situs trust. Such trusts have been established in foreign jurisdictions which have limited fraudulent conveyance remedies and permit settlors to retain enjoyment or control of their own trusts while protecting the trust from their future creditors. While the statutes in each jurisdiction vary, in general, they incorporate significant procedural and substantive barriers that will impact a creditor's decision as to how far to go to attach assets.

Although the optimum protection is achieved by physically transferring assets offshore into a trust, many clients wish to retain control and

§ 24.86

1. *See* Chapter 2 "Non-corporate Entities: Limited Liability Companies and Partnerships," *supra*.

2. Partnership Law § 111.

§ 24.87

1. This rule, known as the self-settled trust doctrine, is set forth in *Restatement (Second) of Trusts* § 156 (1957) and has been codified in EPTL § 7-3.1. Alaska and Delaware have enacted legislation permitting self-settled spendthrift trusts, providing similar benefits to those available previously only with foreign trusts.

2. Income beneficiaries are protected by statute even without an express spendthrift provision. EPTL § 7-1.5(a).

3. *See* Chapter 23 "Elder Law," *supra*.

avoid liquidating their assets until the need arises. Therefore, some attorneys utilize a combined domestic partnership/foreign trust structure to enable the client to retain control until a problem develops.[1]

§ 24.89 Powers of Attorney

In the event that a person becomes physically or mentally disabled, it is important to have legal tools in place to provide for the proper management of their affairs. This is particularly true where either *inter vivos* gifts, as part of prudent estate planning or as part of "Medicaid planning," becomes necessary.[1]

A commonly used tool to provide for the management of one's financial affairs is a durable power of attorney. By signing a power of attorney, a person designates another to act as his "attorney-in-fact," *i.e.*, as his agent. By establishing an agency relationship, the person permits another to act for him with either broad or limited degrees of power.

Under general agency doctrines, an agency relationship terminates upon the incapacity of the principal.[2] However, a "durable" power of attorney that meets the requirement of the statute will survive the incapacity of the principal.[3] The form, which must provide the language included in the statute, provides for a series of broad powers which the principal may choose to give the attorney-in-fact. For short form powers of attorneys executed after January 1, 1997, the principal need only initial the last box providing that the enumerated powers therein are delegated to the attorney-in-fact.[4] In addition, other powers, not necessarily required by statute, that the draftsman may deem important to spell out should also be included. A suggested durable power of attorney form may be found at the end of the chapter.[5]

When a client executes a durable power of attorney, the agency relationship comes into effect *immediately*. This means that, for example, that an unscrupulous attorney-in-fact might use the power immedi-

---

§ 24.88

1. For a more thorough discussion on using foreign trusts and limited partnerships see G. Rothschild, *Asset Preservation: Legal and Ethical Strategies,* N.Y.L.J., 3/11/94, p.1, col.1.

§ 24.89

1. *See* Chapter 23 "Elder Law," *supra*, regarding preservation of assets in the event of the necessity for long term care.

2. *See* Matter of Ciervo, 124 A.D.2d 583, 507 N.Y.S.2d 868 (2d Dep't 1986) (contract signed by attorney-in-fact pursuant to power of attorney which was not "durable" when principal was incompetent was voidable at option of conservator).

3. General Obligations Law §§ 5–1501.

4. General Obligations Law § 5–1501.1.

5. *See infra*, § 24.100. **CAVEAT:** If the power to make gifts is not limited or restricted in some manner, the Internal Revenue Service may argue that the agent is the donee of a general power of appointment, which could make the principal's estate subject to estate tax as part of the *donee's* estate if the donee predeceases the principal. Therefore such power should be limited to gifts to other persons, limited by an ascertainable standard or a 5% or $5,000 limitation. I.R.C. §§ 2041(b)(1)(A), (2).

ately to transfer assets from the principal.[6] Because of this possibility, some people prefer to execute a "springing power of attorney" instead. A short form springing power of attorney is similar to a short form durable power of attorney, except that the powers granted do not come into effect *until* the principal becomes disabled.[7] However, as a practical matter, by providing that the power of attorney does not become effective until the principal is disabled, the attorney-in-fact may have significant problems and delays involving proving that the principal is, in fact, incapable of managing his or her affairs, particularly where the person suffers from a form of dementia.[8]

Library References:

West's Key No. Digests, Principal and Agent ⚖10(1).

§ 24.90 Advance Directives

Another issue which an estate planning attorney should address with clients is the need to provide for someone to make medical decisions on their behalf in the event that they are incapable of doing so. The range of decision-making includes decisions relating to medicines and medical procedures, as well as whether to "pull the plug."[1] The failure to provide for this can result in unwanted medical care, such as being kept alive on a respirator, being continued indefinitely or can result in contentious and expensive litigation between medical providers and family members.[2]

A New York resident can avoid these problems through the use of "advance directives." There are two types of advance directives:

(1) a health care proxy, and

(2) a living will.

---

6. PRACTICE POINTER: The planner should be particularly sensitive to this in second marriage situations, or potentially unstable relationships, and may need to advise the client of the potential for abuse.

7. General Obligations Law § 5–1506.

8. PRACTICE POINTER: For persons who are fearful that an attorney-in-fact may abuse his authority if given a durable, as opposed to a springing, power, consider drafting a durable power of attorney that requires *two* agents to act jointly. In this manner, as long as one of the agents has the principal's best interests in mind, the power cannot be abused.

§ 24.90

1. In Cruzan by Cruzan v. Director, Missouri Dept. of Health, 497 U.S. 261, 110 S.Ct. 2841, 111 L.Ed.2d 224 (1990), the Supreme Court inferred a privacy right of an adult with decisional capacity to accept or reject medical treatment. *See also,* Schloendorff v. Society of New York Hospital, 211 N.Y. 125, 129–130, 105 N.E. 92, 93 (1914) ("[e]very human being of adult years and sound mind has a right to determine what shall be done with his own body . . .").

2. *See* Grace Plaza of Great Neck, Inc. v. Elbaum, 82 N.Y.2d 10, 603 N.Y.S.2d 386, 623 N.E.2d 513 (1993), where the lack of medical directives resulted in liability for ongoing medical services.

§ 24.91 Advance Directives—Health Care Proxy

A health care proxy designates another adult as a health care agent to make health care decisions on behalf of the principal once the principal is incapacitated.[1] A health care proxy must meet the following requirements:

(1) it must name the principal and the agent,

(2) it must state that the principal intends that the agent make health care decisions on the principal's behalf,

(3) it must be signed and dated by the principal, and

(4) two witnesses must sign below a statement that "the principal appeared to execute the proxy willingly and free from duress."[2]

The health care agent is supposed to make decisions consistent with the principal's wishes if the principal's wishes are "reasonably known," and if they are not, such decisions are to be made consistent with the principal's best interests.[3] The one exception to this rule involves the cessation of artificial hydration or nutrition, for which the agent may not decide to cease such life sustaining measures unless the principal's wishes are reasonably known or ascertainable.[4]

West's McKinney's Forms, appropriate to this section, are available.[5]

Library References:

West's Key No. Digests, Physicians and Surgeons ⚖42, 44.

§ 24.92 Advance Directives—Living Will

A living will is another form of advance directive that has been recognized in New York.[1] A living will evidences an individual's wishes concerning medical decision making. It does not name a health care agent, but rather provides evidence as to what the person's wishes are regarding medical treatment if mentally incapacitated. Generally, a living will contains a "personal threshold," namely the set of circumstances under which the living will comes into effect, and the person's choices concerning medical treatments.

---

§ 24.91

1. Public Health Law § 2980(8).
2. Public Health Law § 2981(2)(a), (5).
3. Public Health Law § 2982(2).
4. Public Health Law § 2982.2(b).

PRACTICE POINTER: In order to give the health care agent authority to make decisions regarding artificial nutrition or hydration, a health care proxy must state that the principal has discussed this matter with the agent, and that the agent is aware of the principal's wishes.

5. *See* West's McKinney's Forms—Estate and Surrogate's Practice § 7:704 (health care proxy).

§ 24.92

1. There is no statute governing living wills in New York, but they have been recognized in Matter of Westchester County Medical Center on Behalf of O'Connor, 72 N.Y.2d 517, 534 N.Y.S.2d 886, 531 N.E.2d 607 (1988), and addressed in New York Health Department regulations. 10 NYCRR §§ 400.21(b)(3), 700.5(b)(3).

§ 24.92 ESTATE PLANNING Ch. 24

Note that the existence of a living will and a health care proxy might result in difficulties for the health care agent, especially if a health care provider could argue that the language of a living will *requires* continued medical treatment.[2]

West's McKinney's Forms, appropriate to this section, are available.[3]

Library References:

West's Key No. Digests, Physicians and Surgeons ⟲45.

§ 24.93 Ethical Considerations in Estate Planning

Under the best of circumstances, estate planning can be a remarkably satisfying and conflict-free exercise in which the attorney acts as a true family counselor. Under those idyllic circumstances, the family is united in goals, and looks to the attorney for the best manner to achieve those results. Unfortunately, not every situation that an attorney may find himself in will be so free of conflict. Thus, an attorney must be cognizant of the ethical issues which might arise in the course of representing one or more members of a family.

In addition, it is incumbent upon an attorney to follow all pertinent rules of conduct relating to his representation of an estate planning client and to beware of ethical pitfalls, particularly as it pertains to testamentary gifts to an attorney-draftsman or the appointment of the attorney-draftsman as an executor of the estate.

§ 24.94 Ethical Considerations in Estate Planning—Multiple Clients

Generally, an attorney who is engaged in estate planning will be asked to represent, at a minimum, both a husband and wife. Generally, this is not problematic. However, where there is dual representation, the attorney cannot favor one over the other.[1] All information provided by one spouse would have to be supplied to the other, including scope of

---

2. *See, e.g.*, Evans v. Bellevue Hospital, N.Y.L.J., 7/14/93, p. 11, col. 1 (Sup.Ct., N.Y. County, 1989) (court found language of living will ambiguous and ordered continued treatment of AIDS related complex victim because illness was potentially treatable and term "meaningful quality of life" was undefined by document).

PRACTICE POINTER: Although it is advisable to provide both a health care proxy and living will, clients should provide a copy of only the health care proxy to their physician or hospital and use the living will to provide guidance to their agent.

3. See West's McKinney's Forms—Estate and surrogate's Practice §§ 7:439 and 7:710 (living will).

§ 24.94

1. An attorney has a duty not to accept employment and not to continue multiple employment if his exercise of independent professional judgment on behalf of a client will be or is likely to be adversely affected. DR 5–105(A), (B). The exception, in which a lawyer may represent multiple clients, is where "it is obvious that he can adequately represent the interest of each and if each consents to the representation after full disclosure of the possible effect of such representation on the exercise of his independent professional judgment on behalf of each." DR 5–105(C).

assets, gifts made previously, etc. This can be problematic, for example, where a spouse has hidden assets from the other, or where one spouse has made surreptitious gifts to children from another marriage or to a paramour.[2] Similarly, in the case of second marriages, interests may diverge because one or both spouses want to preserve assets for children from a prior marriage. Under such circumstances, full disclosure of the potential conflicts must be made, and the attorney must consider carefully whether he can adequately represent the interests of both parties. Some practitioners believe it is prudent to have married clients sign a letter acknowledging that conflicts may arise in such dual representations and the lawyer's obligation to share all information with both parties.[3]

One of the primary sources of ethical vexation for estate planners is the identity of the client. For example, suppose adult children bring their frail, elderly parents into an attorney's office because, up to that point, the parents had not engaged in any estate planning. The children want to ensure that as much of the parent's estate will pass to them without being lost to taxes. On the other hand, the parents are reluctant to cede control of their affairs to their children, although they are easily swayed by them. Again, under those circumstances, it would appear that no matter who is paying the actual bill for the parent's estate planning, the attorney should clearly disclose to all parties that he represents the parents, rather than the children.

The lawyer also has a duty in this regard to ensure that the client exercises his own free will regarding his testamentary plan, and is not subject to undue influence. "Undue influence" does not refer to the normal and expected influences that a spouse in a long-enduring marriage might exercise to ensure that she is taken care of. Rather, the influence must be of the type that is not considered to be reasonable under the circumstances, and, as a result, the testamentary scheme reflects the judgment and desire of another instead of that of the testator.[4] Where frail parents, for example, are brought into the attorney's office, the attorney should satisfy himself, and make notes of the precautions taken, to ensure that the will to be executed reflects the desires of the parents rather than those of the children.[5]

2. PRACTICE POINTER: If the lawyer becomes aware of such a situation, the only conceivable course of action for the attorney would be to resign from representation of *both* clients.

3. See infra, § 24.102 for a sample conflicts letter.

4. See, e.g., Matter of Callahan, 155 A.D.2d 454, 547 N.Y.S.2d 113 (2d Dep't 1989), where the testator's will was not admitted to probate where the 90-year-old testator suffered from physical disabilities and was mentally frail, and where the petitioner limited the testator's contact with his family and would not permit him to discuss the will.

5. PRACTICE POINTER: The draftsman should be particularly cautious where the will would make disproportionate bequests to descendants or would significantly alter past testamentary schemes. Videotaping will executions is often advisable in such situations.

§ 24.95 Ethical Considerations in Estate Planning—Attorney/Draftsman as Fiduciary or Beneficiary

A common ethical dilemma faced by practitioners arises when a client seeks to name the attorney/draftsman as a fiduciary under a will. Since a fiduciary is entitled to commissions for his services, a potential for abuse exists.[1] Prior case law certainly indicates that, although under circumstances where the attorney-draftsman had an ongoing relationship with the client such appointment might be reasonable, the appointment of an attorney-draftsman might be invalidated as a constructive fraud, especially where the client was unaware that the attorney would receive statutory commissions.[2] Now, SCPA § 2307A provides that attorneys who are named as executors in wills that are either prepared by them or by an attorney affiliated with them must meet certain disclosure requirements.[3] Specifically, the client must be informed of the following prior to the execution of the will:

(1) Generally, any person (with limited exceptions) may serve as an executor,

(2) Absent an agreement to the contrary, such person, *including an attorney*, will receive a statutory commission for serving as executor; and

(3) If an attorney serves as an executor, the attorney is entitled to *both* statutory commissions and reasonable compensation for legal services.

The client must acknowledge that this disclosure has been made in a signed writing executed prior to, contemporaneously, or subsequent to the execution of the will. The failure to obtain written acknowledgement of this disclosure will result in the attorney's commissions being reduced by one-half.

A more troublesome ethical quandary arises when an attorney is named as a beneficiary of the client's estate. Where the attorney-draftsman is also named as a beneficiary, an inference of undue influence will arise, and the attorney will be obligated, in the first instance to rebut such inference.[4] It has been held that holding a "Putnam hearing" to determine the facts relating to a bequest to such draftsman does not

---

§ 24.95

1. Under the Code of Professional Responsibility, an attorney must avoid even the appearance of impropriety, and is prohibited from consciously influencing a client to name the attorney/draftsman as executor. EC 5-6.

2. *See* Matter of Weinstock's Estate, 40 N.Y.2d 1, 386 N.Y.S.2d 1, 351 N.E.2d 647 (1976).

3. SCPA § 2307A applies to all wills and codicils executed on or after January 1, 1996 and to all estates of decedents dying after December 31, 1996.

4. In re Putnam's Will, 257 N.Y. 140, 177 N.E. 399 (1931). An attorney is generally required to submit an affidavit explaining the circumstances involving the bequest and if the court is not satisfied, a hearing is held (a "Putnam hearing").

violate a will's *in terrorem* clause.[5] In general, unless the client is a relative and the bequest does not favor the draftsman vis a vis relatives of the same or a closer degree, an attorney who will become a beneficiary of the client's estate should heed the Court of Appeals' advice: "Attorneys for clients who intend to leave them or their families a bequest would do well to have the will drawn by some other lawyer. Any suspicion which may arise of improper influence used under the cover of the confidential relationship may thus be avoided."[6]

Note that where a testator leaves a substantial bequest to an attorney, an inference of undue influence does not arise where the will was drafted by an unaffiliated attorney, but where that unaffiliated attorney does not independently counsel the client, a surrogate may allow a hearing to determine whether the attorney-beneficiary exercised undue influence over the testator.[7]

§ 24.96 Forms

The sections which follow include essential forms for handling an estate planning matter. Included are a checklist, an introductory letter to clients, a client questionnaire and a conflict letter to be used when representing both husband and wife. Also set forth are a statutory short form durable general power of attorney, a Crummey notice and a sample spousal conflicts setter. The practitioner must adapt the forms to the particular facts in the specific estate planning matter.

§ 24.97 Forms—Estate Planner's Checklist

1. Preliminary

    • Have client complete questionnaire. (*See* § 24.99)

    • Update client's estate plan, review existing will, trusts, and power of attorney.

---

5. In re Zurkow's Estate, 74 Misc.2d 736, 345 N.Y.S.2d 436 (Surr.Ct., N.Y. County, 1973).

6. In re Putnam's Will, 257 N.Y. at 143, 177 N.E. at 400. *See also*, New York State Bar Association Committee on Professional Ethics, Opinion 610–6/20/90 (2–90), which, in discussing EC 5–5 of the Code of Professional Responsibility's admonition against drafting an instrument which makes the attorney a beneficiary except in exceptional circumstances. "Exceptional circumstances" is defined to include situations where there is a close family relationship between the testator and the draftsman, or where the gift is relatively small compared to the size of the estate and the professional relationship between the testator and the attorney is longstanding.

7. Matter of Henderson, 80 N.Y.2d 388, 590 N.Y.S.2d 836, 605 N.E.2d 323 (1992) (draftsman relied upon notes prepared by attorney-beneficiary without inquiring why testator was leaving substantial bequest to attorney while virtually excluding testator's sister).

PRACTICE POINTER: Obviously, an attorney should discuss, in detail, all of the considerations regarding testamentary dispositions, both as a matter of prudent planning and to satisfy himself that undue influence has not been exercised on the testator.

- Determine if family circumstances have changed, *i.e.*, through divorce, birth, or death.
- Does present will have proper attestation clause and self-proving affidavit? (*See* §§ 24.7–24.8)

2. Will Drafting and Execution.
   - Is there a need for direction for the payment of debts and administrative expenses? (*See* § 24.10)
   - Are any testamentary or nontestamentary bequests to be exempt from tax apportionment? (*See* § 24.10)
   - Should a specific devise of real property be included to avoid DNI? (*See* § 24.11)
   - Has the client considered a contingent "wipeout" clause? Should it provide for one-half to each spouse's heirs? (*See* § 24.17)
   - Are any persons to be specifically disinherited? If a will contest can be anticipated, consider a revocable trust to avoid probate.

3. Dispositions in Trust.
   - Consider that the estate may be too small to justify a trust in view of administration costs. Provide for termination at trustee's discretion if less than a sum certain.
   - Consider retaining principal in simple trust before dividing into separate shares.
   - Does client wish to stagger distributions to children?
   - If children are financially independent, consider multi-generation trust with discretion to pay to children or grandchildren or provide child with a life estate.
   - If protection from a beneficiary's creditors or failed marriages are a concern, consider a discretionary trust rather than mandatory distributions. Include a spendthrift clause.
   - Consider whether to give beneficiaries a limited or general power of appointment.

4. Tax Planning.
   - Consider splitting assets to take advantage of the unified credit. (*See* § 24.21)
   - Should the credit shelter trust provide for the spouse only or be a "sprinkling trust"? (*See* § 24.21)
   - Consider use of a disclaimer trust if estate is not substantial. (*See* § 24.69)

- Compute estate tax liability utilizing optimum marital deduction. Discuss advantage of not using optimum marital deduction. (*See* § 24.22)
- Is there sufficient estate liquidity to pay taxes, debts and administration expenses? (*See* § 24.2)
- Does client wish to leave marital bequest outright or in trust? If in trust, it must meet I.R.C. § 2056 requirements to qualify for marital deduction. (*See* § 24.22)
- If spouse is not a U.S. citizen consider QDOT provisions. Also consider lifetime gifts to the non-citizen spouse. (*See* § 24.58)
- Consider whether to use fractional or pecuniary bequests. (*See* § 24.23)
- Has the client been informed of generation skipping transfer tax exemptions and planning to minimize such tax, including providing for a "reverse QTIP" election? (*See* §§ 24.24–24.31)
- Does client own life insurance on his or spouse's life? If so, consider insurance trust. (*See* §§ 24.34–24.36)
- Does client wish to make any charitable bequests? If yes, is it an outright, remainder trust, lead trust, or pooled fund bequest? (*See* §§ 24.54–24.55)

5. Planning With Certain Assets.
    - Does client have substantial retirement plan assets? (*See* § 24.37)
    - Review beneficiary designations. If client is approaching age 70, discuss benefits of non-recalculation method. (*See* § 24.37)
    - Does client own a closely held business? Is there a buy-sell agreement? (*See* §§ 24.38–24.39)
    - Consider benefits available under I.R.C. § 6166 (to extend time to pay estate tax), I.R.C. § 303 (stock redemption), and I.R.C. § 2032A (special use value). (*See* §§ 24.40–24.42)
    - Consider transfer of ownership interests and reorganization to obtain benefits of valuation discounts. (*See* § 24.41)
    - Is income in respect of decedent a concern? For example, does client own installment obligations, copyrights, employee benefits, or IRAs which require special consideration. (*See* §§ 24.37, 24.43)

6. Lifetime Planning.
    - Discuss advantages (and disadvantages) of making lifetime gifts. (*See* § 24.44)
    - Does client have assets which are expected to highly appreciate? (*See* § 24.46)

- Consider personal residence trust for larger estates. (*See* § 24.47)
- Is client taking advantage of annual gift exclusions, including medical and education expenses? (*See* § 24.49)
- Consider alternatives to gifts to minor children—UTMA accounts, "Crummey" trusts, I.R.C. § 2503(c) trusts, and family partnerships. (*See* §§ 24.50–24.53)
- If client is charitably inclined, discuss charitable trusts. (*See* §§ 24.54–24.55)

7. Special Situations.
   - Is client terminally ill? (*See* § 24.56)
   - Does client have a non-citizen spouse? (*See* § 24.58)
   - Does client have children from a prior marriage or desire to leave less than minimum elective share to spouse? (*See* §§ 24.59–24.62)
   - Is client divorced or involved in divorce proceedings? (*See* §§ 24.63–24.65)
   - Is client co-habiting with a "significant other"? (*See* § 24.66)

8. Postmortem Planning.
   - If client is a beneficiary of an estate, consider use of disclaimer. (*See* §§ 24.68–24.71)
   - Consider making a partial QTIP election to equalize estate values. (*See* § 24.72)
   - Consider electing alternate valuation date. (*See* § 24.73)

9. Probate Avoidance.
   - Consider using a revocable trust where client is concerned about incapacity, confidentiality, or expects a will contest due to unequal treatment of heirs. (*See* § 24.81)
   - If real property situated in other states, consider revocable trust to avoid ancillary probate. (*See* § 24.81)
   - Who will be responsible for funding the trust?

10. Asset Protection
    - Is client concerned about future litigation/creditor claims? Review methods available to protect assets from such claims. (*See* §§ 24.84–24.88)

11. Planning for Incapacity.
    - Discuss benefits of durable power of attorney vs. springing power of attorney. (*See* § 24.89)
    - Consider including gift giving powers. (*See* § 24.89)

- Discuss health care proxy and living will issues. If minimum life sustaining measures desired, state that agent knows of principal's desire with respect to artificial nutrition and hydration. (*See* §§ 24.91–24.92)

12. Ethical Considerations.
    - Identify who the client is and obtain engagement letter. (*See* § 24.94)
    - Have clients sign conflicts letter if representing both husband and wife. (*See* § 24.94)
    - If client wishes to appoint attorney/draftsman as fiduciary obtain required acknowledgment. (*See* § 24.95)

§ 24.98 Forms—Sample Information Request Letter[1]

Mr. John Smith
1111 Main Street
New York, New York

Dear Mr. Smith:

I'm looking forward to meeting with you and your wife on June 1st at my office. The attached form requests information which is important for the planning and administration of your estate. Please try to complete the form as fully as possible (using approximate values is adequate) prior to our meeting. This form will facilitate some consideration of your circumstances at our meeting, and should expedite the process. The contents will, of course, be kept confidential.

Please bring the completed form to our meeting along with the pertinent documents from the enclosed list.

This form and the information it provides will assist me in helping you to fulfill one of the primary goals of estate planning, which is to provide for the disposition of your assets in accordance with your wishes, with a minimum of administration expenses and estate and inheritance taxes.

Many times questions are raised during the estate planning process which require careful consideration and discussion. If this is done in advance of the conference, time will be saved and the likelihood of arriving at the best solutions improved. These include the following. (Your conclusions would cover the eventuality of the death of both as well as one of you).

   a. Who will you designate to act as your personal representative and alternates (the person or corporation who will see to the administration of your estate)?

---

§ 24.98
1. *See supra,* § 24.2.

b. If the creation of a trust to arise at your death appears possible, what person, or persons or corporation would you wish to act as trustee and alternate trustee?

c. Are there any specific items of real or personal property you would wish to go to particular persons?

d. Who would you wish to take the responsibility of the care of your minor children, if any?

e. At what age or ages would you feel your children should receive substantial assets (as opposed to contributions for their health, education and welfare)?

I look forward to working with you in the development of a comprehensive and meaningful estate plan.

Sincerely,

DOCUMENT CHECKLIST

___ 1. Most current personal tax return

___ 2. Most current corporate tax returns (if applicable)

___ 3. Most recent financial statement for your business

___ 4. Copies of your will(s) and trust agreements (if applicable)

___ 5. Copies of durable general powers of attorney

___ 6. Copies of life insurance policies and annuity contracts in force

___ 7. Copies of partnership and shareholder agreements

___ 8. Antenuptial or separation agreements

___ 9. Prior gift tax returns filed

___ 10. Copies of deeds to real property

___ 11. Copies of all IRA, pension and retirement benefit beneficiary designations

§ 24.99 Forms—Client Questionnaire[1]

ESTATE PLANNING QUESTIONNAIRE

Date Prepared _____

Full Name _____ Date of Birth _____

Spouse's Full Name _____ Date of Birth _____

Address _____

City, State & Zip Code _____

Phone (Area Code) (H) Work _____ Residence _____
(W) Work _____

§ 24.99 1. See supra, § 24.2.

Ch. 24   SAMPLE INFORMATION REQUEST LETTER   § 24.98

- Discuss health care proxy and living will issues. If minimum life sustaining measures desired, state that agent knows of principal's desire with respect to artificial nutrition and hydration. (See §§ 24.91–24.92)

12. Ethical Considerations.
- Identify who the client is and obtain engagement letter. (See § 24.94)
- Have clients sign conflicts letter if representing both husband and wife. (See § 24.94)
- If client wishes to appoint attorney/draftsman as fiduciary obtain required acknowledgment. (See § 24.95)

§ 24.98 Forms—Sample Information Request Letter[1]

Mr. John Smith
1111 Main Street
New York, New York

Dear Mr. Smith:

I'm looking forward to meeting with you and your wife on June 1st at my office. The attached form requests information which is important for the planning and administration of your estate. Please try to complete the form as fully as possible (using approximate values is adequate) prior to our meeting. This form will facilitate some consideration of your circumstances at our meeting, and should expedite the process. The contents will, of course, be kept confidential.

Please bring the completed form to our meeting along with the pertinent documents from the enclosed list.

This form and the information it provides will assist me in helping you to fulfill one of the primary goals of estate planning, which is to provide for the disposition of your assets in accordance with your wishes, with a minimum of administration expenses and estate and inheritance taxes.

Many times questions are raised during the estate planning process which require careful consideration and discussion. If this is done in advance of the conference, time will be saved and the likelihood of arriving at the best solutions improved. These include the following. (Your conclusions would cover the eventuality of the death of both as well as one of you).

   a. Who will you designate to act as your personal representative and alternates (the person or corporation who will see to the administration of your estate)?

§ 24.98
1. See supra, § 24.2.

b. If the creation of a trust to arise at your death appears possible, what person, or persons or corporation would you wish to act as trustee and alternate trustee?

c. Are there any specific items of real or personal property you would wish to go to particular persons?

d. Who would you wish to take the responsibility of the care of your minor children, if any?

e. At what age or ages would you feel your children should receive substantial assets (as opposed to contributions for their health, education and welfare)?

I look forward to working with you in the development of a comprehensive and meaningful estate plan.

Sincerely,

DOCUMENT CHECKLIST

___ 1. Most current personal tax return

___ 2. Most current corporate tax returns (if applicable)

___ 3. Most recent financial statement for your business

___ 4. Copies of your will(s) and trust agreements (if applicable)

___ 5. Copies of durable general powers of attorney

___ 6. Copies of life insurance policies and annuity contracts in force

___ 7. Copies of partnership and shareholder agreements

___ 8. Antenuptial or separation agreements

___ 9. Prior gift tax returns filed

___ 10. Copies of deeds to real property

___ 11. Copies of all IRA, pension and retirement benefit beneficiary designations

§ 24.99 Forms—Client Questionnaire[1]

ESTATE PLANNING QUESTIONNAIRE

Date Prepared _____

Full Name _____   Date of Birth _____

Spouse's Full Name _____   Date of Birth _____

Address _____

City, State & Zip Code _____

Phone (Area Code) (H) Work _____   Residence _____
            (W) Work _____

§ 24.99

1. See supra, § 24.2.

Ch. 24   CLIENT QUESTIONNAIRE   **§ 24.99**

Referred by: _____

Citizenship: (H) _____   Social Security No.: (H) _____
             (W) _____   (W) _____

Children:

Full Names	Living?	Date of Birth	Married?	Number of His/Her

* List number of any step-children not formally adopted by your child in parentheses ( ).

FINANCIAL INFORMATION:

If you are married, please list totals in appropriate columns. Approximate totals are adequate. If additional space is needed, attach schedules.

                                            Husband   **Wife**   **Joint**

CASH/BANK ACCOUNTS   _____ _____ _____
STOCKS/BONDS/MUTUAL
   FUNDS   _____ _____ _____
EMPLOYEE BENEFITS:
   Pension/Retirement Plan   _____ _____ _____
   401–K Plan   _____ _____ _____
   IRA   _____ _____ _____
   Other   _____ _____ _____

ANNUITIES   _____ _____ _____

REAL ESTATE:
Property #1 Location: _____
   Estimated Value   _____ _____ _____
   Mortgage Liability   (_____) (_____) (_____)
Property #2 Location: _____
   Estimated Value   _____ _____ _____
   Mortgage Liability   (_____) (_____) (_____)
   Partnership Interest   _____ _____ _____
   Closely–Held Business Interests   _____ _____ _____
   Personal Effects   _____ _____ _____
   Other Property Interests   _____ _____ _____

§ 24.99 ESTATE PLANNING Ch. 24

LIFE INSURANCE:

Name of Co. & Policy #	Insured	Face Amount	Policy Type	Owner	Beneficiary	Cash Value

LIABILITIES: List Loans, Guarantees, Contingent Liabilities.

ANNUAL INCOME FROM ALL SOURCES: $_____

FUTURE INHERITANCES—Do you, your spouse or children expect to inherit property?

ADVISORS:

1. Accountants

2. Broker(s)/Financial Planners

3. Life Insurance Agent(s)

4. Bank(s)

ADDITIONAL INFORMATION NEEDED FOR ESTATE PLANNING:

1. Executor(s)/Trustee(s)
   Original
   Name:

   Address:

Successor
Name: _____

Address: _____
_____
_____

2. Guardian
Original
Name: _____

Address: _____
_____
_____

Successor
Name: _____

Address: _____
_____

6. Contingent Beneficiaries—If your immediate family were all to be deceased, to whom would you wish your property to pass (for example, you might want to have it go one-half to the heirs of each of you, or to charity).
_____
_____
_____

7. Special Instructions
_____
_____

8. Funeral/Burial Instructions (if any)
_____
_____
_____

9. Person(s) to be given power to make health care decisions in the event of incapacity.
Original _____
First Alternate _____
Second Alternate _____

10. Do you have a pre or post-nuptial agreement?
   ____ Yes. If so, provide copy.
   ____ No.

11. How important is the minimization of estate taxes to you?

12. The following questions relate to your children, if any:
    a. How will the estate assets for the benefit of your minor children be managed?
    b. Do any of your children have special living, educational, or medical needs?
    c. Are your children financially responsible?

§ 24.99   ESTATE PLANNING   Ch. 24

    d. At what age do you expect your children to be able to manage an inheritance?

13. Have you and your spouse lived in any of the following states during your marriage: Arizona, California, Idaho, Louisiana, Nevada, New Mexico, Texas, Washington, or Wisconsin? Give dates.

14. Do you have property in other states or foreign countries?

15. Describe any separately held property that you accumulated before your marriage or that you received as gifts or inheritances.

16. Do you contribute to or expect to contribute to the support of anyone other than your immediate family, such as your parents or your spouse's parents?

17. Have you or your spouse made any gifts in excess of $10,000 to any one person in any one year? _____ Please attach copies of the last gift tax returns that you and your spouse filed, if any.

18. Do you or your spouse plan to make substantial charitable gifts during your lifetime or in your will?

19. Have you or your spouse created any trusts that still exist? _____ If yes, please attach a copy of the trust agreement and amendments.

20. Describe any powers of appointment that you or your spouse possess.

21. If you own any closely held business interests, describe:

    —How you plan to dispose of them during your lifetime.

    —How you plan to dispose of them in your will.

22. Describe any other information that you believe may affect your estate plan.

    _____
    _____
    _____

23. Is there any litigation pending which may adversely affect you or your spouse's estate?

    _____
    _____

§ 24.100   Forms—"Durable" Power of Attorney Form[1]

Durable General Power of Attorney
(NEW YORK STATUTORY SHORT FORM)

THE POWERS YOU GRANT BELOW CONTINUE TO BE EFFECTIVE SHOULD YOU BECOME DISABLED OR INCOMPETENT

§ 24.100   1. *See supra*, § 24.89.

Ch. 24   "DURABLE" POWER OF ATTORNEY FORM § 24.100

(CAUTION: THIS IS AN IMPORTANT DOCUMENT. IT GIVES THE PERSON WHOM YOU DESIGNATE (YOUR "AGENT") BROAD POWERS TO HANDLE YOUR PROPERTY DURING YOUR LIFETIME, WHICH MAY INCLUDE POWERS TO MORTGAGE, SELL, OR OTHERWISE DISPOSE OF ANY REAL OR PERSONAL PROPERTY WITHOUT ADVANCE NOTICE TO YOU OR APPROVAL BY YOU. THESE POWERS WILL CONTINUE TO EXIST EVEN AFTER YOU BECOME DISABLED OR INCOMPETENT. THESE POWERS ARE EXPLAINED MORE FULLY IN NEW YORK GENERAL OBLIGATIONS LAW, ARTICLE 5, TITLE 15, SECTION 5–1502A THROUGH 5–1503, WHICH EXPRESSLY PERMIT THE USE OF ANY OTHER OR DIFFERENT FORM OF POWER OF ATTORNEY.

THIS DOCUMENT DOES NOT AUTHORIZE ANYONE TO MAKE MEDICAL OR OTHER HEALTH CARE DECISIONS. YOU MAY EXECUTE A HEALTH CARE PROXY TO DO THIS.

IF THERE IS ANYTHING ABOUT THIS FORM THAT YOU DO NOT UNDERSTAND, YOU SHOULD ASK A LAWYER TO EXPLAIN IT TO YOU.)

THIS is intended to constitute a DURABLE GENERAL POWER OF ATTORNEY pursuant to Article 5, Title 15 of the New York General Obligations Law:

I, JOHN DOE do hereby appoint:

JANE DOE, residing at 4747 Any Avenue, New York, New York 12111

(If 1 person is to be appointed agent, insert the name and address of YOUR agent above)

_____
_____
_____

(If 2 or more persons are to be appointed agents by you insert their names and addresses above)

My Attorney(s)-in-Fact TO ACT

(If more than one agent is designated, CHOOSE ONE of the following two choices by putting your initials in ONE of the blank spaces to the left of your choice:)

[ ] Each agent may SEPARATELY act.

[ ] All agents must act TOGETHER.

(If neither blank space is initialed, the agents will be required to act TOGETHER)

IN MY NAME, PLACE AND STEAD in any way which I myself could do, if I were personally present, with respect to the following matters as each of them is defined in Title 15 of

§ 24.100   ESTATE PLANNING   Ch. 24

Article 5 of the New York Obligations Law to the extent that I am permitted by law to act through an agent:

(DIRECTIONS: Initial in the blank space to the right of your choice any one or more of the following lettered subdivisions as to which you WANT to give your agent authority. If the blank space to the right of any particular lettered subdivision is NOT initialed, NO AUTHORITY WILL BE GRANTED for matters that are included in that subdivision. Alternatively, the letter corresponding to each power you wish to grant may be written or typed on the blank line in subdivision "(qq)", and you may then put your initials in the blank space to the right of subdivision "(qq)" in order to grant each of the powers so indicated)

(A) real estate and cooperative transactions; .... [ ]
(B) chattel and goods transactions; .... [ ]
(C) bonds, shares and commodity transactions; ..... [ ]
(D) banking transactions; ..... [ ]
(E) business operating transaction; .... [ ]
(F) insurance transactions and litigation; .... [ ]
(G) creation of trusts and estate matters; .... [ ]
(H) claims and litigation, including appeals and settlements; .... [ ]
(I) personal relationships and affairs; .... [ ]
(J) military/veterans' benefit claims; .... [ ]
(K) records, reports and statements; .... [ ]
(L) full and unqualified authority to my Attorney(s)-in-Fact to delegate any or all of the powers listed hereunder to any person or persons my Attorney(s)-in-Fact shall select; .... [ ]
(M) access to safe deposit boxes/vaults/safes; .... [ ]
(N) power to sign tax returns and Internal Revenue Service powers of attorney and deal with all federal, state and local tax authorities on all claims, litigation, settlements and other matters; .... [ ]
(O) power to deal with all pension, retirement, incentive, I.R.A./Keogh/SEP and similar type plans, programs and annuities; [ ]
(P) power to create and fund standby and other *inter vivos* trusts for principal; .... [ ]
(Q) power to borrow funds to avoid forced liquidation of principal's assets; .... [ ]
(R) power to handle life, medical, long-term care, homeowners, vehicle and other insurance, including litigation and settling claims and actions; .... [ ]
(S) power to deal with Medicare and Medicaid claims, litigation and settlements; .... [ ]
(T) power to enter into buy and sell transactions; ... [ ]
(U) power to forgive and collect debt; .... [ ]
(V) power to endorse, collect, negotiate, deposit and withdraw Social Security/Veterans and/or other pension, annuity or benefit checks and/or negotiable instruments; ..... [ ]
(W) power to claim, negotiate, obtain and settle claims and actions for government entitlements and benefits of all kinds with

Ch. 24   "DURABLE" POWER OF ATTORNEY FORM § 24.100

(X) power to make statutory elections and disclaimers; .... [ ]
(Y) power to pay salaries of employers and to employ and pay household help and health aides for the principal and the principal's dependents; .... [ ]
(Z) power to make support payments to spouse, dependent children, and others previously dependent on principal; ...... [ ]
(aa) power to provide principal with personal health care services from others; .... [ ]
(bb) power to change the domicile of the principal for any and all purposes; ... [ ]
(cc) power to purchase flower bonds for estate tax purposes; .... [ ]
(dd) power to oversee the management of the principal's business; .... [ ]
(ee) power to retain and dispose of commercial and/or corporate interests; .... [ ]
(ff) power to make and implement tax savings decisions; .... [ ]
(gg) power to retain attorneys, accountants, investment counsel and similar professionals concerning the principal's property and affairs and to pay the same; .... [ ]
(hh) power to fulfill principal's charitable pledges; ..... [ ]
(ii) power to seek a declaratory or damages judgment against any person or entity refusing to honor this durable Power-of-Attorney; .... [ ]
(jj) power to exercise this unrevoked durable Power-of-Attorney any time after execution and lawful delivery thereof to Attorney-in-Fact; .... [ ]
(kk) power to make an orderly disposition of a professional practice; .... [ ]
(ll) power to pay Attorney-in-Fact for services performed as such agent; ... [ ]
(mm) power to make gifts to such agent(s) where agent is a relative of the principal, acts in good faith, not to the exclusion of others, nor to principal's detriment; ... [ ]
(nn) power to make family gifts for estate planning or long-term care planning; .... [ ]
(oo) I hereby designate my attorney(s)-in-fact to serve as the guardian of my person and property, to serve without bond, in the event that I shall be declared unable to manage my affairs pursuant to Article 81 of the Mental Hygiene Law of the State of New York or any statute corresponding thereto; .... [ ]
(pp) all other matters allowed by law; .... [ ]
(qq) each of the above matters identified by the following letters:

_____

_____

_____ .... [ ]

(Special provisions and limitations may be included in the statutory short form power of attorney only if they conform to the requirements of section 5–1503 of the New York General Obligations Law.)

_____

_____

541

§ 24.100   ESTATE PLANNING   Ch. 24

_____
_____

This Durable Power of Attorney shall not be affected by my subsequent disability or incompetence.

If every agent named above is unable or unwilling to serve, I appoint _____ to be my agent for all
(Insert name and address of successor)

purposes hereunder.

TO INDUCE ANY THIRD PARTY TO ACT HEREUNDER, I HEREBY AGREE THAT ANY THIRD PARTY RECEIVING A DULY EXECUTED COPY OR FACSIMILE OF THIS INSTRUMENT MAY ACT HEREUNDER, AND THAT REVOCATION OR TERMINATION HEREOF SHALL BE INEFFECTIVE AS TO SUCH THIRD PARTY UNLESS AND UNTIL ACTUAL NOTICE OR KNOWLEDGE OF SUCH REVOCATION OR TERMINATION SHALL HAVE BEEN RECEIVED BY SUCH THIRD PARTY, AND I FOR MYSELF AND FOR MY HEIRS, EXECUTORS, LEGAL REPRESENTATIVES AND ASSIGNS, HEREBY AGREE TO INDEMNIFY AND HOLD HARMLESS ANY SUCH THIRD PARTY FROM AND AGAINST ANY AND ALL CLAIMS THAT MAY ARISE AGAINST SUCH THIRD PARTY BY REASON OF SUCH THIRD PARTY HAVING RELIED ON THE PROVISIONS OF THIS INSTRUMENT.

This Durable General Power of Attorney may be revoked by me at any time.

In Witness Whereof, I have hereunto signed my name this ____ day of _____, 1997.

(YOU SIGN HERE) = = >   _____ (Seal)

JOHN DOE

STATE OF NEW YORK   )
)   SS: ACKNOWLEDGMENT
COUNTY OF   )

On the _____ day of _____, 1997, before me personally appeared JOHN DOE, to me known and known by me to be the individual described in and who executed the foregoing instrument and he acknowledged to me that he executed the same.

_____
NOTARY PUBLIC

§ 24.101 Forms—Crummey Notice[1]

Dear :

I am writing to you as Trustee of the Greta Grantor Irrevocable Trust, created under an agreement dated _____, 1996 ("the Trust") of which you are a beneficiary.

This letter is to inform you that a gift valued at _____ has been made to the trust. Under Article Two of the trust, you have a right to withdraw from the trust your pro rata portion (but not exceeding $5,000 per year until fully withdrawn) of the gift. If you wish to exercise this right of withdrawal, you should send me written notice of such intention within thirty (30) days of receipt of this letter. If you do not exercise your right of withdrawal within this period, your right to withdraw will lapse.

If you have any questions about your rights under this trust, please do not hesitate to call or write me. Please acknowledge receipt of this letter by signing below and returning a copy to me.

Sincerely,

Trudy Trustee

I HEREBY ACKNOWLEDGE RECEIPT OF THIS NOTICE.

_____

§ 24.102 Forms—Spousal Conflicts Letter[1]

Dear _____ :

We are scheduled to meet on _____ to review your estate planning needs. We appreciate the opportunity of representing you and want to provide you with the highest level of service. Although it is common for a husband and wife to be represented by one law firm, it is important that you understand that husbands and wives may have conflicting interests where estate planning is concerned. Obviously, there is a cost benefit and efficiency of having one attorney represent both of you.

If we are to represent both of you, however, we must remain neutral in making our recommendations. My obligation is to give you complete advice on the planning alternatives available. Such process could make it more favorable to one than the other. Generally, that is not a problem between spouses since your goals will be mutual.

Although you may not have any conflicting interests at present, the ethical rules require us to advise you of such potential for conflict in representing both of you and obtain your consent. We must also obtain your consent that if either of you share a confidence with me, I must

---

§ 24.101

1. *See supra,* § 24.36.

§ 24.102

1. *See supra,* § 24.94.

disclose it to the other party. Of course, such communications remain privileged from disclosure to third parties.

If you wish us to proceed with representing both of you please sign the copy of this letter to reflect your consent and return one copy to me. Of course, if at any time you wish to have separate counsel you may notify me.

Very truly yours,

    Attorney

We have read the foregoing disclosure and consent to having you represent both of us in our estate planning. We understand and agree that between the two of us, with respect to information provided to you, there shall be no confidential communications.

_____   _____

Chapter 25

PROBATE AND ESTATE ADMINISTRATION

by
Hon. Bertram R. Gelfand

Table of Sections

- 25.1 Scope Note.
- 25.2 Explanation of Basic Legal Terms in Estate Practice.
- 25.3 Strategy.
- 25.4 Who May Commence the Estate of a Person Who Dies Without a Will.
- 25.5 Who Is Entitled to Letters of Administration.
- 25.6 Who May Commence the Estate of a Person Who Dies With a Will.
- 25.7 Documents Required on Application for Letters of Administration.
- 25.8 Who Must Be Cited on an Application for Letters of Administration.
- 25.9 When a Guardian *Ad Litem* Must be Appointed.
- 25.10 Denial or Revocation of Letters of Administration.
- 25.11 Letters of Temporary Administration.
- 25.12 Venue.
- 25.13 Duty of the Fiduciary to Expeditiously Seek Probate.
- 25.14 When a Beneficiary Should Petition for Probate.
- 25.15 When a Creditor Should Petition for Probate.
- 25.16 When a Person in Litigation with an Estate Should Petition for Probate.
- 25.17 Information to Be Gathered by Attorney.
- 25.18 Contents of Petition for Probate.
- 25.19 Documents Required to Accompany Probate Petition.
- 25.20 What to Do If Your Client Cannot Produce the Original Will.
- 25.21 Requirements and Procedure for Proving a Will Where the Original Is Lost.
- 25.22 How to Get a Will Admitted to Probate If None of the Witnesses to the Will are Available.
- 25.23 When a Court Must Appoint a Guardian *Ad Litem* in a Probate Proceeding.
- 25.24 Who May Oppose the Admission to Probate of a Will By Filing Objections.
- 25.25 When Objections Must Be Filed.
- 25.26 How to Start an Estate Administration Where There Will Be a Delay in Getting a Will Admitted to Probate.
- 25.27 Form of Objections to Probate.
- 25.28 Burden of Proof
- 25.29 Requirement of a Notice of Objections to Complete Jurisdiction in a Contested Probate.

PROBATE & ESTATE ADMINISTRATION   Ch. 25

25.30   Right to a Trial by Jury.
25.31   Right to Discovery in a Probate, Administration or Accounting Proceeding.
25.32   Who Is Entitled to Letters of Administration When a Person Dies Without a Will.
25.33   Procedures to Follow in Administering the Estate.
25.34   How to Force an Estate Administration to Be Completed—Compelling an Accounting.
25.35   Concluding an Estate Administration Without an Accounting Proceeding.
25.36   Obtaining a Decree Concluding the Estate Based on Filed Receipts and Releases.
25.37   Concluding an Estate by a Formal Judicial Accounting.
25.38   Objections to an Account.
25.39   Prosecuting Objections to an Account.
25.40   Claims Against an Estate by a Creditor.
25.41   Representing a Claimant Against an Estate.
25.42   Obtaining Information About Estate Assets and Recovering Estate Property.
25.43   How to Proceed When Your Client Has a Claim Against an Estate.
25.44   A Special Provision for an Estate Beneficiary Obtaining Funds for Education.
25.45   Who Is Entitled to Assets When Two or More Fiduciaries Are in Dispute.
25.46   Compensation of Executor and Administrator, When Payable.
25.47   Attorney's Fees.
25.48   Declining to Serve as an Executor or Trustee.
25.49   Renouncing an Inheritance.
25.50   Construction of a Will.
25.51   Forms.
25.52   ____ Probate Petition.
25.53   ____ Affidavit Proving Correct Copy of Will.
25.54   ____ Citation in Probate.
25.55   ____ Affidavit of Service of Citation.
25.56   ____ Affidavit of Mailing Notice of Application for Letters of Administration.
25.57   ____ Waiver and Consent.
25.58   ____ Notice of Probate.
25.59   ____ Deposition Affidavit of Subscribing Witness.
25.60   ____ Objections to Probate.
25.61   ____ Decree Granting Probate.
25.62   ____ Receipt and Release Agreement Concluding an Estate Without an Accounting Proceeding.
25.63   ____ Receipt and Release (Legacy).
25.64   ____ Petition to Judicially Settle Executor's Account.
25.65   ____ Citation to Executor to Show Cause Why Judicially Executor Should Not Account.
25.66   ____ Accounting Form.
25.67   ____ Petition for Letters of Administration or Limited Letters of Administration or Temporary Administration.
25.68   ____ Decree Appointing Administrator.
25.69   ____ Affidavit Asking Court to Fix Amount of Administrator's Bond.

25.70 ____ Waiver of Citation, Renunciation of Signer's Claim to Letters and Consent to Appointment of Administrator. 💾
25.71 ____ Notice of Application for Letters of Administration. 💾
25.72 ____ Citation That Can Be Adopted for Use in Any Proceeding. 💾

WESTLAW Electronic Research

See WESTLAW Electronic Research Guide preceding the Summary of Contents.

§ 25.1 Scope Note

This chapter will address the most common areas in which persons interested in the affairs of a decedent will consult an attorney. It will include commencing an estate where a person dies with[1] or without a will,[2] admitting a will to probate,[3] administering[4] and concluding an estate, recovering property for or from an estate, pursuing the rights of a beneficiary of an estate, and pursuing the rights of creditors of an estate. It will also include a discussion of fiduciary compensation,[5] attorney's compensation,[6] and how to deal with a situation where the language in the will is not clear or is susceptible to more than one meaning.[7]

§ 25.2 Explanation of Basic Legal Terms in Estate Practice

An impediment to the non-specialist in estate matters is an absence of familiarity with the terminology unique to this area of law. Some basic definitions and explanations follow:

Citation. A citation is the equivalent to a summons in general litigation. It is the document that must be served upon all parties against whom you seek relief.[1]

Necessary Party. A necessary party is any person who would be adversely affected by the relief you seek.

Petition. A petition in estate practice is the equivalent of the complaint in general litigation pursuant to Civil Practice Law and Rules ("CPLR"). A petition must be verified by the person seeking relief and sets forth the relief sought and the basis of the relief. In probate and administration proceedings, it is prepared on forms

§ 25.1
1. See infra, § 25.13 et seq.
2. See infra, § 25.4 et seq.
3. See infra, § 25.14.
4. See infra, § 25.33.
5. See infra, § 25.47.
6. See infra, § 25.46.
7. For further discussion of all of these issues, see Preminger, et al., *Trusts and Estates Practice in New York* (West 1997).

§ 25.2
1. See infra, § 25.72 for the form entitled "Citation That Can Be Adopted for Use in Any Proceeding."

supplied by the court. In all other proceedings, it is a document to be created by counsel.

Distributee. A distributee is a person who will inherit the property of a decedent who dies without a will. The order of inheritance in the absence of a will is determined by statute.[2]

Legatee. A legatee is a person who is entitled to inherit property pursuant to the provisions of a will. A person may be a distributee and a legatee. However, his interest as a legatee may be different from his interest as a distributee. A person who receives a legacy under a will that is in a lesser amount than would be received if the decedent had died without a will, is an adverse party in a probate proceeding who must be cited. If a legatee under a will receives an equal or greater amount than would be inherited in the absence of the will, he is not an adverse party who must be cited and he may merely be given a Notice of Probate.[3]

Executor. An executor is a fiduciary, nominated under a will to administer an estate, whose appointment is accepted by the court issuing letters testamentary to the nominee.

Administrator. An administrator is a person appointed by the court to administer the estate of a person who dies without a will.

Administrator C.T.A. An administrator C.T.A. is the person appointed to administer the estate of a person who died with a will, where none of the nominated executors is available to serve.[4]

Preliminary Executor. A preliminary executor is a person nominated to administer an estate of a person who has died with a will that has not yet been admitted to probate and who is given temporary authority, usually under bond, to proceed with the administration during the pendency of the probate proceeding.

Temporary Administrator. A temporary administrator is a person appointed to administer the estate of a person who has died without a will and where permanent letters of administration have not been granted, or to administer the estate of a person who has died with a will that has not yet been accepted for probate in a circumstance where none of the nominated executors is available to serve as preliminary executors.

Ancillary Administration. An ancillary administration is a proceeding to collect and distribute property in New York State that belongs to a non-resident decedent whose estate is being administered in another jurisdiction.[5]

2. *See* EPTL § 4–1.1.
3. *See infra,* § 25.19.
4. For a discussion of who is entitled to letters of administration C.T.A., and the priority in right to such letters, *see* SCPA § 1418.
5. See SCPA Art. 16.

Objections. Objections are the equivalent of an answer in general litigation. It sets forth in verified form the items of relief sought in a petition that the objectant opposes and the basis for this opposition.[6]

§ 25.3 Strategy

An attorney consulted by a party in an estate matter must gather the facts needed as the basis for giving meaningful advice. The writer has witnessed a multitude of attorneys frustrate themselves and their clients by uselessly taking a matter down a long and expensive path that could have been avoided by simply gathering and appropriately analyzing all of the facts at the inception of the matter.

The first fact to ascertain is the status of a potential client in relationship to the estate. It should be determined whether the client is a distributee of the decedent by dint of a blood relationship, a surviving spouse who has not contracted away the right of inheritance or election by a valid antenuptial agreement, a beneficiary under a will, a nominated executor under a will, a creditor, or a person involved in litigation with the estate. One should always be sensitive to the fact that in estate matters status by dint of relationship with the decedent, except for a spouse, only arises from a blood relationship, and not by marriage. A person may call the sister of her husband's father "aunt" for 50 years, but for estate purposes she is not her aunt. She is only the aunt of her husband. In-laws have no right to inherit in intestacy.

To blindly accept without further inquiry that a potential client is the decedent's surviving spouse, because the person asserts this status, is a course fraught with hazards. For inheritance purposes, a person enjoys the status of the decedent's surviving spouse only if he was united in matrimony in a ceremonial marriage in accordance with the laws of the jurisdiction where the marriage was performed or if they entered into a common law marriage in a jurisdiction that recognizes common law marriages.[1] A person asserting the existence of a common law marriage must establish by a preponderance of credible and admissible evidence[2] that at some time when both the decedent and the alleged

---

6. The most common objections are objections to admitting a will to probate, objections to the issuance of letters testamentary or letters of administration, objections to the content of an account which may go to the financial data, the claim of a fiduciary to commissions, legal fees or other expenses, or the conclusion set forth in the account as to who is entitled to the net estate.

§ 25.3

1. New York State does not sanction common law marriages, but does recognize as married individuals who entered into a common law marriage in a state that recognized common law relationships as legal marriages at the time of the acts that result in the existence of a common law marriage. *See* Chapter 20, "Domestic Relations," *supra*. *See also* Scheinkman, *et al., New York Law of Domestic Relations* (West 1996).

2. CAVEAT: In attempting to prove a common law marriage, sensitivity must be shown to the provisions of CPLR 4519 (Dead Man's Statute). This statute, if asserted by an adverse party, will prevent the surviving spouse from testifying to the acts that created the common law marriage. This will leave the party alleging the com-

surviving spouse were free to marry,[3] they were present together in a common law marriage jurisdiction and complied with the criteria fixed by the laws of that state for creating a common law marriage.[4]

After ascertaining the existence of a lawful marriage, counsel consulted by the spouse or by a person who would benefit from extinguishing the surviving spouse's right to inherit must explore other areas of inquiry pertinent to the inheritance status of a surviving spouse. If the decedent or the alleged surviving spouse were previously married, and if the prior marriage of either of them was not lawfully dissolved when they married[5] the subsequent marriage between them would not be valid. Similarly, a party under another disability, such as infancy or incompetence, is prevented from entering a lawful marriage. Of course, a determination must also be made as to whether a surviving spouse has forfeited his or her inheritance rights by a binding agreement,[6] by abandonment,[7] or by renouncing an inheritance.[8] Proving abandonment by a spouse requires more than a mere showing that they lived separately and apart. Basically it must be established that the abandoning spouse left the decedent without cause, without an intent to return and not pursuant to a separation agreement.[9] The burden of proof is on the party alleging abandonment.

The absence of a lawful status as a spouse will not necessarily void a legacy by a decedent to "my spouse" even if that person is not, in fact, a spouse. If the person is referred to by name, then there is usually no question as to his or her right to the legacy. However, if the will simply refers to "my wife" or "my husband," and the person is not, in fact, a spouse, a construction proceeding may be required for the court to determine the person the decedent meant by his or her reference to "my wife" or "my husband."

After ascertaining the client's status, inquiry should be made as to the goal the client seeks to achieve in retaining counsel. Upon establishing your client's status and goals, a determination should be made, by a

mon law marriage with the burden of proving its existence by documents or witnesses other than the alleged surviving spouse.

3. Individuals married to another, or otherwise under a disability that would not allow them to enter into a lawful ceremonial marriage, cannot conclude a common law marriage.

4. The most common requirements for a common law marriage are cohabiting as husband and wife with the other party and openly representing that the parties are spouses.

5. See EPTL § 5–1.2(a)(3).

6. *See* Chapter 24 "Estate Planning," *supra*, and its discussion of antenuptial agreements.

7. *See* EPTL § 5–1.2(a)(5), (6) (abandonment by spouse) and EPTL § 4–1.4 (abandonment by parent). The issue as to whether a parent has abandoned the child, so as to have no right of inheritance from the child or a right to share in a wrongful death recovery, arises most often when there is a recovery for the death of the infant and the custodial parent and the parent who did not have custody have a dispute over the proceeds.

8. *See infra*, § 25.49.

9. *See* Estate of Prince, 36 A.D.2d 946, 321 N.Y.S.2d 798 (1st Dep't 1971), aff'd 30 N.Y.2d 512, 330 N.Y.S.2d 61, 280 N.E.2d 888 (1972).

review of the following sections as to the procedure which could attain that goal, its likelihood of success, its approximate cost, and the time it will likely take to prosecute the matter to an end. The existence of a remedy whose attainment is disproportionately expensive, in relation to the benefit that the client is likely to realize, constitutes a remedy that exists only in theory, and it does not constitute an avenue to relief in reality. Giving a client an honest appraisal of the likelihood of success, cost against benefit, and time required to complete a task, is critical to a good ongoing attorney-client relationship. Leading a client down a path whose expense does not justify even a successful result benefits neither attorney nor client. Not underestimating the time factor in a task also is critical to maintaining client confidence. An honest evaluation of the time it takes to complete a procedure must encompass the reasonable time required to gather the requisite information, to prepare the papers, to obtain a citation or order to show cause from the surrogate's court, to serve the process, to have the matter reached on the calendar, and to have the court hear and determine the matter. This will vary from county to county. It will necessarily be longer in busy urban and suburban counties than in rural counties with lesser caseloads. The best course for determining the time gap, from submission of papers to a matter being reached and determined, is to inquire at the law department or of the clerk of the surrogate's court involved. In rural counties where the surrogate's court is not continuously in session, the length of time until the court next sits is also a factor to be evaluated in advising a client as to the course litigation will probably follow.

§ 25.4 Who May Commence the Estate of a Person Who Dies Without a Will

Any person with a beneficial interest in the estate may petition for letters of administration where a decedent has died without a will. At the top of the list of individuals with a beneficial interest are the persons who, as a matter of statute, have the right to inherit the decedent's property. EPTL § 4–1.1 specifically delineates the order of inheritance by virtue of relationship to the decedent. A surviving spouse's right to inherit and status to petition for letters of administration depend on her not having forfeited this right by virtue of a pre-nuptial agreement, a separation agreement, or abandonment of the decedent during his lifetime without cause and without having ever resumed cohabiting with the decedent prior to his death.[1] A parent, like a spouse, may forfeit the right to inherit that the parent would otherwise possess if, during the life of the decedent, the parent failed or refused to provide for, or abandoned such child, while the child was under the age of 21 years, unless the parental relationship and duties were resumed subsequent to the abandonment and continued until the death of the child.[2] Non-marital children have the same right to inherit from the parent as

§ 25.4
1. *See* EPTL § 5–1.2(a)(3), (5), (6).
2. *See* EPTL § 4–1.4.

children born in wedlock.[3] However, for a child to establish his relationship to a father in order to obtain the right to inherit, the child must establish his status as a descendant of the deceased male by complying with one of the specific requirements for establishing status that are delineated in EPTL § 4–1.2(a)(2).[4]

Library References:

West's Key No. Digests, Executors and Administrators ⟲15, 17, 18, 21, 22, 24.

§ 25.5 Who Is Entitled to Letters of Administration

SCPA § 1001 sets forth a statutory order of priority in the granting of letters of administration.[1] When consulted by a person with a right to letters of administration equal to other people, such as one of several surviving children, or one of several surviving siblings, a determination should be made as to whether your client can reach an understanding with those with equal rights to letters of administration or whether a conflict exists which will require litigation. Where individuals have equal rights to letters of administration, the court has discretion to grant the letters to one or more of these individuals or may make a factual determination at the hearing as to the person best qualified to receive the letters.[2]

Library References:

West's Key No. Digests, Executors and Administrators ⟲15, 17, 18, 21, 22, 24.

§ 25.6 Who May Commence the Estate of a Person Who Dies With a Will

The acceptance of a will for probate may be sought by any person who:

---

3. *See* EPTL § 4–1.2.

4. A non-marital child obviously has a more difficult time establishing his relationship to his father than to his mother. Maternal status is apparent by the mother giving birth while establishing the male with whom the mother conceived the child is much less apparent in most cases.

§ 25.5

1. **PRACTICE POINTER:** Unless your client is a person likely to receive letters of administration, it is usually foolish to undertake the burden of an application except where:

(1) It does not appear that any other interested party is moving to commence the administration of the estate, and

(2) Your client may have an inheritance interest which requires commencement of the estate even though your client will not receive the letters of administration.

Before petitioning in a situation where your client is not likely to receive the letters of administration, consideration should be given to whether:

(1) Your client should become a petitioner, or

(2) The most economic course would be to report the estate's existence to the public administrator or county treasurer of the pertinent county and have that person undertake to petition for letters of administration and administer the estate.

2. *See infra,* § 25.71 for the form entitled "Notice of Application for Letters of Administration."

(1) Benefits from the will;

(2) Is the fiduciary of a person under a disability who benefits from the will;

(3) Is named in the will as an executor or a trustee;

(4) Is a creditor of the decedent;

(5) Is a party to a lawsuit to which the decedent would be a party if living; or

(6) Is the public administrator in those counties that have a public administrator, or the county treasurer or Commissioner of Finance in those counties that have no public administrator.[1]

The authority of the public administrator and county treasurer to seek probate is limited to those situations where a will has been filed with the court and no one has diligently acted to seek probate. Before the public administrator or county treasurer can act, he must seek authority from the court alleging that probate of a filed will has been neglected. This application must be on notice to all parties with an interest in the estate and can probably be successfully opposed by a nominated executor or other qualified person interested in the estate if the person can offer a plausible reason for the delay and commit himself to promptly proceed with probate. The public administrator or county treasurer is the fiduciary of last resort who is not usually authorized to administer an estate where there is another party in interest ready, willing, and eligible to be the fiduciary.

The most appropriate and usual person to act as petitioner in seeking the probate of a will is the person, or persons, nominated in the will to serve as executors. When consulted by any other party in interest as to why a will is not probated, the course to pursue is to communicate in writing with the nominated executor or executors, at their last known address. Advise them of the interest of your client, inquire as to when they expect to seek probate, and insert a warning that if probate is not sought by a given time, your client will petition for probate and you would seek legal fees from the estate for the cost of the proceeding. The cost of probate is a proper estate charge[2] and any attorney discharging its functions is entitled to seek compensation for the necessary work from the estate's assets.[3] An attorney for a petitioner seeking probate is entitled to be compensated by the estate even if the effort to attain probate is unsuccessful, so long as he and his client had proceeded based upon a good faith belief that they were seeking acceptance of a valid instrument.[4] However, an attorney representing a beneficiary, a creditor

§ 25.6
1. See SCPA § 1402.
2. SCPA § 2301.
3. Matter of DiJurico, 134 Misc.2d 263, 510 N.Y.S.2d 465 (Surr.Ct., Nassau County, 1987); see also, Matter of the Estate of Watts, 49 A.D.2d 961, 373 N.Y.S.2d 898 (3d Dep't 1975).
4. See id.

§ 25.6   PROBATE & ESTATE ADMINISTRATION   Ch. 25

or a litigant, seeking compensation for initiating a probate proceeding would not be viewed favorably by the surrogate, unless he had first given the executors and their counsel a reasonable opportunity to initiate the proceeding.

Library References:

West's Key No. Digests, Executors and Administrators ⚖15, 17, 18, 21, 22, 24.

§ 25.7   Documents Required on Application for Letters of Administration

Prepare the petition and accompanying documents on an application for letters of administration on forms issued by the respective courts which are obtainable from the administration clerk of each surrogate's court. The information required is essentially the same as on an application seeking probate of a will.[1] All of the same supporting documents are required except of course, there is no copy of any will and no notice of probate is required.[2]

Library References:

West's Key No. Digests, Executors and Administrators ⚖20(5).

§ 25.8   Who Must Be Cited on an Application for Letters of Administration

On an application for letters of administration, citation to show cause, why letters of administration should not be issued to the petitioner, must be served on all of the decedent's distributees. If any of those distributees are not known, or if the distributees are of a relationship no closer than cousins, the public administrator (in counties where there is a public administrator, or the county treasurer in other counties), and the Attorney General of the State of New York, must also be joined as necessary parties and served with citation. The rationale requiring the waivers and consents of all distributees even where the petitioner has a statutory priority to letters of administration, is to afford all interested parties an opportunity to present to the court any contention that there is a legal reason, pursuant to SCPA § 707 or SCPA § 711, why the petitioner should be declared to be ineligible to receive letters of administration thereby allowing letters to issue to a person with a lower priority right than petitioner.[1]

§ 25.7

1. See infra, § 25.18.
2. See infra, § 25.67 for the form entitled "Petition for Letters of Administration or Limited Letters of Administration or Temporary Administration"; § 25.68 for the form entitled "Decree Appointing Administrator"; and § 25.69 for the form entitled "Affidavit Asking Court to Fix Amount of Administrator's Bond."

§ 25.8

1. See infra, § 25.70 for the form entitled "Waiver of Citation, Renunciation of

Library References:

West's Key No. Digests, Executors and Administrators ⊙—20(4.5).

§ 25.9 When a Guardian *Ad Litem* Must Be Appointed

SCPA § 402 delineates who may appear in a proceeding on behalf of an infant or other person under a disability. SCPA § 403(2) sets forth the power of the court to appoint a guardian *ad litem*.

A difference of opinion exists as to the need for a guardian *ad litem* on an application for letters of administration where any of the decedent's distributees are under the disability of either infancy or incompetence. Some courts will not appoint a guardian *ad litem* for a person under a disability, reasoning that that person cannot receive letters in any event. Other courts will reason that a necessity exists for a guardian *ad litem*, who can present to the court appropriate arguments as to the eligibility of the petitioner to receive letters, should a legal reason exist why the petitioner is not eligible. Where the interested party is under a disability that precludes him from appearing on his own, in the absence of such guardian *ad litem*, the court is in effect accepting the contention of the petitioner as to eligibility, without these contentions being subject to adversarial tests by other interested parties. If your client is the petitioner, clearly the view that no guardian *ad litem* is required is in the client's best interest. If you are consulted by a person such as a parent on behalf of an infant beneficiary, where the parent himself has no interest in the Estate, and he wishes you to appear in a proceeding to oppose the issuance of letters of administration to a petitioner, it would be necessary for you to have that parent appointed guardian of the property of the infant, and to then retain you as attorney for such guardian, or in the alternative, for you to present the issues to the court with the request that the court appoint you or another lawyer as a guardian *ad litem* to represent the infant's interest.[1]

Library References:

West's Key No. Digests, Infants ⊙—78(3).

Signer's Claim to Letter and Consent to Appointment of Administrator."

§ 25.9

1. **CAVEAT:** Under SCPA § 403(1) an infant over the age of 14 years or his or her parent or guardian may request by petition, before the return date of process, that a particular attorney be appointed as guardian *ad litem*. The petition must be accompanied by an attorney's affidavit satisfying the requirements of SCPA § 403(1)(a)(i) and (ii). This is necessary so that the court can ascertain whether the appointment of the nominated attorney as guardian *ad litem* is appropriate under the circumstances of the matter at issue. The first question an attorney seeking to be appointed guardian *ad litem* should consider is whether his request involves a conflict of interest. Clearly if the attorney represents a parent and the parent's interest is adverse to the infant's interest, the appointment of a guardian *ad litem* selected by the parent, or in privity with the parent's attorney, is not appropriate.

§ 25.10 Denial or Revocation of Letters of Administration

Where a petitioner has a priority right to letters of administration under SCPA § 1001, the only basis on which a court can deny the issuance of letters of administration is if it is established that one of the reasons set forth in SCPA § 707 for declaring a person ineligible to receive letters, or one of the reasons set forth in SCPA § 711 for revoking letters of administration, renders the petitioner ineligible. SCPA § 707 and SCPA § 711 must be read in conjunction with each other, despite their dealing with different subjects. SCPA § 707 addresses ineligibility to receive letters. SCPA § 711 addresses reasons why letters of administration that are already issued should be revoked. Although the provisions do not mirror each other, a petitioner clearly is as ineligible to receive letters of administration when objections fit within the category of a person whose letters should be revoked, as when he fits within the criteria of ineligibility set forth in SCPA § 707. The burden of proof in establishing ineligibility rests on the person alleging the ineligibility. While the surrogate has certain discretionary powers to revoke letters testamentary or letters of administration issued by the court in order to protect an estate, it is a discretion that is severely circumscribed by the statutory bases for ineligibility and the need for the facts supporting statutory ineligibility to be established at an adversarial hearing.[1]

SCPA § 719 confers on the surrogate the power to remove a fiduciary without a proceeding. Essentially it gives the surrogate the power of summary removal when it appears that one of the same criteria justifying removal that are set forth in SCPA § 711 appear to exist and that unless there is immediate action the estate or trust will suffer a loss. It must be a situation where the delay of serving process and a formal proceeding represents a danger to the estate. *Matter of Doris Duke*[2] makes it clear that when the surrogate chooses to proceed pursuant to SCPA § 719, the surrogate should give the fiduciary being removed an opportunity to defend his or her conduct at the earliest reasonable opportunity.

SCPA § 718 explains how to deal with a situation where an executor, trustee or administrator has to go off to war and leave his duties.

Library References:

West's Key No. Digests, Executors and Administrators ⊜20(8, 8.5).

§ 25.10
1. *See* Matter of Doris Duke, 87 N.Y.2d 465, 640 N.Y.S.2d 446, 663 N.E.2d 602 (1996).

2. *Id.*

§ 25.11 Letters of Temporary Administration

Often the protection of the decedent's estate requires the issuance of fiduciary authority with greater speed than an application for letters of administration in intestacy could be completed, unless the petitioner is proceeding with waivers and consents from all necessary parties. The time required to simply complete the service of process, let alone the immense delay which occurs where a contest arises, may be too long to leave the assets of the decedent unadministered without the danger of the estate suffering significant losses. SCPA § 902 authorizes the court to appoint a temporary administrator on such notice to other parties interested in the estate as the court may direct. Within the framework of this section, the court may issue letters immediately and authorize the notice to be served thereafter where urgency for the prompt granting of authority over the decedent's assets is established. Invariably, before granting temporary administration, the court will fix the prerequisite of a surety bond in such sum as is required to protect the assets. The court may also fix such limitations on the powers of the temporary administrator as it deems appropriate to protect the assets of the estate while awaiting the opportunity to hear from parties interested in the estate other than the temporary administrator.[1] Even when representing the temporary administrator, an attorney may choose to have the court limit his powers, as this will facilitate the filing of a bond in a lesser amount than would be necessary if the administrator had broad powers over all of the assets of the decedent.[2] To illustrate, it might be necessary simply to get temporary letters of administration with reference to a specific asset such as the decedent's business or residence.

Library References:
West's Key No. Digests, Executors and Administrators ⊙—22.

§ 25.12 Venue

The county where a decedent had his legal residence is the proper venue for commencing an estate administration.[1] Where he had more than one legal residence, the county to be selected should be the one that the decedent used as his domicile or principal place of residence.[2]

§ 25.11

1. SCPA § 903 sets forth the general powers of the temporary administrator. These powers are subject to being enlarged or limited by the court as the circumstances provide. An attorney may request such limitations or expansion of the powers of the temporary administrator as he deems appropriate and necessary.

2. **PRACTICE POINTER:** Limiting the amount of the bond not only reduces the cost of the premium, but it is easier to obtain a bond in a lesser amount than a greater sum. A client's net worth could limit the amount of the bond that a surety will issue.

§ 25.12

1. SCPA § 205.

2. **PRACTICE POINTER:** Where a number of residences presents a choice of venue, consideration should be given to tax consequences. To illustrate, if one county has a local income tax and another county does not have a local income tax, selecting the county without a local income tax may

§ 25.12   PROBATE & ESTATE ADMINISTRATION   Ch. 25

The place of death of a decedent does not control venue. The death of a decedent in a hospital or a nursing home in other than his county of residence still leaves the county of residence the proper venue for the administration of his or her estate.[3] A person who gives up his residence to enter a nursing home under circumstances which indicate that the nursing home is now his permanent residence would be deemed to be a resident of the county where the nursing home is located.[4]

Commencing an estate administration in the wrong county is no longer viewed to be a jurisdictional defect. However, upon an application from any party in interest or on the court's own motion, an estate administration commenced in the wrong county will be transferred to the proper county for the continuation of the administration.[5] As much of the administration as has transpired before the estate is transferred to the proper county is good and valid and need not be repeated. After transfer, the matter continues from the point it was at the time of transfer.

The proper venue for ancillary administration of the assets of a decedent whose estate administration is pending in another jurisdiction is the county where the assets are located. If they are in more than one county, you may select from them the county of your choice. As in the case of regular administration, letters of ancillary administration issued in any county in New York are valid as to assets in any part of New York State.[6]

Library References:

West's Key No. Digests, Executors and Administrators ⚖20(.5).

§ 25.13 Duty of the Fiduciary to Expeditiously Seek Probate

A person named in the will as a nominated executor has a duty to expeditiously commence the administration of an estate in order to protect its assets. This duty includes diligently petitioning for probate, and where probate cannot be quickly completed by the consent of all parties, filing with the petition for probate a petition for preliminary

significantly reduce the taxes on the income of a sizable estate. Other considerations to be weighed are often the ability to have papers processed more quickly in the court with a lighter case load and your preference in the surrogate who would determine any contested issues.

3. In re Webber's Will, 187 Misc. 674, 64 N.Y.S.2d 281 (Surr.Ct., Kings County, 1946).

4. Cf. Matter of Urdang, 194 A.D.2d 615, 599 N.Y.S.2d 60 (2d Dep't 1993) (appellate division held that sale of residence while decedent was institutionalized did not establish that decedent intended to abandon her long-standing domicile).

5. See SCPA § 209(3).

6. SCPA § 206.

letters testamentary.[1] Undue delay by an executor or his attorney in petitioning for probate can have several adverse effects on the nominated executor:

1. It can become a license for other parties interested in the estate to commence the probate proceeding;

2. It can be the basis for sustaining an application to disqualify the executor for want of understanding;[2] and

3. It can result in a loss of estate assets, and the charging of this loss to the nominated executor due to his failure to act expeditiously.

Library References:

West's Key No. Digests, Executors and Administrators ⊱1.

§ 25.14 When a Beneficiary Should Petition for Probate

A beneficiary should petition for probate where:

1. The nominated executor is dead or incapacitated;

2. It is believed that the nominated executor should be disqualified for any of the reasons set forth in SCPA § 707 or SCPA § 711; or

3. He has written to the executor to ascertain when he will proceed to seek probate, and he has not responded or proceeded with reasonable diligence.

A circumstance under which an immediate petition on behalf of a beneficiary in order to commence the administration of an estate is dictated, without any prior notice to the nominated executor, is where there is a danger that the slightest delay will jeopardize estate assets. This situation arises where the executor has not acted to commence the estate administration or the client believes the nominated executor is dishonest or incompetent and gives proof that supports the likelihood that the nominated executor can be disqualified as being statutorily ineligible. A petition on behalf of the beneficiary is usually prepared where there is a residence containing items of great value which must be safeguarded, an operating business, an interest in assets subject to highly volatile market conditions, or assets susceptible to being lost. When consulted by a beneficiary in such cases, unless counsel is prompt-

§ 25.13

1. See SCPA § 1412. For a fuller discussion of preliminary letters testamentary, see infra, § 25.26.

2. See SCPA § 707(1)(e).

ly satisfied that the nominated executor is immediately moving to obtain the authority to administer the estate, and the client is satisfied to let the nominated executor take over, a petition for probate on behalf of the client should be prepared and an order to show cause submitted to the surrogate as to why the client should not receive temporary letters of administration pursuant to SCPA § 901(1).[1] This order to show cause must be addressed to the executor nominated in the will, all beneficiaries, and such other persons as the court may direct.[2] Upon an application for temporary letters of administration, in the absence of showing good cause why someone other than the nominated executor should be appointed, it is likely that the court will issue the preliminary letters to a nominated executor who:

1. Appears;
2. Does not appear to be otherwise disqualified; and
3. Offers a plausible excuse as to why it fell to another person to bring before the court the necessity to commence the administration of the estate.

§ 25.15 When a Creditor Should Petition for Probate

The circumstances under which a creditor should undertake the expense and burden of petitioning for probate are few. The creditor should be advised to undertake the burden and expense of probate only where it is clear that:

1. The decedent had sufficient assets to satisfy the debt;
2. The debt is of sufficient size to justify the action;
3. There has been undue delay by other parties in interest in seeking probate; and
4. Further delay in probate will prejudice the creditor by endangering, or unduly delaying, his potential for collecting the debt.

If the estate has assets and it is apparent that the nominated executor and other parties in interest are unduly delaying probate, a creditor petitioning for letters will undoubtedly be compensated for his legal expenses in so proceeding. It is a rare case in which a creditor will actually be granted letters, if there are other individuals with a greater interest in the estate, such as the executor or beneficiaries, appearing in the proceeding and requesting such letters, assuming that they have not otherwise disqualified themselves by lack of diligence or other legal reasons.

---

§ 25.14
1. See supra, § 25.11 for a discussion of temporary letters of administration.

2. See SCPA § 902(2)(b).

§ 25.16 When a Person in Litigation With an Estate Should Petition for Probate

The existence of litigation against the decedent when he was alive can become the genesis of a reluctance, on the part of either an executor or anyone else interested in the estate, to facilitate the litigation by commencing the administration. A lawsuit is cast into abeyance by the death of a party.[1] That party's estate may conclude that delay will prejudice an adverse party in the litigation. Clearly a litigant against the estate who knows a decedent died testate, and who wishes to pursue pending litigation or commence litigation against the estate, should advise the nominated executor that the litigant will seek probate or administration unless the nominated executor proceeds with diligence to complete probate. Whether the surrogate will allow the attorney for a litigant fees from the estate for petitioning for probate will depend on whether the petition benefitted the estate in any way or simply benefitted the litigant represented by the petitioner.[2] If the petition benefitted the estate, the estate should pay the attorney's fees involved. If the petition is only a benefit to the litigant so that he could proceed with his lawsuit, the cost of the proceeding should rest on the person benefitting from it. If the probate benefitted beneficiaries as well as the litigant, the estate should pay the cost of the probate proceeding.[3]

§ 25.17 Information to Be Gathered by the Attorney

A. Date of death and place of death.

B. If the decedent had a will, the location of the original will if the client does not have it.

C. The family tree of the decedent with all information required for completing the kinship affidavit.[1]

D. The current names and addresses of all distributees, the witnesses to the will, and all legatees.

E. Information as to whether any witness to a will is dead or incapacitated.

F. Any information as to whether any legatee or distributee is under the disability of infancy, incompetence or any other disability.

G. Information as to whether a legatee or a distributee under a disability has a fiduciary such as a guardian, conservator or committee.

---

§ 25.16

1. See CPLR 1015.
2. See Matter of Greatsinger, 67 N.Y.2d 177, 501 N.Y.S.2d 623, 492 N.E.2d 751 (1986); In re O'Brien's Trust, 28 A.D.2d 1040, 283 N.Y.S.2d 926 (3d Dep't 1967).
3. See Matter of Burns, 130 Misc.2d 317, 496 N.Y.S.2d 921 (Surr.Ct., Broome County, 1985)(all beneficiaries under will were benefitted by legal services rendered by intervenor and intervenor's attorney was entitled to be paid from assets of estate), aff'd 126 A.D.2d 809, 510 N.Y.S.2d 732 (3d Dep't 1987).

§ 25.17

1. See infra, § 25.19(D) for a discussion of kinship affidavits.

H. All information the client possesses as to legatees or distributees whose whereabouts are unknown.

I. Information as to whether any legatee is dead and whether the legatee died before or after the decedent. If the legatee died before the decedent, determine if the legacy lapsed.[2] If it did not lapse, determine the names and addresses of those now entitled to the legacy. If the legatee died after the decedent, determine if he or she has an estate under administration. The post-deceased legatee's estate succeeds to his interest.[3]

§ 25.18 Contents of Petition for Probate

SCPA § 1402(2) sets forth the required contents of a petition. The surrogate's courts in most counties require that the petition be on its printed form. These forms are obtainable from the probate clerk of each court. The requirements of their content are self-explanatory and, under the Uniform Rules for surrogate's courts, their content should be the same in every county.[1] To the extent that SCPA § 1402(2) denotes as necessary parties persons named in prior wills as either a beneficiary or a nominated fiduciary, these individuals become necessary parties only if the prior will has been filed with the court. Parties named in prior existing wills that are not filed with the surrogate's court are not necessary parties to a probate proceeding. If you represent a person whose only interest in an estate is by virtue of being named a beneficiary or nominated executor in a prior will, and you wish the client to become a necessary party to the proceeding, you should file with the court the original prior will and/or codicil, if you control it. If you do not control it, you should take the appropriate steps to compel it to be filed with the court.[2]

Library References:

West's Key No. Digests, Wills ⬄272–286.

§ 25.19 Documents Required to Accompany Probate Petition

Along with the verified probate petition, the following documents must be filed with the court:

A. *The original will.* The original will and the original of all codicils

---

2. *See* EPTL § 3–3.3.

3. PRACTICE POINTER: If the post-deceased legatee does not have an estate, his next of kin should be advised of the inheritance. Should they take no action to establish an estate to collect the inheritance on an accounting, counsel should provide for its deposit as an unclaimed inheritance with the Finance Director in New York City or the county treasurer in counties outside of New York City.

§ 25.18

1. *See infra,* § 25.52 for the form entitled "Probate Petition."

2. *See infra,* § 25.20 for a discussion of what to do if your client cannot produce the original will.

must be filed with the probate petition.[1]

B. ***Copies of the original will.*** In addition to the original will and original codicil, a copy of the original will and all codicils for which probate is sought must be annexed to the petition. In making copies of the original document, the staples should not be removed since an original document that reflects that the staples have been removed will not be accepted for probate without an affidavit explaining the circumstances under which the staples were removed and that at the time the staples were removed for photostating the document did not reflect holes indicating that the staples had been previously removed. Multiple staple holes in a will raises an issue as to whether pages were substituted after execution.

C. ***Death Certificate.*** A certified copy of the decedent's death certificate must be filed.

D. ***An affidavit of kinship.*** An affidavit of kinship must reflect the family tree of the person who has died to the extent that it shows who is entitled to inherit from the decedent if he had died without a will. Only in this way can the court be satisfied that the petition has named as necessary parties all individuals who would benefit from the decedent's estate if his will were not admitted to probate. Persons who will benefit if the will is not admitted to probate are those who would receive the estate in intestacy under EPTL § 4-1.1, or who would benefit from the estate under any prior will filed with the court. The affidavit of kinship must be made by a person familiar with the facts who is not a party to the proceeding. To illustrate, in the case of a decedent who is survived by a wife, children and grandchildren, the affidavit could be appropriately made by a sibling of the decedent, or of the wife. In the case of a person survived by brothers, sisters, nieces and nephews, any one of their spouses who are familiar with the family tree could execute the affidavit of kinship. To lend credibility to the affidavit, it should state the source of affiant's knowledge.[2] The situation becomes much more complex where the decedent's surviving distributees are cousins, and cousins on one side of the family do not know who is a surviving cousin on the other side of the family.[3] In the event the

---

§ 25.19

1. **PRACTICE POINTER:** Where a will is offered for probate and a codicil exists that is not offered for probate, a nominated executor or beneficiary under the codicil can petition for probate of the codicil. However, probate of a codicil cannot be sought unless a petition to probate the will it modifies is also presented to the court. An executor named in a codicil would have priority in seeking preliminary letters over an executor named in the original will.

2. **PRACTICE POINTER:** To illustrate, a sister-in-law of the decedent might state how long she has known and been member of the family and that from this acquaintanceship and conversations with the decedent and other members of the family she is familiar with the membership of the decedent's family.

3. **PRACTICE POINTER:** If obtainable, this often requires separate affidavits from a person familiar with the maternal family and from another person familiar

decedent was married and divorced, it will be necessary to indicate the date, jurisdiction and place of divorce and to produce a copy of the divorce decree.[4] Where a decedent's spouse is pre-deceased, it is necessary to indicate the place and date of death. Some courts will require a death certificate for the spouse or proof in affidavit form as to why a death certificate cannot be obtained.[5] In those cases where there is no one who can supply the information as to kinship who is eligible to sign an affidavit, it will be necessary for the attorney to conduct a diligent search to gather this information. This search can be done by the attorney or by hiring an investigator experienced in kinship matters.[6] This search will involve the pursuit of birth records, death records, estate administration records, marriage records, divorce proceedings, census records and any other documents or records which would disclose the family tree of the decedent. The diligence required is circumscribed to a degree by the size of the estate. It is not necessary in order to satisfy due diligence to embark on a search for kinship records to an extent that the expense is disproportionate to the size of the estate. If a diligent search does not disclose a decedent's family tree, the person conducting the search should prepare an affidavit indicating that a diligent search for information has been made, the details of the search, the information, if any, discovered, and that it is impossible to fully establish the decedent's family tree. This circumstance will then require adding to the petition as a necessary party, and obtaining jurisdiction over, unknown heirs by service of the citation upon them by publication.[7]

Where service by publication is required, an order of publication must be submitted with the probate petition. The court will insert in the order where the citation must be published. Publication is best accomplished by giving the order and citation to an advertising agency which will arrange for the publication and supply counsel with the proof of publication that must be filed with the court in

---

with the paternal family. It is rare that members of the paternal side of a decedent's family have more than a cursory knowledge of the maternal side and vice-versa.

4. If the decree not found among the decedent's possessions this may require research as to the court granting divorce and the obtaining of a certified copy of the judgment from that court. If, despite due diligence, the judgment cannot be found, the divorce may be proven by credible extrinsic evidence such as an affidavit from a person familiar with the divorce.

5. An illustration of where the absence of a death certificate can be explained is if the pre-deceased spouse was a person of the Jewish faith who lived in Nazi-occupied Europe during World War II and he or she was last seen being deported to a death camp and was never heard from again. Naturally there is no death certificate obtainable for such a person. *See* Matter of Tien, 72 Misc.2d 650, 340 N.Y.S.2d 249 (Surr.Ct., Bronx County, 1973).

6. PRACTICE POINTER: Unless counsel has experience in this area, the latter choice is usually the more effective and economic option.

7. *See* SCPA §§ 307(2)(a), 309(2)(d).

order to acquire jurisdiction. There is no additional cost to counsel or the estate in using an advertising agency instead of dealing directly with the publication. The advertising agency is compensated by the commission it receives from the publication.

E. *Citation.* A citation addressed to all necessary parties directing them to show cause why the will should not be probated must be filed. If it is large enough, the citation can be prepared on a form supplied by the court. If the blanks on the printed form are not large enough to meet your needs in a particular situation, a citation can be duplicated on a word processor as long as it follows the basic format of the court's form.[8] The citation must be filed with the petition. It must be signed and issued by the court before it can be served. Copies of the citation must be served:

1. On all individuals residing within the State of New York either personally or by the alternate means provided for in CPLR 308;
2. By publication pursuant to court order on all persons who are unknown or whose whereabouts are unknown; or
3. By mail on all persons residing outside the State of New York.

Since 1995, an order of mailing is no longer required.[9] Service by mail must be completed by mailing the citation at least 20 days prior to the return date of the citation on individuals residing in the United States, its territories and possessions, and at least 30 days prior to the return date of the citation on individuals residing in foreign countries.[10]

F. *An affidavit of comparison.* An affidavit must be submitted indicating that the copy of the will annexed to the probate petition has been compared with the original document and that the copy is complete and correct.[11]

G. *Waivers and consents.* An alternative to citation is a waiver and consent on the form provided by the court.[12] The waiver and consent signed by an interested party before a notary public indicates he consents to the probate of the will and that he waives service of citation. If all interested parties execute waivers and consents, the probate petition can be submitted with the necessary accompanying

---

8. *See infra,* § 25.54 for the form entitled "Citation in Probate."

9. *See* SCPA § 307(2)(b).

10. A citation served within the State of New York must be served at least 10 days prior to the return date of the citation.

SCPA § 309 delineates when process is deemed to be completed.

11. *See infra,* § 25.53 for the form entitled "Affidavit Proving a Correct Copy of the Will Filed for Probate."

12. *See infra,* § 25.57 for the form entitled "Waiver and Consent."

documents and a proposed decree admitting the will to probate.[13] If some of the parties sign waivers and consents, and others do not, those who have not signed waivers and consents must be served with citation. Only a competent adult, or the fiduciary of a person under a disability, can sign a waiver and consent. An infant or other person under a disability, who has no court appointed fiduciary, cannot waive service of citation.

H. *Proofs of service.* Proofs of service must be filed with reference to all interested parties who have not executed a waiver and consent in order to complete jurisdiction. The proofs must be filed prior to the return date of citation. The proofs of personal service must conform to the provisions of the CPLR. With reference to individuals served by mail, the person posting the mail must prepare an affidavit indicating the time, date and place of mailing.[14] Service of citation by mail should be by certified mail, return receipt requested. Proof of the completion of service should include the original return receipt signed by the person being served. In those cases where the return receipts are not received, and the mail is not returned, an affidavit to that effect should be prepared and the stamped receipt of the post office that it had accepted the mail should be annexed. It is wise to mail certified mail at the post office so that a stamped receipt can be received from the post office affirming that the papers were actually mailed.[15] If a citation served by certified mail is returned as "delivery refused," many courts will accept this as jurisdiction completed. Some courts will require an additional attempt to complete jurisdiction by some alternate means such as remailing the citation by ordinary mail. If it is too late to timely remail the original citation, a supplemental citation, returnable on a new date in the future, will have to be obtained from the court.[16]

I. *Notice of Probate.* SCPA § 1409 sets forth the requirements of the Notice of probate and on whom it must be served. Basically the notice of probate is designed to advise beneficiaries under the will, who are not adversely affected by the will, of its existence and the pending probate proceeding. Without the notice of probate many beneficiaries would not be aware of their inheritance and could not monitor the progress of the estate. Letters will not issue without a notice of probate with the proof of service on all necessary parties

---

13. See infra, § 25.61 for the form entitled "Decree Granting Probate."

14. See SCPA § 308.

15. If all the receipts are not returned, you may be able to prevail on the court to accept the post office receipt, and an affidavit that the mail was not returned, as proof of service. Return receipts often do not come back from foreign countries and are not always returned on domestic mail.

16. See infra, § 25.55 for the form entitled "Affidavit of Service of Citation" and § 25.56 for the form entitled "Affidavit of

annexed thereto.[17]

Library References:

West's Key No. Digests, Wills ⟺272–286.

§ 25.20 What to Do if Your Client Cannot Produce the Original Will

Often a client is unable to produce the original will but has knowledge or a belief that such a will exists and is in the possession of another person. This knowledge may flow from a variety of circumstances. Your client may have seen the original, been told of its existence by the decedent, or may have seen a copy of the will. Where the problem is as simple as the original will being in the possession of the attorney-draftsman, demand should be made on the attorney-draftsman to deliver the will or to file it with the court. An attorney-draftsman has no right to retain an original will and on demand of any interested party, subsequent to the death of the decedent, must surrender it to the party in interest or file it with the court.

If the person you believe to have the will, or information as to its whereabouts, declines to produce the will or supply the information, a petition to the surrogate's court with venue over the matter should be prepared to be verified by your client.[1] The petition should state the basis for his belief that a person possesses the original will, or has knowledge with reference to such original will, and should demand that that person be ordered to produce the will and/or appear before the court to be examined under oath with reference to his knowledge as to the decedent's will.[2] This petition should be accompanied by an order to show cause directing the respondent to produce the will before the court and/or appear to be examined under oath with reference to knowledge as to the will. A certified copy of the order to show cause must be served personally or in such other manner as the court directs.[3] If the court determines that a person has unreasonably withheld a will or codicil, it can impose on that person the reasonable attorney's fees expended to compel production of the document.[4] Since 1993, the court can also *sua sponte* direct a will to be filed where it has knowledge of the existence of such a will that is being withheld.[5]

SCPA § 1401 can also be used to compel the production and filing of a prior will. If your client is not a distributee, but is a legatee under a prior will, you can make your client a necessary party to the proceeding

Mailing Notice of Application for Letters of Administration."

17. *See infra*, § 25.58 for the form entitled "Notice of Probate."

§ 25.20

1. *See* SCPA § 1401.
2. *See* SCPA § 1401.
3. *See* SCPA § 1401.
4. *See* SCPA § 1401.
5. *See* SCPA § 1401.

to probate the later will, by compelling the prior will be filed with the court. This filing gives him the status, he otherwise does not possess, to file objections and, perhaps, to negotiate a settlement of his claims.

§ 25.21 Requirements and Procedure for Proving a Will Where the Original Is Lost

SCPA § 1407 allows the probate of a missing will if the petitioner can establish:

1. That the missing will was in fact executed as required by EPTL § 3–2.1;
2. The exact terms of the missing instrument; and
3. That it was not revoked by the decedent during his lifetime.

Where the proof indicates that the decedent possessed the original will at the time of his death, a petitioner seeking to establish a lost will must overcome a rebuttable presumption that if a person possessed his will and it cannot be found, the person revoked the will by destruction.[1] This is a difficult presumption to rebut, and requires credible testimony explaining why the instrument is missing for a reason other than its revocation by the testator by destruction. Testimony that would assist in overcoming this presumption are:

1. That the decedent at or about the time of his death referred to the instrument as his will or exhibited a copy of his will; or
2. That there was a fire, flood or other occurrence in the decedent's home which would account for its absence.

The easiest circumstance under which a lost will can be established is when a copy is found among the decedent's possessions and it appears that the original was retained by a lawyer who:

1. No longer is alive;
2. Cannot be found;
3. Is no longer in practice; or
4. Will acknowledge that he had the original will but cannot locate it, or believes it was destroyed or lost (in a fire, flood, when he moved his offices, etc).

The contents of a lost will can be established by producing a copy of the will, a draft of the will, or by the testimony of two persons who can credibly establish all of the provisions of the will.[2] When relying upon a draft or copy, there must be supporting testimony that the draft or copy is, in fact, the same as the document that was executed by the decedent.

---

§ 25.21
1. See Estate of Passuello, 169 A.D.2d 1007, 565 N.Y.S.2d 281 (3d Dep't 1991).
2. SCPA § 1407(3).

The copy need not be a photostat and need not be conformed, but it must be established that its content is the same as the original.

When relying on the testimony of an individual to prove the provisions, the individual must be capable of credibly setting forth all of the provisions.[3] Except under exceptional circumstances, this is a task whose credible discharge is virtually impossible. One of the few circumstances where it could be credibly accomplished is if the draftsman or his secretary testifies from notes that were used in preparing the original instrument.[4]

Once revocation by destruction has been rebutted and content has been established, there still remains the duty to prove the will, to the same extent as an original will, by establishing that it was executed by the decedent in the presence of at least two witnesses and that the decedent had testamentary capacity at the time of execution.[5]

§ 25.22 How to Get a Will Admitted to Probate if None of the Witnesses to the Will Are Available

Basically, for a will to be admitted to probate, due execution and testamentary capacity must be attested to by at least two witnesses appearing before the court. Pursuant to SCPA § 1406, the witnesses can offer the required information without appearing before the court by an affidavit executed at the request of the testator when he was alive, or at the request of the petitioner seeking probate after the testator's death.[1] Where the affidavit is made after death, a court certified copy of the original will must be exhibited to the witness before he executes the affidavit. Establishing a will by affidavit, without the witness appearing before the court to be examined, is not acceptable if there are objections to probate, or if for any other reason the court requires the appearance of the witness. The latter circumstance is rare in the absence of objections, and will only arise where the instrument is suspect on its face, or suggests a circumstance where inquiry by the court is required because the instrument benefits a person who was in a fiduciary relationship with the decedent, such as his lawyer, accountant, clergyman, or physician.[2] If at the time of the probate proceeding only one witness is

---

3. See SCPA § 1401.

4. See Matter of Kalenak, 182 A.D.2d 1124, 583 N.Y.S.2d 332 (4th Dep't 1992) (Provisions of will were adequately established, where attorney draftsman stated that conformed copy was identical to original will he had prepared, and attorney's former secretary testified her handwriting was on copy of will and that she conformed copy to original.).

5. SCPA § 1407(2).

§ 25.22

1. See infra, § 25.59 for the form entitled "Deposition Affidavit of Subscribing Witness."

2. **PRACTICE POINTER:** Where a person in a fiduciary relationship to a decedent is named as a beneficiary of the decedent's will, the court will direct a "Putnam Hearing," at which the court must be satisfied that the beneficiary did not become a legatee as a product of abuse of his fiduciary relationship with the decedent. Individuals with a fiduciary relationship to a dece-

available because the other witnesses cannot be found within the state despite due diligence, or are dead, incompetent or physically or mentally unable to testify, the court may dispense with the testimony of the unavailable witness and admit the will to probate on the testimony of the attesting witness who is available.[3] If none of the witnesses is available because all of them are dead, incompetent, unable to testify by reason of physical or mental condition or are absent from the state, the court may admit the will to probate by petitioner proving the handwriting of the testator and of at least one of the attesting witnesses.[4] Proof of the handwriting of the testator and one attesting witness may be by affidavits from individuals familiar with the signature of the testator and the witness. The affiant proving the signature of the testator and the affiant proving the signature of the witness need not be the same person. Usually they will be different individuals.[5]

§ 25.23 When a Court Must Appoint a Guardian *Ad Litem* in a Probate Proceeding

The court must appoint a guardian *ad litem* in a probate proceeding, where there is any party interested in the proceeding who is under a disability and who is prejudiced by the will being admitted to probate.[1] A party would be prejudiced where the will being admitted to probate would leave that party in a poorer financial position than he would be in if the will were not accepted for probate. This circumstance arises where the person under a disability would receive a greater share in the decedent's estate in intestacy, or under a prior will. In those cases, a guardian *ad litem* must be appointed to represent the person under a disability by examining whether there is a justification exists for opposing probate of the will. If the person is not placed at any disadvantage by the will being admitted to probate, no necessity exists for the appointment of a guardian *ad litem*.[2]

The fee of the guardian *ad litem* is fixed by the court on the guardian *ad litem*'s affidavit of services.[3] The fee is usually directed to be paid from the general estate, but it may be charged to the interest of the

---

dent include the decedent's doctor, nurses, lawyer, accountant, clergyman, and the administrator of the nursing home where he resides. Once the relationship raises an inference of possible undue influence by one in a fiduciary relationship with the testator, the burden is on the legatee to satisfactorily explain that the legacy for him is a product of the decedent's own desire free of any abuse of the fiduciary relationship. A court can disallow a legacy which flows from a breach of fiduciary duty. If your client would benefit from such a disallowance and you do not wish to otherwise oppose the probate of the will, you can request that the court order a Putnam hearing. *See* Matter of Putnam, 257 N.Y. 140, 177 N.E. 399 (1931); Matter of Miller, 220 A.D.2d 591, 632 N.Y.S.2d 817 (2d Dep't 1995); Matter of Delorey, 141 A.D.2d 540, 529 N.Y.S.2d 153 (2d Dep't 1988).

3. *See* SCPA § 1405(1).

4. SCPA § 1405(4).

5. *See* Turano, Practice Commentary to SCPA § 1405.

§ 25.23

1. SCPA § 402(2).

2. *See* SCPA § 402(2).

3. SCPA § 405.

person under a disability or to any other party such as the party who started the proceeding necessitating the appointment of the guardian *ad litem*.[4]

Library References:

West's Key No. Digests, Infants ⚖︎78(3).

§ 25.24 Who May Oppose the Admission to Probate of a Will by Filing Objections

Any person who will sustain a pecuniary loss of an interest which he would otherwise inherit except for the will may file objections to probate pursuant to SCPA § 1410. A person whose only pecuniary loss is that he was named as an executor or trustee in a prior will, and he is not so named in the will offered for probate, or by a codicil, does not have an absolute right to file objections. The absolute right to file objections to probate is limited to the pecuniary loss of an inheritance interest.[1] However, a person named as the fiduciary in a prior will, who is not named in the will offered for probate, or whose nomination is extinguished by a codicil, may make an application to the court, on notice to all interested parties, seeking permission to file objections to probate. This application must be based on good cause shown.[2] The circumstances under which a court will allow a fiduciary under a prior will to file objections are limited to those situations where the presentation of good cause indicates reasonable grounds to believe that the instrument offered for probate should not be accepted and there are no other parties in interest who are in a position to file objections.[3] The inability of other parties in interest to file objections can be a product of their all being of advanced age, under disability, living in distant jurisdictions, or their interest being so fragmented as to render economically not feasible for any one of them to file objections.

Another situation in which the court may sanction an executor nominated in a prior instrument to file objections is where an *in terrorem* clause in the will or in a codicil would place a beneficiary in danger of losing his inheritance by filing objections,[4] *i.e.*, where the legatees would have to assume a jeopardy in filing objection to which the executor was not subject. If an issue is raised as to a person's status to raise objections to probate, the court will conduct a hearing to determine status as a preliminary matter in a probate proceeding, before it burdens the estate with the expense of proceeding on the merits of the objections.[5]

4. *See* SCPA § 405.

§ 25.24

1. SCPA § 1410.
2. *See* SCPA § 1410.

3. *See, e.g.,* Matter of Doyle, N.Y.L.J., 2/14/90, p.22, col. 5.

4. *See id.*

5. *See* Matter of Schultheis, N.Y.L.J., 3/17/89, p.26, col.3.

§ 25.25 When Objections Must Be Filed

While SCPA § 1410 commences by stating that objections to probate must be filed on or before the return date of the citation seeking probate, in practice, the exceptions to this deadline routinely extend the date to file objections beyond the return date of the citation. A potential objectant can obtain an automatic extension of the deadline to file objections by advising the court on the return date of citation that he is exercising his right to request an examination of the attesting witnesses to the will pursuant to SCPA § 1404. Such a request automatically extends the deadline for filing objections until 10 days after the completion of the oral examination by deposition of the attesting witnesses.[1] The time to file objections may also be further extended either by the court or by stipulations between the potential objectants and the petitioners seeking probate.

The most economic and effective approach to filing objections is to first complete discovery with reference to the potential issues upon which probate will be opposed. A court will usually grant a reasonable application for the extension of the time to file objections until the completion of specific discovery. Economy also makes it sensible for the parties to stipulate to such an extension without even burdening the court with an application. Filing objections after discovery is completed will avoid the necessity to amend objections, will frequently narrow the issues, and will potentially lend itself to a resolution of the issues with a minimum of avoidable pleadings. A trade-off for an extension of time to file objections that should be considered is for the objectant to consent to the nominated executor being granted preliminary letters under bond, in order to commence the administration of the estate while discovery and a potential probate contest proceeds. All extensions of time to file objections by agreement should be in writing.

Library References:
West's Key No. Digests, Wills ⊜377.

§ 25.26 How to Start an Estate Administration Where There Will Be Delay in Getting a Will Admitted to Probate

Quite often the protection of a decedent's assets requires the issuance of fiduciary authority with greater speed than it takes for a probate

---

§ 25.25
1. **PRACTICE POINTER:** If the party who requests an SCPA § 1404 examination does not diligently examine the witnesses, despite petitioner making them available, the petitioner can move the court to fix a deadline by which the SCPA § 1404 examinations are to be completed or deemed to be waived.

proceeding, particularly a contested probate proceeding, to be completed. Unless the petitioner is proceeding with waivers and consents from all necessary parties, the time just to complete the service of process, let alone the immense delay which occurs where a contest arises, may be too long to leave the assets of a decedent unadministered without the danger of the estate suffering a significant loss. To address this problem, SCPA § 1412 allows the issuance of preliminary letters testamentary to a nominated executor upon the filing of the petition seeking probate, except where the instrument sought to be probated is lost or destroyed.[1]

Ordinarily the request for preliminary letters must be made at the time of the issuance of citation.[2] However, the court, on written request, has the power to issue preliminary letters even prior to the issuance of citation.[3] This discretion would ordinarily be exercised where there will be a delay in the issuance of citation because the petitioner requires further time to prepare the documentation required for citation to issue, such as to complete the information as to the decedent's distributees.

The determination of persons entitled to notice of an application for preliminary letters is within the discretion of the court and the service of such notice may be required before or after the issuance of preliminary letters.[4] Where it appears that delay will prejudice the estate, notice within a given number of days will be allowed after the issuance of preliminary letters. Notice that preliminary letters have issued has no exact form except that it must state:

1. The title of the matter;
2. That the person has made an application for preliminary letters based upon being the nominated executor;
3. The date of the will; and
4. That it has been offered for probate.

Where the propounded will names more than one executor, and the application for preliminary letters is made by only a single executor, he will be required to give notice to the other nominated executors of the application, and the other executors may request that preliminary letters also issue to them at the time of or after the issuance to the first executor requesting preliminary letters.[5] The right of the other nominated executors also to receive preliminary letters is absolute in the absence of any showing that they are ineligible.[6]

Where there is a will of the same testator on file with the court that is later in date than the propounded instrument, notice must be given to

§ 25.26
1. SCPA § 1412(1).
2. See SCPA § 1412(1).
3. See SCPA § 1412(1).
4. SCPA § 1412(2)(a).
5. See SCPA § 1412(2)(a).
6. See SCPA § 1412(2)(a).

all persons nominated executor in the later will. The nominated executors in the later will have a prior right to preliminary letters.[7] In the absence of ineligibility or other good cause, the nominated executors in the later will have an absolute right to preliminary testamentary letters before the nominated executor in the earlier will. However, the nominated executor in the later will cannot assert this right until he has also filed a petition seeking probate of the later will or later codicil that gives him his status as nominated executor.[8]

§ 25.27 Form of Objections to Probate

There are no printed forms for objections. The objections are verified statements setting forth the general reasons why the objectant believes the will should not be admitted to probate.[1] The objections need not set forth factual events, but may generally state the basis for rejection of the will. The most usual objections are:

1. That the will was not executed by the testator in the presence of at least two witnesses;
2. That at the time of execution the testator lacked testamentary capacity;
3. That the will is the product of undue influence;
4. That the will is the product of fraud;
5. That the will is a forgery; or
6. That the will was altered subsequent to execution.

A petitioner served with general objections may serve the objectant with a demand for a bill of particulars requesting the factual basis for the objections. An objectant can seek to defer service of his bill of particulars until after the completion of discovery. If forced to serve a bill of particulars prior to completing discovery, the objectant may reserve his right to amend the bill of particulars if new information is learned during discovery.

Library References:

West's Key No. Digests, Wills ⚖︎277.

§ 25.28 Burden of Proof

On the trial of objections, the burden of proving, by a preponderance of credible evidence, that the will was duly executed and that at the time of execution the decedent had testamentary capacity rests upon the

---

7. SCPA § 1412(2)(b).
8. *See id.*

§ 25.27
1. *See infra*, § 25.60 for the form entitled "Objections to Probate."

proponent who is asking the court to accept the will.[1] He must prove that the decedent signed the will at the end in the presence of at least two witnesses who then both signed the will in the presence of each other (or in the alternative that the decedent signed it and within 30 days after signing it showed his signature to at least two witnesses, and asked them to sign it as witnesses).[2] The petitioner seeking probate must also establish that at the time of execution, the decedent had testamentary capacity. It is not required that the witnesses knew what was in the will or that the decedent understood its contents. It is necessary that the witness know that the decedent is aware of the fact that the paper he is asking them to witness is a will and that it appears that the decedent at the time of execution was not under any disability which would preclude him from understanding a will. This does not require any particular level of intelligence and could even extend to an individual who is confined to a psychiatric hospital.[3] Testamentary capacity is no more than the ability to understand the nature of your assets, who are the natural objects of your bounty, and to be possessed of the capacity to decide what you would like to do with your assets. The mere fact that a person is of little education, low IQ, may be schizophrenic or suffer from other mental disease, does not necessarily mean that he lacks testamentary capacity.[4] However, these elements can be considered in the determination of whether in fact a testator did have testamentary capacity.

The burden of proof on all other issues except due execution, publication[5] and testamentary capacity rests on the objectant who must establish them by a preponderance of credible evidence. In evaluating the ability to establish undue influence, sensitivity must be shown to distinguishing between influence, and undue influence. Obviously, a spouse, a child, a respected advisor, or a friend, may influence what a person decides to do in his will. This only rises to a level of undue influence when it deprives that person of the freedom of choice in making a decision by the influence exerted overcoming that person's free will.[6] To establish fraud it must be proven that the decedent executed the will in reliance upon a false statement that was known by the person advancing the falsehood to be untrue, and that the statement was made for the purpose of inducing the decedent to benefit that person by making a will.[7] The mere fact that the decedent may have relied on

---

§ 25.28

1. In re Will of Westover, 145 Misc.2d 469, 546 N.Y.S.2d 937 (Surr.Ct., Fulton County, 1989).

2. *See* EPTL § 3–2.1(c)(4).

3. Matter of Brody, N.Y.L.J., 4/8/74, p. 394 (Surr.Ct., Bronx County).

4. *See* Matter of Hedges, 100 A.D.2d 586, 473 N.Y.S.2d 529 (2d Dep't 1984).

5. Publication is the testator declaring to the witnesses either orally or by the attestation clause, or both, that this is his will. EPTL § 3–2.1.

6. *See* Matter of Burke, 82 A.D.2d 260, 268, 441 N.Y.S.2d 542, 547 (2d Dep't 1981). *See also* Matter of Walther, 6 N.Y.2d 49, 188 N.Y.S.2d 168, 159 N.E.2d 665 (1959).

7. *See* In re Reilly's Will, 139 Misc. 732, 249 N.Y.S. 152 (Surr.Ct., Westchester County, 1931).

incorrect information does not render a will invalid.[8]

Library References:

West's Key No. Digests, Wills ⚖287.

§ 25.29 Requirement of a Notice of Objections to Complete Jurisdiction in a Contested Probate

SCPA § 1411 mandates that once objections are filed, the proponent who seeks to admit the will to probate must serve a notice of objections on all parties on whom the citation was served, plus all persons who would be receiving any property under the will. This notice must comply with SCPA § 1411 in setting forth:

1. The name of the decedent;[1]
2. The name and address of the proponent;[2]
3. The name and address of each person named or referred to in the will who has not already appeared in the proceeding;[3]
4. Such other persons as are directed to be notified by the court;[4]
5. That the will has been offered for probate;[5]
6. That objections have been filed, when such objections will be heard by the court, or that they will be heard on a date to be fixed by the court in the future;[6] and
7. That the objections may be determined at a hearing or settled at a conference on a date to be fixed by the court.[7]

Furthermore, the notice must also advise the parties that if a settlement is entered into, or agreed to by all parties appearing at said hearing or conference:

1. It will be binding on all those served with the notice of probate, but who have not appeared;
2. It will be binding on all those who defaulted in appearing; and
3. That a defaulting party may be required to contribute to such a settlement an amount that bears the same proportion to the total amount of the settlement as his or her interest in the estate bears to the aggregate of the interest of all other persons required to contribute to the settlement.[8]

---

8. *See* In re Guidi's Will, 259 App.Div. 652, 20 N.Y.S.2d 240 (1st Dep't 1940)(incorrect factual recitals in will).

§ 25.29
1. SCPA § 1411(1)(a).
2. SCPA § 1411(1)(b)(i).
3. SCPA § 1411(1)(b)(ii).
4. SCPA § 1411(1)(b)(iii).
5. SCPA § 1411(1)(c)(i).
6. SCPA § 1411(1)(b)(ii).
7. SCPA §§ 1411(1)(c)(ii), (iii).
8. SCPA § 1411(1)(c)(iii).

EXAMPLE: If some parties agree to a settlement under which their inheritance is reduced by 10%, a defaulting party who has received a notice of probate will be bound by the settlement and his inheritance will likewise be reduced by 10%, even though the defaulting party did not consent to the specific settlement or participate in a trial of the issues.

The notice of objection must be served by the proponent within 30 days of the filing of the objection in the same manner as other process in the proceeding was required to be served pursuant to SCPA § 307. If the proponent fails to serve such notice, it may be served by the objectant, or any other party to the proceeding may be authorized by the court to serve the notice of objections.[9]

The notice of objections adds a whole new litany of parties to the probate proceeding. Until objections are filed, the only necessary parties to the proceeding were those adversely affected by the will. The filing of objections adds to this group those who would benefit from the will. Before the objections were filed, those who would benefit from the will need not be joined in the proceeding because the petitioner asking the court to accept the will is advocating their position. Once objections place admission of the will at issue, it is necessary to afford the beneficiaries the right to participate in the probate proceeding since an adjudication or a settlement may diminish that which they would otherwise receive under the will. Any settlement or adjudication that adversely affects a beneficiary or other party who has not been served with a notice of objection, is jurisdictionally defective with reference to that person, and he is not bound by the adjudication or the settlement.[10] Accordingly, to complete a matter, the notice of objection is a critical document to legitimatizing the result of an adjudication or a settlement.[11]

Library References:
West's Key No. Digests, Wills ⚖︎277.

§ 25.30 Right to a Trial by Jury

A probate proceeding is one of the few proceedings in which there is a right to trial by jury in the surrogate's court. The procedure for asserting a right to trial by jury is circumscribed by the requirement of strict compliance with SCPA § 502. This section requires that any respondent demanding a jury trial must do so in his answer or objections, and pay the required fee for a jury trial.[1] A proponent who wishes

---

9. SCPA § 1411(2).
10. *See* Turano, Practice Commentary to SCPA § 1411.
11. **PRACTICE POINTER:** An omission in serving a notice of objection may be cured by an order directing the parties not served with a notice of objections to show cause why the adjudication or settlement should not be binding upon them.

§ 25.30
1. SCPA § 502(2)(a).

a trial by jury, without regard to whether or not an objectant has made such a demand, must serve and file on his own behalf a demand for jury trial within six days after service upon him of an answer or objections.[2] No party can rely on receiving a jury trial because another party has filed a jury demand. SCPA § 502(5)(b) specifically authorizes any party filing a jury demand to withdraw the demand without the consent of any other party. A proponent who wants a jury trial and fails to demand a jury because the objectant has demanded a jury trial, will find the issues tried by the court without a jury if his time to demand a trial by jury has expired at the time an objectant has opted to withdraw his jury demand.[3] The statute is specifically designed to discourage requests for jury trials. Accordingly, if either a proponent or objectant desires such a trial, he should timely file a jury demand and pay the fee without regard to what has been done on the subject by another party.[4]

SCPA § 502(2)(b) provides a different standard for making a jury demand where a case is transferred from another court to the surrogate's court. It appears that under the provisions of this section, the person making a motion for a transfer should incorporate a jury demand in the motion papers and all other parties have ten days to demand a jury after being served with the order of transfer. The right of both the movant and other parties to assert the right to a trial by jury in a transferred case is dependent upon their not having otherwise waived their right to a trial by jury. If they have otherwise waived their right to a trial by jury, they cannot resurrect this right upon the transfer of the case to the surrogate's court from another court.[5]

§ 25.31 Right to Discovery in a Probate, Administration or Accounting Proceeding

Both the petitioner and objectant in a probate, administration or accounting proceeding have the same broad discovery rights as in any other litigation.[1] Additionally, in a probate contest, a potential objectant has a specific statutory right under SCPA § 1404 to examine the attesting witnesses to the will.[2] It is the duty of the petitioner seeking

---

2. SCPA § 502(2)(a).

3. Matter of James, 139 Misc.2d 179, 527 N.Y.S.2d 707 (Surr.Ct., Monroe County, 1988).

4. *But see* In re Mirsky, 81 Misc.2d 9, 365 N.Y.S.2d 122 (Surr.Ct., N.Y. County, 1975), the court relieved a party of the failure to timely file a jury demand by relying on the provisions of CPLR 4102(e).

CAVEAT: The soundness of a surrogate's court utilizing a provision of the CPLR to dispose of a subject specifically covered in a different manner in the SCPA is questionable. There are no appellate decisions on this subject. At best, the reliance of the surrogate's court on CPLR 4102(e) left the matter to the discretion of the court, and did not constitute an automatic avenue to ensure that a late application for a jury trial would be successful.

5. *See* Turano, Practice Commentary to subdivision 2 of SCPA § 502.

§ 25.31

1. *See* SCPA § 102. *See, e.g.*, Will of Devine, 130 Misc.2d 933, 498 N.Y.S.2d 280, 283 (Surr.Ct., N.Y. County, 1986).

2. SCPA § 1404(1).

probate to produce the attesting witnesses for examination by all other parties before the court.[3] These witnesses may be fully examined as to all circumstances surrounding the execution of the will and their knowledge of the decedent's testamentary capacity, including the source of that knowledge. Additional parties whom an objectant in a probate contest should examine include the attorney-draftsman.[4] An attorney-draftsman should be examined as to:

1. His representation of the decedent before and after the preparation of the decedent's will;
2. How it came about that he was retained by the decedent to draft his will;
3. Any relationship, personal or as an attorney, he may have had with any person who benefits under the will;
4. His experience in drafting wills;
5. The detailed circumstances under which he received his instructions to draft the will;
6. Any notes he took with reference to the terms of the will;
7. How soon after he received his instructions did he draft the will;
8. Whether the decedent received a draft of the will for review prior to its finalization;
9. Whether the decedent had the opportunity to carefully read the will before it was executed;
10. Information the attorney obtained from the decedent before he drafted the will;
11. Whether this information was obtained in person, by mail, or on the telephone, and if by obtained by mail, request his copies of the correspondence;
12. All discussions between the attorney and his client relative to the preparation and execution of the will; and
13. All of the details surrounding the execution of the will.

Hospital and medical records related to the decedent are also discoverable.[5] Remoteness in time will circumscribe the extent of discovery. Ordinarily in the absence of special circumstances, examination of events more than three years before the date of execution of a contested instrument or two years after execution will not be allowed.[6] A propo-

---

3. SCPA § 1404(1).
4. *See* SCPA § 1404(4).
5. In re Rauh, 156 N.Y.S.2d 862 (Surr. Ct., N.Y. County, 1952).
6. *Id. See* Matter of Du Bray, 132 A.D.2d 914, 518 N.Y.S.2d 245 (3d Dep't 1987)(special circumstances found where a scheme of fraud or a continuing course of conduct or undue influence was alleged and was evidenced by facts); In re Brady's, 273 App.Div. 968, 77 N.Y.S.2d 916 (4th Dep't 1948)(same). *Cf.* Matter of Partridge, 141 Misc.2d 159, 532 N.Y.S.2d 814 (Surr.Ct., Rockland County, 1988)(consideration of

nent should depose all objectants as to their knowledge of facts which would support the objections. Often, objectants are proceeding more on suspicion than knowledge, and are hopeful of establishing their cases from information gained in discovery. Motions for summary judgment by proponents will not be successful until objectants have had a reasonable opportunity to conclude all discovery.[7]

In administration contests, discovery is limited to the issue of ineligibility pursuant to SCPA § 707 and SCPA § 711, of a petitioner who has a prior right to letters of administration. Where there is a contest for letters of administration between two people with an equal right to letters of administration, such as two children of the decedent, discovery may be used to explore which person is better qualified to serve as administrator.[8] This discovery may include examination as to the education, business experience and other qualifications of the contestants seeking letters of administration. Inquiry may also be had as to who is better qualified to serve by dint of familiarity with the decedent's affairs, location,[9] age, physical disability, other obligations limiting the giving of the time required to serve as administrator, and any conflicts of interest.[10]

Discovery in an accounting proceeding extends to a party in interest examining the accounting party as to any subject encompassed within the account. The accounting fiduciary may examine an objectant as to the basis for any objection interposed.[11]

§ 25.32 Who Is Entitled to Letters of Administration When a Person Dies Without a Will

SCPA § 1001 sets a strict order of priority among a decedent's distributees as to who is entitled to letters of administration. The pecking order runs through a surviving spouse, the children, grandchildren, a parent, brothers and sisters, followed by other distributees. The provision for granting letters to other distributees is limited to aunts and uncles, since SCPA § 1001(1)(f)(ii) directs that letters shall issue to the public administrator, or county treasurer in counties where there is no public administrator, if the distributees are not in the category of persons specifically delineated in SCPA §§ 1001(1)(a)—(e), or an aunt or uncle.

tape recordings made six to nine years before execution of the will).

7. See e.g., Will of Bartel, 214 A.D.2d 476, 625 N.Y.S.2d 519 (1st Dep't 1995).

8. Cf. Matter of Schwartz, 130 Misc.2d 786, 497 N.Y.S.2d 834 (Surr.Ct., Nassau County, 1986)(Surviving husband and parents of deceased wife filed competing petitions for letters of administration. Discovery denied under the Freedom of Information Law.).

9. A local resident can more easily serve than a person residing in a distant location.

10. Conflicts of interest will not necessarily disqualify a person from serving as a fiduciary. See Matter of Ziegler, 157 Misc.2d 423, 596 N.Y.S.2d 963 (Surr.Ct., N.Y. County, 1993).

11. Cf. In re Kaplan's Estate, 49 Misc.2d 335, 267 N.Y.S.2d 345 (Surr.Ct., Nassau County, 1966).

The order of priority in the issuance of letters confers an absolute right based on that priority so long as the person is eligible and chooses to qualify. In order for a person of lesser priority to succeed in getting letters in preference to someone of higher priority, the objecting party must assert that the petitioner for letters of administration is ineligible for one of the reasons specifically delineated in SCPA § 707 or SCPA § 711.

The court may name more than one person in the same class as an administrator. Within a given class, the court has discretion as to whom it will select as the person most qualified to serve as fiduciary. Subjects which the court will consider in determining a contest between parties of equal priority for letters of administration are the education and experience of the respective parties, their presence in the jurisdiction, any special familiarity they have with the affairs of the decedent which will assist them in discharging their responsibility, and their general ability to best serve as administrator. Thus, it will be more likely that the court would select a son or a daughter of the decedent who is fully familiar with his affairs as a result of a long business association before another child who lacks that familiarity and who may live in a distant jurisdiction.

§ 25.33 Procedures to Follow in Administering the Estate

After the court signs a decree granting letters testamentary or letters of administration, the attorney for the executor or administrator should obtain from the court as many certificates evidencing the letters as will be required in order to collect all of the property of the decedent. The actual collection of the assets is a fiduciary function; the attorney will not be compensated for rendering legal services for the performance of that function.[1] Nevertheless, counsel will often assist or perform this task for their clients. This involves presenting the certificates with proof of the decedent's ownership of the assets to whomever holds these assets. Proof of ownership would include a bank book, bank statement, stock certificate or bond. In negotiating a security, such as a stock or bond, the original bond must be endorsed by the fiduciary or seller to the same extent as the owner would endorse it if he were alive. The fiduciary should be advised to open an estate checking account, and if necessary, a

---

§ 25.33

1. **CAVEAT:** Generally, an attorney may only be compensated from an estate for rendering necessary legal services. The duties of the executor or administrator are to be performed by that person and his payment is statutory commissions. To the extent that an attorney undertakes performance of the fiduciary's tasks, he must be paid by the fiduciary personally, if there is an express or implied agreement by the fiduciary to personally pay the attorney for performing fiduciary tasks. In the absence of an enforceable agreement for the fiduciary to personally pay the attorney, the attorney's performance of fiduciary duties will be viewed as the non-compensable acts of a gratuitous volunteer. Application of Elias, Schewel & Schwartz, 55 A.D.2d 448, 452, 390 N.Y.S.2d 739, 742 (4th Dep't 1977).

brokerage account to negotiate securities. A federal identification number for the estate should be obtained from the Internal Revenue Service and should be used on behalf of the estate in all transactions.

If the court has fixed a bond, the attorney for the estate should contact a bonding agency and facilitate his client's obtaining the required bond, having it executed by the fiduciary, and filing the original bond with the court. No letters will be issued until the bond is filed. The attorney for the estate should familiarize himself with EPTL Article 11 setting forth the powers and limitations of a fiduciary in order to properly advise his client as to his powers, duties and limitations. Counsel should advise his client of his right to avail himself, particularly in significant estates, of investment advice, and his responsibility to make determinations as to whether assets held by the decedent should remain intact to be distributed in kind, or whether they should be liquidated. These decisions essentially involve business determinations giving consideration to the intent of the decedent. Primarily, liquidation is controlled by the need for cash to pay estate obligations and taxes. Beyond this primary consideration, weight must be given to:

1. The intent of the testator as expressed in the will;
2. The impact of a liquidation of securities in generating capital gains tax liability;
3. The preservation of the assets to as great an extent as possible;
4. The desires of the heirs; and
5. All other business decisions which a prudent man would make in seeking to preserve his own assets, as limited by the provisions of EPTL Article 11.[2]

All debts of the decedent considered to be valid obligations should be promptly paid. Claims against the estate viewed as not being valid should be rejected. The fiduciary should be advised to maintain a ledger setting forth all assets received and disbursements made in order to facilitate a final account. The fiduciary should be advised to make a payment on account of federal estate taxes within 6 months of the date of death and on account of New York State estate taxes within 3 months of the date of death.[3] Where required, a Federal Estate Tax Return Form 706 should be prepared and filed, a New York State Estate Tax Return

---

2. **EXAMPLE:** If a decedent left real estate or a business that he would like his children to inherit, an executor should not sell it, except to the extent required to pay administration expenses, taxes and debts. The fiduciary should be advised to give consideration to the wishes of the heirs. Satisfied heirs are less likely to file objections to an account or oppose an attorney's reasonable fee request.

3. **CAVEAT:** Failure to timely pay a deposit on account of estate taxes will result in substantial interest being assessed against the estate. Additionally, substantial penalties will be assessed if the fiduciary cannot show a valid reason why penalties should be waived, such as no cash in the estate and a good reason why assets could not be timely liquidated to raise cash. Interest can never be waived. Failure to advise a fiduciary to make a timely payment on account of taxes may shift the responsibility for the payment of avoidable interest and

ET-90 should be filed, and in the event the Federal return is changed on audit, an amendment to the New York Tax Return should be filed.

§ 25.34 How to Force an Estate Administration to Be Completed—Compelling an Accounting

Any party with a beneficial interest in an estate, either as an heir or as a creditor, can bring on a petition to the court to compel the fiduciary to file his account for judicial settlement. This is a proceeding pursued where the fiduciary does not appear to be concluding the estate with appropriate expedition. It can also become the framework for litigating a disputed claim by a creditor. Whether an accounting should be compelled pursuant to SCPA § 2206 is within the discretion of the court and will be governed by what is in the best interest of the estate. If on the facts presented, it appears appropriate that an accounting be compelled, it will be directed. Should it appear that burdening the estate with an accounting is either premature or unnecessary, the petition to compel an accounting will be denied.[1] If it appears justified, the court can direct an intermediate accounting even if the estate is not concluded. Courts will be reluctant to burden an estate with the legal cost of an intermediate accounting, in addition to a final accounting, in the absence of necessity and good cause being shown by the party seeking the accounting.[2]

§ 25.35 Concluding an Estate Administration Without an Accounting Proceeding

An estate administration may be concluded by presenting, to the parties in interest, an informal accounting of what has transpired and having the parties execute a receipt indicating their satisfaction with the administration and releasing the fiduciary.[1] This instrument may be recorded in accordance with SCPA § 2202. Where the person receiving a distribution or other payment from the estate is an infant or incapacitated person, the receipt and release may be executed by his guardian, or the person receiving the payment, such as the parent of an infant who has no guardian appointed by a court.

§ 25.36 Obtaining a Decree Concluding the Estate Based on Filed Receipts and Releases

Pursuant to SCPA § 2203, a fiduciary may present to the court a petition seeking a decree concluding the estate based on receipts and

penalties from the fiduciary personally to counsel.

§ 25.34

1. *See* Matter of Taber, 96 A.D.2d 890, 466 N.Y.S.2d 50 (2d Dep't 1983).

2. *See infra,* § 25.64 for the form entitled "Citation to Executor to Show Cause Why Executor Should Not Account."

§ 25.35

1. *See infra,* § 25.62 for the form entitled "Receipt and Release Agreement Concluding an Estate without an Accounting Proceeding"; and § 25.63 for the form entitled "Receipt and Release (Legacy)."

releases. While this process may be used with reference to distributions to an infant or incapacitated person who does not have a guardian or a committee of his property, courts will be reluctant to enter a decree discharging a fiduciary and his surety without a formal accounting in which parties under a disability, who do not have a fiduciary, would be represented by a guardian *ad litem*. Unless the interest of the infant or incapacitated person is too insignificant to justify the expense and burden of a formal accounting, and all other parties are consenting competent adults, the better practice is to petition for the judicial settlement of the account and a formal accounting proceeding under which the court will appoint a guardian *ad litem* for persons under a disability. While this imposes an expense on the estate, it precludes any question as to the estate being concluded with finality, after appropriate jurisdiction has been obtained over all parties in interest who are under a disability.

§ 25.37 Concluding an Estate by a Formal Judicial Accounting

A formal judicial accounting should contain separate schedules setting forth:

1. The assets initially received;
2. All transactions involving any change in assets by sale, purchase or exchange;
3. All income received;
4. All expenses incurred;
5. All disbursements paid, including for debts of the decedent;
6. All outstanding expenses or debts that are not paid, but are allowed;
7. All disallowed claims;
8. A computation of fiduciary commissions;
9. The assets remaining on hand, including their form and location; and
10. The parties interested in the estate, and the distribution to which they will be entitled.

In addition, a petition must be prepared seeking acceptance of the account as filed and seeking the discharge of the fiduciary upon his making the payments directed in the decree settling the account. Annexed to the account must be an affidavit pursuant to SCPA § 2209, stating that the information contained in the account is accurate and correct. The account may be accepted by parties in interest by a receipt and release. Those parties not accepting it by a receipt and release must be served with citation obtained from the court directing these parties to show cause why the account that is annexed to the citation should not be judicially settled as presented and the executor discharged.

To the extent that the judicial settlement of the account requires fixing and allowing attorney's fees and/or accounting fees, the citation should specifically contain a direction that the respondent show cause why the fees for the named person performing the services should not be fixed and allowed in the specific amounts requested. The citation must reflect the name of the attorney and the accountant, the amounts of their fees, the amount that has already been paid and the amount that remains unpaid. Additionally, the citation should reflect with reference to a rejected claim, why such claim should be disallowed. If an issue exists as to a right of election or the status of a person to receive a distribution, the citation should specifically set forth the relief requested on those issues. SCPA § 2210 sets forth all of the parties to whom process must issue in a formal accounting.[1]

§ 25.38 Objections to an Account

Any person with a pecuniary interest that is adversely affected by the account filed by a fiduciary, or the Attorney General with reference to any charitable interest, has the right to file written objections setting forth the issue he wishes to raise as to the accuracy or propriety of a filed accounting.[1] The objections must be filed in writing[2] and verified by the objectant.[3] The original objection should be filed with the court with a proof of service by mail upon the attorney for the accounting party.[4] The requisite filing fee for objections must be paid to the court.[5]

§ 25.39 Prosecuting Objections to an Account

The objectant to an account is entitled to full discovery of relevant documents and oral deposition of the accounting party. The accounting party is entitled to depose the objectant as to the basis for his or her objections.[1] At the completion of discovery, either the accounting or objecting party should file a note of issue placing the matter on the calendar of the court for trial. Objections to an account are tried without a jury by the judge. No right to trial by jury exists in an accounting

---

§ 25.37

1. *See infra,* § 25.64 for the form entitled "Petition to Judicially Settle Executor's Account" and § 25.66 for the form entitled "Accounting Form."

§ 25.38

1. SCPA § 2210.
2. In re Silverman's Will, 144 Misc. 675, 259 N.Y.S. 272 (Surr.Ct., Orange County, 1932).
3. SCPA § 303. *See e.g.,* In re Gross, 79 Misc.2d 204, 205, 359 N.Y.S.2d 484, 485 (Surr.Ct., Queens County, 1974).
4. SCPA § 307.
5. SCPA § 2402(10).

§ 25.39

1. *See* In re Kaplan's Estate, 49 Misc.2d 335, 267 N.Y.S.2d 345 (Surr.Ct., Nassau County, 1966).

proceeding.[2] The burden of proof on all issues raised by objections is on the person filing the objections. With few exceptions, the person filing the objections must prove by a preponderance of credible evidence that what is alleged in the objection is correct. The exceptions to this rule are on issues with reference to attorney's fees and claims against the estate by the executor or administrator. If an objection is filed to the fee of an attorney, the burden of proof is on the attorney to convince the court that his fee is fair and reasonable.[3] If the person filing the account disagrees with the fee request of his or her attorney, he or she can request that the court fix the attorney's fee.[4] If the executor or administrator who is filing the account states in the account that the estate owes him or her money and there is an objection to this claim, the burden of proof is on the executor or administrator to establish the validity of his or her claim against the estate.

§ 25.40 Claims Against an Estate by a Creditor

In rare cases, the time to file a claim is fixed by a published notice to creditors pursuant to SCPA § 1801. The time to file and present claims against an estate is usually governed by the alternate provision of SCPA § 1802 that provides that the fiduciary is not responsible for any claim that was not presented within seven months of the date of issuance of letters, where he has in good faith otherwise paid out the assets of the estate. A fiduciary should show great sensitivity to the provision in this section relieving him of responsibility only when he has paid out the assets in good faith. A fiduciary can be held personally responsible for a claim filed even after seven months if the claimant establishes that the liquidation of the estate by the fiduciary was not in good faith, in that he should have known of the existence of the claim even without receiving a formal notice.

> EXAMPLE: A question of fact exists as to whether the liquidation of an estate was in good faith where:
>
> 1. Rent, which had obviously accrued on the decedent's residence, was not paid; or
>
> 2. No inquiry was made as to the existence of a Medicaid lien,[1] even though the decedent had been hospitalized

---

2. In re Nelson's Will, 105 Misc.2d 747, 433 N.Y.S.2d 314 (Surr.Ct., Westchester County, 1980)(children had no right to a trial by jury in the accounting proceeding); In re Filipiak, 66 Misc.2d 742, 321 N.Y.S.2d 973 (Surr.Ct., Erie County, 1971).

3. Matter of Gajeway, 159 A.D.2d 837, 553 N.Y.S.2d 64 (3d Dep't 1990); In re Potts' Estate, 213 App.Div. 59, 209 N.Y.S. 655 (4th Dep't 1925)(burden is on executor's attorneys presenting claim for services to establish reasonableness and value of services), aff'd 241 N.Y. 593, 150 N.E. 568 (1925).

4. See infra, § 25.47 for a discussion of attorney's fees.

§ 25.40

1. See Chapter 23, "Elder Law," supra § 23.82 for a discussion of Medicaid liens.

for a protracted period of time and payment was obviously being made by Medicaid, or

3. In any other situation where the executor or the administrator should have been sensitive to the possible existence of the claim.

A fiduciary should be advised that it is foolish to attempt to evade a claim simply because he has not received formal notice if reasons exist to believe a possibly valid claim may be outstanding. The claim should be ascertained. If it is not paid or its validity is in doubt, upon a formal accounting, it should be viewed as a rejected claim, the claimant cited, and the burden shifted to the claimant to establish the validity of the claim.

There are situations where the accounting party sets forth in the account that the estate owes him a sum of money or that he has a right to an estate asset. If there is an objection filed to the claim being made by the accounting party, the burden of proof is on the accounting party to establish by a preponderance of the credible evidence that the claim against the estate is valid.[2]

Library References:
West's Key No. Digests, Jury ⚖14(1).

§ 25.41 Representing a Claimant Against an Estate

When representing a person with a claim against an estate, a formal written claim, verified by the claimant, should be served upon the executor or administrator, and the original filed with the court. This will make a claimant a party to any accounting proceeding and would require that the executor or administrator serve the claimant with process to show cause why the claim should not be rejected. Only by filing a formal written claim with the court under the index number of the estate can a claimant be certain that he will be viewed as a necessary party to an accounting.

Claims for services rendered may be filed whether the services were rendered to the decedent prior to his death or to his estate subsequent to his death. An attorney, of course, may always file an application to have his legal fees fixed pursuant to SCPA § 2210. This is usually done outside the framework of an accounting only when an attorney has ceased to represent the fiduciary before the estate is completed and an agreement as to compensation cannot be reached.[1]

---

2. Matter of Holmberg, 206 A.D.2d 479, 614 N.Y.S.2d 751 (2d Dep't 1994).

§ 25.41
1. **PRACTICE POINTER:** Before agreeing to pay an attorney's fee, consideration should be given to whether persons with an interest in the estate other than your client will object to the fee upon an accounting. Unless the fee has been fixed by the court pursuant to SCPA § 2110, an objection on an accounting can lead to the fee being found excessive and your client surcharged for paying the fee. Payment of an excessive fee to outgoing counsel for part of the work may not leave sufficient room for approval of a fair fee to successor counsel for the remainder of the work.

§ 25.42 Obtaining Information About Estate Assets and Recovering Estate Property

Often, a person who holds personal property belonging to the decedent refuses to surrender it when a decedent dies. Even more frequently, a suspicion may exist that a person holds such property but the executor or administrator has no information as to the validity of the suspicion or the nature of the specific property that may be at issue. The fiduciary may commence a proceeding to discover property or information pursuant to SCPA § 2103. This is called a discovery proceeding. It is a two tier proceeding. The initial aspect of the proceeding is a petition seeking to examine a person under oath based upon a belief that that person has knowledge or information, or possession, of a decedent's property and should submit to examination under oath on the subject. Examination of such a person is granted on minimal grounds and is one of the few areas of discovery where a fishing expedition is permitted.

The petition should be accompanied by an order to show cause directing the party to appear at the court to be examined. Service of the order must be made by delivery of a certified copy of the order to the person whose examination is sought and the payment or tender to such person of the same fees required to be paid when subpoenaing a witness to testify at a trial.[1] Payment of the fee is critical. Failure to pay the fee will render the service of process incomplete.[2] If a person served with such an order and fee fails to appear to be examined, an application should be brought on to punish that person for contempt for failing to obey an order of the court. If the person whose examination is sought fails to answer the application to show cause why the person should not be held in contempt, the court can hold him or her in contempt, and issue an order directing that unless he appears for examination at the court at a fixed time, that a warrant may issue to the sheriff of the county where this person resides to place him in civil custody and deliver him to the court.[3]

§ 25.43 How to Proceed When Your Client Has a Claim Against an Estate

SCPA § 2102 provides for a proceeding that is often referred to as a reverse discovery proceeding. This is a proceeding by a person against a

---

§ 25.42

1. See SCPA § 2103(5).

2. SCPA § 2301(5). Cf. In the Matter of Freitag, 123 Misc.2d 266, 473 N.Y.S.2d 334 (Surr.Ct., Nassau County, 1984).

3. **PRACTICE POINTER:** Where the information needed is in possession of an entity such as a bank or stock broker, and the entity will not otherwise supply it, the issue can often be resolved by joining the entity in the discovery proceeding, directing it to produce any and all records relating to the issue, and then agreeing that in lieu of appearing, the entity can mail you copies of the records reserving your right to oral examination after you review the records. This limits the time and expense of a reporter to simply transcribe a delivery of documents. It further allows a more prepared oral examination, if one is necessary, after you have had an opportunity to review the records under more considered circumstances than if they were handed to you at a deposition.

fiduciary, seeking to obtain property or information as to property held by the estate that belongs to him. This section provides for multiple relief. A petitioner may request information that affects his interest where the fiduciary has failed, after a request is made upon him in writing, to supply this information.[1] Use of the section for this purpose is rare. A court will mandate a fiduciary to supply information only where the information is required for good reason that goes beyond mere curiosity.[2] More commonly, the proceeding is used;

1. To obtain exempt property to which a surviving spouse or child is entitled;
2. To collect funeral expenses;
3. To obtain payment of a specific bequest, a legacy, a distributive interest, a trust interest, or an administration expense; or
4. To obtain property held by the decedent in connection with his vocation.[3]

§ 25.44 A Special Provision for an Estate Beneficiary Obtaining Funds for Education

SCPA § 2102(5) has a special provision that can be used to facilitate a beneficiary's obtaining a distribution for support or education before the estate is otherwise ready to distribute to beneficiaries. On application, at least a partial distribution of so much of the interest to which the beneficiary is entitled as exceeds the known net estate by at least one third may be granted. Basically, this provides that a beneficiary can force a distribution if all other rights to the estate's assets that are greater or equal to his do not total more than two thirds of the assets held by the fiduciary.[1]

§ 25.45 Who Is Entitled to Assets When Two or More Fiduciaries Are in Dispute

SCPA § 2102(6) creates a procedure that can be useful if there is more than one executor and they do not get along. It allows one fiduciary to petition the court to have another fiduciary deliver property to him. The court will make such direction as is appropriate. The circumstances in which this section is used would involve a:

§ 25.43
1. SCPA § 2102(1).
2. Matter of Apuzzo, N.Y.L.J., 9/14/95, p.32, col.3.
3. **ILLUSTRATIONS:** A furrier dies holding valuable coats belonging to his customers and the fiduciary is reluctant to release the property without a court order establishing the customers' rights to the coats; a deceased art dealer who may have property on consignment that his fiduciary cannot distinguish from property owned by the decedent leading the fiduciary to be reluctant to deliver any property without title first being ascertained in a judicial proceeding.

§ 25.44
1. SCPA § 2102(5).

§ 25.45 PROBATE & ESTATE ADMINISTRATION Ch. 25

1. Concern by one fiduciary over the safety of assets held by another unbonded fiduciary; or
2. Direction necessary for the operation of a decedent's business; or
3. Fear that records needed in the future will not be properly preserved by a fiduciary for any variety of reasons.[1]

§ 25.46 Compensation of Executor and Administrator, When Payable

The only compensation that an executor or an administrator is entitled to, is the statutory sums set forth in SCPA § 2307. This section creates specific percentages to be applied to all assets received by the executor or administrator and all assets paid out by him. In computing commissions, one half of the statutory rate should be applied to all sums received by the fiduciary and one half to all sums paid out by the fiduciary. This procedure is used because the amount paid out may differ from the amount received as a result of the value of an asset increasing or decreasing during the administration of the estate.

> **EXAMPLE:** An asset with a value of $100,000 when received by the administrator, may only be worth $50,000 when he pays it out. The percent due as a receiving commission would be applied to the $100,000 value and the amount of paying out commissions would be applied to the $50,000 value. In each case the percent applied will be one half of the amount set forth in SCPA § 2307.

In computing commissions, the attorney should be sensitive to the fact that specifically bequeathed property under a will is not subject to statutory commissions.[1] However, if a building is administered by the executor for any period of time before it is turned over to the beneficiary, the income collected would be subject to commissions.[2]

If there is more than one fiduciary and the gross value of the principal of the estate exceeds $300,000, each fiduciary is entitled to a full commission up to a maximum of three full commissions. If the principal of the estate exceeds $300,000 and there are more than three fiduciaries, the maximum of three commissions would be divided in equal shares among the fiduciaries.[3] Where there is more than one fiduciary and the estate is less than $300,000, in the case of a person

---

§ 25.45

1. **CAVEAT:** Hostile co-fiduciaries should be made sensitive to the likelihood of their both being removed if they are incapable of submerging their differences to the extent required to properly administer the estate.

§ 25.46

1. See SCPA § 2307(2). **ILLUSTRATION:** If a watch or a specific piece of real property is given to a person and the watch or property is delivered in kind to the beneficiary, the value of the watch or realty is not subject to commission. Attorneys should also be sensitive to this fact before agreeing to a legal fee equal to one commission. Commissions can be very small in a large estate if there is a great deal of specifically bequeath or devised property.

2. SCPA § 2307(6).
3. See SCPA § 2307(5).

who died after August 31, 1993, the multiple fiduciaries must divide a single commission. In estates of individuals who died before August 31, 1993, if the estate exceeds $100,000 in principal, each fiduciary, up to three, is entitled to a full commission. If there are more than three fiduciaries, they must divide a maximum of three commissions. If the estate is less than $100,000, only a single commission is payable, to be divided among all the fiduciaries.[4]

A fiduciary may not pay himself commissions prior to the completion of an estate administration without a court order.[5] A fiduciary who pays himself commissions without a court order is acting improperly and subjecting himself to revocation of his letters, or at the least to a surcharge for interest.[6] A partial payment on account of commission can be obtained by an ex-parte application for a court order pursuant to SCPA § 2310. Orders for partial payment of commissions are routinely granted upon a showing that a tax advantage to the fiduciary or to the Estate will occur by paying a portion of the commission in a given year. Hardship is also a basis for obtaining a partial payment. The fiduciary receiving the partial payment must file a bond, at his own expense, in the amount of the payment guaranteeing its repayment should commissions not be allowed at the conclusion of the estate.[7] An application for payment of commissions on notice to all interested parties may also be prosecuted pursuant to SCPA § 2310. The easier and more economic course is to make an ex-parte application pursuant to SCPA § 2311. The one economy under SCPA § 2310 is that it allows the court to dispense with a bond, if the will does not require a bond, and under certain other circumstances. However, the cost of the bond will often be substantially less than the legal services required to pursue an application on notice.

In addition to statutory commissions, a fiduciary is also entitled to reimbursement of necessary expenses incurred by him in the performance of his duties.[8] This includes actual out-of-pocket disbursements, and not the routine charges such as taxi fare, carfare, postage, and telephone calls related to the performance of his duties as these charges are expenses incorporated within a statutory commission.[9] A fiduciary who lives in a distant location will not be granted the cost of coming to New York to do his job, in the absence of a specific showing that a decedent designated such a person to serve as executor knowing he lived at a distant location and that special expenses would be involved in

4. *Id.* **PRACTICE POINTER:** In determining if more than one commission is payable, sensitivity must be shown to the $100,000 or $300,000 figure being principal and not including income. Even if the funds handled by the fiduciary exceed $100,000, as a result of income earned during the administration, this does not trigger a right to multiple commissions.

5. In re Crippen, 32 Misc.2d 1019, 224 N.Y.S.2d 116 (Surr.Ct., N.Y. County, 1961).

6. *See* Matter of Dubin, 166 Misc.2d 971, 636 N.Y.S.2d 991 (Surr.Ct., Bronx County, 1995).

7. SCPA § 2310(5). The cost of such a bond is relatively small.

8. *See* SCPA § 2307(1).

9. Estate of Picker, 103 Misc.2d 594, 426 N.Y.S.2d 688 (Surr.Ct., Bronx County, 1980).

having this person serve as executor.[10] In those cases, reasonable travel expenses might be allowed. In all other cases, a person who lives in a distant location, who chooses to serve as an executor or administrator, must determine for himself whether he wishes to incur the expenses against the commission he can earn in discharging the responsibilities of being a fiduciary.

§ 25.47 Attorney's Fees

Attorney's fees in the administration of an estate are always subject to court approval.[1] On an accounting, approval of the fee need not be specifically requested: the court may *sua sponte* review and fix counsel fees.[2] An attorney is entitled to fair compensation for the necessary legal services rendered in representing the fiduciary of an estate.[3] For many years there was a rule of thumb that the legal fees were to be fixed in an agreed percentage related to the gross estate or in a sum equal to a single commission. These blanket percentile fees are no longer universally viewed with favor by courts in fixing and allowing fees. An attorney is entitled only to his reasonable and regular hourly charges based upon an affidavit of services showing the exact services rendered, when they were rendered, and the time expended.[4] The services must be necessary and of a nature that requires they be performed by a lawyer.[5] Picking up mail and making bank deposits are not legal duties. Time expended must be within the framework of what is reasonably required to complete the task. An attorney who takes longer to complete a task due to inexperience or limited expertise will be compensated at a lesser hourly rate than more experienced colleagues. Conversely, an experienced lawyer who can complete tasks with greater efficiency of time is entitled to a higher hourly rate. The maintenance of time sheets is critically important in sustaining the claims of an attorney for compensation. While an attorney will not be allowed compensation in excess of his regular time charges, he will not be allowed his regular time charges where the amount of time expended is disproportionate to the value of the estate, or to the reasonable time that it would take an attorney to perform the tasks required.[6]

10. *Id. See also* Matter of Steinberg, 208 Misc. 135, 143 N.Y.S.2d 341 (Surr.Ct., Kings County, 1955); Matter of Schneider, 198 Misc. 1017, 1030, 96 N.Y.S.2d 652, 664 (Surr.Ct., N.Y. County, 1950).

§ 25.47

1. SCPA §§ 2110, 2307(1).

2. Matter of Wiggins, 200 A.D.2d 813, 606 N.Y.S.2d 423 (3d Dep't 1994). *See also*, Turano, 1991 Supp. Practice Commentary to SCPA 2307.

3. Matter of Wiggins, 200 A.D.2d 813, 606 N.Y.S.2d 423 (3d Dep't 1994).

4. Robison v. von Langendorff, 221 A.D.2d 189, 633 N.Y.S.2d 303 (1st Dep't 1995).

5. Estate of Gillespie, 145 Misc.2d 542, 547 N.Y.S.2d 531, 534 (Surr.Ct., N.Y. County, 1989).

6. In re Estate of Freeman, 34 N.Y.2d 1, 9, 355 N.Y.S.2d 336, 341, 311 N.E.2d 480, 484 (1974).

On a formal accounting, an attorney must file an affidavit of legal services with the court, and his fees must be specifically approved. The citation seeking the judicial settlement of an account must specifically set forth the amount of fees being requested by the attorney so that all parties are notified in the citation of the amount of legal fees and disbursements that the court is being asked to approve for payment from the estate.[7] Accountants must likewise file an affidavit of services and have their fees approved by the court.[8] The citation must specifically indicate the amount of the accountant's fees that are requested to be allowed from the estate.[9] Usually, courts will not allow to an attorney, who is also receiving a statutory commission as an executor or administrator, as large a fee as would be allowed if he is serving only as the attorney. While an attorney is only compensated for legal services, there are so many services with reference to the administration of an estate that fall into the grey area of being partially administrative and partially legal, that in fixing legal fees, the court will give consideration to the amount of compensation the attorney is also receiving in statutory commissions.

§ 25.48 Declining to Serve as an Executor or Trustee

No person can be forced to serve as executor or trustee simply because the will nominates him. A person nominated as executor or trustee in a will may renounce his right to letters testamentary or letters of trusteeship by signing an acknowledged instrument setting forth that he does renounce his right to letters testamentary and/or letter of trusteeship.[1] A renunciation may also be used if a decision is made to have the alternate executor serve instead of the person named in the will as executor. In that case the nominated executor will have to execute a renunciation. An executor who wishes to serve cannot be forced to sign a renunciation.[2] A renunciation may be retracted at any time before letters are issued to another person. It may also be retracted should a future vacancy occur during the administration requiring the appointment of a new fiduciary.[3]

---

7. SCPA § 306(1)(d).

8. *See, e.g.,* In re Roese's Will, 36 Misc.2d 643, 232 N.Y.S.2d 592 (Surr.Ct., Westchester County, 1962).

9. SCPA § 306(1)(d).

§ 25.48

1. SCPA § 1417.

2. For the basis and procedure for disqualifying a nominated executor or trustee who refuses to step aside, *see supra*, § 25.10.

3. **PRACTICE POINTER:** In light of the increasingly stringent limitations on an attorney/executor or attorney/administrator receiving both a full commission and a full legal fee, before qualifying to serve as executor or as administrator, an attorney should evaluate if it might not be more profitable to simply serve as the attorney and to renounce appointment as an executor. Of course, the new executor has the right to retain any attorney he wishes, so before an attorney renounces in favor of being the attorney for the estate rather than the executor, he should be reasonably certain that the alternate executor will retain him as counsel. An executor has an absolute right to fire his attorney at any time during the administration and the at-

§ 25.49 Renouncing an Inheritance

There may be tax or business reasons, some involving saving significant sums of money, why an heir named in a will would prefer not receiving all or part of an inheritance. A person may renounce his interest in an estate by signing an acknowledgement of renunciation in accordance with the requirements of EPTL § 2–1.11. However, EPTL § 2–1.11 must be strictly adhered to. A renunciation must be served and filed with the court within nine months of the date of death. The time to file and serve such a renunciation may be extended in the discretion of the court on a petition showing reasonable cause and on notice to such persons, and in such manner, as the court may direct. Unless a will directs to the contrary, when a beneficial interest in an estate is renounced, it is disposed of as if that person had predeceased the decedent.[1] A beneficiary may renounce all or part of an inheritance.

If the person renouncing an inheritance is an infant, or a person otherwise under a disability, an application must be made to the court to authorize the renunciation.[2] This should be done with expedition. Sensitivity must be shown to the time it will take the court to consider the application and the time limitations in EPTL § 2–1.11. On a renunciation application, the court will appoint a guardian *ad litem* for the infant or disabled heir. This must be weighed in considering the time and cost required to complete the application.

§ 25.50 Construction of a Will

If the language of the will is subject to more than one meaning or its intent is not clear, any person having an interest in the issue may bring on a proceeding pursuant to SCPA § 1420 asking the court to construe the meaning of the will. Where will language is subject to more than one interpretation, the executor must obtain a construction before the estate is distributed, if he is going to be protected from reaching a conclusion as to meaning which may not ultimately be accepted by the court. Otherwise, the executor may find himself faced with a circumstance where he has paid out a legacy to the wrong person that cannot be recovered and he is personally responsible for the amount of the legacy, or his attorney is held ultimately responsible in a malpractice action for failing to advise him to obtain a construction.

An attorney pursuing a construction proceeding is entitled to reasonable compensation from the estate for the value of his services, even torney is entitled to no greater compensation than *quantum meruit*.

§ 25.49
1. EPTL § 2–1.11(d).
2. EPTL § 2–1.11(c).

if the construction he advocates is not accepted.[1] The rationale for compensating the attorney from the estate is that if the construction was required, his presenting the issues to the court was a necessary service to the estate, even if his interpretation, if advanced in good faith, is not ultimately embraced by the court. Upon the conclusion of the matter, the party initiating a construction proceeding, must ask the court to allow fair and reasonable compensation to his attorney, and payment of the disbursements incurred in initiating the proceeding.

A construction proceeding is initiated based on a petition requesting the relief and obtaining either a citation or order to show cause addressed to all parties who would be affected by the construction issue.[2] Any affected party not joined in the proceeding would not be bound by the determination.[3] In practice, the court would not issue a citation or enter an order to show cause unless it is addressed to all interested parties. The petition must necessarily incorporate a representation as to who the necessary parties to the proceeding are, their interest, and their addresses.[4] It should also present the alternative interpretations that can be applied to the language of the will and why clarification is necessary at this time. A court will only address a construction issue when a present need for interpretation exists.[5] It will dismiss as premature a request to construe a provision where the need will not arise until a future time or where possible circumstances arising with the passage of time may eliminate the need for a construction.[6]

§ 25.51 Forms

The following forms will aid the practitioner and are discussed *supra*.

§ 25.50

1. Matter of Estate of Greatsinger, 67 N.Y.2d 177, 181–83, 501 N.Y.S.2d 623, 626–27, 492 N.E.2d 751 (1986); Matter of McNab, 163 A.D.2d 790, 558 N.Y.S.2d 751 (3d Dep't 1990).

2. SCPA § 1420.

3. SCPA § 1420(4).

4. SCPA § 1420(1).

5. In re Lederer's Will, 4 A.D.2d 623, 168 N.Y.S.2d 343 (1st Dep't 1957). *See also*, Matter of Di Siena, 178 A.D.2d 720, 576 N.Y.S.2d 952 (3d Dep't 1991); Will of Swett, 52 A.D.2d 330, 383 N.Y.S.2d 770 (4th Dep't 1976).

6. *See* Matter of Mount, 185 N.Y. 162, 77 N.E. 999 (1906); Matter of Stout, 1 A.D.2d 901, 149 N.Y.S.2d 897 (2d Dep't 1956); Matter of Suydam, 139 Misc. 845,

§ 25.52   PROBATE & ESTATE ADMINISTRATION   Ch. 25

§ 25.52   Forms—Probate Petition[1]

For Office Use Only
(Filing Fee Paid $_____)
(_____ Certs: $_____)
(_____ Certs: $_____)
($_____ Bond, Fee: $_____)
(Receipt No: _____ No:_____)

P–1
(4/95)

DO NOT LEAVE ANY ITEMS BLANK

SURROGATE'S COURT OF THE STATE OF NEW YORK
COUNTY OF

..........................X
PROBATE PROCEEDING,   PETITION FOR PROBATE AND:
Will of   [ ] Letters Testamentary
                               [ ] Letters of Trusteeship
                               [ ] Letters of Administration
    a/k/a   [ ] Preliminary Letters
                               [Submit Schedule E]
            Deceased.
..........................X   File No.

TO THE SURROGATE'S COURT, County of [ ]

It is respectfully alleged:

1. The name, citizenship, domicile and interest in this proceeding of the petitioner, who is of full age, are as follows:

Name: _____ Citizenship [ ] U.S.A.
                             (check one): [ ] Other _____
                                                  (specify)

Domicile or, if a financial institution, principal office: (specify)

_____
(Street Address)   (City/Town/Village)

_____
(County)   (State)   (Zip)   (Telephone   Number)

Mailing address: _____
(if different from domicile)

248 N.Y.S. 431 (Surr.Ct., N.Y. County, 1925).

§ 25.52
1. See supra § 25.18.

Ch. 25   **PROBATE PETITION**   § 25.52

Name: _____ Citizenship [ ] U.S.A.
                                      (check one): [ ] Other _____
                                                              (specify)

Domicile or, if a financial institution, principal office: (specify)

_____
(Street Address)   (City/Town/Village)

_____
(County)   (State)   (Zip)   (Telephone   Number)

Mailing address: _____
(if different from domicile)

Interest of Petitioner (check one):

[ ] Nominated Executor   [ ] Proposed Administrator c.t.a.

[ ] Other (specify) _____

The proposed Executor/Administrator c.t.a. [ ] is [ ] is not an attorney. [If an attorney, submit statement pursuant to Uniform Rule 207.19(g); see also, Uniform Rule 207.60 (Accounting of attorney-fiduciary).]

2. The name, domicile, date and place of death, and citizenship of the decedent are as follows: [The Death Certificate must be filed with this proceeding. If the decedent's domicile is different from that shown on the death certificate, check box [ ] and attach an affidavit explaining the reason for this inconsistency.]

Name: _____
        (Name must be the same as the signature on the will)
a/k/a (if required)_____
Domicile: _____
        (Street Address)   (City/Village/Town)

_____
        (State)   (Zip Code)

Township of:_____ County of:_____
Date of Death:_____ Place of Death:_____

Citizenship (check one):   [ ] U.S.A.
                           [ ] Other (specify)_____

3. (a) To the best of the knowledge of the undersigned, the estimated gross value of the decedent's testamentary estate is greater than $_____ but less than $_____, consisting of the following:

Personal property $_____ Improved real property in New York State $_____ Unimproved real property in New York State $_____ Estimated gross rents for a period of 18 months $_____

§ 25.52   PROBATE & ESTATE ADMINISTRATION   Ch. 25

3. (b) No other testamentary assets exist in New York State, nor does any cause of action exist on behalf of the estate, except as follows: [Enter "NONE", or specify] _____

4. (a) The Last Will, herewith presented, relates to both real and personal property and consists of an instrument or instruments dated as shown below and signed at the end by the decedent and the subscribing witnesses as indicated below:

(Date of Will)	(List all Witnesses to Will)
(Date of Codicil)	(List all Witnesses to Codicil)
(Date of Codicil)	(List all Witnesses to Codicil)

4. (b) The Last Will, herewith presented: [Check applicable statement(s)]

[ ] does not affect any inter vivos trust or any other testamentary substitute;
[ ] revokes or modifies an inter vivos trust or any other testamentary substitute; [Refer to Paragraph 7]
[ ] distributes assets to an inter vivos trust. [Refer to Paragraph 8]

[SUBMIT COPY OF TRUST INSTRUMENT]

5. No other will or codicil of the decedent is on file in the Surrogate's Court, and upon information and belief, after a diligent search and inquiry, including a search of any safe deposit box, there exists no will, codicil or other testamentary instrument of the decedent later in date to any of the instruments mentioned in paragraph 4(a), except as follows: [Enter "NONE" or LIST EACH PRIOR INSTRUMENT WITH ITS DATE]

6. The decedent was survived by distributees classified as follows: [Information is required only as to those classes of surviving relatives who would take the property of decedent pursuant to EPTL 4–1.1 and 4–1.2. State "number" of survivors in each class. Insert "No." in all prior classes. Insert "X" in all subsequent classes].

a. [ ] Spouse (husband/wife). (If the decedent was divorced, see Uniform Rule 207.50 (22 NYCRR)).

b. [ ] Child or children and/or issue of predeceased child or children. (Must include marital, nonmarital, and adopted)

c. [ ] Any issue of the decedent adopted by persons related to the decedent (DRL Section 117).

d. [ ] Mother/Father.

e. [ ] Sisters and/or brothers, either of whole or half blood, and issue of predeceased sisters and/or brothers (nieces/nephews, etc.).

Ch. 25   PROBATE PETITION   § 25.52

Name: _____ Citizenship [ ] U.S.A.
                                       (check one): [ ] Other _____
                                                                          (specify)

Domicile or, if a financial institution, principal office: (specify)
_____

(Street Address)   (City/Town/Village)

_____

(County)   (State)   (Zip)   (Telephone   Number)

     Mailing address: _____
     (if different from domicile)

Interest of Petitioner (check one):

     [ ] Nominated Executor   [ ] Proposed Administrator c.t.a.

     [ ] Other (specify) _____

     The proposed Executor/Administrator c.t.a. [ ] is [ ] is not an attorney. [If an attorney, submit statement pursuant to Uniform Rule 207.19(g); see also, Uniform Rule 207.60 (Accounting of attorney-fiduciary).]

     2. The name, domicile, date and place of death, and citizenship of the decedent are as follows: [The Death Certificate must be filed with this proceeding. If the decedent's domicile is different from that shown on the death certificate, check box [ ] and attach an affidavit explaining the reason for this inconsistency.]

Name: _____
          (Name must be the same as the signature on the will)
a/k/a (if required)_____
Domicile: _____
           (Street Address)   (City/Village/Town)

_____
               (State)   (Zip Code)

Township of:_____ County of:_____
Date of Death:_____ Place of Death:_____

Citizenship (check one):   [ ] U.S.A.
                             [ ] Other (specify)_____

     3. (a) To the best of the knowledge of the undersigned, the estimated gross value of the decedent's testamentary estate is greater than $_____ but less than $_____, consisting of the following:

     Personal property $_____ Improved real property in New York State $_____ Unimproved real property in New York State $_____ Estimated gross rents for a period of 18 months $_____

3. (b) No other testamentary assets exist in New York State, nor does any cause of action exist on behalf of the estate, except as follows: [Enter "NONE", or specify] _____.

4. (a) The Last Will, herewith presented, relates to both real and personal property and consists of an instrument or instruments dated as shown below and signed at the end by the decedent and the subscribing witnesses as indicated below:

(Date of Will)	(List all Witnesses to Will)
(Date of Codicil)	(List all Witnesses to Codicil)
(Date of Codicil)	(List all Witnesses to Codicil)

4. (b) The Last Will, herewith presented: [Check applicable statement(s)]

[ ] does not affect any inter vivos trust or any other testamentary substitute;
[ ] revokes or modifies an inter vivos trust or any other testamentary substitute; [Refer to Paragraph 7]
[ ] distributes assets to an inter vivos trust. [Refer to Paragraph 8]

[SUBMIT COPY OF TRUST INSTRUMENT]

5. No other will or codicil of the decedent is on file in the Surrogate's Court, and upon information and belief, after a diligent search and inquiry, including a search of any safe deposit box, there exists no will, codicil or other testamentary instrument of the decedent later in date to any of the instruments mentioned in paragraph 4(a), except as follows: [Enter "NONE" or LIST EACH PRIOR INSTRUMENT WITH ITS DATE]

6. The decedent was survived by distributees classified as follows: [Information is required only as to those classes of surviving relatives who would take the property of decedent pursuant to EPTL 4–1.1 and 4–1.2. State "number" of survivors in each class. Insert "No." in all prior classes. Insert "X" in all subsequent classes].

a. [ ] Spouse (husband/wife). (If the decedent was divorced, see Uniform Rule 207.50 (22 NYCRR)).

b. [ ] Child or children and/or issue of predeceased child or children. (Must include marital, nonmarital, and adopted)

c. [ ] Any issue of the decedent adopted by persons related to the decedent (DRL Section 117).

d. [ ] Mother/Father.

e. [ ] Sisters and/or brothers, either of whole or half blood, and issue of predeceased sisters and/or brothers (nieces/nephews, etc.).

f. [ ] Grandmothers/Grandfathers. [Include maternal and paternal]

g. [ ] Aunts and/or uncles, and children of predeceased aunts and/or uncles (first cousins). [Include maternal and paternal]

h. [ ] First cousins once removed (children of predeceased first cousins). [Include maternal and paternal]

[Note: If there is only one distributee or where distributees are of a more remote relationship than issue of brothers and sisters, proof must be submitted pursuant to Uniform Rule 207.19(c) [22 NYCRR]].

7. Set forth in subparagraphs (a) and (b) below are the names, relationships, domicile and addresses of: (a) all distributees indicated in paragraph 6; (b) all persons designated as primary executors in the propounded will; (c) any person designated in the will as beneficiary, executor, trustee, or guardian whose rights or interests are adversely affected by any other instrument offered for probate that is later in date of execution or which amends or modifies an instrument offered for probate; (d) any person designated as beneficiary, executor, trustee, or guardian in any other will of the testator filed in this court whose rights or interests are adversely affected by the instrument offered for probate; and (e) [if the propounded will purports to exercise a power of appointment] all persons named in any instrument creating a power of appointment who are adversely affected by the instrument offered for probate. [See instructions, item 6]

[ ] The propounded will purports to revoke or modify an inter vivos trust or any other testamentary substitute, and the names, relationships, domicile and addresses of the trustee and beneficiaries affected by the will are set forth in subparagraphs (a) and (b) below. [Check if applicable and attach trust agreement]

[Note: Show clearly how each person is related to decedent. If relationship is through an ancestor who is deceased, give name, date of death, and relationship of the ancestor to the decedent. Use additional sheets if space in paragraph 7 is not sufficient. See Uniform Rules 207.16(b) [22 NYCRR]. If any person listed in paragraph 7 is a nonmarital child of a male ancestor, or descended from a nonmarital person, attach a copy of the order of filiation or Schedule A. If any person listed in paragraph 7 was adopted by any persons related by blood or marriage to decedent or descended from such persons, attach Schedule B. If the will revokes or modifies an inter vivos trust or any other testamentary substitute, check the above box and complete the information below.]

(a) The following are of full age and under no disability, or are corporations or associations: (If nonmarital or adopted-out person, so indicate and attach Schedule A and/or B]

Name and Relationship	Domicile and Mailing Address	Description of Legacy; Other Interest; Nature of Fiduciary Status

§ 25.52   PROBATE & ESTATE ADMINISTRATION   Ch. 25

(b) The following are infants and/or persons under disability: [Attach applicable Schedule A, B, C and/or D]

Name and Relationship	Domicile and Mailing Address	Description of Interest

8. Other than those named in paragraph 7, the names, domiciliary and mailing addresses and interests of all substitute or successor executors and of all trustees, guardians, legatees and devisees, and other beneficiaries named in the propounded Will, and/or trustees and beneficiaries of any inter vivos trust designated in the propounded will are as follows:

(a) The following are of full age and under no disability, or are corporations or associations:

Name and Relationship	Domicile and Mailing Address	Description of Legacy; Other Interest; Nature of Fiduciary Status

(b) The following are infants and/or persons under disability: [Attach applicable Schedule A, B, C and/or D]

Name	Domicile and Mailing Address	Description of Interest

(c) (If decedent is survived by a spouse and parent(s), but no issue, and there is a claim for wrongful death, check here [ ] and furnish name(s) and address(es) of parent(s) below. See EPTL 5–4.4.]

Name	Domicile and Mailing Address	Relationship

(d) No beneficiary named in paragraph(s) 7 or 8 is subject to the Putnam Rule (257 N.Y. 140), except: [Enter "NONE" or specify and attach affidavit for each]

9. No persons, corporations or associations are interested in this proceeding other than those mentioned above.

10. Upon information and belief, no other petition for the probate of any will of the decedent or for letters of administration or affidavit of voluntary administration of the decedent's estate has heretofore been filed in any court, except: [Enter "NONE", or specify]

WHEREFORE, your petitioner(s) pray(s) (a) that process be issued to all necessary parties to show cause why the Will and Codicil(s) set forth in paragraph 4 and presented herewith should not be admitted to probate; (b) that an order be granted directing the service of process, pursuant to the provisions of Article 3 of the SCPA, upon the persons named in paragraph 7 who are not domiciliary natural persons, or whose names or whereabouts are unknown and cannot be ascertained or who may be persons on whom service by personal delivery cannot be made; and (c) that such Will and Codicil(s) be admitted to probate as a Will of real and personal property and that letters issue thereon as follows: [Check and complete all relief requested]

    [ ] Letters Testamentary to _____
_____

    [ ] Letters of Trusteeship to _____ of the following trusts: _____
_____
_____

    [ ] Letters of Administration c.t.a. to _____
    [ ] Preliminary Letters to _____
_____

and that petitioner(s) "have such other relief as may be proper."

1. _____ 2. _____
   (Signature of Petitioner)   (Signature of Petitioner)

   _____   _____
       (Print Name)   (Print Name)

3. _____
   (Name of Corporate Petitioner)
   _____ (Signature of officer)

COMBINED VERIFICATION, OATH AND DESIGNATION

[For use when petitioner is an individual]

STATE OF NEW YORK)
) ss.:
COUNTY OF   )

The undersigned, the petitioner(s) named in the foregoing petition, being duly sworn, say(s):

1. VERIFICATION: (I)(We) have read the foregoing petition subscribed by (me)(us) and know the contents thereof, and the same is true of (my)(our) own knowledge, except as to the matters therein stated to be alleged upon information and belief, and as to those matters (I)(we) believe it to be true.

2. OATH OF [ ] EXECUTOR(S) [ ] ADMINISTRATOR(S) c.t.a. [ ] TRUSTEE(S) PRELIMINARY EXECUTOR(S) as indicated above: (I am) (We are) over eighteen (18) years of age and (a) citizen(s) of the United States and (I)(we) will well, faithfully and honestly discharge the duties

of Fiduciary of the goods, chattels and credits of said decedent according to law. (I am) (We are) not ineligible to receive letters and will duly account for all moneys and other property that will come into (my) (our) hands.

3. DESIGNATION OF CLERK FOR SERVICE OF PROCESS: (I)(We) hereby designate the Clerk of the Surrogate's Court of _____ County, and his/her successor in office, as a person on whom service of any process, issuing from such Court may be made in like manner and with like effect as if it were served personally upon (me)(us), whenever (I)(we) cannot be found and served within the State of New York after due diligence used.

My domicile is: _____
                (Street Address) (City Town Village) (State) (Zip)

My domicile is: _____
                (Street Address) (City Town Village) (State) (Zip)

_____   _____
(Signature of Petitioner)   (Signature of Petitioner)

_____   _____
(Print Name)   (Print Name)

On _____, 19__, before me personally came _____ to me known to be the person(s) described in and who executed the foregoing instrument. Such person(s) duly swore to such instrument before me and duly acknowledged that he/she/they executed the same.

_____

Notary Public
Commission Expires:
(Affix Notary Stamp or Seal)

Name of Attorney: _____ Tel. No.: _____
Address of Attorney: _____

COMBINED VERIFICATION, CONSENT AND DESIGNATION
[For use when a petitioner to be appointed is a bank or trust company]
STATE OF NEW YORK   )
) ss.:
COUNTY OF   )

I, _____ the undersigned, a _____ of
                                                 (Title)

_____
(Name of Bank or Trust company)

being duly sworn, say:

1. VERIFICATION: I have read the foregoing petition subscribed by me and know the contents thereof, and the same is true of my own

knowledge, except as to the matters therein stated to be alleged upon information and belief, and as to those matters I believe it to be true.

2. CONSENT: The above named designated fiduciary, a corporation/national banking association under the laws of _____ hereby accepts its appointment as [ ] Executor [ ] Administrator c.t.a. Trustee [ ] Preliminary Executor of the Will described in the foregoing petition and consents to act as such fiduciary.

3. DESIGNATION: The above named designated fiduciary, having an office at _____ hereby designates the Clerk of the Surrogate's Court of _____ County, and his/her successor in office, as a person on whom service of any process issuing from such Court may be made, whenever one of its proper officers cannot be found and served within the State of New York after due diligence used.

_____   _____
(Name of Bank or Trust Company)   (Name of Bank or Trust Company)
BY _____   _____
         (Signature)   (Signature)

_____   _____
(Print Name and Title)   (Print Name and Title)

On _____, 19__, before me personally came _____ to me known, who duly swore to the foregoing instrument and who did say that he/she resides at _____ and that he/she is a _____ of _____ the corporation/national banking association described in and which executed such instrument, and that he/she signed his/her name thereto by order of the Board of Directors of the corporation.

Notary Public

Commission Expires:

Name of Attorney:_____Tel. No._____

Address of Attorney:_____

§ 25.53 Forms—Affidavit Proving Correct Copy of Will 🗄

SURROGATE'S COURT OF THE STATE OF NEW YORK
COUNTY OF

_____X

PROBATE PROCEEDING,

Will of

AFFIDAVIT OF COMPARISON
(Note: Attach a copy of the Will/Codicil to this Affidavit of Comparison executed by any two persons; if a photocopy of the will is used, only one person need make the affidavit.)

§ 25.53   PROBATE & ESTATE ADMINISTRATION   Ch. 25

                                          File No. _____
Deceased.
_____X

STATE OF NEW YORK   )
) ss.:
COUNTY OF   )

   I/We _____ (and) _____
being duly sworn, say, that he/she has carefully compared the copy of decedent's Will/Codicil propounded herein to which this affidavit is annexed with the original Will dated the _____ day of _____, 19__ (and the original Codicil dated the _____ day of _____, 19__ about to be filed for probate, and that the same is in all respects a true and correct copy of said original Will/Codicil and of the whole thereof.

                              _____
                                      Signature

                              _____
                                      Print Name

Sworn to before me this _____
day of _____, 19__

_____
Signature
Notary Public

§ 25.54   Forms—Citation in Probate[1]

                                          P-11
                                          (4/95)
                                          File No._____
SURROGATE'S COURT—
COUNTY

CITATION

THE PEOPLE OF THE STATE OF NEW YORK,
By the Grace of God Free and Independent

TO

   A petition having been duly filed by _____, who is domiciled at
_____

YOU ARE HEREBY CITED TO SHOW CAUSE before the Surrogate's Court, _____ county, at _____, New York, on _____ 19__, at __

§ 25.54
1. See supra 25.19.

604

o'clock in the ___ noon of that day, why a decree should not be made in the Estate of _____ lately domiciled at _____ admitting to probate a Will dated _____ (a Codicil dated _____)(a Codicil dated _____), a copy of which is attached, as the Will of _____ deceased, relating to real and personal property, and directing that

    [ ] Letters Testamentary issue to: _____

    [ ] Letters of Trusteeship issue to: _____

    [ ] Letters of Administration c.t.a. issue to _____

             (State any further relief requested)

Dated, Attested and Sealed,

_____, 19__

                  HON. _____
                                   SURROGATE

(Seal)

_____   _____
                                 Chief Clerk

Attorney for Petitioner   Telephone Number

_____

Address of Attorney

(Note: This citation is served upon you as required by law. Your are not required to appear. If your fail to appear it will be assumed you do not object to the relief requested. You have a right to have an attorney appear for you.)

§ 25.55 Forms—Affidavit of Service of Citation

P–15
(4/95)

SURROGATE'S COURT OF THE STATE OF NEW YORK
COUNTY OF

_____X

PROBATE PROCEEDING,

                                   Note: File Proof of Service at least 2 days before return date. State clearly date, time and place of service and name of Estate and of person served.
                                   (Uniform Rule 207.7(c))
                                   (22 NYCRR)

a/k/a   AFFIDAVIT OF SERVICE OF CITATION

Deceased.

_____X   File No. _____

§ 25.55 PROBATE & ESTATE ADMINISTRATION Ch. 25

STATE OF NEW YORK)
) ss.:
COUNTY OF   )

_____ of _____ being duly sworn, says that I am over the age of eighteen years; that I made personal service of the citation herein dated _____, 19__, and a copy of thee Will/Codicil on each person named below, each of whom deponent knew to be the person mentioned and described in said citation, by delivering to and leaving-with each of them personally a true copy Of said Citation and Will/Codicil, as follows:

_____, description: sex _____, color of skin _____, color of hair _____, approximate age _____, weight _____ height _____, at _____ o'clock _____.m. on the _____ day of _____, 19__ at _____,

_____ description: sex _____, color of skin _____, color of hair _____, approximate age _____, weight _____ height _____, at _____ o'clock _____.m. on the __ day of _____, 19__, at _____,

_____ description: sex _____, color of skin _____, color of hair _____, approximate age _____, weight _____ height _____, at _____ o'clock _____.m. on the __ day of _____, 19__, at _____

That none of the aforesaid persons is in the military service as defined by the Act of Congress known as the "Soldiers' and Sailors' Civil Relief Act of 1940" and in the New York "Soldiers' and Sailors' Civil Relief Act."

                                               Signature

Sworn to before me this _____
day of _____, 19__
_____

Print Name
Notary Public
Commission Expires:
(Affix Notary Stamp or Seal)

Name of Attorney: _____

Tel. No.: _____

Address of Attorney: _____

§ 25.56 Forms—Affidavit of Mailing Notice of Application for Letters of Administration

Form A-4

SURROGATE'S COURT OF THE STATE OF NEW YORK
COUNTY OF

_____X
ADMINISTRATION PROCEEDING   AFFIDAVIT OF MAILING
Estate of   NOTICE OF APPLICATION
                                   FOR LETTERS OF ADMINIS-
                                   TRATION
a/k/a   (SPCA 1005)
                    Deceased.   File No. _____
_____X

STATE OF NEW YORK
                         ss.:
COUNTY OF

_____, residing at _____, New York, being duly sworn, deposes and says that deponent is over the age of eighteen years; that on _____, 19__, deponent mailed a copy of the foregoing Notice of Application for Letters of Administration, contained in a securely closed postpaid wrapper, directed to each of the persons named in paragraph 4(b), respectively, as follows:

whose post office address is _____
whose post office address is _____
whose post office address is _____
whose post office address is _____
whose post office address is _____
whose post office address is _____
whose post office address is _____
whose post office address is _____

by depositing the document in a letter box or other official depository under the exclusive care and custody of the United States Post Office, located at: _____

_____
Signature

Sworn to before me this
_____ day of
_____, 19__

Notary Public
Commission Expires:
(Affix Stamp or Seal)

§ 25.57 Forms—Waiver and Consent

P-9
(4/95)
SURROGATE'S COURT OF THE STATE OF NEW YORK
COUNTY OF
_____X
PROBATE PROCEEDING,
Will of

a/k/a

Deceased.
_____X

WAIVER OF PROCESS;
CONSENT TO PROBATE

File No._____

To the Surrogate's Court, County of

The undersigned, being of full age and sound mind, residing at the address written below and interested in this proceeding as set forth in paragraph 7a of the petition, hereby waives the issuance and service of citation in this matter and consents that the court admit to probate the decedent's Last Will and Testament dated _____, 19__ (and codicils, if any, dated), a copy of each of which testamentary instrument has been received by me, and that

[ ] Letters Testamentary issue to _____

[ ] Letters of Trusteeship issue to _____ of the following trusts:

_____
_____

_____   _____
Date   Signature
Relationship

_____   _____
Print Name   Street Address Town/State/Zip

STATE OF NEW YORK
                                          ss.:
COUNTY OF

On _____, 19__, before me personally appeared _____ to me known and known to me to be the person described in and who executed the foregoing waiver and consent and duly acknowledged the execution thereof.

Ch. 25 NOTICE OF PROBATE § 25.58

Notary Public
Commission Expires:
(Affix Notary Stamp or Seal)

Name of Attorney: _____

Tel. No.: _____

Address of Attorney: _____

§ 25.58 Forms—Notice of Probate

P-13
(4/95)
SURROGATE'S COURT OF THE STATE OF NEW YORK
COUNTY OF
_____ X
PROBATE PROCEEDING,

ESTATE of   NOTICE OF PROBATE

                                                    (SCPA 1409)
a/k/a
Deceased.   File No. _____
_____ X

Notice is hereby given that:

1. The Will dated _____ (and Codicil dated _____) (and Codicil dated _____) of the above named decedent, domiciled at _____ County of _____, New York, has been/will be offered for probate in the Surrogate's Court for the County of _____.

2. The name(s) of proponent(s) of said Will is/are _____ whose address(es) is/are _____
_____
_____

3. The name and post office address of each person named or referred to in the petition who has not been served or has not appeared, or waived service of process, with a statement whether such person is named or referred to in the will as legatee, devisee, trustee, guardian or substitute or successor executor, trustee or guardian, and as to any such person who is an infant or an incompetent, the name and post office address of a person upon whom personal service of process may be made on behalf of such infant or incompetent is as follows:

NAME   MAILING ADDRESS   NATURE OF INTEREST OR STATUS
                                 (USE ADDITIONAL SHEETS IF NECESSARY)

§ 25.58 PROBATE & ESTATE ADMINISTRATION Ch. 25

Date _____, 19___

[Note: complete Affidavit of Mailing. If serving infant 14 years of age or older, list and mail to infant as well as parent or guardian.

Name of Attorney: _____

Tel. No.: _____

Address of Attorney: _____

AFFIDAVIT OF MAILING NOTICE OF PROBATE

STATE OF NEW YORK   )
) ss.:
COUNTY OF   )

_____ residing at _____ being duly sworn, says that he/she is over the age of 18 years, that on the _____ day of _____, 19__, he/she deposited in the post office or in a post office box regularly maintained by the government of the United States in the _____ of _____, State of New York, a copy of the foregoing Notice of Probate Contained in a securely closed postpaid wrapper directed to each of the persons named in said notice at the places set opposite their respective names.

_____
Signature
Print Name

Sworn to before me this _____
day of _____, 19__

_____
Notary Public
Commission Expires:
(Affix Notary Stamp or Seal)
Name of Attorney: _____
Tel. No.: _____
Address of Attorney: _____

§ 25.59 Forms—Deposition Affidavit of Subscribing Witness 💾

P-8
(4/95)
SURROGATE'S COURT OF THE STATE OF NEW YORK
COUNTY OF
_____X

PROBATE PROCEEDING,   AFFIDAVIT OF ATTESTING
                                  WITNESS
Will of   (After Death)

Ch. 25   DEPOSITION OF SUBSCRIBING WITNESS   § 25.59

Pursuant to SCPA 1406
a/k/a
Deceased.   File No. _____
_____X

STATE OF NEW YORK   )
) ss.:
COUNTY OF   )

     The undersigned witness being duly sworn, deposes and says:

(1) I have been shown [check one]

( ) the original instrument dated _____,

( ) a court-certified photographic reproduction of the original instrument dated _____, purporting to be the last Will and Testament/Codicil of the above-named decedent.

(2) On the date indicated in such instrument, I saw the decedent subscribe the same at the place where decedent's signature appears, and I heard the decedent declare such instrument to be his/her last Will and Testament/Codicil.

(3) I thereafter signed my name to such instrument as a witness thereto at the request of the decedent and in the presence of the decedent, and I saw the other witness(es) _____ _____ sign his/her/their name(s) at the end of such instrument as a witness thereto.

(4) At the time the decedent subscribed and executed such instrument the—decedent was to the best of my knowledge. and belief upwards of 18 years of age, and in all respects appeared to be of sound and disposing mind, memory and understanding, Competent to make a Will, and not under any restraint.

(5) The decedent could read, write and converse in the English language, and was not suffering from defects of sight, hearing or speech, or any other physical or mental impairment, that would affect his/her capacity to make a valid Will. The purported instrument was the only copy of said Will/Codicil executed on that occasion, and was not executed in counterparts.

(6) I am making this affidavit at the request of_____.

_____ (Witness Signature)

_____ (Print Name)

_____ (Street Address)

Sworn to before me this
_____ day of
_____, 19__

(Town/State/Zip)

Notary Public
Commission Expires:
(Affix Notary Stamp or Seal)

(Note: Each witness must be shown either the original Will or a Court certified Reproduction thereof. The Notary Public subscribing to this affidavit may not be a party or witness to the will.)

§ 25.60 Forms—Objections to Probate

SURROGATE'S COURT OF THE STATE OF NEW YORK
COUNTY OF _____
-----------------------------------x
In the Matter of the Probate of   A JURY TRIAL IS DEMANDED
the Last Will and Testament of   File No.

_____,   OBJECTIONS
                                      TO PROBATE
         Deceased.
-----------------------------------x

Respondents _____ and _____ object to the probate of the written instrument dated _____, purporting to be the Last Will and Testament of the above-named decedent and offered for probate herein, and allege, upon information and belief, as follows:

1. Respondents, respectively the _____ and _____ of the above-named decedent, are interested in the estate as the sole heirs at law of the decedent, and who will benefit by the rejection of the purported Last Will and Testament of _____, the above-named decedent.

2. The alleged Will dated _____ was not duly executed by _____, deceased, in that he did not sign the same at the end thereof, nor was such signature affixed by the said decedent in the presence of each of the attesting witnesses nor published the same as his Will in the presence of the witnesses whose names are subscribed thereto, that he did not request the said witnesses to be witnesses thereto, that the said alleged witnesses did not sign as witnesses in his presence or in the presence of each other.

3. On _____, the said decedent, _____, did not know the nature, extent or value of his assets, and was not of sound mind or memory and was not mentally competent to make a Will.

4. The purported Will was not freely or voluntarily made or executed by the said _____, as his Last Will and Testament, but that the said paper writing purporting to be his Will was obtained and the subscription and publication thereof, if in fact subscribed and published by him, was procured by fraud and undue influence, by over-reaching and by the violation of a confidential relationship, all practiced upon the decedent

by one _____, the principal legatee and devisee named in said paper, or by some other persons acting in concert or privity with _____, whose name or names are at the present time unknown to the respondents.

PLEASE TAKE NOTICE, that the respondents demand that the issues of fact raised in this proceeding be tried by a jury in this Court.

WHEREFORE, respondents _____ and _____ pray that this proceeding be dismissed, and that this Court grant respondents such other and further relief as it deems just and proper, including the costs and disbursements of this proceeding.

_____, ESQ.
Attorney for Respondents
Office & P.O. Address
_____, NY
Tel.No.

VERIFICATIONS

STATE OF NEW YORK   )
) ss.:
COUNTY OF   )

_____, being duly sworn, deposes and says:

I am an objectant/respondent in the within proceeding; I have read the foregoing objections and know the contents thereof; the same is true to my own knowledge, except as to those matters herein stated to be alleged upon information and belief, and as to those matters I believe it to be true.

Sworn to before me this
_____ day of _____, 199__

Notary Public

STATE OF NEW YORK   )
) ss.:
COUNTY OF   )

_____, being duly sworn, deposes and says:

I am an objectant/respondent in the within proceeding; I have read the foregoing objections and know the contents thereof; the same is true to my own knowledge, except as to those matters herein stated to be

§ 25.60   PROBATE & ESTATE ADMINISTRATION   Ch. 25

alleged upon information and belief, and as to those matters I believe it to be true.

_____

Sworn to before me this
_____ day of _____, 199_

_____
Notary Public

§ 25.61   Forms—Decree Granting Probate 💾

At a Surrogate's Court held in and for the County of _____, at the Surrogate's Office, in the City of _____, on the _____ day of _____, 19_.

Present: Hon. _____,
SURROGATE
_____

Probate Proceedings, Will of _____)
)   DECREE GRANTING
)   PROBATE
           Deceased.   )   File No. _____
)
_____)

SATISFACTORY PROOF having been jurisdiction has been obtained of all the necessary parties and that the necessary notice has been given; AND the witnesses to said last Will bearing date

having been sworn and examined, their examination having been reduced to writing and filed, or their affidavits having been filed, and it appearing by such proof that said Will was duly executed, and that the Testator, at the time of executing it, was in all respects competent to make a Will, and not under restraint; and the Court being satisfied of the genuineness of said Will of _____, and the validity of its execution:

IT IS ORDERED, ADJUDGED AND DECREED, that the instrument offered for probate herein be, and the same is hereby admitted to probate as the Last Will and Testament of said _____ deceased, valid to pass real and personal property, that the said Will and this decree be recorded, and that Letters Testamentary be issued to the executor who may qualify thereunder.

_____
Surrogate

§ 25.62 Forms—Receipt and Release Agreement Concluding an Estate Without an Accounting Proceeding

SURROGATE'S COURT—STATE OF NEW YORK
COUNTY OF _____X
In the Matter of the Settlement of the
Final Account of Proceedings of _____
_____ and _____ _____, as   File No.
Executors under the Last Will and
Testament of   RECEIPT AND RELEASE
                                              AGREEMENT
_____ _____,

                    Deceased.
_____X

WHEREAS the testator, _____, died on _____, a resident of _____, in the _____, and State of New York, leaving a will dated _____, which was duly admitted to probate and Letters Testamentary thereon were issued to _____ _____ and _____ by the Surrogate's Court of said County on _____; and

WHEREAS, said _____ and _____, as such Executors, have duly administered the estate of the testator; have paid his debts, his funeral expenses, the expenses of administering said estate, the cash bequests provided for in Article of said will and the Foreign, Federal and New York State estate taxes due from said estate; have distributed the tangible personal and real property interest owned by the testator in _____, New York, in accordance with the provisions of Article _____ of said will; and, said Executors now desire to make final distribution of the assets comprised in said estate; and

WHEREAS Article Fifth of said will provides in relevant part as follows:

FIFTH: All the rest, residue and remainder of my property of whatever kind and wherever situated (herein referred to as "my residuary estate"), I give, devise and bequeath as follows:

(1) To my secretary, _____, if she shall survive me, one fourth (25%) of my residuary estate.

(2) The balance I give, devise and bequeath in three equal shares: one share to my brother, _____ and his wife _____, as tenants by the entirety, one share to my sister, _____ and one share to my friend, _____, provided they survive me. If my brother _____ and my sister-in-law _____ should predecease me, then the share they would have received, if living shall be transferred and paid over to their children surviving me in equal parts per stirpes. If my friend _____ should predecease me, I direct that _____'s

mother and father jointly or their heirs be given the sum of $100,000.00.

and

WHEREAS the testator was survived by his said secretary, _____, his said sister, _____, his said sister-in-law, _____ and his friend _____, all of whom are adults and under no disability; and

WHEREAS, in order to avoid the expense and delay of a judicial accounting, the undersigned have requested said Executors to settle their account of proceedings by means of this Receipt and Release Agreement instead of by formal judicial settlement thereof; and

WHEREAS an account of proceedings of said Executors covering the period from _____, to and including _____, has been prepared, which is annexed hereto and made a part hereof;

NOW, THEREFORE, the undersigned, _____, individually, _____, _____ _____ and _____, do hereby represent that they have not assigned, encumbered or otherwise disposed of their respective interests in said estate or any part thereof; and the undersigned, _____, individually and as Co-Executor under said will, _____, _____ _____ and _____, do hereby certify that they have each been represented by counsel and that they have each examined said account of proceedings of said Executors with counsel, and that the same is true, accurate and correct in all respects and is approved and accepted by each of them as an account stated, final and conclusive as regards all the assets comprised in the estate of said _____ _____, deceased, and as regards all the acts, proceedings, and transactions of said Executors in the administration and distribution thereof to the closing date of said account and do further waive judicial settlement of said account of proceedings; and the undersigned do hereby approve the payment of the commissions of said Executors in the sum of $___,___.00 to _____ and $___, ___.00 to _____, of which $_____ was previously paid to each executor on account pursuant to an order entered in the Surrogate's Court of the County of _____ dated _____, as set forth in Schedules _____ of said account, and the payment of attorneys' fees and disbursements to the law firm of _____, _____, _____ & _____, Esqs., together with such additional fees and disbursements as may be incurred prior to the settlement of said account, all as set forth in said Schedules _____; and the undersigned _____, _____, _____ and _____, do hereby acknowledge receipt of all property comprised in the residuary estate to which said beneficiaries are now entitled, as set forth in Schedules _____, of said account of proceedings, after payment therefrom of said commissions, attorneys' fees and disbursements, in full payment and satisfaction of any and all assets due or that may be due said beneficiaries from the Estate.

IN CONSIDERATION of the premises and of the receipt of said property by the undersigned, and the mutual agreement to waive judicial settlement of said account of proceedings, the undersigned do by these presents, for themselves and their respective executors, administrators, distributees, successors and assigns, release and forever discharge said _____ and _____ individually and as such Executors, from any and all liability, responsibility or accountability with respect to the administration of said estate, with respect to their acts and transactions and their omissions, if any, as said Executors, and with respect to the assets due the undersigned, as set forth in the annexed Account and as covers the period _____ through _____; and the undersigned do further agree, to the extent of their respective interests, to indemnify, exonerate and hold harmless said Executors, individually and as such Executors, their executors, administrators, distributees, successors and assigns, from and against any and all taxes, expenses, liabilities, claims or demands which said Executors may at any time have incurred or which at any time may be asserted by anyone against them in consequence of their administration of said estate, during the period _____ through _____, together with the expenses (including attorneys' fees) of any litigation, settlement or other proceedings, judicial or otherwise, that may be incidental to determining or avoiding liability for any such taxes or claims.

THIS INSTRUMENT may be executed in one or more counterparts, but all such counterparts shall together constitute but one and the same instrument.

IN WITNESS WHEREOF, the undersigned have hereunto set their respective hands and seals this day of _____, 19__.

_____

_____

_____

_____

ACKNOWLEDGMENT

STATE OF NEW YORK)
) ss:
COUNTY OF)

On the day of _____ before me personally appeared _____, known to me to be the person described in and who signed the above instrument and who duly acknowledged to me that _____ executed the same.

_____
Notary Public

§ 25.63 Forms—Receipt and Release (Legacy)

SURROGATE'S COURT STATE OF NEW YORK
COUNTY OF

---------------------------------------x
In the Matter of the Judicial   File No.
Settlement of the Account of
_____ _____ and _____ _____,
as Executors under the
Last Will and Testament of   RECEIPT & RELEASE
                                                   (Legacy)

_____ _____,

                         Deceased.
---------------------------------------x

     I, _____ do hereby acknowledge that I have received from _____ _____ and _____, as Executors under the Last Will and Testament of _____, deceased, the sum of _____ Dollars ($_____), in cash, in full payment of the legacy bequeathed to me by Clause _____ of said Will.

     Full payment and satisfaction of said legacy is hereby acknowledged and I do, for myself, my heirs, executors, administrators and assigns, remise, release and forever discharge said _____ and _____, individually and as Executors as aforesaid, of and from any and all claims and demands which I may now have or hereafter may have against said Executor, in respect of said legacy and I do further declare that I have not heretofore prior to the receipt thereof assigned, conveyed or otherwise in any way alienated or encumbered my interest in said legacy.

     In consideration of the receipt thereof prior to the settlement, judicial or otherwise, of the account of the Executors, I do for myself, my heirs, executors, administrators and assigns, hereby agree that if the Executors or their successors and assigns, shall hereafter be required to pay or defend any claim or obligation of any kind, including, without limitation, debts of _____ or of his Estate or other taxes of any kind, which shall be properly chargeable in whole or in part against the foregoing sum transferred to me, then and in that event and to the extent of the portion of such claim or obligation so chargeable, I will reimburse the Executors or their successors and assigns, or the Estate, as the case might be.

     I do hereby waive the issue and service of a citation in the matter of the judicial settlement of any account of the Executors, or their successors and assigns, and consent that a decree may be judicially entered settling any such account without further notice to me.

Dated: _____, ___, 199__

Ch. 25 PETITION TO SETTLE ACCOUNT § 25.64

STATE OF NEW YORK)
) ss.:
COUNTY OF)

On the day of _____, before me personally came _____, to me known and known to me to be the individual described in and who executed the foregoing instrument and she duly acknowledged to me that she executed the same.

_____
Notary Public

§ 25.64 Forms—Petition to Judicially Settle Executor's Account

SURROGATE'S COURT OF THE STATE OF NEW YORK
COUNTY OF
_____x
Proceeding for the Judicial Settlement
of the Account of Proceedings of   File No. _____
_____ as the
Executor of the Last Will of   PETITION TO JUDICIALLY SETTLE
                                             EXECUTOR'S ACCOUNT
_____,

Deceased.
_____x

TO THE SURROGATE'S COURT, COUNTY OF _____:

The petition of _____, by her attorney _____, _____, alleges as follows:

1. Petitioner _____ resides and is domiciled at _____, New York.

2. _____, the decedent, died a resident and domiciliary of _____, County on _____, leaving a Last Will and Testament which was duly admitted to probate by the Surrogate's Court of the County of _____ on _____, a copy of said last will is annexed to the accompanying account as an exhibit thereto.

3. Letters Testamentary pursuant to said last will of the decedent, were granted by this Court to petitioner on the _____ day of _____, 19__ and the petitioner duly qualified and has thereafter acted and is still acting as executor under said last will.

4. More than _____ months have expired since said letters were issued to petitioner.

5. Following is set forth the names and addresses of all interested parties to this proceeding upon whom service of process is required or concerning whom this Court is required to have information:

____ ____ ____, a ____ ____ Street
of decedent, a one-half ____, New York
residuary beneficiary

____ ____ ____, a ____ of ____ Drive
decedent and the alternate ____, New York
executor

____ ____ ____, a ____ ____ Avenue
of the decedent, a beneficiary and al- ____, New York
ternate executor

6. There are no persons other than those mentioned interested in this application or proceeding. All of the persons herein before named are of full age and sound mind.

7. Petitioner is desirous of rendering to said Surrogate's Court an account of her proceedings.

8. The estate herein amounts to more than $____.

9. An estate tax of $____ was paid to the federal government and an estate tax of $____ was paid to the State of New York. Closing letters have been received from the IRS and from New York State, copies of which are annexed hereto. All fiduciary income tax returns have been timely filed and all taxes due thereon have been paid.

10. Petitioner retained the services of ____, Esq. to serve as attorney for the estate. Counsel has represented petitioner in various proceedings in this Court, has probated the decedent's last will and testament, assisted in the marshaling of estate assets, prepared a Federal Estate Tax Return (Form 706), as well as other fiduciary income tax returns. Counsel has prepared this account and will continue to represent petitioner in this proceeding through release and discharge. Counsel has estimated that his legal fees will be $____. Approval for the payment of these legal fees is now requested.

11. No previous application for the relief requested herein has been made to this Court, or to any court or judge.

WHEREFORE, petitioner ____ prays (i) that ____ account as execut__ be judicially settled, (ii) that legal fees of $____ be awarded to ____, Esq., (iii) that this Court direct upon whom and the manner in which notice of this application shall be given, and (iv) that this Court grant such other relief as it deems just and proper.

____, ESQ.
Attorney for Petitioner
Office & P.O. Address
____, NY
Tel.No.____

VERIFICATION

STATE OF NEW YORK)
) ss.:
COUNTY OF)

_____, being duly sworn, deposes and says:

I am the petitioner herein; I have read the foregoing Petition and know the contents thereof and the same are true to my own knowledge, except as to those matters therein stated to be alleged upon information and belief, and as to those matters, I believe them to be true.

_____

Sworn to before me this
___th day of _____, 19__

_____

NOTARY PUBLIC

§ 25.65 Forms—Citation to Executor to Show Cause Why Judicially Executor Should Not Account

File No. _____, 19__

CITATION

THE PEOPLE OF THE STATE OF NEW YORK,

BY THE GRACE OF GOD FREE AND INDEPENDENT,

To [*Insert names of parties required to be cited under SCPA § 2210*]

A petition having been duly filed by _____, who is domiciled at _____,

YOU ARE HEREBY CITED TO SHOW CAUSE before the Surrogate's Court, _____ County, at _____ in the County of _____ on _____, 19__, at ___[a.m.][p.m.], why a decree should not be made in the estate of _____ who died domiciled at _____, in the County of _____, judicially setting the account of said _____, as [Executor of the Last Will and Testament][Administrator of the Estate] of _____.

Dated, Attested and Sealed, _____, 19__

[L.S.]

Surrogate
Clerk

ATTORNEY

Name of attorney: _____ Tel. No. _____

Address of attorney: _____

This citation is served upon you as required by law. You are not obliged to appear in person. If you fail to appear it will be assumed that you do not object to the relief requested. You have a right to have an attorney-at-law appear for you.

§ 25.66 Forms—Accounting Form

SURROGATE'S COURT OF THE STATE OF NEW YORK
COUNTY OF _____

_____
   Accounting of _____
as [Executor][Administrator] of   File No. _____
the Estate of   19___
_____, Deceased.

_____

TO THE SURROGATE'S COURT OF THE COUNTY OF _____:

The undersigned does hereby render the account of proceedings as follows:

Period of account from _____ to _____.

This is [a final] [or an intermediate] account.

SCHEDULE 1
STATEMENT OF PRINCIPAL RECEIVED

INSTRUCTIONS. This schedule must contain an itemized statement of all the moneys and other personal property constituting principal for which each accounting party is charged, together with the date of receipt or acquisition of such money or property. If real property has been sold by the fiduciary, this schedule must set forth the proceeds of sale of such property.

SCHEDULE 1–1
STATEMENT OF INCREASES ON SALES, LIQUIDATION OR DISTRIBUTION

INSTRUCTIONS. This schedule must contain a full and complete statement of all realized increases derived from principal assets whether due to sale, liquidation or distribution or any other reason. It should also show realized increases on new investments or exchanges. In each instance, the date of realization of the increase must be shown and the property from which said increase was derived must be identified.

SCHEDULE 1–2
STATEMENT OF ALL INCOME COLLECTED

INSTRUCTIONS. This schedule must contain a full and complete statement of all interest, dividends, rents and other income received, and the date of each receipt. Each receipt must be separately accounted for and identified, except that where a security has been held for an entire year, the interest or ordinary dividends may be reported on a calendar year basis.

SCHEDULE 2
STATEMENT OF DECREASES DUE TO SALES, LIQUIDATION, COLLECTION, DISTRIBUTION OR UNCOLLECTIBILITY

INSTRUCTIONS. This schedule must contain a full and complete statement of all realized decreases on principal assets whether due to sale, liquidation, collection or distribution or any other reason. It should also show decreases on new investments or exchanges and also sales, liquidations or distributions that result in neither gain nor loss. In each instance, the date of realization of the decrease must be shown and the property from which said decrease was incurred must be identified. It should also report any asset which the fiduciary intends to abandon as worthless, together with a full statement of the reasons for abandoning it.

SCHEDULE 3
STATEMENT OF FUNERAL AND ADMINISTRATION EXPENSES

INSTRUCTIONS. This schedule must contain an itemized statement of all moneys chargeable and paid for funeral, administration and other necessary expenses, together with the date and the reason for each expenditure.

Where the will directs that all inheritance and death taxes are to be paid out of the estate, credit for payment of same should be taken in this schedule.

SCHEDULE 3–1
STATEMENT OF UNPAID ADMINISTRATION EXPENSES

INSTRUCTIONS. This schedule must contain an itemized statement of all unpaid claims for administration and other necessary expenses, together with a statement of the basis for each such claim.

SCHEDULE 4
STATEMENT OF ALL CREDITORS' CLAIMS

INSTRUCTIONS. This schedule must contain an itemized statement of all creditors' claims subdivided to show:

1. Claims presented, allowed, paid and credited and appearing in the Summary Statement, together with the date of payment.
2. Claims presented and allowed but not paid.
3. Claims presented but rejected, the date of and the reason for such rejection.
4. Contingent and possible claims.
5. Personal claims requiring approval by the court, pursuant to SCPA § 1805.

In the event of insolvency, preference allowed various claims should be stated and the order of their priority.

SCHEDULE 5
STATEMENT OF DISTRIBUTIONS MADE

INSTRUCTIONS. This schedule must contain an itemized statement of all moneys paid and all property delivered to the legatees, trustees, surviving spouse or distributees of the deceased, the date of payment of delivery thereof, and the name of the person to whom payment or delivery was actually made. Mention if distributions are in full or partial satisfaction.

Where estate taxes are required to be apportioned and payments have been made on account of said taxes, the amounts apportioned in Schedule H against beneficiaries of the testamentary estate shall be charged in this schedule against the respective individual's share.

SCHEDULE 5-1
STATEMENT OF UNDISTRIBUTED AND ACCRUED INCOME ON HAND _____, 19__, TO DATE OF DEATH OF _____

This schedule must show undistributed and accrued income due the estate of any deceased beneficiary to date of death during accounting period.

SCHEDULE 6
STATEMENT OF ALL PERSONAL PROPERTY REMAINING ON HAND

INSTRUCTIONS. This schedule must contain an itemized statement showing all personal property remaining on hand, including a statement of all uncollected receivables and property rights due to the estate. This schedule must show the assets at market and inventory values. If the accounting is a final one, the increases or decreases should be transferred to Schedules A–1 and B, respectively. The schedule must further show the date and cost of all such property that was acquired by purchase, exchange or transfers made or received, together with the date of acquisition and the cost thereof.

SCHEDULE 7
STATEMENT OF INTERESTED PARTIES

INSTRUCTIONS. This schedule must contain the names of all persons entitled as legatee, devisee, trustee, surviving spouse, distributee or otherwise to a share of the estate or fund, with their post office addresses and the degree of relationship, if any, of each to the deceased, a statement showing the nature of and the value or approximate value of the interest of each such person.

Also a statement that the records of the Surrogate's Court have been searched for powers of attorney and assignments and encumbrances made and executed by any of the persons interested in or entitled to a share of the estate and a list detailing each power of attorney, assignment and encumbrance, disclosed by such search, with the date of its recording and the name and address of each attorney in fact and of each assignee and of each person beneficially interested under the encumbrance referred to in the respective instruments, and also whether the accounting party has any knowledge of the execution of any such power of attorney or assignment not so filed and recorded.

SCHEDULE 8
STATEMENT OF ESTATE TAXES PAID AND ALLOCATION THEREOF

INSTRUCTIONS. This schedule must contain a statement showing all estate taxes assessed and paid in respect of any property required to be included in the gross estate of the decedent under the provisions of the New York Tax Law or under the laws of the United States. The final New York Estate Tax receipt or an order of exemption from tax must be presented with the decree settling the final account. This schedule must also contain a computation setting forth the proposed allocation of taxes paid and to be paid and the amounts due the estate from each person in whose behalf a tax payment has been made and also the proportionate amount of the tax paid by each of the named persons interested in this estate or charged against their respective interest, as provided in EPTL § 2–1.8.

Where an allocation of taxes is required, the method of computing the allocation of said taxes must be shown in this schedule. When taxes are to be paid from residue, the article of the will stating such should be quoted.

SCHEDULE 9
STATEMENT OF COMPUTATION OF COMMISSIONS

INSTRUCTIONS. This schedule must contain a computation of the amount of commissions due upon this accounting.

SCHEDULE 10
STATEMENT OF OTHER PERTINENT FACTS AND OF CASH RECONCILIATION

INSTRUCTIONS. This schedule must contain a statement of all other pertinent facts affecting the administration of the estate and the rights of those interested therein. It must also contain a statement of any real property left by the decedent which it is not necessary to include as an estate asset to be accounted for, a brief description thereof, the gross value and the amount of mortgages or liens thereon at the date of death of the deceased. A cash reconciliation must also be set forth in this schedule so that verification with bank statements and cash on hand may be readily made.

THE FOLLOWING IS A SUMMARY STATEMENT OF THIS ACCOUNT

Charges:

Amount shown by Schedule "A" (Principal received) .... $_____

Amount shown by Schedule "A-1" (Realized increases on principal) .... $_____

Amount shown by Schedule "A-2" (Income Collected) .... $_____

    Total charges .... $_____

Credits:

Amount shown by Schedule "B" (Realized decreases on principal) .... $_____

Amount shown by Schedule "C" (Funeral and administration expenses) .... $_____

Amount shown by Schedule "D" (Creditors' claims actually paid) .... $_____

Amount shown by Schedule "E" (Distributions to legatees, distributees, etc.) .... $_____

    Total credits .... $_____

Balance on hand _____, 19__ as shown by Schedule "F," at market or inventory value $_____

The foregoing balance of $_____ consists of $_____ in cash and $_____ in other property on hand as of the _____ day of _____, 19__. It is subject to deduction of estimated principal commissions amounting to $_____ shown in Schedule I and to the proper charge to principal of expenses of this accounting.

The attached schedules are part of this account.

                                            [Executor][Administrator]

Ch. 25 LETTERS OF ADMINISTRATION § 25.67

AFFIDAVIT OF ACCOUNTING PARTY

STATE OF NEW YORK)
) ss.:
COUNTY OF _____)

_____ being duly sworn says: That the foregoing account contains according to the best of [my][our] knowledge and belief a true statement of all [my][our] receipts and disbursements on account of the estate and of all moneys or other property belonging to the estate which have come into [my][our] hands or been received by any other person by [my][our] order or authority for [my][our] use and that [I][we] do not know of any error or omission in the account to the prejudice of any creditor of, or person interested in, the estate.

Sworn to before me this _____
day of _____ 19__

NOTE: An affidavit of accounting party must be attached to every accounting filed with the Surrogate's Court, whether in voluntary or compulsory accounting proceedings or in an informal accounting proceeding under SCPA § 2202.

§ 25.67 Petition for Letters of Administration or Limited Letters of Administration or Temporary Administration

For Office Use Only
(Filing Fee Paid $)(Certs: $)($Bond, Fee: $)
(Receipt No:)

DO NOT LEAVE ANY ITEMS BLANK

SURROGATE'S COURT OF THE STATE OF NEW YORK
COUNTY OF
_____X

ADMINISTRATION
  PROCEEDING

Estate of

PETITION FOR LETTERS OF:
[ ] Administration
[ ] Limited Administration

§ 25.67   **PROBATE & ESTATE ADMINISTRATION**   Ch. 25

a/k/a
    Deceased.

[ ] Administration with Limitations
[ ] Temporary Administration
File No. _____
(as of 3/93)

_____ X

TO THE SURROGATE'S COURT, County of _____

It is respectfully alleged:

1. The name, domicile and interest in this proceeding of the petitioner, who is of full age, is as follows:

Name: _____ Citizenship (check one): [ ] U.S.A. [ ] Other (specify)

Domicile: _____

       (Street Address)   (City/Town/Village)

_____

   (County)   (State)   (Zip)   (Telephone Number)

Mailing address is: _____

   (if different from domicile)

Interest of Petitioner (check one):
   [ ] Distributee of decedent (state relationship) _____
   [ ] Other (Specify) _____

Is proposed Administrator an attorney? [ ] Yes [ ] No [If yes, submit statement pursuant to 22 NYCRR 207.19(g); see also 207.60 (Accounting of attorney-fiduciary).]

2. The name, domicile, date and place of death, and national citizenship of the above-named decedent as follows [**The Death Certificate must be filed with this proceeding.** If the decedent's domicile is different from that shown on the death certificate, check box [ ] and attach an affidavit explaining the reason for this inconsistency.]:

   Name: _____

   Domicile: _____

       (Street Address)   (City/Town/Village)

_____

  (County)   (State)   (Zip)   (Telephone Number)

Township of: _____ County of: _____
Date of Death: _____ Place of Death: _____
Citizenship (check one): [ ] U.S.A. [ ] Other (specify) _____

[NOTE: For Items 3a through c: Do not include any assets that are jointly held, held in trust for another, or have a named beneficiary.]

3.(a) The estimated gross value of the decedent's personal property passing by intestacy is less than $_____

(b) The estimated gross value of the decedent's real property, in this state, which is [ ] improved, [ ] unimproved, passing by intestacy is less than $_____

A brief description of each parcel is as follows:

(c) The estimated gross rent for a period of eighteen (18) months is the sum of $_____

(d) In addition to the value of the personal property stated in paragraph (3) the following right of action existed on behalf of the decedent and survived his/her death, or is granted to the administrator of the decedent by special provision of law, and it is impractical to give a bond sufficient to cover the probable amount to be recovered therein: **[Write "NONE" or state briefly the cause of action and the person against whom it exists, including names and carrier].**

(e) If decedent is survived by a spouse and a parent, or parents but no issue, and there is a claim for wrongful death, check here [ ] and furnish name(s) and address(es) of parent(s) in Paragraph 7. See EPTL 5–4.4.

4. A diligent search and inquiry, including a search of any safe deposit box, has been made for a will of the decedent and none has been found. Petitioner(s) (has)(have) been unable to obtain any information concerning any will of the decedent and therefore allege(s), upon information and belief, that the decedent died without leaving any last will.

5. A search of the records of this Court shows that no application has ever been made for letters of administration upon the estate of the decedent or for the probate of a will of the decedent, and your petitioner is informed and verily believes that no such application ever has been made to the Surrogate's Court of any other county of this state.

6. The decedent left surviving the following who would inherit his/her estate pursuant to EPTL 4–1.1 and 4–1.2:

a. [ ] Spouse (husband/wife). [**If the decedent was divorced, see Uniform Court Rule 207.50**].

b. [ ] Child or children or descendants or predeceased child or children. [**Must include marital, nonmarital, and adopted**].

c. [ ] Any issue of the decedent adopted by persons related to the decedent (DRL Section 117).

d. [ ] Mother/Father.

e. [ ] Sisters or brothers, either of whole or half blood, and issue of predeceased sisters or brothers.

f. [ ] Grandmother/Grandfather.

§ 25.67 PROBATE & ESTATE ADMINISTRATION Ch. 25

 g. [ ] Aunts or uncles, and children of predeceased aunts and uncles (first cousins).

 h. [ ] First cousins once removed (children of first cousins).

[Information is required only as to those classes of surviving relatives who would take the property of decedent pursuant to EPTL 4–1.1. State "**number**" of survivors in each class. Insert "**No**" in all prior classes. Insert "**X**" in all subsequent classes.].

 7. The decedent left surviving the following distributees, or other necessary parties, whose names, degrees of relationship, domiciles, post office addresses and citizenship are as follows:

[Note: Show clearly how each person is related to decedent. If relationship is through an ancestor who is deceased, give name, date of death, and relationship of the ancestor to the decedent. Use rider sheet if space in paragraph (7) is not sufficient. See Uniform Rules 207.16(b).

If any person listed in paragraph (7) is a nonmarital person, or descended from a nonmarital person, attach a copy of the order of filiation or Schedule A. If any person listed in paragraph (7) was adopted by any persons related by blood or marriage to decedent or descended from such persons, attach Schedule B.]

 7a. The following are of full age and under no disability: [If nonmarital or adopted-our person, so indicate by attaching Schedule A and/or B]

Name	Relationship	Domicile and Mailing Address	Citizenship

 7b. The following are infants and/or persons under disability: [If nonmarital or adopted-out person, so indicate by attaching Schedule A and/or B]

Name	Relationship	Domicile and Mailing Address	Citizenship

 8. There are no outstanding debts or funeral expenses, except: [Write "NONE" or state name]

 9. There are no other persons interested in this proceeding other than those hereinbefore mentioned.

 WHEREFORE, your petitioner respectfully prays that: [Check and complete all relief requested]

( ) a. process issue to all necessary parties to show cause why letters should not be issued as requested;

( ) b. an order be granted dispensing with service of process upon those persons named in Paragraph (7) who have a right to letter prior or equal to that of the person nominated, and who are nondomiciliaries or whose names or whereabouts are unknown and cannot be ascertained;

( ) c. a decree awarding Letters of:
[ ] Administration to _____
[ ] Limited Administration to _____
[ ] Administration with Limitation to _____
[ ] Temporary Administration to _____

or to such other person or persons having a prior right as may be entitled thereto; and

( ) d. That the authority of the representative under the foregoing Letters be limited with respect to the prosecution or enforcement of a cause of action on behalf of the estate, as follows: the administrator(s) may not enforce a judgment or receive any funds without further order of the Surrogate;

( ) e. That the authority of the representative under the foregoing Letters be limited as follows:

( ) f. [State any other relief requested].

Dated:

1. _____ 2. _____
   (Signature of Petitioner)   (Signature of Petitioner)

_____ _____
(Print Name)   (Print Name)

STATE OF NEW YORK
                              ss.:
COUNTY OF _____

COMBINED VERIFICATION, OATH AND DESIGNATION

[For use when petitioner is to be appointed administrator]

I, the undersigned, the petitioner named in the foregoing petition, being duly sworn, say:

1. VERIFICATION: I have read the foregoing petition subscribed by me and know the contents thereof, and the same is true of my own knowledge, except as to the matters therein stated to be alleged upon information and belief, and as to those matters I believe it to be true.

2. OATH OF ADMINISTRATOR as indicated above: I am over eighteen (18) years of age and a citizen of the United States; and I will

§ 25.67   PROBATE & ESTATE ADMINISTRATION   Ch. 25

well, faithfully and honestly discharge the duties of Administrator of the goods, chattels and credits of said decedent according to law. I am not ineligible to receive letters and will duly account for all moneys and other property that will come into my hands.

  3. DESIGNATION OF CLERK FOR SERVICE OF PROCESS: I do hereby designate the Clerk of the Surrogate's Court of County, and his/her successor in office, as a person on whom service of any process, issuing from such Surrogate's Court may be made in like manner and with like effect as if it were served personally upon me, whenever I cannot be found and served within the State of New York after due diligence is used.

My domicile is

_____
(Street Address) (City/Town/Village) (State) (Zip)

_____
Signature of Petitioner

  On the day of _____, 19__, before me personally came _____, known to me to be the person described in and who executed the foregoing instrument. Such person duly swore to such instrument before me and duly acknowledged that he/she executed the same.

_____

Notary Public
Commission Expires:
(Affix Notary Stamp or Seal)

Name of Attorney: _____ Tel. No.: _____
Address of Attorney: _____

_____

§ 25.68 Decree Appointing Administrator 💾

       At a Surrogate's Court of the
       State of New York held in and
       for the County of _____
       at New York on _____, 19__.

PRESENT:
  Hon.
  Surrogate.

_____

ADMINISTRATION PROCEEDING	DECREE APPOINTING ADMINISTRATOR
Estate of a/k/a_____	
	File No.
Deceased.	*(as of 3/93)*

_____

Ch. 25   FIX AMOUNT OF BOND   § 25.69

A petition having been filed by praying that administration of the goods, chattels and credits of the above-named decedent to granted to ; and all persons named in such petition, required to be cited, having been duly cited to show cause why such relief should not be granted or having duly waived the issuance of such citation and consented thereto; and it appearing that is in all respects competent to act as administrator of the estate of said deceased, and a

[ ] bond having been filed and approved in the amount of $_____
[ ] bond having been dispensed with

and such representative(s) otherwise having qualified therefor; now, after due deliberation, with no one appearing in opposition thereto, it is

ORDERED AND DECREED that Letters of Administration issue to
_____

ORDERED AND DECREED, that the authority of such representative(s) be restricted in accordance with, and that letters herein issued contain, the limitation, if any, which appears immediately below.

_____

_____
Surrogate

§ 25.69 Affidavit Asking Court to Fix Amount of Administrator's Bond

SURROGATE'S COURT OF THE STATE OF NEW YORK
COUNTY OF _____

_____
| In the Matter of   )
| Application for   )
| _____   )
|)
|)
|)   Bond Affidavit
| of   )   File No. _____
| _____,   )
| Deceased.   )
|_____)

STATE OF NEW YORK   )
) ss.:
COUNTY OF   )

_____ BEING DULY SWORN, DEPOSES AND SAYS:

That (he)(she) is over the age of _____ years and resides at _____.

§ 25.69   PROBATE & ESTATE ADMINISTRATION   Ch. 25

That _____ is the _____ of the deceased and the petitioner in the above proceeding;

That the value of all the personal property, wheresoever situated, of which the said decedent died possessed amounts to _____ dollars and consists of _____

That the deceased, at the time of _____ death, was _____ seized of real estate consisting of _____

THE MARKET value of which is _____ dollars, subject to mortgages in the amount of _____ held by _____ and the estimated gross rentals for 18 months is $_____

ORDERED, that the petitioner be authorized and directed to file an additional bond of _____ ($_____) Dollars for the purpose of taking into his hands the agency funds held by the deceased at the time of his death, as recited in the petition.

§ 25.70 Forms—Waiver of Citation, Renunciation of Signer's Claim to Letters and Consent to Appointment of Administrator

SURROGATE'S COURT OF THE STATE OF NEW YORK
COUNTY OF _____

ADMINISTRATION PROCEEDING,   WAIVER OF CITATION,
Estate of   RENUNCIATION AND
a/k/a   CONSENT TO
                                     APPOINTMENT OF
              Deceased.   ADMINISTRATOR
                                     (INDIVIDUAL)
                                     File No.
_____   (as of 3/93)

The undersigned, a distributee or creditor of the above named decedent and being full age and sound mind hereby voluntarily appears in the Surrogate's Court of County, New York, and waives the issuance and service of citation in this matter, renounces all right to Letters of Administration of the above captioned estate and consents that

  [ ] Letters of Administration
  [ ] Letters of Administration with Limitations
  [ ] Limited Letters of Administration be issued to or any other person or persons entitled thereto without any notice whatsoever to the undersigned, and consents
  [ ] a bond be dispensed with
  [ ] a bond in the amount of $_____ be posted and hereby specifically release any claim I might have under any bond that may be filed.

Date	Signature	Street Address	Relationship
	Print Name	Town/State/Zip	

STATE OF NEW YORK

ss.:

COUNTY OF _____

On _____, 19__, before me personally appeared _____, to me known and known to me to be the person described in and who executed the foregoing waiver and consent and each duly acknowledged the execution thereof.

Notary Public Commission Expires: (Affix Notary Stamp or Seal)	Name of Attorney Address Telephone No.

§ 25.71 Forms—Notice of Application for Letters of Administration 💾

SURROGATE'S COURT OF THE STATE OF NEW YORK
COUNTY OF

ADMINISTRATION PROCEEDING, Estate of a/k/a _____ Deceased. _____	NOTICE OF APPLICATION FOR LETTERS OF ADMINISTRATION (SPCA 1005) File No. _____ (as of 3/93)

NOTICE IS HEREBY GIVEN THAT:

(1) an application for Letters of Administration upon the estate of the above-named decedent, has been made by _____, petitioner, whose post office address is:

(2) each and every name of the intestate decedent known to the undersigned is as indicated in the above caption.

(3) petitioner prays that a decree be made directing the issuance of Letters of Administration to _____

§ 25.71 PROBATE & ESTATE ADMINISTRATION Ch. 25

(4) the name and post office address of each and every distributee of the above-named decedent, as set forth in the petition and known to the undersigned, are as follows:

(a) Distributees who have been duly cited, have waived citation or have appeared in this proceeding:

Name of Distributee   Domicile and Post Office Address
_____   _____
_____   _____

(b) Other Distributees:
Name of Distributee   Domicile and Post Office Address
_____   _____
_____   _____

[CONTINUE ON REVERSE SIDE IF MORE SPACE NEEDED]

(5) That the undersigned does not know of any other distributees of the said decedent.

(6) That Letters of Administration will issue on or after _____, 19__.

Dated: _____

_____
Signature of Petitioner or Attorney

_____   _____
Attorney for Petitioner   Print Name

_____   _____
Address (Office)   Address
Tel. No. _____

§ 25.72 Forms—Citation That Can Be Adopted for Use in Any Proceeding

File No. _____, 19__

CITATION
THE PEOPLE OF THE STATE OF NEW YORK,
BY THE GRACE OF GOD FREE AND INDEPENDENT,

To [Insert names of parties]

A petition having been duly filed by _____, who resides at _____,
YOU ARE HEREBY CITED TO SHOW CAUSE before the Surrogate's Court, _____ County, at _____ in _____, New York on _____, 19__, at __[a.m.][p.m.], why a decree should not be made in the estate of _____ who died domiciled at _____, in the County of _____, [Set forth fully all relief prayed for in petition].

Ch. 25   CITATION THAT CAN BE ADOPTED   § 25.72

Dated, Attested and Sealed, _____, 19__

[L.S.]

Hon. _____
Surrogate
Clerk.

Name of attorney: _____

Address: _____

Tel. No. _____

This citation is served upon you as required by law. You are not obligated to appear in person. If you fail to appear it will be assumed that you do not object to the relief requested unless you file formal legal, verified objections. You have a right to have an attorney-at-law appear for you.

Address of attorney: _____

This citation is served upon you as required by law. You are not obliged to appear in person. If you fail to appear it will be assumed that you do not object to the relief requested. You have a right to have an attorney-at-law appear for you.

Chapter 26

PERSONAL INJURY

by
James E. Reid

Table of Sections

26.1	Scope Note.
26.2	Strategy.
26.3	___ Client Interview.
26.4	___ Valuing the Case.
26.5	___ Skills and Ethics.
26.6	___ Retainer.
26.7	___ ___ Retainer Statement.
26.8	___ Expenses.
26.9	Investigation.
26.10	___ Premises Liability.
26.11	___ Medical Malpractice.
26.12	___ ___ Hospital.
26.13	___ ___ Dental and Podiatric Malpractice.
26.14	___ Products Liability.
26.15	___ Dog Bites.
26.16	___ Chemical Exposure.
26.17	___ Automobile Accidents.
26.18	___ ___ Police Report.
26.19	___ ___ Witness Statements.
26.20	___ ___ MV104.
26.21	___ ___ Application of No–Fault.
26.22	___ ___ Medical Records.
26.23	___ ___ Photographs.
26.24	___ ___ Insurance Policies and Coverage.
26.25	Claims Procedure for Automobile Accidents.
26.26	___ Filing Notice of Claim With the Motor Vehicle Accident Indemnity Corporation.
26.27	___ ___ Procedure for Cases in Which There Is No Insurance.
26.28	___ ___ Procedure for Cases in Which There Is No Insurance and the Identity of the Wrongdoer Is Not Ascertainable (Hit and Run).
26.29	___ ___ Procedure for Cases in Which Insurance Initially Is Believed to Exist, But There Is No Insurance After Later Disclaimer.
26.30	___ ___ Late Claims.
26.31	Theories of Liability.
26.32	Filing the Action.
26.33	___ When.

26.34 ___ Where.
26.35 ___ Potential Defendants.
26.36 The Summons and the Complaint.
26.37 The Answer.
26.38 Actions Against Municipal Corporations.
26.39 ___ Notice of Claim.
26.40 ___ ___ Content.
26.41 Actions Against the State.
26.42 Discovery—Generally.
26.43 ___ Depositions.
26.44 ___ Interrogatories.
26.45 ___ Document Discovery and Inspection.
26.46 ___ Bills of Particulars.
26.47 ___ Demand for a Bill of Particulars.
26.48 Settlement.
26.49 Liens.
26.50 Alternative Dispute Resolution.
26.51 Trial Preparation: Introductory Note.
26.52 Trial.
26.53 ___ Subpoenas.
26.54 ___ Exhibits.
26.55 ___ *Voir Dire*.
26.56 Disbursement of Proceeds of Settlement or Recovery.
26.57 Drafting Checklists.
26.58 ___ Complaint.
26.59 ___ Answer.
26.60 ___ Demand for Bill of Particulars.
26.61 ___ Responses to Demand for Bill of Particulars.
26.62 Forms—Client's Retainer Agreement.
26.63 ___ Retainer Statement.
26.64 ___ Department of Motor Vehicles MV104 Form.
26.65 ___ Summons and Complaint.
26.66 ___ Amended Answer, Counterclaim and Cross Claim.
26.67 ___ Defendant's Demand for a Verified Bill of Particulars.
26.68 ___ Defendant's CPLR 3101 Demands.
26.69 ___ Plaintiff's Demand for a Verified Bill of Particulars.
26.70 ___ Plaintiff's CPLR 3101 Demands.
26.71 ___ Closing Statement.

WESTLAW Electronic Research

See WESTLAW Electronic Research Guide preceding the Summary of Contents.

§ 26.1 Scope Note

This chapter covers basic information for an attorney who is or will be handling personal injury litigation in New York. Beginning with basic considerations, including whether or not it is economically feasible to accept the case,[1] the chapter progresses to a discussion of ethical considerations connected with the decision whether or not to take the case[2] and a "how-to" approach toward investigation,[3] pleadings,[4] discovery,[5] trial strategies,[6] motions,[7] and jury selection.[8] Specialized areas of personal injury law, *e.g.*, products liability,[9] legal malpractice[10] and medical malpractice[11] are touched on in this chapter, but are covered in greater detail elsewhere in this publication, as are issues related to damages[12] and insurance.[13]

§ 26.2 Strategy

The handling of a personal injury case requires careful planning in order to obtain a successful resolution, either by settlement or verdict. As a successful resolution is not always possible, part of counsel's initial strategy should be to consider past cases and fact patterns in which a successful resolution was not obtained, or in which the claim could not be handled economically, to help with the decision whether or not to take the case. If counsel decides to accept the case, he or she must constantly evaluate the case's strengths and weaknesses to maximize the opportunity for obtaining a successful resolution.

§ 26.3 Strategy—Client Interview

The initial investigation of the case begins with the client interview. It is important to always allow sufficient time for the interview.[1] This is the first opportunity for the client to meet with counsel and to develop a relationship. Counsel should not take calls while interviewing the client so as not to interrupt the client or become sidetracked.

In an appropriate case, counsel should record the initial interview or, perhaps, videotape it. Notes should be taken, but most importantly, clients should be listened to carefully. What do they claim is the wrong done to them? How would they go about seeking a recovery? How do they feel that they have been injured? Are their expectations reasonable?

§ 26.1

1. *See infra*, § 26.4.
2. *See infra*, § 26.5.
3. *See infra*, §§ 26.9–26.24.
4. *See infra*, §§ 26.30—26.31, 26.46—26.50.
5. *See infra*, §§ 26.34—26.36.
6. *See infra*, §§ 26.37—26.41.
7. *See infra*, § 26.41. For helpful discussions of this topic, *see also*, Bensel, Frank, McKeon, *et al.*, *Personal Injury Practice in New York* (West 1997) ¶¶ 9:22–9:226.
8. *See infra*, § 26.44. *See also*, Haig, *et al.*, *Commercial Litigation in New York State Courts*, Ch. 28 "Jury Selection."
9. Chapter 27, "Products Liability," *infra*. *See also*, Kreindler, Rodriguez, *et. al.*, *New York Law of Torts* (West 1997) Ch. 5; Bensel, Frank, McKeon, *et al.*, *Personal Injury Practice in New York* (West 1997) ¶¶ 2:135ff.
10. Chapter 28, "Legal Malpractice," *infra*.
11. Chapter 29, "Medical Malpractice," *infra*.
12. Chapter 30, "Damages," *infra*.
13. Chapter 31, "Insurance," *infra*.

§ 26.3

1. *See also*, Bensel, Frank, McKeon, *et al.*, *Personal Injury Practice in New York* (West 1997) Ch. 1.

Do they seek compensation for injuries and damages, do they seek vindication or do they seek retribution? Do they have a genuine claim for damages or is this a personal vendetta?

If there are injuries that are visible, counsel should obtain photographs of the injured area. Obviously, if the plaintiff is a different gender than counsel, and the area of injury is a sensitive area, a professional photographer or attorney or paralegal of the same sex as the plaintiff should take the photographs. If the injury involves a limitation of movement, that limitation should be documented photographically or by making a videotape of the client's movement, and a physician should be asked to document the limitation in the patient's chart.

It must be determined if there are any witnesses known to the client. If so, the name and address of each such witness should be obtained and, if known, a telephone number. Each witness should be sent an accident questionnaire with a self-addressed, stamped envelope for convenient return.

The client should sign medical authorizations, if he or she received medical treatment, and the name and address of every hospital, physician and therapist who provided treatment should be obtained, together with the approximate dates of treatment. It should be determined how the medical bills were paid and what, if any, insurance coverage applied. It should also be determined if there are any potential liens.[2]

Also, basic information should be obtained from the client, including name, address, date of birth, social security number, date of marriage, children's names and dates of birth, employment information (including duties and wage rate), spouse's employment, education and insurance policy numbers. Of special, and indeed critical, importance is information concerning any previous injuries, particularly if they involve the same area of the body claimed to be injured in this case. Determine if any prior claims have been made by the client, including personal injury or workers' compensation claims.[3]

It should be determined if the client has been contacted by any representative of any insurance company. Did he or she give a statement, either over the telephone or in person? If a statement was given, was the client provided with a copy? Where was the statement given and how soon after the injury did it occur?

---

2. *See infra*, § 26.38. *See also*, Chapter 32 "Workers' Compensation," *infra*; Bensel, Frank, McKeon, *et al.*, *Personal Injury Practice in New York* (West 1997) ¶¶ 1:89–1:94; Kreindler, Rodriguez, *et. al.*, *New York Law of Torts* (West 1997).

3. PRACTICE POINTER: There is a service available to insurance carriers, known as the CIB (Central Index Bureau). Many carriers will send a form to the CIB whenever a claim is received to learn of previous claims filed by the client. Counsel should know this information before the defendant's representatives do.

§ 26.4 Strategy—Valuing the Case

One of the primary considerations of any personal injury attorney in deciding whether or not to take a case is whether the case can be handled economically.[1] In making this determination, two key economic considerations are involved. First, what is the gross value of the injury? Second, what, if any, culpable conduct is the plaintiff guilty of, and by what percentage is this likely to reduce the recovery. After these determinations are made, counsel must also consider the strength of the claim—the chances of recovery—as well as costs and time factors. An example of this process might be the following:

Gross Value	$ 10,000.00
Plaintiff's Culpable Conduct	20%
Net Recovery	$ 8,000.00
Chance of Plaintiff Winning	75%
Potential Recovery	$ 6,000.00
Predicted Costs After Trial	$ 2,125.00
Net	$ 3,875.00
Attorney's Fees	$ 1,291.00
Net to Client	$ 2,584.00
Hours of Time	100
Hourly Renumeration to Attorney	$ 12.91

What this example indicates is that this case cannot be handled economically from initial interview through trial. Given this situation, the attorney should discuss with the client the possibility of engaging in settlement negotiations, but should not agree to undertake a trial of the matter. One should remember, however, that the injury and overall posture of the case may change as the matter is developed.

§ 26.5 Strategy—Skills and Ethics

Another consideration when deciding whether or not to take a case is a determination whether counsel possesses the skill and training to complete that case successfully. An attorney is ethically bound to handle only those cases that he or she is capable of handling.[1]

For example, if the client asks to be represented in a complex products liability or medical negligence case, counsel must determine

---

§ 26.4

1. Bensel, Frank, McKeon, et al., *Personal Injury Practice in New York* (West 1997) Ch. 1 "First Steps in Handling a Personal Injury Case."

§ 26.5

1. The Code of Professional Responsibility was published by the American Bar Association in August of 1969 and adopted by the New York State Bar Association, effective January 1, 1970 as to attorneys in New York State. The Disciplinary Rules, or DR's, of the Code of Professional Responsibility were made effective September 1, 1990 in the Rules of the Appellate Divisions of the New York Supreme Court. *See* Rule 1.1; DR6–101(A).

whether he or she has the knowledge and resources to undertake the review, investigation, work-up and trial of such a case. If the answer is "no," counsel should associate with an attorney who does have that experience or refer the matter completely to such an attorney or firm.[2]

§ 26.6 Strategy—Retainer

There are generally two methods used to compensate attorneys for work on personal injury cases in New York. The first is an hourly contract. In this arrangement, the attorney agrees to work on a matter for a certain rate of pay per hour, and the client agrees to pay the same. Disbursements are billed and paid separately, that is, they are not included in the hourly fee. Note, however, that the hourly fee is not often used in personal injury cases.

The most common form of retention of an attorney in a personal injury matter is the contingency fee retainer agreement. In a personal injury case (except cases of medical, dental or podiatric malpractice) there are two approved contingency fee schedules that may apply.

The most common contingency fee arrangement is the one-third fee agreement, *i.e.*, the attorney's fee is one-third of the amount recovered.[1] The second approved method for calculating a contingency fee in a personal injury case in New York is application of a sliding scale, as follows:

(i) 50% of the first $1,000 of the sum recovered;

(ii) 40% of the next $2,000 of the sum recovered;

(iii) 35% of the next $22,000 of the sum recovered;

(iv) 25% of any amount over $25,000 of the sum recovered.

The percentage must be calculated on the *net* value of the sum recovered,[2] and any contingency fee in a personal injury case in New York must not exceed the maximum limitations on compensation as established by the appellate division.[3]

Whether a case is referred to you for trial, or you refer a case to a trial attorney, there is always a question of responsibility for the file and

---

2. DR6–101(A)(1); EC2–22 and 6–3.

§ 26.6

1. CAVEAT: The law and rules of the various departments of the appellate division of the supreme court require that an attorney's fee be calculated on the *NET* recovery, rather than the gross amount recovered. For example:

Gross Recovery	$10,000.00
Costs/Disbursements	$ 1,000.00
NET	$ 9,000.00
Attorney's fees	$ 3,000.00 *NOT* $3,333.33

22 NYCRR § 603.7(e)(2),(3) (1st Dep't); § 691.20(e)(2),(3) (2d Dep't); § 806.13(b),(c)(3d Dep't); § 1022.31(b),(c) (4th Dep't) *See also* Judiciary Law § 474.

2. 22 NYCRR § 603.7(e)(2) (1st Dep't); 22 NYCRR § 691.20(e)(2) (2d Dep't); 22 NYCRR § 806.13(b) (3d Dep't); 22 NYCRR § 1022.31(b) (4th Dep't).

3. 22 NYCRR § 603.7 (e) (1st Dep't); 22 NYCRR § 691.20 (e) (2d Dep't); 22 NYCRR § 806.13 (3d Dep't) and 22 NYCRR § 1022.31 (4th Dep't).

the division of fees. Although previous rules regarding the division of fees among attorneys required that the division of fees be in proportion to the labor of each attorney, often a straight percentage was utilized between the referring attorney and the trial counsel. Current rules permit the referring attorney and the trial attorney to agree to a division of fees provided that the client is advised that there will be a division of the fees between the retaining/referring attorney and the trial attorney and that both attorneys or firms agree to be responsible for the case.[4]

If the client gives the attorney a retainer (deposit) for disbursements before any actual disbursements are incurred, these funds should be deposited in the attorney's escrow account and segregated until such expenses are incurred and paid. A detailed record, including escrow check number, item, date paid and amount paid, should be kept for each file.

In a case alleging medical, dental or podiatric malpractice, a mandatory sliding-scale contingency fee will be applied. This fee is also *net* of any expenses and is subject to the following maximums.

30% of the first $250,000 recovered;

25% of the next $250,000 recovered;

20% of the next $500,000 recovered;

15% of the next $250,000 recovered;

10% of any amount over $1,250,000.[5]

§ 26.7   Strategy—Retainer—Retainer Statement

The retainer statement is a completely different document than the retainer agreement. As discussed, the retainer agreement is the agreement between the client and the attorney. It governs that relationship and sets forth the terms by which the attorney is to be compensated for the time put in on the case in the event a recovery is made for the client.

The *retainer statement*, on the other hand, is a court document that is required *in every personal injury or property damage contingent fee case*.[1] It is to be filed with the Office of Court Administration of the State of New York ("OCA") within 30 days from the date any such retainer or agreement is made. If the retainer statement is filed by mail, it *must* be accompanied by a self-addressed, stamped post card, containing the words "Retainer Statement," the date of the retainer and the name of the client. The Office of Court Administration will stamp this card with

---

4. *See* DR2–107.

CAVEAT: In any negligence case, the expenses/disbursements are always the responsibility of the client. 22 NYCRR § 603.18. While this is clearly the rule in New York, only the First Department has placed it in its Rules of Court.

5. Judiciary Law § 474–a(2).

§ 26.7

1. 22 NYCRR § 603.7 (1st Dep't); 22 NYCRR § 691.20 (2d Dep't); 22 NYCRR § 1022.2 (4th Dep't). *See infra*, § 26.62 for a form client retainer agreement.

a case number and return it to counsel for inclusion in the file. If more than thirty days have elapsed from the date of the retainer agreement, OCA may return the retainer statement with a request for an affidavit as to the reason why the retainer statement was not timely filed. The retainer statement should be addressed to:

Office of Court Administration—Statements
Post Office Box No. 2016
New York, New York 10008

§ 26.8 Strategy—Expenses

The client should be kept informed, as much as possible, concerning expenses related to the case. This will prevent surprises later in the relationship, particularly if a trial of the matter results in a "no cause of action," and expenses are still outstanding.[1]

Expenses generally can be put into three distinct categories: (1) general administrative expenses, found in every file, including postage, copies, long-distance telephone and the like; (2) expenses necessary to get the case to the courthouse door, including the cost of photographs, investigation expenses, expert review expenses, costs of obtaining medical records, MV104's,[2] and police reports, deposition transcript expenses, filing fees, service of process fees and travel expenses; and (3) costs attendant to trial, including subpoena fees, expert witness fees, document/exhibit production costs, costs of photographic enlargements and similar trial expenses.

Many clients are reluctant to bear the expenses of a lawsuit. While an attorney may advance expenses toward the file, the expenses are *always* the responsibility of the client, as noted above.[3]

A discussion of how the expenses will be paid in the event there is a finding of "no cause of action" should be had with the client, and the agreement should then be reduced to writing.[4] It is also often a good idea to discuss with the client costs that may be assessed after the verdict, including costs allowed by statute[5] and allowable disbursements.

§ 26.9 Investigation

Thorough investigation is clearly the key to the successful prosecution of an action. This is true whether the action is a medical malpractice case, a products liability case, an automobile negligence matter or a

---

§ 26.8

1. *See* Bensel, Frank, McKeon, *et al.*, *Personal Injury Practice in New York* (West 1997) ¶ 1:95.

2. *See infra*, § 26.20.

3. *See also* Bensel, Frank, McKeon, *et al.*, *Personal Injury Practice in New York* (West 1997) ¶¶ 1:228–1:231, 1:235.

4. *See id.*

5. CPLR 8201.

§ 26.9   **PERSONAL INJURY**   Ch. 26

premises liability case. The investigation should begin early in the case,[1] proceed through to the preparation of the case for trial, and often will even continue during the trial.

A determination should be made as to whether an outside investigator should be retained or whether the investigation can be performed by the attorney or by paralegals on staff.[2] If an outside investigator is retained, care should be taken to retain a competent and ethical investigator who is knowledgeable in the area to be investigated, and the retention should be discussed with the client as this expense will be a disbursement against the file.

§ 26.10   Investigation—Premises Liability

When a client comes into an attorney's office after having suffered injuries on real property, counsel must first determine how the client believes he or she was injured, and then must determine if his or her belief comports with reality. More importantly, counsel must decide if the client's version of the facts makes sense from a practical perspective.

In a slip-and-fall case, it is critical that the client be able to describe what it was that caused the fall. The facts should be gone over in great detail. Photographs should be obtained of the area, in order to identify the defect and to establish notice, including constructive notice, *i.e.*, does the defect appear to have existed for a number of months/years, or was the design improper or violative of code(s).[1] Also, it should be determined if there were any witnesses to the accident.[2]

Counsel must attempt to determine whether others have been injured at that location. Were statements made by the defendant's employees indicating knowledge of a problem? If possible, counsel should ascertain the identity of the employee(s) who made the statement.

The ownership of the property in question and the identity of those who had control over the particular premises must be determined. Is there a management company that supervises the premises? In determining ownership, check with the county clerk's office for a certified copy of the deed and for a copy of the lease, if applicable. Also, the assessor's office should be checked to see who pays the taxes on the building.

§ 26.9

1. *See* Bensel, Frank, McKeon, *et al.*, *Personal Injury Practice in New York* (West 1997) Ch. 2 "Prelitigation Investigation Claim Analysis and Employment of Experts."

2. *See* Bensel, Frank, McKeon, *et al.*, *Personal Injury Practice in New York* (West 1997) ¶¶ 2:45–2:134.

§ 26.10

1. *See* Bensel, Frank, McKeon, *et al.*, *Personal Injury Practice in New York* (West 1997) ¶ 2:33.

2. *See* Bensel, Frank, McKeon, *et al.*, *Personal Injury Practice in New York* (West 1997) ¶ 2:95.

If the owner of the premises is a municipality, it must be determined if there is an ordinance requiring prior written notice of the defect, and, if so, whether it is applicable to the case.[3]

If the premises in which the plaintiff was injured are leased, the owner may not be responsible, as a landlord is not ordinarily responsible for the negligent acts of a tenant.[4] However, under certain circumstances landlords may be liable, *e.g.*, if they contracted to repair, and the failure to repair created an unreasonable risk to persons on the land.[5]

If the defect complained of was trivial and slight in nature and possesses none of the characteristics of a trap or a snare, it may not be reasonably foreseen to cause an accident and thus liability may not be predicated on such a defect.[6]

§ 26.11 Investigation—Medical Malpractice

Medical malpractice cases are discussed in detail elsewhere in this publication.[1] A decision as to the value of the case is extremely important in medical, dental and podiatric malpractice cases. An example would be a case involving a complaint of appendicitis. Assume that the appendicitis is not diagnosed. A short period of time goes by and the patient returns to the physician feeling sicker. An exploratory laparotomy is performed, the ruptured appendix is removed, but peritonitis has developed, which is then appropriately treated with antibiotics. Assume that negligence can be easily shown. What are the damages? A scar, a removed appendix, surgery, and a period of recuperation. Yet all of these may have occurred, even without the negligence. There is also a serious issue of proximate cause as to the connection between the damages and negligence.

Many times a prospective client will say, "But I could have ... [been killed], [really hurt], etc." The fact remains, however, that, with the exception of a slightly longer hospital stay, the result in a case such as the one described would have been the same had the appendicitis been diagnosed in the first instance. Thus, where an initial review by a physician is necessary, as is required in medical negligence cases, the costs may quickly exceed the value of the case.

---

3. Holt v. County of Tioga, 56 N.Y.2d 414, 452 N.Y.S.2d 383, 437 N.E.2d 1140 (1982). *See also*, Bensel, Frank, McKeon, *et al.*, *Personal Injury Practice in New York* (West 1997) ¶¶ 5:1–5:99.

4. Blake v. Gardino, 35 A.D.2d 1022, 315 N.Y.S.2d 973 (3d Dep't 1970), aff'd 29 N.Y.2d 876, 328 N.Y.S.2d 442, 278 N.E.2d 649 (1972).

5. Putnam v. Stout, 38 N.Y.2d 607, 381 N.Y.S.2d 848, 345 N.E.2d 319 (1976).

6. Mascardo v. State, 46 A.D.2d 941, 362 N.Y.S.2d 78 (3d Dep't 1974), aff'd 38 N.Y.2d 870, 382 N.Y.S.2d 742, 346 N.E.2d 543 (1976)(trivial defect rule).

§ 26.11

1. Chapter 29, "Medical Malpractice," *supra*. *See also*, Bensel, Frank, McKeon, *et al.*, *Personal Injury Practice in New York* (West 1997) ¶¶ 5:100–5:114; Kreindler, Rodriguez, *et. al.*, *New York Law of Torts* (West 1997).

§ 26.11 PERSONAL INJURY Ch. 26

In 1986, the Legislature amended the CPLR to require that before any medical malpractice action is commenced (unless the time is too short under the Statute of Limitations), the potential cause of action must be reviewed for merit, and a certificate of merit must be attached to the summons and complaint.[2]

Thus, early in any medical malpractice action, a determination must be made as to whether the case can be handled economically. Counsel must bear in mind that medical malpractice cases are perhaps the most difficult and time-consuming of any type of personal injury claim, with the possible exception of a products liability action. Additionally, such claims are extremely expensive to prosecute because of the need for an expert at the inception of the action. Therefore, if the action is not one of sufficient value, the attorney must carefully consider whether the case should be undertaken.[3]

Once the decision to take the case has been made, it will be necessary to assemble all of the medical records. In some cases, particularly orthopaedic cases, it will be necessary for counsel to assemble the X-rays in addition to the medical records. The hospital records should also be obtained, and, if a death resulted, any coroner's reports and autopsy results. Often, the county coroner's office can be an invaluable source of information with regard to the cause of death in a wrongful death action.

After the medical records have been assembled, they should be submitted for review by a physician believed to be knowledgeable in the matter under consideration. While it is not necessary that this physician be a specialist in the area that the case involves, it is better to utilize the services of this type of expert so that the case will not need to be reviewed more than once.

In evaluating the action, counsel must also bear in mind that a mere error in judgment is not ordinarily medical malpractice.[4] Therefore, an issue that should be addressed with the expert early in the case is whether or not what appears to be negligence may, in fact, be merely an error in judgment. This argument is frequently made by the defense, contending that if there was a bad result, it was only the result of an error in judgment and otherwise well within the accepted methodologies of treatment. This argument is often accepted by juries. A second likely defense will relate to the issue of proximate cause, *i.e.*, even if there is an injury, was the defendant's negligence the proximate cause of the injury.[5]

2. CPLR 3012–a. For further discussion of the certificate of merit *see* Chapter 29, "Medical Malpractice," *infra. See also*, Bensel, Frank, McKeon, *et al.*, *Personal Injury Practice in New York* (West 1997) ¶¶ 5:100, 5:284.

3. Chapter 29, "Medical Malpractice," *supra. See also*, Bensel, Frank, McKeon, *et al.*, *Personal Injury Practice in New York* (West 1997) ¶¶ 2:630ff.

4. Oelsner v. State, 66 N.Y.2d 636, 495 N.Y.S.2d 359, 485 N.E.2d 1024 (1985).

5. Eisele v. Malone, 2 A.D.2d 550, 157 N.Y.S.2d 155 (1st Dep't 1956).

After the medical records have been assembled and the expert review performed, counsel should consider obtaining a very short letter from the expert indicating that the records have been reviewed and stating that the expert finds the case to be meritorious.[6] This may be preferable to a detailed report, which might serve as the basis for impeachment of the expert.

Once the summons and complaint have been prepared, the certificate of merit must be attached at the time that the summons and complaint are filed. Note, however, that if the client comes to you at a time close to the running of the Statute of Limitations, and thus there is too little time to have the case reviewed, the case can still be filed with a certificate of merit that indicates that the time was too short to have a review undertaken. Thereafter, the review must be completed within 90 days after the case has been filed.[7]

§ 26.12 Investigation—Medical Malpractice—Hospital

An action against a hospital, unlike an action brought only against a physician, has the potential to involve both medical and ordinary negligence claims, and the two should be differentiated.[1]

At times, physicians in hospital emergency rooms are employees of the hospital, and this determination should be made early in the action. Additionally, some hospitals are municipal corporations and, as such, there may be Notice of Claim requirements under the General Municipal Law[2] or pursuant to the Public Authorities Law. Both of these sources should be checked to make a determination as to the applicable Statute of Limitations.

A determination should also be made as to whether or not the negligence is specifically related to medical treatment, *i.e.*, whether or not it will be necessary to retain an expert because the negligence alleged is outside of the knowledge of the average juror, or whether it is a case of ordinary negligence or, perhaps, a premises liability case, *e.g.*, someone mopped a floor or applied too much wax, and an injury resulted. The mere fact that negligence occurred in a hospital does not necessarily mean that the case is one involving medical negligence that would require expert review and testimony.

If an action is brought against a hospital allegedly based on medical negligence, a medical review should be undertaken, even though CPLR 3012–a refers specifically only to actions for "medical, dental or podiatric

---

6. Chapter 29, "Medical Malpractice," *infra*.

7. CPLR 3012–a(a)(2).

§ 26.12

1. *See also*, Chapter 29, "Medical Malpractice," *infra*.

2. *See generally* General Municipal Law §§ 50–e, *et seq. See also*, Chapter 3, "Municipal Law," *supra*.

§ 26.12 PERSONAL INJURY Ch. 26

malpractice." There is no particular mention in the statute of hospital negligence requiring the pre-suit review, but clearly it is much safer to have the review done and to attach a certificate of merit to the summons and complaint.

§ 26.13 Investigation—Medical Malpractice—Dental and Podiatric Malpractice

In dental and podiatric malpractice actions, the same approach that would be used in a medical malpractice action should be followed.[1] That is, the records should be obtained, reviewed and sent to a dentist, dental surgeon, oral surgeon or podiatrist for review before commencement of an action.[2] A certificate of merit is required in both of these types of cases.[3]

§ 26.14 Investigation—Products Liability

As noted above, medical negligence and products liability actions[1] are the two most time-consuming and expensive types of personal injury actions that can be brought. It should be noted that often a products liability action will arise from a workers' compensation claim. For example, a client may come into counsel's office with a job-related injury for which workers' compensation benefits may be claimed, and he or she may say that the injury occurred when a machine malfunctioned.[2]

It is critical early in a products liability action to identify the particular product involved, including information concerning the make and model of the product. Any manuals or handbooks that exist should be obtained. The year that the product was manufactured is also important, as is information concerning the length of time the employer had the machine. It also will be important to discover how many previous owners of the machine or product there were and who they were.

Another area to discuss with the client, who may be the person with the most knowledge of the machine, is whether or not the machine had been modified in any way prior to the accident, *e.g.*, were any safety devices removed. It should also be determined, if possible, exactly how the machine malfunctioned. Photographs and, perhaps, pre-litigation discovery and inspection may be necessary.[3]

§ 26.13
1. See § 26.12, *supra*.
2. *Id.*
3. CPLR 3012–a.

§ 26.14
1. *See* Chapter 27, "Products Liability," *infra*. *See also*, Bensel, Frank, McKeon, et al., *Personal Injury Practice in New York* (West 1997); Kreindler, Rodriguez, et. al., *New York Law of Torts* (West 1997) Ch. 16 "Products Liability."

2. *See* Chapter 32, "Workers' Compensation," *infra*.

3. *See also*, Bensel, Frank, McKeon, et al., *Personal Injury Practice in New York* (West 1997); Kreindler, Rodriguez, et. al., *New York Law of Torts* (West 1997).

If the product is available, it should be preserved and reviewed, but destructive testing should not be undertaken. A chain of custody should be determined, if at all possible. Early review by an expert should be made.

The Consumer Products Safety Commission may be contacted to determine if the product at issue has been reviewed for dangerousness or has been subject to a recall. Additionally, the Association of Trial Lawyers of America ("ATLA") has a data bank containing information concerning products which have caused injury which can be consulted by members of that organization.

While the preceding suggestions with regard to investigation are certainly not comprehensive, they will provide counsel with a basic approach to get started in a products liability action.

§ 26.15 Investigation—Dog Bites

With regard to dog bite cases, the primary issue is whether or not there was prior notice of the dog's vicious propensity.[1] Thus, when a client comes into your office alleging that he or she was bitten and/or attacked by a dog, the first consideration should be whether or not the plaintiff is aware of any prior notice on the part of the dog's owner. If the dog lives in the client's neighborhood, he or she may have such information. Interviews of neighbors may lead to information about the dog and whether or not there was any prior notice. The local dog warden should also be consulted to ascertain whether the dog was previously cited for biting anyone. Also, a check with the local police department may yield similar information.

If counsel is unable to uncover any information with regard to the owner's knowledge of the vicious propensity of the dog, a second approach would be to focus on a violation of the local leash law. Certainly, if the defendant had been cited for a violation of the leash law, and had entered a plea of guilty, plaintiff's counsel could request the trial court to charge the jury that they could find that violation of the leash law was a proximate cause of the accident and also that the violation of the local ordinance may be considered as some evidence of negligence. This may be an alternative to proof of prior notice of the dog's vicious propensity.

§ 26.16 Investigation—Chemical Exposure

The principal concern in a chemical exposure case is proof of causation, *i.e.,* there must be scientific proof that the type of chemical to which the plaintiff was exposed could cause the disease and/or sympto-

---

§ 26.15
1. Fontecchio v. Esposito, 108 A.D.2d 780, 485 N.Y.S.2d 113 (2d Dep't 1985). See also, Kreindler, Rodriguez, *et. al.*, *New York Law of Torts* (West 1997).

§ 26.16 PERSONAL INJURY Ch. 26

matology incurred by the client.[1] Related issues that must be investigated are the exact nature of the contamination and where the chemical came from. What was contaminated? In other words, was the plaintiff exposed to paint that contained lead, hydrocarbons that leaked into an aquifer and then into the plaintiff's water supply? Was the toxic substance an airborne contaminant emanating from, for example, a furnace?

The length of the exposure should be determined, including the date that the exposure ended. Particular attention should be paid to the relevant Statute of Limitations.[2] Obviously, a toxicologist and an engineer would be of great benefit in determining the source, amount and location of any chemical contaminant. Soil, air and other samplings and testings would also be of great benefit. Additionally, it should be determined whether or not the entity responsible for the client's exposure to the contaminants is viable, *i.e.*, whether or not there are sufficient assets or coverage with regard to the claim, taking into account the economic considerations outlined above.

§ 26.17 Investigation—Automobile Accidents

Investigation of an automobile accident case begins with the client interview, as discussed above. It should be noted that in automobile negligence cases in New York, plaintiff must prove:

a. The defendant(s)' negligence;

b. The plaintiff's serious injury;[1]

c. That the plaintiff's injury was proximately caused by the defendant's negligence; and

d. The plaintiff's damages.[2]

This is an A+B+C=D equation. *Both* negligence *and* serious injury must be proved. Thus, particular attention must be paid to the way in which serious injury can be proved.

After the decision is made to take the case, the initial interview has been completed, the retainer agreement signed and the retainer statement prepared and sent for filing and the file opened, certain basic information should be obtained, as discussed below.

§ 26.18 Investigation—Automobile Accidents—Police Report

The police report of a motor vehicle accident is known as the MV104A. It is prepared by the police officer on the scene. It may consist

---

§ 26.16
1. See Kreindler, Rodriguez, et. al., New York Law of Torts (West 1997).
2. CPLR 214–c.

§ 26.17
1. Insurance Law § 5102(d).

2. *See also*, Bensel, Frank, McKeon, et al., *Personal Injury Practice in New York* (West 1997) Ch. 3 "Damages"; Kreindler, Rodriguez, et. al., New York Law of Torts (West 1997).

of one or more pages, and *all* pages should be obtained. Important information may be contained in the police report, including:[1]

a. Whether or not photographs were taken by the police department;

b. The negligent driver's name and address;

c. The owner's name and address;[2]

d. Contributing factors in the accident;

e. A description of the accident;

f. Possible witnesses;

g. Tickets issued;

h. Restraints used (seat belts);

i. Road contour;

j. Weather conditions;

k. Traffic control devices; and

l. Insurance information.

§ 26.19 Investigation—Automobile Accidents—Witness Statements

The police report should be reviewed to determine if any witnesses are listed, and if there are, a witness statement form should be sent to each.[1]

§ 26.20 Investigation—Automobile Accidents—MV104

An MV104 is a separate document from the MV104A. This form is required to be filed with the New York State Department of Motor Vehicles if a personal injury has been incurred in a motor vehicle accident, or if the property damage exceeded two hundred fifty dollars ($250). The MV104 is often signed by the adverse party and is, therefore,

---

§ 26.18

1. **PRACTICE POINTER:** Counsel should make sure that the information, particularly that attributed to the client, is accurate. If it is not, counsel should consider asking the officer to correct the report or to note the client's objections in an addendum to the report.

If photographs were taken, counsel should either order the photographs or the contact sheet, and, from the contact sheet, it should be determined which photographs should be purchased.

2. **PRACTICE POINTER:** If the owner of the car was not driving at the time of the accident, note that the owner is still vicariously liable for the driver's negligence pursuant to Vehicle and Traffic Law § 388.

§ 26.19

1. *See also*, Bensel, Frank, McKeon, *et al., Personal Injury Practice in New York* (West 1997) Forms 2–5, 2–6, for a form Letter Asking for a Witness Statement and a Witness Statement Checklist.

§ 26.20 PERSONAL INJURY Ch. 26

a statement concerning which that party can be examined.[1]

If the client was operating a vehicle involved in the accident and is thus required to complete and file an MV104, counsel should assist the client with the description of the accident, making sure that the information is accurate.[2] If the client has filed the MV104 and counsel does not have a copy of it, one should be obtained.

Counsel should obtain the defendant's MV104. If it has not yet been filed, the Department of Motor Vehicles will send a notice to the defendant, advising that the form must be completed within thirty (30) days or the defendant's license will be suspended. Also, if the accident is a multiple vehicle accident, the MV104 form of the other operators should be obtained as well, as those statements may provide insight into the accident. The fee to obtain an MV104 is twenty dollars ($20).

§ 26.21 Investigation—Automobile Accidents—Application of No–Fault

When a person is injured in an automobile accident in New York, his or her medical bills are paid under the No–Fault provision of the automobile policy that covers the vehicle in which he or she was an occupant.[1] The attorney is not required to assist the client in completing the No–Fault claim form or, thereafter, in processing bills or claims for lost wages. In fact, many attorneys will decline to assist the client with any processing of medical bills or lost wage claims, because these are extremely time consuming and are not fee-generating *per se*.

The No–Fault process begins with the client's completion of an application for benefits, which must be filed within ninety (90) days of the occurrence of the accident.[2] This application requires basic background information on the claimant, along with wage and employment information, medical information and, importantly, a description of the accident. Also included are authorization forms for the release of employment and medical records, which must be signed.

Whether or not the attorney chooses to assist with the completion of the No–Fault application, he or she should always make sure that the description of the accident is accurate and that it is consistent with other statements, particularly the police report and MV104.

§ 26.20

1. A sample MV104 can be found *infra*, § 26.53. *See* Barker and Alexander, *Evidence in New York State and Federal Courts* (West 1996) § 801(1).2.

2. **PRACTICE POINTER:** The MV104 form completed by the client or by the adverse party may be obtained from the Department of Motor Vehicles in Albany, New York at the following address:

Department of Motor Vehicles
Public Services Bureau
Empire State Plaza
Albany, New York 12228–0232

§ 26.21

1. Bensel, Frank, McKeon, *et al.*, *Personal Injury Practice in New York* (West 1997) Ch. 7 "No–Fault and Uninsured Motorist Law."

2. 11 NYCRR § 65(11); No Fault Arbitration Decision 1781.

§ 26.22 Investigation—Automobile Accidents—Medical Records

The client's hospital record, particularly the admission history, discharge summary, X-ray and laboratory reports, should be obtained and reviewed to determine if there is anything in the records that might be harmful to the case, such as a description of the accident, whether or not seat belts were used, and whether or not alcohol or drug screens had positive results. Also, since a fracture qualifies under the statute as a serious injury,[1] the X-ray reports are crucial to proof of such an injury.

§ 26.23 Investigation—Automobile Accidents—Photographs

If possible, counsel should personally photograph the accident scene, as one never knows what others may have missed. If the injury to the client includes scarring, photographs of the scarring should be obtained. The same applies to severe bruising.

If there is a question whether or not there was a second impact inside the vehicle, counsel should consider taking photographs of the interior of the vehicle. Access to the inside of the defendant's vehicle should be obtained, if possible. This may yield helpful information, such as the presence of loose beer cans, for example, which would provide a useful photograph.

§ 26.24 Investigation—Automobile Accidents—Insurance Policies and Coverage

Previously, an automobile negligence case was considered to be a straight-forward case. Generally, liability insurance coverage could be readily determined, liability defined and damages considered in a direct fashion, with trial or settlement to follow. The passage of the No–Fault provisions of the Insurance Law complicated the picture somewhat, however, particularly with regard to the requirement to prove "serious injury" in order to bring an action in tort.

The most important, and indeed the most complicated, issues today are issues related to insurance coverage, including the coverage available under No–Fault. This section will set forth the various types of coverage and their applicability to an automobile accident case.

No–Fault First Party Benefits. Basic No–Fault coverage (referred to as "Personal Injury Protection" or "PIP") will be applied on the basis of the policy covering the vehicle in which the claimant was an occupant or, if the claimant was a pedestrian, on the basis of the policy covering the vehicle that injured him. The basic No–Fault policy provides cover-

---

§ 26.22
1. Insurance Law § 5102(d).

age in the amount of fifty thousand dollars ($50,000). This coverage includes causally related:

- medical bills (hospital and physician);
- diagnostic testing (X-ray, laboratory, MRI, CT);
- physical and occupational therapy;
- dental treatment;
- chiropractic treatment;
- wages, calculated at eighty percent (80%) of the normal wage, minus disability and/or Social Security disability payments, up to a maximum of two thousand dollars per month for up to three years after the accident;[1]
- mileage to and from medical treatment during the first year after the injury;
- prescription reimbursement;
- household assistance if prescribed by a physician (up to $25 per day); and
- child care assistance if prescribed by a physician (up to $25 per day).

Additional First Party Benefits. Additional No–Fault coverage may be available. "Additional Personal Injury Protection" or "APIP" generally extends coverage to a level of one hundred thousand dollars ($100,000). Of importance, however, is the fact that an APIP lien is created under the policy to the extent APIP benefits are paid. Many insurance carriers require the claimant to sign a subrogation agreement recognizing the lien before APIP benefits will be paid.[2]

If there is APIP coverage, certain coverage situations may arise that will create settlement problems. Consider the situation, for example, where the defendant's liability policy has a mere fifty thousand dollar limit and, due to the serious nature of the client's injuries, the APIP benefits have been paid in the amount of fifty thousand dollars and a lien created. If the lien is then paid in full, the claimant receives nothing, despite serious injuries.

Optional Basic Economic Loss. Certain optional coverages must be made available for purchase by the policyholder. These optional coverages will reimburse the claimant an additional twenty five thousand dollars ($25,000) for either medical benefits or lost wages. This coverage is referred to as "Optional Basic Economic Loss" or "OBEL."

§ 26.24

1. Insurance Law § 5102(a)(2) raised the maximum from $1,000 per month to $2,000 per month, effective November 12, 1991.

2. **PRACTICE POINTER:** If counsel knows that there is an "APIP" lien, the front of the file should be marked accordingly and no payout of any settlement proceeds made until the APIP lien has been resolved with the No-Fault carrier.

A question that often arises with regard to No–Fault coverages, particularly when the claimant was a passenger and has a separate automobile policy on his own vehicle, is whether the No–Fault coverage in his own policy is available when the coverage on the vehicle in which he was a passenger has been paid? This question has been answered in the negative, *i.e.,* No–Fault coverage cannot be "stacked" (aggregated).[3]

Claims against the Motor Vehicle Accident Indemnification Corporation (MVAIC) and Uninsured Motorist Claims. Motor vehicle insurance became mandatory in New York on February 1, 1957. Provisions for coverage for underinsured, financially irresponsible and unknown negligent motorists became effective on January 1, 1959. The problems that led to this legislation have not decreased since that date.

The Motor Vehicle Accident Indemnification Corporation Act is found in Article 52 of the Insurance Law of the State of New York.[4] This Act was designed to provide compensation to persons injured in motor vehicle accidents caused by:

a. Uninsured motor vehicles registered in a state other than New York;

b. Unidentified motor vehicles that leave the scene of an accident;

c. Motor vehicles registered in New York that have no policy of liability insurance in effect at the time of the accident;

d. Stolen motor vehicles;

e. Motor vehicles operated without the permission of the owner;

f. Insured motor vehicles where the insurer disclaims liability or denies coverage; and

g. Unregistered motor vehicles.

The MVAIC Act establishes two distinct groups, each of which must follow a different claims procedure. These procedures must be strictly adhered to if the injured person is to obtain benefits. These two groups are:

a. *Insured Persons*: These are automobile owners, their family members and others defined in the automobile policy endorsement who have suffered personal injuries or death as a result of an accident caused by an uninsured motorist. Insured persons are covered by the endorsements in their own policies, as each insurer contracts on behalf of MVAIC for payment of losses not exceeding the policy limits for that coverage.

b. *Qualified Persons*: Qualified persons are residents of New York, other than an insured or the owner of an uninsured motor vehicle, and

---

3. *See, e.g.,* Powers v. General Accident Ins. Co., 109 A.D.2d 830, 486 N.Y.S.2d 764 (2d Dep't 1985).

4. *See also,* Bensel, Frank, McKeon, *et al., Personal Injury Practice in New York* (West 1997) Ch. 7 "No-Fault and Uninsured Motorist Law."

his spouse when a passenger in such vehicle, or his legal representative, or a resident of another political entity in which recourse is afforded to New York residents of substantially similar character to that provided for in this state.[5]

Uninsured policy coverage is mandatory in New York and includes the same minimum bodily injury limits of coverage requirement as does the basic minimum liability policy. For accidents occurring after January 1, 1996, these limits are $25,000 per person, $50,000 per accident, or in the case of death, $50,000 per person, $100,000 per accident. The mandatory uninsured motorist provision of a motor vehicle liability policy in New York is known as the MVAIC endorsement.[6]

The Insurance Law also provides for the recovery of so-called "no-fault" benefits to qualified persons for basic economic loss arising out of the use and operation in New York of an uninsured motor vehicle.[7]

Coverage under the MVAIC endorsement occurs when a person is injured through the negligence of a motorist, the injured person has coverage available to him for such negligence, but the negligent operator has no coverage on the vehicle he was operating and has no other coverage available to him.

Certain questions should be asked by the attorney regarding claims pursuant to such coverage:

a. Was there any insurance coverage on the vehicle driven by the negligent driver?

b. Was coverage in effect on the date of the injury?

c. If coverage was disclaimed, was the disclaimer proper?

d. Did the negligent operator have coverage available to him other than through the vehicle owner. That is, did the operator have a policy of his own for a vehicle that he owned or that was available in his household? The attorney should review all policies of the owner, operator and others with whom the owner and operator reside(s).

e. If there is no coverage available to the negligent owner/operator, does the injured party have coverage available either through a policy he owns or another policy that could provide coverage, *i.e.*, his own uninsured coverage?

Underinsured Coverage (Supplemental Uninsured Motorist Coverage). The third type of coverage that is important in an automobile accident case is coverage known as Supplemental Uninsured Coverage ("SUM"), also known as *under*insured coverage.

---

5. Insurance Law § 5202(b).
6. Bensel, Frank, McKeon, *et al.*, *Personal Injury Practice in New York* (West 1997) ¶ ¶ 7:169–173.
7. Insurance Law § 5201(b).

SUM coverage is optional. Therefore, it may or may not be a factor in a particular automobile case. However, there are general procedures that should be followed in all cases where SUM coverage may be a factor.

As soon as possible, counsel should ascertain the limits of coverage for bodily injury contained in the negligent owner and/or operator's policy or policies. Counsel should attempt to ascertain if there is any additional stackable liability coverage for the defendant operator, if different from the owner. It should be determined, to the extent possible, if there is any umbrella or excess coverage available. Counsel should remember that it is always a good idea to confirm this in writing with each carrier involved, as it will provide good documentation for the file.

At times it may be difficult to learn from the negligent owner/operator's carrier the limits of coverage. Unfortunately, some carriers and their representatives take the position that policy limits will not voluntarily be disclosed, but will only be given, if required, after suit has been commenced.[8] This can result in the needless serving of a summons and complaint, merely to ascertain coverage. Counsel should thus write to the liability carrier, requesting that the limits be provided and explaining that coverage must be determined and that an underinsured coverage claim will be filed. A note of caution is indicated, however. In some cases, the excess or umbrella coverage is provided under the homeowner's portion of the policy. Thus, where there is the potential existence of umbrella coverage, counsel should demand to see the declaration pages of the automobile policy, the homeowner's policy, if any, and any umbrella or excess or catastrophic loss policies.

If it is clear that the injuries the client sustained are in excess of the potential liability limits, counsel should not hesitate to put the client's insurance carrier on notice of an underinsured motorist claim. This can be done when the No–Fault Application for benefits is sent[9] or as soon thereafter as the injuries are determined to be in excess of the liability limits. If put on notice of a potential claim at that time, it will be difficult for the carrier to successfully claim that it received late notice.

The following checklist may be helpful in processing an underinsured motorist claim:

a. Ascertain the policy limits of any negligent operator and owner.

b. Obtain the client's policy, particulary the declaration pages for all vehicles the client owns. Also obtain the policy and declaration pages for all vehicles owned by others in the client's household.

c. Send a letter to each carrier advising each that the client has been injured and that a claim for underinsured/uninsured coverage is being made.

---

8. CPLR 3101(f).

9. *See supra*, § 26.21.

d. Check with the client's carrier immediately to determine if underinsured coverage is contained in the policy. Often, the only coverage listed on the declaration page is uninsured coverage, and the presence of such coverage is no guarantee that underinsured coverage exists. Remember, uninsured coverage, at least at minimum limits, is mandatory, but underinsured coverage must be purchased separately.

e. Confirm each coverage limit in writing.

f. If required, complete a notice of intention to make a claim and return it to the client's underinsured motorist carrier.

g. Cooperate with the underinsured carrier and provide medical records and other evidence of the seriousness of the injury. Document the severity of the injury to prove that, in fact, the injury merits the implementation of the underinsured coverage.

h. In order to obtain benefits under any underinsured coverage, the claimant must first obtain a recovery of all the available liability coverage.[10] Often the underinsured carrier will demand a letter from the liability carrier(s) stating the limits of coverage and a copy of the check to the claimant before proceeding to discuss payment of the underinsured claim.

i. Caution: Before the case with the owner and operator's liability carrier is settled, counsel must obtain the permission of the underinsured carrier and reserve any rights it may have.[11]

j. The underinsured claim may be negotiated with the carrier. If, however, the case cannot be settled, the claim must be arbitrated in accordance with the terms of the policy. Arbitration may be carried out in the American Arbitration Association forum, private arbitration with one arbitrator, or arbitration where each party selects an arbitrator and the two chosen arbitrators select a third. In any event, arbitration of the underinsured claim will be governed by the terms of the policy.

k. Counsel should remember that at an arbitration, the relevant issues are fault and damages. The arbitration, therefore, should be prepared for and presented as if it were a trial, although obviously in shorter form. As to the issue of fault, diagrams, police reports, witnesses and MV104's will be beneficial.

When dealing with the issue of damages, counsel must consider which witnesses will be of benefit. Generally, medical reports are used,

---

[10]. Insurance Law § 3420(f)(2); Guerra by Guerra v. Fernandez, 149 Misc.2d 25, 562 N.Y.S.2d 1020 (Sup.Ct., Queens County, 1990).

[11]. State Farm Mutual Ins. Co. v. Donath, 164 A.D.2d 889, 559 N.Y.S.2d 567 (2d Dep't 1990); State Farm Mutual Ins. Co. v. Taglianetti, 122 A.D.2d 40, 504 N.Y.S.2d 476 (2d Dep't 1986); State Farm Mutual Ins. Co. v. Isler, 38 A.D.2d 966, 331 N.Y.S.2d 547 (2d Dep't 1972).

although live medical testimony should be considered. Any particular limitations of the claimant requiring special needs should be identified, and if a cost is attached, it will be necessary to prove that cost.

At present, two sets of rules govern supplemental uninsured motorist ("SUM") claims, depending upon the effective date of the relevant policy.[12] For policies effective prior to October 1, 1993, coverage issues are to be determined by the policy language and case law. However, all policies *issued* with effective dates on or after October 1, 1993, and all policies *renewed* to become effective between October 1, 1993 and September 30, 1994,[13] are governed by Regulation 35–D, also known as the Supplemental Uninsured Motorist Insurance Regulation.

Actions that should be taken with regard to claims arising under policies that were *effective before October 1, 1993* include:

a. Review the claimant's policy to determine if there is underinsured coverage available.

b. Put the underinsured carrier on notice as soon as practicable. Some policies require that the carrier be notified within 90 days. As a practical matter, however, it is often impossible to determine if there is an underinsured claim within 90 days, particularly if the liability carrier refuses to disclose its insured's policy limits within that time frame. It is suggested, therefore, that a letter be sent to the underinsured carrier within the 90 day period, informing the carrier of a potential claim.

c. DO NOT provide a release to the liability carrier without the *written permission* of the underinsured carrier. If a release is given to the liability carrier without the written permission of the underinsured carrier, the underinsured carrier can disclaim coverage for violating the terms of the policy and for interfering with its subrogation rights.

Other important considerations applicable to losses that occurred prior to October 1, 1993 and with regard to policies that were effective before that date:

a. SUM coverage is extra-territorial in that it covers the insured in any state or Canadian province.[14] This differs from uninsured coverage, which only applies to losses occurring in New York.[15]

b. The coverage must be "triggered" to be effective. Originally, there was a great deal of confusion as to which limits were to be compared in order to determine whether coverage applied. Rather than discuss the entire confusing scenario, it is now clear that coverage is triggered when a comparison of the *liability limits* of

---

12. Insurance Law § 3420(f)(2).
13. Regulation 35–D has been codified at 11 NYCRR § 60–2.
14. Insurance Law § 3420(f)(2).
15. Insurance Law § 3420(f)(1).

§ 26.24 PERSONAL INJURY Ch. 26

the two vehicles reveals that the claimant has a higher liability limit than does the tortfeasor.[16] If multiple vehicles are involved in an accident, the limits of one policy only must be tendered, rather than all, to trigger an underinsured motorist claim.

c. No set–off will be made for amounts paid by liability carriers. That is, the underinsured motorist coverage will not be reduced by amounts paid by tortfeasors.[17]

d. Stacking of underinsured coverage has been permitted,[18] as has stacking of underinsured motorist coverage and uninsured motorist coverage in the same policy for the same injuries.[19]

Rules for losses subject to Regulation 35–D. The new regulation that governs underinsured motorist coverage is Regulation 35–D. This regulation, contrary to prior case law, allows a set-off on behalf of the underinsured carrier for amounts paid by the tortfeasor. Also, no stacking of coverage is permitted.

The regulation requires that the claimant give written notice of the claim as soon as practicable, which may shorten the 90 day period previously existing in policies. Of importance, however, is the fact that 30 days after the underinsured carrier has received written notice of an offer of the available limits of liability coverage, the plaintiff may execute a release, unless, within that time, the underinsured motorist carrier agrees to advance the amount of such settlement in return for the insured's cooperation in the underlying law suit pursued by the carrier.

As noted above, the police report will show the name of the insurance company that was on the card handed to the police officer at the scene of the accident. Although the carrier any have issued an insurance card that shows a policy period of one year, if the insured did not make the premium payments, the policy will have been canceled. Therefore, counsel should send the carrier listed on the police report a letter of representation and confirm that coverage is still in place. In addition, counsel should have the client bring in the policy and declarations page of his or her policy that was in effect at the time of the accident. Then, the client's carrier should be placed on notice of a potential uninsured or underinsured claim, as necessary.

§ 26.25 Claims Procedure for Automobile Accidents

The time within which an insured person must file a claim is controlled by the terms of the endorsement to his own policy. Generally,

16. Maurizzio v. Lumbermens Mut. Cas. Co., 73 N.Y.2d 951, 540 N.Y.S.2d 982, 538 N.E.2d 334 (1989).

17. United Community Ins. Co. v. Mucatel, 127 Misc.2d 1045, 487 N.Y.S.2d 959 (Sup.Ct., N.Y. County, 1985), aff'd 119 A.D.2d 1017, 501 N.Y.S.2d 761 (1st Dep't 1986), aff'd 69 N.Y.2d 777, 513 N.Y.S.2d 114, 505 N.E.2d 624 (1987).

18. DiStasi v. Nationwide Mutual Insurance Co., 132 A.D.2d 305, 522 N.Y.S.2d 340 (3d Dep't 1987).

19. Reichel v. GEICO, 66 N.Y.2d 1000, 499 N.Y.S.2d 385, 489 N.E.2d 1287 (1985).

Ch. 26   FILING NOTICE OF CLAIM WITH THE MVAIC § 26.26

the insured must notify his carrier within 90 days of the occurrence or as soon thereafter as is practicable. In the event that the carrier disclaims coverage due to late notice, counsel may argue that the carrier had knowledge through the police report, no-fault application or perhaps a property damage or subrogation claim.

Uninsured policy claims are submitted directly to the claimant's own insurer. It should be noted that this should be done as soon as possible (within the policy terms) as the insurer need not show prejudice in asserting a defense of failure to comply with the notice requirement.[1]

The attorney should take the following steps for a potential "insured person:"

1. Upon contact by the client, obtain the police report of the accident and ascertain who is the defendant's carrier. If the carrier information is not on the police report, or if the operator was ticketed for not having insurance,[2] proceed to step 5.

2. If the negligent owner's carrier is listed in the police report, contact the carrier directly, advise the claim department of the client's representation, and determine if coverage exists. If so, have the insurer confirm coverage in writing.

3. If coverage is not confirmed by the owner's liability carrier, contact the owner and have him or her have the liability carrier contact counsel. Again, if there is coverage, it should be confirmed in writing.

4. If coverage is confirmed, proceed directly against the owner/operator, but keep in mind the possible need to go against underinsured motorist coverage.

5. If it cannot be determined that the owner or operator has coverage available, put the client's own carrier on notice of a claim for uninsured motorist benefits under the client-insured's policy. This should be done in writing.

Library References:

West's Key No. Digests, Automobiles ⟐251.5–251.9.

§ 26.26 Claims Procedure for Automobile Accidents—Filing Notice of Claim With the Motor Vehicle Accident Indemnity Corporation

A "qualified person"[1] must file a Notice of Claim with the Motor Vehicle Accident Indemnity Cororation ("MVAIC"). This is a condition precedent to the presentation of a claim. When there has been a delay in

§ 26.25
1. State Farm v. Romero, 109 A.D.2d 786, 486 N.Y.S.2d 297 (2d Dep't 1985).
2. Vehicle and Traffic Law § 319(1).

§ 26.26
1. See definition of "qualified person" supra, § 26.24, note 4, and accompanying text.

§ 26.26

giving such notice, the reasonableness of the delay will depend upon the insured's diligence in ascertaining the insurance status of the other operator and then in giving notice once the lack of insurance was discovered.[2]

The Notice of Claim must be presented within 180 days of the accrual of the cause of action. For each of the three categories of "qualified persons," there is a different procedure that must be followed. Simply stated, the categories are: no insurance; no insurance and identity of wrongdoer not ascertainable; and insurance initially believed to exist, but no insurance after disclaimer by carrier.

Library References:

West's Key No. Digests, Automobiles ⚍251.6.

§ 26.27 Claims Procedure for Automobile Accidents—Filing Notice of Claim With the Motor Vehicle Accident Indemnity Corporation—Procedure for Cases in Which There Is No Insurance

The Notice of Claim affidavit must contain the following information:[1]

a. A statement that the claimant has a cause of action for damages arising out of the accident and setting forth the facts in support.

b. A statement that the cause of action is against the owner or operator of a designated uninsured motor vehicle; and

c. An averment that the claimant is making a claim for such damages.

Library References:

West's Key No. Digests, Automobiles ⚍251.6.

§ 26.28 Claims Procedure for Automobile Accidents—Filing Notice of Claim With the Motor Vehicle Accident Indemnity Corporation—Procedure for Cases in Which There Is No Insurance and the Identity of the Wrongdoer Is Not Ascertainable (Hit and Run)

The accident must have been reported within twenty-four hours after the occurrence to a police, peace or judicial officer in the vicinity, or

---

2. Nasello v. MVAIC, 30 A.D.2d 1041, 294 N.Y.S.2d 851 (4th Dep't 1968).

§ 26.27

1. Insurance Law § 5208(a)(3)(A)(i-iii).

§ 26.29 Claims Procedure for Automobile Accidents—Filing Notice of Claim With the Motor Vehicle Accident Indemnity Corporation—Procedure for Cases in Which Insurance Initially Is Believed to Exist, But There Is No Insurance After Later Disclaimer

The notice of claim, in affidavit form, in this case should state that:

a. The claimant has a cause of action for damages arising out the accident and setting forth the supporting facts;

b. The insurers of the person alleged to be liable for the damages have disclaimed liability or have denied coverage because of some act or omission of the person alleged to be liable, including a denial of coverage based upon the lack of a policy of insurance in effect at the time the cause of action arose; provided, however, that in case of a denial of coverage based upon the lack of a policy of insurance in effect at the time the cause of action arose, timely reasonable efforts must have been made to ascertain coverage;

c. The claimant is making a claim for those damages.[1]

In this situation, the affidavit must be filed within 180 days of the affiant's receipt of notice of the disclaimer or denial of coverage.[2]

Library References:

West's Key No. Digests, Automobiles ⚖=251.6.

§ 26.30 Claims Procedure for Automobile Accidents—Filing Notice of Claim With the Motor Vehicle Accident Indemnity Corporation—Late Claims

Relief may be granted under certain circumstances by the MVAIC or by the court for late filing by a qualified person of the affidavit required under Insurance Law § 5208 (a)(1), when the affidavit is not filed:

a. Within 180 days; or

b. The qualified person is an infant or is mentally or physically incapacitated or is deceased; or

c. The qualified person fails to file within 180 days of the accrual of the action due to receipt of erroneous information from the Department of Motor Vehicles, or from a police report with respect to the identification of a vehicle.

§ 26.29
1. Insurance Law § 5208(a)(3)(A)(i-iii).
2. Insurance Law § 5208(a)(3)(B).

to the Commissioner of Motor Vehicles.[1] The notice of claim, in affidavit form, must contain the following statements:[2]

a. The claimant has a cause of action for damages arising out of the accident and setting forth the supporting facts;

b. The cause of action is against a person whose identity is unascertainable; and

c. The claimant is making a claim for those damages.

However, the fact that the accident was not reported within twenty-four hours after the occurrence, as required by Insurance Law § 5208(a) will not prejudice the rights of the person if it is shown that it was not reasonably possible to make such a report, or that it was made as soon as was reasonably possible.[3]

This portion of the MVAIC statute is also known as the "hit and run" part. The driver or motor vehicle must be unidentified or unidentifiable.[4]

"Hit and run" vehicles are also covered in cases in which the identity of the negligent motorist cannot be determined because of deceit, change of address or immediate failure to appreciate the injury.[5] There is a requirement in this category, however, that there be proof that the injuries suffered arose out of physical contact with the motor vehicle that caused injury to the qualified person, or with the motor vehicle that the qualified person was occupying at the time of the accident.[6] Indeed, physical contact between the hit and run vehicle and the "uninsured" or insured vehicle is a condition precedent to arbitration under the endorsement.[7] Proof of contact may be satisfied with evidence of contact with an intervening object, *e.g.*, another vehicle.[8]

Library References:

West's Key No. Digests, Automobiles ⟸251.6.

§ 26.28

1. Insurance Law § 5208(a). *See also,* Bensel, Frank, McKeon, et al., *Personal Injury Practice in New York* (West 1997) Ch.7.

2. Insurance Law § 5208(a)(1)(A–C).

3. *See generally,* Dimas v. MVAIC, 18 A.D.2d 761, 235 N.Y.S.2d 461 (4th Dep't 1962); Dixon v. MVAIC, 56 A.D.2d 650, 391 N.Y.S.2d 898 (2d Dep't 1977).

4. De Puccio v. MVAIC, 30 A.D.2d 1015, 294 N.Y.S.2d 113 (3d Dep't 1968).

5. Riemenschneider v. MVAIC, 20 N.Y.2d 547, 285 N.Y.S.2d 593, 232 N.E.2d 630 (1967); Allstate Insurance Co. v. McGouey, 42 A.D.2d 730, 346 N.Y.S.2d 115 (2d Dep't 1973).

6. Insurance Law § 5217.

7. Aetna Casualty and Surety Co. v. Smith, 100 A.D.2d 751, 474 N.Y.S.2d 17 (1st Dep't 1984).

8. MVAIC v. Eisenberg, 18 N.Y.2d 1, 271 N.Y.S.2d 641, 218 N.E.2d 524 (1966).

Upon a filing within 31 days of receipt of written notice of correction of the error by the Department of Motor Vehicles or discovery of the mistake contained in the police report, the MVAIC may accept the filing of the affidavit if accompanied by proof satisfactory to it of the facts that caused the delay, that it was not reasonably possible to file the affidavit within the specified period, and that the affidavit was filed as soon as was reasonably possible.[1] In the alternative, a court may, upon like proof, grant leave to file the affidavit within a reasonable time after the expiration of the specified period. In making its decision, the court will, in particular, consider whether the MVAIC acquired actual knowledge of the essential facts constituting the claim within the time specified in Insurance Law § 5208(a)(1) (e.g., within 180 days of the accrual) or a reasonable time thereafter. It shall also consider all other relevant facts and circumstances, including whether:

a. The claimant failed to file a timely affidavit by reason of the claimant's justifiable reliance upon settlement representations made by a person believed to be the insurance carrier representative of the financially irresponsible motorist;

b. The claimant in filing made an excusable error concerning the identity or existence of the corporation against which the claim should or could be filed; and

c. The delay in filing substantially prejudiced the MVAIC in maintaining a defense on the merits.[2]

Application to the court for leave to file a late claim must be made within one year from the beginning of the period for filing the affidavit (date of accrual). The application must include an affidavit showing evidentiary facts in support of the proof required by Insurance Law § 5208(b) for late filing of the claim with the MVAIC, and a copy of the proposed Notice of Claim affidavit. A copy of the application must be served upon the MVAIC by delivery to the person designated by law as a person to whom a summons in an action in the supreme court issued against such party may be delivered. In addition, notice of the return time, together with a copy of the application, must be served at least eight days before the time set for the hearing.[3]

It is recommended that the affidavit averring the evidentiary facts in support of the late filing of claim satisfy the requirements of an affidavit sufficient to defeat a motion for summary judgment.[4] Thus, the affidavit should set forth proof in evidentiary form from a person with personal knowledge. A mere conclusory affidavit from an attorney would not be sufficient.

§ 26.30
1. Insurance Law § 5208(b)(1).
2. Insurance Law § 5208(b)(2)(A), (B), (C).
3. Insurance Law § 5208(c).
4. CPLR 3212.

§ 26.30   PERSONAL INJURY   Ch. 26

Insured's claims. Procedures related to an *insured*'s claim may include the following elements:

a. The claim may be settled by the carrier without court approval unless the injured person is an infant, is adjudicated incompetent, or the claim is for wrongful death.

b. If the claim cannot be settled, *i.e.*, the parties cannot agree, the matter will be arbitrated as to the issues of fault and damages.

c. Either party may make a demand for arbitration.

d. Generally, the arbitration will be held in the county where the insured resides.

e. American Arbitration Association arbitration is mandated by the Insurance Department for uninsured arbitration.

f. If there is any question as to whether the claimant was injured by an insured or uninsured vehicle, the issue must be resolved by a court on a motion to compel arbitration.

g. Other issues to be determined by the court, rather than by arbitration include:

    1. Which insurance is primary;

    2. Which insurance is excess;

    3. What state's limits apply;

    4. Whether the uninsured motorist endorsement permits double coverage; and

    5. Whether payments under one policy can be credited against another.

h. The insured may be required to be examined by the carrier's medical consultant.

i. As with any other hearing procedure, the case must be carefully prepared. A settlement brochure will be useful, both for the claimant's attorney and the arbitrator. This settlement brochure should include:

    1. A brief and concise statement of the liability, paying particular attention to the facts that support a lack of culpable conduct on the part of the claimant;

    2. A complete documentation of all favorable medical proof that has been generated, including the emergency room and other hospital records, particularly the admission and discharge summaries and radiological reports, physicians' office charts, operative reports, physical therapy records, narrative reports and no-fault medical reports and examinations of carriers' physicians;

3. Any photographs of the scene, the vehicles and the injuries, particularly scarring and deformities;
4. The police report and witness statements; and
5. A statement of law, if necessary.

Witness preparation is extremely important and should not be overlooked. Careful witness preparation on the issues of liability, culpable conduct and damages will increase the effectiveness of the presentation before the arbitrator.

Qualified person's claims. Procedures related to a *qualified person*'s claim include the following elements:

a. Once the claim has been filed, the MVAIC may settle any claim (except infants, incompetents or death cases) without court approval.[5]

b. If the MVAIC and the claimant cannot agree on issues of liability and/or damages, these issues may be submitted to arbitration, but questions relating to coverage are issues for the court.

c. If the matter cannot be resolved, the claimant must proceed to judgment against the financially irresponsible motorist, and the MVAIC must be put on notice of the action.

d. The MVAIC may appear through counsel and may defend any action on its own behalf and on behalf of the defendant.[6]

e. Once a judgment has been entered, remains unpaid and appeals have been completed, the injured person must file a verified petition in the court in which the judgment was entered and apply to the court for an order directing payment by the MVAIC of the amount of the judgment.

f. In a "hit and run" case, the following procedure must be followed:[7]

   1. The qualified person must bring a petition before the court;
   2. Show that the petitioner is a qualified person (it is not sufficient to introduce a conclusory statement);[8]
   3. State that the petitioner is a resident of New York State or of a state granting reciprocal relief to New York;
   4. Establish compliance with statutory requirements by showing that the petitioner (i) filed his or her Notice of Claim within 180 days, and (ii) reported the accident to

---

5. Insurance Law § 5213(a).
6. Insurance Law § 5209.
7. Insurance Law § 5218.
8. Bonavisa v. MVAIC, 21 Misc.2d 963, 198 N.Y.S.2d 332 (Sup.Ct., N.Y. County, 1960).

§ 26.30   PERSONAL INJURY   Ch. 26

a police, peace, judicial officer or the Commissioner of Insurance within 24 hours after its occurrence, or provided a substantial explanation for the delay if the accident was not reported within 24 hours;

5. Show that the injured person or deceased was not, at the time of the accident, operating an uninsured motor vehicle or operating a motor vehicle in violation of an order of suspension or revocation;

6. Allege that petitioner has a cause of action against the owner or operator of the motor vehicle;

7. Set forth all reasonable efforts made to ascertain the identity of the motor vehicle and the owner and operator, or of the operator operating it without the owner's consent, and that all such efforts have been unavailing; and

8. State that the application is not made by or on behalf of an insured or surety liable for the payment of all or part of a judgment by reason of any motor vehicle liability insurance policy or indemnity bond, or that no part of the amount is to be paid.

The plaintiff or innocent victim has the burden to establish that the injuries were caused by an unidentified vehicle and operator or owner. If there is the slightest evidence that the person responsible for the damage is known or identifiable, the application to sue MVAIC will be denied, and the injured claimant will be required to pursue his remedy against the defendant.[9]

If the above stated requirements are complied with to the satisfaction of the court, it will grant the claimant permission to proceed with the action directly against the MVAIC.

Library References:

West's Key No. Digests, Automobiles ⇐251.6.

§ 26.31 Theories of Liability

When considering which theories of liability to pursue, it should first be determined if the facts of the case are sufficient to establish all of the necessary elements of the proposed causes of action, as revealed by a review of the governing case law. It is important, however, for counsel not to feel limited by existing theories of law, but rather to use his or her expertise, if necessary, to develop a new theory from existing case law, *i.e.*, a reasonable extension of the existing law. When a reasonable

---

9. Insurance Law § 5218; Frankl v. MVAIC, 53 A.D.2d 614, 384 N.Y.S.2d 20 (2d Dep't 1976); Villanueva v. Muniz, 136 A.D.2d 546, 523 N.Y.S.2d 167 (2d Dep't 1988).

argument can be made to extend the current case law into a new area, the attorney should not be subject to sanctions.[1]

It is important to note, also, that conflicting or multiple theories of liability can be pled in the complaint and, set forth in the bill of particulars. However, when the matter is brought on for trial, the attorney should select the strongest of the theories and proceed with that particular theory. If multiple theories are not inconsistent, they can be used to strengthen each other. For example, in a products liability case, both a design defect claim and a failure to warn claim can be alleged and tried. Of course, each theory of liability must be carefully tied to the damages with proof of proximate cause, for even though a defendant may be negligent, if that negligence is not the proximate cause of the injury, the attorney should consider whether or not to forego that cause of action and concentrate on a theory of liability for which the proof of proximate cause of the injuries and damages sustained is the strongest.

§ 26.32 Filing the Action

Before the commencement by filing law was enacted in 1992,[1] the service of a summons served two functions. It both began the lawsuit and operated to secure personal jurisdiction over the defendant. Now, the initiation of the suit and the obtaining of personal jurisdiction over the defendant are accomplished by *two* separate acts. In supreme and county courts, the action is commenced by the filing of a summons and complaint, or a summons with the required notice pursuant to CPLR 305(b), with the clerk of the court in the county in which the action is brought.[2] At the time the summons and complaint are filed, the index number and date of filing must be stamped on the summons.

Proof of service. The proof of service of the summons and complaint must be in a form of a certificate if the service is made by a sheriff or other authorized officer, in the form of an affidavit if made by any other person, or in the form of a signed acknowledgment of receipt of the summons and complaint or summons with notice.[3] The proof of service should set forth the place and manner of service and that service of process was made by an authorized person in an authorized manner. Whenever service is made by delivery of the summons to the defendant

§ 26.31
1. CPLR 8303–a.

§ 26.32
1. L.1992, Ch. 216, effective July 1, 1992.
2. CPLR 304.

PRACTICE POINTER: The plaintiff or third party plaintiff must purchase an index number for the summons and complaint or summons with notice to be filed in the county clerk's office. The current cost of an index number is $170. It is advisable at the time of filing to have additional copies of the summons and complaint stamped by the clerk's office, showing that the summons and complaint were, in fact, filed before the expiration of the Statute of Limitations.

3. CPLR 306(d).

or the person to be served, the proof of service must also include a description of the person upon whom service was made, including (but not limited to) sex, color of skin, hair color, approximate age, approximate weight and height and any other identifying features.[4]

When service is made pursuant to CPLR 308(4) (the so-called "nail and mail" provision), proof of service must also specify the dates, addressed and times of attempted service.

Service on a corporation and filing proof of service thereof is sometimes a problem when the corporation cannot be located. It should be noted that where service on an individual or a corporation is impracticable, application can be made to the court to fashion a manner of service designed to give a defendant notice of the action.[5] Formerly, there was no provision in CPLR 311 which related to corporations. To remedy this situation, CPLR 311(b) was enacted to provide:

> If service upon a domestic or foreign corporation in time to secure and file proof of service called for by subdivision (a) of section three hundred six-b [306–a(b)] of this article is impracticable under paragraph one of subdivision (a) of this section or any other law, service upon the corporation may be made in such manner, and proof of service may take such form, as the court, upon motion without notice directs.

Thus, in those situations where service cannot be effected under the provisions of Section 311(a), the plaintiff may move the court to fashion a method of service as would be allowed if the defendant were a person pursuant to CPLR 308(5).

Filing proof of service. CPLR 306–a has been amended[6] to eliminate the requirement that proof of service be filed with the clerk of the court. Evidently there was some confusion in New York City as to who the clerk of the court is in actions pending in supreme and county courts. The clerk of the supreme and county courts for the purposes of CPLR 306–a is the county clerk and any summons and complaint, summons with notice, or third party summons and complaint must be filed in the county clerk's office and the index number purchased and affixed to the summons.

CPLR 306–b has also been amended, effective January 1, 1998, to give courts the discretion to extend the current 120–day period for the service of a summons and complaint in civil actions. The new law is, however, silent on the effect of a court denying the motion to extend the 120–day service period and the right to commence a new action. However, since the dismissal is without prejudice, it would seem that the ability to bring a new action with a new filing is still available. This issue is raised by the omission of the language in old Section 306–b which

---

4. CPLR 306(b).
5. CPLR 308(5).

6. L. 1996, Ch. 606, § 3, effective September 1, 1997.

expressly provided for an additional filing and service within 120–days even if the Statute of Limitations had expired. Currently, it appears that if service is not effected within 120 days and the Statute of Limitations has expired within the 120–day period, the best practice after January 1, 1998 would be to file a motion within the 120–day period, outlining the attempts to serve the defendant and why it has not been practicable, and asking the court to extend the time, and perhaps fashion a remedy pursuant to CPLR 308(5).

Improper service as an affirmative defense. Effective January 1, 1997, if the answer contains an affirmative defense of lack of personal jurisdiction,[7] based only on an objection to improper service, a defendant who asserts an affirmative defense based on a claim of improper service, must, within 60 days afterwards, move for judgment on that ground.[8] That motion would obviously be in the form of a summary judgment motion under the provisions of CPLR 3212.

§ 26.33 Filing the Action—When

An action should be filed when it has reasonably been determined that the case cannot be settled or that it is otherwise necessary to proceed to trial. Obviously, the action must be filed before the Statute of Limitations expires. Therefore, Article 2 of the CPLR should be carefully checked to determine the appropriate Statute of Limitations for the particular type of case involved. In this regard, a determination must be made as to the date that the claim accrued so that it will be clear when the Statute of Limitations will have run.

§ 26.34 Filing the Action—Where

The action must be filed in the county in which the action is venued. This will be the county where the defendant or plaintiff resides. In the case of a municipal defendant, the action must be venued in the county in which the municipality is located.[1]

§ 26.35 Filing the Action—Potential Defendants

Prior to the passage of the commencement by filing statute[1] requiring an index number to be obtained for each action, it was often possible and expedient to commence an action within the appropriate Statute of Limitations against the identified defendants, and, if additional defendants became known thereafter, they could be added in a separate action and the actions joined. Today, however, an index number must be purchased for each action commenced. It is economically advisable,

---

7. CPLR 3211(a)(8).
8. CPLR 3211(e).

§ 26.34
1. CPLR 504.

§ 26.35
1. *See supra*, § 26.32.

therefore, to commence an action against any known defendant or potential defendant and to determine as the discovery proceeds whether or not each is a responsible party, and if not, whether to drop him or her as a defendent.

It is recommended, however, that, if potential defendants are thought not to be culpable, they should be stipulated out of the action on the consent of all parties. This procedure should be followed instead of giving the defendants releases in the event that liability ultimately is assessed against them pursuant to the provisions of the General Obligations Law.[2]

If, after the commencement of the action, additional defendnts are identified, and counsel does not want to commence a separate action, a motion can be made, on notice to amend the summons and complaint and to serve the amended or supplemental complaint in the original action.

§ 26.36 The Summons and the Complaint

A summons is not a pleading, but it is the paper by which, through proper service, the court acquires jurisdiction over a party.[1] The complaint, which is the initial pleading, may be served with the summons. If the summons is served without a complaint, it must contain proper notice of the nature of the action and the relief sought, and, except in an action for medical malpractice, it must state the sum of money for which judgment may be taken in case of default.[2]

There are general rules that apply to pleadings. These include the following:

a. Statements should be made with particularity in a pleading.[3]
b. Conditions that should be specifically stated include:
   1. Conditions precedent;
   2. Corporate status;
   3. The existence of a judgment, decision or determination affecting the action;
   4. Signatures (each signature on a negotiable instrument is admitted unless specifically denied);[4] and
   5. Licenses to do business.[5]
c. Separate causes of action or defenses must be separately stated and numbered and may be stated regardless of consistency. Causes of action may be stated alternatively or hypothetically.

2. General Obligations Law § 15–108.

§ 26.36
1. CPLR 3012(a).
2. CPLR 305(b).
3. CPLR 3013; CPLR 3014.
4. CPLR 3015(d).
5. CPLR 3015(e).

When certain types of claims are brought or factual allegations made, particular information may have to be included in the complaint.[6] These claims and allegations include:

a. Libel or slander;
b. Fraud or mistake;
c. Separation or divorce;
d. Judgment;
e. Law of a foreign country;
f. Sale and delivery of goods or performing of labor or services;
g. Personal injury;[7] and
h. Gross negligence or intentional infliction of harm by certain directors, officers or trustees of public corporations, associations, organizations or trusts.

Each complaint must contain a demand for relief to which the pleader deems himself entitled.[8] However, in an action for medical or dental malpractice or an action against a municipality, a demand for relief may not state an amount of general damages sought.[9]

§ 26.37 The Answer

Three types of responses to the allegations set forth in the complaint may be interposed in the answer. An allegation contained in the complaint should be either:

a. Admitted;
b. Denied; or
c. Denied due to lack of knowledge or information to form a belief as to the truth of the allegation.

Any statement to which no response is offered is deemed admitted.[1]

The answer must also set forth those matters that, if not pleaded, would take the other party by surprise. Affirmative defenses that must be set forth in the answer include:

a. Arbitration and award;
b. Collateral estoppel;

---

6. CPLR 3016.
7. **PRACTICE POINTER:** In a case involving an automobile accident in which one covered person brings an action against another covered person, the complaint must state that the plaintiff has sustained a serious injury, as defined in Insurance Law § 5102(d), or that plaintiff has sustained economic loss greater than basic economic loss, as defined in Insurance Law § 5102(a).

8. CPLR 3017.
9. CPLR 3017(c).

PRACTICE POINTER: Actions for podiatric malpractice seem to be excluded from the limitations of CPLR 3017(c)

§ 26.37
1. CPLR 301(8).

§ 26.37   PERSONAL INJURY   Ch. 26

c. Culpable conduct claimed in diminution of damages, as set forth in CPLR 1411;

d. Discharge in bankruptcy;

e. Factors showing illegality either by statute or common law;

f. Fraud;

g. Infancy or other disability of the defendant;

h. Payment;

i. Release;

j. *Res judicata*;

k. Statute of Frauds; and

l. Statute of Limitations.

Other common affirmative defenses include an allegation that certain collateral source payments should reduce damages,[2] and an averment that liability for non-economic loss should be limited when there are joint and several tortfeasors.[3] Defenses must be separately stated and numbered and need not be consistent with one another. Defenses may be stated alternatively or hypothetically.

§ 26.38   Actions Against Municipal Corporations

Claims against municipal corporations, *i.e.*, cities, towns, villages and school boards, are generally covered by the provisions of the General Municipal Law.[1] Actions against authorities, including regional transit systems, are generally governed by the Public Authorities Law, which sets out filing requirements and time limitations. It should be noted, however, that, pursuant to various provisions of the Public Authorities Law, the time frame within which an action must be commenced may be shorter than one year and ninety days. This is often the case with regional transit authorities, against whom the action generally must be commenced within one year from the date of the occurrence.

§ 26.39   Actions Against Municipal Corporations—Notice of Claim

A notice of claim is required to be filed in all actions against a public corporation, officer, appointee or employee of that public corporation.[1]

---

2. CPLR 4545.

3. CPLR Art. 16. Under Article 16, the liability of persons jointly liable for non-economic loss, which is defined to include "pain and suffering, mental anguish, loss of consortium or other damages for non-economic loss," is limited to each defendant's equitable share of the loss, provided the defendant bears fifty percent or less of the total liability. CPLR 1601.

§ 26.38

1. General Municipal Law § 50. *See* Chapter 3, "Municipal Law," *supra*.

§ 26.39

1. General Municipal Law § 50–e(1)(a).

The notice of claim must be filed within 90 days of the time within which the claim arose. However, for wrongful death actions, the 90 day notice of claim provision begins to run from the date of the appointment of the representative of the decedent's estate.[2]

§ 26.40 Actions Against Municipal Corporations—Notice of Claim—Content

The notice of claim must include the name and address of each claimant, together with the name and the address of the attorney, if any. The claim must also state the location, the time, and the manner in which the claim arose. The nature and extent of injuries then known must be provided, together with items of damages claimed to have been sustained, so far as then known. Note that the notice must not state the amount of damages to which the claimant deems himself entitled.[1] The claim must be in writing and must be subscribed and sworn to by the claimant.[2]

The notice of claim must be served personally or by registered or certified mail.[3] In order to determine upon whom the notice of claim should be served, the relevant local law should be checked, as there are different designated agents for service depending upon which municipality is being sued.

If the notice is served within the time period specified, but it is not done in a manner that complies with the provisions of the General Municipal Law, the service will still be valid if the public corporation against which the claim is made demands that the claimant or any other person interested in the claim be examined in regard to it,[4] or if the notice is actually received by the proper person within the time frame specified and the public corporation fails to return the notice specifying the defect in the manner of service within thirty (30) days after it is received.[5]

If the notice is served within the time specified, but not in accord with the manner provided in the statute, and the notice is returned within the time provided, the claimant may serve a new notice in a manner complying with the provisions of the General Municipal Law within ten days after the return notice is received.[6] If a new notice is served within that period, it will be deemed to be timely served.[7]

If the notice of claim is not served within the statutory time frame, the claimant may move the supreme court to permit the filing of a late notice of claim. However, an extension cannot exceed the time within

---

2. *Id.*

§ 26.40
1. General Municipal Law § 50–e(2).
2. *Id.*
3. General Municipal Law § 50–e(3)(a).
4. General Municipal Law § 50–h.
5. General Municipal Law § 50–e(3)(c).
6. General Municipal Law § 50–e(3)(d).
7. *Id.*

which to commence an action against the public corporation.[8] In determining whether or not to grant an extension, the court must consider a number of issues, including:

a. Whether the public corporation, its attorney or its insurance company acquired actual knowledge of the essential facts underlying the claim within the time specified or within a reasonable time thereafter.[9]

b. The court must consider all other relevant facts and circumstances, including:

1. Whether the claimant was an infant;
2. Whether the claimant was mentally or physically incapacitated;
3. Whether the claimant died before the time service notice of claim was required;
4. Whether the claimant failed to timely serve a notice of claim because of his justifiable reliance upon settlement representations made by an authorized representative of the public corporation or its insurance carrier;
5. Whether the claimant, in serving a notice of claim, made an excusable error concerning the identity of the public corporation against whom the claim could be asserted; and
6. Whether the delay in serving the notice of claim substantially prejudiced the public corporation in maintaining its defense on the merits.[10]

The application for leave to serve a late notice shall not be denied on the ground that it was made after commencement of an action against a public corporation.

The municipality can demand, within ninety (90) days of the receipt of the notice of claim, that the claimant be examined under oath with regard to the facts surrounding liability, injuries and damages.[11] A record will be made, as at a deposition. The claimant may appear with counsel, if counsel has been retained. The claimant may also be required to undergo a physical examination.[12]

---

8. General Municipal Law § 50–e(5).

9. Id.

10. Id.

11. General Municipal Law § 50–h. The purpose of an examination at this stage is to give the municipality the opportunity to depose the claimant twice, first at the claim stage and again during pretrial discovery, providing an opportunity for the claimant to make inconsistent statements. Should the municipality choose to forego an examination at the claim stage, the municipality would proceed, and either accept or reject the claim.

12. Id.

After the notice of claim has been filed, the case can proceed with the filing of a summons and complaint.[13] The summons and complaint must be served, in most instances, within one year and ninety days after the act that is the basis of the complaint. Service must be effected in the same manner as set forth in the CPLR.

The complaint must indicate that the notice of claim was served within the time set forth in General Municipal Law § 50–e, that more than 30 days have elapsed since the service, and that the municipality has failed to settle or has otherwise ignored the claim.

§ 26.41 Actions Against the State

Actions against the state are governed by the Court of Claims Act[1] and the rules of the Court of Claims.[2] The requirements for filing a "notice of intention to file a claim" and the filing of the claim itself are covered in the Court of Claims Act.[3]

The first document described in the Court of Claims Act is a "notice of intention to file a claim." This document is the equivalent of the "notice of claim" that must be filed against a municipal corporation under the General Municipal Law.[4] There are, however, differences between the two documents.

The notice of intention to file a claim does not initiate the lawsuit against the state, but rather merely provides notice of the facts that may lead to a suit. The notice of intention to file a claim must be filed within 90 days after the event that is the basis of the notice. However, in a wrongful death action, notice of claim must be filed within 90 days of the appointment of an executor or administrator.[5]

If a claimant fails to file or serve upon the Attorney General a notice of intention to file a claim within the time prescribed for such filing, the court may, in its discretion, permit the claimant to file such claim at any time before an action asserting a like claim against a citizen of the state would be barred under the provisions of CPLR Article 2.[6]

If the notice of intention to file a claim is filed in a timely fashion, the claim itself must be filed and served within two years of the date of the underlying event. This establishes, in essence, a two-year Statute of Limitations for actions against the state. However, if a notice of intention to file a claim is timely filed, but thereafter the claim itself is not timely filed or served, a saving provision may keep the claim alive. The claimant may make a motion to the court for permission to treat the

---

13. General Municipal Law § 50–i.

§ 26.41

1. Court of Claims Act. *See* Court of Claims Act § 8 (partial waiver of the state's sovereign immunity).
2. 22 NYCRR Pt. 206.
3. Court of Claims Act § 10.
4. *See* § 26.32, *supra*.
5. Court of Claims Act § 10(2).
6. Court of Claims Act § 10(6).

notice of intention to file the claim as the claim itself. It is important to note, however, that the court will not grant such an application unless:

   a. It is made before an action asserting a like claim against a citizen of the state would be barred under the provision of CPLR Article 2;
   b. The notice of intention was timely served and filed;
   c. The notice contained facts sufficient to constitute a claim; and
   d. Granting the application would not prejudice the defendant.[7]

Although the notice of intention to file a claim need not state the items of damages or injuries or the sum claimed, it is better practice to include this information in the notice of intention to file a claim. If this information is contained in the notice of intention to file, and the other requirements of the Court of Claims Act are satisfied,[8] the court may consider the document to be a sufficient claim.

There is a provision of the Court of Claims Act analogous to the provision in General Municipal Law § 50–e permitting an examination of claimants when notice of intention to file a claim has been made.[9] Also, a physical examination of the claimant is permitted.

It is important to note that, effective August 2, 1995, it no longer is necessary to file a notice of intention to file a claim with the Clerk of the Court of Claims in Albany. However, service on an Attorney General is still required.[10]

The claim itself is a separate document that is the functional equivalent of a complaint in a civil action. The claim must contain the following information:

   a. The time when the claim arose;
   b. The place where the claim arose;
   c. The nature of the claim;
   d. The items of damage or injuries claimed to have been sustained;
   e. The total sum claimed; and
   f. The post office address of each claimant and the post office address of each attorney.[11]

The claim must be filed with the Clerk of the Court of Claims within 90 days of the accrual of the claim, unless a notice of intention to file a claim has been filed, in which case the claim must be filed within two years of the date that the incident occurred.[12] The state has 40 days within which it must submit an answer. A copy shall be served personal-

---

7. Court of Claims Act § 10(8)(a).
8. Id.
9. Court of Claims Act § 17–a.
10. L. 1995, Ch. 466.
11. Court of Claims Act § 11; Rules of the Court of Claims § 206.6; 22 NYCRR § 206.6.
12. Court of Claims Act § 10(3).

ly or by certified mail return receipt requested upon the Attorney General within the times provided for filing with the Clerk of the Court.

It is not sufficient that the claim or notice of intention to file a claim be mailed within the 90 day period. If it is received by the Clerk of the Court *after* the 90 day time period has expired, the claim is not timely filed. The filing requirements are jurisdictional, and a failure to comply with them will bar the claim.

Filing. A claim must be filed by delivering it to the Office of the Clerk or upon receipt thereof at the Clerk's Office by mail. The claimant must file in the Clerk's Office the original and two copies of the claim. Proof of service on the defendant must be filed with the Clerk within ten days of such service.[13] The address and telephone number of the Clerk's Office is:

Chief Clerk
Court of Claims
Governor Nelson A. Rockefeller Empire State Plaza
Justice Building
Box 7344, Capitol Station
Albany, NY 12224

(518) 465-8881

All papers must be filed with the Clerk and not sent directly to the judge or staff unless counsel is directed by the court or its clerk to do so.

The Attorney General must also be served with a copy of the notice of intention to file a claim or with the claim itself. Service must be made personally on the Attorney General within the state or on any Assistant Attorney General at any local office within the times provided.[14] Affidavits of service must be completed and filed with the Clerk's Office as noted. In order to place the case on the trial calendar, a note of issue must be filed.[15]

§ 26.42   Discovery—Generally

Discovery and disclosure are generally governed by Article 31 of the CPLR. The purpose of discovery is to eliminate surprise, to narrow the issues and to allow each party to discover the nature of the opponent's claim and the evidence underlying each claim.[1] The statute requires full

---

13. 22 NYCRR § 206.5(a).
14. CPLR 307.

PRACTICE POINTER: If the time within which to file a notice of intention to file a claim or within which to file the claim itself has expired, but the principal defendant is an employee of the state and an active tortfeasor, that defendant can be sued individually and a jury trial obtained.

Morell v. Balasubramanian, 70 N.Y.2d 297, 520 N.Y.S.2d 530, 514 N.E.2d 1101 (1987).

15. 22 NYCRR § 206.12.

§ 26.42

1. Spectrum Systems International Corp. v. Chemical Bank, 78 N.Y.2d 371, 575 N.Y.S.2d 809, 581 N.E.2d 1055 (1991). *See also*, Bensel, Frank, McKeon, *et al.*, *Person-*

disclosure of all evidence "material and necessary" to the prosecution or defense of an action.[2] "Material and necessary" is a standard that encompasses "any facts bearing on the controversy which will assist in preparation for trial."[3] Admissibility of the discoverable materials is not a consideration in determining whether it is discoverable if that material may *lead* to the admissibility of discoverable proof.[4]

Discovery of information concerning expert witnesses is authorized by the CPLR for actions commenced on or after July 1, 1985.[5] However, a demand for the expert witness information must be made.[6] Particular requirements are set out for actions other than medical, dental or podiatric malpractice actions. The identity of each person expected to be called as an expert witness at trial must be supplied, and the statute also provides for disclosure in reasonable detail of:

a. The subject matter about which the expert is expected to testify;

b. The substance of the facts and opinions on which each expert expected is to testify;

c. The qualifications of each expert witness; and

d. A summary of the grounds for each expert's opinion.[7]

It is important to note that in medical, dental and podiatric malpractice actions, it is not required that the names of the experts be disclosed.[8] A party may be required to disclose the expert's educational background, the hospital where his or her internship and residency were served, the hospitals where admitting privileges have been granted, the states where the expert is licensed to practice, the societies of which the expert is a member, and his or her board certifications.[9]

Generally, a deposition of the expert witness is not allowed in the absence of special circumstances.[10] It should be noted that the disclosure relating to experts discussed above provides general information only. The question thus arises whether or not the expert's *report*, if one was prepared, is discoverable. Generally, the expert's report is conditionally

---

al *Injury Practice in New York* (West 1997) Ch. 6 "Disclosure."

2. CPLR 3101.

3. Allen v. Crowell–Collier Publishing Co., 21 N.Y.2d 403, 288 N.Y.S.2d 449, 235 N.E.2d 430 (1968).

4. Martinez v. CPC International, Inc., 88 A.D.2d 656, 450 N.Y.S.2d 528 (2d Dep't 1982); Baxter v. Orans, 63 A.D.2d 875, 405 N.Y.S.2d 470 (1st Dep't 1978).

5. CPLR 3101(d).

6. Collins v. Greater New York Savings Bank, 194 A.D.2d 514, 598 N.Y.S.2d 544 (2d Dep't 1993).

7. CPLR 3101(d)(1)(i).

8. CPLR 3101(d)(1)(i).

9. Hamilton v. Wein, 132 Misc.2d 1023, 506 N.Y.S.2d 387 (Sup.Ct., Kings County, 1986). *See also*, Jasopersand v. Rho, 169 A.D.2d 184, 572 N.Y.S.2d 700 (2d Dep't 1991); Morris v. Clements, 228 A.D.2d 990, 644 N.Y.S.2d 850 (3d Dep't 1996); *contra* McGoldrick v. Whitney M. Young, Jr. Health Center, Inc., 135 Misc.2d 200, 514 N.Y.S.2d 872 (Sup.Ct., Albany County, 1987).

10. CPLR 3101(d)(1)(iii); Barnes v. P & C Food Markets, Inc., 132 A.D.2d 921, 518 N.Y.S.2d 478 (4th Dep't 1987).

immune from discovery if a proper showing is made.[11] However, the expert's report is discoverable if the material or item relevant to the report is no longer available for inspection.[12] Dates of reports have been held to be immune from discovery.[13]

Other material that is discoverable includes a party's own statement, a copy of which must be provided.[14] Insurance information is discoverable; a party must disclose the existence and contents of any insurance agreement under which the carrier may be liable to satisfy all or any part of a judgment that may be entered in the action.[15]

The plaintiff should request the following insurance information:

a. All liability policies, including the face sheet or declarations page and the policy itself;

b. Any policy that may be used to satisfy a judgment (stackable coverage);

c. Any umbrella policies;

d. The effective dates of any such policies;

Medical reports and authorizations may be discovered also. It is important for the plaintiff to understand that when a person commences an action for personal injury, his or her medical condition and status are open to discovery, virtually from his or her date of birth to the present, with limited exceptions.[16] Note, however, that information concerning the *defendant*'s physical condition is not discoverable unless the defendant asserts the condition in a counterclaim or the defendant's physical or mental condition is otherwise in controversy.[17]

Physical examinations of the plaintiff are permitted,[18] although objection may be made to the location of the examination.[19] The physician giving the examination may be objected to, although such objections are rarely upheld.[20] Such objections must be set forth with specificity and at length.

If a physical or mental examination is to be held, the attorney has an absolute right to attend with the client, even if the physician does not want the attorney to be present. However, the only person with standing

---

11. Landmark Insurance Company v. Beau Rivage Restaurant, Inc., 121 A.D.2d 98, 509 N.Y.S.2d 819 (2d Dep't 1986). See also generally CPLR 3101(d)(2).

12. Beauchamp v. Riverbay Corporation, 156 A.D.2d 172, 548 N.Y.S.2d 215 (1st Dep't 1989).

13. Pizzi v. Muccia, 127 A.D.2d 338, 515 N.Y.S.2d 341 (3d Dep't 1987).

14. CPLR 3101(e).

15. CPLR 3101(f).

16. Braynard v. Morgan, 50 A.D.2d 810, 376 N.Y.S.2d 575 (2d Dep't 1975).

17. Koump v. Smith, 25 N.Y.2d 287, 303 N.Y.S.2d 858, 250 N.E.2d 857 (1969); see also, Dillenbeck v. Hess, 73 N.Y.2d 278, 539 N.Y.S.2d 707, 536 N.E.2d 1126 (1989).

18. CPLR 3121.

19. Rakowski v. Irmisch, 46 A.D.2d 826, 361 N.Y.S.2d 68 (3d Dep't 1974).

20. Crawford v. Investors Planning Corp., 21 A.D.2d 888, 251 N.Y.S.2d 723 (2d Dep't 1964).

§ 26.42   PERSONAL INJURY   Ch. 26

to object to the attorney's presence is the client.[21] If the attorney attends the physical examination with the client, he or she should note the beginning and concluding times for the client's medical history, as well as of the examination itself, and specific notes should be kept concerning what is done.

§ 26.43   Discovery—Depositions

Depositions are one of the principal discovery devices provided by Article 31. Generally, the deposition on oral questions, or as it is also known, the examination before trial ("EBT"), is governed by the CPLR.[1] Notice of a deposition is required to be in writing, with 20 days notice required.[2] Five days must be added to this time frame if service is by mail.

Generally, the defendant has the priority of noticing the deposition, as the plaintiff cannot serve such notice until the time to serve a response to a pleading has expired.[3] Note, that if the defendant is a corporation, the plaintiff may designate the person to be examined.[4] The general rule is that the person who sends out the notice first deposes first.[5]

Obviously, thorough preparation for all depositions is extremely important. Consideration should be given as to how the witness being deposed can support counsel's theory of the case. In other words, can this witness establish elements of the causes of action alleged? Secondly, what does this witness contend was done appropriately or properly?

The deposition should also include questions concerning the standard of conduct that the witness believes is proper, if relevant, any negligence or deviations from this standard, and any documents that could be used to support the particular action.

A non-party witness can also be deposed. The procedure for obtaining such a deposition is service of a subpoena on the non-party witness, together with the appropriate fee and travel expenses. The parties to the action should be served with a deposition notice that specifies the reasons for deposing the non-party.[6]

The location of the deposition depends, in part, on the identity of the person to be deposed. Parties, or officers, directors, members or employees of a party, can be deposed in the county in which they reside or have

---

21. Jakubowski v. Lengen, 86 A.D.2d 398, 450 N.Y.S.2d 612 (4th Dep't 1982).

§ 26.43
1. CPLR 3106.
2. CPLR 3107.
3. CPLR 3106(a).

4. CPLR 3106(d).
5. Business Envelope Manufacturers, Inc. v. Williams, 40 A.D.2d 597, 336 N.Y.S.2d 62 (1st Dep't 1972).
6. CPLR 3101(a)(4).

an office for the regular transaction of business. A deposition can also be conducted in the county where the action is pending.[7]

Non-parties who are residents of New York State can be deposed within the county where they reside, where they are regularly employed, or where have an office for the regular transaction of business.[8] In contrast, non-New York State residents can be deposed in the county in which they are served, where they are regularly employed, or where have an office for the regular transaction of business.[9]

If the deponent is a public corporation, or any officer, agent or employee thereof, the deposition may only be taken in the county where the action is pending and, unless otherwise agreed, only at the courthouse in that county.[10]

A claimant in an action involving the State of New York may only be examined in the county in which he resides.[11] New York City is considered one county for the purposes of determining the location of a deposition.[12]

The manner in which the deposition is conducted is of some importance. At the outset, counsel should determine what the local practice is with regard to the "usual stipulations" and objections that are to be made at the time of the deposition. Occasionally, there will be an instruction by counsel not to permit a witness to answer a question. Note that counsel is generally without authority to direct a client not to answer a question at a deposition.[13]

A demand for the production of documents may be incorporated into the deposition notice.[14] However, there must be a reasonable connection between the items noticed to be produced and the witness' testimony. There are three criteria that will justify compelling the production of documents:

a. The witness used the document to refresh his recollection;

b. The witness will testify as to matters set forth in the document; or

c. The document will assist the examiner or the deponent in the deposition.[15]

It is the better practice to mark all exhibits used during the deposition and attach them to the original transcript.[16]

7. CPLR 3110(1).
8. CPLR 3110(2).
9. Id.
10. CPLR 3110(3).
11. Court of Claims Act § 17.
12. CPLR 3110.
13. Spatz v. Wide World Travel Service, Inc., 70 A.D.2d 835, 418 N.Y.S.2d 19 (1st Dep't 1979); Ferraro v. N.Y. Telephone Co., 94 A.D.2d 784, 463 N.Y.S.2d 31 (2d Dep't 1983).
14. CPLR 3111.
15. Arett Sales Corp. v. Island Garden Center of Queens, Inc., 25 A.D.2d 546, 267 N.Y.S.2d 623 (2d Dep't 1966).
16. CPLR 3116(c).

§ 26.44 Discovery—Interrogatories

Another method of disclosure, although one not frequently used in state court practice in New York, are interrogatories. Interrogatories may relate to any matter embraced in the disclosure requirements of CPLR 3101. However, a party may not serve interrogatories in an action to recover damages for personal injury, injury to property or wrongful death, based solely on a cause or causes of action for negligence, and also take a deposition of the same party without leave of the court.[1]

The main purpose of interrogatories is to discover hard factual material and documents. An answering party may be required to check all sources of information, including employees and records, and compile the information in an orderly answer to the interrogatory.[2] Note that a plaintiff cannot serve the defendant with interrogatories until twenty (20) days after the service of the complaint.[3] The form of interrogatories is governed by CPLR 3131. If there are objections to the interrogatories, such objections must be made by serving a response stating with reasonable particularity the reasons for each objection.[4] If objection is made to part of an item or category, the part shall be specified. Next, the party seeking disclosure may move for an order under CPLR 3124 with respect to any objection to, or other failure to respond to or permit inspection as requested by the notice or any part thereof.[5]

Information previously supplied in a pleading or other disclosure device need not be included in the response to an interrogatory. Also, questions that seek information as to a matter of law are objectionable.[6]

§ 26.45 Discovery—Document Discovery and Inspection

Document discovery and inspection is also permitted by the CPLR.[1] If a party does not object to document discovery and inspection, the objection is waived.[2] If document discovery is sought, the documents must be specifically designated. Alternatively, the discovery and inspection request may involve premises or an item such as a vehicle or a particular piece of machinery. If discovery and inspection of any of the latter is sought, preparation, with the aid of an expert, will be necessary, and a procedure should be established for conducting the discovery and inspection.

---

§ 26.44

1. *See also* CPLR 3107.
2. Clifton Steel Corp. v. County of Monroe Public Works Dep't, 74 A.D.2d 715, 425 N.Y.S.2d 672 (4th Dep't 1980).
3. CPLR 3132.
4. CPLR 3122.
5. CPLR 3122.
6. Brooklyn Bureau of Social Serv. v. Transamerica Ins. Co., 28 A.D.2d 841, 281 N.Y.S.2d 708 (1st Dep't 1967).

§ 26.45

1. CPLR 3120, CPLR 3122. *See also* Bensel, Frank, McKeon, *et al.*, *Personal Injury Practice in New York* (West 1997).
2. Brewer v. Jamaica Hospital, 73 A.D.2d 851, 423 N.Y.S.2d 188 (1st Dep't 1980).

§ 26.46 Discovery—Bills of Particulars

Although technically not a pleading, provisions concerning bills of particulars are contained in Article 30 of the CPLR, which is entitled "Remedies and Pleading" at CPLR 3041 through 3044. A bill of particulars is a device to amplify the pleadings in a particular case.

A party may require any other party to give a bill of particulars concerning such party's claim.[1] The bill of particulars must be demanded in a writing, stating the items concerning which particulars are desired.[2] The bill of particulars that is produced must be complete and must provide all information requested. If information is demanded, but is willfully withheld when it ought to have been disclosed, the court may issue an order:

1. That the issues to which the information is relevant shall be deemed resolved for purposes of the action in accordance with the claims of the party obtaining the order compelling discovery; or

2. Prohibiting the disobedient party from supporting or opposing designated claims or defenses, from producing in evidence designated things or items of testimony, or from introducing any evidence of the physical, mental or blood condition sought to be determined, or from using certain witnesses; or

3. Striking out pleadings or parts thereof, or staying further proceedings until the order is obeyed, or dismissing the action or any part thereof, or rendering a judgment by default against the disobedient party.[3]

§ 26.47 Discovery—Demand for a Bill of Particulars

The demand must be served in a writing stating the items concerning which particulars are desired.[1] Within 30 days of receipt of the demand, the party upon whom the demand was made must serve the bill of particulars, complying with each item of the demand except as to any item to which the party objects, in which event the reasons for the objection shall be stated with reasonable particularity.[2]

The assertion of an objection to one or more of the items and demands does not relieve the party of the obligation to respond in full within 30 days of the service of the demand to the items to which no objection is made.[3]

§ 26.46
1. CPLR 3041.
2. CPLR 3042.
3. CPLR 3042(d), CPLR 3126.

§ 26.47
1. CPLR 3042(a).
2. Id.
3. Id.

PRACTICE POINTER: A bill of particulars is a device to amplify the pleadings in a particular case. It cannot be used as a basis for obtaining evidentiary information. Thus, where evidentiary information is sought, objections should be made to the bill of particulars in that regard.

§ 26.48 Settlement

The settlement of any case ordinarily will benefit the client. If the case can be settled at a pre-trial conference, the client may be able to save the expenses connected with expert witness fees, exhibit preparation, and other matters. When the attorney attends the pre-trial conference, he or she should have a firm commitment from the client as to an amount that will be acceptable to settle the case. In a significant case, it would be advisable for the attorney to have the client present in court so that, if the matter is settled, the matter can be placed on the record with the client in court, expressing his or her full permission.

If an offer is made, but there are liens that are outstanding, the attorney may wish to ask the court to schedule a follow-up conference or conferences, so that the issue of the liens can be discussed and resolved at that time.[1] This will often have a salutary effect on the ability to settle the case.[2]

If the matter is settled, it is suggested that the defendants be asked to specify the exact identities of the individuals or entities that they wish to have released, so that such release can be processed expeditiously.

Once the matter has been settled and the release transmitted to the defendant, a certified letter, including a copy of the release, should be sent to the insurance company or to the insurance company's attorney, stating that the release is being tendered pursuant to CPLR 5003–a and that the check is to be provided within 21 days.[3] The significance of such a letter is that if the check is not tendered within twenty-one days, the plaintiff may enter a bill of costs with regard to the costs encountered in the case.[4]

§ 26.49 Liens

Three principal types of liens must be considered when resolving a personal injury case, although additional liens should be considered and all case law checked before settling a case. The principal liens are those of the worker's compensation carrier, the no-fault carrier, and the public welfare official.

The workers' compensation carrier may have a lien pursuant to Workers' Compensation Law § 29. There is no lien for first-party benefits paid in lieu of no-fault benefits, up to fifty thousand dollars ($50,000), and for lost-wage amounts equal to amounts covered under the no-fault statute. Should the amount of workers' compensation paid for

---

§ 26.48

1. A case cannot be settled without the permission of the worker's compensation carrier. Workers' Compensation Law § 29. See, e.g., Durham v. Barker Chemical Corp., 151 A.D.2d 887, 543 N.Y.S.2d 182 (3d Dep't 1989).

2. Insurance Law § 50–h.

3. PRACTICE POINTER: The attorney should carefully check for liens on the settlement proceeds before distributing funds to the client.

4. CPLR 5003–a(e).

wages be greater than the no-fault amount, however, a lien will be created as to the difference.

As to other workers' compensation payments made, a lien is created for benefits paid. This lien is ordinarily net of the attorney's fees, on the theory that the employee has created a common fund that partly enures to the benefit of the employer's compensation carrier and that the employer must therefore pay an equitable share of the attorney's fees incurred in creating the common fund. Also, the matter, whether it involves an automobile accident or other type of loss, cannot be settled without the written permission of the worker's compensation carrier.

The attorney should also carefully consider potential offsets with regard to future compensation and an award. The net effect often will be that the settlement of a claim will result in ending workers' compensation benefits.

The second type of lien is the no-fault lien. If the defendant, such as a municipality or a dram shop, is not a covered party, and a recovery is obtained from such defendant, a lien for the no-fault benefits paid will exist.[1] The no-fault carrier should be contacted and an agreement reached with regard to a reduction of that lien early in the course of the litigation if the no-fault attorney intends to proceed with a claim of its own against the uncovered defendant on behalf of the no-fault carrier. As noted, to the extent that any APIP benefits have been paid, a lien is created.

The third type of lien with which counsel should be familiar is a lien for public assistance.[2] Where a person has received public assistance and care subsequent to a personal injury, a lien is created in favor of a public welfare official, not to exceed the total amount of such assistance and care furnished by the public welfare official on and after the date when such injuries were incurred. No such lien will be effective, however, unless a written notice containing the name and address of the injured recipient, the date and place of the accident and the name of the person, firm or corporation alleged to be liable to the injured party for such injuries, together with a brief statement of the nature of the lien, the amount claimed, and that a total lien is claimed upon the right of action is served by registered mail before the payment of any monies to the injured party. This notice must be served on the person, firm or corporation, on counsel, if known, and upon any insurance carrier that has insured such person, firm or corporation against such liability prior to the payment of any money to the injured person.[3] Additionally, a copy

§ 26.49
1. Aetna Life and Cas. Co. v. Nelson, 67 N.Y.2d 169, 501 N.Y.S.2d 313, 492 N.E.2d 386 (1986). See also Chapter 32 "Workers' Compensation," infra.

2. Social Security Law § 104–b.

3. Social Security Law § 104–b(2).

§ 26.49   PERSONAL INJURY   Ch. 26

of the lien should be filed in the county clerk's office.[4] Obviously, these provisions should be carefully checked before any settlement proceeds are distributed.

Any release that is given must protect the subrogation rights of any party that has a lien.[5]

§ 26.50 Alternative Dispute Resolution

There are three types of alternative dispute resolution: mediation; advisory arbitration; and binding arbitration.

Mediation generally is a device whereby the parties agree to discuss the matter in front of a mediator, to whom they will put their relative positions forward and then ask the mediator to help resolve the matter or offer suggestions as to the chances of recovery or total damages.

Advisory arbitration is less common, but it is used. An advisory arbitration is a procedure whereby an arbitrator is selected, acceptable to both sides, and then proof is presented, either by stipulation or through live testimony. When the introduction of proof has concluded, the arbitrator renders a decision that is advisory in nature only, *i.e.*, it has no binding effect. The benefit of this procedure is that it offers the parties at least one person's view of the issues of liability and damages, without either party being bound by the result.

The third type of alternative dispute resolution is binding arbitration. In binding arbitration, the parties agree on the number of arbitrators, generally from one to three. The parties also agree on the issues that will be presented to the arbitrator and on the scope of the arbitrator's authority to decide factual issues and damages issues. Matters may be stipulated to, witnesses may be called or a combination of both. At the conclusion of the proofs, the arbitrator will render a decision that is binding on the parties.

A type of binding arbitration is a procedure known as a "high/low" arbitration. Under this procedure, the parties agree that they will arbitrate the matter in lieu of a trial, within certain parameters. These parameters are usually not known by the arbitrator. The parties agree that in the event that an arbitrator's decision is below a certain amount, the "low amount" agreed upon will become the award of the arbitrator. Conversely, if the arbitrator awards more than the "high amount," the "high amount" agreed upon will become the award. For example, assume that the parties have agreed to arbitrate a matter, agreeing on a low amount of $5,000 and a high amount of $25,000. If the arbitrator returns a decision of no cause of action or any amount below $5,000, the $5,000 amount automatically becomes the award. If, on the other hand,

4. Social Security Law § 104–b(3).

5. Weinberg v. Transamerica Insurance Company, 62 N.Y.2d 379, 477 N.Y.S.2d 99, 465 N.E.2d 819 (1984).

the arbitrator awards any amount over $25,000, the $25,000 amount becomes the award of the arbitrator.

The benefits of an arbitration proceeding are that all sides save time and money. Usually, an arbitration can be heard quickly; if a good deal of the material in a negligence case is stipulated before the arbitrator, the arbitration can generally be completed in half a day or less. Obviously, the more complex the issues, the longer the arbitration will take. Nonetheless, with the agreement of the parties, the proof can be shortened and the arbitration allowed to proceed quickly. An additional benefit of arbitration may be that neither side will have to call expert witnesses if there is an agreement that the reports of the experts, particularly physicians, will be stipulated to before the arbitrator. An additional benefit of arbitration is that it allows both sides to litigate smaller cases without the time and expense of a jury trial.

The principal risk of an arbitration comes with use of the high/low format of binding arbitration. The plaintiff should agree, preferably in writing, to the high/low numbers prior to the arbitration. This is particularly important, from the plaintiff's counsel's perspective, with regard to the cap on the high portion of the arbitration. The risk to the plaintiff obviously is that if the arbitrator awards a high number, and the agreed cap is significantly below that number, the plaintiff may complain that the cap was set too low.

Preparation for an arbitration should be as complete as it would be for a trial. A notebook or settlement brochure should be prepared as if done for a pre-trial conference.

The presentation of the claim is important. A well prepared, attractive brochure, containing the relevant material for the arbitrator to consider, obviously will make a good impression. If your client is going to testify, he or she should be prepared well in advance of the hearing. If the client has any habits or manner of speaking that may detract from the case, these should be pointed out and remedied, to the extent possible.

A brief or legal memorandum, if there are any issues of particular significance or difficulty, should be provided to the arbitrator. Usually, the arbitrator who will hear the case will be a trial attorney who is probably quite busy. It is, therefore, a good idea to keep the presentation simple and direct and to provide the paperwork a sufficient time before the arbitration so that the arbitrator will have an opportunity to review the papers before the arbitration is held.[1]

§ 26.51 Trial Preparation: Introductory Note

The purpose of this section is to describe the pre-trial settlement conference and to offer suggestions with regard to the preparation and

§ 26.50
[1]. Bensel, Frank, McKeon, et al., Personal Injury Practice in New York (West 1997) Ch. 11 "Mandatory Submission of Certain Actions to Arbitration; Health Care Arbitration."

conduct of that conference. This section does not cover mandatory pre-trial scheduling conferences. It should also be noted that pre-trial conferences vary from district to district and from county to county within the state. This section concerns the pre-trial settlement conference with a judge, prior either to a trial date being set or to the beginning of jury selection.

In the Fourth Department, it is generally the practice to hold the settlement conference well in advance of trial—before the case is sent from the IAS judge to the General Trial Calendar or before a trial date is set, if the IAS judge retains jurisdiction over the particular matter.[1]

Preparation for the pre-trial conference should include a comprehensive review of the pleadings, with particular attention paid to the bill of particulars. The attorney should ensure that the complaint does, in fact, set forth the cause of action that has been prepared for trial and that the complaint does, in fact, state a cause of action. Plaintiff's counsel should make sure that the complaint has a "wherefore" clause and that this clause sets forth an amount of damages adequate in relation to the proof. In reviewing the bill of particulars, counsel should ensure that the injuries claimed to exist and that are medically supportable are included. Plaintiff's counsel should also ensure that all claims of negligence are included in that particular section of the bill of particulars. If any violations of statutes or ordinances were alleged, these must be included in the bill of particulars. If special damages are claimed, counsel should make sure that the bill of particulars is up-to-date with regard to these. If demands were served pursuant to CPLR 3101, counsel should make sure that these have been updated, particularly with regard to any witnesses, especially experts.

Counsel should make sure that all medical records have been received and reviewed, including narrative reports from any physician with regard to any injuries, including permanent injuries or information

§ 26.51

1. 22 NYCRR § 202.3 establishes the individual assignment system ("IAS") in New York, which governs all civil actions and proceedings in the supreme court and county court. The IAS system provides for the continuous supervision of each action and proceeding by a single judge. Except as otherwise authorized by the Chief Administrator or otherwise provided for in the rules, every action and proceeding is assigned and heard pursuant to the individual assignment system. Assignments are made by the clerk of the court pursuant to a method of random selection authorized by the Chief Administrator. The judge thereby assigned is known as the "assigned judge" with respect to that matter and, except as otherwise provided, conducts all further proceedings. The Chief Administrator may authorize the establishment in any court of special categories of actions and proceedings, including but not limited to matrimonial actions, medical malpractice actions, etc., for assignment to judges specially assigned to hear such actions or proceedings. The Chief Administrator may also authorize the establishment in any court or county or judicial district of a dual track system of assignment. Under such system each action and proceeding is supervised continuously by the individually assigned judge until the note of issue and certificate of readiness have been filed and the pre-trial conference, if one is ordered, has been held. The action or proceeding then may be assigned to another judge for trial in a manner prescribed by the Chief Administrator.

concerning any long-term prognosis. Any photographs that might be of benefit should be assembled and the list of special damages, including lost wages and medical bills, should be updated.

There are three basic methods of presentation at the settlement conference. The first is a very informal presentation wherein the attorney appears before the judge, having previously presented a copy of marked pleadings, and advises the judge concerning the nature of the case and the demand.

The second method of presentation is to provide, prior to the conference, a one-or two-page synopsis of the case, setting forth the nature of the case, the negligence claimed, the injuries sustained, the special damages alleged to date, including both medical expenses and lost wages, and violations of any laws or statutes, together with pleas entered thereto, the date of birth of the plaintiff, the life expectancy and the work-life expectancy, as contained in the respective tables in the Pattern Jury Instructions. If photographs are beneficial, particularly in a case involving scarring, photostatic color copies should be attached to this presentation. In an automobile case, a copy of the police report could be attached, together with a narrative report, if one exists, from any orthopaedic surgeon. This will give the judge a very brief, but good, overview of the case before the attorneys come into chambers. This synopsis can be sent to the judge a day or two before the pre-trial conference, with a copy provided to the adversary. It can also be delivered to the court and to the adversary on the day of the pre-trial conference.

The third method of presentation is more involved. It involves preparation of a cover sheet, not dissimilar to method two above, but more detailed exhibits are attached to the brochure, and the presentation is broken down into sections on liability, injuries and damages.

In the liability portion of the presentation, a police report and copies of convictions based upon a plea would be included. Second, under the injury part, all medical records and narrative reports would be included. Under the damages section, an economist's report and detailed information with regard to lost wages and medical bills would be provided, as would photographs, if beneficial, and also work-life and life-expectancy tables. A brief might accompany this third presentation, if any issues of law are involved. In addition, behind the brochure would be copies of all pleadings, bills of particulars, discovery demands and responses in the case. It is often best to put this brochure into a three-ring binder. It is also, at times, helpful to include copies of depositions, if they will be used if the matter is not settled. This third method generally is used in a case involving more serious damages, where it is likely that the matter may go to trial.

§ 26.52 Trial

A case can be tried as a single unit, *i.e.*, both liability and damages tried at the same time before the same factfinder, or the trial may be bifurcated.[1] If the jury is to try only the issue of liability, and not damages, no reference to damages will be permitted during the selection of the jury to determine liability.[2]

It is recommended that a trial notebook be prepared. Trial notebooks can consist of the file organized in a logical fashion or in an actual notebook format. Generally, three-ring binders are utilized. If the case is extensive, one binder may be employed for pleadings, another for depositions, another for exhibits and another for questions, opening statement, jury selection considerations, closing argument and jury instructions. Each section is separated by a divider tab, and subsections are prepared as necessary. Counsel must ensure that all witnesses are prepared and, if necessary, are under subpoena.

Before setting a trial date, it is recommended that the physician's schedule be consulted and a firm date arranged for his/her testimony.

§ 26.53 Trial—Subpoenas

The use of subpoenas is governed by CPLR 8001.[1] There are two types of subpoenas. The first type is the subpoena *duces tecum*, which requires the production of books, records and things. If a governmental agency is being subpoenaed, it may require that the subpoena be signed by a judge. Most of the form subpoenas are designated as judicial subpoenas, even though they are signed by an attorney. As noted, however, some entities require that the subpoena either be marked so ordered or actually signed by the judge who is assigned to the case or by the *ex parte* judge.

The second type of subpoena is a testimonial subpoena, which, of course, requires a person to be present and to give testimony.[2] A person whose attendance is compelled by a subpoena, whether or not they actually testify, must receive, for each day's attendance, $15.00 for attendance fees and $0.23 as travel expenses for each mile from the place where they were served and the return. There is no mileage fee for travel within a city.

---

§ 26.52

1. *See generally*, Bensel, Frank, McKeon, *et al.*, *Personal Injury Practice in New York* (West 1997) Ch. 9 "Trial of a Personal Injury Case."
2. 22 NYCRR § 1026.4.

§ 26.53

1. *See* Bensel, Frank, McKeon, *et al.*, *Personal Injury Practice in New York* (West 1997) ¶¶ 8:143–8:165.

2. **PRACTICE POINTER:** After a subpoena has been served (personal service is recommended), a copy of the subpoena, together with the affidavit of service, should be put in the trial notebook. If the witness fails to appear, the affidavit of service and copy of the subpoena can be marked and given to the court with a request to the judge to direct the sheriff to compel the attendance of the subpoenaed witness.

§ 26.54 Trial—Exhibits

To the extent possible before trial, counsel should carefully consider which exhibits will be used at trial and in what order they will be presented.

Exhibits may consist of simple documents, complex models, videotapes, photographs or virtually anything within the attorney's imagination. A list should be compiled of the exhibits to be offered into evidence so that when an exhibit is marked, a notation can be made in the trial notebook exhibit section with regard to the exhibit number or letter, whether it was marked or offered, and if offered, whether it was admitted. The purpose of this procedure is to allow the attorney, when the proof is concluded, but before resting, to review the notes and quickly discern whether or not all of the exhibits that were offered or marked were admitted into evidence. If there is any question in this regard, the court should be consulted for a determination as to whether or not a particular record or exhibit was admitted.[1]

§ 26.55 Trial—*Voir Dire*

The most difficult part of jury selection is actually doing it. Put another way, what many attorneys want to know is, "How do I select a jury that will be favorable to my cause?" The purpose of this text is not to suggest the manner of jury selection, but to suggest a few salient points with regard to the selection of a jury.

Most jury selection begins with the attorney telling the prospective jurors that he or she is interested in selecting a jury that will be impartial and fair and that will see that justice is done. In reality, of course, the attorney wants a jury that will be favorable to his client's cause. The purpose of jury selection is to eliminate those jurors who are not likely to be favorably disposed to the client's cause.

Much has been written about jury selection, both about techniques and about the psychological factors involved.[1] In some recent trials, hundreds of thousands of dollars have been spent by trial lawyers on juror consultants.

The best way to determine if prospective jurors are likely to be favorable to your client is to talk with them. If questions are asked that can only be answered by the panel as a whole or with a "yes" or a "no" answer, the attorney does not have an opportunity to speak with the jurors, to get to know them, to develop a rapport, and through that

---

§ 26.54

1. **PRACTICE POINTER:** If there is any question concerning the admissibility of an exhibit, the attorney should prepare questions to establish the foundation for the admissibility of the exhibit.

§ 26.55

1. *See e.g.*, Bensel, Frank, McKeon, et al., *Personal Injury Practice in New York* (West 1997) ¶¶ 9:92–9:226.

§ 26.55   PERSONAL INJURY   Ch. 26

rapport, to determine if they are jurors who will be sympathetic to the cause.

However, in civil trials today, judges are increasingly taking over the role of jury selection, depending upon the venue in which the case is brought. In some venues, even within the New York State court system, the trial judge will ask a series of preliminary questions, not dissimilar to a criminal trial, and then give the attorneys a very limited opportunity to ask follow-up questions.[2]

Before beginning jury selection in any court, the attorney should speak with the court clerk and the trial judge to determine the method of jury selection that will be employed and to make sure that the attorney is familiar with how the peremptory challenges will be employed.[3]

When beginning jury selection, the attorney should be absolutely truthful with regard to the case. Any time that the attorney exaggerates a case during jury selection, it can have a negative effect on the jury. If there is some issue that is considered to be a weakness in the case, it is suggested that this be discussed with the jury during jury selection. If there is an issue about the client's background, *e.g.*, a prior conviction, it is suggested that the admissibility of that matter be discussed with the trial judge, perhaps by filing a motion in limine, to determine what the court's ruling would be in that regard before the start of the trial.

If the court is inclined to admit evidence of the negative issue, then it should be addressed during jury selection. If the court is willing to make a ruling before trial, the attorney should seek such a ruling, because if the issue will *not* be allowed into evidence, there is no reason to discuss it in front of the jury. The most difficult scenario is where the court decides to take a wait-and-see attitude with regard to the negative issue, thereby putting the attorney on the horns of a dilemma as to whether or not it should be mentioned during jury selection.

Before the start of jury selection, consideration should be given to use of the peremptory challenges.[4] If the attorney is faced with the situation of trying to save a peremptory challenge, but wanting to have a juror excused, counsel should attempt to have the juror excuse himself or

---

2. PRACTICE POINTER: The New York Pilot Jury Project has now been completed, and rules have been promulgated by the Chief Judge of the Court of Appeals with regard to the issue of jury selection. *See* Uniform Rules for the New York State Trial Courts § 202.33. There are three methods of selection that are authorized under today's system. One is the struck method, the second is the so-called White method and, in certain districts, the "strike and replace method." Check with the court clerk before jury selection begins to determine which procedures are followed in the venue in which you are trying the case.

3. PRACTICE POINTER: It goes without saying that the attorney should know how many peremptory challenges he or she has when jury selection begins. Pursuant to CPLR 4109, each side shall have three peremptory challenges and one peremptory challenge for each two alternate jurors. If there is more than one defendant, the plaintiff may ask the court for additional peremptory challenges. This should be done before jury selection begins.

4. PRACTICE POINTER: Consideration should be given during this process toward saving a preemptory challenge.

herself. This is done by questioning the juror in such a way that the juror will indicate that this is not a case that he or she would feel comfortable sitting in judgment on. Perhaps, you may elicit a response that the juror knows a party or has some preconceived feeling about the matter. If this information can be elicited, the attorney seeking to remove the juror may have grounds to exclude the juror for cause. When jurors are excluded, a race and gender-neutral reason must be provided by counsel before excusing a member of the panel.

§ 26.56 Disbursement of Proceeds of Settlement or Recovery

When the proceeds of a settlement or recovery are received, the check should be endorsed by the client and a client accounting, in the form of a closing statement, should be provided. This accounting should be consistent with the accounting procedure set forth in the retainer agreement. For example, if there is a contingent fee arrangement and costs are advanced by counsel, the accounting should set forth the amount of the gross recovery and deduct the costs advanced, and then apply the attorney's contingent fee percentage to the net amount.[1] The check should then be deposited in the attorney's escrow account until the funds clear. Distribution of attorney's fees and the client's recovery are then made from the escrow account. Further, a closing statement will have to be filed with the Judicial Conference, just as the retainer statement is filed.[2]

§ 26.57 Drafting Checklists

Drafting checklists may be of benefit in the preparation of any type of case. Representative checklists will be provided below.

§ 26.58 Drafting Checklists—Complaint

In a complaint, there are certain items that must be covered, some of which have been discussed above. The following items are of significance:

1. State that the action is properly venued as to the residence or location of a party. (See § 26.34)

2. If the case involves a motor vehicle accident, identify the operators and owners of the respective vehicles.

3. Identify the location where the accident occurred and the nature of the negligence of the defendant and owner.

§ 26.56
1. See Bensel, Frank, McKeon, et al., *Personal Injury Practice in New York* (West 1997) ¶¶ 1:239–1:240.

2. See supra, § 26.7.

§ 26.58   PERSONAL INJURY   Ch. 26

4. Include a provision indicating that the plaintiff sustained a serious injury, as that term is defined in § 5102(d) of the Insurance Law of the State of New York. (*See* §§ 26.17, 26.24)

5. Provide a statement that this action falls within one or more of the exceptions of CPLR 1602.

6. Provide a statement that the injuries as sustained by the plaintiff were proximately caused by the defendant's negligence. (*See* § 26.36)

7. Include an amount or items of damages and specifically plead any special damages alleged. (*See* § 26.36)

8. Determine if there is a derivative claim and, if so, set it forth as a separate claim.

9. Ensure that the *ad damnum* (*i.e.*, the "wherefore") clause includes all items of damages. (*See* § 26.51)

Medical Malpractice: (*See* §§ 26.11—26.13)

1. Set forth the appropriate venue by location of the parties.

2. Set forth that the physician is a physician licensed to practice in the State of New York and that a doctor/patient relationship existed.

3. Set forth the dates of negligence.

4. Set forth the items of negligence.

5. State that the negligence was the proximate cause of the plaintiff's damages.

6. Set forth the damages in general terms and plead specific special damages, if known.

7. If a derivative action exists, include that cause of action.

8. Prepare a "wherefore" clause that does not set forth a specific amount of general damages, but that does include special damages, if they are being pled and proved.

Premises Liability: (*See* § 26.10)

1. Set forth the venue.

2. Set forth whether the defendant was the owner or lessor of the premises.

3. State the type of notice that is alleged, whether actual or constructive notice or both.

4. Set forth the negligence of the defendant(s).

5. Set forth a statement relating to proximate cause.

6. Set forth the damages, general and special.

Ch. 26   DEMAND FOR BILL OF PARTICULARS   § 26.60

7. If a derivative cause of action exists, set forth and include all damages in all causes of action in the "wherefore" clause.

§ 26.59   Drafting Checklists—Answer[1]

1. All allegations set forth in the plaintiff's complaint must be responded to in the answer. The responses may be by way of admission, denial, or denial on information and belief.
2. A paragraph should be included stating that any claim in the plaintiff's complaint not otherwise specifically admitted or denied or otherwise controverted is denied.
3. Include all affirmative defenses that are known.

§ 26.60   Drafting Checklists—Demand for Bill of Particulars[1]

The bill of particulars demand in a personal injury action is governed by the CPLR.[2] The following items should be requested:

1. The date and approximate time of the occurrence;
2. The approximate location of the occurrence;
3. A general statement of the acts or omissions constituting the negligence claimed;
4. If notice of a condition is a prerequisite to the action, whether actual or constructive notice is claimed;
5. If actual notice is claimed, a statement of when and to whom it was given;
6. A statement of the injuries and a description of those claimed to be permanent, and, in an action designated in Subsection (a) of Section 5104 of the Insurance Law for personal injuries arising out of the negligence in the use or operation of a vehicle in this state, in what respect the plaintiff has sustained a "serious injury" as defined by Subsection (d) of Section 5102 of the Insurance Law, or economic loss greater than basic economic loss as defined in Subsection (a) of Section 5102 of the Insurance Law;
7. The length of time confined to bed or house;
8. The length of time incapacitated from employment;
9. Total amounts claimed as special damages for physician services and medical supplies;
10. Loss of earnings, with the name and address of the employer;

§ 26.59
1. See supra, § 26.37.

§ 26.60
1. See, supra, § 26.47.
2. CPLR 3043.

§ 26.60   PERSONAL INJURY   Ch. 26

   11. Hospital expenses;
   12. Nurses' services;

In addition, any other amplification of the pleadings can be requested.

For the plaintiff, when an answer contains an affirmative defense, particularly when it alleges culpable conduct under Article 14 of the CPLR, a demand for a bill of particulars should be served upon the defendant demanding to know what damages are claimed to have been caused by the plaintiff's negligence and specifically asking what the plaintiff's negligence was.

§ 26.61 Drafting Checklists—Responses to Demand for Bill of Particulars

1. Each of the items in a demand for a bill of particulars, when received, should be carefully reviewed.

2. The proper response to a demand for a bill of particulars is one that is demand-specific. That is, each item should be answered unless legally objectionable.

3. The greater the detail, the greater the ability to have proof introduced at the trial of the action. It is far better to be very specific in the bill of particulars than to be more general.

§ 26.62 Forms—Client's Retainer Agreement[1]

CLIENT'S RETAINER AGREEMENT

_____, herein called the CLIENT, of _____, hereby retains _____, Attorneys at Law, as the Client's attorneys to represent the Client regarding the accident/occurrence of _____, for a sum equal to thirty-three and one-third percent (33 1/3%) of any recovery in this matter by way of settlement, judgment or otherwise, and on the following terms and conditions:

   1. The Client authorizes and empowers the attorneys to take all steps deemed advisable by the attorneys regarding the above matters, including the instituting of legal proceedings and all other appropriate steps.

   2. The Client shall deposit [$_____] as a cost retainer at the time of execution hereof. All costs and expenses regarding the above matter will be paid by the client regardless of the outcome of the matter, and from time to time shall be itemized to the Client.

   § 26.62

   1. *See, supra.* § 26.6. For use in matters other than medical, dental and podiatry malpractice cases.

3. The attorneys shall not settle or compromise the above matter without the consent of the Client, but shall have a lien for the agreed upon fee and disbursements made upon any money received on behalf of the Client and shall subtract same therefrom to the extent herein agreed. Further, pursuant to the New York Code of Professional Responsibility, particularly DR2–107, the client hereby agrees to employ both the law firm of _____ and the law firm of _____. Moveover, both the law firm of _____ and the law firm of _____ agree to assume joint responsibility for the representation of the client. In the event of a successful recovery, there will be a division fees between the referring attorney and _____.

4. In the event the Client and the attorneys agree that an appeal shall be taken in the above matter, the legal fees shall then be subject to renegotiation.

5. No fee shall be payable if no recovery is obtained, but Client acknowledges that the attorneys have made no guarantee regarding successful termination of said matter or any dollar value thereof.

6. Receipt of a copy of this retainer agreement is hereby acknowledged.

Executed at: ___ [Location] ___
Dated: _____

ATTORNEY _____

CLIENT _____

Address: _____

Address: _____

Telephone: _____

Telephone: _____

§ 26.63 Forms—Retainer Statement[1]

RETAINER STATEMENT

TO   THE OFFICE OF COURT   For Office Use:
        ADMINISTRATION
        STATE OF NEW YORK
        Box 2016
        New York, New York 10008

1. Date of agreement as to retainer _____
2. Terms of compensation _____
3. Name and home address of client _____
4. If engaged by an attorney, name and office address of retaining attorney _____

---

§ 26.63
1. See supra, § 26.7.

§ 26.63   PERSONAL INJURY   Ch. 26

5. If claim for personal injuries, wrongful death or property damage, date and place of occurrence _____

6. If a Condemnation or change of grade proceeding:

   (a) Title and description _____

   (b) Date proceeding was commenced _____

   (c) Number or other designation of the parcels affected _____

7. Name, address, occupation and relationship of person referring the client _____

Dated: _____, N.Y. _____ day of _____, 19__
        Yours, etc.

        _____
        Signature of Attorney

        _____
        Attorney

        _____
        Office and P.O. Address
        _____ Dist. _____ Dept. _____ County
        (Print or Type)

NOTE: COURT RULES REQUIRE THAT THE ATTORNEY FOR THE PLAINTIFF FILE A STIPULATION OR STATEMENT OF DISCONTINUANCE WITH THE COURT UPON DISCONTINUANCE OF AN ACTION.

§ 26.64 Forms—Department of Motor Vehicles MV104 Form[1]

(Form image: New York State Department of Motor Vehicles REPORT OF MOTOR VEHICLE ACCIDENT, MV-104 (11/93))

§ 26.64
1. See supra, § 26.20.

§ 26.64 PERSONAL INJURY Ch. 26

MV-104 (11/93)

SECTION A

You must report within 10 days any accident occurring in New York State causing death, personal injury or damage over $1000 to the property of any one person. Failure to do so within 10 days is a misdemeanor. Your license and/or registration may be suspended until a report is filed. You **must fill in all requested information on the report.**

INSTRUCTIONS
PLEASE PRINT OR TYPE ALL INFORMATION - USE BLACK INK
First - fold along this line.
Then fill in the 11 boxes to the right by entering the number of the item which best describes the circumstances of the accident. If a question does not apply, enter a dash (-). If an answer is unknown, enter an "x".

1. If you were involved in an accident with a pedestrian, enter the pedestrian information in the DRIVER block of the space provided for OTHER VEHICLE NO. 2, and print "PEDESTRIAN" in the OWNER block.

   If you were involved in an accident with a vehicle other than a motor vehicle, e.g., snowmobile, mini-bike, aircycle, all-terrain vehicle, trail bike, or other non-motor vehicle, enter the driver, owner and vehicle information as you would normally for OTHER VEHICLE NO. 2.

   If a vehicle is unoccupied, enter all available information. Be sure to enter the correct vehicle plate number and vehicle type in the appropriate VEHICLE block.

2. Enter driver information EXACTLY as it appears on each driver's license. Enter owner information EXACTLY as it appears printed on the registration of each vehicle involved in the accident.

3. If more than two vehicles were involved in this accident, fill out additional accident reports. On these reports, place the information for the third vehicle in the space marked YOUR VEHICLE NO. 1 and mark it No. 3. Use the space marked OTHER VEHICLE NO. 2 for the fourth vehicle, and mark it No. 4 and so on. Additional forms are available at Motor Vehicle issuing offices.

4. Enter the street or route name, the distance and direction from the nearest intersection, and the name or route number of that intersecting street. For example:

   Route Number or Street Name ☐ Miles ☐ N ☐ E Route Number or Street Name
   on _____ ☐ Feet ☐ S ☐ W of _____
   ☐ At Intersection With

5. If the accident occurred on a State highway, you will find a small green sign called a reference marker somewhere near the crash site. The reference marker section should include the number EXACTLY as it appears on the sign.

6. For each person injured in the accident, describe the injuries and check the injury code K, A, B, or C that applies. If the injured is a pedestrian, place a "P" in the box labeled IN VEH. NO.; if a bicyclist, enter a "B". Injuries are defined as follows:

   K   A
   Any injury that results in death   Severe lacerations, broken or distorted
                                    limbs, skull fracture, crushed chest,
                                    internal injuries, unconscious when
                                    taken from the accident scene, unable to
                                    leave accident scene without assistance

   B   C
   Lump on head, abrasions,   Momentary unconsciousness, limping,
   minor lacerations.   nausea, hysteria, complaint of pain (no
                                    visual injury).

   If more than four persons are injured, another report is needed. In the injury section of that report, record the required information for all additional injured persons.

7. Attach additional reports to page one. Each page of the report must be numbered in the upper right corner. Date and **sign** on the bottom line and submit **original** to:

   ACCIDENT RECORDS BUREAU
   PO BOX 2925
   EMPIRE STATE PLAZA
   ALBANY NY 12220-0925

   PLEASE DO NOT SEND PHOTOCOPIES

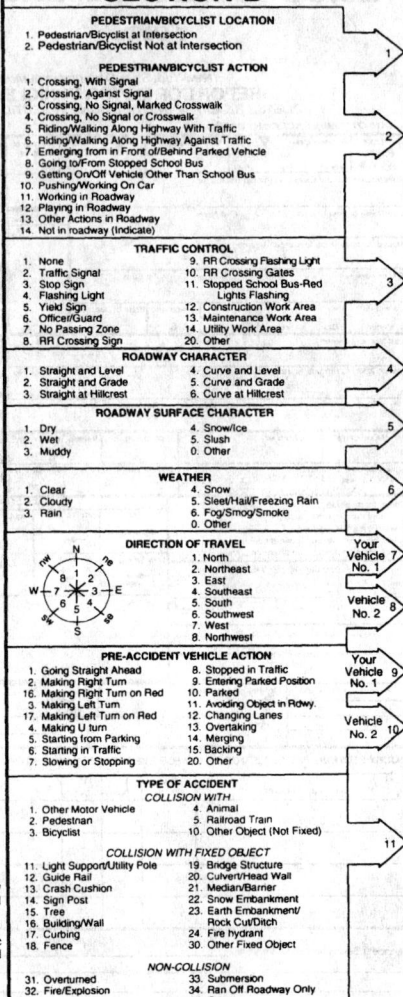

704

§ 26.65 Forms—Summons and Complaint[1]

SUPREME COURT OF THE STATE OF NEW YORK
COUNTY OF _____

_____)
)
_____,   )
                          Plaintiff,)   Summons
)
       -against-   )   Index No. _____
)
_____,   )
                          Defendant.)
_____)

THE PLAINTIFF DESIGNATES _____ COUNTY AS THE PLACE OF TRIAL.
THE BASIS OF THE VENUE IS [PLAINTIFF'S/DEFENDANT'S] RESIDENCE.
THE PLAINTIFF RESIDES AT _____, COUNTY OF _____.

To the above named Defendant

YOU ARE HEREBY SUMMONED to answer the complaint in this action and to serve a copy of your answer, or, if the complaint is not served with this summons, to serve a notice of appearance, on the Plaintiff's Attorney(s) within twenty (20) days after the service of this summons, exclusive of the day of service (or within 30 days after the service is complete if this summons is not personally delivered to you within the State of New York); and in case of your failure to appear or answer, judgment will be taken against you by default for the relief demanded in the complaint.

Dated: _____

                                                      _____
                                                      Attorneys for Plaintiff

                                                      _____
                                                       _____

Defendant Address:

AFFIDAVIT OF SERVICE
STATE OF NEW YORK, COUNTY OF   **SS.:**

being duly sworn, deposes and say, that deponent is not a party to the action, is over the age of 18 and resides at

that on   19
at

§ 26.65
1. See supra, § 26.34.

§ 26.65   PERSONAL INJURY   Ch. 26

deponent served the within subpoena on

[ ]SERVICE ON INDIVIDUAL by delivering a true copy of each to said defendant personally; deponent knew the person so served to be the person described as said defendant therein.

a
corporation, by delivering thereat a true copy of each to

[ ]SERVICE ON CORPORATION
a   corporation, the witness therein named, by delivering a true copy thereof to
personally, whom deponent knew to be the
of said corporation, and at the same time paying (or tendering) in advance $, the authorized travelling expenses and one day's witness fee: deponent knew the corporation so severed to be said corporate witness.

[ ]SUITABLE AGE PERSON by delivering thereat a true copy of each to
a person of suitable age and discretion. Said premises is defendant's actual place of business, dwelling house, usual place of abode, within the State.

[ ]AFFIXING TO DOOR, ETC. by affixing a true copy of each to the door of said premises, which is defendant's actual place of business, dwelling house, usual place of abode, within the state. Deponent was unable, with due diligence to find defendant or a person of suitable age and discretion, thereat, having called there

[ ]MAILING USE WITH SUITABLE AGE PERSON OR AFFIXING TO DOOR, ETC.
Deponent also enclosed a copy of same in a postpaid sealed wrapper properly addressed to defendant at defendant's last known residence at

and deposited said wrapper in a post office or official depository under exclusive care and custody of the United States Postal Service within New York State.

DESCRIPTION USE WITH INDIVIDUAL OR SUITABLE AGE PERSON

[ ]White Skin	[ ]Under 5'	[ ]Under 100 lbs.	[ ]Black Hair	[ ]14–20 Yrs.
[ ]Black Skin	[ ]5'0—5'3"	[ ]100—130 lbs.	[ ]Brown Hair	[ ]21–35 Yrs.
[ ]Yellow Skin	[ ]5'4"—5'8"	[ ]131—160 lbs.	[ ]Blond Hair	[ ]36–50 Yrs.
[ ]Brown Skin	[ ]5'9"–6'0"	[ ]161—200 lbs.	[ ]Gray Hair	[ ]51–65 Yrs.
[ ]Red Skin	[ ]Over 6'	[ ]Over 200 lbs.	[ ]Red Hair	[ ]Over 65 Yrs.
			[ ]White Hair	
			[ ]Balding	

Other identifying features:

Sworn to before me on

_____

Notary Public

SUPREME COURT OF THE STATE OF NEW YORK
COUNTY OF _____

_____
)
)
)
_____,   Plaintiff(s),   )   Complaint
)
    -against-   )   Index No. _____
)
_____,   )
              Defendant.   )
)
_____

Plaintiff(s), _____, by their attorneys, _____, as and for his/their complaint against the defendant herein allege and state to the Court as follows:

1. At all times hereinafter mentioned, Plaintiff(s) was/were and still is/are resident(s) of the County of _____, State of New York.

2. Upon information and belief, the Defendant, _____, at all times relevant herein was and still is a resident of the County of _____, State of New York.

3. Upon information and belief, on _____, the Plaintiff, _____, was the owner and operator of a certain _____ automobile bearing license number _____ for the year _____.

4. Upon information and belief, the Defendant, _____, was, on _____, the owner and operator of a certain _____ automobile bearing license number _____ for the year _____.

5. Upon information and belief, _____ Avenue, at it's intersection with _____ Avenue in the Village of _____, County of _____, is a much traveled public highway running at a generally easterly and westerly direction.

6. On _____, the Defendant, _____, operated his vehicle in such a careless, reckless and negligent fashion as to cause it to collide with the rear of the vehicle owned and operated by _____, the Plaintiff herein.

7. As a result of the Defendant's negligence, carelessness and recklessness as aforesaid, the Plaintiff has sustained a serious injury as that term is defined in Section 5102(d) of the Insurance Law of the State of New York, and has sustained economic loss greater than basic economic loss.

8. By reason of the foregoing, the Plaintiff has been caused to and has endured pain and suffering and injuries which are permanent.

9. By reason of the foregoing, the Plaintiff has been injured and damaged in an amount of $_____.

AS IN FOR A SECOND CAUSE OF ACTION

10. Plaintiff(s) repeat and reallege each and every paragraph in the complaint numbered "1" through "9" as if more fully set forth at length herein.

11. That on _____ and at all times relevant herein, the Plaintiff, _____, was and still is the husband of the Plaintiff, _____, and as such he was entitled to the society, companionship, services and consortium of the Plaintiff, _____.

§ 26.65   PERSONAL INJURY   Ch. 26

12. That by reason of negligence, carelessness, and recklessness of the Defendant as set forth, the Plaintiff, _____, has been caused to suffer the loss of services, society, companionship and consortium of the Plaintiff, _____, without any fault on her part contributing thereto.

13. By reason of the foregoing, the said Plaintiff, _____, has been damaged and injured in an amount of up to $_____.

WHEREFORE, by reason of the foregoing, the Plaintiff(s) demand(s) judgment against the Defendant in the amount of up to $_____ in the first cause of the action and up to $_____ on the second cause of action together with such other and further relief as to the Court may seem just and proper.

Dated: _____

                                              Attorneys for Plaintiff(s)

§ 26.66 Forms—Amended Answer, Counterclaim & Cross Claim

SUPREME COURT OF THE STATE OF NEW YORK
COUNTY OF _____

_____)
)
_____,   )
             Plaintiff(s),   ) Amended Answer, Counter-
) claim and Cross Claim
    -against-   ) Index No. _____
)
_____,   )
           Defendant(s).)
)
_____)

Defendant(s), _____, by his/her/their attorney(s), _____ _____, as and for his/her/their answer to the complaint of plaintiff(s) herein allege(s) as follows:

1. **ADMITS** the allegations contained in the paragraph numbered "__" of plaintiff's/plaintiffs' complaint.

2. **DENIES KNOWLEDGE OR INFORMATION** sufficient to form a belief as to the truth of the allegations set forth in the paragraphs

marked and numbered "__", "__" and "__" of plaintiff's/plaintiffs' complaint.

3. **DENIES** each and every allegation contained in the paragraphs marked and numbered "__", "__" and "__" of plaintiff's/plaintiffs' complaint.

AS AND FOR A FIRST, SEPARATE AND DISTINCT AFFIRMATIVE DEFENSE, DEFENDANT(S) REPEAT(S) AND REALLEGE(S) THE PARAGRAPHS MARKED AND NUMBERED "1" THROUGH "3" ABOVE (BOTH INCLUSIVE) AND FURTHER ALLEGE(S):

4. Upon information and belief, the alleged injuries were brought about in whole or in part by reason of the culpable conduct of the plaintiff(s) herein.

5. By reason of the foregoing, this/these answering defendant(s) demand(s) that the amount of damages otherwise recoverable, if any, be reduced in the proportion to which the culpable conduct of the plaintiff(s) bear(s) to the culpable conduct, if any, of this/these answering defendant(s) pursuant to Section 1411 of the Civil Practice Law and Rules.

AS AND FOR A SECOND, SEPARATE AND DISTINCT AFFIRMATIVE DEFENSE, DEFENDANT(S) REPEAT(S) AND REALLEGE(S) THE PARAGRAPHS NUMBERED "1" THROUGH "5" ABOVE (BOTH INCLUSIVE) AND FURTHER ALLEGE(S):

6. That the plaintiff's/plaintiffs' complaint fails to state a cause of action against this/these answering defendant(s) for which relief can be sought.

AS AND FOR A THIRD, SEPARATE AND DISTINCT AFFIRMATIVE DEFENSE, DEFENDANT(S) REPEAT(S) AND REALLEGE(S) THE PARAGRAPHS NUMBERED "1" THROUGH "6" ABOVE (BOTH INCLUSIVE) AND FURTHER ALLEGE(S):

7. Upon information and belief, the plaintiff(s) has/have been and will be indemnified and reimbursed for some or all of the damages alleged in the complaint by such collateral sources as are defined in CPLR Section 4545 and as such, this/these answering defendant(s) is/are entitled to a set-off against the amount of any verdict of any money collected from a collateral source of payment as set forth.

AS AND FOR A FOURTH, SEPARATE AND DISTINCT AFFIRMATIVE DEFENSE, DEFENDANT(S) REPEAT(S) AND REALLEGE(S) THE PARAGRAPHS NUMBERED "1" THROUGH "7" ABOVE (BOTH INCLUSIVE) AND FURTHER ALLEGE(S):

8. The plaintiff(s) has/have not sustained a serious personal injury as defined in Section 5102(d) of the insurance law of the state of New York, and by virtue thereof, the planitiff's/plaintiffs' complaint does not state a viable and enforceable cause of action against this answering defendant.

AS AND FOR A CROSS CLAIM AGAINST DEFENDANT(S), _____, THIS/THESE ANSWERING DEFENDANT(S) REPEAT(S) AND REALLEGE(S) EACH AND EVERY PARAGRAPH OF THIS ANSWER NUMBERED "1" THROUGH "8" (BOTH INCLUSIVE) AND FURTHER STATE(S):

9. If the plaintiff(s) sustained any injuries and damages at the time and place alleged in the complaint through any acts or omissions other than the plaintiff's/plaintiffs' own, such damages were caused by the acts or omissions of the co-defendant(s), _____, and if any judgment is obtained against this/these answering defendant(s), then this/these answering defendant(s) demand(s) judgment over against said co-defendant(s) for any part of all of said judgment as may be found to be due and owing.

AS AND FOR A COUNTER CLAIM AGAINST THE PLAINTIFF(S), THE DEFENDANT(S) REPEAT(S) AND REALLEGE(S) EACH AND EVERY PARAGRAPH OF THIS ANSWER MARKED AND NUMBERED "1" THROUGH "9" (BOTH INCLUSIVE) AND FURTHER ALLEGE(S) UPON INFORMATION IN BELIEF:

The damages claimed in the complaint were caused by or contributed to by the culpable conduct of the plaintiff(s) and, therefore, the amount of damages otherwise recoverable must be diminished in the proportion to which such culpable conduct including contributory negligence, want of care, and assumption of the risk attributable to set plaintiff(s) bears to the culpable conduct which caused the injury in damages.

WHEREFORE, the defendant(s) _____, demand(s) judgment dismissing the complaint, or in the event judgment is rendered against him/them that he/they have judgment over against the plaintiff(s), _____ and the defendant(s), _____ _____, for such amounts as he/she/they are entitled to under the applicable laws of the state of New York, together with the costs and disbursements of this action.

Dated: _____

                                    _____
                                    Attorneys for Defendant(s)
                                    _____
                                    _____

TO: _____
    Attorneys for Plaintiff(s)
    _____

§ 26.67 Forms—Defendant's Demand for a Verified Bill of Particulars[1]

SUPREME COURT OF THE STATE OF NEW YORK
COUNTY OF _____

_____,	)	
	)	
Plaintiff,	)	Demand for a Verified
	)	Bill of Particulars
-against-	)	Index No. _____
	)	
_____,	)	
Defendant.	)	

PLEASE TAKE NOTICE that pursuant to Article 30 of the Civil Practice Law and Rules, demand is hereby made upon the Plaintiff herein that he/she serve within twenty (20) days from the date of service of this notice, a Verified Bill of Particulars setting forth the following:

1. The full name, age, place of residence and marital status of the Plaintiff.

2. The date, time of day and exact location of the occurrence alleged in the Complaint.

3. A statement showing each act or omission on the part of the Defendant which the Plaintiff will claim constituted negligence.

4. The particular statutes of the State of New York and ordinances, rules or regulations, together with the sections and paragraphs thereof, which the Plaintiff will claim were violated by said Defendant.

5. Specify how the Plaintiff sustained a serious injury as defined in Section 5102 of the Insurance Law of the State of New York.

§ 26.67
1. See supra, § 26.4.

6. Set forth a description of each and every injury sustained by the Plaintiff, together with the nature, extent, location and duration thereof.

7. Set forth a particular description of each and every permanent injury sustained by the Plaintiff, together with the nature and extent thereof.

8. Specify the length of time the Plaintiff was confined to hospital, bed and home.

9. State by name the particular physicians, institutions or health service providers that treated the Plaintiff and for which particular and separate injury, complaint or condition they treated said Plaintiff.

10. State the number of times and the dates thereof that the Plaintiff called upon each and every attending physician or health provider; and the dates the Plaintiff was first attended and last attended.

11. Specify the total amounts claimed as special damages for the following:

   (a) Physicians' services, giving names, addresses and amounts;

   (b) Hospital expenses, giving names, addresses and amounts;

   (c) Nurses' services, giving names, addresses and amounts;

   (d) Specific amounts charged for physiotherapy;

   (e) All other expenses.

12. Specify in what respect and to what extent further sums will be expended in the future for the aforesaid items.

13. A statement setting forth the following:

   (a) The name and address of the Plaintiff's employer;

   (b) A description of the Plaintiff's duties in said employment;

   (c) The length of time the Plaintiff was incapacitated from said employment and the dates thereof;

   (d) The amount of the Plaintiff's weekly wages, salary or other commission;

   (e) The total amount of the Plaintiff's loss of earnings.

14. A statement of each and every other item or loss or damage claimed by the Plaintiff.

Dated: _____

Ch. 26   DEFENDANT'S CPLR 3101 DEMANDS   § 26.68

_____
Attorneys for Defendant
_____
_____

TO: _____
Attorneys for Plaintiff
_____
_____

§ 26.68 Forms—Defendant's CPLR 3101 Demands[1]

SUPREME COURT OF THE STATE OF NEW YORK
COUNTY OF _____

_____
)
)
_____,   )
)
              Plaintiff(s),   )   CPLR 3101 Demands
)
     -against-   )   Index No. _____
)
_____,   )
)
              Defendant(s).   )
)
_____

(I) MEDICAL REPORTS

PLEASE TAKE FURTHER NOTICE, that Defendant(s) demand(s) that copies of any and all medical reports, including office notes of all physicians who have previously treated or examined the Plaintiff(s) and which have come into the possession of the Plaintiff(s) be served upon the attorneys for the Defendant(s) including x-rays and technicians' reports and physical therapy reports, within twenty (20) days from the date of service of this demand. AND YOU WILL FURTHER TAKE NOTICE, that the Defendant(s), hereby demand(s) that you furnish the undersigned within twenty (20) days of the service of this demand, duly executed and acknowledged authorizations permitting the Defendant(s) to obtain a copy of all hospital records, X-ray reports and all other records referred to in any physician's report in connection with the injuries for which recovery is sought.

(II) WITNESSES

PLEASE TAKE FURTHER NOTICE, that you are required to serve upon the attorneys for the Defendant(s) the names and addresses of any

---
§ 26.68
1. See supra, § 26.42.

and all witnesses to the occurrence alleged in this action, including witnesses to admissions made by the parties, names and addresses of witnesses to any acts, omissions, or conditions which allegedly caused the occurrence alleged in the Complaint, and names and addresses of witnesses to the nature and duration of any alleged condition which allegedly caused the occurrence alleged in the Complaint.

(III) STATEMENTS

PLEASE TAKE FURTHER NOTICE, that you are hereby required to serve upon the undersigned pursuant to CPLR 3101(e) a copy of any statements made by Defendant(s) in this action.

(IV) PHOTOS, FILMS, TAPES

PLEASE TAKE FURTHER NOTICE, that you are required to serve upon the undersigned copies of any photos, films, audio and/or video tapes in your custody or control, of the occurrence and of all instrumentalities involved in this action before, on the day of, and after the accident, and of all involved body parts before, on the day of and after the accident.

(V) EXPERTS

PLEASE TAKE FURTHER NOTICE, that the undersigned hereby demands pursuant to CPLR 3101(d) that the Plaintiff(s):

1. Identify and state the qualifications of each person whom the plaintiff(s) expect(s) to call at trial as an expert witness;

2. State the subject matter in reasonable detail, upon which the expert is expected to testify; and

3. Provide the substance of the facts and opinion upon which the expert is expected to testify;

4. Provide a summary of the grounds of each such opinion.

AND YOU WILL FURTHER TAKE NOTICE, that upon your failure to comply with the terms of this demand, the undersigned will object to the use of any experts and/or experts' reports for any purpose upon the trial of this action.

(VI) PARTIES AND ATTORNEYS

PLEASE TAKE FURTHER NOTICE, that demand is hereby made that you serve upon the undersigned attorneys a list of the names of all the parties that have appeared in the action, together with the names and addresses of their respective attorneys, pursuant to CPLR 2103(e).

(VII) SURVEILLANCE PHOTOGRAPHY AND RECORDINGS

PLEASE TAKE FURTHER NOTICE, that pursuant to CPLR 3120, demand is hereby made that you serve, within twenty (20) days after receipt of this demand, upon the undersigned attorneys at their office address listed herein, unedited copies of any and all films, videotapes, photographs, audio recordings of the Plaintiff(s) including surveillance recordings depicting Plaintiff(s)' activities before, at the time of, or subsequent to the accident or incidents complained of, including but not limited to, (A) all "out takes" from such recordings, (B) the names of the individuals, corporations, partnerships or other entities which made the records, (C) the time records of the individuals or entities who made the recordings, including the date, time and place when each portion of said recordings were made, and (D) copies of edited versions of said recordings.

(VIII) ACCIDENT REPORTS

PLEASE TAKE FURTHER NOTICE, that you are required to serve upon the undersigned, pursuant to CPLR 3101(g), any written accident or incident reports related to this case prepared in the regular course of business operations of any person, firm, corporation, association or other public or private entity.

PLEASE TAKE FURTHER NOTICE, that all these demands are continuing demands during the pendency of this action, including any trial herein. In the event of your refusal or failure to comply herewith, the undersigned shall seek to preclude the use at trial of any information requested but not furnished, the testimony of any witnesses whose identity has not been disclosed, and the contents of any statement furnished.

Dated: _____

_____
Attorneys for Defendant(s)
_____
_____

TO: _____
Attorneys for Plaintiff(s)
_____
_____

§ 26.69 Forms—Plaintiff's Demand for a Verified Bill of Particulars[1]

SUPREME COURT OF THE STATE OF NEW YORK
COUNTY OF _____

_____)
_____,)
Plaintiff,) Demand for a Verified
) Bill of Particulars
-against-) Index No. _____
)
_____,)
Defendant.)
_____)

PLEASE TAKE NOTICE that the Plaintiff herein, by her attorneys, _____, hereby demands that the Defendant serve upon the undersigned, within twenty (20) days from the date of service of this demand, a Verified Bill of Particulars specifying the following:

1. As to the Defendant's second affirmative defense found in paragraphs 7 and 8 of the Defendant's Answer:

    (a) A statement setting forth the particular acts or omissions constituting the alleged negligence of the Plaintiff, which allegedly caused or contributed to the injuries and damages which she sustained.

    (b) A statement setting forth the injuries sustained by the Plaintiff herein which were caused by said culpable conduct.

2. As to the Defendant's third affirmative defense found in paragraphs 9 and 10 of the Defendant's Answer:

    (a) A statement setting forth the injuries sustained by the plaintiff due to his/her alleged non-use of a seat belt and/or shoulder restraint.

    (b) A statement setting forth the basis of the second affirmative defense that Plaintiff was not wearing a seat belt and/or shoulder restraint.

    (c) A statement setting forth the injuries claimed which would have been prevented by the Plaintiff's use of a seat belt and/or restraining device.

PLEASE TAKE FURTHER NOTICE that in the event of your failure to furnish said bill of particulars as above demanded, the under-

---

§ 26.69
1. *See supra*, § 26.47.

signed will move for an order in the above-entitled action precluding the giving of evidence at the trial herein with reference to the items of which the particulars have not been delivered.

Dated: _____

_____
Attorneys for Plaintiff
_____

TO: _____
Attorneys for Defendant
_____

§ 26.70 Forms—Plaintiff's CPLR 3101 Demands[1]

SUPREME COURT OF THE STATE OF NEW YORK
COUNTY OF _____

_____,	)))	
Plaintiff,	))	CPLR 3101 Demands
-against-	))	Index No. _____
_____,	))	
Defendant.	)))	

(I) INSURANCE COVERAGE

PLEASE TAKE NOTICE, that pursuant to CPLR 3101(f) Plaintiff hereby demands that copies of all insurance agreements under which any person carrying on an insurance business may be liable to satisfy part or all of a judgment which may be entered in this action or to indemnify or reimburse for payments made to satisfy the judgment, be served upon the attorneys for the Plaintiff within twenty (20) days from the date of service of this demand.

(I.a) EXCESS OR SUPPLEMENTAL INSURANCE COVERAGE

PLEASE TAKE NOTICE, that Plaintiff demands pursuant to CPLR 3101(f) that copies of any and all insurance agreements under which any person carrying on an insurance business may be liable to provide excess or supplemental coverage to satisfy part or all of a judgment which may

---

§ 26.70
1. See supra, § 26.42.

be entered in this action or to indemnify or reimburse for payments made to satisfy the judgment be served upon the attorneys for the Plaintiff within twenty (20) days from the date of service of this demand. In cases of automobile negligence, provide copies of policies covering each and every one of any other vehicles owned by Defendant in addition to the vehicle or vehicles which were involved in the accident complained of herein.

(II) MEDICAL REPORTS

PLEASE TAKE FURTHER NOTICE, that Plaintiff demands that copies of any and all medical reports including office notes of all physicians who have previously treated or examined the Plaintiff and which have come into the possession of the Defendant be served upon the attorneys for the Plaintiff including x-rays and technicians' reports and physical therapy reports, within twenty (20) days from the date of service of this demand.

(III) WITNESSES

PLEASE TAKE FURTHER NOTICE, that you are required to serve upon the attorneys for the Plaintiff the names and addresses of any and all witnesses to the occurrence in this action, including witnesses to admissions made by the parties, names and addresses of witnesses to any acts, omissions, or conditions which allegedly caused the occurrence alleged in the Complaint, and names and addresses of witnesses to the nature and duration of any alleged condition which allegedly caused the occurrence alleged in the Complaint.

(IV) STATEMENTS

PLEASE TAKE FURTHER NOTICE, that you are hereby required to serve upon the undersigned pursuant to CPLR 3101(e) a copy of any statements made by Plaintiff in this action.

(V) PHOTOS, FILMS, TAPES

PLEASE TAKE FURTHER NOTICE, that you are required to serve upon the undersigned copies of any photos, films, audio and/or video tapes in your custody or control, of the occurrence and of all instrumentalities involved in this action before, on the day of, and after the accident, and of all involved body parts before, on the day of and after the accident.

(VI) EXPERTS

PLEASE TAKE FURTHER NOTICE, that the undersigned hereby demands pursuant to CPLR 3101(d) that the Plaintiff:

1. Identify and state the qualifications of each person whom the party expects to call at trial as an expert witness;

2. State the subject matter in reasonable detail, upon which the expert is expected to testify;

3. Provide the substance of the facts and opinion upon which the expert is expected to testify; and

4. Provide a summary of the grounds of each such opinion.

AND YOU WILL FURTHER TAKE NOTICE, that upon your failure to comply with the terms of this demand, the undersigned will object to the use of any experts and/or experts' reports for any purpose upon the trial of this action.

(VII) PARTIES AND ATTORNEYS

PLEASE TAKE FURTHER NOTICE, that demand is hereby made that you serve upon the undersigned attorneys a list of the names of all the parties that have appeared in the action, together with the names and addresses of their respective attorneys, pursuant to CPLR 2103(e).

(VIII) SURVEILLANCE PHOTOGRAPHY AND RECORDINGS

PLEASE TAKE FURTHER NOTICE, that pursuant to CPLR 3120, demand is hereby made that you serve, within twenty (20) days after receipt of this demand, upon the undersigned attorneys, at their office address listed herein, unedited copies of any and all films, videotapes, photographs, audio recordings of the Plaintiff including surveillance recordings depicting Plaintiff's activities before, at the time of, and subsequent to the accident or incidents complained of, including but not limited to, (A) all "out takes" from such recordings, (B) the names of the individuals, corporations, partnerships or other entities which made the records, (C) the time records of the individuals or entities who made the recordings, including the date, time and place when each portion of said recordings were made, and (D) copies of edited versions of said recordings.

(IX) ACCIDENT REPORTS

PLEASE TAKE FURTHER NOTICE, that you are required to serve upon the undersigned, pursuant to CPLR 3101(g), any written accident or incident reports related to this case prepared in the regular course of business operations of any person, firm, corporation, association or other public or private entity.

PLEASE TAKE FURTHER NOTICE, that all these demands are continuing demands during the pendency of this action, including any trial herein. In the event of your refusal or failure to comply herewith, the undersigned shall seek to preclude the use at trial of any information requested but not furnished, the testimony of any witnesses whose identity has not been disclosed, and the contents of any statement furnished.

§ 26.70   PERSONAL INJURY   Ch. 26

Dated: _____

                              _____
                              Attorneys for Plaintiff
                              _____
                              _____

TO: _____
Attorneys for Defendant
_____
_____

§ 26.71   Forms—Closing Statement[1] 💾
CLOSING STATEMENT
                                            For Office Use:

TO: THE OFFICE OF COURT
       ADMINISTRATION
       STATE OF NEW YORK
       Box 2016
       New York, New York 10008

1. Code number appearing on Attorney's receipt for filing of retainer statement. (If statement filed with Clerk of Appellate Division prior to July 1, 1960, give date of such filing.)

                       _____
                         Code Number

2. Name and present address of client _____.
3. Plaintiff(s) _____.
4. Defendant(s) _____.
5. If action commenced, state date _____, 19__, _____ Court, _____ County. Was note of issue or notice of trial filed? _____ If "Yes," was action disposed of in open courts?_____ If not disposed of in open court, state date stipulation of discontinuance was filed with CALENDAR CLERK of the court in which the action was pending _____, 19__.
6. Check items applicable: Settled ( ); Claim abandoned by client ( ); Judgment ( ).

     Date of payment by carrier or defendant _____ day of _____, 19__ Date of payment to client _____ day of _____, 19__.

§ 26.71
1. See supra, § 26.56.

7. Gross amount of recovery (if judgment entered, include any interest, costs and disbursements allowed) $_____ [of which $_____ was taxable costs and disbursements].

8. Name and address of insurance carrier or person paying judgment or claim and carrier's file number, if any _____.

9. Net amounts: to client $_____; compensation to undersigned $_____; names, addresses and amounts paid to attorneys participating in the contingent compensation _____.

10. Compensation fixed by: retainer agreement ( ); under schedule ( ); or by court ( ).

11. If compensation fixed by court: Name of Judge _____, Court _____ Index No _____ Date of order _____.

12. Itemized statement of payments made for hospital, medical care or treatment, liens, assignments, claims and expenses on behalf of the client which have been charged against the client's share of the recovery, together with the name, address, amount and reason for each payment _____.

13. Itemized statement of the amounts of expenses and disbursements paid or agreed to be paid to others for expert testimony, investigative or other services properly chargeable to the recovery of damages together with the name, address and reason for each payment _____.

14. Date on which a copy of this closing statement has been forwarded to the client _____, 19__.

NOTE: COURT RULES REQUIRE THAT THE ATTORNEY FOR THE PLAINTIFF FILE A STIPULATION OR STATEMENT OF DISCONTINUANCE WITH THE COURT UPON DISCONTINUANCE OF AN ACTION.

Dated: _____, N.Y., ___ day of _____, 19__

Yours, etc.

_____
Signature of Attorney

_____
Attorney

_____
Office and P.O. Address
_____ Dist. _____ Dept.
_____ County
(Print or Type)

Chapter 27

PRODUCTS LIABILITY

by
Stuart A. Schlesinger
and
David B. Turret

Table of Sections

27.1 Scope Note.
27.2 Strategy.
27.3 Historical Overview.
27.4 Bases of a Products Liability Claim.
27.5 Theories of Liability.
27.6 ___ Manufacturing Defect or Mistake in the Manufacturing Process.
27.7 ___ Defective Design.
27.8 ___ ___ Burden of Proof.
27.9 ___ ___ Defense.
27.10 ___ Failure to Warn or Inadequate Warnings.
27.11 ___ ___ Burden of Proof.
27.12 ___ ___ Duty to Warn.
27.13 ___ ___ Adequacy of Warning.
27.14 ___ ___ Jury Question.
27.15 ___ ___ Informed Intermediary Defense.
27.16 ___ ___ Duty to Warn the Unusually Sensitive.
27.17 ___ ___ Non-Commercial Cases.
27.18 ___ Failure to Test.
27.19 ___ ___ FDA Approval.
27.20 ___ ___ Jury Question.
27.21 ___ ___ Preemption Defense.
27.22 Distributors' or Sellers' Liability.
27.23 ___ Sale Must Be Part of Ordinary Business.
27.24 ___ Service v. Sales.
27.25 ___ Medical Care Providers.
27.26 Successor Liability.
27.27 ___ Burden of Proof.
27.28 ___ Punitive Damages.
27.29 Liability of the Manufacturer of Component Parts.
27.30 Liability of the Manufacturer of the Complete Product.
27.31 Introducing Evidence of Post Accident Modification or Repairs.
27.32 Introducing Evidence of Other Incidents.
27.33 Effect of Destruction of the Product Upon Plaintiff's Ability to Prove a Defect.

27.34	Proof of Causation.
27.35	____ Question for the Jury or Question for the Judge.
27.36	Foreseeability of Harm.
27.37	Discovery Issues.
27.38	____ Confidentiality Orders or Stipulations.
27.39	Statute of Limitations.
27.40	Intervening Acts of Negligence—Plaintiff's Misuse of the Product.
27.41	____ Alteration of the Product After it Has Left the Hands of the Manufacturer.
27.42	Preemption of Private Claims.
27.43	____ Old Rule.
27.44	____ New Rule.
27.45	____ National Traffic & Motor Vehicle Safety Act and Its Savings Clause.
27.46	____ Public Health Cigarette Labeling & Advertising Act of 1965 and the Public Health Cigarette Smoking Act of 1969—The *Cipollone* Decision.
27.47	____ Federal Insecticide, Fungicide and Rodenticide Act (FIFRA) and Its Impact on Labeling Requirements.
27.48	____ Medical Device Amendments to FDA Regulations.
27.49	____ Limits on Preemption and Statutory Defenses.
27.50	____ Validity of the Safety Standard or Regulatory Statute.
27.51	____ Checklist.
27.52	Imposing Liability when the Manufacturer of a Fungible or Generic Product Is Unknown (Concert of Action/Market Share Liability).
27.53	Collateral Estoppel in Products Liability Cases.
27.54	Proof of Allegations Checklist.
27.55	Drafting Checklist—Complaint.
27.56	____ Answer.
27.57	Forms—Products Liability Complaint.
27.58	____ Products Liability Answer.

WESTLAW Electronic Research

See WESTLAW Electronic Research Guide preceding the Summary of Contents.

§ 27.1 Scope Note

Over the years, tort law has undergone sweeping changes to introduce a theory of liability consonant with the wide reaching distribution of products.[1] This theory of recovery, known as the law of products liability, provides several avenues through which an injured person, no matter how remote his or her contact is with the manufacturer or distributor, may seek redress for the injuries sustained. While products liability law had its genesis in contract claims for breach of warranty, what has now evolved is essentially a pure tort cause of action. However,

---

§ 27.1

1. *See generally*, Kreindler, Rodriguez, et al., *New York Law of Torts* (West 1997).

contract principles still co-exist with tort concepts. The precise manner in which they may influence a products liability claim will be discussed in this chapter, since the application of—and interplay between—basic tort and contract principles will have a significant impact upon the nature of the claim and the facts that underlie it.

One purpose of this chapter is to provide the reader with an understanding of the different theories of liability available under products liability law, and the legal issues that may arise in connection with those theories. Sections 27.5 through 27.30 treat the various liability theories, potential parties, burdens of proof, defenses and other significant legal issues. Section 27.54 through 27.58 contain a proof-of-allegations checklist, drafting checklists for a complaint and an answer, as well as illustrative model forms for these pleadings, all of which are provided to assist the practitioner in the prosecution or defense of a products liability case.

The chapter also examines evidentiary and procedural matters in the products liability case. Different rules have been developed regarding the admissibility of evidence, the scope of discovery and the burden of proof in the products liability context.[2] A lawyer representing a client in a products liability case should be familiar with these rules since they impact upon the entire litigation from inception to verdict. Sections 27.31 through 27.36 discuss special evidentiary issues; Sections 27.37 and 27.38 treat discovery issues; and Sections 27.39 through 27.51 treat the defenses of Statute of Limitations,[3] intervening acts of negligence and preemption.

Imposition of liability where the manufacturer of the offending product is unknown, under a theory of concert of action or market share liability,[4] is discussed in Section 27.52, and the use of collateral estoppel where multiple lawsuits are brought against a defendant is covered in Section 27.53.

In order to appreciate the uniqueness of products liability claims, it is important to understand the derivation of such claims. Section 27.3 presents an historical overview of the subject, and Section 27.4 explores the bases of product liability claims.

§ 27.2 Strategy

When first presented with a products liability case, counsel should carefully elicit facts and information as to the nature of the product involved, the type of injury sustained and how the product was being

---

2. See also, Barker and Alexander, *Evidence in New York State and Federal Courts* (West 1996).

3. See also, Bensel, Frank, McKeon, et al., *Personal Injury Practice in New York* (West 1997) Ch. 5 "Filing Suit: Time Bars and Pleading Concerns."

4. See also, Bensel, Frank, McKeon, et al., *Personal Injury Practice in New York* (West 1997) ¶¶ 2:450–2:466.

used. Each fact bears directly upon the theories of liability that will be used and the defenses that will be asserted or confronted.

What Type of Product Was Involved? Was it a dangerous instrumentality, such as a piece of heavy machinery or a chain saw, or was it something which is expected to be harmless, such as a toy or piece of furniture? Did the injury occur because the product, such as a food, beverage or drug, was ingested? The answers to these questions will impact upon your investigation and concerns about the adequacy of warnings,[1] the foreseeability of harm,[2] and whether the injury was causally related to the product.[3]

What Type of Injury Was Sustained? Again, the issue of the adequacy of the warnings for this particular injury and whether such injury was foreseeable is pertinent.

How Was the Product Being Used? It is important to ascertain whether the product was being used in the manner intended by the manufacturer or whether it was being misused by the injured party.[4] It is also necessary to find out whether the product was used on the advice of a prescribing physician.[5] It is similarly important to determine whether the product was used during the course of the injured person's employment.[6]

Who Was Responsible for the Defect? Depending upon the facts, counsel for the injured person may want to include as defendants the manufacturer and distributor of the product, or a particular component part thereof.[7] There may be affiliate, predecessor or successor companies who should be included as defendants.[8] A defendant may want to base a defense or a cross-claim or third-party action upon the fact that after the product left its hands it was altered by some third-party, such as the plaintiff's employer.[9]

The answers to all of these questions frame the scope of the products liability lawsuit. Research at the intake stage of the case will provide information as to what Statute of Limitations applies, when the cause of action accrues, and whether the cause of action can be framed in such a way so as to take advantage of a longer Statute of Limitations.[10] Additionally, research will yield information as to particular defenses

---

§ 27.2

1. *See infra*, §§ 27.10, *et seq.*
2. *See infra*, § 27.36.
3. *See infra*, § 27.34.
4. *See infra*, § 27.40, discussing the defense of plaintiff's misuse of the product.
5. *See infra*, § 27.15, as to the informed intermediary defense.
6. *See infra*, § 27.41, treating the related topic of alteration of the product after its manufacture.

7. *See infra*, § 27.22, as to liability of distributors and sellers; § 27.29, examining the potential liability of the manufacturer of component parts; and § 27.30, as to liability of the manufacturer of the complete product.

8. *See infra*, §§ 27.26, *et seq.*
9. *See infra*, § 27.41.
10. *See infra* § 27.39.

§ 27.2 PRODUCTS LIABILITY Ch. 27

that can be anticipated or raised, such as whether the claim is preempted by a particular statute or regulation.[11]

§ 27.3 Historical Overview

Perhaps the best way to describe the birth of products liability law is to discuss the erosion of the citadel of privity. In early actions it was first urged that liability for a defective product emanated from the manufacturer's breach of a warranty, expressed or implied. The courts refused to impose any liability or duty unless the injured person was in privity with the defendant. Thus, absent a specific sale between the defendant manufacturer or seller and the plaintiff, it was held that there was no duty or liability for any consequential injury. A contract of sale between the parties was a prerequisite to a successful claim. It was reasoned that the seller of a defective product was not liable for the injury to anyone but its immediate buyer, since the seller's duty grew exclusively out of its contract of sale with its vendee; the seller's duty was owed to its vendee alone and to no one else.

The first deviation from the rule requiring a sale between the manufacturer and the injured person can be found in cases involving inherently dangerous products. In *Thomas v. Winchester*,[1] for example, the defendant, a dealer in poisonous drugs mislabelled a poison as a harmless medicine. The sale was made to another dealer in such drugs and not directly to the injured consumer. Since the defendant's negligence put human life in imminent danger, and since the injury was not likely to fall upon the seller or upon his vendee, but rather upon a remote consumer, the court determined that liability should be imposed since the dealer's duty arose out of the nature of its business and "the danger to others incident to its mismanagement."[2] The court made it very clear that the duty did not arise out of the contract of sale but rather out of the negligent act of sending the falsely labeled poison into the market place.

The courts determined that liability would attach, absent privity, as long as the product was inherently dangerous. For example, in *Statler v. George A. Ray Mfg. Co.*,[3] a coffee urn sold to a restaurant by a manufacturer exploded and injured a customer. The plaintiff had successfully urged that the product "was of such a character inherently that, when applied to the purposes for which it was designed, it was liable to become a source of great danger to many people if not carefully and properly constructed."[4] The Court of Appeals found that this theory was accurately presented to the jury, stating:

11. *See infra*, §§ 27.42, *et seq.* regarding preemption of private claims.

§ 27.3
1. 6 N.Y. 397 (1852).
2. *Id.* at 410.
3. 195 N.Y. 478, 88 N.E. 1063 (1909).
4. 195 N.Y. at 480, 88 N.E. at 1064.

"Any one who leaves a dangerous instrument, as a gun, in such a way as to cause danger, or who without due warning supplies to others for use an instrument or thing which to his knowledge, from its construction or otherwise is in such a condition as to cause danger, not necessarily incident to the use of such an instrument or thing, is liable for injury caused to others by reason of his negligent act."[5] This rule distinctly recognizes the principle that in the case of an article of an inherently dangerous nature, a manufacturer may become liable for a negligent construction which, when added to the inherent character of the appliance, makes it imminently dangerous, and causes or contributes to a resulting injury not necessarily incident to the use of such an article if properly constructed, but naturally following from a defective construction.[6]

The Court of Appeals, however, reversed on other grounds and remanded for a new trial because it found "that errors were committed in rulings on evidence which were ... pronounced ... and prejudicial to the rights of the defendant...."[7]

This principle of applying liability without privity of contract was extended in the landmark case of *MacPherson v. Buick Motor Co.*[8] There, the Court held that the principles of *Thomas* and *Statler* would not be limited to products which in their normal operation are "implements of destruction."[9] Rather, the court imposed the following standard:

> If the nature of a thing is such that it is reasonably certain to place life and limb in peril when negligently made, it is then a thing of danger. Its nature gives warning of the consequences to be expected. If to the element of danger there is added knowledge that the thing will be used by persons other than the purchaser, and used without new tests, then, irrespective of contract, the manufacturer of this thing of danger is under a duty to make it carefully.[10]

MacPherson sounded the death knell for privity as a pre-requisite to tort liability for a defective product. However, privity continued to preclude non-purchasers from the warranty protection afforded to purchasers. This distinction eventually was eliminated when the Court of Appeals equated strict tort liability to strict liability in warranty, thereby considering a breach of implied warranty involving a dangerous product as a tortious wrong, separate and distinct from a breach of a sales contract.[11] In *Mendel v. Pittsburgh Plate Glass Co.*,[12] the Court of Appeals clarified that the concept of privity was eliminated *in toto* by

---

5. Torgesen v. Schultz, 192 N.Y. 156, 159–60, 84 N.E. 956, 957–58 (1908) quoting Lord Justice Cotton in Heaven v. Pender, 11 Q.B.D. 503.

6. 195 N.Y. at 482, 88 N.E. at 1064.

7. Id.

8. 217 N.Y. 382, 111 N.E. 1050 (1916).

9. 217 N.Y. at 389, 111 N.E. at 1050.

10. 217 N.Y. at 389, 111 N.E. at 1050.

11. *See* Goldberg v. Kollsman Instrument Corp. 12 N.Y.2d 432, 240 N.Y.S.2d 592, 191 N.E.2d 81 (1963).

12. 25 N.Y.2d 340, 305 N.Y.S.2d 490, 253 N.E.2d 207 (1969).

§ 27.3   PRODUCTS LIABILITY   Ch. 27

holding "strict liability in tort and implied warranty in the absence of privity are merely different ways of describing the very same cause of action."[13] Nonetheless, products liability decisions continued to recognize the existence of separate causes of action for breach of warranty and strict liability.[14] It was unclear whether the two causes of action were really the same, and whether it would be impossible or inconsistent to find a manufacturer or distributor liable for breach of implied warranty even though a claim of strict products liability could not be established.

Any confusion has been eliminated by the decision of the Court of Appeals in *Denny v. Ford Motor Co.*[15] where the Court succinctly stated:

> [T]he causes of action for strict products liability and breach of implied warranty of merchantability are not identical in New York and ...the latter is not necessarily subsumed by the former.[16]

That case involved a rollover accident in which plaintiff was severely injured when she slammed on the brakes of her Ford Bronco II to avoid striking a deer that had wandered into her vehicle's path.

On her strict products liability claim, the plaintiff sought to prove that the vehicle should have been designed with a higher stability index. Ford argued that not only were the vehicle's design features necessary for its off-road capabilities, but that the vehicle had not been designed for sale as a conventional passenger vehicle. Introduced into evidence by plaintiff was Ford Bronco II's marketing manual which noted that many people would be attracted to this automobile because it was "suitable to contemporary life styles" and was "considered fashionable in certain suburbs." After reviewing the evidence presented at the trial, the Court of Appeals observed:

> According to this manual ..., the vehicle's ability to switch between two-wheel and four-wheel drive would "be particularly appealing to women who may be concerned about driving in snow and ice with their children."[17]

Plaintiff and her husband testified that the safety benefits arising from the vehicle's ability to operate in four-wheel drive impacted upon their decision to select and use this vehicle. They further stated that they were not interested in using the vehicle off-road.

The trial court submitted both the strict products liability claim and the breach of implied warranty claim to the jury, over Ford's objection that the two causes of action were identical. The jury found for plaintiff

---

13. 25 N.Y.2d at 345, 305 N.Y.S.2d at 494.

14. Victorson v. Bock Laundry Mach. Co., 37 N.Y.2d 395, 373 N.Y.S.2d 39, 335 N.E.2d 275 (1975).

15. 87 N.Y.2d 248, 639 N.Y.S.2d 250, 662 N.E.2d 730 (1995).

16. 87 N.Y.2d at 263, 639 N.Y.S.2d at 259, 662 N.E.2d at 739 (1995).

17. 87 N.Y.2d at 252, 639 N.Y.S.2d at 252, 662 N.E.2d at 732 (1995).

§ 27.4 PRODUCTS LIABILITY Ch. 27

In *Codling,* the Court of Appeals specifically held that the contributory fault of the plaintiff was a defense to an action for strict products liability. It should be noted that under the provisions of Article 14–A of the CPLR, culpable conduct of the injured party no longer bars recovery, but the amount of damages otherwise recoverable are diminished by the comparative fault of the plaintiff.[3]

The rationale for the strict products liability theory enunciated in *Codling* rested upon public policy. By marketing its product, a manufacturer or seller undertook a responsibility toward consumers who may be injured by the use of that product. In later cases the Court of Appeals reaffirmed that the burden of accidental injury caused by products intended for public use should be placed on those who market them, since such parties are in the best position not only to protect against defective products but also to bear the costs of injury when such products fail.[4]

Library References:
West's Key No. Digests, Products Liability ⚖1.

§ 27.5 Theories of Liability

While an injured party may have a single claim arising from an incident which caused harm, such claim may generate several causes of action or theories of liability: contract—express or implied,[1] negligence, and/or strict products liability.[2] The *Victorson* Court recognized that all of these claims, no matter how they are labeled, sound in tort rather than contract.[3]

---

3. *See* CPLR 1411.

4. Sage v. Fairchild–Swearingen Corp., 70 N.Y.2d 579, 523 N.Y.S.2d 418, 517 N.E.2d 1304 (1987). *See generally* Sukljian v. Ross & Son Co., 69 N.Y.2d 89, 95, 511 N.Y.S.2d 821, 823, 503 N.E.2d 1358 (1986); Codling v. Paglia, 32 N.Y.2d 330, 345 N.Y.S.2d 461, 298 N.E.2d 622 (1973); *Restatement (Second) of Torts* § 402A, cmt.c.

§ 27.5

1. The claim is really one for breach of warranty which is "not only a violation of the sales contract out of which the warranty arises but ... a tortious wrong suable by a noncontracting party whose use of the warranted article is within the reasonable contemplation of the vendor or manufacturer." Goldberg v. Kollsman Instrument Corp., 12 N.Y.2d 432, 436, 240 N.Y.S.2d 592, 594, 191 N.E.2d 81, 82 (1963). A manufacturer impliedly warrants that its product will not prove unreasonably dangerous when used for the purpose for which it is made. Tinnerholm v. Parke, Davis & Co., 411 F.2d 48, 53 (2d Cir.1969). *See also,* Denny v. Ford Motor Co.,87 N.Y.2d 248, 639 N.Y.S.2d 250, 662 N.E.2d 730 (1995) for the proposition that a manufacturer impliedly warrants that its product was "merchantable" or "fit" for its "ordinary purpose."

2. Victorson v. Bock Laundry Mach. Co., 37 N.Y.2d 395, 373 N.Y.S.2d 39, 335 N.E.2d 275 (1975).

3. *See* Velez v. Craine & Clark LBR Corp., 33 N.Y.2d 117, 124–25, 350 N.Y.S.2d 617, 623, 305 N.E.2d 750, 754 (1973); Goldberg v. Kollsman Instrument Corp., 12 N.Y.2d 432, 240 N.Y.S.2d 592, 191 N.E.2d 81 (1963). However, in Denny v. Ford Motor Co., 87 N.Y.2d 248, 639 N.Y.S.2d 250, 662 N.E.2d 730 (1995) the Court of Appeals clarified that warranty and strict liability are not identical and that a warranty claim could still be established even if a plaintiff could not establish a strict products liability claim. *See* supra, § 27.3.

on the implied warranty claim even though it found that the defendant was not liable on the strict products liability claim.

The Court of Appeals rejected Ford's argument that the two claims were identical reasoning that the Legislature itself in its enactment of Uniform Commercial Code Section 2–314(2)(c) continued the separate and distinct existence of a breach of warranty cause of action. In so holding, the Court of Appeals wrote:

> ...[I]n the final analysis, the argument is flawed because it overlooks the continued existence of a separate statutory predicate for the breach-of-warranty theory and the subtle but important distinction between the two theories that arises from their different historical and doctrinal root.[18]

Thus, it now appears that if there is privity, a plaintiff may recover under a UCC based warranty claim even absent proof that the product is defective. As the *Denny* Court expressed:

> While the strict products concept of a product that is "not reasonably safe" requires a weighing of the product's dangers against its overall advantages, the UCC's concept of a "defective" product requires an inquiry only into whether the product in question was "fit for the ordinary purposes for which such goods are used" (UCC Section 2–314(2)(c)).[19]

§ 27.4 Bases of a Products Liability Claim

The culmination of the development of product liability law is found in the case of *Codling v. Paglia*.[1] In that case, the Court of Appeals determined that the manufacturer of a defective product could be held liable to a remote bystander *without proof of negligence* for any injuries sustained as a result of a defect in the manufacturer's product. The Court set forth very clear standards that had to be met in order to impose such liability under what it labeled the "Doctrine of Strict Products Liability":

1. That at the time of the occurrence, the product was being used for the purpose and in the manner normally intended;

2. That if the person injured was the actual user of the product, he or she would not by the exercise of reasonable care have discovered the defect and perceived its danger; and

3. That by the exercise of reasonable care, the person injured would not have otherwise avoided the injury.[2]

---

18. 87 N.Y.2d at 254, 639 N.Y.S.2d at 253, 662 N.E.2d at 733 (1995).

19. 87 N.Y.2d at 258, 639 N.Y.S.2d at 256, 662 N.E.2d at 736 (1995).

§ 27.4

1. 32 N.Y.2d 330, 345 N.Y.S.2d 461, 298 N.E.2d 622 (1973).

2. 32 N.Y.2d at 343, 345 N.Y.S.2d at 470.

A claim in strict products liability includes several sub-categories or theories of liability under which a manufacturer or distributor may be held liable. Starting of with the basic tenet—that the manufacturer of a defective product is liable to any person injured or damaged if the defect is a substantial factor in producing the injury—several bases for liability have been spawned. The product can be considered defective (1) if there was a mistake in the manufacturing process[4] or (2) if it was improperly or poorly designed[5] or, (3) if the manufacturer or distributor placed the product into the marketplace without adequate warnings.[6] Integrated into these categories are other theories of liability arising from the manufacturer's or distributor's failure to adequately and properly test its product before placing it into the stream of commerce[7] and/or the manufacturer's responsibility for distributing a product (usually a drug) which lacks efficacy; *i.e.* the product is ineffective for the purpose or usage for which it was marketed.[8]

Depending upon the circumstances, a manufacturer can be held liable in negligence and/or in strict products liability[9] for dangers from unknown or latent defects either in construction or design which are reasonably foreseeable as potentially causing harm.[10]

§ 27.6 Theories of Liability—Manufacturing Defect or Mistake in the Manufacturing Process

Sometimes a product causes harm because something happens in the course of production which causes it to perform improperly. For the most part, such claims are established by showing that the product which caused the plaintiff's injury was manufactured differently from, or not in accordance with, the defendant's own quality standards. The plaintiff must prove that the product was defective in that it did not perform as the manufacturer intended. The defect or flaw arises because

---

4. Victorson v. Bock Laundry Mach. Co., 37 N.Y.2d at 403–04, 373 N.Y.S.2d at 44, 325 N.E.2d at 279 (1975).

5. Micallef v. Miehle Co., Div. of Miehle–Goss Dexter, 39 N.Y.2d 376, 384 N.Y.S.2d 115, 348 N.E.2d 571 (1976).

6. Torrogrossa v. Towmotor Co., 44 N.Y.2d 709, 405 N.Y.S.2d 448, 376 N.E.2d 920 (1978).

7. Roginsky v. Richardson-Merrell, Inc., 378 F.2d 832 (2d Cir.1967).

8. *See* Bichler v. Eli Lilly and Co., 79 A.D.2d 317, 436 N.Y.S.2d 625 (1st Dep't 1981), aff'd 55 N.Y.2d 571, 450 N.Y.S.2d 776, 436 N.E.2d 182 (1982).

9. PRACTICE POINTER: The plaintiff need not choose which theory to pursue. All should be pleaded in the Complaint. *See infra*, § 27.55 for a Form Products Liability Complaint setting forth causes of action in Negligence, Strict Liability, Express Warranty and Implied Warranty.

10. In Bolm v. Triumph Corp., 33 N.Y.2d 151, 350 N.Y.S.2d 644, 305 N.E.2d 769 (1973), the Court went so far as to note that liability could attach even if the defect was not causally connected with the initial occurrence of an accident which ultimately caused injury. In Bolm, the plaintiff was operating a motorcycle which was involved in a collision with an automobile. The injury to the plaintiff arose as a result of his coming into contact with a defective parcel grid on the motorcycle.

the product was "misconstructed."[1]

A claim arising out of a construction flaw is readily distinguished from a defective design case in that the latter case is based upon a product that presents an unreasonable risk of harm no matter how meticulously it has been constructed according to plans and specifications.[2]

Library References:

West's Key No. Digests, Products Liability ⚖8.

§ 27.7 Theories of Liability—Defective Design

A defectively designed product is defined as one that is unreasonably dangerous for its intended use at the time it leaves the seller's hands.[1] The imposition of liability for a defectively designed product requires a weighing of the risks against the utility of the product.

Under this theory, a manufacturer is liable regardless of its actual knowledge of the condition of the product because the manufacturer is in the superior position to discover any design defect and correct it or alter the design before making the product available to the public.[2] The Court of Appeals has stated that a *prima facie* case in strict products liability for design defect can be established by a showing that the manufacturer breached its duty to market a safe product when it marketed a product that was designed so that it was not reasonably safe and that the defective design was a substantial factor in causing the plaintiff's injury.[3]

A product is defectively designed when it presents an unreasonable risk of causing harm. A design defect claim in strict liability is akin to a *prima facie* case in negligence.[4] Evidence capable of sustaining a negligence claim based upon a design defect will also establish strict liability, since the plaintiff must prove that the manufacturer failed to exercise reasonable care in manufacturing its product.[5]

In products liability cases in which this theory of liability is pursued, expert testimony will be necessary in order for the plaintiff to establish that it was feasible to design the product in a safer manner.

§ 27.6

1. Opera v. Hyva, Inc., 86 A.D.2d 373, 450 N.Y.S.2d 615 (4th Dep't 1982).
2. Robinson v. Reed–Prentice Div. Package Machinery Co., 49 N.Y.2d 471, 426 N.Y.S.2d 717, 403 N.E.2d 440 (1980).

§ 27.7

1. Voss v. Black & Decker Mfg. Co., 59 N.Y.2d 102, 463 N.Y.S.2d 398, 450 N.E.2d 204 (1983).

2. *Id.*
3. *Id.*
4. Bolm v. Triumph Corp., 71 A.D.2d 429, 422 N.Y.S.2d 969 (4th Dep't 1979).
5. *Id.*

§ 27.8 Theories of Liability—Defective Design—Burden of Proof

In order to establish a products liability case under a defective design theory, the plaintiff's burden is threefold. Evidence must be presented that (1) the product, as designed, was not reasonably safe because there was a substantial likelihood of harm; (2) it was feasible to design the product in a safer manner; and (3) the design defect in the product was a substantial factor in causing the plaintiff's injury.[1]

The courts have recognized that in order to meet this burden, the plaintiff may deviate from the general rule of evidence and proffer evidence of post-accident modifications.[2] In *Bolm*,[3] the Court rationalized that, provided limiting instructions are given, evidence of post-accident design changes may be used when the defendant manufacturer contests the issue of feasibility. The *Bolm* Court reasoned that such evidence can be probative of "what alternatives were available to the manufacturer at the time the product was made so that the jury may determine whether he acted prudently in deciding upon its final design."[4] *See* Section 27.31 "Introducing Evidence of Post Accident Modifications or Repairs."

Library References:

West's Key No. Digests, Products Liability ⟐75.

§ 27.9 Theories of Liability—Defective Design—Defense

Hoping to defeat attempts to hold them liable, manufacturers frequently offer evidence (a) that the product is a safe product whose utility outweighs its risks, and (b) that the product was designed so that the risks are reduced to the minimal degree possible while retaining the product's inherent usefulness at an acceptable cost.[1] It is the jury's role to weigh the evidence and balance the product's risks against its utility and cost in order to reach a determination as to whether the product as designed was not reasonably safe.[2] The Court of Appeals noted that this utility/risk balancing must take into account several factors:

§ 27.8

1. See Micallef v. Miehle, 39 N.Y.2d 376, 384 N.Y.S.2d 115, 348 N.E.2d 571 (1976).
2. *See infra*, § 27.31 "Introducing Evidence of Post Accident Modifications or Repairs."
3. Bolm v. Triumph Corp., 71 A.D.2d at 437, 422 N.Y.S.2d at 975.
4. *Id.*

§ 27.9

1. Rainbow v. Albert Elia Bldg. Co., 79 A.D.2d 287, 436 N.Y.S.2d 480 (4th Dep't 1981), aff'd 56 N.Y.2d 550, 449 N.Y.S.2d 967, 434 N.E.2d 1345 (1982).
2. Voss v. Black & Decker Mfg. Co., 59 N.Y.2d 102, 463 N.Y.S.2d 398, 450 N.E.2d 204 (1983).

§ 27.9 PRODUCTS LIABILITY Ch. 27

"(1) the utility of the product to the public as a whole and to the individual user; (2) the nature of the product, *i.e.*, the likelihood that it will cause injury; (3) the availability of a safer design; (4) the potential for designing and manufacturing the product so that it is safer but remains functional and reasonably priced; (5) the ability of the plaintiff to have avoided injury by careful use of the product; (6) the degree of awareness of the potential danger of the product which reasonably can be attributed to the plaintiff; and (7) the manufacturer's ability to spread any cost[3] related to improving the safety of the design."[4]

Library References:
West's Key No. Digests, Products Liability ⬖11, 26–27.

§ 27.10 Theories of Liability—Failure to Warn or Inadequate Warnings

The duty to warn is based upon the concept that "[a] product can be dangerous even if it is not defectively designed."[1] A supplier[2] of a product who is aware, or reasonably should be aware, that the product is dangerous when put to a foreseeable use is charged with a duty "to exercise reasonable care to inform the user of the facts which make the product dangerous."[3] If the failure to warn of known dangers associated with the use of the product is a proximate cause of the user's injury, the user may recover against the supplier under basic negligence theory as well as strict products liability theory. It should be noted that the duty of a manufacturer[4] to warn is greater than that of a mere vendor.[5] The New York Courts have held that "inadequate warnings will render a product defective for purposes of warranty and strict products liability."[6]

---

3. In Caprara v. Chrysler Corp., 52 N.Y.2d 114, 115, 436 N.Y.S.2d 251, 256, 417 N.E.2d 545 (1981) the Court of Appeals recognized "economic realities ...among others, the growing market share of the mass manufacturer, the well-nigh universality of insurance, the escalation of governmental regulation...."

4. Voss v. Black & Decker Mfg. Co., 59 N.Y.2d at 109, 463 N.Y.S.2d at 402–03, 450 N.E.2d at 208–09.

§ 27.10

1. Smith v. Hub Mfg., Inc., 634 F.Supp. 1505, 1508 (N.D.N.Y.1986).

2. Generally, a supplier is a party involved in the distribution of a product. See infra, § 27.22 "Distributors' or Sellers' Liability."

3. Young v. Elmira Transit Mix, Inc., 52 A.D.2d 202, 204–05, 383 N.Y.S.2d 729, 731 (4th Dep't 1976) (Cardamone, J.) (citing *Restatement (Second) of Torts* § 388); see also Billiar v. Minnesota Mining and Mfg. Co., 623 F.2d 240, 243 (2d Cir.1980) (also citing Young); McLaughlin v. Mine Safety Appliances, Co., 11 N.Y.2d 62, 68, 226 N.Y.S.2d 407, 411, 181 N.E.2d 430, 433 (1962).

4. For a description of what entities can be defined as a manufacturer for product liability purposes, see infra, § 27.22 "Successor Liability," § 27.29 "Liability of the Manufacturer of Component Parts," § 27.30 "Liability of the Manufacturer of the Complete Product."

5. Cover v. Cohen, 61 N.Y.2d 261, 275, 473 N.Y.S.2d 378, 386, 461 N.E.2d 864, 871 (1984).

6. Ezagui v. Dow Chemical Corp., 598 F.2d 727, 733 (2d Cir.1979) (applying New York law); see also Robinson v. Reed–Prentice Division, 49 N.Y.2d 471, 478–79, 426 N.Y.S.2d 717, 720, 403 N.E.2d 440, 443 (1980); Torrogrossa v. Towmotor Co., 44

§ 27.11 Theories of Liability—Failure to Warn or Inadequate Warnings—Burden of Proof

With a strict products liability claim, unlike a negligence claim, the plaintiff is not required to prove that the defendant "knew or should have known of the harmful character of the product without a warning."[1] Rather than focusing on the fault of the defendant, the jury's attention is directed to the defect in the product arising from the inadequate warning.[2] So great is the duty to provide adequate warnings that the manufacturer may not seek to absolve itself from liability by proving that the plaintiff failed to read the warnings that it had issued.[3]

Library References:

West's Key No. Digests, Products Liability ⚖︎75.

§ 27.12 Theories of Liability—Failure to Warn or Inadequate Warnings—Duty to Warn

However, in some instances where the danger is blatant it has been held that there is no duty to warn.[1] For example, in *Heller v. Encore of Hicksville, Inc.*[2] the Court held there was no duty to warn a patron not to smoke during a break in a hair dye procedure in which absorbent cotton, which the plaintiff knew to be flammable, was used. Thus, a manufacturer may not be held responsible for failing to warn of facts or information which is available to the usual lay person through ordinary experience or common knowledge.[3] In cases where injuries were sustained as a result of a plaintiff diving into shallow water, some courts, after analyzing the facts, have determined that the plaintiff's reckless conduct, rather than the manufacturer's failure to warn, was the *sole* proximate cause of the accident.[4] In dismissing complaints in these

---

N.Y.2d 709, 711, 405 N.Y.S.2d 448, 449, 376 N.E.2d 920, 921 (1978).

§ 27.11

1. Lancaster Silo & Block Co. v. Northern Propane Gas Co., 75 A.D.2d 55, 64, 427 N.Y.S.2d 1009, 1015 (4th Dep't 1980).

2. *See* Caprara v. Chrysler Corp., 52 N.Y.2d 114, 123, 436 N.Y.S.2d 251, 255, 417 N.E.2d 545, 549 (1981).

3. Johnson v. Johnson Chem. Co., 183 A.D.2d 64, 588 N.Y.S.2d 607 (2d Dep't 1992).

§ 27.12

1. Wood v. Peabody Int'l Corp., 187 A.D.2d 824, 589 N.Y.S.2d 960 (3d Dep't 1992).

2. 76 A.D.2d 917, 429 N.Y.S.2d 258 (2d Dep't 1980).

3. Lancaster Silo & Block Co. v. Northern Propane Gas Co., 75 A.D.2d 55, 427 N.Y.S.2d 1009, 1015 (4th Dep't 1980).

4. Boltax v. Joy Day Camp, 67 N.Y.2d 617, 620, 499 N.Y.S.2d 660, 661, 490 N.E.2d 527, 528 (1986); Howard v. Poseidon Pools, Inc., 72 N.Y.2d 972, 530 N.E.2d 1280, 534 N.Y.S.2d 360 (1988).

diving cases, the courts have reasoned that the acts of a plaintiff in voluntarily diving head first into shallow water is "an unforeseeable superseding event absolving" the defendant from liability.[5]

A leading case defining the manufacturer's duty to warn emanates from the State of Washington. In *Ayers v. Johnson & Johnson*,[6] David Ayers, who was fifteen months old, picked up a container of Johnson & Johnson baby oil that his sister had placed in an unmarked container in her purse. The infant started to drink the baby oil which the mother immediately observed; however, the infant had already drawn a small amount of oil into his lungs. The infant's mother examined the original bottle in which Johnson & Johnson sold its baby oil, which alerted her that the only adverse effect of ingesting baby oil might be diarrhea. With this knowledge imparted to her by Johnson & Johnson, she took no immediate action. Later that night, the infant began having difficulty breathing and was hospitalized. There was baby oil in his lungs and the infant suffered cardiac arrest and brain damage.[7] The jury rendered a verdict of $2.5 million in favor of the plaintiff.

The Trial Court, however, set aside the verdict by granting the defendant's motion for judgment n.o.v. The intermediate appellate court reversed and this was affirmed by the Washington Supreme Court.[8]

The appellate court pointed out that when a party manufactures a product such as baby oil, which is composed of 99% mineral oil, thereby creating a special risk of inhalation, the duty to warn is consistent with the risk involved. As the Court stated, "[w]hat makes baby oil unique, and what is the *sine qua non* of our decision, is that baby oil is intended for use on babies."[9]

The Court went on to explain that the ordinary consumer is unaware of the dangers presented by inhalation of baby oil; in fact, the user's misconception is enhanced by the words "pure and gentle" on the baby oil container. The question of whether proper warnings would have avoided the injury to the infant was a question of fact for the jury since the plaintiff's mother had specifically testified that had she known of the danger of aspiration which could be caused by baby oil, the baby oil would have been kept out of the infant's reach.

Library References:

West's Key No. Digests, Products Liability ⟜14.

§ 27.13 Theories of Liability—Failure to Warn or Inadequate Warnings—Adequacy of Warning

Even if a product is not inherently defective, such as a drug that is pure, the failure to provide adequate warnings with respect to the

---

5. Boltax v. Joy Day Camp, 67 N.Y.2d at 620, 499 N.Y.S.2d at 661, 490 N.E.2d at 528.

6. 117 Wn.2d 747, 818 P.2d 1337 (1991).

7. 117 Wn.2d at 750, 818 P.2d at 1339.

8. 117 Wn.2d at 750, 818 P.2d at 1339.

9. 117 Wn.2d at 758, 818 P.2d at 1343.

product renders it unreasonably dangerous and defective for the purposes of a products liability claim.[1] The manufacturer's duty is not only to warn, but to warn adequately.[2] Whether or not the warnings are adequate, except in the clearest cases, is usually a question for the jury.[3] The manufacturer of pharmaceuticals has an even higher duty to warn. In *Baker v. St. Agnes Hospital*,[4] the Court noted:

> The duty to warn assumes great significance in a products liability case involving pharmaceuticals. If the drug is pure and accompanied by adequate warnings, the manufacturer may not be liable. (See *Incollingo v. Ewing*, 444 Pa. 263, 282 A.2d 206). On the other hand, notwithstanding the purity of the drug, a breach of the duty to provide adequate warnings renders the drug unreasonably dangerous and therefore unfit. In such circumstances, it becomes a defective product for the purposes of strict products liability. (See *Davis v. Wyeth Labs*, 9 Cir., 399 F.2d 121, 130; Restatement, Torts 2d, § 402A, comments h, j, k; 2 *Frumer & Friedman, Products Liability*, § 16A(4)(e).)[5]

The manufacturer must make sure that its warning clearly provides notice to the potential user of any dangers that can be caused by its product.[6] If the warning is so general, or "watered down" so as to understate or minimize the consequences of any risk, then the manufacturer can be held responsible for failure to warn.[7] Thus, even though the reactions suffered by the plaintiff after using a defendant's drug are in fact listed in the "adverse reactions" section of the package insert, the defendant can be held responsible when there is qualifying language such as:

> These reactions are usually reversible and disappear when the drug is discontinued.[8]

In refusing to find a warning with such language to be adequate as a matter of law, the Appellate Division found that "the last sentence of the 'adverse reaction' section of [the manufacturer's] package insert tends to qualify and dilute the whole of the sections' admonition."[9]

But the warnings provided by the manufacturer must be read in their totality. In *Martin v. Hacker*,[10] the Court of Appeals found that

---

§ 27.13

1. *See* Baker v. St. Agnes Hospital, 70 A.D.2d 400, 421 N.Y.S.2d 81 (2d Dep't 1979).

2. Wolfgruber v. Upjohn Co., 72 A.D.2d 59, 61, 423 N.Y.S.2d 95, 96 (4th Dep't 1979).

3. Johnson v. Johnson Chem. Co., 183 A.D.2d 64, 588 N.Y.S.2d 607 (2d Dep't 1992).

4. 70 A.D.2d 400, 421 N.Y.S.2d 81 (2d Dep't 1979).

5. Baker v. St. Agnes Hospital, 70 A.D.2d 400, 421 N.Y.S.2d 81, 85 (2d Dep't 1979).

6. McFadden v. Haritatos, 86 A.D.2d 761, 448 N.Y.S.2d 79 (4th Dep't 1982).

7. 86 A.D.2d at 762, 448 N.Y.S.2d at 81.

8. 86 A.D.2d at 762, 448 N.Y.S.2d at 81.

9. 86 A.D.2d at 762, 448 N.Y.S.2d at 81.

10. 83 N.Y.2d 1, 14–15, 607 N.Y.S.2d 598, 604–05, 628 N.E.2d 1308, 1314 (1993).

"[t]he consistent and clear statements in the Actions and Warnings Sections of the insert concerning the post-withdrawal persistence of side effects after reserpine withdrawal negate the effect of whatever ambiguity could arguably result from the Adverse Reactions Section." The court held that when the Warnings Section and the Adverse Reaction Section were read together, they were "sufficient to convey to any reasonably prudent physician an unambiguous and consistent message that reserpine is a slow acting drug ... and that reserpine-induced depression may lead to post-withdrawal suicide but that such depression usually disappears after withdrawal."[11]

Language showing a watered down or unclear warning may serve as a basis for questioning whether the manufacturer has violated certain labeling statutes.[12] The Second Circuit has stated:

> The failure to provide adequate warnings of known risks associated with normal use of the product, moreover, also violates the Federal Food, Drug and Cosmetics Act, 21 U.S.C. § 352, and the New York Education Law § 6815, both of which state that 'A drug or device shall be deemed to be misbranded ... if the labeling is false or misleading in any particular ... The term 'labeling' means all labels and other written, printed, or graphic matter ... accompanying such article.[13]

The duty to warn is a continuing one, so that in assessing whether warnings are adequate, the jury should consider not merely the information available at the time a product is used, but the information that becomes available afterwards. In *Lindsay v. Ortho Pharmaceutical Corp.*,[14] the Court held:

> The manufacturer's duty is to warn of all potential dangers which it knew, or in the exercise of reasonable care should have known, to exist. *Baker v. St. Agnes Hospital, supra.*, 70 App. Div. 2d at 405, 421 N.Y.S.2d 81; *Tinnerholm v. Parke Davis & Co.*, 285 F.Supp. 432, 451 (S.D.N.Y.1968), aff'd on other grounds, 411 F.2d 48 (2d Cir. 1969). The duty is a continuous one, requiring the manufacturer to keep abreast of the current state of knowledge of its product as gained through research, adverse reaction reports, scientific literature, and other available methods.[15]

Evidence of subsequent changes by the manufacturer can be used to establish that information warranting a better warning was available to

---

11. 83 N.Y.2d at 14–15, 607 N.Y.S.2d at 605, 628 N.E.2d at 1315.

12. Food, Drug and Cosmetics Act, 21 U.S.C.A. § 352; Education Law § 6815.

13. Ezagui v. Dow Chemical Corp., 598 F.2d 727, 733 (2d Cir.1979).

14. 637 F.2d 87, 91 (2d Cir.1980).

15. 637 F.2d at 91 citing Baker v. St. Agnes Hospital, 70 A.D.2d at 406, 421

the manufacturer at the time it placed its product on the market.[16] In *Bartlett v. General Electric Co.*,[17] the plaintiff sought to introduce subsequent design changes and warnings to show that the product which caused the injury was unreasonably dangerous as originally designed. In that case, the Court held that the testimony of the plaintiff's expert and the defendant's product safety manager was relevant on the issue that, "General Electric knew or should have known of the dangers inherent in its cord and also of the advisability of the warnings and design changes then available which it adopted some years thereafter."[18] For further discussion, see § 27.31 "Introducing Evidence of Post Accident Modification or Repairs."

Library References:
West's Key No. Digests, Products Liability ⚖14.

§ 27.14 Theories of Liability—Failure to Warn or Inadequate Warnings—Jury Question

In almost all cases where the adequacy of the warnings given by the manufacturer is in dispute, the resolution of the question is a matter for the jury to determine. In *Cooley v. Carter-Wallace, Inc.*,[1] the Fourth Department concluded:

> The failure to warn is essentially a case of negligence and the drastic remedy of summary judgment is rarely granted since the very question of whether a defendant's conduct amounts to negligence is inherently a question for the trier of facts in all but the most egregious instances.[2]

The jury must consider several factors. The extent and language used in the warning must be measured against the risk involved and the use of the product.[3] Similarly, where the warning is placed on the product or its package, the size of the type face used, and the type of injury or side affects warned against, are all factors that must be considered by the jury in determining the adequacy of the warning.[4] There is no require-

---

N.Y.S.2d at 86.

16. *See infra*, § 27.31 "Introducing Evidence of Post Accident Modification or Repairs."

17. 90 A.D.2d 183, 457 N.Y.S.2d 628, 629 (3d Dep't 1982).

18. 90 A.D.2d at 183, 457 N.Y.S.2d at 628.

§ 27.14

1. 102 A.D.2d 642, 478 N.Y.S.2d 375 (4th Dep't 1984).

2. 102 A.D.2d at 647, 478 N.Y.S.2d at 379; *see* Ugarriza v. Schmieder, 46 N.Y.2d 471, 414 N.Y.S.2d 304, 386 N.E.2d 1324 (1979); McFadden v. Haritatos, 86 A.D.2d 761, 762–63, 448 N.Y.S.2d 79–80 (4th Dep't 1982); *see also*, Billiar v. Minnesota Mining & Mfg. Co., 623 F.2d 240 (2d Cir.1980).

3. Cover v. Cohen, 61 N.Y.2d 261, 473 N.Y.S.2d 378, 461 N.E.2d 864 (1984); Martin v. Hacker, 83 N.Y.2d 1, 607 N.Y.S.2d 598, 628 N.E.2d 1308 (1993).

4. Martin v. Hacker, 83 N.Y.2d 1, 607 N.Y.S.2d 598, 628 N.E.2d 1308 (1993); Torrogrossa v. Towmotor Co., 44 N.Y.2d 709, 405 N.Y.S.2d 448, 376 N.E.2d 920 (1978).

§ 27.14 PRODUCTS LIABILITY Ch. 27

ment that the jury be presented with expert testimony in order to reach a determination that the manufacturer's warning is inadequate.[5]

Library References:

West's Key No. Digests, Products Liability ⚖87.

§ 27.15 Theories of Liability—Failure to Warn or Inadequate Warnings—Informed Intermediary Defense

Quite often in prescription drug cases, the defendants urge that the duty to warn is discharged when the prescribing physician is provided by the manufacturer with directions and warnings for use. This "informed intermediary" defense is based upon the allegation that the drug manufacturer has discharged its duty to warn by warning the medical community of those risks of which the manufacturer has knowledge so that the prescribing physician acts as the "informed intermediary" between the manufacturer and the patient assessing the benefits of the drug and advising the patient of the possible risks and side effects.[1] As the Court of Appeals has stated:

> Warnings for prescription drugs are intended for the physician, whose duty it is to balance the risks against the benefits of various drugs and treatments and to prescribe them and supervise their effects.[2]

> The warning to the physician is given in many ways. The most common of which is "(1) the inclusion in the Physicians Desk Reference, the annually updated encyclopedia of medications; and (2) the manufacturer's formal warning in the package insert of a prescription drug ... [which] must be written in accordance with the Food and Drug Administration's recommendation for the proper labeling of prescription drugs. (See. 21 CFR 201.56, 201.57; 21 U.S.C. § 355(e))...."[3]

Library References:

West's Key No. Digests, Products Liability ⚖14.

5. Billiar v. Minnesota Mining and Manufacuting Co., 623 F.2d 240 (2d Cir.1980); Young v. Elmira Transit Mix, Inc., 52 A.D.2d 202, 205, 383 N.Y.S.2d 729, 731 (4th Dep't 1976); Rainbow v. Albert Elia Building Co., 49 A.D.2d 250, 373 N.Y.S.2d 928 (4th Dep't 1975).

§ 27.15

1. Wolfgruber v. Upjohn Co., 72 A.D.2d 59, 423 N.Y.S.2d 95 (4th Dep't 1979), aff'd 52 N.Y.2d 768, 436 N.Y.S.2d 614, 417 N.E.2d 1002 (1980); Lindsay v. Ortho Pharmaceutical Corp., 637 F.2d 87 (2d Cir.1980).

2. **CAVEAT**: Plaintiffs counsel would be wise to include the prescribing physician as a defendant in the action; however, a medical malpractice claim, unlike a product liability claim against the manufacturer of distributor may be time barred. *See infra*, § 27.39 "Statute of Limitations."

3. Martin v. Hacker, 83 N.Y.2d 1, 607 N.Y.S.2d 598, 601–02, 628 N.E.2d 1308, 1311–12 (1993).

§ 27.16 Theories of Liability—Failure to Warn or Inadequate Warnings—Duty to Warn the Unusually Sensitive

Another argument advanced by manufacturers—that numerous persons had previously used the product without harm, and therefore a duty to warn was not reasonably required—has been rejected by the courts.[1] In fact, in one case, *Wright v. Carter Products, Inc.*,[2] the Court pointed out that a manufacturer of a cosmetic product has a duty to warn even those few persons who might suffer serious injury as a result of an unusual sensitivity to the product.[3]

Library References:

West's Key No. Digests, Products Liability ⟜14.

§ 27.17 Theories of Liability—Failure to Warn or Inadequate Warnings—Non-commercial Cases

The duty to warn has extended itself to cases occurring in a non-commercial context. In an informative case arising under a unique set of facts, *Andrulonis v. U.S.*,[1] a rabies researcher contracted rabies while conducting laboratory experiments with a rabies viral strain. The defendants had failed to warn that the vaccine which the researchers were using might not protect against airborne exposures. The case, which was tried without a jury before Judge Munson of the United States District Court of the Northern District of New York, resulted in a verdict of nearly $6 million.[2]

In *Andrulonis*, the Court specifically noted that liability for failure to warn "does not require a commercial transaction."[3] Accordingly, where there was no sale of a product or a commercial transaction, as in the *Andrulonis* case, the law still imposes upon a manufacturer, as well as upon the operator of a business or even a not-for-profit or governmental scientific laboratory, the obligation and duty to warn, and any consequential failure to warn constitutes a breach of duty.

Library References:

West's Key No. Digests, Products Liability ⟜14.

§ 27.16

1. Ayers v. Johnson & Johnson, 117 Wn.2d 747, 818 P.2d 1337 (1991).
2. 244 F.2d 53 (2d Cir.1957).
3. 244 F.2d at 58.

§ 27.17

1. 724 F.Supp. 1421 (N.D.N.Y.1989) aff'd in part, rev'd in part, 924 F.2d 1210 (2d Cir.1991), cert. granted and vacated New York State Dept. of Health v. Andrulonis, 502 U.S. 801, 112 S.Ct. 39, 116 L.Ed.2d 18, on remand 952 F.2d 652 (2d Cir.1991).
2. 724 F.Supp. at 1538.
3. 924 F.2d at 1220.

§ 27.18 Theories of Liability—Failure to Test

Many products liability cases, especially those involving pharmaceutical products, turn upon claims that the defendant manufacturer failed to adequately test its product. Failure-to-test claims have, for example, been presented in cases involving intrauterine devices,[1] DES,[2] and the Norplant birth control device.[3] In *Tinnerholm v. Parke Davis & Co.*,[4] the Court found that the defendant vaccine manufacturer "in its rush to commercialization of its product either overlooked or neglected to consider the possibility that its product Quadrigen was too unstable a vaccine" to be used on the infant plaintiff.[5] In its analysis, the Court considered evidence revealing that defendant Parke–Davis was negligent in failing to test the product under market conditions such as how known variations in temperature during shipping and storage could effect the safety and effectiveness of the vaccine.[6] The Court also considered evidence that in the testing of the product there was an absence of controls of the diagnostic and reporting procedures rendering conclusions with regard to the tests invalid.[7]

Library References:
West's Key No. Digests, Products Liability ⟐13.

§ 27.19 Theories of Liability—Failure to Test—FDA Approval

The failure-to-test theory can be a powerful tool in a products liability action. Often a defendant will urge that its product was approved by the FDA and that this fact should immunize it from liability. The FDA does not conduct its own independent tests; rather, it relies upon the information and test results provided to it by the applicant. Therefore, if a plaintiff can show that the testing was unreliable or inadequate, liability may attach, even though the FDA approved a drug.[1]

This failure-to-test theory of liability was successfully used in DES cases. In *Bichler v. Eli Lilly and Co.*,[2] the plaintiff was injured as a result of her *in utero* exposure to the defendant's drug, DES, which was ingested by her mother. The defendant urged that it had obtained FDA

---

§ 27.18

1. Odom v. G.D. Searle & Co., 979 F.2d 1001 (4th Cir.1992).

2. Bichler v. Eli Lilly & Co., 79 A.D.2d 317, 436 N.Y.S.2d 625 (1st Dep't 1981), aff'd 55 N.Y.2d 571, 450 N.Y.S.2d 776, 436 N.E.2d 182 (1982).

3. In re Norplant Contraceptive Prod. Liability Litigation, 886 F.Supp. 586 (E.D.Tex.1995).

4. 285 F.Supp. 432 (S.D.N.Y.1968), modified on other grounds 411 F.2d 48 (2d Cir.1969).

5. 285 F.Supp. at 448.

6. *Id.*

7. *Id.*; *see also* Roginsky v. Richardson–Merrell, Inc., 378 F.2d 832 (2d Cir.1967).

§ 27.19

1. *But see infra*, § 27.28 "Preemption of Private Claims."

2. 79 A.D.2d 317, 436 N.Y.S.2d 625 (1st Dep't 1981), aff'd 55 N.Y.2d 571, 450 N.Y.S.2d 776, 436 N.E.2d 182 (1982).

approval prior to marketing its product which was administered to pregnant women to prevent miscarriages. In support of its failure-to-test theory, plaintiff produced expert testimony as to the availability of tests on mice which, if conducted, would have demonstrated that within six months of ingestion there was a danger of cancer developing in the fetus after it reached maturity. Such testimony was introduced to convince the jury that had the manufacturer performed this simple and available test, it could have easily discovered that its drug would or could cause harm to the fetus of a human mother using that drug during her pregnancy.

Library References:
West's Key No. Digests, Drugs and Narcotics ⇔17.

§ 27.20 Theories of Liability—Failure to Test—Jury Question

Resolution of the failure-to-test issue is for the jury. The Court's charge on the failure-to-test theory in the *Bichler* case required the jury to first determine whether, at the time of the plaintiff's mother's pregnancy when she ingested DES, a reasonably prudent manufacturer should have foreseen that DES might cause cancer in the pregnant user's offspring, considering the state of scientific knowledge and techniques then existing. If the jury concluded that this was foreseeable, the jury was then to determine whether a prudent manufacturer would have tested the drug on pregnant mice and whether the results of such tests would have prevented the manufacturer from manufacturing its drug.[1]

Reference should be made to the Court of Appeals decision in *Bichler*. The interrogatories[2] submitted to the *Bichler* jury demonstrate a logical means by which the jury could assess the evidence and determine that the defendant was liable under a failure-to-test theory:

(1) Was DES reasonably safe in the treatment of accidents of pregnancy when it was ingested by plaintiff's mother in 1953? (2) Was DES a proximate cause of plaintiff's cancer? (3) In 1953 when plaintiff's mother ingested DES, should the defendant, as a reasonably prudent drug manufacturer, have foreseen that DES might cause cancer in the offspring of pregnant women who took it? (4) Foreseeing that DES might cause cancer in the offspring of pregnant women who took it, would a reasonably prudent drug manufacturer test it on pregnant mice before marketing it? (5) If DES had been tested on pregnant mice, would the tests have shown that DES causes cancer in their offspring? (6) Would a reasonably prudent

---

§ 27.20

1. 79 A.D.2d at 333, 436 N.Y.S.2d at 635.

2. **PRACTICE POINTER:** Positive answers to interrogatories can be used to collaterally estop the same manufacturer from relitigating the failure-to-test theory in later cases. *See infra,* § 27.53 "Collateral Estoppel in Product Liability Cases."

§ 27.20 PRODUCTS LIABILITY Ch. 27

drug manufacturer have marketed DES for use in treating accidents of pregnancy at the time it was ingested by the plaintiff's mother if it had known that DES causes cancer in the offspring of pregnant mice? (7) Did defendant and the other drug manufacturers act in concert with each other in the testing and marketing of DES for use in treating accidents of pregnancy?[3]

Library References:

West's Key No. Digests, Products Liability ⚖︎87.

§ 27.21 Failure to Test—Preemption Defense

It should be expected that in failure-to-test cases, manufacturers and distributors will attempt to invoke recent decisions regarding the defense that a state tort claim for injuries sustained by a particular product is preempted by certain federal legislation or administrative approval.[1] For a more detailed discussion, *see infra*, Section 27.48 "Preemption of Private State Claims—Medical Device Amendments (MDA) to FDA Regulations."

Library References:

West's Key No. Digests, States ⚖︎18.65.

§ 27.22 Distributors' or Sellers' Liability

New York Law is clear that a retailer and/or seller of merchandise is responsible for a product which it sells if that product is defective.[1] The doctrine of strict products liability, applies to the sale of used, as well as new, products pursuant to *Restatement (Second) of Torts*, § 402A. However, there is an exception if the sale of the product is not part of the ordinary business of the seller. *See* Section 27.23, *infra*.

Library References:

West's Key No. Digests, Products Liability ⚖︎23.1, 25.

---

3. Bichler v. Eli Lilly Co., 55 N.Y.2d at 587, 450 N.Y.S.2d at 783 fn. 10. For examples of other drug cases, *see* Moehlenbrock v. Parke Davis & Co., 141 Minn. 154, 169 N.W. 541 (1918); Gielski v. State, 3 Misc.2d 578, 155 N.Y.S.2d 863 (Ct.Cl.1956); *see* outcome of later case, 9 N.Y.2d 834, 216 N.Y.S.2d 85, 175 N.E.2d 455 (1961). For cases involving products other than drugs, *see* Braun v. Roux Distrib. Co., 312 S.W.2d 758 (Mo.1958) (hair dye); Holland v. St. Paul Mercury Insert 1:. Co., 135 So.2d 145 (La. App.1961) (pesticide); Foley v. Pittsburgh Des Moines Co., 363 Pa.1, 68 A.2d 517 (1949) failure to make adequate tests of safety of product, a tank.

§ 27.21

1. *See* King v. Collagen Corp., 983 F.2d 1130 (1st Cir.1993); LaMontagne v. E.I. Du Pont De Nemours & Co., 41 F.3d 846 (2d Cir.1994).

§ 27.22

1. Meade v. Warner Pruyn Div., 57 A.D.2d 340, 394 N.Y.S.2d 483 (3d Dep't 1977); Cover v. Cohen, 61 N.Y.2d 261, 473 N.Y.S.2d 378, 461 N.E.2d 864 (1984); Giuffrida v. Panasonic Indus. Co., 200 A.D.2d 713, 607 N.Y.S.2d 72 (2d Dep't 1994).

§ 27.23 Distributors' or Sellers' Liability—Sale Must Be Part of Ordinary Business

A distributor or seller of a defective product will not be deemed strictly liable for injuries resulting from its use if the sale of the product is not part of the distributor's or seller's ordinary business (such as in the case where a manufacturer or company seeks to divest itself of one particular machine or piece of equipment).[1] In *Sukljian v. Charles Ross & Son Co., Inc.*,[2] New York's Court of Appeals, in defining what type of sale would be considered incidental to the seller's ordinary business, determined to include in the definition a sale of equipment no longer needed by General Electric for its own use. The Court of Appeals found that since General Electric was not regularly in the business of selling such equipment, the doctrine of strict products liability did not apply to any claim against General Electric arising out of a defect in that equipment.

In *Sukljian*, the Court of Appeals relied upon the case of *Gobhai v. KLM Royal Dutch Airlines*.[3] In *Gobhai*, the plaintiff was injured while using complimentary slippers provided by an airline during her son's first class KLM flight. The Court found that KLM was not in the business of selling slippers and that its providing an incidental amenity to its passengers did not subject it to strict products liability. The First Department noted that the slippers had not been purchased from the defendant; since the slippers had been provided as an incidental service during the plaintiff's son's flight on KLM, strict liability did not apply to the airline's distribution of the defective slipper.[4]

A careful analysis of the facts of a particular case must be made when considering the liability of the entity that does not, in the regular course of its business, manufacture or distribute the particular product that causes injury. For instance, in *Nutting v. Ford Motor Co.*,[5] the defendant regularly purchased a substantial number of automobiles for use by its employees. Since that company regularly disposed of such cars by auction sales to used car dealers for eventual resale to the public, it was found liable under strict products liability law notwithstanding that it was not in the business of manufacturing or selling such products.[6] The regular and yearly bulk sale of used goods was a factor that

---

§ 27.23

1. Sukljian v. Charles Ross & Son Co., Inc., 69 N.Y.2d 89, 511 N.Y.S.2d 821, 503 N.E.2d 1358 (1986) where the Court of Appeals laid down the "incidental" or "casual" seller defense.

2. Id.

3. 85 A.D.2d 566, 445 N.Y.S.2d 445 (1st Dep't 1981), aff'd 57 N.Y.2d 839, 455 N.Y.S.2d 764, 442 N.E.2d 61 (1982).

4. 85 A.D.2d at 567, 445 N.Y.S.2d at 447. See also, Welch v. Dura-Wound, Inc., 894 F.Supp. 76, 79 (N.D.N.Y.1995).

5. 180 A.D.2d 122, 584 N.Y.S.2d 653 (3d Dep't 1992).

6. 85 A.D.2d at 567, 445 N.Y.S.2d at 447.

apparently convinced the court to impose liability under strict products liability law.

§ 27.24 Distributors' or Sellers' Liability—Service v. Sales

Often, a defendant will argue that a products liability theory is inapplicable since it did not sell the product but rather merely serviced it. In *Perazone v. Sears Roebuck & Co.*,[1] the plaintiff had purchased a garden tractor sold by Sears. Some five years later, the defendant, Hubbel Brothers, serviced the tractor for the plaintiff and also replaced the gas tank cap with a standard replacement cap. The plaintiff suffered serious burns approximately one year thereafter when the gas cap blew off the tank, causing gasoline to ignite while the plaintiff was using the tractor. Although the plaintiff obtained a verdict on some of his claims, the trial court dismissed the strict products liability claim against Hubbel, the servicer of the tractor and the supplier of the gas cap. Hubbel's defense was that it was in the business of repairing, not selling, machinery and that its servicing of the tractor and providing the gas cap was in the nature of a "service" rather than a sale.[2]

The Third Department ruled that the plaintiff was not barred from bringing a products liability claim against Hubbel. While the relationship between Hubbel and the plaintiff may have been "primarily service oriented," it was clear that Hubbel was in the business of selling lawnmower parts at retail, and that one could purchase the gas tank cap involved in the case without having any repairs performed. Thus, plaintiff had a valid products liability claim even if the relationship was "primarily service oriented."[3]

As seen in *Perazone*, the distinction between sales and service is not always a clear one.[4] If the plaintiff's injuries are caused by a party who is not a direct manufacturer or distributor of the product causing harm, counsel must analyze and distinguish whether the potential defendant's role was "tangential,"[5] "peripheral,"[6] "casual" or "incidental."[7] If a

---

§ 27.24

1. 128 A.D.2d 15, 515 N.Y.S.2d 908 (3d Dep't 1987).
2. *Id.*
3. *But cf.* Van Iderstine v. Lane Pipe Corp., 89 A.D.2d 459, 455 N.Y.S.2d 450 (4th Dep't 1982), appeal dismissed 58 N.Y.2d 610, 462 N.Y.S.2d 1028, 449 N.E.2d 427 (1983).
4. **PRACTICE POINTER:** Plaintiffs who desire the benefits of a strict products liability claim should be careful to properly plead the allegations, obtain proof of sales independent of service during discovery, and at trial, prove a sale rather than a service.
5. Blackburn v. Johnson Chem. Co., 128 Misc.2d 623, 490 N.Y.S.2d 452, 455 (Sup. Ct., Kings County, 1985) (where court found that can manufacturer was not responsible for inadequate warning it had lithographed on insecticide container since it had not been hired to design the label and did not have expertise "equal to or greater than the label's designer" to discern the inadequacies of the warnings).
6. Brumbaugh v. CEJJ, Inc., 152 A.D.2d 69, 547 N.Y.S.2d 699 (3d Dep't 1989) (exclusive marketing agent's role in placing product in stream of commerce was too peripheral to manufacturing and marketing to warrant imposition of liability).
7. Sukljian v. Charles Ross & Son Co., Inc., 69 N.Y.2d 89, 511 N.Y.S.2d 821, 503 N.E.2d 1358 (1986).

plaintiff can show that the defendant was actively involved in the sale or manufacture of the defective product or a component thereof, liability may be imposed.

§ 27.25 Distributors' or Sellers' Liability—Medical Care Providers

Quite often physicians or other medical care providers are involved in the dissemination of defective products. Plaintiff's counsel should consider whether these parties can be held responsible under products liability law for their participation in the distribution of a product. In *Detwiler v. Bristol–Myers Squibb Co.*,[1] strict products liability causes of action were sustained against a physician where the plaintiff claimed injuries as a result of periodic injections of silicone into her body. Since the action was commenced approximately twelve years after the last treatment, a medical malpractice claim was time barred under the two-and-one-half year Statute of Limitations contained in CPLR 214–a. Relying upon *Simcuski v. Saeli*,[2] the plaintiff argued that her physician should be estopped from asserting the Statute of Limitations defense based upon his failure to disclose his malpractice and/or the dangers inherent in the treatment. Observing that the fraudulent acts alleged by the plaintiff were based upon the same acts upon which the malpractice was claimed, the Court held that the doctrine of equitable estoppel did not apply since "it may be invoked only when a physician conceals his prior malpractice...."[3]

Accordingly, the only avenue upon which plaintiff Detwiler could recover, as a result of her doctor's use of a harmful product, was under a products liability theory which was subject to a three year Statute of Limitations running from the discovery of the injury.[4]

In response to the pleadings, which alleged that the defendant doctor had "designed, manufactured, tested, inspected, advertised, marketed, distributed and/or sold" the silicone he injected into the plaintiff's face, the *Detwiler* Court noted that ordinarily physicians should not be held responsible for the administration of a defective product since they are neither a direct manufacturer nor distributor of the product:

> New York courts appear to have developed a rule that a physician cannot be liable in strict products liability for a defective product he administers when his provision of the product is incidental to the medical services. *See Goldfarb v. Teitelbaum*, 149 A.D.2d 566, 540 N.Y.S.2d 263, 264 (2d Dep't. 1989) (insertion of dental prosthesis was "only a procedure incident to medical treatment"); *Probst v.*

§ 27.25
1. 884 F.Supp. 117 (S.D.N.Y.1995).
2. 44 N.Y.2d 442, 406 N.Y.S.2d 259, 377 N.E.2d 713 (1978).
3. 884 F.Supp. at 120.
4. 884 F.Supp. at 121.

§ 27.25 PRODUCTS LIABILITY Ch. 27

Albert Einstein Medical Center, 82 A.D.2d 739, 440 N.Y.S.2d 2, 3 (1st Dep't.1981) (insertion of metal rod into plaintiff's spinal column was "incidental to the medical services provided"); *Perlmutter v. Beth David Hospital*, 308 N.Y. 100, 106, 123 N.E.2d 792, 795 (1954) (in breach of warranty action, hospital not liable for tainted blood transfusion because the "supplying of the blood by the hospital was entirely subordinate to its paramount function of furnishing trained personnel and specialized facilities in an endeavor to restore plaintiff's health") ... [T]hose cases (and the ones they cite) held that a physician who uses a product in the course of medical treatment is not a "seller" of that product.[5]

However, the *Detwiler* court distinguished those cases from the instant case, noting that in none of them did the plaintiff claim that the physician manufactured or processed the product, whereas, in *Detwiler*, an issue of fact existed as to whether the defendant physician was liable under a products liability theory since the plaintiff had come forth with evidence linking the physician to the manufacture and distribution of the harmful product, to wit: a 1981 document issued by the defendant doctor's medical group conceding that it pharmaceutically refined locally available liquid silicone in order to make it suitable and safe for tissue augmentation.[6]

The *Detwiler* decision demonstrates how a particular party can be held to be a manufacturer, distributor or seller so as to be subject to liability on a products liability cause of action. Invoking a products liability theory was critical to the *Detwiler* plaintiff since the medical malpractice claim was time barred.

§ 27.26 Successor Liability

Very often a company that has manufactured a product that causes harm has subsequently sold its business or product line to another corporation or company. The injured party in such cases will look to both the predecessor company and the successor company for recompense.[1]

Liability of a successor company which takes over the company that manufactured the defective product becomes critical if the original manufacturer is no longer in existence. Our courts will impose liability on a successor corporation if certain standards are met:

(1) the successor corporation expressly or impliedly assumed the predecessor corporation's tort liability; (2) there was a consolidation or merger of the seller and the purchaser (successor corporation); (3)

---

5. 884 F.Supp. at 121.
6. 884 F.Supp. at 121–22.

§ 27.26
1. Grant–Howard Associates v. General Housewares Corp., 63 N.Y.2d 291, 482 N.Y.S.2d 225, 472 N.E.2d 1 (1984). *See also*, Kreindler, Rodriguez, et al., *New York Law of Torts* (West 1997) Ch.16 "Products Liability."

the successor corporation was a mere continuation of the selling corporation; or (4) the transaction was entered into fraudulently to escape outstanding obligations of the original corporation.[2]

In order to establish a continuity of enterprise,[3] certain factors demonstrating a continuity of corporate responsibility must be demonstrated. The *Schumacher* Court suggests, as examples, a continuity of management, key personnel and physical location. Thus, successor liability may be imposed where the successor corporation uses the predecessor corporation's factory, name and office personnel to produce the same product as the predecessor corporation.[4]

In pursuing a claim against a successor corporation, one should not limit the cause of action to products liability. Indeed, in *Schumacher*, while the Court found no strict products liability claim available, it held that a negligence cause of action for failure to warn could exist if it could be shown that the acquiring corporation possessed knowledge of the risk of injury created by the operation of the machine which its predecessor put into the stream of commerce. In *Schumacher*, the Court focused upon the fact that in addition to making one service call, the successor corporation knew of the location and owner of the machine and had actively offered to service it. The successor corporation had held itself out to plaintiff's employer as having expertise in the product line it had acquired and, while it had not formally assumed the manufacturers's service contracts, it offered to service the machine to its potential economic advantage.[5]

Notwithstanding the agreements or writings between the successor and predecessor corporation, successor liability may also be imposed if evidence of a "*de facto* merger" exists. In *Sweatland v. Park Corp.*,[6] several factors were identified:

(1) continuity of ownership; (2) a cessation of ordinary business and dissolution of the predecessor as soon as practically and legally possible; (3) assumption by the successor of the liabilities ordinarily necessary for the uninterrupted continuation of the business of the predecessor; and (4) a continuity of management, personnel, physical location, assets and general business operations.[7]

The *Sweatland* Court noted that the courts have flexibility in determining whether a transaction constitutes a *de facto* merger.

2. Schumacher v. Richards Shear Co., 59 N.Y.2d 239, 464 N.Y.S.2d 437, 451 N.E.2d 195 (1983).

3. *See* Turner v. Bituminous Cas. Co., 397 Mich. 406, 244 N.W.2d 873 (1976).

4. *See* Schumacher v. Richards Shear Co., 59 N.Y.2d 239, 464 N.Y.S.2d 437, 451 N.E.2d 195 (1983) (where the Court referred to Ray v. Alad Corp., 19 Cal.3d 22, 136 Cal.Rptr. 574, 560 P.2d 3 which discussed what is termed a "product line" line theory).

5. 59 N.Y.2d at 248–49, 464 N.Y.S.2d at 442.

6. 181 A.D.2d 243, 587 N.Y.S.2d 54 (4th Dep't 1992).

7. 181 A.D.2d at 246, 587 N.Y.S.2d at 56.

§ 27.26

It is imperative that in the course of discovery the plaintiff obtain detailed information regarding the negotiations and contract which resulted in the successor corporation's acquisition of the assets of the predecessor company. Sometimes the two corporations contractually determine who should bear the financial burden in the event any claim is made by one exposed to the subject product.[8]

Library References:
West's Key No. Digests, Corporations ⚖445.1.

§ 27.27 Successor Liability—Burden of Proof

In order for successor liability to be imposed, evidence meeting the above standard must be produced. The mere sale of corporate property from one company to another does not make the purchaser responsible for the pre-existing tort liability of the seller.[1] If the predecessor corporation continues to remain responsible for warranty claims made against its product during the time it manufactured that product, the successor corporation may not be held responsible for the product that was manufactured prior to its purchase of the predecessor's business.[2]

Library References:
West's Key No. Digests, Corporations ⚖519(1).

§ 27.28 Successor Liability—Punitive Damages

A successor corporation may even be liable in punitive damages for a product placed into the market by its predecessor. In *In re New York State Silicone Breast Implant Litigation*,[1] successor corporations Baxter International Inc., and Baxter Health Care Corp. unsuccessfully sought summary judgment, arguing that there could be no punitive damage claim as a matter of law because they were successor corporations that did not design, manufacture or sell the silicone breast implants which the plaintiffs claimed were defective. In denying the defendants' motion, the Court referred to a New Jersey case, *Brotherton v. Celotex Corp.*,[2] where the Superior Court had determined that punitive damages would be appropriate against a successor corporation upon a showing by the plaintiff that there existed "such a degree of identity of the successor with the predecessor as to justify the conclusion that those responsible

---

8. *See* Grant-Howard Associates v. General Housewares Corp., 63 N.Y.2d 291, 482 N.Y.S.2d 225, 472 N.E.2d 1 (1984).

§ 27.27

1. Flecha v. Seybold Machine Co., 146 A.D.2d 515, 536 N.Y.S.2d 455 (1st Dep't 1989).

2. Heights v. U.S. Electrical Tool Co., 138 A.D.2d 369, 525 N.Y.S.2d 653 (2d Dep't 1988).

§ 27.28

1. N.Y.L.J., 6/1/95, p.27, col.2 (Sup.Ct., New York County). For further discussion of punitive damages, *see infra* Chapter 30 "Damages," §§ 30.31–30.36.

2. 202 N.J.Super. 148, 493 A.2d 1337 (1985).

for the reckless conduct of the predecessor [should] be punished, and the successor ...be deterred from similar conduct."[3] The *Brotherton* Court stated that the key factor to be considered was the degree to which a predecessor's business entity remained intact. Applying *Brotherton*, the New York Court held that "the determination of whether the actions of the Baxter defendants in connection with their *continued* involvement in breast implant products were culpable is an issue to be determined by a jury, not by this Court."[4]

Library References:

West's Key No. Digests, Damages ⚖︎87-94.

§ 27.29 Liability of the Manufacturer of Component Parts

Many products are comprised of several component parts which may have been manufactured or supplied by another. In addition to naming as defendants the manufacturer and supplier of the product which caused the injury, plaintiffs' counsel should also include as a defendant the manufacturer or supplier of the particular component part that caused the product to be defective. The party that supplies the defective part which causes an accident is liable under negligence and strict liability.[1] For instance, a person injured as a result of a fire inside an automobile could pursue a claim against the automobile's manufacturer as well as the entity that manufactured the flammable materials used in the vehicle's interior.[2]

Library References:

West's Key No. Digests, Products Liability ⚖︎23.1.

§ 27.30 Liability of the Manufacturer of the Complete Product

In *Delzotti v. American LaFrance*,[1] the manufacturer and distributor of the whole or complete product sought to avoid liability by claiming the plaintiff's injuries were caused by a defective component part manufactured by another. The Appellate Division, First Department, did not agree and found the manufacturer of the complete product liable. In

3. 202 N.J.Super. at 156, 493 A.2d at 1341.

4. N.Y.L.J. 6/1/95, p.27, col.2 (emphasis added).

§ 27.29

1. Smith v. Peerless Glass Co., 259 N.Y. 292, 181 N.E. 576 (1932), 259 N.Y. 292, 181 N.E. 576, rearg. denied 259 N.Y. 664, 182 N.E. 225 (1932) For decisions under a theory of strict products liability *see* Yates v. Dow Chem. Co., 68 A.D.2d 907, 414 N.Y.S.2d 200 (2d Dep't 1979); Clark v. Bendix Corp., 42 A.D.2d 727, 345 N.Y.S.2d 662 (2d Dep't 1973); Sanders v. Quikstak, Inc., 889 F.Supp. 128, 131 (S.D.N.Y.1995).

2. 68 A.D.2d at 908, 414 N.Y.S.2d at 201-02.

§ 27.30

1. 179 A.D.2d 497, 579 N.Y.S.2d 33 (1st Dep't 1992).

§ 27.30   PRODUCTS LIABILITY   Ch. 27

Delzotti, the plaintiff fire fighter was injured when he was caused to fall as a result of the collapse of a folding step on a fire truck manufactured by defendant American LaFrance. Plaintiff claimed that the step had broken because of a manufacturing defect caused by metallurgical deficiencies.[2]

American LaFrance defended the case by urging that since it was not the manufacturer of the step, it could not be held responsible for the step's collapse.[3] The First Department rejected this argument, stating:

> As to the defendant American LaFrance, the record indicates that the step may very well have been defectively manufactured. While American LaFrance asserts that it was not the manufacturer of the step, this does not relieve it of liability as ultimate manufacturer of the fire engine.[4]

The *Delzotti* decision eliminates any equivocation on the issue of whether the manufacturer of a complete or whole product should be held responsible for a defective component. It is fundamentally clear that even if a manufacturer does not produce the defective component part which directly causes the injury, it will not be relieved of liability as the ultimate manufacturer of the complete or whole product.

Library References:
   West's Key No. Digests, Products Liability ⌐24.

§ 27.31   Introducing Evidence of Post Accident Modification or Repairs

Perhaps one of the most important distinctions between a strict products liability case and a negligence case is the fact that the evidentiary rule precluding proof of a post-accident repair, improvement or modification which applies to negligence actions is inapplicable to a products liability case.[1] In *Barry v. Manglass*,[2] the appellate division provided a very compelling reason for this distinction:

> Thus, while it may be sound to exclude evidence of postinjury remedial safety measures in negligence cases because the repairs reflect hindsight rather than foresight and might militate against the making of such repairs (see 2 Harper & James, Torts (1956 ed.), p.981 and Harper & James Torts, Supp. to Vol.2, pp. 64–65 and Smyth v. Upjohn Co., 529 F.2d 803), to extend the rule to cases of strict products liability would, without basis in reason, permit an arbitrary exclusionary rule to operate in the field of consumer

---

2. 179 A.D.2d at 497, 579 N.Y.S.2d at 34.

3. 179 A.D.2d at 497, 579 N.Y.S.2d at 34.

4. 179 A.D.2d at 497, 579 N.Y.S.2d at 34.

§ 27.31

1. Caprara v. Chrysler Corp., 52 N.Y.2d 114, 125–26, 436 N.Y.S.2d 251, 256–57, 417 N.E.2d 545 (1981).

2. 55 A.D.2d 1, 389 N.Y.S.2d 870 (2d Dep't 1976).

protection. In such cases we are not dealing with *fault* or *negligence* or *culpability*, but, regardless of any of them, with a defect which existed in the product. The former deal with the defendant's conduct, the latter with the product (see 54 Calif.L.Rev. 1550).[3]

§ 27.32 Introducing Evidence of Other Incidents

While depending upon the circumstances, the fact that other persons have used the product without harm may be admissible, it is certainly not dispositive. As stated by the Court of Appeals in *Orlick v. Granit Hotel & Country Club*,[1] continued usage without incident does not "negate negligence," but is simply something for the jury to consider.[2] Similarly relevant and admissible is proof that other persons suffered the same injury from using the product which allegedly caused the plaintiff's injury.[3]

In *E.I. du Pont De Nemours & Co. v. White*,[4] an action by a person who claimed to have been injured as a result of exposure to poisonous gases in the work place, the court permitted testimony of other employees that the gases had a similar affect upon them. Also, in *Bolm v. Triumph Corp.*,[5] where the plaintiff claimed his injuries arose from a defectively designed motorcycle, the court received testimony from a witness that he had sustained a similar accident while using one of the defendant's motorcycles; the court found that "proof of similar accidents may be received to establish a dangerous condition."[6] Evidence of prior incidents may also be used to show that the defendant had notice of a dangerous and defective condition.[7] However, evidence of a subsequent incident may only be used to establish the existence of the dangerous condition.[8]

§ 27.33 Effect of Destruction of the Product Upon Plaintiff's Ability to Prove a Defect

Quite often the person injured by the defective product is not the owner of that product. After an incident, immediate steps should be taken to safeguard and/or preserve the integrity of the subject product so that the plaintiff's ability to establish a claim is not compromised. If there is concern about the potential loss or destruction of evidence, the

---

3. Id. 55 A.D.2d at 7, 389 N.Y.S.2d at 875.

§ 27.32

1. 30 N.Y.2d 246, 331 N.Y.S.2d 651, 282 N.E.2d 610 (1972).

2. 30 N.Y.2d at 250, 331 N.Y.S.2d at 654, 28 N.E.2d at 612 (1972).

3. Zenkel v. Oneida County Creameries Co., 104 Misc. 251, 171 N.Y.S. 676, (Sup.Ct., Monroe County, 1918) aff'd without opinion 188 App.Div. 905, 176 N.Y.S. 927 (1918).

4. 8 F.2d 5 (3d Cir.1925).

5. 71 A.D.2d 429, 422 N.Y.S.2d 969 (4th Dep't 1979).

6. 71 A.D.2d at 439, 422 N.Y.S.2d at 975 (1974).

7. Sawyer v. Dreis & Krump Mfg. Co., 67 N.Y.2d 328, 502 N.Y.S.2d 696, 493 N.E.2d 920 (1986).

8. Galieta v. Young Men's Christian Assoc., 32 A.D.2d 711, 300 N.Y.S.2d 170, 173 (3d Dep't 1969).

plaintiff should commence a proceeding to obtain pre-action discovery[1] to prevent the product from being destroyed; within that application plaintiff should also seek to obtain information as to the identity of the manufacturer or distributor of the product.

A court order compelling the preservation and/or production of evidence, if subsequently violated by the party in possession of such evidence, can be aggressively used to seek preclusion or sanctions. In *Strelov v. Hertz Corp.*,[2] the plaintiff alleged that she was injured due to defective steering and brake mechanisms in the lessor's vehicle. When, during the course of discovery, Hertz's counsel advised at a deposition that the subject car was in "an official legal hold status," plaintiff's counsel requested that the car remain in such status and that notice be given of when the vehicle would be available for inspection.[3] Nonetheless, the lessor sold the vehicle, keeping only the tires. Plaintiff was not advised of that sale until over six months had passed. The appellate division found that based upon this conduct, which the lessor tried to excuse as "law office and claims adjuster failure," it was appropriate to preclude defendant from rebutting plaintiff's claims of possible defects in the automobile component parts that were no longer available for inspection.[4] It is important to note that the *Strelov* Court imposed the remedy of preclusion even though no formal notice or order to produce had yet been served. When there is a destruction of evidence in violation of a court order or as an intentional attempt to evade compliance with a discovery notice, the courts are more inclined to grant an even broader order of preclusion.[5]

An example of obstructionist conduct resulting in the most severe sanction—the entry of a default judgment on the issue of liability—is presented in the case of *Carlucci v. Piper Aircraft Corp.*[6] In that case the defendant manufacturer had perpetuated a policy of destroying engineering documents "with the intention of preventing them from being produced in lawsuits ...[a] practice [which] continued after the commencement of [the] lawsuit...."[7]

Even where the actual product which caused the injury is destroyed other than by the defendant, a plaintiff may still be able to establish a case. In *Otis v. Bausch & Lomb, Inc.*,[8] for example, the appellate division found that the fact that the plaintiff had disposed of her contact lenses

§ 27.33
1. CPLR 3102(c).
2. 171 A.D.2d 420, 566 N.Y.S.2d 646 (1st Dep't 1991).
3. 171 A.D.2d at 420, 566 N.Y.S.2d at 647.
4. 171 A.D.2d at 420, 566 N.Y.S.2d at 646.
5. Ferraro v. Koncal Assocs., 97 A.D.2d 429, 467 N.Y.S.2d 284 (2d Dep't 1983) (display rack which caused infant's injuries was destroyed after the plaintiff had served a discovery notice and an inspection date had been set).
6. 102 F.R.D. 472 (S.D.Fla.1984).
7. 102 F.R.D. at 485.
8. 143 A.D.2d 649, 532 N.Y.S.2d 933 (2d Dep't 1988).

which had caused her injuries, while perhaps precluding her from proving a manufacturing defect in those very lenses, would not affect her right to show that the manufacturer's lenses, as a whole, were defectively designed or distributed without adequate warnings. Furthermore, as discussed at length in Section 27.34 "Proof of Causation," a defect in the product can be established by circumstantial evidence.

Library References:

West's Key No. Digests, Products Liability ⚛82; Torts ⚛13.

§ 27.34 Proof of Causation

In order to establish a claim under a products liability theory, the plaintiff does not have to offer direct evidence of the specific defect that caused the injury.[1] Proof of such defect may be circumstantial; *i.e.*, that the product did not perform as intended.[2] While the mere happening of an accident does not prove that the subject product was defective, a defect in the product may be inferred if the failure to perform as intended can be shown.[3]

One of the early cases is *Jackson v. Melvey*.[4] In that case a relatively new car veered off the highway and onto a shoulder causing the injuries which were the subject of the lawsuit. Plaintiff claimed that the accident occurred because the steering mechanism was defective. No expert witness was produced and plaintiff relied exclusively upon circumstantial evidence. The appellate court reversed the granting of the manufacturer's motion for summary judgment noting:

> ... the plaintiff is not required to prove the specific product defect and his proof may be circumstantial in nature. Thus, the defect may be inferred from proof that the product did not perform as intended by the manufacturer.[5]

The *Jackson* case expanded the holding in the seminal case on the subject, *Codling v. Paglia*, where the Court of Appeals had stated:

> Though the happening of the accident is not proof of a defective condition, a defect may be inferred from proof that the product did

---

§ 27.34

1. Codling v. Paglia, 32 N.Y.2d 330, 345 N.Y.S.2d 461, 298 N.E.2d 622 (1973). *See also*, Kreindler, Rodriguez, *et al.*, New York Law of Torts (West 1997) § 16.73.

2. Yager v. Arlen Realty & Dev. Corp., 95 A.D.2d 853, 464 N.Y.S.2d 214 (2d Dep't 1983).

3. Caprara v. Chrysler Corp., 52 N.Y.2d 114, 436 N.Y.S.2d 251, 417 N.E.2d 545 (1981); Halloran v. Virginia Chemicals, Inc., 41 N.Y.2d 386, 393 N.Y.S.2d 341, 361 N.E.2d 991 (1977); Markel v. Spencer, 5 A.D.2d 400, 171 N.Y.S.2d 770 (4th Dep't 1958), aff'd 5 N.Y.2d 958, 184 N.Y.S.2d 835, 157 N.E.2d 713 (1959).

4. 56 A.D.2d 836, 392 N.Y.S.2d 312 (2d Dep't 1977).

5. 56 A.D.2d at 836, 392 N.Y.S.2d at 314. *See* Landahl v. Chrysler Corp., 144 A.D.2d 926, 534 N.Y.S.2d 245 (4th Dep't 1988). *See also* Hunter v. Ford Motor Company, 37 A.D.2d 335, 325 N.Y.S.2d 469 (3d Dep't 1971).

§ 27.34 PRODUCTS LIABILITY Ch. 27

not perform as intended by the manufacturer.[6]

Demands that plaintiff come forth with proof of a specific defect are usually first raised in the pleading or discovery stages of the litigation. In one case, *Speed v. Avis Rent–A–Car*,[7] the trial court adopted the defendant's position that the plaintiff should be precluded from offering evidence at trial with regard to its defective steering or suspension system since the supplemental bill of particulars was allegedly not specific as to the claimed defects. Noting that the plaintiff had not been able to examine the vehicle before it had been destroyed by the defendant, the First Department found that the bill of particulars was sufficient, and that there was no basis for the order of preclusion since the plaintiff could prove her case by circumstantial evidence. Citing *Codling v. Paglia*,[8] the unanimous court held:

> Thus, despite plaintiff's inability to specifically describe defective conditions in or specific acts of negligent design and manufacture of the steering, suspension, and brake systems other than in the power brake booster she is not precluded from attempting to demonstrate through circumstantial evidence that such defects caused the automobile to behave as she alleged.[9]

In *Abar v. Freightliner Corporation*,[10] the plaintiff truck driver was injured when the grab bar that he was using to hoist himself up into the cab of his truck gave way causing him to fall and sustain severe back injuries. Plaintiff commenced a products liability action against Freightliner which had designed and manufactured the truck ten years earlier. Freightliner in turn commenced a third-party action against Abar's employer. Plaintiff's expert concluded that the grab rail assembly (comprised of a 20 inch tube attached to upper and lower brackets by fastening devices) failed when the lower bracket gave way and the tube came out of the upper bracket leaving Abar with nothing to hold onto. The expert offered the opinion that the lower bracket gave way because the bolts that had been used to attach it to the cab were inadequate. Since it was undisputed that the lower bracket which the plaintiff's expert actually inspected was not the original bracket that had been installed by the defendant, the defendant argued that plaintiff's action must be dismissed due to his failure to prove that the bolts which failed were the actual ones that had been installed by the defendant when it manufactured the truck.

The court readily rejected this argument stating:

6. 32 N.Y.2d 330, 345 N.Y.S.2d 461, 298 N.E.2d 622 (1973).

7. 172 A.D.2d 267, 568 N.Y.S.2d 90 (1st Dep't 1991).

8. 32 N.Y.2d 330, 345 N.Y.S.2d 461, 298 N.E.2d 622 (1973).

9. 172 A.D.2d at 268, 568 N.Y.2d at 91.

10. 208 A.D.2d 999, 617 N.Y.S.2d 209 (3d Dep't 1994).

This, however, is not fatal to plaintiffs' action since "* * *the existence of a product defect as well as the identity of the manufacturer of the product are issues of fact capable of proof by circumstantial evidence." (*Treston v. Allegretta*, 181 A.D.2d 470, 471, 581 N.Y.S.2d 289, quoting *Otis v. Bausch & Lomb*, 143 A.D.2d 649, 650, 532 N.Y.S.2d 933).[11]

The circumstantial evidence in the *Abar* case included the testimony of the plaintiff's expert that when he removed the new lower bracket, he found that in addition to the two holes used to install and attach the new bracket, there were two other holes with broken bolts still in them. The expert was thus able to conclude that these broken bolts were the original ones since experience showed that there was generally no reason to replace such bolts. The expert also explained that the new holes were drilled because if the original bolts had previously failed, it would have been extremely difficult to extricate those broken bolts to permit use of the original holes. Accordingly, the court held:

> In our view this evidence, along with the absence of definitive proof that the grab rail assembly had been altered prior to Abar's accident, provided sufficient evidence for the jury to conclude that the bolts that failed were the ones installed by defendant.[12]

Finding that such evidence was sufficient to establish a *prima facie* case, the court wrote:

> To establish such a case in a strict products liability action predicated upon design defects, "a plaintiff must show that the manufacturer marketed a product which was not reasonably safe in its design, that it was feasible to design the product in a safer manner and that the defective design was a substantial factor in causing the plaintiff's injury." (*DeMatteo v. Big V Supermarkets*, 611 N.Y.S.2d 970, 971).[13]

In another case, *George Larkin Trucking Co. v. Lisbon Tire Mart, Inc.*,[14] a trucking company brought suit to recover for property damage that was caused to its truck engines from contaminated oil that it alleged had been sold to it by the defendant.[15] The complaint set forth causes of action sounding in negligence, strict products liability and breach of warranty. The jury verdict in plaintiff's favor was unanimously affirmed with the reasoning that the evidence that had been presented was "sufficient to enable the jury to infer that the product was defective and unfit when sold by the defendant." The plaintiff had presented evidence that the product had malfunctioned during normal use, so that the jury

11. 208 A.D.2d at 1000, 617 N.Y.S.2d at 212.
12. 208 A.D.2d at 1000, 617 N.Y.S.2d at 212.
13. 208 A.D.2d at 1000, 617 N.Y.S.2d at 212.
14. 210 A.D.2d 899, 620 N.Y.S.2d 654 (4th Dep't 1994).
15. 210 A.D.2d at 900, 620 N.Y.S.2d at 655 (4th Dep't 1994).

was able to infer that the product or its packaging was defective when it left the defendant's hands.

The *Larkin* Court noted that the plaintiff had presented proof that all four of its trucks had experienced similar engine problems within a short time of the oil changes in which defendant's oil was used. This factor, coupled with evidence that the oil drum was sealed before it was sold by the defendant to the plaintiff and had remained sealed until the plaintiff tapped the drum several months later in order to change the oil in its vehicles, supported the inference that the oil was defective at the time it left the defendant's hands. In support of its finding, the *Larkin* Court referred to the seminal cases in products liability law:

> A plaintiff in a strict products liability action may predicate its claim entirely upon circumstantial evidence (*Halloran v. Virginia Chems*, 41 N.Y.2d 386, 388, 393 N.Y.S.2d 341, 361 N.E.2d 991; *Codling v. Paglia*, 32 N.Y.2d 330, 337–338, 342, 345 N.Y.S.2d 461, 298 N.E.2d 622; 1 Weinberger, N.Y. Prod. Liab. §§ 14.08.50, 20.03, 20.04). A plaintiff need not adduce direct evidence of a specific defect, but, depending on the circumstances, may rest on proof that the product did not perform as intended by the manufacturer (*Codling v. Paglia*, supra; *Landahl v. Chrysler Corp.*, 144 A.D.2d 926, 927, 534 N.Y.S.2d 245).[16]

The court rejected the defendant's anticipated argument that the plaintiff's trucks had been damaged by other means since the defendant had failed to come forth with logically supported evidence which would absolve it of responsibility.

Library References:

West's Key No. Digests, Products Liability ⚖15.

§ 27.35 Proof of Causation—Question for the Jury or Question for the Judge

It must be remembered that the question of causation—whether the defendant's product caused the plaintiff's injury—is to be determined by the jury. While the cases previously discussed show that expert testimony is not always necessary to establish causation, there are certain situations, especially those involving drugs or toxic substances where expert testimony is essential.

No matter how difficult or sophisticated the expert testimony may be on a particular subject, the weight to be afforded such testimony, and a consideration of the credibility of the witness presenting it, rests exclusively within the province of the jury. In *Kallenberg v. Beth Israel*

---

16. 210 A.D.2d at 900, 620 N.Y.S.2d at 655.

Medical Center,[1] several experts testified on the medical issue of whether the defendants' failure to give the decedent the prescribed drug of choice prevented her from reaching an operable condition, thereby causing her to deteriorate and ultimately die. On appeal, the defendants urged that the appellate court consider all of the factual and expert testimony and make its own finding with regard to whether the decedent's demise was caused by the defendant's negligence. In its *per curiam* decision, the appellate division quite succinctly stated, "[t]he question of proximate cause is a jury question, and a jury alone may weigh conflicting evidence and determine the credibility of witnesses and the weight to be accorded expert testimony."[2]

Recently the Supreme Court of the United States addressed the issue of the court's role in assessing the expert's testimony that is to be presented to a jury. In *Daubert v. Merrell Dow Pharmaceuticals, Inc.*[3], the court discussed the role of a federal trial judge in assessing expert testimony for admissibility purposes.

In construing Section 702[4] of the Federal Rules of Evidence, the Supreme Court in *Daubert* laid down the precept that the trial judge is assigned "the task of ensuring that an expert's testimony both rests on a reliable foundation and is relevant to the task at hand."[5] The *Daubert* Court rejected the use of the "general acceptance" standard for admissibility—that expert opinions fall within the generally accepted scientific community of thought.[6] Instead, it determined that the trial judge should apply "[r]ule 702's 'helpfulness' standard [which] requires a valid scientific connection to the pertinent inquiry as a precondition to admissibility."[7] The Supreme Court thus stated:

> Faced with a proffer of expert scientific testimony, then, the trial judge must determine at the outset, pursuant to Rule 104(a), whether the expert is proposing to testify to (1) scientific knowledge that (2) will assist the trier of fact to understand or determine a fact in issue. This entails a preliminary assessment of whether the reasoning or methodology underlying the testimony is scientifically valid and of whether that reasoning or methodology properly can be applied to the facts in issue.[8]

§ 27.35

1. 45 A.D.2d 177, 357 N.Y.S.2d 508 (1st Dep't 1974), aff'd 37 N.Y.2d 719, 374 N.Y.S.2d 615, 337 N.E.2d 128 (1975).

2. 45 A.D.2d at 181, 357 N.Y.S.2d at 511.

3. 509 U.S. 579, 113 S.Ct. 2786, 125 L.Ed.2d 469 (1993).

4. If scientific, technical, or other specialized knowledge will assist the trier of fact to understand the evidence or to determine a fact in issue, a witness qualified as an expert by knowledge, skill, experience, training, or education may testify thereto in the form of an opinion or otherwise. Fed. R.Evid. 702.

5. 509 U.S. at 597, 113 S.Ct. at 2799. *See* Barker and Alexander, *Evidence in New York State and Federal Courts* (West 1996) § 702.2.b.

6. Frye v. United States, 293 F. 1013 (App.D.C.1923).

7. 509 U.S. at 591, 113 S.Ct. at 2796.

8. 509 U.S. at 591, 113 S.Ct. at 2796.

§ 27.35 PRODUCTS LIABILITY Ch. 27

While the *Daubert* decision specifically states that the judge's role is limited exclusively to a preliminary assessment and determination of the admissibility of expert testimony, defense counsel have used it to seek preclusion of expert testimony in its entirety and/or to have the court substitute its judgment for that of the jury as to the weight and credibility to be afforded expert testimony. Needless to say, *Daubert* has had an impact on products liability cases where there are serious issues as to whether the injuries sustained were in fact caused by the defective product. Particularly subject to *Daubert* scrutiny are those cases where the injury suffered is caused by the alleged ingestion or exposure to a drug or toxic substance.

In *In Re Joint Eastern & Southern District Asbestos Litigation*, (Asbestos Litig. IV),[9] the Second Circuit was presented with a case it defined as marking "the convergence of epidemiological evidence, probabilistic causation in carcinogenic torts, and the important issue of the extent to which a trial court may assess the sufficiency of scientific evidence in light of the Supreme Court's recent holding in *Daubert v. Merrell Dow Pharmaceuticals Inc.*"[10] At issue was whether the decedent's chronic exposure to fireproof asbestos spray had caused the decedent's injury and death from colon cancer. The case involved a battle of experts as to whether a causal link existed between asbestos and colon cancer. Initially, the district court had found in favor of the defendant, granting summary judgment on the ground that the epidemiological and clinical evidence of causation was insufficient.[11] On appeal, the Second Circuit reversed the granting of summary judgment and remanded for further proceedings.[12] The jury awarded its verdict to the plaintiff in the sum of $4,510,000, of which the jury found the non-settling defendant, United States Mineral Products Company (USMP), fifty percent responsible.

Thereafter, USMP moved for judgment as a matter of law on the ground *inter alia* that the evidence was insufficient. The District Court judge in addressing this issue, interpreted *Daubert* as "speak[ing] to the sufficiency required of scientific evidence and the gate keeping role of the trial judge with regard to misleading evidence."[13] Interpreting the Agent Orange cases[14] and the Bendectin litigation[15] as requiring greater proof of

9. 52 F.3d 1124 (2d Cir.1995).

10. 52 F.3d at 1126.

11. In re Joint Eastern & Southern District Asbestos Litigation, 758 F.Supp. 199 (S.D.N.Y.1991) ("Asbestos Litig. I"), reargument denied, 774 F.Supp. 113, and reconsideration denied 774 F.Supp. 116 (S.D.N.Y. 1991).

12. In Re Joint Eastern & Southern District Asbestos Litigation, 964 F.2d 92, 96–97 (2d Cir.1992) ("Asbestos Litig. II").

13. In Re Joint Eastern & Southern District Asbestos Litigation, 827 F.Supp. 1014, 1025 (S.D.N.Y.1993) ("Asbestos Litig. III").

14. In Re Agent Orange Prod. Liab. Litig., 597 F.Supp. 740, 785 (E.D.N.Y.1984) ("Agent Orange I") aff'd 818 F.2d 145 (2d Cir.1987) cert. denied, 484 U.S. 1004, 108 S.Ct. 695, 98 L.Ed.2d 648 (1988).

15. Brock v. Merrell Dow Pharmaceuticals, Inc. 874 F.2d 307 (5th Cir.1989), modified on reh'g 884 F.2d 166 (5th Cir.1989),

epidemiological evidence in mass tort cases, the *Asbestos Litig. III* Court determined that the epidemiological evidence presented was insufficient to support a causal connection between asbestos exposure and colon cancer since "[t]he causal relationship is not established by the statistical analyses of the two events, exposure to asbestos and developing colon cancer, and as such, the epidemiological evidence[16] falls far short of the requisite level of sufficiency to support the jury's verdict."[17] The district court determined that there was an absence of affirmative clinical evidence and labeled the plaintiff's evidence as "nothing more than a superficial and insignificant differential diagnosis."[18] In rather harsh words, the District Court concluded that the opinions of the plaintiff's experts asserting a causal connection between asbestos and colon cancer "were nothing more than 'sheer surmise and conjecture'[19] masquerading behind the guise of sound science."[20] On appeal, the Second Circuit was presented with the primary issue of whether a trial judge's role in assessing the admissibility of scientific evidence in a federal trial as articulated by *Daubert* extended to a consideration of the *sufficiency* of the scientific evidence *that had already been admitted*. The Second Circuit concluded that the District Court went far beyond the *Daubert* principles by "impermissibly cross[ing] the line from assessing evidentiary reliability to usurping the role of the jury."[21] In the Asbestos Litigation cases, the sufficiency inquiry bore directly on the factual question of causation, *i.e.* "whether the body of the plaintiff's evidence was sufficient to persuade a rational jury that [the decedent's] exposure to asbestos more likely than not caused his colon cancer."[22] It is interesting to note that the Second Circuit Court of Appeals' decision amounts to a reiteration of the precept adopted in New York years ago in *Kallenberg v. Beth Israel Hospital*[23]—no matter how difficult or sophisticated the expert testimony may be on a particular subject, the weight to be afforded such testimony, and a consideration of the credibility of the witness presenting it, rests within the exclusive province of the jury. Indeed, the Second Circuit in *Asbestos Litig. IV*, specifically noted that a

cert. denied 494 U.S. 1046, 110 S.Ct. 1511, 108 L.Ed.2d 646 (1990).

16. As the district court noted in Asbestos Litig. III, in toxic carcinogenic tort cases, the study of disease patterns in human populations, known as epidemiology is necessary to set forth a relationship between a specific toxin or carcinogenic and the disease claimed to have been caused by it. The purpose of epidemiological studies is to formulate statistical means for detecting abnormally high incidents of disease in a certain population so as to thereby associate such incidents with unusual exposures to questionable environmental factors. *See* In Re Orange Product Liability Litigation, 611 F.Supp. at 1231. Epidemiological studies are not the exclusive means by which causation can be established. "The plaintiff may rely on conclusions derived from experimental studies involving animals or discrete groups of persons, or from clinical evidence including the medical, personal and family history of the individual suffering from the disease." 827 F.Supp. at 1026, 1028.

17. 827 F.Supp. at 1050.

18. 827 F.Supp. at 1051.

19. Samuels v. Air Transport Local 504, 992 F.2d 12, 14 (2d Cir.1993).

20. 827 F.Supp. at 1050.

21. 52 F.3d at 1131.

22. 52 F.3d at 1130.

23. 357 N.Y.S.2d at 511.

§ 27.35   PRODUCTS LIABILITY   Ch. 27

trial judge "is not to 'assess the weight of conflicting evidence, pass on the credibility of the witnesses, or substitute its judgment for that of the jury.' "[24]

There is no question that *Daubert* generated confusion as to the exact role the trial judge should play in the assessment of expert testimony. That role has been clarified by *Asbestos Litig. IV*, wherein the Second Circuit acknowledged "that sufficiency poses unique difficulties for trial courts in toxic or carcinogenic tort cases ... which hinge on competing interpretations of epidemiological evidence."[25] However, the Second Circuit in *Asbestos Litig. IV* was able to recognize that the case before it was not about the admissibility of the evidence but rather its sufficiency, which raised the question "whether the collective weight of a litigant's evidence is adequate to present a jury question...."[26]

The Asbestos Litigation cases, and more particularly the Second Circuit Court of Appeals decision therein, demonstrates how the trial court should treat the scientific evidence of the relationship between an injury and the product claimed to have caused it, so the jury can make the ultimate determination as to causation. As the Second Circuit noted:

> Causation in toxic torts normally comprises two separate inquiries: whether the epidemiological or other scientific evidence establishes a causal link between c (asbestos exposure) and d (colon cancer), and whether plaintiff is within the class of persons to which inferences from the general causation evidence should be applied. *See In Re Agent Orange Product Liability Litigation*, 611 F.Supp. 1223, 1261–62 (E.D.N.Y.1985) ("Agent Orange II"), *aff'd*, 818 F.2d 187 (2d Cir.), *cert. denied*, 487 U.S. 1234 (1988).[27]

While epidemiological evidence does not ordinarily lead the fact finder toward a definitive answer as to causation since it deals with statistical *probabilities* and the *possibility* of confounding causal factors,[28] the trial court cannot substitute its own determination for that of the jury. In dealing with the inherent uncertainty of causation in toxic or carcinogenic tort cases, the role of the trial court on a post-verdict motion addressed to the sufficiency of the evidence is to determine "whether, viewed in the light most favorable to the non-moving party, 'the evidence is such that, without weighing the credibility of the witnesses or otherwise considering the weight of the evidence, there can be but one conclusion as the verdict that reasonable [jurors] could have reached.' "[29]

24. 52 F.3d at 1131, citing Mattivi v. South African Marine Corp., "Huguenot," 618 F.2d 163, 167 (2d Cir.1980).

25. 52 F.3d at 1133.

26. 52 F.3d at 1132.

27. 52 F.3d at 1130.

28. *See* Brock v. Merrell Dow Pharmaceuticals, Inc., 874 F.2d at 311.

29. 52 F.3d at 1133 at 504; Samuels v. Air Transport Local 992 F.2d 12, 14 (2d Cir.1993) (quoting Simblest v. Maynard, 427 F.2d 1, 4 (2d Cir.1970)).

Since the trial court itself, in *Asbestos Litig. III*, had considered the weight of the conflicting evidence and the credibility of the witnesses, thereby substituting its judgment for that of the jury, the Second Circuit in *Asbestos Litig. IV* reversed and reinstated the jury verdict in favor of the plaintiff.

The decision of the Second Circuit in *Asbestos Litig. IV* provides a formidable ally for plaintiffs in toxic or carcinogenic tort cases. Once the admissibility test is met, the plaintiff is placed in the stronger position. When confronted with a challenge to the sufficiency of scientific evidence, the evidence must be viewed in a light most favorable to the plaintiff where there is conflicting testimony on the issue of causation. The trial judge, after determining that certain evidence meets the *Daubert* standard for admissibility, cannot then make an independent assessment as to the weight of that evidence and the comparative credibility of the witnesses presenting it. Sufficiency is for the jury, not the judge.

Library References:

West's Key No. Digests, Products Liability ⚖=87.

§ 27.36 Foreseeability of Harm

The plaintiff does not have the unduly heavy burden of proving that it was foreseeable that he or she would suffer his or her particular injury from use of the defendant's product. Defendant need not have foreseen the precise nature or consequences of the risk, or the exact injury.[1] It is liable if, in the exercise of reasonable care, it should have foreseen that *some* serious risk or danger was attendant upon the marketing or use of its product.[2]

In the *Poplar* case, the Court of Appeals held that the defendant's liability for negligence turns upon "the foreseeability of *any* harm resulting from the careless conduct" and not upon the foreseeability of the *exact nature of the accident or injury which does, in fact, ensue* (emphasis added).[3] In the *Beckusen* case, the Court of Appeals made it clear that a manufacturer is liable for failure to warn of foreseeable danger even if the actual injury does not occur in the precise manner which could or should have been foreseen.[4]

§ 27.36

1. *See* Beckhusen v. E.P. Lawson Co., 9 N.Y.2d 726, 214 N.Y.S.2d 342, 174 N.E.2d 327, reversing 9 A.D.2d 536, 196 N.Y.S.2d 531 (1960); Schubart v. Hotel Astor, 168 Misc. 431, 5 N.Y.S.2d 203, aff'd 255 App. Div. 1012, 8 N.Y.S.2d 567, aff'd 281 N.Y. 597, 22 N.E.2d 167(1939); Poplar v. Bourjois, 298 N.Y. 62, 80 N.E.2d 334 (1948).

2. Butler v. Sonneborn Sons, Inc., 296 F.2d 623 (2d Cir.1961).

3. Poplar v. Bourjois, 298 N.Y. at 67, 80 N.E.2d at 336.

4. 9 N.Y.2d at 726, 214 N.Y.S.2d at 342,

§ 27.36   PRODUCTS LIABILITY   Ch. 27

In *Butler v. L. Sonneborn Sons, Inc.*[5] the court, in confirming that a manufacturer need not have foreseen the exact manner in which the injury occurred to be held liable, stated "[e]ven slight foreseeability" of injury, in whatever manner, may warrant a conclusion by the jury that prudence required the manufacturer to give appropriate warnings.[6]

In *Del Cid v. Beloit Corp.*,[7] the plaintiff sustained severe workplace injuries when his right leg was crushed while a machine manufactured by the defendant was cycling. The plaintiff alleged that the machine was defectively designed in that it was not equipped with an appropriate device to guard a pinch or shear point at the top of the machine. The manufacturer claimed that its machine was manufactured in full compliance with all applicable industry safety standards and that the actions of the plaintiff which caused the injury—climbing on top of the operating machine to reposition an entangled chain hoist—were not foreseeable. In denying the defendants' motion to set aside the verdict in favor of the plaintiff, the Eastern District Court applied New York law, and held:

> As with proximate cause, negligence and foreseeability normally are questions of fact, and are rarely suitable for determination as a matter of law. See, e.g., *Derdiarian v. Felix Construction Corp.*, 51 N.Y.2d 308, 314–15, 414 N.E.2d 666, 670, 434 N.Y.S.2d 166, 169 (1980); *Rotz v. City of New York*, 143 A.D.2d 301, 304, 532 N.Y.S.2d 245, 247 (1st Dep't 1988).[8]

The court further explained:

> [A]lthough foreseeability is an issue in design defect cases, all that is required is the foreseeability of the general type of risk to which the user was exposed; the precise misuse of the product need not have been foreseen. *Parsons, supra*, 929 F.2d at 905; *Grant v. Westinghouse Electric Corp.*, 877 F.Supp. 806, 818–19 (E.D.N.Y.1995); *Derdiarian, supra*.[9]

Library References:

West's Key No. Digests, Products Liability ⟸1, 15.

§ 27.37   Discovery Issues

Discovery in products liability actions is quite broad. Ordinary limitations on the production of information of other accidents or alternative methods of design are not available. While it may be burdensome for a defendant to search its offices and records for information regarding other incidents involving the same model as the one that caused the

174 N.E.2d at 327.
5.   296 F.2d 623 (2d Cir.1961).
6.   296 F.2d at 626 (2d Cir.1961).
7.   901 F.Supp. 539 (E.D.N.Y.1995).
8.   901 F.Supp. at 549–50.
9.   901 F.Supp. at 550.

plaintiff's injuries, the courts generally do not tolerate such an excuse.[1] Broad disclosure concerning testing and safety design is available to a plaintiff.[2] Evidence of design alternatives is also discoverable.[3]

In addressing discovery issues, courts refer to the broad evidentiary rules which permit the admissibility of evidence. As one appellate court noted:

> Evidence of design modifications are admissible to show what other designs were feasible at the time of manufacture.[4]

Thorough discovery in a products liability case is crucial. Information regarding testing, design, feasibility of alternative designs, and defendant's knowledge of the hazards inherent in its product is readily available through the liberal discovery afforded under the Federal Rules of Civil Procedure and the CPLR. As long as the plaintiff's claim relates to the tangible and/or continual defect or breach of duty by the defendant in the design or manufacture of the subject product, discovery of other claims is readily available. If resistance is met to such discovery, plaintiff's counsel should point out that the issue is not whether such information is admissible but whether it may lead to relevant evidence.[5]

In *Mendelowitz v. Xerox Corp.*,[6] the plaintiff claimed that his cancer was caused by the inhalation of asbestos dust emanating from the defendant's copying machines. The court permitted the plaintiff discovery of a list of all health claims by defendant's workers in which adverse health effects were reported as a result of exposure to asbestos used in the manufacturing of defendant's copying machines. The defendant's argument that the plaintiff should be limited to information about lawsuits involving the same models of copiers that had been used by the plaintiff was rejected by the First Department, which held:

> The weight to be given evidence of other injuries or deaths on the issues of notice and causation, and indeed the very admissibility of such evidence for whatever purpose plaintiff may want it introduced, are not of concern in the context of disclosure. At this juncture, the concern is with the usefulness and reasonableness of the list plaintiff asks defendant to compile in aiding preparation for trial (*Allen v.*

§ 27.37

1. Parry v. Pyramid Crossgates Co., 158 A.D.2d 787, 551 N.Y.S.2d 77 (3d Dep't 1990).

2. Valet v. American Motors, Inc., 105 A.D.2d 645, 481 N.Y.S.2d 364 (1st Dep't 1984).

3. Baleno v. Jacuzzi Research, Inc., 93 A.D.2d 982, 461 N.Y.S.2d 659, 660 (4th Dep't 1983).

4. *Id.*, citing Rainbow v. Elia Bldg. Co., 79 A.D.2d 287, 436 N.Y.S.2d 480, aff'd 56 N.Y.2d 550, 449 N.Y.S.2d 967, 434 N.E.2d 1345 (1982); Lancaster Silo & Block Co. v. Northern Propane Gas Co., Inc., 75 A.D.2d 55, 427 N.Y.S.2d 1009 (4th Dep't 1980); Bolm v. Triumph Corp., 71 A.D.2d 429, 422 N.Y.S.2d 969 (4th Dep't 1979), mot. for lv. to app. dsmd. , 50 N.Y.2d 801, 430 N.Y.S.2d 1025, 407 N.E.2d 1353; *cf.* Opera v. Hyva, Inc., 86 A.D.2d 373, 377, 450 N.Y.S.2d 615, 618 (4th Dep't 1982).

5. Wiseman v. American Motors Sales Corp., 103 A.D.2d 230, 479 N.Y.S.2d 528 (2d Dep't 1984).

6. 169 A.D.2d 300, 573 N.Y.S.2d 548 (1st Dep't 1991).

§ 27.37   PRODUCTS LIABILITY   Ch. 27

Crowell–Collier Publishing Co., 21 N.Y.2d 403, 406–407, 288 N.Y.S.2d 449, 235 N.E.2d 430); with that in mind, we think the list should be supplied if only because it could be useful in facilitating communication among persons who have good reason to think of themselves as similarly situated.

In another case, the plaintiff sought information with regard to other accidents involving a ten-inch radial arm saw which did not contain a lower blade guard as part of its equipment.[7] The defendant manufacturer was required to produce information with regard to various other models of its ten-inch radial-arm saw and such disclosure was not limited to only those accidents, complaints or lawsuits involving the type of accident (a particular rip cut) in which the plaintiff was injured. Here, broad discovery was available as a result of the broadness of the pleadings. The plaintiff had not confined himself to an issue of whether the absence of a blade guard rendered the machine dangerous, so that the court found all other accidents pertinent, regardless of the particular task being performed with the defendant's saws.

During the discovery phase of the case, the plaintiff is entitled to obtain information relevant to complaints, both before and after the injury by the product at issue. Excluding production of evidence merely because it post dates the accident or the date of manufacture of the product gives, as one court put it, "undue and artificial significance to an essentially arbitrary line of demarkation."[8]

Yet quite often defendants seek to cut off discovery at the date the plaintiff was injured; the argument is advanced that injuries occurring after plaintiff's accident are not relevant and therefore should not be disclosed. However, such information is certainly discoverable and in fact may be relevant to establish causation and/or to rebut the defendant's claim that the plaintiff could not have been injured by the defendant's product in the manner claimed by the plaintiff.[9]

In *Dollar v. Long Mfg. N.C., Inc.*,[10] the plaintiff's decedent was killed when he was crushed between a control panel of a backhoe and the roll bar canopy of a tractor. Critical to the case was the question of what caused the backhoe to come off the ground resulting in the operator being crushed between the control panel and the roll bar. In his

---

7. McKeon v. Sears, Roebuck & Co., 190 A.D.2d 577, 593 N.Y.S.2d 519 (1st Dep't 1993).

8. Jackson v. Firestone Tire & Rubber Co., 779 F.2d 1047, 1063 (5th Cir.1986).

9. PRACTICE POINTER: A notice for discovery and inspection or a notice to produce may be used to demand information about the defendant's product—such as adverse reaction reports, other incidents and/or modifications or alterations to the product and/or its warnings. The time frame of counsel's request should include a reasonable period of time preceding the accident (five or ten years) up to the date of the demand. It should also be stated in the notice that this discovery request is a continuing one, to ensure that plaintiff will be provided with information that comes into the defendant's hands after the demand is initially responded to.

10. 561 F.2d 613 (5th Cir.1977).

interrogatories, the plaintiff sought to obtain the identity of other persons who had filed a claim for injuries caused by the backhoe. In response, the defendant limited its answer to the date of plaintiff's accident, thereby concealing that at least two other persons had been injured after the date of plaintiff's accident and prior to the date of plaintiff's interrogatory responses. In strong language the Fifth Circuit held:

> "...we start with the proposition that discovery '...together with pretrial procedures make a trial less a game of blind man's bluff and more a fair contest with the basic issues and facts disclosed to the fullest practicable extent.'"[11]

Finding the defendant's interrogatory response "evasive as well as incomplete,"[12] the court held that such information was highly relevant with respect to the issues of causation even though it could not be used to show the defendant's prior knowledge or notice of a defect.[13]

Library References:

West's Key No. Digests, Federal Civil Procedure ⚖1261–1686; Pretrial Procedure ⚖11–486.

§ 27.38 Discovery Issues—Confidentiality Orders or Stipulations

Very often the manufacturer or distributor will argue that before their disclosure of information, the plaintiff should sign a stipulation of confidentiality. The usual grounds for such contention is that trade secrets could be revealed.[1] The initial showing of the need for confidentiality must be made by the party seeking it and the mere statement of its attorney is usually insufficient.[2] Confidential proprietary information has been defined as trade secrets, business secrets, secret processes or research.[3]

Stipulations of confidentiality can be resisted by reference to those lines of cases which provide that the distribution of a product containing a trade secret constitutes a public disclosure thereby defeating any claim of confidentiality where the nature of the trade secret may be ascertain-

---

11. 561 F.2d at 616.
12. 561 F.2d at 617.
13. **PRACTICE POINTER:** Plaintiff's counsel should use this logic to push for full discovery.

§ 27.38

1. Snyder v. Parke, Davis & Co., 56 A.D.2d 536, 391 N.Y.S.2d 579 (1st Dep't 1977). The court determined that confidentiality was not necessary to protect "trade or business secrets, secret processes or research or any other confidential material."

2. Bristol, Litynski, Wojcik v. Town of Queensbury, 166 A.D.2d 772, 562 N.Y.S.2d 976 (3d Dep't 1990).

3. *See* Ball Memorial Hospital, Inc. v. Mutual Hospital Ins., Inc., 784 F.2d 1325, 1346, (7th Cir.1986), rehearing denied 788 F.2d 1223; Snyder v. Parke, Davis & Co., 56 A.D.2d 536, 391 N.Y.S.2d 579 (1st Dep't 1977).

able by inspection of the product.[4] Quite often, however, engaging in time consuming litigation on the issue of confidentiality will not serve the best interests of the plaintiff's case.

Nevertheless, and apparently in recognition of those decisions finding that stipulations of confidentiality and the sealing of court records can wrongly chill the sharing of information vital to other people who may have been injured by the same product,[5] rules and regulations addressed to this very issue have recently been enacted. The sealing of court records is now the subject of a rule in the Uniform Rules of Trial Courts in the State of New York.[6] The purpose of the rule is to make it clear that not only should the interests of the litigants be taken into account—since the defendants will always claim this information is confidential and plaintiff is usually unable to advance any interest in not having the information kept confidential—but the interests of the public must be taken into account as well.

Thus, in a case where there is a question of a defective product such as the Dalkon Shield, breast implants or a defective automobile, the defendant must not be permitted to have the records sealed, for that would require successive plaintiffs with similar claims to start discovery anew. Any court that does seal a file should limit the "sealing" to permit the information to be shown to any other plaintiff's attorney and expert so that the defendants cannot use the claim of confidentiality as a means of preventing the plaintiffs' lawyers from sharing information.[7]

Library References:

West's Key No. Digests, Federal Civil Procedure ⊙⇒1355; Pretrial Procedure ⊙⇒41.

§ 27.39 Statute of Limitations

Prior to 1986, it was clearly the law in New York that a person exposed to a hazardous substance, drug or product causing harm, whether immediately or many years later, was subject to a three year Statute of Limitations which would commence to run from the date of plaintiff's exposure.[1] The result was that in many cases, plaintiff's time to file suit expired before plaintiff even knew he/she was injured.[2] Plaintiffs sought to take advantage of the longer Statute of Limitations for contract cases.

4. Midland–Ross Corp. v. Sunbeam Equipment Corp., 316 F.Supp. 171 (W.D.Pa. 1970).

5. United States v. Hooker Chemicals & Plastics Corp., 90 F.R.D. 421, 426 (W.D.N.Y.1981).

6. 22 NYCRR § 216.1.

7. *See Public Access to Court Records in Civil Proceedings: The New York Approach,* 54 Albany L.Rev. 93 (1989).

§ 27.39

1. CPLR 214.

2. Schwartz v. Heyden Newport Chemical Corp., 12 N.Y.2d 212, 237 N.Y.S.2d 714, 188 N.E.2d 142 (1963); Lindsey v. A.H. Robins Co., 91 A.D.2d 150, 458 N.Y.S.2d 602 (2d Dep't 1983).

However, the Court of Appeals in *Victorson v. Bock Laundry Mach. Co.*[3] applied the three year period of limitations for personal injury and property damage, which ran from the date of the injury, rather than the six year contract Statute of Limitations which ran from the date of sale.[4]

Recognizing the difficulty in applying the usual three year Statute of Limitations for personal injury actions contained in CPLR 214, the Legislature determined to enact certain exceptions. CPLR 214–b was enacted in 1982 to protect Vietnam veterans exposed to Agent Orange; the period of limitations pursuant to this statute was made to run from the date of discovery of the injury. In 1986, CPLR 214–c was enacted to protect people exposed to certain toxic substances or drugs such as DES and asbestos. That statute was then amended in 1992 to add the word "implantation" in order to dispel any doubt that the date-of-discovery rule would apply to breast implant cases.[5]

Library References:

West's Key No. Digests, Limitation of Actions ⚙=30–32, 55.

§ 27.40 Intervening Acts of Negligence—Plaintiff's Misuse of the Product

Many times an injury results when the manufacturer's product is misused. A defendant will use this circumstance to argue that the misuse was not foreseeable or that it constituted an intervening act which insulates it from liability. In *Derdiarian v. Felix Contr. Corp.*[1] the Court of Appeals set forth a very stringent standard with regard to what type of intervening conduct or act would relieve another from responsibility. In that case, an automobile driven by an epileptic motorist, who had failed to take medication, crashed into an excavation site, striking a laborer who was then splattered by boiling liquid from a kettle. In finding that the conduct of the motorist did not automatically preclude a

---

3. 37 N.Y.2d 395, 373 N.Y.S.2d 39, 335 N.E.2d 275 (1975).

4. The Victorson Court expressly overruled its earlier determination in Mendel v. Pittsburgh Plate Glass Company, 25 N.Y.2d 340, 305 N.Y.S.2d 490, 253 N.E.2d 207 (1969) where the Court of Appeals had held that the six year Statute of Limitations for contract actions applied to a claim for injuries caused by a faulty door installed by the defendant. Determining that such Statute of Limitations ran from the date of the sale, the Mendel Court believed that applying the negligence period of limitations which ran from the date of injury would expose the manufacturer to liability indefinitely. However, in Denny v. Ford Motor Co., 87 N.Y.2d 248, 639 N.Y.S.2d 250, 662 N.E.2d 730 (1995) the New York Court of Appeals has clarified the existence of a separate breach of warranty claim which is contractually and UCC based. It seems that Victorson's imposition of a three year negligence Statute of Limitations to all products liability claims may now be modified so that a four year warranty or six year contract Statute of Limitation will apply to the cause of action sounding in express or implied warranty.

5. *See also*, Kreindler, Rodriguez, *et al.*, *New York Law of Torts* (West 1997) §§ 19.1–19.38.

§ 27.40

1. 51 N.Y.2d 308, 434 N.Y.S.2d 166, 414 N.E.2d 666 (1980).

finding of liability for the general contractor's failure to provide safety precautions at the worksite, the Court of Appeals held:

> Where the acts of a third person intervene between the defendant's conduct and the plaintiff's injury, the causal connection is not automatically severed. In such a case, liability turns upon whether the intervening act is a normal or foreseeable consequence of the situation created by the defendant's negligence. (citations omitted) If the intervening act is extraordinary under circumstances, not foreseeable in the normal course of events, or independent of or far removed from the defendant's conduct, it may well be a superseding act which breaks the causal nexus. (citations omitted) Because questions concerning what is foreseeable and what is normal may be the subject of varying inferences, as is the question of negligence itself, these issues generally are for the fact finder to resolve.[2]

In another case, *Del Cid v. Beloit Corp.*,[3] decided under New York law the court recognized:

> Although the foreseeability of the misuse of a product is relevant to the issue of whether the manufacturer adequately designed the product to guard against the risk, the precise chain of events preceding the misuse need not have been foreseen to require the manufacturer to guard against the consequence of that misuse. *Parsons, supra*, 929 F.2d at 905–06. Rather, "foreseeability includes the probability of the occurrence of a general type of risk involving the loss, rather than the probability of the occurrence of the precise chain of events preceding the loss ..." *Tucci v. Bossert*, 53 A.D.2d 291, 293, 385 N.Y.S.2d 328, 331 (2d Dep't 1976).[4]

Establishing that an intervening cause severs the liability of the manufacturer for placing a defective product into the market place is a difficult burden to meet. For instance, in a case where an infant sustained severe injuries when he opened the door of a front loading washing machine and thrust his hand inside while the machine was in a spin cycle, the appellate division affirmed the trial court's refusal to charge the jury on intervening or superseding cause since the plaintiff's theory of liability included a claim that the machine was defective in that it was not equipped with an interlock mechanism which would have prevented the door from opening while the machine's drum was spinning.[5]

Thus, if the misuse of the product is foreseeable, a defendant manufacturer may not even be entitled to present to the jury its defense

---

2. 51 N.Y.2d at 315, 434 N.Y.S.2d at 169–70.

3. 901 F.Supp. 539 (E.D.N.Y.1995).

4. 901 F.Supp. at 544–45.

5. Martinez v. Gouverneur Gardens Housing, 184 A.D.2d 264, 585 N.Y.S.2d 23 (1st Dep't 1992).

of intervening cause or superseding events.[6] In assessing the misuse of the product, consideration should be given not only to the nature of the misuse but to the person who has misused the product. A manufacturer of products to be used by children is charged with the duty to foresee that the toy or product, when "placed in the hands of inexperienced children who may seek to enlarge their knowledge by experimentation of various and sometimes unexpected character . . . may be a source of peril . . . ."[7] Additionally, the manufacturer's own conduct in promoting its product may either directly or indirectly encourage the product to be misused in a dangerous manner. In one case,[8] a toy was marketed to conform with a character on an animated cartoon series regularly seen on television. This character fought his enemies with a star shaped weapon with eight sharp points. An infant playing with a toy marketed to resemble this character was injured when a detachable piece of the toy (the star shaped weapon) struck her in the eye. The appellate division in sustaining the denial of summary judgment rejected the manufacturer's argument that it could not be held liable since its product conformed to certain federal toy safety regulations and because the type of harm that occurred was an "obvious risk" that did not require any special warning. As to the first contention, the appellate division noted that mere compliance with a safety statute, while constituting some evidence of due care, does not automatically preclude a finding of negligence.[9] As to the obvious risk argument, the appellate division held:

> Under New York Law . . . the extent to which a risk may be deemed to have been obvious is simply another factor in determining the degree of reasonable care exercised by the parties and, as such, must be reserved for the trier of the facts.[10]

The finding of the appellate division is consistent with the principle that in products liability cases, as in any negligence case, the fact that a plaintiff may have been partially at fault does not bar recovery, but rather affects the amount of recovery pursuant to the jury's apportionment of fault.[11]

Library References:

West's Key No. Digests, Products Liability ⚖15, 27.

6. *See* Sutherland v. Elpower Corp., 923 F.2d 1285 (8th Cir.1991) (battery for child's rideable toy exploded when charged with an automobile type battery charger).

7. Crist v. Art Metal Works, 230 App. Div. 114, 243 N.Y.S. 496, 499 (1st Dep't 1930), aff'd 255 N.Y. 624, 175 N.E. 341 (1931).

8. Lugo by Lopez v. LJN Toys, Ltd., 146 A.D.2d 168, 539 N.Y.S.2d 922, 924 (1st Dep't 1989).

9. 146 A.D.2d at 170, 539 N.Y.S.2d at 924 citing Sherman v. M. Lowenstein & Sons, Inc., 28 A.D.2d 922, 282 N.Y.S.2d 142 (1967).

10. 146 A.D.2d at 170, 539 N.Y.S.2d at 924.

11. CPLR Art. 14–A.

§ 27.41 Intervening Acts of Negligence—Alteration of the Product After It Has Left the Hands of the Manufacturer

The general rule is that the manufacturer of a product cannot be held liable if there is a substantial modification or alteration of the product after it leaves the possession and control of the manufacturer, which modification is shown to be the cause of plaintiff's injury.[1] For instance, in *Lovelace v. Ametek, Inc.*,[2] the plaintiff was injured when he was dragged into a machine used to extract water from fabric by centrifugal force. When the machine left the manufacturer, it was equipped with three safety devices, one of which was a locking mechanism which prevented the opening of the machine while the drum was spinning. At the time of the plaintiff's injury, none of the three safety devices were operative; it was undisputed that had these features been working, the accident would not have occurred. The evidence indicated that someone other than the manufacturer had removed the machine's protective covers and rotated an interference rod, thus "forestalling [the] workability of the safety feature requiring the covers to be closed before the extractor started...."[3] Having been presented with evidence from the manufacturer's director for products reliability analysis that the repositioning of the safety feature was not an "easy feat," the appellate division held:

> Even if such tampering and defeat of the extractor's protective devices was foreseeable during the 60-year interval between its manufacture and the accident, the responsibility for injuries therefrom would not fall on defendant.[4]

However, if a plaintiff can establish that the modification or alteration was foreseeable by the manufacturer, then liability will still be imposed against that manufacturer. In *Lopez v. Precision Papers, Inc.*,[5] the plaintiff was injured on the job while operating a forklift from which an overhead safety guard had been removed. In finding that such a modification was not the type of alteration which would absolve the manufacturer from liability, the *Lopez* Court held:

> Because of the ease with which the overhead guard could be removed and the forklift's added versatility when operated without the guard, there is a legitimate jury question as to the scope of the forklift's intended purposes. (citations omitted)[6]

§ 27.41

1. Robinson v. Reed–Prentice Div. of Package Mach. Co., 49 N.Y.2d 471, 479, 426 N.Y.S.2d 717, 720, 403 N.E.2d 440 (1980).

2. 111 A.D.2d 953, 490 N.Y.S.2d 49 (3d Dep't 1985).

3. 111 A.D.2d at 954, 490 N.Y.S.2d at 51.

4. 111 A.D.2d at 954, 490 N.Y.S.2d at 51.

5. 107 A.D.2d 667, 484 N.Y.S.2d 585 (2d Dep't 1985).

6. 107 A.D.2d at 668, 484 N.Y.S.2d at 587.

Thus, if the modification could be easily accomplished and if it was foreseeable that the product would be modified or used without a particular safety feature, the manufacturer can still be held responsible.

Library References:
West's Key No. Digests, Products Liability ⚖15, 16.

§ 27.42 Preemption of Private Claims

The typical products liability claim raises questions with regard to the adequacy of the manufacturer's warnings and whether the subject product was sufficiently tested prior to being marketed. The defendant will usually urge that its product has complied with all federal regulations. In many products liability cases governmental regulations or standards address the product in question. Obviously, whether such standards are applicable and whether defendants have complied with them are issues that have a significant impact on the outcome of each case. The issue of whether the product violated or complied with a particular standard is one to be resolved by the jury. Expert testimony containing conclusions as to whether there was compliance is not permitted.[1]

Library References:
West's Key No. Digests, States ⚖18.65.

§ 27.43 Preemption of Private Claims—Old Rule

Traditionally, the fact that a manufacturer had complied with government regulations could not exculpate it from liability in a negligence and strict liability case since government rules set forth only minimal protective measures.[1] In *Sherman v. Lowenstein*, the plaintiff was injured by a flammable pajama and the defendant sought to relieve itself of liability by urging that it had complied with flammability testing as had been prescribed by law. In rejecting this contention, the Appellate Division, Second Department held:

> ... [I]n reversing the judgment, we reject defendant Lowenstein's argument that it cannot be held liable because in manufacturing the fabric used in making the pajamas, it complied with the flammabili-

---

§ 27.42

1. *See* United States v. Bilzerian, 926 F.2d 1285, 1294–95 (2d Cir.1991); Payne v. A.O. Smith Corp., 627 F.Supp. 226, 228 (S.D.Ohio 1985); Rodriguez v. New York City Hous. Auth., 209 A.D.2d 260, 618 N.Y.S.2d 352, 353 (1st Dep't 1994); Ross v. Manhattan Chelsea Associates, 194 A.D.2d 332, 598 N.Y.S.2d 502 (1st Dep't 1993). *See also See also*, Kreindler, Rodriguez, *et al.*, *New York Law of Torts* (West 1997) § 19.50.; Barker and Alexander, *Evidence in New York State and Federal Courts* (West 1996) Ch. 7 "Opinions and Expert Testimony."

§ 27.43

1. Sherman v. Lowenstein, 28 A.D.2d 922, 282 N.Y.S.2d 142 (2d Dep't 1967); Dorsey v. Honda, 655 F.2d 650 (5th Cir.1981); Hubbard–Hall Chem. Co. v. Silverman, 340 F.2d 402 (1st Cir.1965).

§ 27.43 PRODUCTS LIABILITY Ch. 27

ty-testing method prescribed by law (Tit. 15 U.S.C. § 1191; General Business Law, § 502). While a defendant's compliance with a statute 'is some evidence of the exercise of due care' (*Phillips v. Roux Labs.*, 286 App.Div. 549, 551, 145 N.Y.S.2d 449, 451), it does not preclude a conclusion that he was negligent (see 2 Harper & James The Law of Torts, § 17.6, p.1014 (1956)).[2]

Under the old rule, if one violated the statutes and regulations governing the manufacture of a product and the nature and scope of the requisite warnings, such conduct constituted negligence *per se*.[3] In fact, some courts would even allow punitive damages to be awarded, even where there was compliance with a government standard, if it was shown that the manufacturer knew the standard was inadequate and willfully failed to correct the dangerous condition.[4]

Library References:
West's Key No. Digests, Products Liability ⚖71; States ⚖18.65.

§ 27.44 Preemption of Private Claims—New Rule

All of that has now changed. Under the doctrine of Federal Preemption, which has in large part been accepted by the courts, defense counsel have successfully taken the position that so long as there is compliance with the federal standard, the plaintiff and the public can and should expect nothing more than what the statute or regulation requires. This defense is premised upon the argument that a manufacturer who does what the statute requires should be immunized from liability and should not be subjected to a private state tort claim brought by a person injured by the defendant's product.[1]

§ 27.45 Preemption of Private Claims—National Traffic & Motor Vehicle Safety Act and Its Savings Clause

Sometimes an act or federal standard contains language, known as a savings clause, providing that compliance with the act or standard does not preempt a common law tort claim.[1] Despite this type of provision in the National Traffic & Motor Vehicle Safety Act, defendant manufacturers have sought to convince the courts that such a savings clause in the

2. 28 A.D.2d at ___, 282 N.Y.S.2d at 143–44.
3. Martin v. Herzog, 228 N.Y. 164, 126 N.E. 814 (1920).
4. Dorsey v. Honda, 655 F.2d 650 (5th Cir.1981).

§ 27.44
1. Worm v. American Cyanamid, 970 F.2d 1301 (4th Cir.1992); Papas v. Upjohn Co., 926 F.2d 1019 (11th Cir.1991); Arkansas-Platte & Gulf Partnership v. Van Waters & Rogers, Inc., 959 F.2d 158 (10th Cir.1992); Warner v. American Fluoride, 204 A.D.2d 1, 616 N.Y.S.2d 534 (2d Dep't 1994). Kreindler, Rodriguez, et al., *New York Law of Torts* (West 1997) §§ 16.81–16.86.

§ 27.45
1. *See, e.g.*, National Traffic & Motor Vehicle Safety Act, 15 U.S.C.A. § 1397(c).

§ 27.47 PRODUCTS LIABILITY

FIFRA product (such as an insecticide) upon either... at large, the public or a private person. According... FIFRA:

> ... acts to ensure that the States could continue to... sales even where, such as with regard to the banning... products, a narrow preemptive overlap might occur. As... discussion of express preemption, it is doubtful that Co... tended to exclude localities from the scope of § 136v(a)'s au... tion, but however this may be, the type of local regulation at... here would not fall within any impliedly preempted field.[8]

The *Wisconsin* decision on the non-preemptive effect of FIFRA cannot be clearer. It stated:

> As we have made plain, the statute does not expressly or impliedly preclude regulatory action by political subdivisions with regard to local use.[9]

In another situation it was determined that federal regulations did not preempt review of a state statute addressing the same labeling that was addressed by FIFRA. In *New York State Pesticide Coalition v. Jorling*,[10] Judge Kaufman, writing for the bench, held that a New York State statutory regulations,[11] which obligated pesticide applicators to take certain steps to warn the general public, did not constitute "labeling" of a pesticide so that it could not be construed to conflict with and violate the "preemption" provision of FIFRA. The court specifically held that the issue of whether a member of the public should be notified of the dangers of a FIFRA pesticide was a proper subject for action by a state, and was not preempted by FIFRA labeling requirements. The court rejected the preemption argument that the additional requirements of the New York statute amounted to an additional "labeling" precluded by FIFRA.[12] The court carefully distinguished the labeling obligation from the notification obligation, the latter of which is designed to insure that members of the public are warned of the dangers associated with the use of the product. While labeling requirements insured a proper warning, notification requirements insured that the proper warning would be disseminated among those who might come into contact with the product. The court's careful analysis is worth repeating:

> The appellants claim that New York's notification provisions constitute 'labeling' since those provisions require additional 'written, printed or graphic matter' which 'accompan[ies] the pesticide or device at anytime.' Because the notification materials are present in some spatial and temporal proximity to the applied pesticide, it is asserted they 'accompany' it. But this definition is rather strained.

---

8. 501 U.S. at 614, 111 S.Ct. at 2486.
9. 501 U.S. at 615, 111 S.Ct. at 2487.
10. 874 F.2d 115 (2d Cir.1989).
11. 6 NYCRR Pt. 325 (1987); ECL § 33–1001(1).
12. 874 F.2d at 120.

Ch. 27 PREEMPTION OF PRIVATE CLAIMS § 27.46

Act does not mean what it says, and that so long as the manufacturer complies with the federal minimum standards, it need do no more to be sufficiently protected from liability.

In *Myrick v. Freuhauf*,[2] an important case originating in the district court in Georgia, defense counsel had persuaded the district court that although the subject tractor-trailers did not have anti-lock brakes (which were not specifically required by the federal act), and although the act specifically provided that compliance with it would not prevent a person from seeking to recover under common law standards, the plaintiffs were preempted from claiming that the absence of anti-lock brakes caused the trucks to go out of control and seriously injure them. The Eleventh Circuit Court reversed, and the United States Supreme Court affirmed that determination.[3] The Eleventh Circuit, as affirmed by the United States Supreme Court, found that since the National Traffic & Motor Vehicle Safety Act contained a specific provision that compliance with the federal safety standards does not exempt or do away with a common law claim for negligence,[4] there should be no preemption as was made clear by the United States Supreme Court in *Cipollone v. Liggett Group, Inc.*[5]

Library References:

West's Key No. Digests, Products Liability ⇔35–40; States ⇔18.65.

§ 27.46 Preemption of Private Claims—Public Health Cigarette Labeling & Advertising Act of 1965 and the Public Health Cigarette Smoking Act of 1969—The *Cipollone* Decision

In *Cipollone v. Liggett Group, Inc.*,[1] the United States Supreme Court was called upon to determine whether state tort claims were preempted under the Public Health Cigarette Labeling and Advertising Act ("1965 Act") and the Public Health Cigarette Smoking Act of 1969 ("1969 Act"). Section 5 of the 1965 Act, captioned "Pre-emption" provided:

(a) No statement relating to smoking and health, other than the statement required by section 4 of this Act, shall be required on any

---

2. 795 F.Supp. 1139 (N.D.Ga.1992), rev'd 13 F.3d 1516 (11th Cir.1994), reh. en banc den. 24 F.3d 256 (11th Cir.1994), aff'd Freightliner v. Myrick, 514 U.S. 280, 115 S.Ct. 1483, 131 L.Ed.2d 385 (1995).

3. 13 F.3d 1516 (11th Cir.1994), reh. en banc den. 24 F.3d 256 (11th Cir.1994), aff'd Freightliner v. Myrick, 514 U.S. 280, 115 S.Ct. 1483, 131 L.Ed.2d 385 (1995).

4. 15 U.S.C.A. 1397(k).

5. 505 U.S. 504, 112 S.Ct. 2608, 120 L.Ed.2d 407 (1992) (discussed in this section).

§ 27.46

1. 505 U.S. 504, 112 S.Ct. 2608, 120 L.Ed.2d 407 (1992).

§ 27.46 PRODUCTS LIABILITY Ch. 27

cigarette package.[2]

(b) No statement relating to smoking and health shall be required in the advertising of any cigarette the packages of which are labeled in conformity with the provisions of this Act.[3]

The 1969 Act not only strengthened the warning but also revised Section 5(b) to read:

(b) No requirement or prohibition based on smoking and health shall be imposed under State law with respect to the advertising or promotion of any cigarettes the packages of which are labeled in conformity with the provisions of this Act.[4]

In distinguishing the provisions of each act and scrutinizing the very language used, the *Cipollone* Court found that Section 5 of the 1969 Act preempted state tort failure to warn claims while Section 5 of the 1965 Act did not.[5] In *Cipollone*[6] the United States Supreme Court made it clear that a common law claim would only be preempted if there was a specific Congressional intent to preempt; the issue of whether such a claim was preempted was to be narrowly construed. The Supreme Court held that since there were specific warnings required by the Act,[7] the plaintiff's claim with regard to those warnings would be preempted since in order to prove them, the plaintiff would have to rely upon a state law requirement or prohibition which was additional to or different from what was required under the Act.[8] However, the Supreme Court quite clearly stated that the Act *does not preempt* plaintiff's claims that rely upon the cigarette company's *"testing or research practices or other acts unrelated to advertising or promotion."*[9]

Library References:

West's Key No. Digests, States ⚖18.65.

§ 27.47 Preemption of Private Claims—Federal Insecticide, Fungicide and Rodenticide Act (FIFRA) and Its Impact on Labeling Requirements

To help convince a court reviewing a preemption issue, to allow the action to proceed, it would be wise for plaintiff's counsel to cite *Ferebee*

---

2. Section 4 of the 1965 Act provided: "Caution: Cigarette Smoking may be Hazardous to Your Health." Cipollone, 60 U.S.L.W. at 4706.

3. 15 U.S.C.A. § 1334(b).

4. Id.

5. 505 U.S. at 513, 112 S.Ct. at 2616.

6. 505 U.S. 504, 112 S.Ct. 2608, 120 L.Ed.2d 407 (1992).

7. 15 U.S.C.A. § 1334.

8. **CAVEAT:** When a statute expressly preempts state authority in a particular area, a reviewing court must narrowly construe its terms to assess the scope of the intended preemption.

9. 505 U.S. at 525, 112 S.Ct. at 2622 (emphasis added).

IMPACT ON LABELING REQUIREMENTS § 27.47

Chevron Chem. Co.,[1] one of the early cases to address the issue of federal preemption as it applied to the labeling requirements for pesticides set forth in the Federal Insecticide, Fungicide and Rodenticide Act ("FIFRA").[2] In that decision, the court presented a very logical reason why a state claim would not undermine FIFRA's purpose:

> [S]tate damages actions of the sort at issue here do not stand as an obstacle to the accomplishment of FIFRA's purposes. Such a conflict would exist only if FIFRA were viewed not as a regulatory statute aimed at protecting citizens from the hazards of modern pesticides, but rather as an affirmative subsidization of the pesticide industry that commanded states to accept the use of EPA-registered pesticides. That interpretation of FIFRA, however, is precluded by both the explicit savings clause at 7 U.S.C. Section 136v(b) and by the entire legislative history of the Act. Of equal importance, federal legislation has traditionally occupied a limited role as the floor of safe conduct; before transforming such legislation into a *ceiling* on the ability of states to protect their citizens, and thereby radically adjusting the historic federal-state balance, *United States v. Bass*, 404 U.S. 336, 349, 92 S.Ct. 515, 523, 30 L.Ed.2d 488 (1971), courts should wait for a clear statement of congressional intent to work such an alteration.[3]

After *Cipollone*, courts have departed from the *Ferebee* logic and have held that FIFRA precludes a private claim.[4] In New York, the Appellate Division, Second Department, dismissed a state tort action finding that the negligence, strict liability and breach of implied warranty claims were expressly preempted by FIFRA since they were dependent upon proof that the manufacturer's labeling and packaging were factors in causing the plaintiff's injuries.[5]

However, not all claims involving products regulated by FIFRA will be preempted.[6]

The United States Supreme Court in *Wisconsin Public Intervenor v. Mortier*,[7] held that FIFRA does not preclude a state (by its legislature or by a court addressing a plaintiff's claim) from considering the effect of a

---

§ 27.47

1. 736 F.2d 1529 (D.C.Cir.1984).
2. 7 U.S.C.A. §§ 135 *et seq.*
3. 736 F.2d at 1542–43.
4. Worm v. American Cyanamid, 970 F.2d 1301 (4th Cir.1992); Papas v. Upjohn Co., 926 F.2d 1019 (11th Cir.1991); Arkansas-Platte & Gulf Partnership v. Van Waters & Rogers, Inc., 959 F.2d 158 (10th Cir.1992); Warner v. American Fluoride, 204 A.D.2d 1, 616 N.Y.S.2d 534 (2d Dep't 1994).
5. Warner v. American Fluoride, 204 A.D.2d at 12, 616 N.Y.S.2d at 54; *See* June v. Laris, 205 A.D.2d 166, 618 N.Y.S.2d 138 (3d Dep't 1994).

6. **PRACTICE POINTER:** When facing a defense of preemption, plaintiff's counsel should consider the remedy sought, determine how the injury was caused, and then examine the language of any act or standard that may apply. Each factor has a dispositive role in determining whether preemption is available.

7. 501 U.S. 597, 111 S.Ct. 2476, 115 L.Ed.2d 532 (1991).

'Labeling' is better understood by its relationship, rather than its proximity, to the product.

* * *

By contrast, the target audience of the New York notification program is those innocent members of the general public who may unwittingly happen upon an area where strong poisons are present as well as those who contract to have pesticides applied. The mere proximity of the warning for example, notices posted around enclosed field or copies of the EPA's labeling information provided to the contracting parties, does not transform the admonition into 'labeling' within the meaning of FIFRA § 2(p).[13]

Library References:

West's Key No. Digests, Agriculture ⚖9.13; States ⚖18.65.

§ 27.48 Preemption of Private Claims—Medical Device Amendments to FDA Regulations

In a case *King v. Collagen*,[1] involving the Food and Drug Administration ("FDA") regulations under the Medical Device Amendments ("MDA"),[2] the plaintiff was preempted from bringing a failure to warn claim, as well as a claim that the defendant had fraudulently obtained FDA approval of the subject product and its labeling, even though such approval was based exclusively upon information that had been provided to the FDA by the defendant manufacturer.[3] In *Medtronic, Inc. v. Lohr*,[4] the Supreme Court of the United States determined that the MDA does not preempt private state court design defect claims against a pacemaker manufacturer under either negligence or strict liability theories. The court also determined that the plaintiff could pursue claims based upon defective labeling and marketing.

Library References:

West's Key No. Digests, Products Liability ⚖46; States ⚖18.65.

§ 27.49 Limits on Preemption and Statutory Defenses

A district court in Florida rebuffed an attempt by a manufacturer to avoid and/or minimize its liability by claiming that the plaintiff's employer's statutory violation was the proximate cause of the injury. In *Tierney*

---

13. 874 F.2d at 119(emphasis added).

§ 27.48

1. King v. Collagen, 983 F.2d 1130 (1st Cir.1993). *See* Kreindler, Rodriguez, *et al.*, *New York Law of Torts* (West 1997) § 16.85.

2. 21 U.S.C.A. §§ 360 *et seq.*

3. *See* Becker v. Optical Radiation Corp. 66 F.3d 18 (2d Cir.1995) where the court found that the MDA preempted state tort law claims against the manufacturer of an intraocular lens since that product had to go through a pre-market approval process.

4. __ U.S. __, 116 S.Ct. 2240, 135 L.Ed.2d 700 (1996).

v. Black Brothers Company,[1] the fifteen year old plaintiff was injured while using a glue spreader manufactured and designed by defendant Black Brothers. The complaint alleged that the manufacturer was strictly liable for designing and selling a defective product and that it negligently designed the glue spreader. In response, the defendant, Black Brothers, set forth the affirmative defenses that both the infant plaintiff as well as his employer were comparatively negligent pursuant to a Florida statute which prohibited an employer from employing a person of the plaintiff's age for work with power driven machinery. The court instructed the jury that it could not consider the statute with regard to the negligence of the plaintiff, but it could consider that statute with respect to the negligence, if any, of his employer. The jury returned a verdict finding the defendant manufacturer ten (10%) percent negligent, and his employer comparatively negligent in the amount of ninety (90%) percent. No fault was attributed to the plaintiff.[2]

The court, however, granted plaintiff's motion for judgment as a matter of law, and held the defendant manufacturer liable for the entire damage award. In its analysis, the court determined that any party basing its claim (or defense) upon a violation of a statute must establish that it is a member of the class the statute was designed to protect. Since the subject statute entitled "Hazardous Occupations Prohibited" specifically provided "no minor fifteen years of age or younger ... shall be employed or permitted or suffered to work in any of the following occupations: (a) [Occupations Involving] power-driven machinery.",[3] the court found that the subject statute was designed to protect a particular class of people—workers under a certain age, and not an employer who violated that statute or the manufacturer whose product injured the underage worker. The court buttressed its holding by noting that even if the statute were to be construed as a general one (not designed to protect a particular class) the defendant manufacturer would still not be able to claim the benefit of such statute since there was "a complete paucity of proof relating to a proximate cause between Plaintiff's minority age and his injuries."[4]

In attempting to defeat a preemption claim, plaintiff's counsel may, in appropriate circumstances be in a position to direct the court's attention to the different causes of action asserted, since not all of them may be preempted. For example, in *Jillson v. Vermont Log Bldgs., Inc.*,[5] the plaintiff claimed that her injuries arose from exposure to pentachlo-

§ 27.49

1. 852 F.Supp. 994 (M.D.Fla.1994).
2. 852 F.Supp. at 998.
3. Fla. Stat. Ch.450.061(1)(a)(1993).
4. 852 F.Supp. at 1001.

PRACTICE POINTER: The Tierney logic should be used by plaintiffs' counsel whenever defendants attempt to invoke either statutory or decisional law to limit their liability. If the particular statute or principle is intended to benefit a certain class of which a defendant manufacturer is not a member, then a clear and convincing argument can be made that it is not entitled to benefit from such statute or decision.

5. 857 F.Supp. 985 (D.Mass.1994).

rophenol in her log home which had been supplied by the defendant. Referring to *Cipollone*, the court determined that FIFRA preempted plaintiff's claims for breach of implied warranty and failure to warn but did not preempt plaintiff's claims "with respect to the breach of express warranty ... which does not arise under state law, and the negligent design and manufacture claims, which do not relate to product labeling."[6] In reaching its determination, the *Jillson* court noted:

> The claims of negligent design and manufacture do not relate to labeling or packaging, which is the only realm FIFRA occupies. This court must assume, consistent with *Cipollone*, that matters outside the realm of the statute's express preemption provision are not preempted. __ U.S. at __, 112 S.Ct. at 2618. By recognizing the negligent manufacture and design claims, the state is not requiring information on the Woodlife label "different from" or "in addition to" the information FIFRA requires. The state is simply imposing an affirmative duty on manufacturers of potentially dangerous chemicals to guard against design or manufacturing defects in their chemicals, and to be liable for damages if injuries are caused by such defects. This does not interfere with FIFRA's purpose of requiring uniform national standards of labeling.[7]

In applying the *Cipollone* restrictions and the specific savings provisions of FIFRA, the *Jillson* Court noted:

> By recognizing claims for negligence such as plaintiff's here, the state is requiring only that fungicides such as Woodlife be safely designed. This sort of indirect regulation falls neatly within the FIFRA "savings" clause: "A State may regulate the sale or use of any federally registered pesticide or device in the State, but only if and to the extent the regulation does not permit any sale or use prohibited by this subchapter." 7 U.S.C. § 136v(a). Imposition of a common law duty of care in the design and manufacture of harmful chemical products does not permit any sale or use prohibited by FIFRA; nor does it in any way frustrate the will of Congress. In sum, FIFRA does not preempt Vermont Log's claim for contribution from DAP for negligent design and manufacture.[8]

Library References:

West's Key No. Digests, Products Liability ⚖26, 71; States ⚖18.65.

§ 27.50 Preemption of Private Claims—Validity of the Safety Standard or Regulatory Statute

Some standards or regulations provide administrative means for reviewing their application or validity to those adversely affected by the provision. A party who failed to avail itself of such remedies may be

---

6. 857 F.Supp. at 992.
7. 857 F.Supp. at 991.
8. *Id.*

precluded from subsequently urging the invalidity of such regulation or standard in a private action. In *Contini v. Hyundai Motor Company*,[1] the plaintiffs contended that Hyundai's defective seatbelt design caused one plaintiff to move within the vehicle so as to strike the infant plaintiff's head. Plaintiffs alleged that defendant's seatbelt violated Federal Motor Vehicle Safety Standard ("FMVSS") 209 S4.1(b) (Pelvic Restraint). The *Hyundai* defendants attempted a collateral attack upon the validity of the safety standard, arguing that FMVSS 209 S4.1(b) was a nullity under the enabling statute because it did not have objective testing criteria to determine compliance.

Rejecting the contention on the merits, the court also found that Hyundai was barred under principles of estoppel and waiver from challenging the standard on the eve of trial. Noting that Hyundai could have challenged the validity of the regulation and asked for a ruling during the five years the litigation was pending, the court stated that "principles of estoppel and waiver weigh heavily in favor of rejecting Hyundai's challenge to the standard on the eve of trial."[2] In addition, Hyundai had failed to challenge the standard in an appropriate proceeding such as the one set up by Congress for judicial review of a safety standard whereby a "person adversely affected by an order prescribing a motor vehicle safety standard" may file a petition for judicial review in a Court of Appeals prior to the sixtieth day after such order is issued.[3]

Library References:

West's Key No. Digests, Products Liability ⋘2; States ⋘18.65.

§ 27.51 Preemption of Private Claims—Checklist

If there is concern whether a particular statute or regulation preempts a private tort claim, the following questions should be considered.

1. What language is used in the act or statute, and in particular is there any savings clause which does not exempt a person from liability under common law?[1] (*See* § 27.45)

2. Does the language of the act or its enabling legislation reveal a

---

§ 27.50

1. 876 F.Supp. 540 (S.D.N.Y.1995).
2. 876 F.Supp. at 546. The court expressed its skepticism as to the sincerity of Hyundai's challenge to the validity of the standard. Hyundai and other car manufacturers had been certifying their compliance with the standard for several years without voicing any alleged inability to do so. Its sudden complaint that the standard was invalid was obviously generated by its concern that the jury would find that the vehicle in which the plaintiffs were injured did not comply with the standard.
3. 49 U.S.C.A. § 30161.

§ 27.51

1. Myrick v. Freuhauf Corporation, 13 F.3d 1516 (11th Cir.1994), reh. en banc den. 24 F.3d 256 (11th Cir.1994), aff'd Freightliner v. Myrick, 514 U.S. 280, 115 S.Ct. 1483, 131 L.Ed.2d 385 (1995).

specific legislative intent to preempt?[2] (See § 27.46)

3. What claims are preempted by the act or standard? If the act addresses itself only to labeling or warning requirements, then the failure to test and/or the breach of express warranty claims may not be preempted even though the failure to warn claims are.[3] (See id.)

4. What is the purpose of the statute? If the statute regulates labeling, it may not address a claim addressed to notification requirements[4] or requirements regulating the use of the product.[5] (See § 27.47)

5. Is the party claiming the benefit of the preemptive statute part of the class the statute is designed to protect?[6] (See id.)

6. Is the preemptive statute valid and can its validity, or lack thereof, be challenged in the private state action?[7]

Library References:
West's Key No. Digests, States ⚖18.65.

§ 27.52 Imposing Liability When the Manufacturer of a Fungible or Generic Product Is Unknown (Concert of Action/Market Share Liability)

The person who seeks recompense for injuries sustained by a particular product is usually required to prove that the product which caused harm was one that was manufactured or distributed by the defendant.[1] A market share theory[2] permits a finding of liability and an apportionment of damages in cases where identification of the manufacturer of the subject product is impossible. Such liability is joint, not several, and imposes liability upon a particular defendant manufacturer based upon its share of the national market for that product.[3] Since a plaintiff seeking recovery on a market share basis can only recover from a

---

2. Cipollone v. Liggett Group, Inc., 505 U.S. 504, 112 S.Ct. 2608, 120 L.Ed.2d 407 (1992).

3. 505 U.S. at 525, 112 S.Ct. at 2622; Jillson v. Vermont Bldgs. Inc., 857 F.Supp. 985 (D.Mass.1994). See Wallace v. Parks Corp., 212 A.D.2d 132, 629 N.Y.S.2d 570 (4th Dep't 1995).

4. New York State Pesticide Coalition v. Jorling, 874 F.2d 115 (2d Cir.1989).

5. Wisconsin Public Intervenor v. Mortier, 501 U.S. 597, 111 S.Ct. 2476, 115 L.Ed.2d 532 (1991).

6. Tierney v. Black Brothers Company, 852 F.Supp. 994 (M.D.Fla.1994).

7. Contini v. Hyundai Motor Company, 876 F.Supp. 540 (S.D.N.Y.1995).

§ 27.52

1. Bauer v. Raymark Industries, Inc., 849 F.2d 790, 792–93 (2d Cir.1988); Hymowitz v. Eli Lilly & Co., 73 N.Y.2d 487, 504, 541 N.Y.S.2d 941, 945, 539 N.E.2d 1069, cert. denied 493 U.S. 944, 110 S.Ct. 350, 107 L.Ed.2d 338 (1989).

2. Hymowitz v. Eli Lilly & Co., 73 N.Y.2d 487, 504, 541 N.Y.S.2d 941, 945, 539 N.E.2d 1069, cert. denied 493 U.S. 944, 110 S.Ct. 350, 107 L.Ed.2d 338 (1989).

3. 73 N.Y.2d at 511, 541 N.Y.S.2d at 950, 539 N.E.2d at 1078 (the drug DES used to prevent miscarriages during pregnancy was involved in that case).

§ 27.52   PRODUCTS LIABILITY   Ch. 27

defendant based upon its share of the market, there will not be a full recovery if any one of the participants in the manufacture and distribution of the product is not included in the lawsuit.

Market share liability will only be imposed if the product is fungible or generic; *i.e.* there are no distinguishing features or characteristics (such as pill color or size) that will enable the manufacturer to be identified.[4] While the Court of Appeals in *Hymowitz* specifically limited the application of market share liability to DES cases,[5] a plaintiff who is injured by another product or substance may be able to convince a court to employ a market share theory of liability where the product is fungible, generic and/or incapable of being identified because of the manner in which it was marketed.

A concert of action theory of liability provides another means for obtaining a plaintiff's verdict even though the manufacturer of the product can not be identified. In *Bichler v. Eli Lilly & Co.*,[6] the New York Court of Appeals affirmed a verdict in favor of a plaintiff against a defendant manufacturer on a concert of action theory of liability. In recognizing the viability of such a theory, the Court of Appeals held:

> Concerted action liability rests upon the principle that [a]ll those who, in pursuance of a common plan or design to commit a tortious act, actively take part in it, or further it by cooperation or request, or who lend aid or encouragement to the wrongdoer, or ratify and adopt his acts done for their benefit, are equally liable with him (Prosser, Torts 4th ed., § 46, at p.292; see also, Restatement, Torts 2d § 876). An injured plaintiff may pursue any one joint tort-feasor on a concerted action theory (*see Graphic Arts Mut. Ins. Co. v. Bakers Mut. Ins. Co. of N.Y.*, 45 N.Y.2d 551, 410 N.Y.S.2d 571, 382 N.E.2d 1347). Such tort-feasor may, in turn, seek contribution from others who acted in concert with him *see Dole v. Dow Chem. Co.*, 30 N.Y.2d 143, 331 N.Y.S.2d 382, 282 N.E.2d 288.[7]

The Court of Appeals in *Bichler*, however, did not rule on the validity of such a theory of liability in New York since that issue had not been preserved for appellate review. Though not explicitly rejecting the concert of action theory in New York, the Court of Appeals in *Hymowitz*, in finding that a market share theory of liability would be more suitable in DES cases, held that a concert of action theory would be appropriate only if "the precise identification of a wrongdoer is impossible."[8]

4. Sindell v. Abbott Laboratories, 26 Cal.3d 588, 163 Cal.Rptr. 132, 607 P.2d 924 (1980).

5. 73 N.Y.2d at 506, 541 N.Y.S.2d at 947.

6. 55 N.Y.2d 571, 450 N.Y.S.2d 776, 436 N.E.2d 182 (1982).

7. 55 N.Y.2d at 580–81, 450 N.Y.S.2d at 780.

8. 541 N.Y.S.2d at 945, 539 N.E.2d at 1073.

Library References:

West's Key No. Digests, Products Liability ⚙⇒23; States ⚙⇒18.65.

§ 27.53 Collateral Estoppel in Products Liability Cases

When a particular product causes harm to many people generating a multitude of lawsuits, it is a waste of judicial resources to require each plaintiff to separately establish the liability of that product's distributor or manufacturer. The courts have thus held that the doctrine of collateral estoppel may be used by other plaintiffs to preclude a manufacturer or distributor from re-litigating issues which it unsuccessfully litigated in another earlier action.[1] This doctrine of collateral estoppel will preclude the re-litigation of an issue which was previously decided against a party in a proceeding in which that party "had a fair opportunity to fully litigate the point."[2]

In order for this doctrine to be invoked, the party seeking its benefit must meet two requirements:

> First, the identical issue necessarily must have been decided in the prior action and be decisive of the present action, and second, the party to be precluded from re-litigating the issue must have had a full and fair opportunity to contest the prior determination.[3]

The party seeking to defeat the application of collateral estoppel must prove that there was an absence of a full and fair opportunity to litigate the issue in the prior action.[4] In the *Kaufman* case, the plaintiff, who was injured as a result of the drug DES, sought to preclude the drug company from re-litigating the jury's finding in *Bichler v. Eli Lilly & Co.*[5] In *Bichler*, the jury's answers to the questions propounded by the Court conclusively determined the liability of the drug company for failing to test its product. Accordingly, it was easy for the *Kaufman* Court to apply the doctrine of collateral estoppel to impose liability upon the drug company for its failure to test the same product that caused the injuries to Ms. Bichler and Ms. Kaufman.

Library References:

West's Key No. Digests, Judgment ⚙⇒634–751.

§ 27.54 Proof of Allegations Checklist

1. Manufacturing defect or mistake in the manufacturing process:

§ 27.53
1. Kaufman v. Eli Lilly and Co., 65 N.Y.2d 449, 492 N.Y.S.2d 584, 482 N.E.2d 63 (1985).
2. 65 N.Y.2d at 455, 492 N.Y.S.2d at 588; Gilberg v. Barbieri, 53 N.Y.2d 285, 291, 441 N.Y.S.2d 49, 50, 423 N.E.2d 807 (1981).
3. 65 N.Y.2d at 455, 492 N.Y.S.2d at 588.
4. Id.
5. 55 N.Y.2d 571, 450 N.Y.S.2d 776, 436 N.E.2d 182 (1982).

§ 27.54   PRODUCTS LIABILITY   Ch. 27

- Was the product manufactured in accordance with the defendant's own quality standards?
- Did the product perform as the manufacturer intended? (*See* § 27.6)

2. Defective design:
   - Was the product as designed not reasonably safe because there was a substantial likelihood of harm?
   - Was it feasible to design the product in a safer manner?
   - What are the risks of the product as opposed to the utility of the product?
   - Was the design of the product a substantial factor in causing injury? (*See* §§ 27.7, 27.8)

3. Failure to warn or adequate warnings:
   - Does the warning provide notice to potential users of any dangers that can be caused by the product?
   - Is the warning specific or general?
   - Where is the warning placed on the product? (*See* §§ 27.10, 27.11, 27.12, 27.13)

4. Failure to test:
   - Was the product properly tested before it was placed on the market?
   - How was the testing performed? Did the testing take into account market conditions? (*See* § 27.18)

5. Causation:
   - Is the product still available, or was it destroyed in the accident or thereafter? (*See* § 27.33)
   - Is there circumstantial evidence that can be used to prove that the product was defective? The defect may be inferred from the fact that the product did not perform as intended by the manufacturer. (*See* § 27.34)

6. Foreseeability of harm:
   - The defendant does not have to foresee the precise manner in which the accident happened.
   - The defendant does not have to foresee the type of injury that the plaintiff suffered. (*See* § 27.36)

7. Collateral Estoppel:
   - Was the defendant unsuccessful in a prior litigation concerning the same product? Consider whether the determinations in the prior litigation collaterally estop the defendant from relitigating certain issues. (*See* § 27.53)

§ 27.55 Drafting Checklist—Complaint

1. How many defendants are involved and what are their roles in placing the product into the stream of commerce?
2. Is the defendant a manufacturer, and if so did it manufacture the whole or complete product (*See* § 27.30); or, did it manufacture only a component part which rendered the product defective? (*See* § 27.29)
3. Is the defendant a distributor or seller of the product (*See* § 27.22), and if so was the sale of the product, or a component thereof, part of the ordinary business of the defendant? (*See* § 27.23)
4. Did the defendant itself put the product into the marketplace, or is it a successor to the company that actually did? (*See* § 27.26)
5. What is the defect in the product that is responsible for the plaintiff's injury?
   - Was there a manufacturing defect or mistake in the manufacturing process? (*See* § 27.6)
   - Was the product defectively designed? (*See* § 27.7)
   - Was the product marketed without adequate warnings? (*See* § 27.10)
   - Was the product properly tested before it was placed into the marketplace?[1] (*See* § 27.18)
6. What express warranties accompanied the product when it was placed into the stream of commerce? (*See* § 27.5)
7. What implied warranties would be applicable under the common law or the Uniform Commercial Code. (*See* § 27.5)
8. Is there privity of contract (a sale) between the plaintiff and the defendant? (*See* §§ 27.3, 27.4, 27.5)
9. Are there any governmental standards, regulations or statutes which address the product which caused the plaintiff's injury? (*See* § 27.42)
10. Can you identify the manufacturer or distributor of the product, and if not, is this because the product is fungible or generic? (*See* § 27.52)

Library References:
West's Key No. Digests, Products Liability ⟺72.

§ 27.56 Drafting Checklist—Answer

1. What was defendant's role in placing the product into the stream of commerce? Consider the nature of defendant's business and its

---

§ 27.55
1. **PRACTICE POINTER:** Typically, the plaintiff will not know, until all discovery is completed, the answer to these questions. It is important to plead all of these possible ways the product may be found to be defective.

§ 27.56   PRODUCTS LIABILITY   Ch. 27

connection with the product or the company that actually placed the product into the marketplace.

2. Was defendant properly served with process?
3. Is defendant subject to the jurisdiction of the court?
4. Was the product misused? (*See* § 27.40) Consider the foreseeability of the manner in which the product was used by the plaintiff and/or the way the accident happened. (*See* § 27.36)
5. Did some other party alter or modify the product? (*See* § 27.41) Consider a third-party complaint against the plaintiff's employer, or a party that serviced and/or repaired the product, or a party that manufactured/ supplied a defective component part. (*See* § 27.29)
6. Did the plaintiff contribute in whole, or in part to the happening of the occurrence?
7. Did the plaintiff, in using the product, assume the risk of injury?
8. What statutes of limitations apply to each cause of action? (*See* § 27.39) If there are warranty claims, when was the product purchased?
9. Does the complaint state a cause of action? Consider whether your client merely serviced the product or a component part thereof, rather than participated in its sale. (*See* § 27.24)
10. Is the plaintiff's claim preempted by a statute, rule or regulation which concerns the subject product or the warnings accompanying it? (*See* § 27.42)
11. Is another party named as a defendant? Consider that party's responsibility and whether a cross-claim may be appropriate.

Library References:
  West's Key No. Digests, Products Liability ⇐72.1, 73.5.

§ 27.57   Forms—Products Liability Complaint

SUPREME COURT OF THE STATE OF NEW YORK
COUNTY OF _____

_____

_____,

                    Plaintiff,
                                    Verified Complaint
       -against-
                                    Index No._____

_____,

                    Defendant.

_____

788

§ 27.55 Drafting Checklist—Complaint

1. How many defendants are involved and what are their roles in placing the product into the stream of commerce?
2. Is the defendant a manufacturer, and if so did it manufacture the whole or complete product (*See* § 27.30); or, did it manufacture only a component part which rendered the product defective? (*See* § 27.29)
3. Is the defendant a distributor or seller of the product (*See* § 27.22), and if so was the sale of the product, or a component thereof, part of the ordinary business of the defendant? (*See* § 27.23)
4. Did the defendant itself put the product into the marketplace, or is it a successor to the company that actually did? (*See* § 27.26)
5. What is the defect in the product that is responsible for the plaintiff's injury?
   - Was there a manufacturing defect or mistake in the manufacturing process? (*See* § 27.6)
   - Was the product defectively designed? (*See* § 27.7)
   - Was the product marketed without adequate warnings? (*See* § 27.10)
   - Was the product properly tested before it was placed into the marketplace?[1] (*See* § 27.18)
6. What express warranties accompanied the product when it was placed into the stream of commerce? (*See* § 27.5)
7. What implied warranties would be applicable under the common law or the Uniform Commercial Code. (*See* § 27.5)
8. Is there privity of contract (a sale) between the plaintiff and the defendant? (*See* §§ 27.3, 27.4, 27.5)
9. Are there any governmental standards, regulations or statutes which address the product which caused the plaintiff's injury? (*See* § 27.42)
10. Can you identify the manufacturer or distributor of the product, and if not, is this because the product is fungible or generic? (*See* § 27.52)

Library References:
West's Key No. Digests, Products Liability ⟿72.

§ 27.56 Drafting Checklist—Answer

1. What was defendant's role in placing the product into the stream of commerce? Consider the nature of defendant's business and its

---

§ 27.55
1. **PRACTICE POINTER:** Typically, the plaintiff will not know, until all discovery is completed, the answer to these questions. It is important to plead all of these possible ways the product may be found to be defective.

§ 27.56   PRODUCTS LIABILITY   Ch. 27

connection with the product or the company that actually placed the product into the marketplace.

2. Was defendant properly served with process?
3. Is defendant subject to the jurisdiction of the court?
4. Was the product misused? (*See* § 27.40) Consider the foreseeability of the manner in which the product was used by the plaintiff and/or the way the accident happened. (*See* § 27.36)
5. Did some other party alter or modify the product? (*See* § 27.41) Consider a third-party complaint against the plaintiff's employer, or a party that serviced and/or repaired the product, or a party that manufactured/ supplied a defective component part. (*See* § 27.29)
6. Did the plaintiff contribute in whole, or in part to the happening of the occurrence?
7. Did the plaintiff, in using the product, assume the risk of injury?
8. What statutes of limitations apply to each cause of action? (*See* § 27.39) If there are warranty claims, when was the product purchased?
9. Does the complaint state a cause of action? Consider whether your client merely serviced the product or a component part thereof, rather than participated in its sale. (*See* § 27.24)
10. Is the plaintiff's claim preempted by a statute, rule or regulation which concerns the subject product or the warnings accompanying it? (*See* § 27.42)
11. Is another party named as a defendant? Consider that party's responsibility and whether a cross-claim may be appropriate.

Library References:
    West's Key No. Digests, Products Liability ⟳72.1, 73.5.

§ 27.57   Forms—Products Liability Complaint 💾

SUPREME COURT OF THE STATE OF NEW YORK
COUNTY OF _____

_____

_____,
                     Plaintiff,
                                   Verified Complaint
    -against-
                                   Index No._____

_____,
                     Defendant.
_____

Plaintiff, *JANE PLAINTIFF*, complaining of the defendant, by her attorney(s), *[ATTORNEY(S)]*, respectfully alleges, upon information and belief, as follows:

THE PARTIES

1. Plaintiff resides at *[Plaintiff's address]*.

2. Defendant *DEFENDANT MANUFACTURER, INC.*, (hereinafter referred to as "*MANUFACTURER*") is a foreign corporation duly organized and existing under and by virtue of the laws of the State of Delaware.

3. Defendant *MANUFACTURER*, by and through its agents, servants, employees, affiliates, subsidiaries and/or sister corporations, does business in the State of New York and derives substantial revenue therefrom.

4. Defendant *MANUFACTURER* maintains a principal place of business located at *[Defendant's address]*.

THE UNDERLYING FACTS

5. Defendant *MANUFACTURER* was, and still is, in the business of designing, assembling, manufacturing, selling, marketing, distributing, leasing, servicing and repairing *[product type]* machines, their appurtenances and component parts.

6. Defendant *MANUFACTURER* designed, assembled, manufactured, sold, marketed, distributed, leased, serviced and repaired a *[product type]* machine commonly known as the *[Product Name]*, Model Number *[1234]*, and/or its appurtenances and component parts.

7. Defendant *MANUFACTURER* sold and distributed said *[Product Name]*, Model Number *[1234]*, and/or its appurtenances and component parts, for use by the public at large.

8. Prior to *[date of occurrence]*, defendant *MANUFACTURER* caused, directly or indirectly, the aforesaid *[Product Name]*, Model Number *[1234]*, and its appurtenances and component parts, to enter the stream of commerce.

9. Defendant *MANUFACTURER* was, and still is, in the business of adding and distributing parts for, maintaining, servicing, repairing, and/or rebuilding, copy machines, their appurtenances and component parts.

10. On or about *[date of occurrence]*, and prior and subsequent thereto, *[DEFENDANT MANUFACTURER]* was in possession of the aforesaid *[Product Name]*, Model Number *[1234]*.

§ 27.57   PRODUCTS LIABILITY   Ch. 27

11. The aforesaid *[Product Name]*, in the possession of *[DEFENDANT MANUFACTURER]* was serviced, repaired and maintained by defendant *MANUFACTURER*.

12. On or about *[date of occurrence]*, and prior and subsequent thereto, plaintiff, *JANE PLAINTIFF*, was lawfully upon *[place of occurrence]*.

13. On or about *[date of occurrence]*, while plaintiff *JANE PLAINTIFF* was properly using the aforesaid *[Product Name]*, Model Number *[1234]*, she was caused to sustain severe and permanent personal injuries, including, among other things, *[list injuries]*; and this plaintiff was otherwise damaged, all of which damages and injuries are permanent in nature and continuing into the future.

AS AND FOR A FIRST CAUSE OF ACTION (NEGLIGENCE) ON BEHALF OF PLAINTIFF, JANE PLAINTIFF

14. The aforesaid occurrence and injuries sustained by plaintiff, *JANE PLAINTIFF*, were caused by the carelessness, recklessness and negligence of the defendant in the design, assembly, manufacture, sale, distribution, maintenance, servicing, repairing, and/or rebuilding of the aforesaid *[Product Name]*, Model Number *[1234]*, its appurtenances and component parts, including, among other things, in defectively designing and manufacturing the aforesaid *[Product Name]*; in defectively designing and manufacturing said *[Product Name]* so that it could be readily altered and/or modified; in defectively designing and manufacturing said *[Product Name]* so that it could be operated without the use of safety devices; in negligently representing and warranting that repairs and/or alterations made to said machine were done properly; in failing to adequately test said *[Product Name]* for proper *[defect causing injury]*; in failing to insure that said *[Product Name]* was safe for use by the general public and, more particularly, the plaintiff herein; in failing to properly and adequately service, repair and maintain said *[Product Name]*; in recklessly and negligently altering the aforesaid machine so that it could be operated without the use of safety devices; in failing to warn that said machine was or could be easily made unsafe and unfit for its intended use; in failing to warn of the dangers and hazards of using said *[Product Name]*; in failing to provide warnings or information despite knowledge of the dangers and hazards, more particularly, *[defect causing injury]*; in failing to conform with industry regulations and standards; in selling and distributing for use by the general public and placing into the stream of commerce an unsafe and unreasonably dangerous product; in causing the occurrence complained of herein; and this defendant was otherwise careless, reckless and negligent.

15. The aforesaid occurrence and injuries resulting therefrom were caused solely by the carelessness, recklessness and negligence of the

defendant, without any fault or negligence on the part of the plaintiff contributing thereto.

16. By reason of the foregoing, plaintiff, *JANE PLAINTIFF*, has been damaged in an amount not to exceed the sum of *[money amount]*.

AS AND FOR A SECOND CAUSE OF ACTION (STRICT LIABILITY) ON BEHALF OF PLAINTIFF, JANE PLAINTIFF

17. Plaintiff repeats, reiterates and realleges each and every allegation contained in the paragraphs of this complaint numbered "1" through "15," inclusive, with the same force and effect as if the same were more fully set forth at length herein.

18. Defendant knew, or had reason to know, that the ultimate users of their *[Product Name]*, would be exposed to a risk of electrical hazard arising from the use of the defendant's *[product type]* machine.

19. Defendant placed said *[product type]* machine into the stream of commerce when it knew, or had reason to know, that said *[product type]* machine was not reasonably safe for use by members of the general public.

20. The ordinary and foreseeable use of defendant's *[product type]* constituted a dangerous and unreasonable risk of *[defect causing injury]* hazard to members of the public at large and, more particularly, to the plaintiff herein.

21. As a result of the foregoing, plaintiff, *JANE PLAINTIFF*, was caused to sustain the severe and permanent personal injuries as set forth above.

22. By reason of the foregoing, plaintiff, *JANE PLAINTIFF*, is entitled to recover against the defendant under the Doctrine of Strict Products Liability.

23. By reason of the foregoing, plaintiff, *JANE PLAINTIFF*, has been damaged in an amount not to exceed the sum of *[money amount]*.

AS AND FOR A THIRD CAUSE OF ACTION (EXPRESS WARRANTY) ON BEHALF OF PLAINTIFF, JANE PLAINTIFF

24. Plaintiff repeats, reiterates and realleges each and every allegation contained in the paragraphs of this complaint numbered "1" through "15" and "18" through "22," inclusive, with the same force and effect as if the same were more fully set forth at length herein.

25. Defendant, by and through its agents, servants and/or employees, sold and distributed its *[Product Name]*, Model Number *[1234]*, and expressly warranted that it was of merchantable quality and fit for its intended purpose.

26. The aforesaid *[product type]* machine was defective, was not of merchantable quality and was not fit for its intended purpose.

27. Defendant's breach of warranty was a cause of plaintiff's injuries, as aforesaid.

28. By reason of the foregoing, plaintiff, *JANE PLAINTIFF*, has been damaged in an amount not to exceed the sum of *[money amount]*.

AS AND FOR A FOURTH CAUSE OF ACTION (IMPLIED WARRANTY) ON BEHALF OF PLAINTIFF, JANE PLAINTIFF

29. Plaintiff repeats, reiterates and realleges each and every allegation contained in the paragraphs of this complaint numbered "1" through "15," "18" through "22," and "25" through "27," inclusive, with the same force and effect as if the same were more fully set forth at length herein.

30. Defendant, by and through its agents, servants and/or employees, sold and distributed its *[product type]* machine, *[Product Name]*, Model Number *[1234]*, and impliedly warranted that it was of merchantable quality and fit for its intended purpose.

31. The aforesaid *[product type]* machine was defective, was not of merchantable quality and was not fit for its intended purpose.

32. Defendant's breach of warranty was a cause of plaintiff's injuries, as aforesaid.

33. By reason of the foregoing, plaintiff, *JANE PLAINTIFF*, has been damaged in an amount not to exceed the sum of *[money amount]*.

WHEREFORE, plaintiff demands judgment in the First, Second, Third and Fourth Causes of Action against the defendant in an amount not to exceed the sum of *[money amount]*, together with the costs, disbursements and attorneys' fees[1] of this action.

[Attorney(s)' name and address]

VERIFICATION

STATE OF NEW YORK)
) SS:
COUNTY OF)

JANE PLAINTIFF, being duly sworn, deposes and says:

That I am the plaintiff in the within action; that I have read the foregoing Complaint and know the contents thereof; that the same is

---

§ 27.57
1. **PRACTICE POINTER:** In the course of discovery, it may be learned that the defendant violated a statute or regulation. Since that statute or regulation may provide for an award of attorneys' fees to the injured party, it is wise to include a prayer for such an award in the complaint so as to dispense with the need to later amend the complaint.

true to my own knowledge, except as to the matters therein stated to be alleged upon information and belief, and that as to those matters, I believe them to be true.

JANE PLAINTIFF

Sworn to before me this
___ day of _____, 199__

_____
Notary Public

Library References:

West's Key No. Digests, Products Liability ⊃73, 73.5.

§ 27.58 Forms—Products Liability Answer

SUPREME COURT OF THE STATE OF NEW YORK
COUNTY OF _____

_____,
               Plaintiff(s),   ) Verified Answer
        -against-   ) Index No._____
_____,
             Defendant(s).)

Defendant, _____, as and for its Verified Answer to the Verified Complaint herein, by its attorney(s), _____, respectfully alleges, upon information and belief:

1. Denies having knowledge or information sufficient to form a belief as to the allegations contained in paragraphs "___", "___", "___" and "___".

2. Denies each and every allegation contained in paragraph "___".

AS TO THE FIRST CAUSE OF ACTION

3. Denies each and every allegation contained in paragraphs "___", "___" and "___".

AS TO THE SECOND CAUSE OF ACTION

4. Defendant repeats, reiterates and realleges each and every denial and denial of knowledge or information sufficient to form a belief as to

793

each of the allegations of the complaint reiterated and realleged by the plaintiff in paragraph "___" with the same force and effect as if more fully set forth here at.

5. Denies each and every allegation contained in paragraphs "___", "___", "___", "___", "___" and "___".

AS TO THE THIRD CAUSE OF ACTION

6. Defendant repeats, reiterates and realleges each and every denial and denial of knowledge or information sufficient to form a belief as to each of the allegations of the complaint reiterated and realleged by the plaintiff in paragraph "___" with the same force and effect as if more fully set forth here at.

7. Denies each and every allegation contained in paragraphs "...", "___" and "___".

AS TO THE FOURTH CAUSE OF ACTION

8. Defendant repeats, reiterates and realleges each and every denial and denial of knowledge or information sufficient to form a belief as to each of the allegations of the complaint reiterated and realleged by the plaintiff in paragraph "___" with the same force and effect as if more fully set forth here at.

9. Denies each and every allegation contained in paragraphs "___", "___" and "___".

AS AND FOR A FIRST AFFIRMATIVE DEFENSE

10. This Court lacks jurisdiction over the person of the answering defendant herein.

AS AND FOR A SECOND AFFIRMATIVE DEFENSE

11. That plaintiff's Complaint fails to state a cause of action.

AS AND FOR A THIRD AFFIRMATIVE DEFENSE

12. Upon information and belief, the [product type] described in the verified complaint was misused.

AS AND FOR A FOURTH AFFIRMATIVE DEFENSE

13. Upon information and belief, the [product type] described in the verified complaint was installed, repaired and/or maintained improperly.

AS AND FOR A FIFTH AFFIRMATIVE DEFENSE

14. Upon information and belief, any damages sustained by plaintiff as alleged in the complaint were caused by parties other than the answering defendant.

AS AND FOR A SIXTH AFFIRMATIVE DEFENSE

15. That the damages of the plaintiff were caused in whole or in part by the culpable conduct of the plaintiff which either bars the claim completely or else diminishes the damages by the proportion that such culpable conduct of the plaintiff bears to the total culpable conduct causing the damages.

AS AND FOR A SEVENTH AFFIRMATIVE DEFENSE

16. By the exercise of reasonable care, plaintiff would have discovered the alleged defect, perceived and observed its danger and avoided its danger and avoided the alleged damages.

AS AND FOR AN EIGHTH AFFIRMATIVE DEFENSE

17. [Defendant's] liability in this action, if any, is several and not joint.

AS AND FOR A NINTH AFFIRMATIVE DEFENSE

18. In the event that any person or entity liable or claimed to be liable for the damages alleged in this action has been given or may hereafter be given a release or covenant not to sue, [Defendant] will be entitled to protection under General Obligations Law § 15–109 and the corresponding reduction of any damages which may be determined to be due against [Defendant].

AS AND FOR A TENTH AFFIRMATIVE DEFENSE

19. The warranty claims of plaintiff against [Defendant] are barred by reason of lack of privity of contract between the parties.

AS AND FOR AN ELEVENTH AFFIRMATIVE DEFENSE

20. Certain claims and damages sought herein are limited and excluded by the express terms of any applicable warranties.

AS AND FOR A TWELFTH AFFIRMATIVE DEFENSE

21. The warranty claims of plaintiff [or if other claims so state] against [Defendant] are barred by the applicable Statute of Limitations.

AS AND FOR A THIRTEENTH AFFIRMATIVE DEFENSE

22. Plaintiff was cognizant and had full knowledge of all facts, circumstances and conditions of its workplace, including the requirements, standards and procedures for the use of the product in the environment of its workplace, and thus voluntarily assumed the risks, if any, arising from and attendant to such use, including any misuse or overuse occurring under such facts, circumstances, conditions, standards, procedures and workplace environments.

AS AND FOR A FOURTEENTH AFFIRMATIVE DEFENSE

23. [*Defendant*] denies that plaintiff's damages were caused by the use of its product. To the extent that it is determined that any such damages are related to the use of such product, then these damages were caused by the superseding and intervening acts and/or negligence of other parties over whom [*Defendant*] had no control and for whose acts and/or omissions this defendant is not liable.

AS AND FOR A FIFTEENTH AFFIRMATIVE DEFENSE

24. [*Defendant*] denies that plaintiff's damages were caused by the use of its product. To the extent that it is determined that any such damages are related to the use of such product, at the time this product left the control of [*Defendant*] there was not a practical and technically feasible alternative design that would have prevented the harm without substantially impairing the reasonably anticipated and intended function of this product.

AS AND FOR A FIRST CROSS–CLAIM AGAINST CO–DEFENDANTS

25. Upon information and belief, if plaintiff was caused to sustain damages at the time and place and as otherwise set forth in the Complaint through any acts, carelessness, recklessness, breach of warranty and/or negligence other than its own, then said damages were sustained by reason of the carelessness, recklessness and or affirmative acts of omission or commission by [*Co-Defendants*] without any fault of answering defendant.

26. By reason of the foregoing, defendants will be liable in indemnification and/or contribution to answering defendant in the event and in the amount of any recovery by the plaintiff herein or in such amounts as the Court or jury may decide and [*Defendant*] will be entitled to such judgment over and against [*Co-defendants*].

AS AND FOR A SECOND CROSS–CLAIM AGAINST CO–DEFENDANT

27. That if plaintiff was caused to sustain damages at the time and place and in the manner and due to the circumstances set forth in the plaintiff's complaint through any carelessness, recklessness and/or negligence or other culpable conduct other than that of the plaintiff himself, then said damages were caused and/or said damages were contributed to by reason of the carelessness, recklessness, and/or negligence and/or acts of omission or commission or other culpable conduct of the co-defendant and if any judgment is recovered herein by the plaintiff against this answering defendant, this answering defendant will be damaged thereby and this answering defendant will be entitled to recover all or part of that judgment by reason of the foregoing, and thus the defendant will be